DATE DUE

			PRINTED IN U.S.A.

CLASSICAL AND MEDIEVAL LITERATURE CRITICISM

Guide to Gale Literary Criticism Series

For criticism on	Consult these Gale series
Authors now living or who died after December 31, 1959	*CONTEMPORARY LITERARY CRITICISM (CLC)*
Authors who died between 1900 and 1959	*TWENTIETH-CENTURY LITERARY CRITICISM (TCLC)*
Authors who died between 1800 and 1899	*NINETEENTH-CENTURY LITERATURE CRITICISM (NCLC)*
Authors who died between 1400 and 1799	*LITERATURE CRITICISM FROM 1400 TO 1800 (LC)* *SHAKESPEAREAN CRITICISM (SC)*
Authors who died before 1400	*CLASSICAL AND MEDIEVAL LITERATURE CRITICISM (CMLC)*
Black writers of the past two hundred years	*BLACK LITERATURE CRITICISM (BLC)*
Authors of books for children and young adults	*CHILDREN'S LITERATURE REVIEW (CLR)*
Dramatists	*DRAMA CRITICISM (DC)*
Hispanic writers of the late nineteenth and twentieth centuries	*HISPANIC LITERATURE CRITICISM (HLC)*
Native North American writers and orators of the eighteenth, nineteenth, and twentieth centuries	*NATIVE NORTH AMERICAN LITERATURE (NNAL)*
Poets	*POETRY CRITICISM (PC)*
Short story writers	*SHORT STORY CRITICISM (SSC)*
Major authors from the Renaissance to the present	*WORLD LITERATURE CRITICISM, 1500 TO THE PRESENT (WLC)*

ISSN 0896-0011

Volume 18

CLASSICAL
AND MEDIEVAL
LITERATURE
CRITICISM

Excerpts from Criticism of the Works of World
Authors from Classical Antiquity through the
Fourteenth Century, from the First Appraisals
to Current Evaluations

Jelena O. Krstović
Editor

GALE

DETROIT · NEW YORK · TORONTO · LONDON

STAFF

Jelena Krstović, *Editor*
Mary L. Onorato, James E. Person, Jr., *Contributing Editors*
Ondine LeBlanc, *Associate Editor*
Susan Trosky, *Managing Editor*

Marlene S. Hurst, *Permissions Manager*
Margaret A. Chamberlain, Maria Franklin, Kimberly F. Smilay, *Permissions Specialists*
Diane Cooper,
Edna Hedblad, Michele Lonoconus, Maureen Puhl, Susan Salas, Shalice Shah,
Barbara A. Wallace, *Permissions Associates*
Sarah Chesney, Margaret McAvoy-Amato, *Permissions Assistants*

Victoria B. Cariappa, *Research Manager*
Alicia Biggers, Julia Daniel, Tamara C. Nott, Michele P. Pica, Tracie A. Richardson, Cheryl Warnock, *Research Associates*

Mary Beth Trimper, *Production Director*
Deborah Milliken, *Production Assistant*

Barbara J. Yarrow, *Graphic Services Manager*
Sherrell Hobbs, *Macintosh Artist*
Pamela A. Hayes, *Photography Coordinator*
Randy Bassett, *Image Database Supervisor*
Robert Duncan, *Imaging Specialist*

™
This book is printed on acid-free paper that meets the minimum requirements of American National Standard for Information Sciences—Permanence Paper for Printed Library Materials, ANSI Z39.48-1984.

Library of Congress Catalog Card Number 88-658021
ISBN 0-8103-9981-4
ISSN 0896-0011
Printed in the United States of America

10 9 8 7 6 5 4 3 2 1

Contents

Preface   vii

Acknowledgments   xi

Preface

Since its inception in 1988, *Classical and Medieval Literature Criticism* has been a valuable resource for students and librarians seeking critical commentary on the writers and works of these periods in world history. Major reviewing sources have assessed *CMLC* as "useful" and "extremely convenient," noting that it "adds to our understanding of the rich legacy left by the ancient period and the Middle Ages," and praising its "general excellence in the presentation of an inherently interesting subject." No other single reference source has surveyed the critical reaction to classical and medieval literature as thoroughly as *CMLC*.

Scope of the Series

CMLC is designed to serve as an introduction for students and advanced readers of the works and authors of antiquity through the fourteenth century. The great poets, prose writers, dramatists, and philosophers of this period form the basis of most humanities curricula, so that virtually every student will encounter many of these works during the course of a high school and college education. By organizing and reprinting an enormous amount of commentary written on classical and medieval authors and works, *CMLC* helps students develop valuable insight into literary history, promotes a better understanding of the texts, and sparks ideas for papers and assignments. Each entry in *CMLC* presents a comprehensive survey of an author's career, an individual work of literature, or a literary topic, and provides the user with a multiplicity of interpretations and assessments. Such variety allows students to pursue their own interests; furthermore, it fosters an awareness that literature is dynamic and responsive to many different opinions.

CMLC continues the survey of criticism of world literature begun by Gale's *Contemporary Literary Criticism (CLC)*, *Twentieth-Century Literary Criticism (TCLC)*, *Nineteenth-Century Literature Criticism (NCLC)*, *Literature Criticism from 1400 to 1800 (LC)*, and *Shakespearean Criticism (SC)*. For additional information about these and Gale's other criticism series, users should consult the Guide to Gale Literary Criticism Series preceding the title page in this volume.

Coverage

Each volume of *CMLC* is carefully compiled to present:

- criticism of authors and works which represent a variety of genres, time periods, and nationalities

- both major and lesser-known writers and works of the period (such as non-Western authors and literature, increasingly read by today's students)

- 4-6 authors or works per volume

- individual entries that survey the critical response to each author, work, or topic, including early criticism, later criticism (to represent any rise or decline in the author's reputation), and current retrospective analyses. The length of each author or work entry also indicates relative importance, reflecting the amount of critical attention the author, work, or topic has received from critics writing in English, and from foreign criticism in translation.

An author may appear more than once in the series if his or her writings have been the subject of a substantial amount of criticism; in these instances, specific works or groups of works by the author will be covered in separate entries. For example, Homer will be represented by three entries, one devoted to the *Iliad*, one to the *Odyssey*, and one to the Homeric Hymns.

Starting with Volume 10, *CMLC* will also occasionally include entries devoted to literary topics. For example, *CMLC*-10 focuses on Arthurian Legend and includes general criticism on that subject as well as individual entries on writers or works central to that topic—Chrétien de Troyes, Gottfried von Strassburg, Layamon, and the Alliterative *Morte Arthure*.

Organization of the Book

An author entry consists of the following elements: author heading, biographical and critical introduction, principal English translations or editions, excerpts of criticism (each preceded by a bibliographic citation and an annotation), and a bibliography of further reading.

- The **Author Heading** consists of the author's most commonly used name, followed by birth and death dates. If the entry is devoted to a work, the heading will consist of the most common form of the title in English translation (if applicable), and the original date of composition. Located at the beginning of the introduction are any name or title variations.

- A **Portrait** of the author is included when available. Many entries also feature illustrations of materials pertinent to the author or work, including manuscript pages, book illustrations, and representations of people, places, and events important to a study of the author or work.

- The **Biographical and Critical Introduction** contains background information that concisely introduces the reader to the author, work, or topic.

- The list of **Principal Works** and **English Translations** or **Editions** is chronological by date of first publication and is included as an aid to the student seeking translated versions or editions of these works for study. The list will focus primarily on twentieth-century translations, selecting those works most commonly considered the best by critics.

- **Criticism** is arranged chronologically in each entry to provide a useful perspective on changes in critical evaluation over the years. All titles by the author featured in the critical entry are printed in boldface type to enable the user to ascertain without difficulty the works being discussed. Also for purposes of easier identification, the critic's name and the publication date of the essay are given at the beginning of each piece of criticism. Anonymous criticism is preceded by the title of the journal in which it appeared. Publication information (such as publisher names and book prices) and parenthetical numerical references (such as footnotes or page and line references to specific editions of works) have been deleted at the editors' discretion to provide smoother reading of the text. Many critical entries in *CMLC* also contain translations to aid the users.

- A complete **Bibliographic Citation** provides original publication information for each piece of criticism.

- Critical excerpts are also prefaced by **Annotations** providing the reader with information about both the critic and the criticism, the scope of the excerpt, the growth of critical controversy, or changes in critical trends regarding an author or work. In some cases, these notes include cross-references to excerpts by critics who discuss each other's commentary. Dates in parentheses within the annotation refer to a book publication date when they follow a book title, and to an essay date when they follow a critic's name.

- An annotated bibliography of **Further Reading** appears at the end of each entry and lists additional secondary sources on the author or work. In some cases it includes essays for which the editors could not obtain reprint rights. When applicable, the Further Reading is followed by references to additional entries on the author in other literary reference series published by Gale.

Topic Entries are subdivided into several thematic rubrics in which criticism appears in order of descending scope.

Cumulative Indexes

Each volume of *CMLC* includes a cumulative **author index** listing all authors who have appeared in Gale's Literary Criticism Series, along with cross references to such biographical series as *Contemporary Authors* and *Dictionary of Literary Biography*. For readers' convenience, a complete list of Gale titles included appears on the page prior to the author index. Useful for locating an author within the various series, this index is particularly valuable for those authors who are identified with a certain period but who, because of their death date, are placed in another, or for those authors whose careers span two periods. For example, Geoffrey Chaucer, who is usually considered a medieval author, is found in *Literature Criticism from 1400 to 1800* because he died after 1399.

Beginning with the tenth volume, *CMLC* includes a cumulative index listing all topic entries that have appeared in the Gale Literary Criticism Series *Classical and Medieval Literature Criticism, Contemporary Literary Criticism, Literature Criticism from 1400 to 1800, Nineteenth-Century Literature Criticism,* and *Twentieth-Century Literary Criticism.*

Beginning with the second volume, *CMLC* also includes a cumulative nationality index. Authors and/or works are grouped by nationality, and the volume in which criticism on them may be found is indicated.

Title Index

Each volume of *CMLC* also includes an index listing the titles of all literary works discussed in the series. Foreign language titles that have been translated are followed by the titles of the translations—for example, *Slovo o polku Igorove (The Song of Igor's Campaign)*. Page numbers following these translated titles refer to all pages on which any form of the title, either foreign language or translated, appears. Titles of novels, dramas, nonfiction books, and poetry, short story, or essay collections are printed in italics, while those of all individual poems, short stories, and essays are printed in roman type within quotation marks. In cases where the same title is used by different authors, the author's name or surname is given in parentheses after the title, e.g. *Collected Poems* (Horace) and *Collected Poems* (Sappho).

Critic Index

An index to critics, which cumulates with the second volume, is another useful feature of *CMLC*. Under each critic's name are listed the authors and/or works on whom the critic has written and the volume and page number where criticism may be found.

A Note to the Reader

When writing papers, students who quote directly from any volume in the Literary Criticism Series may use the following general forms to footnote reprinted criticism. The first example pertains to material drawn from a periodical, the second to material reprinted from books.

Rollo May, "The Therapist and the Journey into Hell," *Michigan Quarterly Review,* XXV, No. 4 (Fall 1986), 629-41; excerpted and reprinted in *Classical and Medieval Literature Criticism,* Vol. 3, ed. Jelena O. Krstović (Detroit: Gale Research, 1989), pp. 154-58.

Dana Ferrin Sutton, *Self and Society in Aristophanes* (University of Press of America, 1980); excerpted and reprinted in *Classical and Medieval Literature Criticism,* Vol. 4, ed. Jelena O. Krstović (Detroit: Gale Research, 1990), pp. 162-69.

Suggestions Are Welcome

Readers who wish to make suggestions for future volumes, or who have other comments regarding the series, are cordially invited to write or call the editors (1-800-347-GALE, Fax: (314) 961-6815).

Acknowledgments

The editors wish to thank the copyright holders of the excerpted criticism included in this volume and the permissions managers of many book and magazine publishing companies for assisting us in securing reprint rights. We are also grateful to the staffs of the Detroit Public Library, the Library of Congress, the University of Detroit Mercy Library, Wayne State University Purdy / Kresge Library Complex, and the University of Michigan Libraries for making their resources available. Following is a list of the copyright holders who have granted us permission to reprint material in this volume of *CMLC*. Every effort has been made to trace copyright, but if omissions have been made, please let us know.

COPYRIGHTED EXCERPTS IN *CMLC*, VOLUME 18, WERE REPRINTED FROM THE FOLLOWING PERIODICALS:

Arethusa, v. 25, Fall, 1992. © 1992 by Department of Classics, State University of N.Y. at Buffalo. Reprinted by permission of the publisher.—*The Hebrew Annual Review*, v. 10, 1986 for "Gender Imagery in the Song of Songs" by Carol Meyers. Reprinted by permission of the author.—*Italica*, v. 63, Autumn, 1984. Reprinted by permission of the publisher.—*Journal of Biblical Literature*, v. LXXXVI, June, 1967. Reprinted by permission of the publisher.—*Medieval & Renaissance Texts & Studies*, v. 23, 1983. © Copyright 1983 Center for Medieval & Early Renaissance Studies, SUNY Binghamton. Reprinted by permission of the publisher.—*Studies in Religion/Sciences Religieuses*, v. 3, 1973-74. Reprinted by permission of the Canadian Corporation for Studies in Religion/Sciences Religieuses.

COPYRIGHTED EXCERPTS IN *CMLC*, VOLUME 18, WERE REPRINTED FROM THE FOLLOWING BOOKS:

Alter, Robert. From *The Art of Biblical Poetry*. Basic Books, Inc., Publishers, 1985. Copyright © 1985 by Robert Alter. Reprinted by permission of the author. In the U.S., Canada and Philippine Islands by permission of Basic Books, a division of HarperCollins Publishers, Inc.—Blum, Rudolf. From *Kallimachos: The Alexandrian Library and the Origins of Bibliography*. Translated by Hans H. Wellisch. The University of Wisconsin Press, 1991. Copyright © 1991. All rights reserved. Reprinted by permission of the publisher.—Falk, Marcia. From *The Song of Songs: A New Translation and Interpretaiton*. Harper San Francisco, 1990. Copyright © 1973, 1977, 1990 by Marcia Lee Falk. All rights reserved. Repinted by permission of HarperCollins Publishers, Inc.—Ferguson, John. From *Catullus*. Oxford at the Clarendon Press, 1988. © Oxford University Press, 1988. Reprinted by permission of the publisher.—Goold, G. P. From an introduction to *Catullus*. Edited and translated by G. P. Goold.—Duckworth, 1983. © 1983 by G. P. Goold. All rights reserved. Reprinted by permission of Gerald Duckworth and Co. Ltd.—Havelock, E. A. From *The Lyric Genius of Catullus*. B. Blackwell, 1939. Reprinted by permission of the Literary Estate of Eric A. Havelock.—Korte, Alfred. From *Hellenistic Poetry*. Translated by Jacob Hammer and Moses Hadas. Columbia University Press, 1929. Copyright 1929 Columbia University Press, New York. All rights reserved. Reprinted with permission of the publisher.—Lee, Guy. From an introduction to *The Poems of Catullus*. Edited and translated by Guy Lee. Oxford at the Clarendon Press, 1990. © Guy Lee 1990. All rights reserved. Reprinted by permission of Oxford University Press.—Luther, Martin. From "Lectures on the Song of Solomon," translated by Ian Siggins, in *Luther's Works, Vol. 15*. Edited by Jaroslav Pelikan and Hilton C. Oswald. Concordia Publishing, 1972. Copyright © 1972 by Concordia Publishing House. Reprinted by permission of the publisher.—Lyne, R. O. A. M. From *The Latin Love Poets: From Catullus to Horace*. Oxford at the Clarendon Press, 1980. © R. O. A. M. Lyne. All rights reserved. Reprinted by permission of Oxford University Press.—Martin, Charles. From an introduction to *The Poems of Catullus*. Translated by Charles Martin. Johns Hopkins University Press, 1990. © 1979 Charles Martin. © 1990 The Johns Hopkins University Press. All rights

PHOTOGRAPHS AND IMAGES APPEARING IN *CMLC*, VOLUME 18, WERE RECEIVED FROM THE FOLLOWING SOURCES:

Piraeus Athena, photograph. German Archaeological Institute. Reproduced by permission.

Ptolemy II, photograph. British Museum. Reproduced by permission.

Text of the *Song of Songs*, illustration. Shalom Asch Collection. Courtesy of The Beinecke Rare Book and Manuscript Library, Yale University.

Callimachus

c. 310/305 B.C.-c. 240 B.C.

Greek poet and scholar.

INTRODUCTION

Callimachus was a poet and scholar of great influence during a major transition in Greek history. After the death of Alexander the Great in 323 B.C. the influence of Greek culture began to extend beyond Greece eastward to Persia and Asia; scholars have typically referred to this as the beginning of the Hellenistic Age. Many classicists have identified Callimachus as one of the forces that helped shape the literature of the age, even going so far, in the case of Bruno Snell, to dub Callimachus the "father of Hellenistic poetry." Callimachus was a highly prolific writer—producing an estimated 800 volumes of poetry and scholarship— and a substantial record of his work survives either in manuscript fragments or in citations by other writers. Scholars have devoted particular attention to his *Hymns,* all six of which are extant in complete form, most or all of his epigrams, the *Iambi,* and two of his longer works, the *Aitia* and *Hecale.* He is also well known, albeit less often studied, for his scholarship, conducted during his tenure as a cataloguer at the Alexandrian royal library. There he prepared exhaustive bibliographies—*Pinakes*—of the library's contents.

Biographical Information

Scholars date Callimachus's birth between 310 and 305 B.C.; he was born in Cyrene, a Greek colony situated in the part of North Africa that is now Libya. Callimachus sometimes carries the name Battiades, or "son of Battus", in reference to his father's name and the royal lineage that that name designates: until about 450 B.C., the names of the colony's rulers alternated between Battus and Arcesilaus. His family, however, was probably middle-class. When he was a young man, Callimachus moved to Alexandria, Egypt, then a focal point of Greek culture and the home of the royal family. He initially took a position as a teacher in a suburb of the city, but eventually was offered a place in the royal library maintained by the ruler Ptolemy II Philadelphus, who wanted the volumes in his extensive library catalogued. Scholars still debate the exact nature of the position that Callimachus took on. Whether he was a cataloguer only or also the library director, there is no doubt that the work he did was substantial and significant. The bibliographies of the library's holdings that he created exceeded 120 volumes.

Callimachus's work for the library necessarily exposed him to literary and non-literary works from preceding generations, making him a tremendously learned writer. Critics regularly have noted the influence of this reading in Callimachus's poetry. Although he is not known for producing critical works, Callimachus nonetheless became a voice to be reckoned with in the poetics—or literary conventions—of his day, becoming enmeshed in heated feuds with other scholars and poets. The most significant of these was actually one of his own students, Apollonius Rhodius, who went on to hold the library director position. Evidence of these debates, which were often hostile rather than rational, shows up consistently in Callimachus's poetry. Scholars have found little information about his later years, determining only that he continued to work at the library and that he composed poetry until close to the end of his life.

Major Works

Although the works Callimachus is known to have composed greatly exceed what has survived, there is still a substantial body of his work available for readers and scholars to examine. Because the *Hymns* are intact they win a good deal of study, as do the *Aitia* and *Hecale,* both of which have survived in substantial fragments. The *Hymns* are six in number, each addressed to a different deity: 1 to Zeus, 2 to Apollo, 3 to Artemis, 4 to Delos, 5 to Athena, and 6 to Demeter. In structure all closely imitate Homeric Hymns, typically composed for oral presentation at festivals; however, critics concur that Callimachus followed these conventions without ever presenting at such events. Callimachus apparently prepared his work for a small and elite audience, although some critics disagree, noting the dramatic and humorous elements that would seem to appeal to a broader audience, and arguing that seemingly esoteric allusions would in fact be familiar to the average Greek theater- or festival-goer. The *Hymns* were generally shorter compositions and, like Callimachus's other works, incorporated his considerable knowledge of his poetic predecessors while introducing innovative and sometimes parodic elements.

Scholars have had to reconstruct the matter of the other major works from fragments. The *Aitia,* which translates as "causes", seems to compile and—for Callimachus's contemporaries—update various myths and local legends that the author would have encountered in his extensive reading. The work consists of four books, collected in discrete poems, totalling about 7,000 lines of verse. The last poem, *The Lock of Berenice,* became famous in its own right, eventually being translated by the Roman poet Catullus and providing the ground-work for Alexander Pope's 1712 mock epic, *The Rape of the Lock.* The *Aitia* also gives evidence of Callimachus's involvement in debates on poetics, since his introduction doubles as an *Answer to the Telchines*—a rebuttal of his literary critics.

One of the debates in which Callimachus engaged concerned the conventions of epic poetry. Callimachus, opposing his student Apollonius, advocated marked changes in the genre, contending that new poems should be shorter than tradition demanded, and more simple and concise. His *Hecale,* estimated to have totalled about 1,000 lines, put into practice many of his ideas about epic. The poem tells a traditional tale—the story of Theseus's journey to fight the bull at Marathon. Along the way, the young hero encounters a storm that compels him to take refuge in the hut of an old woman named Hecale. Callimachus's rendition of this tale, while using a traditional basis, turned convention on its head by effectively putting Hecale rather than Theseus in the spotlight. The story she tells Theseus of her life—a fall from aristocracy to her present condition—occupies the lion's share of the poem. Furthermore, her death after Theseus's victory at Marathon marks the end of the poem, particularly since Theseus bestows on her a hero's funeral.

While the preceding poems have garnered the bulk of critical attention, fragments of many shorter works have allowed scholars to round out their impression of Callimachus's work as a whole. Thirteen iambi and various lyrics reinforce the image of Callimachus presented in the major works and supplement it with love poems and more satire. He is also acclaimed for the sixty-one epigrams that demonstrate his skill with this form.

Textual History

Although what is available from Callimachus's corpus appears to be only a fraction of the prolific writer's works, it still provides a substantial sample. Many of his works were transmitted through the centuries because they were so broadly admired: writers imitated, quoted, and translated his works for hundreds of years after his death. Consequently, the six *Hymns* remain fully intact, preserved by their transcription in medieval manuscripts. Scholars assume that the sixty-one epigrams, mostly collected in Byzantine anthologies, represent Callimachus's contribution to the genre. The *Aitia, Hecale, Iambi,* and various lyrics became available for contemporary readers only in the twentieth century, when fragments of the works came to light with the discovery of papyri manuscripts.

Critical Reception

Since his own age, Callimachus has been an object of critical debate. Typically, his admirers have applauded his innovative twists on convention, the polished concision of his style, and the breadth of his knowledge. His detractors have ranged from those who condemn his break with tradition—particularly because his poetry was too short and because it embraced mundane rather than elevated subject matter—to those who find his allusions too obscure. Callimachus's reputation grew with writers of following ages, who found much to admire and imitate in his innovations: the Romans Catullus, Propertius, and Ovid declared their debt and English poets of recent eras—including Alexander Pope, William Cory, and Lord Byron—have also attested to his influence.

Debate among twentieth-century scholars recreates, to some degree, that original critical divide, with some valuing Callimachus's originality and learnedness and others arguing that that learnedness made his work elitist. Moving beyond these stances, some critics have pursued historical analysis, investigating the influence of political environment and literary heritage on Callimachus's work. Historical studies of Callimachus's immediate circumstances typically stress his relationship to the Alexandrian court—especially his need to win continued patronage from the rulers Ptolemy II and Ptolemy III. Rudolf Pfeiffer's work, one of several studies that looks at the *Pinakes* as well as the poetry, has explored the breadth of Callimachus's learning. Combined, these approaches emphasize the interrelatedness of all aspects of the poet's life in the creation of his poetry.

PRINCIPAL WORKS

Aitia
Epigrams
Hecale
Hymns
Iambi
The Lock of Berenice
Pinakes

PRINCIPAL ENGLISH TRANSLATIONS

The Works of Callimachus (translated by H. W. Tytler) 1793

Poems of Callimachus (translated by Robert Furness) 1931

The Epigrams of Callimachus (translated by Gerard Mackworth Young) 1934

Hymns and Epigrams (translated by A. W. Mair) 1955

Aetia, Iambi, lyric poems, Hecale, minor epic and el-

egiac poems and other fragments by Callimachus (translated by C. A. Trypanis) 1975
Hymn to Zeus (translated by G. R. McLennan) 1977
Hymn to Apollo (translated by Frederick Williams) 1978
Hymn to Demeter (translated by N. Hopkinson) 1984
The Fifth Hymn [*Bath of Pallas*] (translated by A. W. Bulloch) 1985
Callimachus: hymns, epigrams, select fragments (translated by Stanley Lombardo and Diane Rayor) 1988
Hecale (translated by A. S. Hollis) 1990

CRITICISM

Alfred Körte (essay date 1929)

SOURCE: "The Elegy," "The Epic," and "The Epigram," in *Hellenistic Poetry*, translated by Jacob Hammer and Moses Hadas, Columbia University Press, 1929, pp. 94-150, 150-257, 350-406.

[*The following excerpt, drawn from his* Hellenistic Poetry, *presents Körte's summation of Callimachus as a writer of elegy, epic, and epigram. Examining Callimachus' work largely in the context of his biography and the social and political environment in Alexandria, Körte finds certain qualities constant in Callimachus across the genres. Körte emphasizes especially the poet's aptitude for originality and novelty, remarking that "precisely what was obscure, untouched and neglected had the greatest attraction for Callimachus." The excerpt also includes extended quotations in translation.*]

THE ELEGY

Callimachus is the most significant and the most fascinating personality among the Alexandrian poets. He therefore deserves a detailed treatment.

Of his life we know, unfortunately, very little. He was born not much before 330 in the old Graeco-African city, Cyrene, which belonged after 322, with short intermissions, to the empire of the Ptolemies. His father bore the same name as the mythical founder of the city, Battus. From Battus the poet claimed descent; he therefore belonged to the old nobility of Cyrene. His grandfather, also named Callimachus, had occupied an eminent position in his native community. So the poet himself, as an old man, tells us in an imaginary epitaph for his father:

> Whoever near this peaceful tomb art passing,
>   Stranger! see
> Callimachus's son and sire, Cyrene-born in
>   me.

> Both you may know. Her general, one led his
>   country's host,
> One sang what even Envy own'd superior. For
>   such boast
> There is no Nemesis: whom once the Muses
>   with kind eye
> Greet as their friend they ne'er discard when
>   hoary hairs are nigh.
>
> —R. G. MacGregor

In the ever recurring civil wars of Cyrene the family seems to have become impoverished. This appears from the fact that Callimachus, after a sojourn at Athens as student, lived for some time apparently in needy circumstances as a teacher of an elementary school in Eleusis, a suburb of Alexandria.

To this period, probably, we owe the majority of his charming epigrams, in which he occasionally complains of poverty, as, e.g., in the bitter lines:

> I know my hands are bare of gold;
>   For Heaven's sake, my dear,
> Chant not the too familiar tale
>   For ever in my ear.
>
> I'm sick at heart when all day long
>   I hear the bitter jest;
> Of all thy qualities, my love,
>   This is unloveliest.
>
> —Walter Leaf

But greater poetic works also belong to the period during which for a paltry remuneration he taught reading and writing to the children of the suburb. A recently found papyrus presents us with hardly intelligible scraps of an elegy celebrating the athletic victories won at the games by a certain Sosibius, son of Dioscorides, who played a part at the inauguration of the cult of Serapis. The poem must be dated before 280. Its noteworthy feature is that Callimachus dared to clothe such a poem in the form of an elegy; during the classical period, Pindar and Bacchylides composed epinician odes in the pretentious strophes of choral lyric. Callimachus' epinicion is intended not to be sung but to be recited; with the Alexandrians we find again and again verses intended for song replaced by verses intended for speech, since all their poetry was then meant to be recited. About 280 also was composed the first of the six extant hymns of Callimachus, namely the *Hymn to Zeus*. These hymns again, unlike the older cult-songs, were intended not for choral singing but for recitation; for this reason they were composed in epic hexameters, except the fifth hymn, which is written in elegiac distichs. That the *Hymn to Zeus* was not destined to be delivered at a festival in honor of the gods as a ceremonial act its opening lines immediately and clearly reveal:

At Jove's high festival, what song of praise
  Shall we his suppliant adorers sing?
To whom may we our pæans rather raise
  Than to himself, the great Eternal King?
  Who by his nod subdues each earth-born
    thing;
Whose mighty laws the gods themselves
    obey?
But whether Crete first saw the Father
    spring,
Or on Lycæus's mount he burst on day,
My soul is much in doubt, for both that praise
    essay.

Some say that thou, O Jove, first saw the
    morn
  On Cretan Ida's sacred mountain-side;
Others that thou in Arcady wert born:
  Declare, Almighty Father—which have lied?
  Cretans were liars ever: in their pride
Have they built up a sepulchre for thee;
  As if the King of Gods and men had died,
And borne the lot of frail mortality.
No! thou hast ever been, and art, and aye
    shalt be.

                —Fitzjames T. Price

Every Greek drinking bout commenced with a libation to Zeus. The poem is therefore intended for de-
livery at a symposium, and, indeed, for an educated
and intellectual circle, which would be in a position
to appreciate the combination of mythographical erudition, apparent naïveté and gentle irony. None of the
circle, of course, believed in the gods of the people.
Zeus, conceived in Stoic fashion as the embodiment
of a cosmic order, may have excited religious emotion; such a feeling is echoed in the third, fourth and
fifth verses. But an euhemeristic Zeus, who was born
and fought battles and whose tomb, even, is shown,
is for the educated purely a creation of poetic fancy,
in which people are interested only for the sake of
the older poets. Now, Hesiod represents Zeus as born
in Crete, and this was the prevailing tradition; when,
therefore, Callimachus declares that he harbors serious doubts concerning the god's birthplace and then
decides in favor of Arcadia, he both surprises and
charms his audience by such a turn. The decision is
wittily based on the declaration of a Cretan, the
mythical seer Epimenides, whose verse, "The Cretans
are always liars, evil beasts, idle bellies," is quoted
by the Apostle Paul in his Epistle to Titus; still more
facetious is the candor with which father Zeus himself is first asked to reveal which of the two parties
in question falsified. Then a confirmation of his immortality is granted to the god, whence it must needs
follow that the tomb of Zeus, shown by the Cretans,
is fraudulent. Thus one sees that the religious spirit is
utterly absent from this hymn; it is, to use Lessing's

expression, a product of wit but not of feeling.

The poets and their audiences were interested, to be
sure, in the naïveté of the myths current among the
people, but they hardly felt the devotion with which
our own romanticists steeped themselves in folk-be-
lief. Theirs was rather an aesthetic joy in the colorful
profusion of lively forms. No translation can render
the chief charm which the poem had for its audience,
namely the perfection of its metrical form. By a whole
series of carefully contrived rules, adopted more or
less by all contemporary poets, Callimachus bestowed
upon epic verse a refinement, suppleness and sonority
hitherto unknown. As compared with the Hellenistic
verses, Homer's efforts impress one as almost devoid
of art; judged by Alexandrian standards, the very first
verse of the *Iliad* contains no fewer than three mistakes!

But let us return to the **Hymn to Zeus**. The poet first
follows the established custom of hymns to gods in
relating Zeus's birth in Arcadia; he summons to his aid
a rich store of geographic names which, indeed, must
not be examined as to their correct application. He
then reports how the divine babe was conveyed to Crete
and was suckled on the hills of Ida by the she-goat
Amaltheia and how the Curetes drowned the infant's
cries with their noisy dances and thus protected him
from the snares of his father, Cronus. Now, in accordance with the prevailing usage, the deeds of the gods
should have followed, the tale of the downfall of his
father, Cronus, and of his allies, the Titans, the combat
with Typhon and the Giants. But of all this we hear
nothing. The poet continues:

Fair was the promise of thy childhood's
    prime,
  Almighty Jove! and fairly wert thou reared:
Swift was thy march to manhood: ere thy
    time
  Thy chin was covered by the manly beard;
  Though young in age, yet wert thou so
    revered
For deeds of prowess prematurely done,
  That of thy peers or elders none appeared
To claim his birthright;—heaven was all
    shine own,
Nor dared fell Envy point her arrows at thy
    throne.

Poets of old do sometimes lack of truth;
  For Saturn's ancient kingdom, as they tell,
Into three parts was split, as if forsooth
  There were a doubtful choice 'twixt Heaven
    and Hell
  To one not fairly mad;—we know right well
That lots are cast for more equality;
  But these against proportion so rebel
That naught can equal her discrepancy;

If one must lie at all—a lie like truth for me!

No chance gave thee the sovranty of heaven;
  But to the deeds thy good right hand had
  done,
And thine own strength and courage, was it
  given;
  These placed thee first, still keep thee on
  thy throne.

—Fitzjames T. Price

Why does the poet here suddenly and peremptorily brush aside Homer's story that Zeus, Poseidon and Hades, the three sons of Cronus, divided by lot heaven, sea and lower world? Why is the whole matter treated so broadly? Because the poet intends to proceed from the king of the gods to the earthly king, Ptolemy Philadelphus. Like Zeus, Ptolemy was not the eldest son of his father, and it is a fine compliment to the king that the older sons of Cronus recognized of their own accord the supremacy of the youngest brother—a free invention on the part of Callimachus. The suggestion is that the elder son of Ptolemy Soter should have acted similarly, something he had in fact failed to do. More and more clearly the poem points to the earthly king. Of mankind, only kings were the especial care of Zeus; lesser persons were assigned to minor divinities: the artisans to Hephaestus, the warriors to Ares, the hunters to Artemis, the singers to Phoebus. Under Zeus's guidance kings rule over nations; upon them he bestowed wealth and power—but not in equal measure upon all; upon Ptolemy in particular abundance. And now comes the surprising conclusion, which is related in form to the ancient hymns of the rhapsodes and clearly indicates what Callimachus and his colleagues needed:

Callimachus wrote one of his hymns to the god Zeus.

All hail, Almighty Jove! who givest to men
  All good, and wardest off each evil thing.
Oh, who can hymn thy praise? he hath not
  been,
  Nor shall he be, that poet who may sing
In fitting strain thy praises—Father, King,
All hail! thrice hail! we pray to thee, dispense
  Virtue and wealth to us, wealth varying—
For virtue's naught, mere virtue's no defense;
Then send us virtue hand in hand with
  competence.

—Fitzjames T. Price

The earthly counterpart of the king of heaven understood how to appreciate this poem, a masterpiece of its kind, better than modern classical scholars, who for centuries deemed this esthetic titbit unpalatable. Ptolemy commissioned Callimachus to catalogue the library and thereby gave him a distinguished and secure position.

About ten years later than the ***Hymn to Zeus*** is the song in commemoration of the death of Queen Arsinoë, sister and wife of Philadelphus (July, 270). Of this song we have remains in a Berlin papyrus. This poem shows a style quite different from that of the hymn. Even the meter is very peculiar. It consists of anapaestic verses with iambic endings, and a caesura observed as a rule after the third anapaest produces a certain passionately emotional effect. The language has a Doric coloring; short and almost abrupt sentences indicate the stormy agitation. There is no trace of the waggish and easy-going conversational tone, of the droll irony of the hymn; everything is serious and there is genuine pathos.

After a short invocation of the god, without whom the poet is unable to fulfill his task, he immediately plunges *in medias res*. The soul of the deified queen has already passed the moon and has ascended into the sphere of unchanging constellations, when a pitiful cry resounds: "Our queen is gone!" What follows is hopelessly mutilated, but then comes a magnificent scene. Philotera, a sister of Arsinoë, who died a maiden, and who was likewise deified, happens to be setting out from Henna in Sicily, where she dwelt in the retinue of Demeter, to Lemnos, the seat of Hephaestus and his spouse, Charis. Across the sea she espies the dusky clouds of the funeral pyre or of the sacrifices offered to the dead. Full of anxiety she beseeches Charis to take her stand on Athos, the highest mountain of the Thracian sea, and to discover what these volumes of smoke may mean. Charis soon reports that "the smoke comes from Libya, from thine own city; a great misfortune must have befallen. Indeed, it is not as if the lighthouse of Pharus (the mechanical wonder of the age) were wrapped in flames; but the entire folk weep and wail, they bewail the loss of thy sister. The cities of the land have arrayed them in mourning." Here the papyrus breaks off. This certainly is courtly poetry and courtly mourning. But the feeling is not a pretense, for the death of the exceptionally clever and energetic queen must have been felt as a serious misfortune, especially in the circle of Callimachus. Further, the elaborate apparatus of gods and goddesses, the mighty picture of the clouds of smoke which drift from Egypt over the Thracian sea, the lookout from the lofty watchtower of Athos are all features that are still fresh and not outworn. We have here true baroque style, the conscious exaggeration of all forms and all feelings into colossal and gigantic proportions—a tendency with which we have long been acquainted in the plastic art of this period. The effects of baroque art are, always, gradually blunted because one artist tries to outdo the other and in the course of time mighty means are employed for petty themes. But as long as baroque art is fresh, its effect is indisputably strong.

That Callimachus pursues in this poem a course so different from that of the **Hymn to Zeus** must not be interpreted as desertion of his artistic principles. The bold impetus of the baroque style and the ingenious conversational tone with its popular touches were alike new; they were alike remote from the beaten track of an aging classicism. It was such novelty that was our poet's chief concern. Nothing is so objectionable to him as the faded and outworn. This sentiment he expressed most clearly in an epigram which is hardly translatable:

> I detest the cyclic poem, I delight not in the
> way
> That carries hither, thither all the traffic of the
> day;
> I loathe a hackneyed beauty, and never will I
> drink
> At the public drinking-fount; from all banality
> I shrink.
>
>   —Walter Leaf

To a somewhat earlier date appears to belong the most voluminous accomplishment of the poet, on which his renown with posterity chiefly rests—the four books of

Aitia (Origins). In this work, also composed in elegiac distichs, he treats the origins of all possible festivals, games, ceremonial usages, customs, also the foundations of cities and sanctuaries. It was a selected array of legends and myths, for the most part very remote, which the poet made with great erudition and then presented in an attractive poetical form. The subject matter belonged in great measure to the province which we nowadays call folklore; precisely what was obscure, untouched and neglected had the greatest attraction for Callimachus.

Famous in antiquity was the prooemium, which the Roman poets Ennius and Propertius imitated. In a dream the poet envisions himself translated to Helicon, Hesiod's mount of the Muses; the Muses give him a draught from the spring Hippocrene and prescribe his theme. In the extant epilogue to the entire poem he makes Zeus grant him definite assurance that he had successfully followed in the path of Hesiod. This relationship with Hesiod, twice referred to by Callimachus, is surprising; Hesiod is an epic poet, while in the *Aitia* we have elegiac verse. It is plainly seen that the verse form is of little consequence to the Alexandrian; he can narrate an epic theme even in elegiac distichs, just as he employed in the majority of his hymns the hexameter and only once the distich. His selection of Hesiod, not of Homer, for his godfather, so to speak, is to be explained, first, by the fact that Callimachus' choice of theme causes the lack of an unified action; and, secondly, by the oft expressed preference of the Hellenists for the Boeotian poet: his contact with nature and his more prominent personality were especially congenial to them.

For the clear conception which we are able to form at present of Callimachus' narrative manner in the *Aitia* we are again indebted to a series of newly discovered papyri. Of these, two from Oxyrhynchus make the greatest contribution. One papyrus sheet stood apparently at the beginning of a book and neatly shows how the poet, in an easy conversational tone, introduces his theme to the reader. As we know from another source, he spoke of a wealthy merchant, Pollis, an Athenian who settled in Alexandria and who even on the banks of the Nile celebrated Athenian festivals:

> Nor did the morn of the Broaching of the Jars pass unheeded, nor that whereon the Pitchers of Orestes bring a white day for slaves. And when he kept the yearly festival of Icarius' child, thy day, Erigone, lady most sorrowful for Attic women, he invited to a banquet his familiars, and among them a stranger who was newly visiting Egypt, whither he had come on some private business. An Ician he was by birth, and I shared one couch with him—not by appointment, but not false is the saw of Homer that God ever brings like to like; for he, too, abhorred the wide-mouthed Thracian draught of wine and liked a little cup. To him I said, as the beaker was

going round for the third time, when I had learnt
his name and lineage: "Verily this is a true saying,
that wine wants not only its portion of water but
also its portion of talk. So—for talk is not handed
round in ladles, nor shalt thou have to ask for it,
looking to the haughty brows of the cup-bearers, on
a day when the free man fawns upon the slave—let
us, Theogenes, put talk in the cup to mend the
tedious draught; and what my heart yearns to hear
from thee, do thou tell me in answer to my question.
Wherefore is it the tradition of thy country to
worship Peleus, king of the Myrmidons? What has
Thessaly to do with Icos? And why with a leek and
. . . loaf does a girl . . . at the procession in honour
of the hero?"

—A. W. Mair

A few similarly mutilated questions follow. Then the
deep sigh with which the Ician begins his reply is still
distinguishable:

"Thrice blessed, verily thou art happy as few are, if
thou hast a life that is ignorant of sea-faring. But
my life is more at home among the waves than is
the sea-gull."

—A. W. Mair

Here we have an altogether realistic scene from the
personal life of the poet. For the knowledge of the
cults and ritual usages of the small island Icos which
he intends to relate he is not indebted to divine inspiration; he had the cults recounted to him at a banquet,
by a merchant of Icos. This banquet, which is surely
imaginary, is described with easy-going garrulity and
gives the poet an opportunity to insert a few highly
erudite remarks about Attic festivals, which, for a
modern reader at least, call for commentary.

The first two days of the oldest Attic Dionysus festival, the Anthesteria, were called Pithoigia or the
Broaching of Jars, and Choes, Pitchers or Jugs; on
these two days the slaves were permitted to carouse
and feast with the free men. The aetiological legend
connected Orestes with the establishment of the Feast
of Pitchers. The Attic king Demophon was supposed
to have received Orestes hospitably, although he was
still polluted by matricide, and, in order to protect his
citizens from pollution, to have ordered, in addition to
the closing of the sanctuaries, a pitcher of wine to be
set before every Athenian. The next-mentioned festival, that of Erigone, is the Aiora, the Swing Festival.
According to the legendary form followed here, Erigone is the daughter of Icarius. To him Dionysus had
given the vine, but Icarius was killed by intoxicated
peasants to whom he had offered the first wine. After
a long search, his daughter found his body and hanged
herself on the tree under which the body lay. Dying
she utters a curse, praying that the daughters of the
Athenians shall suffer a similar death, and a suicide
epidemic breaks out among the Athenian maidens.

Thence she receives the appellation, "lady most sorrowful for Attic women." By order of the Delphic god,
the Athenians atone for their offense by the introduction of the Swing Festival: on ropes fastened to trees
the Athenian maidens swing to and fro in imitation of
the corpse of Erigone stirred by the wind, and they
accompany their swinging with the chant of a ritual
song.

A similar transition to leisurely narrative from terse
allusion intelligible only to scholars is found also in
the longest papyrus fragment of the *Aitia*, which begins in the midst of the story of Acontius and Cydippe.
It is a happy chance that from Ovid's *Heroides* and
from the letter of the late, affected epistle-writer Aris-
taenetus the story of Acontius' love for Cydippe and
the saga of the race of the Acontiadae, a distinguished
family of Ceos, were already more fully known to us
than is any other part of the *Aitia*. The handsome youth
Acontius catches sight in the temple of Delian Artemis
of the charming Naxian maiden Cydippe and falls madly
in love with her. In order to win the maiden of another
race he contrives a peculiar expedient: he scratches on
a beautiful "Cydonian apple" (i.e., the quince) the
words: "I swear by Artemis to marry Acontius." This
fruit he let fall in the maiden's path; she took it up and
in amazement read the inscribed words. Unsuspecting-
ly she uttered aloud, "I swear by Artemis to marry
Acontius," and thus unwittingly and unintentionally
bound herself by this oath in the sanctuary of the goddess. She returns to Naxos and conceals the event from
her parents. Soon afterwards her father decides to give
her in marriage to a Naxian youth; the wedding is
being prepared, but on the day of the ceremony the
bride falls ill. After her recovery the date for the wedding is set for the second time, but again the maiden
is seized by an obstinate fever; the same thing is repeated for the third time. The alarmed father goes to
consult the Delphic Apollo, who reveals to him that
his daughter is bound by the oath uttered in the sanctuary of Artemis and may marry none other than Acontius of Ceos. Now Acontius is fetched to Naxos; the
two lovers celebrate their wedding and become pro-
genitors of a flourishing Cean family. I have set the
whole narrative forth in advance because it is quite
difficult to follow the thread of this simple tale as
related in the account of Callimachus. The extant portion begins with the preparation for the first wedding,
namely with the mention of the very strange Naxian
nuptial custom, the origin of which is only hinted at:

And already the maid had been bedded with the
boy, even as ritual ordered that the bride should
sleep her prenuptial sleep with a male child both
whose parents were alive. Yea, for they say that
once on a time Hera—thou dog, thou dog, refrain,
my shameless soul! thou wouldst sing of that which
is not lawful to tell. It is a good thing for thee that
thou hast not seen the rites of the dread goddess:
else wouldst thou have uttered their story too. Surely

much knowledge is a grievous thing for him who controls not his tongue: verily this is a child with a knife.

In the morning the oxen were to tear their hearts in the water, seeing before them the keen blade. But in the afternoon an evil paleness seized her: seized her the disease which we banish to the goats of the wild and which we falsely call the holy disease. And then that ill sickness wasted the girl even to the gates of death. A second time the couches were spread: a second time the maid was sick for seven months with a quartan fever. A third time they bethought them again of marriage: a third time a deadly chill settled on Cydippe. A fourth time her father abode it no more but set off to Delphian Phoebus, who in the night spake and said. "A grievous oath by Artemis thwarts thy child's marriage. For my sister was not vexing Lygdamis, neither in Amyclae's shrine was she weaving rushes, nor in the river Parthenius was she washing her stains after the hunt: nay, she was at home in Delos when thy child sware that she would have Acontius, none other, for her bridegroom. But if thou wilt take me for thy adviser, thou wilt fulfil all the oath of thy daughter even as she announced. For I say that Acontius shall be no mingling of lead with silver, but of electrum with shining gold. Thou, the father of the bride, art sprung from Codrus: the Cean bridegroom springs from the priests of Zeus Aristaeus the Lord of Moisture: priests whose business it is upon the mountain-tops to assuage stern Maera when she rises and to entreat from Zeus the wind whereby many a quail is entangled in the linen mesh." So spake the god. And her father went back to Naxos and questioned the maiden herself; and she revealed to him the whole matter. And she was well again. For the rest, Acontius, it will be her business to go with thee to her own Dionysias.

So faith was kept with the goddess, and her fellows straightway sang their comrade's marriage hymn, deferred no longer. Then I deem, Acontius, that for that night, wherein thou didst touch her maiden girdle, thou wouldst not have accepted either the ankle of Iphicles who ran upon the corn-ears nor the possession of Midas of Celaenae. And my verdict would be attested by all who are not ignorant of the stern god. And from that marriage a great name was destined to arise. For, O Cean, your clan, the Acontiadae, still dwell, numerous and honoured, at Iulis. And this thy passion we heard from old Xenomedes, who once enshrined all the island in a mythological history. . . .

—A. W. Mair

Here I break off. The story of Acontius and Cydippe comes to an end. But the mention of Xenomedes, a local historian of Ceos of about the Periclean age, affords the poet opportunity to give, in the space of twenty-two lines, a bird's-eye view of the whole earlier history of the island of Ceos, until the establishment of its four cities, just as Xenomedes had com-

posed it. This appended catalogue, which of course is inserted only to enumerate other Cean *Aitia,* namely the foundation of certain cities, is without poetic charm, and hardly suitable for translation into modern verse if only because of the perplexing abundance of proper names; I count about thirty in these few lines. But what a mass of erudite material is forced into the story of Acontius and Cydippe! We have at the very beginning a mention of the peculiar Naxian custom that the bride must spend her prenuptial night with a boy both of whose parents are alive, and who is therefore especially suitable for ritual purposes. It is not a question of that prenuptial intercourse which Immermann describes in his *Oberhof* as a rustic custom; for the boy is not the bridegroom, but perhaps the human representative of a god to whom, at some early period, the right to the virginity of all maidens of the island was conceded. Such symbolic nuptials with a divinity are not unusual elsewhere in Greek religion; each year at Athens during the Anthesteria, the "king's wife," the Basilinna, was married to Dionysus. The aetiological legend to which Callimachus barely alludes is of much later origin than this ritual custom, which, certainly, is very ancient. We know it from the Homeric scholia, and it has left a trace in the *Iliad* itself: Zeus and Hera were united before the celebration of their sacred marriage.

But this is not the only piece of folklore with which the poet regales us. In passing he touches upon a custom of transferring to wild goats the so-called holy disease, i.e., epilepsy, just as Christ banished the spirits of those possessed into Gadarene swine. Again, the prophecy of Apollo affords the poet the opportunity of elucidating the origin of the name Parthenius as "virgin-river"; it bears this name because the maiden goddess Artemis is wont to bathe in its stream after the hunt. The lineage of Acontius is traced to a peculiar cult of Zeus Aristaeus of Ceos, whose priests were obliged to obtain by entreaty the blowing of the Etesian winds in midsummer on the appearance of the Dog Star, to assuage the heat of the dog days, and again in the early spring to pray for the favorable north wind which drives swarms of birds of passage into the nets of the island Greeks. This last feature is especially characteristic of the life of the inhabitants of the Cyclades, and I should not be surprised if even today some saint, instead of Zeus, is asked for favorable weather for quail catching. The very description of Acontius' fortune in love is also embellished with an erudite flourish. That the youth would not have exchanged the possession of his beloved for the gold of Phrygian Midas seems to us so commonplace a figure that one is almost surprised to find it in this connection. But it was only through the Hellenistic poets and particularly Ovid that the story of Midas became so familiar. Even stranger is the other boon for which Acontius would be unwilling to exchange his bride, namely, the swiftness of foot of Iphicles. Hesiod had told of him who, vying with the winds, ran so swiftly over a grainfield that the ears did not bend under his steps. Only the immense importance which the Greeks attached to all accomplishments relating to sport made it comprehensible that such athletic ability could possibly be mentioned as the equivalent of a bride.

In spite of all its erudition, Callimachus' narrative is by no means dry. Everything he relates presents vivid pictures. The sacrificial oxen doomed to death, which on the festal morning spent the force of their rage in the sea, the suffering maiden, the goddess Artemis weaving rushes on the banks of the Eurotas and washing away the dust of the hunt in the river Parthenius, the priests on the rocky shore with their prayer for help in quail catching, the maidens singing at the marriage ceremony and the bridegroom beaming with happiness we see, every one, clearly, before us. The language too is quite simple and strives for the popular tone by means of such proverbial expressions as "knives are not befitting boys" or "no mingling of lead with silver." In giving the oracle of Apollo the poet succeeded best in reproducing the tone of fable, which makes the great of earth and heaven speak the language of common folk. In his outspoken simplicity this Olympian matchmaker anticipates Tieck's fairy kings. But in fact this popular simplicity is as little sustained by Callimachus as by our own older romanticists, and doubtless he did not aspire to uniformity of tone any more than they aspired to it. When the poet immediately before a climax of his story sets about giving an explanation of a peculiar ritual custom and then suddenly leaves this explanation to moralize at length on the dangers of garrulity, or when he appends the dry statement that he read all this in Xenomedes to the bright conclusion of the tale, we have conscious violations of atmosphere such as Tieck was so fond of, and which Friedrich Schlegel emphatically praises as an artistic expedient. Callimachus carries this peculiarity furthest in a small Berlin papyrus fragment of the *Aitia*, in which he coolly advises the reader to imagine for himself the further action and thus to reduce the length of the poem. Never to be tedious, never to be commonplace, always to charm and to surprise were obviously the guiding principles to which the poet adhered in the course of composition of his long work. The endless store of scholarly material is articulated and dovetailed with the highest art. The mood is now a leisurely andante, now a headlong presto; at one time the tone has the simplicity of a fairy tale, at another it is ingeniously pointed, and always the clever and smiling face of the poet peeps through the richly variegated array of his characters. In regard both to art of composition and to narrative, Ovid's *Metamorphoses,* alone of ancient works, can be put side by side with the *Aitia*. In the *Metamorphoses,* however, Ovid's personality is by no means as prominent as is that of Callimachus in the *Aitia*. Of modern poems, as von Wilamowitz has rightly observed, Byron's *Don Juan*

shows the closest resemblance.

With the *Aitia* Callimachus intended to terminate his poetic career; to this he gave clear expression at the end of the work. After Zeus has endorsed the Hesiodic character of his work, as we have said, and the god takes leave of him with the friendly wish that he may fare better in life than did the Boeotian poet, Callimachus subjoins these lines:

> . . . Hail, greatly hail to thee also, O Zeus! do thou save all the house of our kings! and I will visit the haunt of the Muses on foot.
>
> —A. W. Mair

To understand the last line, we must remember that, both in Greek and in Latin, 'pedestrian language' can signify only prose; and the learned work in the library, to which the poet intended to devote himself entirely, was as much in the service of the Muses as was his poetry.

> **[A]lways the clever and smiling face of the poet peeps through the richly variegated array of his characters**
> **—Alfred Körte**

Callimachus, however, did not live up strictly to the resolution which he had made. It is true that some of his poems, which I have as yet not taken into consideration, e.g., his epyllion *Hecale* . . . and the hymn *The Bath of Pallas*, belong to the period before the conclusion of the *Aitia;* other poems, however, are with probability or even with certainty to be put later.

Among these the book of *Iambi* is very peculiar. The same Oxyrhynchus papyrus which gave us the *Cydippe* contains more than two hundred and fifty verses of the *Iambi* which, unfortunately, are in many places hopelessly mutilated. Their form is the so-called halting iambic (scazon), a trimeter the last foot of which is inverted, i.e., a trimeter ending in ∪--∪ instead of in ∪ -∪-. This inversion gives the verse a lame, even vulgar effect. Hipponax of Ephesus had introduced this meter into poetry in the sixth century, and it was well suited for his vulgarly realistic, abusive and beggarly poetry. Because he was as unlike as possible an Attic youth such as we find on the Parthenon frieze, this uncouth proletarian aroused great interest among the Alexandrians, and Callimachus adopted not only his meter, which, in fact, he manages more artistically and vigorously than the Ephesian had managed it, but also the Ionic popular dialect. This is not the language which was spoken in the streets of Miletus and Ephesus in the time of Callimachus, but, as we learn from Ionic inscriptions, a dialect which for a long time had been obsolete, a language therefore which the Dorian Callimachus learned out of books. This is not so surprising as may appear to us today, for Greek poetry since Homer had almost always made use of a literary language which was never actually spoken anywhere. The Cyrenean had also to learn the language of his elegies and hymns; though in the fifth and the sixth hymn he gives a Doric tone to the epic dialect, the Doric element is, after all, but a varnish laid over the epic. At the opening of the *Iambi* he introduces as speaker Hipponax, who comes from Hades, "where they sell an ox for a penny," to tell a story. How far Hipponax is retained as a narrator cannot be exactly determined; he is not retained throughout the whole book, for in a later passage we hear, "This is the tale of Aesop of Sardis, whom, when he sang his story, the Delphians received in no kindly wise." The book has no unity, and one story or tale is quite loosely linked with another. After the story of the golden cup of Bathycles, which was passed from one to another of the Seven Sages because none of them was willing to consider himself the wisest, the tale of the quarrel of the Laurel and the Olive is humorously narrated. It is in good preservation. First the haughty laurel speaks and disdainfully looks down upon the "foolish olive." It boasts of the beauty of its foliage and, above all, of its position in religious worship. Laurel branches decorate every doorpost; every seer and every priest wears them; the Pythia is surrounded with laurel branches; Branchus cleansed the plague-stricken Ionians with laurel and abracadabra. Laurel is used at festive banquets and by the choruses of Apollo, nay, the laurel is made the prize of victory at the Pythian games and is fetched from the Vale of Tempe for this express purpose. The laurel is pure and therefore has naught to do with mourning; the olive, on the other hand, is spread beneath corpses. But the olive is not easily intimidated by the laurel's boast. That which the laurel cites as a reproach, its use in the service of the dead, constitutes the olive's chief pride. The olive accompanies those gloriously slain in battle, as well as aged women and men on their last journey, and is more desirable for them than is the laurel for those who fetch it from Tempe. Even in the games the olive is more highly esteemed than the laurel, for the former is the prize at Olympian games, the latter only at Delphi—the very birds in the trees have long been twittering of this. Who brought forth the laurel? Earth, sun and rain, just as they created other plants; the olive was created by Athena when she contended with Poseidon. The fact that both are pleasing to the gods the olive does not wish to dispute. But now she plays her trump. The fruits of the laurel are useless, while the fruits of the olive yield a highly esteemed food and furnish delicious oil. Further, suppliants carry olive branches, and the Delians preserve most carefully the olive's stump. The olive remains triumphant!

Even during the olive's speech the birds in the branches were so boisterous that the olive had impatiently to bid them keep silence. The laurel is furious and wants to boast anew; but a bramble bush intercedes and, assuming an air of equality with the nobler trees, urges peace. But this intervention was ill received by the haughty laurel: "Art thou one of us?" says she, and is all the more eager to quarrel.

At this point, the continuity is broken. We have here a genuine example of Ionian story telling—a merry tale with a didactic touch, such as was told in the market places and palaces of Ionia as far back as the seventh century, and such as may be heard even today in Anatolian bazaars.

It is therefore very remarkable that on the two following, hopelessly mutilated sheets, the poet suddenly turns to questions of poetic technique, mixture of dialects, use of certain meters and limitation to certain classes of poetry—apparently, throughout, in an irate tone. Thus even in the innocent Ionic tales the personality of the poet obtrudes, by way of expressions that have to do with his literary quarrels.

The third and fourth hymns, those to Artemis and to Delos, will be touched upon only briefly; both are rich in original invention and both often treat the gods with as little respect as did the Old Attic Comedy. The opening scene of **the Artemis hymn** is delightful. The little divine babe sits in the lap of her father, Zeus, and begs him, with a mixture of naivete and precociousness, to grant her all the gifts which she will later need as an adult goddess:

> "O grant me, father," thus the goddess said,
> "To reign a virgin, an unspotted maid.
> To me let temples rise and altars smoke,
> And men by many names my aid invoke;
> Proud Phœbus else might with thy daughter
>   vie,
> And look on Dian with disdainful eye.
> To bend the bow and aim the dart be mine,
> I ask no thunder nor thy bolts divine;
> At your desire the Cyclops will bestow
> My pointed shafts and string my little bow.
> Let silver light my virgin steps attend,
> When to the chase with flying feet I bend,
> Above the knee be my white garments roll'd
> In plaited folds, and fring'd around with gold.
> Let Ocean give me sixty little maids
> To join the dance amid surrounding shades;
> Let twenty more from fair Amnisius come,
> All nine years old, and yet in infant-bloom,
> To bear my buskins, and my dogs to feed,
> When fawns in safety frisk along the mead,
> Nor yet the spotted lynx is doom'd to bleed.
> Be mine the mountains and each rural bower,
> And give one city for thy daughter's dower;
> On mountain-tops shall my bright arrows
>   shine,

And with the mortal race I'll only join,
When matrons torn by agonizing throes
Invoke Lucina to relieve their woes;
For at my birth the attendant Fates assign'd
This task to me, in mercy to mankind,
Since fair Latona gave me to thy love,
And felt no pangs when blest by favouring
  Jove."

  She spoke, and stretch'd her hands with
  infant-art,
To stroke his beard, and gain her father's
  heart;
But oft she rais'd her little arms in vain.
At length with smiles he thus reliev'd her
  pain.
  "Fair daughter, lov'd beyond th' immortal
  race,
If such as you spring from a stol'n embrace,
Let furious Juno burn with jealous ire,
Be mine the care to grant your full desire,
And greater gifts beside . . ."

                              —H. W. Tytler

In this graceful nursery scene the request of the little maid for eternal maidenhood and for sixty daughters of Oceanus, who should be unmarried though already nine years of age, approaches travesty very closely. Father Zeus resembles the Raphaelite portrait in which he is represented as pinching the cheek of Ganymede. The poet almost oversteps the bounds of good taste in describing the wild Cyclops smiths, of whom all divine children are in dread: when they are naughty, their mothers quickly call for Arges and Steropes; in the place of these, Hermes blackened with soot comes out from his corner and the divine children cry and hide their heads in their mothers' robes. And yet the charm of this hymn rests entirely on the genre scenes, freely invented, and not on the scholarly catalogue of all the mountains, islands and cities where the Artemis cult flourished, which forms the conclusion of the poem.

In the ***Hymn to Delos***, Callimachus enters into a dangerous competition with the first Homeric Hymn; but his poem contains such a rich flood of new ideas that, so far as his contemporaries were concerned, he no doubt forced the older poem into the background.

Among other things, the Celtic invasions and their menace to the Delphic sanctuary in 279 are effectively depicted in this poem. The poet knew these dangerous barbarians from personal observation. Ptolemy had procured a detached band of Celts to serve him as mercenaries and, finding that they proved insubordinate, he had them destroyed by fire on a small island in the Sebennytic mouth of the Nile. Callimachus describes "the Titans of a later day" and their strange weapons with a mixture of horror and admiration, just as do the Pergamene sculptors in their masterly statues of the Celts. It was on account of this Celtic adventure

in Egypt that Callimachus admitted the Celts into his poem. To be able to do so, he resorts to a rococo contrivance: while the pregnant Leto seeks in vain for a place to bear her divine progeny—out of fear of the anger of jealous Juno all countries, cities and islands refuse to receive her—Apollo, yet unborn, utters from his mother's womb quite a long prophecy; he does not want to be born in Cos, because another god is destined to be born there in the future (King Ptolemy Philadelphus), with whom, in days to come, he will make common cause against the Celts, he himself at Delphi, Ptolemy on the Nile. For this reason Leto is bidden to go to the floating island of Delos and to give birth to him there! And this is not the first but the second prophecy of the unborn; he had already threatened Thebes, where in days to come he was to inflict destruction upon the offspring of Niobe.

Some twenty years after the completion of the ***Aitia***, Callimachus composed the second hymn, that to Apollo, his only hymn with a political background.

Already Ptolemy I had appointed his stepson Magas viceroy of Cyrene. Magas later (about 274) rebelled against his stepbrother, Ptolemy Philadelphus, invaded Egypt, and achieved full independence, although the formal suzerainty of Ptolemy was preserved. To secure the restoration of Cyrene, at least after Magas' death, Philadelphus betrothed his son and heir apparent, the later Euergetes, to Magas' only daughter, Berenice. But when Magas died (about 250), his widow, Apame, a daughter of the Syrian king Antiochus, wished to dissolve the arrangement; she offered the hand of Berenice and with it the throne of Cyrene to a Macedonian prince, the young and handsome Demetrius. He promptly came to Cyrene and assumed the kingship; he appeared even more desirable to his mother-in-law, however, than to his bride. The very youthful princess became the head of a court conspiracy; Demetrius was slain in the bedroom of the dowager queen; the latter, however, was spared. Thereupon Berenice consummated her marriage to the Egyptian heir apparent, Euergetes, and shortly thereafter (246) ascended the throne of Egypt. Callimachus' ***Hymn to Apollo*** belongs, therefore, to the period between Magas' death and Berenice's marriage with Euergetes. The poet relates in detail the colonization of the country and the foundation of the city of Cyrene by the Greeks, and states emphatically that Apollo, the protector of the Greek colony, had solemnly promised to give it to "our kings," and Apollo is wont always to keep his promise. The hymn is, therefore, at the same time a poetic manifesto against the threatened defection of Cyrene from the empire of the Ptolemies. The personality of the poet stands out in incomparably bolder relief in the ***Hymn to Apollo*** than in the older hymns; in this respect a resemblance to the choral odes of Pindar is noticeable. In the ***Bath of Pallas*** Callimachus had already attempted to make his audience share in the emotions of those participating fully in a lengthy ritual, and in the present poem he resumes this manner of representation. At the beginning of the hymn we stand with the poet amid the crowd of worshipers in front of the temple and experience the expectant awe which precedes the appearance of the god. I quote the first few lines:

> What force, what sudden impulse, thus can
> make
> The laurel-branch, and all the temple shake!
> Depart, ye souls profane; hence, hence! O fly
> Far from this holy place! Apollo's nigh;
> He knocks with gentle foot; the Delian palm
> Submissive bends, and breathes a sweeter
> balm:
> Soft swans, high hovering, catch th'
> auspicious sign,
> Wave their white wings, and pour their notes
> divine.
> Ye bolts, fly back; ye brazen doors, expand,
> Leap from your hinges, Phœbus is at hand.
> Begin, young men, begin the sacred song,
> Wake all your lyres, and to the dances
> throng . . .
>
> —H. W. Tytler

But the epiphany of the god which we are led by the thrilling proclamation to expect does not take place. In the following verses, which render praise to the god, we sometimes think that the chorus is singing, but then again the poet bids the ritual cry to be uttered and speaks of the chorus in the third person. From the glorification of Apollo's varied manifestations of power uninterrupted by any interposition of genre-like or even parodic features there gradually develops the story of Cyrene's foundation under Apollo's guidance. And here again verses are found which could only have been spoken by the poet, not by the chorus:

> To tuneful Phœbus, sacred god of song,
> In various nations, various names belong;
> Some Boëdromius, Clarius some implore,
> But nam'd Carneüs on my native shore.
>
> —H. W. Tytler

The Dorian god, Apollo Carneius, is the true racial god for the Cyrenean Callimachus, but not for the Alexandrian chorus. What is more, the poet does not want us to distinguish sharply his own utterances from those of the chorus; he would have us feel with him the mood of Apollo's festival. This mood is genuine, even if its true source be love of his native country rather than faith in the gods. The slaying of the Pythian dragon, which in other ceremonial songs in honor of Apollo forms the central theme, constitutes in this affectionate account of Cyrene an incidental appendix, as it were; the conclusion, however, shows a surprisingly personal touch:

> An equal foe, pale Envy, late drew near,
> And thus suggested in Apollo's ear:
> "I hate the bard who pours not forth his song
> In swelling numbers, loud, sublime, and
> strong;
> No lofty lay should in low murmurs glide,
> But wild as waves, and sounding as the tide."
> Fierce with his foot indignant Phœbus spurn'd
> Th' invidious monster, and in wrath return'd.
> Wide rolls Euphrates' wave, but soil'd with
> mud,
> And dust and slime pollute the swelling flood:
> For Ceres still the fair Melissae bring
> The purest water from the smallest spring,
> That softly murmuring creeps along the plain,
> And falls with gentle cadence to the main.
> Propitious Phœbus! thus thy power extend,
> And soon shall Envy to the shades descend.
>
> —H. W. Tytler

Here we are suddenly thrust out of the religious mood and thrown into the midst of the battle waged by Alexandrian poets over the justification for the existence in their age of the heroic epic. Already in antiquity it had been recognized that these lines are a rough rejoinder to the reproach uttered in the circle of Apollonius of Rhodes, that Callimachus rejected heroic epos only because he himself lacked power to create one. The fact that Callimachus adds this strange appendage to the hitherto harmonious unity of the *Hymn to Apollo* shows clearly enough that this disruption of harmony affords him conscious pleasure, quite in the spirit of Friedrich Schlegel. The quarrel with Apollonius was probably the cause of a smaller, apparently far from pleasing poem, the *Ibis*. With reference to Callimachus, Ovid composed an elegiac poem of six hundred and forty-four verses under the same name, in which he curses an unnamed enemy, quoting a large number of purposely veiled stories of divine punishments and misfortunes. Ovid's *Ibis* is not, as was formerly believed, a free adaptation of Callimachus' poem. Of the latter we know only that it was substantially shorter, but similar to Ovid's in construction; not even the meter is certain. I maintain that Callimachus' poem bears a relationship to Apollonius Rhodius, in spite of recent doubts on the subject. I mention this work, although for us it is only a phantom, because of the considerable influence it exerted upon later poets. . . .

The **sixth hymn**, to Demeter, is closely related to the *Hymn to Apollo* in mood, style of narrative, and verse technique; the two hymns cannot be far apart in time of composition. I give a short introduction. Again we witness a great ritual celebration, the Procession of the Sacred Basket of Demeter, in Alexandria. We are among women standing along the street, who, excited and exhausted by fasting, eagerly await the approach of the procession and the appearance of the evening star which is to put an end to their fast. To shorten the hours of waiting, the women chat about the sufferings and might of the goddess. From this conversation there develops the long burlesque, yet gruesome, legend of Erysichthon, who was punished with a voracious and unquenchable appetite—a legend which occupies the larger part of the hymn. This gruesome example of the great goddess's power is related quite in the popular tone. To be sure, the waggish poet applies his colors so generously that what seemed ghastly to the pious appeared facetious to his readers; the worst part, the death by starvation, he suppresses. But this legend is kept within the frame of the ceremonial rite; the procession draws near and the women join it. The poet himself withdraws to the background and the final prayer is also in perfect accord with the harmony of the whole.

> The basket swift-descending from the skies,
> Thus, thus, ye matrons, let your voices rise:
> "Hail! Ceres, hail! by thee, from fertile ground
> Swift springs the corn, and plenty flows
>   around."
> Ye crowds, yet uninstructed, stand aloof,
> Nor view the pageant from the lofty roof,
> But on the ground below; nor matrons fair,
> Nor youth, nor virgins, with dishevell'd hair,
> Dares here approach: nor let the moisture flow
> From fasting mouths to stain the mystic show.
> But radiant Hesper from the starry skies
> Beholds the sacred basket as it flies:
> Bright Hesper only could persuade the power
> To quench her thirst, in that unhappy hour,
> When full of grief she roam'd from place to
>   place,
> Her ravish'd daughter's latent steps to trace.
> How could thy tender feet, O goddess, bear
> The painful journey to the western sphere?
> How couldst thou tread black Æthiop's
>   burning climes,
> Or that fair soil, in these distressful times,
> Where, on the tree, the golden apple beams,
> Nor eat, nor drink, nor bathe in cooling
>   streams?
>   Thrice Achelous' flood her steps divide,
> And every stream that rolls a ceaseless tide.
> Three times she press'd the centre of that isle,
> Where Enna's flowery fields with beauty
>   smile.
> Three times, by dark Callichorus, she sat,
> And call'd the yawning gulf to mourn her
>   fate:
> There, faint with hunger, laid her wearied
>   limbs,
> Nor eat, nor drank, nor bath'd in cooling
>   streams.
>   But cease, my Muse, in these unhallow'd
>   strains,
> To sing of Ceres' woes, and Ceres' pains;
> Far nobler to resound her sacred laws,

> That bless'd mankind, and gain'd their loud
>   applause.
> Far nobler to declare how first she bound
> The sacred sheaves, and cut the corn around,
> How first the grain beneath the steer she laid,
> And taught Triptolemus the rural trade.
> Far nobler theme (that all his crime may shun)
> To paint the woes of Triopas' proud son;
> How meagre famine o'er his visage spread,
> When her fierce vengeance on his vitals fed.
>   Not yet to Cnidia the Pelasgi came,
> But rais'd at Dotium to bright Ceres' name
> A sacred wood, whose branches interwove
> So thick, an arrow scarce could pierce the
>   grove.
> Here pines and elms luxuriant summits rear;
> Here shone bright apples, there the verdant
>   pear:
> A crystal fountain pour'd his streams around,
> And fed the trees, and water'd all the ground.
> With wonder Ceres saw the rising wood,
> The spreading branches, and the silver flood,
> Which, more than green Triopium, gain'd her
>   love,
> Than fair Eleusis, or bright Enna's grove.
> But when, incens'd, his better genius fled
> From Erysichthon, rash designs invade
> His impious breast: he rush'd along the plain
> With twenty strong attendants in his train,
> Of more than mortal size, and such their
>   power,
> As could with ease o'erturn the strongest
>   tower.
> With saws and axes arm'd they madly stood,
> And forc'd a passage through the sacred
>   flood.
> A mighty poplar rais'd his head on high
> Far o'er the rest, and seem'd to touch the sky
> (The nymphs at mid-day sported in the shade).
> Here first they struck: on earth the tree was
>   laid,
> And told the rest her fate in doleful moans;
> Indignant Ceres heard the poplar's groans,
> And thus with anger spoke: "What impious
>   hand
> Has cut my trees, and my bright grove
>   profan'd?"
> She said, and instant, like Nicippa, rose,
> Her well-known priestess, whom the city
>   chose;
> Her holy hands the crowns and poppy bore;
> And from her shoulder hung the key before.
> She came where Erysichthon's rage began,
> And mildly thus address'd the wretched man.
>   "My son, whoe'er thou art that wounds the
>   trees,
> My son, desist, nor break high heaven's
>   decrees:
> By thy dear parent's love, recall thy train,

Retire, my son, nor let me plead in vain:
Lest Ceres' wrath come bursting from above,
In vengeance for her violated grove."
　　She said: but scornful Erysichthon burn'd
With fiercer rage, and fiercer frowns return'd,
Than the gaunt lioness (whose eyes they say
Flash keener flames than all the beasts of
　　prey)
Casts on some hunter, when, with anguish
　　torn,
On Tmarus' hills her savage young are born.
"Hence, hence," he cried, "lest thy weak body
　　feel
The fatal force of my resistless steel:
Above my dome the lofty trees shall shine,
Where my companions the full banquet join,
And sport and revel o'er the sparkling wine."
　　He said. Fell Nemesis the speech records,
And vengeful Ceres heard th' insulting words;
Her anger burn'd: her power she straight
　　assum'd,
And all the goddess in full beauty bloom'd:
While to the skies her sacred head arose,
She trod the ground, and rush'd amidst her
　　foes.
The giant woodmen, struck with deadly fear,
That instant saw, that instant disappear,
And left their axes in the groaning trees:
But unconcern'd their headlong flight she
　　sees;
For these t' obey their lord the fences broke,
To whom with dreadful voice the goddess
　　spoke.
　　"Hence, hence, thou dog, and hasten to thy
　　home;
There shape the trees, and roof the lofty
　　dome:
There shalt thou soon unceasing banquets join,
And glut thy soul with feasts and sparkling
　　wine."
　　Her fatal words inflam'd his impious breast;
He rag'd with hunger like a mountain-beast:
Voracious famine his shrunk entrails tore,
Devouring still, and still desiring more.
Unhappy wretch! full twenty slaves of thine
Must serve the feast, and twelve prepare the
　　wine;
Bright Ceres' vengeance and stern Bacchus'
　　rage
Consum'd the man who durst their power
　　engage:
For these combine against insulting foes,
And fill their hearts with anguish and with
　　woes.
His pious parents still excuses found
To keep their son from banquets given
　　around.
And when th' Ormenides his presence call
To Pallas' games, by sacred Iton's wall,

Th' impatient mother still their suit denied.
"The last revolving day," she swift replied,
"To Cranon's town he went, and there
　　receives
An annual tribute of a hundred beaves."
Polyxo comes, the son and sire invites,
To grace her young Actorion's nuptial rites:
But soon the mournful mother thus replies,
With tears of sorrow streaming from her eyes:
　　"The royal Triopas will join thy feast;
But Erysichthon lies with wounds opprest;
Nine days are past, since, with relentless
　　tooth,
A boar on Pindus gor'd the unhappy youth."
　　What fond excuses mark'd her tender care!
"Did one the banquet or the feast prepare?
My son is gone from home," the mother cries:
Was he invited to the nuptial ties?
A discus struck him, from his steed he fell,
Or numbers his white flocks in Othrys' dale.
Meanwhile the wretch, confin'd within the
　　rooms,
In never-ending feasts his time consumes,
Which his insatiate maw devour'd as fast,
As down his throat the nourishment he cast;
But unrequited still with strength or blood,
As if in ocean's gulfs had sunk the food.
　　As snows from Mima's hills dissolving run,
Or waxen puppets melt before the sun,
So fast his flesh consum'd, his vigour gone,
And nervous fibres only cloth'd the bone.
His mother mourn'd; his sisters groans
　　resum'd;
His nurse and twenty handmaids wept around:
The frantic father rent his hoary hairs,
And vainly thus to Neptune pour'd his
　　prayers:
　　"O power divine, believ'd my sire in vain;
Since thou reliev'st not thy descendant's pain:
If I from beauteous Canace may claim
My sacred birth, or Neptune's greater name;
Behold a dire disease my son destroy:
O! look with pity on the wretched boy.
Far happier fate, had Phœbus' vengeful dart
Struck, with resistless force, his youthful
　　heart;
For then my hands had funeral honours paid,
And sacred rights to his departed shade.
But haggard famine with pale aspect now
Stares in his eyes, and sits upon his brow.
Avert, O gracious power, the dire disease,
Or feed my wretched son in yonder seas.
No more my hospitable feasts prevail,
My folds are empty, and my cattle fail.
My menial train will scarce the food provide;
The mules no more my rushing chariot guide.
A steer his mother fed within the stall,
At Vesta's sacred altar doom'd to fall,
This he devour'd, and next my warlike horse,

So oft victorious in the dusty course.
Ev'n puss escap'd not, when his fury rose,
Herself so dreadful to domestic foes."

　Long as his father's house supplied the feast
Th' attendants only knew the dreadful waste.
But when pale famine fill'd th' imperial dome,
Th' insatiate glutton was expell'd from home,
And, though from kings descended, rueful sat
In public streets, and begg'd at every gate:
Still at the feast his suppliant hands were
　spread,
And still the wretch on sordid refuse fed.
　Immortal Ceres! for thine impious foe
Ne'er let my breast with sacred friendship
　glow.
Beneath my roof the wretch shall never prove
A neighbour's kindness, or a neighbour's love.
Ye maids and matrons, thus with sacred song,
Salute the pageant as it comes along.
"Hail! Ceres, hail! by thee from fertile ground
Swift springs the corn, and plenty flows
　around."
As four white coursers to thy hallow'd shrine
The sacred basket bear; so, power divine,
Let Spring and Summer, rob'd in white,
　appear;
Let fruits in Autumn crown the golden year,
That we may still the sprightly juice consume,
To soothe our cares in Winter's cheerless
　gloom.
As we, with feet unshod, with hair unbound,
In long procession tread the hallow'd ground;
May thus our lives in safety still be led,
O shower thy blessings on each favour'd
　head!
As matrons bear the baskets fill'd with gold,
Let boundless wealth in every house be told.
Far as the Prytaneum the power invites
The women uninstructed in the rites;
Then dames of sixty years (a sacred throng)
Shall to the temple lead the pomp along.
Let those who for Lucina's aid extend
Imploring arms, and those in pains attend
Far as their strength permits; to them shall
　come
Abundant bliss, as if they reach'd the dome.
　Hail, sacred power! preserve this happy
　town
In peace and safety, concord and renown:
Let rich increase o'erspread the yellow plain;
Feed flocks and herds, and fill the ripening
　grain:
Let wreaths of olive still our brows adorn,
And those who plough'd the field shall reap
　the corn.
　Propitious, hear my prayer, O Queen
　supreme,
And bless thy poet with immortal fame.
　　　　　　　　　　　　　—H. W. Tytler

The last poem of Callimachus, so far as our knowledge goes, is ***The Lock of Berenice,*** a courtly occasional poem which shows the poet's art at its zenith. In 346 Ptolemy Euergetes ascended the Egyptian throne, together with the young and beautiful queen, Berenice, to whose determined intervention the empire of the Ptolemies owed the recovery of Cyrene.

Immediately upon his ascension the young king set out for Asia to wreak his vengeance upon the Syrian king Seleucus for the murder of his sister. His wife, Berenice, vowed to the gods a lock of her hair for his safe return. After a brilliant and triumphant expedition which brought him farther east than any Ptolemy before him had penetrated, revolts in Egypt induced the king to return; he brought with him rich booty, and the queen fulfilled her solemn vow. But on the next day, to the consternation of all, the royal lock disappeared from the temple. Thereupon the famous court astronomer, Conon, contrived an exquisite means of rendering homage to the adored queen. As he had just discovered a new constellation among the fixed stars in the heavens, he named it the *Lock of Berenice* and invented the myth that the gods themselves had carried off the lock from the temple and placed it in the heavens, just as once upon a time they had vouchsafed eternity to Ariadne's crown in the heavens. Even today the constellation retains this name: it lies between the Great Bear and the Virgin.

This gallant invention of the astronomer, which must certainly have interested the court circles of Alexandria, Callimachus now glorified in a grand elegy. We possess it only in the Latin translation of Catullus, which can hardly be literal, but doubtless faithfully reproduces the poetic style. Recently, mutilated fragments of the original turned up in a papyrus from Oxyrhynchus. In Catullus' poem, which I give in translation, the lock itself is the speaker.

　Who first discerned the heavenly lights, the
　　rise
　And set of stars, the pageant of the skies,
　How wanes the splendour of the striding sun,
　How stars set duly, when their course is run,
　How from her orbit through the sky sweet
　　love
　To Latmos' caves can Trivia remove,
　'Twas he, 'twas Conon who me too descried
　A lock of Berenice's hair enskied,
　A glory, which to many a god in prayer
　She vowed, outstretching arms so smooth and
　　fair,
　What time the newly-married king arose
　To leave his home and clash with Syrian foes.
　Is Venus hated by new brides? Or is
　It all to cheat fond bridegrooms of their bliss,
　The tear-drop in the bower, the wail of woe?
　So help me all the gods 'tis idle show.

My queen that lesson taught me on the day
When to grim war her bridegroom went away.
Or will you say you mourned not for your
    dear, But for your kinsman's absence shed
    the tear?
What! when the sorrow pierced your inmost
    soul!
When every sense was ravished, and your
    whole
Heart fainted in sore trouble! Yet I knew
No girl so valiant from a child as you.
Have you forgot the gallant deed which won
Your royal wedlock? Braver deed was none.
Then the last parting! All you tried to say!
Dear God! how oft you brushed the tears
    away!
What Power could change you so? You only
    prove
That lovers need the presence of their love.
'Twas then for your sweet husband's
    homecoming
To all the gods you vowed that you would
    bring
This lock of hair, with blood of bulls. Anon
Asia for Egypt by his arms was won.
Therefore, O queen! in duty bound I pay
Your ancient vow to heav'n's high host to-
    day.
Unwillingly, my queen, I left you; I
Swear by your life, your head, unwillingly
(And may whoe'er to these makes false appeal
Have due reward): but who could cope with
    steel?
Not ev'n the crest of all the crests that on
Earth's shores are traversed by bright Thia's
    son,
When through mid Athos Persian chivalry
Floated upon their new-created sea.
Shall locks of hair stand fast, when mountains
    fall?
God whelm the Chalybes, whelm one and all,
Him most, who foremost rifled earth, and 'gan
Draw out hard iron bars, the curse of man.
While still the sister locks made moan for me,
Lo! the winged courser of Arsinoe,
Ev'n Ethiopian Memnon's brother dear,
Striking the earth with waving wings drew
    near:
'Twas he who bore me through the darkling
    sky,
In Aphrodite's holy lap to lie,
When the Zephyrian queen with this intent,
Greek dweller on Canopus' shores, had sent.
So, on the threshold of the spangled skies
Lest Ariadne's golden crown should rise
And stand alone, that I no less might shine,
Spoil of that sunny head, with light divine,
Me, a new star in heaven, dripping yet
With brine, among old stars the goddess set.

For I beside Lycaon's child, between
The Maiden and the Lion's angry sheen,
Slope to my setting, slow Bootes' guide,
Who long delays to dip in Ocean's tide.
But though the gods by night beside me pace,
Though at the dawn I see white Tethys' face,
(Maiden of Rhamnus, suffer me to say
The word no craven fear shall hide to-day,
Though angry stars should scold and rend me,
    lest
The secret of my soul should be confessed)
Less joy have I herein than agony
To know my lady ever far from me,
With whom when she was maid, I drank
    untold
Abundance of sweet perfumes manifold.
But, lady mine, when on the stars you gaze,
While festal lamps in Venus' honour blaze,
Since I am yours, to me abundance sweet
Of perfume give, till all the stars repeat
With one accord: "O! were your lady mine!
Orion by Aquarius might shine."

                —Hugh Macnaghten

The modern reader will not find it easy to adapt himself to the baroque style of this elegy; it is possible that the ancient reader was at first similarly affected. What surprises us most is the fact that the lock is made the speaker in a long poem, but this would not strike an ancient reader as strange, since the epigram had accustomed the ancients to speeches by inanimate objects. From the earliest times, poetic inscriptions were freely put into the mouths, as it were, of graves and votive offerings. As early as the sixth century we find in the epigrams tombs, statues, athletic implements, drinking cups and bowls speaking; why should not a consecrated lock utter speech? The only difference is that, while votive offerings are wont to be concise, the lock becomes diffuse in almost a hundred verses. We have already become acquainted with the rise of human relations and feelings to superhuman heights . . . in the dirge in honor of Arsinoë, with which the present poem is, in many respects, the most closely related of all of Callimachus' works. But what was set forth there with weighty gravity is here frequently turned into mirth and frivolity. The liberty which the old and renowned poet and scholar takes in teasing his young and royal compatriot is amazing. The description of the nuptial night and the amorousness of the queen, which strikes modern taste as being unduly coarse, was probably somewhat coarsened by Catullus. But, even if the tone be softened, as is done in the translation I have cited, the fact remains that Callimachus says things to his princess which no poet would have dared to say to a queen or a princess at the court of Louis XIV. The pathos, too, in places is so exaggerated that it calls forth a smile, especially in the comparison of the tunneling of Mount Athos with the cutting of the lock; but again there occur serious passages. Truly Callimachean is the entirely unexpected end, where the lock is so overcome with longing for its old place on Berenice's head that the entire arrangement of the fixed constellations in the heavens is of no consequence to it.

Here we see again united all those variegated elements which make Callimachus' art so inconsistent and so fascinating: spirit, wit, imagination, taste, mastery of form. Of all qualities that go to make a poet, he was denied but one—that, to be sure, the greatest of all— intense and lofty feeling; thus Ovid's verdict upon him is justified:

> Even throughout all lands Battiades's name
>   will be famous;
> Though not in genius supreme, yet by his art
>   he excels.

. . . . .

THE EPIC

Among the Hellenes the stream of epic poetry was never entirely dried up. Around the *Iliad* there arose the poems of the epic cycle, which related the happenings which preceded and followed the action of the *Iliad;* this entire epic mass bore the name of Homer until about the end of the fifth century. Aristotle was the first to limit the work of Homer to the *Iliad* and the *Odyssey* (though he let the mock epic *Margites* pass as Homeric), a view which later gained general acceptance. And now there began a diligent search for names for the authors of the cyclic poems, which had in fact been anonymously transmitted. The mythological and genealogical poetry like Hesiod's similarly continued into the fifth century. But in this instance a clear distinction between the *Theogony* of Hesiod and the genealogical poetry connected with it was not drawn as it was in the case of epic poetry between Homer and the poets of the *Cycle*. The late *Catalogues of Heroines* continued to be read as Hesiodic, and for this reason the Egyptian papyri restore to us an ever increasing quantity of these epics of the Epigoni, while not a scrap from the epic cycle has turned up in Egypt. Besides the two great spirits, Homer and Hesiod, who continued productive even in death, there were in Ionia poets of more tangible personality who lived in historic times. I will mention only Panyassis, an older relative of Herodotus, who composed a *Heracleia* about the middle of the fifth century, and Antimachus, the author of the *Lyde,* who composed a *Thebais* about the year 400. Bolder was the venture of Choerilus of Samos (about the end of the fifth century), who treated the Persian Wars in the epic meter. But though this attempt may have attained a certain success, on the whole the later epic was of little consequence in the literature of the fifth and fourth centuries; it paled into insignificance beside the shining splendor of the Attic Tragedy. When the Alexandrians consciously attempt-

ed to create a new poetry in tacit opposition to the Attic, the important question arose as to what attitude should be taken toward the Ionic epos. The want of new epic poetry was felt. Alexander had taken in his train the epic poet, Choerilus of Iasos, in the hope that he would become a new Homer for the new Achilles— a hope in which he was wretchedly disappointed. There were those who held it possible and desirable for the great heroic epic to be resumed in the style of the cyclic poets, somewhat modernized perhaps, under the influence of Antimachus. Against this view Callimachus and his school waged vehement war. Time and again he insists on the rejection of the cyclic epic. When he says, "A big book is a big evil," he is thinking of corpulent epic. "I hate a cyclic poem," he says in an epigram, and another shows how lightly he esteems even the productions of the older cyclic poets. He lets the epic of Creophylus of Samos, *The Sack of Oechalia,* speak for itself, and adds a disparaging verse at the close:

> A Samian gave me birth, the sacred bard
> Whose hospitable feast great Homer shar'd;
> For beauteous Iole my sorrows flow,
> And royal Eurytus oppress'd with woe:
> But mightier names my lasting fame shall
>   crown,
> And Homer give Creophilus renown.
> —H. W. Tytler

Callimachus' pupil Theocritus harps on the same chord:

> For, even as I detest the artificer who essays
> High as Oromedon's crest a mansion of men
>   to upraise,
> So the birds of the Muses I hate, who weary
>   themselves in vain,
> Cackling early and late, to rival the Chian's
>   strain.
> —A. S. Way

One must not believe that Callimachus would enter the lists against Homer himself. Parthenius . . . later dared to do so and called the *Iliad* "muck" and the *Odyssey* "mud." But Callimachus was convinced that any attempt at a great epic would be wrecked on the comparison with the *Iliad* and the *Odyssey,* and that compared to these the older cyclic epics were worth little, an opinion which Aristotle had already expressed. He would by no means abandon epic treatment of the materials of the saga, but the new epic must differ from the cyclic in every respect. Here he considers three points of special importance. First, the subject matter must not be taken from the sagas which had been dealt with innumerable times and were familiar to everyone, but it was necessary to discover new and untouched material in the immense abundance of Greek legends. Second, the compass of the poem must be reduced, so that it might be possible to achieve finished mastery of form, which to Callimachus was a necessary requirement of the poetic art. Third, the tone of the treatment must be entirely individual, and such as to bring the people of former ages near to the modern reader.

As a model of this new epic style Callimachus himself composed the small epic *Hecale*. Of the characteristics of this poem finds in Egypt have now given us a somewhat clearer idea, although the total number of the new verses amounts to only about seventy. The subject is an episode from the adventures of Theseus, the conquest of the bull of Marathon. The poem begins with an entertainment at the home of the poor but hospitable Hecale. The name of this heroine survived in that of a small Attic rural community and in that of a festival of Zeus, the Hecalesia, celebrated by the population of the surrounding country. The conclusion of the poem is devoted to the establishment of this festival. Hecale had prayed for the success of her bold young guest and had vowed a sacrifice to Zeus. But before Theseus returned victorious with the conquered monster, the good old woman had died, and the hero performed in her stead the sacrifice she had vowed. This saga, which the poet owed to some local chronicle of Attica, bears an aetiological character, and the poet might as well have included it in his *Aitia*.

The affectionate portrayal of detail with which the poverty of Hecale and her humble cheer are described was particularly effective. Ovid borrowed from the *Hecale* the colors for his idyllic pair, Philemon and Baucis. This pair has survived in Goethe's *Faust*. That the great heroes of antiquity could be placed in unpretentious, even needy circumstances was not altogether unheard of. The home of the godlike swineherd Eumaeus is luxurious compared to the hut of Hecale, but even so it showed rustic simplicity. But in general one is accustomed to see the Homeric heroes with all the circumstance of pomp and splendor, a splendor which had acquired its fairylike glitter through the dim recollection of the luxuriant Cretan-Mycenaean culture, and had made a powerful impression upon the Greeks of the seventh and sixth centuries. But in the meantime the standard of living had risen to extreme luxury. Even the palaces of Alcinous and Menelaus could hardly impress the courtly circle of Alexandria. It was much more effective for the audience of Callimachus to see' the heroes of the past represented as living under conditions which would appear quite unendurable to an educated Alexandrian.

An important point with reference to the style of composition of the *Hecale*, deduced from an Egyptian wooden tablet, is that about a hundred verses were devoted to a conversation between two birds, a considerable part of a poem that was surely not very long. The poet has inserted a rather detailed episode, whose motivation we are not able to discover, into the simple action of his poem. A crow relates to another bird the story of the birth of Erichthonius and the consequent wrath of Athena against the crows. She foretells further that the raven, heretofore white, would receive black feathers from the furious Apollo. Quite surprising is the conclusion of this bird episode:

> While she spoke thus sleep seized her and seized her hearer. They fell asleep but not for long; for soon came a frosty neighbour: "Come, no longer are the hands of thieves in quest of prey: for already the lamps of morn are shining; many a drawer of water is singing the Song of the Pump and the axle creaking under the wagon wakes him that hath his house beside the highway, while many a thirled smith, with deafened hearing, torments the ear."

> —A. W. Mair

This bold somersault of the imagination is very characteristic of Callimachus. The custom was for the birds to report the new day to mankind; the poets had many times used the cock's crow and the song of the lark to announce the dawn. Callimachus now turns the tables and has his birds deduce the coming of a new day from the restless activity of men. But the men whose early clamor was heard by the birds of the Attic mountains in the time of Theseus are in reality the inhabitants of the noisy metropolis of Alexandria. The noises which may often enough have disturbed his own morning slumbers—the song of the water carrier, the creaking of wagons and the smithy's clangor—Callimachus cleverly puts into the mouths of his mythical birds. Therefore, even in that class of poetry which least favors the portrayal of the personality of the poet and his period, Callimachus knew how to introduce modern and subjective elements.

. . . . .

THE EPIGRAM

Next to Asclepiades, Callimachus is by far the most important master of the Alexandrian epigram. He is not quite as simple as Asclepiades in language and thought, but is his equal in vigor and perfection of form, and superior in the art of saying much in a few words. . . .

Of the sixty-three epigrams which we have from his hand the majority, it is certain, belong to his youth, when he was teaching boys in Eleusis. But as an old man he occasionally harked back to the epigram with undiminished skill, as in the graceful homage to his young compatriot, Queen Berenice, in celebration of whom the last of his great elegies was also written:

> Four are the Graces: three we know
> And Berenicë here below.
> See how she holds their linkéd hands,

And wet with perfume by them stands.
Without her now who shines afar
Not e'en the Graces graces are.
                                    —F. A. Wright

Callimachus shows a somewhat richer variety of form than Asclepiades and his companions. In addition to the customary elegiac distich, he employs other measures in four epigrams, one of which I quote:

Menoetas' quiver, with his bow,
    Serapis, at thy feet cloth lie.
No shafts are here—the stricken foe
    Of Hesperis shall tell thee why.
                                    —J. A. Pott

This little poem, which also belongs to the poet's later years, under the reign of Ptolemy Euergetes, is in no wise as artless as it appears at first blush. Much history is involved in it. The Cretan archer Menoetas served in the king's army, and with him subdued the insubordinate inhabitants of Euhesperides in the territory of Cyrene. Now the war is over; Menoetas gives up his military service and dedicates his weapons, which had become useless to him, to Serapis, the great god of Alexandria. In the candid address to the god the bow is slightingly referred to by the name of its material, horn; we see that its possessor no longer values it highly. He can give up his bow and quiver, but not his arrows, for with them he has unerringly smitten the inhabitants of Euhesperides, and thereby faithfully discharged his warrior's duty. All this is told without a trace of boasting. We can hardly believe, yet can scarcely deny with certainty, that the famous old poet could at that time really be induced to compose a dedicatory epigram for a simple soldier.

But that in his youth Callimachus composed dedicatory and sepulchral epigrams to order seems to me indisputable. In contrast to Asclepiades, the number of his poems which give the impression of being real inscriptions is quite large. In fact many of those extant give only the necessary names and the statement of the dedication or burial. The charm of these little poems lies only in their conciseness of expression and the skillful arrangement of names. It is a charm which can hardly be rendered by translation; I venture, however, a few citations. First, I give the dedicatory inscription of a statue of a young maiden in the temple of Isis:

Fair Æschylis, from Thales sprung,
In Isis' fane an offering hung;
And thus the vow her mother made,
Irene's vow, is fully paid.
                                    —H. W. Tytler

The only information given here beside the bare statement of the facts is that the mother and not the father vowed the statue.

Next comes a sepulchral inscription:

Who pass this tomb of Elean Cymon, know
The son of old Hippæus sleeps below.
                                    —R. G. MacGregor

The second verse serves only to emphasize the father's name.

To be sure, Callimachus often understands how to sound a short but sharp note of sentiment even in the briefest form:

His son, now twelve years old, Philippus sees
Here laid, his mighty hope, Nicoteles.
                                    —Lord Neaves

By being placed at the close of the verses the two names are emphasized, and thereby a contrast is drawn between the tender youth of the deceased and the high hopes his father lost in him, a motif which is ever suitable for graves of children at all times and in all places.

And now I give the pearl of all the poet's sepulchral epigrams:

Here Dicon's son, Acanthian Saon lies
In sacred sleep: say not a good man dies.
                                    —Lord Neaves

I know that the second verse with its unexcelled simplicity of spirit has seemed to German fathers in our own day the best expression of mourning for a hopeful son.

Even when the poems become somewhat longer and more pretentious in content and expression, they may yet have been composed for the practical end of being inscribed. Note the pretty dedication of a brazen gamecock for a sporting victory, probably in cockfighting. The fowl itself speaks, with waggish candor:

I am a bronzen game-cock—thus
My donor says, Eusenetus;
For of myself I know not aught—
Unto the Great Twin brethren wrought,
In gratitude for victory won;
I take the word of Phaedrus' son.
                                    —Walter Leaf

How the confidence of the cock in the veracity of his donor Euaenetus makes it possible for the father and the grandfather of the dedicant to be mentioned is as unexpected as it is clever.

One of Callimachus' epigrams on cenotaphs of victims of the sea may also have been a real inscription:

Would there had never been a ship to run
    The hazard of the deep:
We had not wept for Diocleides' son
    As vainly now we weep.
Dead in the dreary waste, dear Sopolis,
    You drift upon the wave,
And nought is left us but your name, and this
    Only an empty grave.

                  —J. A. Pott

In the case of the epigram for the cenotaph of the Cyzican Critias we have already seen . . . that it was only an elaboration of an Asclepiadean poem and that in reality its presuppositions were impossible. Callimachus, therefore, used the form of the sepulchral inscription for clever pastime just as Asclepiades had done. Sometimes an epigram has the effect of an interpretation, occasioned by the poet's mood, of an actual epitaph.

> Timonoe! Who art thou? By Heav'n! I should
>   not thee have known,
> But for thy sire Timotheus' name carv'd on
>   thy fun'ral stone,
> Methymna's too, thy natal town. Well wet I,
>   losing thee
> Great of thy lord Euthymenes the pain and
>   grief must be!
>
>   —R. G. MacGregor

Apparently the poet approached the grave and at first read only "Timonoe." The name alone told him nothing, but he reads also the name of the father and the home, and he realizes that he has known the deceased and her husband. The poet's positive assertion that the surviving husband will be affected with great sorrow is a tribute to the dead.

A form of sepulchral inscription which in later times was repeated with variations *ad nauseam* and was often actually carved on stone was the dialogue between a passerby and the grave or the dead. Callimachus has an example of this form:

>   A
> Rests Charidas beneath this tomb?
>   B
>   Here I,
> Son of Arimnas of Cyrene, lie.
>   A
> Charidas! what's below?
>   B
>   Eternal night.
>   A
> What your returns to earth?
>   B
>   A falsehood quite.
>   A
> And Pluto?

>   B
> But a fable: all as one,
> Body and soul are ended and undone.
> Soft words you'd have of me, I speak the
>   true,
> An ox in Hades fares as well as you.
>
>   —R. G. MacGregor

The poet first addresses the grave, which then replies, after the manner of a doorkeeper. Then the dead himself enters into the conversation. His replies to the curious questioning of the living regarding conditions in the hereafter are delightful. At first his utterances are brief and bitter, but when the stranger expresses shocked surprise at the complete evanescence of the amiable and hopeful pictures of the world below he is moved to a long and very incisive response. Myths, philosophical speculations and popular imaginings are amusingly intermingled in the few verses. Callimachus also had Hipponax say in his collection of *iambi* . . . that he comes from the place where they sell an ox for a penny. . . .

Callimachus' love epigrams, like those of Asclepiades, deal with either his own or others' love affairs. The following, for example, deals with a comrade:

> To Fair Ionis Callignotus said:
> 'None will I love but thee, nor man nor
>   maid.'
> So did he vow; but lovers' oaths, men say,
> Reach not the ears of gods, they go astray.
> Now for a youth he burns; and she, forlorn,
> Is like poor Megara a thing of scorn.
>
>   —F. A. Wright

The last verse contains an allusion to a well-known oracle. The Megarians had complacently inquired of the Delphian god what rank they held among the Greeks. But they came off badly, for Apollo enumerated various states and peoples who took first place respectively in various domains and then closed:

> But as for you, men of Megara, not third, not
>   fourth, nor yet twelfth
> Can ye be reckoned, nor come ye at all into
>   possible counting.

In Callimachus' own amatory experiences handsome lads played a larger role than did girls. Probably his best love poem, a companion piece to the Amyntas epigram of Asclepiades, treats of his love for Archinus with a tenderness and warmth that is not surpassed by the work of any other epigrammatist:

> If I did come of set intent
> Then be thy blame my punishment;
> But if by love a capture made
> Forgive my hasty serenade.

Wine drew me on, Love thrust behind,
I was not master of my mind.
And when I came I did not cry
My name aloud, my ancestry;
Only my lips thy lintel pressed;
If this be crime, the crime's confessed.

　　　　　　　　　　　—F. A. Wright

In love as in poetry Callimachus contemns anything trivial, or light of attainment; he is attracted only by the unusual and the difficult. To this feeling he gives open and impressive utterance:

The hunter, Epicydes, will not spare
To follow on the trace of fawn and hare
Through snow and frost, so long as still they
　　fly;
But if one say "'Tis hit," he passes by.
Even so my love, winged for no willing prize,
Follows what flees, and flees what fallen lies.

　　　　　　　　　　　—Richard Garnett

Of his own love for a girl he speaks in only one poem, which is a skillful compression of a *paraclausithyron* into the narrow frame of an epigram:

O Cruel, cruel! As I lie
　Upon this ice-cold stone,
So may you sleep whose lovers sigh
　In misery alone—
The very neighbours grieve to see
How here I lie in agony.

So may you sleep! Within your heart
　No shade of pity lives;
Your pride in mercy has no part,
　To love no kindness gives.
Soon will the grey hairs come—and they
Perchance will make you rue this day.

　　　　　　　　　　　—F. A. Wright

The repetition of the identical expressions was intended to echo the artless manner of the serenade before the door of the beloved, which comprised only few motifs often repeated. . . .

Bruno Snell (essay date 1948)

SOURCE: "Art and Play in Callimachus," in *The Discovery of the Mind: The Greek Origins of European Thought,* translated by T. G. Rosenmeyer, Cambridge, Mass: Harvard University Press, 1953, pp. 264-80.

[*In the following excerpt from his book* The Discovery of the Mind: The Greek Origins of European Thought, *originally published in German in 1948, Snell declares Callimachus the "father of Hellenistic poetry" and compares him at length to Germany's Goethe. Accord-*

ing to Snell, Callimachus's defining characteristic was his "post-philosophical" enhancement of technique and playfulness above moral instruction, the province of earlier eras in Greek literature.]

Father Bromius!
Thou art genius,
Century's genius,
Art what inward glow
To Pindar was,
What to the world
Is Phoebus Apollo . . .

Jupiter Pluvius!
Not by the elm tree
Didst thou visit him,
With his brace of doves
In his affectionate arm,
Crowned with the friendly rose,
Playful him, flower-revelling
Anacreon,
Storm-breathing deity!

Not in the poplar grove
On the Sybaris' banks,
Nor at the mountain's
Sunlight-radiant brow
Didst thou seize him
Singing of bees,
Prattling of honey,
Genially beckoning
Theocritus.

When the wheels rattled
Quickly wheel upon wheel around the goal,
Up soared
Victory-flushed
Youths' cracking of whips,
And dust was rolling
As from the mountains
Downward the shower of stones,
Thy soul glowed perils, Pindar,
Heart . . .

When the twenty-two year old Goethe was 'passionately singing to himself this half-nonsense', the *Wanderer's Storm Song,* he probably did not reflect that there was a literary precedent for his distinction between the sublime grandeur of Pindar and the playfulness of Anacreon and Theocritus. And yet the turning-point from the age of the rococo to the era of the 'untutored genius' stands in a significant relation to that other turning-point, in the history of Greek literature, when the contrast between playfulness and pathos was first officially enunciated. Goethe himself, granted that he had been willing to acknowledge this literary debt, could have referred only to the Roman middleman who supplied him with his Greek concept. For the Greek work which may be regarded as his ultimate model has only recently become known through an Egyptian papyrus. It is all the more significant that Goethe in many respects came closer to the spirit of the original than the derivative work with which he was acquainted.

In his poem, Goethe looks at Pindar through the spectacles of a literary tradition rather than with his own eyes. He admits this much himself, for in the following year, in the middle of July 1772, he tells Herder: 'I have now made Pindar my home, and if the splendour of the palace could make a man happy, I should be so.' He goes on to confess: 'Yet I feel what Horace was able to say, what Quintilian praises'. In point of fact the image: 'As from the mountains downward the shower of stones,' is a quotation, or a variation, of Horace's poem (4.2) which has fixed our conception of Pindar since the Renaissance:

> Monte decurrens velut amnis, imbres
> Quem super notas aluere ripas,
> Fervet.

Following this model, the writers of the baroque and the rococo identified Pindar with the grand or sublime style, unfettered by the strict rules of prosody. Again, Goethe's view of Theocritus as the representative of pastoral poetry, and of Anacreon as a light-hearted singer of wine and love; both standing at opposite poles from Pindar, is purely conventional. To cite an example which happens to occur to me: Goldoni says in his *Memoirs* (1.41) about Metastasio's arias, that 'some are written in the spirit of Pindar, others after the manner of Anacreon'. This shows, incidentally, that at that time the name of Anacreon was associated less with the genuine lyrics of the archaic poet than with the so-called Anacreontic poems which were ascribed to him.

But although Goethe fell in with the literary jargon of his time, he went much further. Nor did his readings in Horace, who deprecated his own trifles by comparison with the grandeur of Pindar, set a limit to his thought. In more than one way, Goethe managed to return to an ancient source whence the tradition in which he moved had first sprung up.

Horace, in his ode on Pindar, refuses to celebrate the deeds of Augustus in the solemn accents of a Pindaric song; instead he selects a slender and graceful form. Like other Romans who voice the same idea he thus follows the lead of Callimachus, the father of Hellenistic poetry. . . . Both Callimachus and Goethe stood on the threshold of a new age. After more than a century of enlightenment in the course of which the ancient religious beliefs had been dissolved, they had finally become weary of the spirit of rationalism. A new important era of poetry was about to begin. Still, so radically did the rhythm of antiquity differ from the trend of the modern age that Callimachus, and with him his age, decided in favour of a slender delicacy in poetic writing, whereas Goethe, and he too as the leader of his contemporaries, turned in the opposite direction, toward pathos and emotional fervour.

Despite some external similarities, the early Hellenistic age differed greatly in its intellectual situation from the last phase of the eighteenth century. For one thing, it lacked the storm and stress, the revolutionary ardour, of the later period. When, beginning with the third century B.C., after a century of prose writing . . . , poetry re-entered the scene with productions of high calibre and great authority, it kept intact the ancient poetic forms, particularly the spoken verse of the archaic period. Its spirit was new, but this newness was not of the sort to be proclaimed as a revelation, or to be championed with impassioned zeal. These Hellenistic poets are, if we may say it in one word, post-philosophical, while the earlier poets are pre-philosophical. The earlier poetry is ever intent to stake out new areas of the mind, and philosophy and science, the rational assimilation of the newly-found material, formed its natural sequel. In the realm of the epic, the heroic sagas furnished the seeds for Ionian historiography, and the theogonies and cosmologies opened the way for Ionion natural philosophy and its search for the *arche.* The lyric led to Heraclitus, the drama to Socrates and Plato. But with the beginning of Hellenistic poetry, the great age of continuous philosophical creation approached its end. The fourth century had witnessed the achievements of Plato, Aristotle and Theophrastus; its close coincides with the foundation of the two schools of philosophy which were to remain sovereign in the generations which followed: the Garden of Epicurus and the Stoa of Zeno. Greek philosophy, that is, had reached the point which, generally speaking, it was not destined to surpass. That was the moment when in a new intellectual centre, in Egyptian Alexandria, the residence of the Ptolemies, a number of poets, among them Theocritus and Callimachus, their most important figure, joined together in a circle which carried poetry to new heights.

These poets are post-philosophical in the sense that they have ceased to believe in the possibility of mastering the world by a theoretical control. As against Aristotle who had credited poetry with a philosophical nature . . . they have no use for the universal in poetry, and so they devote their special attention to details. Callimachus in particular shows himself to be post-philosophical because he entertains theories concerning the potentialities of poetry in his age. This is his innovation in the history of literature; he lays down his views regarding the art of writing in the form of programmatic utterances, especially in the lines against his foes with which he prefaced his longest and most important work, the *Aitia.* Similar statements appear also in the body of other works, and finally in a few single epigrams. Callimachus raises the question: What sort of poetry should we write? This implies that there are various genres of poetry, and in fact the writers of the period were engaged in the composition of epic as well as dramatic and lyric poetry. We consider it only natural, but an earlier age would have found it hard to understand, that there should be one 'literature' comprising a number of categories; that the poet could exercise his own free choice of the genre to which he wanted to devote his skill.

This first theoretical argument by a poet on behalf of his own art was, of course, preceded by numerous discussions of other people's works, such as Aristophanes' biting criticism of Euripidean tragedy, Plato's reflections on the value of poetry, the *Poetics* of Aristotle, and many other examples which are now mostly lost to us. Callimachus readily avails himself of some of these earlier critiques; his defence of the brevity of his poetry tallies with the opinion of Aristotle, and his justification of the delicate and unimpassioned style—the ideal which through Horace remained in force long after him—is intimately connected with certain motifs in Aristophanes. . . .

Nor were the influences which moulded the thought of Callimachus restricted to the field of literary criticism. In the prologue to his *Aitia* (lines 25 ff.) he says that Apollo warned him at the outset of his poetic undertaking not to take the broad, much-travelled roads, but to hew out his own path, however narrow. The notion that man has two roads before him, and the behest not to take the one which is easy and populous, but that which is narrow and deserted: this idea derives ultimately from the *Works and Days* of Hesiod (lines 287 ff.), whence Prodicus took it and worked it into his fable about Heracles. In Hesiod and Prodicus the narrow path leads to virtue, the broad avenue to vice; similarly Callimachus decides that the narrow path is the right one, but he fails to tell us where the two roads lead. This shows that he has dropped the moral for whose sake the image had originally been invented; even Apollo does not inform him why he should choose the one path and not the other.

Earlier he had said: a victim should be fat, but a poem slender. Aristophanes, in his *Frogs,* had taken the opposite stand and preferred the grand and imposing to the delicate. Again Callimachus fails to produce a reason such as had served Aristophanes to justify his opinions. Aristophanes had rated the grandiose style of Aeschylus higher than the refined manner of Euripides because, in his view, Euripides corrupted the people, while Aeschylus instructed them in noble thoughts. In Callimachus we look in vain for similar moral evaluations. Once more, therefore, we must ask the question: What are the motives of Callimachus for the choice he makes? His answer appears in the words (lines 17 f.): 'Judge my poetry (literally: my wisdom, *sophie*) by

its art (*techne*), not by the Persian cubit.' The only criterion which he acknowledges is that of his skill, of art itself; the two words *sophie* and *techne* are so closely related as to be practically synonymous; art is to be measured in no terms but its own

In the earlier period all Greek poetry strove for some meaning lying beyond the limits of the writing itself. Even after poetry, in the course of time, had relinquished more and more of its social function, the poets endeavoured to seize upon a new concrete reality. In the end this objective became progressively more elusive, so that finally the poet abandoned his search to the philosopher. This element in art which points beyond art was, by Aristophanes, narrowed down to the didactic function of poetry. He thus attached to art a moral purpose; it was his way of preserving for poetry a task transcending its own boundaries even though this task was no longer founded in fact. Callimachus gives all that up, and proceeds to gauge art by itself. He addresses himself to a new audience all his own; for while Attic tragedy had still spoken to the mass of the people, Callimachus calls upon a small circle of cultured men to pass judgment on him. Plato's insistence that the experts should do the judging is here applied to a wisdom which is not the knowledge of the ultimate good, but culture, education, and good taste.

The wisdom of Callimachus is, above everything else, a matter of form. He manipulates his verse with the same delicacy and purity of line which Archilochus espoused, but which had been observed neither in the hexameters of the epic nor in the trimeters of drama. His ear is exceptionally sensitive to the effect of sounds, his vocabulary is rich and varied, and he chooses his words with a masterly feeling for cadence and emphasis, constantly reminding the educated reader of some significant reference. His skill in varying his diction, composition, and metrical scheme is unrivalled. Whenever Callimachus speaks of his wisdom, these are the things which he has chiefly in mind; the content is of lesser importance.

He was a scholar; his immense and careful learning is everywhere present in his work. But he did not employ it to write a didactic poem, as might be expected of an artist who cites the example of Hesiod for his art. The only use he makes of his erudition is to introduce a wealth of colourful and interesting material. He is a collector, with a preference for curiosities; he exhibits his wide knowledge less in order to teach his listeners a lesson than to entertain or even confuse them. Instead of talking about things generally known he surprises us by turning up a rare variant, by playing hide-and-seek, guessing-games and all sorts of tricks and pleasantries. His sense of humour provokes him to combine matters which in actuality are entirely unrelated. In his *Hymn to Zeus* he asks the question: Was Zeus born at the Cretan mount Ida or at mount Lycaeus in Arcadia? Since the former version was the one commonly accepted, he naturally decides for the other, far-fetched as it is, and cites in support of his choice the famous words of Epimenides of Crete: 'All Cretans are liars.' And then he scores once more with the remark that the Cretans also show a grave of Zeus, although everybody knows—and this has been skilfully anticipated in the invocation—that Zeus is immortal. His wit, his spirited handling of the sources, is obviously based on a great deal of learning, but this learning is not made to further the case of knowledge; its only service is to bask in its own glory. Later in Seneca, who inherited this amalgamating of myths from Callimachus through the mediation of Ovid, the learning is used to embellish and aggrandize the style; in Callimachus who loathes pathos it is a source of fun and sparkling ingenuity.

In his iambic verses Callimachus brings on the stage the Seven Sages who since the archaic period had, for the Greeks, embodied the ideal of wisdom. Callimachus, however, does not tell any of the numerous stories in which they were shown searching for knowledge, passing just judgment, or doing any of the noble things for which they were famous. In his view, their claim to wisdom is proved by their lack of vanity. The Arcadian Bathycles has left a golden bow which after his death is to become the property of the wisest man. His son carries it around from sage to sage, each one of them remonstrating that not he, but the next man was the wisest, until ultimately Thales, when the bowl reaches him the second time, dedicates it to Apollo. The reason why Callimachus tells the story is to upbraid the Alexandrian scholars for their quarrels; as far as he was concerned the savants disagreed not because each of them took his convictions and findings seriously, but because they were tainted with pretentiousness and vanity, the congenital vices, as he thought, of the world. In his story about the strife between the olive and the laurel he succeeded once more in taking his stand against presence and ostentation, two evils which have always lain in wait for those who, without following an objective task, possess enough cleverness and talent to live only for the effect. Of the one and only protection against these vices, self-irony, Callimachus is a past master.

He often stresses the playful nature of his poetry by casting himself in the role of the *ingénu.* The tale of Berenice's lock, for instance, which was sacrificed by the queen on the altar of Aphrodite and thence translated into the sky, is reported by the innocent little lock itself. Ancient myths whose truth he finds hard to credit, and stories invented by himself, he tells with a semblance of childish seriousness. This is one of the most peculiar forms of his wit. In his *Hymn to Delos* he describes how Hera, in her anger at Leto, issues an order to all places in Greece not to offer the unhappy mother a haven for bringing Apollo into the world. All

cities, rivers, and mountains are, according to the old religious belief, supposed to possess their own divinities. This is the concept which Callimachus, in his own waggish way, seems to take seriously: no sooner does Leto appear at any one place than the nymphs and demons take to their heels. The result is a general exodus of all localities, until there is no place left for Apollo to be born.

In these poems, and others like them, Callimachus is not just acting the clown. His exaggeratedly ironical pathos is so lively and rich in nuances, and behind it all there is so much genuine joy in the naive and the primitive, so much charm and grace in spite of his raillery, that the finished product is as intriguing as it is hard to puzzle out. He himself calls his poetry 'childish play' (*paizein* and *paignion*). He constructed his slender works 'like a child' (*pais hate*), as the Telchines say of him in the prologue to the *Aitia* (line 6).

Because Callimachus is genuinely filled with the spirit of childhood, he was the first among Greek poets to be able to picture the behaviour of children in true colours, though, of course, with an admixture of irony which guarded him from losing himself entirely to the world of the child. In his *Hymn to Artemis* he introduces the goddess as a little girl sitting on the lap of her father Zeus and begging him (lines 6 ff.):

> Please, daddy, let me keep my virginity for ever and let me have many names, so that Apollo cannot keep up with me. And give me arrows and bow— or no, father, I do not ask for a quiver, and I do not want a big bow from you. The Cyclopes will rightaway make the shafts for me, and also a well-curved bow. But allow me to carry torches and to wear a knee-high dress with a bright hem, so I may kill off the wild beasts. Also give me sixty Ocean-daughters for my companions in the dance. . . .

and so she prattles on and produces one request after another. All this furnishes a picture, and in part a very learned picture, of the nature and activities of Artemis. But the way in which Callimachus looks at the little Artemis has something grandfatherly about it; yet he is not sentimental about her, he does not dispense with the superior perspective of the grown-up: he does not become an artificial child himself.

With the same slightly ironical delight in simple and naive things Callimachus relates in his *Aitia* the scurrilous customs of primitive cults, exotic tales, and rare events. With impressive seriousness, and yet not with a wholly straight face, he pours out a wealth of information. If we were to look for a unifying idea, for an intellectual objective or a programme of enlarging the mental horizon of his listeners, we would not find them. Instead we find a keen sense for the colourful variety of all the strange happenings around us, and this sense Callimachus possessed in a greater measure than any Greek writer since the archaic period. It is, however, no longer the genuinely child-like amazement of the earlier writers who took the wonders of life to heart, and who felt themselves sustained by the significant forces which they discovered about them. The amazement of Callimachus is of the head-wagging sort: Isn't life full of odd goings-on?

The world of play, which since the days of tragedy had been part and parcel of all Greek literature, is here blended with mature learning, and it is this genial mixture of youthful emotion and intellectual scepticism which makes for the ripe grace of this distinguished art.

The lack of a concrete objective, and altogether of all higher commitments, is evident also in his love poetry. There the beloved person, and the desire for the happiness of possession, fade into the background, and a new element which merits the label *erotic* in a very modern sense comes to the fore. In one epigram we read this (*ep.* **41**):

> One half of my soul has made its getaway. I wonder whether she has once again gone to a boy? And yet, I have so often sent out the order: 'Do not receive the runaway, youths!' . . . She deserves to be stoned to death (i.e., because she is a deserter) and she is in league with wicked Eros; I know that she is on the loose somewhere there.

This love of Callimachus differs from the love which reigned in the earlier works, for in the writers before him it had always been directed to a beloved person; it had been a 'love for somebody', as Plato's Diotima puts it (*Symp.* 199 D). The love of Callimachus, on the other hand, lacks this orientation. A part of his soul has made itself independent, and he does not know where it may have strayed. He is in love without really knowing whom he would love.

Another epigram (*ep.* **31**) conveys roughly the following idea: 'The huntsman in the mountains pursues every hare and every deer and delights in the snow. But when he is told: "There, the animal is hit!" he does not want it. My love is like that: it pursues the fleeing prey, but it hurries past that which is readily available.' This happens to be a rebuff to a boy named Epicydes whom Callimachus addresses in the first line, but at the same time it serves him for a general statement of his view on love. Like the huntsman who is more interested in the sport itself than in his quarry, he devotes more attention to the game of pursuing than to that of catching his object. The two epigrams have this in common that the goal, the direction of the love instinct is declared to be unimportant by comparison with the subjective feeling; in the one case it is the mere impulse, in the other the pleasure of the chase which ranks highest in his scale of values.

Two further epigrams (**30** and **43**) are rather alike in the point which they are designed to make; on both occasions Callimachus notices that someone else is in love, once because of the expression of his features, and the other time because he fetches a deep sigh. His reaction is: I understand, for I feel the same way. Thus Callimachus chooses to confess his own love via the description of another; but he does not do so in the presence of his beloved, to influence him. In the one case he conveys his sympathy to a rival, and the other epigram is addressed to nobody in particular. The indirect form helps him to avoid the open confession 'I love' with its pathos and inelegance, and to deflect his admission into irony. He creates an impression as if this reminder of his passion were merely a passing comment which he had not really intended.

In the last two epigrams which we have discussed, the playful nature of Callimachus' art manifests itself in the lack of seriousness with which his problem is voiced; in the other two it is shown in the fact that his love exists only for its own sake—and in this it, of course, resembles his art which is only for art's sake. All four epigrams, however, agree in one thing, viz. that love is but the subjective psychological state of being in love, and not the intercession of a deity as it had appeared in Archilochus, Sappho, and even Anacreon. Nor is it the love which we encounter in tragedy, the violent passion which stirs up the innermost soul of a man, nor again the metaphysical search for perfection, as Plato thinks of it. On the other hand, it is decidedly not, as might be expected after all this, a base desire for transitory pleasures of the flesh. Obviously the love of Callimachus is not of the sort to inspire him to ponder the mysteries of god, the world, or human existence. All it does is to make him aware of his own sensibilities.

But in spite of the egocentric character of his poetry, Callimachus does not advance to a genuine self-reflexion or self-analysis. Neither in the field of psychology nor in any other area of the human mind does he deserve to be called an innovator or discoverer, unless we are to regard it as a discovery that he was able to look at himself with a smile and to state: So this is what you are like. By stepping back and viewing himself from a distance, he adds an abstract dimension to his consciousness; but neither Callimachus nor his successors combined this abstractness with sufficient philosophic vitality to make it fruitful as a beginning of new thought.

Callimachus' resolve not to take things too seriously, particularly those matters which exceed the horizon of man, is a sign of post-philosophical exhaustion. If he does take anything seriously, it is that which is already known. Though he made merry with the rich literary tradition of Greece supplied to him by the Alexandrian library, he still retains a genuinely scholarly interest in the tracing and preserving of that material. The rules of his sport command him not to disclose the seriousness and the labour expended on his research, and not to allow the dust of the library to tarnish the brilliance of his wit and his fiction. But his poetry would be unthinkable if he had not had a deep sympathy for learned studies, or if he had not enjoyed rummaging in old sources. Among his audience, too, Callimachus expects a wide acquaintance with tradition; they must understand his allusions, and show an interest in far-fetched curiosities. Because he himself moves about with ease and comfort in the vast halls of learning, so he demands that his public too feel at home in them. It is only natural that his public can never be large; his art is decidedly exclusive, choice fare for connoisseurs.

The language in which he couches his *jeux d'esprit* owes its light touch to its rhetorical background. It is the birthright of Greek rhetoric to incline toward spirited pleasantries and to be less interested in content than in form. The excessive employment of vocal effects for which its founder Gorgias had striven was soon dropped, for reasons of good taste rather than from any conviction that the form of speech ought to be determined by its concrete objective. Euphony and its stimulus upon the emotions, and a playfully contrived richness of word relations, i.e. antithesis, anaphora and so forth, remained the principal goal. The highly developed prose writing of the fourth century had achieved a perfection of these stylistic features, and it had demonstrated how they could be used with discretion. In Callimachus they are less obvious even than, e.g. in Ovid's *Metamorphoses,* but without a training in the theory of rhetoric his easy mastery of diction could not have been accomplished. This is one case, therefore, in which prose exercised a decisive influence upon poetry. Callimachus is, of course, careful not to adopt the characteristic traits of that prose, such as the overt expression of logical connexions; on the contrary, his thought associations are imbued with a kind of Homeric naïveté.

We have seen that in the time of Callimachus the best minds began to turn away from philosophy and to devote themselves to antiquarian and philological studies, and also to the writing of poetry. Like all earlier attempts of the Greeks to break with the past and to discover new territory, this also was a reaction designed to force a new immediate contact with reality. The philosophers had tried to control the world and life by means of a rational system; the new writers rediscover the great appeal of non-reflective simplicity, and so they turn to the earliest speech of man, to poetry. The cultured men from the big cities are fascinated by primitive customs, by unspoiled manners, by the simple life which is best described by Theocritus, but which also appears in the pages of Herodas and others. But just as in his portrayal of children Callimachus never forgets himself to the point of affecting a false infantility, so also in all other respects he never abandons his irony and his superior wit. Without setting up theories or programmes, he stands for a new, a knowing naiveté; his playfulness stems from the strength of his intellect; it is the genial spirit of one who surveys a lost treasure from the heights of his scepticism rather than weeping sentimental tears.

There were other attempts during his time, as well as the preceding age, to return to an immediate experience of the simple life. The factor which puts Callimachus in a special category is that he does not sacrifice the intellect. He does not want the primitivism of the Cynics; he does not admire the Scythian Anacharsis. Conversely he does not preach culture and humaneness, terms which only too easily betoken a spirit of hollow show and self-applause.

Because Callimachus was on the whole a derivative poet it is not legitimate to speak of him as a discoverer. But his contributions came to be so important for the formation of our European culture that he must be counted among its pioneers. Education or culture is for him tantamount to the faculty of recollection which, aside from cleverly fitting together disparate pieces and thus diverting the listener with surprising effects, enables a man to look down upon the varied manifestations of life with a catholic and sympathetic mind. The cultured man, the scholar, delights in his sensation of standing above the world, without being committed to it. From Callimachus this concept was, through the agency of the Romans, and again primarily through the services of Ovid, handed down to the humanists of the Renaissance. The only difference was that the Romans infused into it the idea of a higher realm of the spirit, of poetry and culture, to which they looked up with a longing admiration. Callimachus lacks this humility; he is too certain of himself, too much at home in his intellectual habitat. His refusal to acknowledge an overall goal of knowledge is matched by his failure to follow any ethical, political, or even simply educational directive. He would be the last to wish to admonish anyone to adopt his cultural convictions. The domain of the spirit in which he dwells is airy and attractive enough to compel the voluntary allegiance of anyone who has a mind for it.

In his *Wanderer's Storm Song* Goethe had contrasted the grand poetry of Pindar with Anacreon and Theocritus. This was not only a declaration of faith in favour of one of the two styles which baroque literary criticism had posited, nor was it merely a renunciation of the rococo literature with which he himself had been identified a little earlier. It was also his break with the heritage of the traditional humanistic creed.

In his *Dichtung und Wahrheit* (2.10) Goethe says he had learned from Herder 'that poetry is a possession of the whole world, of the people, and not just the private property of a few refined, cultured men'. These last words are an exact definition of what poetry had become through Callimachus. Since the Renaissance, this exclusive heirloom had been entered upon and cherished by those educated in the classics with many variations, and blending with a good many other influences, the tradition may be detected in Ariosto's *Orlando Furioso,* in Pope's *Rape of the Lock,* in Wieland's verse tales, and in Byron's *Don Juan.* Thus we have the paradox that Goethe, in a situation which in many respects resembled that in which Callimachus found himself, turned against the very things which owed their existence to him.

Theocritus and Anacreon—that is, the author of the *Anacreontea*—the playful, genially beckoning Hellenistic poets, are not visited by the deity, not by Zeus (Jupiter), Apollo, or Dionysus (Bromius). Dionysus is 'genius'—behind this we sense the concept of the untutored, the original genius—he is 'what inward glow to Pindar was, what to the world Phoebus Apollo is.' The 'inward glow' is the poet's participation in the divine spirit. In a letter dated Sept. 13th, 1774, written to K. Schmidt, Heinse describes Goethe himself as a new Pindar: 'Goethe stopped off with us, a beautiful young man of twenty-five, who from top to toe is genius and power and strength, a heart full of feeling, a spirit full of fire with eagle's wings, *qui ruit immensus ore profundo'*—this being the sequel of Horace's ode on Pindar from which we quoted above. These words are more significant than similar statements about other poets of the period who are praised as a new Pindar or, if a lady, as a new Sappho. Goldoni, for example, says about the *improvvisatore* Perfetti: 'The poet sang for about fifteen minutes stanzas in the manner of Pindar. Nothing finer than his song. He was Petrarch, Milton, Rousseau . . . no, Pindar himself.' By way of contrast with so affected and banal an application of historical names, Goethe tries to establish contact with the original experiences of the artist: 'When the wheels rattled . . . thy soul glowed perils, Pindar, heart.' True, this also has little to do with the real Pindar, for that poet nowhere refers to himself as being passionately involved in the contests which he celebrates, nor does he ever talk of 'victory-flushed youths' cracking of whips.' What we have is, rather, a vague concept of Pindar's victory hymns, constructed on the basis of Horace's simile of the mountain stream, and brought into line with certain views on the role of 'experience' in poetry which were current in Goethe's own time.

And yet in one point Goethe's new image of Pindar comes close to the truth. Goethe emphasizes the religious aspect of that poetry, following the teaching of Herder that genuine poetry does not spring from privacy, from refinement or education, but from the divine. This is the essential difference between Callimachus and Goethe, and between their two ages, that the reaction against rationalism takes two different shapes; once

it explodes as religious emotion, as enthusiasm and pathos and dithyrambic excitement, whereas in Alexandria its manifestation was the *jeu d'esprit*. The elements which Callimachus introduced into poetry were those same evils to which Goethe in his day objected, for rococo poetry was erected on the ideals of good taste and refined wit. In the age of rationalism the poets had managed to move closer than ever to the wellspring of the humanistic tradition, to Callimachus.

The new religious fervour of the *Storm and Stress* is no return to the ancient beliefs which had ruled supreme prior to the age of enlightenment. Goethe, to be sure, invokes the classical gods. In taking his leave of the humanistic tradition he attaches himself to an even older Greek heritage. But what transpired was not the re-establishment of a religious cult, but the creation of an independent secularized faith which traces the divine powers in the workings of nature and in the soul of the individual. Art furnished a very special revelation of these divine forces; and the Greeks were the great artists *par excellence.* That is why Winckelmann was able to find in Homer and in classical sculpture an expression of the divine on earth. This recollection of a distant past whose significance had been temporarily obscured made it possible to overcome rationalism without a recourse to scepticism or sleight-of-hand. In the age of Callimachus also, new religious needs had come to the fore and sought satisfaction outside the traditional forms of the native cults. This led to the acceptance of Asiatic and Egyptian gods, to an influx of barbaric material which could not but clash with the Greek culture. Wincklelmann, in a later age, was in a position to return to the foundations of European thought. He went outside the seemingly exhausted tradition of religious beliefs, to look for the revelation of the deity in the visible world. And thus he found himself able once more, despite enlightenment and scepticism, to arouse himself and others to an enthusiastic and passionate acclaim of the significant achievements in history and art. Among the Greeks this reversal from playfulness to seriousness was no longer feasible. But Goethe, in his age, repeated that distinction between the grand and the slender art which Aristophanes had been the first to promulgate

The poetry of the period of *Storm and Stress* is therefore not post-philosophical in the same sense as we saw it to be true of Callimachus. In its wake there developed a philosophy which was in many respects opposed to rationalism and which, unlike the philosophy of the enlightenment, succeeded in integrating history in its plan. Another consequence of it was— and here again the contrast with the age of Callimachus is evident—a tremendous upsurge of the historical sciences. This development, whatever other stimuli may have been operative to bring it about, owed its chief impulse to the new approach toward antiquity. Moreover, it was probably due to the new understanding of the Greek world as a historical phenomenon, that in the lyric poetry which at the time overran England and France as well as Germany, self-reflexion did not at once turn into the playful irony of Callimachus; that all poets, however personal the sentiments they expressed, acknowledged their membership in a meaningful world and in a life which in spite of all conflicts deserves to be taken seriously. The romantics may have longed for the age of childhood, they may have yearned for a return to the simple and artless forms of life; at the same time, however, Greek culture was, in some shape or other, their ultimate goal. In the course of the nineteenth century we often find a violent rejection of all things classical, and here we may detect the echoes of certain *Storm and Stress* ideas regarding the primitive genius. But we ought not to overlook the subtle irony of the circumstance that even the raving half-nonsense of the primitive genius is intimately linked with a tradition, a tradition, to boot, which derives from the opposite pole. Let us therefore console ourselves with the knowledge that the tradition of European culture is a reservoir which gives us the strength we need to overcome our spiritual crises. The Greeks did not yet have this reservoir at their disposal; it is all the more imperative that we exploit its energies. In this way, with the help of the Greeks, we shall perhaps be even more successful than they in fighting shy of the wrong turns and blind alleys which hamper our progress.

K. J. McKay (essay date 1962)

SOURCE: "A Glance at the Hymns," in *The Poet at Play: Kallimachos, "The Bath of Pallas,"* E. J. Brill, 1962, pp. 10-25.

[*In his book-length study of Callimachus's* Bath of Pallas, *classicist K. J. McKay begins with an overview, excerpted below, of the poet's six hymns. In an effort to determine date of composition and what some of Callimachus's sources might have been, McKay considers the poems, especially their imagery, in relation to earlier works and in the context of the history of the Alexandrian court.*]

We owe the preservation of the **Hymns** to the tidy mind of an early scribe who brought together the Hymns of Homer, Kallimachos, Orpheus (and the Orphic *Argonautica*) and Proklos. It is worth bearing in mind what we would now possess but for this fortunate circumstance. Of the 95 lines of the **first Hymn** we would have some thirteen complete lines, parts of ten others and tatters of papyrus. But this would be sheer luxury compared with the lot of **Hymns 5** and **6**. Of the latter we would be able to identify only three lines with confidence from ancient testimonia, with fragmentary relics on papyrus. *Of the former, the subject of this study, we could not place a single line.* Lines are not

assigned to the **Hymn** on the rare occasions on which they are quoted, and—presumably by accident—the **Hymn** is not represented among the papyri. Among the hymns fewest ancient testimonia survive for **Hs. 5** and **6** and, even if Poseidippos . . . does really demonstrate an early regard for the *Bath of Pallas*, beyond an allusion or two in Propertius and Tibullus we have little to show that its merits continued to be recognized.

It is frequently regretted today that the **Hymns** are the only complete work of the poet to survive (for we have only a selection of his epigrams). This complaint is not difficult to appreciate. The sizable fragments of the *Hecale* and *Aitia* which are now accessible to us give an impression of greater relaxation from the point of view of style and content. But, for good or ill, with all their richness, variety and the obscurity which time, no less than design, has stamped upon them, the **Hymns** remain the most substantial surviving relics of the poet's work. As I have mentioned, we could have had a great deal less. Let us be grateful for so fortuitous a transmission, and draw from them what illumination we can.

The **Hymns** are six in number, and there is no shred of evidence to suggest that Kallimachos ever wrote more. Their subjects are **1. Zeus 2. Apollo 3. Artemis 4. Delos 5. Athene** (*The Bath of Pallas*) and **6. Demeter**. At every level their variety becomes painfully obvious. Five of the hymns are written in dactylic hexameters, one, the fifth, in elegiac couplets. Four of the hymns are written in epic-Ionic, but the fifth and sixth in literary Doric. Three (**Hs. 1, 2, 4**) flatter the Ptolemies. Again three (**Hs. 2, 5, 6**) plunge us into an atmosphere of excited expectation, the reactions of the faithful awaiting a divine epiphany. Again, the poems differ in purpose. **Hymn 1**, which ends with a prayer for both virtue and wealth, is often construed as the artful dodge of Kallimachos in his early days of poverty to gain recognition from Ptolemy Philadelphos, in the spirit of the American parody: 'Alleluia, give us a handout to revive us again'. **H. 2** is assumed, certainly wrongly, to be designed to reconcile Kallimachos' native city, Cyrene, to the overlordship of Egypt. **H. 4**, a glorification of Delos and built around the story of Leto's search for a land which would have the courage to ignore Hera's hostility and assist at the birth of Apollo, contains a deification of Philadelphos which may be more important than its subordinate position suggests. **Hymns 3, 5** and **6** (at least) have a literary purpose.

Again, **Hymns 1, 2, 5** and (in a special way) **6** may be separated from the other two by the way in which the poet superimposes images. This point is worth elaborating. If I say more in this chapter about **Hymns 1** and **2** than **3** and **4** it is because the former have more significant points of contact with **Hs. 5** and **6**. Moreover one can extract more from them, even if one cannot lay claim to understanding them. In truth—something about which it pays to be frank—**H. 3** is an enigma to me, and also part of the purpose of **H. 4**. I can take comfort only in the fact that, even in this year of grace and with an author as diligently studied as Vergil, it would be unwise to risk money on behalf of another's claim that he understood the *Eclogues*.

It was the Ptolemaic ruler-cult which provided a ready-made opportunity for studies in ambivalence. Where kings and queens became gods and goddesses by royal decree, and enterprising parts of the empire were prepared to pay them such honours during their lifetimes (and Ptolemy Philadelphos was to legitimize the practice), a poet—particularly a court poet—had ample opportunity to garnish the hymnal form with judicious overlapping of images. It is a reflection of Kallimachos' mischievous spirit that he does not sustain the device throughout the first two hymns. I know that there have been scholars with a differing viewpoint, but if this study establishes anything, it draws attention to Kallimachos as 'the mischievous poet', who delights in the ebb and flow of images and challenges us to detect when his semantic tide is on the turn. I trust, also, that the reader will notice in retrospect that it is *a priori* likely that both **Hs. 1** and **2** precede **Hs. 5** and **6**, precisely because the identification of god and ruler calls for no display of the imagination, whereas the nature of the levels of reference in **Hs. 5** (taken from popular piety) and **6** (taken from literature) suggests that they are developments of the feature.

The **first hymn** starts with Zeus. The image is quite clear, for the poet debates whether the god was born in Crete or Arcadia. Arcadia, he says, must win, for Cretans are notorious liars, and they prove this by exhibiting Zeus' grave. But what of lines 57 ff., in which Kallimachos quarrels with the common sense of the orthodox view that Zeus, Poseidon and Pluto drew lots for Heaven, Sea and Earth? Only fools, argues the poet, would draw lots for unequal prizes, for Olympos and Hades. The truth is that Zeus' elder brothers magnanimously recognized his merits as a warrior and installed him in Heaven. This seems to me to involve transparent flattery. 'The suggestion is that the elder son of Ptolemy Soter should have acted similarly, something he had in fact failed to do' (Körte, *Hellenistic Poetry . . .*). The fact that Homer (*Il.* 15. 190 ff) presents the view of the partition which Kallimachos rejects, and Hesiod (*Theog.* 881) that which the poet accepts, has invited the conclusion that **H.** 1.57 ff. is simply an exercise in literary polemics. But Kallimachos protests too much; he is a little too anxious to establish his case. After all is not . . . 'It is proper to cast lots on equal terms' . . . a piece of special pleading? If Hades is to be thought of as a booby prize, then only a fool would accept it without a chance at a higher prize. When the poet talks of 'equality' he argues

from the premise that each party has offered a region *as his stake;* but we should know better.

When Kallimachos flatters Ptolemy as a mighty warrior (66 f.) he follows a course which Theokritos also considered diplomatic (*Id.* 17.56 f., 103). To be sure history tells another story (Gow *ad locc. cit.*), but the conceit was harmless. However reference to the troubled rise of Philadelphos to power was a risky business; Ptolemy might misconstrue his meaning. And so the poet has provided the allusion with a perfectly respectable facade, a suggestion of that new respect for Hesiod which is a characteristic of the age. If Ptolemy takes umbrage Kallimachos is ready with his bearing of injured innocence. Zeus is now Ptolemy Philadelphos and, we may conclude, freshly risen to power. We may notice it as a curiosity— although no part of the poet's plan—that Zeus' brothers may very properly be deemed *philadelphoi*. But Callimachean images are seldom simple; the poet prefers kaleidoscopic variety. And so he retraces his steps. 'From Zeus come kings, since nothing is diviner than the kings of Zeus' (78-9), and most highly blessed of all is 'our ruler' (84-9). That is to say, kings are *diogeneis,* and especially Philadelphos. Is Zeus now Philadelphos' father, Ptolemy Soter? Possibly. At least he is not Philadelphos. But the poet moves forward again.

The *envoi* (91-6) contains a prayer to the divinity for virtue and wealth. From Hom. Hymn 15. 9, 20. 8 and Buck, *Greek Dialects* (1955), we gather that it is a traditional formula. But Kallimachos uses repetition in a way which is highly suspicious: 'not wealth without virtue, nor virtue without wealth, but virtue and wealth'. We now have no doubt that the earthly king is uppermost in the poet's thoughts. The distinctive result is that the poem contains two levels of reference, but the pattern is not so thorough-going that we can think of simple and consistent allegory. The one image is at one moment elevated, at another subordinated, and consistently within the confines of a formal harmony. This is the principal way in which Kallimachos exploits the hymnal form, by weaving sporadically into his hymn an alien strand, but of similar texture to the general composition. It is a strand which transforms the composition, either announcing the poet's purpose (as here) or, as in the 'epiphany' hymns (where it constitutes a special device which I have called later, for want of a more inspired name, a *sophisma*) safeguarding the poet, and the reader, from excessive attention to the rich emotional content of that type of composition.

Although an 'epiphany' hymn, **H. 2** is a companion piece to **H. 1**. Both Zeus as king and Apollo as patron of the arts have earthly counterparts. At the opening Apollo is returning from his holidays. Nature falls silent before the paean of welcome; also those who perpetually mourn, Thetis for her Achilles, and metamorphosed Niobe. This leads artistically, *via* the thought that Niobe's grief over her children, slain by Apollo and Artemis, was the result of her boast that she was superior to Leto in fecundity, to the utterance: 'Cry Hié! Hié! It is an ill thing to vie with the Blessed Ones. He who fights with the Blessed would fight with my king; he who fights with my king would fight also with Apollo'. Apollo and king are set side by side, bound together by a mysterious, ill-defined bond which excites our interest: Apollo and Ptolemy are ὁμοφρονέοντες. In lines 97-103 an aition is provided for the ritual cry ἰὴ ἰὴ παιηον, based on ἴει, ἴει 'shoot, shoot', the cry raised by the Delphians when Apollo joined battle with the dread Python. 'A helper from the first your mother bore you, and ever since that is your praise' (103-4). Kallimachos finishes with an example of Apollo's help:

> Envy spoke furtively into the ear of Apollo: "I don't think much of the poet who does not sing the loud song of the sea". Apollo kicked Envy away and retorted: "Mighty is the current of the Euphrates, but it carries on its waters much litter and garbage. And not of every water do her priestesses carry to Demeter, but of the water pure and undefiled that springs up from a hallowed fountain, a trickling stream, the finest flower of water".

The *envoi,* short and crisp, prays that Blame may join Envy, expelled from the Heavenly circle.

Of course this literary quarrel is not conducted at a celestial level. Envy and Blame stand for definite, although unknown, critics of Kallimachos. We cannot help thinking of the critics pilloried by the poet as the Telchines, malevolent Rhodian spirits, in the preface to his *Aitia,* the more so as in the same passage Apollo presents to the poet his literary manifesto. Hence Apollo assuredly stands for a Ptolemy, Ptolemy the patron, the champion; and, we may suspect, **H. 2** is the poet's paean to him. We find ourselves then wondering exactly how much of the poem really is divorced from a retrospective double reference. The sight of Apollo ensures greatness (10). 'We shall see you, Farworker, and we shall never be lowly' (11). Is Ptolemy definitely excluded? The alien strand is so similar in texture to the material of the form that we cannot be sure. There are some who have not been able to identify it at all. . . . In a sense, we are all interlopers here. **H. 2** is not written for us, no *monumentum aere perennius;* it was all for Ptolemy's benefit. What mattered most was to give his flattered patron opportunity to find his reflection mirrored in the poem at the second reading. Here we may merely note how the poet invites our confusion by a formal respect for the type of composition which he employs. Even Apollo's act in expelling Envy with a kick, which Bethe noted as most ungodlike, is *formally* balanced by line 3; the god who kicks the door in welcome kicks Envy in dismissal. It is the

departure in sense from the Homeric hymn which indicates the poet's mischievous intervention.

If then **H. 1** is reasonably regarded as an early plea for royal favour and recognition, **H. 2** seems a later act of thanksgiving for royal protection. There is a distinctly personal tone to the poem: 'my king' (26-7) . . . 'my city' (65) . . . 'our kings' (68) . . . 'But I call you Karneios; such is the manner of my fathers' (71). As Chamoux [*Cyrène sous la monarchie des Battiades*] observes: 'Le ἐμοὶ πατρώιον οὕτω sonne très haut'. It is particularly unfortunate that our complete understanding of the imagery of **H. 2** is crippled by chronological problems. I would gladly bypass them completely, for this is not a suitable moment to ventilate the subject adequately, but at least the choice confronting us must be mentioned. It is generally, but not always, assumed that the hymn is late, an idea which has recently been challenged by Prof. Von der Mühll [*Museum Helvetica,* vol. 15, 1958]. An early date suggests Philadelphos again as the human term of reference, while a late date may turn our thoughts to his successor, Ptolemy Euergetes, who became sole ruler in 247. The ***Lock of Berenice*** establishes that the poet was still productive after this date, but, according to the theory, **H. 2** could have been written before the death of Philadelphos.

The scholiast at line 26 took 'my king' to refer to Euergetes, διὰ δὲ τὸ φιλόλογον αὐτὸν εἶναι ὡς θεὸν τιμα. Perhaps this is no more than a guess, and may be based on the line which gives the identification most point: δύναται γάρ, ἐπεὶ Διὶ δεξιὸς ἧσται (29). Now a reference to the source of the divinity's power is traditional, and Kallimachos plays upon this fact again at **H. 5**. 131 ff. We may compare Pindar fr. 146 Snell, where Athene sits on the right hand of Zeus and receives his commandments for the gods. The problem is the question of whether both Zeus and Apollo are allegorical terms at this point, or whether only Apollo has an earthly counterpart. If the former, we recall that in **H. 1** Zeus and Philadelphos are identified. The poet would hark back to his earlier hymn. In fact the equation of Zeus and Philadelphos is almost canonical. For example, at Theocr. *Id.* 7. 93 Simichidas, representing Theokritos in his youth, says that he would not be surprised if his poems had already been brought by report to 'the throne of Zeus'. Meleager (*Anth. Pal.* VII. 418.3) talks of 'Kos which reared Zeus', for Philadelphos was born on that island. Theokritos (*Id.* 17. 131) compares Philadelphos' married life with his sister Arsinoe to the *hieros gamos* of Zeus and Hera. We would then have to seek in Apollo a co-regent of Philadelphos.

Now we do hear of a co-regent from 267/6, but he is always 'Ptolemy the son'. Since the title Euergetes was not assumed until between the third and fifth year of his reign, it was once supposed that 'Ptolemy the

Athena, the subject of The Bath of Pallas.

son' is Euergetes. To this identification, in the present state of our knowledge, Volkmann, who has recently studied the evidence in *R.E.* xxiii, 2 (1959), 1666.26 ff. and 1668. 35 ff., has raised serious objections. Again, Apollo as Euergetes seems to give special significance to the poet's historical sketch of the foundation of Cyrene under Apollo's guidance, for Euergetes was betrothed to Berenice, the daughter of Magas, king of Cyrene. But Kallimachos had valid reasons for discussing Cyrene since it was his native city. Moreover that this episode is so important that the opening epiphany scene is to be localised in Cyrene is a quite unnecessary assumption. And yet Apollo may still be Euergetes, promoted to a partnership, which he did not formally enjoy, by a grateful poet. Such a liberty would fall short of being outrageous, for Philadelphos, as Zeus, would not be deprived of his meed of honour.

The alternative is to assume Apollo to be Philadelphos the patron, the counterpart of Zeus as Philadelphos the king in **H. 1**. Here again we meet a choice. Is Zeus then his father, Ptolemy Soter, who had been deified along with his wife as the 'Saviour Gods'? Hardly likely, when Philadelphos' co-regency was as early as 285-283 and the tense of ἧσται demands a present reality; but Soter may now be Zeus Soter, enthroned in Heaven. Or is Zeus simply his celestial self? Philadelphos then becomes Zeus' most honoured son, just as at one stage in **H. 1** this king is the divinest of kings, honoured by Zeus. If we could be confident of this identification, we might find it of a little use for chronological purposes. In **H. 1** the image fluctuates between Zeus, Ptolemy=Zeus and *Ptolemy* who derives his power from Zeus, in **H. 2** between Apollo, Ptolemy=Apollo and *Apollo=Ptolemy* who derives his power from Zeus. That is to say, there would be a development in the imagery. At this stage in the first hymn Ptolemy is 'divinest of the kings of Zeus', while in the second he is unequivocally a god. This would suggest that **H. 1** precedes, while **H. 2** follows, Philadelphos' open assumption of divine honours (c. 271/0 B.C.).

Much more could be said, but it would serve no purpose. Better to practice angelic, even archangelic, caution, for the elucidation of Kallimachos from Ptolemaic chronology is the explanation of the obscure *per obscurius*. And yet, whether Philadelphos or Euergetes is involved, the fact of the double level of reference stands firm.

We have examined at some length the interaction of dominant images in the first two hymns because **Hymns 5** and **6** also feature a similar play. But the technique is also used at a lower level. For example, at **H. 4**. 47-9 Delos, when a wandering island under the name of Asterie, swam to the 'water-drenched *maston* of the island Parthenie (for it was not yet Samos)'. Μαστός is at the same time 'breast' and 'hill'. As Prof. C. del

Grande (*Filologia Minore,* p. 244) reminds us, a double image is possible because of the poetic conceit that an island is a giant nymph lying in the sea. Particularly one with so feminine a name as Parthenie. The device had already been noted as Pindaric by G. Norwood (*Pindar,* pp. 35, 38) and J. Duchemin (*Pindare,* pp. 141-2). Pindar liked to blend the images of a city and its eponymous nymph, as at *Pyth.* 4. 8, where Battos is sent to found Cyrene ἐν ἀργινόεντι μαστῷ. It is interesting to find him applying the same technique to Delos, and then in an unequivocal form (*Paean* 5. 39-42):

> ἐρικυδέ τ᾽ ἔσχον
> Δᾶλον, ἐπεί σφιν Ἀπόλλων
> δῶκεν ὁ χρυσοκόμας
> Ἀστερίας δέμας οἰκειν.

We may justly say of Kallimachos what H. Fränkel (*Ovid,* p. 99) found good reason to say of Ovid's interest in metamorphosis: 'The theme gave ample scope for displaying the phenomena of insecure and fleeting identity, of a self divided in itself or spilling over into another self'.

The Hellenistic circle had a special regard for the ambivalent in language, or what could pass for ambivalence, for this, after all, is the stuff of metaphor. When we find in Kallimachos a rare word, we shall learn nothing if we merely catalogue the use as recherché, and close our minds to the factors which prompt the use. When words cease to be affective they often cease to be effective for the poet. He finds himself obliged to reestablish the imagery, perhaps in a different direction, or to restore lost sonority, perhaps on the basis of principles of which an earlier age was not conscious. He had above all to overcome the handicap of a lingua franca, the *Koine,* which gave little encouragement to poetic endeavour. The rare word, then, may convey a desirable sound or may add a new dimension to the imagery. The common word may equally be renovated by changing its associations or by recalling it to an etymology which it had by lapse of time outgrown. In Kallimachos it pays to be sensitive to both new and old, for we have the added complicating factors of the degree of conformity of the language to a particular type of composition (e.g. the language of the *Epigrams* and **H. 5** is rather different from that of the *Aitia*), and of the strong possibility of pointed literary reference. Again and again we are driven back to our lexica to find the antecedents of a usage; the results are so rewarding that we can only regret the more keenly the passing of so much literature which must have been exposed to the poet's excerpting passion.

In **H. 5** there is not a good deal in the way of special verbal effects. The language is refined because too many distractions will put Kallimachos' purpose beyond our recall. But there are some effects. For example, at lines 75-6. There could not have been a poet of any standing who had not had occasion more than once to describe the bloom of youth; the subject must have been a continual challenge to a clever poet. Kallimachos swings into the image in the hexameter with ἄρτι γένεια and when the pentameter opens we are surprised to find περκάζων as the verb, for it is appropriate to ripening grapes. In fact he is appropriating, with characteristic modification, an image from Euripides' *Cretans . . .* (of Pasiphae's bull!). One of a quieter kind occurs in line 12, where the horses' mouths are χαλινοφάγοι. He might have said χαλινοδάκοι . . . , but the frothing of the horses' mouths suggested mastication, not mere biting. English has the same transfer in 'to champ the bit', for which verb the Oxford English Dictionary defines the primary meaning as 'munch (fodder) noisily'. Latin is no different with its *mandere,* e.g. Verg. *Aen.* 4. 135: stat sonipes ac frena ferox spumantia mandit.

There are clearer examples in **H. 6**. At lines 94-5 we are told: 'His mother wailed, and his two sisters lamented bitterly, and the breast that he used to drink and the many tens of handmaids'. 'The breast that he used to drink' is of course Erysichthon's wet-nurse, but it is more than a simple case of *synecdoche,* the part for the whole. The logical verb for 'breast' in the sentence is 'lamented'. . . . We then begin to remember that beating the breast was a regular way for women to express grief, and that Kallimachos is again playing upon two levels of reference. Again at line 105. Through the insatiable hunger of Erysichthon the food supply of the palace is rapidly being exhausted. 'The cattle stalls are empty', but the adjective used by the poet is . . . 'widowed'. The idea of 'bereavement' adds a pathetic overtone to Triopas' plea to Poseidon. Lastly we shall notice one not so successful. Erysichthon's parents try to conceal their disgrace, but this is impossible ὄκα τὸν βαθὺν οἶκον ἀνεξήραναν ὀδόντες. The house is . . . 'prosperous', 'wealthy'. Kallimachos associates this metaphorical idea of 'depth' with a pit or well, hence the forceful . . . 'they dried up the (deep)house'. This is bearable, but the subject is 'his teeth', which must then be thought of as a searing wind drying up even a deep well. This is venturesome, to say the least, but perhaps we should bear in mind that the Erysichthon tale is burlesque, and humorous exaggeration must consequently enjoy some concession.

We shall also find it useful to consider some of the elements which make the amalgam of a Callimachean hymn. At the summit Homer reigns, but precisely because he is a colossus of unique power no Hellenist sought merely to be stamped as *Homerikotatos.* While many Hellenistic scholars are known to have been keen commentators on the Homeric texts, both those who approved of an epic canvass of its original dimensions and those who did not strove to innovate. It was customary to modify when borrowing, as at **H. 5**. 104, where the thought of *Il.* 20. 127-8 (Αἶσα / γιγνομένῳ ἐπένησε λίνῳ, ὅτε μιν τέκε μήτηρ) and *Il.* 24. 209-210 (Μοῖρα κραταιὴ / γιγνομένῳ ἐπένησε λίνῳ, ὅτε μιν τέκον αὐτή) appears in the form: Μοῖραν ὧδ᾽ ἐπένησε λίνα, / ἁνίκα τὸ πρατόν νιν ἐγείναο. The most surprising thing is the rise of Hesiod; not simply as a more approachable standard, but for positive reasons. He was to them a polymath with wide interests, a didactic poet who paid careful attention to sound, and, as the supposed author of the *Catalogue of Women,* a mythological mine, a model for narrative art, with even a curious reputation for love poetry.

But far more important was the Hellenistic eagerness to give new life to limp traditional forms by blending the Classical genres. Kallimachos' formal model, the Homeric Hymn, was heavily indebted to the epic and, generally speaking, breathed the atmosphere of an earlier age of piety. It does not do to overstate the latter point. They are not religious outpourings, and the Hymn to Hermes, for example, is as modern in its playfulness as a Callimachean production. The deep dependence on Homer, which strengthened the tradition that Homer was their author, at any rate stamped them collectively as archaic. The most obvious importation into Kallimachos' hymns is a pronounced lyrical flavour. We need not think of it as a preserve of our poet. I think particularly of an attractive fragment of a kind of *partheneion* to Demeter, in a mixture of Aeolic and Doric, almost certainly of the Hellenistic period.

> Ἤνθομεν ἐς μεγάλας Δαμάτερος ἐννέ
> ἐάσσαι,
> παῖσαι παρθενικαί, παῖσαι καλὰ
> ἔμματ᾽ ἔχοισαι,
> καλὰ μὲν ἔμματ᾽ ἔχοισαι, ἀριπρεπέας
> δὲ καὶ ὅρμως
> πριστω ἐξ ἐλέφαντος, ἴδην ποτεοικότας

'We are nine young maids who went to Church, all wearing our Sunday best'. It is hard not to think of Gilbert and Sullivan.

A lyrical element in the hymnal form reminds us that lyricists also wrote hymns. Apart from Pindar, whose influence is almost omnipresent, it is only seldom that we have the means to gauge the extent of their influence upon Kallimachos; but what we find suggests that it was strong. For example, **H. 3** opens with forty lines of discussion between a wheedling three-year-old Artemis and her indulgent father, 'das Baby Artemis auf Papa Zeus' Schoss', in which the goddess prattles about the presents she would like, and finds a responsive ear. A few lines of Lesbian poetry, attributed without certainty to Alkaios, provided the inspiration:

"I vow that I shall ever be virgin, a huntress on the peaks of lonely mountains. Come, grant these favours for my sake." So she spoke; and the father of the blessed gods nodded assent.

More important for us, because of the epiphany motif, is Alkaios' Hymn to Apollo, of which only the first line survives. Fortunately the contents are summarized for us by Himerius (*Or.* xiv. 10 f. = xlviii. 10 f. Colonna). Apollo, sent by Zeus to Delphi to speak as prophet of justice and right to Hellas, disobediently spends a year among the Hyperboreans. The Delphians compose a paean and beseech the god to come back. Eventually he does.

> Now it was summer, and indeed midsummer, when Alkaios brings Apollo back from the Hyperboreans. And so, because the summer was aglow, and Apollo was at home . . . , even the lyre puts on a summer-dress, so to speak, in honour of the god. . . . The nightingales sing him the kind of song you expect of birds in Alkaios; swallows and cicadas sing, forgetting to tell of their own sufferings among men, and devoting their songs wholly to the god. Kastalia flows, in poetic vein, with streams of silver, and the waves of Kephisos heave and surge, like Homer's Enipeus. For Alkaios, like Homer, perforce makes even the water capable of perceiving the gods' presence. . . .

The interest which this has for Kallimachos' **H. 2**. 1-24 becomes obvious.

> How the laurel sapling of Apollo trembles! How the whole shrine trembles! Away, away, he that is sinful! Now surely Phoibos is striking the door with his lovely foot. Don't you see? The Delian palm nods merrily all at once, and the swan sings sweetly in the air! Now of yourselves swing back, you bars of the gates, swing back of yourselves, you bolts! For the god is no longer distant. And do you, young lads, prepare yourselves for song and dance.

> Not to every man does Apollo appear, but to him who is good. He who sees him, he is great; who sees him not is of low estate. We shall see you, Farworker, and we shall never be lowly. The lads are not to keep lyre silent or tread noiseless when Apollo is at home . . . , if they wish to accomplish marriage and cut hoary locks, and the wall to stand upon its ancient foundations. Well done, lads! For the lyre is no longer idle. Be hushed as you hear the song to Apollo. Hushed even the sea, when singers glorify the lyre or bow, the weapons of Lycorean Apollo. Not even Thetis wails a mother's lament for Achilles, when she hears the cry 'Hié Paiéon! Hié Paiéon!' And the tearful rock defers its grief, the wet stone that is set in Phrygia, a marble rock in the stead of a woman, uttering sorrowful words from an open mouth.

Both hymns concern an *epidemia* of Apollo, and in both the excitement runs high. What is particularly interesting is the complete diversity of illustration within common themes. There is the same excited reaction of Apollo's impersonal associates, but in Alkaios it is his lyre (given to him at his birth, whence he invented lyre playing, Alc. α 1 (b) Lobel-Page—perhaps from this same hymn), in Kallimachos the sacred laurel, palm and the whole of the shrine. In both birds also react. Alkaios features the nightingales, Kallimachos the swans. (In Alkaios Apollo has a chariot of swans.) Gloom is dispelled in both versions. In Alkaios the swallows and cicadas forget their sufferings (immortalized in the Prokne-Philomela and Tithonos stories); in Kallimachos it is Thetis and Niobe. We notice, incidentally, that the former react to the presence of Apollo, the latter to the paean itself. In both versions water reacts. In the earlier Kephisos heaves and surges with joy, in the latter the sea is reverently hushed. When Alkaios' Kastalia flows with streams of silver, there is probably the same honorific intention that we find in H. 5. 49. ff., where Inachos brings down gold and blossoms on its waters, and in Moschos 3. 1-3, where Alpheus courts Arethusa, his waters bearing beautiful leaves and blossoms and holy dust from the race-course at Olympia.

Such unity in diversity admits of only two explanations: either Kallimachos is completely remodelling Alkaios, or there is a specialized lyric hymn centring upon the *epidemia* of Apollo, either inaugurated by Alkaios or a common possession of both poets. In either case, the parallel invites the conclusion that **H. 2** is earlier than **Hs. 5** and **6**. These three hymns feature an arresting dramatic-mimetic opening to an epiphany. **Hs. 5** and **6**, we shall see, are closely connected and highly specialised compositions. **Hymn 2** stands apart from both in dialect, and from **H. 5** in metre. Either **H. 2** precedes, or follows, **Hs. 5** and **6**. The clue is, I think, given by the fact that in the last two hymns the epiphany is incidental to the poet's purpose. He does not say to himself 'I shall construct an epiphany hymn'. He says instead 'I shall do something with this story of Teiresias' (**H. 5**) and 'I shall do something more with this Doric dialect' (**H. 6**). If the rest of this study has any merit, in **Hs. 5** and **6** Kallimachos is using the epiphany motif as something already found satisfying and successful. And it was earlier found successful in a composition which borrowed the excitement of an epiphany from a lyric hymn. In other words, since we know of a hymn by Alkaios featuring an epiphany of Apollo, it is *a priori* likely that Kallimachos developed the idea first in his **Hymn to Apollo**, for which the basic idea came readymade, and then maintained the technique in **Hs. 5** and **6**. At the same time (a matter of intuition, I fear), I would not be inclined to put **H. 2** *much* earlier than the later pair.

In the face of the variety which I have been illustrating, it is unlikely that we shall ever find a master-key to unlock the door of every hymn. Certainly every

attempt hitherto has failed. Cahen (*Callimaque,* pp. 247 95.) disposes of them all—that they were written by royal command, were allegorical glorifications of the Ptolemies, were liturgical poems, were poems written for poetic contests held during religious festivals. Cahen's own theory is equally involved in their fall. He believed that the hymns have a basis in 'une espèce d'ἐπίδειξις, de lecture solennelle, en rapport direct avec la fête religieuse, en dehors pourtant de son programme' (*Callimaque,* pp. 281 f.). He does not help his idea by wedding it to the belief that each poem was declaimed at the very places where the festival was celebrated, and that therefore the poems were directed to a genuine public—but not the *profanum uulgus,* rather 'un public de dévots, capable d'émotion religieuse et d'émotion littéraire aussi'. . . . Kallimachos would have been appalled (or, perhaps more characteristically, entertained) by the prospect. We may at the present day feel confident that Kallimachos wrote in Alexandria for his friends (including some in the highest places), and for them alone; but for the answers to more particular questions we must weigh each poem individually. . . .

T. B. L. Webster (essay date 1964)

SOURCE: "Kallimachos," in *Hellenistic Poetry and Art,* Barnes & Noble, Inc., 1964, pp. 98-121.

[*In the following excerpt from his* Hellenistic Poetry and Art, *Webster considers Callimachus's reputation during his career and his aesthetic criteria, simultaneously providing an extensive examination of the poet's works, including the hymns, the iambi, Hecale, and the epigrams. Webster's discussion entails a summary of the "hostilities" concerning aesthetics that Callimachus found himself engaged in with other poets. In his final assessment, Webster attributes Callimachus with "elegance, humour, learning, and variety."*]

Kallimachos certainly lived through the reign of Ptolemy Philadelphos and died in the reign of Ptolemy Euergetes. He came from Cyrene to Alexandria; he was first a schoolmaster in the suburb of Eleusis, then was in charge of the catalogue at the Library. The fixed points for his production are given by Pfeiffer [*Callimachus*]: *Epigram 20* is very early, about 300, and was written at Cyrene; it probably takes *Epigram 54,* also for a Cyrenaean, with it. *Hymn 1,* according to Wilamowitz, contains a reference to Philadelphos early in his reign, i.e. about 280 B.C.; this therefore will have been written soon after Kallimachos came to Alexandria. The *Galateia* (fr. 378-9) is probably not long after 278 B.C. The *Marriage of Arsinoe* (fr. 392) is about 276/5 B.C., and the *Deification of Arsinoe* (fr. 228) in 270 B.C. The *Hymn to Delos* (IV) is dated by Wilamowitz 269/5, after the death of Arsinoe and before the outbreak of the war with Antigonos Gonatas. If, as he argues, Kallimachos had visited Delos when he wrote this hymn, fr. 114 (probably from bk. III of the *Aitia*), fr. 203 (*Iambos* **XIII**), and *Ep. 62* derive from the same visit: fr. 178 (*Aitia*) in which Kallimachos denies knowledge of seafaring should be earlier.

Theokritos' dated poems belong to the years 273/70, and according to our argument presuppose a first edition (in whatever form) of Apollonios' *Agronautika*, as do also the *Aitia* and the *Hekale* of Kallimachos. The likely echoes of Theokritos in Kallimachos are two in the *Hekale,* one in the third book of the *Aitia*; the introduction to the eleventh idyll is clearly echoed in *Epigram 46*, which is itself dated well before 240, because, as Pfeiffer notes, the doctor consoled in that epigram has a son who is referred to as an authoritative person in a papyrus of 240. It is at least tempting to put fairly near 270 B.C. some other poems recalling the manner rather than the wording of Theokritos, particularly *Hymns V* and *VI* which have the same spirit as Theokritos' *Adoniazousai* (XV). Four further epigrams may also belong here; *Ep. 30* (note also the name Kleonikos) and *43* recall the unhappy lover of Theokritos XIV; *Ep. 22* is bucolic, not only in matter but also in the bucolic anaphora, which is found again in the first book of the *Aitia* (fr. 27); *Ep. 52* may be a compliment to the young Theokritos.

After 265 B.C. we have no firm dates again until the beginning of the reign of Euergetes in 246 B.C. It can at least be suggested that most of the last two books of the *Aitia*, the *Hekale*, and the third hymn belong here; and *Iambos* IV with its pair of birds has perhaps a reminiscence of the *Hekale.* For the last period *Hymn II* is dated by its reference to Euergetes (26). The *Coma Berenices* belongs to 246/5 B.C. with fr. 388 rather earlier and fr. 387 rather later. The prologue of the *Aitia*, written when Kallimachos had lived 'many decades', must belong to this time, and the reference to Parmenion's Serapieion in the first *Iambos* may place this here too. Possibly also the Sosibios poem (fr. 384) is very late; it is as frigid as the *Coma Berenices*.

The late dating of the first *Iambos,* if it can be maintained, is extremely interesting as it may be Kallimachos' last word on literary disputes. He pictures Hipponax returning from the dead to summon the *philologoi* to the new Serapieion to hear the story of the Seven Sages: Thales was offered the cup which had been bequeathed to the wisest, and passed it on to Bion; so it went the rounds until it came back to Thales, and he dedicated it to Apollo at Branchidai. The Alexandrian scholar-poets are not only told the story of the Seven Sages by a revenant; they are also told it among the statues of wise men in the Serapieion, if Professor Rees'[*Classical Review*, vol. 75, 1961] attractive interpretation is right. Euhemeros in the poem is a statue, presumably one of a group like the remark-

able collection of Homer, Pindar, Demetrios of Phaleron, Orpheus, Hesiod, Protagoras, Thales, Herakleitos, and Plato from the Exedra of the Serapieion at Memphis; similar groups are known in mosaics, which presumably derive from Hellenistic paintings. The presence of two Early Hellenistic figures, Euhemeros and Demetrios of Phaleron, in these groups of classical and mythical figures shows how strongly the Alexandrians felt themselves the heirs of the whole tradition of Greek poetry and wisdom. Thales at Memphis is explaining a globe with his stick; Thales in the first *Iambos* is also an astronomer and is scratching geometrical diagrams on the ground with his stick. The metre and the language and the manner of this poem come from Hipponax, but Kallimachos has given the expression an Alexandrian obscurity: Thales is drawing a figure invented by his junior, Pythagoras; Pythagoras is therefore called by the name of the Trojan war hero, Euphorbos, whose incarnation Pythagoras claimed to be. This learned allusion is matched by an equally learned vocabulary. But this learnedness is varied with direct flashes: 'my good man, don't wrinkle your nose. I have not much time myself.' But the general purpose must be a demand to cease hostilities, and the revenant Hipponax, who in his lifetime drove the sculptor Boupalos to suicide by his abuse, as he reminds us at the beginning, is the most powerful possible advocate. The solidarity of learned poets is also the message of the fourth *Iambos,* the story of the two trees, which may also belong to this time, if it is later than the *Hekale.*

The hostilities themselves are mentioned during this late period at the end of *Hymn II*, in the prologue to the *Aitia*, and in *Iambos* **XIII**, which is certainly later than the Delian hymn (270/65) and may have been composed as a pendant to *Iambos* **I**. The *Diegesis* to *Iambos* **XIII** says that Kallimachos answered those who blamed him for the variety of his poems by saying that he copied Ion of Chios and that nobody blames the craftsman for making many different sorts of object. What is left of *Iambos* **XIII** gives first the criticism Kallimachos writes Ionic without going to Ephesos, mixes old and new vocabulary, mixes dialects— then the answer that no one made a rule 'one poet, one genre', then probably the passage about the craftsmen (36) and Ion of Chios (41 f.). The Muses loved him, but now the poets abuse each other so violently that the Muses fly past for fear of being abused. 'Do not wonder then if I sing limping iambics, although I have never been to Ephesos.' The charge against Kallimachos is variety of metre, dialect, and vocabulary; his countercharge is mutual abuse and lack of inspiration.

The abuse poured out by rival poets in *Iambos* **XIII** is personified by Phthonos and Momos of *Hymn II* (105): 'Envy said in Apollo's ear, "I do not like the singer who does not sing as the sea." Apollo kicked Envy out and said: "The Assyrian river's stream is great but carries most of the filth of the land and much rubbish on its waters. Demeter's bees do not bring water from everywhere but the little water, finest flower, which wells clean and undefiled from a holy spring." Farewell, Lord. May Criticism dwell where Envy is.' Viewed with the charge, the defence is an admission of writing many kinds of poetry, a claim that each poem is comparable to the finest, purest spring water, and a countercharge that the large poem contains a lot of filth and rubbish (this elaborates the lack of inspiration alleged in *Iambos* **XIII**). It sounds as if Kallimachos has been in danger of losing some position and that, although Phthonos has been defeated, criticism (Momos) remains. Wilamowitz suggests that the reference may be to Apollonios' withdrawal to Rhodes; chronologically this seems unlikely, and as the scholiast (on l. 26) says that Kallimachos gives divine honours to Euergetes as a scholar, the patronage of Euergetes would seem to be what Kallimachos achieved against his rivals and detractors; with the new king as his patron he could adopt towards others the lofty attitude of the first *Iambos,* and call his own song 'stronger than the evil eye' as he does in *Epigram 21* (perhaps the concluding epigram of a collection of epigrams). In the context of the historical situation, Berenike of Cyrene's defeat of Demetrios, and her marriage with Euergetes, the whole hymn makes sense: Kyrene as the bride of Apollo defeating the lion (90 f.) is a divine parallel to the story of Berenike, Demetrios, and Euergetes, just as Apollo's rejection of Phthonos is a divine parallel to Euergetes' giving patronage to Kallimachos in spite of his detractors. We should not simply identify Apollo and Euergetes: we should rather say that the human event has a divine parallel (which in the case of Apollo and Kyrene lies in past history). A rather similar kind of near-identification is to be seen on the later Archelaos relief: Homer's fame is eternal and ubiquitous, but Time and the World are given the faces of Ptolemy Philopator and Arsinoe, because they made the Homereion in Alexandria and so ensured Homer's immortality in the Greek-speaking world. Apollo may work through Euergetes but he is also for Kallimachos the god of poetry; the *Hymn to Apollo* is therefore a very personal poem. Like *Hymns V* and *VI* it is a dramatic presentation, and here too the god is going to appear. The other two hymns describe a ritual procession with statue or emblem, but here the laurel, the walls, the doors, the palm-tree, and the swan all feel that the god himself is coming (like Hekate in Theokritos II) and the young men must sing. It is their song that Kallimachos gives in his hexameters, an elegant cult hymn, telling of Apollo's powers and prowess and so leading to the founding of Cyrene, which Apollo pointed out to Kallimachos' ancestor Battos and promised to 'our kings', presumably Philadelphos and Euergetes (65 ff.). Such a hymn from the time of Homer's Delian hymn could always finish with a *Sphragis* containing a reference to the poet, and this tradition formally justifies the allusion to Kallima-

chos' own position at the end.

Apollo is quoted again in the late prologue of the *Aitia* (I, 21): 'when I first put the tablet on my knees, Apollo said to me: "The victim must be fat but the Muse fine (*leptalee*); don't take the high-road but the untrodden path, even if it is narrower".' Originality is emphasized more obviously here than in the *Hymn [to Apollo],* but there too the clean spring is only known to Demeter's priestesses, just as here Kallimachos claims to sing among those who love the shrill sound of the cicada and not the braying of asses. After Apollo's advice the poem comes to its conclusion with a curse upon old age and an assertion that the Muses will not desert their own when he grows grey: this is the confident spirit of the first *Iambos.* The beginning part of the poem with the ancient commentary goes into greater detail: 'The Telchines grumble at my song (ignorant of the Muse, they are not beloved by her), because I never completed a single continuous song in many thousands of verses to reverend kings or former heroes, but spin my song small, like a child, though the decades of my years are not few. I say this to the Telchines: "Prickly tribe, knowledgeable at wasting away your own hearts, I am truly oligostichic. Bounteous Demeter defeats the tall oak; the fine (*lepton*) sayings taught that Mimnermos is the sweeter of the two poets, the large woman failed. Let the Massagetai shoot far at their man. Koan nightingales like ours are sweeter. Away, horrid children of the evil-eye. Judge wisdom again by art not by the Persian measure. Don't ask me to father a loud sounding song. Thunder does not belong to me but to Zeus."' Here the contrast is very clear between the short fine poems (*leptos*), which vary in dialect and metre, and the single continuous lone poem, which the jealous critics say that Kallimachos has not written. (The scholiast on *Hymn II,* 106, says that the *Hekale* was written in answer to such criticism; if this is true, the criticism must have been made much earlier and the answer was evidently not accepted.)

The poem is more valuable still for its examples of ideals and critics. Kallimachos admires Mimnermos and Philitas. He dislikes Antimachos' *Lyde,* as we know from an epigram (fr. 398): '*Lyde,* a thick and unclear book'. In this poem (12) the large woman, unfavourably contrasted with Mimnermos' 'fine sayings', must be the *Lyde* (and the reader is meant to supply Mimnermos' Nanno as a small woman). The objection to the *Lyde* is presumably that what started as a poem lamenting the loss of the poet's beloved became a jumble of mythology, the Argonauts, Bellerophon, Oedipus, the Sun's cup, etc. But for Hermesianax these were 'holy books' (Ath. 13, 598a), for Asklepiades (*Anth. Pal.* IX, 63) 'the joint writing of the Muses and Antimachos' made Lyde more noble than any Ionian aristocrat and Poseidippos (*Anth. Pal.* XII, 168) names her in the same breath as Mimnermos' Nanno. Asklepiades and Poseidippos are named by the scholiast on *Aitia* fr. 1 as two of the Telchines, the jealous critics. If it is surprising to find two elegiac poets, Asklepiades and Poseidippos, attacking Kallimachos, the answer must lie partly in the dispute over the *Lyde*. The other author known to us in the scholiast's list is Praxiphanes of Mitylene. Praxiphanes was himself attacked by Kallimachos in a prose work, ***Against Praxiphanes***. Praxiphanes was a pupil of Theophrastos, and Professor Brink [*Classical Quarterly,* vol. 40, 1946] convincingly argues that as a Peripatetic he would believe in the long poem with organic unity covering its digressions, and the scholiast sums up his list of critics by saying that they blamed Kallimachos because his style was emaciated and he had no length. With length goes the full-bloodedness of the grand manner, which allows digressions within the general scheme; 'emaciated' and 'thick' deprecate the qualities which 'fine' and 'full-blooded' appreciate. The fragment of Kallimachos' ***Against Praxiphanes*** (460) throws another name into the battle: 'Kallimachos mentions Aratos as his elder not only in the epigrams but also in ***Against Praxiphanes***, praising him as learned and a first-rate poet'. The epigram (27) cannot be dated: 'Hesiod's the song and the manner. Not the furthest of singers I fear the man of Soli copied but the most honey-sweet of poems. Hail fine sayings, sign of Aratos' sleeplessness.' For Praxiphanes Aratos presumably came into the same category as Empedokles does for Aristotle (*Poet.* 1447b, 17, 'there is nothing shared by Homer and Empedokles except metre; therefore Homer may be called a poet and Empedokles a physiologist rather than a poet'). Kallimachos answers: he was copying Hesiod and not Homer. Hesiod was Kallimachos' own model; at the beginning and end of the *Aitia* (fr. 2; 112) he tells of Hesiod receiving his song as he pastured his sheep on Helikon and in the earlier passage he claims that in a youthful dream he himself received the *Aitia* from the Muses on Helikon. One other epigram should be quoted here. The beginning of the Aratos epigram suggests a book-title; *Epigram 6* is also a parody of a book-title for Kreophylos' *Sack of Oichalia;* the best that can be said of the poem is that it is called Homeric. And with this can be associated *Epigram 28:* 'I hate the cyclic poem and the high-road and the prostitute; I don't drink from the fountain; I loathe everything public. Lysanias, you are beautiful, yes, beautiful. But before Echo has got this out, someone says, "Another has him".' In this parody of a love poem the comparison of the cyclic poem to high-road and public fountain recalls the prologue of the *Aitia* and *Hymn II*. It looks as if 'cyclic' already means (as in Horace, *A.P.* 136) not only conventional but poem of the Epic Cycle; it would thus cover both Kreophylos and Antimachos.

The epigrams are not dated. The prologue of the *Aitia* is a late affirmation of Kallimachos' doctrine. Of the critics listed by the scholiast Poseidippos was writing as late as 264/3, but Asklepiades is associated as much with Ptolemy I as with Ptolemy II and Theokritos equates him with Philitas (VII, 40). The *Phainomena* of Aratos must have been published soon after his arrival at Antigonos' court in 276 B.C., if Apollonios Rhodios already knew it when he wrote the first version of the *Argonautika.* Praxiphanes need not, of course, have criticized it immediately; the two firm dates for Praxiphanes are the Delian inscription dated epigraphically (270/60 B.C.) and the fact that he was Theophrastos' pupil before 288/7 B.C.; Professor Brink puts his birth about 340 B.C. It seems therefore unlikely that the work which Kallimachos answers in *Against Praxiphanes* was written much later than 270. Another piece of early evidence for the clash of two poetic ideals is in Theokritos, not only in his rewriting of Apollonios in *Idylls* XIII and XXII but in his criticism of the 'birds of the Muses' who 'toil vainly, crowing against the Chian singer' (VII, 47). The echoes of Theokritos in Kallimachos have already been noticed, and it is at least possible that the love epigram (52) is a pretty compliment to an ally. On the evidence of *Idyll* VII Theokritos had declared himself by 270, and Timon's knowledge of the struggles in the bird-cage is certainly not later.

The prologue to the *Aitia* is therefore a late stage in an action which had been going on for thirty years. The name Telchines suggests not only malice but Rhodes. Among the known critics of the scholiast's list only Praxiphanes could be called a Rhodian, and he may have migrated to Rhodes before the death of Theophrastos. If Praxiphanes was in Rhodes from about 290 onwards and as an Aristotelian was in favour of long poetry, was it to him or to his entourage that Apollonios went when he retired from Alexandria and did Kallimachos include Apollonios in the Telchines? One of the links between the two may have been a veneration for Antimachos, whom Apollonios edited and used as a source . . . and whom Praxiphanes as a Peripatetic would venerate out of loyalty to Plato. Praxiphanes, like Asklepiades, was probably dead before the prologue to the *Aitia* was written but Apollonios was still Librarian when Kallimachos feared that he would not get the patronage of Euergetes. Apollonios' name is not in the scholiast, but this may only mean that there was no record of his having attacked Kallimachos in writing, and does not exclude the possibility that Kallimachos meant the name Telchines to include the Rhodian writer of long epic. The *Ibis* (fr. 381-2) is our evidence that Kallimachos did attack Apollonios, but this may belong rather to the earlier date before Apollonios retired to Rhodes.

Kallimachos claims for himself short poetry, in many metres (Pfeiffer's index lists sixteen), original, learned, only appreciated by connoisseurs. One quality more he gives in his own epitaph (*Ep. 35*): 'You walk past the tomb of Battiades who was skilled in song and skilled in laughter attuned to the wine'. Gabathuler suggests that this may be the concluding epigram of a collection (like 21). He claims not only serious poetry but also the light touch evident in the asides in the first *Iambos*. Although some of his poetry is obviously pretty occasional verse (e.g. *Iambos* **XII**, fr. 227, 399-401), his light touch makes him sometimes difficult for us to interpret, particularly in the *Epigrams*. The poem to Theokritos (52) is a pretty compliment rather than an exaggerated declaration of love. And none of the symposion poems (*Ep.* 1, 8, 25, 28, 29, 31-2, 41-2, 44-6, 52, 59) need be taken very seriously whether they have an obvious literary reference or not: *Ep.* **43** with its Aristotelian terminology might be the apology of any young hero of Menander and ends with a near-quotation of the *Dyskolos* (303). But is the poem to Lysanias (28) primarily a condemnation of Lysanias or a condemnation of long poetry? Is the ninth *Iambos* primarily aetiology or primarily a condemnation of Philetades? And does the charming poem about Orestes (59) imply that Kallimachos lost all his friends by writing an unsuccessful drama? The Suda credits him with dramas, and another epigram (8) prays Dionysos for the short word 'I conquer'. The epigram on Theaitetos (7), who is probably the epigrammatist of that name, is a mock epitaph, but the ideal of pure poetry which theatre audiences reject is Kallimachos' own ideal. It is not an easy ideal, and in *Iambos* **III**, another difficult poem in which it is not clear to us whether the real object of attack is a prostitute or the society which lets the poet starve, he writes: 'It would have been profitable to toss my hair to the Phrygian flute in honour of Kybele or in a long frock to wail Adonis as a slave of the goddess. But I madly fumed to the Muses: I must eat the bread I baked.' Theokritos' Adonis festival does not contain a male performer, but Galloi are well known from the Anthology, and later in the third century Dioskorides contrasts the success of Aristagoras dancing Gallos with the disaster of his own poem on the *Temenidai*.

Herakleitos had lived true to the high ideal, and his 'nightingales' will live (*Ep.* **2**). It is not technically an epitaph because it was meant for the circle of Herakleitos' friends, not for his tombstone; but it has the same simplicity and seriousness as the poems which may be accepted as epitaphs, e.g. *Ep.* 9, 12, 14-20, 26, 40, 58, 60, 61. Take for instance *Ep.* **15**: '"Timonoe". But who are you? By the gods I should not have known you, if the name of Timotheos your father had not been on the stele and Methymna, your city. Your husband Euthymenes surely grieves deeply in his widowhood.' Here the genuine feeling suggests a real epitaph; but the poem (13) in which the dead man says that Ploutos is a myth and life is cheap in the underworld is epigram rather than epitaph (cf. 3, 4, 7, 11, 21-3, 30, 35, 43, 61, some of which have been already discussed), and the eleventh *Iambos* is aetiology cast into the form of an epitaph. The same problem arises

with the dedications: the interpretation of the pinax with a standing hero as the gift of a man who was angry with a cavalryman (24) is surely a joke (cf. also 47). The dedication for a temple in Thermopylae (39) was presumably commissioned by the Naucratite who dedicated his tithe there. But did the Rhodian comic actor Agoranax, who dedicated the double-sided mask of Pamphilos, commission Kallimachos to say that the mask was 'not totally ravaged by love, but half like a roast fig and the lamps of Isis' (49)? The other mask epigram (48)—the tragic Dionysos in the schoolroom, which gapes twice as wide as the Samian Gaping Dionysos—is also surely occasioned by seeing Dionysos in a schoolroom and is not a dedication written for the mask.

In the *Epigrams* Kallimachos wears his learning lightly. The scanty prose fragments (403-64) give some idea of the extent of this learning: he wrote among other things on Contests, Winds, Barbarian customs, National names (which seems to have been a lexikon of names given in different parts of the Greek world), Wonders of the world (chiefly rivers), Names of months, Foundation of cities and changes of name, Nymphs, Birds, and the hundred and twenty volumes of *Pinakes*, which was a catalogue of all writers giving their lives and their works. This learning shows more obviously in the *Hymns* and the *Hekale* than in the *Epigrams* and most obviously in the *Aitia* and the *Iamboi*.

The *Hymns* are hymns only in two senses: their subjects are gods and a cult place, and like the Homeric hymns all except one are in hexameters. The Homeric hymns were meant for performance at a festival, these hymns are literature to read, and though they have a dramatic setting this setting must not be examined too closely. In the second *Hymn* as we have seen the poet imagines the holy place quivering in anticipation of Apollo's appearance, then he writes the choral hymn to the god ending as such hymns may with the poet's own view of his art. The introduction suggests Delphi and the hymn ends with the slaying of Pytho, but the emphasis is on Cyrene and even in the introduction the palm-tree is Delian. Perhaps we should think of a temple of Apollo in Cyrene and the audience would know the statue with golden chiton, himation, lyre, bow quiver, and sandals. Kallimachos is only interested in the gold and gives no hint of the posture of the statue. In the other statue-poems also we have no evidence that he made his readers see the statue: *Iambos* **VI** gives the dimensions and cost of the Olympian Zeus; the Leukadian Artemis (fr. 31b), the Hera at Samos (fr. 101) and the Delian Apollo (fr. 114) interest him because of their unexpected attributes.

The fifth and sixth *Hymns* have no personal reference but are more like the *Adoniazousai* of Theokritos. The identification must not be pressed too far, but essentially the speaker of *Hymn V* (the only hymn in elegiacs) purports to be a priestess of Athena at Argos instructing and talking to the girls who are to bathe the statue of Athena. Of course she speaks of the statue as if it were the goddess; that is natural for the priestess. She tells the girls to come out because the horses of the goddess' chariot are already neighing. She tells them not to bring cosmetics because Athena did not use cosmetics at the Judgment of Paris. 'Come out, Athena.' She tells diem the story of Eumedes. 'Come out, Athena.' She warns all of the dangers of river-water today because Athena is to bathe in it. 'Come out, Athena.' She tells them the story of Teiresias who saw the goddess bathing. 'At last Athena is coming.' This is essentially a simple poem: the stories come from Kallimachos' learning but they are the right stories for the Argive priestess to tell her girls. The speaker of *Hymn VI* purports to be the instructor of the women who sing to the Basket of Demeter as it goes in procession from the Alexandrian Eleusis. Because this is a festival designed to bring plenty she refuses to tell them of the wanderings of Demeter but tells them instead of the punishment of Erysichthon which is again treated in a highly individual and ironic way. The scheme here is the same as in *Hymn V.*

The first *Hymn* is a hymn to Zeus to be sung at the libation; in so far as it has a setting, the setting is a symposion. It is a learned poem: the Arcadian story of the birth of Zeus is to be preferred to the Cretan story. Zeus did not divide the world with his brothers; he won his kingdom by force; he is the god of kings, and therefore of Ptolemy Philadelphos. The *Hymn to Artemis* (III) is in form like a Homeric hymn. 'We sing of Artemis . . . Farewell, Queen, and kindly accept our Song.' But except for the brief solemn passage about the city of unjust men (122 f.), when Artemis takes over the functions of the Hesiodic Zeus (*Op.* 225 ff.), the learned list of islands, nymphs, and cities, and the farewell with its four mythological examples of the disaster which ensues from dishonouring Artemis, the poem, as Professor Herter [*Kallimachos und Homer*, 1929] has shown in detail, may be described as a pleasant trifling with Homeric themes. The technique is known from Apollonios Rhodios: not only translation into Hellenistic terms (as in the *Hekale* and the divine scenes at the beginning of Apollonios' third book) but direct contrast with the original, as when Apollonios turns Kirke into a nervous aunt. The tone is set in the second line, where Artemis is introduced as hunting hares. Then she appears as a child on the knees of Zeus and makes her demands: behind this scene is Thetis' appeal to Zeus. When she goes to get her weapons from the Kyklopes the contrast with Thetis' visit to Hephaistos is clear: child and monsters instead of goddess and god; and the metalwork which is being made when she arrives is Poseidon's horse-trough instead of tripods for the banquets of the gods. Once (53) a piece of Alexandrian science intrudes; the Kyk-

lops' eye is compared to a shield with four (instead of the Homeric seven) ox-hides, because Herophilos had recently discovered the four skins of the eye. After the serious passage about the unjust city, Herakles on Olympos (144 ff.) is pure comedy: a traditional glutton, he urges Artemis only to shoot the largest animals including oxen. The succeeding sections on islands, nymphs, and cities are full of learning. Not only learned but whimsically obscure is the passage about the dancers (170 ff.): 'when the nymphs surround you in dance . . . may not my oxen be ploughing another man's field . . . for the Sun never passes by that fair dance but stops his chariot to watch and the days lengthen.' This involved way of emphasizing the beauty of the dance recalls two lines in the *Aitia* (ff. 75, 10 f.), where instead of saying 'in the morning the oxen were going to be sacrificed', he says 'in the morning the oxen were going to rend their hearts, seeing the sharp knife in the water'. This is the 'narrow path' of originality in expression.

The fourth *Hymn*, to Delos, is the longest and perhaps the least interesting: in shape it is like a Homeric hymn and it is packed with learning. It has its political reference to Ptolemy Philadelphos and the Gauls (160 ff.). It has its Homeric reminiscences. Delos 'a fitter coursing ground for gulls than horses' (12) clearly recalls Homeric Ithaka (*Od. 4,* 605 ff.). In the Homeric hymn to Apollo the story is told shortly (III, 30): all the places visited by Leto refuse her except Delos, who stipulates that Apollo shall build his temple there. All the goddesses are there except Hera and Eileithyia, whom Hera has kept on Olympos. The goddesses send Iris to offer Eileithyia a gold necklace; Eileithyia comes and Apollo is born. What the Homeric hymn does in ninety lines takes two hundred in Kallimachos. Hera puts Ares on Haimos and Iris on Mimas to watch and threaten all the places visited by Leto. (Not long before in the *Deification of Arsinoe* (fr. 228) Kallimachos had sent Charis to the top of Athos to look over the sea and discover the meaning of the smoke rolling over the sea from Arsinoe's pyre.) Leto visits the places one by one. Twice the unborn Apollo speaks to threaten Thebes (88), to warn her off Kos (162) (because Ptolemy Philadelphos is to be born there), and, extremely late, to suggest Delos as a suitable place. Before this Peneios (121) had been prepared to receive her in spite of the threats of Hera and Ares, but she refused this sacrifice and turned to the islands who fled in terror before Iris. 'They all at her bidding fled in a body down the stream, whichever island Leto approached' (159). There seems to be a contradiction between this conception of islands that run away and the other conception of Delos as the wandering island among fixed islands (190 ff.). Presumably Kallimachos would answer that the island nymph is not bound to her island, as when the islands dance round Delos, but the juxtaposition of the two conceptions is unfortunate and perhaps argues a lack of visual imagination in the poet. Delos defies Hera's anger. Iris flies to tell Hera. Then (228) she sits beneath Hera's throne, like one of Artemis' hunting dogs, ears pricked, always ready for orders; she sleeps beside the throne with her head lolling on her shoulders. This is one of the few passages where Kallimachos seems to be thinking of a work of art. Hera, after a taunt at Zeus' women who give birth on deserted rocks, pardons Asterie (Delos) in spite of her criminal conduct, because in the past she preferred the sea to Zeus. This is in Kallimachos' best manner.

The one poem in which Kallimachos employs his technique on a larger scale is the **Hekale**. Its length has been estimated at a thousand lines, and the scholiast to **Hymn II**, 106 says that it was an answer to those who charged him with being incapable of writing a large poem. Even if the estimate is right, it is considerably shorter than any of Apollonios' four books. The ancient *Summary* tells us that Theseus, having escaped the plot of Medeia, was carefully guarded by his father, having unexpectedly returned from Troizen. Wanting to go and attack the bull of Marathon, he had to escape secretly in the evening. Suddenly a storm broke and he took refuge in the hut of Hekale. In the morning he went out and overcame the bull and returned to Hekale. He found her dead and lamented her. He rewarded her by bringing together the people into a deme which he called after her and established a precinct of Zeus Hekaleios. Plutarch, *Thes.* 14, adds the point that Hekale vowed a sacrifice to Zeus if Theseus returned. The *Priapea* 12, 3 says that Theseus actually found her on the pyre. Ovid tells us that she was never married (*rem. Am.* 747). Statius *(Theb. xii,* 581) speaks in a single sentence of Marathon Crete, and Hekale's tears. Many fragments survive, and it is justifiable to follow every hint in placing them.

The poem starts with Hekale living on the Eastern slopes of Pentelikos, honoured because she is hospitable, comely in her broad shepherd's hat, with a shepherd's crook in her hand and a stick of heath to prop her aged steps. The picture recalls the realistic old figures of Hellenistic art, but perhaps Kallimachos felt that he was getting too sentimental (having used all his powers of alliteration and assonance in this description) and pulled himself up with the word ποιηφάγον (fr. 365), normally used of 'grass-eating' animals but here of the old woman, whose diet was vegetables. How he managed the transition to Theseus is unknown; perhaps Hekale foresaw the storm because of the snuffs on the wick of her lamp (fr. 269), and perhaps the poet addressed Adrasteia here (fr. 299, 687) because Hekale's life was near its end.

Theseus, like Hekale, is described: he wears a new Thessalian hat and a long chiton (fr. 304, 293). Presumably the various fragments referring to the Argolid come here and his journey was narrated, perhaps with

considerable aetiological digression. Medeia recognizes him and tries to poison him, but Aigeus has also recognized him and prevents him drinking: someone curses Medeia. Here the story evidently follows the same lines as in Plutarch's *Theseus* (ch. 12). The account of Theseus' recognition tokens, sword and boots, is given by the poet, partly in narrative, partly as a speech by Aigeus to Aithra, which continues to within thirty lines or so of the point where Theseus sets out to find the Marathonian bull. This must therefore be a flashback to the time when Aigeus was with Aithra in Troizen, and perhaps fr. 359, Aigeus 'picks up his armour and says', marks the return to the story: Aigeus forbids Theseus to leave Athens. As far as we can appreciate this part it is elegant narrative with Homeric echoes and a fair proportion of rare words.

The papyrus resumes with a description of clear weather while it was still midday; in the evening when daughters ask their mothers for the evening meal (a Hellenistic elaboration of the simple term, evening; so later the poet gives an elaborate description of dawn) then the storm gathered over all the mountains of Attica and the North wind fell upon the clouds. Surely the effect which Kallimachos wants here is that the storm, coming over Parnes, thyme-clad Aigaleos, rough Hymettos, chases Theseus up the road, and therefore Theseus has already started 'while it was still midday'; this is not really inconsistent with the *Summary*'s 'about evening' because it is evening before Theseus has got far.

Theseus finds shelter in Hekale's hut: 'Be the craftsman of my life and conqueror of my hunger' (fr. 267). Pfeiffer has shown that the model here is Odysseus' visit to Eumaios in the second half of the *Odyssey,* but this is Hellenistic genre-painting with all the colours of assonance and alliteration and with rare words. Hekale answers 'There is water and earth and a baking stove' (fr. 268). He takes off his cloak, she sits him down, she makes up the fire, she heats water for washing, she gives him olives, vegetables, and bread.

A papyrus fragment (fr. 253) gives on one side the end of Theseus' speech and on the other side part of Hekale's answer. Theseus told her who he was and that he was going to Marathon but perhaps not much more, before he asked who she was. She probably accused him of waking sleeping tears (fr. 682, perhaps also fr. 313 belongs here). She had been well off and of good family (fr. 254). She was turned out of her property and complained to the kings, and she was brought from Kolonos here, where she lives among poor farmers (this seems a possible way of putting the fragments together and may fill the gap in fr. 253). She goes back to her prosperity: 'I was watching the oxen circling my threshing-floor, when a chariot brought him from Aphidnai, like the kings who are sons of Zeus or god himself. I remember he had a fair cloak, held by golden pins, work spider-fine.' The abrupt introduction without a name shows that the man from Aphidnai must be a known character, and Pfeiffer's suggestion of Aigeus seems almost certain. Then she goes on to describe the fine down on his face, like helichryse (fr. 274), and his fair hair, which waved about his head, whereas Theseus' hair is cropped close (fr. 361, 376, 281). Nevertheless the likeness is amazing (fr 367). Here too the background is Homeric, the youthening of Odysseus in the sixth book of the *Odyssey* and Helen's recognition of Telemachos in the fourth. Perhaps she leads on to the rest of the story by wishing she had never met Aigeus (fr. 619).

We cannot here be far from two overlapping papyri, which place nine book fragments. Hekale speaks of two children whom she brought up in every kind of luxury. Then a gap probably of at least twenty-five lines, in which presumably the sentiment 'God did not give mortals laughter without tears' (fr. 298) belongs. Then, 'Did I refuse to hear death calling me a long time ago that I might soon rend my garments over you too.' There are two possible interpretations: 'I failed to die when one (or both) of the children died, and therefore now I shall have also to see you, Theseus, die', or she transposes herself into the past 'I failed to die when the first of the children died in order that shortly after I might see you, X (the other child), die'. With the second interpretation the death of the first child (and therefore probably the front of *Ox. Pap.* 2377) must come in the gap. With the first interpretation Hekale fears that Theseus, who is so like the young Aigeus of long ago, will be killed by the Marathonian bull of which he had just told her. Hekale goes on to speak of Kerkyon, who fled from Arcadia and dwelt near, a bad neighbour to us. 'May I dig out his eyes and eat him raw!', and presumably soon afterwards 'May I die when I hear of him dead' (fr. 591). Hekale does not know that Kerkyon has already been killed by Theseus, and this is a wish which comes true, because she dies the day after Theseus has told her. On the first interpretation Hekale's narrative may be broken here, and Theseus may tell her of Kerkyon. Then she goes on to describe the death of the other child: 'this was my blackest day' (fr. 348). The front of *Ox. Pap.* 2377 has something about Peteus, son of Orneus, about fetching horses from Eurotas, possibly about Cape Malea, and about sailing with a hostile omen, and something about kings. It is a reasonable conjecture that the second child was sent on an expedition by Peteos and died in a disaster at sea. But who were the children? Ovid's evidence that Hekale was never married must be trusted. She may have been raped by Aigeus or another; but her account of bringing up the children sounds more like a nurse than a mother. A possible clue is given by fr. 527: 'whom a concubine bore to him'. The children may have been illegitimate sons of Aigeus whom he left with Hekale to bring up. At the end of this scene Hekale presumably reproached

herself for garrulity (fr. 310, 483).

Hekale went to bed (fr. 256). Theseus perhaps lay outside with his head on a stone (fr. 375). Hekale saw him get up (fr. 257) and presumably then prayed to Zeus for his safe return (Plutarch). Theseus went to Marathon and captured the bull, which had tried to escape up a valley. As he brought the bull back, the villagers were terrified, but he told them to send a messenger to Aigeus; then they sang a paian and pelted him with leaves, and the women wound their girdles round him (fr. 260). Is it perhaps here that someone sings a hymn to Aithra among the assembled women? (fr. 371).

After a gap of twenty-two lines the crow is speaking and the crow goes on speaking till nearly dawn. It follows therefore that Theseus spent the night wherever the victory was celebrated (Marathon?) and only next day found Hekale on her pyre. (It is true that on fr. 351, which is tied to this passage by *P. Oxy.* 2398, the Suda says 'Hekale said', but as there is no break in front of this passage and the lines continue with another story about the crow, this must be a corruption for 'Kallimachos said in the *Hekale*'). The preserved sequence then is the crow's account of Pallas, Erichthonios, and the daughters of Kekrops. This is followed by another gap of twenty-two lines in which belong certainly fr. 261, 'I met Athena as she was coming to the Acropolis' (and told her that the daughters of Kekrops had disobeyed her), and probably frs. 320, 332, 374, Athena's anger. The crow goes on 'Athena's anger is always heavy. I was there when I was quite young eight generations ago.' This ends the Erichthonios story. Then after a gap of about twelve lines, now reduced by the two lines of *P. Oxy.* 2398, the crow continues with the prophecy of the Thriai that the crow will be turned black for informing Apollo about Koronis. Then the crow and her listener go to sleep before dawn. The listener may be the owl, which seems to speak in the first person in fr. 529 (cf. also 326, 608).

But how does the crow come into the *Hekale*? Gentili [*Gnomon,* vol. 33, 1961] suggests that as the crow's story quotes two instances of punishment for bringing bad news, the occasion must be the bad news of Hekale's death. The last word before the Koronis story is . . . 'messenger of evil', and this is the end of the difficult passage which seems to be an interlude between the two stories. In the gap after the Erichthonios story the text picks up with fr. 346, 'may I but have a defence against cruel famine for my belly', then an unintelligible line, then a line which it is tempting to read as ἀλλ' Ἑκάλη λίπε λιτὸν ἔδος, then an unintelligible line, then 'and groats that dripped from the posset upon the earth . . . no one be brave enough (?) to go . . . messenger of evil'. It looks as if, after the story of the crow's exclusion from the Acropolis for bringing the news about Erichthonios, the crow returned to the theme of Hekale's death before going on with the Koronis story. The sequence must be something like this: the crow needs food and now Hekale is dead, and the food is dripping on the ground; no one will be brave enough to tell Theseus. This means that the death of Hekale had already been told to the crow in the gap before the Erichthonios story, and it is at least possible that the owl had brought the news. The announcement must have been brief because this first twenty-two-line gap has also to include the end of the rejoicing over Theseus and the beginning of the crow's story.

Kallimachos' scholarly knowledge of early Attic legend and cult has burst out exuberantly for some ninety lines here. This is the poet of the *Aitia*, but he laughs at himself by putting his knowledge into the mouth of the crow, now aged about 250 years. The fourth *Iambos* is another instance of this technique: there Simos was warned to keep out of Kallimachos' circle by the story of the laurel and the olive, who stopped their quarrel to round on a bramble. The laurel praises itself but the olive puts its learned eulogy into the mouth of two birds chattering among its leaves. (The reference to the *Hekale* in l. 77 does not quite certainly put it later; it may merely show that Kallimachos was already thinking of *Hekale*. If it is later, the message of the fourth *Iambos* prepares for the first *Iambos*.)

After this excursion into scholarship, Kallimachos puts the birds to sleep with another reminiscence of Odysseus and Eumaios. The dawn is frosty; the thieves have ceased to prowl; lamps are lit; the water-carrier sings; the waggon-axles squeak; the smiths start their deafening noise. Here sound is much more important than light; Apollonios on the other hand was more interested in light. But this is again a typical Hellenistic genre description. The birds presumably did not tell the news to Theseus as he had to ask whom the neighbours were burying (fr. 262); fragments remain of the neighbours' lament (fr. 263) and of Theseus' lament (fr. 264). Then must have followed the establishment of the Deme and of the temenos of Zeus Hekaleios. Perhaps Aiaeus himself was there, having come out to meet Theseus as a result of the message sent after the capture of the bull.

The cause of the poem is the name and cult of an Attic deme. Kallimachos may have taken the story from his contemporary Philochoros (who was used by Plutarch). He is exposed then to two conflicting forces, the desire to tell a human story which reminds him of the meeting of Odysseus and Eumaios in the *Odyssey*, and the desire to put in the maximum of Attic legend and cult. The human story is told in more detail than by Homer: the descriptions of clothing and food are more elaborate; the storm is more realistic; midday and dawn awake a variety of pictures or sounds instead of a single formula; Hekale and Theseus are probably softer than Eurykleia and Telemachos. The atmosphere is conveyed by mellifluous verse, full of alliteration and assonance. Against the sweetness is the astringency of learned words and jokes: ἀμάζονες is not Amazons but men without bread, ποιήφαγον is not cattle but Hekale with her diet of vegetables. The greater difficulty is to find a place for the learning; and here Kallimachos uses two devices—the flashback when Aigeus tells of his instructions to Aithra and the flashback given by the crow's knowledge of Athens eight generations before the date of the story. This is a brilliant conception; how successful it was is hard to say without the whole of the poem.

The *Aitia* is a great outpouring of scholarship. The interesting question is how far the individual poems came alive. The question is difficult to answer, partly because the passion for aetiology, which was obviously present in the audiences of Apollonios and Kallimachos, is lost to us, partly because the poems are so fragmentary that we can only sometimes see how Kallimachos treated his subjects. The prologue is a late addition. The Dream (fr. 2) gives the framework: just as Hesiod was given the *Theogony* and the *Erga* by the Muses on Helikon, so Kallimachos dreamt in his youth that the Muses gave him the *Aitia*. The method was an interrogation of Kleio and Kalliope by Kallimachos. So the poems are written as questions by Kallimachos answered by the Muses. But, although in the last poem of the *Aitia* Hesiod's conversation with the Muses is again recalled, Kallimachos seems to have changed the form after the second book; in the third and fourth books he tells the stories himself and sometimes quotes his human sources (fr. 75, 53; 92), but even in the *Akontios*, where he quotes Xenomedes as his authority, he ends 'whence the story hastened to my Kalliope' (fr. 75, 77), showing that he has not forgotten the fiction of the first two books.

Where we can see a longer passage, the poems have all the elegance, humour, learning, and variety which we expect from Kallimachos. In the Anaphe poem, in which the Muse tells the story of the Argonauts, probably as we have seen, borrowing from Apollonios, the day of the sacrifice begins (fr. 21): 'Then Tito woke from the embraces of Laomedon's son to chafe the neck of the ox'. This is a learned variation on the Homeric dawn formula: 'Eos rose from the bed of noble Tithonos' (*Iliad* 11, 1, etc.). Tithonos is the son of Laomedon. Eos in Hesiod is the daughter of Hyperion and Theia, children of Ouranos, and so a Titan. Agricultural work starts at dawn, and Kallimachos here remembers Hesiod's advice to work early—'Dawn, who appearing puts many men on the road and the yokes on many oxen' (*Op.* 581). Variation on a Homeric theme we have noticed already in the *Hymn to Artemis* as well as in the *Hekale*. Another very elegant instance is in the *Akontios*, where Apollo replies to Keyx (75,

22): 'My sister was not then harassing Lygdamis nor was she plaiting rushes in Amyklai nor washing off the dirt of the chase in the river Parthenios, but she was at Delos'. Here the scheme is given by Chryses' prayer to Apollo at his different addresses in the first book of the *Iliad* (37). But for simple addresses we here have allusions to history, cult and myth. The story of Theiodamas has the nice touch of the hungry young Hyllos tearing the hair on Herakles' chest, like the little Artemis with the Kyklops (fr. 24, *Hymn* 3, 76). A long recital of Sicilian cities starts with the scholarly sentiment 'the garlands on my head do not keep their scent, the food that I eat does not stay in my body. Only what I put in my ears remains in my possession' (fr. 43). A discussion of the worship of Peleus on Ikos starts at a dinner party given by an Athenian in Alexandria, at which Kallimachos sits next to a congenial Ikian (fr. 178), who satisfies his curiosity.

The poem of which we know most is the *Akontios* (fr. 67-75) which ends with an abbreviated history of Keos from Xenomedes. Till then Kallimachos narrates the story of the two lovers. They met in Delos, he from Keos, she from Naxos. Then he describes their beauty. 'No one came to the welling spring of shaggy old Seilenos nor put delicate foot to the dance of sleeping Ariadne with a more dawn-like face than she.' We think of the girls fetching water or dancing on Greek vases; again the Homeric comparison of a beautiful woman to a goddess is in the background and, nearer in date the lovely Theokritean 'Nycheia with spring in her eyes' (XIII, 45). Kallimachos makes it a negative comparison with Naxian ladies fetching water or dancing: Seilenos is a natural figure for an island which worshipped Dionysos, and elsewhere Seilenos springs are known; Kallimachos may have known sculptured Seilenoi as fountain figures. The dance must have been to wake Ariadne in her capacity as an earth-goddess. After Akontios has been described and then his passion, which hurt him as much as his beauty had hurt others (fr. 70), the story continues with the ruse of the apple and then the three attempts of Keyx to marry off Kydippe (fr. 75). In Naxos the bride slept with a boy the night before her marriage. Kallimachos stops himself from telling the origin of this rite in the pre-nuptials of Zeus and Hera: 'Dog, dog, stop, wanton soul, you will sing what is not holy. You are lucky that you have not seen the rites of the terrible goddess. You would even have poured out their story. Learnedness is a great danger for an unrestrained tongue: truly this boy has a knife.' Then the lines quoted above about the oxen seeing the sacrificial blade reflected in the water. Then the story runs swiftly to the consultation of the oracle of Apollo and the marriage and the naming of Xenomedes as source. The narrative is a simple story told in elegantly decorative language. The learned man appears for a moment in person but mockingly checks himself and goes on with the tale; only when he has named his source does he go over to pure for-

mation. The fascination of Kallimachos is this struggle between the scholar and the poet, a struggle which with ironical humour he makes no attempt to conceal.

Rudolf Pfeiffer (essay date 1968)

SOURCE: "Callimachus and the Generation of his Pupils," in *History of Classical Scholarship: From the Beginning to the End of the Hellenistic Age,* Oxford at the Clarendon Press, 1968, pp. 123-51.

[*One of the most-cited Callimachus scholars, Pfeiffer presents an in-depth study of ancient Greek scholarship in his* History of Classical Scholarship: From the Beginning to the End of the Hellenistic Age. *The chapter excerpted below looks at Callimachus as a primary contributor to the scholarship, especially in his role as cataloguer for the Alexandrian royal library. Pfeiffer also offers a detailed view of the* Pinakes, *or bibliographies, Callimachus prepared for the library, and considers their impact on Callimachus's poetry.*]

There was no distinguished textual critic in the generation after Zenodotus; only Aristophanes of Byzantium at the end of the third century was his equal if not his superior in this field. The outstanding representatives of scholarship between Zenodotus and Aristophanes were two men from Cyrene, Callimachus and Eratosthenes.

After Alexander's death Ptolemy I ruled over the old Dorian colony of Cyrene as the western part of his Egyptian kingdom (perhaps 322 B.C.); then his stepson Magas was given a kind of independent regency (about 300 B.C.?), and there was a time of considerable trouble between Egypt and Cyrene in the seventies. But at length the only daughter of Magas and Apame, Berenice, was betrothed to the son of Ptolemy II, and on their marriage and accession in 247/6 B.C. Cyrene was finally united with Egypt. Although we cannot fix a precise date for the arrival of the two Cyreneans in Alexandria, there is no doubt that it was after the Ionians had started the 'new movement'. For literary men were attracted, not all at once—but in the course of several generations—by the splendour of the new capital and the patronage of its kings. Callimachus' *Encomion on Sosibius* (fr. 384) may have been one of his earliest elegiac poems, written under Ptolemy I in Alexandria; the only well-attested facts are that he celebrated the marriage of Ptolemy II to his sister Arsinoe (between 278 and 273, perhaps 276/5 B.C.) by an epic, and the apotheosis of the queen (shortly after July 270 B.C.) by a lyric poem. This was apparently in the prime of his life; towards its end he composed the *Lock of Berenice* (246/5 B.C.) in honour of the Cyrenean princess recently married to Ptolemy III. It was this king who sent for the other native of Cyrene, Eratosthenes, called a 'pupil' of Callimachus, to be librarian and probably tutor to his son. Both the Cyreneans, very different from each other in age and spirit, seem to have been peculiar favourites of the young royal pair.

There is a complete unity of the creative poet and the reflective scholar in Callimachus. We found this combination first in Philitas. Between him and Callimachus, however, Zenodotus had made a contribution of a new kind to scholarship, and institutions for its promotion had been founded by the kings and especially favoured by a king who was the pupil of Philitas and Zenodotus; so the younger generation started from a better position and was enabled to reach a higher degree of that unity than the older one. There is every reason to believe that Callimachus began to write poetry in his early years in Cyrene. We read on Cyrenean coins of the end of the fourth and the beginning of the third century the same names of members of a noble family as in one of his epigrams in which he mourned their misfortunes. He was apparently still in his mother country when, as he tells us himself, he first put a writing tablet on his knees, and the Lycian Apollo addressed him as 'poet' and 'dear friend' and advised him on the art of poetry. A few lines later he implies that he is one of those 'on whom the Muses have not looked askance in their childhood'. In the poem to his greatest poetical achievement, the four books of the *Aitia,* he pictures himself transferred in dream from 'Libya' to Mount Helicon 'when his beard was just sprouting'; and 'Libya'—supposing that the anonymous epigram quotes him exactly—can mean Cyrene more easily than Alexandria. When and why he left Cyrene for Alexandria we do not know; we are only told that he started modestly as a schoolmaster in a suburb of the Egyptian capital called Eleusis. This may have been under Ptolemy I; since in the seventies, during the reign of Ptolemy II and his sister Arsinoe, Callimachus already moved in the court circle, celebrating royalty in the two poems we have mentioned, and he was probably still a 'young man' of the court when he was given a responsible commission in the royal library. This swift career seems to have been due entirely to the extraordinary gifts of a masterful personality.

Callimachus' poems, in spite of their novelty, were informed by an exact and wide knowledge of the earlier poetry from which he drew his models. Practising his craft and reflecting on it went together. This reflection quite naturally extended to the literature of the past, to all the various forms of metre and language, and to the recondite sources of its subject-matter. Only the most passionate study could result in exquisite poetical workmanship, and only boundless curiosity could open the untrodden ways (fr. I. 28) to new fields of learning. Ironically the poet hints at the danger of 'much knowledge' . . . in certain cases; on the other hand, the mere pleasure of listening and learning is to him the least perishable of pleasures in human life.

Two points should be kept in mind. If his verse very often sounds like charming word-play, the poet is never tired of reminding us that everything he is going to tell is true because it is well attested . . . ; the Muses, who once taught Hesiod and now answer Callimachus' questions, always utter the truth. In another case he refers to a local writer by name (fr. 75. 54) as his reliable source. In speaking of 'recondite sources', 're-liable source', we apply this word, which originally means the fountain of a stream or a river, figuratively to literature. In the beautiful finale of Callimachus' **hymn to Apollo** (*hy.* II 108-12) the god contrasts the filthy water of a great river with the clear droplets the bees carry to Demeter from the pure and undefiled fountain-head. In these metaphorical lines spoken by Apollo the poet condemns the lengthy traditional poem with its conventional formulae, but praises brevity and novelty in verse. This meaning is quite obvious. But there seems to be implied another piece of advice, hardly recognized by modern interpreters of the hymn: poets should draw from the original pure source, not from its polluted derivatives. Callimachus was, as far as I can see, the first to use this image in a literary sense. This demand of the scholar poet applies equally to poetry and to scholarship. It became a favourite image in the age of humanism and a fundamental concept of scholarship in the modern world.

If we consider Callimachus' general attitude, occasionally revealed in some lines of his poems, the remarkable feat of scholarship that he achieved in the library is perhaps not quite incomprehensible. His task was to find a system for arranging the texts of all the writers collected for the first time in the royal library (or libraries). When we glanced at the prehistory and early history of script and book in Greece, we observed the oriental background and commented cautiously on the relations between the orient and Greece. Now in Alexandria a Greek library was founded on a grand scale; and this reminds us of the enormous Babylonian and Assyrian libraries of old. It is natural to inquire whether there may have been direct influence, since the door of the east had been opened by Alexander much wider than before, and recent research has at least put this question more urgently; but the answer so far is not very definite. The layout of the papyrus-rolls in the Alexandrian library seems to have resembled that of the clay tablets in the oriental libraries in one or perhaps two significant points. The title of a work was regularly placed at the end of the roll and of the tablet (in contrast for instance to the practice in the Egyptian papyri), and in 'catalogues' not only this title, but also the 'incipit' was cited. On tablets and rolls the number of lines was occasionally counted, and these 'stichometrical' figures were put at the end and sometimes as running figures in the margins; they appear again in library-catalogues. The earliest example of title and number of lines placed at the end of a roll turned up in a recent publication of Menander's *Sicyonius;* the date of the papyrus seems to be the last third of the third century B.C., very near to Callimachus' lifetime. Even a personal remark of the scribe in verse is added, and these notes altogether may be properly called a 'colophon'. There is very scanty evidence for libraries in the Ionic and Attic periods; but the same technical devices as in the east, or similar ones, may have been used in Greek private houses or in philosophical schools.

Whatever may have been achieved before the third century B.C., Callimachus had no real model for his immense undertaking. Though his task was probably not so much to create as to develop an appropriate method, he did it so successfully that his 'lists', called Πίνακες, were generally acknowledged as a model for the future. Besides the **Pinakes**, he assembled a variety of learned material helpful for the understanding of the ancient texts and invaluable for the writing of poetry in the new style; in these books he resumed the labours of the younger Sophists and the Peripatos with a new purpose.

For the Πίνακες Tzetzes is again our authority; after giving the number of books in the two libraries he goes on to say: ὧν τοὺς πίνακας ὕστερον Καλλίμαχος ἀπεγράψατο. This sentence is slightly enlarged in another later version: ὡς (?) ὁ Καλλίμαχος νεαείσκος ὢν τῆς αὐλῆς ὑστέρως μετὰ τὴν ἀνόρθωσιν τοὺς πίνακας αὐτῶν ἀπεγράψατο; then a reference to Eratosthenes follows and finally the remark: ἀλλὰ τὰ Καλλιμάχου καὶ τοῦ Ἐρατοσθένους μετὰ βραχύν τινα χρόνον ἐγένετο τῆς συναγωγῆς τῶν βίβλων, ὡς ἔφην, καὶ διορθώσευς κἂν ἐπ᾽ αὐτοῦ τοῦ Πτολεμαίου τοῦ Φιλαδέλφου. Obviously it is the sequence of events that is stressed in both versions of the *Prolegomena*: ὕστερον—ὑστέρως μετὰ τ.ἀ.—μετὰ βραχύν τινα χρόνον. Therefore the change of ὑστέρως to ἱστορεῖ ὅς, proposed by Dziatzko and accepted by most modern editors, is not justified. This conjecture would enormously enhance the authority of Tzetzes' report, as it makes Callimachus himself the ultimate source of at least a part of the *Prolegomena*. The unfortunate Italian humanist had no scruples about producing the following 'translation' on the margin of his Plautine codex: 'sicuti refers Callimacus aulicus regius bibliothecarius qui etiam singulis voluminibus titulos inscripsit.' *Hinc illae lacrimae*. Here we have Callimachus not only quoted as a literary authority, but also elevated to the official rank of court-librarian; there is no evidence that he held this position except this slip of the 'translator', and there is not even room for him in the well-known series of librarians.

Tzetzes apparently had in mind a sort of catalogue of books extant in the library. Hesychius-Suidas' biographical article Καλλίμαχος, once probably the introduction to an edition of Callimachus' collected poems (of

Ptolemy II ruled during Callimachus's career.

which therefore very few titles were mentioned in the biography) points to a comprehensive 'bibliography': . . . **'Tables of all those who were eminent in any kind of literature and of their writings in 120 books'.** The previous generation had done some quite respectable scholarly work in the library at least on the foremost poets, without waiting for catalogues and bibliographies, and this may have been very helpful now in the completion of the **Pinakes**. It is Suidas' description—as we should expect from his much better sources—not Tzetzes' that is correct; this is confirmed by the fragments still preserved. The distinction between a mere library catalogue and a critical inventory of Greek literature is sometimes obscured in modern literature on Callimachus' great work; it was certainly based on his knowledge of the books available in the library, but he also had regard to works only mentioned in earlier literature and to questions of authenticity.

The entire body of Greek literature, the πᾶσα παιδεία, was divided into several classes: only three are attested by verbal quotations: ῥητορικά (fr. 430-2, cf. 443-8), νόμοι (fr. 433), παντοδαπὰ συγγράμματα (fr. 434/5). From references to epic (fr. 452/3), lyric (fr. 441, 450), tragic (fr. 449?, 451), comic poets (fr. 439/40), to philosophers (fr. 438?, 442), historians (fr. 437), and medical writers (fr. 429?) registered in the *Pinakes* we may conclude that seven further classes existed; there were probably many more and a number of subdivisions. It is now fairly certain that the individual authors of every class were arranged in alphabetical order; each name was accompanied by a few biographical details, and later writers were sometimes disappointed by what they considered deficiencies (fr. 447). Less conscientious, even sensational, the vast biographical work of Hermippus of Smyrna, who is called 'peripateticus' as well as ΚαλλιμῬχειος, be regarded as a more popular supplement to the esoteric *Pinakes*. But we may doubt if his master Callimachus liked it; he had confined himself to the reliable evidence for the lives and works of literary men. The list of their writings which followed the biography cannot always have been arranged in the same way, but the alphabetical system seems to have prevailed. The little we know of some minor epics and all we know of the dramatic poems leads to this assumption, if indeed the order in the lists of later antiquity is derived from the *Pinakes*. The best example is the famous κατάλογος τῶν Αἰσχύλου δραμάτων which was once obviously an appendix to the life of the poet and still presents to us the titles of seventy-three plays, tragedies, and satyr-plays, in strictly alphabetical order. For Euripides there were only fragments of two inscriptional catalogues, until recently published papyri brought very welcome new evidence for titles of his plays arranged in order of the initial letter. In the most important of these papyri, which gives summaries of the plots, the title is followed by the formula οὗ (ἧς, ὧν) ἀρχή and the citation of the first line. This 'incipit' had been introduced by Callimachus in his *Pinakes*, for instance: ἐπικὸν δὲ τὸ ποίημα, οὗ ἡ ἀρχή, followed by the opening verse of the poem (fr. 436). A mere title might have been ambiguous, particularly in the case of prose writings; the 'incipit' made the identification easier. A list similar to that of Aeschylus' plays is preserved in two manuscripts of Aristophanes, where brief details of his life are followed by an alphabetical catalogue of his comedies. Menander may have found a place in the *Pinakes*, like Alexis (fr. 439) and Diphilus (fr. 440); for the beginning of an alphabetical list of his plays (titles only) is preserved in a papyrus.

Cataloguing the lyric poetry . . . must have presented thorny problems. Callimachus divided the great triadic poems (which we usually call 'choral', although we often cannot tell whether they were actually sung by a choir) into special groups. . . . Simonides' songs of victory, for instance, were called ἐπίνικοι and subdivided according to the type of contest (foot-race, pentathlon, etc.); for we know that Callimachus (fr. 441)

had described a part of the *Epinicia* as . . . 'for runners'. Pindar's *Epinicia* must also have been divided into several groups, but in a different way, according to the place of the contests (Olympia, Nemea, etc.); otherwise it would not have been possible to say that Callimachus (fr. 450) placed the second Pythian ode, as it was later named although it actually celebrated a local victory of Hieron, among the Nemean odes. Finally Bacchylides' dithyrambs seem to have been separated from his paeans; for Callimachus was blamed for having entered among the paeans a poem which Aristarchus declared to be a dithyramb and entitled *Cassandra*. We know these classifications from references to the editions of lyric texts, begun by Aristophanes of Byzantium, and from later grammatical sources; but it is easily forgotten that some fundamental terms and formulae were, if not coined, at least first attested in the Callimachean *Pinakes*. Although we can recognize certain groups of choral songs, we still cannot guess how the individual poems were arranged. No doubt they were registered somehow, as the references to Pindar's second Pythian ode and Bacchylides' *Cassandra* demonstrate. Because the dithyrambs and probably the νόμοι had titles like the plays, they could easily have been listed in alphabetical order. But what about all the others, especially the monostrophic poems of Sappho, Alcaeus, Anacreon? They had no titles; and therefore the only way to register them, it seems, was according to the 'incipit', a method still applied in modern indexes of lyric poems of an author or of an anthology.

Callimachus lavished his efforts also upon the classification of the prose writers; the different classes, as far as we can make out their names, have been noted above. In principle the arrangement followed the same lines as in the poetical section; but the difficulties were greater than in the *Pinakes* of the poets, as the case of Prodicus shows; Callimachus listed him with the orators (quite correctly, I should say), but others objected that he belonged to the philosophers (fr. 431). The names of writers in every class were given in the usual alphabetical order (fr. 435). The works of each author may have been subdivided into several groups, such as public and private speeches; subdivision was unavoidable in the case of πολυείδεια (fr. 449; 429?). Individual speeches that had titles, for instance Περὶ Ἀλοννήσου (fr. 443), Περὶ τῶν συμμοριῶν (fr. 432) of Demosthenes, or Περὶ Φερενίκου (fr.448) of Lysias, could be listed alphabetically, though the 'incipit' was usually added (fr. 443, 444). But in cases where there was no title, or where the authorship of speeches (fr. 444-7) or whole books (fr. 437) was a matter of dispute, we have no clue to the arrangement. It seems to be over-optimistic to see in the famous complete list of Theophrastus' writings (Diog. L. v 42-50) a sort of enlarged copy of Callimachus' *Pinakes*; the very complicated tradition does not recommend this simple solution. Neither can we trace the list of

Aristotle's writings (Diog. L. v 22-27) back to Callimachus as the ultimate source. As regards the philosophers in the *Pinakes* our knowledge is deplorably poor. Our information is much more precise on the 'Miscellanea' (. . . fr. 434-5); under this heading a number of writings were registered that did not fit into the main categories of literature. For instance, Athenaeus in his *Deipnosophists,* being particularly concerned with books about 'dinners', has preserved an excerpt with the name of the author of one (a well-known Athenian parasite), the title, the opening words and the number of lines (fr. 434), and another excerpt containing an alphabetical list of four writers on pastry cooking (fr. 435). The intention was clearly to omit nothing from this inventory of the πᾶσα παιδεία, not even books on cookery.

Besides the general *Pinakes* two special ones are known that differ totally from the main work in being one chronological, one linguistic. Both titles are extant only in Suidas' article. The first is . . . **'Table and register of the dramatic poets in chronological order and from the beginning'**. This Pinax must have been based on Aristotle's διδασκαλίαι taken from the documents in the archon's archives. Alexander Aetolus and Lycophron had busied themselves with the tragic and comic texts in the Alexandrian library in the early third century; in its second half Eratosthenes and Aristophanes devoted major works to the Attic drama. Between them Callimachus compiled his record, the great scale of which we can still guess from fragments of three inscriptions found in Rome, where they had probably occupied a wall in a great library. Körte's suggestion that the inscriptions are a more or less exact apographon of the Callimachean Pinax has been universally accepted. The parts preserved enumerate the Dionysiac and Lenaian victories of comic poets from 440 to 352 B.C.; but if the title given by Suidas is correct the Pinax extended back to the ἀρχή, that is, to the introduction of comedy into each of the two festivals, the City Dionysia in 486 B.C. and the Lenaia in 442 B.C. The second special Pinax was apparently a list of glosses, and it is not surprising to find Callimachus following Philitas and Zenodotus as glossographer; what surprises is the wording in Suidas: Πίναξ τῶν Δημοκράτους γλωσσῶν καὶ συνταγμάτων (?). Whatever is meant by συντάγματα (probably 'writings'), its connexion with γλῶσσαι is strange, as 'a list of writings' should belong to the great general *Pinakes*. It is, of course, easy to change the proper name to Δημοκρίτου. Democritus was a bold innovator in the language of philosophy, but it can hardly be said that his own language is distinguished by obsolete words. We must also remember that he wrote something himself on Homer's language and his glosses, although only the title remains, as in the case of Callimachus' Democritean Pinax.

We have taken pains to call attention to many dry and sometimes baffling titles. Inconspicuous as the individual headings may look, the impression of the whole is overwhelming. To amass hundreds of thousands of rolls in the library would have been of little use without a sensible classification that enabled the prospective reader to find the books he needed. For the first time in history the *Pinakes* of Callimachus made the greatest treasures of literature accessible by dividing poetry and prose books into appropriate classes and by listing the authors in alphabetical order. Only the most passionate desire to save the complete literary heritage of the past from oblivion and to make it a permanent and fruitful possession for all ages could have provided strength and patience for this immense effort. Querulous critics of the scholar poets, Philitas, Callimachus, and their followers in ancient and modern times, may carp at the excessive learning of their poetry and at the amateurish deficiencies of their scholarship. But they should not undervalue the fervent devotion to learning that sprang from the enthusiasm of a great poet.

No doubt the 120 books of the *Pinakes* gave plenty of scope for additions and corrections; even our short quotations have revealed this again and again. Aristophanes of Byzantium published a whole book Πρὸς τοὺς Καλλιμάχου πίνακας. Πρός is ambiguous and often means 'against' in titles, but there is not the slightest reason to assume that Aristophanes ever wrote *'Against* Callimachus' Pinakes';* his book was meant to be a supplement, which certainly was very welcome about fifty years afterwards, and he made use of Callimachus' chronological tables of the Attic dramatists for the summaries of plays in his editions. This was the immediate effect; but everyone who needed biographical material, who undertook editions of texts, who wrote on any literary subject had to consult the great work; it has never been superseded by a better one. The anonymous Πίνακες of the rival library in Pergamum, very rarely quoted, once for a comic poet and twice for orators, did not compare in importance with the Alexandrian *Pinakes* of Callimachus upon which they were probably modelled.

A number of titles, some of them found only in Suidas' article, and some short quotations give an idea of the variety of learned books published under Callimachus' name; in preparing them he may have been assisted by friends and pupils. A throng of students was drawn to Alexandria by the new longing for unlimited knowledge and the fact that incomparably richer material was now offered there than ever before in Athens or elsewhere. The Sophists had had epideictic-oratorical aims in their treatment of literary, especially poetical, subjects, and the great Attic philosophers and their schools had had their philosophical purposes. Now for the first time we find wide literary knowledge being acquired for the sake of the literary tradition itself, that is, for the works to be written in the present age and for the preservation and understanding of the works written in past ages. This is the new separate discipline of scholarship.

The books of Callimachus the scholar . . . are often regarded as mechanical compilations of antiquities. As a matter of fact they are not restricted at all to antiquarian matter; we can apply our old scheme to them, though perhaps in a different sequence, briefly reviewing his books on antiquities, on language, and on literary criticism, and finally considering how far he may be regarded as an interpreter of earlier Greek poetry.

The Νόμιμα βαρβαρικά were an antiquarian collection of **'Non-Greek Customs'**, possibly supplementing Aristotle's book with the same title. A general book Περὶ ἀγώνων probably belongs to the same group, since some of the Sophists and Aristotle and his school frequently compiled material 'On games'. The forty-four excerpts in Antigonus of Carystus, *Hist. mirab.* 129-73, from Callimachus' Παράδοξα show him as a writer on marvels; his keen curiosity for 'Incredibilities' led him to make this **Collection of marvels in all the earth according to localities** from historical, geographical, and antiquarian sources. There is no earlier example of paradoxography as a distinct literary genre. Like Philitas and Zenodotus he was not scientifically minded, as this work reveals better than any other; there is no recognizable intercourse between science and scholarship in Alexandria before Eratosthenes.

From a book entitled . . . **Local nomenclature**, special names for fishes in different cities (Chalcedon, Thurii, Athens) are quoted; as there was a chapter on fishes, the arrangement of the whole must have been by subjects. Though unproven, it is not impossible that the titles Περὶ ἀνέμωά (fr. 404), Περὶ ὀρνέων (fr. 414-28), Μηνῶν προσηγορίαι κατὰ ἔθνος καὶ πόλεις (p. 339, *Local Month-names*) are only the sub-titles of other chapters in the same comprehensive Onomastikon. This vocabulary was certainly not arranged in alphabetical order like Zenodotus' *Glossai*. The relation of names to things was a philosophical problem, discussed at length in Plato's *Cratylus* and also by Aristotle. But Callimachus listed and disposed all the names he could find for the purely literary reasons which we have just stated; it was the first vocabulary of its kind, as far as we know, and was eagerly used by Aristophanes of Byzantium and later generations. It can hardly be decided whether works entitled Κτίσεις νήσων καὶ πόλεων καὶ μετονομασίαι (p. 339) and Περὶ τῶν ἐν τῇ οἰκουμένῃ ποταμῶν (fr. 457-9) belong to the books on antiquities or to the books on language; 'changes of name' rather point to the second group. There remain a few headings and fragments for which we are completely at a loss to find a place, or even to understand the titles. But the important fact is that we are able to find traces of nearly all the learned collections of Callimachus in his

poems: fair sounding names of rivers and islands, of winds and nymphs and birds were picked out of them to embellish the verses, and a number of fine local stories was found in them and saved from oblivion.

One book has been left out of this cursory survey, Callimachus' **Against Praxiphanes** . . . (fr. 460); we mentioned it earlier, when we were pointing out non-Aristotelian features in the whole new movement in Alexandria. The only fragment quoted from this book is clear evidence of literary criticism in so far as it asserts the high poetical qualities of the work of his contemporary Aratus. . . . As we know of no other similar book by Callimachus, the polemics against the Peripatetic Praxiphanes may have included both his judgement on Plato's incompetence as a literary critic, (the more so as Praxiphanes' Περὶ ποιητῶν was a dialogue between Plato and Isocrates), and also his famous maxim: τὸ μέγα βιβλίον ἴσον τῷ μεγάλῳ κακῷ. Whatever βιβλίον here means, μέγα κακόν, a 'great evil', is a sort of old formula (*O* 134, ι 423), and μέγας with reference to literature is always vituperative; we may compare the filthy μέγας ῥόος in contrast to the pure ὀλίγη λιβάς (*hy.* II 108), or the μεγάλη γυνή of a poem contrasted with subtle small-scale ones, κατὰ λεπτόν (fr. 1. 12). As in the case of Aratus the statement in the prose book has its exact parallel in an epigram, so also there are obvious parallels in the poems to the two other passages tentatively ascribed to the same prose writing. Plato was deemed an incompetent critic . . . ; the reason was that he appreciated the poetry of Antimachus, whose *Lyde* Callimachus condemned in an epigram (fr. 398) as 'a fat and not lucid book'. The general disapproval of the μέγα βιβλίον uttered in the prose maxim is a common topic in Callimachus' poems and is the particular theme of his introductory elegy to the **Aitia** against his adversaries, whom he calls 'Telchines'.

A list of these adversaries compiled by a learned scholiast includes the name of Praxiphanes the Mytilenean; this is invaluable evidence for the opposition between the poet and a leading Peripatetic and shows that the ambiguous Πρός in the title means *'against* Praxiphanes'. There is no tradition that Praxiphanes had personally attacked Callimachus in his writings. The learned collections and also the **Pinakes** may give the impression of being rather Aristotelian in subject-matter, despite their new purpose; but in literary criticism Aristotle's theory and Callimachus' views are plainly incompatible. As the one relevant prose book is almost lost, we have to rely mainly on the poems. Again and again, charmingly as well as firmly, he put forward his clear and consistent opinions. He is never pedantic, but rather humorous and ironical or even of a lively aggressive spirit. Aristotle, we remember, in the severest of styles demanded organic unity of every artistic work: ἕν, ὅλον, τέλος, μέγεθος were the decisive terms. All parts must have a definite relation to the whole work, which itself is distinguished by completeness and magnitude. The *Iliad* and *Odyssey*, but not the other epics, are living organisms of this kind; they and the masterpieces of Attic tragedy alone fulfil these requirements. If it were possible for any further poetical works to be produced at all, they must somehow conform to this standard prescribed by Aristotle. Now Callimachus regarded Homer with the same devotion and affection as Aristotle had done, in contrast to everything 'cyclic' (*Ep.* 28), which lacked organic unity, but abounded in traditional formulae. For that very reason he esteemed Homer inimitable, even unapproachable. It would be a vain ambition to vie with him and the other great poets of the past; if poetry lived on, it was bound to follow principles quite different from those inferred by Aristotle from the ancient poems. . . . For years poetical criticism had been in the hands of Sophists and theorizing philosophers; the time had come for a return to its originators, the practicing poets.

The new poetical school of Callimachus and his followers was ostentatiously anti-Aristotelian. Rejecting unity, completeness, and magnitude, it consciously aimed at a discontinuous form (fr. 1. 3 . . .) in a more or less loose series of pieces of a few lines (fr. 1. 9 . . .). The proper quality of a poem was to be . . . 'subtle'. It has been rightly noticed that this key term and a few other ones had already occurred in Aristophanes' comedies, especially in the critical passages of the *Frogs*: τέχνη / [κρίνετε] . . . τὴν σοφίην (Call. fr. 1. 17 f.) is almost a verbal quotation. But the truth of this observation was overlaid by two hypotheses: namely that Aristophanes borrowed his phrases from a Sophistic source, probably Gorgias, and that Callimachus used a rhetorical source on the *genera dicendi*. No proof of these hypotheses has yet been produced; they remain a strange but typical example of the modern quest for hidden sources. The natural assumption is that the Hellenistic poets derived their critical terminology directly from the poets of the fifth century, whom they knew so well. Substantial parts of Callimachus' *Iambi* are indebted to Attic comedy; there is no need to invent intermediate handbooks. The meaning of the word λεπτός underwent a characteristic change; while it was once used disapprovingly of over-refinement of spirit or diction, for instance, that of Euripides in contrast to the vigour that Aeschylus achieved through the magnitude . . . of his words, the Alexandrians, Callimachus, Hedylus, Leonidas, employed it as a term of the highest praise to describe the style they were eager to achieve in their poems. We find another significant epithet in the Praxiphanes pamphlet, where Aratus was praised as a poet of the highest rank: πολυμαθής. 'Much learning' was in archaic times a reproach against those who had no true wisdom; but this word also came to have the opposite connotation in the Hellenistic age; unlimited knowledge of subject-matter and language was now deemed

an indispensable requisite for the new poetry called σοφίη (Call. fr. 1. 18).

Looking back on Callimachus' own πολυμαθίη amassed in his prose works, we may ask whether they can be assigned to a particular epoch of his life. When the epilogue of the *Aitia* came to light, the first editor saw in the concluding line Callimachus' 'formal farewell to poetry' and a declaration 'that he will now devote himself to prose'; indeed his appointment at the Alexandrian library was regarded as the point in his career at which he turned from poetry to prose. But αὐτὰρ ἐγὼ Μουσέων πεζὸν [ἔ]πειμι νομόν indicates the *Musa pedestris* of the *Iambi* which followed the *Aitia* in the final edition arranged by the poet himself; the pentameter gives no answer to this or any other question of chronology.

When we divided Callimachus' prose works into three groups, on antiquities, on language, and on literary criticism, we asked whether there was not a fourth one on interpretation. As far as we know, he never edited a text or wrote a commentary; the few fragments of his Ὑπομνήματα seem to indicate a collection of mythological, linguistic, and geographical material. But in many passages of his poems he discloses his acquaintance with the *Iliad* and *Odyssey* and occasionally allows us to guess not only what text he chose but also how he understood its meaning. In this sense only he may with reserve be called an 'interpreter' of Homer.

First of all we should like to know how far Callimachus used Zenodotus' new critical edition of Homer and how far he relied on pre-critical texts, . . . such as Timon recommended to Aratus. Several Callimachean readings of the Homeric text seem to agree with those known to us only as Zenodotean. The beautiful Naxian girl, Cydippe, took part in 'the dance of sleeping Ariede, Ἀριήδης / [ἐς χ]ορὸν εὑρούσης, Callimachus tells us (fr. 67. 13); in the famous Homeric passage to which he alludes, χορόν . . . οἶον . . . Δαίδαλος ἤσκησεν . . . Ἀριάδνη (Σ 592), only Zenodotus read Ἀριήδη. This certainly is a most remarkable coincidence; but as Zenodotus constituted his text on earlier manuscripts that he found reliable, the same sources may have been accessible to Callimachus. Although it is possible or even very probable that he followed Zenodotus, the coincidence in this and about ten similar cases is not conclusive proof. At least one example proves that Callimachus also consulted other texts older than the Zenodotean edition: only the 'city-editions' had the unique variant reading νήσων ἔπι θηλυτεράων (Φ 454 and Χ 45), from which he transferred the epithet to another noun, θηλύτατον πεδίον (fr. 548), 'the most fertile plain'. By connecting θηλύτατον with πεδίον Callimachus gave his 'interpretation' of the Homeric phrase: it does not mean 'island where females reign', like Lemnos and Imbros, but 'island that is . . . with good soil, fertile.' It is possible that he consulted the elementary explanatory notes that must have accompanied the Homeric text for a long time and finally became a substantial part of our so-called D-Scholia, in which they were mixed up with more learned grammatical comments. When he took over τοῖος from *H* 231 in the sense of ἀγαθός (fr. 627), his interpretation possibly was in accordance with Aeschylus, certainly with the glossographers; when he called a messenger ἀπούατος (fr. 315), he was induced by whatever source not to read ἀπ᾽ οὔατος in E 272, but a compound meaning 'bringing the tidings'. These may be rather odd examples of Homeric epithets; but there are more common epic words too that have been puzzling in all ages. We can still distinguish how Callimachus understood some of these adjectives . . . , nouns . . . , or verbs . . . , or controversial etymologies of proper names. . . .

We started from the fact that the creative epic poets were their own interpreters and that the rhapsodes continued the self-interpretation of the poets. The Sophists can be regarded as the heirs of the rhapsodes in so far as they tried to explain poetry for their new purpose, and the great Attic philosophers and their schools completed this development. Now once again poets became active in this field; there were no commentaries produced in the first generations of the Hellenistic age, but these poets were the immediate forerunners of the writers of continuous interpretations. . . . It is from Callimachus and his pupils that a line runs to the true ἑρμηνεία τῶ ποιητῶν by the Alexandrian γραμματικοί of the following generations. In contrast to them, Crates and his pupils in Pergamum renewed in a way the ancient allegorical method and forced their own philosophical, particularly Stoic, views upon the Homeric and other poems. But the not infrequent quotations from Callimachean verses in our Scholia to Homer show how helpful they were for the other, the scholarly way of interpreting old epic poetry.

G. Zanker (essay date 1987)

SOURCE: "The Practice of Pictorial Realism" and "The Everyday and the Low in Alexandrian Poetry," in *Realism in Alexandrian Poetry: A Literature and Its Audience,* Croom Helm, 1987, pp. 55-112, 155-227.

[*In the following excerpt, Zanker studies the use of pictorial realism among Alexandrian poets, looking at Callimachus alongside Appollonius, Theocritus, and Herodas. Zanker's discussion of Callimachus considers many of his works, including the* Aetia *and the* Hymns, *but his thesis rests primarily on an extended study of the* Hecale, *which he finds particularly demonstrates the meaning of pictorial realism. He argues that Callimachus uses the style for a specific meaning—to show "that appearances may be deceptive and that moral nobility can be found in people of lowly*

circumstances"—and that he achieved "a totally new tone . . . in epic" with his use of pictorial realism.]

THE PRACTICE OF PICTORIAL REALISM

. . . In the case of Callimachus of Cyrene, . . . we have indisputable evidence of a keen yet judicious interest in pictorial realism, even though two works of great importance to this book, the *Aetia* and the *Hecale,* are in a fragmentary state,

To consider the *Aetia* first, it must first be noted that cult origins will not have been a theme naturally conducive to pictorial description. Callimachus is in general more interested in the brief delineation of the history which led to the founding of cults. Even so, *Fr.* 114.1-17 takes the form of a dialogue between Callimachus and a statue of Apollo, and in the course of the conversation an explanation is given of why Apollo is carrying a bow in his left hand and the Graces in his right; a definite picture of the statue emerges, though it appears to have been meant only as the occasion for Callimachus' explanation of its peculiarities.

The *Hymns* yield much interesting evidence for Callimachus' approach to pictorialism and the contexts to which he thought it appropriate. The third, that to Artemis, claims our particular attention. The poem opens with a family tête-à-tête, where little Artemis, still a child, is seated on her father Zeus' knee and in a forthright, ironically naive manner asks for her divine attributes as maiden goddess of the hunt and of childbirth and for polyonymy:

> . . . Of Artemis we sing, . . . beginning at the time when, still a little child, she was sitting on her father's knees and addressed her parent with these words: 'Daddy, grant that I may keep my virginity forever, and grant me many names, so that Phoebus won't vie with me, and grant me arrows and a bow . . .' With these words the child wanted to touch her father's beard, and she kept stretching her hands in vain so that she might touch it. With a laugh her father nodded assent and said, caressing her, 'When goddesses bear me children like this, little need I bother about Hera's jealous anger.'

The homely visual details of the little goddess, repeatedly straining to touch her father's beard and being unable to reach, Zeus' delighted laugh and his spite for his wife, Hera, are carefully emphasised. Now one of Callimachus' models is a scene in the *Iliad* and a brief comparison will prove instructive. In Homer, Artemis, who is unlike her counterpart in Callimachus in that she is adult, has been put in her place by her stepmother, Hera, for meddling in the affairs of gods greater than herself in the divine struggle over Troy. She flies home to her father and sits weeping on his knee, her robe trembling with her sobs; Zeus makes her look at him and with a smile asks her who is troubling her and she tells him it is Hera and blames her for the gods' dissension (*Il.* 21.505-13). The pose of the daughter on her father's knee, Zeus' laughter and the family frictions are already present in Homer, but Callimachus' version is even more intent upon highlighting amusing domesticities, again of a predominantly visual nature, and upon giving the scene individuality and vividness by so doing; its aim is to dwell on the particular, individualising detail, whereas the Homeric passage gives the impression of stylisation, not only because of its formulaic phraseology, but also because a sense of decorum is preserved to a greater degree; Callimachus dwells upon characterising, homely strokes and invests the portrayal of the behind-the-scenes dealings of the gods with a feeling of *tout comme chez nous.* Another main model seems to be a hymn to Artemis by Alcaeus (304 Lobel-Page (= Sappho 44A Voigt)) in which Artemis makes her vow of chastity with a solemnity which contrasts pointedly with the tone of the Callimachean Artemis' request, and in which the pictorial is scarcely discernible at all. The comparison with these two models thus reveals Callimachus' heightened concern with visual detail; it also illustrates the close connection between pictorialism and the depiction of the everyday which of course lends the scene its humour. The fusion of vividly pictorial representation of realistic matter and momentous grandeur of setting is curiously paralleled in baroque art.

The second chief section of the hymn maintains a pronounced emphasis on the pictorial. At lines 46ff. Artemis goes to Hephaestus' workshop to ask the Cyclopes for a bow, arrows and a quiver. The giants are at work around a red-hot mass of iron and an anvil (48f.). The attendant nymphs are terrified at the sight of them, and Callimachus does not miss the opportunity to give a vivid picture of the Cyclopes' appearance: they are 'dread monsters that look like the crags of Mount Ossa and beneath their brow their single eyes, like a shield with four folds of hide, glare fearfully' (51-4). The nymphs are frightened, too, by the noise the smiths make and, once again, we are given a picture of the Cyclopes as they swing their hammers above their shoulders and strike the iron or bronze hissing from the furnace, their hammer blows falling in alternate succession (59-61). But no shame to the nymphs, Callimachus remarks, for not even the goddesses who are already past their childhood look upon the Cyclopes without a shudder (64-5). Moreover, he says, divine mothers bring their disobedient daughters to heel by calling the Cyclopes to frighten them; or Hermes comes out from inside the house, all stained with ashes, and plays bogy with the child, who covers her eyes with her hands and runs to her mother's lap (66-71). But Artemis is different from the nymphs. On an earlier occasion, when she was only three years old (72) and needed her mother, Leto, to carry her (73), she had visited Hephaestus who had promised her the presents customarily given to a new-born child when an adult

sees him for the first time . . . ; the little goddess sat on Brontes' knees and tore a handful of hair from his chest (76f.); 'even to this day', we are told, there remains a bald patch on Brontes' chest, just as when a man gets mange and loses his hair (78-9). So now Artemis finds no difficulty in framing her request boldly (80). Homely realistic detail and thoroughgoing pictorial portrayal of it form the appeal of the passage and humorously contrast with the grandeur of the metre and the dignity of treatment normally expected in a hymn.

Though Callimachus' pictorialism is evidenced most clearly in the ***Hymn to Artemis,*** it is by no means exclusively confined to that poem. Consider Callimachus' account in the ***Hymn to Delos*** of the crucial moment when Leto finally gives birth to Apollo: she comes to rest and sits by the River Inopus, undoes her girdle and, wearied by her pain, leans backwards with her shoulders supported by the trunk of a palm-tree; her whole body is covered in sweat; she addresses her unborn child and begs him to come forth (205-12). The visual elements here employed to heighten the pathos of the scene may certainly be called realistic. Callimachus' model is the *Homeric Hymn to Apollo* and a comparison will illustrate the Alexandrian poet's realism. In the Homeric hymn, the birth of the god is mentioned briefly at lines 25-7, but is treated at greater length ninety lines later (115-19). Eileithyia visits Delos and Leto longs to give birth; she throws her arms around the palm-tree, kneeling on the soft meadow, and the earth smiles beneath; Apollo springs forth into the light of day and all the goddesses shout for joy. The scene is pictorial enough, though perhaps less precisely observed, but the birth is an easy one and Eileithyla is allowed to help Leto, whereas Callimachus makes no mention of her presence at the birth. Callimachus has invested the scene with a dramatic force and pathos absent from his model; his choice of pictorial detail from actual childbirth with its emphasis on pain and particularly his alteration of Leto's pose to one realistically evocative of utter exhaustion are the main means of achieving his effect. And . . . we have evidence of just how closely the aims of *enargeia* and *mimēsis biou* are connected.

Now this passage is set in an account of Leto's flight in which Callimachus has gone far out of his way to introduce incidents which are realistically quite fantastic and incredible. We can hope to understand the motivation behind his procedure only once we have analysed, in their proper place, the other aspects of the scene's realism.

Also in the ***Hymn to Delos*** is the description of Iris, where the messenger-goddess sits down after informing Hera that Leto has given birth to Apollo:

   . . . So she spoke and sat at the foot of the golden

throne like a hunting hound of Artemis which, after the swift chase, sits at her feet, its ears pricked up, always ready to receive the goddess's call; like that, Thaumas' daughter sat at the foot of the throne. She never neglects her post, not even when sleep brushes its wing of forgetfulness against her, but there by the corner of the great throne she sleeps tilting her head aslant a little. She never undoes her girdle or her swift hunting-boots in case her mistress gives her even a sudden command.

Pindar's passage on Zeus' eagle being lulled to sleep by the phorminx (*P.* 1.6-10) is in some ways interestingly comparable. The eagle's external appearance is clear enough: the bird is perched on Zeus' sceptre, its wings relax, its head droops, its eyes are closed, and its supple back rises and falls as it breathes. But Pindar moves easily from this external picture to the less pictorial imagery of the dark cloud which the phorminx spreads over the eagle's head, 'a sweet seal for his eyelids', and of the dream and enchantment that the phorminx induces. Callimachus is far more pictorial and, moreover, limits his less visual sleep-imagery to the motif of the brushing of sleep's wing. The lines present an image of Iris so graphic and precise in its detail that scholars have claimed that they are inspired by particular works of plastic art, though unanimity has never been reached over which. The picture may well have been influenced in its general conception and composition by works of art and the poet's eye may have been opened to the possibilities of pictorialism by his contemplation of art, a point I have already argued, but there is no need to postulate the influence of any particular statue or the like, given the fact that for Callimachus and his movement pictorialism, which we have found denoted in second-century criticism by the word *enargeia,* was in itself a well-attested aim in literature. Still, in the case of the description of Iris one may agree with a modern scholar that 'in general Callimachus' imagery is less static than this'. As we shall see, however, other Alexandrian poets, notably Apollonius and Theocritus, offer us even more detailed and extended descriptive passages.

One further aspect of the *Hymns* deserves mention here. It is the 'mimetic' approach of the *Hymn to Apollo, The Bath of Pallas* and the *Hymn to Demeter.* The most recent editors of these poems agree that they are literary pieces and are meant only to create the illusion that they accompany actual rituals: the audience, consequently, was not present at them. The narrators, who are identifiable with the masters of ceremonies at the different festivals, realistically evoke for Callimachus' audiences an atmosphere of religious excitement by reporting the different stages of the rites, by urgent commands to the participants, by addresses to the deity and by expressions of awe at his or her epiphany. This realism is not pictorial, but it is analogous to pictorial realism as a style lending immediacy to its subject.

It is now time to examine a poem by Callimachus which exhibits, despite its fragmentary state, all the major aspects of Alexandrian realism and may be called the centre-piece of this book. It is the *Hecale*. The fragments provide ample evidence that Callimachus throughout the epyllion aimed at pictorially realistic description.

We possess a fragment which appears to have described the weather on the day Theseus left (*Fr.* 238.15-30). It describes first, I take it, the weather as it was at noon:

> . . . So while it was still noon and the earth was warm, the bright sky was clearer than glass and not a wisp of cloud appeared anywhere, and the heavens stretched cloudless.

Evening is described as 'the time when girls take the wool they have spun to their mother, ask for their evening meal and take their hands from their work' (19-20), in itself a picturesque scene. It is then that the storm suddenly breaks over Attica; the clouds, the wind and the lightning are described; and the mountains of Attica over which the storm passes, Parnes, Aegaleos and Hymettus, are detailed (21-30). This will be the storm which forced Theseus to lodge with Hecale, and it is evident that Callimachus has taken much care over presenting a vivid picture of it and the time it occurred. Moreover, the storm he describes motivates Theseus' taking refuge in Hecale's hut.

Callimachus' portrayal of Hecale herself is of key importance to this book. Her person, life and milieu are described with a remarkable visual realism, and her poverty is emphasised largely by means of it; *enargeia* and *mimēsis biou* are therefore once again inseparable. Callimachus' presentation of her as a figure of low realism in fact depends for its impact on his vivid description of her, so that the real point of his pictorialism is only intelligible once the background to low realism has been explored. Discussion of the description of Hecale must therefore wait till that has been done. It is sufficient here to note that the 'heroine' of the epyllion—who, after all, gives it its name—is described extensively and in arresting detail, and that the poem's real point (aside from its formal, aetiological one), namely that appearances may be deceptive and that moral nobility can be found in people of lowly circumstances, actually depends upon pictorialism.

It looks as if Theseus' victory over the bull of Marathon was also described. One fragment tells how Theseus 'forced the terrible horn of the beast down to the ground' (*Fr.* 258). We learn from *Fr.* 288.1 *S. H.* (= *Fr.* 260.1 Pf.) that Theseus probably broke off one of its horns with his club. Another fragment describes how after the struggle Theseus 'dragged [the bull] and it followed, a reluctant travelling-companion' (*Fr.* 259).

A more substantial fragment (*Fr.* 288.1-15 *S.H.* = *Fr.* 260.1-15 Pf.) depicts Theseus' triumphal procession, dragging the bull by its remaining horn, and relates how the country-folk grew frightened at the sight of the hero and the animal and showered him with leaves in a ritual φυλλοβολία; the simile describing the number of the leaves, and hence the people's relief, is also graphic:

> . . . The south wind does not spread so great a fall of leaves, nor even the north wind itself when it is the month of falling leaves, as the country folk then showered Theseus with, around and on both sides of him, . . . surrounded by the crowd[?], and the women . . . crowned him with girdles . . .

The fragments permit us, surely, to conclude that Callimachus' narration of the victory was pictorially vivid.

The description of the dawn at which Theseus returns to Hecale is a charming mixture of everyday and pictorial detail. Dawn is called the time when burglars have given up searching for loot; the early morning lanterns are beginning to appear and many a water-bearer is singing the Song of the Well; people whose house is on the road-side are woken by the axles squeaking under wagons; and blacksmiths are either being troubled for a light or are troubling others for it (*Fr.* 288.65-9 *S.H.* = *Fr.* 260.65-9 Pf.).

There is only one more poem of Callimachus that need be discussed here to demonstrate that pictorialism was by no means limited to the poet's epos. In *Iambus 6* (*Fr.* 196) Callimachus goes to inordinately painstaking lengths to describe the statue of Zeus at Elis to a friend sailing off to see it. The Diegete tells us that he describes the length, height and width of the base, the throne, the footstool and the god himself, and how much the whole group cost. The fragments mention the winged Victory in Zeus' hand (39), the Horae (42) and, conjecturally, the Graces (44f.), attested elsewhere as adornments of the statue. The poem, as we know it, looks like a monstrous display of erudition, and its joking point may have been to render Callimachus' friend's visit to Elea unnecessary.

We have now surveyed sufficient evidence to allow us to conclude that pictorial realism is used extensively by Callimachus. Whenever we have been able to compare Callimachus' treatment of earlier, especially Homeric models, we have seen that he extends the everyday, low and pictorialist elements in his version. Sometimes pictorialism is used to give high-flown material an impression of immediacy or ironic *tout comme chez nous*, as in the **Hymns**, sometimes it is integral to his thematic point, as in the case of the **Hecale**, but it is always an important aspect of his poetry. . . .

THE EVERYDAY AND THE LOW IN ALEXANDRIAN POETRY

The Alexandrians' literary-critical thinking on the content appropriate to the genres can be reconstructed quite clearly. The movement's central figure, Callimachus, provides us with the most direct evidence. This is found in the proem to the *Aetia*, which is written in elegiacs, but by this time narrative elegiac and hexameter poetry were both viewed as epic, so that the prologue's programme is relevant to Callimachus' thought on hexameter epic as well. Callimachus claims that his poetry is criticised 'because I did not accomplish one continuous poem of many thousands of links on . . . kings or . . . heroes, but I unroll a tale . . . for a short time, like a child' (*Fr.* 1.3 6). The comment is valuable to us because it explicitly shows that readers of Callimachus' poetry missed in it the 'kings and heroes' of traditional epic. Nor does the poet reject these charges. Moreover, the statement implies that his interest was perceived to have been fixed on people of another kind. That these are ordinary, everyday folk like Acontius and Cydippe and their non-heroic encounter, or low folk like Molorchus, or heroes in uncharacteristically domestic settings like Heracles, will become evident in the following pages. Callimachus' reply to his critics that Apollo taught him to tread untrodden poetic paths (25-8) is probably in part a defence against their objections to his avoidance of traditional themes and subject matter. Perhaps the concern with such people is a reason for Callimachus' interest in Hesiod, whom he seems to have taken over as the authority for his literary doctrine when he rejected traditional epic on the scale of Homer's poems and the bombast that he apparently viewed as the standard epic tone. Quite apart from certain stylistic features of Hesiodic poetry, like its comparative shortness, its continual change of subject, its disjointed, seemingly illogical sequence of thought and its personal tone, Hesiod's celebration of the farmer and not the kings in the *Works and Days* may have struck Callimachus as particularly congenial and fruitful.

It appears from the *Aetia*-prologue, then, that Callimachus was consciously subverting traditional expectations of epic subject-matter. Perhaps he was thinking of Aristotelian notions of epic in particular. But Callimachean thinking can be discerned elsewhere in the Alexandrian movement. Apollonius, for example, yields clear evidence in the *Argonautica* that his conception of the material appropriate to epic was untraditional. He makes the seer Phineus prophesy to the Argonauts that the success of their expedition depends on Aphrodite (2.423f.). Now Phineus is like Teiresias who advises Odysseus which deity should be supplicated (*Od.* 11.101-3, 130ff., and with *A.R.* 2.310 compare *Od.* 10.539f.), but, while Teiresias directs Odysseus' attention to his persecution by Poseidon, Phineus alerts Jason to the special role to be played by the goddess of love. Love is an emotion which post-Euripidean poets and especially the Alexandrians seem to ahve viewed as a more human and familiar and hence a more compelling motive for action than a desire for glory or the like. Apollonius makes his intention even more plain in his proem to Book 3. There he calls upon Erato, the Muse of love poetry, to tell 'how Jason brought the fleece to Iolcus through the love of Medea', and makes much of the Muse's close connections with Aphrodite (3.1-5). And he shares Callimachus' misgivings over the traditional status of the epic hero, for . . . in his characterisation of Jason he scales down traditional ideas of heroic grandeur to a more emphatically everyday level.

Theocritus' agreement with Callimachus' programme cannot reasonably be doubted. There is the interesting passage in *Idylls* 16, the *Graces* or *Hiero*, in which he shows very clearly what he really thinks to be the material appropriate to modern epic. At lines 48-57 he cites examples of poetry's power to confer immortality on men, and it is interesting to see what caught is eye. He devotes three lines to heroes connected with the Trojan war, but he devotes no less than seven to the *Odyssey* (51-7), thereby showing a preoccupation with an epic which refused to fit into the neat categorisations of literary criticism as an epic of unequivocal heroic grandeur. But, most interestingly for us, the list of persons and events in the *Odyssey* culminates with the swineherd Eumaeus and the neatherd Philoetius, and with Laertes, whom we most readily picture at work in his orchard. Theocritus, then, is interested in the *phauloi* of the tradition, in particular those of the countryside. Moreover, he expresses this interest in poetry by making a reluctant patron say 'Who would listen to another? Homer is enough for everybody' (20). Poetry, Theocritus suggests, is not 'written out' provided that it strikes out in new directions, and, although Homer is certainly pre-eminent, there are aspects of his poetry which are worth closer attention. Figures like Eumaeus, who stand on the periphery of the heroic main narrative, become the literary legitimation of his pastoral poetry, a specimen of which he makes later in the poem (90-7), and it is to such *phauloi* that he wished to give the centre stage in his new epos. This is tantamount to saying that in his pastorals he crosses the traditional genres, though that observation is true also of the other main branches of his *oeuvre*. The passage became something of a manifesto for later pastoral. The *Lament for Bion*, for an example, claims that while Homer sang of heroic persons Bion eschewed warlike themes and opted instead for Pan, pastoral song and love (70-84).

One of the problems of particular concern to the Alexandrians was clearly, then, the nature of the hero appropriate to contemporary epic. Callimachus, Apollonius, Theocritus, and the author of the *Lament* all show a distaste for traditional concepts of what constitutes a literary hero, and their literary-critical utter-

ances indicate that they were predisposed towards everyday and low heroes in epic and hence towards the violation of generic expectations like those formulated by Aristotle.

Our main field of inquiry in what follows will be epic. It will pay to heed the reminder of Ziegler and others that Alexandrian epic was in fact an isolated branch of the epic written in the Hellenistic period and that the hexameter-poetry of the age continued to deal with grand themes, whether mythological, historical or encomiastic. Evidently, the grand associations of the genre and its metre were still the norm. Further proof of this is provided (if it were still needed) by the fact that later in the third century Ennius chose to introduce the metre into Latin poetry and to employ it in his *Annales*: if its acoustic grandeur had been dissipated, would he have taken such an enormous step? In investigating the Alexandrians' use of the everyday and low in epic, we must place their generic experimentation within the context of contemporary epic as a whole in order to try to appreciate their poetry's impact on people's minds and ears.

One of the chief aims of this chapter will be to establish the tones and effects which the Alexandrians created through their deployment of everyday and low material. Tone is a notoriously labile commodity, and I am aware that many readers may disagree with my judgements. I have, however, at least tried to relate these to the aesthetic, cultural, political and moral sensibilities of the period as I understand them. But in my attempt to ascertain the tone that might have been perceived by an Alexandrian audience I am aware that here too responses were probably multiple. I can only hope that my readings will not contradict what is known of the Alexandrian audiences' tastes and that they will approximate to the responses of a reasonable section of the original readership.

A poet obviously preoccupied with the everyday and the low is Herodas. His bawds, panders, child-delinquents, sadistic schoolmasters, chattering housewives, jealous mistresses of sexually disobedient slaves, and his dildo-stitching cobblers are realistic enough as subject-matter, but Herodas makes no attempt at an analytical presentation of their circumstances, or, we may add, of their psychology: the characters are designed simply to provoke our laughter. We may, in other words, conclude that in his poems the separation of genres remains intact.

We need examine only one of the *Mimiambi* in order to substantiate these conclusions. The second, *The Pandar,* is as instructive as any. In his legal suit before the Coan jury Battarus, the Pandar, is, for comic effect, repeatedly made to revert to well worn phrases and arguments in Attic oratory. So, for instance, he solemnly reminds the court of their duty to judge him and the sea captain, Thales, as equals before the law, despite the latter's superior wealth (1-10), argues that judgement on his suit will determine the security of the state and the rights of non-citizens like him (25-7, 92-4), and appeals to the legendary glories and deeds of the jury's Coan ancestors to stimulate pride of country (95-8). He even offers his own body to be tortured as if he were a slave, provided that Thales places before the court the compensation-money. This is an impudent and avaricious perversion of the law that the accuser had to pay damages to the master of a slave tortured before giving evidence on a charge which proved false (87-91). The Pandar's claptrap rhetoric is a means of characterising him, rather than simply a parody of legal rhetoric.

Another aspect of Battarus' characterisation is his continual use of proverbs, on occasion supremely sordid. Proverbs had long been an integral part of mime and Sophron himself is attested as having used them extensively. So, for example, when the Pandar asks the clerk to stop the clepsydra, he is reminded of a proverb running something like 'lest the anus is incontinent and the bedcovers are stained' (44-5). Again, he complains that he was treated by Thales 'like the mouse in the pitch-pot' (62-3).

The story of how Battarus was wronged is skilfully unfolded detail by detail, from his own mouth, but in such a way that it becomes perfectly plain that his presentation of himself as a poor, law-abiding metic in Cos is a total sham and that his charge, for all its bullying abuse of rhetoric, cannot stand. We do not get a real idea of what has happened until lines 33ff., when we are told that Thales, in what was evidently a rowdy revel, stole one of Battarus' girls from his establishment by night, setting fire to his house with torches. Finally, and almost incidentally, the Pandar lets it out that Thales abducted the girl because he was in love with her (79). He goes on to claim that all Thales has to do is to pay him for Myrtale's services and there the matter will rest. He thereby reveals that his indignation over the sailor's treatment of her is insincere and that he is bringing suit merely because one of his girls is being used free of charge and because he stands to win a fast buck if he is successful or bludgeons Thales into a settlement out of court.

The characterisation of Battarus is achieved by means of what has been called the 'mosaic' technique. It is the method of the New Comedy and Theophrastus: a general type is selected and then individualized by realistic traits and details. Within the bounds of ancient comic character-portrayal, then, we do not have any difficulty in calling the chief character of *Mimiamb* 2 realistic. However, there are other aspects of the poem which are not at all realistic. Battarus' oratory is a perverted imitation of Athenian legal rhetoric, but the scene of the poem is Cos (95-8). Since the

scene is Doric-speaking Cos, the dialect in which Battarus speaks is unrealistic, being an imitation of Hipponax' Eastern Ionic and thus obsolete. The metrical form of the poem, a revival of Hipponax' choliambs, makes it much more stylised than the prose of traditional mime. If, as seems probable, Herodas wanted to catch his audience's interest by presenting a scene from contemporary Coan low life in a revived and confessedly archaic form, one which had originally been used for satirical rather than mimic purposes, and in a defunct form of Greek, then *Mimiamb* 2 must to some extent have represented a literary in-joke: the philological-learnedness of the piece (and of the collection as a whole) must have been perceived as colliding ironically with the lowness of the subject-matter. Herodas' aim in selecting and portraying low material like the Pandar is the unswerving pursuit of comic effect, and we can now see how absurd it is to try to label the poet a prototype social realist or the like.

Callimachus' *Iambi* have a moral earnestness absent from Herodas. Callimachus, too, revives Hipponax' choliambic metre and, in modified form, his Ionic, but everyday and low material is firmly subordinated to the comparatively contemplative character of the poems. The first *Iambus* will illustrate my point. The Diegete (*Dieg.* VI.1-21) informs us that the purpose of Hipponax' appearance among the living was to forbid the literati of Alexandria from jealous feuding. Thus the poem is moralistic in intention. Hipponax' speech has a colloquial tone. For example, he expostulates in lively terms at the size of the crowd of scholars who have gathered to listen to him: 'Apollo, these people are swarming in droves like flies on a goatherd or wasps from the ground or Delphians from a sacrifice; Hecate, what a crowd! The old baldy over there will burst his lungs trying to keep his measly cloak from being torn off' (26-30). Secondly, he is repeatedly made to resort to common proverbs. His comments on the crowd, for instance, contain a reference to the Delphians who were proverbial for the way they filched meat from other people's sacrifices. Such proverbs are doubtless intended to give a realistic flavour to Hipponax' speech. True, by this period proverbs had become a field of scholarly research and their use was perhaps to some extent a self-conscious literary device, but this need not detract from a realistic effect. Thirdly, it is worth noting how carefully Callimachus sets the scene. He refers to places and personages of topical interest and makes Hipponax call the scholars outside the city walls to the Serapeum dedicated by Parmenio, where 'the old babbler who fabricated the ancient Panchaean Zeus scribbles his impious scriptures' (9-11), referring to Euhemerus. The 'old baldy' crutching at his cloak in the bustle seems meant to be a Cynic philosopher. The realistic setting of the imaginary scene is wittily ironic. Fourthly, the poet appears keen to make his characterizations as dramatically vivid as possible by means of realistic touches. So Hipponax calls his audience to silence and commands them to begin note-taking (31), interrupting his lecture by abusing some-one whom he sees turning up his nose at the thought of a long harangue (32-5). The same concern is present in Hipponax' cautionary tale about the Seven Wise Men. There is, for instance, the picturesque, everyday piece of scene-setting when the cup which Bathycles bequeathed to the best of the Wise Men is offered to Thales. The philosopher, who has been discovered characteristically pondering mathematical problems and drawing diagrams on the ground (52-63), apparently scratches the ground with his stick and with his free hand thoughtfully strokes his beard (69f.)

Among the poems on sex (3, 5, 9, 11), the third is an attack on the materialism of the times and the venality of a boy whom Callimachus is inconclusively lusting after, but, in contrast with what Herodas might have done, the poet apparently refrains from the obvious humour that the theme might lend itself to. The other poems, like *Iambus* 13, with Callimachus' defence of his writing in different genres and his dialect-mixing, also demonstrate how much more reflective the choliambic tradition became in Callimachus' hands.

. . . . .

In the first two lines [of the **Hymn to Artemis**] there is a jarring note for the reader expecting a traditional hymn. In the manner of the *Homeric Hymn to Artemis* . . . Callimachus begins by saying 'we hymn Artemis'. But, while the older poet mentions the goddess' golden arrows and her attribute of 'stag-hunter' . . . and draws a magnificent picture of her as she hunts, the Alexandrian talks of her love of the bow—and hare-hunting. . . . He has picked out the least of her quarries and established a tone which is deliberately lower than that of the Homeric poem. This tone persists, more-over, for, after a brief mention of her love of dance and sport in the mountains (3), we are immediately led into the scene of Artemis and Zeus' tête-à-tête in which Artemis first asks 'daddy' . . . for no less than eternal virginity (6). The poet does not specify the goddess' age, though we may assume from her expressed desire for nine-year-old Oceanids as her companions (14) that she is about the same age, perhaps a little older. In any case, her naive precociousness astounds us. Callima-chus has, however, carefully prepared us for the mo-ment with a deliberate shift of emphasis in his depic-tion of the goddess, displacing traditional sublimity with a homely, domestic detail of a child seated on its father's knee. The altered perspective is all the more striking when we consider the solemnity with which Artemis expresses to Zeus her vow of chastity in the Aeolic hymn (Alcaeus 304 Lobel-Page = Sappho 44A Voigt) which appears to have served as Callimachus' model for his Artemis' request, for he makes her voice her wish with a frankness which is borne of truly child-like innocence. It is matched by her desire for polyon-ymy, which she wants 'so that Phoebus may not rival her' (7). This sibling-rivalry is also a detail taken straight from life.

When she asks for a bow and arrows, but interrupts her request by saying that she won't ask them of '*you*, father', for the Cyclopes will provide her with them 'immediately' (8-10), this is again humorously realis-tic, for the little girl assumes with an infant's imperi-ousness that the Cyclopes will have nothing else to do and will drop tools on any other project just for her. Her request for her hunting-dress (11f.) and for no less than sixty Oceanids to dance with has the specification that all of them should be nine years old and all still virgins, which reminds us of her earlier display of precociousness (13-14). Her demand for twenty nymphs, who are to be her attendants in the hunt and will perform the humdrum task of looking after her boots and hounds after it (15-17), also juxtaposes the marvellous and the banal. Her request for 'all moun-tains' as her domain is typically childlike in its hyper-bole, but when she says that she'll only visit cities when she is called upon to assist women in childbirth (18-25), we notice once more her precociousness over sex, which she talks about in the most matter-of-fact way.

Artemis' whole speech is, therefore, a masterpiece of comic characterisation. This extends to linguistic fea-tures. So, for instance, quite apart from her address to 'daddy' . . . at line 6, we have the five-fold repetition of the phrase 'give me' . . . and her reference to herself in the third person when she says 'Artemis will rarely go to town' (19), a trait typical of 'naive' speech in ancient Greece.

We have already compared the scene of Artemis' sup-plication of Zeus with one of its models, the passage in the *Iliad* which depicts Artemis being comforted by Zeus after her rough treatment at the hands of Hera (*Il.* 21.505-13). The comparison demonstrated Callimachus' concern to outdo Homer's use of pictorialism and humorously realistic material. (The Aeolic poem by Sappho or Alcaeus is outstripped in this respect by far.) But there is a reference in the scene to another passage of the *Iliad,* that famous moment in which Thetis supplicates Zeus for revenge for Achilles (*Il.* 1.495-532). Thetis sits at Zeus' feet and takes hold of his knee with her right hand and his chin with her left (*Il.* 1.499-502); but Artemis sits on her father's knee and grabs in vain at his beard. Thus Callimachus ne-gates the grandeur of the supplicatory gestures in his second model from the *Iliad.* Moreover, Homer's Zeus refers to the strife that he will have to face with Hera if he accedes to Thetis' request, and this is no doubt meant to lend humour to the characterisation of the grand god. But, whereas Homer makes him express his foreboding 'greatly troubled', Callimachus gives the motif a new complexion by making the god voice his claim that with spirited daughters like Artemis he need have no fear of Hera, and by making him laugh with delight and affectionately caress his little daughter. He has expanded the motif of Zeus and Hera's marital friction and relaxed the element of tension contained in the Homeric Zeus' frustrated anger; the god is characterized like a husband or father in the New Comedy.

But what precisely is Callimachus aiming at with this extraordinary mixture of Homeric citation and everyday matter? In his redeployment of moments in the epic tradition he emphasizes everyday detail which is already present in them, thus effectively deheroising them. Simultaneously, he cites more elevated moments in the tradition to give, by contrast, even greater prominence to the domestic elements in his poem, so that they thus become comic. In this way he is subverting his contemporaries' received expectations of the epic and hymnal tradition. The use of the hexameter, with all its associations, will have contributed still further to his design. In short, far from committing mere unconscious lapses of taste in the first part of his hymn as he has been charged with doing, Callimachus is experimenting with his audience's notions of appropriateness in order to produce deliberate artistic effects. The result is not simply travesty or parody of either the Homeric passages or the epic genre in general, but rather an episode to which Herter originally applied the phrase 'Idyll der Kleinwelt', which we have found aptly describes other moments in Callimachus. Thus a totally new tone has been created in epic. Moreover, as we have noticed, the poet gives us a precise mental picture of the whole scene which contributes effectively to its special character.

The scene of Artemis' visit to the Cyclopes is no less a conscious study in contrasts. We have already noted its emphatic pictorialism. It is obviously modelled on the episode in the *Iliad* where Thetis visits Hephaestus to ask for arms for Achilles. Now there is light, everyday matter even in the Iliadic passage: so, for instance, Charis greets Thetis by remarking what a long time it's been since they've seen the goddess; she hasn't visited for ages (*Il.* 18.385-7). But Callimachus goes to infinitely greater trouble to bring out such details. The giants of Lipara are making a horse trough for Poseidon. This is rather a humble project, one would have thought, for the poet to have called it a 'mighty task'; already the episode is placed in an unexpectedly everyday context (46-50). The nymphs' terror at the sight and sound of the Cyclopes at work is pardoned by the poet when he adduces another homely detail of everyday life on Olympus, the role played by the Cyclopes and Hermes as bogy-men for naughty little goddesses (64-71). Artemis' contrasting boldness is stressed by the reference to her willingness to sit, as a three-year-old, on Brontes' knee when she visited him to collect gifts and pulled out a handful of chest-hair (72-9). So now she has no shyness in framing her request for arrows and a quiver like those of her brother, a detail

which again suggests her sibling-rivalry. And, as she has self-confidently assumed, the Cyclopes fulfil her wish immediately, by which we may infer that they do indeed drop their tools on the 'mighty task' for Poseidon!

The impression which the scene leaves upon the reader is the same as that of the preceding. The incongruity of so much homely detail and human characterisation in the framework of a hymn which, moreover, deliberately invites comparison with scenes in Homer, again creates an episode which may be called an 'Idyll der Kleinwelt'. We now see the rules according to which Callimachus is operating: he is 'crossing the genres' to secure a brilliant new literary effect.

Yet even though the Alexandrian evidently enjoys his achievement in humour, he is still concerned in other parts of the hymn to present his subject in its serious aspect. Artemis receives from Pan a pack of hounds, which, incidentally, conform with specifications for the very best hounds as laid down in the hunting treatises of Callimachus' own day (87-97). Next she captures with her own hands huge hinds to draw her chariot (98-109). The hymn here begins to leave behind the domestic tone of the earlier scenes. She tests her bow, first choosing as her target an elm tree, then an oak, then a wild animal, but finally turning her arrows on a city of unjust men. Thus the hymn proceeds from the levity of its earlier scenes, via the comparatively non-serious motif of target-practice with the bow, to the grave moment where the goddess exercises her supreme moral oversight over men's actions and is revealed in her traditional grandeur. The picture of the unjust city and of that on which Artemis looks with favour (122-37) is directly modelled on Hesiod's description of the unjust and just cities in the *Works and Days*. Here, of course, the subject-matter is in concord with the traditional expectations of its hymn-frame, and Callimachus shows his mastery of the orthodox conception of *to prepon* just as he has shown in the hymn's opening scenes how brilliantly he can subvert it.

But directly after he has conformed with his audience's expectations he proceeds to undermine them again, once more demonstrating his love of contrasting tones. In his description of Artemis' return to Olympus from the hunt Hermes and Apollo meet her, though the latter's task of collecting the goddess's booty has now been usurped by Heracles since his arrival on Olympus. The 'Tirynthian anvil', as he is heroically styled to contrast with the comic labour in which we are about to see him engaged, now stands before the gates, on the alert, as always, in case she brings meat. He is the laughing-stock of the Olympians, especially his mother-in-law Hera, when he drags some animal, a bull or a wild boar, from Artemis' chariot. He 'cunningly' (152) advises her to shoot at boars and bulls, animals which harm man, not harmless deer or hares; in that way men will call her a helper, even as they do to him. It is, of course, implied that his 'cunning' actually consists of his attempt to get more food. The poet explains that though Heracles is dead he still has the hungry stomach with which he faced Theiodamas ploughing (142-61). The nymphs attend to the hinds which draw her chariot while she goes into Zeus' house to sit next to her brother, even though others ask her to sit next to them (162-9).

It is clear that Heracles is presented here in his role as the comic glutton, and again low detail clashes with grand form. This comic tone seems meant as an ironic foil to an impressive episode in earlier epic, the opening scene of the *Homeric Hymn to Apollo* (2-13), where Apollo enters the house of Zeus, all the other gods jumping up from their seats in welcome, and his mother Leto takes his hunting-weapons and leads him to his seat where Zeus welcomes him. Apart from the comic business with Heracles, Callimachus makes his Phoebus attend on Artemis, so that the theme of sibling-rivalry is continued, even if this becomes apparent only once it is recognised that the welcoming-scene is a literary counterpiece to that in the Homeric hymn and that now Apollo is doing the welcoming. The result is again an 'Idyll der Kleinwelt', especially as regards Apollo and Artemis; in the depiction of Heracles we have outright burlesque. The range of comic effects in the passage is thus extraordinarily wide. Integral to it is the poet's skill in crossing the genres.

In *Hymn 6*, the *Hymn to Demeter*, Callimachus again makes extensive use of everyday matter. In the scene depicting Demeter's punishment of Erysichthon we are presented with a domestic comedy of manners. As a result of the bulimia with which the goddess has punished him, we are told, Erysichthon constantly craves for another meal of the same size as the one he has just consumed; it takes twenty cooks to prepare his food and twelve waiters to draw off his wine (68f.). In his present state he will inevitably be a disgrace at any dinner that he attends, and his parents invent every excuse for his not accepting dinner invitations. This is simply because they are socially embarrassed. . . . Erysichthon's mother is characterized as worried not so much about her son as about her family's reputation. Her bourgeois concerns are matched by the excuses which she fabricates: her son is said to be involved in all the sorts of activities that any son of a well-to-do family might be expected to (72-86). Her embarrassment would be entirely appropriate in a scene from the New Comedy. Likewise, when Triopas prays to his father, Poseidon, it is far from obvious that his words are motivated by pity for Erysichthon's plight, because he concludes the prayer with the wish that Poseidon either get rid of Erysichthon's disease or feed him himself, for the cooks have emptied Triopas' tables, folds and byres. His real feelings are thus ones of pique at the impoverishment of his household. This is

made even clearer in the remainder of his speech: the cooks have slaughtered the wagon-mules and Erysichthon has eaten the heifer which his mother was fattening for Hestia, the prize race-horse, the warhorse and even the ancient equivalent of the cat at which the mice trembled (96-110). We are also told how as long as Triopas' provisions held out only the household knew of the scandalous business, but when Erysichthon had got through them, the scandal was a secret no longer: 'the son of the king' sat in the very crossways begging for crusts and scraps (111-15). This, then, is the 'bourgeois denouement to the story'; the parents' shame is complete and so is the comedy. The humour of this part of the story (Callimachus, we note in passing, has kept his version of the tale as light as possible by toning down the more gruesome elements in the legend) will have been increased by the clash of the domestic material with the hymnal form and metre.

The poet's aim in incorporating so much comical domesticity in the hymn seems once again to lie in his love of contrasts. The description of Erysichthon's punishment and his parents' reaction to it is immediately preceded by the episode of his crime. There the tone is anything but comic, and the crime is presented as a very serious affair indeed. Erysichthon is depicted as a wilfully wicked man and is characterized as such by his ruthlessness in the attack on the sacred grove and by his angry and arrogant defiance of the gentle admonitions of Demeter who has disguised herself as one of her own priestesses, Nicippe. Demeter, on the other hand, is both patient and reasonable. When her request that he stop his tree-felling is refused, she assumes her divine form, her feet touching the earth, her head Olympus. She mercifully exempts from her wrath Erysichthon's attendants, who had been acting under their master's orders, but curses Erysichthon, ominously proclaiming that he will indeed have many banquets in future, picking up his hot-headed retort to her that he intended to use the wood from the grove to make a dining-hall for banquets. The narrator tells us that the aim of the cautionary tale is 'so that one may avoid transgression' (22), and Erysichthon's crime is an indisputable instance of transgression. The story is one of crime and punishment and Callimachus couches the crime in serious terms. The scene of punishment, therefore, stands in stark tonal contrast with it. It is unthinkable that such a contrast could be unintentional, and we may conclude that the poet has intended his comedy of manners to act as a foil to the scene with Demeter. Nor do the everyday elements necessarily undermine the seriousness of the narrator's moral or the prayer 'May he be no friend or neighbour of mine who is hated by you, Demeter; I hate evil neighbours' (116f.): Callimachus' approach resembles that of *spoudaiogeloion*-literature like certain of his own *Iambi*.

Finally, there is the *Hymn to Delos*. Apart from the pictorial and scientific elements in the scene of Leto's parturition, consider Leto's cry to Apollo to come forth. It is realistically representative of how a woman sounds in labour, for she speaks in short gasps; each word in the line that she utters, *geineo, geineo, koure, kai ēpios exithi kolpou* (214), corresponds with the metrical divisions, and a strong sense-break occurs at the caesura. This is *mimēsis biou* indeed, and is in stark contrast with the traditional grandeur of the episode which we find in the *Homeric Hymn to Apollo* (89-139). It contributes impressively to the pathos of the scene. But what is such everyday detail doing in a poem in which, among other things, an unborn god prophesies from his mother's womb (88-98, 162-95), an island turns into gold (260-3) and, apparently metamorphosing into a nymph, nurses the baby god (264-74)?

The exuterine prophecies are the basic problem. Callimachus is evidently building on the moment in the Homeric hymn where the god, just born, pronounces to the goddesses in attendance on Leto that music, archery and prophecy will be his particular care (131f.). This is greeted by the goddesses' wonder (135). I suggest that the poet is putting the motif of the god's precociousness, which is a teasing mixture of the everyday and the miraculous, back one stage further, and is thus, as with the birth-scene, trying to outdo his model, with the result that the everyday motif of a child's precocity is put on a miraculous plane indeed, as is under-lined by the words 'in his mother's womb' (86) and 'the prophet still in the belly' (189). There may have been a special piquancy for an Alexandrian audience in all this, for they would have been familiar with prophets who made their voice come from the bellies of other people, the point here being that Apollo is presented as a god performing the human practice, from within his own mother's belly! But having got the prophecies into the realm of the truly miraculous, he proceeds to place them in a strikingly immediate relation with his audience's experience. The forward reference to the event of the god's slaughter of Niobe's children is hardly especially immediate, though its accuracy does vindicate the god's exemplary prophetic powers. But when he makes Apollo prophesy the birth of Philadelphus on Cos, the victory over the Gauls in 279 BC, in which the god himself was supposed to have taken part, and Philadelphus' punishment of the Gallic mercenaries in around 274-2 BC (160-95), he touches on matters of direct, even sensational interest to an audience at Alexandria. Thus actual history and the world of myth and miracle are tantalisingly presented as compatible, just as in the birth-scene of Apollo the everyday and the scientific, and the mythical and miraculous are brought into a piquant unison. This is clearly part of the thinking behind Apollo's statement that in their dealings with the Celts he and Philadelphus will be united in a 'common struggle' (171). This, I further suggest, is the rationale of Callimachus' deployment of everyday and topical material in *Hymn 4*: it establishes a relationship between the world of myth and contemporary life, and in the process confers authenticity on Philadelphus' claim to a special and direct link with the Olympians.

Thus in the *Hymns* of Callimachus the incorporation of everyday, realistic detail is an important means of subverting generic expectations, which is evidently one of the poet's special preoccupations and one over which he shows a sure mastery. It also helps the poet to put the grand personages and events of myth into a new perspective. Topical matter is employed to bring the mythical past and the present into close relation with one another, to the enrichment of historical and contemporary people and events. Common to each of these functions is the poet's desire to put a new perspective on the Alexandrians' cultural heritage.

Mention of the *Hymn to Delos* has raised the question of encomiastic poetry again, and we may now inquire into the Alexandrian inclusion of realistic material in the poems written in praise of the Ptolemies. Theocritus' *Heracliscus* and Callimachus' *Victoria Berenices* have taught us that the Ptolemies were quite happy to be celebrated even where everyday and low material created an ironical effect. This is also true of *Idyll 15*, but the effect is striking in *Idyll 14*, where Thyonicus recommends that Aeschinas join Ptolemy's army to get over his shattered love-life. So too with Herodas' first *Mimiamb*, where Gyllis the go-between paints a picture of the pleasures of Ptolemaic Egypt (23-36) designed to convince Metriche that her Mandris is not going to come back to her and that she had better accept Gyllis' proposal of a substitute. Machon felt at liberty to refer to Soter and Philadelphus in the company of parasites and courtesans (*Frr.* 1,5,18 Gow). Sotades' fatal expression of revulsion at Philadelphus' incestuous marriage (*Fr.* 1 Pow.), however, shows that there was a line beyond which you could not go when commenting on the Ptolemies' personal lives. More restrained is the use of everyday matter in Callimachus' *Lock of Berenice* (*Fr.* 110), where the lock deprecates the frosty honour of catasterism since it will never again touch Berenice's head and enjoy the creature comforts of oils and myrrh.

The approach is adopted in the formal encomium, Theocritus' *Idyll 17*. Irony must have been perceived in passages like that on the Ptolemies' ancestor, Heracles (13-33), or in that on the personified Cos (58-71), which is comparable with the motif in Callimachus' *Hymn to Delos*. We may infer that such treatment was to the regents' taste and was actively encouraged by them, if only because they wanted to show they were 'with it' in their appreciation of realistic material in poetry. In any case, the savants of the Alexandrian court for whom these poems were meant would have been diverted by the sophisticated allusiveness of an *Encomium for Ptolemy*. The Ptolemies knew that the masses wanted a Pompe, but they were clearly happy to let their poets indulge in a modicum of irony to amuse the intelligentsia. When Theocritus turns in *Idyll* 16 to another Hellenistic monarch, Hiero II of Syracuse, his approach is perhaps significantly different. To be sure, he parades the *phauloi* of the *Odyssey,* arguably as an announcement of his pastoral poetry, but Hiero himself is portrayed in exclusively heroic terms, indeed as 'the like of the heroes of old' (80). The vignette of the peace in the countryside that will follow Hiero's expulsion of the Carthaginians from Sicily (90-7) is motivated by the belief that peace in the day-to-day life of the ordinary man reflects the prowess of the ruler. And the humour in the scene of the Graces' empty-handed return (8-12) is at Theocritus' expense alone. His failure to 'humanise' Hiero contrasts with his strategy with the Ptolemies. Perhaps this is further evidence of the uniqueness of the Egyptian monarchs' taste for the humorous realism of their court-poets.

But humour is not the only result of the Alexandrians' deployment of humble material in their encomia. In the fragments of Callimachus' **Apotheosis of Arsinoe** (*Fr.* 228), which laments in the unusual iambo-lyric archeboulean metre the death of Queen Arsinoe in 270 BC and celebrates her deification, the Queen's younger sister, Philotera, who apparently predeceased her, is depicted in congenial human terms. When she sees the smoke rolling over the Aegean from Arsinoe's pyre (40-5), she sends Charis to find out the cause and expresses anxiety whether 'her Libya', Egypt, is being harmed (45-51). Charis, too, is very human in her grief when she sees that the smoke is coming from Alexandria (52-5) and in the sympathetic way she assures Philotera that her country is safe and gently breaks the news about Arsinoe, 'her only sister' (66-75). Here the poet is exploring the more serious side of the humanity that Charis exhibits when she welcomes Thetis at *Iliad* 18.382ff. These touches invest the two new deities with real pathos and humanity.

. . . . .

Callimachus' **Hecale** exhibits a realism unprecedented in Greek literature both in its nature and its extent.

The old woman, Hecale, is the figure central to our inquiry. To judge from the fragments, Callimachus described her humble appearance in some detail. She is apparently said to have 'the ever-moving lips of an old woman' (*Fr.* 490). Another fragment describes her broad-rimmed hat, 'the felt headgear of a shepherd' . . . and her walking-stick (*Fr.* 292). The word for 'hat', πίλημα, which harks back to Hesiod's advice to the farmer to wear a πῖλος 'so as to keep your ears from getting wet', is typically Callimachean in that it is a technically precise word from the life of the peasant-farmer (*W.D.* 545f.). The stick is mentioned again as 'the support of her old age' (*Fr.* 355). Thus Callima-

chus appears to have used pictorialism to emphasise Hecale's lowly situation.

The old woman's generosity was celebrated right at the poem's opening, for we possess a fragment from there which says that 'all travellers honoured her for her hospitality, for she kept a house which was never closed' (*Fr.* 231). Her generous nature and humble circumstances are prominently displayed throughout the scene in which she receives Theseus in from the storm (the description of which itself contains domestic matter, already noticed, like the simile of the weaving girls laying aside their work for their evening meal: *Fr.* 238. 19f.). The hero casts off his cloak, wet from the storm, Hecale makes him sit down on her pauper's couch, having snatched a small tattered garment from her bed (presumably to spread over the couch), takes down dry wood that she has stored long ago and cuts it (*Frr.* 239-43). Callimachus' model here is the episode in the *Odyssey* in which Eumaeus gives shelter to Odysseus (*Od.* 14.48ff., 418ff.). Next follows the scene in which Hecale washes Theseus' feet. She brings a hollow, boiling pot (*Fr.* 244), empties the bowl and draws another draught (*Fr.* 246). Though the fragments of the foot-washing scene are, to say the least, meagre, it is plain enough that Callimachus' model is this time the moment in the *Odyssey* in which the second great *phaulos* of the epic tradition, Eurycleia, washes Odysseus' feet (*Od.* 19.386ff.). Thus the poet carefully places his heroine in the tradition of paradigmatic *phauloi* of canonical epic. Our fragments give us an idea of the humble meal which Hecale serves, 'olives which grew on the tree, wild olives and white olives which she had laid down in autumn to swim in brine' (*Fr.* 282.4-5 *S.H.* = *Fr.* 248 Pf.), wild vegetables and cabbage (*Frr.* 249, 250), and many bread-loaves 'of the kind which women store up for herdsman', which Hecale now takes from her bread-basket (*Fr.* 251). Mention is possibly made of her pauper's table (*Fr.* 284 *S.H.* = 252 Pf.).

Her moral goodness and straitened circumstances are further described in the conversation which she and Theseus apparently strike up after the meal. Theseus then asks her why she, an old woman, dwells in such a lonely place. It is likely that she begins by asking Theseus why he wants to 'awaken a sleeping tear' (*Fr.* 682); certainly there is much pathos in what follows. She evidently goes on to tell Theseus of her former life, possibly prefacing her story with the statement 'my poverty is not hereditary nor am I a pauper from my grandparents' (*Fr.* 254). She mentions men who guarded her threshing-floor which her oxen trod in a circle, an indication of her wealth. She describes the arrival from Aphnidae of what must be her husband. He was godlike in appearance and dressed in a rich mantle (*Fr.* 285.8-12 *S.H.* = *Fr.* 253.8-12 Pf.). Hecale talks about her two sons, whom she reared in an abundantly rich household, with slaves, in all probability, to bathe them in warm baths (*Fr.* 287.1-6 *S.H.*). She says that the two of them grew up like towering poplars beside a river, . . . (*Fr.* 287.7-9 *S.H.*). This is a clear reminiscence of Thetis' words about Achilles, doomed to die, at *Iliad* 18.56f.: 'he shot up like a sapling; I nursed him, like a tree in the rising ground of an orchard'. . . . Hecale is now being compared with one of the noble personages of traditional epic, and the pathos of her situation is greatly enhanced by the comparison. After another gap, we find her bewailing the death of her younger son; the death of the older (*Fr.* 287.12f. *S.H.*) was probably described in the lacuna. Apparently, this son was killed by the robber, Cercyon, in his horrid wrestling-matches (*Fr.* 287.18 *S.H.*). She wishes that she might pierce Cercyon's eyes with thorns while he is still alive and eat his raw flesh (*Fr.* 287.24-6 *S.H.*). There seems to be a connection between the fates of Hecale and Theseus, for Theseus killed Cercyon and presumably told Hecale that her son's death had been avenged. And again Hecale is compared with grand characters from the *Iliad.* Her refusal to die 'when death had been calling for a long time' (*Fr.* 287.12 *S.H.*) recalls Hector's recognition that 'the gods have called me deathward' (*Il.* 22.297) and her threat of cannibalism reminds us of Hecuba's wish to eat Achilles' liver for the death of her son (*Il.* 24.212f.). Thus in her description of the death of her remaining son, on whom she had concentrated all her hopes, the pathos of her characterisation is deepened by association with figures of intense suffering from traditional epic.

It is clear, then, that Callimachus' depiction of Hecale's misfortune is movingly serious, and that in her grief she is raised to the stature of the grand people of the epic tradition. Yet this is the woman whom the poet has evidently wished us to view in terms of a Eumaeus and a Eurycleia. She is, like them, a *phaulos,* despite the fact that she came from a rich family, but her fall from prosperity is described with far greater pathos than Homer depicts those of Eumaeus and Eurycleia (or, for that matter, than Euripides does in the case of the Farmer). And in this important respect she is markedly different from her earlier counterparts. The New Comedy may have been influential here with its recurrent motif of the kind-hearted slave, menial or prostitute who turns out to be of noble birth. Again, as with Eumaeus, Eurycleia and the Farmer, it seems likely that Callimachus tries to some extent to account for Hecale's generosity by appeal to traditional Greek thought on the matter, but her present position in society, illustrated so amply, remains that of a *phaulos* from whom such nobility was not normally to be expected. In any case, it looks as if the poet is more intent upon extracting the pathos inherent in the motif than in using it to account for his heroine's unexpected moral goodness.

After their conversation, Theseus and Hecale retire, and Hecale says that she will sleep in the corner of the room where there is a bed ready for her (*Fr.* 256). In this way she once more resembles Eumaeus, who prepares a bed for Odysseus near the fire while he himself goes to his usual bed near the pigs to be able to keep guard over them (*Od.* 14.518-33). When Theseus rises she is already awake (*Fr.* 257). Thus Callimachus depicts Hecale in her treatment of Theseus as generous and considerate, while reminding us throughout of her lowly literary antecedents.

Fr. 288 *S.H.* (= Fr. 260 Pf.), which relates the puzzling conversation between two birds, probably a crow and an owl, closes with the description of the dawn of Theseus' return to Hecale, in which Callimachus indulges in further *genre*-painting, as we have seen, with his reference to robbers, lanterns being lit, water carriers singing, wagons with squeaking axles, and blacksmiths or other people fetching fire for the day (*Fr.* 288.64-9 *S.H.*). If, as is likely, the conversation of the birds occurred near Hecale's hut, then the poet is again sketching in the details of her milieu, and using his pictorialist skill for the purpose.

We possess part of the funeral-speech pronounced over her grave by Theseus or her neighbours. The speaker claims that they 'will often remember [her] hospitable hut, for it was a common shelter for everybody' (*Fr.* 263). We know that Theseus fully recognised the old woman's goodness and rewarded her by creating a deme named after her and establishing a shrine to Zeus Hecaleios (*Dieg.* XI.5ff.). Thus the poem began and ended with Hecale and her moral nobility.

Callimachus has indeed given a serious and prominent role to his *phaulos*. But he has not neglected Theseus, a hero who would in traditional thought have been considered a quite appropriate figure in epic. *Frr.* 232 and 233 come from the episode in which Medea attempts to poison Theseus. *Frr.* 234-7 are what remains of the episode in which Theseus unexpectedly appears to Aegeus after being reared in Troezen. *Fr.* 238.1-14 is part of a conversation between the two, Theseus urging his father to let him go out to face adventures; his impetuosity and bravery seem to have been stressed. As we have seen, the victory over the bull of Marathon was described. *Fr.* 288.1-15 *S.H.* (=Fr. 260.1-15 Pf.) describes Theseus' triumphal procession, how no one dared to look straight at the 'great hero and the monstrous beast', but eventually greeted him with a ritual shower of leaves. Here we see the commoners' reaction to the conquering hero. Finally, as we have just observed, his slaying of Cercyon is mentioned and appears to have had bearing on his relationship with Hecale. Theseus is, therefore, presented as a traditional epic hero, a true *spoudaios*. Apparently, Callimachus means us to regard him as a foil to Hecale, who is a *phaulos* and yet is elevated to a central role in the epic. Thus, on the one hand, Theseus' gratitude to Hecale and the honours which he posthumously bestows upon her confirm her true moral worth despite her lowly station. On the other, her untraditional status as an epic hero is thrown into sharp relief by juxtaposition with a hero of the traditional type.

Callimachus has brought her and her goodness into remarkable prominence. The seriousness with which he portrays her is striking. In the *Victoria Berenices* he had created a *phaulos*, Molorchus, whose goodly but humble life is set in deliberate contrast with the grand myths and events which frame it, and he had put this contrast to comic effect. But this is not at all the case in his portrayal of Hecale. Certainly, there is a deliberate superficial incongruity in the contrast between her lowly social status and the heroic context in which she is placed, but this is given emphasis only to demonstrate that appearances can be deceptive and that in a deeper ethical sense she is entirely worthy of the world of epic. The poet makes her describe her family's fate and her own emotions with evident pathos and presents her moral goodness as seriously as he does Theseus' traditional heroism. She is, of course, unlike Eumaeus and Eurycleia, with whom we are continually invited to compare her, in that she is portrayed as acting in a way which is spontaneously good. The acceptance of the idea that a *phaulos* might initiate independent moral action had been made possible by developments in Greek thought which we saw evidenced in Euripides' treatment of the Farmer in the *Electra*. But she is significantly unlike that figure as well in the way in which she is presented. Euripides may have defended the integrity and moral worth of low characters like the Farmer, but he was still precluded by the genre in which he was working from giving them a *main* role. Here Callimachus has gone one step further than the tragedian. He has given Hecale the central role in his epic and has made her goodness the poem's real point. Thus for the first time in extant Greek poetry the *spoudaios* has been displaced from the centre stage and is made to share it with a *phaulos*.

. . . The implication that by removing the *spoudaioi* from their traditional central position in epic Callimachus deliberately intended to leave room for everyday and low heroes is borne out by the poet's practice in the *Hecale* even more strikingly than by that in the *Aetia* or the *Hymns*. The poem represents an instance of genre-crossing which is a significant exception to Auerbach's generalisations about the separation of the genres in ancient literature, and its realism in this respect comes quite close to that of modern literature. Because of this the *Hecale* is one of the poet's most remarkable achievements and one of the most important poems in our inquiry. We should remark, finally, that it is also realistic in a manner that we have come to regard as typical of Callimachus and of the Alexandrian movement as a whole. It attempts to bring the heroic world of myth down to earth and hence help its

audiences to relate to their heritage in an arresting new way. But the seriousness of tone with which Hecale is portrayed makes the poem realistic in a sense unique even in Alexandrian poetry.

Rudolf Blum (essay date 1991)

SOURCE: "Kallimachos and His Lists of Greek Authors and Their Works," in *Kallimachos: The Alexandrian Library and the Origins of Bibliography*, translated by Hans H. Wellisch, The University of Wisconsin Press, 1991, pp. 124-81.

[*In the excerpt that follows, Blum focuses his attention on Callimachus the scholar rather than Callimachus the poet. Blum carefully reconstructs the history of the royal library at Alexandria, attempting to determine the post Callimachus held there and the years of his tenure.*]

Accounts of the life and work of Kallimachos are neither particularly extensive nor are they particularly sparse. Our main source is the article "Kallimachos" in the *Suda* which contains some biographical data and a selective bibliography of his works. The article is based on an epitome of the *Onomatologos* (Nomendator), a lost bibliographic lexicon compiled from older reference books by Hesychios of Miletos in the 6th century A.D. The abridgment of the *Onomatologos* affected also the article "Kallimachos". This explains some of its defects. Thus, we learn from it, for example, what was the name of Kallimachos's father-in-law, but we do not know what position he himself occupied at the court of the Ptolemies in Alexandria. Nevertheless, this article supplies interesting information not contained in any other source. The data of Hesychios which were incorporated in the *Suda* are corroborated and augmented only by some scattered notes of other ancient scholars. Kallimachos himself inserted into his extant works only a few personal remarks; the most important ones relate to the criticism to which his poetic works had been subjected.

The following is a translation of the article in the *Suda* (necessary or probable corrections suggested by earlier researchers are in brackets).

> Kallimachos, son of Battos and Mesatma [Megatima], from Kyrene, grammarian, pupil of the grammarian Hermokrates of Iasos, married the daughter of Euphrates [Euphraios] of Syracuse. His sister's son was the younger Kallimachos who wrote about islands in verse. He was so zealous that he wrote poems in every meter and many books in prose. And he wrote more than eight hundred books. He lived in the time of Ptolemaios Philadelphos. Before he was introduced to the king, he was a teacher in an elementary school in Eleusis, a suburb of Alexandria. And he lived until the time of

Ptolemaios Euergetes, the 127th [133rd] Olympiad, in the second year of which Ptolemaios Euergetes began his reign.

Among his books are the following: *The arrival of Io; Semele; The colony[?] of the Argonauts; Arcadia; Glaukos; Hopes;* satyr plays; tragedies; comedies; songs; *Ibis* (a poem on obscurity and slander against a certain Ibis, who had become the enemy of Kallimachos; that was Apollonios, the author of the *Argonautika*); *Museion; Lists of those who distinguished themselves in all branches of learning and their writings*, in 120 books; *Table and register of playwrights, arranged chronologically from the beginning; A list of glosses and writings by Demokrates* [Demokritos], *The names of months according to peoples and cities; Foundation of islands and cities, and changes of their names; On the rivers of Europe; On marvels and natural curiosities in the Peloponnesos and in Italy; On changes of names* [rather naming] *of fishes; On winds; On birds; On the rivers of the world; Collection of the marvels of the world appearing in certain places.*

According to this article, Kallimachos is classified as a grammarian (i.e. a philologist) who wrote more than eight hundred works in verse and prose. The selective bibliography lists, however, only a few poetic writings, in part even only the kinds of such writings (which may have been headings of sections in the original) and a few scholarly works; none of his known poetic works is listed, except his abusive poem against Apollonios Rhodios, *Ibis.* All other listed poems are unknown. The first ones were perhaps parts of the famous *Aitia* (Causes), narrative elegies on the mythical origin of worship rites and other customs. On the other hand, the scholarly works of Kallimachos named in the list are sometimes also mentioned by other authors. They begin with three *pinakes:* first, there are the *pinakes* of Greek authors and their works. The arrangement of the other titles is mixed up. Among others there are collective titles and partial titles of two works, and two partial titles of one work whose collective title is not mentioned, all of which are separated from each other by other titles.

Only some of his poetic works have been preserved. Six hymns and 63 epigrams have come down to us in manuscripts from the 14th and 15th century. Fragments of other poetic works by Kallimachos were found on papyri which were discovered during the past decades in Egypt, among them fragments of his *Aitia.* His scholarly works, however, which were used by several later authors are lost, and we can only get a vague idea about some of them from quotations. The poems of Kallimachos have often been dealt with, and they have been duly appreciated as masterpieces of Alexandrian literature; for those, I therefore refer the reader to the relevant literature. My investigation does not deal with the poet Kallimachos but with his achievements as a scholar.

The fame of Kallimachos as a poet is documented by many works, the Romans also held him in high esteem. Kallimachos the scholar is relatively often quoted. Cicero once even put him on the same level as the most celebrated men of Greek science: medicine is represented by Hippokrates, geometry by Euclid and Archimedes, musical theory by Damon and Aristoxenos. According to the *Suda,* the lifetime of Kallimachos coincided nearly with that of his patron, king Ptolemaios II Philadelphos (308-246 B.C.) under whose reign he lived. According to Gellius, Kallimachos became a renowned poet at the court of that king shortly after the outbreak of the first Punic War (264 B.C.), that is, he reached the highest point in his career, his akme (which is thought to have occurred in his fortieth year) around 263 B.C. Accordingly, he was probably born in 303 B.C. Since he wrote a poem that can be dated with certainty to the year 246/245 B.C., namely the elegy *Plokamos Berenikes* (The lock of Berenike [the wife of Ptolemaios III]), he outlived Ptolemaios II, but probably only by a few years. It is therefore true, as the *Suda* says, that his lifetime extended into the era of Ptolemaios III.

He was born in Kyrene, an old Greek (Doric) colony situated not far from the coast in that part of Libya still named Cyrenaica after that city. The city was under the rule of Ptolemaios I since 322 B.C. Kallimachos came from a noble family, his grandfather, after whom he was named, had held the position of a *strategos* (army commander), as the poet says in an epitaph for the grave of his father. The name of his father was Battos, the name of the founder and first king of Kyrene. According to Strabo, Kallimachos claimed to have been descended from that first Battos. In an epitaph for his own grave he referred to himself as a Battiad, and later poets, especially Roman ones, also called him by that name. The term is, however, ambiguous. But no doubt the family of Kallimachos belonged to a group of Greeks who ruled over a north African region long before Alexander conquered Egypt. Kallimachos himself also lived always among Greeks. As far as he was concerned, Alexandria as well as Kyrene belonged to Hellas. Hellas was everywhere where Hellenic settlements and culture existed. Even in Alexandria Kallimachos was not noticeably touched by Egyptian culture.

The *Suda* names as teacher of Kallimachos the grammarian Hermokrates of Iasos, of whom it is only known that he wrote about the theory of accents (prosody). But the tradition that he studied in Rhodos together with Aratos under the Peripatetic Praxiphanes, whose ideas on literary esthetics he later attacked in a special work, is not trustworthy. A sojourn of the young poet and scholar in Athens has also not been established. It seems that Kallimachos was largely self educated. He was evidently an avid reader, like Aristotle, but he was also an attentive listener who, as he once said, lent his ear to those who wanted to tell a story. Already in Kyrene there was much to read and to hear; in Alexandria there was, of course, that much more.

We do not know when he moved to the capital. In an epigram he says that his hands "are empty of wealth." His family was probably impoverished. In a suburb of Alexandria he worked, according to the *Suda,* as a teacher in an elementary school, until he was introduced to king Ptolemaios II Philadelphos, who was sole ruler since 283/82 B.C. The lexicon is silent about his further career. But in his notes on the beginnings of the Alexandrian library Tzetzes says that Kallimachos, a young man at the court, compiled the *pinakes* of the books acquired by the king. Accordingly, Kallimachos was called to the court of the king, who presumably liked the poems of the young teacher, around 280 B.C. There he worked in the library. In the course of time he certainly became a member of the Museion. At any rate, he stayed at the court until his death.

We may believe Tzetzes that Kallimachos began already as a young man to compile *pinakes* of the books acquired by the kings, that is, catalogs of the library in the Museion. But these were by no means a youthful work, as the Byzantine scholar seems to think: rather, they were the work of a lifetime, because the library was already at that time quite large and grew constantly. The *Pinakes* of Greek authors which evolved from the *pinakes* of the library and filled 120 books, according to the *Suda,* were therefore not of an even quality throughout, as the critical remarks of Dionysius of Halikarnassos show. But this was not because Kallimachos lacked help. Quite to the contrary: seven scholars, some of which were quite well known, are indicated as pupils of Kallimachos, and it is unlikely that all of them worked together with Kallimachos in the library. This seems to me to be important. We do not know of so many pupils of any other Aiexandrian grammarians of the third and second century B.C., except for Aristarchos of Samothrake, who was the director of the library under Ptolemaios VI Philometor (180-145 B.C.).

According to Athenaios, Kallimachos once said that a big book is a big evil. Unfortunately we do not know in what context he made that remark. Perhaps he did not speak as a librarian or generally as a scholar, and did not mean scrolls but works, and not just any works, but only poetical ones.

Whether Kallimachos wrote his other scholarly works before or at the same time as the *Pinakes,* or perhaps in part before and in part at the same time is impossible to say. Some interpreters concluded from the last verse of the *Aitia* that Kallimachos intended to devote himself in the future only to the compilation of the *pinakes;* the verse is, however, ambiguous. No doubt Kallimachos wrote poetry until the end of his life. This is attested to not only by the **Lock of Berenike** but also by the (afterwards inserted) prologue to **Aitia** in which he deplores the burden of old age. He has even been described as poet laureate, because he wrote a poem on the occasion of the marriage of Ptolemaios II with his sister Arsinoe (276/275 B.C.), and dealt in another poem with the deification of the queen who had died after only a few years (270 B.C.), and of course also because of the **Lock of Berenike**. It seems to me that this designation is inappropriate. Kallimachos was honored by the Ptolemies, as Strabo says; he enjoyed their patronage and reciprocated with proofs of his devotion.

Whether he became the director of the royal library is in dispute. This question has often been discussed. But in my opinion, some important facts have been neglected or have been misinterpreted. As indicated above, Zenodotos, the literature teacher of the future Ptolemaios II, was appointed as director of the royal library by Ptolemaios I after the end of his teaching career. Demetrios of Phaleron continued, however, to devote himself to the development of the collection, which was not the task of the *bibliophylax,* the Keeper of the library. After he had been banished from the court by Ptolemaios II, the "friends" of the king acquired books for the library. Zenodotos was probably relieved of his official duties when the king, his former pupil, asked him to reconstruct, together with Alexandros Aitolos and Lykophron, the text of the classical works with the aid of the copies available in the library. The books were at that time probably already arranged by literary genres, authors, and works. When Kallimachos now began to compile lists of those books, he performed exactly the duty of a library director. No one can say what he would have had to do if somebody else had cataloged the collection. The scholars who are named as his pupils also make it seem as if he had been the head of a school. But such a position belonged only to the director of a library. All Alexandrian grammarians of the third century and the first half of the second century B.C. who are named as teachers of other grammarians, beginning with Zenodotos, of whom three pupils are known, were also directors of the royal library. But most modern experts think that, according to the sources, Kallimachos had not been appointed to the position of library director as Zenodotos's successor and as teacher of the crown prince, the future Ptolemaios III Euergetes (born ca. 284 B.C.), because these two positions were linked to each other. They assume either that Kallimachos himself renounced the office of library director in order to avoid having to teach the crown prince, or else, that the king himself found Kallimachos to be unfit for that task, although he was otherwise favorably inclined towards him. Instead, the king appointed one of his pupils, namely Apollonios, born ca. 300 B.C. in Alexandria, who was named the Rhodian after his adopted country, and who was the author of the *Argonautika*. When Apollonios had recited this epic for the first time, Kallimachos had criticized it sharply. This led to a bitter dispute between them which spilled over from the literary to the personal domain, and was the cause for a defamatory poem (now lost but mentioned in the *Suda*) against his former pupil, entitled **Ibis** (after the dirty bird). Apollonios ultimately relinquished his post or was forced to resign, and moved to Rhodos. Ptolemaios III Euergetes (246-222) appointed as his successor a younger compatriot of Kallimachos and queen Berenike, namely Eratosthenes of Kyrene, one of the greatest scholars of the third century. Kallimachos and Apollonios were, by the way, not the only members of the court who quarreled with each other; it was notorious that not everything in the Museion was sweet harmony. But the quarrel between the two famous poets has always been of particular interest to scholars. However, in the framework of the present investigation we are concerned only to find out whether Kallimachos cataloged the library in his capacity as its director or whether he merely participated in this work as "one of the scientific assistants under the direction of Apollonios" as [Friedrich] Schmidt presumes [in *Die Pinakes des Kallimachos,* 1922].

Neither the article in the *Suda* nor any other source indicates that Kallimachos was the director of the library and the teacher of the crown prince, but that does not mean very much, because the information on his career is incomplete. In the article of the *Suda* on Eratosthenes there is no hint either that he was director of the library, we know that only from the article on Apollonios and from the notes of Tzetzes on the beginnings of the library. Apollonios does not appear in those notes at all. His two *bioi* which have come down to us together with his *Argonautika* do not indicate either that he was director of the library and teacher of the crown prince. The first one says that he was born in Alexandria, lived under the Ptolemies (which is certainly corrupted), was a pupil of Kallimachos (the second *bios* says "of the grammarian Kallimachos") and lived first with his teacher. It should be noted that Apollonios also wrote scholarly works: he wrote against Zenodotos (because of his version of the text of Homer) on Hesiod (defending the authenticity of the *Aspis*) and on Archilochos. The author of the first *bios* then continues: Apollonios had begun to write poems only at a late time, but others had claimed that he had recited his *Argonautika* when he was still an ephebe but had not been successful. Because of this humiliation and the criticism by other poets he had left his home town Alexandria and had moved to Rhodos. There he had rewritten his epic, had become famous and honored as a teacher and had even been made a citizen. The author of the second *bios* adds that some people say that

Apollonios had returned to Alexandria, and that he had recited his *Argonautika* there with great success, had been found worthy of the library of the Museion, and had finally been buried alongside Kallimachos. In the past, these words were interpreted to mean that Apollonios had been appointed as director of the Alexandrian library after his return from Rhodos. Only [Rudolf] Pfeiffer [in *History of Classical Scholarship,* 1968] recognized that the expression "he had been found worthy of the library of the Museion" referred to Apollonios as an author, and did not mean more than that his *Argonautika* had been found worthy of inclusion in the library, as shown by parallel cases. But this statement was probably misunderstood already in Antiquity. It is also unhistorical, because the Ptolemies sought to include in their collection all books written in Greek, including cookbooks, and did not make any selection.

The whole story of Apollonios's return to Alexandria is implausible, as [Hans] Herter ["Zur Lebensgeshichte des Apollonios von Rhodos," *Rheinisches Museum für Philologie,* 1942] and others have stressed.

The brief article "Apollonios" in the *Suda* mentions, however, his library post:

> Apollonios of Alexandria, epic poet, dwelt in Rhodos, was the son of Silleus, pupil of Kallimachos, contemporary of Eratosthenes, Euphorion and Timarchos, lived under Ptolemaios Euergetes, and became the successor of Eratosthenes as director of the Alexandrian library.

The lifetime of Apollonios Rhodios is here indicated in the traditional manner first, by the synchronism with Eratosthenes and the poet and scholar Euphorion, whose birth occurred, according to the relevant articles in the *Suda,* during the 126th Olympiad (276/72 B.C.) (it is not known who was Timarchos); secondly, by the *akmē* under Ptolemaios III, who ruled from 246-222 B.C. For a contemporaneity in the narrower sense one would assume that Apollonios Rhodios was also born during the 126th Olympiad, and that was probably indeed the intention of Hesychios or the authority on whom he relied. If so, the learned poet would have reached his *akmē* about ten years after the beginning of Ptolemaios III's reign. These data are compatible with each other, but they yield only approximate dates.

The article says in the beginning that Apollonios, who was born in Alexandria, dwelt in Rhodos, that is, he lived there after he left Alexandria. The last sentence presupposes, however, his return to Alexandria because it says that he became the successor of Eratosthenes as director of the library. According to the *Suda* Eratosthenes had been called to Alexandria by Ptolemaios III (after 246). We do not know how long he held the office of library director; he reached the age of eighty.

But it is unlikely that he was succeeded by a man his own age.

An explanation of this peculiar statement comes from a papyrus fragment from the first half of the second century B.C., found in Oxyrhynchos, which contains, among other things, a list of directors of the great Alexandrian library. In order to evaluate and reconstruct this important document, it is necessary to know certain facts. The fragment consists of six columns: the first one is destroyed, except for a few remnants; the second, third, fourth, and fifth are for the most part well preserved (each has 36 lines with an average of 22 letters); of the sixth only about half still exists. The text of the fragment was part of an anthology compiled in the first century. B.C. or A.D., a collection of all kinds of interesting facts in the form of lists or abstracts. In column one, lines 1-5, some famous sculptors and painters are listed (only the ends of lines have been preserved). On a scrap of papyrus which apparently belongs to the same column (according to Hunt, one of the editors, it contained lines 14-17, but there too only the ends of the lines remain) one can read *grammati[koi]* and *[Phila]delphu.* That is all that remains of this column. It certainly contained a new section dealing with famous grammarians, but apparently only the Alexandrian ones which were indeed the oldest (except for their precursor Praxiphanes). Since the most important among them were also directors of the Alexandrian library, I presume that the list stated first and foremost that it had been founded by Ptolemaios II Philadelphos (with the help of Demetrios of Phaleron?). The column had enough space for this. Furthermore, the grammarians who had been entrusted with the administration of the royal book collection were listed with annotations, certainly first Zenodotos, then perhaps Kallimachos, but none of this has been preserved. Our text starts only in column two, lines 1-21:

> [Apollo]nios, son of Silleus, of Alexandria, named the Rhodian, pupil of Kallimachos. He was also the teacher of the first king. He was succeeded by Erathosthenes. Thereafter, [came] Aristophanes, son of Apelles, of Byzantium, and Aristarchos, then Apollonios of Alexandria, named the Eidographer, after him Aristarchos, son of Aristarchos who was from Samothrake. He was also the teacher of the children of Philopator. After him Kydas of the lance bearers. But under the ninth king flourished the grammarians Ammonios and Zeno[dotos] and Diokles and Apollodoros.

This is the end of that section. The next one deals with inventors in the field of warfare. The former section contains a regular list of successors in the office of library director, as Hunt already recognized. It extends to an officer in the royal guard by the name of Kydas who apparently took over the office of Aristarchos when he, together with many other scholars, left Alexandria

in 145 B.C. because they feared the ruthless Ptolemaios VIII. It seems that the four last-named grammarians never became directors of the library.

The list contains three obvious mistakes, besides mentioning Aristarchos two times, which is odd: 1. Apollonios Rhodios cannot have been the teacher of the first king; the editor therefore changed *prōtu* (first) to *tritu* (third), which was approved by all other researchers. Apollonios, who according to the *Suda* was about ten years younger than Ptolemaios III (born ca. 284 B.C.) became thus his teacher; therefore, he must have been born at least 15 years earlier, that is, ca. 300 B.C. 2. Aristarchos did not teach the children of Ptolemaios IV Philopator but, according to the *Suda,* those of Ptolemaios VI Philometor; Hunt corrected the papyrus also in this passage accordingly. 3. Ammonios and Apollodoros—assuming that these are the famous pupils of Aristarchos, which can hardly be doubted— flourished not under the ninth but under the eighth Ptolemaios.

All researchers were surprised to find in the list besides Apollonios Rhodios a second Apollonios with the epithet *eidographos* (classifier). This man was until then only known from two remarks of ancient and Byzantine scholars who had said that he was a talented librarian and dealt with the classification of old lyric poems. But it had not been known that he came from Alexandria and that he had been the director of the library.

The list also mentions Aristarchos both before the second Apollonios (only by his name) and after him (by his name and with other data). The original sequence of library directors is here evidently disrupted. The report can be interpreted in various ways. The most likely interpretation is, that Apollonios the Eidographer was originally listed before Aristophanes, but was first omitted from the exemplar from which the Oxyrhynchos papyrus was made, was then added in the margin and was finally inserted by the copyist of this papyrus who had already begun with the Aristarchos entry, after its beginning (which was to be erased), i.e. after Aristophanes. The following reasons support his assumption: 1. In the article "Aristophanes Byzantios" in the *Suda* an Apollonios is mentioned as his predecessor. 2. In the article "Apollonios Alexandreios" of the *Suda* he—apparently the later Rhodian—is listed as the successor of Eratosthenes and therefore also as predecessor of Aristophanes. 3. The most famous pupil of Aristophanes, Aristarchos of Samothrake, was most probably his immediate successor in the office of library director. But if this office was held by an Apollonios after Erathosthenes, and then by Aristophanes and Aristarchos, the Apollonios named in the *Suda* as successor of Eratosthenes cannot have been the Alexandrian scholar who emigrated to Rhodos, but his namesake who was also from Alexandria, Apollonios the Eidographer. But it seems to me that there was not only a mix-up of two men born in the same city and bearing the same name, but that even parts of the articles dealing with the two homonymous persons were confounded. Such confusions of articles in the lexicon have already been found in several instants. They are generally not to be blamed on the editor of the lexicon nor on his authority Hesychios (or his epitomator) but they were caused by the reference works used by Hesychios, and are only seldom due to copyist's errors but rather to conjectures of scholars. The Hellenistic biographers and bibliographers had great difficulties distinguishing among the many bearers of the same name; sometimes, they made one person out of two homonymous ones, but the opposite also happened.

In the case of the two men named Apollonios the following reasons support my conjecture: 1. The original article "Apollonios I" probably contained, like many other articles, at the end a summary of the works of that author who was an eminent scholar as well as a poet. But the extant article does not mention any of the works of Apollonios, not even his most famous one, the preserved epic on the Argonauts. The last sentence says instead that Apollonios became the successor in office (*diadochos*) of Eratosthenes, his purported contemporary, whereas in reality he was succeeded by Apollonios II (the Eidographer). This sentence, with the *diadochē* statement came therefore most likely from the article "Apollonios II". 2. In the *Suda* a statement about the *akmē* (So-and-so lived under . . .) generally precedes that of a *synchronismos* (So-and-so was a contemporary of . . .) which makes sense. In the "Apollonios" article it is the other way around: the *akmē* follows the *synchronismos.* This is easiest to explain by the assumption that not only the last sentence (the statement of the *diadochē*) but also the last but one sentence (the *akmē* statement) came from the article "Apollonios II". The antepenultimate sentence, however, (the *synchronismos* statement) relates to Apollonios I, because a man the same age as Erathosthenes would hardly have become his successor. The seam between the two parts of the confounded Apollonios articles would therefore lie between the *synchronismos* and the *akmē.* But there was probably also an *akmē* statement in the "Apollonios I" article—before the *synchronismos* statement—namely the same as the one in the "Apollonios II" article. Although the second Apollonios was somewhat younger than the first one, the two namesakes from Alexandria could nevertheless have had their *akmē* in the same era, under Ptolemaios III Euergetes, say, the first ca. 235 and the second cat 225 B.C. I think that this is the reason why they were, according to a particular biographic tradition, erroneously thought to be the same person. When the two Apollonios articles were confounded, the first *akmē* statement before the *synchronismos* was omitted and the

last two sentences in the article "Apollonios II" were substituted for the list of works.

Thus, according to the papyrus, Apollonios was born ca. 300 B.C., i.e. soon after Kallimachos, but according to the *Suda* he was born ca. 275 B.C. Here we have two opposing statements. The question is, which one is more reliable? The answer will decide not only how to reconstruct the career of Apollonios but also that of Kallimachos. The list in the papyrus is said to be based on a reliable tradition, and this is certainly true for most of the entries—we must here disregard the mistakes of the copyists—but we are by no means forced to accept everything in it. The data in the *Suda* which are summarily dismissed by some are generally also based on sound tradition; this is evident from the data in the article "Kallimachos". The currently accepted opinion, according to which Apollonios was almost the same age as Kallimachos, is supported solely by the remark in the papyrus "he was also the teacher of the first [rather: the third] king". But is this remark so reliable that we should dismiss the chronological data in the *Suda* which are doubly corroborated by the *synchronismos* and the *akmē,* according to which Apollonios was at best of the same age as the future Ptolemaios III? Apollonios was not at all the teacher of the third king, but possibly the teacher of the son of the second king. A later passage in the list says: "Aristarchos was the teacher of Philopator's children" [rather: Philometor's]. This is correct. Should now the text for Apollonios be amended accordingly, or is that only an incorrect wording? It seems to me that a third explanation is more likely. Towards the end of the third century, when the second Apollonios was very likely in charge of the Alexandrian library, a boy was king, namely Ptolemaios V Epiphanes, born 210 B.C., who reigned from 204-180 B.C. The library director who educated him was indeed the teacher of a king, namely the fifth one. One cannot dismiss the suspicion that the source of the papyrus had instead of *prōtu* (first) not *tritu* (third), as Hunt thought, but *pemptu* (fifth). Thus, Apollonios Rhodios may have owed his title as teacher of a king to his namesake, the Eidographer. Under these circumstances I think that one must rely on the data of the *Suda.*

Although it is therefore likely that Apollonios Rhodios taught the future Ptolemaios III, who was the same age, he may still have been the director of the Alexandrian library before Eratosthenes, as indicated in the papyrus. According to the prevalent opinion, there would then indeed be no room in the list of of Alexandrian library directors for Kallimachos because, according to Tzetzes, Aristarchos was the fourth or fifth (not the fifth or sixth) director after Zenodotos. The Byzantine scholar refers, however, in those passages no doubt not to the library directors but to the textual critics of Homer's epics. In his opinion, Zenodotos was the first corrector of Homer, Aristarchos the fourth or fifth. He does not say who were the others. Among those, there were presumably also scholars from places other than Alexandria, for example, Aratos or the Cretan Rhianos.

It is therefore entirely possible that Kallimachos was mentioned in the list of Alexandrian library directors before the first Apollonios. The designation of the Rhodian as a pupil of Kallimachos would even indicate that he had been named in the list, because if a grammarian followed his teacher immediately in the office of library director, this was a special case of *diadochē* (succession) which may perhaps have been unique in the third century. This does not prove, of course, that Apollonios was indeed the successor of Kallimachos.

The researchers who determined the birthdate of Apollonios at ca. 300 B.C. had to explain why he was preferred over his teacher Kallimachos when Zenodotos had to be relieved as library director. They always presupposed that the office of library director was linked to that of the teacher, or more precisely, the literature teacher of the crown prince. But if Apollonios was born only in ca. 280 B.C. or even later, he was not a competitor of Kallimachos. It is therefore quite possible that he taught literature to the crown prince; after all, he had once been a school teacher. But he did not have to teach in order to become, or to remain library director, because it is very doubtful whether the two offices were then indeed linked to each other, as is always claimed. When Philitas taught the future Ptolemaios II there was presumably as yet no library to speak of in the Brucheion. But his successor Zenodotos was probably entrusted with the administration of the royal book collection only after he had finished his career as a teacher ca. 291 B.C. We do not know when he was relieved of his office as *bibliophylax,* in order to devote himself to textual criticism of Homeric and other poems. Assuming even that the crown prince had at that time already needed a literature teacher, it is not evident that a scholar was then expected to deal both with the cataloging of innumerable scrolls and with the literary education of a royal prince. Ptolemaios II was also not bound to appoint the library director as teacher of his son, or to make the teacher a library director, much less did he need to fill the two offices with a man who was able to carry out both tasks, just because his father had appointed the scholar who had been his own teacher to the post of library director. No tradition existed as yet at that time which would have recommended to the king to link the two offices. Was there such a tradition later on? There is no evidence that the library director Eratosthenes also taught the future Ptolemaios IV Philopator. His successor Apollonios the Eidographer was perhaps the teacher of Ptolemaios V Epiphanes. It is not known whether his successor Aristophanes also held this office. It is only documented that Aristarchos as library director also

taught the children of the fifth and sixth Ptolemaios. It should therefore not be taken for granted that the office of library director was linked to that of the literature teacher of the crown prince.

There is thus no valid reason not to assume that Kallimachos, who performed the duties of a library director at least during the second quarter of the third century, was indeed appointed as director of the library. It is unlikely that Zenodotos, who had reached the midpoint of his life already in 295, when he became the teacher of the future Ptolemaios II, remained nominally the library director until the appointment of Eratosthenes (after 246 B.C.). His successor could only be Kallimachos, because Apollonios was born only ca. 275 B.C. It is possible that Apollonios relieved Kallimachos when he had become weary of his office, and that he served for a few years as library director until he quarreled with his former teacher and moved to Rhodos. But it is not impossible that he was included in the list of the Alexandrian library directors only as a pupil of Kallimachos because he had been mistaken for the other Apollonios, the Eidographer. What happened to the facts in the process of being transmitted to us is no longer possible to reconstruct, but this is immaterial for our present investigation.

From the *Suda* and other works we know the titles of fifteen scholarly works by Kallimachos. All of these are lost, but a few can be reconstructed in outline with the aid of later authors who had used them. Thus we may get an approximate idea of Kallimachos as a scholar.

Even in his poetic works it is sometimes possible to discern some scholarly character traits. The Alexandrian *poetae docti* sought to give artistic expression to subjects which had never or seldom been dealt with, as is well known. Kallimachos used his studies in the libraries also in order to collect material for his poetic production. Thus, he may have encountered some peculiar customs whose mythical origin he later retold in his *Aitia.* In one known case he said so expressly. After having told the story of Akontios of Keos and Kydippe of Naxos, the most famous part of the *Aitia,* he says that he found the subject in an old (and not fictitious) author by the name of Xenomedes who had written the history of Keos. He then relates in broad outline the contents of Xenomedes's work. Among other things, one could read there that Keos has originally been called Hydrussa, and how it had acquired its later name, an information that interested Kallimachos very much, as we shall see. To us it seems peculiar that the poet wished to document, as it were, a harmless love story with a happy ending (a well-known family of Keos claimed to have been descended from Akontios and Kydippe), but that was quite in tune with his maxim, transmitted to us out of context: *amartyron uden aeidō* (I sing of nothing that has not been witnessed).

We would assume that he did the same in his scholarly works and particularly in those, even if the 44 excerpts made by a certain Antigonos of Karystos from Kallimachos's collection of marvelous and unusual natural phenomena would not show this quite clearly. This collection is cited as *Eklogē tōn paradoxōn* (Selection of natural curiosities) and as *Thaumasia* (Marvelous things) by Stephanos of Byzantium. In the Kallimachos article of the *Suda* we find (a) **Thaumatōn tōn eis hapasan tēn gēn kata topus ontōn synagōgē (Collection of the marvels of the world appearing in certain places)** and (b) separated from the first by several other titles, a specific title **Peri tōn en Peloponnēsō kai Italia thaumasiōn kai paradoxōn (On marvels and natural curiosities in the Peoloponnesos and in Italy)**. In the list of works by Kallimachos at least a second work on the *thaumasia* and *paradoxa* was probably also named. We do not know whether Kallimachos published these writings as parts of one work, or whether they were combined to a larger unit at a later time. The cumbersome title given in the *Suda* was hardly the one assigned by Kallimachos.

If we did not know the name and the position of the author we would have to conclude from the work alone that he had a very large collection of books at his disposal. It is obvious that Kallimachos perused the relevant departments of the Alexandrian library, noted on sheets unusual local curiosities reported in the books (trees that grow in the sea, mice that live in springs, and the like) with an indication of the author's name, and then arranged those sheets geographically. With the publication of his collection he started a long line of paradoxagraphers, whose works were very popular in Antiquity and in the Middle Ages. Two things are noteworthy: 1. Kallimachos did not list observations which he himself had made in nature, but only descriptions of curiosities which he had found in the literature. 2. He conscientiously listed the authors from whose works he had excerpted his notes. Among those were famous natural scientists such as Aristotle and Theophrastos, whose works are partially still extant, but most of these authors are merely names for us.

His collection was almost a documentation of curiosities with one restriction: he mentioned the titles of works from which he had taken his statements only in some exceptional cases, as for example when he indicated a certain Megasthenes as the author of *Indika,* and a certain Philon as the author of *Aithiopika.* He never criticized the sources from which he took his material, nor did he try to discover the causes (*aitiai*) of the curiosities. He was not a scientist like Aristotle, but was he really a courtier with a penchant for oddities, a collector in the grand manner, driven by refined curiosity, as [Ernst] Howald [*Der Dichter Kallimachos von Kyrene,* 1943] and with him most later literary historians thought? [Alfred] Körte-Händel [*Die hellenistische Dichtung,* 1960] hesitated, however, to agree

with Howald; according to them, we are still uncertain about the nature of Kallimachos's scholarship. I think that this is correct. But we can obtain a better insight only through a more detailed investigation of Kallimachos's scholarly endeavors, including his achievements in library-related and bibliographic fields.

The quotations from other works of Kallimachos are unfortunately far less numerous and extensive than those from his collection of curiosities. Not all works listed in the *Suda* are quoted by ancient or Byzantine authors, and conversely, not all quoted works appear in the incomplete bibliography transmitted to us by the *Suda.* The titles of works known to us are as follows:

Pere tōn en tē oikumenē potamōn (**On the rivers of the world**). As in the case of the collection of curiosities, the *Suda* lists in addition a part of this work which was also arranged geographically: **Peri tōn en Europē potamōn** (**On the rivers of Europe**). An author of a scholium cites another part: **Peri tōn kata tēn Asian potamōn** (**On the rivers of Asia**).

Peri orneōn (**On birds**). This work in several books, frequently quoted by later scholars, was compiled from the works of Aristotle and other scientists and arranged by species.

Peri agōnōn (**On contests**). *Nomina barbarika* (**Customs of the barbarians**). *Peri nymphōn* (**On nymphs**). On the subjects of these three works, which are not listed in the *Suda,* there were also works by earlier scholars. Hellanikos had already compiled *Nomina barbarika,* and so had Aristotle.

Ktiseis nēsōn kai poleōn kai metonomasiai (**Foundation of islands and cities and changes of their names.**) Kallimachos was very much interested in the subject of this work which is listed only in the *Suda,* and he dealt with it also in his poems whenever there was an opportunity. Since changes in the names of places were often connected with their colonization, he dealt also with this issue. His predecessors, among whom was again Hellanikos, had done the same.

Ethnikai onomasiai (**Designations according to peoples**) [i.e. the inhabitants of regions, islands and cities]. This collective title is cited by Athenaios. The *Suda* does not list it but mentions two titles which were apparently parts of this work: **Peri onomasias ichthyōn** (**On the names of fishes**), also cited by Athenaios, and **Mēnōn prosegoriai kata ethnē kai poleis** (**The names of months according to peoples and cities**). Perhaps **Peri anēmon** (**On winds**) was also part of this work. The *Ethnikai onomasiai* listed dialectal names of fishes, months and winds. Thus, Kallimachos was interested not only in the various names that a place had had in the course of time, but also in different designations for the same concept which were in use in the Greek language community. He probably took the dialectal terms mainly from the lists of glosses compiled by scholars such as Philitas and Simias (and perhaps also Zenodotos). But his work was apparently the first *onomastikon* (vocabulary) arranged by subject groups.

We may assume that Kallimachos used in all the works mentioned here the material collected by his predecessors and that he added notes which he had made while reading the works. But it is not impossible that he also used oral information in his works on changes in place names and dialectal names of fishes, etc.

In addition to these works, ancient and Byzantine scholars mention four times the *hypomnēmata* of Kallimachos, which are not listed in the *Suda*. Modern researchers are unsure about the character of these *hypomnēmata*. But there is no reason to assume that they were different from the *hypomnēmata* bequeathed by Aristotle to Theophrastos and continued by the latter, so that it was later not known whether they should be ascribed to him or to his teacher. These were collections of notes, excerpts, sketches and the like. The lexicon of Harpokration (2nd century A.D.) has an entry for *Akē* which says that Kallimachos had explained in his *hypomnēmata* that this was the city now named Ptolemais. This note was probably found in Kallimachos's work on the foundation of islands and cities and the changes of their names. The indication of this work as a *hypomnēma* is not dubious, rather the opposite. The work on marvelous and unusual natural curiosities partially reported by Antigonos was certainly a *hypomnēma* in the same sense then used, because it contained nothing but excerpts from various authors. His work on birds, of which we have a somewhat more precise idea than of his other scholarly works thanks to some quotations, was also based on excerpts from Aristotle and other natural scientists. It is likely that all of Kallimachos's works listed above were thought to be *hypomnēmata* because they only presented the material that he had found in the library, sometimes with an indication of authors, but in an unpretentious literary form, and they displayed neither a scientific conception nor did they establish a theory. Incidentally, Istros and Philostephanos, who were pupils of Kallimachos, also compiled *hypomnēmata*.

Nevertheless, Kallimachos was not just a collector, much less was he a hunter of curiosities. It was not enough just to collect, to find and note down interesting information from the literature. The notes had to be filed according to their purpose and had to be arranged by some rational principles. This was not so easy, especially since Kallimachos certainly took notes for several different collections while perusing the literature. Evidently, he knew not only how to collect but also how to classify scientific material. Even if he had not compiled the **Pinakes** of Greek authors, we

could imagine him only as a scholar surrounded by many boxes full of sheets with notes. Since then, there have been innumerable scholars of this kind. Among the ancient ones, the best known is Plinius. The author of the *Naturalis historia* excerpted, as he assures us in his foreword, more than 2,000 scrolls, and he began his work with long lists of the Latin and Greek authors on which he had relied for each chapter, among whom was also our Kallimachos and a physician by the same name from the second century B.C.

What was the purpose of Kallimachos's collections? Philitas and Simias probably intended their glossaries as aids for the explanation of old poetic works, perhaps also as a mine of information for new poets. Was this also the intention of Kallimachos? The ancient commentators on the *Birds* of Aristophanes relied on Kallimachos's work on birds when they did not know which birds had been meant by Aristophanes. Kallimachos had indeed written about some but not all birds mentioned in the comedy. It was thus not his intention to explain the relevant passages in the *Birds.* On the other hand, his collections went much further than necessary for the explanation of old poets and for the creation of new poetic works. Since Kallimachos collected material from many fields and certainly compiled also collections other than those of which we know by chance, we may presume that he as director of the royal library intended to compile the knowledge on diverse subjects contained in the books, first of all those in which he himself was most interested, and to present it to the world of scholarship in an orderly fashion. Thus, his *hypomnēmata* are different from those seemingly similar writings of other scholars. Because of their strict adherence to the literature they are to be considered as attempts by a librarian to utilize the collection of books in his care, and to exploit its riches through compilations. Thus, his compendium on birds may have had a purpose that was not the same but similar to that of a modern librarian who compiles a special catalog of the ornithological literature in his library.

It will be easier to understand the main work of Kallimachos, the compilation of the **Pinakes** of Greek authors, if we conclude from his *hypomnēmata* that he was capable to peruse and utilize large masses of literature, and that he has mastered the techniques of collection and classification of scientific material which had been developed by Aristotle and Theophrastos.

FURTHER READING

Bulloch, Anthony W. "The Future of a Hellenistic Illusion: Some Observations on Callimachus and Religion." *Museum Helveticum,* Vol. 41, No. 4, October, 1984, pp. 209-30.

Addresses the "sense of paradox and even puzzlement" readers often have in response to Callimachus's religious poetry in order to work out some of the complexities in the Hellenistic view of the human rulers' relationship to the gods.

Bundy, Elroy L. "The 'Quarrel between Kallimachos and Apollonios' Part I: The Epilogue of Kallimachos's *Hymn to Apollo.*" *California Studies in Classical Antiquity,* Vol. 5, 1972, pp. 39-94.

Uses the ambiguity of Callimachus's feud with Apollonius and a careful examination of language to demonstrate the hymn's "artistic integrity."

Cameron, Alan. *Callimachus and his Critics.* Princeton: Princeton University Press, 1995. 534 p.

An exhaustive overview of Callimachus's work, the work of his contemporaries, and the critical discussion that has surrounded Hellenistic poetry.

Dawson, Christopher M. "The *Iambi* of Callimachus. A Hellenistic Poet's Experimental Laboratory." *Yale Classical Studies,* edited by Harry M. Hubbell, Vol. 11, 1950, pp. 1-168.

Comments exhaustively on each of the *Iambi,* the history of the manuscripts, and suggests a possible "coherent view of the *Iambi* as a whole."

Hutchinson, G. O. "Callimachus." In *Hellenistic Poetry.* Oxford: Oxford at the Clarendon Press, 1988, pp. 26-84.

Refutes some of the common criticisms of Callimachus and concludes instead that the poet used his scholarship toward a dramatic and effective purpose.

Klein, T. M. "The Role of Calllimachus in the Development of the Concept of the Counter-Genre." *Latomus,* Vol. XXXIII, No. 2, April-June, 1974, pp. 217-31.

Considers Callimachus's place in the discussions of philosophy of his age, particularly as they relate to his ideas about epic.

Mair, A. W. "Callimachus." In *Callimachus, Hymns and Epigrams,* translated by A. W. Mair. Cambridge, Mass: Harvard University Press, 1955, pp. 1-33.

Introduces his translation with information about Callimachus's life and the manuscript of the *Hymns.* Also provides commentary on the *Hymns,* including a synopsis of each, and a summary of the critical history.

Zanker, G. "Callimachus's Hecale: A New Kind of Epic Hero?" *Antichthon,* Vol. 11, 1977, pp. 68-77.

Analyses *Hecale* as a "break with the whole of Greek epic tradition," specifically by virtue of Callimachus's focus on the life of an ordinary woman and the "subtle and restrained" language he chose for the portrayal.

Catullus

c. 84 B.C. - c. 54 B.C.

(Full name Gaius Valerius Catullus.) Latin poet.

INTRODUCTION

Catullus is best known for his love poetry, in which eloquent expression of emotion is combined with a technical agility. Seeking inspiration from the Greek Alexandrian poetry tradition, Catullus experimented with new themes and forms in poetry and became the founder of a new school of Latin poetry that favored brief, witty compositions. Technically, Catullus is praised for his virtuistic use of a range of poetic meters, including the lyric, the elegiac, and iambic. Many critics regard the influential group of poems inspired by his tumultuous relationship with a woman to whom he referred as "Lesbia" as his greatest achievement.

Biographical Information

Catullus was born in about 84 B.C. in Verona into a well-known local family. He does not directly mention his family in his poetry, except to express sorrow over his brother's untimely death. The circumstances of Catullus's education are unknown, but the characteristics of his work indicate that he was most likely tutored in Greek and Latin literature. Some critics have suggested that Catullus may have studied under the grammarian Valerius Cato, who at that time lived in Verona. From 62 B.C. onward Catullus lived primarily in Rome, returning to Verona only occasionally. In Rome Catullus traveled in exclusive but decadent literary circles and became enamored with a married woman whom he called Lesbia in his poetry. Scholars believe that Lesbia was probably Clodia, the wife of Q. Metellus Celer and the sister of P. Clodius Pulcher, infamous enemy of Cicero. Catullus became a leader of a loose-knit literary group called the New Poets (*neoterici*), which included Helvius Cinna and Licinius Calvus, and who were influenced by the ideals of the Greek Alexandrians. Catullus greatly admired the Greek poet Callimachus and translated at least one of his poems. In 57 B.C. Catullus travelled to Asia with the Roman governor Gaius Memmius, possibly to visit his brother's grave, or as a lucrative business venture; whatever the reason for the trip, it did not make Catullus wealthy. The date of his death is uncertain , but it is known that he died young, probably in about 54 B.C.

Textual History

Scholars are certain that at least some of Catullus's poems circulated before his death; there is evidence, for example, that Caesar was acquainted with some poems directed at him. Some literary historians believe that a small collection of poems might have been published privately by Catullus himself. Other than fragments quoted by fellow writers, the first poem of Catullus preserved in a manuscript was Poem 62, in the *Codex Thuanneus*, a ninth-century anthology of Latin poetry. The rest of his known texts were preserved in the *Codex Veronensis*, which surfaced in Verona in the 1200s, was copied twice, and disappeared in the fourteenth century. Only one of these copies, the *Codex Oxoniensis*, survived and is housed at Oxford University. Two copies were made from the second, lost copy. All modern Catullus editions are based on these three surviving codexes. Manuscripts based on the codexes number Catullus's poems from 1 to 116, but most critics agree that this is not necessarily the order in which they were written. The poems are organized into three distinct groups: 1-60 are polymetric poems (mostly short pieces written in a variety of meters, including some fragments); 61-68 are long poems; and 69-116 are elegiac fragments (shorter elegies and epigrams, and couplets). Kenneth Quinn has argued that it is possible that the first 60 were published by Catullus and the rest arranged by someone else, an editor or a literary friend of Catullus's in Rome. The careful arrangement still leaves scholars puzzled and many theories have been advanced to explain it. The three extant manuscripts contain many trivial errors and are inexact as scholars have added and deleted alternative readings of their predecessors' work. Though there have been numerous modern translations and editions of Catullus's work, those by Quinn and Thomson are regarded as among the best.

Major Works

Deemed a *doctus poeta* ("learned craftsman") by his contemporaries, Catullus was able to tightly organize his poems to maximize the effectiveness of his ideas. Although they are highly structured, Catullus's poems create the illusion of spontaneous, conversational Latin, and he uses common language and verbal irony, especially in his shorter pieces, to great effect. The most successful of his poems seem sincere and light, full of heartfelt sentiment, but it is the combination of elaborate structure and well-chosen language that produces this response. Catullus's subject matter belies his technical brilliance and the scholarly drive to perfection which imbue all his work. The most important theme in Catullus's work concerns his obsession with Lesbia—their doomed attachment, love, hate, frustration, and betrayal—and he returned to this relationship repeatedly in his poetry until his death. In allowing the ruling passion of his life to be fully expounded on in his work, Catullus gave Latin poetry a new direction: this honest, personalized vision, rooted in Greek tradition, opened up new possibilities in Latin poetry and gave rise to a new school of poets that profoundly influenced Vergil, Propertius, Tibullus, Ovid, and Horace.

Critical Reception

Catullus was well known among his generation of Romans and in later antiquity was commonly read and discussed. Cornelius Nepos found the quality of his poetry to be equal to that of Lucretius's. Literary critics like Quintilian admired Catullus as a poet in the iambic tradition, but made no mention of him as a lyricist. Discussing this unusual occurrence, E. A. Havelock has suggested that the problem may have been that Catullus was too intensely subjective for his contemporaries to appreciate fully. Other classical poets thought Catullus extravagant and did not respect his use of diminutives in poetry. Although he was highly influential, he was essentially forgotten from the late first century to the fourteenth. Catullus's influence can again be seen in such Elizabethans as Ben Jonson and William Shakespeare, and the nineteenth-century poets Lord Byron and Alfred Tennyson. Modern critics are divided on the merit of the poetry of Catullus: some find his work uneven in quality, while others find much to praise in every line.

PRINCIPAL ENGLISH TRANSLATIONS

Catullus, Tibullus, and Pervigilium Veneris (translated by Francis W. Cornish, John P. Postgate, and John W. Mackail) 1912

Odi et Amo: The Complete Poetry of Catullus (translated by Roy A. Swanson) 1959

The Poems of Catullus (translated by James Michie) 1969

The Poems of Catullus (translated by Peter Whigham) 1969

Catullus: The Poems (translated by Kenneth Quinn) 1970

Catullus: The Complete Poems for American Readers (translated by Reney Meyers and Robert J. Ormsby) 1972

Catullus: A Critical Edition (translated by D. F. S. Thomson) 1978

The Poems of Catullus (translated by Frederic Raphael and Kenneth McLeish) 1979

CRITICISM
James Davies (essay date 1877)

SOURCE: "Hymen, O Hymenæe!" and "The Roman-Alexandrine and Longer Poems of Catullus," in *Catullus, Tibullus, and Propertius,* J. B. Lippincott & Co., 1877, pp. 62-75, 76-92.

[*In the following chapters from his* Catullus, Tibullus, and Propertius, *Davies offers a discursive reading of Catullus's most notable poems among the poet's epithalamia and alexandrines.*]

[Catullus may be seen, at first glance] rather as the writer of passionate love-verses to Lesbia, or *vers de société* to his friends, literary or light, as the case might be. There are yet two other and distinct aspects of his Muse. That which he borrowed from the Alexandrian school of poetry will [be considered later]; but in the present it will suffice to give some account of his famous epithalamia, the models of like composition for all time, and the *loci classici* of the ceremonial of Roman marriages, as well as exquisite pictures of the realisation of mutual affection. It [may be readily seen] how fully, notwithstanding his own blighted hopes, Catullus was able to conceive the life-bond between his friend Calvus and his helpmeet Quinctilia. A longer and more lively picture presents the ecstasy of Acme and Septimius in lines and words that seem to burn. The two doting lovers plight vows, and compare omens, and interchange embraces and kisses that inspire with passion the poet's hendecasyllables. The conclusion of the piece is all we can quote, and is given from a translation by the author of 'Lorna Doone,' but it may serve to show that Catullus was capable of picturing and conceiving the amount of devotion which his nuptial songs connect with happy and like-minded unions:—

> Starting from such omen's cheer,
> Hand in hand on love's career,
> Heart to heart is true and dear.
> Dotingly Septimius fond
> Prizes Acme far beyond
> All the realms of east and west—
> Acme to Septimius true,
> Keeps for him his only due,
> Pet delights and loving jest.
> Who hath known a happier pair,
> Or a honeymoon so fair?

One image from the rest of the poem cannot pass unnoticed—that of Acme bending back her head in

Septimius's embrace, to kiss with rosy mouth what Mr. Blackmore translates "eyes with passion's wine opprest"; but the whole piece deserves to the full the unstinted praise it has met with from critics and copyists.

The Epithalamium of Julia and Manlius, however, is a poem of more considerable proportions; and at the same time that it teems with poetic beauties, handles its subject with such skill and ritual knowledge as to supply a correct programme of the marriage ceremonial among the Romans. Strictly speaking, it is not so much a nuptial ode or hymn in the sense in which the playmates of Helen serenade her in Theocritus, as a series of pictures of the bridal procession and rites, from end to end. The subjects of this poem were a scion of the ancient patrician house of the Torquati, Lucius Manlius Torquatus, a great friend and patron of our poet, and Vinia, or Julia Aurunculeia, one of whose two names seems to have been adoptive, and as to whom the poet's silence seems to imply that her bridegroom's rank was enough to dignify both. It was not so long afterwards that Manlius sought our poet's assistance or solace in the shape of an elegy ["**Poem lxviii**"] on her untimely death; but in the present instance his services are taxed to do honour to her wedding: and it may be interesting to accompany him through the dioramic description which his stanzas illustrate. The poem opens with an invocation to Hymen, child of Urania, dwelling in his mother's Helicon, bidding him wreathe his brows with sweet marjoram or amaracus, fling round him a flame-coloured scarf, and bind saffron sandals to his feet, in token of going forth upon his proper function and errand. Other accompaniments of his progress are to be song, and dance, and pine-torch,— each of them appropriate in the evening fetching-home of the bride from her father's house; and his interest is bespoken in one who is fair, favoured, and fascinating as Ida's queen, when she condescended to the judgment of Paris:—

> As the fragrant myrtle, found
> Flourishing on Asian ground,
> Thick with blossoms overspread,
> By the Hamadryads fed,
> For their sport, with honey-dew—
> All so sweet is she to view.

It is this paragon, proceeds the ode, for whose sweet sake the god is besought to leave awhile his native grottos and pools, and lend his aid in binding soul to soul to her husband—yea, closer than clasping ivy twines meshy tendrils round its naked elm. To welcome her too, as well as to invite Hymenæus to his wonted office with the readier alacrity, are bidden the blameless maidens of the bride's train, with a series of inducements adapted to bespeak their sympathy—his interest in happy nuptials, his blessing so essential to the transfer of the maiden from one home and name to

another, his influence on the prospects of an honoured progeny; and strong language is used, in vv. 71-75, of such nations as ignore the rites and ordinances of marriage.

And now the bride is bidden to come forth. The day is waning; the torch-flakes flicker bright in the gloaming; there is no time for tears of maidenly reluctance; the hour is at hand:—

> Dry up thy tears! For well I trow,
> No woman lovelier than thou,
> Aurunculeia, shall behold
> The day all panoplied in gold,
> And rosy light uplift his head
> Above the shimmering ocean's bed!
>
> As in some rich man's garden-plot,
> With flowers of every hue inwrought;
> Stands peerless forth, with drooping brow,
> The hyacinth, so standest thou!
> Come, bride, come forth! No more delay!
> The day is hurrying fast away!

Then follow encouragements to the bride to take the decisive step over the threshold, in the shape of substantial guarantees of her bridegroom's loyalty; and of course the elm and the ivy are pressed, for not the first time, into such service. More novel, save that the text of Catullus is here so corrupt that commentators have been left to patch it as they best may for coherence,— is the stanza to the bridal couch. All that Catullus has been allowed by the manuscripts to tell us is that its feet were of ivory, which is very appropriate; but if the render's mind is enlisted in the question of upholstery, it may be interested to know that collateral information enables one critic to surmise that the hangings were of silver-purple, and the timbers of the bedstead from Indian forests. But anon come the boys with the torches. Here is the veil or scarf of flame colour, or deep brilliant yellow, capacious enough, as we learn, to shroud the bride from head to foot, worn over the head during the ceremony, and retained so till she was unveiled by her husband. Coincidentally the link-bearers are chanting the hymenaeal song, and at intervals, especially near the bridegroom's door, the rude Fescennine banter is repeated; whilst the bridegroom, according to custom, flings nuts to the lads in attendance, much as at a Greek marriage it was customary to fling showers of sweetmeats. The so-called Fescennine jests were doubtless as broad as the occasion would suggest to a lively and joke-loving nation; and another part of the ceremonial at this point, as it would seem from Catullus, though some have argued that it belonged rather to the marriage-feast, was the popular song "Talassius" or "Talassio," said to have had its origin in an incident of the "Rape of the Sabine Women." Catullus represents the choruses at this point as instilling into the bride by the way all manner of good advice as to wifely duty and obedience, and auguring for her, if she takes their advice, a sure rule in the home which she goes to share. If she has tact, it will own her sway—

> Till hoary age shall steal on thee,
> With loitering step and trembling knee,
> And palsied head, that, ever bent,
> To all, in all things, nods assent.

In other words, a hint is given her that, though the bridegroom be the *head* of the house, she will be herself to blame if she be not the *neck*.

As the poem proceeds, another interesting ceremonial, which is attested by collateral information, is set graphically before the reader. Traditionally connected with the same legend of the carrying off of the Sabine women, but most probably arising out of a cautious avoidance of evil omens through a chance stumble on the threshold, was a custom that on reaching the bridegroom's door, the posts of which were wreathed in flowers and anointed with oil for her reception, the bride should be carried over the step by the *pronubi*— attendants or friends of the groom, who must be "husbands of one wife." This is expressed as follows in Theodore Martin's happy transcript of the passage of Catullus:—

> Thy golden-sandalled feet do thou
> Lift lightly o'er the threshold now!
> Fair omen this! And pass between
> The lintel-poet of polished sheen!
> Hail, Hymen! Hymenæus hail!
> Hail, Hymen, Hymenæus!
>
> See where, within, thy lord is set
> On Tyrian-tinctured coverlet—
> His eyes upon the threshold bent,
> And all his soul on thee intent!
> Hail, Hyinen! Hymenæus, hail!
> Hail, Hymen, Hymenæus!

By-and-by, one of the three prætexta-clad boys, who had escorted the bride from her father's home to her husband's, is bidden to let go the round arm he has been supporting; the blameless matrons (*pronubæ*), of like qualification as their male counterparts, conduct the bride to the nuptial-couch in the atrium, and now there is no let or hindrance to the bridegroom's coming. Catullus has so wrought his bridal ode, that it culminates in stanzas of singular beauty and spirit. The bride, in her nuptial-chamber, is represented with a countenance like white parthenice (which one critic suggests may be the camomile blossom) or yellow poppy for beauty. And the bridegroom, of course, is worthy of her; and both worthy of his noble race, as well as meet to hand it on. The natural wishes follow:—

> 'Tis not meet so old a stem
> Should be left ungraced by them,
> To transmit its fame unshorn
> Down through ages yet unborn.

The next lines of the original are so prettily turned by Mr. Cranstoun, that we forbear for the nonce to tax the charming version of Martin:—

> May a young Torquatus soon
> From his mother's bosom slip
> Forth his tender hands, aim smile
> Sweetly on lids sire the while
> With tiny half-oped lip.
>
> May each one a Manlius
> In his infant features see,
> And may every stranger trace,
> Clearly graven on his face,
> His mother's chastity.

Of parallels and imitations of this happy thought and aspiration, there is abundant choice. Theodore Martin's taste selects a graceful and expanded fancy of Herrick from his "Hesperides"; while Dunlop, in his 'History of Roman Literature,' quotes the following almost literal reproduction out of an epithalamium on the marriage of Lord Spencer by Sir William Jones, who pronounced Catullus's picture worthy the pencil of Domenichino:—

> And soon to be completely blest,
> Soon may a young Torquatus rise,
> Who, hanging on his mother's breast,
> To his known sire shall turn his eyes,
> Outstretch his infant arms awhile,
> Half-ope his little lips and smile.

The poem concludes with a prayer that mother and child may realise the fame and virtues of Penelope and Telemachus, and well deserves the credit it has ever enjoyed as a model in its kind.

Of the second of Catullus's Nuptial Songs—an hexameter poem in amœbæan or responsive strophes and antistrophes, supposed to be sung by the choirs of youths and maidens who attended the nuptials, and whom, in the former hymn, the poet had been exhorting to their duties, whereas here they come in turn to their proper function—no really trustworthy history is to be given, though one or two commentators propound that it was a sort of brief for the choruses, written to order on the same occasion for which the poet had written, on his own account, the former nuptial hymn. But the totally different style and structure forbid the probability of this, although both are remarkable poems of their kind. This one, certainly, has a ringing freshness about it, and seems to cleave the shades of nightfall with a *réveillé* singularly remarkable. The youths of the bridegroom's company have left him at the rise of the evening star, and gone forth for the hymenæal chant from the tables at which they have been feasting. They recognise the bride's approach as a signal to strike up the hymenæal. Hereupon the maidens who have accompanied the bride, espying the male chorus, enter on a rivalry in argument and song as to the merits of Hesperus, whom they note as he shows his evening fires over Œta—a sight which seems to have a connection; wish some myth as to the love of Hesper for a youth named Hymenaeus localised at Œta, as the story of Diana and Endymion was at Latmos, to which Virgil alludes in his eighth eclogue. Both bevies gird themselves for a lively encounter of words, from their diverse points of view. First sing the virgins:—

> Hesper, hath heaven more ruthless star than
>   thine,
> That canst from mother's arms her child
>   untwine?
> From mother's arms a clinging daughter part,
> To dower a headstrong bridegroom's eager
>   heart?
> Wrong like to this do captured cities know?
> Ho! Hymen; Hymen! Hymenæus, ho!
>
>   —D.

The band of youths reply in an antistrophe which negatives the averment of the maidens:—

> Hesper, hath heaven more jocund star than
>   thee,
> Whose flame still crowns true lovers' unity
> The troth that parents first, then lovers plight,
> Nor deem complete till thou illum'st the
>   night?
> What hour more blissful do the gods bestow?
> Hail! Hymen, Hymen! Hymenæus ho!
>
>   —D.

To judge of the next plea of the chorus of maidens by the fragmentary lines which remain of the original, it took the grave form of a charge of abduction against the incriminated evening star. If he were not a principal in the felonious act, at least he winked at it, when it was the express vocation of his rising to prevent, by publicity, such irregular proceedings. But now the youths wax bold in their retort, and wickedly insinuate that the fair combatants are not really so very wroth with Hesper for his slackness. After a couplet which seems to imply, though its sense is obscure and ambiguous, that the sort of thieves whom these maidens revile, and whose ill name is not confined to Roman literature (for in the Russian songs, as we learn from Mr. Ralston's entertaining volumes, the bridegroom is familiarly regarded as the "enemy," "that evil-thief," and "the Tartar"), speedily find their offences condoned, and are received into favour, they add a pretty plain

charge against the complainants that—

> Chide as they list in song's pretended ire,
> Yet what they chide they in their souls desire.

This is such a home-thrust that the virgins change their tactics, and adduce an argument *ad misericordiam,* which is one of the most admired passages of Catullus, on the score of a simile often imitated from it. The following version will be found tolerably literal.—

> As grows hid floweret in some garden closed,
> Crushed by no ploughshare, to no beast
>   exposed,
> By zephyrs fondled, nursed up by the rain,
> With kindly sun to strengthen and sustain:
> To win its sweetness lads and lasses vie:
> But let that floweret wither by-and-by,
> Nipped by too light a hand, it dies alone.
> Its lover lads and lasses all are flown!
> E'en as that flower is lovely maiden's pride,
> In her pure virgin home content to bide;
> A husband wins her,—and her bloom is sere,
> No more to lads a charm, or lasses dear!
>
>   —D.

The last line is undoubtedly borrowed from a fragment of the Greek erotic poet, Mimmermus; and the whole passage, as Theodore Martin shows, has had its influence upon an admired canto of Spenser's *Faery Queen* (B. ii. c. xii.).

Will the boys melt and give in, or will they show cause why they should not accept this sad showing of the mischief, for which Hymen and Hesper have the credit? Let us hear their antistrophe:—

> As a lone vine on barren, naked field
> Lifts ne'er a shoot, nor mellow grape can
>   yield,
> But bends top-heavy with its slender frame,
> Till root and branch in level are the same:
> Such vine, such field, in their forlorn estate
> No peasants till, nor oxen cultivate.
> Yet if the same vine with tall elm-tree wed,
> Peasants will tend, and oxen till its bed.
> So with the maid no lovers' arts engage,
> She sinks unprized, unnoticed, into age;
> But once let hour and man be duly found,
> Her father's pride, her husband's love
>   redound.
>
>   —D.

The epithalamium ends with an arithmetical calculation of the same special pleaders, which the maidens apparently find unanswerable, and which is of this nature—namely, that they are not their own property, except as regards a third share. As the other two shares belong to their parents respectively, and these have coalesced in transferring their votes to a son-in-law, it is obviously as futile as it is unmannerly to demur to the nuptial rites. And so the poem ends with the refrain of "Hymen, O Hymenæe!" It has with much plausibility been conjectured by Professor Sellar to be an adaptation of Sappho or some other Greek poet to an occasion within Catullus's own experience. Certainly it does not exhibit like originality with the poem preceding it. It might be satisfactory, were it possible, to give, by way of sequel to the epithalamium of Julia and Manlius, trustworthy data of the young wife's speedy removal; but this is based upon sheer conjecture, and so much as we know has been already stated. If we might transfer to the elegiacs addressed to Manlius before noticed a portion of the story of Laodamia, which has sometimes been printed with them, but is now arranged with the verses to Manius Acilius Glabrio, we should be glad to conceive of Julia's wedded life as matching that of Laodamia, and offering a model for its portrayal.

> Nor e'er was dove more loyal to her mate
> That bird which, more than all, with clinging
>   beak,
> Kiss after kiss will pluck insatiate—
> Though prone thy sex its joys in change to
>   seek,
>
> Than thou, Laodamia! Tame and cold
> Was all their passion, all their love to shine:
> When thou to thy enamoured breast didst fold
> Thy blooming lord in ecstasy divine.
>
> As fond, as fair, as thou, so came the maid,
> Who is my life, and to my bosom clung;
> While Cupid round her fluttering, arrayed
> In saffron vest, a radiance o'er her flung.
>   —(C. lxviii.) M.

. . . . .

That portion of the poetry of Catullus which has been considered hitherto is doubtless the most genuine and original; but, with the exception of the two epithalamia, the poems now to be examined, as moulded on the Alexandrine form and subjects, are perhaps the more curious in a literary point of view. Contrasting with the rest of his poetry in their lack of "naturalism essentially Roman and republican," they savour undisguisedly of that Roman-Alexandrinism in poetry which first sprang up in earnest among the contemporaries of Cicero and Caesar, and grew with all the more rapidity owing to the frequent visits of the Romans to the Greek provinces, and the increasing influx of the Greek *literati* into Rome. Of the Alexandrine literature at its fountain-head it must be remembered that it was the substitute and successor on the ruin of the Hellenic nation, and the decline of its nationality, language, literature, and art of the former national and popular literature of Greece. But

it was confined to a limited range. "It was," says Professor Mommsen, "only in a comparatively narrow circle, not of men of culture—for such, strictly speaking, did not exist—but of men of erudition, that the Greek literature was cherished even when dead; that the rich inheritance which it had left was inventoried with melancholy pleasure or arid refinement of research; and that the living sense of sympathy or the dead erudition was elevated into a semblance of productiveness. This posthumous productiveness constitutes the so-called Alexandrinism." Originality found a substitute in learned research. Multifarious learning, the result of deep draughts at the wells of criticism, grammar, mythology, and antiquities, gave an often cumbrous and pedantic character to laboured and voluminous epics, elegies, and hymnology (a point and smartness in epigram being the one exception in favour of this school), whilst the full genial spirit of Greek thought, coeval with Greek freedom, was exchanged for courtly compliment, more consistent with elaboration than freshness. Among the best of the Alexandrian poets proper—indeed, the best of all, if we except the original and genial Idyllist, Theocritus—was the learned Callimachus; and it is upon Callimachus especially that Catullus has drawn for his Roman-Alexandrine poems, one of them being in fact a translation of that poet's elegy "On the Hair of Queen Berenice"; whilst another, his **"Nuptials of Peleus and Thetis,"** has been supposed by more than one critic to be a translation of Callimachus also. This is, indeed, problematical; but there is no doubt that for his mythologic details, scholarship, and other features savouring of ultra erudition, he owes to Callimachus characteristics which his intrinsic poetic gifts enabled him to dress out acceptably for the critics of his day. The singular and powerful poem of **"Atys"** belongs to the same class, by reason of its mythological subject. A recent French critic of Catullus, in a learned chapter on Alexandrinism, defines it as the absence of sincerity in poetry, and the exclusive preoccupation of form. "He," writes M. Couat, "who, instead of looking around him, or, better, within himself, parades over all countries and languages his adventurous curiosity, and prefers *l'esprit* to *l'ame*—the new, the pretty, the fine, to the natural and simple—such an one, to whatever literature he belongs, is an Alexandrinist." Alexandrinism in excess is what in this writer's view is objectionable; and whilst we are disposed to think that few will demur to this moderate dogma, it is equally certain that none of the Roman cultivators of the Alexandrine school have handled it with more taste and less detriment to their natural gifts than Catullus. With him the elaborateness which, in its home, Alexandrinism exhibits as to metre and prosody, is exchanged for a natural and unforced power, quite consistent with simplicity. As is well observed by Professor Sellar, "His adaptation of the music of language to embody the feeling or passion by which he is possessed, is most vividly felt in the skylark ring of his great nuptial ode, in the wild hurrying agitation of the 'Atys,' in the stately calm of the '**Epithalamium of Peleus and Thetis**'." Herein, as indeed in the tact and art evinced generally in these larger poems, we seem to find ground for dissent from the opinion of several—otherwise weighty critics of Catullus, that they were the earlier exercises of his poetic career—a subject upon which, as there is the scantiest inkling in either direction, it is admissible to take the negative view. As a work of art, no doubt the "**Nuptials of Peleus and Thetis**" are damaged by the introduction of the episode of Ariadne's desertion within the main poem—an offence obviously against strict epic unity. But it is not by any means sure that this is so much a sign of youthful work as of an independence consistent with poetic fancy, and certainly not amenable to the stigma of Alexandrinism, which must be *en règle,* if anything. It is with this largest, and in many respects finest, sample of Catullus's epic capacity, that we propose to deal at greatest length, reserving space for a glance or two at the "**Atys**" and the "**Hair of Berenice.**" "The whole poem" ('**Peleus and Thetis**'), to quote Mr. Sellar once more, "is pervaded with that calm light of strange loveliness which spreads over the unawakened world in the early sunrise of a summer day." If here and there a suspicion of overwrought imagery and description carries back the mind to a remembrance of the poet's model, it must be allowed that, for the most part, this poem excels in variety, in pictorial effects, in force of fancy, and clever sustentation of the interest. It begins with the day on which, in the hoar distance of mythic ages, the Pelion-born Argo was first launched and manned, and the first sailor of all ever burst on the realm of Amphitrite—a statement which we must not criticise too closely, as the poet elsewhere in the poem tells of a fleet of Theseus prior to the Argonautic expedition:—

> Soon as its prow the wind-vexed surface crave,
> Soon as to oarsmen's harrow frothed the wave,
> Forth from the eddying whiteness Nereids shone,
> With faces set-strange sight to look upon.
> Then, only then, might mortal vision rest
> On naked sea-nymph, lifting rosy breast
> High o'er the billows' foam. 'Twas then the flame
> Of love for Thetis Peleus first o'ercame:
> Then Thetis deigned a mortal spouse to wed,
> Then Jove approved, and their high union sped.
>
>   —D.

The poet having thus introduced the betrothal, as it were, of the goddess and the hero, pauses, ere he plunges into his subject, to apostrophise heroes and heroines in general, and more especially the twain immediately concerned: Peleus, for whom the very susceptible father of the gods had waived his own *penchant* for Thetis; Peleus, the stay and champion of Thessaly; and Thetis, most beautiful of ocean's daughters, and grandchild of earth-girding Tethys and her lord Oceanus—a fitting proem to the action of the poem, which commences with no further delay. We see all Thessaly come forth to do honour and guest-service to the nuptials, gifts in their hands, and joy and gladness in their countenances. Scyros and Phthia's Tempe, Cranon, and Larissa's towers are all deserted on that day, for the Pharsalian home where high festival and a goodly solemnity is kept. A lively description follows of the country and its occupations given over to complete rest and keeping holiday; and this is seemingly introduced by way of contrast to the stir and splendour and gorgeous preparations within the halls of Peleus. But the poet without delay presses on to one of his grand effects of description—the rich bridal couch, with frame of ivory and coverlet of sea-purples, on which was wrought the tale of Ariadne's desertion by Theseus. She has just awakened to her loss, and the picture is one of passionate fancy and force. To give a transcript of this is impossible; and though Mr. Martin's handling of the whole passage is admirably finished, yet where the best comes far short of the original, it seems justifiable to introduce a distillation of its spirit, without attempting metrical likeness. The following version is by the Rev. A. C. Auchmuty ["**Poem LXIX**," vv. 52-75]:—

> There, upon Dia's ever-echoing shore,
> Sweet Ariadne stood, in fond dismay,
> With wild eyes watching the swift fleet, that bore
>   Her loved one far away.
> And still she gazed incredulous; and still,
> Like one awaking from beguiling sleep,
> Found herself standing on the beachy hill,
>   Left there alone to weep.
> But the quick oars upon the waters flashed,
> And Theseus fled, and not a thought behind
> He left; but all his promises were dashed
>   Into the wandering wind.
> Far off she strains her melancholy eyes;
> And like a Maenad sculptured there in stone
> *Stands as in act to shout,* for she espies
>   Him she once called her own
> Dark waves of care swayed o'er her tender soul
> The fine-wove turban from her golden hair
> Had fallen; the light robe no longer stole
>   Over her bosom bare.
> Loose dropped the well-wrought girdle from her breast,
> That wildly struggled to be free: they lay
> About her feet, and many a briny crest
>   Kissed them in careless play.
> But nought she reeked of turban then, and nought

Of silken garments flowing gracefully.
O Theseus! far away in heart and thought
   And soul, she hung on thee!
Ay me! that hour did cruel love prepare
A never-ending thread of wildering woe
And twining round that heart rude briars of
 care,
   Bade them take root and grow;
What time, from old Piraeus' curved strand
A ship put forth towards the south to bring
Chivalrous-hearted Theseus to the land
   Of the unrighteous king.

A comparison of the above with the Latin text will show that, as in the italicised passages, the translator has been careful to preserve, as much as might be, the expressions, metaphors, and similes of the author. That author proceeds from this point to explain the causes of Theseus's visit to the home of Minos, and to unfold the legend of the monster, the labyrinth, the clue to it supplied by Ariadne, and the treachery of Theseus, who, when he had vanquished the monster, and led the princess to give up all for him, forsook her as she lay asleep in Dia's sea-girt isle. The lament of Ariadne on discovering her desolation is a triumph of true poetic art in its accommodation of the measure to the matter in hand; the change from calm description to rapid movement and utterance, as, climbing mountain-top, or rushing forth to face the surges upplashing over the bench to meet her, she utters outbursts of agony and passion intended to form a consummate contrast to the ideal happiness of them on whose coverlet this pathetic story was broidered. Two stanzas from Martin's beautiful and ballad-like version must represent tile touching character of this lament, in which, by the way, are several turns of thought and expression which Virgil seems to have had in mind for the 4th Book of the 'Æneis':—

Lost, lost! where shall I turn me? Oh, ye
 pleasant hills of home,
How shall I fly to thee across this gulf of
 angry foam?
How meet my father's gaze, a thing so doubly
 steeped in guilt,
The leman of a lover, who a brother's blood
 kind spilt?

A lover! gods! a lover! And alone he cleaves
 the deep,
And leaves me here to perish on this savage
 ocean steep.
No hope, no succour, no escape! None, none
 to hear my prayer!
All dark, and drear, and desolate; and death,
 death everywhere!
      —(C. lxiv. vv. 177-187.)

The lines in which she declares that, had Ægeus ob-

jected to her for a daughter-in-law, she would have been his to spread his couch and lave his feet, have more than one echo in English poetry; and the climax of the lament, in a deep and sweeping curse on her betrayer, is a passage of terribly realistic earnestness:—

Yet ere these sad and streaming eyes on earth
 have looked their last,
Or ere this heart has ceased to heat, I to the
 gods will cast
One burning prayer for vengeance on the man
 who foully broke
The vows which, pledged in their dread
 names, in my fond ear he spoke.

Come, ye that wreak on man his guilt with
 retribution dire,
Ye maids, whose snake-wreathed brows
 bespeak your bosom's vengeful ire!
Come ye, and hearken to the curse which I, of
 sense forlorn,
Hurl from the ruins of a heart with mighty
 anguish torn!

Though there be fury in my words, and
 madness in my brain,
Let not my cry of woe and wrong assail your
 ears in vain!
Urge the false heart that left me here still on
 with headlong chase,
From ill to worse, till Theseus curse himself
 and all his race!
         —M.

It is not to be denied that it would have been more artistic had the poet here dismissed the legend of Theseus and his misdemeanors, or, if not this, had he at least omitted the lesson of divine retribution conveyed in his sire's death as he crossed the home threshold, and contented himself with the spirited presentment of Bacchus and his attendant Satyrs and Sileni in quest of Ariadne, on another compartment of the coverlet. So far, the reader of the poem has represented one of the crowd gazing at the triumphs of needlework and tapestry in the bridal chambers. Now, place must be made for the divine and heroic guests, and their wedding-presents: Chiron, with the choicest meadow, alpine, and aquatic flowers of his land of meadows, rocks, and rivers; Peneius, with beech, bay, plane, and cypress— to plant for shade and verdure in front of the palace; Prometheus, still scarred with the jutting crags of his rocky prison; and all the gods and goddesses, save only Phoebus and his twin sister, absent from some cause of grudge which we know not, but which the researches of Alexandrine mythologists no doubt supplied to the poet. Anon, when the divine guests are seated at the groaning tables, the weird and age-withered Parcae, as they spin the threads of destiny, in shrill strong voices pour forth an alternating song with apt and mystic refrain, prophetic of the bliss that shall follow this union, and the glory to be achieved in its offspring. Here are two quatrains for a sample, relating to Achilles the offspring of the union:—

> His peerless valour and his glorious deeds
> Shall mothers o'er their stricken sons confess,
> As smit with feeble hand each bosom bleeds,
> And dust distains each grey dishevelled tress.
>
> Run, spindles, run, and trail the fateful
>   threads.
>
> For as the reaper mows the thickset ears,
> In golden corn-lands 'neath a burning sun,
> E'en so, behold, Pelides' falchion shears
> The life of Troy, and swift its course is run.
>
> Run, spindles, run, and trail the fateful
>   threads.
>
>   —D.

At the close of this chant of the fatal sisters, Catullus draws a happy picture, such as Hesiod had drawn before him, of the blissful and innocent age when the gods walked on earth, and mixed with men as friend with friend, before the advent of the iron age, when sin and death broke up family ties, and so disgusted the minds of the just Immortals that thenceforth there was no longer any "open vision"—

> Hence from earth's daylight gods their forms
>   refrain,
> Nor longer men's abodes to visit deign.

It is by no means so easy to give any adequate idea of the **"Atys,"** which is incomparably tile most remarkable poem of Catullus in point of metrical effects, of flow and ebb of passion, and of intensely real and heart-studied pathos. The subject, however, is one which, despite the praises Gibbon and others have bestowed on Catullus's handling of it, is unmeet for presentment *in extenso* before English readers. The sensible and correctly judging Dunlop did not err in his remark that a fable, unexampled except in the various poems on the fate of Abelard, was somewhat unpromising and peculiar as a subject for poetry. In a metre named, from the priests of Cybele, Galliambic, Catullus represents—it may be from his experience and research in Asia Minor—the contrasts of enthusiasm and repentant dejection of one who, for the great goddess's sake, has become a victim of his own frenzy. A Greek youth, leaving home and parents for Phrygia, vows himself to the service and grove of Cybele, and, after terrible initiation, snatches up the musical instruments of the guild, and incites his fellow-votaries to the fanatical orgies. Wildly traversing woodlands and mountains, he falls asleep with exhaustion at the temple of his mistress, and awakes, after a night's repose,

to a sense of his rash deed and marred life. The complaint which ensues is unique in originality and pathos. "No other writer"—thus remarks Professor Sellar—"has presented so real an image of the frantic exultation and fierce self-sacrificing spirit of an inhuman fanaticism; and again, of the horror and sense of desolation which a natural man, and more especially a Greek or Roman, would feel in the midst of the wild and strange scenes described in the poem, and when restored to the consciousness of his voluntary bondage, and of the forfeiture of his country and parents and the free social, life of former days." The same writer acutely notes the contrast betwixt "the false excitement and noisy tumult of the evening and the terrible reality and blank despair of the morning," which, with "the pictorial environments," are the characteristic effects of this poem. In the original, no doubt these effects are enhanced by the singular impetuosity of the metre, which, it is well known, Mr. Tennyson, amongst others, has attempted to reproduce in his experiments upon classical metres. Such attempts can achieve only a fitful and limited success. English Galliambics can never, in the nature of things or measures, be popular. And even supposing the metre were more promising, it is undeniably against the dictates of good taste to make the revolting legend of Atys a familiar story to English readers of the ancient classics.

Curiosity, however, would dictate more acquaintance with **"Berenice's Lock of Hair,"** a poem sent, as has been already stated, by Catullus to Hortalus, and purporting to be the poet's translation of a court poem of his favourite model, the Alexandrian poet Callimachus. The metre of both is elegiac; but of the original only two brief fragments remain so brief, indeed, that they fail to test the faithfulness of the translator. The subject, it should seem, was the fate of a tress which Berenice, according to Egyptian tables of affinity the lawful wife and queen of Ptolemy Euergetes, king of Egypt, although she was his sister, dedicated to Venus Zephyritis as an offering for the safety of her liege lord upon an expedition to which he was summoned against the Assyrians, and, which sadly interfered with his honeymoon. On his return the vow was paid in due course: the lock, however, shortly disappeared from the temple; and thereupon Conon, the court astronomer (of whom Virgil speaks in his third eclogue as one of the two most famous mathematicians of his time), invented the flattering account that it had been changed into a constellation. So extravagant a compliment would naturally kindle the rivalry of the courtly and erudite Alexandrian poet; and the result was soon forthcoming in an elegiac poem, supposed to be addressed to her mistress by the new constellation itself, in explanation of her abduction. To judge by the fragments which are extant, Catullus appears to have paraphrased rather than closely translated the original of Callimachus, though how far he has improved upon or embellished his model it is of course impossible to say. In some degree this detracts from the interest of the poem—at any rate, when viewed in connection with the genius of Catullus. Still, it deserves a passing notice: for its art and ingenuity, as employed after Catullus's manner, in blending beauty and passion with truth and constancy. It is curious, too, for its suggestive hints for Pope's "Rape of the Lock." The strain of compliment is obviously more Alexandrian than Roman; and readers of Theocritus will be prepared for a good deal in the shape of excessive compliment to the Ptolemys. But even in the compliment and its extravagance there is a considerable charm; and it is by no means uninteresting to possess, through the medium of an accomplished Latin poet, our only traces of a court poem much admired in its day. If, after all, the reception of Berenice's hair among the constellations forming the group of seven stars in Leo's tail, by the Alexandrian astronomers, is a matter of some doubt, it is at least clear that Callimachus did his best to back up Conon's averment of it, and that it suited Catullus to second his assertion so effectually, that it has befallen his muse to transmit the poetic tradition. The argument of the poem may be summarised. The Lock tells how, after its dedication by Berenice, if she received her lord from the wars safe and sound, Conon discovered it a constellation in the firmament. He had returned victorious; the lock had been reft from its mistress's head with that resistless steel to which ere then far sturdier powers had succumbed—

> But what can stand against the might of steel?
> 'Twas that which made the proudest mountain
>   reel,
> Of all by Thia's radiant son surveyed,
> What time the Mede a new Ægean made,
> And hosts barbaric steered their galleys tall
> Through rifted Athos' adamantine wall.
> When things like these the power of steel
>   confess,
> What help or refuge for a woman's tress?
>   —(42-47.) M.

Need we suggest the parallel form Pope?—

> What time could spare from steel receives its
>   date,
> And monuments, like men, submit to fate.
> Steel could the labours of the gods destroy,
> And strike to dust the imperial towers of
>   Troy;
> Steel could the works of mortal pride
>   confound,
> And hew triumphal arches to the ground.
> What wonder then, fair nymph, thine hairs
>   should feel
> The conquering force of unresisted steel?

The tress proceeds to describe her passage through the air, and her eventual accession to the breast of Venus,

thence to be transferred to an assigned position among the stars. A high destination, as the poem makes Berenice's hair admit, yet one (and here adulation takes its finest flight) which it would cheerfully forego to beonce more lying on its mistress's head:—

> My state so glads me not, but I deplore
> I ne'er may grace my mistress's forehead
>   more,
> With whom consorting in her virgin bloom,
> I bathed in sweets, and quaffed the rich
>   perfume.

In conclusion, the personified and constelled lock, with a happy thought, claims a toll on all maids and matrons happy in their love and nuptials, of an onyx box of perfume on the attainment of each heart's desire; and this claim it extends, foremost and first, to its mistress. Yet even this is a poor compensation for the loss of its once far prouder position, to recover which, and play again on Berenice's queenly brow, it would be well content if all the stars in the firmament should clash in a blind and chaotic collision:—

> Grant this, and then Aquarius may
> Next to Orion blaze, and all the world
> Of starry orbs be into chaos whirled.
>   —M.

After a survey of the larger poems . . . it would be especially out of place to attempt the barest notice of all that remains—a few very scurrilous and indelicate epigrams, having for their object the violent attacking of Cæsar, Mamurra, Gellius, and other less notable names obnoxious to our poet. By far the most part of these are so coarse, that, from their very nature, they are best left in their native language; and in this opinion we suspect we are supported by the best translators of Catullus, who deal with them sparingly and gingerly. Here and there, as in Epigram or Poem **"84,"** Catullus quits this uninviting vein for one of *purer* satire in every sense, the sting of it being of philological interest. Arrius, its subject; like some of our own countrymen, seems to have sought to atone for clipping his h's by an equally ill-judged principle of compensation. He used the aspirate where it was wrong as well as where it was right. The authors of a recent volume already alluded to—'Lays from Latin Lyres'—have so expressed the spirit and flavour of Catullus's six couplets on this Arrius, that their version nay well stand for a sample of one of the most amusing and least offensive of his skits of this nature. It is, of course, something in the nature of a parody:—

> Whenever 'Arry tried to sound
> An H, his care was unavailing;
> He always spoke of 'orse and 'ound,
> And all his kinsfolk had that failing.

Peace to our ears. He went from home;
But tidings came that grieved us bitterly
That 'Arry, while he stayed at Rome,
Enjoyed his 'oliday in Hitaly.

And so we bid adieu to a poet who, with all his faults, has the highest claims upon us as a bard of nature and passion, and who was beyond question the first and greatest lyric poet of Italy.

Arthur Leslie Wheeler (essay date 1934)

SOURCE: "The Elegies," in *Catullus and the Traditions of Ancient Poetry,* University of California Press, 1934, pp. 153-82.

[*In the essay below, Wheeler demonstrates that Catullus was a pioneer and signal influence in the genre of the classical elegy.*]

In elegy the Romans achieved one of their greatest literary successes. Three quarters of a century after the death of Ovid, the last of the great Augustan elegists, Quintilian, a sober critic, comparing the Roman achievement with the Greek, briefly expresses his verdict in the words, *elegia . . . . Graecos provocamus,* "in elegy we challenge the Greeks." It is a verdict from which the modern critic, after studying all the remains of Greek and Roman elegy—and the material is abundant—is not likely to dissent. Undoubtedly the Romans possessed a remarkable gift for this kind of poetry, and even if we had before us today the entire product of all the Greeks and Romans, it is probable that we should still regard the elegy of the Augustan Age, with its four great names—Gallus, Tibullus, Propertius, and Ovid—as on the whole the acme of the *genre.*

Like all other kinds of Roman poetry, Augustan elegy is compounded of both Greek and Roman elements. Among the Greeks the *genre* had a very long development and they had brought it to the highest degree of perfection of which they were capable some two centuries before the Romans began to practice it. The first Roman elegies appear in Catullus only a generation earlier than the most perfect example of the *genre* in the Augustan Age. Clearly if we would understand how it came about that the Romans achieved such perfection, it is necessary to study the elegies of Catullus, the pioneer.

But what was the general character of elegy in antiquity? We of modern times have inherited the term, but we have greatly restricted its meaning. Elegy is now defined as "a short poem of lamentation or regret, called forth by the decease of a beloved or revered person, or by a general sense of the pathos of mortality," or as "a song of grief . . . it can look forward to death as well

as back."

These definitions fit only one type of ancient elegy—an important type because, in accordance with the predominant ancient view, elegy was originally a lament; the word ἔλεγοι (Latin *elegi*), "couplets" or "an elegy," and the adjective ἐλεγεῖος from which came the noun ἐλεγεία (Latin *elegeia* or *elegia*), "an elegy" or "elegy" (the *genre*), were connected, perhaps rightly, with the noun ἔλεγος, a "lament." But if elegy was ever exclusively restricted to a content of mourning, sorrow, and consolation, it must have been at a period antedating the earliest extant examples of the *genre,* which occur in Archilochus and Callinus sometime between 700 and 650 B.C. The actual (and abundant) remains of elegy reveal no such restriction. On the contrary from the seventh century to the end of the Augustan Age the lament was at some periods rare and was never the most important type of elegy. In fact so; far as content and tone are concerned ancient elegy had an extremely wide range. But to an ancient nothing was elegy unless it was written in the elegiac couplet, which consisted, in the words of Diomedes, of a (dactylic) hexameter and a pentameter placed alternately. In English the movement of this meter is fairly well represented by Coleridge's translation of Schiller's couplet:

> In the hexameter rises the fountain's silvery
>   column,
> In the pentameter aye falling in melody back.

This meter was used by the ancients for such a wide range of themes that we may almost agree with Mackail that it was a meter "which would refuse nothing." But we cannot fully agree, for the couplet was regarded as a weaker, less dignified, metrical vehicle than the hexameter alone. The Greeks and Romans often called the pentameter "soft," "tender" . . . , peculiarly adapted to the theme of love. Ovid wittily illustrates this conception in the second poem of his *Amores.* He had begun a lofty epic, he says, and the second verse was equal in length to the first, for he was using the regulation epic meter, the hexameter. But Cupid, who was resolved that Ovid should be a love poet, stole a foot from the second verse, thus changing it into a pentameter, whereupon the poet in his tirade against the thief exclaims, "My fresh page began with a splendid first line, but that second line removed all my vigor!" And so perforce he had to sing of love in a meter better adapted to the subject.

Efforts to reproduce classical meters in English are rarely successful, although with the employment of extreme care in the choice of words and syllables some fairly good results can be attained. In English the pentameter is bound to be monotonous and tends 'to degenerate into a mere jingle. Tennyson, who was in the best sense an imitator of the classics, greatly admired the hexameter and the Alcaics of Horace, but he did not like the Sapphic stanza with the little Adonic at the end "like a pig with its tail tightly curled," as he expressed it, and for the pentameter he suggested the outrageous parody:

All men alike hate slops, particularly gruel.

The metrical form of ancient elegy was fixed; in modern elegy it is free. The themes of ancient elegy had a very wide range; in modern elegy they are rather closely limited. The ancient elegists put some curious subjects into elegiac form. For example, Nicander wrote on snakes, Archelaus on plants, Xenothemis on travel, and Ovid during the long years of his exile wrote nine books of elegiac verse, mostly letters to his friends in Rome. All these things were, from the ancient point of view, elegy, but they were bypaths, not the main highway. Anybody who will follow the course of elegy for more than six hundred and fifty years from Archilochus and Callinus to Ovid will be impressed by the great variety of its content and its purpose. He will be still more impressed by the fact that love, for the first three hundred years an infrequent theme, became important in the fourth and third centuries and dominant in the Augustan Age. From early Greek elegy—ending about 400 B.C. or somewhat later—we have remains of over thirty elegists, but only two, Mimnermus (*ca.* 600 B.C.) and Antimachus (*ca.* 400 and later) are really important as erotic elegists. During most of the fourth century the history of elegy cannot be followed; the remains are too meager. Toward 300 B.C., however, fragments become more numerous, so that we can form some conception, imperfect though it is, of the so-called Alexandrian elegy from Philetas and Callimachus, its acknowledged leaders, to Parthenius, sometimes called the last of the Alexandrians. Toward the end of this period Rome became the literary center of the world. Parthenius lived at Rome and his long life made him a contemporary of both Catullus and the Augustan poets. He was intimately associated with Gallus and Vergil, and he dedicated to the former a collection of mythological love stories in prose to be used, as he says, in the composition of epic and elegy. This little book is still extant, but the poetical work of Parthenius is in tatters.

This association in Rome of Greek writers composing in Greek with Romans composing in Latin is, I think, one of the most striking proofs of the continuity of Greek and Roman literature. Parthenius was only one of many. For nearly two hundred years there had been Greek men of letters residing in Rome. A long list of these Greeks is known, including in the second century B.C. such prominent names as Panaetius, the philosopher, and Polybius, the historian, who were members of the literary circle of the younger Scipio, the conqueror of Carthage, and in the first century besides Parthenius the epigrammatists Philodemus and Crinag-

oras. Cicero knew and befriended a number of Greek literary men, among whom the name of Archias is known (or used to be known!) to every schoolboy. The surviving work of Archias, however, does not measure up to the estimate which Cicero gives of his ability as a poet.

From these Greeks the Romans learned much and they learned to such good effect that by the Augustan Age they had wrested from them the supremacy in most departments of poetry which were being practiced at that time. They were freed at last from Greek leading strings although they did not wish to be freed from Greek influence.

Elegy was one of the greatest Roman successes, and although other themes were by no means excluded, it was to a very large extent erotic. In the Tibullus collection, for example, there are, excluding the little erotic epigrams, twenty-eight elegies of which twenty-two belong to the thorough-going erotic type, while in four others love is an important theme, and the non-erotic themes, such as love of country life, hatred of war, are often intimately connected with the erotic. In Propertius and Ovid there is greater variety, but love continues to be by far the most important theme. Gallus wrote four books of elegies of which only one line survives, but there is not the slightest doubt that they too were predominantly erotic.

It is not surprising then that when the ancient critics of this and later periods spoke of elegy they thought first of erotic elegy. Fine elegies were written on other themes, for example; the seventh of Tibullus' first book celebrating at once the Aquitanian triumph and the birthday of the great Messalla, or Propertius, III.18, mourning the untimely death of young Marcellus; but such elegies were outside the main current. And so we find that when in the first century of the Empire Quintilian alludes to elegy he has in mind primarily erotic elegy. In his famous canon of the elegists he characterizes Ovid as *lascivior,* "more wanton," a word which applies only to the erotic elegies of that poet. Elsewhere he remarks that elegy is not suitable reading for schoolboys.

At the outset we must distinguish two main groups of erotic elegies: (1) those in which the poet deals with his own love; (2) those in which he deals with the love of others—friends, mythological characters, etc. The first variety is often called by the clumsy but expressive name subjective-erotic elegy, and it is by far the more important because here the Romans are probably most original, certainly at their best. If we are to determine what contributions Catullus made to elegy it will be well to bear in mind what were the salient characteristics of this type in the period of its highest development. And so it is worth while to attempt a definition or concise description of the Augustan erotic elegy. In the sphere of poetry, definitions are never very satisfactory, but the attempt to define may serve to clarify our ideas.

A subjective-erotic elegy was a poem of considerable length, usually addressed to an individual or to readers, in which the poet communicates the thoughts and feelings which are suggested by some experience or aspect of his own love. It is usually serious or sad, but on occasion it may be joyous or even gay. Humor and wit are not excluded. It may be gracefully familiar, but it is rarely comic or vulgar, for it possesses a certain dignity of tone and style. Some comments will make this definition clearer. The length of such an elegy may vary between some sixteen lines (Propertius, II.31) and one hundred and sixty (Catullus, "LXVIII"). The average is between fifty and sixty lines. Longer pieces are found among Ovid's *Heroides* or *Tristia* and of course in the three books of his *Ars amatoria,* but these are not of the subjective-erotic type and I have excluded them. When a composition is very short it tends to pass into the field of the epigram, as, for example, Propertius, I.21 or 22 (10 lines) or Tibullus, IV.14 (4 lines). This point will be considered later. Ordinarily, however, there is no difficulty in distinguishing an elegy from an epigram.

The address, which had been a common feature of elegy from the earliest times, is ordinarily to the loved one or to friends (*sodales, amici*) of the poet, less often to patrons—Messalla, Maecenas, etc. Sometimes no name is used and we have a mere *amici* or *vos* or an address to readers generally. This feature is not confined to elegy; it occurs in many other forms—lyric, satire, etc., but it is a noteworthy characteristic of elegy—part of its intimate nature.

The course of true love never did run smooth—it would not be very interesting if it did—and so the tone of elegy is usually serious or sad. Exultation there is, but gloom and despair are far more common. Sometimes there are flashes of humor, as in Tibullus, or of wit, as in Ovid. But Ovid's excessive display of gaiety and wit show that in him the elegy is already beginning to decline.

The general dignity of this type of Augustan elegy is striking. The poet-lover maintains in general a gallant, romantic, almost a chivalrous attitude which lifts this love poetry far above most of the stuff which the Greeks, so far as we know, produced. In the last analysis this tone is due to the general attitude of the Roman toward the Roman woman, whose position was superior to that held by woman among the Greeks. With this attitude the style of elegy conforms; there is a general decency, not to say nobility of language.

Elegy, says Reitzenstein, speaking of the earlier Greek period, is "talk." Solon, for example, talks to his audi-

ence. This is much more true of Roman elegy. It is *sermo,* often very much like the *sermones,* the "talks," of Horace, except that its style is more dignified, and it deals for the most part with different themes. The elegist like the satirist often thinks or reflects out loud. This produces a loose quasi-extemporaneous structure, and logic often goes by the board. It is as if the reader received only those impressions of the poet's mood which happen to become oral.

There is an endless variety in human love affairs and the novelists of our day have by no means exhausted them. If you survey the whole range of Roman elegy you will find that these ancient poets made a very fair beginning and many a passage in the modern novel, particularly if the story happens to be told in the first person, need only be translated into Latin elegiacs to become a good Roman elegy. I have noted such passages all the way from Henry Fielding to Arnold Bennett. But of course there is an enormous difference in the impression of sincerity produced by a Roman elegist pouring forth his own sentiments about his own passion and the impression produced by a modern novelist presenting the sentiments of a character—the same difference which exists between Tibullus' subjective-erotic elegies and those pretty pieces in the fourth book in which he deals with the love affair of Sulpicia and Cerinthus, or between these same pretty pieces and their sources, the startlingly sincere little elegiac letters of Sulpicia herself.

The best Roman elegies create the impression of reality and sincerity. The heroine is real flesh and blood and the poet's moods and sentiments have a real basis. At times he displays a bit of humor but for the most part he is in dead earnest. We must not forget this when we read one of those humorous summaries of the elegiac love story which it is easy for the observant bystander to compose. The scoffing bystander is indeed a character in Roman elegy, for the elegists, especially Propertius, were quite aware that their preoccupation with love was in the eyes of the average Roman folly and worthlessness (*nequitia*). This confession renders the picture of their slavery all the more convincing. The true elegist is the slave of love and he cannot help it, and it is precisely because Ovid was in reality a witty bystander that he is not so good an elegist as Tibullus and Propertius.

If you will bear in mind the importance of love to the elegist himself, it will do no harm to read the outline of a typical affair composed by one who saw at once its pathos and its humor—the late Kirby Smith.

> The bacillus amatorius generally penetrates the poet by way of his eyes, and the period of incubation is ridiculously short. Among the first symptoms one of the most notable is an utter inability to sleep. It

is useless to struggle. The arrows of Dan Cupid are unerring and burn to the bone. His victim is an ox at the plow, and the worst is yet to come; he is a soldier detailed for special service, always leading the forlorn hope. To overcome the girl's disdain is only one of his troubles. Frequently there is a selfish and tactless "husband" in the way. Then follow all the varieties, moods, and motives of an intrigue.

The emotional temperature is far above the danger point. Clothes torn, hair forcibly removed, faces scratched, black and blue spots—these are all marks of affection. As the observant Parmeno remarks—

in amore haec omnia insunt vitia: iniuriae,
suspiciones, inimicitiae, indutiae,
bellum, pax rursum, etc.

"A bitter-sweet passion at best," says Burton, after consulting all the books in and about Oxford—"dolentia delectabilis, hilare tormentum—fair, foul, and full of variation."

Jove's book for recording lovers' oaths is running water. And "la donna è mobile"—her promises are sport for the winds and seas. The poet is always poor. His mistress however is not only a pearl, but a pearl of price. He promises her immortality in his verses; she is more concerned about her immediate future in this life. He learns as did the Abbé Voisenon that—

Sans dépenser
C'est en vain qu'on espère
De s'avancer
Au pays de Cythère.

He is therefore the natural enemy of wealth, greed, and present-day luxury. His ideal is the Golden Age, when men were so happy and so poor. He takes no part in politics, is not ambitious to get on in affairs; war is as unpopular with him as seafaring and similar short cuts to death. He observes omens, frequently consults witch-wives and Thessalian moon specialists, and generally makes them responsible for the sins of his mistress. She herself has a decided leaning for ritualism. She is devoted to Isis and sows dissension by her periodical attacks of going into retreat.

She is earnestly advised not to mar her great natural beauty by artificial means. In the course of the affair she never fails to have an illness. The poet nurses her and afterwards writes a poem about it. He too falls ill. Maybe he is going to die. If so, will she see to it that the following directions with regard to his funeral are carried out?

Like Anakreon he must love, and is made to sing of love alone. To expect him to write epic is quite out

of the question. Indeed the gods themselves sometimes serve notice on him to that effect.

Such then in outline was the most important type of elegy at the height of its development in the Augustan Age. Its chief basis was life and experience, but the poets were trained artists and they drew freely on all kinds of literature, Greek and Roman, which could help them in the artistic presentation of their love. They did not limit themselves to elegy but made use of epic, lyric, epigram, Greek New Comedy, bucolic poetry, and even prose—remember, for example, the little prose book of love stories which Parthenius dedicated to Gallus "for use in epic and in elegy." Whatever useful material they found they poured into the form of elegy, each poet of course modifying it to suit his own purpose.

Now the most important feature of this elegy is the fact that the poet employs all his material, whether he drew it from life or from literature, in the presentation of his own love. He depicts the varying aspects of his love at length; he dwells on them. He causes the reader to grasp the elements which enter into his varying moods. Often he is highly lyric, often he narrates, describes or illustrates, still more often he reflects, as it were, out loud. Many details of this elegy have been traced to ultimate sources in Greek literature, but the whole—the developed treatment by a poet of his own love—has no counterpart there, even in elegy. If any Greek elegist wrote poems of this kind, they have not survived.

From the point of view of literary history we have here a question which has divided scholars into two camps. The Alexandrian elegists, Philetas and Callimachus, were greatly admired by Catullus, Propertius, and Ovid, and the last two often acknowledge a debt to them. Although Tibullus names no Greek poet, his obligation to the Greeks is none the less clear. Philetas is said to have written some kind of poetry concerning a sweetheart Bittis, but the few fragments of his work allow us to form no conception of it. Callimachus is called by Quintilian the leader of elegy (*princeps elegiac*). He wrote many elegies of which we have fairly numerous fragments—one of eighty-odd lines—together with the Latin translation of a complete elegy by Catullus, but no sweetheart's name is mentioned in connection with him, and all his elegies seem to have been of the etiological variety, narrative poems in which it would have been very difficult to insert passages about his own love. In fact neither the fragments of Alexandrian elegy nor the numerous statements by Greek and Roman writers about it prove that any of these Greek poets composed elegies of the Roman type. And yet many scholars have believed that subjective-erotic elegies were composed by the Alexandrian poets and that the Romans found in them direct models which they adapted to their own situations. These scholars believe that the Greek elegists utilized the new comedy, lyric, epic, epigram, etc., and that the presence in Roman elegy of motive traceable to these *genres* is best explained on their assumption. When, for example, Propertius and Ovid pose as experts in the art of love, it has been asserted that they did not get the idea directly from the New Comedy where it was first developed, but from some Greek elegist who had used the New Comedy.

The work of Catullus throws considerable light, in my opinion, on this central problem of elegy and I shall keep it in mind throughout the following discussion. Catullus was not generally thought of as an elegist, for he wrote few poems of this kind. Moreover, his fame as a writer of the very short types of poetry was so great that men were prone to forget the rest of his work. In the Augustan Age Propertius alone connects him with elegy, placing him with Varro of Atax at the head of his fist of Roman elegists. Varro was a contemporary of Catullus but he did not turn to elegy until he had completed a long epic on the Argonauts and so it is probable that Catullus is to be regarded as actually the first Roman elegist. Certainly as a poet he ranked far above Varro.

We have from Catullus only five elegies (including the translation from Callimachus): **"LXV-LXVIII,"** and **"LXXVI"**—a total of 402 lines. Two of these (**"LXV,"** **"LXVIII"**) can be dated *ca.* 59 B.C. In 59 B.C. Gallus was a boy of nine or ten, and Tibullus and Propertius began to write nearly thirty years later, about 31-30 B.C. Ovid began to make public his *Amores* about 25 B.C. In round numbers a period of about seventy-five years—from the earliest datable work of Catullus to the death of Ovid, 17 A.D.—will include the beginning, the perfection, and the decline of the best Roman elegy.

When we compare the work of Catullus with Augustan elegy, we see at once that the Augustans developed the *genre* in many ways. What part Gallus took in this development it is impossible to say since his four books of elegies are lost, but his contribution was certainly important and, since he died 26 B.C. and had for some time been actively engaged in affairs, his work was probably completed before Tibullus and Propertius began to write. At any rate even the earliest elegies of the last two poets are finished products. It is with their work and that of Ovid that we must compare the elegies of Catullus. To what extent did he anticipate them in content and in form? What was his conception of elegy and how did it influence the Augustans? And, finally, what elements of Greek elegy did Catullus make his own? These are some of the questions which I shall try to answer and the result will enable us to define the position in this department of Catullus himself. He is a much more important figure, I am convinced, than most scholars have believed him to be,

and even the few who have recognized in him the founder of Roman elegy have not given an adequate account of his contributions to the development of the *genre.*

Meter is too technical a subject to be fully discussed here, but perhaps I can make one or two points clear. The first Roman to employ the elegiac couplet was, so far as we know, Ennius, over one hundred years earlier than Catullus. He did not write elegy, but, as we have had occasion to note again and again, the couplet was the favorite meter of epigram and in tracing the history of the meter all occurrences of it must be included. The hexameter and pentameter were adapted from the Greek and they were difficult for the Romans because their movement is dactylic (- / /) and for this the Latin language was not by nature well suited; it had too many long vowels and syllables, not enough words and combinations of two short syllables. Moreover the Latin accent had a strong element of stress which had to be reckoned with in working out a verse agreeable to the ear. From the metrical point of view Roman poetry is a curious phenomenon. Almost every one of the meters was taken over from the Greek, which had a so-called musical accent, into a language whose accent was to a large extent one of stress. It was a transfer from one medium into another in which the original elements were not present in the same degree or the same proportions. Necessarily the results were different in kind. The Roman poets strove to compose verses which to their ears reproduced the movement of the Greek originals. The results could only be approximate since the media were different.

And so generation after generation of Roman poets contributed to the development of this meter. As we follow the history of the meters from the third century B.C. to the Augustan Age, they become more and more perfect in form. In fact the Romans rather overdid the thing and developed ideals of perfection unknown to the Greeks or at least unpracticed except as *tours de force.* To my taste the meters of Horace's odes are too perfect. They sacrifice freedom for a perfection of form which incurs the risk of artificiality.

The history of the elegiac couplet follows the usual course, and it is to a large extent a struggle to secure a dactylic movement. In this Ovid was the first Roman to succeed. The verses of Catullus are heavy with spondees. In other respects also the Augustan poets produced lighter, smoother, more flexible verses. They have fewer and less harsh elisions and they were far more successful in adapting the word order, the syntax, and the sense to the meter.

Yet we must remember that all the poets who wrote elegiac couplets were trying to perfect the meter and that the Augustans could not have succeeded in their achievement without the work of a long line of predecessors among whom Catullus was foremost. We may, I think, go a step farther. Catullus, with all his metrical skill, was unable to perfect the couplet. He came too early. But if we compare his work with that of the earlier centuries (Greek and Roman) on the one hand, and with that of the Augustan Age on the other, we see that if he could have carried out his ideas with the requisite technical skill, his couplets would have reached a perfection different from that of Tibullus and especially of Ovid whose couplets are usually regarded as the norm. His successors followed a number of the principles which he had laid down, others they rejected, and they developed some new things, notably the "Law of the Distich," in accordance with which each distich or couplet became more or less a unit of thought. Neither the Greeks nor Catullus observed this last principle and I doubt whether it was a real improvement. The same may be said of the strong Augustan tendency to end the pentameter with a word of two syllables. Both these principles tend to make the verse schematic, monotonous. Catullus held more closely to the Greeks and as a result he strove to produce a freer couplet. The Augustans, although they had greater technical skill, restricted its freedom. It is all a matter of taste, but I agree with the greatest commentator on Catullus, Robinson Ellis, that a Vergil might have molded a better couplet than that of Ovid by following along the lines marked out by Catullus. Propertius indeed started to do this but later he went over to the camp of Ovid.

Thus Catullus helped to develop the metrical technique of elegy; but his chief contributions are of a different character. The first of these is his development of the epigram into an elegy. We have already noted that elegy and epigram run closely parallel courses in Greek and Latin. The favorite meter of epigram was the elegiac couplet and the themes were often the same as the themes of elegy. Almost all the extant collections of Roman elegies—Catullus, Tibullus, Propertius, Ovid's *Amores*—include epigrams, sometimes imbedded in an elegy. Many an elegy was in a sense an expanded epigram or, if you prefer, the same theme was worked up in both epigram and elegy. The difference was one of length and especially of treatment.

Ordinarily if we wish to study the difference between an elegy and an epigram on the same subject it is necessary to compare the work of two different poets. Excellent examples of this may be found in the fourth book of the Tibullus collection where some of the little epigrams of Sulpicia are worked up by a real poet presumably Tibullus himself, into elegies. In each case the elegy is three or four times the length of the epigram on which it is based. In Catullus however we have the unique opportunity of comparing an elegy with epigrams on the same situation all written by one

and the same poet. Moreover these poems all concern the poet's own love, and so they throw a great light on one way at least in which the most important type of elegy originated and developed.

The eighty fifth poem ["**Poem 85**"] consists of only two lines, but it is one of the unforgettable things of poetry:

> Odi et amo: quare id faciam fortasse requiris.
> nescio, sed fieri sentio et excrucior.

Hate and love—torture that I do not understand—a whole human life in a couplet, as Moritz Haupt said. But soon the poet begins to understand. In the seventy-fifth poem ["**Poem 75**"] the same situation is treated still epigrammatically, but a little more fully: "My heart has been brought to such a pass through your fault, Lesbia, and has suffered such ruin through its own devotion that I could no longer wish you well, should you become the best of women, nor cease to love you, no matter what you do." Here the hate—(in the tempered form of "not wishing her well") and the love persist, but there is more; there is the inability to cast the feelings aside, and above all there is some explanation: Lesbia's faithlessness (*culpa*) and the poet's devotion have caused his conflicting passions. The poet has begun to reflect. He has taken the first step toward that extended presentation of a situation and a mood which characterizes subjective-erotic elegy in its purest form. And in the seventy-sixth poem ["**Poem 76**"] we have the elegy. The situation is the same—the poet-lover convinced of the girl's faithlessness but unable to break the fetters of his love. The brief suggestions of the epigrams appear in expanded form: his devoted loyalty, her faithlessness, his persistent love and torture; the recognition that his own strength is so slight that he must appeal to the gods for pity and aid. There are many more finished poems in Latin and in Catullus, but none can approach this elegy in the gripping power and sincerity with which the torture of a human heart is laid bare. Propertius and Ovid have dealt with the same theme but their elegies are very inferior to that of Catullus.

Thus Catullus had begun to work into subjective-erotic elegy by way of epigram. In this he anticipates an important method of Augustan elegy. Before Catullus no Greek or Roman poet, so far as we know, had attempted it, but it would be rash to assume that the method as a method originated with Catullus.

The only other subjective-erotic elegy is the long sixty-eighth poem ["**Poem 68**"]. In this elegy Catullus combines three themes: his friendship for Allius, his grief for his brother's death, and his love for Lesbia. He had gone home to Verona crushed by his grief when his friend Allius, who was suffering from some misfortune in love, wrote to him requesting consolatory poetry. Catullus at first declares that his grief makes it impossible for him to write, and then suddenly he launches forth into a long poem of more than one hundred lines in which he mourns his brother and praises Allius for aid in his own love affair with Lesbia. As a whole the poem is a curious composition. Its structure, for example, is unique. The poet has three main themes: friendship, love, sorrow. He works through the friendship to the love and so to the sorrow and then back again in reverse order: sorrow, love, friendship. The structure may be represented by the letters A B C B A, and the parts also of each main theme are arranged with equal symmetry. As we read from the beginning to the central lines we may compare the poem to one of those nests of boxes cunningly wrought by some Chinese workman, the sorrow representing the core of the whole. Whether this highly artificial structure was suggested to Catullus by some lost Greek poem, or by the Pindaric ode, or whether he invented it himself, we do not know. To me it appears to be an extreme development of the old Homeric digression or the tale within the tale, but since it was never imitated it throws no light on the development of elegy and I need not discuss it here.

The three themes—grief, friendship, love—taken in the broadest sense all appear both in Greek and in Augustan elegy. Catullus' lament for his brother continues one of the oldest themes of elegy—perhaps, as we have seen, the original theme. But the other two themes stand on a different basis. They are closely connected with each other, and the friend (Allius) is thanked and praised for services connected with the poet's own love. Praise (encomium) as such is not uncommon in Greek elegy, but nowhere is it rendered for services in love. Catullus connects the encomiastic element with the subjective-erotic and in this also he anticipated Augustan elegy. Like Tibullus and Propertius he had begun to reflect in elegy the love affairs of himself and his friends, and the services for which he thanks Allius are of the same type as the services which Propertius, for example, promises to Gallus.

In the use to which he puts the story of Laodamia Catullus anticipates an important feature of Augustan elegy. He makes of the myth an illustration of his own love: Laodamia came to Protesilaus as Lesbia came to Catullus and her motive also was love. The Greeks— Theognis and Antimachus, for example—had begun this use of myth, but they had not developed it in the same way. In Augustan elegy however and especially in Propertius the phenomenon is so common as to require no illustration, but it is worth while to note that Propertius employed the same myth.

Another mythological parallel occurs in vv. 138-140 and suggests an interesting point. In this passage the poet compares his own forbearance toward Lesbia's flirtations with the attitude—enforced, to be sure—of

Juno toward Jupiter. Both the attitude and the manner in which it is expressed became common in Augustan elegy, but the Augustans developed them into the principle of complaisance (*obsequium*) and made it part of their didactic system. Catullus knows nothing of such a system.

I have referred above to the generally elevated tone and style of Augustan erotic elegy—one of its most striking characteristics. In this also Catullus led the way. He felt his love for Lesbia to be of the purest type like that of a father for his children. When he came to a full realization of her perfidy his epigrams and lyrics express hate and loathing in the most violent terms. Not so the elegies. In his elegies he preserves a certain decency and dignity. Lesbia possessed for him much more than physical charm. She was dearer to him than his life and he regarded their relation as bound by a compact like that of wedlock. Nothing is more significant of his conception of elegy than the style in which the erotic details are expressed. The sixty-eighth poem ["**LXVIII**"] contains many such details but they are clothed in language which does not endanger the dignity of the whole composition. Clearly Catullus felt that elegy should maintain a certain dignified level, and this is all the more striking because in the rest of his subjective-erotic work he follows no such principle. In addition to the principle itself every one of the details which I have mentioned can be paralleled in Augustan elegy. But I must pass on to other things.

The remaining elegies ("**LXV**"-"**LXVII**") do not represent the most important type, but they contribute a number of interesting points to our knowledge of Catullian elegy as a whole.

The sixty-seventh poem ["**LXVII**"], the tale of a bit of Veronese scandal, lies so far outside the general course of ancient elegy that I need not dwell long upon it. It has, however, two details of form which are interesting because they appear again in Augustan elegy. The story is told in dramatic dialogue between the poet and a house door. Speaking tombstones, statues, chaplets— even, as we shall see in a moment, locks of hair—are common enough in ancient poetry, but this is the first appearance of the device in elegy. Propertius continued it in the sixteenth elegy of his first book and he employs the dramatic dialogue also in the first poem of his fourth book. But the form was exceptional. When a character was made to speak, the instinct of the elegists was correct in choosing the informal method which allowed the poet also to speak and to comment at will. The dramatic dialogue was too rigid to suit the general character of elegy.

The sixty-sixth poem, the "**Tress of Berenice**" ["**LXVI**"], is a translation of Callimachus' [poem of the same name], a complimentary elegy of the etiological type. The Greek poet told how the queen vowed one of her tresses to the gods if her husband Ptolemy should return safely from war, and how the tress, as the astronomer Conon had professed to discover, became a constellation. This is the only complete elegy of Callimachus that has survived and in spite of the Latin form it throws a great deal of light upon the Greek poet's art as an elegist, for Catullus' translation is on the whole so faithful that we may rely on the Latin poem as representing the structure, the run of the thought, and the general character of the Greek, though not always the verbal details.

In the history of elegy the sixty-sixth poem contributes chiefly to our knowledge of Callimachus, not Catullus. But Catullus admired Callimachus; he must have seen something to admire in this elegy or else he would not have translated it. Since Callimachus was regarded by both Catullus and Propertius as the leader among Alexandrian elegists it is worth while to examine the sixty-sixth poem in order to determine what qualities appealed to Catullus. The answer is in short this: Catullus was interested chiefly in the poetic art with which Callimachus told a love story, the same art—the "modern" art—which is displayed in the long papyrus fragment of the great Alexandrian's *Cydippe,* his most famous elegy. Let us glance at some of the details.

The **"Tress of Berenice"** is a narrative elegy. The ostensible theme is the dedication and the deification or, if I may use such a term, the "starification" of the tress. But the erotic element, which is logically subordinate, becomes in the actual telling of the storymuch more important then the mere narrative theme. It is the love of Berenice for Ptolemy which prompts her to make and to carry out her vow, and it is love for Berenice which is the chief feeling of the Tress as she tells the story—for Callimachus makes of the tress a person and puts the whole tale into her mouth. This device is of the same kind as that employed by Catullus and Propertius when they personify the house door. Callimachus found in it a convenient means of complimenting the royal pair. The elegy is court poetry, but it has other aspects which are of much greater interest.

The elegy is full of learning, especially in the astronomical passages. Some of the allusions are so obscure that in spite of the labors of scholars they are not yet fully understood. Callimachus knew and his cultured readers understood him, but we do not wonder that in later times his elegies proved to be so difficult that they were called the "exercising ground of the grammarians." Catullus and the other *docti poetae* were attracted by this idea of inserting bits of learning into poetry. More important is the manner in which it was done. Often there was just an allusion; the reader was expected to know the rest, as when Callimachus just alludes (5-6) to the tale of Endymion. If such a tale did not happen to be well known, obscurity might result, but the poets were at no pains to be clear. It was a

method widely practiced by the well trained Roman poets and they learned it from Callimachus and other later Greeks.

Still more important is the way in which the erotic element is managed. Berenice's feelings as she parts weeping from her husband are analyzed—in fact the feelings of brides in general are analyzed—by a series of insinuating questions and answers (15-32) which prove that her acts are due to love. The passage is worthy of Ovid. Berenice becomes one of those heroines who, like the Arethusa of Propertius, are forced to part from their lovers. All the details are familiar to readers of Augustan elegy—the tears, the vow, the longing for the lover's return, the parting words, although Callimachus spares us the actual speech.

Similarly the feelings of the Tress are emphasized— her unwillingness to leave Berenice, her yearnings to be once more with the queen, her despair. These reflections of feeling are skilfully connected with the narrative, and the manner in which Callimachus passes from one to the other, dwelling rather on the feeling, is a marked characteristic of Roman elegy. It is part of the modern Greek method of telling a love story which is better illustrated in the *Cydippe* of Callimachus than anywhere else because there the poet is himself telling the tale, not, as in the **"Tress of Berenice,"** putting it into the mouth of a character. In the *Cydippe* also the narrative advances, as it were, by fits and starts. The poet breaks off to address himself and to reflect, he apostrophizes Acontius, gives his source for the story (Xenomedes), and expresses his own resolve. In a word, the personality of the poet is constantly felt—we might almost say intruded—in this modern fashion of telling a story. Many details of this technique appear also, as I have shown, in the short epic, the hexameter narrative. But in elegy the poets made of it something more natural, and as regards style more colloquial. What a world of difference there is between this intimate, modern way of telling a story and the old-fashioned style and how quickly it developed can best be seen by comparing the long fragment of Alexander of Aetolia (*ca.* 300 B.C.), in which the story of Antheus and Cleobeia is told, with the *Cydippe,* which must have been written hardly fifty years later.

Here then in the art of Callimachus we have the secret of his influence on Roman elegy. This alone is sufficient to explain why Catullus liked the **"Tress of Berenice,"** why Callimachus is mentioned much more often by Propertius and Ovid than any other Greek elegist. The Romans undoubtedly utilized the material they found in Callimachus, but their chief obligation was one of poetic craftsmanship. Callimachus wrote no subjective erotic elegies—he confined this content to his epigrams—but many details of the art which he employed in narrative elegy were easily transferred by the Romans to elegies and other forms in which they presented love. In this Catullus made a good beginning.

In a brief lecture it is impossible to present all the details or even all the classes of details which contribute to our estimate of Catullus as an elegist. I have omitted much—for example, all comment on the sixty-fifth poem ["LXV"]. But enough has been said, I think, to prove that Catullus in the department of elegy was a real pioneer laying the foundations and in many ways clearly indicating the lines which his successors were to follow. In elegy as in his other work he owed much to the Greeks, but his indebtedness, stated in general terms was an indebtedness of form, not content. The entire content of the sixty-seventh ["LXVII"] and seventy-sixth ["LXVI"] poems and the major parts of the sixty-fifth ["LXV"] and sixty-eighth ["LXVIII"] were derived from his own observation and experience. He learned from the Greeks not so much what to say as how to say it.

His own elegies are few—only four, if we exclude the translation of Callimachus—and yet they anticipate Augustan elegy in a surprising number of characteristics. By far the most important of these is the expression of the poet's own love, for this became the striking feature of Augustan elegy. It is quite possible that his services here were even more important than the meager extant evidence indicates that he was not only the first Roman poet, but the first poet, Greek or Roman, to enter this field. As one scans the long centuries of elegiac writing from Archilochus to Catullus, searching for the beginning or at least the elements of that modern, extended treatment by a poet of his own love which is the great achievement of the Augustan elegists, several tendencies seem to converge on Catullus. From the earliest times certain elements persist to the very end, for example the address to friend, or patron, or reader—a form not peculiar to elegy but nevertheless very characteristic of it—or the mythological parallel. Such elements may be called permanent traits of the *genre;* they pass from the early to the later Greeks, to Catullus, and so to the Augustans. I have amused myself by making a collection of these permanent traits. Among the themes of elegy the lament is such a trait; love for woman is another. But the mere mention of these reminds one that during the course of six hundred years such elements were subject to modification and development. Love of woman first appears as a theme of elegy in Mimnermus *ca.* 600 B.C., then in Antimachus *ca.* 400 B.C. or later, then in a number of elegists at the end of the fourth century and the beginning of the third—Philetas, Hermesianax, Alexander Aetolus—and finally in Callimachus and his successors who lead us on to Catullus and the Augustans in the first century. "Mimnermus burned with love for Nanno," says Hermesianax, a somewhat dubious authority, "inventing amid his woes the breath of the soft pentameter." Subjective-erotic, then, in elegy.

But how did Mimnermus deal with love; In almost eighty lines of fragments he touches on love: life is nothing without love; love is the tender flower of youth; let me die when love is no longer possible for me. Love and youth are the great blessings of humanity, old age and death are its evils. He generalizes; his attitude is that of the philosopher surveying human life and finding love an important element. There is nothing of that intimate personal treatment which characterizes the Roman elegy.

Antimachus also dealt with his own love. The nine broken lines which have survived from his poetry give no hint of his treatment, but we know something about It from the statements of other writers, especially Plutarch. He consoled himself (says Plutarch) for the loss of his wife Lyde by enumerating, in an elegy named after her, the unfortunate affairs of mythology. The *Lyde,* then, was a long composition in at least two books, chiefly narrative, not subjective; the myths, not the poet's love, were the main theme. It was a catalogue poem. Of its method we can form a good idea by reading the long fragments of Hermesianax and Phanocles who continued this form. All is objective narrative-story tacked on to the story by means of the old formulae "such as", "or as," etc. It is certain, I think, that these earlier elegists did not work out in detail the vicissitudes and moods of their own love, and I have already noted that in objective narrative the earlier manner persisted into the third century, when Philetas and Callimachus revolted against it Callimachus (and Catullus too) condemned Antimachus, and Callimachus at least knew how to tell the tale of another's love in modern fashion. His own love he restricts to epigram, in which probably Asclepiades had preceded him. And this brings me to the second point. When we search extant Greek poetry for traces of subjective-erotic we find it not in elegy, but in lyric and especially in epigram, forms which did not afford opportunity for the extended treatment which is characteristic of elegy. The epigram and the lyric have something more than the mere germs of it; there the situations, the moods, the sentiments are often the same as in elegy. But the Greeks did not develop the epigram into a true elegy. Just before and during the period of Catullus certainly they were still confining their subjective-erotic poetry to the short forms, witness Meleager, Philodemus, and others.

It is significant that the first attempts of the Romans in this kind of erotic—the attempts of Valerius Aedituus, Porcius Licinus, end: Lutatius Catulus, which I described in the third lecture—are also in epigram, and still more significant that Catullus continued the same type of epigram. But as we have just seen, he was the first, so far as we know, to develop such epigrams into elegies. We see him feeling his way from one *genre* into another, a *genre* that is richer in every way—a better medium for the expression of a poet's own erotic feeling. It seems to me that in Catullus we may discern the chief-type of elegy coming into existence. If, as many scholars have believed, the Greeks had written elegies of this type, it is difficult to understand why Catullus did not write more of them. They were an excellent form, as his two examples show, in which to express his love for Lesbia.

But Catullus did not choose to persist in elegy, and if such a course would have curtailed his other work, we may on the whole congratulate ourselves that he did not persist. The briefer and more, varied forms were better suited to his genius and he used them with a much more perfect technique than he displays in elegy. Nevertheless we must not allow the brilliance of these little jewels to obscure their author's importance in the field of elegy.

The Augustan specialists developed elegy in every way. They perfected its form and they greatly extended its scope. Elegiac erotic became a system in which countless situations, countless moods were reflected in whole cycles of poems and the poet lover posed as an erotic expert able to aid other lovers although he admits on occasion that he cannot aid himself. This system does not exist in Catullian elegy but many of its elements and much of the art with which it was presented are there. Like Catullus the Augustan elegists were expressing for the most part their own experiences and sentiments. Like him they utilized any suitable material which they found in any kind of Greek literature. They greatly extended the field in which such material could be found, turning, for example to Greek New Comedy and bucolic poetry which (in elegy) Catullus had not used. All these suggestions they poured into the elegiac mold. But, so far as the sources of elegy were bookish, the Augustans had an advantage over Catullus; in addition to the Greek writers they had at their disposal a group of artistic Roman poets among whom Catullus himself was foremost, whereas Catullus had found no stimulus in the art of his own Roman predecessors. In fact the Augustan elegists, not Horace or Vergil, were the real heirs of Catullus. They were stimulated not only by his elegies but by all parts of his work. But if we consider the influence of his elegy alone, it is fair to say that the Augustans achieved their success in this field by following the lead of Catullus.

E. A. Havelock (essay date 1939)

SOURCE: "Lyric and Liberty," in *The Lyric Genius of Catullus,* 1939. Reprint by Russell & Russell, 1967, pp. 161-84.

[*In the following essay, Havelock places Catullus within the context of his time, explaining the poetic tradition of which he was a part and his influence upon the Roman poetry of the classical age.*]

(i) The *Poetae Novi* and their Significance

Though Catullus is best understood in detachment from the rest of the Latin poets, he is no isolated freak. His poetry occupies indeed a peculiar and ambiguous position, exercising a powerful influence on the young Virgil, remembered grudgingly by Horace but gratefully by the elegists, imitated by Martial, discussed by Quintilian—yet among these not one shows any signs of catching or understanding the direct inspiration of his lyrics. This fact reveals something of the fate of Latin poetry. Two things in the history of Latin literature it is difficult to understand. The first is its decline. Poetry had exhausted its vigour when Juvenal died, yet the imperial system still had several centuries to run out. To the glaring contrast between the political effectiveness of that system, and the paucity of imaginative literature produced within it, recorded history offers no parallel. The loss of political liberty can scarcely be the explanation, for the Caesars did not and could not exercise dictatorship over their peoples in the manner of a totalitarian state. Daily life and local politics over most of the empire's vast area were comparatively free, and society was certainly secure enough during long periods to support a leisured and, one would have thought, a creative class. But while these conditions produced culture and scholarly writing, they did not create literature. Failure revealed itself in the lack of emotional content put into forms which rapidly became mechanical.

The second thing difficult to comprehend is the significance of what is known as the Alexandrian movement in Roman literature, led by Catullus and his contemporaries. This is generally represented as in the main a false move in the direction of artificial sources, the mannered verse, elaborate epics and learned allusions of Hellenistic grammarians. We have seen how little of such pedantry there is in Catullus. Not only in him, but in the fragments of his contemporaries, and in the record of them preserved by the next generation, lingers a strong flavour of originality and emotional vigour and spontaneity. However artificial they sometimes allowed themselves to be, surely it is Horace who thirty years later seems to resent the daring of his predecessors, deploring in the *Satires,* for example, the preference shown by Valerius Cato, once leader of the new movement, for the rough vigour of Lucilius, refusing anywhere to acknowledge his passionate contemporary Propertius, and exhorting the writers of Rome, in his *Ars Poetica,* to discipline emotions and trim them to suit the exact forms handed down from the past. Who in fact should stand convicted of formalism—the Alexandrians or some of the Augustans?

Each of these problems however—the curious status of the *poetae novi* and the later decline of Latin poetry—can be used to shed light on the other. There is I believe a connection between them, which can be appreciated only when the nature of the poetic revolution attempted by Catullus' school is appreciated also. The literary remains of that school, if we except Catullus, are as scanty as those of earlier Latin literature, and this, combined with the fact that we read the Latin writers as it were backwards, from the point of view of Horace and the Augustans, has obscured the entire perspective. To correct it I am going to offer a reinterpretation of Roman literary history. But by the very nature of the evidence it must remain a controversial and tentative hypothesis.

First let us remind ourselves of what seems to be the relation between matter and form in poetry. The first is the fruit of the poet's emotions. Unless these are powerful and sincere, he cannot write powerful verse. If they are, then they have to find expression in image-language and in rhythm; they have to attain form. Here it seems to be a law of poetry that the elements of form should be borrowed from tradition. It is as though the poet refused to concern himself directly with intellectual construction, and merely looked around for the readiest medium in which to express his feeling. But to be completely successful his instincts must guide him to choose such forms as will least impede his feeling with artificial effort. These having been chosen will in the process of use undergo some transformation at his hands; he will produce variations which constitute his own claim to originality. If we may guess at the poet's psychological process, his manipulation of form may be compared to the motions of driving a car. These, complicated and severe in their discipline, are nevertheless in the complete car driver performed in his unconscious, leaving the conscious mind free to enjoy the scenery or emulate a rival's speed according to mental capacity. Such conscious activity corresponds to the play of feeling in the poet's mind, which summons from the unconscious an appropriate form of expression. If the relation is reversed, and the motions of driving or of poetic composition themselves remain conscious, they may be equally precise, but they will not be sustained as long, and the total process will lack verve and enjoyment.

With this rough analogy in mind, consider the course taken by the Roman poets. From the time when we first hear of them in the middle of the third century B.C., they are translating Greek epics, and adapting Greek plays, turning from the attempt to use native rhythms like the rough Saturnian, ignoring the stress accent of Latin, seeking to import Greek quantitative methods into Roman poetry. As for Italian lyric, we do not hear of it at all. The songs and ballads and rough spontaneous verse in which early Italy had presumably expressed its feelings survived neither in their original form, nor—and this is more important—as an influence on the first literary poets. From its recorded origins Roman literature marks an artificial attempt to imitate foreign tradition. The comic dramatists with

sound instinct used Greek models which were practically contemporary in their appeal; the epic writers did not even do this, but sought to revive in Latin a Greek epic style which in the passage of time had already become slightly archaic even among the Greeks. The general result was that Roman poetry completely missed that kind of direct feeling, which distinguishes Homer and the Greek lyrists and dramatists. It could not sing, just at that stage in its development when it was proper for it to sing. Moreover, the attempt to wrest Greek forms and metres to the uses of the Latin tongue produced, in the compromise between native and foreign, a roughness and clumsiness which the new poets of the first century instinctively disliked.

Rapid economic expansion, by greatly enlarging the leisured class in Italy in the first century B.C., created the soil from which sprang the 'neoterics', the new school of Latin poetry. They like their predecessors borrowed their forms from foreign tradition, though not, as we shall see, precisely the same tradition. But before this debt is considered, the first thing to realize is that the mainspring of the movement was an emotional release, which produced at last in the Roman breast a direct spontaneous sort of personal feeling which poets desired to express in verse. Without this emotional inspiration, the movement becomes inexplicable. Why were its leaders nearly all from Cisalpine Gaul? The list is impressive: Valerius Cato, the theorist who guided the movement, and his devoted disciple Furius Bibaculus, both of whom lived long enough to cross swords with Horace and the Augustans after their own star had set; Alfenus Varus, Quintilius Varus, Cornelius Nepos, Publius Varro of Atax, perhaps Cinna, and of course Catullus himself, besides a few others mentioned in his own verses, such as Caecilius and 'Volusius.' Calvus is the only prominent name among the neoterics which cannot be included in this list. Now, one might expect to find cultured learning and artificial mannerism overstressed at the capital, but scarcely in the provinces.

The movement however though emotionally powerful was not naive; it did not spring from the soil. It came too late in the history of the race for that. It represented, as we can see from Catullus himself, the most distinguished but a not untypical member of the school, a marriage between spontaneity and sophistication. These poets were capable of direct emotion, but urbanized, inspired pre-eminently by personal relationships, as illustrated, for example, by the various fragments in which they celebrate and attack each other and by the recurring references to similar exchanges in Catullus' own verse. Especially they felt the urge to translate sex-interest into poetry, a fact witnessed not only by Catullus' verse, but by those epyllia composed by the school whose titles survive. There was the *Lydia* of Valerius Cato, which perhaps celebrated his own mistress, and the famous *Smyrna* of Cinna, a study of passion, incestuous, it is true, but still for poetic purposes romantic. Calvus wrote a poem on the loves of Io and Jupiter, and then, coming nearer home, an elegy on his own wife's death, a landmark in Roman literature, which reveals the new and more romantic attitude now possible in marital relationships between men and women of the same class. Catullus (no. **"35"**) also mentions the *Cybele* of his friend Caecilius in terms which suggest that it was a work tinged with erotic feeling. In all this there is a flavour of feminism and of introspection; Catullus himself had to offer defence, as we have seen, against the charge of *mollities,* a charge which was apparently directed against his lyrics. As for his longer studies, every one of them concerns itself, directly or indirectly, with erotic themes—the marriage of Peleus and Thetis, the betrayal of Ariadne, the loves of Ptolemy and Berenice, the self-mutilation of Attis. The emotional atmosphere of the period can be compared to that of an earlier one which in Greece produced Alcaeus end: Sappho, a period equally leisured, sophisticated, and yet emotionally direct, a period when poetry dealt with personal and inner feeling, when poets exchanged verses and spoke often in the vocative.

And now we face the question which these new poets were forced to face for themselves. Where were they to look for the necessary forms in which to express these emotions—forms which, as I have said, are never invented overnight, but have to be borrowed and adapted from tradition. At once the fact confronts us that fate had denied them a native lyric tradition on which to build. It seems incredible. Catullus himself is a highly finished product requiring a literary ancestry, and yet, if we greet him as the first lyric voice of Rome, we must assume that his poetic ancestry was not Latin. Was the Latin tongue then so impoverished? Searching the record before him, we discern a few doubtful names like Aedituus, Licinus, Catulus, Matius and Laevius. These, on the strength of a few meagre fragments and notices, are presumed to have written short poems in the century preceding his birth, but the fragments reflect no native vigour, no soil and sun of Italy; rather they seem to be anticipating Catullus in the imitation of Hellenistic epigrams and light verse. The story of Roman poetry in fact stands on its head; it had produced a sophisticated sort of drama patterned on Greek models before producing a single song. What native song-tradition Italy may once have fostered had now long perished through neglect. So, just as Plautus, Terence and Ennius had turned to Greek models to inspire their drama and epic, the *poetae novi* were now forced to turn to Greek sources even for lyric, and thence borrowed their metrical patterns of eleven-syllables, iambics, glyconics and elegiacs, as well as the older sapphics and asclepiads in which Catullus made his few experiments. Thence too they borrowed the literary genres of epigram epyllion and hymn. The common denominator of all such poetry was its sub-

jectivity and emotionalism, that personal feeling which transformed even the old-fashioned epic form into 'little epics'. On Catullus and his school was therefore laid a double burden, of expressing feelings of affection, hate, joy or sorrow more direct and powerful than any Roman had cared to express in poetry before, and yet also of achieving a literary revolution in order to do this. In order to sing in Latin, Catullus and his contemporaries had to read Greek first, and if we fail to sympathize with their enormous task, that is because we judge them by the standards of their successors rather than of their predecessors.

But finally, what tradition was it that these new poets chose for their own inspiration? Deprived of a native source, they did the next best thing and chose one which was foreign but contemporary. The significance of this choice is completely obscured in modern histories. The instinct which led these poets to Alexandria was essentially sound, because Alexandrian literature was not an archeological curiosity, it was not 'classical,' it was alive and exciting and contemporary; it belonged to the same world. If one is to express vital emotion, the forms borrowed for it must somehow have an emotional meaning which is contemporary. A painter for example working in a foreign manner may create a new native standard, remoulding the influence he has caught. The actual foreign painters he imitated might be second-rate men; but they would be expressing an idiom which as we say is 'modern'. The past can provide 'higher', more classical standards. But for present creative purposes they are dead. A pre-Raphaelite movement will never succeed in conveying an archaic manner wholesale into a modem setting and make a success of it. Either the original mould is abandoned, or the result has to remain artificial.

The occasional verse, epigrams and idylls of Alexandria may all have been second-rate; they were Greek and foreign anyway. But they were still alive, still being written, when Catullus grew up. The Romans listened to the lectures of men who were writing these things, conversed in Greek with them at the table, felt the touch of contemporary enthusiasm for this or that poet—it had to be a Greek poet, for where was the native Roman poetry? So they joined cliques and praised or damned each other's work, reading Sappho and Sophocles a little, but thinking and writing and arguing in the prevailing mode of their teachers and their Greek friends, the foreigners they could still visit and admire. Though Callimachus was long dead, Philodemus for example was writing lovely verse in the tradition of Callimachus, and so were dozens more.

By contrast, the models provided by Homer, the Greek tragedians and the early Greek lyrists seemed to these new poets to be archaic, and I think that one of the reasons for this lay in the gradual shift in the pronunciation of Greek. By the time that the Alexandrian grammarians had to invent the accent marks to preserve the memory of the Greek pitch accent, we may guess that in common speech that pitch was already being extinguished. Instead of being sung like Chinese, the 'common Greek' in which for example the New Testament is written was being pronounced much more like any modern European tongue, with a stress accent. The rhythms however of hexameter, of the old Aeolic poets, and of Pindar were, we can assume, such as seemed natural and came readily to the ear only in a tongue which was sung in pitch. Once the pitch was dropped, iambic metres and metres close to iambic became necessary if emotion was not to be impeded by artificial structure. As I have earlier said of the eleven-syllables and iambic metres of Catullus, they managed to convey authentic lyric because they lent themselves to improvisation, which is as it were the necessary raw material of finished verse, supplied in the unconscious mind. But no poet of the Hellenistic period was able to improvise Sapphics, Alcaics or Asclepiads. This the instinct of the Alexandrian school had already recognized. It retained, it is true, the dactylic rhythms for epic and epigram and elegy, but even these made too severe a demand on the intellect of the poet. To sustain them in long poems without sacrificing emotional sincerity became increasingly difficult. This explains why only the short epigram retained emotional vitality, alongside the occasional lyrics, while epic, even when shortened to epyllion, could not lift itself above the level of mannered exercise; the metre itself had become too stilted: one cannot write sincerely in such artificial rhythm, unless one has the peculiar and indeed unique genius of a Virgil, who was content to let a line cost him a day's effort. In so far, therefore, as the *poetae novi* made: the eleven syllables and iambics their own they were being moved by a perfectly sound instinct to give the conversational accent of the Latin tongue its normal play in verse; they were seeking to undo the original error whereby accentual scansion had been dismissed, as too primitive, in favour of Greek quantities. The dactylic rhythm offered a stiffer problem) though even here Catullus managed to make the rhythm of his epigrams eminently conversational, if judged by Augustan standards of elegy. The fate however of these forms in Augustan hands we shall consider presently.

And apart altogether from metrical reasons, Hellenistic poetry gave the Romans a direct emotional contact with historical romance, for it brought the past down to the present, as the works of the earlier and greater poets, to whom the label 'classical' is often restricted, never could. We can summarize the situation by saying that however artificial were the products of the Alexandrian movement, it was not artificial for Romans to imitate them. An apt parallel is provided by the case of the Elizabethan poets. They too were children of a prosperous commercial age which increased the leisured class and also enlarged the historical horizon

through commercial expansion. They too fertilized their native inspiration by resorting to foreign sources and models, and so produced a new poetry. But these had to be the contemporary sources of renaissance Italy, which, though they were founded on the classical authors, were intrinsically inferior to them, just as the Alexandrians had been inferior to their own predecessors. But they had a living meaning for the sixteenth century, could be discussed in London taverns and read not as 'classical' but as exciting contemporary stuff designed to amuse, not instruct, just remote enough to be romantic, and sophisticated enough to provide forms and models and a style which, it was felt, English poetry needed at that time. The result, in Spenser and Sidney and Raleigh and a dozen lyrists, not to mention Shakespeare himself, was that same combination of learning and lyric, historical and geographic romance, wit and epigram, foreign and exotic forms blended with personal emotion, which distinguished the work of the *poetae novi.*

There happens to be extant a couplet composed by Furius Bibaculus in honour of Valerius Cato, the critic who led this lyric movement to Alexandria and schooled or inspired Roman poets to imitate Hellenistic verse:

> Cato grammaticus, Latina siren,
> Qui solus legit ac facit poetas—
>
> Dear master, who alone cost make
> Bards of the lads who to thee throng,
> Take these poor verses for my sake,
> Thou siren of the Latin tongue.

To those with a historical imagination, this testimony to the poetic leadership of a professor would seem, judged by any modern standards, to be at first sight incredible. But a little more imagination still may assist us to catch the note of emotional release in these lines, and to realize that here, in this praise of a scholar of Greek, a teacher of metre and form, is the voice of Roman lyric, denied any native traditional forms, thwarted in its expression, well-nigh strangled at its birth, yet finding a sudden miraculous and artificial release by resorting to Greek forms and trying to sing in them. It was a second best, but it served to create a body of verse which mirrored the emotions of a brief brilliant age. The verses and epigrams of Cato and Bibaculus, of Catullus, Calvus and Cinna, the little metrical romances so vividly conceived, yet so carefully executed in Greek colours, were forced hot-house plants, soon to die as such plants do, but while they lived they dazzled with a special sort of brilliance and alarm; and after Cornelius Gallus in the next generation had committed suicide, and Virgil had turned to the composition of official epic, the brilliance and the alarm were never recaptured.

Thus we have the lyrics of Catullus, emancipated by

Alexandrianism from the clumsiness and the ugliness of the Latin tradition, breathing, instead of its crude and musty atmosphere, a free air. The results are to be sampled in *Vivamus, mea Lesbia, atque amemus; Miser Catulle, desinas ineptire; Dicebas quondam solum te nosse Catullum;* and the marriage hymn . . . composed for Manlius and Vinia—

> Collis o Heliconii
> Cultor, Uraniae genus,
> Qui rapis teneram ad virum
> Virginem, o Hymenaee Hymen,
> O Hymen Hymenaee . . .

This vivid and alarming poem is a kind of example displaying all the paradoxical qualities which distinguished the school of *novi poetae* at their best. The metre is Greek, but its conversational rhythm does not flag for two hundred and thirty-five lines. The invocation to Hymen, the order of themes, the conclusion are formally Greek, yet completely fitted to the Roman marriage scene and to the poet's own spontaneous emotions. The Greek learning, the foreign history and geography, are there, but the allusions are light and swift and add romantic glamour to the native situation. The poem is closer to Shelley's lyrical mood than anything else that survives from antiquity.

To the next generation the neoterics thus left a threefold legacy; of naive emotional power, which found expression particularly in easy lyrical rhythms; of neat exact form, both of theme and metre; and a fondness for historical romance which issued in geographical and mythological allusion. The Augustans and their successors remembered the last two, and gradually forgot the first—as indeed modern scholarship has forgotten it—and this is the secret of those twin puzzles, the ambiguous position of the 'neoterics' in the eyes of Roman posterity, and the slow decline of Latin poetry. Not that the emotional legacy was at once forgotten. The young Virgil responded to it readily, not only in his occasional pieces, but in the *Eclogues* and above all in the great episode of Orpheus and Eurydice which closes the *Fourth Georgic.* This tale of romantic regions under the sea, of passionate love and tragic separation, is too rarely recognized for what it is—an example of what the epyllion could become in Latin when handled with emotional sincerity and sure taste. Constructed on the sort of mechanical plan perfected by Callimachus, of a plot within a plot within a plot, in the manner of Catullus' *Peleus and Thetis* and *Epistle to Allius,* it yet manages to combine romantic mystery, prettiness, passion and pathos in a kind of literary tapestry. Virgil never spoke again of love and death with the same direct feeling, and his contemporary Cornelius Gallus, who shared this romantic mood, did not live long enough to leave his impression on Latin poetry. Propertius too represents the same traditions of subjective emotion, but spontaneity has already begun

to abandon his slightly mannered verse. *Haec quoque lascivi cantarunt scripta Catulli* he says of his own productions: the graceful acknowledgment does not undo the fact that he is taking up an attitude towards himself as a professional love-poet. Thus he betrays that historical manner of the Augustans, which made them too conscious of themselves and their literary role, but produced as its finest and most typical products the *Aeneid,* the *Odes* of Horace and the studies in history and mythology undertaken by Ovid. These were all written in the old rhythms of Greece, which however close they had once been to the rhythms of common speech, had now in Latin to be treated as severe literary exercises, and accordingly were pruned with Alexandrian meticulousness. Such formal modes demanded a formalized content, and the result was the *Aeneid,* carefully planned, painfully written, some of it splendid, but half of it dead; the *Odes* of Horace, imitations of the old Aeolic measures more exact than the original, with skittish eroticism or moral commonplace for content; the *Metamorphoses* and elegies of Ovid, fluent, elegant and unemotional, or else morbid.

Sheer form has scarcely been seen again practiced to such exquisite degree, but poetry paid the price. Such of the emotional inheritance left from the neoteric creed as lingered on was unacknowledged for the most part, and by Horace definitely disparaged. It was not the emphasis on careful form that he could deplore in his immediate predecessors. What he instinctively feared and disliked in them was their enthusiasm, their extravagance, so often productive of mistakes and absurdities which his cautious mind could satirize, but nevertheless to be recognized by the more sympathetic as 'the real thing'. Thus it was that the poetic instincts of Valerius Cato, the surviving champion of the neoterics, supported Lucilius' vigour and verve against Horace's cautious style, and incurred Horace's hostility for it. Thus it was that Horace on the contrary strove in the *Ars Poetica* to excise the emotional purple patch from Latin literature. His condemnation of it if applied to particular cases might be technically correct, and yet his general emphasis was disastrous. 'If, as we read in Mimnermus', he says contemptuously in the *Epistles,* 'there is no pleasure without love and laughter, then try living on love and laughter' It is a safe guess that the emotionalism in Propertius repelled him, for he never mentions him. Meanwhile Furius Bibaculus and one or two more tried to continue for a time the previous tradition, writing lyrics and lampoons and championing Valerius Cato. Such productions may well have looked clumsy beside Horace's deft craftsmanship. But they had a germ of growth and progress in them if they had been developed by successors, and Horace's work had not. Hence he also gives in the *Ars Poetica* that disastrous advice, uncritically swallowed by modern literary historians, to stick to classical lyrical rhythms, those tested by antiquity, and use each for its appropriate material. Such advice reveals the enormous gulf between Horace and the true lyric temper, which, as we can see in Catullus, not only chose rhythms without regard to their antiquity, but twisted them to serve new and more serious moods. Horace followed his own advice only too well, turning his back on what seemed the frivolous occasional verse of his day, imposing his own standards as the true standards of Latin lyric and thereby assisting in the gradual extinction of Latin poetry.

For Roman poetry unhappily continued to follow in the footsteps of the Augustans in every essential respect. Neglect of native lyric by the earliest writers had shorn it of Italian inspiration. In the neoteric school it had sought to find a substitute in a foreign but vital tradition. Then it gave it up and having in the Augustan period reverted to classicism remained stuck there. For some centuries poetry was now exalted—so it seemed—to the status of a cultured exercise in Greek classical quantities and forms. It produced one more powerful writer in Juvenal, but his secret is his rhetoric, essentially a prosaic gift. Lyric emotion fumbled for expression in Statius, and did not kind it. 'Culture' is fatal to authentic lyric, and occasional verse, like Hadrian's address to his soul, forms only an aberration in the dull record. Serious poetry never again dared to revive and develop the occasional style for serious purposes. Those that used it apologized for it, and without Catullus' irony. As a result, the empire suffered from a fatal class-distinction in literature, between the polite writing of the cultivated who knew Greek and the vulgar polyglot talk of the market-place, the ribald songs of soldiers, the crude verse of pantomime. If polite and vulgar had mated, lyric would have revived and all poetry been reinvigorated. As it was, poetry continued to languish, until, the power of polite Latin having disintegrated, a new beginning could be made, in ecclesiastical Latin scanned by the accent of common speech, and then in the vernaculars which produced the early songs and ballads of the romance tongues.

As spontaneous emotion abandoned poetry, disciplined and subdued by artificial form, cultured Romans themselves lost the power to understand that in their own poet Catullus, and in his school, a miracle had struggled to achieve itself—passion, humour, hate, straining to sing, and forcing scholarship to be their handmaid. Posterity remembered with gratitude only the scholarship, which it assiduously imitated. The recondite allusiveness of the neoterics, which marked where they failed, was the lasting influence they left on Latin poetry. In the pages of Quintilian, Rome's: great professor and literary critic of the first century A.D., Catullus is cited seven times, and never once as a lyrist. The omission conveys a judgment on the limitations of the Roman temper as severe as any that could be pronounced by modern taste.

Such is the story of Roman poetry. It has a fourfold moral. First, that Virgil and Horace, despite their individual greatness, led poetry up a blind alley; the forms they selected for it were incapable of further creative development; all that remained was repetition in a minor key. Only their very special genius, devoted to the special cause of reconstructing a culture shattered by civil war, could have moulded powerful verse out of such archaic forms as they chose to work in. The force of their example made spontaneity in Roman poetry for the future impossible; they took away liberty of emotion, and lyric consequently perished, but its loss meant the petrification of all poetry. Second, the neoterics, in submitting to the attraction of a contemporary tradition, showed sounder poetic instinct than the Augustans. But we should not claim more for them than this. The road they took, had it been followed, might have led further, but probably not far enough. Their own failure to kind vital form for narrative poetry, seen for example in Catullus' *Peleus and Thetis,* indicates that the inspiration of Alexandria was too specialized and narrow to fertilize Roman poetry as a whole. We should therefore go on to conclude, in the third place, that the Alexandrianism of the neoterics and the classicism of the Augustans were both desperate attempts to replace from foreign sources a native tradition long since destroyed; the result was only heron failure. The fatal blow had been dealt Roman poetry in those obscure centuries when the native modes were dropped and Livius Andronicus thought it a fine thing to educate the masters of Tarentum by translating Homer wholesale. Fourth, and last, we do not see this story in perspective because we read Roman poetry upside down. We read the Augustans, take their own estimate of their efforts at face-value, model our taste on them, and so form our conception of what was proper and artistically inevitable for Latin poetry, forgetting that the very metres they perfected, so far from reflecting any native instincts in rhythm and form, were an artificial importation, so that for example, they could never conceivably be sung as their Greek models had been in their heyday. Measuring a poet like Catullus against such standards, we notice only a roughness here, a greater license there, and an emotional power which we ascribe to individual eccentricity. Here for example is a sentence from a recent critical essay on the poet, remarkable otherwise for its sympathetic treatment of his work: 'Catullus showed true instinct when he went back to Sappho for his poem on Lesbia; but he lost his great discovery apparently because he had in his youth grown so, much more familiar with easier metres and found the Aeolian forms fettering his impatient utterance'. This kind of judgment is the result of adopting Horace's notions of poetry, and of reading his odes as though they were the real thing. Important lyric is not disqualified by being written in 'easier metres', but rather the contrary. Modem critiques of contemporary poetry would never dream of adopting such pedantic formulas; only classical scholarship still obediently strives to model its taste on Augustan practice. But the gulf between scholarship and poetry is (alas!) now far greater than it was in Catullus' own day. Should we not very properly rebel if we were required to read Dryden and Pope as a prerequisite for mastering the Elizabethans?

(ii) Catullus and Horace

This review of Latin literature has had to cast a very wide net, and its conclusions will be recognized as contentious. Let me therefore close it by comparing more closely the lyric achievements of Catullus and Horace. It is a comparison which must occur to all who know something of Roman literature, for these two represent very nearly all there is of Roman lyric, and yet even within this restricted field they appear as opposed and even hostile forces.

Comparison soon makes it plain not only why Horace is the only other Roman lyrist, but why the claim must always remain doubtful. I have already suggested that Catullus' two Sapphics, read beside his other lyrics, would wear in the eyes of his contemporaries a slightly archaic air, imitations of a great but dead tradition. The same would be true of his single plaintive but rather moving experiment in Asclepiads (no. "30") a rhythm Sappho had also used extensively. Three is not a very high total for these experiments, and we may guess that instinct warned him of the emotional limitations of the Aeolic rhythms. But Horace, about whom there was always a touch of the schoolmaster, deliberately set himself the historical task of studying the original lyrics of the Greek tradition, the Sapphics, Alcaics and Asclepiads, and of 'marrying them to Italian measures'. His proud boast of achievement stands justified; he accomplished a *tour de force,* composing three books of perfectly charming museum pieces, laborious studies which were polished till the labour was hidden, in metres mathematically regular. His achievement was in a sense dead as soon as it was born, but it immediately became the perfect school-book for the Romans themselves.

Modern criticism has lately gone so far as to suggest that Horace, to assist his readers in following these compositions of his in artificial rhythms, incorporated a sort of metric guide in the collection by introducing his readers to each new metre through a careful translation of a Greek original, which could be recognized by the Hellenists and thus serve as a pattern of the metre of similar poems to follow. This if true only underlines what he himself felt to be the extreme artificiality of his task.

Such an achievement was to prove of perennial value and charm, but it required a stamp of mind totally different from the Catullan temper. Only by the accident of following certain archaic metres is Horace a lyrist at all. His whole inspiration and outlook is the reverse of lyrical. This is no defect in him. Rather it is

true that he brought to the task of verse-composition a special sort of literary tact, ·exactly the right instincts to achieve success. His odes are historical studies in form. But form needs some appropriate content, however slim. This Horace with careful taste could supply, in one of his three moods. He could deal in the less tragic symptoms of erotic emotion with ironic detachment; he could moralize gently over friendship, Epicureanism and the sober life. Or he could abandon the presence of lyric altogether, and compose short heroic odes in celebration of national virtue. None of these emotions are powerful except in the imagination of professional commentators. Horace was not a powerful person. He is a master of phrase and form and of sententious wisdom, products of what I have called the historical attitude in the Augustans. For these he lives when Catullus finds survival harder.

Yet Catullus in his inspired moments can make Horace's careful art look insignificant. Take for example the very Sapphics in which Catullus bids bitter farewell to Lesbia. His use in this particular poem of historical and geographic romance—India, Parthia, the Nile, Alps, etc.—seems to have left an impression on Horace, for twice in his odes he writes what looks like a reminiscence of it. The parallels are instructive, because, showing as they do the two poets working with the same sort of material, they expose the gulf between them. The first echo occurs in the *Integer vitae* ode: I quote enough of it in paraphrase to reveal the technique:

> To hearts from guilt set free, to lives lived
>   purely,
> The strength of Moorish spear and flying dart,
> The poisoned arrow's deadliness, are surely
> An empty art:
>
> Across the Caucasus though they should
>   wander,
> Or where on Afric sands the breaker roars,
> Or where Hydaspes' fabled streams meander
> By shadowy shores.
>
> For once when I, the woodland's call obeying,
> Forgot my cares, and sang my love instead,
> A wolf beyond my boundaries saw me
>   straying
> Helpless—and fled.
>
> Yet mightier far was he than all the races
> Of monsters that the Daunian woodlands hem,
> Or lions of Juba's land, in desert places
> That mother them . . .

The two concluding stanzas invite anyone interested to place the poet either in the Arctic circle or at the equator; the discomforts of neither situation will prevent him from loving his Lalage:

Still in my heart shall linger her sweet
   laughter
And her sweet speech.

Thus Horace too tries a little globe-trotting before
coming to his amatory theme, underlining his attempt
to manipulate historical romance in this way with the
epithet in '*fabulosus Hydaspes*.' But his amatory theme,
unlike Catullus, is too thin to stand being combined
with the sweeping effects of the Hydaspes, Caucasus,
and the rest of the apparatus, and the result is a poem
of incongruities which has puzzled the tastes of critics
ever since. It reads like a parody because Horace's
emotions are not equal to his conception. His second
attempt to reproduce a similar effect is, however, happier, and I paraphrase it in full:

Friend, if I go, you too will go with me
To far Cadiz or wild north Spain, you say,
Or that grim shore where the Moroccan wave
   Clamours for aye.

But I still turn to Tivoli. To come
One day to that old town the Greeks built
   there,
And rest at last from war and wayfaring—
   Such is my prayer.

If fate forbids, I have another home
Where the dear waters of Galesus flow
And sheep in skins go clad, where Spartan
   kings
   Reigned long ago.

I love that laughing corner of the world:
The honey there—you cannot get as good
In Greece, and olives are the finest grown
   On native sod.

There summer lingers, and the winter days
Are long, and vale of Aulon, that dear name,
Grows grapes that have but little need to fear
   Falernum's fame.

Those happy heights are calling you and me.
There by my grave you'll linger at the end
With tribute for a poet, and a tear
   Shed for a friend.

This charming poem succeeds, where the previous one
failed, because the poet abandons the ambitious Catullan conception of geographic romance used as a setting for personal passion, and restricts himself to the
contrast between distant scenes and some local associations of his own Italy—among which he characteristically includes food. On this lower emotional key he
manages to maintain harmony throughout the poem.

A good deal of nonsense is often talked about the

immortality of poetry. I have already said something
of its impermanence, and pointed out that the more
vivid the poet's emotions and their expression, the more
they tend to rely on the idiom of his own age. Nothing
reveals this more clearly than the respective fates of
Horace's odes and Catullus' lyrics. The former are
exclusively a work of the intellect, the latter were born
from the heart. But it is the works of the intellect that
live longest. Because Horace composed what even in
his own generation were careful historical studies, they
demanded from the first a mood of detachment in order to be written at all, and hence display qualities
which have the same timeless appeal as mathematics.
His work-order and cunning phrasing are mathematical, and intoxicate us intellectually by their skill, as
the less obvious skill of Catullus' epigrams also intox-
icates when it is perceived. But Horace does not make
the mistake, from the point of view of survival, of
writing in the quick idiom of the table and street; his
vocabulary is never colloquial. Passing endearments,
diminutives, and slang were totally unsuited to such
formal composition as his. His sentiments again never
depend wholly on personal occasions; they are always
generalized. One cannot in any case express much
personal feeling in a literary strait-jacket, however
cunningly contrived.

So the lesser poet with the bookish method wears better.
He is the sort of poet who might fulfil the Platonic
demand that poetry should embody something exact,
some timeless and philosophical essence, or else be
banished from Utopia Having put together three books
of odes, graven with a passionless skill, endowed with
an abstract life more lasting than the quick breath of
poetry, he could safely compose their grandiloquent
epilogue, written this time not without emotion—the
most sincere feeling of which he was capable, his hope
of fame:

My Monument abides
My Task is ended
The royal pyramids
Not so ascended,
The brass wrought in the flame
Sooner shall perish
Than my immortal name
That nations cherish.

The rain's devouring blight
Cannot deface it:
The wind's unbridled might
Cannot abase it.
The centuries may deal
Their mortal wages:
My monument stands real
To all the ages.

Not all of me shall die.
My greater portion

Shall flee death, and defy
His vain extortion.
So shall the future time
Crown my example,
While the processions climb
To Rome's high temple. . . .

His boast stands justified. Flawless poetic masonry has a survival value. Economy and precision, pattern and prettiness and dignity—they are all there in the *Odes;* only the emotion is absent. But Catullus is all emotion, fitted to the tight thin glove of contemporary fashion. For this he fascinated his own generation: '*nil praeter Calvum et doctus cantare Catullum*'—the deft gibe is Horace's. Horace could never be sung around the dinner table. But by this also was Catullus entangled in fleeting time, a writer of *nugae,* sparingly honoured by posterity, and forgotten altogether for five hundred years. He knew himself, and his probable fate:

So here's my book. I know
   It isn't much—
A bit of a thing—and yet
   O may it stay,
My lady Muse, awhile,
   Though men decay?

The prayer was as far as he dared go. A poet of his temper is ill occupied with self-conscious ambitions for immortality. But occasionally we still notice and feel his love and hate and grief, preserved in the cunning shape of lyric and epigram. Ephemeral emotions these, when spent so extravagantly on mere persons, 'dear, dead women' and dead men. But we become aware at least of a heat which while it burnt was very hot, and feeling it, are perhaps grateful if for a moment it warms us.

Macaulay (1800-1859) on the emotional power of Catullus's poetry:

I have pretty near learned all that I like best in Catullus. He grows on me with intimacy. One thing he has—I do not know whether it belongs to him or to something in myself—but there are chords of my mind which he touches as nobody else does. The first lines of *Miser Catulle*; the lines to Cornificius, written evidently from a sick-bed; and part of the poem beginning *Si qua recordanti,* affect me more than I can explain. They always move me to tears.

Thomas Babbington Macaulay, quoted in
Ancilla to Classical Reading, edited by Moses
Hadas, Columbia University Press, 1954.

Kenneth Quinn (essay date 1959)

SOURCE: "Characteristics of the New Poetry," in *The Catullan Revolution,* Melbourne University Press, 1959, pp. 44-69.

[*Below, Quinn examines the features of what he terms "the Catullan movement" in classical Roman literature, focusing upon the poetry of youth and reaction, meter and structure, and the language of Catullus and the* poetae novi.]

DID THE POETAE NOVI FORM A SCHOOL?

One piece of significant biographical information that emerges clearly from the Catullan poems is that their author was one of a group deeply interested in poetry. It is tantalizing to know so little of Catullus' relationships with his fellow revolutionaries and his stature among them. The common view is that there existed a clearly recognized school of *poetae novi,* its most prominent members (after Catullus) being the orator Licinius Calvus and the minor politician Helvius Cinna. Cinna's *Zmyrna* is praised by Catullus in '**Poem 95**', and the name of Calvus is linked by him with the discussion of the new poetry in two of the four poems where his name is mentioned—'**Poem 14**', and especially '**Poem 50**'. Only small crumbs of their verse survive. Others usually reckoned among the *poetae novi* and mentioned (probably) by Catullus are Cornificius, Valerius Cato and Furius Bibaculus. We have only a line or so of Cornificius and most likely nothing at all of Cato, though some ascribe to him the authorship of the *Dirae* of the Virgilian *Appendix.* Furius Bibaculus, however, is in some ways the best represented of the lot: in addition to a handful of fragments we have two complete poems, the longer extending to eight lines. Both poems unfortunately are confined by their subject, literary gossip, to a level of intent that makes them of little value as a guide to what Furius may have achieved when he was really trying. Catullus asks Cornificius for some verses to comfort him in '**Poem 38**'. The Cato of '**Poem 56**' could be Valerius Cato. The Furius of Poems '**11**', '**26**', '**23**' and '**26**', also referred to in '**Poem 24**', is likely to be Furius Bibaculus; the usual interpretation of these poems, that Catullus is attacking this Furius, is perhaps the result of looking at them somewhat uncritically: exaggeratedly abusive language is not uncommon among friends, particularly if they are of Catullus' violent temperament, and there are hints in the Furius poems, and in other violent poems, that the abuse was not meant to wound—as it clearly was meant to in other poems, for example '**28**', '**29**', '**47**', or '**59**'. Then there is the Caecilius of '**Poem 35**' (not otherwise known); nor is it unreasonable to imagine that common interests in poetry, as well as in what Horace calls 'iuuenum cures et libera uina', linked Catullus with the Flavius of '**Poem 6**' (otherwise unknown); the Varus of '**Poem**

10' (various candidates proposed); the book-loving Don Juan, Camerius, of Poems **'55'** and **'58B'** (who may have been Cornificius' brother-in-law, but is otherwise unknown); and others besides. The only new poet of whose work fragments survive, but who is not named by Catullus, seems to be Ticidas. We need not, of course, doubt that many more existed of whom we know nothing.

Three passages of Cicero are customarily used to prove that the existence of a school was recognized by a contemporary. . . . [One of these] comes from a letter written to Atticus at the end of the year 50 B.C. The letter begins:

> Brundisium uenimus VII Kalend. Decembr. usi
> tua felicitate nauigandi; ita bella nobis
> Flauit ab Epiro lenissimus Onchesmites. . . .

The term 'neoteric', often applied by modern scholars to the new poets, owes its origin to this passage. The neoteric flavour of Cicero's hexameter is usually supposed to reside only in the spondaic fifth foot, but the line has a lot of the ring of Catullus' **'Poem 64'** about it stylistically, as well as metrically. The five-word hexameter is frequent in **'Poem 64'**. So, too, is the trick of the learned name: *Onchesmites* is the wind that blew from Onchesmus in Epirus towards Italy (Horace's *Iapyx*). Compare (on all these points) line 28 of **'Poem 64'**:

> tene Thetis tenuit pulcerrima Nereine.

Both here and in line 395 the epithet chosen by Catullus (*Nereine* may not be right) is so obscure that the manuscript tradition has been confused.

The third quotation contains another term much used by modern critics, *poetae novi*. It deals with the dropping by these poets of the old licence that allowed a final 's' before an initial consonant to be disregarded metrically:

> Quin etiam, quod iam subrusticum uidetur, olim autem politius, eorum uerborum, quorum eaedem erant postremae duae litterae quae sunt in *optimus,* postremam litteram detrahebant, nisi uocalis insequebatur. Ita non erat ea offensio in uersibus quam nunc fuguint poetae noui. Sic enim loquebamur:
>
> > qui est omnibu' princeps
> > non *omnibus princeps,* et:
> > uita illa dignu' locoque
> > non *dignus.*

Cicero need not, of course, be pointing to anything more than a difference in practice between contemporary poets and older poets in general. This view is consistent with Cicero's own practice, as far as we can judge from the fragments of his verse. The device occurs only in his earliest verse. He seems therefore to have already abandoned it before Catullus began writing. Any special colour that we read into the phrase *poetae novi* can only come therefore from our associating this passage with the other two.

The view that a school existed has been strongly attacked. It seems that whether there was a clear-cut 'school', and whether its members were commonly referred to as the *poetae novi* or the *neotori,* are matters that must, at least, remain in doubt. (We need not for that reason avoid the convenient term *poetae novi* which modern use has made familiar.) It should be noted, incidentally, that none of the quotations from Cicero comes from a work written during Catullus' lifetime. The earliest (the letter to Atticus) was probably written several years after Catullus' death, and the other two are four to five years later still. The existence of a clear-cut Catullan school in the formative years of Virgil and Horace is, of course, an exciting possibility and fits in well enough with the view that Calvus (who died, probably, in 47 B.C.) and Cinna (who was assassinated, probably, in 44 B.C.) were members of it. Our concern here, however, must be not with the state of affairs in the middle forties, but with a period twenty to twenty-five years earlier, at the outbreak of the Catullan revolution.

Even if the existence of some sort of school is admitted, there is nothing to indicate that Catullus was its head. His relationship in terms of leader and disciple to the poets he names is undeterminable. Some hold the leader was Valerius Cato, basing their view on a passage in Suetonius, where Cato is called *peridoneus praeceptor* and an epigram quoted which is usually attributed to Furius Bibaculus, where Cato is clearly regarded as an authority on poetry, though it is not clear whether in the phrase 'solus legit ac tacit poetas' *facit* means 'rightly evaluates' or 'establishes the reputation of'. Valerius Cato is lavishly praised by other *poetae novi,* but, unless he did write the *Dirae,* we have no way of testing their judgments. Even if he wrote little of any worth, this would not be the only instance known of a critic directing tyrannically a new poetic movement, though himself an indifferent poet

Still less determinable is to what extent these shadowy figures took their poetry seriously. Did their work possess only the elegant triviality of Laevius, or was it pervaded with the new spiritual atmosphere that wrenched the *nugae* away from the level of scholarly persiflage and their longer poems from the level of erudite dullness up to the level of front-rank poetry?

What should be incontestable (though it has been contested is that Catullus wrote, and discussed with other poets in poems that are extant (e.g. Poems **'14', '22'**,

'35', '36', '50', '65', '95', '116'), a kind of poetry that had certain highly novel overall features. Wrongheadedness and formalism have in the past sometimes obscured this truth, though it is today more generally admitted. Catullus and his friends must, of course, have had some realization of where they were heading, though, once again, the distant critic may have a clearer view of the contours of the terrain—clearer certainly than many contemporaries, clearer perhaps than the poets had themselves.

Despite these unresolvable uncertainties, Catullus' own poems make it clear that he was one of a group of poets who shared confidences, aspirations and ideas about poetry and literary criticism. It is also clear that these ideas had a permanent influence on Roman poetry. Inevitably we must try to guess at their shape from the surviving work of the one poet about whose poetry we really know anything. It is difficult to make any sure critical assessment of the surviving fragments of the other new poets, but there is a good deal in them all the same to suggest that, in both tone and style, they were close to Catullus.

THE POETRY OF YOUTH AND REACTION

Beginning a recent discussion on Catullus, a French scholar, J. Bayet, sets out from an overall generalization about the contours of the new movement (as we should, perhaps, call it in order to avoid the word 'school'). It was, he says, 'un phénomène de jeunesse. . . . Des jeunes gens, peu nombreux, instruits, curieux, . . . complices . . . contre la génération précédente, celle de Cicéron'. The first factor—youth with its independence, its recklessness, its singleness in enthusiasm—emerges clearly from the poems. Catullus himself tells us he had just assumed the toga of manhood when his first experiences of love came—and he began writing:

> tempore quo primum uestis mihi tradita pure
> est,
> 　iucundum cum aetas florida uer ageret,
> multa satis lusi: non est dea nescia nostri,
> 　quae dulcem curis miscet amaritiem.
> 　　　　　　　　　　　　**('Poem 68'**, 15-18)

> There was the time when I had just been
> 　given my plain white toga.
> I was the age to feel like the flowers do that
> 　are filled with the joy of spring.
> I took my fall share of life's fun. My name is
> 　well known to the goddess
> who concocts the bitter-sweet anguish of love.

Bayet's second point, that the Catullan movement was a movement opposed to Cicero and his generation, may be restated more elaborately. Because of Cicero's long life and Catullus' short one, we tend to lose sight of the fact that the poet was something like twenty to twenty-five years younger than the orator. In terms of poetic tradition, it is the representatives of the epic-tragic stream that Cicero valued highest among Roman poets and it was their style he had himself followed and in some technical matters improved. Cicero is sometimes supposed to have passed through a neoteric phase himself. It is certainly possible, though we may suspect he was too old before the movement began. Aratus (whom Cicero translated) was an Alexandrian, but an interest in his learned didactic poetry did not necessarily make Cicero an adherent of the new movement taking shape in Rome in Cicero's own time. If we look at the Catullans in terms of personalities, then Bayet is clearly tight. But we should remember that the enmities and friendships of good poets are more transitory than their poetry. If, therefore, we try to think instead in terms of the evolution of the Roman poetic tradition, we should perhaps say the generation of Cicero placed highest the epic-tragic stream of that tradition, whereas Catullus represents a fusion of the three streams of tradition that reached him.

THE POETRY OF CATULLUS: ITS UNDERLYING UNITY

But it is time we passed from the poets themselves and their attitudes to an examination of some of the distinctive qualities of what they wrote. In the previous chapter, I tried to show the shallowness of the view that there are two Catulluses ('learned' and 'lyric'), and to substitute for that notion the notion of levels of poetic intent. The notion of levels of intent, however, if left unqualified, tends to suggest a disintegrated, discontinuous view of Catullus' poetry. We need a formula to tune our thinking, to give us some feeling for the overall shape of the new poetry and what was new in it. We can get this, perhaps, by lifting a phrase from a recent study of a single poem. J.-P. Boucher, seeking such a formula in order to integrate **'Poem 64'** with the remainder of Catullus' work, calls it the kind of poetry where 'la sensibilité du poète est engagée'. Catullus is not a professional poet or a dilettante, he says, but a writer whose personal reactions are involved in the story he tells in **'Poem 64'**, and it is these reactions that dictate the whole layout of the poem. It is not simply that Catullus lets us feel he cares about Ariadne. We are made constantly to feel the *presence* of the poet by the way in which he directs the story, altering its tempo, imposing on stylized ancient legend an ironical overlay of modern realistic detail, giving the poem constantly. the imprint of his own personality.

This personal involvement of the poet is something new that the Roman temperament brought to ancient poetry at this stage. The Greeks were capable of the acutest analysis of passion and able to frame it in high poetry. The Hellenistic poets exploited deliberately and obviously clever arrangement and layout of a poem.

But about both ages of Greek literature there was always something external and intellectual. Even when Hellenistic poetry introduced the fashion of writing in the first person, a coldness, a withholding of self persisted. Any wholesale condemnation of Greek literature for its impersonal character would obviously be absurd. It results in some departments of literature in a nobility and an objective purity the Romans never matched. Its limitations only appear when Hellenistic poets start writing of themselves.

One notices the same intrusion of the personal when one compares Roman sculpture with Greek. Catullus, like Keats, was a barbarian who so transformed the raw material of his own life in his poetry that it attained heroic stature, and who contrariwise experienced the excitement of personal involvement in re-creating what a modern poet has called approvingly

> legends that strut in verses out of the past,

because the stuff of legend has an organized tension about it that the rawer material of contemporary life seems to the poet to lack.

Interaction between the elements of self and legend is constant. The long poems are vitalized by this feeling of participation, the short poems are often thereby made to soar from the level of conversation improved upon (when urbanity and sophistication are the predominant qualities of the verse) to the level of very real poetry by a single evocative phrase. This need not involve straightout employment of mythological material—rare in Catullus, compared with the elegiac poets. As an example of how the unreal, romantic world surges up at the slightest touch, consider the effect of the two words *candida puella* in '**Poem 13**':

> Cenabis bene, mi Fabulle, apud me
> paucis, si tibi di fauent, diebus,
> si tecum attuleris bonam atque magnam
> cenam, non sine candida puella
> et uino et sale et omnibus cachinnis.

> You'll dine in style, dear Fabullus, when you
>   come to me,
> any day now, if the gods are kind to you.
> So long as you bring a good square meal
>   along as well.
> And don't forget that lovely fair-haired
>   creature—
> and a bottle of wine, some salt and a full
>   supply of stories.

Into the narrow world of this elegantly worded invitation, in which pure form is at once the stimulus of genius and the justification of the poem as literature, is suddenly thrust the vision, heavy with overtones, of the radiant beauty of an unknown girl. Compare Cat-

ullus' use of the same word, applied to a woman, in '**Poem 35**', 8, and especially '**Poem 68**', 70 (*mea candida diua*), where he chooses this epithet at the moment when he likens his mistress to a goddess.

Consider also how much is built into '**Poem 7**' while answering the question 'How many kisses are enough?' The question could have been treated on a purely intellectual plane of metaphysical wit—as it would have been if, for example, the opening two lines of '**Poem 7**' had been followed by lines 7-13 of '**Poem 5**', and that poem deprived of its lyrical overtones by removing lines 3-5. We should then have a poem like this:

> Quaeris, quot mihi basiationes
> tuae, Lesbia, sint satis superque. ('**Poem 7**', 1-
>   2)

> da mi basia mille, deinde centum,
> dein mille altera, dein secunda centum,
> deinde usque altera mille, deinde centum.
> dein, cum milia multa fecerimus,
> conturbabimus illa, ne sciamus,
> aut ne quis malus inuidere possit,
> cum tantum sciat esse basiorum. ('**Poem 5**', 7-
>   13.)

> You ask me, Lesbia, how many kisses it will
>   take
> to make me really satisfied.
> Give me a thousand kisses, followed by a
>   hundred;
> another thousand then, and a second hundred.
> Then a further thousand, plus a hundred.
> Finally, when we've made it many thousands,
> please muddle all the accounts and forget the
>   total.
> Then no nosey nasty person will be able to be
>   envious
> through knowledge of such heavy transacting
>   in kisses.

This combination of the more purely intellectual parts of two poems would have given us a perfectly acceptable non-lyric, non-imaginative epigram. Instead in '**Poem 7**' we have:

> Quaeris, quot mihi basiationes
> tuae, Lesbia, sint satis superque.
> quam magnus numerus Libyssae harenae
> lasarpiciferis facet Cyrenis
> oraclum Iouis inter aestuos
> et Batti ueteris sacrum sepulcrum;
> aut quam sidera multa, cum tacet nox,
> furtiuos hominum uident amores:
> tam te basia multa basiare
> uesano satis et super Catullo est,
> quae nec pernumerare curiosi
> possint nec male fascinare lingua.

You ask me, Lesbia, how many kisses it will
  take
to make me really satisfied.
As many as the sands of Libya's desert
that lies round Cyrene where the silfium
  grows,
stretching between the oracle of sweltering
  Jove
and the holy tomb of Battus long ago
  departed.
Or as many as the stars that in night's quiet
look down on as mortals stealing love.
That is the total of the kisses that will make
your passionate Catullus really satisfied.
A sum like that the nosey couldn't reckon up,
or evil tongues weave spells around.

The poem is laden with the qualities that controlled imagination can impart. Jove's ancient shrine in the sweltering desert. The magic of night that Virgil recaught in his

ibant obscuri sola sub nocte per umbram.

But night's magic is always easily evoked and it would have been a blemish in so short a poem to use as a second image of countless number a thing so commonplace—if it had not been given special appropriateness. The lyric and imaginative impulse is strengthened, therefore, by our sharing with the poet the thrill of an ironical reference to the poet's own *furtiuus amor* with Lesbia.

The term *controlled lyricism* may serve to label what is going on in this poem and others like it (for example, **'Poem 31'** . . .). The lyrical impulse is tightened by an intellectual awareness of significance and proportion, which controls, and organizes what is said. Even in the poems of completest surrender to emotion we can have the feeling that Catullus is aware of the course the poem must take if it is to remain the sort of poem this tension between intellect and emotion best produces. Contrast the surrender to the lyric impulse in Tibullus and his uncritical acceptance of emotion. Poetry can be written the Tibullan way, too, but its characteristic will be charm rather than strength. In Horace and Ovid, on the other hand, the intellect has a sort of non-*engagé* effect, framing the emotional vignette that teach ode or elegy constitutes, suggesting a judgment (often, in Horace, of a scene involving others and not, on the surface, personal at all) and a point of view.

This is perhaps the point for a word about 'sincerity'. The common view rightly stresses the sincerity of Catullus' poetry, but tends to confuse poetic sincerity with autobiographical truth. The following judgment on poetry, for example, would, I think, still win ready acceptance among many students of classical literature, not only for the eloquence with which it is expressed:

> the Lesbia cycle cannot be paralleled in ancient literature for sincerity of passion, passing through all the stages of joyous contentment, growing distrust, and wild despair to the poignant adieu of the disillusioned lover.

Few modern literary critics, however, would accept the doctrine of *Dichtung und Wahrheit* in so ingenuous a form. They would deny that sincerity of this sort is vital to good poetry. And, conversely, that Catullus' poetry must be good because it seems to record authentic experience. Sincerity, like other forms of emotion, is no more than an ingredient of poetry, essential to securing the temperature of fusion of the poet's raw material into poetry. It is at best a poor criterion of quality, and its relationship to factual truth is complicated. A measure of *insincerity* even is not incompatible with good poetry, though in Roman poetry we have to wait till Horace for the studied exploitation of attitudes so complex in the poet to his subject-matter.

METRE AND STRUCTURE

Another characteristic of the new poetry is its exploitation of the possibilities of metrical variety. The course of the old Roman tradition here has already been indicated, from the *cantica* of Plautus through the polymetric *nugae* of Laevius. In the *poetae novi* this is first and foremost a matter of intense interest in metrical experiment. The excitement it could produce in Catullus is dear from **'Poem 50'**:

Hesterno, Licini, die otiosi
multum lusimus in meis tabellis,
ut conuenerat esse delicatos:
scribers uersiculos uterque nostrum
ludebat numero modo hoc modo illoc,
reddens mutua per iocum atque uinum.
atque illinc abii tuo lepore
incensus, Licini, facetiisque,
ut nec me miserum cibus iuuaret
nec somnus tegeret quiete ocellos,
sed toto indomitus furore lecto
uersarer, cupiens uidere lucem,
ut tecum loquerer simulque ut essem.
at defessa laboret membra postquam
semimortua lectulo iacebant,
hoc, iucunde, tibi poema feci,
ex quo perspiceres meum dolorem.
nunc audax caue sis, precesque nostras,
oramus, caue despuas, ocelle,
ne poenas Nemesis reposcat a te.
est uehemens dea: laedere hanc caueto.

The poem ends with an elaborately pathetic entreaty for another meeting. Licinius Calvus is to be supposed as receiving the poem first thing the next morning. This becomes clearer if we change the past tenses in the second half to presents it was common in Latin letters for the writer to adopt in matters of time the standpoint of the recipient. Indeed 'yesterday' in the first line, by our conventions, should perhaps be 'today' though we may keep 'yesterday' for convenience and assume the poem was written after midnight. Two further points should be noted: the way in which Catullus consciously suggests the tone of a love-letter, even in details of vocabulary (e.g. *miserum; dolorem*) in order to convey an intellectual or artistic excitement that is as acute as sensual excitement; and the degree to which this ostensibly spontaneous poem has been arranged for publication, by sketching in the circumstances in the opening lines—Calvus did not need to be told what Catullus tells him. The poem is more complex than might at first appear.

> How well spent, Licinius, the idle hours of
>   yesterday!
> I'd my notebook with me and we had glorious
>   fun,
> sophisticated by arrangement.
> Each of us took his turn at versifying,
> gaily experimenting with metre after metre,
> vying with the other while we joked and
>   drank.
> I left for home, fascinated,
> Licinus, by the elegance of your wit.
> My dinner gave me no comfort. I was in a
>   torment.
> Nor could sleep lid my eyes or bring me rest.
> Gripped by excitement I cannot tame, I've
>   been tossing
> all around my bed, impatient for the day,
> hoping we can be together and I car' talk with
>   you.
> Finally, exhausted with fatigue, extended
> on my bed, half-way now to death,
> I've made, dear friend, this poem for you,
> so you can understand the torture I've been
>   through.
> Take care, please do not be foolhardy;
> do not say No, dearest friend, to my request,
> lest avenging Nemesis exact her retribution.
> Don't provoke the goddess. She can be
>   violent.

The fascination that metrical problems have for front-rank poets is hard, perhaps, for those of us who are not poets to understand. We have still to resist a tendency to equate interest in technique with inferior genius—a carry-over of the romantic doctrine of lyrical inspiration. Though, rather curiously, it is more fashionable to disparage Horace for a preoccupation with metre than Catullus. Yet the importance attributed to metre by leading poets today is easy to gather from their readiness to discuss this and other aspects of tech-

nique, and from the confessions poets occasionally make to us about their methods of composition. In Roman literature these enthusiasms for technique were novel. The old craftsman-poet was conservative and rightly so, because cleverness: was not his business. Cleverness that went beyond the very occasional special effect would thrust the personality of the artist into the work of art, and in epic and tragedy the artist should remain anonymous.

All the same, the way in which the short poems of Catullus fall into two groups is remarkable: Poems '1' to '60' are written *numero modo hoc modo illoc,* but Poems '69' to '116' are all in elegiacs. As far as we can tell, Catullus practiced the two genres simultaneously, not at any stage abandoning either for the other as his successors did: the polymetric poems prepared the way for the *Epodes* and the *Odes* of Horace, the elegiac poems for Augustan elegy. In Catullus, the subject-matter of both genres is often the same, though the treatment of it is usually very different, except at the lowest level of intent where an abusive epigram in hendecasyllabics may not differ greatly from an epigram in elegiacs. On the higher levels of composition, the polymetric poems display greater surges of emotion, more spontaneous writing we may say—provided by spontaneous we mean an effect of art, and do not suppose spontaneity to exclude long preparation—or structural complexity. The elegiacs are less exuberant in their wording, though they often display a restrained ferocity. There are elements of tradition latent in this distinction, though not enough to make it clear why Catullus chose to develop the distinction so sharply.

Coupled with metrical experiment is a new attention to structural problems. In epic poetry the canvas is so vast that the quality of the structure is less important. In the drama and in the didactic poetry of Lucretius, there is necessarily an overall layout of the material, but nothing approaching the structural tightness that a good short poem must have. In Catullus, the qualities of concision and slickness are so apparent that it is hardly necessary to quote examples from the short poems. Even in the longest poems, e.g. '64' and '68', there is a new attention not only to overall structure, but, instead of a loose string of purple passages, an effect of carefully calculated contrast (e.g. in '**Poem 64**' between description of scene and direct speech), as well as studied exploitation of the unexpected angle and of the diversity of layout in description, extremely detailed description contrasting sharply with succinct résumé. In structure, too, the polymetric poems and the elegiac poems differ, the latter displaying a more closely knit logical sequence of thought, as opposed to the cyclic effect that we get—often in the polymetric poems, where a single idea is enunciated, expanded, and then reiterated.

LANGUAGE

With the new poets came a remarkable renovation in the language of Roman poetry. The language of serious poetry, that of epic and tragedy, had really changed very little since the days of Ennius. An effective poetic style (and Ennius was that) tends, once formed, to persist until its remoteness from living language deprives it of vitality to a degree that is felt to be intolerable and to make it unfit for the effective expression of any sincerely felt emotion.

Differences between the two kinds of poetic language are obvious. Though of course there are common features. Catullus keeps, for example, in his more serious writing (in Poems '63' and '64', in the more seriously intended elegies) to the rugged, highly alliterative style which goes back to the very origins of Roman poetry. Unfortunately, apart from studies of points of detail, little has been done to investigate the differences adequately—or the relationship of epic language and Catullan language to other Roman poetic styles. Moreover, the usual approach is based on an ancient grammatical tradition that treats the language of poetry as merely the vehicle of the sense—as though there existed first a body of material to be communicated which is then wrapped in a garb of poetic language. Any good poetry is more than this sort of product of versifying ideas. Such an approach becomes, however, hopeless when we have to deal with the intensely cohering compositions of the *poetae novi,* where every detail of word, sound and metre, and the organization of these into an integrated whole, are active constituents of the poetry. Though this is almost a commonplace of modern literary criticism, it is perhaps worth reiteration here.

The new climate in literary criticism is, of course, the outcome of changes in the way poetry has been written in our time. The nature of the phenomenon with which we have to deal in Catullus can be more readily understood, therefore, today than fifty years ago as a result of the comparable renewal that we have seen in the language of poetry in our own literature. The similarity between the two movements is at least sufficient to make it worth taking advantage of the acuter feeling we necessarily possess for our own language in order to get some feeling for what happened with the *poetae novi.*

The source of these renovations when they occur is the living, everyday language. In Roman literature, the elements of a style drawing upon everyday speech already existed in the comic-satiric stream of tradition. What the *poetae novi* had to do was to adapt the racy directness of speech so that it could be used for serious poetry. The degree of adaptation depended on the level of poetic intent. The colloquialism of Catullus is, of course, well recognized by scholars, though it is seldom adequately represented by Catullus' many translators in recent years. Indeed the gulf that separates the *poetae novi* from their Alexàndrian 'models' is perhaps deepest here. The diction of Hellenistic poetry is, by comparison, an odd jumble of worn, pretentious literary archaism. Despite the many technical achievements of that brilliant movement, we see here a symptom of disease, the result of making poetry in a kind of literary laboratory.

Of course, even at the lowest levels of intent the new poetry, like the dialogue of Oscar Wilde's comedies, contains a great deal of artistic improvement upon the conversation of the most brilliantly sophisticated set. In Catullus, the language of conversation is improved upon in two directions. Firstly, as in Wilde, by a heightened tension, giving the appearance, still, of naturalness, but bringing about a sustained brilliance which is the effect of art. Quite apart from metre, we may be sure the *poetae novi* never talked in this way. This improvement upon conversation is so straightforward we need not do more than mention it, as a warning against those who put the case for colloquialism too simply. It cannot, alone, make poetry out of speech. If we are to get the right feeling for Catullus, we must grasp a second way in which his language (despite its colloquial raciness), by a subtle infiltration of the unobtrusively archaic, the unusual and even the exotic, assumes the evident tone, the solemnity almost, that serious poetry requires. Again, a look at modern poetry may help us to get our bearings. Let us take Robert Graves's poem 'The Cool Web' as an illustration of one kind of poetic language, concentrating our attention on that aspect only:

> Children are dumb to say how hot the day is,
> How hot the scent is of the summer rose,
> How dreadful the black wastes of evening
>   sky,
> How dreadful the tall soldiers drumming by.
>
> But we have speech, to chill the angry day,
> And speech, to dull the rose's cruel scent.
> We spell away the overhanging night,
> We spell away the soldiers and the fight.
>
> There's a cool web of language winds as in,
> Retreat from too much joy or too much fear:
> We grow sea-green at last and coldly die
> In brininess and volubility.
>
> But if we let our tongues lose self-possession;
> Throwing off language and its watery clasp
> Before our death, instead of when death
>   comes,
> Facing the wide glare of the children's day,
> Facing the rose, the dark sky and the drums,
> We shall go mad no doubt and die that way.

There is hardly a detail in this poem of which we could say that it belonged to literature only and not to living language. Even the omission of the relative pronoun in the first line of the third stanza occurs in colloquial language, in addition to its regional and archaic overtones. There are whole lines that we might without difficulty use in conversation. Yet, quite apart from the obvious structural qualities of the poem: the incantatory effect, for example, of the patterns of repetition (remember what prominent features anaphora and circular composition are of Catullan style); quite apart from the special exploitation of certain words (the deliberate ambiguity of 'spell' for example, the personifying effect of applying the epithet 'cruel' to a rose's scent, or the unusual syntax of 'dumb to say'); apart from all these apparent devices, the poem is pervaded by both a tightness of tone and a solemnity that make it quite unlike prose. And this is a comparatively neutral example, because we have chosen a poem which contains no dialogue.

Stylistic comparisons between any modern poet and an ancient one should not be pushed too far, though most of the devices in this poem could, I think, be paralleled from Catullus. What we want from Graves's poem is an overall impression of style to tune our reactions to Catullus. Almost any Catullan poem that is more than a few lines long can make us feel the power a comparable *crispness* of diction possesses to create the atmosphere of poetry. The effect is discreetly heightened by the unusual turn of phrase or word. The alternation of colloquialism and elaborate polysyllable should particularly be noted.

The most instructive poems are those whose raw material (that which becomes the subject-matter when the poem has been made) provides no obvious poetic impulse. Consider what Catullus does with the situation he deals with in **'Poem 6'**:

> Flaui, delicias tuas Catullo,
> ni sint illepidae atque inelegantes,
> uelles dicere nec tacere posses.
> uerum nescio quid febriculosi
> scorti diligis hoc pudet fateri.
> nam te non uiduas iacere noctes
> nequiquam tacitum cubile clamat
> sertis ac Syrio fragrans oliuo,
> puluinusque peraeque et hic et ille
> attritus, tremulique quassa lecti
> argutatio inambulatioque.
> nam nil stupra ualet, nihil tacere
> cur? non tam latera ecfututa pandas,
> ni tu quid facias ineptiarum.
> quare, quidquid haloes bond malique,
> dic nobis. uolo te ac tuos amores
> ad caelum lepido uocare uersu.

The situation is a stock one the young man who won't produce his girl for inspection. Smartness and sophistication are the key-notes of the poem.

> Flavius, you've a sweetheart, but she must
> be just a bit uncouth, not entirely U perhaps,
> or you'd want to talk of her, couldn't help it
> even.
> I expect it's some baggage feverish for a man
> that you're in love with, and ashamed of
> owning up.
> They're no celibate nights you're passing.
> Your room,
> though tongueless, shrieks its testimony just
> the same.
> All those flowers, that oily Syrian scent,
> those pillows crumpled just as much on either
> side,
> that rickety bed, so knocked about it emits
> falsetto creaks as it wanders round the room.
> Not the slightest use refusing to talk.
> Why, you're an obvious case of shagger's
> back.
> There must be funny business going on.
> So tell us who she is you've got—whether
> good
> or bad. I want to poeticize your love and you
> and raise you to the sky in polished verse.

To confine ourselves to diction: consider the contribution of the striking polysyllables febriculosi (with a deliberately coarse word juxtaposed), *argutatio, inambulatio* (two extravagant abstract nouns, that make up a line between them) and that of the personification implied by *clamat* or *uiduas*. Exuberant fantasy is allowed to run its delicious course, and then at the end the poem wheels round on to a more seriously poetic note: there is perhaps the stuff of poetry in this affair between Flavius and his mistress, and Catullus is eager to exploit it.

The atmosphere of a poem like this is difficult to create and Catullus is not always successful in his choice of language. Contrast the opening half of **'Poem 39'**:

> Egnatius, quod candidos habet dentes,
> renidet usque quaque. si ad rei uentum est
> subsellium cum orator excitat fletum,
> renidet ille; si ad pii rogum fili
> lugetur, orba cum flet unicum mater,
> renidet ille. quidquid est, ubicumque est,
> quodcumque agit, renidet: hunc habet morbum,
> neque elegantem, ut arbitror, neque urbanum.

> Egnatius has got teeth that are shining white,
> and so breaks
> on every conceivable occasion into a flashing
> grin. The prisoner's
> in the dock. His counsel's working at our
> tears. Egnatius

breaks into a flashing grin. Or at a funeral:
   grief on every side
the mother who's bereaved laments her model
   son. Egnatius
breaks into a flashing grin. On every
   conceivable occasion,
no matter what he's doing, that flashing grin.
   It's a complaint he suffers from
and one that's neither smart, I think, nor
   sophisticated.

Here the attempt to transform prose statement by the structural force of repetition (e.g. the *renidet ille,* repeated at the same position in the line, the parallel cum clauses) somehow fails.

It is this effect which I have been calling *crispness* (to denote something that is fairly evident in illustration, but hard to analyse) that Havelock felt, perhaps, when he called these poems 'lyrical'. But even taken in this way, that term narrows too much the range of tone that we find in Catullus. Consider **'Poem 10'**, where this same crispness of language gives life to a poem where anything approaching emotional outburst is carefully held in check in order to achieve a mixture of narrative and urbane comment that was to prepare the way for the best hexameter writing of Horace. On the other hand, discreetly strengthened with some of the traditional devices of poetry, it contributes to the success of Poems **'63'** and **'64'**. Even in these long narrative poems, the straightout inflation of rhetoric and the artificial intensity of rhetoric are avoided—except in the set speeches (a prominent feature of both. poems), which acquire thereby a deliberately archaic, 'epic' tone with which the mannered slickness of the narrative sections is set in calculated contrast. Consider this passage of **'Poem 63'**:

> ita de quiete molli rapida sine rabie
> simul ipsa pectore Attis sue facta recoluit,
> liquidaque mente uidit sine quis ubique fores,
> animo aestuante rusum reditum ad uada tetulit.
> ibi maria pasta uisens lacrimantibus oculis,
> patriam allocuta maestast ita uoce miseriter.
> 'patria o mei creatrix, patria o mea genetrix . . .
> ubinam aut quibus locis te positam, patria,
>   reor?'

> (**'Poem 63'**, 44-50, 55)

The narrative opening of this section, unadorned by traditional rhetorical devices other than alliteration, but drawing vigour from forceful, unconventional words, contrasts with the loose declamatory style of Attis' speech, which is almost a pastiche of tragic style:

> Then, when after soft repose, free from
>   madness' grasp,
> Attis himself in mind reviewed kiss situation,
> and with intellect cleared perceived where he

was and what he lacked,
thought once more seething he returned to the
   water's edge,
and scanning with tear-brimmed eyes the
   ocean's vast extent,
pitifully addressed with sorrowing voice his
   native land:
'O land where I was conceived, land where I
   was born . . . .
where, in what place, shall I think you
   situate?'

A detailed analysis of Catullan language cannot, however, be attempted here, though there is urgent need both for intensive research into points of language that have never been looked at, and for bringing together the studies of detail that have been made, in order to give meaning to dry lists of words and points of syntax in terms of what poets really do. It is obviously not enough, for example, to say that diminutives are a feature of Catullus' style and give a list of them. It is still not enough to say their effect is colloquial. Take **'Poem 64'**, line 131:

> frigidulos udo singultus ore cientem

> with tearful face summoning chilly sobs

or line 316:

> laneaque aridulis haerebant morsa labellis

> and from the dried-up lips hang wisps of
>   wool, bitten off.

In these contexts the diminutives have the power both to create pathos and to heighten the interpenetration of legend and reality that we have spoken of earlier.

The archaism of Catullus has been sometimes exaggerated. The language of his contemporary Lucretius is much more deeply penetrated with archaism. Nevertheless, archaic touches exist, producing, among other effects, simplicity and solemnity. And archaism is, of course, a constant device in Poems **'63'** and **'64'**, where their strength comes largely from a basic archaism and non-naturalism of tone (emphasized by static, heavily detailed pictures: e.g. **'Poem 64'**, 52-70) given a fresh subtlety by gentle but conscious touches of ironical realism.

A more complicated clement of Catullan language is the employment of Greek words and constructions. Often Greek words (e.g. *mnemosynum, pathscus, catagraphus,* and, probably, *strophium*) are part of the sophisticated slang of the circle of the *poetae novi*. An example of a more complicated trick (the sort of thing we might associate more with Virgil than Catullus) is given by Ronconi:

nutricum tenus exstantes e gurgite cano
                                        (**'Poem 64'**, 18)

In this line, use of *nutrix* for *mamma* probably depends on the reader's knowing that a Greek word for *nutrix* also means *mamma*.

Lastly, we may mention the Graecisms of syntax: the use of an accusative after a passive participle, for example,

non contecta leui uelatum pectus amictu,
non tereti strophio lactentis uincta papillas
                                        (**'Poem 64'**, 64-5)

giving an effect that is novel, that draws upon the hearer's erudition. The sense in which this construction may be called a Graecism needs to be precisely stated. It should be obvious that a writer of any skill will not simply import from another language a wholly alien piece of syntactical idiom. The requirements are best met stylistically when the alien construction is comprehensible, offers positive advantage (freshness, concision), and is only just not normal syntax. For example, 'From the worth-nothing that he was he is become a personage' is a series of syntactical Gallicisms in English obvious to those who know French ('Du vaurien qu'il était, il est evenu un personnage'), but offering stylistic possibilities whether this is recognized or not; whereas, say, 'I demanded of him how it did itself that this should be arrived' completely lacks these possibilities of stylistic exploitation. The same conditions apply to the stylistic exploitation of Greek syntax in Latin. In the case of the example quoted: there are traces of a middle past participle with a direct object in Latin from early times, just enough for the Greek construction to be understood and felt as a kind of Latin, unusual but effective. It therefore becomes possible to exploit the much greater use made in Greek of this construction and its affinity with the accusative of respect in Greek, a construction that is not Latin at all.

Another example from Catullus is his use of *ut* with the subjunctive in imitation of Greek σς, for example:

sed quid ego a primo digressus carmine plura
commemorem, *ut* linquens genitoris filia
    uultum,
ut consanguineae complexum, *ut* denique
    matris,
quae misera in gnata deperdita laetabatur,
omnibus his Thesei dulcem praeoptarit
    amorem:
aut *ut* uecta rati spumosa ad litora Diae
uenerit, aut *ut* eam deuinctam lumina somno
liquerit immemori discedens pectore coniunx?
                                        (**'Poem 64'**, 116-23)

Once again what Catullus says is possible Latin, though the construction is much commoner in Greek, and the concentrated repetition of *ut* here could hardly fail to sound somewhat exotic. The normal Latin equivalent of the Greek construction is the accusative and infinitive, so that here there is the added advantage of conciseness, because we escape from the heavy prose construction.

Both these Graecisms caught on and are frequent in Augustan poetry. Others, like the use of the nominative and infinitive,

ait fuisse nauium celerrimus
                                        (**'Poem 4'**, 2)

proved less popular.

These details of language, like the new attention to structure and the interpenetration of simple sense with elaborate imagery (as in **'Poem 7'**), build up a picture of a movement about which two final generalizations are, perhaps, useful. Firstly, this is hard poetry—not for the general public, but for the lettered *élite* who have the culture needed to appreciate its subtleties and the enthusiasm for tracking them down. Secondly, it is the poetry of art for art's sake, the poetry of *littérature pure:* above all in its most serious productions at the highest level of intent (Poems **'63'**, **'64'**, **'66'**), but also in the *nugae,* the uselessness of which is deliberately emphasized. The antithetical force and the programmatic character of the words in **'Poem 1'**

namque tu solebas
meas esse aliquid putare nugas.

For you used to think
these little scraps of verse had real worth.

are often missed. There is some evidence that in this matter of art for art's sake the *poetae novi* followed a conscious doctrine, provided mainly by Philodemus, the Greek philosopher and poet who lived in Italy and was a contemporary of Catullus. Philodemus was the theorist of a movement to launch a doctrine of the conscious uselessness of poetry.

Both innovations succeeded: Roman poetry remained 'hard', and Roman poets fought to maintain *littérature pure,* despite the efforts of patrons to put poetry again to the service of the community. This is true even of Horace. Despite the occasional high-quality *engagé* political poem and his decision in the last years of his life to support a compromise (the famous *omne tulit punctum qui miscuit utile dulci*), Horace was, in his most creative years as a serious poet, on the whole an adherent of *littérature pure,* just as much as he was, almost everywhere in the *Odes*, an adherent of 'hard' poetry.

On both counts, again, the parallel with our own day is close, and in both contexts we might ask ourselves at what point the heightened possibilities offered to poetry cease to outweigh the consequences of divorce from large sections of the educated public.

Peter Whigham (essay date 1966)

SOURCE: An introduction to *The Poems of Catullus,* translated by Peter Whigham, University of California Press, 1969, pp. 9-46.

[In the following essay originally published in 1966, Whigham surveys what he deems the highlights of Catullus's poetic canon.]

The date of Catullus's introduction into Roman society is of interest in helping to assess how much of his younger, formative life was spent in what he refers to as 'the province'. It is, unfortunately, likely to remain an unsolved query. If Metellus Celer was responsible, Catullus would not be likely to have left home before the spring of 62. On the other hand, his father, who must have been a wealthy man, was probably just as capable of arranging the matter for himself. In which case, there is no knowing when he left. There is a third alternative—of no help from the point of view of dates, but worth considering for other reasons. It is not impossible that he was provided with introductions to Roman literary circles by Publius Valerius Cato, the Veronese teacher, poet and critic, known not only to Catullus but to at least three other of the 'new poets', Ticidas, Gaius Cinna and Furius Bibaculus, all Cisalpines and all, at one time or another, pupils of his. It is likely, but unprovable, that Catullus was another. Cato was the author of a work on grammar, now lost, and probably of a poem called Dirae, which is still extant. A line of Cinna's refers to a poem called Diana, and a line of Ticidas', although not quite so certainly, to one called *Lydia.* Bibaculus speaks of him as though he were not only a master but an exemplar. He calls him 'the sole maker of poets', and laments the poverty of so discerning an individual. The warmth and personal element in Bibaculus's tributes, together with Catullus's poem ('**56**'), give us a hint of the mingled feelings of equality and respect which these men seem to have felt for him. If, as most scholars believe, Cato was the moving force behind the 'new poets', it would help to explain the number of Cisalpines among them. It would also explain, perhaps, something of the urgency and iconoclasm—although that word may be too strong—that they brought to their work. It would be misleading to suggest that, because they came from across the Po, an area which had not yet acquired full Roman status, they were what we should call 'provincials'. But there would be a freshness about them, and this—as in the case of Catullus— would give a bite to their Roman manners. Cato himself outlived all his pupils, dying as late as 25 B.C. only eight or nine years before Propertius, whose work, if he read it, he must certainly have approved of.

When we speak of the 'new poets' and the inspiration they derived from Cato, it should be remembered that we are in effect speaking of the work of Catullus and a tradition about Cato. The surviving fragments of the works of Calvus, Cinna, Cornificius, Bibaculus and Ticidas occupy barely three pages of print. Fortunately, in at least ten of his poems Catullus gives some very direct indications of what he and his friends felt about poetry, what their prejudices were and what they expected from it. Most of these poems are written to fellow poets and cast in the form of imaginary letters. (Catullus was fond of this convention: the opening lines of poem '**13**' follow the actual wording of a formal invitation to dinner.) Some of these 'letters' promise, or enclose, or make excuses for not enclosing translations of Greek models. Others are humorously abusive of poets of whom Catullus disapproves. Others are tributes to friends. We gather that the followers of the old-fashioned tradition of Roman epic were not popular with the 'new poets', that long-windedness was to be avoided, and anything pompous, stilted or affected. We are told, or it is implied, that gaiety should be a concomitant of the arts, that the psychological and personal approach was to be preferred to the formal or public one, and that elegance (*venustas*), taste and learning (*doctrina*), were among a poet's most precious jewels. Perhaps the most illuminating poem of this genre is '**No. 50**', where we see Calvus and Catullus, like any two poets who are also friends, playing at poetry together. We are aware that their poetry was a very close part of their lives. This was something new in Roman letters.

There is always the danger that the literary historian will invest the past with a more or less spurious unity. Life, we feel, is more haphazard than most biographers or historians would like it to appear. The documentary evidence for the idea that there was a new movement at all rests on three brief passages of Cicero, in one of which appears the term 'new poets'—and, as an ironic allusion to their literary ancestry, 'new poets' is written in Greek. To some people this has seemed insufficient proof of the existence of a literary movement, and they have consequently denied that the so-called 'new poets' worked together or formed a school. And yet one of the strongest impressions left from a reading of the dozen or so poems mentioned above is that Catullus, and the other writers with whom he mixed, felt themselves united, in an almost arrogant manner, *for* certain things in poetry, and *against* others, and this seems to me stronger evidence than Cicero's. When Catullus started writing in 69 or 68 B.C. he had three traditions to draw on: Roman epic and tragedy Roman comedy and satire; and the Roman love epigram which was an importation from Alexandrian Greek. This third element was comparatively new, with a history of not more than fifty years. The examples we have are elegant but brittle; slight in accomplishment and small in quantity. The weightier traditions of tragedy and epic were not with out Greek influence; but beside them the love epigram is like an exotic that had not taken root. By setting out these trends, in this way, I do not wish to imply that they were of equal importance, either in themselves or to Catullus. They were not. The exact nature of his debt to each is a matter of dispute. In general terms, however, it is safe to say that he drew his ability to convey grandeur (the Aegeus passage in **'Poem 64'**) from the language of epic and tragedy, that he guessed at the uses to which colloquialism and realism might be put from the comico-satiric tradition, and that it was in the last, the somewhat precious form of the love epigram, that he saw the opportunity for original development. But a poet's greatness rests largely on the extent to which he is able to effect a synthesis of preceding traditions while producing something that has not been achieved before. This provides the fourth element: the constant and individual interplay between the three traditions. Fused in the oeuvre, it is what gives Catullus's poetry its immediacy and, as far as Latin literature is concerned, its originality. Before Catullus, colloquialism had been confined to comedy; the elevated manner to epic or tragedy. In his poetry, for the first time, grandeur is heightened by unexpected realism. Colloquial diminutives express tenderness, which rubs shoulders with an equally colloquial grossness. The subject matter of the Roman epigram is broadened and shifted to the entirely new field of the personal lyric with a wide variety of metres, many of which are used for the first time. As for his own epigrams, he confined these, for the most part, to elegiacs and, in so doing, made the brittleness of the epigrammatic technique, once a limitation of the poetic sensibility, an end in itself, so that his most vitriolic fantasies become disembodied and intellectualised: imagery and metaphor are discarded and a startling directness of language takes their place. But the most important thing Catullus does for the Alexandrian Greek epigram is to make it personal.

The Greek stimulus sought by the 'new poets' came mainly from Alexandria. The reason for this was natural enough. Ever since its foundation by Alexander in 332 B. C., and the subsequent building of the great library by Ptolemy I (323-283), it had been the principal centre of Greek culture and learning. It represented what Greece meant to a contemporary. It would be unrealistic to expect writers to have gone behind Alexandria to Greece itself. Her judgements (in literary matters) were regarded judgements of Greece, or the Greek cities. Added to this, Alexandria had in the second century B.C., come under Rome's sphere of influence, and as recently as the year 80 had actually, been bequeathed to Rome by Ptolemy X in his will. The focal point for the scholars and poets of Alexan-

dria was, of course, the magnificent library, the greatest in the world carefully nursed, for their own political ends, by the Ptolemies. Callimachus himself, whom the 'new poets' seem to have held in especial regard, worked and taught there from c. 260 B.C. to his death in 250. Apollonius Rhodius (*c.* 295-*c.* 230), whose *Argonautica,* so sympathetic to modern tastes, was clearly known to Catullus, was a pupil of his. This was where the 'new poets' derived their ideal of the scholar-poet. It was here that they learnt to attach as much importance to the complexity of a poet's attitudes as to their consistency; it was here that they learnt their love of allusion and the oblique manner, and to cultivate an almost eighteenth-century type of artistic sensibility. It was here they learnt their respect for craftsmanship and their devotion to form and structure. But the 'new poets' applied these Alexandrian principles and techniques to a very un-Alexandrian situation. The Alexandrian school had been engaged in resuscitating, and to some degree had succeeded in embalming, an old tradition; the 'new poets' were endeavouring to found a new one. When considering the Alexandrian school as a whole, it is permissible to regret the lack of (apparent) spontaneity which characterised the earlier age of the Greek lyric. But spontaneity, or its appearance, is by no means the *sine qua non* of a successful poem. We regret its absence only in certain moods. To compare a poem of T. S. Eliot's to 'Go Lovely Rose' and find Eliot wanting, is to indulge in an extra-literary judgement. Only a prejudice against Alexandrianism, as such, could lead us to deplore its deep and widespread influence over Catullus and his circle. They or Catullus—had plenty of 'spontaneity', and if his more substantial works, such as **poems 64 and 68**, do at times read a little like *The Waste Land,* they seem none the worse for that.

The longer works (**'61-8'**) stand in the middle of the volume of his poems as it has come down to us, and deserve special mention. But first there is the volume itself, which is curiously arranged. It is in three parts: mixed lyrics, long poems and epigrams. The epigrams are nearly all quite short. **'Poem 76'**, the longest, runs to no more than twenty-six lines, and may more properly be called a love elegy. With **'68'**, it represents the first example of its kind in Latin This section is introduced, metrically, by the second half of the long poems, **'65-8'**, which are all in elegiacs. The lyrics (**'1-60'**) are in various metres, sapphics, choliambics, iambic trimeters, and the metre which Catullus made peculiarly his own, the Phalaecian hendecasyllable, which appears to be calculatedly inserted between the others. **'Poem 34'**, the hymn to Diana, is the only one in this group to be written in glyconics, and, as with the elegiacs and poems **'65-8'**, so here we find that the first of the long poems is also written in glyconics. It is clear that whoever arranged the poems did so on an almost exclusively metrical basis. This would suggest that the arrangement was at least post-Augustan. But the decisive factor is the length of the whole book—approximately 2,300 lines. This was enough to fill nearly three rolls; and the roll did not give place to our book form until the third or fourth century A.D. A likely theory is that poems '1-60' were originally a collection on their own, perhaps arranged by Catullus and preceded by the dedication to Cornelius Nepos. Various of the long poems, notably '64,' would have been published as individual items, while the poems at the end may only have been passed round privately among intimates. There is no means of knowing whether they are complete, or whether they are a selection. While they contain some of Catullus's best and most characteristic work, they are of varying worth, and are certainly more scrappily arranged than the lyrics.

Turning to the long poems, we see that '61' is in the form of a personal epithalamium. Its recipient was Lucius Manlius Torquatus, a close friend of Catullus; about the wife we know nothing. 'Poem 62' is another epithalamium, but generalised. Taken with poem '34', it is one of the only two non-personal or public poems that he ever wrote. It is written in hexameters. 'Poem 63' is the celebrated *Attis*. The subject is again the relationship between male and female but it is treated psychologically, in terms of Catullus's own experience, which he projects into the world of myth. It is written in the galliambic metre, so-called from the priests of Cybele, the *galli,* from whose ritual cries and dance movements it was said to be derived. It is the only poem to have survived in this metre either in Latin or Greek. Poem 64 blends each of the foregoing elements: it is mythological; love is a public, official affair (the marriage of Peleus and Thetis), and a private one (Ariadne's elopement, desertion and consolation). Like '62' it is in hexameters; they are the only two poems he wrote in this metre, and it will be seen that they neatly sandwich the unique galliambics. 'Poem 65' introduces three new subjects: poetry itself friendship and the loss of his brother. It is a dedicatory epistle to '66' and is addressed to Q. Hortensius Hortalus. It initiates the series written in elegiacs. 'Poem 66' itself is a direct translation from a poem of Callimachus', an elegant piece of court poetry verging on persiflage. Nothing—or little—is accidental in Catullus, least of all the subject matter of a translated poem. ('Poem 51', his other direct translation, is further proof of this.) In 'No. 66' he chose a poem in which the protagonist—a woman's lock of hair—laments the fact that it was severed from its mistress's head on her wedding night, before she had had time to experience the pleasures of married love. The lock recounts the occasion and its circumstances, concluding with a request for votive offerings of the scents used by married women, since it never experienced these in life. If wives preface the 'chaste dalliance of the marriage bed' with libations such as these, they will be blest with arts which will keep their husbands faithful to them. I believe that

Catullus has exaggerated the element of persiflage that he found in the original and used his subject matter as an opportunity to turn the poem he is translating inside out and thus make a personal poem out of a quasi official one. (Callimachus wrote the piece very soon after the events which it describes.) 'Poem 67', set in 'the province', consists of a dialogue between Catullus and the door of an unnamed woman. The Caecilius who is spoken of as having right of access to the house may be the fellow poet of 'No. 35', who had written a poem, presumably not unlike the *Peleus and Thetis,* on Cybele. Unfortunately, the local allusions are lost on us. We are confronted with (at the least) incest and adultery, and an attempt to swindle an inheritance out of someone under the Lex Voconia, whereby a daughter was unable to inherit a substantial sum unless she produced a male child, in which case she could hold the money in trust. (The same reference is found in 'Poem 68'.) The poem is amusing, coarse, realistic, and presents us with the obverse of '61' and '62'. 'Poem 68' is addressed to Manlius Torquatus. I accept the theory that Manlius's wife, Aurunculeia, has died, and that the poem is principally one of consolation. But Manilus's love and loss is intricately interwoven with Catullus's own loss (of his brother) and love (of Lesbia). The themes of friendship and poetry make their reappearance. If '67' was local and realistic, '68' is local and romantic. Mythology is used again, but not now as a framework, as in '64'. In '64' the mythological landscape was touched with realistic detail. Here, the world of reality is irradiated by myth. The poem has a trancelike quality.

Enough should have been said to show that this middle section contains poems that are essential to an understanding of Catullus and that cannot be regarded separately from the rest of his work. If this seems a curious statement to the reader who has read my translations but is no Catullan scholar, then one of the purposes of my version will have been achieved. Not only do these poems form a unity in themselves but in their unreal and, in the *Attis,* violent and catastrophic, handling of the sexual relationship, they cast backwards to the extremes of tenderness, in the lyrics, and forwards to the obscenities of the Gellius sequence. (There are 'obscene' poems in section '1-60', and warm and tender poems in section 69-116; but as a generalization the distinction may be allowed to stand.) Catullus is, of course, a lyric poet. But, as far as the middle section is concerned '61' is nothing if not lyric; '65' and '68' both have very great lyrical beauty of a grave and meditative kind: while no man should imagine he can fully apprehend the spirit which informs the sparrow or the kissing poems, unless he has the *Attis* in his other hand. The objection to the longer poems would seem to resolve itself into an objection to '64'. Since '64', together with '68', were doubtless the poems which he himself regarded most highly, another look at both of them would seem to be indicated.

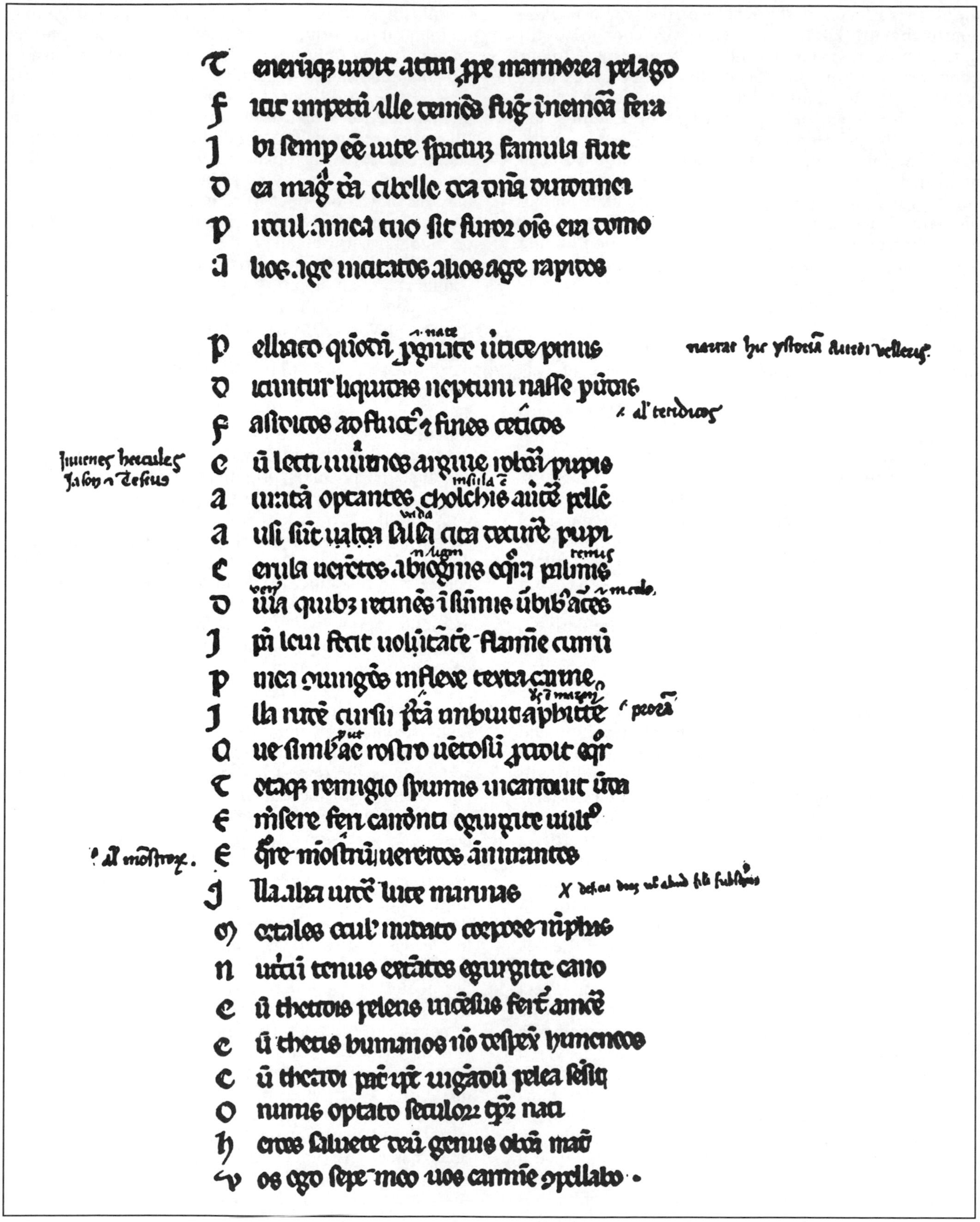

A page from the "Codex O" manuscript of Catullus's poetry.

'**Poem 64**' is the centrepiece of the *Carmina*. It is a window on the world of the gods. If to-day we look back over our shoulders a thousand years or so we do not, even if we are G. K. Chesterton Distributists, feel that we have missed-out on Eden. But a similar idea does appear to have haunted both Greeks and Romans round about the beginning of the Christian era. It was no mere accident of literary fancy that insisted that all genealogies, whether of city, state or hero, should be traced back to the time when the gods still walked the earth. This feeling was the inspiration of the Evander passages in the *Aeneid,* of the whole of Ovid's sprawling *Metamorphoses* and, of course, of the *Peleus and Thetis*. Although the part played by Crete in the early history of the Aegean basin was then unknown, it is plain from both myth and legend that the Minoan age was in some obscure way recognised as the time when this desirable state obtained. In the *Peleus and Thetis* Catullus employs all the resources of a highly eclectic and allusive use of myth to depict its passing. In a sense, his method allows him to have things both ways. He can pin-point details which serve his purpose, but even while he is doing this the body of the material he does *not* use still exerts its influence over the reader's mind. Taking the Argonautic expedition as a whole, the fact that Peleus leant over the side of the ship and saw and fell in love with the sea-nymph Thetis, is of such slight importance that it might well pass unmentioned; while Ariadne, deserted on Naxos, and Aegeus, committing suicide because of the wrong coloured sail, are traditionally, and rightly, regarded as postscripts to the Minotaur myth. Yet it is from the interlocking of details such as these, taken from quite separate mythological cycles, that Catullus conjures his orderly, consistent and convincing narrative. His points of departure are pre-Homeric Crete, the marriage of Peleus and Thetis, and Troy. The connection between them is effected (backwards to Crete) by the wedding quilt, and (forwards to Troy) by the ill-omened epithalamium. We are shown how the fall of Minoan Crete marked a process which, via the birth of Achilles, found its conclusion in the fall of Troy. As though this were not enough, Catullus also manages to tell us what the golden age once meant in terms of human happiness and what the future held in terms of human distress. He describes how a goddess marries a man, and a woman marries a god. A life of heroic action is rewarded in the first instance, and love is eased of its passion in the second. (Ariadne, as a victim of faithlessness and unrequited love, is a mouthpiece for Catullus's own feelings.) He also shows Nemesis overtaking evil (Aegeus's suicide), a foretaste of the state into which the world is about to lapse. The way in which the whole poem folds inwards on itself to the seventy lines of Ariadne's lament, which represents the 'personal' centre of the poem, is perhaps best shown in tabulated form.

ll. 1-49: The Argonautic expedition on which Peleus

first sees Thetis; the wedding day; the Palace; the coverlet on the marriage bed.

ll. 50-264: Description of the scenes woven on the coverlet. This section is divisible as follows:

ll. 50-75: Ariadne on the beach at Naxos; the intrusion of evil in the shape of human faithlessness;

ll. 76-123: flashback of Theseus' expedition to Crete, the slaying of the Minotaur and Theseus' subsequent elopement with Ariadne;

ll. 124-31: return to Ariadne on Naxos;

ll. 132-201: Ariadne's lament and curse;

ll. 202-14: the Gods, as Theseus nears Greece, hear Ariadne's curse;

ll. 215-37: flashback of Aegeus's instructions to Theseus before he set sail for Crete, and Aegeus's feelings on that occasion;

ll. 238-48: return to the present; Theseus forgets his instructions; Aegeus commits suicide; Theseus' state of mind is compared to

ll. 249-50: that of Ariadne as she stands gazing out to sea after him;

ll. 251-64: the scene passes forward to the advent of Bacchus which ends the description of the coverlet.

ll. 265-77: Departure of the mortal guests.

ll. 278-304: Advent of the immortals—the Olympians, Jupiter and Juno, attended by the three demi-gods particularly associated with the bride and bridegroom. First: Chiron, the local deity of the chief mountain of Thessaly, Pelion, and the future tutor of Achilles;secondly, Peneus, spirit of the principal river and related to Thetis; and thirdly, Prometheus, who foreseeing the glory that will accrue from the marriage has persuaded Jupiter to sanction it. Apollo, who is to be the author of Achilles' death is mentioned as staying behind on Olympus.

ll. 305-22: Description of the Parcae.

ll. 323-81: Hymn of the Parcae, constituting the epithalamium; the scene moves forward as the Fates foretell the birth of Achilles and the subsequent fall of Troy.

ll. 382-408: Final peroration on the fallen state of man and the vanished golden age with which the poem has opened.

The total effect is cinematic. We have glimpses of

paradisal landscapes emerging from the clear, primal world of sea and sky. But the clarity is deceptive and the landscapes and figures dissolve into one another and are never fully revealed. All is a little mysterious; which is as it should be for without mystery there is no paradise.

The second of Catullus's Alexandrian pieces ('**68**') is even more complex. Unfortunately, the text is very corrupt. We do not even know for certain whether it is one poem or two. (In the original codex, now lost, there was no indication where one poem ended and another began, and the copyist, after a break in his work, was quite capable of taking up his pen again at the wrong place.) It is unlikely that the string of queries which the poem prompts will ever be satisfactorily resolved. If it is one poem, is it addressed to 'Allius', or 'Mallius', and is this person identifiable with L. Manlius Torquatus of poem '**61**'? Is the *domina* of the house which has been lent to Catullus for his meetings with Lesbia(?) its *châtelaine,* or Torquatus's mistress or both? And is his wife, Aurunculeia, dead? And is her death really the main subject of the poem or, more accurately, the core around which the poem is built? As elsewhere, I have taken different readings from different texts, and different suggestions from different scholars—usually I have found that it has been the more traditional interpretation that has attracted me—and having selected my material on the basis of what I found most stimulating poetically, I have then tried to rewrite the poem as I imagined Catullus might have written it had he been alive to-day and writing in English. As a poem is more than the sum of its constituent parts, a certain ruthlessness over details is often necessary. It is the whole poem which has to be captured and rewritten. One is, of course, grateful for whatever donne's fall into one's lap, passim. But the details of a poem are to be digested so that they become a part of the living grain of the new poem, not embalmed like flies in ointment. Since '**68**' is not a narrative poem, a table setting out the various strands of which it is composed will need to be a little more explanatory than was the case with '**64**'.

ll. 1-40: Preface. Manlius has written to Catullus asking him for 'gifts of Love and the Muses' to console him in his sorrow. Catullus replies by saying that his own sorrows match Manlius's, and that he cannot comfort him as he would wish. Manlius's sorrow consists of the loss of his young wife, Aurunculeai; Catullus's of the loss of his brother.

ll. 41-74: Catullus nevertheless decides to record the debt that he owes to Manlius, weho once provided him with a house in which he could meet Lesbia and in which they could make love. She comes to him as a 'bright-shining goddess'.

ll. 74-86: His own love for Lesbia, and the dead Au-

runculeia's for Manlius are fused in the image of Laodamia, the symbol of wifely passion.

ll. 87-90: Troy, where Laodamia lost her husband, Protcsilaus, is apostrophised in the first of two bridge pasages as a source of widespread sorrow. (There may be a connection here with the 'historical' view of Troy expressed in 64, where its fall marks the end of the golden age.) Through Troy, Laodamia's loss is linked to Catullus's and so to Manlius's. In the intensity of her love she represents Aurunculeia, and of her grief, Manlius.

ll. 91-100: Catullus's brother was buried near Troy. The theme of his dead brother was broached in the first section of the poem; it is taken up again and expanded. Catullus repeats the original lines (20-4) nearly word for word.

ll. 101-4: The second of the bridge passages about the Trojan War. It is worth noting that Helen is mentioned by name in the first, and Paris in the second. In themselves the two passages constitute a laconic reflection from outside the body of the poem—on the inherently calamitous nature of mortal love.

ll. 105-30: Catullus passes from the cause of Leodamia's grief to an analysis of her love. He does this by means of three sustained similes, each to do with a different sort of bird: the Stymphalian birds of Hercules's Sixth Labour, the vulture, and mating doves. The poetic significance of the passage has puzzled commentators. Catullus's technique is similar to that of our seventeenth-century Metaphysicals. In lines 74-86, Laodamia's love is evoked in such a way that we are intended to participate in it, here the intention is that we should understand it. The passages complement each other.

To take the similes in order: I read the caverns under Mount Cyllene as a reference to the consummation of the marriage. Hercules can stand only for Manlius. We cannot know what his Sixth Labour suggested to a man of Catullus's day: but there can be no doubt that in the context of the poem the derivation of the word 'Stymphalus' (. . . the male and female members) is of peculiar significance. The reference to Hebe, goddess of eternal youth, whom Hercules marries on his apotheosis, indicates that Aurunculeia, still young, will be reunited with Manlius in the next world. In the second simile, the vulture symbolises death. The woman's gifts that the bride (Laodamia) brings will keep even death at bay. In the third simile, Isis's vulture gives place to Venus's doves which symbolise the enjoyment of sexual love. In brief, we have *(a)* ritualistic loss of virginity; *(b)* the expectations and the transforming power of love; *(c)* sexual pleasure.

ll. 131-48: Reintroduction of the theme of Catullus

and Lesbia's love for each other. Their illicit relationship is compared with that of married love.

II. 149-60: Epilogue. Catullus has, after all, written a poem to Manlius. Not a formal piece, such as he sent to Hortalus in '66', but an account of their relations with each other. The poem ends with a final evocation of Lesbia as 'she who endows Catullus with the quality of vision'.

I have often felt that the poem reads like an expansion of '65'. Both poems consist of a similar, elaborate interweaving of the themes on which Catullus felt most deeply. Both have the same slow-trailing movement of successive clauses loosely drawn out. But what made the poem new in Latin, and remains its outstanding virtue, is the calculated and delicate of use to delineate specific psychological states. It is a reminder what we may well have lost in the works of Calvus, Cinna and the other 'new poets'.

There remains the *Attis*. Walter Savage Landor's comment with which he concludes his long survey of Doering's second edition of the *Carmina* (published nearly fifty years after his first, Leipzig, 1788) provides a fitting and amusing prelude to any discussion of the poem.

> They who have listened, patiently and supinely, to the catarrhal songsters of goose-grazed commons, will be loth and ill-fitted to mount up with Catullus to the highest steeps in the forests of Ida and will shudder at the music of the Corybantes in the temple of the Great Mother of the Gods.

The poem is a strange one, both violent and barbaric, full of odd coinings and archaisms, and written in the breakneck metre known as 'galliambic'. The youth Attis is described as crossing the sea to Asia Minor and there castrating himself in the frenzy of his devotion to the Mother Goddess. The act is accompanied in the original Latin by a change of gender. Attis calls to the other initiates of Cybele's cult to join him at her shrine on Mount Ida. There he falls into a coma. On waking, his immediate reaction is to regret what he has done. He returns to the beach and looks back over the sea. There follows a twenty-three-line lament for the civilised patrimony which he has abandoned. This patrimony is described in Greek terms not Roman, a fact which has led some scholars to presume a Greek model, even a Greek original, and to read the whole as an expression of conflict between civilised and barbaric values. Even if such an interpretation is correct, it still leaves the core of the poem untouched. Following Attis's lament, Cybele unyokes one of her lions and instructs it to drive Attis back into the thickets on the slopes of Ida, where he is to remain for the rest of his life, a helpless devotee. In the last three lines, Catullus prays to Cybele to protect him from such desires; 'goad

others to rabid madness keep your fury from my house'. The lines are spoken as though he has woken from a nightmare (the preceding ninety lines) and recognized, with horror, himself in the figure of the unfortunate Attis. To emphasise this reading I have placed the last four lines of my version in direct quotes.

When considering the significance of this poem, I have always found it suggestive that the Temple of Cybele stood not far from Clodia's house, on the Palatine. The clashing cymbals, the drums and the peculiar ululating cries of the worshippers must on occasion have been audible to the members of Metellus Celer's household. Whether the initial stimulus that Catullus found in the myth lay simply in an accident of locality such as this, or whether it weas the result of his trip to Asia Minor, it is impossible to say. The worship of Cybele had been introduced into Rome in the year 204 B.C., during the Second Punic War. A black stone representing the Goddess had been brought up the Tiber and placed, temporarily, in the Temple of Victoria, since the new temple which was designed to house it had not yet been completed. The cult was of Anatolian origin and was ecstatic like that of Dionysus, some of the terms being interchangeable. The general effect of both has been described as not unlike a latter-day Dervish dance. The worshippers inflicted wounds on themselves, were liable to despatch anyone who stumbled on their devotions, and, in the rites of the Mother Goddess, actually underwent voluntary castration. The fundamentally grave Romans viewed the cult with suspicion, and it was not allowed to spread.

On many occasions, in moments of intense emotion Catullus expresses his feelings in the guise of a woman. The fact that homosexuality was not then considered either as a vice, an aberration or a disease, as it is now, is attendant but not cardinal to the point that I wish to make, which is that there was in Catullus a strain of femininity which went deeper than 'normal' adherence to the bisexual conventions of his class and time. His Iuventius poems strike exactly the same note as the heterosexual poems such as '32', that were not written to Clodia. The absence of 'guilt' is matched by a similar absence of 'spirituality'—of anything that is not a straightforward satisfaction of desire. With Clodia, lust is at a discount. It is she, to speak from the evidence of the poems, who displays the animality, not him. In '**No. 72**' he even compares his feelings for her with those of a fisher for his daughter: an attitude unique in Roman poetry. '**Poem 51**' is a translation from Sappho. It is the poem in which he gives Clodia the name of 'Lesbia'. In it, not only does he speak to her in the person of Sappho but the poem he has chosen to translate is one in which Sappho describes the physical sensations she experiences from the close presence of her beloved, in her case, if we accept the tradition, another woman. In the beautiful, tentacular '**65**', the startling, bright little vignette at the end (which is in itself a brilliant switch from the inclusive to the elliptical) represents an identification of himself with a young girl who is caught harbouring a guilty secret, the secret being her awareness of her own sexuality, symbolised by an apple. In poem '2', he wishes he were able to play with Lesbia's sparrow, *as Lesbia does,* and imagines that if he were, he would feel like Atalanta, when she stooped to pick up the apple and so lost the foot-race and, with it, her virginity. In 'No. 66', we have observed how he assumes the *persona* of a woman's lock of hair; while in 'No. 68' we noted a similar switch of sexes in the passages where he describes Manlius's and his own grief in terms of Laodamia's. But there is an obverse to this side of Catullus's nature. It is to be found in his obsession with the more repulsive aspects of sexuality. ('Poem 97' and the Gellius sequence.) His male drives found their outlet here, and the more disagreeable the news they could report, the more justification they provided for his invert fantasies. In poem 11 he refers to Lesbia as 'dragging the guts' out of him in the love act; and elsewhere there are references to the way in which a woman 'drains' a man of virility. It is as though Catullus felt that at the moment of orgasm a man became like Cybele's priests behind Metellus Celer's house. This I believe to have been the significance of the Attis myth for Catullus. Woman has, as it were, a lien on man's sex, an attitude expressed in the priests' castration and in the dramatic change of gender in the poem. It is the reason why Catullus was both repelled and attracted by the myth. The hate which Attis proclaims for Venus in line 17 is identical with that which Catullus in poem '85' expresses for Clodia. It has nothing to do with the antipathy of discordant elements, but arises from the repulsion from which attraction draws its strength, each succeeding the other in the love-hate see-saw. The experience is, of course, that of the manic depressive. And the *Attis*, as is now generally accepted, is a document of that state.

As a footnote to the poem, it is worth recalling the story of how an ancestress of Clodia's vindicated her chastity by using her *zona* or girdle, to secure the image of the Holy Mother when the ship bringing it up the Tiber ran aground in shoal water. It is unclear exactly how she did this, but the garment in question was evidently used to bring the image (it was probably a meteorite) safely to dry land. Clodia must have known the tradition. And Catullus too. Did he perceive and, if so, relish, the irony it contained for him?

The hills around Lake Garda can have altered little since Catullus's day, and the waters of the lake not at all. Garda is subject to very swift changes of weather. The wind off the Dolomites blows down over Trento to Riva at the head of the lake. The hills which stand close in to the northern shore conduct the wind from one end of Garda to the other. Suddenly the water will be curled into steep, crested waves, so that the lake

looks like the open sea. A very slight shift of wind and the waters will be smooth again. The pleasure boats which in the tourist season ply north and south between Riva, Malcesine and Desenzano wisely hug the coast. The violent and abrupt changes of mood which characterise the lake are also characteristic of Catullus's poetry. They are each as unpredictable as the other. But the lake could be called—is invariably and justly called 'beautiful', and that is not the aptest word to apply to Catullus's poetry. There is immediacy and vitality and pathos and nobility. He riddles away with words, juggling them about, a dozen times in half as many lines: eyes, apples, stars, numbers and then more numbers. The primitive is sometimes surprisingly near the surface. He has made his own mirror, not of life but of himself, and in this of course he is a Romantic. The tributes to him in English poetry are innumerable. They start with Ben Jonson, and go through Lovelace to Landor and Tennyson, Swinburne, Arthur Symons, Yeats and Ezra Pound. And when I think how I shall conclude this tribute of mine, I turn again to Walter Savage Landor whom I have just quoted and whose paraphrases and adaptations stand second only to those of Ben Jonson. The lines touch on the problem of Catullus's 'obscenity'. Landor, whom no one could accuse of laxity in this respect, saw that the question was of little or no importance in itself, and existed only in an incidental relationship to the whole work. The picture is a charming one, and not without relevance in these days of hasty and intemperate opinions on the subject of what should and should not be printed.

> Tell me not what too well I know
> About the bard of Sirmio—
>   Yes, in Thalia's son
> Such stains there are—as when a Grace
> Sprinkles another's laughing face
>   *With nectar, and runs on.*

Kenneth Quinn (essay date 1972)

SOURCE: "The Poetry of Social Coment," in *Catullus: An Interpretation,* B. T. Batsford Ltd., 1972, pp. 204-82.

[*In the following essay, Quinn explores Catullus's poems that focus upon political and social commentary: those poems which, in the main, "establish a norm (if one can speak of a norm in connexion with a segment of society whose habits are often so abnormal), set against which the Lesbia affair stands out in sharp contrast, without any more needing to be said."*]

There are only something like twenty-five to thirty Lesbia poems in a collection which numbers in all one hundred and thirteen poems. Among the rest are old favourites such as 'Catullus' Yacht' ('Poem 4'), 'Sirmio' ('Poem 31') and **'Arrius and his Aitches' ('Poem 84')**. And then of course there are the **'Attis' ('Poem 63')** and the **'Peleus and Thetis' ('Poem 64')** and the two marriage hymns (Poems **'61'** and **'62'**). Anyone who knows his Catullus could easily list a score of poems, some equally well known, others poems which just happen to appeal to him personally. But one does this very much in the frame of mind of a man who is making up a supplementary list: it is the Lesbia poems, we feel, that matter; the rest are sometimes striking, not infrequently obscene, often poems we haven't read for years. No doubt it was all part of the urbane casualness with which Catullus presents his collection in Poem 1 to offer the reader a very mixed bag, in which the Lesbia poems, however much they stood out, were deliberately classed as *nugae* along with the rest. It is easy to forget that 'the rest' means three quarters of the collection.

If we look only at the figures (one in four a Lesbia poem), it may seem paradoxical to claim that the Lesbia poems form the really important part, not just of the first group of sixty poems, but of the total of one hundred and thirteen, and to relegate the rest to the status of background. Yet I doubt very much that any critic would want to deny primacy of importance to the Lesbia poems, at any rate in the two groups of short poems, **'1-60'** and **'69-116'**. What puzzles some is the presence in such numbers of other poems, and the apparent triviality of many of these. Even when allowance has been made for the unusual range in the level of intent—the result of the way in which Catullus became, so to speak, a serious poet by accident—the trivial pieces seem to outnumber needlessly the pieces we can take seriously as poems. Most critics resolve their puzzlement by assuming a haphazard collection, in which everything that has survived got preserved, simply because Catullus was known to have been the author. . . .

[My own view] is that, in the collection which Catullus planned, the Lesbia poems were placed in a contrasting context against which the poet's affair with his mistress stands out in sharp, implicit relief. The mixed bag isn't the result of a haphazard collection gathered together by somebody else: it is an effect planned by Catullus himself; more thought has been devoted to the contents of the bag than is obvious on first inspection; the mixed bag, in short, is largely an illusion.

That is not to say of course that the other poems were written to form this contrasting background. Still less that they were written to compose Catullus' picture of social life and politics, say, in his day. Each poem is self-contained and self-sufficient. At first reading, the poems break up into small, apparently unrelated subseries—the Bithynia poems, the Juventius poems, and so on; others don't seem to fit in particularly anywhere. There is no hope of piecing all the background poems together into a single picture: however much those who find the game attractive rack their brains over the jig-saw puzzle, there aren't enough pieces to form anything you could call a comprehensive background, and there are always pieces left over that can't be fitted in at all.

I believe none the less that the picture—a tantalizing, fragmentary sort of picture—was the guiding principle of the collection. Here and there a poem may have been revised, or specially written (though I imagine there was more of this with the Lesbia poems than with the rest). But in the main the picture is built up by poems already written. I am confident all the same that when Catullus came to arrange his poems for publication, some such guiding principle dictated choice and arrangement of the pieces which were to provide the background to the Lesbia poems. Perhaps people were already saying of Lucilius what Horace was to say a generation later *(Satires* 2.1.30-4):

> ille uelut fidis arcane sodalibus olim
> credebat libris, neque si male cesserat umquam
> decurrens alto, neque si bene; quo fit ut omnis
> uotiua pateat ueluti descripta tabella
> uita senis. . . .

> He used to confide secrets to his books, as if
> they were trusted friends, turning nowhere
>   else, whether
> things had gone badly, or gone well. So that
>   old Lucilius'
> whole life, as if painted on a votive tablet,
>   was there
> for all to see. . . .

Cicero said much the same of the poems of Philodemus in 55 B.C., just at the time when Catullus may be supposed to have been putting his collection together: they constituted a picture, or as Cicero put it, a mirror, of the way of life of Philodemus' patron Piso. It didn't occur perhaps to Lucilius that his poems, taken together, built up a picture of a personality and a way of life. Nor does Cicero mean Philodemus intended his poems to mirror his patron's way of life; it hadn't perhaps occurred to Philodemus either that a collection of poems written at different times and in different circumstances could be used in this way. Both poets perhaps simply thought of themselves as writing poems about what went on around them. It was only when collections came to be made that the collective force of such poems became apparent.

By 55 B.C., however, the idea that a collection of poems could work this way was in the air. I find it easy to believe that Catullus, casting round for a guiding principle for a collection of poems traditionally too slight to be taken seriously, should have hit upon the principle of a picture of the way of life of a section .

of society, as a background against which he could set the poems about himself and his mistress. He need not have taken the idea very seriously. It would be absurd to suppose a rigid principle of selection and arrangement, strictly adhered to. But that Catullus did set himself some such principle to work to in selecting and arranging the poems he had written is hardly a rash hypothesis: it would help him in deciding which to keep and which to reject, as well as helping in his decisions about the order in which to place the poems he chose.

There are a few cases where the function of a poem as social comment may fairly be pointed to. Political poems, such as **'Poem 29'** (*Quis hoc potest uidere, quis potest pati? . . .*) or **'Poem 52'** (*Quid est, Catulle, quid moraris emori? . . .*) are cases in point. Their function as social comment is clear because in them Catullus is following a recognized tradition of political lampoon. At the same time they form part of the picture of the world in which Catullus moved, and his reactions to it. Or take Poems **'43'** (*Salue, nec minimo puella nave . . .*) and **'86'** (*Quintia formosa est multis . . .*). Here the social comment lies in the explicitly stated contrast: in **'Poem 43'** it is 'fools compare Ameana with Lesbia'; in **'Poem 86'** it is 'Quintia has good looks, but lacks Lesbia's personality'. In both poems Catulllls opposes his own standards to conventional standards, scornfully rejecting the latter. Mostly, however, the social comment is implicit: the function of the background poems is to establish a norm (if one can speak of a norm in connexion with a segment of society whose habits are often so abnormal), set against which the Lesbia affair stands out in sharp contrast, without any more needing to be said.

A familiar name frequently provides an easy transition from the Lesbia poems to their context. Plainly the Egnatius of **'Poem 39'** (39. 1-2):

> Egnatius, quod candidos habet dentes,
> renidet usquequaque. . . .

> Egnatius' teeth are shining white, and so he breaks
> on every conceivable occasion into a flashing grin. . . .

is also the Egnatius who is the subject of the thumbnail sketch in the concluding lines of **'Poem 37'**, where he is singled out for special attention among the lovers of Lesbia who frequent the *salax taberna*. To miss the connexion with **'Poem 37'** is to miss the reason for the savagery which lies so near the surface in the fantasy of **'Poem 39'**.

Of the five Caelius and Rufus poems, **'Poem 58'** (*Caeli, Lesbia nostra. . . .*) is a Lesbia poem; so too, possibly,

is **'Poem 7'**, (*Rufe mihi frustra ac nequiquam credite amice . . .*). **'Poem 69'** (*Noli admirari, quare tibi femina nulla . . .*), **'Poem 71'** (*Si cui lure bono sacer alarum obstitit hircus . . .*) and **'Poem 100'** (*Caelius Aufillenum et Quintius Aufillenam . . .*) belong, like the second Egnatius poem, to the background; they are part of the poetry of social comment. But at the same time we feel we know why Rufus is being got at in Poems **'69'** and **'71'**: like Egnatius, he is now one of the 'small-time back-street lechers' (37. 16 *pusilli et semitarii moechi*), however close a friend of Catullus he may have been once. The first and the third of the elegiac fragments (Poems **'69'** and **'71'**) are addressed to Rufus, while the second and the fourth (Poems **'70'** and **'72'**) are addressed to Lesbia. Then in **'Poem 77'** Rufus is bitterly reproached for betraying his friend: I find the obvious inference hard to avoid, that Rufus, like Gellius in **'Poem 91'** (*Non ideo, Gelli, sperabam te mihi fidum . . .*) has betrayed his friend by stealing his mistress. When we come to **'Poem 100'** (100. 1-4):

> Caelius Aufillenum et Quintius Aufillenam
> flos Veronensum depereunt inuenum,
> hic fratrem, ille sororem. hoc est, quod dicitur, illud
> fraternum uere dulce sodalicium. . . .

> My story is of Caelius and Quintius, cream of Verona's
> youth: the one's madly in love with Aufillenus, the
> other with Aufillenus' sister. That's what they mean
> when they talk of true, sweet brotherly solidarity. . . .

the reader who knows his Catullus stretches out to bridge the gap between Catullus' feelings for Caelius once (100. 5-8):

> cui faueam potius? Caeli, tibi: nam tua nobis
> perspecta est igni tum unica amicitia,
> cum uesana meas torreret flamma medullas.
> sis felix, Caeli, sis in amore potens.

> Whom shall I back? Why, you, Caelius, for your outstanding friendship for me has stood the test of fire, that time
> when mad passion's flame scorched the marrow of my bones.
> Good luck to you, Caelius! Much success in love!

and his feelings, left so eloquently unexpressed, for that friend who has stood the test of fire, on another occasion (**'Poem 58'**):

> Caeli, Lesbia rostra, Lesbia illa,
> illa Lesbia, quam Catullus unam

plus quam se atque suos amauit omnes,
nunc in quadriuiis et angiportis
glubit magnanimi Remi nepotes.

Lesbia, Caelius, this Lesbia of ours,
this Lesbia, no one else, whom Catullus loved
more than self, more than all to whom he
   owed love,
now on street corners and in back alleys
peels Remus' generous descendants bare.

There is no way of lining these five poems up in a chronological sequence. We can only guess at the circumstances, at Catullus' attitude to Caelius at the time of writing each. As biography the poems are of little use. But that they reflect widely different circumstances and sharply different attitudes is evident.

Or take the Furius and Aurelius poems. We have seen the extent to which an apparent shift in attitude has worried commentators on **'Poem 11'**. The Furius and the Aurelius of **'Poem 11'**, however, are no less friends of Catullus, in my view, than they were in Poems **'15'**, **'16'**, **'21'**, **'23'** and **'26'**. But the circumstances and the level of intent are different. Friends can be teased (**'Poem 26'**—Furius' family have had to raise the wind on their villa), even teased a little unmercifully (**'Poem 23'**—Furius, his father and his stepmother are incredibly hard up, so . . . let them make a virtue of poverty: they aren't at any rate going to get any money out of Catullus). Or abused with that lurid extravagance in abuse which is possible between friends, especially if the charges border on literary fantasy (Poems **'15'** and **'21'**—Aurelius is accused of making passes at Juventius): as Cicero said, of comparable libellous accusations levelled at Caelius when he was younger, such insinuations, so long as they are wittily expressed and innocent of malice, are a mark of *urbanitas*. **'Poem 16'** is a *prise de position*: it is unreasonable, protests Catullus, to assume a man is a queer simply because he writes risqué homosexual verse; but the lines are also outrageously witty, and therefore an example as: well of *urbanitas*. In **'Poem 11'**, speaking of matters where *urbanitas* has no role to play (because the abuse is directed this time against Lesbia and is meant to hurt), Catullus perhaps feels both closer to his friends, and at the same time a little resentful at their uncomprehending anxiousness to help.

These changes in attitude are one of the things that lend the collection an exciting quality of depth. When Catullus selected and arranged his poems for publication, there must have been many which expressed attitudes to friends, former friends and acknowledged enemies that no longer corresponded to the way he' felt. Where his mistress was concerned, it was important to put on record the way he felt at the end, and **'Poem 11'** does this. But she was a special case. Where the rest were concerned, didn't matter if circumstances

and attitudes had altered. There was certainly no more need to reject poems on that account than there was to reject poems to and about Lesbia. The reader senses the clash in attitudes from one poem to another. Often it is plain enough. But usually he can do no more than guess the reasons for the change: he has something to go on, but never quite enough. The effect is oddly moving. I am inclined to think Catullus knew what he was doing.

I. The urbani

'Poem 37' (*Salax taberna uosque contubernales. . . .*) is both a Lesbia poem and a satirical picture of the members of a smart set and the life they live within the confines of their self-conscious non-conformity: Lesbia prefers the company of tines fatuously arrogant Don Juans to that of Catullus (37 14-20):

> hanc boni beatique
> omnes amatis, et quidem, quod indignum est,
> omnes pusilli et semitarii moechi
> tu praeter omnes, une de capillatis,
> cuniculosae Celtiberiae fili
> Egnati, opaca quem bonum facit barba
> et dens Hibera defricatus urine.

> Her you fine gentlemen love—
> the lot of you; and what's more to be
>   ashamed about,
> all you small-time back-street lechers too.
> You especially, O uniquely hairy one,
> son of Celtiberian bunny-land,
> Egnatius, all black-bearded distinction
> and teeth that gleam with Spanish piss.

Egnatius, though singled out (17 *tu praeter omnes. . . .*), is summarily disposed of, no doubt because he had already been dealt with at length in **'Poem 39'**, which begins with a string of vignettes of Egnatius—occasions when he succeeds in making himself conspicuous, without quite succeeding in being a social success (39. 1-8):

> Egnatius, quod candidos habet dentes,
> renidet usquequaque. si ad rei uentum est
> subsellium, cum orator excitat fletum,
> renidet ille; si ad pii rogum fili
> lugetur, orba cum flet unicum mater,
> renidet ille. quidquid est, ubicumque est,
> quodcumque agit, renidet: hunc habet morbum,
> neque elegantem, ut arbitror, neque urbanum. . . .

> Egnetius' teeth are shining white, and so he
>   breaks
> on every conceivable occasion into a flashing
>   grin. The prisoner's
> in the dock, his counsel's working on our
>   tears: Egnatius

breaks into a flashing grin. Or a funeral; grief
  on every

side, mother bereaved laments her only son:
  Egnatius

breaks into a flashing grin. On every
  conceivable occasion,

no matter what he's doing—flashing grin. It's
  a disease,

and one that's neither smart, I feel, nor
  sophisticated. . . .

Compare with these sketches of Egnatius and his friends the fuller picture we get from a different pen. Writing to his friend Atticus in February 61 B.C., Cicero describes a meeting of the Assembly called to pass a bill providing for the trial of Clodius (Clodia Metelli's brother) on a charge of desecrating the rites of the Bona Dea the previous year. A special bill was necessary because the case did not fall within the jurisdiction of any of the standing courts. The meeting was thrown into well organized chaos:

> When the day came for submitting the bill under the terms of the Senatorial decree, there was a crowd of young men with little beards charging around— all the Catilinarian gang, with that little queer, young Curio, as ring-leader—demanding that the people should throw the bill out. . . . Clodius' thugs had occupied the gangways; when the voting tablets were distributed, nobody got one with FOR THE BILL on it. . . .

These young men with their little beards are the smart young debauchees whom Cicero, when the Catilinarian affair came to a head a couple of years before, had grouped along with the bankrupts, the ex-soldiers and the criminals among the supporters of Catiline:

> Finally comes that group which is so typical of Catiline, not just in numbers but in its whole way of life. This is the group that really appeals to him, the one he embraces and holds onto with affection. You see them with their combed hair, all dolled up, beardless and fully bearded, long-sleeved, ankle-length tunics—or dressed in sails, you'd think, not togas; the one great purpose in their lives, the labour of their waking hours, to organize dinner parties that last till dawn's early light. Mixed up in their gangs are all the gamblers, all the adulterers, all the foul perverts in Rome. For these charming, precious youngsters are not only versed in the arts of making love and being loved, in dancing and in singing; they are also versed in dagger-play and in slipping a dose of poison in your cup. You can take it from me that, unless they are exiled or killed, our state will be a breeding ground of Catilines, even when Catiline himself is dead and gone. But what on earth do these poor fools think they're doing? Surely they can't take their girl friends along with them when they join Catiline's private army? But if they don't, how will they be able to stand it without them, the

nights being what they are at this time of year? How will they be able to endure the Apennine frosts and snows? Do they think that dancing in the nude at parties is good training for standing up to winter? What a war it's going to be: I'm scared to death when I think of General Catiline with whores on his staff! . . .

Catiline *was* dead of course by the time of Cicero's letter to Atticus, but the phrase 'all the Catilinarian gang' (*totus ille grex Catilinae*) was too useful a label to pin on young men whose ways and ideas he disliked for Cicero to abandon it simply because Catiline was dead and the threat of a *coup d'état* by Catiline a thing of the past. Had he not predicted that, even when Catiline was dead and buried, Rome would be 'a breeding ground of Catilines' (*scitote hoc in re publica Catilinarum seminarium futurum*)? Ten years later, on the eve of Caesar's crossing of the Rubicon, these will be 'the lost generation' (*tam perdita iuuentas*) whom Cicero lists among the supporters of Caesar.

Circumstances alter cases, of course, and in another letter to Atticus, a few months after the letter in which he described the breaking up of a meeting of the Assembly, Cicero preens himself at the thought that 'our friends' the goatee-bearded cafe revolutionaries' (*nostri isti commissatores coniurationis*) are linking his name with that of Pompey. And when he returned from exile (in September 57 B.C.), anxious for proof that he had not become a political has-been, it gave him pleasure to fancy the smart young men about town felt some grudging respect for an elder statesman like himself. Indeed, within six months of his return, he found himself defending one of these smart young men against the machinations (as Cicero would have us believe) of his ex-mistress Clodia. It was a forensic operation that called for some skilful footwork on thin ice, for there was no getting round the fact that Caelius had been, to say the least, one of the Catilinarian gang, and the cognoscenti must have admired Cicero's display of sympathetic indulgence towards those who had been unable to resist the undeniable charm of that, in so many ways, attractive swine:

> He was a supporter of Catiline, you say, some years after entering public life? So were many, of all ages and ranks of society. The fact is that Catiline, as I expect you remember, showed very many signs of admirable qualities, even if the signs were only sketched in outline, not clearly printed. There was a time, to be frank, when he came close to deceiving *me*. . . . If, among such crowds of friends, Caelius was also a friend of his, it is rather for him to regret his mistake, just as I sometimes regret the mistake I made about Catiline. . . .

It is characteristic of such groups of sophisticated young men everywhere that their individual commitment to the common interests of the group varies: if some are passionately involved in politics, the interest of other members of the group in politics is lukewarm, or non existent; for them, all that matters. in life is poetry, or women, or the demonstration of their emancipation from convention by the simple fact of belonging to a smart set. Cicero's picture of Catiline's supporters isn't that of a band of committed revolutionaries: there are determined, ruthless men among them, Cicero would have is believe, but for the rest toying with revolution is clearly just another way of breaking with convention. We may suspect that some of the *habitués* of the *salax taberna* of '**Poem 37**' talked politics as much as of wine, women and song; while others (Catullus, among them, perhaps, till he quarrelled with the group) were savagely contemptuous of politics and politicians.

These are the *urbani,* the elegant young men about town. It is very noticeable how the key words of their jargon, as reflected in Catullus (words like *lepidus* and *delicatus*), are taken up by Cicero to deride their preciousness; *urbanitas* itself, however, was a different matter. It is a quality ('wit', but with; overtones suggesting that the wit expresses the values of a socially acceptable group) frequently spoken of with approval by Cicero. He prided himself on possessing *urbanitas,* and was anxious that the credit should not be denied him for his witty remarks, complaining if the bad jokes of others were attributed to him. But *urbanitas* wasn't just a matter of cracking jokes, even good ones, it was a way of behaving, of being able to use ridicule effectively but without malice or meanness.

We can call these elegant young men, if we like, the members of a leisured class, though that term, to the modern ear, lays too strong an emphasis upon social background. The words used by Roman writers are *luxuria* ('soft living') and *otium* (half-way—because *otium* always suggested *negotium*—between 'leisure' and 'idleness'); the former if you were against it, the latter if you were not. For the *urbani, otium* meant that freedom to take life easy which is guaranteed by independent means or by patronage. The idea that one could lead a life of leisure was still comparatively novel in a society upon which, at one end, poverty weighed heavily (and continued to weigh heavily, of course, throughout antiquity) and, at the other end, extreme social constraint, the need (expressed through family pressure, or simply through the pressure of convention) to serve the republic as a member of her citizen armies in time of war or provincial uprising. To say nothing of the moral responsibility, amounting for those of any rank or standing in the old republic to something close to moral obligation, to serve the state as *patronus,* or as a member of an amateur administrative hierarchy that extended from such relatively minor offices as the curule aedileship to the higher 'magistracies' of the state. For Catullus' comments on the sort of people into whose hands these exalted offices sometimes fell, see '**Poem 52**' (52. 2-3):

sella in curuli struma Nonius sedet,
per consulatum peierat Vatinius. . . .

In the curule chair that boil Nonius sits;
by his consulship Vatinius swears, and lies. . . .

For many of the *urbani,* the pursuit of *otium* was no more than a brief period of social irresponsibility. Even during that period, we have seen that some at any rate of the *barbatuli iuuenes* took politics seriously enough to demonstrate at meetings called for the transaction of public business. Calvus and Cinna, friends of Catullus and, like him, poets, followed the traditional path of public service and public office, as did Caelius Rufus, about whose career we know a good deal, chiefly as a result of his letters to Cicero and Cicero's letters to him. Catullus himself 'served' (the word hardly exaggerates the Roman view of the matter, at any rate in theory) as a member of the personal staff of C. Memmius in Bithynia—and perhaps served again, three years later, under Crassus or Caesar. His friends Veranius and Fabullus served in similar fashion, once in Spain ('**Poem 9**') and then a second time, it seems, in Macedonia (Poems '**28**' and '**47**'), under Calpurnius Piso. We are still a generation removed from Horace's life-long commitment (after his early adventures in politics, military life and administration) to a career as man of letters; from the dedicated craftsmanship of Virgil; or from the life of acknowledged *desidia* of the poet-lover Propertius.

The key concepts of the *urbani* occur more often as adjectives than as nouns. In addition to the adjective *urbanus* itself, there are *elegans, lepidus, salsus* and *uenustus,* and the corresponding negatives—for it is not given to all to be *elegans, lepidus, salsus* or *uenustus;* or because it can be modestly asserted of a person or a thing approved of that the person or thing, far from being *insulsus* (say) is really *non inelegans,* or *non illepidus,* or *non inuenustus.* Varus' girl friend, for example, seemed (on first impression) *non sane illepidum, neque inuenustum* (10. 4), a phrase which is repeated in '**Poem 36**' of the view the goddess of love will take, Catullus hopes, of his proposal to substitute the Annals of Volusius as a burnt offering in place of some verses of his own (36. 17). We should add *ineptus* and *infacetus* (only the negative form is used in this connexion, though both *facetiae* and *infacetiae* occur); from *ineptus* comes the verb *ineptire* (8. 1 *Miser Catulle? desinas ineptire.* . . .) and a noun *ineptiae,* used as a suitably depreciatory description of Catullus' poems on an occasion when he was immodest enough to reckon with the possibility that they might survive ('**Poem 14b**'):

Si qui forte mearum ineptiarum
lectores eritis manusque uestras
non horrebitis admouere nobis. . . .

You (if such there are) who may chance to
  read
this poor stuff of mine, you whose hands
may without repugnance turn these pages. . .

Catullus had in mind perhaps the 'obscene' *jeux d'esprit*
which follow; but he assumes the same urbane tone in
'Poem 1'—the tone of a man who can speak lightly of
things that matter to him none the less.

To miss out on these qualities elicited urbane rejection. **'Poem 86'** (*Quintia formosa est multis* . . .) for
example: poor Quintia, though people rave about her
good looks, is utterly devoid of *uenustas*. Or **'Poem
12'** (*Marrucine Asini, manu sinistra non bella uteris .
. .*): Asinius Pollio's brother thinks going round souve-
niring people's table napkins is smart, whereas in fact
it is a shabby trick, not in the least *uenustus* (*5 qua-
muis sordida res et inuenusta est*). Or, to take a more
serious case, there is Suffenus: one might think, just to
meet the man and hear him talk, that he deserved to be
ranked among the *urbani* (22. 1-2):

> Suffenus iste, Vare, quem probe nosti,
> homo est uenustus et dicax et urbanus. . . .

> Friend Suffenus, Varus, you know him well of
>   course,
> a charming fellow, good talker, man about
>   town. . . .

Suffenus, however, prides himself as a poet. He writes
the stuff by the yard, publishes it in éditions de luxe.
And it's tripe (22. 9-11 and 12-14):

> haec cum legas tu, bellus ille et urbanus
> Suffenus unus caprimulgus aut fossor
> rursus uidetur. . . .

> . . . qui modo scurra
> aut si quid hac re scitius uidebatur,
> idem infaceto est infacetior rure. . . .

> When one reads the stuff, this elegant man
>   about town
> Suffenus seems just any ordinary goat-milker
> or ditch-digger. . . .

> . . . the man who just now
> seemed a wit or whatever there is that's
>   slicker than that—
> that's the man who's now uncouther than the
>   uncouth
> countryside. . . .

On a par, in fact, with the Annals of Volusius (36. 19-
20):

> pleni ruris et infacetiarum

> annales Volusi, cacata carte.

> you countrified, uncouthness-stuffed
> Annals of Volusius, paper shat upon.

When it comes to bad verse, Catullus' feelings almost
get the better of him. Passionate denunciation, however, is reserved for more extreme cases—Caesar's hang-
ers-on in **'Poem 54'**, or the bath-house pickpocket
Vibennius and his obscene son in **'Poem 33'**; or Aemilius, the unspeakable Don Juan of **'Poem 97'**.

The key-words express a code of behaviour in terms
that are external and conventional within the group;
they are flung out casually, with no claim to moral
seriousness or philosophical system. For the urbani they
express judgments which imply deliberate, apprecia-
tive restraint in approval. Or which damn.

II. The Pursuit of Love

Nearest to the Lesbia poems among the poems of social comment are those which build up a picture of
typical relationships between the *urbani* and their mistresses. These are:

'Poem   6' *Flaui, delicias tuas Catullo* . . .
'Poem 10' *Varus me meus ad suos amores* . . .
'Poem 17' *O Colonia, quae cupis ponte ludere longo*
. .
'Poem 32' *Amabo, mea dulcis Ipsitilla* . . .
'Poem 35' *Poetae tenero, meo sodali* . . .
'Poem 41' *Ameana, puella defututa* . . .
'Poem 45' *Acmen Septimius suos amores* . . .
'Poem 55' *Oramus, si forte non molestum est* . . .
'Poem 58b' *Non custos si fingar ille Cretum* . . .
'Poem 69' *Noli admirari, quare tioi femina nulla* . .
.
'Poem 71' *Si cui lure bono sacer alarum obstitit
hircus* . . .
'Poem 74' *Gellius audierat patruum obiurgare sol-
ere* . . .
'Poem 78' *Gallus habet fratres* . . .
'Poem 88' *Quid facit is, Gelli, qui cum matre atque
sorore.* . .
'Poem 90' *Nascatur magus ex Gelli matrisque nefan-
do* . . .
'Poem 94' *Mentula moechatur* . . .
'Poem 97' *Non (ita me di amens) quicquam referre
putaui.* . . .
'Poem 100' *Caelius Aufillenum et Quintius Aufille-
nam* . . .
'Poem 103' *Aut sodes mihi redde decem sestertia,
Silo* . . .
'Poem 110' *Aufillena, bonae semper laudantur ami-
cae* . . .
'Poem 111' *Aufillena, uiro contentam uiuere solo* . . .
'Poem 113' *Consule Pompeio primum duo, Cinna,
solebant* . . .

Naturally, these poems form a group only in the sense that it is critically useful to consider them together because in them certain themes preponderate. It is no more sensible to detach the group arbitrarily from the rest of the collection than it is to detach the Lesbia poems. Like any other such list we might make, it imposes decisions which are quite artificial. For example, I have included poems which involve Catullus himself (Poems '32', '103', '110')—he is after all one of the *urbani;* but I have omitted three poems in which Lesbia figures by name or certain allusion:

'Poem 43' *Salue, nec minimo puella nave . . .*
'Poem 86' *Quintia formosa est multis . . .*
'Poem 91' *Non ideo, Gelli, sperabam te mihi fidum . . .*

It is a good example of how the collection resists attempts at rigid classification. The list, like the list of Lesbia poems, also cuts across any prosopographical grouping: it includes only some of the Mamurra poems, for example. One can argue even that it should (again like the list of Lesbia poems) cut across the division into short and long poems, since we might very reasonably add **'Poem 67'** (*O dulci iacunda uiro, iacunda parenti. . .*)—the shortest of the long poems (apart from **'Poem 65'**, which is only an introductory note to **'Poem 66'**); or even the two marriage hymns (Poems **'61'** and **'62'**), since marriage and *furtiuus amor* are themes that go very much hand in hand in Catullus. It is also the place, I think, to consider **'Poem 63'**, as I hope to show.

To call these poems about the urbani and their mistresses 'poems about love' or 'poems about social life' is to define too loosely, or too arbitrarily, the area within which they move. A moral standard is clearly discernible: it challenges, or rather, it runs counter to, contemporary morality (which young men in all ages tend to shun as sham); but Catullus substitutes his own standards, and claims the right to be morally outraged when these are transgressed. It is probably exaggerated to speak of a moral intent: Catullus, I suspect, was too much influenced by Philodemus' doctrine of the conscious uselessness of poetry to allow himself to preach; at any rate this is the attitude flaunted. The fact remains that many of the poems on the list have the bitter, tight-lipped tone of Brechtian satire: the picture of a corrupt society is set as à background to the record of a shattered personal ideal.

The Human Comedy: the urbani and their mistresses in **Poems 1-60**

When Catullus writes about the relationships of young men and their mistresses in the poems which make up the first of the three groups in the Catullan collection, he presents an urbanely ironical picture of contemporary mores. At least he purports to do this. For the picture, though plainly presented as a picture of life in contemporary Rome (with occasional glances at Verona), is surprisingly like that painted by Plautus and Terence a century and more earlier; and the picture they paint is based on that painted by Menander and the writers of Greek New Comedy of life in fourth-century Athens: indeed, Athens, or at any rate Greece, is the ostensible setting of the comedies of Plautus and Terence. Admittedly we hear nothing in Catullus of domineering, skinflint fathers (and if there are references to censorious uncles, the uncles are quickly reduced to silence, as in **'Poem 74'**); nor do we hear anything of ingenious, witty slaves (the ancient-world version of P. G. Wodehouse's Jeeves), quick to put right all that goes wrong when a young master's ability to cope with the problems of life is reduced even further by infatuation with a pretty girl. That this remained the comic plot par excellence as long as Roman comedy survived (which is to say, until the Augustan age) is indicated by Horace's summary of a typical plot from a comedy of Fundanius, thee leading comic writer of the time. But the skinflint father and the witty slave are the result of the exigencies of plot-construction: their function is to produce the bewildering sequence of hopeless complication hard on the heels of hopeless complication. Their absence from the pages of Catullus isn't surprising, therefore. As far as the young men and their mistresses are concerned, little seems to have changed in a century to a century and a half.

The tempo of **'Poem 10'** is more relaxed than that of comedy, but Varus, his unnamed girl friend and Catullus move essentially in the same world:

Varus me meus ad suos amores
uisum duxerat e foro otiosum—
scortillum (ut mihi tum repente uisum est)
non sane illepidum neque inuenustum;
huc ut uenimus, incidere nobis
sermones uarii, in quibus, quid esset
iam Bithynia, quo modo se haberet,
et quonam mihi profuisset acre.
respondi id quod erat—nihil neque ipsis
nec praetoribus esse nec cohorti,
cur quisquam caput unctius referret—
praesertim quibus esset irrumator
praetor, nec faceret pill cohortem.
'at certe tamer,' inqulunt 'quod illic
natum dicitur esse, comparasti
ad lécticam homines.' ego (ut puellae
unum me facerem beatiorem)
'non' inquam 'mihi tam fuit' maligne,
ut, prouincia quod male incidisset,
non possem octo homines parare rectos.'
(at mi nullus erat nec hic neque illic,
fractum qui ueteris pedem grabati
in collo sibi collocare posses.)
hic illa, ut decuit cinaediorem,
'quaeso', inquit 'mihi, mi Catulle, paulum

istos commode: nam uolo ad Serapim
deferri.' 'mane,' inquii puellae,
'istud quod modo dixeram me habere . . .
fugit me ratio: meus sodalis—
Cinna est Gaius—is sibi parauit;
uerum utrum illius an mei, quid ad me?
utor tam bene quam mihi pararim—
sed tu insulsa male et molesta uiuis,
per quam non licet esse neglegentem!'

Varus had taken me off to meet his girl,
finding me in the Forum with time upon my
    hands.
An attractive wench, my first impression was
agreeable to talk to and not without a certain
    charm.
Well, when we got there, we began to discuss
a variety of subjects, including the sort
of place Bithynia was, the present state of it
and how I'd done in terms of cash while I
    was there.
I told them the facts: nothing in it for either
natives, chiefs of mission or their entourage,
not a hope of coming home with pocket
    lined—
specially when you had a bugger of a praetor
who didn't give a damn for his entourage.
'All the same', they said, 'you must have got
    a team
of men to haul your litter round. It's
the local product, so they say.' Just to
make her suppose I wasn't too badly off, I
    said,
'I've got to admit things were really not so
    bad—
even though I'd landed a rotten province—
that I couldn't round up eight able-bodied
    men.'
In fact, neither then nor now had I a single
    man
that could have loaded on his neck as much
as a second-hand bedstead's broken foot.
Then she (it's the sort of shameless bitch she
    was)
said, 'Do me a favour, please, Catullus. Let
    me have
those men of yours a bit. I'd like them to take
    me
to Serapis' service.' 'Wait,' I said to the girl,
'when I said just now I had these chaps, there
    was
something I forgot. Actually, a close friend of
    mine,
Cinna—Gaius Cinna—got them together.
    They're his.
The position is that, his or mine, it's all the
    same:
I can use them just as if I'd bought them
    myself.

Really, what a tiresome, tactless creature you
    are!
The way a man's got to watch his words if
    you're around!'

The characters in this little drama might slip so easily into the pages of a Roman comedy, one asks to what extent Catullus and the *urbani* are living up to an ideal—attempting to create, to thrust into the ruder reality of contemporary life, a code of behaviour that existed only in imaginations fed by the traditions of the Hellenizing stage. I think the answer must be that, if it is an ideal, it is an ideal in the sense that the world created by Cicero's letters (his letters to Atticus in particular) is an ideal. A world that is witty, well read, ironically frank about its own ambitions and shortcomings. A world in which Cicero can write with graceful cynicism about a day in the Senate, urbanely tolerant of the motives and foibles of others, and even of his own. A world whose affectionate intimacy with all the best writers, Greek and Roman is so much a common possession that that knowledge can be aired without self-consciousness or pedantry. A world that is no less proud of its humanity, its involvement in what is going on, than it is of its *doctrina.* A world which can boast urbanely, like Terence's Chremes, *humani nihil a me alienum puto* and believe the boast, unconscious of the limitations of its humane vision.

What of the mistresses of these young men? Here Cicero's letters are of limited assistance. True, Clodia appears in them a number of times; but it is chiefly her relations, political and otherwise, that interest Cicero; for the more public side of her career we have to turn to the *Pro Caelio.* We can, however, appeal to Horace, if with some caution (Horace's mistresses somehow lack substance), and once again it is surprising how little different the picture is from that we find in Roman comedy.

'**Poem 10,**' taken by itself, tells us little about Varus' girl friend. We do not even learn her name—Catullus simply refers to her as a *scortillum,* a 'bit of a wench'. The word is scarcely complimentary, but the overtones, I think, are of tolerant approval, as when Horace proposes sending a message to Lyde to come and join the picnic, not forgetting to bring her lyre along with her (*Odes* 2. 11. 21-4):

quis deuium scortum eliciet domo
Lyden? eburna dic age cum lyre
    maturet, in comptum Lacaenae
    more comam religata nodum.

Who will get Lyde, that shy, retiring wench
away from home? Tell her to be quick and
    bring
her lyre, her hair tied back neatly in a knot,

in Spartan style.

To suppose Horace and his friend have in mind only to satisfy their lust is clearly a gross misreading of the text. Lyde is no slave girl, at Horace's beck and call: for plainly, since she has to be enticed, she is free to refuse to join the party, if she is not in the mood. But at the same time the word *scortum* rules out social equality: the girl's standing in society is not that of the men who seek the pleasure of her company. Her role is to amuse and be decorative. The situation in **'Poem 10'** seems very similar. One can presume the social standing of the girl is not that of the young man who has fallen in love with her—whether Varus is the lawyer Alfenus Varus (the Alfenus, probably, of **'Poem 30'**), or the Quintilius Varus who was to become the friend of Horace and Virgil: her interest in attending the rites of Serapis suggests she was a foreigner, not a native born Roman, just as Lyde's hair-style places her. A real-life girl doesn't have to come from Sparta simply because she favours Spartan hair-styles, nor is there any reason why a Roman girl in real life mightn't somehow have developed an interest in Serapis: but competent poets don't drop false, or worthless, clues. We must not, however, read too much into Catullus' *scortillum.* After all, Catullus does not call her that to her face, any more than Horace calls Lyde a *scortum* to her face: these are the private thoughts of men in a men's world about the women who grace that world, but are not of it.

But if she might be a character out of Plautus or a girl we meet in an ode of Horace, there can be no doubt that Varus' girl friend existed. **'Poem 10'** is set firmly in contemporary time and space: Varus and Catullus meet in the Forum; when they join the girl and the conversation gets going, it quickly turns to Bithynia and Catullus' recent tour of duty there. It all has the ring of something that actually happened, and happened the way Catullus tells it. One cannot say this of Horace's Odes. And note that the girl joins in the conversation; and note too that, if Catullus is annoyed when she asks him to lend her his team of litter-bearers, it isn't because she has no right to ask, but because her request puts Catullus on the spot—in a situation from which he can't gracefully extricate himself—and that annoys him. What shows her less *uenusta* and *lepida* than on his first appraisal of her is her failure to respect the limitations of her role within a man's world; to appreciate that men are entitled to boast without being embarrassed by a nuisance of a girl (33 *sed tu insulsa male et molesta uiuis*) who hasn't the sense to realize that what a man says in conversation (especially when there's a pretty girl present) isn't to be pressed.

Then there is Flavius' girl friend, of whose existence we have such abundant evidence (the facts speak for themselves), even though Flavius is at pains to keep her out of sight (**'Poem 6'**)

> Flaui, delicias tuas Catullo,
> ni sint illepidae atque inelegantes,
> uelles dicere nec tacere posses.
> uerum nescio quid febriculosi
> scorti diligis: hoc pudet fateri.
> nam te non uiduas iacere noctes
> nequiquam tacitum cubile clamat
> sertis ac Syrio fragrans oliuo,
> puluinusque peraeque et hic et ille
> attritus, tremulique quassa lecti
> argutatio inambulatioque.
> nam nil stupra ualet, nihil tacere.
> cur? non tam latera ecfututa pandas,
> ni tu quid facias ineptiarum.
> quare, quidquid habes boni malique,
> dic nobis. uolo te ac tuos amores
> ad caelum lepido uocare uersu.

> Flavius, you've a sweetheart, but she must be
> just a bit uncouth, a graceless lass perhaps,
> or you'd want to talk of her, couldn't help it
>   even.
> I expect it's some hot little piece or other
> you're cherishing, and ashamed of owning up.
> They're no celibate nights you're passing.
>   Your room,
> though tongueless, shrieks its testimony just
>   the same.
> All those flowers, that oily Syrian scent,
> those pillows crumpled just as much on either
>   side,
> that rickety bed, so knocked about it emits
> falsetto creaks as it wanders round the room.
> Not the slightest use refusing to talk.
> Why, you're an obvious case of shagger's
>   back.
> There must be funny business going on.
> So tell us who she is you've got—whether
>   good
> or bad. I want to poeticize your love and you
> and raise you to the sky in polished verse.

The reason Flavius' leg is being pulled isn't that he has fallen in love with a *scortum;* it is because the *scortum* is nothing to write home about—or so Catullus is quick to insinuate, since Flavius hasn't produced the girl (as Varus did) for inspection by his friends. The strategy of **'Poem 6'** is the reverse of that employed by Horace in *Odes* 2. 4: there the joke lies in suggesting that the maid-servant Horace's friend is in love with is really perhaps some exotic foreign princess who has fallen on evil days; that the *ancilla* was in fact a princess isn't a suggestion which is thrown out any more seriously than Catullus' suggestion that the girl on whom Flavius is lavishing his affection (5 *diligis*) is just 'some hot little piece or other' (4-5 *nescio quid febriculosi scorti*), and pretty ill-favoured to boot

(2 *illepidae atque inelegantes*). The closing lines come nearer the truth of the matter. If the affair were as sordid as lines 4-5 make it sound, there'd hardly be any question of 'celebrating the affair to the skies in polished verse'.

'**Poem 45**' provides a useful corrective to hasty assumptions about Poems '**6**' and '**10**'. We shift from ironic realism to something we can perhaps describe as an ironic study in Romantic love ('**Poem 45**'):

> Acmen Septimius suos amores
> tenens in gremio 'mea' inquit 'Acme',
> ni te perdite amo atque amare porro
> omnes sum assidue paratus annos,
> quantum qui pote plurimum perire,
> solus in Libya Indiaque tosta
> caesio ueniam obuius leoni.'
> hoc ut dixit, Amor sinistra ut ante
> dextra sternuit approbationem.
> at Acme leuiter caput reflectens
> et dulcis pueri ebrios ocellos
> illo purpureo ore suauiata,
> 'sic', inquit 'mea uita Septimille,
> huic uni domino usque seruiamus,
> ut multo mihi major acriorque
> ignis mollibus ardet in medullis.'
> hoc ut dixit, Amor sinistra ut ante
> dextra sternuit approbationem.
> nunc ab auspicio bono profecti
> mutuis animis amant amantur.
> unam Septimius misellus Acmen
> mauult quam Syrias Britanniasque:
> uno in Septimio fidelis Acme
> facit delicias libidinesque.
> quis ullos homines beatiores
> uidit, quis Venerem auspicatiorem?

> Holding his sweetheart Acme on his lap,
> Septimius said, 'If I do not, my darling,
> love you to distraction, if I am reluctant
> to love you unswervingly in all the years to
>   come—
> and as distractedly, moreover, as ever human
>   can:
> then may I, among the roasting sands of Lybia
>   or of India,
> run slap into a lion, green eyes and all.'
> When this was said, the god of love, on left
>   hand now
> as previously on right, sneezed his
>   approbation.
> Whereas Acme, head arching gently
>   backwards,
> with those brightly coloured lips began to kiss
> the love-drunk eyes of her darling lover.
> 'Likewise, Septimius my darling, all life to
>   me, may I
> your slave for ever be and you my master.

> For a much greater and far fiercer fire
> *burns within the marrow of my bones!'*
> When this was said, the god of love, on left
>   hand now
> as previously on right, sneezed his
>   approbation.
> With good omen thus they began their journey
>   into love.
> Now each lover's loved with responsive
>   passion.
> Poor Septimius would rather have his Acme
> than all the Syrias and the Britains that there
>   are.
> While Acme, faithful to Septimius alone,
> in all love's delights is co-operative.
> Who ever saw human beings happier,
> or affair embarked on with better omen?

The starting point of '**Poem 45**' is a traditional form which we find idealized in the Idylls of Theocritus and the Eclogues of Virgil—a singing match between two contestants at some rustic festival. Out of this Catullus has made an elegantly structured conversation-piece between two lovers, in which the girl caps the boy's protestations of undying, passionate devotion by an assertion of her even more fiercely burning love for him. A brief comment from the poet sets the scene at the beginning of each speech, and each speech is followed by a kind of refrain reporting how the god of love sneezed in approval. A third stanza, one line shorter than the others, gives the poet's final summing up. Almost everything in this graceful, charming study in romantic love—the lovers' unashamed rhetoric, an unusual descriptive lushness, the almost open irony of the poet's comments in the third stanza—warn against assuming anything like total commitment on Catullus' part to this dextrously executed exercise in *urbanitas*. A date late in 55 B.C. is indicated by the reference to Syria and Britain in line 22—the natural interpretation is that, so long as he can have his Acme, Septimius is willing to renounce thoughts of the glamour of travel to the East with Crassus, or to the Far North with Caesar. '**Poem 45,**' in other words, is not only close in date to '**Poem 11**' (*Furi et Aureli, comites Catulli . . .*), but also, perhaps, an ironic study in what might have been.

These young men, it seems, once they left the paternal household to set up quarters of their own and thus free themselves from paternal surveillance, had to fend for themselves. If there were slaves (and it seems hard to imagine there were none at all, in a society so dependent on slave-labour) they presumably played so minor a part (like the eight Bithynian litter-bearers in Poem lo that Catullus didn't actually have and that his friend Cinna didn't perhaps actually have either), there was normally no place for them in so economically structured a dramatic form as the poems of Catullus. Catullus and his friends had to rely on themselves in getting out of trouble.

Or rather, they relied on one another. The members of a close-knit group are well placed to keep an eye on each other. And, in this man's world which is reflected in the poems of Catullus, they feel the obligation to do so. Your friends form a kind of mutual protection society, on the watch for the latest victim of the folly of love or the predatory female, quick to check on the whereabouts of one of their number if he disappears from circulation, in order to make sure the girl is all right, and perhaps even worthy of something like honorary membership of the group for the duration of her affair with one of its members.

It is a game in which the unwritten rules are well understood, if not always accepted. Varus produces his girl friend for inspection. Flavius doesn't, and is told not to be so secretive. Likewise Camerius in **'Poem 55'**:

Oramus, si forte non molestum est,
demonstres ubi sint tuae tenebrae.
te Campo quaesiuimus minore,
te in Circo, te in omnibus libellis,
te in templo summi Iouis sacrato.
in Magni simul ambulatione
femellas omnes, amice, prendi,
quas uultu uidi tamen serenas.
taueltet, sic ipse flagitabam,
Camerium mihi, pessimae puellae.
quaedam inquit, nudum reduc . . .
'en hic in roseis latet papillis.'
sed te iam ferre Herculi labos est:
tanto te in fastu negas, amice.
dic nobis ubi sis futurus, ede
audacter, committe, crede luci.
nunc te lacteolae tenent puellae?
si linguam clauso tenes in ore,
fructus proicies amoris omnes.
uerbosa gaudet Venus loquella.
uel, si uis, licet obseres palatum,
dum uestri sim particeps amoris.

If it isn't too much trouble, would you please
reveal the location of your hide-out?
I've scoured the lesser Campus, hunting after
    you.
Been to the Circus too, looked in all the little
    books.
Visited the holy temple of all-mighty Jove.
In great Pompey's Portico, my friend,
I interrogated every female, but I saw
not one display an apprehensive look.
'Restore to me', so ran my personal appeal,
'my Camerius, you naughty, naughty girls!'
'Look!' said one, hand raised in full-breasted
    disclosure,
'that's him, hiding in my pinky bosom.'

It's hell's own job putting up with you,
my friend, when you're such an arrogant
    recluse.
Tell us where it is you'll be. Come,
boldly share the secret, give it light of day.
The blondes have got you, have they? Fine!
But if your tongue is held and mouth is
    sealed,
you throw away all love's profit.
It's the man who talks brings Venus joy—
though lock your lips in silence if you will,
so long as I am let into the secret.

If Varus' girl friend was a *scortillum*, we must assume she was a cut above the *pessimae puellae* of **'Poem 55'**, who answer, as far as we can tell (for something has gone wrong with the text) with a ribald rejoinder and a gesture to match when Catullus questions them in the Portico of Pompey's Theatre (the Piccadilly Circus of ancient Rome in Ovid's day, if not in Catullus') concerning the whereabouts of his friend Camerius Though to call a girl *pessima* means that you are cross with her, rather than that you disapprove of her sexual mores (the that any rate seems the way to take Catullus' words when he calls Lesbia *pessima puella* in **'Poem 36'**). Anyway, the blondes have got Camerius, it appears (17 *nunc te lacteolae tenent puellae?*). The plural includes the girl's colleagues from the Portico, one suspects, or perhaps it is what the grammarians call a generalizing plural, or even a mock-heroic 'poetic plural'. Be that as it may, the important thing is to track Camerius down, and get the truth out of him.

The member of the group who drops out of circulation (the Latin word is *latet*) is a theme we find in Horace too. The Sybaris Ode (*Odes* 1. 8) gives it a slightly more serious twist: Sybaris' infatuation with Lydia has made him cut cavalry parades and generally behave like a sissy; but much the same was true (or so Horace archly pretends) of the great Achilles—and he turned out all right in the end.

Poems **'6'** and **'55'** suggest an interpretation of **'Poem 18'** that fits the text better than the usual reading of these lines. For **'Poem 13'** is *not* an invitation to dinner: it is a put-off, a poem wriggling out of inviting Fabullus to dinner with the excuse that the dinner will be forthcoming—any day now, if Fabullus is lucky (2 *paucis, si tibi di fauent, diebus*). One suspects that Fabullus (just back from Spain, perhaps, like Veranius in **'Poem 9'**) is angling for an introduction to Lesbia, and is told he'll have to wait. The fact that Catullus is hard up isn't the reason for delay, since Catullus makes it clear that, even when the invitation eventuates, Fabullus will have to provide everything out of his own pocket. It was fashionable, of course, in the circle in which Catullus moved to boast of being hard up—to be flush with cash stamped you as a Mamurra. But as the poem proceeds, a pretty clear hint is dropped that the reason for the delay (and the reason perhaps why Catullus is completely broke) is . . . Lesbia. Let Fabullus be patient for a day or two, Catullus seems to be saying between the lines, and (provided Fabullus does the decent thing) Catullus will turn on a foursome (Fabullus providing his own girl) at which Fabullus and Lesbia can meet (13. 9-14):

> sed contra accipies meros amores,
> seu quid suauius elegantiusue est:
> nam unguentum dabo, quod meae puellae
> donarunt Veneres Cupidinesque;
> quod tu cum olfacies, deos rogabis,
> totum ut te faciant, Fabulle, nasum.

> In return, I'll offer something irresistible,
> you couldn't imagine anything more charming,
>   more tasteful:
> a perfume I can provide, personally presented
> to my derring by the Powers of Desire.
> When you've had one sniff, you'll ask the
>   gods,
> Fabullus, to turn you into one great big nose.

'Poem 35' utilizes the traditional material but introduces a fresh component. The girl friend of the poet Caecilius is herself interested in poetry. Even so, she mustn't be allowed to stand in the way of a serious discussion about poetry between Catullus and Caecilius:

> Poetae tenero, meo sodali,
> uelim Caecilio, papyre, dicas
> Veronam ueniat, Noui relinquens
> Comi moenia Lariumque litus.
> nam quasdam uolo cogitationes
> amici accipiat sui meique.
> quare, si sapiet, uiam uorabit,
> quamuis candida mikes puella
> euntem reuocet, manusque collo
> ambas iniciens roget morari.
> quae nunc, si mihi uera nuntiantur,
> illum deperit impotente amore;
> nam quo tempore legit incohatam
> Dindymi dominam, ex eo misellae
> ignes interiorem edunt medullam.
> ignosco tibi, Sapphica puella
> muse doctior: est enim uenuste
> Magna Caecilio incohata Mater.

> Please, papyrus, tell the tender poet,
> my good friend Caecilius, I want him to
> come to Verona, abandoning the walls of
> New Comum and the Larian shore, for
> I have certain reflections to impart
> of a friend of his and mine.
> If he's wise, therefore, he'll eat up the road,
> though his blonde mistress call him back

a thousand times, and, clasping both arms
around his neck, beseech him to wait a while.
For she, if the news I have is true,
loves Caecilius madly, uncontrollably;
ever since she read the first draft of his
Mistress of Dindymus, the fire has been eating
into the marrow of the poor girl's bones.
Nor do I blame you, girl more endowed with
   taste
than Sapphic muse: Caecilius' Great Mother
is jolly good, for a first draft.

Pretty obviously, there is an element of leg-pull in the reference to the girl's literary attainments. We needn't doubt it is her passion for Caecilius which makes her so reluctant to let him out of her sight, rather than her passion for poetry. But we are on the edge here of one of the great traditions of Roman love poetry—the *docta puella*. The girl is no blue-stocking: *docta* means something more like 'knowledgeable about literature'— she hadn't just read a lot, she had taste as well. Clearly the Roman love poets liked to think their mistresses could appreciate what they wrote about them. Ovid lays down a formidable reading list for the girl who wants to succeed in society: Callimachus, Philetas, Anacreon, Sappho of course (*quid enim lasciuius illa?*), Menander, Propertius, Cornelius Gallus, Tibullus, Varro of Atax (who wrote a version of Apollonius' *Argonautica*), Virgil (only the *Aeneid,* apparently) . . . and perhaps Ovid's own *Amores.* No doubt, like all reading lists, Ovid's set a standard to aim at rather than one the ordinary *candida puella* about town could be expected to take in her stride. Caecilius' girl friend belongs almost two generations earlier, and she may have been only a local girl whom Caecilius had got to know in Novum Comum. All the same, she is one sign that a love affair, in the group in which Catullus moved, could mean something more than sophisticated sensuality. The *urbani* were getting used to the idea that a girl might provide a young man with the kind of intellectual companionship he had traditionally got only from men. We are on the way to Lesbia, with whom the adventure starts with a translation of Sappho, and to Propertius' Cynthia, who reads her lover's poems while she waits for him to rejoin her. A poet's mistress needs after all special qualifications.

Observe, too, that Caecilius' girl is not referred to as a *scortum* (let alone a *nescioquid febriculosi scorti,* like Flavius' girl friend), or even as a *scortillum* (like Varus' girl friend): she is a *candida puella,* like the girl Fabullus is invited to bring with him to the party. We have to remember that not all not wholly respectable women were *scortilla.* Some were mime actresses, like the famous Cytheris, who was in her time the mistress of several leading figures in Roman public life: the poet Cornelius Gallus (who called her Lycoris in his poetry), Marcus Brutus, Mark Antony, and earlier on the occasion when Cicero dined with her in 46

B.C. (a little taken aback to find himself in such fast company) the mistress of his host Volumnius Eutrapelus, after whom she was known for a time as Volumnia.

Others were married women. The readiness of allegedly respectable women at this time to take lovers is well attested. A generation later Horace thought it worth advising lusty young bloods to stick to *libertinae* (freed slaves), as being safer—husbands of respectable married women were liable to take the law into their own hands.

Some *matronae* were relatively innocent amateurs, like the pretty young wife of **'Poem 17'** whose husband drew down Catullus' angry censure upon his head for not keeping a better eye on her (17. 14-22):

> cui cum sit uiridissimo nupta flore puella,
> et puella tenellulo delicatior haedo,
> adseruanda nigerrimis diligentius uuis,
> ludere hanc sinit ut lubet, nec pili facit uni,
> nec se subleuat ex sua parte; sed uelut alnus
> in fossa Liguri facet suppernata securi,
> tantundem omnia sentiens quam si nulla sit
>   usquam,
> talis iste meus stupor nil uidet, nihil audit,
> ipse qui sit, utrum sit an non sit—id quoque
>   nescit. . . .

> He's got a wife, a girl that's lush with
>   youthful growth,
> tenderer than a tiny baby kid, a girl you'd
>   watch with
> greater care than your ripest, darkest grapes.
>   Well, all
> the fun she wants, she takes. He lets her,
>   doesn't give a hoot.
> Doesn't bestir himself on his own account,
>   lies like an
> alder log left hamstrung in a ditch by a
>   Ligurian axeman,
> no more perception of what's going on than if
>   it didn't exist.
> He does not see, the stolid lump, he does not
>   hear,
> who he is he doesn't know, or whether he's
>   alive at all. . . .

The tone is by conventional standards frankly amoral, despite the presence of scandalized morality. But it is an amorality devoid of cynicism. And in place of conventional morality the poem imposes its own moral perspective, according to which a man who shows no concern whether his pretty young wife is playing fast and loose is a fool—not because he lets himself be deceived, but because his sense of values is false; the point is made, rather more bluntly, with regard to Lesbia's husband in **'Poem 85'**.

The frisky young wife of **'Poem 17'** is a mere *giovan principiante* among married woman. Very different, in age, experience and the quality of the pity one feels for her, is the battered *moecha* of **'Poem 41'**:

> Ameana puella defututa
> tote milia me decem poposcit,
> ista turpiculo puella naso,
> decoctoris amica Formiani.
> propinqui, quibus est puella curae,
> amicos medicosque conuocate:
> non est sane puella, nec rogare
> qualis sit soles aes imaginosum.

> Ameana's a girl who's fucked about a lot
> but ten cool thousand's what she's quoted
>   me—
> That girl with the rather horrid nose,
> friend of the bankrupt from Formiae.
> Relations, on you the care devolves:
> call friends and doctors into conference.
> This girl is sick; she checks her looks no
>   more
> against reflection-crowded mirror made of
>   bronze.

We're not told that Ameana was married. But she sounds more like Lesbia than Varus' unnamed girl friend in **'Poem 10'**, or Flavius' in **'Poem 6'**—a *puella,* not a *scortum,* who has a family that can be appealed to to look after her (rather as Clodia's interests were supposed to be looked after, we gather from Cicero, by a family council after the death of her husband). Indeed a comparison with Lesbia is made specifically in the second Ameana poem (43. 7 *tecum Lesbia nostra comparatur?*)

The type seems to have been not uncommon. Take Sallust's Sempronia. Sallust singles her out as a case among many—one example of the kind of woman Catiline gathered round him in the sixties. Society women who had acquired expensive tastes, and then, as they got older, ran into debt:

> He is said to have attached to himself at that time large numbers of men from all classes and conditions of society. There were some women, too, who had begun by prostituting themselves to meet their enormous expenses, and had then run heavily into debt when age had limited their earning power without limiting their appetite for luxury. . . .

Sempronia was doubtless more interesting than most. She was certainly a woman of exceptional talents:

> Among these was Sempronia. . . . Of good family, attractive, with a husband and children, she had little to complain of; knowledgeable about literature, both Greek and Latin, able to play the lyre and to dance

more elegantly than is indispensable to a woman of virtue, she was in many ways cut out for a life of luxury. . . . It would he hard to decide which worried her less, money or reputation. Her appetite for sex was such that she took the initiative with men more often than they with her. . . . And yet she had a brain that was far from negligible: she could write poetry, raise a laugh, adapt her style of conversation so that it was modest, suggestive, or quite shameless, while never failing to display considerable wit, and even charm. . . .

Then there is poor Rufa ('**Poem 59**'),

Bononiensis Rufa Rufulum fellat,
uxor Meneni, saepe quam in sepulcretis
uidistis ipso rapere de rogo cenam,
cum deuolutum ex igne prosequens panem
ab semiraso tunderetur ustore.

Rufa from Bologna sucks her Rufulus.
Menenius' wife, I mean. You've seen her
   often
in the graveyards, as she grabs up for dinner
a lump of bread tumbling from the burning
   pyre,
the half-shaved slave in charge laying into
   her.

The women we meet in the background poems in the group '**1-60**' vary a good deal, then, though most are types we recognize. We mustn't expect, however, we can synthesize a Lesbia out of any or all of them. Of the nine (leaving out of account, that is, the *pessimae puellae* of '**Poem 55**'—and Lesbia), the gay young wife of '**Poem 17**' and poor Rufa are explicitly described as adultresses; the former is treated with good-natured indulgence—it is her husband who is reproached for not taking proper care of her; as for Rufa, she is treated with the detached contempt appropriate to this vignette from the seamy side of life. The rest—Flavius' girl friend in '**Poem 6**', Varus' girl friend in '**Poem 10**', Ipsitilla ('**Poem 32**'—another Sempronia, or perhaps an Orestilla?), Caecilius' girl friend in '**Poem 35**', Ameana (Poems '**41**' and '**43**'), Septimius' girl friend in '**Poem 45**' and the unnamed teenager (one presumes) in '**Poem 56**'—are set in an ambience which is stripped of all moral censure, explicit or implicit. The ridicule levelled at them implies on the contrary acceptance by Catullus. His only real complaint is that his contemporaries arc tasteless enough to compare Ameana with Lesbia. His attitude in Poems '**1-60**', if more gaily, more exuberantly expressed, is very; much that of those epigrams from the Greek Anthology which J. W. Mackail collected under the apt title 'The human comedy'. Catullus, we feel, isn't greatly concerned to have the world otherwise.

The Sick Society

The elegiac epigrams are a different matter. The pic-

ture we get from the poems about men and their mistresses in Poems '**69-116**' is that of a sick society, drawn by an artist whose pen is sharpened by an anger and a contempt which have blunted his sense of fun, or the inherently absurd in the human situation. '**Poem 86**' (*Quintia formosa est multis . . .*), which reverts to the theme of '**Poem 43**' (*Salue, nec minimo puella naso*), is perhaps alone in recalling the tone of '**1-60**'.

In a sense we are closer to what many would call realism. The basis is the smart world of which we see something in the pages of Sallust's *Catiline,* but on a smaller scale, closer to the kind of everyday gossip which Caelius Rufus reports to Cicero during the latter's absence from Rome as governor of Cilicia:

No news, really, unless you want an account of the following—as no doubt you will. Young Cornificius has become engaged to Orestilla's daughter. Paulla Valeria, Triarius' sister, filed a petition for divorce (with no reasons stated) on the very day her husband was due back from his province; she's going to marry D. Brutus. . . . Many incredible things like this have happened while you've been away. Servius Ocella wouldn't have got anybody to believe he had it in him to be an adulterer, if he hadn't been caught red-handed twice in the space of three days. You will want to know where they caught him. The answer, I'm afraid, is: in the last place I could have wished. I leave it to you to get the details from others: I rather like the idea of General Cicero having to ask everybody he writes to who the lady was with whom so and so was caught *in flagrante delicto.* . . .

But though we find here an urbanity to match that of Catullus (granted the more diffuse form of a prose letter), Caelius' pleasure in witty gossip is superficial and petty by comparison with the incisive scorn we find in Catullus.

Those singled out for the most savage ridicule are more often men than women. Take Aemilius. He is the subject of quite the most hair-raisingly lurid imagery in the whole of Catullus (97. 5-8):

os dentis sesquipedalis,
gingiuas uero ploxeni habet ucteris,
praeterea rictum qualem diffissus in aestu
meientis mulae cunnus habere soles. . .

Catullus is remarkably savage about the laughter of those whom he dislikes—Egnatius in '**Poem 39**', the *moecha putida* of '**Poem 42.**' But nowhere else is there anything like this. Yet this crude creature is a successful lecher who can preen himself at conquest after conquest (9 *hic futuit multas et se facit esse uenustum*)—whereas the girls flee from Rufus in distaste (69. 7—8):

hunc metuunt omnes, neque mirum: nam mala
    ualde est
bestia, nec quicum bella puella cubet . . . .

All the girls are scared of him—and no
    wonder: the
beast's a real stinker, not one any smart girl'd
    go to bed with.

By comparison with **'Poem 97'**, **'Poem 56'**, *The Chain Reaction* (*O rem ridiculam, Cato, et iocosam. . . .*), which must by any conventional criterion be regarded as the most obscene poem in Catullus, is a gay, light-hearted jeu d'esprit. **'Poem 97'** is meant to wound.

Or take Gallus. *His* forte is for *recherché* match-making. The fool (**'Poem 78'**):

Gallus habet fratres, quorum est lepidissima
    coniunx
alterius, lepidus filius alterius.
Gallus homo est bellus: nam dulces iungit
    amores,
cum puero ut bello bella puella cubes.
Gallus homo est stultus, nec se uidet esse
    maritum,
qui patruns patrui monstret adulterium.

Gallus has two brothers. One has an utterly
    charming
wife, the other's got a charming son.
Gallus is a terrific lad. In love's pleasures he
    has joined
the two, sending charming girl to bed with
    charming boy.
Gallus is a fool. That he's married he has
    forgotten, when
showing how to make an uncle cuckold,
    though he's an uncle too.

The first couplet sketches in the basic data; the second presents Gallus' view of himself (*Gallus homo est bellus*) and the evidence in support of that view; the third couplet offers a contradictory assessment (*Gallus homo est stultus*). The sting is in the tail, and it is directed at Gallus. But at the same time the epigram passes judgment on a society in which this sort of thing is reckoned no more than good, clean fun, and in which Gallus' clever scheme can be confidently relied upon to rebound on himself.

The women involved are more often *ingenuae,* it seems, than *scortilla.* Only two (always excepting Lesbia) are mentioned by name (but then only three are mentioned by name in **'1-60'**). Maecilia is a pathetic figure, almost, by comparison with Ameana or Ipsitilla; she is closer to Rufa perhaps (**'Poem 113'**):

Consule Pompeio primum duo, Cinna, solebant

Maeciliam: facto consule nunc iterum
manserunt duo, sed creuerunt milia in unum
singula. fecundum semen adulterio.

In Pompey's first consulship, Cinna, Maecilia
    had
two lovers. Now he's consul for a second
    time,
the two remain, but behind each stand a
    thousand
more who've come of age: fertile business,
    fornication!

Pompey's first consulship was in 70 B.C.; he was made consul for the second time in January 55 B.C. (the elections were late). Maecilia was still going strong, it appears.

Aufillena seems more typical of the rest who are left unnamed. She occurs herself in three different epigrams. In **'Poem 110'** she is perhaps on the threshold of her career as a demi-mondaine and has to be told she can't have it both ways (**'Poem 110'**):

Aufillena, bonae semper laudantur amicae:
accipinnt pretium quae facere instituunt.
tu, quod promisti mihi quod mentita inimica
    es,
quod nec das et fers saepe, facis facinus.
aut facere ingenuae est, aut non promisse
    pudicae,
Aufillena, fuit: sed data corripere
fraudando officiis, plus quam meretricis auarae
    est.
quae sese toto corpore prostituit.

It's the good girl friends, Aufillena, who're
    always praised,
the ones who collect the cash and deliver the
    goods. You
promised me, and broke your promise, so
    you're no friend of mine. Always collecting,
    never giving—it's against the rules.
Decent girls do what they promise, respectable
    girls don't
make promises, Aufillena. But collecting and
    then breaking
the bargain, even a greedy whore who stops at
    nothing
where whoring is concerned doesn't do that.

Catullus' moral instruction is hardly disinterested, and perhaps all that has occurred is that he has failed to persuade Aufillena to exercise her woman's right to change her lover. For in **'Poem 100'** it is Quintius (Catullus' devoted friend of **'Poem 82'**) who is passionately in love with Aufillena. But then Aufillena reappears in **'Poem 111'** as the woman who will stop at nothing, not even incest with an uncle.

These poems are full of riddles. Is Rufus' rival in '**Poem 71**' perhaps that disgusting Don Juan, Aemilius, of '**Poem 97**'? Or did Catullus not intend us to recall Poems '**69**' and '**71**' when we come to stinker Aemilius in '**Poem 97**'? I suspect he did hope we would remember the fastidiousness the *puellae* displayed towards Rufus and compare it with their lack of fastidiousness when faced with the charms of Aemilius. We must know when to stop, however. Anybody who feels that, by putting two and two together, he can discover who has been sleeping with whom is almost certainly wasting his time.

Take Aufillena. We learn from '**Poem 111**' that she is a married woman and a mother (even if her children are not her husband's). Whether the uncle is her uncle or her children's uncle (as well as their father) is not clear. He might in the latter case be the brother of that Aufillena to whom (as we learn from '**Poem 100**') Caelius is passionately devoted, while Quintius is madly in love with the sister. Are we to connect all this with the Gellius poems? For we learn from Poems '**74**' and '**88**' that Gellius is cuckolding an uncle. Is Gellius' uncle's wife the *lepidissima coniunx* of '**Poem 78**'? Apparently not, since *her* lover should be called Gallus, not Gellius (he is the *lepidus filius* of Gallus' brother). The answer, plainly, to questions such as these is that there aren't answers, or aren't answers any more. Catullus and his friends usually knew, no doubt, even if there were occasions when one friend chose to leave another to speculate, as Caelius leaves Cicero to speculate about who had recently been taken *in flagrante delicto* with whom, 'in the last place I could have wished'. It is not the poet's purpose, however, to arouse the curiosity of his more permanent audience about details. We are being presented with a picture of a society in which such goings on went on. Catullus' object is satire, not gossip.

'**Poems 74**' (*Gellius audierat patruum obiurgare solere. . . .*), or '**78**' (*Gallus habet fratres . . .*), or even '**90**' (*Nascatur magus . . .*), taken individually, might suggest Catullus was on the side of the uncle-cuckolders. Set against these the savage condemnation of Gellius in Poems '**88**', '**89**' and '**91**' and that impression is quickly dispelled; the final condemnation is the stronger if Catullus has not pointed the moral at every turn. Set against all these the Lesbia poems in '**69-116**', which run like a deep current of personal anguish through the superficial, perverted antics of those around Catullus and his mistress. That the background picture is intended to be that of a society in which relationships had become hopelessly depraved becomes hard to doubt.

IV. The Homosexual Poems

From the poems about the *urbani* and their mistresses it is only natural that we should turn to the homosexual poems, though I shall argue caution in assessing their contribution to the picture of contemporary society. Their role seems to me rather as light relief. For two reasons.

The first is that the things talked of or threatened so casually, if not exactly beyond accomplishment or belief, are sufficiently so to constitute a warning against taking what is talked of and threatened *au pied de la lettre*. As Michael Holroyd remarked of Lytton Strachey and Maynard Keynes:

> The frankness which Lytton and Keynes exchanged in their letters from this time onwards seems, at a first reading, to uncover a state of affairs within Cambridge which would have produced curiosity in Gomorrah and caused the inhabitants of Sodom to sit up and take note.

The second is the evident tone of these poems, as it seems to me, and the assumptions that tone invites, or inhibits.

First, let us take stock. The homosexual poems are easily identified. There are eleven of them (nine in '**1-60**', two in '**69-116**')—not counting the insinuations thrown out in passing in Poems '**25**', '**28**', '**33**', '**47**' and '**57**'. Seven are built round the character of Juventius, an arrogant youth in whom Catullus proclaims a passionate, unrequited interest. Three of these, Poems '**16**' (*Pedicabo ego uos et irrumabo. . . .*), '**48**' (*Mellitos oculos tuos, Iuuenti . . .*) and '**99**' (*Surripui tibi, dum ludis, mellite Iuuentu . . .*) deal with nothing more wicked than kisses, though it is true that '**Poem 16**', which is a follow-up of '**Poem 48**', might cause some to blink if there were any real indication that the strong words in the opening and closing lines were meant to be taken at their face value. Poems '**24**' (*O qui flosculus es Iuuentiorum. . . .*) and '**81**' (*Nemone in tanto potuit populo esse, Iuuenti . . . ?*) form a pair, both addressed to Juventius: the theme of the former is 'I wish you'd have nothing more to do with that beggar Furius'; the theme of the latter is 'I wish you'd have nothing more to do with that so and so from Pisaurum'. '**Poem 81**' is a little less light-hearted perhaps in tone than the rest of the Juventius poems. The four which remain are a mixed bag. '**Poem 56**' (*Orem ridiculam, Cato, et iocosam . . .*) is a frankly outrageous fantasy, which ranks only technically as a homosexual poem: the joke announced to Cato seems to lie in boasting that the youngster who is so anxious to prove he is a man receives in his turn from Catullus an appropriately virile and witty equivalent of the traditional punishment meted out to those caught *in flagrante delicto* (described in some detail at the end of '**Poem 15**'). '**Poem 106**' is an amusing trifle:

cum puero bello praeconem qui uidet esse,
quid credat, nisi se uendere discupere?

If one sees a pretty boy with an auctioneer in
    tow,
one can only suppose the boy is very keen to
    sell himself.

'Poem 100' involves Caelius in this world of the wittily outrageous, along with Aufillena's brother (100.
1-4):

> Caelius Aufillenum et Quintius Aufillenam
> flos Veronensum depereunt iuuenum,
> hic fratrem, ille sororem. hoc est, quod dicitur,
>   illud
> fraternum uere dulce sodalicium. . . .

> My story is of Caelius and Quintius, cream of
>   Verona's
> youth: the one's madly in love with
>   Aufillenus, the
> other with Aufillenus' sister. That's what they
>   mean
> when they talk of true, sweet brotherly
>   solidarity. . . .

The eleventh, **'Poem 80'** (*Quid dicam, Gelli, quare
rosea ista labella . . . ?*), is a lampoon directed at
Gellius in which Catullus reports rumours accounting
for Gellius' unwonted pallor, and proceeds to fling out
an accusation and to name names.

These eleven poems raise two major problems of interpretation. One is the problem of obscenity, the other is
the problem involved in fixing the level of intent. The
two are related of course.

The problem of obscenity isn't confined to the homosexual poems. It arises also in connexion with something like half a dozen other poems: certainly Poems
'32' (*Ipsitilla*) and **'97'** (Aemilius); probably Poems
'33' (Vibennius *père et fils*) and **'71'** (Rufus), if not
'Poem 25' (Thallus); also, I suppose, Poems **'6'** (Flavius and his girl friend) and **'37'** (the *salax taberna*);
perhaps, if one is to be very squeamish, Poems **'23'**
(the peculiarities of Furius' alimentary system in lines
18-23) and **'39'** (Egnatius' peculiar habits of oral hy-
giene). Poems **'11'** (the final dismissal of Lesbia) and
'58' (*Caeli, Lesbia nostra . . .*) are clearly a different
case, but it can't be denied that the theme of **'Poem
58'** is obscene, or that one passage of **'Poem 11'** (lines
17-20) can reasonably be held to be obscene. Altogether, quite a lot.

The conventional standards of the time did not differ
greatly from ours in the matter of obscene words. The
question is discussed by Cicero in a letter to his friend
L. Papirius Paetus, a learned and witty Epicurean (as
well as a wealthy man). He acknowledges that the
Stoics held one should call a spade a spade (*placet
Stoicis, suo quamque rem nomine appellare*). This isn't

Cicero's view, however, and he proceeds to discuss a
large number of particular words and expressions. Again
in the *De Officiis* he draws the line at words which are
admittedly obscene: he had no objection to innuendo—indeed the point of a witty remark (including many
of Cicero's own sallies) often turns on what one can
succeed in implying, while avoiding actual *uerborum
obscoenitas.* Here intention comes into the matter: to
be witty without being offensive, while it is first of all
a matter of style (one has to be elegant, urbane, ingenious, clever) is also a matter of attitude; one has to
make the sally with detachment (*remisso animo*)—one
mustn't, for example, be activated by anger or malice.
Cicero had made the same point more than ten years
before in his defence of Caelius Rufus, while answering allegations that Caelius had been involved in homosexual attachments. On that occasion Cicero affected to be tolerant: he had in mind to give as good as he
received—before the trial is over he will have the court
rocking with laughter at Clodia's expense, her more
than sisterly affection for her brother included. Innuendoes of the kind which the prosecution are making
such a fuss about, said Cicero, are not to be taken
literally; it isn't as if a formal charge had been laid in
court.

Our own permissive age is less disturbed either by
plain speaking or by outrageous innuendo than Victo-
rian England. Today only the very mealy-mouthed
indeed would want to complain of obscenity when
pressure of emotion causes Catullus to hurl out the
isolated plain word or phrase in a poem whose intent
is plainly serious, as in **'11'**. 17-20:

> cum suis uiuat ualeatque moechis,
> quos simul complexa tenet trecentos,
> nullum amans uere, sed identidem omnium
> ilia rumpens. . . .

> Tell her to live with her lovers and be good
>   riddance—
> those three hundred lechers that share the
>   embraces
> of one who loves no man truly, but lets all
>   time and again
> screw themselves to bits. . . .

or 58.4-5:

> nunc in quadriuiis et angiportis
> glubit magnanimi Remi nepotes.

> now on street corners and in back alleys
> she peels Remus' generous descendants bare.

even though modern translators often miss or obscure
the point, turning Catullus' plain, curt directness into
the explicitly crude, often to produce something far
more obscene than the original. Poems **'56'** and **'97'**

go a good deal further, however. They are calculated provocations of those who let themselves be scandalized. The object is to achieve what Cicero in the *De Officiis* was to hold unforgivable—talking about the unmentionable in so many words (si *rerum turpitudini adhibetur uerborum obscoenitas*)—and get away with it by sheer exuberance (an irrepressible sense of fun), or elegance of form, or both.

We need not doubt that the persons talked about or addressed in the homosexual poems exist: if not all historically identifiable, they are too tightly enmeshed in the known facts of Catullus' life to be fictitious. To that extent, at least, the poems can't be dismissed as literary exercises in the Hellenistic manner. What then of the assertions, expressed or implied? To answer what Cicero answered in respect of Caelius—that this is the sort of thing that's always said about any young man who isn't positively repulsive to look at—seems to me to be dealing with the matter a little unsubtly. Cicero, being in court, could afford nothing short of categorical denial. Catullus' poems move in a world where clear-cut denials and outright rejections aren't called for in the same way. It may even be fun to lay oneself open to accusation—and then jump severely on those who are too simple-minded or too heavy-handed.

That at any rate seems the way to read Catullus' disclaimer in **'Poem 16'**:

> Pedicabo ego uos et irrumabo,
> Aureli pathice et cinaede Furi,
> qui me ex uersiculis meis putastis,
> quod sunt molliculi, parum pudicum.
> nam castum esse decet pium poetam
> ipsum, uersiculos nihil necesse est;
> qui tum denique habent salem ac leporem,
> si sunt molliculi ac parum pudici,
> et quod pruriat incitare possum,
> non dico pueris, sed his pilosis
> qui duros nequeunt mouere lumbos.
> uos, quod milia multa basiorum
> legistis, male me marem putatis?
> pedicabo ego uos et irrumabo.

> I'll bugger the pair of you, one way or
>   another,
> Aurelius you queer, you pansy Furius,
> for jumping to the conclusion, just because
>   my verses
> are on the suggestive side, that I'm not quite
>   nice.
> A decent poet must himself be pure,
> his verse is free from such an obligation.
> In fact, it really can't have wit or charm,
> unless it's on the suggestive side and not
>   quite nice—
> the sort in short that can raise an itch,
> not just in boys, but in those shaggy types

> whose loins are stiffened up, no action in
>   them left.
> Just because you read about kisses by the
>   thousand,
> do you suppose I haven't the makings of a
>   man?
> I'll bugger the pair of you, one way or
>   another.

The poems on homosexual themes, Catullus argues in effect, display characteristic qualities of urbanitas, namely *sal* and *lepos:* they are inherently witty (they have *sal*) and witty also in the presentation of their ideas (they have *lepos*). Admittedly, they are a shade suggestive, verging on the indecent even (8 *molliculi ac parum pudici*) but the poet's confessions mustn't be taken as true confessions. Whatever their effect on those with dirty minds, they are essentially *jeux d'esprit,* poems that toy with things which border on fantasy. Ovid, Pliny and Martial were to make similar disclaimers—Pliny rather self-consciously, Martial disingenuously (he has no objection really to pandering to dirty minds), Ovid in accordance with his usual practice of special pleading. Catullus' disclaimer is more impressive: the key words and phrases are repeated with patient precision, in a way that reminds us of those elegiac epigrams in which he tries to put on record what went wrong: between him and Lesbia.

I don't think all the same we can dismiss the homosexual poems as just *jeux d'esprit.* Moreover, the common tendency to treat these poems as a few odd pieces that happened to get included in the collection along with other waifs and strays is inadmissible once we assume a planned collection. It is clear the homosexual poems have been grouped together with some care: seven of them (the Juventius poems) form a sequence as coherent as the Lesbia poems; four of these stand close together in the collection (Poems **'15'**, **'16'**, **'21'** and **'24'**), and these four are linked by a common name with two more poems (Poems **'23'** and **'26'**). There are too many of them, in short, and they hang together too closely, for them to be swept aside.

In this connexion, three elegies of Tibullus, all in the first book (I. 4, 1. 8 and 1. 9), are interesting. All are confessions, in different circumstances, of a homosexual attachment to a young man whom Tibullus calls Marathus. Along with the Juventius poems of Catullus, they form the main corpus of poems on homosexual themes in Latin. In the first, Tibullus poses to prospective lovers of boys as an authority on the subject—a variation on the familiar theme of the elegiac poet as an authority on love (*praeceptor amoris*). Indeed, Tibullus claims to have been instructed in the subject by Priapus himself, the scarecrow son of Bacchus and Venus (represented by Tibullus as the paederast *par excellence*)—and then wrily confesses that Titius, with whom in mind he underwent this course of instruction, is in love with . . . his wife. One might think that Tibullus might have learnt the fickleness of boyish love, but, no, he is as hopelessly infatuated as ever, this time with Marathus (I. 4. 81-2):

> heu, heu, quam Marathus lento me torques amore!
>
> deficiunt artes, deficiuntque doli. . . .

> Alas! the slow torture of love which Marathus subjects me to:
>
> my skill deserts me, guile deserts me too. . . .

In Elegy 1. 8 it appears that Marathus in his turn, if not' contemplating marriage, is at any rate taking an active interest in the opposite sex. On his behalf Tibullus urges a lady named Pholoe, with whom Marathus is represented as passionately in love, not to show herself uncooperative—a young lover (Marathus isn't yet bearded) is worth his weight in gold (1. 8. 31-2):

> carior est auro iuuenis cui leuia fulgent
> ora nec amplexus aspera barba terit . . .

Pholoe will regret it if she lets such an opportunity slip, and then it will be too late. In the third elegy (1. 9), Marathus is apparently making progress with Pholoe (assuming, as seems natural, that she is the mistress referred to in lines 3950), but Tibullus now regrets the help he gave Marathus, because he has lost the boy—not to the girl, but to another man, a wealthy admirer (the homosexual counterpart of the *diues amator* of Elegy I. 5), whose wife and sister, Tibullus hopes (comforting himself with the thought), will vie with one another in shameless living.

The three elegies appear to tell a connected story, the hypothesis of which can be fairly easily pieced together. We don't have to take the story very seriously. The poems seem to me to offer more than a hint of the way the elegiac tradition will be reshaped in Ovid's hands, into the kind of love poetry whose object is to entertain us and to scandalize us at the same time. It is part of the charm of these three elegies that we feel none of the usual embarrassment about Tibullus' sincerity; they are much better constructed, moreover, than Tibullus can usually manage. And yet a number of verbal echoes reinforce the feeling that we are surprisingly close to Catullus.

Tibullus invites us to take for granted, as something that calls for no special explanation, that a young man (Marathus is described as a *puer* in 1. 8. 27 and as a *iuuenis* in 1. 8. 31) can have a mistress and still be (or perhaps in the case of Titius, who is now married, very recently have ceased to be) the *puer delicatus* of a male lover. This can hardly be pure fantasy. If the notion were completely outlandish, or one that his contemporaries would have found completely repul-

sive, Tibullus would scarcely have written these confessions, or mock confessions. True, Tibullus represents his passion for Marathus as relatively innocent, if too intense for us to describe it as purely Platonic, but he is comparing himself with the man who has stolen Marathus from him, and in such cases, if your rival's motives are *ex hypothesi* suspect, your own are above suspicion.

These three elegies of Tibullus seem to me to be of considerable help in interpreting the homosexual poems of Catullus. They suggest the appropriate gloss to add to Catullus' *molliculi ac parum pudici*—themes that challenge conventional morality, without damning the man who writes about them in the eyes of those who are at all broadminded. More than that, the elegies suggest that the homosexual poems of Catullus and Tibullus correspond to attitudes in real life that are somewhat different from our own. They help too in making sense of **'Poem 63'**. Attis had obviously been a *puer delicatus* (or would have been so regarded if his home had been Rome)—and one much courted at that (63.64-7):

> ego gymnast fui flos; ego eram decus olei;
> mihi ianuae frequentes, mihi limina tepida,
> mihi floridis corollis redimita domus erat,
> linquendum ubi esset orto mihi sole
>   cubiculum. . . .

> I was the flower of the gymnasium, the glory of the oil;
> there were always crowds at the door, the step was still warm,
> the house was encircled with garlands of flowers
> when the sun rose and it was time for me to quit my bed. . . .

He reminds us of those young Athenians whose company Socrates in the dialogues of Plato finds so congenial. Attis' tragedy is that he is no Alcibiades. The poem seems to me really only to make sense if we take it as a study of a young man who, along with others, had found (to their horror, or their shame) that they could not make the transition society demanded from the role of *puer delicatus* to that of husband, or Don Juan (*moechus*) and who abandon civilized life for the wilds of Phrygia and there 'unman themselves through too great hatred of the goddess of love' (17 *corpus euirastis Veneris nimio odio*). Observe the references to Attis' appearance: he has 'snow white hands' (8 *niueis manibus*), 'slender fingers' (10 *teneris digitis*), 'rosy lips' (74 *roseis labellis*). They might be intended to suggest some miraculous change in Attis' appearance following his self-emasculation. But isn't it more likely they point to the sort of young man Attis was?

Catullus, in other words, offers us an ironic reinterpretation of the Attis legend, in line both with his technique of bringing legend up to date (as in the 'realistic' treatment of Ariadne on the beach in **'Poem 64'**) and with the role of **'Poem 63'** in a collection of poems about love and contemporary society. In both cases we can easily suppose Catullus' insight into and his interest in the legend were sharpened by personal experience. Indeed it is tempting to regard Attis' flight to Phrygia as the symbol of Catullus' own expedition to Bithynia, to 'get away from it all'. We can imagine if we like that Attis' 'hatred of sex' (for that is what *Veneris nimio odio* really amounts to) was the result of a disastrous affair with a woman older and more experienced than himself, so long as we remember that this kind of package interpretation of a work of literature in terms of the writer's known (or supposed) personal experience isn't to be taken very seriously, and that the pursuit of correspondences between biographical fact and poetic fiction quickly leads us far away from literary criticism.

If we can grant, however, that **'Poem 63'** makes sense as a poem about a young man who could not make the kind of transition from boy to man which Tibullus' Marathus was able to accomplish so easily, the banter of the *Fescennina iocatio* in the first marriage hymn also starts to make rather more sense (61. 119-43):

> ne diu taceat procax
> Fescennina iocatio,
> nec nuces pueris neget
> desertum domini audiens
>   concubinus amorem.

> 'da nuces pueris, iners
> concubine! satis diu
> lusisti nucibus: lubes
> iam seruire Talasio.
>   concubine, nuces da.

> sordebant tibi uilicae,
> concubine, hodie atque heri:
> nunc tuum cinerarius
> tondet os. miser a miser
>   concubine, nuces da.

> diceris male te a tuis
> unguentate glabris marite
> abstinere, sed abstine.
> io Hymen Hymenaee io,
>   io Hymen Hymenaee.

> scimus haec tibi quae licent
> sola cognita, sed marito
> ista non eadem licent,
> io Hymen Hymenaee io,
>   io Hymen Hymenaee'. . . .

No more holding back the teasing
Fescennine jesting, concubinus can't
refuse the boys their walnuts
now he hears his love for his
master has been rejected.

'Give the boys the nuts, you lazy
concubinus! You've played with nuts
for long enough: now it's fun
to be slave to the Marriage God.
Hand over the nuts, concubinus.

Farm-stewards' wives weren't good enough
for you, concubinus, yesterday and today.
Now the barber comes to shave
your cheeks. Poor, unhappy
concubinus, hand over the nuts.

O groom, all sleek with unguent, they'll say
you don't want to be separated from your
darling, but separated you must be.
Lo! Hymen Hymenaeus, lo!
Lo! Hymen Hymenaeus.

We know your secrets, nothing wrong
in what you did, but you're a husband now
and the same things would be wrong.
Lo! Hymen Hymenaeus, lo!
Lo! Hymen Hymenaeus'. . . .

First the *concubinus* is made the recipient of ribald banter (lines 12-33), then the groom (lines 134-43). The *concubinus* is a slave (122 *domini,* 127 *seruire*), a youngster to whom the groom has been devoted. The scattering of walnuts (used as playthings in children's games) during the wedding procession, like the ritual shaving of the concubinus' cheeks (lines 131-2) are symbols indicating the time has come to put childish things aside. The arch innuendoes addressed to the groom about his relationship with the boy were no doubt also part of the tradition of the *Fescennina iocatio,* though the origins of the form are ancient and obscure. We are not obliged to take the innuendoes very seriously: it is easy to think of innocent and practical reasons why a Roman bachelor of good family might keep a handsome young male slave as his personal servant; nor is it hard to imagine that the slave might occupy the same room as his master—as some kind of body-guard, for example. And if it was the custom, it is natural enough that the custom should be made the subject of more or less good natured speculation; natural enough, too, that the youngster should preen himself on his privileged position—and that he should be teased for behaving as though 'farm-stewards' wives were not good enough for the likes of him' (129 *sordebant tibi uilicae*); and no less natural that such a slave should be dismissed on his master's marriage. Equally the thing may have become by Catullus' time no more than a traditional part of the marriage procession, a symbolic renunciation of one way of life for another: there was perhaps a slave actually present to whom the role of *concubinus* was assigned for the duration of the ceremony.

If the insinuations didn't deal with things that were common and accepted, or which one could pretend were common and accepted, in a spirit of ironical make-believe and in a context where that spirit was felt to be called for and not liable, therefore, to be misinterpreted, they would surely have no place in a marriage hymn. The relationship between groom and *concubinus* seems to me, in short, instructively close to that Catullus boasts of between himself and Juventius—or affects to fear between Furius, or Aurelius, and Juventius. With the Juventius poems we come of course to a different literary tradition. But in neither case is it so very important to disentangle tradition and reality, to separate fantasy from fact: what is important is to recognize that elements of both are present.

A passionate attachment to a *puer delicatus* wasn't exactly something to boast about in all seriousness. The Juventius poems move in an area where confession easily expands into fantasy, in order to inhibit credulity, and in order to make it clear that the reader is being offered a demonstration of *urbanitas,* rather than true confession. The parallel with **'Poem 32'** (*Amabo, mea dulcis Ipsitilla . . .*) and Catullus' cool announcement of the feat of prowess he is contemplating is close. For the reader to suppose, in either case, that Catullus means exactly what he says is to betray a lack of *urbanitas.*

If one puts fantasy and make-believe aside, the Romans (like the Greeks, or rather more than the Greeks) clearly felt little sympathy for the dirty old man. It was the stock smear of politicians. Clearly too it was held shameful for young men to surrender to their importunities. But passionate relationships, so long as they remained relatively innocent, seem to have been extended something approaching tolerant approval. One feels a flirtation with an attractive boy was looked at in much the same light as flirtation with another man's wife: both involved the pursuit of forbidden fruit, and had therefore to be disapproved of, however indulgently in a society where both were common; as Ovid knew well, the fun of a seduction, or at any rate the part to boast about in verse, lies more in the pursuit than in the capture. Where the two cases differed was in the view taken of the man who went too far. Adultery was naturally disapproved of by husbands; stern penalties were provided by law, and presumably sometimes exacted. Society, however, was inclined to be on the side of the adulterer. One gets the impression that considerably less glamour attached to the role of the successful paederast.

Once a youngster passed from the age where he could be described as *puer* to the age where he is described as *iuuenis* or *adolescens,* it seems to have been understood that (as Catullus tells the young slave in the first marriage hymn) the time when he could expect to be the recipient of such attentions was over. It is of course an obvious stage in adolescence, and one often remarked on by the Romans, even if the word *puer* is occasionally applied (like *puella* and our 'boy' and 'girl') to those rather older. The risk then disappeared: once the youngster had assumed the *toga uirilis* he was reckoned a 'man among men'; Cicero insists on the point in defending Caelius, to disprove insinuations about his client's relationship with Catiline. He might have added, if the circumstances had been different (had he not been defending Caelius in court as a young man of unimpeachable character) that Caelius was old enough to start taking an interest in youngsters himself.

Professor Gordon Williams has put the problem of the level of intent in the Juventius poems in an interesting form:

> Three famous poems of Catullus in the same metre are all about the arithmetic of lovers' kisses: two are to Lesbia ('5' and '7') and the third is to the boy Juventius ('48'). Each poem is epigrammatic in form and '48' is structurally the simplest, but it is impossible to give an account of the three poems by which '48' can be separated artistically from the other two. If the important fact about the Lesbia-poems in general is that Catullus' passion for her was so real, how could he write a poem like '48' without its appearing totally artificial?

Williams' question seems to me to be answered by **'Poem 16'** (*Pedicabo ego uos et irrumabo . . .*). The disclaimer is a poetic structure in its own right, a conceit built round the key words *pedicabo* and *irrumabo.* Indignant refutation of the innuendo of being a practicing paederast is expressed in the form of a threat of homosexual attack: the words *pedicabo et irrumabo,* that is to say, if used primarily in their colloquial sense (something like 'you can go to hell'), are put in a context in which the original meaning is drawn to the surface and exploited, even if the threat the words now express is hardly a practical possibility. Catullus' disclaimer underpins, I suggest, what should be our natural reaction to **'Poem 48'** (and **'Poem 99'**). The very brilliance and verve with which passion is flaunted demonstrates that what is being talked about is not passion deeply felt. It is not necessary (and, I think, not right) to seek to excuse these poems as exercises in Greek themes. They are exercises rather in *urbanitas,* all the wittier for being outrageous and because they baffle the *pilosi.* **'Poem 48'** is an elegantly frivolous demonstration of the contrapuntal possibilities of soberly measured syntax and wildly passionate statement; **'Poem 99'** (after **'Poem 76'**, the longest and most elegantly worded of the elegiac pieces in **'69-116'**) is a little like an English sixteenth-century lyric such as Wyatt's 'Alas! madame, for stelyug of a kysse':

> Alas madame for stelyng of a kysse,
> Have I somuch your mynd then offended?
> Have I then done so grevously amysse,
> That by no means it may be amended?
> Then revenge you: and the next way is this:
> An othr kysse shall have my lyffe endid.
> For to my mowth the first my hert did suck,
> The next shall clene oute of my brest it pluck.

It is true some of the things one wants to say about the Juventius poems apply with equal force to Poems '5' and '8'. They too are marked by an urbane, bantering irony. There is much in them too that is little more than wishful thinking. But the tone and attitude of Poems '5' and '7' are surely quite dissimilar. If emotion is held throughout under firm intellectual control, the emotion is real and unmistakable, it provides a justification for the wit: in Poems '48' and '99' wit is its own justification.

Poems '48' and '99' are to be lined up with poems such as Poems '6' (*Flaui, delicias tuas Catullo . . .*) or '32' (*Amabo, mea dulcis Ipsitilla . . .*). Poems '5' and '7' show the same form at a level of intent that was, I think, quite unprecedented in Roman poetry. We are dealing no longer with ideas Catullus found it fun to toy with: we are dealing with things which were carried to their proper, logical conclusion—the possession of Lesbia as his mistress. There is a new earnestness: sentiment, pathos almost, take the place of flippant bravura. To fail to distinguish between Poems '5' and '7' and Poems '48' and '99' is carrying open-mindedness too far. We might as soon refuse to distinguish between Catullus and Ovid.

Charles Martin (essay date 1979)

SOURCE: An introduction to *The Poems of Catullus,* translated by Charles Martin, The Johns Hopkins University Press, 1990, pp. ix-xxv.

[*In the following excerpt from his 1979 introduction to his edition of Catullus's poetry, Martin speaks of Catullus as one whose poetry was unique in its day and notably influential in modern times. Martin adds that Catullus's observations and concerns resonate readily within the contemporary mind.*]

1

Near the end of the seventeenth century, John Dryden could speak of translation, with offhanded assurance, as the act of bringing the thought of one author over into the language of another. In his day, poetic thought was social in nature, as were the rhymed couplets in which it was expressed. As a result, the poet was linked

in thought and expression not only to the community of the living but to the *fabulae Manes* as well, the fabled dead of the literary tradition, whose collective wisdom he guarded and interpreted.

Today, nearly three hundred years after Dryden, we speak of a poet's voice rather than a poet's thought, and we require that voice to be a reflection of the poet's sensibility rather than an expression of the tradition from which it emerges: our poet must deliver original, subjective truths in idiosyncratic utterances. We no longer share Dryden's sense of the wholeness of the past or of its continuity with the present: the modern poet has more in common with the archeologist in the ruins than with the curator of the museum. And, not surprisingly, we give our almost automatic assent to Robert Frost's intimidating proposition that poetry is what gets lost in the translation. As how could it not, when any voice, poetic or otherwise, shares in the evanescence of gesture?

It is the voice part of poetry that is so easily lost in translation.

2

Catullus entered Latin poetry as a voice not at all like those that the ears of his fellow citizens were used to hearing. In Rome during the first century B.C., a long-established tradition of high-minded, socially responsible, didactic verse was being challenged by a new wave from the East. Inspired by the classical postmodernism of Alexandrian poetry, a group of poets known today as the neoterics were writing poems that were playfully cerebral, sophisticated in their sensuality, and emphatically subjective. Nothing like this had happened to Latin verse before this happened to it; and so, when his first audience discovered Catullus among the neoterics, he must have been as much of a shock to his fellow citizens as the early twentieth-century modernists were to ours.

There really had been no one like Catullus writing in Latin before he came along, though he was not original in our sense of the word, which usually implies that a poet so labelled has neither read nor acknowledged the work of either his predecessors or his contemporaries. Catullus was typically neoteric in his erudition, and his voice was certainly shaped by his predecessors, the Latin and Greek poets whose works he carefully studied; nevertheless, what they had done was very different from what he would do.

One important difference, and one of the major reasons he is so attractive a poet in our time, is his way of presenting himself as one voice among other voices—highly competitive, yes, but not privileged, not central to his culture, as the epic poet believes himself to be. Whatever attention his poems get is attention that they have to put up a fight for, which is perhaps why these poems seem so active, with all their questions and answers, projections and provocations. Their author is one poet for whom solitude seems to have had little if any charm. We usually think of writing as a solitary act, but even here Catullus surprises us—in poem **"50,"** we find him composing verses in the company of his friend, Calvus. When he is alone in these poems, his ordinary response is to issue an invitation of one kind or another. One kind invites someone to visit the poet:

> Go, poem, pay a call on Caecilius,
> my friend the master of erotic verses:
> tell him to leave his lakefront place at Comum
> & spend a little time here at Verona. . . .

Another kind requests an invitation from someone else:

> I beg of you, my sweet, my Ipsitilla,
> my darling, my sophisticated beauty,
> summon me to a midday assignation. . . .

Although he said things that no one else would ever say, in ways that no one else could say them, he was also fascinated by the kind of things that other people were always saying, by the extraordinary range of the social registers of the collective Roman voice. Proverbs and cliches, the featureless coins of everyday speech, easily made their way into his verse: Does Dickface fornicate? *The pot gathers its own potherbs.* Aemilius thinks himself clever? *He hasn't the brains to guide a miller's donkey.* (In an age when there were millers, and the millers had donkeys, the latter would move endlessly in a circle around the millstone that ground grain into flour; who could not figure out the route would have been dumb indeed.) Does some poor *nouveau* attempt to put on airs by trying to mouth words as he has heard the notes pronounce them? Catullus is on hand in poem **"84"** to deflate such pretensions:

> Arrius had to have aitches to swell his
>   orations,
> and threatened us all with, *"hateful, hinsidious hach-shuns!"*

In poem **"53,"** he captures the spontaneously indecent observation of an anonymous bystander, overheard at one of the city's open-air courts while the poet's diminutive friend Calvus was orating: "Great gods, this little pecker's sure persuasive!"

Much of the time he wrote a poetry whose strength and attractiveness derives from its openness to the life and language of the streets of Rome and Verona. To paraphrase Paolo Pasolini on Ezra Pound, Catullus' love for the purely phatic aspect of language, its function as chat, is one of the most extraordinary phenom-

ena in classical literature. Gossip enthralls him: he is the poet as representative ear, the not-so-still center of a maelstrom of voices; why, this one will listen to stories about anyone from any source—even, as in poem **"67,"** from a door anxious to disburden itself of a few unsavory secrets. And, of course, he will pass the stuff along to others; why on earth would he keep it to himself? A good story repaid an invitation to dinner, deflated a rival, made you appear more serious, more attractive, or more dangerous in company. Catullus is skilled at passing gossip on with a kind of disclaimer: "Gellius, what shall I tell them? Everyone's asking me why it is that you . . ." He presents himself as someone who knows just what everyone's saying:

> What everyone says of pretentious, babbling
>   asses
> fits you, if anyone, putrescent Victius. . . .

He is wonderfully good at lining up imaginary tropes for real battles, battles in which there is no muck too messy to fling at an enemy, including the sort of messages scratched into walls about people like "RUFA THE BOLOGNESE WIFE OF MENENIUS," whose unsavory activities in the cemetery live on long after her in poem **"59."**

Behind the grotesque, boastful exaggerations of the obscenities, there is often—though not always—a more serious purpose, for Catullus sees himself as a moralist, an arbiter of conviviality, who must often remind others of what constitutes proper behavior in social relationships. In order to make any impression at all on the morally dense, those reminders often had to be pretty savage. Nevertheless, the street fighter rolling up his cloak into a shield does so in order to protect a curious, almost childlike innocent, who is easily (and repeatedly) disappointed because of the high expectations he has for the behavior of others. Catullus believes absolutely in some kind of moral authority apart from and above mere self-interest. That authority resides in such deities as *Fides,* the Roman god of Good Faith, *Nemesis,* the Greek god of retribution, and, ultimately, in the nameless abstractions he calls upon in poem **"76,"** when he wishes to be delivered from the self-described sickness of his passion for Lesbia.

There, as in other poems, with unself-conscious ease Catullus could turn from the pungent obscenities of the streets, from language used in exaggeration, to the ritual pieties of religious expression, in search of another kind of language for his poems, a language whose balance and restraint will redress grievances and help to set the moral universe in order.

3

Of course, if he had been content to say only what everyone else was saying, it is very unlikely that we would be reading him today: his almost miraculous survival was surely the work of an editor who recognized and valued the uniqueness of his gift, passing it on to a long succession of readers who have had the same high regard for it. The uniqueness of any poet whom we find interesting as a person lies in the success with which he or she manages to imprint a communal poetics with the stamp of subjectivity, with what we have been calling the poet's voice.

Catullus is so often immediately accessible to the reader that we tend to think of him as simple, direct, and unaffected; these are, after all, words that are frequently used as terms of praise for a poet nowadays. Most of the time, however, they simply do not apply to Catullus, whose voice and sensibility are more accurately described as complex, duplicitous, artful, and ironic. He is almost always saying more than just one thing. Consider, for example, poem 3, his lament for the dead sparrow of his mistress, which begins with what seems a solemn invocation:

> Lugete, o Veneres Cupidinesque
> et quantum est hominum venustiorum!

> Cry out lamenting, Venuses & Cupids,
> and mortal men endowed with Love's
>   refinement!

But how solemn can this invocation be when the very next line, *"Passer mortuus est meae puellae . . . ,"* reveals the somewhat less than portentous reason behind it: "The sparrow of my ladyfriend is dead." Venuses and Cupids (the plural is meant to suggest the enormity of the poet's grief) are urgently summoned (along with the more refined among mortals) to grieve over the hardly unprecedented death of yet another avatar of the common sparrow, *Passer domesticus.* Does he really mean it? The short answer—there being insufficient room in this introduction for the long answer—is Yes and no, or He does and he doesn't: the playfulness of this poem, as of so many others, makes a direct, unequivocal answer impossible to give.

The main strategy of playfulness is ironic juxtaposition, as in the juxtaposition of high summons and low motive in the opening lines. But here, as elsewhere in the verse of Catullus, there are ironic juxtapositions even on the level of diction. There is, for instance, the line in which he describes the sparrow lighting out for the underworld: *"qui nunc it per iter tenebricosum."* Just eleven syllables: in the first six, we can hear the sparrow chirping along in the poet's own words, an understandably nervous, repetitive, obsessively rhyming little scrap of sensibility: "qui *nunc it per iter.*" Suddenly, out of nowhere comes the second half of the line, a single, polysyllabic monstrosity that stops the bird dead in its tracks: "TENEBRICOSUM!" "It now flits off on its way, goes GLOOM-LADEN . . ." tries, not with-

out losing something, to catch the effect.

Other gestures of his voice are even less possible to reproduce in English. What can a translator do about the opening line of poem 12, against Marrucinus Asinius? At dinner parties, his left hand goes slipping over into his neighbor's lap: Is he just being friendly? No—a moment later, and neighbor's napkin is missing. Catullus pins him to the board with a line that forever marries his name to his left-handed proclivities:

> Marrucin' Asini, manu sinistra . . .

There is the pattern made by the repetition of the three vowel sounds (*a u i / a i i / a u i / i a*), and there is the repetition of all but two of the consonants; there is the insinuating rhyme of name and hand, *Marru'* and *manu,* not to mention the wicked repitition, like gossip being passed on in a whisper from one ear to another, of *cin'/ Asini / sini*; and there is the way in which they together build, in only as much time as it takes to mouth those four words, an unanswerable equation: Asinius is sinister.

4

Catullus is a poet with a wide range of experience: he not only knows life on the streets but has mastered his craft, is a well-taught student of literature and mythology, and an intimate of the rich, the powerful, and the famous. In his poetry he is unwilling to scant any aspect of that experience in favor of any other. He is capable of juxtaposing an ancient cliche with a figure drawn from the world of Roman high finance or from Alexandrian literature. Consider, for example, poem "7," a lyric for Lesbia that begins:

> Quaeris quot mihi basiationes
> tuae, Lesbia, sint satis superque.

> My Lesbia, you ask how many kisses
> would be enough to satisfy, to sate me!

Lesbia has asked Catullus a straightforward question to which this poem is going to be the answer. Or is it? It may indeed be an answer, but it is anything but straightforward. The signal is given with that word *basiationes,* for which the English "kisses" is a woefully pale shadow. Something's already lost in translation, and the poem will lose a little more, since the whole phrase, broken between two lines, *basiationes / tuae,* probably sounded as odd in Latin as the corresponding English phrase, "basiations of you," would sound to us. Yes, there is such a word as "basiation," lovingly laid up in the Oxford English Dictionary, after having been used, once, by George Meredith in 1879. However, the word is perfectly useless to any sane translator, since it's obvious that Meredith got it from

Catullus in the first place; translation ought to be a matter of repaying a debt rather than increasing it, and so, alas, kisses must do.

If the poem has already, in its first two lines, taken something of a leap away from the straightforward, it gets even more indirect when it answers, or appears to answer, Lesbia's question. The first part of the poet's answer is given in a poetic cliche as old as Homer or the Bible, and probably not exactly a novelty then, either:

> quam magnus numerus Libyssae harenae,

as many kisses as there are grains of sand in the Libyan desert. But immediately Catullus goes on to complicate things:

> . . . Laserpiciferis iacet Cyrenis,
> oraclum Iovis inter aestuosi
> et Batti veteris sacrum sepulcrum. . . .

> . . . near Cyrene, where silphium is gathered,
> between the shrine of Jupiter the sultry
> & the venerable sepulchre of Battus!

The playful self-mockery that offers us *basiationes / tuae,* makes Catullus also capable of ironically posing to his mistress as the modern successor of the overeducated Alexandrians. Here is one who not only knows the site of the commercial center for the trade in asafoetida but gives the coordinates of that site with a detail that translates into a literary reference: Callimachus, the pluperfect Alexandrian, to whom Catullus was especially devoted, came from Cyrene and called himself Battiades, son of Battus, the founder of the city. Not only does the poet know all of these things, but he is perfectly capable of including such details in what is sometimes taken as a simple love poem. A love poem it is, but simple it is not; and much of its complexity comes from the poet's need to join together, for the moment at least—and not without the serious qualification of irony—the disparate parts of his own experience.

5

Neither his concern nor his strategies will be unfamiliar to those who have read the English poets of the seventeenth century, especially John Donne, with whom Catullus shares the ability to conceive of a conceit whose intellectual brilliance reflects the intensity of his emotions. He does this never more perfectly than in poem "**5**":

> Vivamus, mea Lesbia, atque amemus,
> rumoresque senum severiorum
> omnes unius aestimemus assis.
> Soles occidere et redire possunt:

nobis, cum semel occidit brevis lux,
nox est perpetua una dormienda.
Da mi basia mille, deinde centum,
dein mille altera, dein secunda centum,
deinde usque altera mille, deinde centum,
dein, cum milia multa fecerimus,
conturbabimus illa, ne sciamus,
aut ne quis malus invidire possit,
cum tantum sciat esse basiorum.

> Lesbia, let us live only for loving,
> and let us value at a single penny
> all the loose flap of senile busybodies!
> Suns when they set are capable of rising,
> but at the setting of our own brief light
> night is one sleep from which we never
>   waken.
> Give me a thousand kisses, then a hundred,
> another thousand next, another hundred,
> a thousand without pause & then a hundred,
> until when we have run up our thousands
> we will cry bankrupt, hiding our assets
> from ourselves & any who would harm us,
> knowing the volume of our trade in kisses.

The poem is an invitation from the poet to his beloved to escape with him from the traditional restraints imposed upon them by Roman society (represented by the gossipmongering elders) and to live entirely for the moment, entirely for the sake of passion. (Is it a shared passion? The reader may very well wonder, for Catullus is anything but explicit here.)

Nevertheless the premise of the poem is that such an escape is indeed possible, and Catullus is wonderfully persuasive here: his voice caresses the Latin, plays with it as who had ever had the wit to do before him? When he wants to illustrate the brevity of life and the longlastingness of death, he takes advantage of the similarity in sound of the Latin words for light and night, *lux* and *nox*. (Here, perhaps, is one of the rare cases where a little something is actually gained in translation, since the rhyme in English is more exact than in Latin.) The *lux* goes out at the end of the fifth line, and *nox* begins at the very beginning of the sixth, which sets that monosyllable in poignant opposition to the polysyllabic words that tell us what it really represents:

> nox est perpetua una dormienda.

Catullus here takes brilliant advantage of the elision that occurs in Latin verse when an unstressed vowel ends a word coming before a word that begins with a vowel, as between *perpetua* and *una;* the last vowel of the first word is omitted, and so the line would actually have been pronounced as:

> nox est perpetu una dormienda

joining *perpetua,* "forever," and *una* "one," into a single cry, a lament for the unending sleep of death.

Nevertheless, against this blissful vision of erotic liberation from the moral restraints imposed by society, the poet sets a very distinctive countermovement, beginning in the third line, where he does not tell us that the rumors generated by the old men are worthless but rather tells us (with a curiously odd precision) that they are not worth an *as* the Roman equivalent of our penny. This is not remarkable in itself, but then, when he asks Lesbia for kisses, he does so by alternating demands for a thousand kisses (*mille*) with demands for a hundred (*centum*) in a way that would have inevitably reminded his audience of fingers shuttling across the columns of an abacus, busily toting up sums in some Roman counting house:

> *da mi basia* mille   *deinde* centum,
> *dein* mille *altera   dein secunda* centum,
> *deinde usque altera* mille   *deinde* centum,

What is he up to here? In his edition of Catullus, Kenneth Quinn suggests that "*da mi* + name of article + quantity was perhaps the formula for placing an order with a merchant (hence *basia mille,* not *mille basia*). We are invited perhaps to imagine the kisses stacked in rows (like sacks of grain, say) as the quantities specified are delivered—and then jumbled up into a single pile." Kisses delivered like sacks of grain, then, with someone keeping track of the deliveries on an abacus. If Quinn's suggestion seems bizarre, it is only because we have simplified Catullus for too long John Donne, addressing his mistress as "[M]y America, my new found land," would have had no problem with the conceit. Quinn is—no pun intended—right on the money here, for when Catullus finishes his sums, he proposes to throw them into confusion, so that no one will ever know the total. But the word he uses, *conturbare,* is according to C. J. Fordyce, "a technical term for fraudulent bankruptcy with concealment of assets." Such language in a love poem must have seemed as curious to his audience as, say, a poem in which a love affair is compared to a leveraged buy-out would be to us.

Nevertheless, the language is indisputably there. Catullus did not allow this theme to enter the poem by accident, and its effect on the poem is to contradict the ostensible message of the poet to his mistress: a poem which at first seems to defy calculation, to throw calculation to the winds, is in fact inextricably bound to the very instrument of calculation, the abacus. And, finally, what are we to make of that word *conturbare?* Does it not convey the disturbing intimation that somewhere down the road, emotional ruin, a bankruptcy of the spirit, is lying in wait for the optimistic lover?

6

Immensely popular for a few centuries after his death, Catullus' work disappeared almost completely in the early Middle Ages; it survived only because of the discovery of a manuscript of his poems at Verona about the year 1300. (Were it not for that manuscript, we would have only poem **"62,"** which was preserved independently.) Poetic influence is very often indirect: Dante Alighieri does not mention Catullus or his poems, though in Sirmione there is a castle, once the property of Dante's great friend Can Grande della Scala, which Dante is said to have visited. Had he walked a mile or so to the end of the peninsula, he could have sat in the ruins of the villa known today as *le grotte di Catullo.* There he might have recited to himself parts of the *Commedia,* which, like many of the poems Catullus wrote, is written in lines of eleven syllables: Dante inherited and shaped a line which Catullus before him had inherited from the poets of Alexandria; after demonstrating its usefulness, Catullus passed it on to other Latin poets, whose work and influence survived into Dante's time. The Italian poets of Dante's age were of great interest to the poets of the English Renaissance, and so the line of eleven syllables (shortened to ten) became one of the continental sources of the ever dependable, ever renewable workhorse of English poetry, the iambic pentameter line: Catullus enters English poetry already lost in translation.

In a more explicit way, Catullus appears on the English scene at the beginning of its Renaissance, in an enormous, sprawly, mock-serious elegy inspired by his two sparrow poems: John Skelton's *The Boke of Phyllyp Sparrowe.* After Skelton, virtually every important poet of the sixteenth and seventeenth centuries who read Latin knew Catullus, but his influence was subterranean enough to make him something of "a poet's poet."

One reason for this was that Callus had gotten off to such a late start. The manuscript that surfaced in Verona was found before Gutenberg's useful invention, and so it took considerable time before its poems could be copied and gotten into circulation in Europe, and of course, even longer for them to find their way to England. Moreover, those poems appeared without the centuries of interpretive commentary that had led to the canonization of poets like Virgil and Horace. In the meanwhile, the neoteric tradition had been lost, and its assumptions were no longer intelligible. As a result, some of the poems, such as poem **"64,"** were very difficult to deal with. Since there were no other poems like this one, the question, What kind of a poem is this? was impossible to answer.

The poet's reception was also slowed down by English prudishness in the face of Catullan licentiousness. In the eyes of the guardians of public morality from the

1600s through the 1800s, the morals of classical authors (with the exceptions of Virgil and Horace) were frequently thought to be unfit to set before children. But our poet was really the worst offender: as Byron's Donna Inez hendecasyllabically opined, "Catullus scarcely has a decent poem." This did not mean that he could not be read, only that hypocrisy made pleasure pay for the privilege, as Byron shows us in his description of the classical education of the young Don Juan:

> Juan was taught from out the best edition,
>   Expurgated by learned men, who place,
> Judiciously, from out the schoolboy's vision,
>   The grosser part; but, fearful to deface
> Too much their modest bard by this omission,
>   And, pitying sore his mutilated case,
> They only add them in an appendix,
> Which saves, in fact, the trouble of an index;
>
> For there we have them all "at one fell
>   swoop,"
>   Instead of being scattered through the
>   pages;
> They stand forth, marshalled in a handsome
>   troop,
>   To meet the ingenuous youth of future
>   ages. . . .

The ingenuous youth of our age might well be disappointed: one recent edition of the poems of Catullus intended for the edification of young scholars not only left out a fourth of the poems, but omitted an appendix as well.

7

Catullus is perhaps the only Latin poet of the classical period to have had an important influence on modern poetry in English, and it is not unreasonable to regard Ezra Pound as the modern discoverer of Catullus, at least for poets writing in English, since he did so much to encourage the young modernists to read and translate the Latin poet.

As George Steiner has pointed out, however, Pound's judgement had been formed by the poets and translators of the nineteenth century. It was, in fact, J. W. Mackail, eminent man of letters (O.M., M.A., LL.D., F.B.A.), in his standard text, *Latin Literature* (1895), who first saw in Catullus what the modems were later to see, praising his "hard clear verse" and the "dear and almost terrible simplicity that puts Catullus in a place by himself among the Latin poets. Where others labour in the ore of thought and gradually forge it out into sustained expression, he sees with a single glance, and does not strike a second time." A high regard for simplicity is certainly not the virtue I would choose to stress for readers of Catullus, but Mackail's appreciation does have a hard, clear, modern ring to it.

And Ezra Pound, himself searching for hardness and clarity in verse, found it in Catullus, whom he read with close attention during the years when he was one of the inventers of free verse. Pound was fascinated by the way in which Catullus had transformed the matter and meter of Sappho in his poem **"51"**; and, setting out from some rather wooden imitations of that poem, he very quickly learned how to write a poem in Sapphics that sounded as though it were *vers libre:*

> Golden rose the house, in the portal I saw
> thee, a marvel, carven in subtle stuff, a
> portent. Life died down in the lamp and
>   flickered,
> caught at the wonder.

The traditional Sapphic line breaks after the fifth or sixth syllable, and is, to a large extent, end-stopped. "Apparuit" sounds like free verse because Pound has enjambed the lines and paused within them at unpredictable places. What I have said about the first stanza of this poem is true of the rest of it. After mastering the Sapphic stanza, Pound fragmented it to create "The Return," a poem in which Sapphics really do meet free verse:

> See, they return; ah, see the tentative
> Movements, and the slow feet,
> The trouble in the pace and the uncertain
> Wavering!

Little of the Catullan influence manages to make its way into Pound's later work, but it is clear that the influence was extraordinarily important to him in his formative years. Pound seems to be paying homage to it in Canto III, where he lovingly evokes the beauty of Sirmione in the passage beginning "Gods float in the azure air," and which concludes with two lines that are a commentary on the first tableau of **'Poem 64'**:

> And in the water, the almond-white swimmers,
> The silvery water glazes the upturned nipple. .
>   . .

Catullus was an influence not only on the formation of free verse in our time, but on the development of traditional verse as well. Robert Frost was a lifelong admirer of Catullus, and you can hear the influence of Catullan hendecasyllabics on Frost's iambic pentameter, which often admits an eleventh syllable to the line. Frost wrote a poem, "For Once, Then, Something," in which he imitated Catullan hendecasyllabic meter in a way that gives us, for once, then, a clear sound of the measure part of the poet's voice:

> Others taunt me with having knelt at well-
>   curbs

Always wrong to the light, so never seeing
Deeper down in the well than where the water
Gives me back in a shining surface picture
Me myself in the summer heaven, godlike,
Looking out of a wreath of fern and cloud
    puffs.

It is not at all accidental, I think, that the two poets
who have made the greatest use of Catullus in our time
and our language saw in him a source of renewal.

Frederic Raphael and Kenneth McLeish (essay date 1979)

SOURCE: An introduction to *The Poems of Catullus,*
translated by Frederic Raphael and Kenneth McLeish,
David R. Godine, Publishers, 1979, pp. 9-24.

[*In the essay below, Raphael and McLeish provide a
portrait in miniature of Catullus's life and enduring
accomplishment, piecing together a likely outline of
the poet's life and that of Lesbia using such sources as
are available.*]

Tennyson called him tender; Harold Nicolson was
unable to understand why. Gaius Valerius Catullus,
the greatest Roman lyric poet, who was said by St
Jerome to have died at the age of thirty, has always
excited contradictory judgments. He is prized by some
for the sincerity and deprecated by others for the crudeness of his feelings; romantics credit him with spontaneity, classics with erudition; his eroticism gives him
a dubious reputation among the austere; the sentimental see in his delicacy the very instance of the sensibility which proves too fine for this world: those whom
the Muses love, they say, die young.

Of the specific nature of his death nothing is known,
and of his life very little. Did the cruelties of his mistress indeed bring on despair and death? He may as
well have died of malaria or in a street accident. (Juvenal, a century and a half later, reminds us that such
things were commonplace.) Perhaps like Cinna, his
friend and the unluckiest of poets, he was killed in
some brawl which did not concern him personally—
or, like Marlowe, in one that concerned him closely,
for Catullus had a savage tongue as well as a tender
heart. He was reckless enough, and brave enough, to
make savage fun of Caesar and of Pompey (poems
'29', '54', '57', etc.) at a time when a dagger in the
back was a more likely response to libel than a civilised injunction. We are promised that Caesar took the
young man's ribaldry in good part, but Catullus hit
with contemptuous accuracy right below the belt, his
favourite target. He saw the republic collapsing into
tyranny and in that collapse of public modesty he read
the ruin of his own hopes of a decent life among decent people, and he raged accordingly. Rome had nev-

er been a just society in any egalitarian sense, but it
had been governed according to conventions of self-
restraint (the consuls yielding power annually to their
elected successors) and respect for the common good,
however narrowly that might be interpreted. The vanity of wealth and the megalomania of conquest were in
the process of rupturing all that, and forever. But though
he was a caustic observer of social degeneration, it
would be quite false to represent Catullus as a revolutionary; like many young aristocrats when they devote
themselves to the arts, he was more disgusted by the
graceless style of *ces princes qui nous gouvernent* than
the advocate of any ideology of social change. He was
a sort of Tory romantic (if one must plump for an
anachronism): like so many ancient poets, he affected
to revere the values of the golden age, whenever that
was. In an age of shifting political and sexual alliances, he dreamed of fidelity and true friendship. His
denunciations of his mistress, pitched at the highest
level of poetic despair, and even of the dinner guest
who stole his napkins pitched somewhat lower, might
prove tiresome in their whining reproach, were it not
that one has a sense always of a dream of true constancy and affection muffled by the sour blanket of reality.
'It need not be like this' is ever at war with 'this is
how it is'. Such tension is at the heart of the Catullan
character; hate and love rise and fall on an eternal see-
saw, each counter-weighted and held in suspense by
the other.

Catullus was probably born about 84 B.C., if we are to
accept Jerome's statement that he died at thirty, since
poem 29 alludes to Caesar's conquest of Britain, which
took place in 55 B.C. (Jerome says that he was born in
87 B.C., but this is incompatible with the text.) But the
date of his death is of merely academic interest, for his
immortality is assured. His best poems speak with a
directness unique in surviving Roman literature. One
need not disparage Horace and Virgil, I.ucretius and
Ovid, or indeed Propertius and Juvenal, to justify the
view that Catullus is a case gloriously apart. It was not
always so. His work disappeared from public knowledge for the best part of a thousand years and he might
easily have shared the fate of Cinna, who not only
perished in the flesh because he happened to be mistaken for a hated politician of the same name, but whose
poems also failed to elude the *oubliette* of time: scarcely
a line remains. Catullus himself survives only because
some wine merchant in his native city of Verona chose',
in the fourteenth century, to stuff a bundle of his poems in an unused measuring vessel. (The story that
they were wedged in a wine cask is a romance.) From
that precarious source—the so-called Veronensis MS—
all our present manuscripts derive.

What proportion of the poet's complete output the
existing 113 poems represent, no one can say. There
are fragments and traces of poems which are not represented in the present *œuvre.* Some scholars believe

that these are the selected works as collated and edited by Catullus himself; others maintain that they cannot be regarded as definitive. Equally, one party declares that it is absurd to suppose that the poet himself arranged them in so haphazard, even silly, an order; the other insists that there is subtle art in the apparently casual interleaving of passion with pretentiousness, of satire with sentiment. Professor J. P. Sullivan has kindly pointed out that Professor Clausen strongly believes that no ancient editor would have classified a poetic corpus by *metre.* No doubt Catullus did indeed issue a *libellus,* but the present text, in both Clausen's and Sullivan's view, is the work of a later editor. This does not, of course, mean that no signs are evident of the poet's own adroit juxtapositions. Certainly Catullus was a master of *variatio:* his poems rang the changes on metre and subject in a manner which was indeed, in a literary sense, revolutionary. He drew his inspiration from the Greek poets of Alexandria, above all Callimachus who, in a famous and prescriptive polemic, pronounced the superiority of the contemporary short poem over the long. Catullus endorsed his view that a thoroughly elaborated small work was in every way better than a sprawling, jerry-built long one (see poems '**22**', '**36**' and '**95**'). It used to be said that he deplored longer poems because he was incapable of writing them: one of the 'problems' of Catullus was that his *œuvre* was broken abruptly into two halves, the successful shorter works and the allegedly inferior longer ones, '**61-68**'. This supposed dichotomy—the idea of 'two Catulluses'—does not endure sympathetic scrutiny, although it remains true that the long poems are longer than the short ones. The same poet is unmistakably at work in both areas and the same obsessions reveal themselves. It has been suggested that poem '**63**', for instance, was written as a kind of exercise, because Catullus was concerned to discover whether or not he could handle the metrical difficulties. If it is true that every conscious artist (and Catullus was certainly that) is likely to present himself with stylistic challenges, like a great golfer who disdains the easy shot as unworthy of his idea of himself, the terrible *donnée* of poem '**63**', the castration theme, has surely a more than academic significance. Catullus' sense of being somehow irrevocably unmanned by his, as they say, ball-crushing mistress gives the Attis poem a characteristic personality. Some scholars have suggested that it is merely a translation from Callimachus, though no Callimachan poem on the theme is known to us. Here again we may say that, even if such a poem existed, Catullus chose this particular one and made it his own, just as the 'Imitations' of Robert Lowell are very much Lowell. An inspired translator does not translate just anything.

The old debating points recur frequently in one's attempts to understand Catullus. Did he write for others or for himself? Did he rely on inspiration or was he hardly more than a gifted *pasticheur?* Was he serious or was he flippant, a unique genius or merely the sole instance to come down to us of a whole school of similar talents? If his generation did indeed boast of several poets of his quality, it must have been uniquely blessed, for its sky blazed with suns. Yet Catullus certainly did belong to a movement, famously labelled by Cicero 'the *neoteroi',* which could mean merely 'the newer/younger ones', though one suspects a sarcastic overtone to the soubriquet. Cicero larded his letters with Greek tags and was an honest admirer of Greek culture, but the Hellenistic affectations of those brilliant young men who looked to Alexandria for their models probably struck him as both suspect and impertinent. The iconoclastic wit of men like Cinna, Calvus (another possible genius lost to us forever) and Catullus gave them, it seemed, an easy *entree* into the highest social circles, where their affectations of disdain for the prosaic platitudes of public life must have added to Cicero's sense of uneasiness. There was, he might be forgiven for thinking, something positively dangerous about a drop-out who could drop in on the smartest people and take his place among them with only an arrogant epigram to serve as a calling card. Cicero himself was regarded by Catullus with ambivalence: witness the two ways of reading '**Poem 49.**' A man capable of celebrating his consulship and the victory over Catiline with a verse like *O fortunatam natam me consule Romam* (lucky Rome, born again with me as consul) can scarcely have been regarded with undiluted admiration by a poet who placed a premium on subtlety. The *neoteroi* formed an aristocracy of taste, with a slang and style of its own, and Cicero—himself a 'new man' socially and politically—must have felt his exclusion with something of the bitterness of one who, having travelled hopefully, liked to think that he had now undoubtedly arrived. That Catullus was soon in love with one of the sisters of Cicero's most implacable enemy salted the wound stingingly. However, it would be wrong to make too much of the antagonism between the Ciceronian and the Catullan view of life and of letters. If Cicero, who had so needed patrons when he began his career, was disposed, in middle age, to patronise the next generation, he recognised Catullus' quality with the grudging condescension of old talent for young genius.

Catullus may have paraded a certain patrician stylishness, but he was hardly less provincial in origin than Cicero himself. He came from Verona, where his father was a landowner sufficiently prominent to entertain Julius Caesar when the great man came through Cisalpine Gaul on official business. Catullus grew up on his father's estates by Lake Garda. As poem '**31**' proves, he remained devoted to the beauties of his native region. He loved his elder brother, whose premature death, in the Troad, occasioned the touching elegy of poem '**101**' and perhaps, by analogy, the consolatory lines of poem '**96**'. There is no direct allusion anywhere to his feeling for his father or mother. Perhaps it is anachronistic to wonder whether or not he loved them. The Roman family was held together by traditional rights and duties rather than by the tenuous bonds of affection. However, one is tempted to see something of Baudelaire in the young poet: he had an appetite for the shocking. His ostentatious insolence towards Caesar suggests a certain desire to scandalise his father by attacking so boasted a guest. (It can equally be argued that there were good reasons for satirising Caesar apart from a wish to embarrass one's parents.) Baudelaire's outrageousness was, of course, directed especially against his step-father and the analogy should not be pressed with any vigour. However, the complexities of the Catullan psychology are perhaps at least made less 'inexplicable' in the light of the Baudelairean syndrome. For Catullus too seems to have pitched himself into a blatantly doomed relationship; he too had a certain fastidious *nostalgie de la boue.* That the object of his notorious passion was a woman of mature years, though scarcely old enough to be his mother, suggests (if such suggestions are illuminating) an Oedipal obsession. So too, though Catullus may sincerely have wished it otherwise, does his fidelity to a married woman notorious for her faithlessness. The hope that he could wrest Lesbia from her husband and from the way of life which she found so amusing may have been genuine enough. Passionate lovers are not in the habit of weighing the odds. Yet to hope, as he did, that he and Lesbia could ever be married, to hope even that she would cease to have other lovers, comes very close to the infantile fantasy that one's mother can become one's sole property, the father displaced from his own bed. Such psychological speculations neither tarnish nor explain the poetry which came of Catullus' eventually ruinous involvement, but they may enable us to see a unity behind the diversity of tone, style and content. Innocence and guilt, fastidiousness and coarseness, tenderness and perversity complement rather than contradict each other in the context of a passionate yet impossible love.

How could he ever have dedicated the purity of his feelings to an affair soon sordid with cynicism and betrayal? What may well have begun as a smart and casual affair—what better way to mark one's arival in smart society than by humping the hostess?—devloped into a dominating obsession. Even when he was supplanted in Lesbia's bed by his erstwhile friend, Caelius Rufus, he could not call it a day. He knew very well what sophisticated convention required—that one accept the transience of love with cynical grace—but he could not keep the rules, much as he may have wished to. Sensible men about Rome put such things down to experience and went on to the next adventure. Catullus was hooked. The apparently chic provincial poet, with his bold confidence in matters of aesthetics, fell victim to a naiveté he could wholly conceal, although he managed to ape the coolness of the in-crowd, to catch their tone and echo it in amusing squibs and sardonic epigrams which seemed to endorse their casualness in sexual matters. His own fervent fidelity to Lesbia did not entirely inhibit him from sexual indulgence in other directions, both with girls and with boys. The females were almost certainly professionals—Ameana and Ipsitilla (see poems '32' and '41')—whose charms were available when more sentimental satisfactions were denied, but the homosexual attachments, especially to Juventius, did not lack their emotional element. It may be said that we have no evidence that Catullus was literally involved with young men. Perhaps he was merely amusing himself by developing a standard erotic theme. The recommendation not to read biographical facts into a writer's work has led some critics to deny that there can be any inference at all from the text to the life. However, can anyone truly believe that Catullus did not actually love a woman whom he addresses as Lesbia but who was almost certainly the infamous Clodia? (T. P. Wiseman maintains in his essay *Lesbia—Who?* that it night as well have been her youngest sister, who also had the hot blood of the family, but his agile arguments are not wholly convincing.) Catullus' poems are lively with the names of actual persons of the day and they would surely have had small point if they did not make equal play with their actual characters and actions. How can his accusation that Vibennius *père et fils* (poem '33') stole from the changing rooms in the public baths have been amusing unless it had some credible foundation in daily life? We should remember that Roman poetry was not written merely to be published but also to be performed; reading aloud was a standard part of poetic practice. Catullus and his clan undoubtedly competed in entertaining and dazzling one another. The reproaches which the anguished poet flings at his faithless friends (he seems to have been singularly ill-served) were not infrequently delivered to their faces, if they cared or dared to show them. The lighter poems in particular were intended to get laughs no less than to prick consciences. They can be best enjoyed, even today, by being spoken aloud. The sometimes abrupt changes of tone, even within the text of a short poem, make better sense if one presupposes an audience, rather than a solitary and silent reader. The dramatic or comic pause is part of the skilful machinery; the habit of taking Latin poetry as a printed text whose complexities must be construed and unravèlled at an even, tortuous pace, has led generations of readers to miss the ironies which Catullus' implied timing was surely designed to emphasise. Often a twist in the last line turns solemnity to laughter, self-pity to self-deprecation.

An instance where the irony is usually missed is poem '35'. The usual interpretation is that Catullus, the earnest critic, secretary-general of the *neoteroi,* writes to his friend Caecilius, who is some hundred miles away, and commands him at once to leave the girl whom he is enjoying in order to some post-haste to a literary tutorial. Catullus has just read his friend's Ode dedicated to the Great Mother and wants to tell Caecilius what is wrong with it. Scholars have assumed the poem to be a serious summons, as if Catullus genuinely expected a young man (a young *Latin*!) to leap from his mistress's bed, having reminded her of Catullus' belief that poetry takes priority over love, and rush to be told what is wrong with his work. Well, of course Catullus took poetry seriously and of course that is one way of reading the poem. But it is precisely because Catullus and his friends did take their craft seriously that the lines also have a comic undertone. Surely they read more entertainingly as an ironic comment on Caecilius' affections of dedication to the Muse and also, perhaps, as an example of Catullan self mockery: how can an inadequate poet like Caecilius be entitled to so enviably delicious a girl? Catullus presents himself here in the role, somewhat inverted, of Stevie Smith's Person From Porlock: he interrupts lovers with the news that a poem has to be worked out. Happiness as Stevie Smith herself remarked, does not make us write, but rather puts thoughts of literature out of one's mind. The comedy of poem **'35'** lies in Catullus' confidence that Caecilius will *not* come. What comedy could have been left in it, had Catullus' audience seriously assumed that the dutiful lad would immediately obey his tutor's summons? There is a kind of final, tragic irony in the fact that Catullus himself whose aesthetic convictions held poetry to be largely a matter of the intellect, proved no more able to abandon his mistress than was Caeilius. Here again the audience must have recognised how badly bitten was the biter We are all good at enjoining sobriety on others, but who can be sure of his own?

Critics of Catullus have often emphasised the distinction between his sober and his scandalous self, without perhaps realising how closely they are linked. It seems incredible to certain prosaic people that Catullus can have been all *that* hurt by his wrecked affair with Lesbia. (The chronology is arguable—and argued about—but he seems to have been her official lover for a short time, during which they enjoyed the idyllic passion he naively imagined would endure forever. After that, he shared her favours for another period, before finally being excluded from them, either by his own belated nausea or by her decisive cruelty.) That he could have continued to be stricken three whole *years* after the collapse of his hopes may seem absurd to hard heads, but to imagine that a single affair cannot dominate a writer's thoughts for that long is to forget that Flaubert, for instance, loved Madame Schlésinger all his life, though he never shared her bed and only briefly her company. The imposition on himself of a rigorous system of impersonal literary endeavour in no way precluded Flaubert from an endless obsession with the woman of his dreams. 'Get over it' is precisely what writers so often cannot do. Affectations of tough-mindedness are often calculated to dissimulate embar-

rassingly persistent, even puerile softheartedness. Cynicism is sentiment that dare not speak its name. Somerset Maugham was notably beady-eyed in his attitude to the sexual and sentimental attachments of others, but he continued to weep over the death of his mother eighty years after the event; Proust's whole sense of life was coloured by the memory of a goodnight kiss. The sexual pathology of Catullus may now, at last, be discussed without false tact; such discussion is not necessarily more important than textual elucidation and need not be unduly prolonged, but it may help to establish an underlying unity which prudishness has obscured. It is generally held that the Lesbia poems are the sincere centre of the Catullan *oeuvre*. Some of them are admittedly peripheral, like that alluding to Lesbia's brother, Lesbius (poem **'79'**), the clearest evidence we have that Lesbia was indeed Clodia, the sister of that notorious Clodius whose appetite for scandal led him to dress up as a female and intrude on the ceremonies of the vestal virgins, thus breaking a taboo in a fashion which all decent Romans, however privately sceptical, were obliged to regard as sacrilegious. Clodia is widely believed to have committed incest with her racy brother, though the main evidence of this, apart from their dissolute reputations, comes from Cicero's speech *Pro Caelio,* in which he was defending Clodia's ex-lover and Catullus' ex-friend. It was essential to his case to blacken Clodia, which he seems to have done to such good effect that her name ceases to be mentioned in any chronicles of the period. Catullus' lampoon suggests that the rumour was generally current, though poem **'79'** too could be regarded as suspect on grounds of *parti pris.* However peripheral it may be, this little poem is the hinge, as it were, joining the 'sincere' side of Catullus, the side most agreeable to moralists, with the morally less sweet-smelling. For it needs no great psychological acuteness to see that Catullus was as much fascinated by betrayal as he was hurt by it. He was obsessed by Lesbia's lovers, about whom there is a considerable number of poems, particularly if one includes her husband among them. We need not regard these poems as symptoms of immaturity in order to see in them a psychological pattern which keeps step very well with the Oedipal syndrome. Catullus' 'confusion'—his inability to be 'grown-up', his incessant havering between one posture and another, between purity and lechery, hard and soft—makes singular sense if we admit that his sexuality was stimulated, however much it may have appalled him, by the very treachery which so painfully soured his love. Why does Catullus both love and hate? Why does he desire Lesbia more but love her less? The conflict between sex and love is less strange to us now than it was to generations of critics with little experience of life and reluctant powers of inferential self-analysis. Proust saw jealousy as the single greatest motive for love. If this view is exaggerated by his own sexual proclivities, it is surely one which enables us to understand Catullus better.

Swann's love for Odette consumes the elegant cosmopolite no less thoroughly, and no less bewilderingly, than did love for Lesbia obsess Catullus; time and again Swann is aware that Odette is not really his type, but his dread of losing her, even when he has ceased to love her in the sentimental sense, makes him a slave to her moods. Jealousy replaces tenderness, but is almost more effective (and painfully tenacious) as an aphrodisiac. Herbert Gold's story *Love And Like* has a striking conclusion when a man, saying goodbye to the wife who is about to divorce him, is suddenly filled with a lust he has not felt for years and virtually rapes her. Many relationships are sustained by that kind of ambivalence. We diminish the complexity of Catullus' character, rather than preserve its integrity, when we choose to ignore the likely pattern of its emotional and sexual nature. Had Lesbia agreed to be as faithful as her lover's courtly side would have liked, had she honoured that notion of a true marriage he seemed so touchingly to desire, would their relationship really have prospered? What future in mundane fact could it ever have had? Clodia was a powerful woman, with a *salon* at the very centre of Roman political and social life. She had a complaisant and elderly husband (who died in 59 B.C.) and she pleased herself, as we have seen, with whatever man she fancied. Could Catullus ever seriously have supposed that she wanted to come and live with him in a country cottage? Even if it played a part in their amorous dialogue, one cannot see Clodia settling down for long to a life of well-water and rural *charcuterie;* even when Catullus seduces us, and convinces himself, most thoroughly with his idyllic visions, they remain manifestly illusory. His choice of Lesbia was, in some sense, perverse from the outset. She did not *become* impossible, but was always so. Was not that her attraction? For though there have indeed been cases in amorous history where sophisticated married ladies have been lured from a life of glittering cynicism, touched and sustained by the purity of their youthful lovers, Clodia was hardly a promising candidate for such redemption. She was too blatantly urban and urbane; to absent herself from her many felicities for the sake of a moon-struck poet, however many kisses he promised, or wanted, was virtually unthinkable. (Oddly enough, there is a vague literary parallel, an exception which hardly embarrasses the rule, in D. H. Lawrence's affair with Baroness von Richthofen, who was married, though in significantly more provincial and discontented circumstances, when the passionate young genius met and carried her off, though Frieda probably did quite as much of the carrying as Lawrence. Those who care to press analogies may diagnose in Catullus' urgent fervour the possibility that he, like Lawrence, was suffering from that frenzy for life which so often inflamed the tubercular.)

The enduring vitality of the Catullan *œuvre* is due not only to the genius of the poet, but also to the ageless immediacy of his predicament. He lends himself to translation both because he is a great poet and because his 'case', however particular and however unchallengeably unique in its original expression, has an undying call on our imaginations. The names of the woman he loved and of those he fucked, the men whom he trusted and who let him down, may bear an antique ring, but his situation has not dated at all. It may be that there are or will be societies where jealousy is unknown, where love and possessiveness have nothing in common, where Oedipus has no taste for Jocasta and where the eternal triangle, in all its contorted forms, is an unknown figure of speech or pattern of life, but until such a society is commonplace, the passion and anguish of Catullus will continue to seem abidingly modern. After that, his genius will have to work its own way with the reader; its chances of survival are unlikely to be very much impaired.

Wiseman on understanding Catullus's poetry:

. . . Why] should we expect his design to be immediately apparent to us? Just because he was capable of writing individual poems of such direct simplicity that they still speak to us face to face after two millenia, it does not follow that he was always simple, much less that his tastes and attitudes necessarily coincide with ours.

Catullus and his friends wrote for a small and intelligent audience, and we must work hard to reconstruct the intellectual climate they inhabited and the standards of sensibility they took for granted. Otherwise we have no chance of properly understanding either the arrangement of his collected works or the full meaning of the poem in which he introduced them to his friend . . . Cornelius Nepos. No doubt Nepos understood both perfectly well, for though he was a historian and Catullus a poet, in the literary world of Hellenistic Rome that distinction did not mean as much as it does to us. One was a great artist, the other not, but their intellectual heritage was the same.

T. P. Wiseman, *Clio's Cosmetics,* Leicester University Press, 1979.

R. O. A. M. Lyne (essay date 1980)

SOURCE: "Catullus," in *The Latin Love Poets: From Catullus to Horace,* Oxford at the University Press, 1980, pp. 19-61.

[*Below, Lyne discusses Catullus's love poetry, focusing closely on the Lesbia poems and demonstrating Catullus's enormous influence on the themes, forms, and style of later poetry.*]

1. Introduction

Catullus was born *circa* 84 B.C. and died about thirty years later. He came from a well-to-do family in provincial Verona but soon moved to Rome, which he henceforth regarded as his home (poem '**68**'.34-5).

I shall now assume that the Lesbia concerned in his finest love poetry is Clodia, wife of Metellus. . . . Catullus therefore loved a lady who acted the courtesan. . . . He wished (he says so: e.g. poem '**109**') to solemnize and perpetuate a kind of 'whole love'; he wanted to commit himself, and he wanted his beloved to commit herself, to their love in the way that conventional Roman society committed itself—in theory—to marriage. A problematic aspiration. Catullus' love and life must have been fraught with tension. Out of it came his love poetry: life transmuted into art.

The more sympathetic we are at the outset to the problems intrinsic in Catullus' love, the more receptive we may he to his poetry. A few more moments of preliminary thought are in order. The personality and impact of Clodia should be pondered. Caelius' and Cicero's fairly vicious picture of her is hardly the whole truth. But it is some of the truth and Catullus often enough shows himself aware of it. On the other hand Clodia can be the 'fair goddess', the light upon which the sweetness of life depends. She must have had qualities to inspire such devotion: we are not simply witnessing the discrepancy between the face the world sees and the hallucinated vision of a sentimental fool. Clodia must have had elements of both the sublime and the abysmal, baffling to her lover. And promiscuity in a lover is a curious thing. It is a strange but psychologically explicable fact (observed by Marcel Proust among others) that the very availability of available and widely attractive women can be just the thing to excite or exacerbate dreams of unique possession among romantic but unfortunate lovers.

Tension is inherent in Catullus' life and love, his aspirations are made up of probably incompatible elements. Here are the sources, or rather the matter, of much of his love poetry. We could say in fact that Catullus' Lesbia love poetry boils down to being *either* an attempt to express his conception of love and his aspirations in it; *or* to an attempt to communicate the wonderfully significant trivia of an affair going well or only marginally badly; *or* to an attempt to express feelings consequent upon a knowledge of failed ideals. But that of course is vastly to over-simplify. And one doesn't boil down poetry. We must shift our mode of approach.

It is vital . . . for us to respond to the fact that Catullus' love poetry springs from his life; it is vital to remember that poetry for Catullus was a medium of communication. But we must not become too focused on what is communicated—on content rather than form,

in so far as these two are separable. Certainly we must not fall a prey simply to abstracting and eulogizing Catullan ideas, ideals, and feelings. Unconventional and remarkable as these may have been, they will hardly have been unique or unrivalled. Other people before Catullus loved and hated simultaneously—and indeed virtually said as much. If we want to find out what is truly great and unique about Catullus, we must study the *process whereby* Catullan life his thoughts and feelings, are transmuted into art. We must study his different methods of fixing the chameleon nature of feelings, the intangible quality of moments, the indefinable essence of an ideal, in the enduring substance of literature.

2. The importance of Lesbia

There is one general feature of Catullus' Lesbia love poetry that we must notice. It is a strikingly original feature which stands out but which is insufficiently remarked. Whereas Catullus the lover of Clodia is special but not of momentous importance, Catullus the poet-lover of Lesbia is unique in his time and incalculably important. Catullus is, so far as we can judge, the first poet in Greek or Latin who decided to write about a particular love-affair in depth in a related collection of poems. Compare and contrast two influential predecessors, the archaic Greek poetess Sappho and the Alexandrian epigrammatist Meleager. The former of course said startling and original things about love in startling and original ways; it is likely enough too that she addressed numbers of poems to favourites like Anactoria and Atthis. Meleager writes numerous epigrams to Zenophila—and Heliodora, and the boy Myiscus. But a profound, systematic, and continuing exploration of a single relationship through poems which relate to and illuminate each other—this is not in these lover-poets' manner or nature. It is not in any ancient poet's manner or nature before Catullus. There is no precedent in ancient literature for Catullus and Lesbia.

And 'Lesbia' we might say (to look ahead for a moment) is Catullus' single most important bequest to Latin (and subsequent) literature. For after Catullus numerous lover-poets found that they too were irresistibly committed to loving a figure like Lesbia and unavoidably compelled to write related cycles of poems about her. Some indeed had to enhance or perhaps invent all-engulfing love-affairs about which then perforce to write. Such can be the influence of art on art and art on life. Such was the influence of Catullus' Lesbia poetry; and a study of the great Latin love poets properly starts with him. Catullus' poems relating the ecstasy, suffering, and ambivalences of a romantic commitment to one dominating mistress set the fashion for other such poetry. And all this, together with the love poetry of anti-romantic reaction, forms a coherent genre of literature: Latin Love Poetry.

3. The Lesbia Epigrams

It is clear that Catullus experimented with different methods of communicating the feelings of love. Interestingly, his most original work is (I think) not his best. I start by looking at his most original work, the Lesbia epigrams. (For convenience's sake I refer to poems '69-116', which are all in elegiac metre, as the 'epigrams', and to poems '1-60', which are in a variety of lyric metres, as the 'polymetrics'.)

Catullus had remarkable ideals in love; he was profoundly interested in the strange and conflicting emotions of love. It is natural that he should want to analyse these ideals and feelings in his poetry. It is also natural, incidentally, that this desire to analyse should become more acute when reality began more obviously to fall short of ideals. That is simple psychology. It is when ideals are might-have-beens that one is impelled to analyse them; it is the feelings consequent upon failure that one scrutinizes, morbidly and obsessively. In the optimism of a present happiness ideals are an irrelevant abstraction and feelings too natural for analysis.

Catullus attempts to analyse ideals and feelings in the epigrams. The desire to analyse (usually morbidly) fuels a succession of poems in this part of his work. Such poems make up most of the Lesbia epigrams. And it is *only* in the epigrams that we find such analyses. The typical Lesbia epigram is therefore *analytical,* endeavouring to isolate what it was that was in the lovers' grasp, what it was that went wrong, what were the feelings that were then in consequence generated.

Catullus' methods in these poems are startlingly original. He takes over but transforms the traditional erotic epigram In the hands of the Greek epigrammatists like Callimachus or their Roman imitators like Q. Lutatius Catulus this had been a vehicle of wit, pathos, or sentiment. Typically it enacted or suggested some often stock little scene or drama which was brought to a neat and pointed end. Epigram's structure lent itself naturally to antithesis (hexameter alternates with pentameter, couplet with couplet, and so on) and this was regularly used to enhance the pointed pathos, sentiment, or wit. Note for instance the following piece by Philodemus, a contemporary of Cicero:

> 'I know, graceful girl, how to kiss when I am kissed,
> and again I know how to bite when I am bitten.
> Don't pain me too much—someone who loves you.
> Don't wish to provoke the grievous anger of the Muses against you.'
> So I continually cried and forewarned
> but you were as deaf to my words as is the

Ionian sea.
So now *you* wail and weep mightily.
I sit in Naias' lap.

Philodemus uses the antithetical pattern of pentameter and hexameter in the first couplet to emphasize the range of his potential amorous response: reciprocation or retaliation as the occasion demands. And he organizes antithesis in the structure as a whole. At the exact turning-point in the poem we are greeted with the surprise that the first four lines were in fact quoted speech from a *past* occasion, a warning that, in the event, has been unheeded (the ancient reader or hearer of course did not get the clue provided by modern quotation marks). Past time is contrasted neatly with present time. The final couplet provides a typically epigrammatic conclusion. Philodemus' present happy state is sketched, and the first girl's folly dramatically (in the literal sense of the word) demonstrated. Again antithesis of hexameter and pentameter accentuates the effect.

This is the form that Catullus chooses for his analytical poetry. But his handling of it transforms it. He almost entirely expels all the dramatic element. The suggestions of situation (as in Philodemus' poem) or other little enacted scenes . . . which typified the genre—these are all jettisoned. Catullus in fact leaves himself with just the bare bones of the epigram form. His motives are comprehensible and recoverable. The epigram thus laid bare offered him opportunities not only for succinct analytical statement; he could also exploit the antithetical structure for his own ends. By (for example) balancing his own ideas against a common view of mankind he could point and emphasize his own originality just as Philodemus accentuates his own felicity by putting it in the balance with the misery of the heedless girl.

However, having evolved himself a clever and promising form, what *language* was Catullus to use? Given that the kind of whole love that he aspired to was hardly a familiar phenomenon, its analytical expression naturally presented problems. He had to evolve his own vocabulary. One method that he hit upon I have already hinted at. Since Roman marriage was founded in theory upon principles of mutual consent and commitment, principles which were basic to Catullus' conception of love, marriage might provide him with some of his needs; and (as we shall see) it did.

But only rather special occasions could be served in this way. Catullus needed a more general vocabulary of commitment. Now if Rome lacked a vocabulary for profound commitment in love, it did have a highly developed code, and therefore language, of *social* commitment. And here Catullus found more of what he was looking for.

Rome was in essence an aristocratic society and possessed an elaborately developed code of social conduct, a code determining the mode and standards of relations and obligations among its upper classes. All aristocratic societies evolve such codes: norms of morality and responsibility upon whose general acceptance (in the relevant classes) they depend for their cohesion, indeed existence. These norms are of course ultimately founded only upon convention; but they are so socially vital that they gather an aura of untouchability, even sacrosanctity. And a virtually technical terminology grows up, a terminology of 'proper behaviour': a vocabulary of highly and particularly charged words, capturing the obligations of aristocracy.

The Roman social code was deeply felt and, as a rule elaborately practiced. Virtually every page of the correspondence of Cicero (to name one obvious source) attests both code and terminology. I mention here simply the essential elements. *Fides* ('fidelity', 'integrity') was, or should be, the foundation of all actions and relationships; one conducted oneself in accordance with *pietas* ('sense of loyalty', 'conscientiousness'). One had a profound sense of *officium* ('service', 'dutifulness'); one was pleased, indeed compelled, to find and to display *gratia* ('favour'). Embracing and applying all these and other ideas was the extensive, sometimes very formal relationship connoted by *amicitia:* a complex and profound 'friendship' implying at best mutual obligation, mutual affection, and mutual pleasure. *Amicitia* was, among the Roman aristocracy, the essence of any proper relationship, private or public, business or pleasure. So: *fides, pietas, officium, gratia, amicitia:* these and other such ideas are the bases of Roman aristocratic conduct and the pillars of its society. (The English glosses are of course woefully inadequate. The nuances of a vocabulary of correct social conduct are very hard to recover and even harder to translate succinctly, once the society in question has vanished or changed.)

It is this language, the highly-charged language of Roman aristocratic fellowship, that Catullus tried to adapt to the purpose of communicating what he saw as important aspects of love. It was an unconventional tactic, but in a way, in the circumstances, natural enough. Lovers had not yet worked out a language of mutual commitment; society had, so Catullus used it. (In an analogous way, English love poets have availed themselves of the language of Christian devotion and commitment.) It is worth stressing, I think, that there is not really any question here of *metaphor.* Catullus did actually conceive of love or part of love as a form of *amicitia;* he did actually think that love ought to involve the sort of ideals and standards that were inherent or theoretically inherent in the aristocratic code; and therefore he used that language. The procedure was rather *faute de mieux* and liable perhaps to incon-

gruity as well as vagueness: there must always have been a danger of prosaicness, of heaviness, in using words like *officium* and *pietas* of love. But because the aristocratic code involved ideas and terms which matched or closely approximated to Catullus' own feelings about love, it was a logical step to talk in the same way—without any thought of metaphor.

I ought to take this opportunity to refute explicitly one highly misleading statement—that in the Lesbia epigrams Catullus uses the 'Vocabulary of Political Alliance', 'the (almost technical) terminology of the workings of party politics and political alliances at Rome', 'the metaphor . . . of a political alliance'. The origin of this seemingly incredible claim (what could induce a romantic lover-poet to picture his relationship metaphorically in terms of the workings of party politics?) is easy to uncover—and to explain. And it has its interest. True, the language of Catullus' Lesbia epigrams does closely resemble the language used by Roman politicians. But that is for a simple reason. Men in political life *also* used the language of aristocratic commitment and obligation; and they did this very naturally. In Roman society government was almost exclusively in the hands of a technically amateur aristocracy; there was no professional machinery of political parties as we know them; there was no profession of politics in the sense that we would mean it. Nobles formed alliances and understandings with each other (which might indeed have the *effect* of parties) following the normal procedures of their society and class, and in theory respecting the usual obligations and standards; and when 'new men' like Cicero came along they fell into the pattern of their betters. Political life in Rome was, in origin and essence, an extension of the normal life of aristocratic society or rather just one department of it. And naturally therefore it followed, or purported to follow, the traditional code of behaviour; and naturally it used the customary terminology: *amicitia, officium,* etc. Political life and Catullus simply had a common source for their terminology. But while politics, being an increasingly cynical business, tended to debase it, Catullus tried to protect and exalt it.

So: to express some of his unconventional ideas about love Catullus sought to adapt the still emotive language of aristocratic obligation; and he deployed it in a stripped-down epigram form. I begin with a convenient but not the most obvious example: poem **'75'**.

> huc est mens deducta tua mea Lesbia culpa
> atque ita se officio perdidit ipsa suo,
> ut iam nec bene uelle queat tibi, si optima
>   fias,
> nec desistere amare, omnia si facias.

> Lesbia, by your wrongdoing my mind has
>   been forced so far

and by its own dutifulness so destroyed itself,
that now, should you become a paragon, it
  could have no affection for you;
and whatever you should do, it could not but
  go on loving you.

In this poem Catullus confronts and attempts to analyse despairing, ambivalent feelings. He reports the confusion of his present mental state, seeking to identify the components of that confusion; and he reports the source of the confusion. We may compare the famous and lauded analysis of ambivalence, poem **'85'**:

> odi et amo. quare id faciam, fortasse requiris?
>   nescio, sed fieri sentio et excrucior.

> I hate *and* love. Perhaps you ask why I do
> this?
> I do not know; but I feel it happen and am in
> torment.

But **'75'** is a more probing analysis of a more complex ambivalence.

In the second couplet of **'75'**, Catullus informs us that even if Lesbia should become a paragon, he could not now feel 'affection' for her; but nothing she might do could stop him 'loving' her. The source of this ambivalence is stated in the first couplet; the second couplet is all in consequence of (*ut*) the first.

In part the ambivalence is due to the effect on Catullus' mental state of Lesbia's 'wrongdoing', *culpa* (*culpa* embraces the notions of blame, offence, and more particularly sexual infidelity); and in part it is due to the effect of his own 'dutifulness'. It should be stressed that both of these items have contributed to both aspects of the ambivalence; that is the implication of the syntax. Only if we appreciate this shall we appreciate the full message of the poem.

Thus the consequence of Lesbia's 'wrongdoing' (line 1) is to be seen in the fact that Catullus is incapable of 'affection' *and* in the fact that he remains irrevocably passionate about her (we infer that 'loving' means in particular *'passionately* loving': see below). The second part of this is striking, though comprehensible. Other people besides Catullus have found that a lover's faithlessness far from diminishes passion, indeed leads to it. More striking perhaps are the implications of line 2. Why should Catullus' own 'dutifulness' lead to his ceasing to feel 'affection' for Lesbia but his continued 'loving'? That seems not so clear. We need a better understanding of terms like *bella uelle* and *officium*. Does Catullus guide us towards such an understanding?

We should first note how the antithetical potential of the epigram form is being exploited to point meaning.

bene uelle is formally contrasted with *amare;* the terms are presumably semantically contrasted. *bene uelle* seems to cover emphatically unsexual affection; so we may assume *amare* covers strongly sexual love: passion. Antithesis in short helps to confine the general and vague term *amare* to a specific function.

But we need more help, with *bene uelle* and *officium*. We need in fact the knowledge that a contemporary reader would have had instinctively and which Catullus presupposes. Both *bene uelle* and *officium* are emotive and charged terms within the language of aristocratic obligation. *officium* covers the duty, the service that one undertakes for *amici*—that one delights to undertake for them; and it covers one's *sense* of that duty. It also carries with it a clear implication of reciprocity: *officium* by definition deserves, and within sincere *amicitia* duly obtains, *officium* in return. Not so clearly in Catullus' relationship with Lesbia. And *bene uelle* is one of the characteristic terms to express the generous feelings that underlie the relationship of *amicus* to *amicus*. It is one of the definitions and one of the splendours of *amicitia* that one *bene uult,* one feels a disinterested warmth for an *amicus*.

The technical terms show the framework in which Catullus is thinking: *amicitia;* the terms were so particular and resonant for a Roman that this patent fact did not have to be stated. Once upon a time, we gather, Catullus had believed that a very special bond of fellowship existed between himself and Lesbia—their own *amicitia*. Because of that belief he assiduously displayed his 'dutifulness'. Evidently, however, Lesbia failed to reciprocate in the manner demanded by such a relationship. The belief in the existence of the relationship had therefore to be abandoned. That meant inevitably that the special generosity of feeling *(beneuolentia)* that he had felt or thought to feel for Lesbia had also to go; for it can only exist in such a relationship. But passion of course could persist, being independent of *amicitia;* and human nature being human nature, no doubt it would. The logic of the poem becomes clearer.

So Lesbia's failure to reciprocate *officium*—and her *culpa*—led to Catullus' abandonment of belief in *amicitia* and to the results consequent upon that, chronicled in the second couplet. But Catullus phrases himself more distinctively, and pathetically, than our summary implies: 'My mind has so destroyed *itself,* by *its own* dutifulness.' Catullus acknowledges that the idea of *amicitia* had been his, that he had behaved with regard to Lesbia according to the exalted standards of a relationship of his creation, of his imagination. His unilateral observance of this ideal led to the demonstration that such an ideal was unfounded; Catullus set himself up for his cruel disappointment and in part therefore caused it. All this he admits, in the powerful and pathetic second line.

I turn now to the famous poem '76'. Again we find a poem riven with ambivalence: a man loathing a relationship has to pray to the gods to help him break it. There is (on more than one account) an interesting comparison to be made between '76' and '8'. . . . In poem '8' Catullus tries to come to terms with Lesbia's loss of interest in him; in '76' he tries to effect a conclusion to the affair himself and come to terms with that. The situation of '76' is more tragic than that of '8'; its utterance is far more bitter suiting its strange and unkind birth.

> siqua recordanti benefacta priora uoluptas
> est homini, cum se cogitat esse pium,
> nec sanctam uiolasse fidem, nec foedere in
>   ullo
> diuum ad fallendos numine abusum homines,
> multa parata manent in longa aetate, Catulle,
> ex hoc ingrato gaudia amore tibi.
> nam quaecumque homines bene cuiquam aut
>   dicere possunt
> aut facere, haec a te dictaque factaque sunt.
> omnia quae ingratae perierunt credita menti.
> quare iam te cur amplius excrucies?
> quin tu animo offirmas atque istinc teque
>   reducis,
> et dis inuitis desinis esse miser?
> difficile est longum subito deponere amorem,
> difficile est, uerum hoc qua lubes efficias:
> una salus haec est, hoc est tibi peruincendum,
> hoc facias, siue id non pote siue pote.
> o di, si uestrum est misereri, aut si quibus
>   umquam
> extremam iam ipsa in morte tulistis opem,
> me miserum aspicite et, si uitam puriter egi,
> eripite hanc pestem perniciemque mihi
> quae mihi subrepens imos ut torpor in artus
> expulit ex omni pectore laetitias.
> non iam illud quaero, contra me ut diligat illa,
> aut, quod non potis est, esse pudica uelit:
> ipse ualere opto et taetrum hunc deponere
>   morbum.
> o di, reddite mi hoc pro pietate mea.

> If there is any pleasure for a man in
>   recollecting his former kindnesses—
> when he reflects on his conscientiousness,
> that he has not outraged sacred fidelity, nor in
>   any pact
> misused the gods' authority in order to
>   deceive his fellow men—
> then there are many pleasures laid up in store
>   for you Catullus,
> in the long life ahead of you,
> resulting from this love of yours that has
>   received no thanks.
> For whatever men can do in the way of
>   kindness of word or deed for anyone
> this you have done, kindnesses of word and
>   deed.
> But it's all been thrown away, an investment
>   in a thankless heart.
> Wherefore, why will you now torture yourself
>   further?
> Why do you not stiffen your resolve, bring
>   yourself back
> and cease to be wretched in despite of
>   heaven?
> It is hard suddenly to set aside a long love.
> It is hard. But achieve it in any way you can.
> This is your one deliverance, it must be
>   completely won.
> Do this—whether it is possible or not.
> Gods, if it is your wont to pity, if ever
> you have brought help at the last to people
>   even in the hour of death,
> look at me in my wretchedness and if I have
>   lived an unstained life
> tear out from me this disastrous disease
> which creeping to the extremities of my limbs
>   like a numbness
> has driven all joy from my heart.
> I do not now ask that she should return my
>   love,
> or want to be what she cannot be, decent.
> I pray that I may be healthy, and set aside
>   this foul disease. Gods, grant me this, for
>   my conscientiousness.

Our first reaction to the beginning of this poem may be one of incredulity. Catullus may seem to be associating himself with people who are *in general* charitable, conscientious, faithful, and scrupulous; if (he seems to be saying) there is pleasure for such saintly folk in mulling over their goodness, there is pleasure in store for him. The suggestion of possible pleasure is of course ironical. But that does not affect the pretentiousness of the apparent claim.

Things are not as bad as they seem. In the sixth line Catullus limits the range of his own virtue to his love-affair: 'there are many pleasures . . . for you . . . resulting from this love of yours'; and it is in fact a very particular company of virtuous people with whom he is associating himself in the first five lines: those who have been virtuous *in the particular relationship of* 'amicitia.' For virtually all the key words in 1-6 (*benefacta, plus, sancta fides,* and indeed *ingratus;* cf. *gratia*) are part of the semi-technical terminology of aristocratic obligation and therefore evoke that particular situation. *benefacta* (cf. *beneficia, benefacere, benigne facere*) *is* the only term yet to be fixed as semi-technical: *benefacta* are the 'kindnesses' that earn one *amici,* that keep *amici,* that are naturally and without solicitation exchanged between 'friends' in formal and informal ways.

Catullus means therefore in the opening lines of '76'

that if anyone can have pleasure from pondering conscientious behaviour *in amicitia,* he can; he, if anyone, has displayed that kind of *pietas.* This he does mean to claim: for he has indeed faithfully observed a very special *amicitia,* one he himself conceived, a relationship of affection and loyalty with a lover. And what is more, he persisted for a long time in the face of lack of proper reciprocity, a leek of due *gratia: ex ingrato amore.* Here is the same sort of statement as in '75' and the same plaint; and Catullus adapts the same type of language to communicate it, only here more extensively.

But now he wishes to end the ill-starred affair. The rest of the poem shows Catullus trying to accomplish and come to terms with such an end, describing the feelings and thoughts involved. So it is a dynamic rather than a static analysis of feeling—and more besides. The poem *enacts* Catullus declaring and trying to impose his will upon intense and ambivalent *shifts* of feeling. We seem to witness this actually happening. Note particularly the questions at lines 10-12 and the prayer at 17, all revealing wavering of purpose. In a sense therefore the poem is, as well as dynamic, dramatic (in the literal sense of the word)—and very immediately so. It almost seems to be itself a drama, an emotional event actually happening, rather than an artistically composed re-enaction.

It is this immediacy that is the cause of certain poetical faults. Catullus is not distanced from feeling in the way that an artist should be, and emotion runs away with language producing laxity of expression, incoherence, and confusing hyperbole.

Our account of lines 1-6 was certainly right. But an initial misunderstanding was forgivable. Catullus leans very heavily on an instinctive appreciation of the scope of his *amicitia* vocabulary. We eventually grasp what he means but the poem's composition in those lines scarcely compels a proper understanding. At line 7 expression is even more lax and more liable to mislead: *nam quaecumque homines . . . ,* 'whatever men can do . . .' Catullus actually says here (whatever he meant) that any good in word or deed that men can perform for anyone (*cuiquam*), this he has done. The range of the couplet is in fact strictly (whatever the intention) unlimited. Note too for example *si uitam puriter egi* (19). In what sense has Catullus led a spotless life? Presumably (or perhaps) he means: in regard to Lesbia. But he does not say so. Nor is there any technical *amicitia* nuance to *puriter* which might help to define and confine it. The effect of such language is to imply an outrageous and implausible self-righteousness. And there is much else at the end of the poem that is clearly emotional and unmeant hyperbole—but I do not think I need to labour examples.

A study of poem '**76**' once more shows us Catullus

attempting to analyse feelings; and once more it shows us him adapting the language of *amicitia* to that end. Interestingly, too, it is dramatic: the analysis and description of feeling occur within an action. But it is a poetic failure. It is itself more of a dramatic event, an emotional and fairly direct description of feeling, than an artistically created drama (examples of which we shall see below). The latter is, the former obviously is not, promising poetry. Because it is an event rather than art we find laxity of expression incompatible with art. We see here, I think, one obvious danger of 'analytical poetry'. A poet who deals with emotions so directly risks letting emotion run away with expression.

In the course of poem '**76**' Catullus uses the word *foedus* ('treaty' or 'pact'). This is a vital word in Catullan love poetry, but unfortunately its implications are disputed. We must identify them. The study will lead us into a general and important topic.

Foedus is used in contexts of *amicitia,* but it is reserved for occasions when an exceptionally strong or formal degree of commitment is at issue. Just as international treaties, *foedera,* were 'ratified by solemn oaths and to break them was perjury', so the same sanctity applied or should apply to pacts of social obligation. For this reason it is much rarer than other *amicitia*-terminology, indeed hardly classes as one of the usual technical terms.

A good place in which to observe its special force as a term of aristocratic obligation is Cicero's letter to Crassus making his peace with the 'triumvirs'. Here Cicero demonstrably intends an especial solemnity, indeed has the full sense 'treaty' in mind: 'I want you to consider that what I write here is going to have the force of a treaty (*foedus*) not of a letter; and what I promise you and take upon myself, I shall observe most sacredly (*sanctissime*) and pursue most diligently.' We can note too the pained passion with which the exiled Ovid reproaches a friend who scorned the 'sacred and venerable name of *amicitia*' while others sympathized with him who had '*not* been joined by any *foedus*'. It suits Ovid, who has an axe to grind, to propound a very elevated view of friendship, and *foedus* in these circumstances is a useful term. And Catullus, in poem '**76**' (line 3), clearly thinks that when a *foedus* exists between *amici* it is literally sacred, protected by the authority of the gods. He himself (he implies) has honoured his relationship with Lesbia as though it were not only *amicitia* but special and sanctified *amicitia:* a *foedus.*

But *foedus* has another and very particular function in Catullus. He uses it directly or indirectly of marriage. His two certain examples of this occur in his mythological poem on the marriage of Peleus and Thetis, poem '**64**'. Line 335: *nullus amor tali coniunxit foed-*

ere amantes,/ qualis adest Thetidi, qualis concordia Peleo ('no love ever joined lovers in such a *foedus*'— as Peleus' and Thetis' love did); and line 373: *accipiat coniunx felici foedere diuam,/ dedatur cupido iam dudum nupta marito* ('let the husband receive the goddess [i.e. his bride] in *happy foedus . . .*'). Now this is a use which is well paralleled after Catullus; but as far as I can judge it is unparalleled before him. It seems therefore that the idea of referring to a marriage as a *foedus* is Catullus' invention—and that later poets are following his precedent. This is plausible enough. *Foedus* is a particularly happy choice for the marriage of Peleus and Thetis and so may well have been made specially for it: the connotations of *foedus* suitably stress the unparalleled degree of reciprocity and sanctity that this romantic, mythical marriage (in Catullus' version) apparently possessed.

Foedus therefore can refer in Catullus to an ideal— 'pact' of marriage. Let us put this fact on one side for a moment, and consider another fact. At times Catullus talks of his own relationship with Lesbia in terms of marriage; marriage, like *amicitia,* afforded him vocabulary to express things in love which were difficult to express in normal erotic terminology. I mentioned this above, and we shall shortly observe a striking and extended example in poem **'68'**. But note too poem **'70'**:

> nulli se dicit mulier mea nubere malle
>   quam mihi, non si se Iuppiter ipse petat.
> dicit: sed mulier cupido quod dicit amanti,
>   in uento et rapida scribere oportet aqua.

> My woman says that she prefers to marry no one
> rather than me, not if Jupiter himself should court her.
> That's what she says: but what a woman says to her passionate lover
> ought to be written on the wind and on rushing water.

One does not imagine that Lesbia meant her stated preference to marry Catullus too seriously, or that she thought very deeply about it. It will have been a casual, romantic indulgence. Why does Catullus react so bitterly, so scornfully? Because, presumably, he did take the idea seriously; he did have a belief that his life with Lesbia might be, or have been, in very true senses, in the best senses, if not in literal senses, marriage. (Notice incidentally how epigram's antithetical structure is again exploited: the second couplet is formally opposed to the first, and the contrast between protestation and reality thereby highlighted.)

So we now have two facts. (1) Catullus idiosyncratically and originally refers to an apparently ideal, mythical marriage as a *foedus.* (2) He is inclined to imagine

his own love-affair as an ideal marriage. We must therefore interpret a poem in which he talks of his own affair as a *foedus* with care.

'Poem 109':

> incundum, mea uita, mihi proponis amorem
>   hunc nostrum inter nos perpetuumque fore.
> di magni, facite ut uere promittere possit,
>   atque id sincere dicat et ex animo,
> ut liceat nobis tota perducere uita
>   aeternum hoc sanctae foedus amicitiae.

> You declare, my life, that this our love
> will be between us 'delightful' and 'eternal'.
> You gods, make it that she be capable of promising truly,
> and that she say this candidly and from the heart.
> Then we may be able throughout life to carry through
> this eternal pact of inviolable friendship.

Here Catullus is (as in **'70'**) echoing a declaration of Lesbia's: 'this love between us will be delightful, eternal.' He seems to be repeating her actual words: *incundus* ('delightful') was probably an *à la mode* word at the time for pleasant things or experiences, the sort of word Lesbia would use. Catullus clearly regards this rather glib declaration with scepticism However, if she *should* mean what she says, and mean it fully— and Catullus prays to that end fervently—then it would be possible for them to live out the Catullan ideal of a reciprocal relationship. And as he makes this point Catullus attempts an analytical description of that ideal: *tota. . . . uita/aeternum hoc sanctae foedus amicitiae.*

A key concept is 'eternity' and the basis of the definition seems, as was to be expected, to be the complex of ideas contained in amicitia (mutual pleasure, trust obligation, etc.). However *amicitia* is here *exalted* by the epithet *sanctae*—so that it is now something *explicitly* beyond the range of normal amicitia; and it also seems in some way to be transformed by *foedus.* Now it is possible that Catullus simply means to emphasize the sanctity and commitment of this special *amicitia* by using a word allied to the terminology that was reserved for exceptional cases. But considering that he is here effectively defining his ideal, considering that ideas of marriage seem to have been very close to his ideal, and considering that he elsewhere uses *foedus* of the pact of an ideal marriage— then I think that that is likely to be the intended significance here. Catullus is talking therefore of a '*marriage*-pact of friendship', a lively phrase which connotes (among much else) a reciprocal relationship possessing the solemnity of marriage but founded on true affection.

If my interpretation is right, which all the pointers suggest it is, then we have an important observation to make. Catullus is, I think, directly confronting the problem facing the Roman lover which I mentioned at the end of the last chapter [not reprinted here], and going some way towards defining a solution. I remarked how some Roman lovers must have been tantalized to see that on the one hand an institution existed (marriage) which was suited to the solemnizing of whole love--but it was abused; meanwhile, on the other hand, relatively whole love was confined to precarious, unformalized circumstances (the *demi-monde*). The 'marriage-pact of friendship', the *foedus amicitiae,* seems to me to be proffered as an at least partial resolution of this paradox. Achieving this a lover would achieve a fair synthesis: a relationship that was permanent, reciprocal, solemnized, and loving and sincere. And it is Catullus' belief, or at least it is his prayer, that it can be achieved.

Before we leave this poem let us note how Catullus, who obviously questions Lesbia's ability to live up to such an ideal, adumbrates his own capability and commitment. The *foedus* is to be maintained *tota uita;* if Catullus calls Lesbia *mea uita* in that context, it is a simple but eloquent statement of where he stands.

It is probable that when *foedus* occurs in other Lesbia epigrams it is meant to suggest not just the pact of a special *amicitia* but the pact of ideal marriage. This may be true of poem '**76**' but if so the ambiguity (for that is what it would have to be) is hardly perspicuous. More significant is poem '**87**'.

> nulla potest mulier tantum se dicere amatam
> > uere, quantum a me Lesbia amata mea est.
> nulla fides ullo fuit umquam foedere tanta,
> > quanta in amore tuo ex parte reperta mea est.

> No woman can say that she has been so truly loved
> as my Lesbia has been loved by me.
> There has never ever been such great fidelity in any pact
> as has been discovered on my part in my love for you.

Catullus is again looking back, analysing the degree and kind of his past devotion. In the first couplet he expresses himself in simple terms, in terms that others might use (*uere amare*). But this is insufficient or liable to be misunderstood: the words are too common. So he defines what he means by *uere amare* in the second couplet.

Two features throw emphasis on this definition. First, antithesis. The conventional language of the first couplet, set in the balance with the very different language of the second, highlights the unconventional and particularly Catullan nature of that second couplet. Antithesis invites us to probe its implications. The second feature is an easy-to-miss apostrophe. As Catullus turns to clarify his special love for Lesbia, he (very suitably) switches from third-person description to a second-person address, to Lesbia. The message becomes personal and particular.

Two formal devices therefore call attention to the individuality of the definition in lines 3-4. Given this I feel sure that the particularly Catullan sense of *foedus* is operative. The language is of course essentially that of 'aristocratic obligation' and one can translate simply in those terms. Thus: 'No fidelity was ever in any pact (of *amicitia*) so great as that discovered in my love for you.' But that must also imply: 'No fidelity was ever in any pact so great as that discovered in *the pact of* my love for you.' Catullus implies a love-*foedus,* that is, *his* conception of a *foedus;* he alludes by a neat and sweet ambiguity to his vision of love as an ideal marriage.

To sum up so far. Catullus has been trying to describe complex ideas and feelings: a special degree and nature of love; feelings of injury consequent upon bitter disappointment, including (very characteristically) ambivalence. To communicate some of his ideals he has used the language of aristocratic obligation. I stress that 'metaphor' is not here the word to apply. Catullus actually means that he feels or felt for Lesbia a kind of *amicitia.* Of course his was an exalted *amicitia* to which the values and therefore the basic, unqualified terms of the more conventional variety might only approximate. But it was *amicitia* none the less. He has also found it relevant to suggest that his relationship was in some senses 'marriage' And it is perhaps wrong, or an oversimplification, to call this metaphor. Catullus *means* that his relationship had, or might have had, the best essence of marriage. His vision *was* marriage—albeit again in an exalted form.

So, two unexpected areas of life are providing language to analyse Catullan erotic ideals. Catullus also made a very interesting attempt to use a third area of life—this time metaphorically: the family. '**Poem 72**':

> dicebas quondam solum te nosse Catullum,
> Lesbia, nec prae me uelle tenere louem.
> dilexi tum te non tantum ut uulgus amicam,
> sed pater ut gnatos diligit et generos.
> nunc te cognoui: quare etsi impensius uror,
> multo mi tamen es uilior et leuior.
> qui potis est, inquis? quad amantem iniuria talis
> cogit amare magis, sed bene uelle minus.

> Once upon a time Lesbia you used to say that
> Catullus was the only lover you knew,

> that you did not wish to possess Jupiter before me.
> I loved you then not just as ordinary people love their girlfriends,
> but as a father loves his sons and sons-in-law.
> Now I know you. Wherefore, although I burn more fiercely,
> you are much cheaper, more paltry in my estimation.
> 'How can that be?', you say. Because such injustice
> compels a lover to love more, to feel the warmth of true affection less.

The similarities of this poem to '**70**' and particularly to '**75**' are obvious. They are interesting too: for at crucial points Catullus says not only more but rather different things, and in different ways.

The structure of '**72**' again offers an antithesis, 'then' (1-4) against 'now' (5-8); and the one sets in relief the other in the usual way. I look at the second half first. It contains a striking use of *amicitia* language.

Nunc te cognoui . . . Now Catullus knows the true nature of Lesbia. In consequence his physical feelings are *more* intense (that is interesting, somewhat unexpected, but one instinctively understands it; cf. '**75**', above, but the *greater* intensity here is to be noted); his respect for her character much less (a more natural reaction). The final couplet purports to explain this ambivalence (*qui potis est*). Here we switch to *amicitia* language. Unlike poem 75, this poem lays the final blame for loss of generous warmth of feeling (*bene uelle*) fairly and squarely on Lesbia: on actions of hers, or rather the spirit informing her actions (*iniuria*, 'injustice'). *Iniuria* is a crucial term: it is precisely what, in the language of aristocratic relations, will destroy *amicitia*, implying severe things about the intent of the offender. Catullus means that Lesbia has not just committed wrongs against him (i.e. acts of infidelity), she has committed them with such wilful and inimical intent that the wholeness of Catullan love (exalted *amicitia*) is now impossible. So warmth of feeling is gone; but passion persists—indeed increases.

The last couplet therefore adds the *cause* of Catullus' paradoxical dilemma. But we might note that it does not explain how or why it takes the form it does, which is rather what *qui potis est* leads us to expect. That is a pity. I should like to have seen Catullus' explanation of why infidelity and offence excite *greater* sexual passion in the lover. However, having added the cause, all Catullus really does is restate his ambivalent dilemma in a tauter, more intimate, though perhaps not fully successful paradox.

To turn to the first half of the poem—to 'once upon a time'. Lesbia was then all specious protestations of devotion. Catullus echoes her words in the first couplet to set in relief an analysis of his own sincere feelings at the same time. 3-4: 'I loved you then not just as ordinary people love their girl-friends, but as a father loves his sons and sons-in-law'—perhaps one of the most famous lines in Catullus It is unique and it is brilliant and it does not quite come off.

What Catullus is trying to do is to communicate an indefinable feeling of unequivocal, committed love. He resorts to simile to illustrate it. And, clearly, an unequivocal, committed love is what a father feels, often enough, for his sons and sons-in-law. (The presence of *generos*, 'sons-in-law', should not trouble us; as Fordyce ad loc. says, their inclusion 'reflects a traditional attitude which puts the sons-in-law within the head of the family's protective concern'.) But the equation cannot be quite true. Paternal love embraces all sorts of other things, all sorts of motivations and feelings, that a lover could not and would not want to have. Catullus really means that some of his love resembled some of a father's; he did not actually love Lesbia as a father loves his sons and sons-in-law. We must interpret the simile selectively, eliminating much of our natural response. It is hardly completely informative, and hardly a complete poetical success. But it is a fascinatingly original attempt by Catullus to express things arguably quite out of his time.

Catullus' work in the Lesbia epigrams was brilliantly original. But it is not his best poetry. There are criticisms to be made which have literary-historical as well as aesthetic relevance. First a relatively minor point.

Analysis like this in epigram, while benefiting from the pointed antithetical form, runs the risk (because of the extreme compression) of inexactness. Analysis is the job of prose and scientists. Catullus tries to be careful about his use of words but he falls into traps. For example his use of *amor* and cognates is careless (and confusion over this word is in the circumstances if most understandable also most undesirable). In poem '**87**' he uses it (I take it) of whole love; in '**75**' of one part of love, passion. In poem '**72**' in the space of two lines he actually uses it in *both* these senses and produces a flawed *sententia* in the process. Or take the lauded *odi et amo* (85): is the sense of *amo* clear there? And what is the force of *excrucior*? Again, is not some of the special Catullan terminology, in particular *foedus*, very liable to be misunderstood? Yes, demonstrably: people have misunderstood it repeatedly.

Description of feelings also runs another risk, that of too immediate involvement, leading not just to inexact but to incoherent expression (poem '**76**').

These one might say are minor quibbles considering the magnitude of Catullus' originality. My next point is more serious. I think that Catullus' venture in the epigrams was bound to fail *as poetry* more or less by definition. If that seems a bold statement, it is one that the practice of later love poets tacitly supports.

Analysis and poetry are essentially conflicting occupations. To define the constituent elements of ideas and feelings can hardly be the proper function of poetry. For if one succeeds in doing it, one will *also* have succeeded in confining words to a particular sense in a tight and static syntax. And that is the character of scientific or philosophical prose, whose job therefore analysis properly is. My remark above ('analysis is the job of prose and scientists') has more profound implications. The poetic art is to stimulate the imagination, to *suggest* not define. All great poetry is a dynamic not a static texture in which words can (as it were) *move,* combining and recombining to yield shifting aspects of meaning. Unlike a successful analysis a great poem is not the same thing each time one picks it up. Nuances have realigned to suggest new aspects and new colours.

The relevance and truth of these comments will be confirmed as we proceed. I conclude my remarks on the Lesbia epigrams by recalling one which was, in one discreet respect, different and arguably more interesting: poem '87'. This is an epigram which I think starts to come alive, to become real poetry. The point to appreciate is the sudden apostrophe in the second couplet. For his very individual description of devotion Catullus suddenly switches from third to second person, and addresses Lesbia. The effect of this unexpected apostrophe is to startle the reader into thinking about the apostrophized person, into thinking about Lesbia. It brings Lesbia's personality suddenly into the reckoning; into indeed the poem. The words are now, suddenly, in an emotive *context:* we cannot call them merely analytical; they are in the literal sense dramatic. They exist in an implicit, artistically created drama—words of idealism addressed to the woman who shatters that idealism. Pathos haunts their utterance, other resonances and adumbrations—and suddenly an epigram is poetry.

4. The Lesbia Polymetrics

Adapting the epigram form for analysis Catullus had by and large ejected the dramatic element that had typified the genre. He had attempted to analyse thought and feeling, exploiting the antithetical structure that the form offered. In his Lesbia polymetrics his practice is completely different, and from one point of view conventional. The poems remain dramatic: each one enacts, suggests, or reacts to some specific 'drama'. It should be stressed that these poems are artistically composed re-enactments, and not veritable events like poem '76'. Now we may in fact—I think we demonstrably do—learn as much or more about Catullus' love and feelings, but we learn it indirectly: through the

interaction of personality with personality or personality with event within a dramatic context. The kind of phenomenon we observed fleetingly in poem '87' is the rule in the Lesbia polymetrics.

What we are observing then is that Catullus decided upon two radically different strategies of love poetry, basically practicing one in the polymetrics and the other in the epigrams. (This is a slight over-simplification, but true in essence.) He therefore drew a sharp distinction between polymetric and elegiac short poems that had hardly existed before. There is a reason why he divided his work in this way. The metres that he favoured in the Lesbia polymetrics (hendecasyllables and scazons) offer less opportunity for pointed antithesis, but they are relatively close to the natural rhythms of Latin speech. They therefore suit dramatic poems, poems that artistically enact life.

Now the approach of the polymetrics is as I say basically more conventional. The feelings informing them tend, too, to be less agonizcd than those analysed in the epigrams. But less agonized feelings are not necessarily less profound or complex; and (of course) a more conventional poetical strategy does not inevitably mean inferior poems. And in fact Catullus transmogrifies his inherited form.

I start by looking at poem '7'.

> quaeris, quot mihi basiationes
> tuae, Lesbia, sint satis superque?
> quam magnus numerus Libyssae harenae
> lasarpiciferis facet Cyrenis
> oraclum louts inter aestuosi
> et Batti ueteris sacrum sepulcrum;
> aut quam sidera multa, cum facet nox,
> furtiuos hominum uident amores:
> tam te basia multa basiare
> uesano satis et super Catullo est,
> quae nec pernumerare curios)
> possint nec male fascinare lingua.

> You ask me, how many kisses
> are enough for me, Lesbia, enough and to
>   spare?
> As many as is the number of grains of Libyan
>   sand
> that lie in Silphium-bearing Cyrene
> between the oracle of sweltering Jupiter
> and the sacred tomb of Battus of old.
> Or as many as the stars that, when night is
>   silent,
> witness people's love-affairs.
> To kiss you so many kisses
> is enough and to spare for mad Catullus,
> kisses which busybodies would not be able to
>   reckon up
> nor an evil tongue bewitch.

The poem is addressed to Lesbia, answering a question from her. It is phrased as a piece of persuasion, aimed at Lesbia in a specific context. Its expression should therefore (we might expect) be tailored to suit her personality and mood. The poem exists in a carefully adumbrated dramatic situation, and Lesbia is part of the drama and therefore part of the poem as she was in a much more rudimentary way a part of poem '87'. The whole poem is *living* in the way that the final couplet of '87' was.

Let us follow the drama—the persuasion—through. We must note that although the piece is an artistic creation, an artifice, it is absolutely vital to respond to it as it is designed: as a drama.

The opening two lines suggest Lesbia's original question, the occasion of the drama. Lesbia has apparently found her lover's lavish attentions (cf. poem '5') a mite too much of a good thing. 'Just how many kisses *do* you want?' she has asked with an edge of impatience. This is the basic, assumed fact governing the shape of the poem. The task of Catullus' persuasion is to win a slightly wearied woman back into good humour and compliance

His basic tactic in response is candour. To the impatient 'How many kisses?' he answers 'An infinity'. In other words, to a question 'Are you insatiable?' he answers 'Yes'. There is obvious potential appeal in such candour. And the way it is deployed and amplified makes it, we must suppose, quite disarming.

Catullus starts the poem lightly. It is kisses (*basia*) which seem to have got on Lesbia's nerves, so he immediately clowns with the word and with her irritable question. He humorously travesties the question she presumably asked, namely *quot basia . . .?*, producing the comically pompous version *quot basiationes . . . ?* (*basium* is the colloquial word for 'kiss'; *basiatio* is a coinage on the analogy of *osculatio,* a word of high diction; it is therefore a colloquial word got up in overformal clothes). In this way he removes any edge to the question, already making Lesbia smile at her own objection.

The subsequent lines express the idea of 'infinity', an infinity of kisses, in two images. Both images are in essence obvious and well-paralleled illustrations of innumerability. But the first, the image of the grains of sand (3-6), has been extraordinarily embellished with learned elaboration. The second, the picture of the stars (7-8), contrasts by virtue of its warm simplicity. Why two so very differently handled images to illustrate one basic idea? Because (and this is vital to appreciate) Catullus is shaping and amplifying his reply to suit Lesbia's personality. He is candidly saying 'infinity', i.e. I am insatiable', but phrasing it in ways that will particularly appeal to her. Since the poem is as it

were trying to win a case with a particular and individual person that is the obvious explanation for such particular and individual phrasing.

In fact the allusive details of 3-6 are so thick—laid as to border on caricature. Catullus embroiders the simple notion 'desert sand' with extravagant vigour. He is striking a pose, to flatter and amuse Lesbia. *She,* it is assumed, has the *doctrina* to see and understand all the allusions provided by the *doctus poeta;* she also has the wit to see through them. She can appreciate the learned coinage *lasarpiciferis,* and the wit and learning in *Iouis aestuosi;* she can detect the allusion to Callimachus in *Batti* and admire the artfully contrived alliteration of s's in the description of the desert (hearing the sound of winds in sand). She also knows the limits to plausible embellishment. Catullus is writing to her presupposing, and adapting to, her cultivation, her aesthetic sensibility, and her sense of humour.

He also presupposes and adapts to a certain warmth and sentimentality. In 7-8 he switches to a tactic of 'appealing to the heart', dressing the idea of infinity in the tender image of the stars. We should note that it is Catullus who has made the image tender, and tender in a particularly relevant way. These are stars which 'witness the love-affairs of mankind when night is silent (and therefore conducive to *furtiuus amor*)'. The lines are attractively redolent of stolen love—love like Catullus' and Lesbia's. Catullus is, while saying 'an infinity', while saying in effect 'my love for you is insatiable', reminding Lesbia of the warm moments of their love-affair—tactfully and pertinently.

In 7-8, I suppose, is the centre of the poem's persuasion and the centre of the poem. But clearly one does not dally long over sentimentality with a woman like Lesbia. In line 9 Catullus returns swiftly to his note of clowning, concluding with a humorous reaffirmation of his insatiability. So many good things (the *basia*) might seem to be inviting nemesis in the shape of the malevolent spells of jealous ill-wishers. But the kisses will simply be too many to count and hence beyond such malevolence.

Such then are the tactics of Catullus' persuasion—a carefully packaged candour. First he casts the whole issue humorously (1); then cuts a dash (3 ff.); then he introduces tones of personal warmth (7-8), but finally returns swiftly to humour and clowning. We have watched these tactics in action; we have seemed to eavesdrop on a drama of persuasion. The poem offers us a living event transmuted into and immortalized by art.

And there is much to be learnt about the personality and psychology of the lovers from it: that should be clear. We have seen what Catullus regards as the right routes to Lesbia's good humour; and so the ingredients of the poem (humour, urbanity, extravagance, warmth, and a touch of sentimentality), and the proportion and ordering of those ingredients, must allow invaluable insight into the personalities of both Catullus and Lesbia and into how the two interact. In fact, if duly pondered, the poem tells us—indirectly—more about two people and their relations with one another than could ever be conveyed adequately by paraphrase. Or for that matter by analytical epigram.

Here is a point that we should identify clearly: the different potential as well as method of the dramatic poem compared with the analytical epigram. The poetical enactment of scene or situation can tell us things about feeling and personality that defy direct analysis. True, we are not given succinct and clear statement but things are adumbrated to us which statement could never encompass. We watch characters in a context and infer our knowledge. And language is expressive, not confined. The dramatic poem by giving its diction a living context encourages a subtle and suggestive verbal texture. That is richer than statement. One very simple example: *amores* in poem '7' occurring in a living exchange between Catullus and Lesbia and hinting persuasively at their stolen love is more suggestive, more emotive, more *meaningful* in the literal sense of that word) than any use of *amor* in any of the analytical epigrams.

Another fine and very interesting example of a dramatic poem is poem '8':

> miser Catulle, desinas ineptire,
> et quod uides perisse perditum ducas.
> fulsere quondam candidi tibi soles,
> cum uentitabas quo puella ducebat
> amata nobis quantum amabitur nulla.
> ibi illa multa cum iocosa fiebant
> quae tu uolebas nec puella nolebat,
> fulsere uere candidi tibi soles.
> nunc iam illa non uolt: tu quoque impotens noli,
> nec quae fugit sectare, nec miser uiue,
> sed obstinata mente perfer, obdura.
> uale, puella. iam Catullus obdurat,
> nec te requiret nec rogabit inuitam.
> at tu dolebis, cum rogaberis nulla.
> scelesta, uae te, quae tibi manes uita?
> quis nunc te adibit? cui uideberis bella?
> quem nunc amabis? cuius esse diceris?
> quem basiabis? cui labella mordebis?
> at tu, Catulle, destinatus obdura.

> My poor Catullus, do stop being foolish,
> and what you see is gone, well realize it's lost.
> Once upon a time the sun shone bright for you,
> when you used to follow where she led

> (a girl beloved by me as no girl will ever be).
> Then, when there were those many playful intimacies,
> which you so wanted and she was not averse to,
> truly the sun shone bright for you.
> Now she is disinclined. So you also, undisciplined fellow,
> don't chase a fugitive, don't live in misery.
> sear up, apply your mind resolutely, be firm.
> Goodbye, girl. Now Catullus is being firm.
> He won't seek you back nor ask favours from you thus unwilling.
> But you'll be sorry when no one asks your favours.
> Wretched girl, pity on you! What life awaits you?
> Who will now approach you? Who will think you pretty?
> Whom will you love now? Whose will you be said to be?
> Whom will you kiss? trite whose lips?
> But Catullus!—be fixed, be firm!

The poem suggests its dramatic background: Lesbia is finished with Catullus. One should not I think get the impression that Catullus regards this as the end to end all ends—the poem is very much tinged with humour which rather precludes such an interpretation. Nevertheless, Catullus must face the worst; and the poem conveys his consequent feelings and reactions. They are of course ambivalent. Catullus wants to be proud and firm in the separation; but he wistfully longs for a return to the old days.

The poem conveys these feelings (and all the subtle ramifications which I shall not try to paraphrase) by, precisely, *dramatizing* them. It is of course difficult to dramatize one man's ambivalence. But Catullus has found a way. His basic tactic is the self-address. A strong Catullus addresses a weak Catullus and the interaction of the two produces a lively and suggestive *event*. So again we have a drama (as in poem '7'), albeit ingeniously contrived; again we witness a piece of action, transmuted into art, from which we intuit our knowledge of feeling.

Strong Catullus bids Weak Catullus be sensible and realistic. He admits that once upon a time things were marvelous; he even evokes those days rather patronizingly (3 ff.): *fulsere quondam candidi tibi soles . . .* ; and he manages to insinuate that the happiness of the time was not only at the expense of some Catullan dignity but regarded with less than total enthusiasm by Lesbia ('when you used to follow where she led'; 'intimacies which you so wanted and she was not averse to', 4 and 7). So Strong Catullus admits that things were once upon a time marvelous. . . . And the memory has been too much for him. Strong Catullus has become lost, at one with Weak Catullus in romantic nostalgia. He repeats his evocation of the time of bliss but now emphatically without the patronizing tone: *'truly* the sun shone bright for you (8)'. Ambivalence, and how its emphases shift, is being clearly—dramatically—conveyed to us. It is worth noting that there was an earlier sign that Strong Catullus' strength was not all it might be. He was addressing Weak Catullus in the separated second person singular in these lines; but he could not dissociate himself from the affecting *cri,* line 5, 'beloved by me as no girl will ever be'. (*nobis* there may in fact be a true plural, 'beloved by us': Strong Catullus associates himself momentarily and as it were unwittingly with Weak Catullus in his adoration.)

However, Strong Catullus reasserts himself and utters a sterner admonition to be firm: *nunc iam illa non uult,* etc. (9-12). After this Catullus seems united in obduracy: *uale puella . . .* He turns and dispassionately— or perhaps, we should rather say, *vindictively*—evokes for Lesbia the implications of a mateless future, a future without Catullus. *at tu dolebis, cum rogaberis nulla./ scelesta, uae te, quae tibi manet uita? . . .* (14 f.). But again sentiment—the Weak Catullus—soon intrudes. The first and glaring equivocation is in fact already there in 13, 'nor ask favours from you *thus unwilling (inuitam)*'. That is after all a formidable qualification of the bald *uale puella.* And we soon feel Catullus palpably slipping into sentiment. It becomes more and more plain that Catullus fears the answer to the repeated questions (*quis nunc te adibit? . . .*) is *not* going to be 'no one', and more and more plain that he wishes it might be himself. Another stern admonition is then required from Strong Catullus: *at tu, Catulle, destinatus obdura*—the end of the poem. Not, we should imagine, of the conflict. How the conflict then progressed is and is meant to be anybody's guess. We have witnessed an intentionally inconclusive event, moments of Catullus' inner life externally dramatized: ambivalence in action.

And that I maintain is a better way to be apprised of the nature and complexity of ambivalence than to read an attempted analysis of it (even the spontaneously dramatic analysis that '**76**' offers; '**76**' is very interesting to compare with poem '**8**'). Of course the famous epigrams of ambivalence deal with a different degree—perhaps even kind—of ambivalence; but to an extent they are tackling the same subject and they do it, I maintain, demonstrably less successfully, certainly less poetically than poem '**8**'. Here in poem '**8**' Catullus again composes an event for us, characters in a context. The event has to be contrived with more artifice than in poem '**7**': this time it is not Catullus and another character on stage, but Catullus and himself, Catullus in two capacities. He has in fact taken great trouble to contrive drama, so we can see what store he set on the poetic medi-

um of drama. And it works. We respond to the interaction of personality with personality, and personality with event, within a context, analogously to poem '**7**'. And we *infer* the necessary messages rather than listen to someone trying to state them. Again language is not confined but encouraged to expressiveness by a living context. *fulsere . . . candidi soles* for example (note that *candidus* has connotations of good fortune as well as brightness, whiteness, and beauty) evokes past happiness better than a thousand paraphrases or epigrams could analyse. It is at once actual and symbolic; it feeds the imagination. Or test the power of *uere* here and in poem '**87**'. Our present context gives it implications of deep wistfulness and in turn (in retrospect) irony. It is, literally, more meaningful here than in poem '**87**'—than it would be in any use outside a living context. And *amata . . . amabitur,* an emotional utterance of total love, with, in context, repercussions of irony and pathos; where can you find such a resonant and therefore meaningful use of *amo* in the epigrams? We note incidentally that the connotations are quite different from those of *amores* in poem '**7**'—because the context is quite different. In both poems Catullus has, by constructing or adumbrating a drama, provided the basis and stimulus for a rich verbal texture—a poetic texture. That is something that an analytical epigram with its lack of context and its pursuit of precision cannot (by definition) do.

These are I think Catullus' best dramatic poems. But other polymetrics could have been selected to illustrate the technique. For instance poem '**2**', one of Catullus' most famous pieces:

> passer, deliciae meae puellae,
> quicum ludere, quem in sinu tenere,
> cui primum digitum dare appetenti
> et acris soles incitare morsus,
> cum desiderio meo nitenti
> carum nescio quid lubet iocari,
> et solaciolum sui doloris,
> credo, ut tum grauis acquiescat ardor:
> tecum ludere sicut ipsa possem
> et tristis animi leuare curas!

> Oh sparrow, my girl's darling!—
> whom she is wont to play with, to hold in her
>   bosom,
> to whom she is wont to give her fingertip
>   (you seek it)
> and provoke eager pecks:
> a favourite game for her
> when her eyes shine with longing for me,
> and a little solace for her anguish
> to make her *grievous* passion abate—
> Would that I could play with you as she
>   does—
> and alleviate the sad cares of my spirit.

(There is irony in *doloris* and *grauis . . . ardor,* and perhaps *desiderio meo nitenti.* I have emphasized 'grievous' in the translation in an attempt to bring out the tone.) Catullus and Lesbia are it seems perforce separated from one another; Lesbia is taking the separation better than Catullus. Through a witty address to Lesbia's pet bird Catullus manages to convey his current feelings: his pain at the separation which is considerably greater than Lesbia's, his rueful awareness of that fact that it is greater than Lesbia's; his jealousy of the fact that she can so easily divert herself in what should be her time of suffering; his jealousy of the way Lesbia casually disposes her affections; and so on. All this is wittily and tactfully communicated to Lesbia herself, and to us, via the dramatized address to Lesbia's pet.

Or take poem '11' (*Furi et Aureli, comites Catulli*). Here Catullus dramatizes a farewell to Lesbia that combines the bitterest of sarcastic repudiations with (I think) an appeal to ignore that repudiation. The feelings that inform such a poem and come across to us are of course highly complex. One could endeavour to spell it all out; but paraphrase would hardly encompass it all. That is one reason why Catullus composed in this dramatic way. A dramatic poem can embody extraordinary complexity, subtlety, or delicacy. It offers us *life,* transmuted into art: deftly selected scenes or moments artfully presented so as to stimulate an imaginative response. We share experience with the poet and thereby come to an intuitive appreciation of often inexpressible things. And that is a richer adventure than being told the expressible.

5. Aspects of 'Poem 68'

On one splendid occasion Catullus makes extensive use of myth in his love poetry. **'Poem 68'** is probably the most extraordinary poem in Latin. It is clearly experimental in many respects and its quality highly uneven, laboured artificiality vying with sublimity. Not a small part of its extraordinariness lies in the disparate facets of Catullus' experience it covers: his relationship with Lesbia, the death of his brother. But I must confine my attentions to its function as a Lesbia love poem and in particular to the role played by the elaborate comparison with Laodamia and Protesilaus. And even here I must comment selectively. I quote some important passages.

> is clausum lato patefecit limite campum,
> isque domum nobis isque dedit dominae
> ad quam communes exerceremus amores.
> quo mea se molli candida diua pede
> intulit et trito fulgentem in limine plantam
> innixa arguta constituit solea,
> coniugis ut quondam flagrans aduenit amore
> Protesilacam Laudamia domum
> inceptam frustra, nondum cum sanguine sacro

hostia caelestis pacificasset ergs.
nil mihi tam ualde placeat, Ramnusia uirgo,
quod temere inuitis suscipiatur eris.
quam ieiuna plum desideret ara cruorem,
docta est amisso Laudamia uiro,
coniugis ante coacta noui dimittere collum,
quam ueniens una atque altera rursus hiems
noctibus in longis auidum saturasset amorem,
posset ut abrupto uinere coniugio,
quod scibant Parcae non longo tempore
    abesse,
si miles muros isset ad Iliacos.

(lines 67-86)

aut nihil aut paulo cui tum concedere digna
lux mea se nostrum contulit in gremium,
quam circumcursans hinc illinc saepe Cupido
fulgebat crocina candidus in tunica.
quae tamen etsi uno non est contenta Catullo,
rare uerecundae furta feremus erae,
ne nimium simus stultorum more molesti.
saepe etiam Iuno, maxima caelicolum,
coniugis in culpa flagrantem concoquit iram,
noscens omniuoli plurima furta Iouis.
atqui nec diuis homines componier aequum
    est—

(lines 131-41)

nec tamen illa mihi dextra deducta paterna
fragrantem Assyrio uenit odore domum,
sed furtiua dedit mire munuscula nocte,
ipsius ex ipso dempta uiri gremio.
quare illud satis est, si nobis is datur unis
quem lapide illa diem candidore notat.

(lines 143-8)

He opened up a fenced field with a broad
    path,
and he gave a house to me, and gave a house
    to a mistress,
a house where we might pursue the love we
    shared.
And my fair goddess betook herself there with
    gentle step;
she set her shining foot on the worn threshold,
halting, her sandal sounding—
Just as once upon a time burning with love
came Laodamia to the house of Protesilaus—
a house that was begun vainly, for not yet
    with holy blood
had a victim appeased the lords of heaven.
May nothing, maid of Ramnus [i.e. Nemesis],
    so mightily appeal to me
that it be undertaken rashly with our lords
    unwilling!
And how hungrily the altar desires the pious
    blood
Laodamia learnt, losing her husband:
compelled to loose her bridegroom from her

arms
before the coming of a first and a second
   winter
had satisfied their eager love in length of
   nights
so that, her marriage sundered, she might bear
   to live.
And *that* the Fates knew was close at hand
if once Protesilaus went to fight at Troy . . .

                       (67-86)

Hardly or not at all worthy to give place to
   her
she who is my light brought herself to my
   bosom.
Cupid, darting round on either side of her,
gleamed brightly in a saffron cloak.
And though she is not happy with Catullus
   alone
I shall bear with the affairs of my mistress,
   for they are rare and she is circumspect,
lest I should be too tedious, in the manner of
   boors.
Often even Juno, greatest of the heaven-
   dwellers
swallows burning anger due to her husband's
   infidelity,
knowing all-loving Jupiter's plenteous affairs.
And yet to compare men with gods is not
   right. . .

                       (131-41)

But she did not, conducted by her father's
   hand,
come to a house fragrant with Assyrian scent,
but granted me stolen favours in a night of
   wonder,
favours taken from her very husband's bosom.
And so it is enough if to me and only me is
   given
the day which she marks out with the whiter
   stone of luck.

                       (143-8)

Catullus is thanking a friend (Allius) for a service rendered. The service sounds relatively small; Allius put at his and Lesbia's disposal a house to make love in. But clearly what it meant to Catullus, the quality of the moments passed there (I shall come back to this), made the service in effect inestimable.

I start by looking at lines 70-2, *quo mea se molli candida diua* . . . These are in fact a fine example of Catullus' exploitation of dramatic situation, the technique of the Lesbia polymetrics; though here Catullus re-creates the drama in a report rather than an enactment. Lesbia is approaching the house lent by Allius; Catullus is already waiting within. We witness Catullus waiting. But the Lesbia he waits for seems posi-

tively numinous, a creature of dreams ('and my fair goddess betook herself there with gentle step. She set her shining foot on the worn threshold . . .'). We must ask, *why?* Why does she seem so numinous? The simple answer to that is: because that is how she seemed to Catullus at the time; because, to put it another way, of the special quality and effect of those particular moments. And Catullus now re-creates those moments for us, to impart understanding of them to us. Dramatic re-creation will give us an understanding of things hard to analyse.

The particularity of these moments is their condition of heightened expectancy. Catullus is in fact touching on a phenomenon which is probably familiar to all. It is by way of being a truth that expectation creates excitement, and excitement can magnify even mythicize the object of excited expectancy. Perhaps no beloved is ever quite so beautiful, so divine, as in the moments just before she arrives. That is a rather sombre but frequent fact of life that lovers with impressionable sensibilities have to face. That is anyway what Catullus is talking about. Lines 70-2 re-create his own romanticizing of Lesbia in the moments of expectation just before she arrived at the *domus*. And by re-creating the moments and the romanticizing, Catullus communicates to us an abundance of knowable but hardly expressible things: the power of romantic expectancy to magnify.

These lines in fact take us to a climactic and pivotal moment: the sound of Lesbia's shoe on the threshold. It is indeed a climactic moment, and it is pivotal. It is the high point of romance; but in seconds Lesbia will enter the house and then she will *change*. She must change. She will be a creature of flesh. However wonderful, she can hardly remain the *candida diua*. That was the creation of expectancy.

What Catullus now does (73 ff.) is remarkable. He holds the pivotal, climactic moment—through 58 lines. Lesbia's foot is frozen on the threshold while a massive simile (plus sundry diversions) develops: Laodamia. Why this huge simile? What does it represent?

For one thing it means (I suppose) that Catullus in his reexperiencing of the events of the *domus* clings very tenaciously to the last seconds of the period of expectancy. That must make us have our doubts or fears about how reality matched romantic expectations. It certainly creates suspense. More importantly it means that Catullus has not yet conveyed all he wants to convey about those final moments. He has dramatically evoked the scene and communicated understanding that way, but still there are things he wants to say which he senses are unsaid. Therefore he enlists the assistance of comparison and myth. Why particularly Laodamia? The basic answer to that lies in Catullus' vision of his relationship with Lesbia as *marriage*. His sense of expectation while waiting not only elevated Lesbia into a goddess; it also set a marriage dream into motion. Therein in fact had lain much of the magic of Allius' service: it had enabled the actualization, for a while, of that dream. Line 68 is crucial. In Catullus' eyes Allius had given them not simply a place for a clandestine meeting but: *isque domum nobis isque dedit dominae,* 'he gave a house to me and to a (or *its* or *my*) mistress.' *domus* connotes 'home', the home of man and wife; and though the interpretation of *dominae* is problematic I think it is certain that it refers to Lesbia and that it means 'mistress'. And it means 'mistress' not in the sense of 'mistress of a slave' but 'mistress of a house', 'the lady': in combination with *domus, domina* can hardly mean anything else. Allius' kindness therefore had allowed the Catullan fancy of marriage to take shape: Catullus was the *dominus* awaiting the arrival of a beloved *domina*. He was a romantic husband waiting for a divine wife. A wife, who was, too, like Laodamia.

In a way Laodamia selected herself. Traditionally she was the loving, passionate wife *par excellence,* the beautiful, faithful wife *par excellence,* devoted to her husband to the extent that life was insupportable without him. In fact without him she was literally unable to live: note 106 *ereptum est uita dulcius atque anima/ coniugium,* 'marriage snatched away that was sweeter than life, sweeter than her soul'; note too line 84. Laodamia is one of the most touching and appealing figures from the resonant world of mythology, certainly the most appealing wife. She connoted more to someone familiar with mythology than could ever have been stated. That is why Catullus used myth at this point—and Laodamia in particular. Since he was trying to illuminate and to maintain the vision he had possessed of Lesbia as a romantic devoted wife, Laodamia did rather suggest herself.

But the myth obviously had other and discordant implications and Catullus has other and profounder purposes in using it. He in fact selected the story of Laodamia because it could serve *two* broad functions. It could illuminate and maintain a romantic vision, as I have just described. It could also simultaneously darker things. At this point it is vital to stress that the use of myth here is not allegory: there is no 'one for one' correspondence between what illuminates and what is illuminated. Rather, the myth generates many implications on various levels. That is its great value. I can of course only hope to point to a few of them here.

And to focus some of them, it will be useful to look ahead: to the point where Lesbia actually crosses the threshold. In a last burst of fancy Catullus describes her entry (131-4). And then in lines that are still tender and loving he confronts the truth (135-48). The magic of expectancy has (as we anticipated) dissipated and

Lesbia is no longer—she no longer could be—the creature of dreams. She is not a goddess, not a mythical faithful wife, not a wife or *domina* at all (emphatically not), and not even faithful in her adultery to Catullus. All this is explicitly stated. But Catullus will not make a fuss or be tediously insistent. He loves her and it is enough. Indeed Lesbia, Lesbia the creature of flesh, is dearer to him than life itself. That is the sense of the very last lines of the poem: *mihi quae me carior ipso est/lux mea qua uiua uiuere dulce mihi est,* 'she who is dearer to me than myself, my light of life; while she is alive, life is sweet for me.'

What we witness here in fact (from 131 on) is the step-by-step collapse of the romantic vision started in 70-2, then maintained and amplified in the myth of Laodamia. All the wonderful things that Laodamia was, Lesbia is not after all and is said not to be. Nevertheless, Catullus loves her—a moving declaration. Let us note in particular the final pathetic irony that the poem delivers. In those last two lines of the poem Catullus affirms precisely the transcending fidelity and devotion that he had attributed to Laodamia and, therefore, wishfully to Lesbia. Compare those lines with lines 84 and 106 mentioned above. It almost sounds as if Catullus chose and narrated the Laodamia myth with the very intention of setting up his own romanticizing for a cruel fall. And that I think is in a way exactly what he did do.

I think simply that Catullus' choice and manner of telling Laodamia's story not only issues from a desire to maintain and amplify a romantic vision of Lesbia; it also evidences a simultaneous awareness in the romancer that the vision is fantasy and bound to collapse. The implications of the myth are too unerringly at odds with truth in crucial respects for Catullus not to have had some sense of the discrepancy from the beginning. The emotional sources of the myth are therefore quite literally ambiguous: romanticizing and insight. Its purpose is to communicate a romanticism compromised by a sense of more sombre reality. And Catullus means us (I think) to have some awareness of the ambiguity in his mythical comparison virtually from the start. As his praises of Laodamia mount, so our awareness of the incongruity of the comparison should mount; and so should our sympathy for Catullus who is also aware of the incongruity but trying to cling to a romantic vision.

Further thought supports this line of interpretation; and both the romanticizing and the pathetic self-knowledge implicit in the myth are more pronounced than I have perhaps so far suggested. In the moments of expectancy of 70-2 and the immediately ensuing myth, Catullus is not just generally assimilating Lesbia to a wife. He sees these moments more precisely as the culmination of a *wedding* and views the future of their whole relationship as a romantic mythical marriage stretching before them. The text is in this respect quite explicit.

The myth opens with Laodamia's arrival at Protesilaus' house as a *bride;* and that (the arrival at a *domus*) is the immediate point of contact between the situation of the myth and the situation of Catullus and I,esbia. And the implication that Catullus imagined specifically a wedding is confirmed by the sequel. When the romantic vision of the myth is demolished, the idea of a wedding is specifically rebutted: note lines 143ff.: *nec tamen illa mihi dextra deducta paterna/fragrantem Assyrio uenit odore domum,/sed furtiua dedit mira munuscula nocte.* (The *mira nox* refers I think to the night in the *domus* of Allius, and Catullus is here emphatically admitting that Lesbia was not then his bride.) So: the expectancy of 70-2 caused Catullus not just to compare Lesbia to a wife (and to a goddess, etc.) but to imagine those moments as the climax of a wedding, and the future of their relationship stretching before them as a whole romantic mythical marriage. Or rather as a marriage like Protcsilaus' and Laodamia's. The comparison is of course disastrously equivocal, as becomes clear when we view it in this more exact way. The marriage of Protesilaus to Laodamia was indeed one of the most romantic and tender in mythology. It was also uniquely tragic, doomed from its inception. And Catullus emphasizes that fact by inventing or highlighting a detail: the *pax deorum,* the agreement of the gods to the marriage, had not been obtained by sacrifice at the outset (75-6); hence inevitably the tragic end followed. So Catullus' choice of myth supports his romantic vision; but it also radiates disaster. A *domus* that was *incepta frustra* (74-5) is an unhappy illustration for someone imagining a romantic *domus* for himself and his beloved. Catullus wishes and tries to believe in his 'marriage' to Lesbia; *and* he knows it is doomed. His choice of so ambiguous a myth implies and communicates just that. There was in fact a presentiment of the fantasy marriage's doom already in the dramatic scene of 70-2. Lesbia's foot knocking on the threshold is, whatever else, an unlucky omen for a bride.

Catullus therefore both in his initial dramatic re-creation and in his myth dreams and sees through his dreaming. Recreated drama allows us to intuit more than could ever be encompassed by statement. And so does myth: this is something we have not met before. Like drama myth allows us to infer the inexpressible; it suggests, adumbrates (it does *not* dictate), stimulating and drawing upon our imaginative response. Like drama, too, myth provides a living context for diction, encouraging a rich verbal texture; I shall not even begin to try to paraphrase the implications and repercussions in context of (for example) *coniugis, amore,* and *domum* in lines 73-4. The use of myth to assist in the illumination of personal feelings is one of the original *and* great accomplishments of this poem.

6. Conclusion

I shall now try to summarize the achievements of Catullus as a love poet. The first must be, in a word,

'Lesbia'. Catullus is the first ancient poet to treat a love-affair with one commanding lover in depth, in a related collection of mutually deepening poems. This had simply not happened before. But it will now be the fashion. Art will imitate art and life will imitate art and we shall observe how Propertius finds himself compelled to write about Cynthia, Tibullus about Delia, and Ovid about Corinna. And before them we know that Varro of Atax wrote about a Leucadia and Cornelius Gallus wrote about Lycoris (Cytheris); but their works are unfortunately lost. In this respect alone Catullus' influence was enormous.

He experimented with different methods of love poetry, some more successful than others; and that meant that lessons were available to be learnt by the next generation. His analytical epigrams, in spite of their originality of form and language, were not successful poetry. But they did pithily advertise his remarkable aspirations and feelings in love. The social implications of these aspirations I shall touch on in chapter four. But let us here note that the epigrams brought into the conscious awareness of succeeding poets something they might only have been unconsciously aware of: a sense of the great ambivalences that love can engender. And (I now make explicit a point so far only implicit) they promulgated the principles of a new erotic romanticism. Formulating a relationship of profound equality (*amicitia, foedus-marriage*) Catullus was in fact making a definably romantic statement. He was sacrificing in exchange for his ideal of love the pride of place that the male in a heterosexual affair might at that time reasonably have expected. It was not just that the object of an upper-class man's passionate love was traditionally his social inferior. She was his psychological inferior too (the constant Greek distinction between *eron* and *eromenos* or *eromene* is implicit in Roman thinking).

Catullus also richly developed the potential of the traditional dramatic poem. And perhaps there is his most consistently good poetry. The success of these poems and how it was achieved must have much impressed his followers. Finally in one poem, poem **'68'**, he treated aspects of his relationship with Lesbia at great length in the elegiac metre; and he exploited not only dramatic re-creation but mythical narrative. The Alexandrian Greek poets had perfected the art of allusive, subjectively told myths in elegiacs. None, however, had used it systematically and explicitly like this to illuminate their own current feelings. This was another example of Catullus' that was to have most important and direct influence.

G. P. Goold (essay date 1983)

SOURCE: An introduction to *Catullus,* edited and translated by G. P. Goold, Duckworth, 1983, pp. 1-18.

[*In the following excerpt, Goold emphasizes Catullus's role as a pioneer in the crafting of effective poetic diction in classical poetry.*]

[Poets] from Ennius onwards had successfully clothed Greek literary forms in a Latin dress but had conspicuously failed to match their originals in elegance and beauty of language. This failure the neoterics sought to redeem, taking as their models the poetry of Ptolemaic Alexandria and of Callimachus in particular. l hey imitated not only formal features like artistic word-order and prosodical precision but also the poetic ideology of their models, who discarded the major genres of drama and epic in favour of compositions on a smaller and even miniature scale, for in these every line and every word could be carefully crafted and the proportions of the whole meticulously calculated. No less did the neoterics cultivate the recondite learning characteristic of the Hellenistic poets and especially the subjective and personal manner in which they recounted abstruse and often novel versions of mythological stories.

Catullus' technical skill is especially noticeable in his handling of the native Roman artifice of matching sound to sense: this abounds in his work and is the more effective for being mostly unobtrusive, like the monosyllables of '**III**' 11 with their voiceless consonants mimicking the pathetic hopping of the sparrow along the road of death or the alliteration, variety of vowels, and spondaic ending of '**LXV**' 23 which arrestingly reproduce the tumbling down of the apple that reveals all. How endearingly in '**XLV**' does Septimius alliterate to Acme with *p* and she to him with *s*, though the latter letter spits out savageness at '**XLIV**' 155f and the former pours forth poison from the first to the last line of '**XXIX**'! Some of his rhetorical figures are possibly overdone, anaphora, for instance, of which he was inordinately fond, though in '**LXIII**' (21ff *ubi*, 63f and 68ff *ego*) we should make allowances for the constraints of the metre.

Two features of Catullus' diction call for comment. Diminutives constituted a rich source of expression in colloquial Latin no less than in modern Italian—how rich we can surmise from the vast yield from our exiguous means of access to it: Plautus and Terence, Cicero's *Letters,* and Petronius. On one occasion ('**XXV**') Catullus used these forms to great effect, exploiting the notion of effeminacy which lurks in their nature; and elsewhere we find in isolation over seventy different diminutives, a greater proportion than any other classical Latin poet has put in his work. Munro deeply regretted the Augustans' banishment of this word-type, which 'made the lyric of the heart impossible'. Yet a little investigation shows that in Catullus the diminutive is often hardly more than a substitute (or the natural word, which we discover to be excluded *by* the metre (e.g. '**LXI**' 174 *bracchiolum* for -

chium; '**LXIII**' 35 *lassulae* for *lassae*; '**LXVI**' 16 *lacrimulis* for *-mis*; '**LXVIII**' 2 *epistolium* for *-tulam*): '**V**' and '**VII**' and '**VIII**' and '**XI**' and '**XIV**' and '**XXXI**' and '**XXXIV**' and '**LI**'—to give a representative selection—scarcely support Munro's contention.

Compound words, which contributed so much to the richness of Greek, were coldly regarded in classical Latin. Early republican poets had freely imitated Greek formations, but how incompatible these were with the very nature of Latin is sharply revealed by an instance like Pacuvius' *Nerei repandirostrum incurvicervicum pecus* (of dolphins). If this sounds grotesque to us, we should reflect that compounds like Ennius' *altivolans* and Lucretius' *lauricomus* (which may appeal to us as highly poetical) probably struck the Romans as being unattractive only in a lesser degree. In fact the only compounds to become thoroughly at home in Latin were noun-object/verb combinations like *signifer*. In his lyrics Catullus has only *buxifer, laserpicifer, pinnipes*, and *plumipes* (the last two in the experimental '**LV**'), and they are seen no more; of the other dozen examples *erifuga, hederiger, nemorivagus, properipes*, and *silvicultrix* all occur in '**LXIII**' and, since they can never enter dactylic verse, probably owe their existence in some measure to metrical exigencies.

The most impressive feature of Catullus' diction, however, is—and here one can do no better than quote from the old school edition (1879) of Francis P. Simpson—'the simplicity and naturalness of his language, which are in great contrast to the later artificial Latin style. . . . However difficult the metre in which he writes, however subtle the thought he would convey, he is never intricate and never obscure. His words seem to have fallen of themselves into metre without leaving their natural order, and would make good prose—if they were not poetry. His language, in the epigrams, lyrics, and elegiacs, is little removed from ordinary speech. He is full of familiar phrases . . . He uses the tongue of the wits of the town, the lips of the lover of real life.'

His humanity needs no comment, but he stands out above most poets of antiquity for his imaginative sympathy with nature and inanimate things. Though his zest for society took him to Rome he never lost his appreciation of the north Italian scenery which we may fancy we detect in such passages as the third stanza of '**XXXIV**' and the first major simile of '**LXVIII**' (57ff). In particular the sea, indeed water generally, which for Lucretius, Virgil, Horace, and the other poets was an element to be feared and shunned, represents for Catullus laughter and gaiety ('**XXXI**' 14; '**LXIV**' 269ff). For him the lopping of a wild-flower was as tragic as the destruction of his own love ('**XI**' 22ff), a sensitivity he displays again in '**LXII**' (39ff).

The verse of Catullus so often implies a situation in

which individual poems were sent on tablets ('**XLII**') or in *feuilleton* ('**XXXV**') that it must have been in this way that the poet's productions were first disseminated and that he himself acquired some celebrity or, it may be, notoriety '**XVI**' 12, referring to '**V**' 10). We also read of reactions experienced on receipt or in the circulation of his poems whether by intimates like Lesbia ('**XXXVI**') or Cornelius Nepos ('**I**') or by prominent public figures like Cicero ('**XLIX**') or Caesar ('**LIV**'). 'Children of the moment' was the happy phrase that Wilamowitz applied to such poems, and it accurately conveys how little at the time of creation the poet was concerned with publication in book-form. That could come later. The tantalizing thing is we do not know how far Catullus was able, to use the modern term, to see his work through the press. He cannot have done more than assemble a collection of his lyrics and prefix a dedication to Cornelius Nepos when death overtook him (and of this he may have had no warning). Improbable even that this lyric collection was published as such: antiquity has no knowledge of a title, and it may be wondered whether, if 'publication' (that is the establishment of a definitive edition) had already taken place, the person responsible for the collected edition which we inherit today would have ventured to insert other poems into it, as he seems to have done. The last year of Catullus' life was prolific, but he died with his work unfinished: his epyllion lacks a title and may lack the author's *imprimatur* as well; nor do the long elegiacs either form a whole or amount to sufficient bulk to constitute a *libellus* on their own. In short, Catullus' poems were published posthumously.

Stuart G. P. Small (essay date 1983)

SOURCE: "The Miniature Epic, No. 64" and "Some Conclusions," in *Catullus: A Reader's Guide to the Poems,* University Press of America, 1983, pp. 135-52, 153-61.

[*Below, Small examines Catullus's most ambitious work, "Poem 64," and draws critical conclusions about the poet and his view of the role of poetry as a vehicle of self-expression, self-understanding, artistic immortality, and power "to celebrate whatever may merit praise . . . , to punish the wicked, to expose the inept, to defend the helpless and to retaliate upon the ungrateful."*]

No. "**64**" is Catullus' longest poem, perhaps his latest, certainly his most ambitious. It is an epyllion or short mythological epic. The epyllion was one of the more important literary innovations of the Hellenistic age. The genre was taken up and naturalized at Rome by the New Poets as part of their reaction against historical epic in the Ennian manner. We have already had occasion to mention in Chapter Two Cinna's epyllion,

the *Zmyrna,* which is praised in no. "**95.**" From other sources we know of an *Io* by Calvus, a *Glaucus* by Cornificius, and a few others. Of these works only a handful of tantalizing fragments survive. Catullus' 64th poem is the earliest Latin epyllion which has come down to us entire. In this masterwork the poet incorporates much of what is most characteristic in his previous writings. As Putnam says, it contains "reflections of almost every major subject which interested him." It expresses the essence of his experience in life and literature, the sum of his discoveries. Hence the old hypothesis that no. "**64**" is a mere translation or paraphrase of a lost Alexandrian original is extremely improbable and has for the most part been laid to rest.

The epyllion usually deals with a love theme and often includes a contrasting "digression." Catullus' poem adheres to this formula. The framework narrative tells of the happy wedding of the Argonaut Peleus and the sea-goddess Thetis. This encloses a contrasting digression of approximately equal length on the disastrous love affair of two mortals, Theseus and Ariadne. I shall try to explain the relationship of these two narratives later on.

Instead of plunging *in medias res,* Catullus begins at the beginning. He gives a brief account of how the ship Argo was constructed from the pines that grew on Mt. Pelion. This is a reminiscence of no. "**4,**" 10-12, where the poet's *phaselus* was also traced back to a stand of timber on a mountain top. But there are differences between the two passages. The *phaselus,* for all its excellences, was but one craft among many, whereas the Argo was the first ocean-going vessel, an unprecedented *monstrum* and a marvel to all beholders. Therefore the building of the Argo is described in high epic style; no. "**4,**" 10-12 on the other hand is a mock-heroic inset in an informal and conversational poem.

In addition, the opening paragraph offers a characterization of the Argonauts in general and goes on to tell us something about the hero Peleus in particular. The Argonauts were men of valor, outstanding among the Argive youth, bold pioneers who had the courage to sail to far-off Colchis. It was because of their heroic excellence that they were honored by the assistance of Athena, for it was she, the goddess of handicraft herself, who built the marvelous Argo for them. During the outward voyage they received another tribute to their surpassing worth when with mortal eyes they were privileged to gaze upon the divine beauty of the unclad Nereids as they rose from the gray waters. It was then that Peleus, the pillar and bulwark of Thessaly, fell in love with Thetis. Thetis accepted him, and Jupiter himself sanctioned their marriage. At this point, Catullus breaks with the convention of epic objectivity in a quasi-lyric outburst modelled upon the closing paragraphs of the Homeric Hymns. He cries out his praise of the whole race of heroes. He says he will often invoke these "excellent sons of excellent mothers." Born in an evil generation, he rejoices to escape, at least in fancy, into the glorious heroic age. The enraptured questions of vv. 25-30 sustain the lyric mood. Peleus' surpassing good fortune in being allowed to marry a goddess is almost too good to be true; Catullus can scarcely believe such a thing ever happened. Yet it did, for ancient tradition affirms it, and tradition does not lie.

In line 31 we leap forward in time from the first meeting of Peleus and Thetis to their wedding at Peleus' palace in Pharsalus. It is just before the meeting of bride and bridegroom. We have here a heightening and intensification of that magic hour which Catullus had glorified in poems **"61"** and **"62."** From all Thessaly the guests arrive with wedding presents, their faces shining with happiness. No one is envious or disaffected; all rejoice that the king is honored, for when he is honored, his subjects are honored as well. Indeed, the whole human race is exalted by Thetis' acceptance of Peleus. On this glorious day, field work ceases for ordinary folk, the curse of labor is lifted, and there is a temporary recovery of the bliss of the Golden Age. Within the palace, all is bright and shining. The color imagery of lines 43-48 matches the primary mood of festal joy. White predominates: this is the color of happiness and the color the Olympian gods love best. Associated with the whites of the palace interior is the sheen of silver, gold and ivory. These are beautiful, precious, and long-lasting materials. Gold and ivory have sacral significance: from these were fashioned some of the holiest and most revered images of the gods, e.g., that of Athena in the Parthenon and that of Zeus at Olympia. Peleus welcomes Thetis and the divine wedding guests with the best that man has at his disposal.

Why does Peleus play such a prominent role in no. **"64"**? It is difficult to be sure about the reason. One attractive possibility is that the Peleus story is related to Catullus' own experience. It has been well said that Catullus approaches myth empathetically, not objectively. He has to be able to see himself in it somehow; otherwise he does not need it. This is evident in the long elegy, no. **"68"**; it is equally evident in no. **"64."** Peleus' marriage to Thetis marks the perfect attainment of a bliss that the poet had imperfectly experienced at the beginning of his relationship with Lesbia. In the long elegy he exalts her as a radiant goddess and compares her arrival at the house of Allius to an epiphany of Venus. But she was a goddess only in the metaphorical sense and only for the duration of the *mira nox.* Thetis on the other hand is a true goddess and according to Catullus' account deeply in love with Peleus. She lived with him in perfect concord, and their union apparently lasted until Peleus' death As we shall see later on, the perfection of their happiness was

eventually marred after the birth of their son, but apart from this their relationship is unflawed. Thetis' condescension to the hero Peleus is the nearly perfect actualization of an ideal approached in some degree and fleetingly experienced by Catullus at the house of Allius. It is because the poet once aspired to and partially attained a felicity analogous to that of Peleus that he chooses the marriage with Thetis as the principal subject of the epyllion.

In the midst of all the chryselephantine splendor within Peleus' palace, there is one object of contrasting hue, the crimson coverlet that is thrown over the marriage bed. This coverlet is embroidered with figures taken from heroic myth. Under the pretext of describing this coverlet Catullus launches into his second subject, the sad story of how Theseus carried Ariadne away from her Cretan homeland and then abandoned her on the island of Dia (Naxos).

He begins the story with a description of Ariadne on the shore of the island. She has just discovered that her lover has betrayed her. She looks out over the uncrossable sea, grieving for all she has lost. Her situation resembles that of Attis in no. **"63."** Both have been driven by passion to take an irreversible step. Ariadne had been impelled by Venus, Attis by hatred of Venus. Ariadne awoke from sleep to discover (too late) that she had been abandoned. Attis awoke from sleep to discover (too late) that he had lost all to Cybele. Ariadne in her distraction rushes to the seashore; so does Attis. At the shore they look out over the sea, Attis in the direction of his far-off *patria,* Ariadne in the direction of the far-off ship of Theseus. Both are surrounded and cut off by hostile nature. In front of them is the vast sea, the uncrossable gulf that separates them from all they love. Behind her Ariadne has the craggy bluffs of Dia. the dwelling place of wild beasts and birds; behind him Attis has the Phrygian mountain where wild creatures make their lairs. Both are alone. Ariadne, after a night of love on the beach, has been forsaken by Theseus. Attis at the shore has left his companions behind him on the mountain top; they are no longer human in any case. Finally, both break into impassioned and pathetic soliloquies by the seashore. The similarities between the two scenes are extraordinary.

However, there are also important differences. In Ariadne's case there is nothing to compare with the symbolic sunrise in the Attis poem. Conversely, the sea imagery of no. **"64"** is much richer in implication than that of no. **"63."** The literal and external sea around Dia cuts the heroine off from her past in Crete and from her hoped-for future with Theseus. It imprisons her in an intolerable present on a desert island (so Dia is conceived by Catullus) to die of starvation. But in addition she is lashed by a metaphorical, inward sea: not merely a sea of troubles as in no. **"68a"** but a high sea raised by Venus and Cupid, which is therefore a sea of passion. Ariadne is a helpless swimmer in this metaphorical sea. Like a person tossed by vast waves she has lost her autonomy, her power of self-determination. The metaphor, first used at v. 62, recurs at v. 97ff. in a heightened and intensified form. In these lines, unless the figure is mixed, she is no longer a swimmer but a ship, a ship on fire, driven by a storm at sea. These images establish her as a victim of the passion of love and as a pathetic figure.

As we said above, Catullus views myth empathetically, not objectively. In the light of that principle, we discerned an analogy linking the poet to Peleus. There is also a significant correspondence between Catullus and Ariadne. He goes out of his way to identify with her. At v. 61 he adds an *eheu* in order to sigh for her and with her. At v. 69 he adds the vocative *Theseu,* calling on Theseus by name, as she did; he is one with her in her affliction. The exclamations *a misera* in v. 71 and *heu* in v. 94 have a similar effect. He knows what she is going through. Her storm-tossed passion, her pathos, reflects his own sufferings as a victim of passion. Her rejection by Theseus is comparable to his own experience of rejection. The infidelity which destroyed her happiness resembles the infidelities that had darkened his life. Ariadne has been humiliated, mistreated, and Catullus' heart goes out to her.

Catullus not only identifies with Ariadne; he also justifies her. In his eyes she is *misera,* pitiable. She is pitiable because she suffers far beyond her deserts. It is true that she turned her back on her father, her family and her homeland. People in her society would say that she had done wrong in forsaking all other loves for one love (v. 120) and in presuming to choose her own husband. Nevertheless, it was impossible for her to do otherwise. She could not be expected to resist the maddening passion which had been visited upon her by the cruelty of Venus and Cupid (vv. 71f., and 95ff.). It was by their prompting that she fell in love with Theseus at first sight (v. 86), the moment he arrived at her father's palace. She was not drawn to him because of his inner qualities or character traits. In personality the two had nothing in common, were in fact direct opposites. She was drawn by his looks alone, his *dulcis forma* (v. 175). It was the sight of that splendid male animal that set Ariadne on fire: Venus willed that it should be so. She sowed in Ariadne's heart a seed which grew into a great thorn-bush (v. 72), signifying all the anxiety and pain *(curae, luctus)* which love inevitably brings, in Catullus' view. Ariadne is not to be condemned for falling in love, believing Theseus' false promises of marriage, and running away with him.

Once Cupid and Venus have done their work, Ariadne is totally transformed. Catullus emphasizes the extent of the transformation in the contrasting images of v.

87ff. Before Theseus' arrival she resembled the chaste unmarried girls of the wedding poems, secluded and protected, safe in her mother's arms. Like them she is compared to a flower, a myrtle that is refreshed by river waters and caressed by spring breezes. After she as gazed upon him she is a woman on fire, burning. Her love is described in terms which had been used to describe Catullus' love for Lesbia. Desire penetrates to the very marrow of her bones; line 93 is reminiscent of the imagery of liquid fire in no. **"51,"** 9-10 (the Sapphic ode). The fire metaphor connotes pain, among other things. Love, to Ariadne, is far from being unalloyed bliss, delight and fulfillment. It is joy mixed with suffering (v. 95) as it had been in Catullus' own experience (cf. no. **"68,"** 17-18). Ariadne's love for Theseus is as distressing and intense as Catullus' love for Lesbia had been.

A large part of her pain comes from humiliation, from the experience of being rejected. This is hard for any lover to bear, but it is especially hard for a royal princess like Ariadne, the daughter of proud Minos. Her pain is still further increased by Theseus' base ingratitude. Because she loved him, she helped him to escape from the labyrinth and return home a hero. Then, believing his false oaths of fidelity, she had given up all she possessed to leave Crete with him. Her assistance, her sacrifices and her trust are repaid with stony-hearted betrayal. Theseus is *immemor,* v. 135. Like the Alfenus of no. **"30,"** he is unmindful of past benefits received, promises given, obligations incurred. In fact he has decided to destroy her. In exchange for the gift of life he gives her death by abandoning her on a desert island. He does this not so much because he hates her as because he hates her cruel and unjust parent. In other words, he carries her off and forsakes her in order to punish his enemy Minos. The innocent daughter pays for the sins of her father.

To Catullus, Theseus is a hero, but he is not a character with whom he can empathize. He does not identify with Theseus in any way. Perhaps that is why he is not given any speeches in the poem. He is known to us not by his words but by his actions and by Ariadne's attitude toward him. Naturally she heaps reproaches on his head, and they are richly deserved. Nevertheless the poet stops short of presenting him as a "villain" motivated by sheer malevolence. The malign and diabolical villain is on the whole a post-classical phenomenon. Theseus cannot be considered diabolical. His heroism is conceded from the start: the crimson coverlet displays *heroum virtutes,* v. 51. Although the plural is somewhat peculiar, it certainly includes Theseus' exploits. As hero, he is *ferox,* "bold" (vv. 73, 247). He thirsts for fame, glory and praise (v. 102, cf. 112). That is perhaps the very essence of heroism. The hero's one overriding purpose in life is to acquire prestige, to make himself worthy of honor by performing deeds of valor, to obtain glory by meeting the challenge of a crisis situation. In determining to free Athens from the burden of paying tribute in human life to an unjust king, Theseus shows heroic devotion (v. 80 ff.). The verb *optauit* in line 82 should not be overlooked. It means "chose." He went to Crete of his own free choice, not because any other person, human or divine, had imposed the task on him. He is motivated not only by love of fame but also by loyalty to Athens. However, his conception of love and loyalty is irreconcilable with Ariadne's. Theseus is loyal to the ancient pieties, devoted to country and to his father Aegeus. His great courage, his willingness to sacrifice himself for the commonwealth, remind us of the Roman heroes of the early Republic. Ariadne is the reverse of this. She is loyal in her personal relationship to Theseus. She deserts father, family, country and the altars of her gods in order to be with the one person whom she perceives as irreplaceable and upon whom she concentrates all her affection and desires. Furthermore, where Theseus is heroic, Ariadne is pathetic. Every kind of hero, good or bad, is the antithesis of the pathos figure. The hero acts, the pathos figure reacts; the hero is the vigorous agent, the pathos figure is the passive victim; the hero in some sense wins, the pathos figure, after struggling feebly against overwhelming odds, goes down to inevitable defeat.

Since Theseus and Ariadne are direct opposites we should not be surprised to discover that the deities associated with each of them are opposites also; for the god who influences and sways any individual is the god who is most in accord with his basic nature and self-hood. By virtue of his birth, upbringing and circumstances, Theseus is under the patronage of Pallas Athena: Athena is controlled and rational, a goddess of warfare, a protectress of city states (especially of Athens, the city state named after her), and a special guardian of heroes (we recall that she built the Argo for the Argonauts); but she is cold, inclined to cruelty, and of course, as virgin goddess, impregnably chaste. Chastity is not one of Theseus' virtues, but apart from this he participates in the qualities perfectly exemplified in the goddess Athena. Ariadne on the other hand is swayed by the deities of instinct, passion and natural human impulse, Venus and Cupid. Moreover, we find out later on that she is loved by Bacchus, another god identified with man's instinctual side. At first her acceptance of natural impulse leads not to happiness and liberation but the opposite: loss of autonomy, rejection, humiliation, pain and despair. In the end, however, she escapes unexpectedly into joy. Theseus, apparently victorious and triumphant, is suddenly thrust into disaster.

His valor peaks at v. 105ff. In answer to Ariadne's prayer the gods grant him victory over the Minotaur. Catullus condenses the story of their fight into seven lines. The end result is given in v. 110: Theseus "laid low" (*prostravit*) the monstrous bull. How this was accomplished is not directly narrated; instead, it is implied in the five-line simile which immediately precedes. The Minotaur is compared to a mighty oak or pine on an exposed mountain top; Theseus is like a still mightier force, the unconquered whirlwind. The whirlwind wrenches the tree up by its roots and throws it flat. The imagery suggests that the adversaries were not duelling with weapons but wrestling with bare hands. Apparently Theseus manages to lift his opponent from the ground and goes into an "airplane spin"; this is followed by a body-slam which has fatal consequences. Guided by Ariadne's clue he emerges from the labyrinth unharmed and exultant. The brevity and obliquity of the account do not detract from Theseus' glory, but it is worth noting that his *aristeia* is bracketed by references to the help Ariadne gave him. Catullus does not want us to forget this.

If Theseus' victory over the Minotaur marks the physical climax of the epyllion, the emotional climax is provided by Ariadne's lament at the shore, vv. 132-201. As we have already suggested, her monologue shows a number of correspondences with the climactic soliloquy of Attis in no. "63" (vv. 50-73). Both speeches are written in the first person singular and may be regarded as lyric insets in a third person narrative; both give pathetic expression to a sense of overwhelming loss. But Ariadne's lament is three times longer than the complaint of Attis. It is a far more varied and complex composition. Attis' speech shows little dramatic progression. He hardly gets beyond self-accusation and the expression of vain regrets. Ariadne does not accuse herself; she accuses Theseus. Her mood evolves continuously; she passes from helpless lamentation to deep despair, then in the end turns to the gods for help and calls down angry curses on her false lover: these curses are not vain. They bring death, not upon the hero himself but upon his father, who suffers for the sins of his son. Although both Attis and Ariadne are presented sympathetically, one senses that the poet projects himself far more deeply into the experiences of the heroine than into those of Cybele's victim; Attis represents to him only a terrifying possibility, but Ariadne recalls the agony of lived experience.

She begins by addressing the absent Theseus in apostrophe. The opening adverb *sicine,* followed by seven lines of rhetorical questions, shows (by a technique now very familiar to us) that she can scarcely believe that he has left her. She is appalled by the sudden revelation of his cruelty, ingratitude and treachery. All his promises were false and worthless; like the assurances of Alfenus in no. "30," 9-10, they have been carried off by the winds. Then at 143ff. she checks herself, tries to make excuses for him. He is not unique, he is just a man; all men are like that, opportunists and deceivers. Catullus had attempted to excuse Lesbia in similar terms in no. "70." But she soon veers back to reproach, remembers her past acts of kindness and how they have been repaid by monstrous cruelty. She calls him the child of a lioness or a sea monster (v. 154ff.). The poet had used comparable imagery in crying out against Lesbia's inhumanity (no. **"60"**), but the present passage is even more vehement. At v. 155 in place of the neutral *genuit,* "bore," she uses the ugly metaphor *exspuit,* "spewed out." The implication is that even such subhuman mothers as Syrtis, Scylla or Charybdis must have rejected with horror and disgust what they had conceived: the birth was a spitting out, a vomiting forth, a throwing up. At v. 158ff. she again shifts and relents, declares that she would be willing to accept almost any humiliation just to be close to him. Passion abases its victims. Already enslaved to him in the figurative sense, she would serve him literally as well. Although a royal princess, she would be glad to make his bed and wash his feet. For her, even foot-washing could be beautiful, an act of love (v. 162).

But there is a limit to her capacity for self-abasement. In line 188 she turns from useless self-address to prayer. She does not pray for healing and release from her love, as Catullus had done in no. **"76"**; she calls down curses in the name of justice. She asks the Furies, those powers of vengeance who take the part of innocent victims, to punish the guilty Theseus in accordance with the law of the talion, measure for measure. She hates him for his cruelty and deception, for giving her death in exchange for the gift of life; she hates him for his injustice. Yet at the same time she curses him against her will. *Cogor,* "I am compelled" (v. 197), makes this clear. The curse is wrenched from her; something within resists. That something is what is left of her love. *Ardens* and *furore* in the same line are usually understood as referring to her wrath, but it is better to take them as functionally ambiguous. They refer both to anger and to love. Ariadne is going through something very like the quintessentially Catullan experience of no. **"85"** (*Odi et amo*). Anger, hatred, love and a sense of outraged justice coexist within her tormented heart.

After Ariadne's soliloquy Jupiter gives solemn assent to her prayer and she is avenged. This is followed by a flashback to the time of Theseus' departure from Athens, The hero's father Aegeus (in the second extended speech of the poem, vv. 215-237) gives his son his final instructions: if he succeeds in killing the Minotaur he is to change his sails from sad violet to joyful white. In its pathos Aegeus' speech resembles that of Ariadne. He is extremely old and feeble; Theseus is his only son, dearer to him than life itself. They had been separated for many years and were only recently reunited. He grieves (vv. 223, 226) that he must now part from him again and expose him to mortal danger in Crete; yet circumstances (*fortuna,* v. 218) and Theseus' bold resolve (*feruida uirtus,* ibid.) tie his hands (vv. 216, 219). He does not expect his son to return; he mourns and pours dust on his head as if he

were already dead (v. 224). Aegeus is presented as wholly sympathetic figure. Ariadne in line 159 had misjudged him, imagining in him a severity which is alien to his character. Certainly Theseus is more eager to go to Crete than Aegeus is to send him. Although Catullus is sometimes hard on the older generation, especially on rigid puritans and killjoys who are envious of the happiness of young people, he shows no animus against Aegeus. On the contrary he sympathizes with him as a lover and a sufferer, as one who suffers through his love and indeed dies because of it. The old can be lovers too. One thinks of the aged grandfather in the simile of no. **"68,"** vv. 119-124. Aegeus is a pathetic expansion of that old man.

The epic is often called the most comprehensive form of poetry on the ground that it creates a whole world. A whole world from the ancient point of view will include a divine dimension. Hence in our epyllion the gods have an important role to play. What is the relationship between men and gods, according to this poem? In the extremity of her pain Ariadne briefly entertains the idea that the world is not governed on any rational basis whatsoever (vv. 169-170). She feels that what she has been through is meaningless. What made it happen, really? What purpose did it serve? Or worse, she suspects that the universe may be ruled by *fors insultans,* diabolical evil, an unpredictable power which is not merely indifferent to human suffering but actively and inscrutably cruel. However she does not hold this view for long. Almost immediately she turns to the gods in supplication. According to the theology of this poem she is right to do so; for the gods do exist, they do rule the universe, they do listen to prayers. Sometimes, to be sure, they grant them to the hurt of the person praying, as at vv. 103-104, where they accept Ariadne's prayer that Theseus may be victorious over the Minotaur. But they also accept prayers that wrongdoing may be punished: Theseus is made to suffer for his perjury. At v. 204 Jupiter nods in solemn assent to Ariadne's prayer for vengeance, and at v. 207ff. Theseus forgets his father's instructions. 'What has happened? Has Jupiter invaded Theseus' personality and forced him to forget? The curiously contorted simile in vv. 238240 hints at an answer. A high and snow-capped mountain (representing either Aegeus and his instructions or Theseus) usually has at its summit a plume of cloud (representing Theseus' thoughts). Just as a blast of wind may blow the cloud away, so an unnamed force analogous to the wind made Theseus forget. All winds are under the control of Jupiter as god of the upper air and of weather generally; likewise the unnamed force operates according to his will. Since there is no discernible motivation at the human level, it is a fair inference that Jupiter alone causes Theseus to forget.

Is justice then done? A very rude and approximate kind of justice at best. Minos pays for his pride cruelty and injustice, as we have seen, and Theseus is not permitted to get away with his perjury. The gods punish the guilty Theseus by direct interference and the guilty Minos by a more circuitous route. That much is understandable. But they do not protect the innocent. Ariadne, the victim of Venus and Amor, who did no voluntary wrong, suffers far beyond her deserts. The gods, in order to get at her father, allow her to endure agony. Likewise Aegeus, through no fault of his own, dies because of the offenses of a son whom he loved more than life itself. The divine justice is flawed and incomplete. The gods cannot bring perfect good out of evil. There is a margin for tragedy in the world. There is a discrepancy between the ideal justice man longs for and the rough-hewn justice which the gods dispense. Nevertheless that discrepancy is far from total Wrongdoing is punished, however clumsily, and the prayers of blameless victims are not ignored. According to Catullus, the powers that govern the universe are not blankly indifferent to our need. Man is not a *passion inutile,* malevolent *fors* is not in control; the world is not absurd.

The story is not over. Theseus' sad end is contrasted with a sudden rebound in Ariadne's fortunes. Her sufferings are ended by the unexpected arrival of the god Iacchus. Iacchus is Dionysus or Bacchus. He is much more than a jolly god of wine and intoxication. Finley rightly calls him a god of liberation, especially a god who frees women from all that restricts and confines them. As a god of release he delivers Ariadne from her imprisonment on the desert isle of Dia. He does not come to her in answer to a prayer: she never prays to be saved, the possibility does not even cross her mind. Nor does he come in the interests of justice or compassion. He comes to her, winging his way across the sea, simply because, for no apparent reason, he is on fire with love for her:

te quaerens, Ariadna, tuoque incensus amore.

(v. 253)

seeking you, Ariadne, and on fire with love
  for you.

Loving her, he must have seen her somewhere, before her flight with Theseus; seeking her, he must have lost her: but Catullus does not go into details. Once he has found her she joins his ecstatic entourage, the *thiasos* or holy company of Satyrs, Sileni and Maenads, and becomes his bride. She is united with Iacchus as Peleus is united with Thetis. The parallelism and contrast between these two major myths helps to fuse the two halves of the epyllion into a thematic unity. Marriage with divinity is the common term. As Thetis condescended to accept Peleus, so Iacchus raised up and glorified Ariadne. Love, which brought her all her sufferings in the first place, finally releases her from the crimson world of her pain.

In the long elegy, no. **"68,"** Catullus uses mythology as a mirror of his own experience. It seems probable that the Ariadne legend also had some private and personal meaning for him. Certainly he never thought of himself as a hero. Theseus is the antithesis of all he valued most, and he must have known that the glory of a Peleus was not available to him. But what of the passionate Ariadne, with whom he so clearly identifies? Having shared her pain did he long to share in some sort of final liberation and joy comparable to hers? Did he ever hope he might be loved without reason or deserving by a god of release and thus share the divine life forever? If so, he must have realized the hope was illusory. In his time, the gods no longer show themselves to man (v. 397ff). Attis in poem no. **"63"** had hoped for a blissful union with the goddess Cybele but in the upshot was subjected to a life of hellish servitude. Catullus knew he could never be a second Ariadne, but the hopeless yearning may still have existed within him, deep down. I suspect that lines 251-264 express that yearning in mythical terms.

The poet breaks off his description of the crimson coverlet at v. 265. The mortal wedding guests, who are not allowed to look upon the gods face to face, and who therefore must not be present when the divine guests arrive, depart from the graced palace of Peleus to resume their normal occupations in the familiar world. Their departure is described in the longest and most elaborate simile of the poem, vv. 269-77. In these lines the guests are compared to the waves of the sea at dawn, which under a freshening wind grow higher and higher, move faster and faster toward the rising sun and make more and more sound as they go, finally reaching a point where they are clearly seen. Likewise the crowd of guests moves slowly at first, then gathers speed as it advances; at first silent, they gradually begin to laugh and speak as they move out of the dusky megaron of Peleus' palace into the bright sunlight. The effect of the simile is to suggest that the collective mood has changed. A moment before they had been gazing with eager intensity at the images of Ariadne's suffering and exaltation which were embroidered on the coverlet (vv. 265-8): now they leave the palace and start home Their state of mind has shifted, the spell is broken they are about to resume their ordinary and unexalted lives as field-laborers.

The most obvious difference between epyllion and epic is that the one is short and the other is long. Because of the ample scale of his genre, the epic poet has to cope with the problem of retardation and expansion; he must know how to provide passages of relaxation between the climaxes. In the miniature epic these problems are less pressing; it is possible to secure continuous concentration and speed. Catullus maintains in poem no. **"64"** a density and richness comparable to that which we find in the best of his shorter poems. But if there is any passage in the epyllion in which a relaxation of intensity is permitted, lines 278-302 seem to provide the likeliest example. This is the verse paragraph in which the gods begin to arrive at the palace. Once again, as in his narrative of the arrival of the Thessalian guests (v. 32ff.), the device of the epic catalogue is utilized. The catalogue is not without a principle of organization. The gods are listed in order of rank, first the lesser and then the greater. Chiron heads the list, followed by Peneus; next comes the Titan Prometheus, and finally the Olympians.

Chiron is the wise centaur who lives on Mt. Pelion. He was famous for his skill in hunting, music, "gymnastics," and the art of prophecy. Many of the most distinguished heroes of Greek mythology were trained by him. Jason, Castor and Pollux were among his pupils; so too were Peleus and Achilles. He brings as a wedding gift not the celebrated Pelian spear but garlands of wild flowers, simple emblems of festivity.

Peneus is the chief river god of Thessaly and as such the source and sustainer of all life in the country. He is also, as it happens, a close relative of Thetis. He has his hands full: he brings five kinds of trees, to be planted at the entrance of Peleus' palace; there they will provide shade for generations yet unborn. Among his sylvan gifts are the poplar and cypress, both of which connote death and are perhaps prophetic of the brevity of Achilles' life.

Prometheus' presence is heavy with significance. It was he who had warned Jupiter not to marry Thetis, as the high god had once intended to do: she was destined to give birth to a son greater than his father. Jupiter therefore renounced her and allowed her to marry Peleus instead (cf. vv. 26-27).

Jupiter and the other Olympian gods arrive last. Like Prometheus they bring no gifts; their mere presence is gift enough. Two of the Olympians are absent, Apollo and his twin Diana. As god of prophecy, Apollo foreknows that Achilles, the future son of Peleus and Thetis, will kill Hector and thus seal the fate of Troy, his favorite city. He also foreknows that he will himself take Achilles' life in retaliation. The absence of the children of Latona, like the earlier references' to poplar and cypress, casts an ominous shadow on the otherwise ideal happiness of the occasion.

After the gods have arrived the Parcae sing their wedding song. . . . [T]he song is double-edged in its effect: while it praises the perfect love of Peleus and Thetis it also prophesies the birth of a terrible son, greater than his father but a shedder of blood, violent, cruel and inhuman. The perfect joy of the wedding day will bring fresh evil into the world.

There is a marked element of paradox in Catullus' portrayal of the Parcae. To the casual observer they are three insignificant little old ladies suffering from something like Parkinson's disease: their infirmity is mentioned twice, vv. 305 and 307. Festively attired for the occasion in crimson and white, they have nevertheless brought with them baskets of fleece and (as Merrill points out) refuse to stop their incessant spinning even during the wedding feast. As they spin, they strip the finished threads clean with their teeth, and flocks of bitten wool cling to their withered lips. But despite their unprepossessing appearance and curious behavior we know that these little old ladies are really all-powerful birth goddesses who foreordain the course and duration of every human life. If they are old and infirm, it is because they have been carrying on their *aeternus labor,* their "everlasting occupation" (v. 310) ever since mankind first appeared on earth. Although the description of their clothing may seem purely ornamental, recent investigation has shown that it is part of a pattern of color contrast which pervades the entire poem; white is insistently associated with happiness and crimson with suffering. In the present passage the combination of the two colors hints at the varying proportions of joy and affliction that the Parcae assign us at birth. It is not over-subtle to say that the white and crimson garments together with the crimson headbands are emblematic of their awesome divine power over the lives of mankind.

They are engaged in the humdrum and unremarkable activity of spinning (described in meticulous detail at vv. 311-14), but their spinning has no ordinary utilitarian purpose. The woollen threads they are forming are obviously symbolic. Since thread is a fragile commodity that has a beginning, grows steadily in length as it is spun, and comes to an end when the fleece on the distaff is exhausted, it is an apt image for the frail brevity of human life. Everyone is familiar with the developed form of the myth according to which one of the Parcae spins, another measures and a third snips the thread. Catullus, however, here follows Homer's earlier and simpler version in which all three spin and the measuring and cutting are not mentioned. Only the spinning matters in the present context.

As they spin they sing; their song is modelled in part upon primitive work songs. Such songs often have a refrain comparable to that sung by the Parcae,

> currite ducentes subtegmina, currite, fusi
>
> run, spindles, run and spin the threads
> 　　　　　　　　　　　　　　　(v. 327 etc.),

in which a tool or utensil is apostrophized as if it were a lazy animal or slave and verbally encouraged to hurry up and get the job finished as soon as possible. Work songs are sung by people engaged in boring and repetitive jobs; the idea is to turn routine into something like play. No doubt the Parcae are rather bored by their everlasting occupation of spinning our innumerable lives into existence; after all we are only "threads", more or less alike, and our minor differences are rather uninteresting. The little old ladies are mainly intent on keeping up their schedule, getting through their quota of fleece on time.

But because it is sung by goddesses the song of the Parcae differs from ordinary work songs. [Their song] is prophetic and inerrant; the point is stressed, vv. 321-3, 336, 383. The threads may fix the length of each life, but it is the song that determines its nature; the Parcae sing our whole future into being, in all its distinctive particularity. As they sing they offer evaluations that jar on the sensibilities of any enlightened human being. Of course we are not disturbed by their praise of the harmonious love shared by Peleus and Thetis, but when they go on to describe the career of Achilles, their comments begin to strike us as alarmingly inappropriate. Indifferent to the sufferings and injustices endured by the vanquished, childishly superficial in their conception of heroic *arete,* they seem malicious or senile or both. Enormous power is seen to rest in irresponsible and incompetent hands, and the three sisters, as Quinn puts it, are at once sinister and absurd. Apart from the Cybele of no. **"63"** and the Orcus of no. **"3"** they represent Catullus' least attractive, most disquieting image of divinity.

After the Parcae have sung their ambiguous epithalamium, one expects to read a description of the arrival of Thetis and the entry of the happy pair into the bridal chamber. However, Catullus omits this and proceeds to draw a contrast between the world-wide *pietas* of the heroic age and the wholesale corruption of human relationships in the present. In olden times, the gods "often" visited the houses of mortal men, showed themselves to human eyes, descended to earth on festal occasions, accepted generous sacrifices, led their worshippers in sacred dances upon the mountain tops, came to their aid in time of war. Men's homes were still *castae;* the family was unstained by impurity and wickedness; *pietas* was not yet scorned; religion and justice were not yet forsaken. Hence men lived on terms of intimacy with the gods in those days. Now, however, all that is changed. We are living in an Iron Age, sodden with sin. Justice is forgotten and evil desires have taken over in the form of avarice, ambition and lust. Family life is defiled. Brother offends against brother as sibling rivalry is pushed to the point of fratricide. Children offend against parents and begin to look forward eagerly to the deaths of their fathers and mothers. Parents offend against children: the father lusting after his son's fiancée desires his death in order to be free to marry the girl himself, thus saddling his remaining children with a stepmother; the mother makes incestuous love with her offspring, daring to pollute by her sin the sanctity of the household gods. The end result has been an irrational overturning of all values

and an alienation of the gods from the human race. Affronted by our universal degeneracy they no longer visit man's world or show themselves to mortal eyes.

The idea that the human race is degenerate was a commonplace in antiquity. Hesiod and Aratus, to mention no others, provide examples of the motif. Catullus follows in their footsteps, yet his version of the myth is generally felt to be unsatisfactory. Some have called it moralistic. If the adjective implies that he is narrow and conventional in his judgments, it is ill chosen. It is not narrowminded to deplore fratricide and incest. The trouble lies elsewhere. Quinn has correctly diagnosed the weakness of the passage. Catullus' denunciation of the age is too direct, too abstract, too unqualified, too heavy-handed. Any opposition of shining virtue to conscienceless depravity is bound to seem melodramatic and Catullus has not managed to escape this trap. Furthermore, one is disturbed by the lack of any rational analysis of the problem. The poet points with alarm, wrings his hands, but goes no further. What has caused this hideous falling away into vice? Is it the fault of the Parcae? Or does time by its very nature mar and degrade the original harmony? What, if anything, can be done to halt and reverse the downward spiral? No answer is given; perhaps no one knows.

Alexandrian in form, no. **"64"** is no mere literary exercise. It is typically Catullan in its approaches, attitudes and preoccupations. An astonishing number of themes taken from the shorter poems are incorporated into its substance. The so-called moral epilogue denounces vices similar to those attacked in the invective poems. The mythical material introduces dramatic con'flicts and expressions of hope and fear analogous to those which we have met in the Lesbia cycle. Ariadne consumed by passion and forsaken by her faithless lover is undoubtedly a surrogate for the poet himself. He takes her part, identifies with her, can see himself in her. Her lyric lament expresses a despair which reminds us of his own anguished disillusionment with Lesbia. Likewise he is personally involved in the story of Peleus and Thetis. The mythical pair represent what he had once hoped for in his relationship with Lesbia, at a time when she still seemed to him to be a goddess on earth. In brief, no. **"64"** recapitulates and expands most of the major themes which appear elsewhere in the body of his poetry. It is so thoroughly Catullan in spirit, so intimately related to his other writings and to his life experience, that it is difficult to see why it was once regarded as a translation from the Greek. Klingner is unquestionably right in regarding it as his greatest achievement, the crown of his literary career.

Some Conclusions

As we have mentioned several times . . . , Catullus was one of the New Poets, a prominent member of that band of brilliant young men who, in the course of a single generation, succeeded in transforming Latin poetry. Until they made their influence felt, the dominant poetic genre at Rome had been the Ennian epic, heavy and long-winded, preoccupied with nationalistic themes, historically oriented and thoroughly impersonal. Departing from this tradition, the young innovators turned to Alexandria for their models and brought over into Latin literature the dominant forms of Hellenistic verse: miniature epic, elegy, and "lyric," i.e. the independent short poem. One of their chief aims was to master the literary erudition and concentrated brevity characteristic of the best Alexandrian writers. Along with high standards of craftsmanship in language and versification, they cultivated a new sophistication of outlook and a new ironic wit. Even more important, they initiated a shift from the state-centered values of their Roman predecessors to a new individualism and a new concern for the subjective and personal. In brief the New Poets effected a radical change in the Roman literary sensibility and gave a different direction to the development of Latin poetry. The effect of their work on subsequent writers was lasting and profound.

It is easy to exaggerate the influence of the Alexandrians on the New Poets and in particular their influence on Catullus. Certainly he was no slavish imitator of the Greeks. He recognized an obligation to "make it new," in Ezra Pound's phrase. He realized that he had to move beyond his models, adapt the tradition to his own talent, carry it forward. To his short poems he brought an intimate and vivid personalism that marks an enormous advance upon the elegant evasive conventionality of the Hellenistic epigram and has no discernible parallel in Greek literature after early iambic and melic verse (e.g., Archilochus, Sappho, Alcaeus, Ibycus and Anacreon). His literary raw materials are purportedly taken from real life experience in the contemporary world. The experience par excellence is of course the madness or disease of passionate love, which strikes arbitrarily and irresistibly and makes its victim *miser,* pitiable, a pathos figure in the fullest sense of the word. In language that often seems to approximate ordinary colloquial usage, Catullus dramatizes the whole course of his affair with Lesbia from its anxious beginnings to its acrid end. It is this series of some two dozen love poems (all short, except for no. **"68"** and no. **"76"**) that, in the opinion of most modern readers, constitutes his most creative innovation and his chief title to literary fame.

Yet his longer poems must not be underestimated. Formerly dismissed as stuffy Alexandrian exercises, they are now recognized as being no less innovative than the Lesbia lyrics. In two of them, nos. **"64"** and **"68,"** Catullus introduces mythological subject matter and adopts a more elevated style to match. The invocation of the heroes in no. **"64,"** 22-30 suggests that mythology offered him an escape from his corrupt present into the ideal splendor of an imagined past. More important than this rather literary nostalgia is his technique of blending myth with autobiography, a procedure that apparently was unknown to the Alexandrian Greeks. Peleus' marriage to Thetis marks the fulfillment of a bliss that Catullus had fleetingly and imperfectly experienced at the house of Allius. Our author repeatedly identifies with the passionate and suffering heroines of legend. He sees correspondences between his own pathos experience and that of an Ariadne, overwhelmed by passion and abandoned by her false lover. He empathizes with the ardent and devoted Laodamia, who lost her irreplaceable Protesilaus at Troy, the very place where his own brother was buried. The interrelation of personal experience with mythical paradigms in no. **"68"** foreshadows Augustan practice, especially that of Propertius; for this reason among many others, this poem has been called the prototype of Roman "subjective" love-elegy.

These are fundamental innovations. Taken collectively they make up the essence of what has been called the "Catullan Revolution." That revolution marks an important advance over Alexandrian precedent, a broadening of the classical sensibility, and a shift in the whole direction of the Graeco-Roman literary tradition. Nevertheless, it does not signal a complete break with the past, and therefore the term "revolution" is perhaps somewhat misleading. Radical discontinuities are hard to find in literary history; probably they do not exist. In many important ways Catullus is linked to his predecessors and is plainly a continuator of established poetic practice. To call him a Romantic, as if he had somehow miraculously anticipated the European literature of the Nineteenth Century, seems to me to be a serious anachronism. Catullus is no Romantic. He is an essentially classical author and by that very fact a literary traditionalist.

He is typically classical in his respect for the *exemplaria Graeca,* the tested and approved models, both Hellenistic and earlier. His debt to Sappho as a monodist and as a composer of wedding-songs is already familiar to us and need not be rehearsed here: the very name Lesbia, "girl of Lesbos," bears witness to his dependence. His invective poems are based not only on Archilochus, Hipponax and other Greeks but on the work of his Roman predecessors in the comic-satiric tradition. Ross has shown that most of the short elegiac pieces are written in the style of pre-neoteric, old-Roman epigram. His close relationship with the Alexandrians, especially Callimachus, requires no further documentation at this point. As a literary traditionalist he accepts without cavil the received genres of classical poetry. He is familiar with the rhetoric taught in the schools of his day add makes expert use of it. In poetic diction, imagery and versification he shows no significant break with established practice. Like all other Latin authors he takes it for granted that the correct method of literary composition is by *imitatio:* the poet's proper task is not to strive for absolute originality but to rival and if possible to excel the form and style of the recognized classics, the great models of achievement in each kind. In addition, he accepts the classical principle of decorum, which prescribes that the style of any given poem must be appropriate to the presumed speaker, the circumstances and the literary genre. This is strikingly evident in the hymn to Diana, no. **"34,"** but may be observed throughout his writings.

Later Roman authors like to call Catullus *doctus,* "polished," "accomplished." For him as for the Alexandrians before him poetry is above all an art *Ingenium,* "innate talent," is of course indispensable; so too is that strange subconscious impulse that we call inspiration. All the same, poetry remains *ars* an acquired skill. Skill is developed by study. We learn from lines 31-36 of no. **"68"** that one needs a whole library of books in order to write a large-scale work. **"No. 1"** with its references to polish and pumice gives us some idea of the importance Catullus attaches to exact and discriminating craftsmanship. In no. **"95"** he expresses his admiration for Cinna's ultra-Alexandrian *Zmyrna,* an epyllion that was nine years in the writing. Significantly, the Muses connote to our author not inspiration but technical expertise. They are *doctae virgines,* "accomplished maidens" (no. **"65,"** v. 2). He confides his thoughts to them; they put his ideas into memorable form and pass the result on to his readers (no. **"68,"** 41-50). So intent was Catullus upon mastering the technical secrets of earlier writers that he even deigned to compose verse translations of Callimachus (the *Coma Berenices,* no. **"66"**), of Sappho (no. **"51"**) and Theocritus (the *Pharmaceutria;* this version has not come down to us, but it is referred to by the elder Pliny. Such exercises no doubt helped him to acquire his distilled and concentrated style. The informal, colloquial manner that he deliberately adopts in so many of the shorter poems must not be mistaken for artless spontaneity; it is evidence for his skill in the difficult art of concealing art. Even the least ambitious poems are workmanlike, competently constructed and not devoid of artifice. We do not regret that they have been preserved.

The average emotional temperature of Catullus' writings is high; hyperbole and rhetorical questions abound. Nevertheless, the artist is invariably in control of his art. He is not thrown off balance by sheer passion. Even when he is in the grip of vehement love or hate, he never dreams of rejecting or undervaluing reason. On the other hand, lyric poetry that is bereft of feeling is a contradiction in terms. Many of Catullus' most unforgettable poems combine intense personal involvement with rational and artistic detachment. The writer is at once the observer and the observed; thought and emotion are intertwined. A similar combination of emotion and unfaltering insight has often been discerned in Sappho.

Non-Sapphic, however, is Catullus' technique of dramatizing inner division by self-address. We have called attention to several poems in which he apostrophizes himself by name: *Catulle, miser Catulle.* Naturally these vocatives are associated with imperatives, jussives or rhetorical questions. They are spoken by a superior self who analyzes and understands to an (unreplying) inferior self who agonizes or endures or is simply unaware. The superior self exhorts, arouses, encourages or warns the inferior self. We are not always sure that he wins out, but he never gives up hope, never stops trying.

Catullus did not write to please a literary patron; he had no need of one. He wrote to please himself and a small circle of like-minded friends. His primary audience was therefore a lettered elite. Wheeler is no doubt correct in supposing that the poems were at first passed around from hand to hand and only at a later date made available to a wider readership. The general public, when they read his published work, found themselves treated as semi-outsiders, not fully informed about what was going on. They were allowed only to overhear the poet's words. Probably they missed many of the elliptical and half-hidden allusions. So do we; it is just this semi-private quality that obscures the meaning of many of the occasional pieces to this very day. Barring the unlikely event of new information turning up, the ultimate intention of many passages will in all probability never be recovered.

Hand in hand with his literary traditionalism goes a distinct conservatism in morals and religion. Unlike his many false friends, Catullus honors the virtues of *fides,* "good faith," and *pietas,* "responsibility." He insists upon loyalty and integrity in personal relationships. He naively expects men and women to stand by their sworn word and to show gratitude for benefits received. In time of crisis he turns to the just and merciful gods in prayer (no. **"76"**). He writes a hymn to Diana, perhaps with a view to public presentation at a religious festival; he prays that she may protect and preserve the people of Romulus. He even offers the archaic *inferiae* at his brother's grave in the Troad, in spite of the fact that he knows the rite is vain and ineffectual. In his wedding-songs he upholds the old-fashioned upper-class view that *par conubium,* "marriage with a fitting and proper partner," is a blessing both to family and nation; he maintains that *iustum matrimonium* is in accordance with nature, reason, law and immemorial custom, and indeed that it is the gods' best gift to the human race.

On the other hand, there is also a strain of nonconformity and rebellion in Catullus. Since he was wealthy and well-born, he could afford a certain independence of outlook. In his invectives he cuts a very different figure from the pathetic *miser* of the poems of complaint. He speaks out with republican forthrightness and blistering obscenity against Caesar and Pompey and their underlings, whom he regards as destroyers of the commonwealth, obsessively intent upon consolidating political power and appropriating the spoils that belong by right to the state. Few would have dared to say so much so openly. Yet he attacks politicians on personal rather than ideological grounds: probably he did not understand the realities of politics very well. Certainly his attitude toward Rome's exploitation of conquered peoples is unenlightened and unreflective. Like the vast majority of his contemporaries, he takes it for granted that the empire exists for the economic advantage of the ruling class.

He is exceptional in his rejection of normal Roman career objectives. Apart from his year in Bithynia, he lived a life of *otium.* He manifested no interest in entering politics, law, the army or public administration The central concerns of his life were poetry and love, in both areas he was a pioneer. Before his time, writers had regarded love as a youthful aberration to be presented in the comic or satiric mode. Catullus insisted upon taking love seriously. At the beginning of the affair, Lesbia was his *domina* and he her servant; or even more hyperbolically, she was his radiant goddess and he her worshipper. Later he dreamt of a perfect relationship with her, grounded in physical passion to be sure, but sanctioned by oaths and marked by *bene velle* and *consensio* on both sides; it was to be a companionship of kindred spirits. He said that he felt for her a responsible and protective affection such as fathers feel for their sons and for their daughters' husbands. Yet in spite of these idealistic yearnings he openly admitted that he was carrying on a love affair with a married woman. How could he square this conduct with his vaunted *pietas is* a puzzling question.

His main concern is with man, not nature. Nature for its own sake does not interest him very much. Of course, he often describes the world around him, but these descriptions serve either as a basis for comparisons (e.g., the mountain cascade in no. **"68,"** 57-62) or as a significant background for hymen speech and action (e.g., the seascapes of no. **"64"**). Like most Latin authors, he is repelled by wild and desolate scenery. The remote woodlands of the Diana hymn inspire a certain awe, but he shudders at the dark snow-clad forests of Cybele's sinister mountain. Even well-cultivated farmland subdued by human labor and ministering to human needs (which Ruskin regarded as the favorite Roman landscape) fails to excite his admiration. We recall how, in his spring poem (no. **"46"**), he flees the rich plowland of sweltering Nicaea for the shining cities of Asia. He simply does not share Horace's enthusiasm for the country life or Virgil's passion for agriculture. It is true that Sirmio appeals to him partly because of its natural beauty, but he values even more

the security it affords and the opportunity for repose after the hardships of travel abroad. Rome, not Sirmio, was his usual place of residence; the metropolis was more attractive than the countryside. At times he seems to sense that nature is positively alien to man. It has no kinship with us. In our sufferings the elements mock us by their indifference, and the endless cycles of the external world taunt our ephemeral hold on existence. Man is not fully at home in his world.

Catullus has a favorable opinion of himself. Notwithstanding his occasional excursions into mild self mockery, he is not troubled by feelings of inadequacy or inferiority. He readily assumes the role of an urbane arbiter of social behavior, and passes confident Judgment on the gaucheries and ineptitudes of his acquaintances. He girds against his *saeclum insapiens et infacetum,* his "witless, tasteless generation" (no. **"43,"** 8). He retaliates against his rivals with scathing invective. In some respects he believes he stands far above other men. Especially does he praise himself as a faithful lover. He compares his love for Lesbia to a beautiful but defenseless flower, nicked and destroyed by the plow of her *culpa.* The world has never seen a *fides* to equal his, nor will it ever again. No one can be his parallel.

Despite this conviction of personal uniqueness, the modern reader ordinarily has little difficulty identifying with him. All poetry worthy of the name fuses the particular with the universal. His thoughts, experiences and emotions are widely shared, especially by young people. Betrayal and rejection are common experiences. Disillusionment is nothing new. Many youthful idealists (Hamlet was not the first) have discovered to their pain that reality does not live up to their expectations, that ingratitude is pandemic, that society is sometimes foolish but more often corrupt, that the flower of love is callously destroyed, that death is final, that this world can show itself a god-forsaken hell, that there are innumerable reasons for pessimism and despair. But Catullus is not always sad. He knows the joy of homecomings, the delight of reunions, the solid satisfactions of true friendship, the sweetness of laughter and kisses, and the exhilaration that comes from plenty of good wine. Excellence does not belong entirely to the past. The wedding songs celebrate fruitfulness, concord and fidelity, happiness in love and in the ongoing continuity of the family. In sum, whether he praises or finds fault, he thinks and feels as many of us still do. He bears witness to the unchanging substratum of human nature. If he did not do so, his poetry would not be classical.

Many classical writers think of man as a paradoxical blend of grandeur and misery. Man is magnificent in his capacity for heroic achievement but pitiable because of the manifold limitations under which life must be lived. Catullus does not altogether accept this formula. He does not deny the possibility of heroism but sees it as belonging to the remote past (Peleus) and as often flawed or spurious even then (Theseus, Achilles). On the other hand, he has a thoroughly classical awareness of human finitude. In his view, our freedom is compromised in a minor sense by other men but in a major sense by time, fortune, fate (the Parcae) and the gods. Against the depredations of the first three he sees no appeal; the gods, however, are ambivalent. He holds that they punish the guilty, but they do not always protect the innocent. At their best they impose obligations of *fides* and *pietas;* if we live up to these obligations we are entitled to call upon them in prayer when trouble comes. Usually we do not live up to them, and therefore the world has become a moral waste land in which even the holiest bonds of affection are regularly dishonored. At their worst they smite us with passion (Venus and Cupid) or inexplicable madness (Cybele). Really, the cards are stacked against us. Man is born to trouble as the sparks fly upward. To live is to suffer, either through our own fault or that of others or through the very structure of reality; and the end of all is total extinction, *nox perpetua.*

This is a dark picture, but I repeat that Catullus is far from being a total pessimist. Life does offer major consolations, though the sort that most men value are vain. Catullus does not believe in transcendence through responsible and devoted service to the commonwealth, as many Romans of his class and status did; or through conversion to philosophy, whether Stoic or Epicurean, with its notorious devaluation of the affective life; or through initiation into one or another of the many oriental mystery cults. He certainly does not believe man can save himself through the pursuit of power, wealth and status. Crass hedonism does not seriously tempt him. Depressed by the decadence of the contemporary world, he has no hopes the process may be reversed and a better age be at hand; he dreamed of no new *saeclorum ordo* such as Virgil foresaw in his Fourth Eclogue. For Catullus, the major sources of satisfaction are true friends (especially fellow poets), conviviality, love in its glorious beginnings, familiar and beloved surroundings (e.g., Sirmio), the joys of a clear conscience, and above all his art.

Not that he believed in art for art's sake. Poetry to Catullus is a *source* of good, both to his readers and to himself. To his readers it is valuable not only because of the pure pleasure it gives but also because of the wisdom it imparts. Poetry can be a way of teaching, advising, exhorting and consoling. As vicarious experience it enhances our understanding of the human predicament. To the poet, his poetry is even more. It is self-expression first, a kind of safety valve for the pent-up emotions. Further it confers power: power to celebrate whatever may merit praise; power to punish the wicked, to expose the inept, to defend the helpless and to retaliate upon the ungrateful. Even more impor-

tant it is a way to self-understanding. One of the best ways to sort out one's experience, to make sense of one's existence, is to try to write a good poem about it. And finally if the *patrona virgo* grants her favor, it is a way to create a series of artifacts which, in a qualified sense at least, will escape the destructive power of time and last *plus uno saeclo*: down through the years.

John Ferguson (essay date 1988)

SOURCE: "The Poems (1)" and "The Poems (2)," in *Catullus*, Oxford at the Clarendon Press, 1988, pp. 24-31, 32-9.

[*Below, Ferguson provides an overview of the Lesbia poems, the elegies, and four long poems; two marriage-hymns ("Poem 61" and "Poem 62"), "Attis" ("Poem 63,"), and "Poem 64."*]

The Lesbia-Poems

Catullus chooses to introduce his readers to the woman central to his life in the two poems about her pet sparrow. She is not there identified even by the pseudonym Lesbia, but, whatever other women there may have been in the poet's life, there is no serious doubt that all the six love-poems in the first eleven refer to the same woman. We have come to appreciate that the first of these ('2') is a hymn, the sparrow who drew Aphrodite's carriage taking on her divinity, that it stands within Hellenistic traditions, and that the language is highly erotic in its details. There is one potent ambiguity: *strouthos* in Greek and its Latin equivalents, *turtur* and the like, are used of the male sex-organ. This gives a strong ambiguity to the second poem ('3'), where G. Giangrande has argued that the death of the sparrow has an underlying meaning of sexual impotence. Not everyone accepts this, but there is no doubt about the ambiguities of *passer, pipiare, mouere, gremium,* and *mors.* The point is not that the poem is about sexual impotence, but that it must be read at more than one level. For the rest the poem shows extraordinary skill: the use of the conversational *male:* the onomatopoeic tinily pattering *it per iter;* the elisions conveying the devouring power of death

> . . . qu(ae) omnia bella deuoratis
> tam bellum mihi passer(em) abstulistis;

the use of hiatus and chiasmus in o *factum male! o miselle passer.*

The two kissing-poems are different from one another. The last part of the first ('5') shows Catullus using finger-gestures which both represent the number of kisses and scorn of the old puritans, adoration of the beloved, the aversion of the evil eye while Lesbia keeps the tally with pebbles on a board, which she finally shuffles to confuse the issue.

This is a poem of happy love. The other is not, and the critic who spoke of 'a novitiate entering an Elysium of love' was grotesquely astray. It is a dark poem, in which *nox* has replaced *lux,* the desert sand leads to the dead tomb, the love is one of many thefts, and Catullus is mad and in need of the silphium used for hysteria and neurotic conditions. The genius of the poem consists in the poet's capacity to distance himself from himself and observe his condition.

The other two poems are both poems of renunciation, set within a recognized *genre.* Here again Lesbia is not named; here alone is directly addressed *puella;* elsewhere she is *mea puella.* The metre, the scazon or limping iambic, does not normally belong to the *genre.* The poem is carefully structured and patterned, the vocative *Catulle* in the first and last lines giving it ring-form. In seeking a mythological precedent he chooses Cyclops in Theocritus, with references also to Callimachus and Sappho. But he does not seek solace in another woman, as mythology and the *genre* demand. In the first line he charges himself with *ineptire:* this is not part of traditional love-vocabulary: it is a failure in cultured urbanity. At the last he turns the *at tu* he has addressed to the woman savagely against himself: the brilliant use of *destinatus* is ambiguous between 'Stand your ground, be steadfast' and 'Stand your ground; there's nothing else left for you to do'.

So the eleventh poem ('**11**') starts with a monumental journey across the world from east to west expressed in high liturgical language. For 16 lines he builds up an effect; in 8 he strikes, first in scathing obscenity, then in tender pathos. The poetically rare word *identidem* ('again, again') appears at the same point of the verse as in the translation of Sappho (51), only here it is linked with brutally harsh elisions. Then at the last the world shrinks to a field and the love which might have changed the world lies broken on the edge of the field (note how *ultimi* echoes the remote Britons), and the hypermetric elision *prat(i) ultimi flos* wonderfully expresses the snapping of the stalk which projects into the path of the plough.

It is neither possible nor necessary to explore in detail all the light which has been shed by modern commentators on all the other poems in the Lesbia-cycle, but one or two must be mentioned.

The '**51st**' is thought by most to be the first poem he wrote to Lesbia, though Wiseman has argued that it is a late poem made sombre by allusions to other poems notably the '**11th**' in the same Sapphic metre. It is mostly a translation from Sappho, in which the poet identifies himself with the poetess: his self-identification with the feminine, in general so alien from Roman

mores, here and elsewhere, is of both poetic and psychological interest. In the very first stanza he adds to the original an allusion to the Roman religious formula fas *sit uidisse* in relation to an epiphany. This is not mythological and Greek; it is Roman and real, and Clodia . . . a real goddess (compare '**68**'.70 *candida diua*). It has been much disputed whether the *otium* stanza is a detached fragment, or a part of the original poem. On the whole opinion favours the latter, though there are contrary voices. Nor is it clear what he is saying: *otium* has been seen as a political term, an ethical term of disapprobation, a linguistic opposite to *negotium,* an ambivalent attitude to an Epicurean ideal, a condition of literary creation, a negative attitude in love. Such diversity almost compels us to see ambiguity in the poet's mind.

It is worth pausing a moment over the little *cri-de-coeur* ('**58**')

> Caeli, Lesbia nostra, Lesbia illa,
> illa Lesbia, quam Catullus unam,
> plus quam se atque suos amauit omnes,
> nunc in quadriuiis et angiportis
> glubit magnanimi Remi nepotes.

with the ritual threefold repetition of the name, and the agonized inverted order of *Lesbia illa illa Lesbia.* In the last line we have come to recognize the mock-heroic tone (applied also to Cicero: '**49**'.1): it is curiously parallel to Caelius's jibe at Clodia as *quadrantaria Clytemnestra* where epic dignity is combined with coarseness. But Catullus mutes his coarseness. Wiseman has observed that he never turns on Lesbia the full vocabulary of obscene invective. *Glubit* is metaphorical: a euphemism, if you like. It means to strip the bark from a tree. So Lesbia strips the nobility of Rome of clothes, money, and potency.

The '**68th**' poem in its complexity will be treated later. Some of the epigrams apply directly to Lesbia. They are beautifully shaped. '**70**' owes something in form to Callimachus. It moves from the particular to the general—with particular implications. 'My woman says she wants to marry me.' 'Women aren't to be trusted by men in love.' The last two lines have a powerful contrast between *cupido . . . amanti* and *rapida . . . aqua.* The lover lusts, but the water commits the rape, and the words embraced by the lusting lover are dissolved in the middle of the speeding stream.

The '**72nd**' is an expression of conflicting emotions, carefully balanced in two quatrains. In the first he is treating her with *amicitia* and *pietas.* In the second he has seen through her: *amicitia* has become a broken bond, but *amor* a more intense yearning. It is a marvellous piece of self-examination mightily expressed.

The next poem is something of a curiosity. The language is again the application of political terminology to personal relations, which fits it firmly into the Lesbia-cycle: *bene uelle, mereri, pium, ingrata, fecisse benigne, unum atque unicum amicum.* The unnamed recipient is one of his rivals, Rufus or Gellius. There are some astonishing sound effects: *quoquam quicquam,* followed by *posse putare pium.* A word is lost from the fourth line: we should perhaps read *immo etiam taedet, taedet obestque magis.* The last line is unique with five elisions in four feet including one across the caesura: *quam modo qui me unum atque unicum amicum habuit.* It is expressive of controlled contempt. Some of the language, *quoquam quicquam* and *unum atque unicum,* make the poem almost a hieratic curse.

The '76th' poem has been, justly, the object of much critical attention. Here we see epigram burgeoning into elegy. A statement of 16 lines is followed by a prayer of 10 lines, each subdivided:

STATEMENT
1-8 General, leading to particular
9-16 Particular

PRAYER
17-22 General, leading to particular
23-6 Particular

Each of these sections is carefully articulated, the cycle of the whole poem being completed by *plum* ('76'.2) being picked up in *pietate* ('76'.27), and that of the prayer by the recurrence of *o di* at start and finish. But 26 lines divide naturally into two blocks divided by the pivotal couplet, which Otto Friess called 'the poem's navel'.

difficile est longum subito deponere amorem.
difficile est, uerum hoc qua lubet efficias.

(It is hard to know whether to punctuate the first line with a query or full stop.) The prayer has none of the accoutrement of the Hellenistic literary prayer—deity, epithet, cult, or site: it is Roman and immediate. The writing is deliberately informal. The first line has a caesura after a trochee in the fourth foot, which is never found in Callimachus or Catullus 64, a violation of Hermann's Bridge. Phrases like *uerum hoc qua lubet efficias* or *siue id non pote siue pote* or *quod non potis est* are conversational. The echoes of his earlier love-poems are clear, but the fever of love has become a fever of disease ('76'.19-22, 51.5-10). Above all, this poem, together with the **'109th'**, applies the language of politics to love.

The Polymetrics

The fourth poem ['4'] is in form an *anathematikon,* a dedication-epigram; only here, as in Callimachus *Epig.* 5 Pf, the speaker is the object dedicated. This allows

for some ingenious ambiguities ('4'.4 *palmulis;* '4'.17 *imbuisse;* '4'.21 *pedem*), and a suggestion that the ship is whispering (*-ss-* comes 11 times in the poem, 3 times in one line); the poet keeps acting as interpreter ('4'.2 *ait;* '4'.6 *negat;* '4'.15 *ait;* '4'.16 *dicit*). The ship is a garrulous slave ('4'.19 *erum*). It is a Greek ship, and uses Greek idiom ('4'.2). It stands on its dignity, a little pompous ('4'.4-5 *siue . . . siue*), boastful of the places it has visited. Unlikely that the boat itself has reached the Lago di Garda: more likely a painting, as in some Greek epigrams. The poem is shaped in *omphalos-form:* it starts in the present, moves backwards in time to the poem's centre and forwards again to the present. Metrically it is a *tour de force,* written in pure iambics with never two consecutive long syllables, no doubt to represent the gentle rocking of the boat. Now the boat has reached haven: the servant has found honourable retirement. What of the poet? 'Dare we think that Catullus is claiming that he too has been tossed on the seas of life, through the darkness of his brother's death and the storm of his love for Lesbia, and has now reached haven? *Senet quiete*—oh! he was young yet, but it is a young man's thought.'

The thirteenth poem ['13'] is technically a *uocatio ad cenam,* a standard *genre.* The first line has all the feel of a genuine dinner invitation, but we soon find that it is whimsical, good-humoured, and parodic. The poet speaks freely, as equal to equal. The first twist is that Fabullus will have a good dinner—if he brings it: food, a pretty girl, wine, salt (a *double entendre* for wit), and laughter. Catullus likes a hypothesis followed by *nam.* Here comes the second twist. His purse is empty? No—full—of cobwebs. Eight lines spell out the situation; six provide the conclusion. Fabullus will receive 'pure love'. What does that mean? A girl? But he has been asked to bring one. No—it is something more delightful and cultivated. It's an unguent given *meae* (i.e. hands off!) *puellae* by all the powers of love. Not then an unguent, but her natural scent. But Fabullus must not touch; he must be content to smell—and he will wish to become all nose (had he a very large or very small nose?).

One of the most brilliantly illuminating critical articles on particular poems was produced by Niall Rudd on a quite minor poem, the **'17th'**. The structure of the poem gives 11 lines on the town he calls Colonia and its rickety bridge (structured 4-3-4), 11 lines on an indolent husband and his attractive wife (arranged: husband-simile-wife-simile-husband), 4 lines of conclusion picking up words and ideas from earlier in the poem. But the parallelism of the first two sections runs deep. The bridge is personified as male and equipped with incompetent legs, the town as female, lively, eager for a festival, and full of sexual desires. Catullus wants to throw the husband into the mud underneath as a propitiatory offering, and at the same time receiving a drastic version of current medical treatment for lethargy. H. Akbar Khan has added to this magnificent analysis the fact that the language is sexually highly charged, as one would expect of a poem in the Priapean metre. We should note also the characteristic use of expressive elision for the tenacious effects of the mud, *praecipit(em) in lutum* ('17'.9), and especially the last two lines

et supin(um) anim(um) in graui derelinquere caeno,
ferre(am) ut soleam tenac(i) in uoragine mula. ('17'.25-6)

The 29th poem ['29']is seen by some commentators as a key poem both for the poet's political stand and for his use of sexual invective. It is not totally clear precisely to whom the poem is addressed—Caesar and Pompey; Caesar, Pompey, and Crassus; Caesar, Pompey, and the people of Rome. The poem (in pure iambics again, and a *tour de force*) is shaped as a riddle, with a series of questions, such as P. Clodius used in political mob-oratory[,] eliciting the answers he wanted from the crowd. But the poem is an attack on Mamurra, lackey to his patrons and the real power behind them. He is called *diffututa mentula* ('a far-fucked cock'), and charged with lust of money, as he is later charged (assuming he is the Mentula of 94, 105, 114-15) with lust for land, other people's wives, and poetic glory. At the end *perdidistis,* expressly of Pompey and Caesar, and a current political term to describe their policies puts them in the same boat as Mamurra.

The hymn to Diana ('34') has been the subject of some interesting recent observations. Wiseman notices how the *lex Gabinia Calpurnia* of 58 B.C. made much of the ancient sanctity of Delos as birthplace of Apollo and Artemis, and the importance of the island practically for the corn-supply as well as religiously, and notes how in Catullus Diana, not normally a goddess of agriculture, 'fills the farmer's barns with grain'. Critical opinion is hardening that this was not a literary exercise but a genuine hymn.

Acme and Septimius ('45') is a good example of a poem in which critical opinion has shifted. Until comparatively recently the normal (but not universal) view was that it was a charming account of mutual love. It is indeed a carefully constructed symmetrical poem with three stanzas, the first two of 9 lines each, 7 followed by a refrain, and a carefully shaped 8—line comment by an observer. The formulaic language of marriage is introduced. In the first line and a half the lovers seem to intertwine: *Acmen Septimius suos amores/tenens in gremio.* But more recent interpreters have noted irony throughout. The omens which form the refrains are odd: is *sinistra* well-omened with Roman use or ill-omened with Greek use, when she bears a Greek name, he a Roman? How many omens

are there? Is the sneeze right and left doubly favourable or ambiguous? The long abstract *approbationem* is an effect Catullus always uses with a dark shadow ('7'.1, '12'.12, '21'.1, '21'.8, '23'.14, '32'.18, '38'.5, '38'.7, '47'.5 and probably '48'.6). Septimius is full of exaggerated rhetoric. Acme is *fidelis,* Septimius is *misellus.* The accounts do not precisely balance. The poem is about Acme, and the poet is identified with her—a psychologically important point which recurs through the poems. The poem is datable to 55 by reference to the lion (Pompey used 600 in the 'games' that year) and Britain. We have another poem from the same year, full of references to India and Africa, Syria and Britain: and it is a bitter rejection of love ('11'). *Acme and Septimius* ends not on an affirmation hut a question. Catullus knows the answer.

Francis Cairns has helped us to understand the next poem ('46'). It is a *syntaktikon,* a poem for a journey, in this instance between two places abroad, though on the way from abroad home. Cairns notes the variants introduced by Catullus. A statement about the spring weather replaces the normal prayer for a safe voyage at the outset. He does not address the people of the province, but himself: this makes the poem much more internalized. He expresses joy instead of the conventional regret at leaving. Wiseman has further noted that here and elsewhere Catullus tends to allude to foreign parts in terms of their economic assets. Cairns suggests that the poet's innovations allow him to use a *genre* not normally associated with pleasure for an expression of joy. This is indeed typical of Catullus's often unexpected use of his medium. There are two other points to notice. Bithynia was the scene of his brother's death and the line which he refers to it is extraordinary in its sound effects: *Nicaeaeque ager uber aestuosae.* The other is the tinge of Epicureanism at the last. The governor, Memmius, was an Epicurean patron; friendship was a strong Epicurean quality; *dulces* a favourite Epicurean term. Like the atoms, the friends are to be scattered; in the end *omnes manet nox.* Pleasure is not unalloyed; happiness is the greatest excess of pleasure over pain—or the smallest excess of pain over pleasure.

It is hard to see how readers have failed to detect the irony which underlies the address to Cicero ('49'), though some have taken it as a literal expression of gratitude. Catullus belonged to a different literary circle to Cicero; he was less compromising towards the triumvirs, and would not have liked Cicero's volte-face over Vatinius; and Cicero's relations with Clodia had oscillated from possible sexual involvement to the exposure of her as a worthless nymphomaniac. The poem begins with a highflown ironic phrase *disertissime Romuli nepotum* (cf. '58'.5); Cicero was *inquilinus ciuis.* It passes into another mock-heroic formula. It uses a mode of address (*Marce Tulli*) appropriate to state occasions and ludicrously incongruous in hendecasyllabics. It pivots on *gratias tibi maximas Catullus* with a grotesque near-rhyme to *Marce Tulli.* It ends with a doubly ambiguous compliment. Catullus does not believe he is *pessimus poeta;* in which case Cicero is not *optimus patronus.* But he was *omnium patronus,* who took all cases, good or bad.

This is a small selection only of recent interpretations of the polymetrics, but sufficiently indicative of contemporary approaches.

The Second Book

The four longer poems which constitute the second scroll have received their share of attention. Apart from the standard commentaries, the wedding-hymn for Manlius Torquatus and Junia Aurunculeia has been the subject of an extended commentary by P. Fideli and some pertinent remarks by Gordon Williams; the second wedding-hymn elicited a major article by no less a scholar than E. Fraenkel; *Attis* and *Peleus and Thetis* have attracted a host of interpreters.

The first of the marriage-hymns is strongly personal, Greek in form, Roman in ritual content, almost as if the poet were creating a new world. The poem is dramatic. The marriage has not yet taken place; we pass from an indeterminate scene via the bride's house to the groom's; the whole is a brilliant literary construct. It is truly hymnic, starting with a formulaic address to the deity, and later uses hieratic, archaic language. There are brilliant visual and colour effects throughout. The poet's characteristic diminutives (and pseudo diminutives such as *tremulus*) express tenderness. Elision is exquisitely used to express union:

> qui rapis tener(am) ad uirum
> uirgin(em), o Hymenae(e) Hymen ('**61**'.3-4)

or

> ment(em) amore reuinciens
> ut tenax heder(a) huc et huc
> arbor(em) implicat errans ('**61**'.33-5)

The repetition of a single word or root is skilfully used, as in *domum dominam uoca* ('**61**'.31) or *quod cupis cupis* ('**61**'.197). But Manlius was at least probably the friend in whose house Catullus enjoyed union with Lesbia ('**68**'.67), and we cannot help but note allusions to his own experience. After all Sappho was the great exponent of the marriage-hymn, and Sappho was inescapably associated with the Lesbia he named after her (see '**61**'.64-5; '**51**'.1 and '**68**'.141; '**61**'.212: '**51**'.5; '**61**'.199-203; '**7**'.3-8; '**61**'.89, '**188**'; '**11**'.23; '**61**'.180: '**68**'.71; '**61**'.225; '**68**'.2). Behind his prayer for his friend's happiness lurks his own pain, and that adds power to his feelings and his writing.

There is less to say about '**62**'. It is less personal, more artificial. The singing competition stands in the traditions of pastoral poetry: it is carefully but not precisely balanced, and contains some magnificent imagery and writing. Catullus has put remarkable imaginative power into differentiating the girls from the boys. Fraenkel's conclusion is an excellent appreciation: 'Lovers of Catullus may disagree about the relative merits of the two wedding poems, **"LXI"** and **"LXII"**. Many will prefer the lyric poem on account of its wealth of realistic detail, its vigorous humour, its precious information about very ancient rituals, and its winged and gay rhythms, which somehow call to mind another song, "Quart' è bella giovinezza, che si fugge tuttavia!" There are others to whom the softer notes of **"LXII"** will appeal with equal force. A scholar must not pretend to be a judge on such matters. I will rather conclude by saying that *Vesper adest* has one important characteristic in common with all that is best in Roman poetry: it could never have come into being without the Greek seed, and at the same time it owes its strength, its freshness, and its particular flavour to the soil of Italy out of which it grew.'

Attis has always fascinated, not least as a metrical *tour de force*. The galliambic metre requires a minimum of 10 short syllables in every 16, 4 or 5 of them consecutive, an exceedingly difficult effect to maintain over all but 100 lines in a language as weighty as Latin. The poem is carefully constructed:

> (a) Narrative introduction 1-5
>   (b) The frenzy of Attis 6-11
>   (c) Attis sings in ecstasy 12-26
>   (d) The frenzy of the Gallae 27-34
> (e) Sleep 35-8
>   (f) Sanity: return to shore 39-47
>   (g) Attis speaks in despair 48-73
>   (h) Frenzy: return to mountain 74-90
> (i) Poet's closing prayer 91-3

The alternation between *narratio* and *oratio* is carefully controlled, and narrative is kept to a minimum. There is a constant seesaw between the subjective and the objective. The poem is about speed, desire, and madness; all three are contained in the opening sentence. *Citatus* is a keyword; there is an astonishing poetical effect in *citato cupide pede tetigit* ('**63**'.2), and throughout a striking succession of verbs of motion.

Nature is the backcloth to this drama. The other keyword is *remora,* areas of the wildwood sacred to its deity. Dawn is symbolic of an awakening to the truth. Attis goes down to the sea. But the sea is *ferum,* and Attis himself *liquida mente* and *animo aestuante.* His words are formally an *epibaterion,* an address on reaching the end of a journey. But it is inverted. He praises the place he has left, its people, its buildings, its life. He attacks the place he has reached, a snowy wilderness, whose only citizens are wild animals, *cerua si-luicultrix* and *aper nemoriuagus*—the compound epithets, generally clumsy in Latin, are brilliantly evocative. Animal imagery dominates the poem. *Citatus* and *stimulatus* are habitually used of animals. A *nemus* was a place for grazing. Attis calls the initiates *uaga pecora* ('**63**'.13). They break into animal noises (*reboant, ululatibus, remugit*). Only he is no herdsman, but to be compared to a heifer ('**63**'.33).

The poem is wrung from the poet's own experience. It is surely a product of his visit to Asia. In '**68**' Asia, his brother's death, and his own unhappy love are intertwined. The *furor* which seized Attis had seized him too in his love ('**7**'.10 *uesano*). Fanatical devotion and despairing disillusion were marks of his own state. This book has comprised two marriage-songs: it will go on to the uncertain blessings of the union between Peleus and Thetis. This too is a marriage-song of a sort, since Attis was consort to Cybele; it is a kind of anti-epithalamium. Catullus can feel the loss of sex; in a curious way he can identify with the female in Attis. Both regret their *furor*. But Attis cannot escape. Catullus can; the final prayer is his, and it is parallel to the prayer for healing in '**76**'.3

The '**64th**' poem is by a long way the longest of the long poems, and almost certainly one of the latest, and has attracted a good deal of attention. Wilamowitz wrote 'This poem is the work in which Catullus wanted to write his masterpiece.' Our evidence is of course internal, but it is clear enough. Richard Jenkyns in a wide-ranging study justified the opinion: 'In *Peleus and Thetis* Catullus aims for a continuous brilliance over a length of four hundred lines; and the extent of his success is astonishing.' Old scholars were less than enthusiastic about it. Positive appreciation starts with a sensitive study by F. Klingner in 1956.

The poem is often called an epyllion or short epic, but that is misleading; it implies that this was a recognized Alexandrian genre, for which the evidence is slight, and that Catullus was writing a work to be judged by the critical canons appropriate to epic, combined with brevity and polish. The poem we have is not really a narrative poem, but a series of tableaux, not a miniature *Iliad* but *sui generis*.

It has two major subjects, the marriage of Peleus and Thetis ('**64**'.151, 265-408) and Ariadne's desertion by Theseus in between. A digression of this sort, producing a literary sonata-form, is not uncommon, but nowhere else does it occupy half the poem.

The whole poem is meticulously shaped.

1 INTRODUCTION 1-30
    (a) The Argonauts 1-11
        (b) Peleus and Thetis 12-21

        (c) The Argonauts 22-30
2 THE WEDDING 31-408
    (i) Human guests 31-277
        (a) Arrival 31-49
            (b) Coverlet 50-266
        (c) Departure 267-77
    (ii) Divine guests
        (a) Arrival 278-302
            (b) Fates 303-83
        (c) Absence today 384-408

Subsections, and especially the Ariadne episode, are planned with a comparable symmetry of structure. Throughout there are careful verbal effects, onomatopoeia, deliberate reminiscences of earlier poets, alliteration and assonance, puns and the like. Jenkyns must be correct in maintaining that this is essentially a poem in its own right, composed with sustained brilliance.

But is that all that can be said? Is it self-contained? J. C. Bramble in an excellent paper pointed to its ambiguities of mood. A number of critics have seen in the poem something more than *l'art pour l'art meme*—a critique of the Rome of the poet's own day, or the concept of the *domus*, or his grief for his dead brother and the ambiguities of his relationship to Lesbia. To suggest that any of these is the theme of the poem is a large overstatement, and Jenkyns for one sweeps them aside. But this allows too little for the ambiguities of tone, the allusions to Lesbia poems (which can hardly be accidental), the darkness which underlies some of the brighter passages. Jenkyns having dismissed Catullus as a moralist, accepts (he can hardly do otherwise) that the conclusion is moralizing: but, if so, it is not impossible that there may be moralizing judgements underlying some of the earlier writing; it would be surprising if there were not.

In short, a poem may serve more than one purpose for a poet. If it is to be his deliberate masterwork he can hardly help pouring into it experiences and attitudes from past and present.

The Elegiac Poems

Catullus began his third volume with a mini-dedication, to Q. Hortensius Hortalus, lawyer, patron, and poet of a very different approach. Catullus had lost his brother. Hortensius tried to encourage him into returning to poetry. Catullus apologized for essaying a translation only, but that translation was of Callimachus. In this way he opens his book of elegiacs with his Greek exemplar, as he will close it with Callimachus and the threat to translate another poem, the vituperative *Ibis*. The opening poem ('**65**') would not be the favourite of many, but there is much to admire in it. He leads gently to his loss: *namque mei nuper Lethaeo gurgite fratris* ('**65**'.5), where the separation of *mei* from *fratris* by the stream of Lethe, and the juxtaposition of *gurgite* *fratris* are equally moving; in the next line we hear the water lapping in *pallidulum . . . alluit.* He uses the language of love: *uitafrater amabilior* ('65'.10). The stock image of the nightingale is not a mere cliche, for he feels that the *domus* has indeed been violated. The glory of the poem is its final image, of the girl who has concealed the love-gift of an apple, jumps up to meet her mother, and to her chagrin sees the apple fall:

> atque illud prono praeceps agitur decursu,
>   huic manat tristi conscius ore rubor.
>   ('65'.23-4)

In the first line the apple seems to hover for an age, then rushes down and bumps heavily on the floor. In the second the bringing together of *tristi conscius* and *ore rubor* shows Latin poetry at its subtlest.

The '**67th**' poem is something of a riddle: of many explanations Giangrande's is the best, especially with the reading *matronae* for *Veronae* ('67'.34) which eliminates a puzzling reference. A man named Caecilius has married. A visitor hears rumours of the wife's infidelity, and questions the house-door, the traditional guardian of faithfulness. The door protests that the lady was deflowered before coming under its protection by her future father-in-law, more vigorous than his son and perhaps even invited to perform the original penetration. But she has been long promiscuous, and that is to be attributed to her character not to the door's negligence. This is an original poem, not least in the portrayal of the door as a garrulous, gossiping, grumbling janitor. It seems to portray a real situation, or there would be no point in the reference to an anonymous adulterer with ginger eyebrows (no doubt identifiable to the readers). The poem ends with a massive *double entendre* (*longus homo est*), and a four-word pentameter forming an ironical contrast between noble form and ignoble content.

The next poem is, as Lachmann once said, the shibboleth of Catullus's interpreters. The basic question (or questions) is: Are '**104**', 41-160 a single poem or two and is the Mallius of the first identical or not with the Allius of the second?

Probably the best explanation is that we have an example of enclosed form, 41-148, addressed to the Muses, being sandwiched between 1-40 and 149-60 (the *munus* of 149 picks up 10 and 32). At '**68**'.41 *me Allius* would be indistinguishable in pronunciation from *Mallius*. At lines 11 and 30 then read with Schöll *mi Alli* for MS *mali*. But this does not prevent Allius, a name in its own right, from being a covername for Mallius or Manlius. There can be no certainty: but this preserves the unity of the poem most economically.

The central section brings together the themes of Laudamia, Troy, the poet's dead brother, and the po-

et's love. It is constructed with a scrupulous care:

41-50 *foedus* of Allius and Catullus—10 lines
51-6 Catullus's own love: torture of desire—6
57-72 Allius's relief compared: epiphany of thedina—16 (13 + 3)
73-86 Laudamia and Protesilaus—14
87-8 Helen—2
89-90 Troy: tomb—2
91-100 dead brother—10
101-2 Greek youth: hearth—2
103-4 Paris—2
105-18 Laudamia and Protesilaus—14
119-34 Laudamia's love compared: epiphany of diua—16 (13 + 3)
135-40 Catullus's own love: torture of self—6
141-60 *foedus* of Catullus and his message—10

Wheeler compared it to a nest of Chinese boxes. Quinn called it an early experiment in stream of consciousness technique, but it is more carefully controlled than that.

Imagery is intensive throughout and leads to the epiphany of the poet's *candida diua*. She was a goddess to him—that goes back to 51 and *candida* goes back to many 'golden' compounds in Sappho. But the omens are not unequivocally favourable. She halts on the threshold, which no bride should do, and her sandal creaks. She reminds the poet of Laudamia, whose husband Protesilaus was doomed to death at Troy—like Catullus's own brother. When the goddess comes back she is identified with Venus. But the mood is strange. She is *lux mea;* but light fades. And then, in an astonishing inversion, she is the promiscuous Jupiter and he the patient Juno. His weary complaisance is a mood unique in Republican poetry, though Propertius can match it. Behind it is a fundamental honesty of outlook. He ends with an assertion of love over infidelity, light over darkness, life over death, joy over sorrow.

An uneven poem, and yet in many ways the climax of the poet's achievement.

A number of the key epigrams have been treated or touched on in other parts of this survey. It remains to mention one or two only of the others.

'**80**' is typical of the poet's eight-line verses, dividing into two quatrains. It is addressed to one of his *bêtes-noires*, Gellius. It is a riddle and answer. The riddle gives no hint of the answer. Gellius's dear little lips, normally rosy, are white as snow. There is one hint only: the day is *mollis,* enervating. The answer starts from rumour, and, as Latin permits, Catullus builds his effect word by word: 'it's big—you do something—it belongs to the middle—it's stiff—you devour it—it belongs to a male.' Gellius is a homosexual practicing fellation, and the final couplet turns the rumour into a certainty, and drives home the obscenity with a pun on *labra* (lips and vats) and agricultural language. Catullus could hate powerfully, and without that we do not understand him.

'**84**' is a poem which continues to fascinate, about a social climber named Arrius. Latin had lost the aspirated consonants which Greek retained. Initial aspirates did exist in Latin, but had tended to drop out in popular speech. The upper classes restored the aspirate: Augustine tells us that in his day it was less serious to hate a *homo* than to pronounce the word *omo*. Sometimes the aspirates were wrongly placed, as in *(h)umidus* and *(h)avere, pulc(h)er* and *triump(h)us*. To place them wrong was the mark of a social climber. Arrius was hoping for a career as an orator: he projected his voice ('**84**'.4, 7) and used the commonplaces of political oratory, *commoda* and *insidias* (*chormmoda* and *hinsidias*): his oratory was a string of mispronounced clichés. So to the point of the poem. A *horribilis* communication has come, that the Ionian waves are now Hionian. It is an elaborate pun. *Horribilis* is used of tossing waves, and chilling news—but there is a further implication that the *spiritus asper,* aspiration or rough wind, has roughened the waves, which have become Hionian or wintry, snowy. And this in turn implies that Arrius's oratory has been a *frigus* or frost. The poem is almost certainly directed against Q. Arrius, 'a man of low birth who without natural ability or higher education, achieved high office, wealth and influence', a hanger-on of Crassus who may have gone to the east with him.

'**93**', a couplet on Caesar, is one of the best-known of the epigrams: Quintilian alluded to it without remembering who wrote it ('**11**'.1.38). The first line is carefully shaped. Caesar is central with three words on either side, the outer words giving the basis emphasis (*nil . . . . placere*). In the second line Catullus does not care to know whether Caesar is *albus an ater homo.* The phrase is said to be proverbial, but Catullus seems to have coined the proverb, borrowing the contrast from wine. Applied to people the words are ambiguous. Perhaps 'brunette' or 'blond', a pleasing thought in the light of Caesar's baldness. Perhaps 'unlucky' or 'lucky': Caesar's luck, like Sulla's, was notorious. The words do not mean 'vicious or virtuous', which is *niger an candidus.* Catullus knows that Caesar is vicious; there is no alternative to that. No need to explore the verses on his henchman Mentula, 'Old Cock' (probably Mamurra); they play wittily on the name.

There is little fresh to say on the moving lines on the poet's dead brother ('**101**'). It is not an epitaph, but it is an adaptation of the *genre.* The poem is an omphalos-form. Catullus starts from his journey, passes through the *inferiae* and his own *munus* to the central couplet which speaks of his loss in language taken from '**68**'.92, and back through the *munus* and the *inferiae* to the final *uale* as he sets out on the journey back. There are some magical touches: the juxtaposition of *mihi tete;* the ambiguity of *indigne* referring both to *miser* and *adempte,* to his brother and himself; the ambiguity of the central couplet, which can follow on from *nequiquam* or anticipate *tamen.* The sound of the poem is carefully contrived. In ten lines twelve words begin with *m* and nine end with *m; it* is a mournful letter, says Quintilian. The *f* and *t* of *frater, fortuna, fletu* add a touch of bitterness. At the last a gentle wind breathes through *aue atque uale.*

Guy Lee (essay date 1990)

SOURCE: An introduction to *The Poems of Catullus,* edited and translated by Guy Lee, Oxford at the Clarendon Press, 1990, pp. ix-xxvi.

[*In the excerpt below, Lee examines Catullus's epigrams, citing the epigrammatist Martial for clarification and comparison.*]

Catullus the Epigrammatist

Because he writes short and intense poems about his own feelings, modern readers tend to think of Catullus as a lyric poet, and indeed Jerome in his *Chronica* (late fourth century A.D.) actually describes him as 'the lyric writer' (*scriptor lyricus*). But Jerome's reason for this label is likely to have been the purely formal one that Catullus used lyric metres (hendecasyllables, sapphics, asclepiads, glyconics, etc.) in Poems '**I-LX**', '**LXI**', and '**LXIII**'. Earlier in antiquity, however, he was classed not as a lyric poet but as an epigrammatist.

Martial, epigrammatist *par excellence,* regards him as the originator of the genre in Latin (see the prose preface prefixed to Book I of his *Epigrams*) despite the fact that Ennius and Lucilius had written epigrams in the second century B.C., and that Calvus and Cinna are known from their Fragments to have written epigrams in the same metres as Catullus. Martial also regards him as the greatest Latin exponent of the genre and his own highest ambition is to be placed second on the list of epigrammatists after Catullus. It should be noted that he counts as epigrams not only the elegiac couplets of '**LXIX-CXVI**' but also the hendecasyllables and iambics of '**I-LX**', because he refers to Catullus' *Passer* as his model, meaning by that word the whole *libellus* whose first word it is, and because he himself includes hendecasyllables and iambics among his elegiacs. Theocritus had done the same in the third century B.C., and Martial's contemporary the younger Pliny states that his own collection of hendecasyllables could just as well be called epigrams. Like Catullus, Martial refers to his verse as *nugae* and to his books as *libelli.*

Martial counts epigram as lowest in the hierarchy of literary genres and specifically states that its subject matter is everyday life: *agnoscat mores Vita legatque suos,* 'Let Life (here) recognize and read about her own behaviour'. According to him epigram as a genre exhibits two features which are likely to repel the squeamish: first, personal abuse; secondly, coarse language (*lasciua uerborum ueritas, id est epigrammaton lingua,* . . . I, *praefatio*). As regards the first of these Martial emphasizes that he himself never attacks real people, even the humblest, in this differing from his predecessors, who did not hesitate to name real names and even great ones (*nomina magna sed et uera*). But as regards the second characteristic, obscenity, he writes: 'I would apologize for it if I were the first to use it, but Catullus, Marsus, Pedo, Gaetulicus, all write like that—so does any epigrammatist worth reading.'

In fact what Martial says about epigram helps us a great deal in understanding Catullus. Admittedly Catullus never mentions the word, but no one would wish to deny that **'LXIX-CXVI'** in elegiacs are epigrams; as Ross has shown they carry on a tradition started in Latin by Ennius. As regards **'I-LX'** the word *iambi,* 'iambics', crops up three times: at **'XXXVI'**. 5 and **'LIV'**. 6 in hendecasyllables, and at **'XL'**. 2 in scazons or limping iambics. Now *iambi* ever since the Greek poet Archilochus' first use of the metre, was a technical term for invective verse, and invective verse, as Martial, tells us, is characteristic of epigram.

Even the reader who reckons that he knows Catullus' work well will be surprised, when he actually counts up its total of obscene and/or abusive poems, to find out how very many of them there are. It is in fact much quicker to list those that contain no element of obscenity or abuse. Among the *Polymetra* they total a mere twenty, viz. **'I-V'**, **'VII-IX'**, **'XIII'**, **'XXXI'**, **'XXXIV-V'**, **'XIV-VI'**, **'XLVIII-LI'**, **'LV'**, **'LVIII B'**—that is, about one third. Among the elegiac epigrams the proportion is even smaller—ten out of forty-nine, viz. **'LXXXV-VII'**, **'XCII'**, **'XCVI'**, **'C-CII'**, **'CVII'**, **'CIX'**, and that includes one (**'LXXXVI'**) which could reasonably be counted out on the ground that it is insulting to Quintia. It must therefore be admitted that at least two-thirds of Catullus' epigrams are such as either 'do not lend themselves to comment in English' (as Fordyce archly observes)or exemplify personal abuse or are at the same time obscene and abusive.

We do not know whether Catullus was the first to lace his collection of epigrams with so much invective or whether this element was already present in similar proportion in contemporary Greek collections. On the one hand, ribald Fescennine verses were a characteristic Latin thing, and Rome was notorious as *maledica*

ciuitas, 'a slanderous community'; on the other hand, Catullus is well known as a *doctus poeta* or scholar-poet (Martial calls him *doctus* on several occasions) and was well acquainted with Greek literature, as is shown by his translations from Sappho and Callimachus, his knowledge of Greek epigram, and his not unlikely connection with the Hellenistic poet Parthenius, a connection emphasized by Clausen. It is perhaps unlikely then that as first of the Latin epigrammatists (if we can trust Martial) naturalizing a fresh Greek genre in Latin he would have departed far from contemporary Greek precedent. This of course is not to deny that his individual epigrams are different from their Greek counterparts, as may clearly be seen by a comparison of Philodemus' invitation to Piso with Catullus' invitation to Fabullus (**'XIII'**), or Meleager's grave-epigram for Heliodora with Catullus' for his brother (**'CI'**). The Latin epigrams have an immediacy and a closeness to the spoken language that is lacking in the more ornate and 'poetical' Greek.

Moreover Catullus attacks real people, his contemporaries, including the great and powerful among them. As Martial implies, this is the cardinal difference between the two poets, and it reflects first of all their different social standing, and secondly the different political state of their times. Both poets were provincials, but Catullus came from a rich and influential family in the neighbourhood of Verona. He had the entrée to high society in Rome and like the satirist Lucilius in the previous century could afford to throw his weight about. Besides, he wrote in the turbulent times of the First Triumvirate of Pompey, Caesar, and Crassus, times marked by political in-fighting, electoral corruption, and public disorder, when he and his friends could safely play the part of a Roman Republican *Private Eye.* Martial, on the other hand, an impoverished citizen from Bilbilis in Spain, lived under the tyranny of the Emperor Domitian, when political freedom was minimal and one had to watch out for informers. Private need and the temper of the times demanded that he attack lay figures. He could count himself lucky to get away with obscenity under an emperor so insistent on public propriety that he buried alive a Chief Vestal Virgin found guilty of immorality.

Catullus' Life and Poetry

A recent book on Catullus begins with this statement: 'We do not know very much about the life of Catullus'. It is true that we have very few hard facts about his life. External information is limited to a mere three or four items. Jerome in his *Chronica* tells us that Catullus was born at Verona in 87 B.C. and died in his thirtieth year in 57 B.C. Unfortunately the second date must be wrong, because there are poems of Catullus which allude to events after 57 B.C.; thus **'CXIII'** refers to Pompey's second consulship, which fell in 55 B.C., and **'XI'** refers to Caesar's invasion of Britain, which took place in the autumn of that same year. It is customary to suppose that Jerome is right about Catullus' age and to choose 54 B.C. as the date of his death and therefore 84 B.C. for his birth.

The one reasonably certain date in his life is that of his service in the province of Bithynia on the staff of the governor Memmius from 57 to the spring of 56 B.C. This date depends on a letter of Cicero to his brother Quintus from which we gather that Memmius is praetor designate for 58 B.C. It was normal for a praetor to remain in Rome during his year of office and in the following year to proceed to a provincial governorship. If Memmius did the regular thing, then the earliest datable poem of Catullus is **'XLVI'**, written in the spring of 56 B.C. when he was on the point of returning from Bithynia to Italy via some of the famous cities of Asia Minor.

Suetonius in his *Life of Julius Caesar* tells us that Catullus' father was accustomed to entertain Caesar, which means that he must have been one of the local aristocrats of Cisalpine Gaul, certainly a land-owner, with a villa on the peninsula of Sirmione on Lake Garda (**'XXXI'**), and Wiseman further suggests that he was a businessman with interests in Spain and Asia Minor. In the same place Suetonius records that Catullus' verses about Mamurra (presumably **'XXIX'** and **'LVII'**) were recognized by Caesar as having brought an indelible stigma on himself, but that when the poet 'made amends' he invited him to dinner.

Apuleius tells us in his *Apologia,* some two hundred years after Catullus' death, the real name of the woman Catullus calls Lesbia, and incidentally provides us with Catullus' own praenomen or first name, thus: 'Gaius Catullus used the name Lesbia for Clodia'. Apuleius will have got this information from Suetonius' *De Poetis,* who in his turn, according to Wiseman, will have had it from Julius Hyginus, librarian of the Palatine Library in the time of Augustus, interested in modern poetry and author of *De Vita Rebusque Illustrium Virorum.*

Apart from these few items of information from other writers we are dependent on Catullus' own poems for knowledge of his life. And in fact they tell us a great deal about the man and the sort of life he led. Indeed it would be true to say that we know more about Catullus from his poetry than about any other classical poet, with the exception of Horace and Ovid. This is because two thirds of his work are concerned with actual moments, incidents, and personalities in his life. Virtually all his epigrams (**'I-LX'** as well as **'LXIX-CXVI'**) are concerned with his emotional reactions to other people, his contemporaries. Even those epigrams concerned with places (**'XXXI'** Sirmio, and **'XLIV'** his farm), things (**'IV'** his yacht, and **'XLII'** his hendecasyllables), or animals (**'II-III'** Lesbia's sparrow)

personify their subjects and treat them as human beings. His reactions to other people usually arise from some event in his daily life: he welcomes a friend back from military service in Spain, records an incident that happened to him in the Forum to his disadvantage, taxes an acquaintance with the theft of some table-napkins, invites a friend to a rather special dinner, complains about being given an anthology of bad poetry at the Saturnalia, advises a friend on a poem, consoles Calvus on the death of his beloved Quintilia, celebrates the publication of Cinna's long-meditated miniature epic. After reading some hundred epigrams about the poet's friends and enemies and about things that happened to him, one feels one knows a good deal about him and the sort of life he led.

Of course this is not to say that one can take everything he tells us as gospel truth. In literary studies, as in most other departments of life, fashion swings from one grotesque extreme to the other. In the nineteenth century many scholars took poetic statements as too literally related to real life; in the twentieth many have believed that poetry has no relation at all to life but exists in a self-referential vacuum or a self-contained world of literary allusion. One even meets sceptics who do not believe that Catullus' Lesbia really existed; and if they mean that the picture of Lesbia one gets from Catullus' poems about her is not a faithful representation of the historical character to whom the pseudonym refers, then they may well be right. But if they mean that the pseudonym is purely fictitious and refers to no historical character at all, then on the evidence of Apuleius they are wrong.

Unfortunately Latin has no definite or indefinite article, so we cannot know whether Apuleius meant 'a Clodia' or *'the* Clodia'. For us *'the* Clodia' is the Clodia attacked by Cicero in his speech *Pro Caelio,* the Clodia married to Metellus Celer, who held the praetorship in 63 B.C. and the governorship of Cisalpine Gaul (Catullus' homeland) the year after that, the Clodia notorious for her sexual licence, who was even rumoured to have murdered her husband Metellus by poison. But this Clodia had two sisters, who also spelt their patrician name of Claudia in the plebeian way as Clodia, following the example of their brother Publius Clodius Pulcher, Cicero's enemy. Which of these three Clodias was Catullus' Lesbia?

Since the Renaissance most scholars have favoured Metellus' Clodia: she was married, which fits with Catullus' admission that the affair was adulterous (**'LXVIII'**. 143-6); she also had an affair with Marcus Caelius Rufus, which fits with Catullus' reference to 'our Lesbia' in **'Poem LVIII'** addresses to a Caelius, and with his hitter complaint in **'Poem LXXVII'** that a Rufus has betrayed him; she would have known Catullus from at least 60 B.C. until 55 when he finally breaks with her in **'Poem XI'**, a space of time which can reasonably allow the affair to be described in **'Poem LXXVI'** as a long love.

The opponents of this identification, however, point out that the first datable poem of Catullus is **'XLVI'**, written just before his return from Bithynia in 56 B.C., and that all the other datable poems (**'IV'**, **'XXXI'**, **'XI'**, **'XXIX'**, **'XLV'**, **'LII'**, **'LV'**, **'LXXXIV'**, and **'CXIII'**) are later than that. Besides, Catullus' Caelius, according to **'Poem C'**, is a native of Verona, whereas Cicero's Caelius Rufus came from the Ancona area; moreover Catullus' Rufus apparently suffers from gout and halitosis (**'LXIX'** and **'LXXI'**), whereas Cicero's Caelius Rufus was an elegant young man about town.

There is also an important metrical argument to be taken into account. It has been pointed out that Catullus' treatment of the first two syllables, or base, of the hendecasyllabic line varies according to an odd pattern. In the 263 hendecasyllables of Poems **'II-XXVI'** there are only four exceptions to spondaic base (two long syllables), viz. **'II'**.4, **'III'**.12 and 17, **'VII'**.2. On the other hand, in the 279 hendecasyllables of Poems **'XXVIII-LX'** there are sixty-three exceptions—thirty-three with iambic base (short, long) and thirty with trochaic (long, short). Now **'Poem I'**, the dedication to Cornelius Nepos, which we can reasonably suppose to have been written last of all the poems **'I-LX'**, has one iambic and three trochaic bases in its ten lines. Professor Otto Skutsch has therefore inferred that Catullus began by sticking strictly to the rule that a hendecasyllable should begin with a spondee, but as time went on gradually relaxed this restriction.

His argument provides a possible means of the relative dating of the hendecasyllabic poems, which Wiseman develops. The earliest datable poem, **'XLVI'**, has spondaic bases only. So too **'Poem X'** (a long one of 34 lines), **'Poem V'** (clearly an early Lesbia poem), and Poems **'VI'**, **'IX'**, **'XII-XV'**, **'XVI'** (clearly later than **'V'**, to which it refers), **'XXI'**, **'XXIII-XXIV'**, **'XXVI'**, **'XXVIII'**, **'XLIII'** (again a Lesbia poem), **'XLVIII'**, **'LVI-LVII'**. In short, according to Wiseman, we have no reason to suppose that any Lesbia poem is earlier than 56 B.C., and therefore Catullus' Lesbia cannot have been Metellus' Clodia, because she was a widow at that time, whereas Catullus states that he was committing adultery.

Fascinating as it may be, the question of Lesbia's identity is not of great importance to Catullus' readers. Its answer leaves his poetry unaffected. He has not wished his readers to identify Lesbia and that is why he has given her a pseudonym. Why did he choose that particular pseudonym? It means literally 'the woman from Lesbos', as *Andria,* the title of Terence's play, means 'the woman from Andros'. Curiously enough a Lesbia occurs in the cast of Terence's *Andria*—as a midwife.

This is not an allusion likely to have occurred to Catullus! Professor Wendell Clausen, who made these points in conversation, believes that Catullus' original readers would have taken Lesbia as the name of a Greek courtesan from Lesbos and that that was what Catullus meant them to do. After all, if we can believe Apuleius, Catullus was committing adultery with an aristocratic Roman lady. He would not wish her to be publicly dishonoured, and moreover he himself disapproved of adultery (**'LXI'**. 97-9). Presumably he first used the pseudonym in **'Poem LI'**, his adaptation of Sappho's famous poem, where it would have most point (for Sappho was a native of Lesbos); so the knowledgeable reader of that poem would naturally associate the name with Sappho. But while this is probably so, Catullus has deliberately concealed the connection from the reader by placing **'Poem LI'** late in his *libellus* and introducing the name without any Sapphic associations in **'Poem V'**. From its appearance in this poem, in which love is implicitly contrasted with money as the thing worth living for, the reader would guess that Lesbia was a Greek courtesan and Catullus not wholly serious. But, on reading on in the collection, he would be amazed by the number, the content, and the quality of the Lesbia poems; for as Lyne has pointed out 'Catullus is the first ancient poet to treat a love-affair . . . in depth, in a related collection of mutually deepening poems', and this treatment was an inspiration to many later poets.

The importance of Lesbia in the life of Catullus, however, must not incline us to underestimate the importance to him of his poet-friends, in particular of Gaius Licinius Calvus (**'XIV'**, **'L'**, **'LIII'**, **'XCVI'**) and Gaius Helvius Cinna (**'X'**, **'XCV'**, **'CXIII'**). In **'XCV'** Catullus greets the publication of Cinna's brief epic narrative poem, or epyllion, the *Zmyrna,* just as the Alexandrian Greek poet Callimachus had greeted the publication of Aratus' *Phaenomena,* and by the epigram's balanced structure and allusive content, by its attack on the verbosity of Hortensius and the *Annals* of Volusius, and by its praise of the small-scale and its scorn for the popular taste for the orotund, indicates, indeed exemplifies, the sort of poetry approved by Cinna and himself. That was the poetry Callimachus had championed, concentrated, subtle, erudite, and allusive, the result of much thought and revision. What Cinna had produced was an epyllion in the contemporary Greek manner, re-telling an out-of-the-way legend about a daughter who fell in love with her own father, deceived him into intercourse, was changed into a myrrh-tree, and in due time split open to bear a son, Adonis. Cinna's bizarre *Zmyrna* (this spelling represents the Greek pronunciation of *Smyrna)* is lost, save for two hexameters, but we have Catullus' own epyllion, **'LXIV'**, as first surviving representative of this new genre in Latin poetry.

No less revealing in its different way than **'XCV'** is

Catullus' epigram '**L**' to Calvus, recording how they spent an evening together drinking and improvising *versiculi* in various metres. Key words here are *ludere, delicati, lepor,* and *facetiae,* pointing to light verse, sophistication and impropriety, elegance, wit, and humour. In fact the poem is intended to be an object-lesson in precisely these qualities, its impropriety being the barefaced declaration of love for Calvus in a poem designed to be read by the general public (Calvus himself would not need to be given the information provided in lines 1-6). The word *versiculi* (for which Quinn in his commentary proposes the translation 'epigrams') has already appeared in '**XVI**', another indecent mock-serious piece, indeed a poetic manifesto intended to justify the sort of poetry that Poems '**I-LX**' represent—and one would not need to justify an already existing type of verse.

Catullus' work mirrors himself, and in it we can clearly see that Lesbia, his brother, his friends, and poetry were the four loves of his life. If he has a message, it can be summed up (surprisingly enough) in that untranslatable word *pietas,* with its overtones of duty, devotion, respect, and even pity. He claims to have shown this quality in his love for Lesbia ('**LXXVI**'.2), in his relationship with an unnamed friend ('**LXXII**'.2), and in his vocation as a poet ('**XVI**'.5). Although the word does not occur in the famous farewell to his brother ('**CI**'), that grave-epigram is unmistakably an embodiment of *pietas.* But his *pietas* goes unrewarded. Lesbia spurns him; his friend betrays him; he loses his brother. His ideal lives on, however, in the mind of Virgil, whose own observation of life may well have combined with his reading of Catullus to extend its scope into the domain of public life and to make it the key to the character of his epic hero Aeneas.

William Fitzgerald (essay date 1992)

SOURCE: "Catullus and the Reader: The Erotics of Poetry," in *Arethusa,* Vol. 25, No. 3, Fall, 1992, pp. 419-43.

[*In the following essay, Fitzgerald develops "an erotics of Catullus's poetry, and especially the polymetrics, because of the fact that these poems are performances that take place in the context of a still self-conscious and developing conception of sophisticated, urban social behavior."*]

When Lucretius says that the purpose of his poetry is to sweeten the bitter draught of a difficult but beneficial philosophy we tend to take him at his word, and have often set ourselves and others the task of showing how Lucretius goes about his purpose. Catullus' statement that his verses are successful (have *sal* and *lepor*) only if they can sexually arouse hairy men has not

generated much in the way of research. Of the various possible reasons for this, one that we can eliminate is that the poem from which this statement comes has not been taken seriously as Catullan poetics. On the contrary, this poem ("**16**") has been used (I think wrongly) to show that Catullus distinguishes between his life and his poems, and that though the latter are *molliculi ac parum pudici* (8), he himself is not. Even if we do take Catullus to be making a distinction between what is proper (*decet,* 5) for the poet and what is proper for his *versiculi,* we should give some attention to the substance, as well as the fact, of the distinction. This means that we should consider the sense in which sexual provocation might be a factor in Catullan poetics, and it means first of all that we must look at the relation of poet to audience.

Of course, poem "**16**" is not a reflection on poetry that stands outside the practice itself, and what it says about the relation between poet and reader needs to be considered in the context of the poetic game that it is playing. In what follows I will be examining a group of poems ("**1**," "**2**," "**15**" and "**16**") that are connected insofar as, directly or indirectly, they put into play the relation between poet and reader in a sexual context. These are particularly important poems because they take us to the heart of that combination of social performance, risqué sexuality and aesthetic sophistication that is the essence of Catullan poetics. To see these poems in relation to each other is to see a peculiarly Roman articulation of spheres that are to us distinct; one of the most intriguing aspects of the Catullan corpus is the way that Catullus explores the situation of being a poet as a new kind of social performance, and in these particular poems we can examine what we might call the erotics of that performance.

The first two poems present us with two delightful objects, almost toys: the *lepidum novum libellum* ("smart new little book," "**1**".1), with its smooth surfaces and the sparrow that is the *deliciae* of its mistress. Not only are these both, as I shall argue, erotic objects, but they are also part of a game that the poet is playing with his audience. Just as there is something ambiguous about the book in "**1**" (physical object or poetic work?) so there is an ambiguity about the sparrow, which may be an innocent pet or the vehicle of a sexual metaphor. There is in both poems a play with surface and depth that eroticizes our relation to these objects which are both offered and withdrawn, which both hide and reveal: the *nugae* might, after all, *be* something ("**1**".3-4) and Lesbia's play with the sparrow might be part of the narrative of a love affair; the poems take their character from the gesture with which these objects are presented to us. It is Catullus' focus on the dynamics of the relation between poet and audience, his exploration of the possibilities of this new kind of relation in the context of the Questionable, which is the category under which any performance falls in Roman culture, it is this that constitutes the distinctiveness of his poetics, and for which there is no equivalent among the Alexandrians.

My second pair of poems also consists of one that is explicitly about the relation between poet and readers ("16") and one that appears to be an episode from the erotic life of Catullus ("15"). In the former Furius and Aurelius are attacked for concluding that Catullus is effeminate from the evidence of all those kisses they have read about in his poetry. It is here that he retorts that his poetry only has the requisite charm *(sal* and *lepor,* "16".7) if it can excite hairy men. In poem "15" Catullus simultaneously commends the boy that is the object of his affections to Aurelius and warns him to keep his hands off. The violent phallic threats with which 15 ends and with which 16 both begins and ends reflect the Roman obsession with relations of dominance and subordination, an obsession that is amply attested by Catullus' poetry. In both cases Catullus has made himself vulnerable by virtue of what he has entrusted to Furius and Aurelius; the combination of entrusting and withholding in "15" recapitulates, as I shall argue, the giving and withholding that characterizes poem "1", but in a much more aggressive context. These poems raise the question of the relation between poet and reader from the standpoint of the poet's vulnerability, his lack of control over the transaction, and so provide the counterpart to poems "1" and "2", which speak from a position of confidence. That the vulnerability of the poet is expressed in relation to a phallic threat from other men has to do with the provocative performance that he stages as poet and with the culture's determination of the particular form of pleasure that he purveys as effeminate. Both here and in the case of poems "1" and "2" I will be considering the Aesthetic as a function of the positionality of agents in a transaction, for the aesthetic sphere is characterized by Catullus as one in which the positionality of agents is more ambiguous, more manipulable than it is in other spheres of the culture.

Poem "1" is the logical place to begin, for it must in some way be programmatic. To call this poem a dedication would be to smother the complexity of its gesture, for what Catullus does in this poem is to put the book into circulation, to give it to its readership, and the nature of the object is to a great extent constituted by the form of this gesture. The giving of the freshly completed book to Nepos is a complicated act because it stands at a nodal point between Nepos' earlier approval of Catullus' *nugae* and the reception of posterity:

> quare habe tibi quidquid hoc libelli
> qualecumque; quod, (o) patrona virgo,
> plus uno maneat perenne saeclo.

> So have this little book for what

it's worth, and, O patron and virgin,
May it stay fresh for more than one
generation.

The phrase *habe tibi* is, as Fordyce points out, "a regular phrase of Roman law in reference to the disposal of property," but both in the legal sense and in the colloquial sense which implies, as Fordyce puts it, "a certain indifference," there is often a contrast between what is given and what is retained. In this case, it is the same thing that is both given and retained (*habe tibi . . . quod maneat*), though *maneat perenne* means that it will not be Catullus who will keep what he has so casually given, but rather a posterity that transcends them both. There is a real connection between the lightness of Catullus' relation to his *nugae* and their continued freshness as aesthetic objects. Catullus keeps nothing, for the book goes on the one hand to anyone who can find something in these trifles and on the other to a posterity that continues to find them fresh. Nepos gets this attractive little book because he made something of the *nugae,* but then he can't get satisfaction because the virgin sees to it that it will remain fresh for future generations. The erotic aspect of the transaction becomes clear if we turn to the opening lines of the poem, where the newly completed book is described as *arida modo pumice expolitum* ("just smoothed with the dry pumice," "2"). The *pumex* has two uses in the literary sphere: to smooth the ends of the scroll in the final stages of the book's preparation and to erase and correct the work prior to publication. The first use of the *pumex* draws attention to the book's attractions and availability; the book becomes an erotic object, as Horace indicates when he berates his book of epistles for its eagerness to prostitute itself to the public:

> Vertumnum Ianumque, liber, spectare videris,
> scilicet ut prostes Sosiorum pumice mundus
> odisti clavis et grata sigilla pudico;

> You seem, book, to look towards Janus and
>   Vertumaus [bookseller's area],
> Wanting to offer yourself smooth with the
>   pumice of the Sosii [booksellers],
> You shun keys and seals, which are welcome
>   to the chaste.

Horace's *pumice mundus* plays on the fact that pumice was used as a depilatory and Catullus' *pumice expolitum* also associates the book's smart and appealing exterior with sexual attractiveness and availability. But this aspect of the book, its immediate appeal and, so to speak, consumability, is conveyed by the same words that also convey the labor of composition and the literary perfectionism implied by liberal use of the eraser, features of the book that ensure its continued life beyond this generation.

Modern commentators have tended to concentrate on showing how this poem is an Alexandrian or Neoteric literary manifesto: the lightness and modesty with which Catullus offers his book is all part of a display of allegiance to Alexandrian principles. This approach usually generates a language of surface and depth which says as much about modern scholarship as it does about the poem: this apparently light and unprepossessing poem conceals references to Alexandrian watchwords and aesthetic attitudes, and once these have been identified by the scholar, the poem reveals itself as a serious work of high art. The work of the scholar protects us from the poem's trivial surface. The conception of this poem as a coded and concealed masterpiece posing a riddle for the learned reader is compatible with much of what we know of the Alexandrians. But there is another dimension to the poem, which is more distinctively Roman, and that is its social gesture. The associations of words like *pumex* and *expolitum* in Latin are not only Alexandrian; smoothness and polish are connected in a literary context by the elder Seneca, who, when he says, *Ite nunc et in istis vulsis atque expolitis et nusquam nisi in libidinibus viris quaerite oratores* ("Go ahead, look for orators among those plucked exquisites, only men in their lust"), reminds us that these qualities have a dubious sexual connotation at Rome. Catullus' book has a teasing sexuality that is provocatively effeminate. What I am suggesting here is that Catullus is playing with the particularly complex relation between poet and reader(s) through the way he relates the giving of the book and the withholding of the book as a kind of teasing. The aesthetics of this poem is not one of surface and depth (Catullus professes an urbane indifference to the trivialities he offers Nepos, but finally reveals his sense of their true worth) or even of paradox (it takes the harsh application of dry pumice to make something that never dries up: *perenne,* 10), but rather of teasing.

Catullus teases Nepos with his book rather as Lesbia teases her sparrow with her finger in the next poem ("**2**".3-4), or perhaps as Catullus teases his readers with intimations of sex, only to turn the tables on them in the final lines, where once again virginity intervenes:

> tecum ludere sicut ipsa possem
> et tristis animi levare curas
> tam gratum est mihi quam ferunt puellae
> pernici aureolum fuisse malum
> quod zonam soluit diu ligatam.

> If I could play with you as she does
> and lighten the gloomy troubles of my mind—
> that is as pleasing to me as they say
> was the golden apple to the swift-footed girl
> which loosened her girdle, so long tied.

We are now told that the game with the *passer* is itself the consummation to be desired; it would be as pleasing to Catullus as the apple that brought the end of virginity to Atalanta, and in being *as* pleasing it denies us the untying of the knot, for the game that suggested sex now becomes its alternative or substitute. Like that "something" which Nepos saw in Catullus' *nugae,* but which immediately fades into the suave surface of the urbane tone, the sexuality of the *passer,* or those who play with it, never comes into focus. Catullus brings up the subject of intercourse only to hold it at a distance, leaving the game with the *passer* suggestive but ambiguous. The sexual innuendo is now transferred to Atalanta, whose virginal mind is no doubt incapable of understanding what *we* know about her reaction to the apple; so the impenetrable and teasing sophistication of Catullus offers us its own supplement, the penetrable, half-innocent mind of Atalanta, whose ambiguity we are in a position to observe knowingly. Of course, the poem I am describing is to be found in none of the modern texts of Catullus, for if we detach the puzzlingly "inappropriate" simile of Atalanta and the apple with which the poem ends in the manuscripts (and call it, say, "2b") then we have a poem that falls into line with one of the most common ways of thinking about Catullus: the trivial Lesbia plays with her sparrow and so assuages her desire for Catullus, which he wishes he could do himself, but being a man and a great poet, he feels more deeply than she. This truncated version of the poem provides a neat parallel to the usual interpretation of the dedication: just as Catullus writes *nugae,* but by virtue of the care he lavishes on them proves himself a dedicated and serious Alexandrian poet, so the intensity of his love for Lesbia transcends its rather trivial object. I doubt that editors would have been so impressed with the problems of the manuscript text of the end of poem "**2**" were they not so satisfied by the kind of reading made possible by detaching the last three lines.

If the reconstituted poem "**2**" ends not with a *cri de coeur* anticipating the serious Catullus of the later love poems ("**8**", "**11**" and the elegiacs), but with a teasing of the audience that exploits rather than transcends female sexuality, then how should we understand the relation between poems "**1**" and "**2**"? My interpretation of poem "**1**" has stressed its gesture, the interplay between giving and withholding, rather than its putative statement (a coded commitment to Alexandrian poetics), and the play with surface and depth rather than the layering of one on the other (an urbane pose on a proud claim to poetic achievement). Similarly, I see poem "**2**" as a teasing of the audience with intimations of sex and hints of a psychological and biographical background to Catullus' interest in Lesbia's play with the *passer.* The truncating of the poem by the editors provides a clear layering of surface and depth, so that the different relations of the characters to the game with the *passer* gives us a reassuring sense of what it is that allows us to say that the trivial is trivial.

In the same way that the gesture of poem "**1**" teases us with the notion that the *nugae are* something, without allowing us a clear separation between what is nugatory and what is something, so the address to the *passer* in 2 suggests that there is something behind this game only to leave us with suggestiveness. The nugatory is not a matter of a particular kind of content or even style; it is a form of game with the audience.

The detachment of Catullus from his book/*nugae* in relation to his audience has two sides: one which makes the book accessible and another which withdraws it; similarly, the teasing sexuality of the game with the *passer* ends up by splitting into the impenetrable mind of Catullus and the penetrable mind of Atalanta. It is the determination of Catullus to remain on the level of the suggestive, and not to resolve the literary and sexual foreplay with the *passer,* that maintains the voyeuristic pleasure of the audience; the male observer who shows us Lesbia at her play does not interpose his desire, instead he teases us to enter his mind (*tam gratum est mihi quam ferunt puellae*) which eludes us as it offers us in exchange the virgin Atalanta. Catullus' non-consummatory desire with respect to Lesbia is the prerequisite for his flirtation with his readership. This is as true of the two *basia* poems that incur the suspicions of Furius and Aurelius as it is of poem "**2**".

As a transition to my next pair of Catullan poems, where the relation between reader and poet is embedded in the more anxious and violent context of sexual relations between men, I would like to consider a passage from one of Pliny's letters. Pliny was a great admirer of Catullus and published, evidently with considerable success, *nugae* in the Catullan style. Writing to Pontius, he explains how a serious man such as himself came to write hendecasyllabics. It happened that one summer morning he had read to him the work of Asinius Gallus in which the latter compares his father to Cicero. In this work there is an epigram of the great man to his slave Tiro in which Cicero complains that Tiro had reneged on his promise of some kisses. This sticks in Pliny's mind and when he retires for his midday nap and finds that he can't sleep he reflects on the fact that great orators enjoyed and respected this kind of poetry; not one to be left behind, Pliny tries his now unpracticed hand at writing verse himself and quickly sketches out an account of what it was that had inspired him to write (*id ipsum, quod me ad scribendum sollicitaverat, his versibus exaravi*). In these verses he describes how he came across the epigram of Cicero, notable for the same genius with which Cicero wrote his serious works and for showing that the minds of great men rejoice in *humanis salibus multo varioque lepore.* He then describes Cicero's epigram and concludes:

> "cur post haec" inquam, "nostros celamus amores

> nullumque in medium timidi damus atque fatemur
> Tironisque dolos, Tironis nosse fugaces
> blanditias et furta novas addentia flammas."

> "After this," I said, "why should I conceal my loves
> and be afraid to make my contribution and confess
> that I know the tricks of Tiro and the teasing flirtation and the cheats that add new flames."

This account of the beginning of the path that led Pliny to Catullan hendecasyllabics is itself clearly influenced by Catullus "**50,**" which also describes how the poet came to be writing the present poem in a fit of insomnia brought on by his excitement with a day spent with his friend Calvus. The spirit of friendly competition in the writing of verse is common to both poems, for Catullus describes how he and Calvus, having agreed to be *delicati,* spent the day swapping verses, which caused Catullus to become inflamed with Calvus' *lepor.* The poems also share a homosexual theme, with Catullus describing his excitement in the language of love and Pliny confessing to his own homosexual experience. There is more to the homosexual element in these poems than the desire to appear sophisticated in the Greek fashion. When Pliny decides to jump on the bandwagon, he asks why he should conceal his love (or love poetry) and timidly avoid making his contribution (*nullumque in medium timidi damus*); he confesses that he too knows the tricks of a Tiro, the flirtation (*fugaces blanditias*) that causes new flames. The logic of the parallel with Cicero's epigram requires that Pliny be saying that he too has been tormented by a provocative and flirtatious boy, but the event that Pliny is describing in this poem, his decision to join in Cicero's *lascivum . . . lusum,* allows us to understand Pliny's statement that he knows Tiro's tricks as a statement of his own flirtatious abilities. To publish erotic poetry is to play a provocative game with one's audience which means adopting the position of the flirtatious Tiro. Pliny's response to Cicero is a kind of blow up of the game that Catullus and Calvus played, a quasi-erotic game of mutual provocation, with Catullus' *tabellae* for a bed (*Hesterno, Licini, die otiosi/ multum lusimus in meis tabellis,* "**50**".1-2); Catullus says that he and Calvus had agreed to be *delicatos,* an adjective that spans the erotic and the aesthetic, but always implies effeminacy. In a sense it is the mark of the great man to feel himself superior enough to the attitudes of common society to be able to play at being the *delicatus;* Pliny here links himself with Cicero by joining in the game, and the game, like the playing of Catullus and Calvus, has to be questionable, risqué; look at the extraordinary phrase he uses of the way his literary activity snowballs from the incident he has just described:

transii ad elegos; hos quoque non minus
celeriter
explicui, addidi alios *facilitate corruptus.*

I moved on to elegies; these too I finished off
quite as
swiftly; I added others, *seduced by my own
fluency/ease.*

In poems **"15"** and **"16"** Catullus addresses directly the sexual connotations of his poetic teasing as they determine the power relations between poet and reader. These poems explore the poet's vulnerability: the homosexual content of the poems and the phallic nature of the threat presented by the reader indicate that the issue here is the positionality of reader and poet, an issue raised by the provocative role of the poet already explored in poems **"1"** and **"2,"** and this provocation or teasing casts the poet in the role of the effeminate or subordinate.

The first of these poems concerns the threat posed by the penis of the addressee to whom the poet's boy is commended; it plays with the very Roman institution of commendation in the same kind of way that poem **"1"** played with legal language (*habe tibi*). To commend someone to somebody is both to draw attention to the commendee's qualities and to entrust that person to the would-be patron. A potential conflict arises when the commendee is an object of desire. Catullus commends himself and his love (*meos amores*, **"15"**.1) to Aurelius, but begs him to keep his hands off the boy. The twist in the commendation is that the boy is to be protected not from the usual external corrupting influences but from the voracious and indiscriminate penis of Aurelius himself. The basic gesture of this poem then is similar to that of poem **"1,"** not only in the combination of giving and withholding, but also in the twist given to a Roman social ritual (the book is dedicated to Nepos, but the Muse is the *patrona;* the boy is commended to Aurelius, but it is Aurelius from whom the boy must be protected). When we consider that the fragment that precedes this poem is addressed to the readers of Catullus' verses, if any should address themselves to his *ineptiae* and not shrink from laying their hands on his work (**"14b"**), and that the poem that follows it, addressed to Furius and Aurelius, is directed against those who have misinterpreted his more risky verses, it appears that the problematic act of entrusting in this poem might also be about publication. Not only are the addressees of **"15"** and **"16"** the same, but the issue of *pudicitia* and *castitas is* also common, for in both cases Catullus is concerned to withhold from Aurelius (along with Furius in **"15"**) some core of purity from what has been entrusted to them (compare *castum* and *pudice* in **"15"**.4-5 to *parum pudicum* and *castum* in **"16"**.4-5).

Catullus' use of an erotic framework to explore the

anxieties and ironies of publication in **"15"** goes back to Theognis, who complains that although he has given Kyrnos wings of fame so that he will be present at all banquets, where he will lie on the lips of men, the boy deceives him with words (237-254 W). Theognis has made Kyrnos available to all except himself and is deceived by the very medium that he has so effectively used on Kyrnos' behalf. The same kind of paradox occurs in Callimachus' famous epigram which begins with his programmatic statement "I hate the cyclic poem," goes on to list other forms of the public (*ta demosia*) that he hates and then concludes: "Lysanie, you are beautiful, yes beautiful—but before the echo has spoken this clearly, someone says 'Another has you'. Here the erotic relation provides the same kind of ironic reflection on the poet's alienation from his own words and intentions as it does in Theognis' lines. The pun between *kalos* (beautiful) and *allos* (another) and the association of the echo with the words of another puts Callimachus' words, like his desires, in the public realm, contradicting the literary principles based on exclusivity; as soon as Callimachus moves from hate to love, from criticism to celebration, he finds himself in the world of *ta demosia,* where he cannot have what he wants: the beautiful boy belongs to another just as certain forms of literary beauty have already been claimed by other authors. Callimachus' sophisticated irony works through juxtaposition and parataxis. We do not know exactly *how* the final erotic couplet reflects on the foregoing; the two voices, the split between desire and power, the mocking echo, all suggest that these lines stand in an ironic relation to the definitive pronouncements that make up the rest of the poem, and that the poet's relation to *ta demosia* is complex: is it sour grapes or a realistic sense of the possible that prompts Callimachus' renunciation of the Public, in view of the fact that what he finds beautiful belongs to another? As in Theognis and Catullus the erotic relation dramatizes the alienation that comes with entering the public world of literature. Callimachus assumes that we don't need things spelled out for us, that this deadpan juxtaposition says it all to those who know, and so he includes us in that Olympian perspective of his so well described by Veyne (1988.18-19). For Catullus, the relation between poet and reader is the issue; in late republican Rome literature has not yet become the institution that it was for the librarians of Alexandria, and to write poetry is still a questionable social activity, so Catullus focuses not on his relation to tradition and to other poets, but to the reader. Catullus embeds his anxious irony in a particular social transaction, for he is interested in the peculiar nature of the contract between reader and poet.

Although the literary issues in these two poems are different, my comparison is warranted by the fact that Catullus recalls Callimachus' poem in his own. Callimachus equates his hatred of the cyclic poem to his dislike of the path that "bears the crowd this way and that" (*hode kai hode,* 2); Catullus tells Aurelius that he is not worried about the threat to his boy from the populace ("**15**".7-8):

> istos, qui in platea *modo huc modo illuc*
> in re praetereunt sua occupati.

> those who pass by on the street now this way
> and now that, engaged in their own affairs.

Callimachus' path, the way of a debased literary convention that accommodates the masses, now contains the workaday Romans who present no threat to Catullus' boy, and the boy himself is derived from the flighty beloved (*periphoiton eromenon*) who features next in Callimachus' list of what he hates, another metaphor for the literary world he rejects. Catullus has changed the issue from the poet's relation to a public tradition to the poet's relation to the audience to whom a poem is *entrusted,* and he has cast this issue in terms of the very Roman institution of the *commendatio.* The drama or irony of the poem, though still a matter of the poet's paradoxical relation to the Public, is quite different from that of Callimachus' epigram because it is located in the peculiar dynamics of this act of (re)commendation or entrusting, where the usual distribution of roles has been turned upside down. The potential threat coming from others in the usual situation where an older man takes on the care of a boy is no longer operative, because the outsiders are here scornfully dismissed as those who mind their own business; it is instead Aurelius who, by virtue of his interest in what is being entrusted to him, is the potential threat.

But what is this threat in terms of the literary situation? In the following poem Catullus is defending his own *pudicitia* and *castitas* against imputations of effeminacy by Furius and Aurelius, who have drawn the wrong conclusions from the *milia multa basiorum* ("many thousands of kisses," "**16**".12) they have read of in his poetry. This pair features in one other poem of Catullus ("**11**"), where their long-winded protestations of friendship are answered with a request to take a short and unpleasant message to Lesbia. In "**16**" the duo appear as readers who have judged Catullus from his *versiculi* ("**16**".3), and again a problem arises from the fact that Catullus must entrust his words to them. Here Catullus is concerned with the power relations between poet and reader, beginning with the phallic threat that reverses the positions that Furius and Aurelius, as readers of Catullus' titillating verse, have adopted in relation to the poet, whom they have fixed as one who speaks in the style of a *mollis.* But Catullus, as performer, sees himself as one who turns his audience, however manly they might think themselves, into excitable pathics. His verses have *sal* and *lepor* only (8-11),

> si sunt molliculi ac parum pudici,
> et quod pruriat incitare possunt,
> non dico pueris, sed his pilosis
> qui duros nequeunt movere lumbos.

> If they're a little soft and not quite straight,
> and can incite a tingling, not in boys,
> I say, but in these hairy types,
> whose stiff flanks don't know how to
> undulate.

Catullus has cleverly given *durus* a meaning ("stiff/clumsy") that upsets the paradigm implied by Furius and Aurelius when they call Catullus *mollis:* the hairy types are not flexible enough for the undulations of the pathic, but Catullus, verse will still get them twitching. This puts his readers in rather a different position from that assumed by Furius and Aurelius, who conclude Catullus' effeminacy from his verses ("**16**".3-4).

Martial, Catullus' greatest imitator, plays a similar game with the relationship between poet and reader in a poem addressed to a certain Chrestillus ("**11**".90). Chrestillus wants Martial to imitate the rough style of the old poets, and he disapproves of poems *molli quae limite currunt* ("which move on a soft track," 1). Martial turns the tables on his critic's implication by concluding, after a review of the kind of poetry that Chrestillus likes, with the words *dispeream nisi scis mentula quid sapiat* ("damn me if you don't know the flavor of prick," 8). Depending on whether we take *sapiat* (tastes) as literal or metaphorical we will interpret Chrestillus' approval of the virility of the ancient poets in different ways, and this brings up the interesting question of how the reader is situated in relation to the poet and the poem. Furius and Aurelius are like Chrestillus in that they understand the words of Catullus as revealing an effeminacy that puts him in the feminine position with respect to his male readership; in an analogous way, Chrestillus adopts the masculine position in relation to Martial by comparing his poetry unfavorably to the "manly" kind that he, Chrestillus, admires. The two poets make a similar kind of move in response, which is to emphasize the need that the poetry serves for the reader: Chrestillus is turned on by the rough masculinity of ancient verse, and Catullus' *risqué* verse titillates his readers, who find themselves reacting like pathics. It is not that the two poets hereby reveal the true nature of the poet-reader relationship, but rather that the fluid, sometimes metaphorical nature of the relationship allows them to *play* with positionality.

This kind of maneuvering reflects a general phenomenon in Roman social life, which is the obsessive concern with the position of one person relative to another in terms of power and obligation in any social transaction. The poetry of both Martial and Catullus is a particularly good example of this, for it emphasizes the transactional character of the poem, and of course in the case of Martial this is related to the fact that he is a dependent whose poetry is his means of livelihood. In Catullus the question of the relation between poet and reader is not colored so much by the complexities of dependency as by the new forms of *urbanitas* with its provocative social persona. It may be that the sophistication to which the members of Catullus' circle aspired acquired its *cachet* from being Greek, but the form it takes in Rome is determined by the fact that in its new home it is *questionable.* The Olympian assumption by Callimachus of a shared sophistication that need never itself become an issue is quite impossible at Rome, where the poet must negotiate the complicated implications of a word like *delicatus.* The juxtaposition of poems **"15"** and **"16"** in Catullus suggests that the issue of **"16"** is not Catullus' morals per se, but the kind of relationship that pertains between reader and poet in the context of this questionable sophistication.

But what is the role of the erotic in this poetics? In what sense does Catullus think of his *basia* poems as prurient, and what is the threat of Aurelius' penis? To address the latter question first, the problem with Aurelius' penis is that it is *infesto pueris bonis malisque* (**"15"**.10); Aurelius, voraciousness makes no distinctions, which is as bad a quality in a reader as in a lover. If we turn to poem **"6,"** in many ways the reverse of **"15,"** we can see the same situation with the roles reversed and the poet firmly in control. Here we find the secretive Flavius challenged by Catullus to reveal his new *deliciae* (lover and lovemaking, **"6"**.1). Taunting Flavius that his silence can only mean that this new love of his betrays his lack of sophistication (**"6"**.2;14), Catullus urges him to entrust his secret to the poet (15-17):

> quare, quidquid habes *boni malique,*
> dic nobis. volo te ac tuos amores
> ad caelum lepido vocare versu.

> So, whatever you have, good or bad,
> tell me. I want to summon to divinity
> you and your love with an elegant poem.

Here the nature of Flavius' love is immaterial to the elegant poet, who can produce *lepor* even out of the silence that betrays the *ineptia* of his friend. Just as the silence of Flavius has not protected him from being pilloried by his sophisticated friend, so his speech would have no control over the poet even if he were to reveal his love. In **"15"** we have the reverse of this situation, for it is the love of the poet that is threatened by the friend to whom it is entrusted. Between them these two poems reveal the two sides of the poem's isolation from real speech: on the one hand, the poet is all powerful because he speaks for others who are not allowed to speak for themselves, but on the other hand he must entrust his words to others, who may find it as

much grist to their mill as he does the "material" that comes from the speech of others.

The omnivorous penis of Aurelius that threatens Catullus' boy is a symbol of the reader's power to use the poet as he will, to make what he wants of what the poet has entrusted to him. The phallic threats that end poem **"15"** and that enclose poem 16 are intended as retaliation, restoration of the balance of phallic power, which of course was the purpose of the punishment for adultery, *rhaphanidosis,* alluded to by the end of poem **"15."** In poem **"16"** Furius and Aurelius present a potential phallic threat to Catullus in that they have taken his *versiculi molliculi* as the speech of a *mollis,* just as they would in everyday speech, a failure of discrimination rather like Aurelius' sexual appetite. Catullus' reply that the poems only have *sal* and *lepor* if they excite the hairy types shifts the issue by giving a determination to the distinction boy/man that has to do with literary ambition rather than the poet's sexuality (7-11):

> qui [sc. versiculi] tum denique habent salem
>   ac leporem,
> si sunt molliculi ac parum pudici,
> et quod pruriat incitare possunt,
> non dico pueris, sed his pilosis
> qui duros nequeunt movere lumbos.

The *mollitia* of Catullus' verses has to do with the fact that it is more difficult to excite men than boys, and therefore becomes an assertion of his poetic ambition rather than a revelation of his effeminacy. A comparison with the corresponding gesture in poem **"15"** will help to bring these lines into focus. When Catullus asks Aurelius to protect his boy he says (5-10):

> conserves puerum mihi pudice,
> non dico a populo-nihil veremur
> istos, qui in platea modo huc modo illuc
> in re praetereunt sua occupati—
> verum a te metuo tuoque pene
> infesto pueris bonis malisque.

> Preserve my boy modestly for me,
> I don't mean from the crowd—I have no fear
> of those on the street who pass this way and
>   that
> intent on their own affairs—
> but from you (that's my fear) and your prick
> gunning for boys good or bad.

The words *non dico a populo* (6) perform the same function as *non dico pueris* in the previous poem (**"16"**.10), for the people who go back and forth on the highway are associated, via Callimachus, with the kind of literary enterprise Catullus rejects. The dismissal of these two groups (boys and the *occupati*) is a concomitant of Catullus' literary ambition and of the risk that he is undertaking with respect to Furius and Aurelius, his readers. Catullus' poetry involves playing with social positions and stances in a provocative way, and it is of the essence of the *poetic* in this connection that the relations between the agents are ambiguous.

The question we have to address now is that of the substance of the accusations of effeminacy made by Furius and Aurelius (*male me marem putatis?* **"16"**.13). Evidently these accusations were provoked by reading poems **"5"** and **"7."** Poem **"5"** would seem to be the natural referent of *milia multa basiorum* (**"16"**.12). It is a poem that has much in common with poem **"2"**, in that the erotic is here associated with foreplay rather than consummation, for the thousands of kisses that constitute Catullus' demand on Lesbia and that seem to be leading to a climax ("and then . . . and then . . . and then . . .") take us only to a final confusion of kisses that slyly provokes the voyeur/reader (**"5"**.10-13),

> dein, cum milia multa fecerimus,
> conturbabimus illa, ne sciamus,
> aut ne quis malus invidere possit,
> cum tantum sciat esse basiorum.

> then, when we've put together thousands,
> we'll mix them up, so as not to know,
> or so no evil man might envy us,
> when he learns there are so many kisses.

Furius and Aurelius read Catullus' apparent lack of interest in "taking" Lesbia as a sign of effeminacy which puts them in a dominant position with respect to Catullus; his thousands of kisses have that non-purposive and playfully exquisite character associated with the *delicatus*.

The eroticism of **"5"** and **"7,"** in which a non-climactic foreplay is connected with a teasing provocation of the audience is in sharp contrast to the *deliciae* of Flavius in the intervening poem; his silence leads Catullus to conclude that he loves some feverish whore (*nescio quid febriculosi/ scorti diligis: hoc pudet fateri,* **"6"**.4-5). In fact, Flavius' silence hides nothing (13-14):

> non tam latera ecfututa pandas
> ni tu quid facias ineptiarum.

> you wouldn't display such fucked-out loins
> if you weren't up to something foolish.

The crudeness of Flavius' lovemaking (*ecfututa*) is associated with the obviousness of what is going on (*pandas*); everything about Flavius is blatant, even the squeaking of the bed. which sounds like an ineffective orator (10-11):

> tremulique quassa lecti
> argutatio inambulatioque.

> the broken squeaking of the bed
> and its pacing back and forth.

This poem that unmasks and speaks for Flavius, whose crude sexuality consigns him to a silence that is itself blatant (*nequiquam tacitum cubile clamat,* "the vainly silent couch cries out,"), is sandwiched between two poems in which extended foreplay is connected with a provocation of the audience that is a mixture of hiding and revealing. By contrast with Flavius in the central poem of this group, Catullus is telling his *deliciae* ("pleasures," "whims") to us, and unlike the blatantly phallic activity of Flavius, which would not admit of a very interesting telling anyway, they are both *lepidae* and *elegantes* (cf. **"6"**.2). But this telling is erotic and provocative because, again by contrast with Flavius, Catullus is teasing.

In poem **"7"** Catullus responds to Lesbia's supposed question, apropos **"5,"** of how many kisses will suffice him. The rather precious and very learned variant on the "numberless as the sands" topos with which he responds is an encore performance for those who want a reprise of poem **"5"**; it is a riddle that withholds its referent . . . while indulging us in exotic and witty periphrasis (**"7"**.3-6):

> quam magnus numerus Libyssae harenae
> lasarpiciferis iacet Cyrenis
> oraclum Iovis inter aestuosi
> et Batti veteris sacrum sepulcrum:

> as many as the sands of Libya that lie
> in silphium-bearing Cyrene
> between the oracle of blazing Jupiter
> and the sacred grave of Battus:

The poem plays with the desire of the audience to hear it again, as the lengthened and neologistic abstract form *basiationes* indicates. The innumerability topos is as much an expression of the fact that the audience can never quite be satisfied as it is of the boundlessness of Catullus' love for Lesbia. After the sands come the stars (8-9):

> aut quam sidera multa, cum tacet nox,
> furtivos hominum vident amores:

> or as many as the constellations in the silent
>   night
> that watch the furtive loves of humans:

These stars, watching the lovers in the silent night, are of course the audience listening with bated breath to Catullus telling of his erotic life, and they find themselves representing the very impossibility of ever hearing the whole thing. Instead, they have the satisfaction of knowing what the four lines on the sands add up to: Callimachus (a native of Cyrene, who claimed descent from Battus).

In this group Catullus the poet remains firmly in control, whether he is frustrating the jealous and the curious whose interest he has piqued, as at the end of poems **"5"** and **"7,"** or offering to make an elegant poem of Flavius' inelegant love (which is what he has already done). In poems **"15"** and **"16"** this command breaks down when the relation between reader and poet is seen from a different angle: Catullus entrusts his *amores* to the indiscriminate and rapacious sensibilities of Furius and Aurelius, who have no respect for the nature of the game that is being played and see Catullus as the performing *cinaedus* sexually subject to his audience. Of course, Catullus needs Furius and Aurelius to establish the riskiness of his performance, which depends on its being questionable. This poem is not a defense of poems **"5"** and **"7,"** or of the aesthetic qualities they exhibit; still less is it a defense of the poet's morals based on a separation between art and life; rather it is a continuation and a filling in of the game between reader and poet.

To return to my opening question about the role of sexual stimulation in Catullus' poetics: to take this seriously we do not necessarily have to explain the relation between Catullus' verse and certain physical symptoms. As I have argued, poem **"16"** needs to be seen as part of a game opened up by the ambiguous and kaleidoscopic potential of the relation between poet, poem and reader. Both this concern with social transactions and positionality and the fact that the activity of the poet of *versiculi* falls in the category of the Questionable, a category which relies heavily on sexual metaphors, are peculiarly Roman aspects of Catullus' poetics. The ambiguities of the relations, gestures and transactions of the aesthetic sphere upset any secure sense of positionality, and it is positionality that is at stake in ancient sexuality. I have spoken several times of the need to develop an erotics of Catullus' poetry, and especially the polymetrics, because of the fact that these poems are performances that take place in the context of a still self-conscious and developing conception of sophisticated, urban social behavior. The language that conveys the values of the group of poets that is implied by Catullus' book reflects a concern for social attractiveness; it is language that often blurs the boundary between social and sexual attractiveness, and it is often language that in the Roman context is provocative, another category that is both social and sexual. We need to think more about what this poetry is doing and less about what it is expressing.

FURTHER READING

Bibliography

Harrauer, Herman. *A Bibliography to Catullus.* Hildesheim: Gerstenberg Verlag, 1979, 206 p.
> Complex bibliography covering translations, commentary, background, and other Catullus-related publications from 1500 to 1978.

Criticism

Copely, Frank Olin. "Emotional Conflict and Its Significance in the Lesbia-Poems of Catullus." *American Journal of Philology* LXX, No. 277 (1949): 22-40.
> Discusses Catullus's struggle with language in the experession of his emotions and of the exact nature of his love for Lesbia.

Goold, G. P. *Interpreting Catullus.* London: H. K. Lewis & Co., 1974, 50 p.
> Discusses a number of controversial and still unsettled points in criticism of Catullus.

Hutchinson, G. O. *Hellenistic Poetry.* Oxford: Clarendon Press, 1988, 374 p.
> Presents a literary picture of third-century B.C. poets, including Catullus and highlighting his "uneasy conjunction of diverging emotions."

Jenkyns, Richard. "Catullus and the Idea of a Masterpiece." In *Three Classical Poets: Sappho, Catullus, and Juvenal,* pp. 85-150. Cambridge: Harvard University Press, 1982.
> Discusses Catullus's Poem 64, arguing that there are similarities between Catullus's shorter pieces and his longer work.

Lateiner, Donald. "Obscenity in Catullus." *Ramus* 6, No. 1 (1977):15-32.
> Comments on the nature of Catullus's obscenity, finding it mostly humorous in nature and "an outlet for Catullus's aggressive impulses."

Lindsay, Jack. Foreword to *Catullus: The Complete Poems,* pp. ix-xxii. London: Sylvan Press, 1948.
> Summarizes Catullus's life and contemporary influences on his work.

Loomis, Julia W. *Studies in Catullan Verse: An Analysis of Word Types and Patterns in the Polymetra.* Leiden: E. J. Brill, 1972, 160 p.
> Studies how Greek and Latin quantitative metrics affected the polymetra of Catullus.

Munro, H. A. J. *Criticisms and Elucidations of Catullus,* 2nd edition. London: George Bell and Sons, 1905, 250 p.

Primarily concerned with codexes and whole, correct language in Catullus's poetry. This work was first published in 1878.

Putnam, Michael C. J. "Catullus." In *Essays on Latin Lyric, Elegy, and Epic*, pp, 3-94. Princeton: Princeton University Press, 1982.
Discusses some of Catullus's poems, linking them by "Catullus's attraction to the theme of separation and desertion."

Quinn, Kenneth, ed. *Approaches to Catullus.* Cambridge: Heffer, 1972,   113 p.
A collection of essays concerned with general theories on Catullus and his poetry; contains articles concerned with specific poems and includes two reviews of the main controversies in Catullan scholarship.

Ross, David O., Jr. *Style and Tradition in Catullus.* Cambridge: Harvard University Press, 1969, 188 p.
Explores Catullus's poetic vocabulary, the relationships between certain poems, and the literary traditions in which they were written.

Thomson, D. F. S. Introduction to *Catullus: A Critical Edition,* pp. 3-43. Chapel Hill: The University of North Carolina Press, 1978.
Outlines the existing codexes of Catullus's poetry, describing their histories and weighing their respective merits; also indexes other relevant sources and information.

Wiseman T. P. *Catullan Questions*. Leicester: Leicester University Press, 1969, 70 p.
Explores questions raised by a variety of Catullus's poems.

————. "Catullus and Cornelius Nepos." In *Clio's Cosmetics*, pp. 143-81. Leicester University Press, 1979.
Background on Catullus's contemporaries' definitions of history and poetry, the source of his knowledge in these areas, and how it affected his poetry.

Song of Songs

c. 500 B.C. - c. 300 B.C.

Hebrew poem.

INTRODUCTION

An erotic poem, the *Song of Songs* (also known as the *Song of Solomon* and the *Canticle of Canticles*) is one of the *Kethubim*, or "Writings," in the third part of the Hebrew Bible. Attributed to King Solomon, the *Song* was admitted to the Hebrew Canon as an allegory of God's relationship with Israel. Its mysterious language has since led to centuries of extensive and sometimes fanciful commentary comprising many different modes of allegorical exegesis and secular interpretation. In some readings, the poem's eroticism is an expression of the love of King Solomon for a young shepherdess—the "Shulamite"—or a celebration of Solomon's wedding. In the Christian era, the *Song* has been read as an allegory of the bridegroom Christ's relationship with his bride, the Church, and it found an important place in Roman Catholic marian theology, especially in the Middle Ages. Subsequent research has revealed possible links with Tammuz cult worship, with Syrian and Egyptian love poetry, and with traditions of folk marriage celebration; but despite much modern and secular focus on the poem's sensuousness and erotic imagery, the *Song* retains its place in the Hebrew Canon as a holy allegory and continues to be used in the liturgy of Passover.

Plot and Major Characters

The *Song of Songs* has been generally considered a love poem which takes the form of a dramatic dialogue concerning the mutual devotion of young, unmarried, heterosexual lovers. Each lover invokes the other's most glorious and delightful qualities in rich imagery taken from the world around them: scents, animals, plants, landscapes, even architecture. In some interpretations additional personae, the girls of Jerusalem, who receive guidance in the ways of love, and the brothers of the main female voice of the poem, function as a choric commentary on the erotic action of the drama.

The plot of the *Song of Songs* is inseparable from the debate over its interpretation. While convention often divides the *Song* into eight parts, and there are recurrences of theme and image in a series of narrative fragments, the number of "poems" believed to make up the work varies from one translator to the next. The lovers use pastoral and regal associations to describe each other, invoking the smell and taste of spices and perfumes, and pleasant images of landscape and nature. The *Song*'s rich metaphorical language avoids straightforward description of physical lovemaking; instead the female is a "lotus among brambles" and the male "resembles a buck, / Or a young stag;" his mouth is "sweetness." The female lover's body, too, is described in metaphor; she is a tended vineyard, her breasts "like two fauns." For the female persona especially, love's pleasures are mitigated by its attendant emotional pain: she twice goes in search of her lover, at night in the city, and is once stopped, and beaten, by the city guards. While love is consistently described as a blissful state, the *Song* also treats the trials of separation, where the lovers pine for each other's presence. But throughout the poem, fulsome descriptions of topography, of fauna and flora, and of the smells and tastes of life in ancient Israel are repeatedly mingled with descriptions of the lovers' bodies to associate sexual love with the pleasure and joy of life.

Major Themes

The ostensible and literal subject of the *Song of Songs* is erotic love, the delight in the presence and in the thought of the loved one. However, thematic interpretations have often depended upon the context in which the *Song* would have been read or performed. The voices of the poem speak of physical beauty and sensuous pleasure, but in early allegorical exegesis the loving relationship thus described is construed to be that of God and Israel; in later Christian readings it describes that between Christ and the Church. In the literal, secular reading, the major theme is one of the celebration and exploration of the delights and difficulties attendant upon sexual love. References to Solomon and to weddings have prompted interpretations of the *Song* as an epithalamium, or poem celebrating marriage, either specifically for the King and his bride, or generally as part of a wider literature of marriage celebration. Claims that the *Song* is part of an ancient pagan cult have prompted speculation that its major theme is fertility, while another modern reading links the *Song* to cult celebrations of the primacy of love and rebirth in the face of death.

Textual History

Although written in biblical Hebrew, the *Song of Songs* contains many traces of other languages: Ugaritic,

Persian, Aramaic, and Mishnaic Hebrew. Much uncertainty surrounds the composition date of the *Song*, and speculations have been dependent upon clues to be found in the text itself. Most scholars believe that the work was written between 500 B.C. and 300 B.C. The *Song* was long attributed to Solomon himself on the basis of the numerous references to him within the poem, and the work has also been attributed to Isaiah and Hezekiah; however, the unity of the work suggests that a later, anonymous editor may have compiled the extant text. There are a series of textual versions: the *Septaguint*, or Greek translation of the Old Testament, probably composed around 100 B.C.; the Vulgate *Canticum Canticorum* (398), by Saint Jerome; and the *Peshitta*. The Masoretic Hebrew version of the *Song* had no stanzaic divisions, and new editions have divided the text into chapter and verse according to the translator's interpretation. English translations of the *Song* have been numerous; notable are those of Henry Ainsworth (1639), Christian David Ginsburg (1857), Marvin H. Pope (1977), and Michael V. Fox (1985).

Critical Reception

The fundamental and continuing debate in interpretation of the *Song of Songs* is whether the poem is a religious allegory, a pagan cult liturgy, or a secular, sensuous work of erotic literature. The admission of the *Song* to the Scriptural Canon by Rabbinical scholars is thought to have depended upon its association with King Solomon and on the allegorical reading of the work's erotic imagery. Reference is made to the the *Song* in the *Talmud* and the *Targum*, and Rabbi Akiba (50-132) gave the *Song* its well-known title, the "holy of holies." In Christian biblical scholarship the subject of the *Song* has been considered either an allegory of Christ's relation to the Church, or of the relationship between the Soul and the Divine Word. The Christian theologian Origen considered the poem a drama played by Solomon and a Shulammite shepherd girl.

Modern readings have focused increasingly on the *Song*'s literal expression of human love and on other mystical meaning. In 1860 Auguste Renan compared the *Song* with modern Syrian wedding poetry, and comparisons with Egyptian love lyrics have located the *Song* within a broader cultural context. Claims have also been made that the *Song* was a cult liturgy, linked either to the Osiris cult or the Tammuz-Istar cult. H. H. Rowley has seen the poem as a collection of several bold love poems with allusions to a cult, but has suggested that the *Song* is not itself a cult liturgy, while Marvin Pope, too, has argued for a secular interpretation of the *Song*'s cult origins. The 1857 interpretation of Ginsburg is considered influential for such feminist readings as that of Carol Meyers.

PRINCIPAL ENGLISH TRANSLATIONS

Solomons Song of Songs, in English Metre: With Annotations and References to Other Scriptures, for the Easier Understanding of It (translated by Henry Ainsworth) 1639

A Brief Exposition of the Whole Book of Canticles; or, Song of Solomon (translated by John Cotton) 1648

Song of Songs: or, Sacred Idyls. Translated from the Original Hebrew with Notes Critical and Explanatory (translated by John Mason Good) 1803

The Song of Songs, Translated From the Original Hebrew with a Commentary, Historical and Critical (translated by Christian David Ginsburg) 1857

The Song of Songs Unveiled: A New Translation and Exposition (translated by Benjamin Weiss) 1859

Solomon's Song: Translated and Explained (translated by Leonard Withington) 1861

The Book of Canticles: A New Rhythmical Translation with Restoration of the Hebrew Text (translated by Paul Haupt) 1902

The Song of Songs, Being a Collection of Love Lyrics of Ancient Palestine: A New Translation Based on a Revised Text, Together with the Origin, Growth, and Interpretation of the Songs (translated by Morris Jastrow, Jr.) 1921

The Song of Songs, Translated and Interpreted as a Dramatic Poem (translated by Leroy Waterman) 1948

The Song of Songs: A Study, Modern Translation, and Commentary (translated by Robert Gordis) 1954; revised 1974

The Song of Songs, Translated from the Original Hebrew with an Introduction and Explanations (translated by Hugh J. Schonfield) 1959

The Song of Songs (translated by Robert Graves) 1973

Song of Songs: A New Translation with Introduction and Commentary (translated by Marvin H. Pope) 1977

The Song of Songs and the Ancient Egyptian Love Songs (translated by Michael V. Fox) 1985

The Song of Fourteen Songs (translated by Michael D. Goulder) 1986

The Voice of My Beloved (translated by E. Ann Matter) 1990

CRITICISM

Origen (essay date 240)

SOURCE: "Commentary: Prologue," in *"The Song of Songs": Commentary and Homilies*, translated by R. P. Lawson, The Newman Press, 1957, pp. 21-57.

[*In the following prologue to his commentary, written in 240, Origen ascribes the* Song of Songs *to Solomon, noting the importance of a cautious distinction between "passionate love" and "charity" to an interpretation of the dramatic poem's "secret metaphors."*]

1. *The* Song of Songs *a Drama of Mystical Meaning*

It seems to me that this little book is an epithalamium, that is to say, a marriage-song, which Solomon wrote in the form of a drama and sang under the figure of the Bride, about to wed and burning with heavenly love towards her Bridegroom, who is the Word of God. And deeply indeed did she love Him, whether we take her as the soul made in His image, or as the Church. But this same Scripture also teaches us what words this august and perfect Bridegroom used in speaking to the soul, or to the Church, who has been joined to Him. And in this same little book that bears the title **Song of Songs**, we recognize moreover things that the Bride's companions said, the maidens who go with her, and also some things spoken by the Bridegroom's friends and fellows. For the friends of the Bridegroom also, in their joy at His union with the Bride, have been enabled to say some things—at any rate those that they had heard from the Bridegroom Himself. In the same way we find the Bride speaking not to the Bridegroom only, but also to the maidens; likewise the Bridegroom's words are addressed not to the Bride alone, but also to His friends. And that is what we meant just now, when we said that the marriage-song was written in dramatic form. For we call a thing a drama, such as the enaction of a story on the stage, when different characters are introduced and the whole structure of the narrative consists in their comings and goings among themselves. And this work contains these things one by one in their own order, and also the whole body of it consists of mystical utterances.

But it behoves us primarily to understand that, just as in childhood we are not affected by the passion of love, so also to those who are at the stage of infancy and childhood in their interior life—to those, that is to say, who are being nourished with milk in Christ, not with strong meat, and are only beginning *to desire the rational milk without guile*—it is not given to grasp the meaning of these sayings. For in the words of the **Song of Songs** there is that food, of which the Apostle says that *strong meat is for the perfect;* and that food calls for hearers *who by ability have their senses exercised to the discerning of good and evil.* And indeed, if those whom we have called children were to come on these passages, it may be that they would derive neither profit nor much harm, either from reading the text itself, or from going through the necessary explanations. But if any man who lives only after the flesh should approach it, to such a one the reading of this Scripture will be the occasion of no small hazard and danger. For he, not knowing how to hear love's language in purity and with chaste ears, will twist the whole manner of his hearing of it away from the inner spiritual man and on to the outward and carnal; and he will be turned away from the spirit to the flesh, and will foster carnal desires in himself, and it will seem to be the Divine Scriptures that are thus urging and egging him on to fleshly lust!

For this reason, therefore, I advise and counsel everyone who is not yet rid of the vexations of flesh and blood and has not ceased to feel the passion of his bodily nature, to refrain completely from reading this little book and the things that will be said about it. For they say that with the Hebrews also care is taken to allow no one even to hold this book in his hands, who has not reached a full and ripe age. And there is another practice too that we have received from them—namely, that all the Scriptures should be delivered to boys by teachers and wise men, while at the same time the four that they call *deuterōseis*—that is to say, the beginning of Genesis, in which the creation of the world is described; the first chapters of Ezechiel, which tell about the cherubim; the end of that same, which contains the building of the Temple; and this book of the **Song of Songs**—should be reserved for study till the last.

2. *The Theme of the* Song of Songs

Before we come to consider the things that are written in this book, therefore, it seems to me necessary to say a few things first about love itself, which is the main theme of this Scripture; then about the order of the books of Solomon, among which we find that this one is put third; then about the name of the book itself, why it is entitled the **Song of Songs**; and, lastly, for what apparent reason it s written in dramatic form and, like a story that is acted on the stage, with dialogue between the characters.

Among the Greeks, indeed, many of the sages, desiring to pursue the search for truth in regard to the nature of love, produced a great variety of writings in this dialogue form, the object of which was to show that the power of love is none other than that which leads the soul from earth to the lofty heights of heaven, and that the higher beatitude can only be attained under the stimulus of love's desire. Moreover, the disputations on this subject are represented as taking place at meals, between persons whose banquet, I think, consists of words and not of meats. And others also have left us written accounts of certain arts, by which this love might be generated and augmented in the soul. But carnal men have perverted these arts to foster vicious longings and the secrets of sinful love.

You must not be surprised, therefore, if we call the discussion of the nature of love difficult and likely to be dangerous also for ourselves, among whom there are as many inexperienced folk as there are people of the simpler sort; seeing that even among the Greeks, who seem so wise and learned, there have none the less been some who did not understand what was said about love in the sense in which it was written, but took occasion from it to rush into carnal sins and down the steep places of immodesty, either by taking some suggestions and recommendations out of what had been written, as we said above, or else by using what the ancients wrote as a cloak for their own lack of self-control.

Lest, therefore, the like should happen to us, and we too should interpret in a vicious and carnal sense the things the ancients wrote with good and spiritual intent, let us stretch out our hands, alike of body and soul, to God; that the Lord, who *gave the word to them that preach good tidings with great power*, may by His power bestow the word also on us; so that we, out of these things that have been written, may be able to make clear a wholesome meaning in regard to the name and the nature of love, and one that is apt for the building up of chastity.

In the beginning of the words of Moses, where the creation of the world is described, we find reference to the making of two men, the first in *the image and likeness of God*, and the second *formed of the slime of the earth*. Paul the Apostle knew this well; and, being possessed of a very clear understanding of the matter, he wrote in his letters more plainly and with greater lucidity that there are in fact two men in every single man. He says, for instance: *For if our outward man is corrupted, yet the inward man is renewed day by day*; and again: *For I am delighted with the law of God according to the inward man*; and he makes some other statements of a similar kind. I think, therefore, that no one ought any longer to doubt what Moses wrote in the beginning of Genesis about the making and fashioning of two men, since he sees Paul, who understood what Moses wrote much better than we do, saying that there are two men in every one of us. Of these two men he tells us that the one, namely, the inner man, is renewed from day to day; but the other, that is, the outer, he declares to be corrupted and weakened in all the saints and in such as he was himself. If anything in regard to this matter still seems doubtful to anyone, it will be better explained in the appropriate places. But let us now follow up what we mentioned before about the inner and the outer man.

The thing we want to demonstrate about these things is that the Divine Scriptures make use of homonyms; that is to say, they use identical terms for describing different things. And they even go so far as to call the members of the outer man by the same names as the parts and dispositions of the inner man; and not only are the same terms employed, but the things themselves are compared with one another. For instance, a person is a child in age according to the inner man, who has in him the power to grow and to be led

onward to the age of youth, and thence by successive stages of development to come to the perfect man and to be made a father. Our own intention, therefore, has been to use such terms as would be in harmony with the language of Sacred Scripture, and in particular with that which was written by John; for he says: *I have written to you, children, because you have known the Father; I have written to you, fathers, because you have known Him who was from the beginning; I have written unto you, young men, because you are strong, and the word of God abideth in you, and you have overcome the wicked one*. It is perfectly clear; and I think nobody should doubt that John calls these people children or lads or young men or even fathers according to the soul's age, not the body's. Paul too says somewhere: *I could not speak unto you as unto spiritual, but as unto carnal, as unto little ones in Christ. I gave you milk to drink, not meat*. A little one in Christ is undoubtedly so called after the age of his soul, not after that of his flesh. And finally the same Paul says further: *When I was a child, I spoke as a child, I understood as a child, I thought as a child; but, when I became a man, I destroyed childish things*. And again on another occasion he says: *Until we all meet . . . unto a perfect man, unto the measure of the age of the fullness of Christ*: he knows that those who believe will *all meet unto a perfect man* and *unto the measure of the age of the fullness of Christ*.

So, then, just as these different ages that we have mentioned are denoted by the same words both for the outer man and for the inner, so also will you find the names of the members of the body transferred to those of the soul; or rather the faculties and powers of the soul are to be called its members. We read in Ecclesiastes, therefore: *The eyes of a wise man are in his head*; and again in the Gospel: *He that hath ears to hear, let him hear*; and in the prophets likewise: *The word of the Lord that was made in the hand of Jeremias the prophet*, or whoever it happens to be. The passage that says: *Let not thy foot stumble*, is another instance of the same; so also is: *But my feet were moved a little less*. The womb of the soul also is plainly designated where we read: *Lord, from fear of Thee we have conceived in our womb*. So likewise who is puzzled when it is said that *their throat is an open sepulchre*, and again: *Cast down, O Lord, and divide their tongues*, and also when it is written: *Thou hast broken the teeth of sinners*, and again: *Break Thou the arm of the sinner and of the malignant?*

But what need is there for me to collect more examples of these things, when the Divine Scriptures are full of any number of evidences? It is perfectly clear that in these passages the names of the members can in no way be applied to the visible body, but must be referred to the parts and powers of the invisible soul. The members have the same names, yes; but the names plainly and without any ambiguity carry meanings proper to the inner, not the outer man. Moreover, this material man, who also is called the outer, has food and drink of like sort with himself—that is to say, corporeal and earthly; but in the same way the spiritual man, who also is called the inner, has for his proper food that *living Bread which came down from heaven*, and drinks of the water that Jesus promises, saying: *Whosoever shall drink of this water, which I will give to him, shall not thirst for ever.*

The same terms, then, are used throughout for either man; but the essential character of the things is kept distinct, and corruptible things are offered to that which is corruptible, while incorruptible things are set before that which cannot be corrupted. It happens in consequence that certain people of the simpler sort, not knowing how to distinguish and differentiate between the things ascribed in the Divine Scriptures to the inner and outer man respectively, and being deceived by this identity of nomenclature, have applied themselves to certain absurd fables and silly tales. Thus they even believe that after the resurrection bodily food and drink will be used and taken—food, that is, not only from that True Vine who lives for ever, but also from the vines and fruits of the trees about us. But concerning these we shall see elsewhere.

Now then, as the foregoing remarks have shown, one person is childless and barren according to the inner man while another has plenty of offspring. And we notice that the saying: *The barren hath borne seven, and she that hath many children is weakened*, is in accord with this; as also is that which is said in the blessings: *There shall not be one among you that is childless or barren.* This being so, it follows that, just as there is one love, known as carnal and also known as Cupid by the poets, according to which the lover sows in the flesh; so also is there another, a spiritual love, by which the inner man who loves sows in the spirit. And, to speak more plainly, if anyone still bears the image of the earthy according to the outer man, then he is moved by earthly desire and love; but the desire and love of him who bears the image of the heavenly according to the inner man are heavenly. And the soul is moved by heavenly love and longing when, having clearly beheld the beauty and the fairness of the Word of God, it falls deeply in love with His loveliness and receives from the Word Himself a certain dart and wound of love. For this Word is *the image* and splendour *of the invisible God, the Firstborn of all creation, in whom were all things created that are in heaven and on earth, seen and unseen alike.* If, then, a man can so extend his thinking as to ponder and consider the beauty and the grace of all the things that have been created in the Word, the very charm of them will so smite him, the grandeur of their brightness will so pierce him as with *a chosen dart*—as says the prophet—that he will suffer from the dart Himself a saving

wound, and will be kindled with the blessed fire of His love.

We must realize also that, just as an illicit and unlawful love may happen to the outer man—as that, for instance, he should love a harlot or adulteress instead of his bride or his wife; so also may the inner man, that is to say, the soul, come to attach its love not to its lawful Bridegroom, who is the Word of God, but to some seducer or adulterer. The prophet Ezechiel plainly states this fact under the same figure, when he brings in Oolla and Ooliba to represent Samaria and Jerusalem corrupted by adulterous love; the actual passage in the prophetic scripture declares this plainly to those who desire a deeper understanding of it. And this spiritual love of the soul does flame out, as we have taught, sometimes towards certain spirits of evil, and sometimes towards the Holy Spirit and the Word of God, who is called the faithful Spouse and Husband of the instructed soul, and from whom indeed the Bride derives her title, particularly in this piece of Scripture with which we are now dealing; this, with the Lord's help, we shall explain more fully when we come to expound the actual words of the book.

It seems to me, however, that the Divine Scripture is anxious to avoid the danger of the mention of love becoming an occasion of falling for its readers; and, to that end and for the sake of the weaker ones, it uses a more respectable word for that which the wise men of the world called desire or passion—namely, charity or affection. For instance, it says of Isaac: *and he took Rebecca and she became his wife, and he loved* (dilexit) *her*; and again the Scripture speaks in the same way about Jacob and Rachel: *But Rachel had beautiful eyes and was fair of face, and Jacob loved* (dilexit) *Rachel and said, 'I will serve thee seven years for Rachel thy younger daughter.'* And the unchanged force of this word appears even more plainly in connection with Amnon, who had a passion for (adamavit) his sister Thamar; for it is written: *And it came to pass after this that Absalom the son of David had a sister who was very fair of face, and her name was Thamar, and Amnon the son of David loved* (dilexit) *her.* The writer has put 'loved' here in place of 'had a passion for.' *And Amnon*, he says, *was so troubled that he fell sick because of Thamar his sister, for she was a virgin, and Amnon thought it a serious thing to do anything to her.* And a little later, with reference to the outrage that Amnon did to Thamar his sister, the Scripture says thus: *And Amnon would not listen to what she said, but overpowered her and humbled her and slept with her. And Amnon hated her with an exceeding great hatred, for the hatred with which he hated her was greater than the love* (dilectio) *with which he had loved* (dilexerat) *her.*

In these places, therefore, and in many others you will find that Divine Scripture avoided the word 'passion' and Put 'charity' or 'affection' instead. Occasionally, however, though rarely, it calls the passion of love by its own name, and invites and urges souls to it; as when it says in Proverbs about Wisdom: *Desire her greatly* (adama) *and she shall preserve thee; encompass her, and she shall exalt thee; honour her, that she may embrace thee.* And in the book that is called the Wisdom of Solomon it is written of Wisdom herself: *I became a passionate lover* (amator) *of her beauty.* I think that the word for passionate love was used only where there seemed to be no occasion of falling. For who could see anything sensuous or unseemly in the passion for Wisdom, or in a man's professing himself her passionate lover? Whereas had Isaac been spoken of as having a passion for Rebecca or Jacob for Rachel, some unseemly passion on the part of the saints of God might have been inferred from the words, especially by those who do not know how to rise up from the letter to the spirit. Most clearly, however, even in this our little book of which we are now treating, the appellation of 'passionate love' has been changed into the word 'charity' in the place where it says: *I have adjured you, O daughters of Jerusalem, if you find my Nephew, to tell Him that I have been wounded by charity.* For that is as much as to say: 'I have been smitten through with the dart of His "passionate love."'

It makes no difference, therefore, whether the Sacred Scriptures speak of love, or of charity, or of affection; except that the word 'charity' is so highly exalted that even God Himself is called Charity, as John says: *Dearly beloved, let us love one another, for charity is of God; and everyone that loveth is born of God and knoweth God; but he that loveth not knoweth not God, for God is Charity.* And although some other time might be more suitable in which to say something about these words that, by way of example, we have cited from John's Epistle, it seems not unreasonable to touch briefly on the matter in this context too. *Let us love one another,* he says, *for charity is of God*; and a little later: *God is Charity.* In saying this, he shows both that God Himself is Charity, and that He who is of God also is Charity. For who is of God, save He who says: *I came forth from God and am come into this world?* If God the Father is Charity, and the Son is Charity, the Charity, that Each One is, is one; it follows, therefore, that the Father and the Son are one and the same in every respect. Fittingly, then, is Christ called Charity, just as He is called Wisdom and Power end Justice and Word and Truth. And that is why the Scripture says that if *charity abideth in you, God abideth in you*—God, that is to say, the Father and the Son, who also come to him who has been perfected in charity, according to the saying of Our Lord and Saviour: *I and my Father will come to him and will make our abode with him.*

We must understand, therefore, that this Charity, which God is, in whomsoever it exists loves nothing earthly,

nothing material, nothing corruptible; for it is against its nature to love anything corruptible, seeing that it is itself the fount of incorruption. For, because God, *who only hath immortality and inhabiteth light inaccessible*, is Charity, it is charity alone that possesses immortality. And what is immortality, except the life eternal which God promises to give to those who believe in Him, the only true God, and in Jesus Christ, whom He has sent? And for that reason we are told that the thing which in the first place and before all else is acceptable and pleasing to God, is that a man should love the Lord his God with all his heart and with all his soul and with all his powers. And because God is Charity, and the Son likewise, who is of God, is Charity, He requires in us something like Himself; so that through this charity which is in Christ Jesus, we may be allied to God who is Charity, as it were in a sort of blood relationship through this name of charity; even as he, who was already united to Him, said: *Who shall separate us from the charity of God which is in Christ Jesus our Lord?*

This charity, however, reckons all men as neighbours. For on that account the Saviour rebuked someone, who thought that the obligation to behave neighbourly did not apply to a righteous soul in regard to one who was sunk in wickedness; and for that same reason He made up the parable that tells how a certain man fell among robbers, as he was going down from Jerusalem to Jericho, and blames the priest and the Levite, who passed by when they saw the man half-dead, but approves the Samaritan who showed mercy. And, by means of the reply of him who raised the question, He affirmed that the Samaritan was the neighbour of the man, and said: *Go, and do thou in like manner.* By nature, indeed, we are all of us neighbours one of another; but by the works of charity a man who has it in his power to do service to another who has not that power, becomes his neighbour. Wherefore also our Saviour became neighbour to us, and when we were lying half-dead from the wounds the robbers had inflicted on us, He did not pass us by.

We must recognize, therefore, that the charity of God is always directed towards God, from whom also it takes its origin, and looks back towards the neighbour, with whom it is in kinship as being similarly created in incorruption. So you must take whatever Scripture says about charity as if it had been said with reference to passionate love, taking no notice of the difference of terms; for the same meaning is conveyed by both. But if anyone should remark that we speak of 'loving' money and harlots and such—like evils, using the same word as that which has obvious reference to charity, you must understand that in such contexts we speak of charity by an improper use, and not according to its basic sense. To take another example, the word 'God' is used primarily of Him *of whom are all things, and by whom are all things, and in whom are all things*; so that it declares plainly the virtue and nature of the Trinity. But by a secondary and so to speak improper usage Scripture describes as gods those to whom the word of God came, as the Saviour affirms in the Gospels. And the heavenly powers also seem to be called by this name when it is said: *God hath stood in the congregation of gods; and, being in the midst of them, He judgeth gods.* And by a third usage, false rather than improper, the daemonic gods of the Gentiles are so styled when Scripture says: *All the gods of the Gentiles are devils.*

Thus, then, the name of charity belongs first to God; and for that reason we are bidden to love God with all our heart and all our soul and all our strength—Him, that is, from whom we have the very power of loving. And this command undoubtedly implies that we should also love wisdom and right-doing and piety and truth and all the other virtues; for to love God and to love good things is one and the same thing. In the second place, we are bidden also to love our neighbour as ourselves by a use of the word that is, as it were, derived and secondary. And the third usage is that by which 'loving' money, or pleasure, or anything that is connected with corruption and error, is called charity by a misnomer. So it makes no difference whether we speak of having a passion for God, or of loving Him; and I do not think one could be blamed if one called God Passionate Love (*Amorem*), just as John calls Him Charity (*Caritatem*). Indeed I remember that one of the saints, by name Ignatius, said of Christ: 'My Love (*Amor*) is crucified,' and I do not consider him worthy of censure on this account. All the same, you must understand that everyone who loves money or any of the things of corruptible substance that the world contains, is debasing the power of charity, which is of God, to earthly and perishable objects, and is misusing the things of God by making them serve purposes that are not His; for God gave the things to men to be used, not to be loved.

We have discussed these matters at some length because we wanted to distinguish more clearly and carefully between the nature of passionate love and that of charity; lest perhaps, because Scripture says that God is Charity, the charity and love that is of God should be esteemed to be in our every attachment, even to corruptible things. And we have seen that though charity is truly the possession and the gift of God, His work is not always appropriated by men for the things of God and for what God wills.

At the same time we ought to understand also that it is impossible for human nature not to be always feeling the passion of love for something. Everyone who has reached the age that they call puberty loves something, either less rightly when he loves what he should not, or rightly and with profit when he loves what he should love. But some people pervert this faculty of passion-

ate love, which is implanted in the human soul by the Creator's kindness. Either it becomes with them a passion for money and the pursuit of avaricious ends; or they go after glory and become desirous of vainglory; or they chase after harlots and are found the prisoners of wantonness and lewdness; or else they squander the strength of this great good on other things like these. Moreover, when this passion of love is directed on to diverse skills, whether manual crafts or occupations needful only for this present life—the art of wrestling, for example, and track running—or even when it is expended on the study of geometry or music or arithmetic or similar branches of learning, neither in that case does it seem to me to be used laudably. For if that which is good is also laudable—and by that which is good we understand not anything corporeal, but only that which is found first in God and in the powers of the soul—it follows that the only laudable love is that which is directed to God and to the powers of the soul.

And that this is the case is shown by Our Saviour's own statement when, having been asked by a certain person what was the greatest commandment of all and the first in the Law, He replied: *Thou shalt love the Lord thy God with thy whole heart and with thy whole soul and with all thy powers; . . . and the second is like unto it: Thou shalt love thy neighbour as thyself*; and He added: *On these two commandments dependeth the whole Law and the Prophets*, showing thereby that true and perfect love consists in keeping these two, and that the entire Law and Prophets hang on them. And the other injunction: *Thou shalt not commit adultery, thou shalt not kill, thou shalt not steal, thou shalt not bear false witness*, and whatever other commandment there may be is summed up in the words: *Thou shalt love thy neighbour as thyself.*

This will be better explained as follows. Suppose, for instance, that there is a woman with an ardent passion of love for a certain man who longs to be admitted to wedlock with him. Will she not act in all respects and regulate her every movement in a manner designed to please the man she loves, lest maybe, if she acts against his will in something, that excellent man may refuse and scorn her society? Will this woman, whose whole heart and soul and strength are on fire with passionate love for that man, be able to commit adultery, when she well knows that he loves purity? Or murder, when she knows him to be gentle, or theft, seeing she knows him to be pleased with generosity? Or will she covet other people's goods, when all her own desires are absorbed in passionate devotion for that man?

That is the sense in which every commandment is said to be comprised in the perfection of charity, and the strength of the Law and the Prophets to depend on it. Because of this good gift of charity or love, the saints are neither straitened in tribulation, nor utterly per-plexed in doubt, nor do they perish when they are cast down; but *that which is at present momentary and light of their tribulation worketh for them above mea-sure an eternal weight of glory*. This present tribula-tion is not described as momentary and light for every-one, but only for Paul and those who resemble him in having *the* perfect *charity of God in Christ Jesus poured out in their hearts by the Holy Spirit*.

In the same way also it was the love of Rachel that kept the patriarch Jacob from feeling the searing of either heat by day or cold by night through seven long years of toil. So too do I hear Paul himself, enkindled by the power of this love, declare: *Charity beareth all things, believeth all things, hopeth all things, endureth all things; charity never falls*. There is, therefore, noth-ing that he who loves perfectly would not endure; but there are many things that we do not endure, simply because we have not got the charity that *endureth all things*. And, if we are impatient under certain burdens, it is because we lack the charity that *beareth all things*. In the struggle that we have to wage with the devil, too, we often fall; undoubtedly because the charity that *never falls* is not in us.

The Scripture before us, therefore, speaks of this love with which the blessed soul is kindled and inflamed towards the Word of God; it sings by the Spirit the song of the marriage whereby the Church is joined and allied to Christ the heavenly Bridegroom, desiring to be united to Him through the Word, so that she may conceive by Him and be saved through this chaste begetting of children, when they—conceived as they are indeed of the seed of the Word of God, and born and brought forth by the spotless Church, or by the soul that seeks nothing bodily, nothing material, but is aflame with the single love of the Word of God—shall have persevered in faith and holiness with sobriety.

These are the considerations that have occurred to us thus far regarding the love or charity that is set forth in this marriage-hymn that is the **Song of Songs**. But we must realize how many things there are that ought to be said about this charity, what great things also about God, since He is Charity Himself. For, as *no one knoweth the Father but the Son, and he to whom it shall please the Son to reveal Him*, so also no one knows Charity except the Son. In the same way also, *no one knoweth the Son*, since He Himself likewise is Charity, *except the Father*. Further and in like man-ner, because He is called Charity, it is the Holy Spir-it, who proceeds from the Father, who alone knows what is in God; just as the spirit of man knows what is in man. Wherefore this *Paraclete, the Spirit of Truth who proceedeth from the Father*, goes about trying to find souls worthy and able to receive the greatness of this charity, that is of God, that He desires to reveal to them.

3. *The Place of the* Song of Songs *among the Works of Solomon*

Now, therefore, calling upon God the Father, who is Charity, through that same charity that is of Him, let us pass on to discuss the other matters. And let us first investigate the reason why, when the churches of God have adopted three books from Solomon's pen, the Book of Proverbs has been put first, that which is called Ecclesiastes second, while the **Song of Songs** is found in the third place. The following are the suggestions that occur to us here.

The branches of learning by means of which men gen-erally attain to knowledge of things are the three which the Greeks called Ethics, Physics and Enoptics; these we may call respectively moral, natural, and inspec-tive. Some among the Greeks, of course, add a fourth branch, Logic, which we may describe as rational. Oth-ers have said that Logic does not stand by itself, but is connected and intertwined throughout with the three studies that we mentioned first. For this Logic is, as we say, rational, in that it deals with the meanings and proper significances and their opposites, the classes and kinds of words and expressions, and gives infor-mation as to the form of each and every saying; and this branch of learning certainly requires not so much to be separated from the others as to be mingled and inwoven with them. That study is called moral, on the other hand, which inculcates a seemly manner of life and gives a grounding in habits that incline to virtue. The study called natural is that in which the nature of each single thing is considered; so that nothing in life may be done which is contrary to nature, but every-thing is assigned to the uses for which the Creator brought it into being. The study called inspective is that by which we go beyond things seen and contem-plate somewhat of things divine and heavenly, behold-ing them with the mind alone, for they are beyond the range of bodily sight.

It seems to me, then, that all the sages of the Greeks borrowed these ideas from Solomon, who had learnt them by the Spirit of God at an age and time long before their own; and that they then put them forward as their own inventions and, by including them in the books of their teachings, left them to be handed down also to those that came after. But, as we said, Solomon discovered and taught these things by the wisdom that he received from God, before anyone; as it is written: *And God gave understanding to Solomon and wisdom exceeding much, and largeness of heart as the sand that is on the seashore. And wisdom was multiplied in him above all the sons of men that were of old, and above all the sages of Egypt*. Wishing, therefore, to distinguish one from another those three branches of learning, which we called general just now—that is, the moral, the natural, and the inspective, and to dif-ferentiate between them, Solomon issued them in three books, arranged in their proper order. First, in Proverbs he taught the moral science, putting rules for living into the form of short and pithy maxims, as was fitting. Secondly, he covered the science known as natural in Ecclesiastes; in this, by discussing at length the things of nature, and by distinguishing the useless and vain from the profitable and essential, he counsels us to forsake vanity and cultivate things useful and upright. The inspective science likewise he has propounded in this little book that we have now in hand—that is, the *Song of Songs*. In this he instills into the soul the love of things divine and heavenly, using for his purpose the figure of the Bride and Bridegroom, and teaches us that communion with God must be attained by the paths of charity and love. But that in laying down these basic principles of true philosophy and establishing the order of the subjects to be learnt and taught, he was neither ignorant of the rational science nor refused to deal with it, he shows plainly right at the beginning of his Proverbs, primarily by the fact that he made *Proverbs* the title of his book; for the word pro-verb denotes that one thing is openly said, and another is inwardly meant. The ordinary use of proverbs shows us this, and John in his Gospel writes of the Saviour saying: *These things have I spoken to you in proverbs; the hour cometh when I will no more speak to you in proverbs, but will show you plainly of the Father.*

So much in passing for the actual tide. But Solomon goes on forthwith to discriminate between the meanings of words: he distinguishes knowledge from wisdom, and instruction from knowledge, and represents the understanding of words as something different again, and says that prudence consists in a person's ability to grasp the shades of meaning in words. He differentiates, moreover, between true justice and right judgement; but he mentions a certain perspicacity as being necessary for those whom he instructs—meaning, I believe, the astuteness of perception by which crooked and fallacious lines of thought may be seen for what they are, and shunned accordingly. And he says, therefore, that subtlety is given by wisdom to the innocent, doubtless lest they should be deceived in the Word of God by sophistic fraud. And in this also it seems to me that he has in mind the rational science, whereby the content of words and the meanings of expressions are discerned, and the proper significance of every utterance is reasonably defined. Children in particular are to be instructed in this science; he enjoins this when he says: *to give perception and the faculty of thought to the younger child.* And because he who is instructed in these matters inevitably rules himself reasonably, because of what he has learned, and preserves a better balance in his life, Solomon says further: *He who understandeth shall acquire government.*

But after all this, knowing that there are different modes of expression and sundry forms of speech in the divine words, whereby the order of living has been transmitted by the prophets to the human race, and realizing that among these there is one figure called a parable, another that is known as dark speech, others that have the name of riddles, and others again that are called the sayings of the wise, he writes: *Thou shalt also understand the parable, and dark speech, and the sayings of the wise, and riddles.* Thus, by these several means, he expounds the rational science clearly and plainly; and, following the custom of the ancients, he unfolds immense and perfect truths in short and pithy phrases. And, if there is anyone who meditates day and night on the law of the Lord, if there is anyone who is as the mouth of the just that meditates wisdom, he will be able to investigate and discover these things more carefully; always provided that he have first sought and knocked at Wisdom's door, beseeching God to open to him and to make him worthy to receive the word of wisdom and the word of knowledge through the Holy Spirit, and to make him a partaker of that Wisdom who said: *I stretched out my words and ye did not hear.*

And rightly does he speak of 'stretching out his words' in the heart of him to whom God had given largeness of heart, as we said above. For the heart of a man is enlarged, when he is able, by taking statements from the Divine Books, to expand by fuller teaching the things that are said briefly and in enigmatic ways. According to this same doctrine of the most wise Solomon, therefore, it behoves him who desires to know wisdom to begin with moral instruction, and to understand the meaning of the text: *Thou hast desired Wisdom: then keep the commandments, and God will give her to thee.* This, then, was the reason why this master, who was the first to teach men divine philosophy, put at the beginning of his work the Book of Proverbs, in which, as we said, the moral science is propounded—so that when a person has progressed in discernment and behaviour he may pass on thence to train his natural intelligence and, by distinguishing the causes and natures of things, may recognize the vanity of vanities that he must forsake, and the lasting and eternal things that he ought to pursue. And so from Proverbs he goes on to Ecclesiastes, who teaches, as we said, that all visible and corporeal things are fleeting and brittle; and surely once the seeker after wisdom has grasped that these things are so, he is bound to spurn and despise them; renouncing the world bag and baggage, if I may put it in that way, he will surely reach out for the things unseen and eternal which, with spiritual meaning verily but under certain secret metaphors of love, are taught in the *Song of Songs*.

This book comes last that a man may come to it when his manner of life has been purified, and he has learnt to know the difference between things corruptible and things incorruptible; so that nothing in the metaphors used to describe and represent the love of the Bride for her celestial Bridegroom—that is, of the perfect soul for the Word of God—may cause him to stumble. For, when the soul has completed these studies, by means of which it is cleansed in all its actions and habits and is led to discriminate between natural things, it is competent to proceed to dogmatic and mystical matters, and in this way advances to the contemplation of the Godhead with pure and spiritual love.

I think, moreover, that this threefold structure of divine philosophy was prefigured in those holy and blessed men on account of whose most holy way of life the Most High God willed to be called *the God of Abraham, the God of Isaac, and the God of Jacob.* For Abraham sets forth moral philosophy through obedience; his obedience was indeed so great, his adherence to orders so strict that when he heard the command: *Go forth out of thy country, and from thy kindred, and out of thy father's house,* he did not delay, but did as he was told forthwith. And he did more even than that: even on hearing that he was to sacrifice his son, he does not hesitate, but complies with the command and, to give an example to those who should come after of the obedience in which moral philosophy consists, *he spared not his only son.* Isaac also is an exponent of natural philosophy, when he digs wells and searches out the roots of things. And Jacob practices the inspective science, in that he earned his name of Israel from his contemplation of the things of God, and saw the camps of heaven, and beheld the House of God and the angels' paths—the ladders reaching up from earth to heaven.

We find, moreover, that for this reason those three blessed men made altars to God, as it was fitting that they should—that is to say, they hallowed the results of their philosophy, no doubt that they might teach us that these fruits must be ascribed, not to our human skills, but to the grace of God. Further, they lived in tents to show thereby that he who applies himself to divine philosophy must have nothing of his own on earth and must be always moving on, not so much from place to place as from knowledge of inferior matters to that of perfect ones. And you will find that this order, which we have pointed out in regard to the books of Solomon, appears in just the same pattern in many other things in the Divine Scriptures too; but it would take too long for us to follow these up, with another matter on hand.

If, then, a man has completed his course in the first subject, as taught in Proverbs, by amending his behaviour and keeping the commandments, and thereafter, having seen how empty is the world and realized the brittleness of transitory things, has come to renounce the world and all that is therein, he will follow on from that point to contemplate and to desire *the things that are not seen*, and *that are eternal.* To attain to these, however, we need God's mercy; so that, having beheld the beauty of the Word of God, we may be kindled with a saving love for Him, and He Himself may deign to love the soul, whose longing for Himself He has perceived.

4. *The Title* 'Song of Songs'

We must now pass on to our next point, and discuss the actual title of '***The Song of Songs.***' You find a similar phrase in what were called *the holies of holies* in the Tent of the Testimony, and again in the *works of works* mentioned in the Book of Numbers, and in what Paul calls *the ages of ages.* In other treatises we have, as far as we were able, considered the difference between *holies* and *holies of holies* in Exodus, and between *works* and *works of works* in the Book of Numbers; neither did we pass over the expression *ages of ages* in the passages where it occurs. Rather than repeat ourselves, therefore, we will let those comments suffice.

But we must now enquire for the first time what are the songs in relation to which this song is called '***The Song of Songs***.' I think they are the songs that were sung of old by prophets or by angels. For the Law is said to have been *ordained by angels in the hand of a mediator.* All those, then, that were uttered by them, were the introductory songs sung by the Bridegroom's friends; but this unique song is that which the Bridegroom Himself was to sing as His marriage-hymn, when about to take His Bride; in which same song the Bride no longer wants the Bridegroom's friends to sing to her, but longs to hear her Spouse who now is with her, speak with His own lips; wherefore she says: *Let Him kiss me with the kisses of His mouth.*

Rightly, then, is this song preferred before all songs. The other songs that the Law and the prophets sang, were sung to the Bride while she was still a little child and had not yet attained maturity. But this song is sung to her, now that she is grown up, and very strong, and ready for a husband's power and the perfect mystery. It is said of her for this reason: *My perfect dove is but one.*

As the perfect Bride of the perfect Husband, then, she has received the words of perfect doctrine. Moses and the children of Israel sang the first song to God, when *they saw the Egyptians dead on the seashore*, and when they *saw the strong hand* and the high arm *of the Lord, and believed in God and Moses His servant.* Then they sang, therefore, saying: *Let us sing to the Lord, for He is gloriously magnified.* And I think myself that nobody can attain to that perfect and mystical song and to the perfection of the Bride which this Scripture contains, unless he first marches *through the midst of the sea upon dry land* and, with *the water becoming to him as a wall on the right hand and on the left,* so makes his escape *from the hands of the Egyptians* that he *beholds them dead on the seashore* and, seeing the strong hand with which the Lord has acted against the Egyptians, believes in the Lord and in His servant Moses. In Moses, I say—in the Law, and in the Gospels, and in all the Divine Scriptures; for then he will have good cause to sing and say: *Let us sing unto the Lord, for He is gloriously magnified.*

A man will sing this song, however, only when he has first been freed from bondage to the Egyptians; but after that, when he has traversed all those things that are written in Exodus and in Leviticus, and has come to be admitted to the divine Numbers, then he will sing another, a second song, when he has emerged from the valley of Zared, which means Strange Descent, and has come to the well of which it is written: *And the Lord said to Moses: 'Gather the people together, and I will give them water to drink from the well.'* For there he will sing and say: *Consecrate the well to Him. The princes dug it, the kings of the Gentiles hewed it out in their kingdom, when they had the rule over them.* But we have already treated more fully of these matters, as far as the Lord gave us, in treating of the Book of Numbers. We must proceed, then, to the well which has been dug by princes and hewn out by kings, on which no common person labours, but all are princes, all are kings—royal and princely souls, that is too say, who search to its depths the well that holds the living water.

After this song we come to that in Deuteronomy, of which the Lord says: *And now write you the words of this song and teach it to the children of Israel, and get them to know it by heart; that this song may be unto me for a testimony among the children of Israel.* And see how great a song and of what sort it is, for which it is not enough that it be sung on earth alone, but heaven too is called upon to listen to it! For it says: *Hear, O heaven, and I will speak: and let the earth give ear to the words of my mouth!* Observe what great and what momentous things are said. *Let my speech*, it says, *be looked for as the rain, and let it come down as the dew upon the grass and as falling snow on the hay; because I have invoked the Name of the Lord*, and so forth.

The fourth song is in the Book of Judges. Of it Scripture says that *Debbora and Barac son of Abinoem sang it in that day, saying: 'Bless ye the Lord for that which the princes undertook, and that which the people purposed. Hear, O ye kings, give ear, ye governors,'* and so forth. But he who sings these words must be himself a bee, whose work is such that kings and commoners alike make use of it for purposes of health. For Debbora means bee, and it is she who sings this song; but Barac sings it with her, and his name means a flash. And this song is sung after a victory, because no one can sing of perfect things until he has conquered

his foes. That is why we sing in this same song: *Arise, arise, O Debbora, rouse up the people in their thousands. Arise, arise, sing a song; arise, O Barac.* But you will find further discussion of these questions too in the little addresses that we published on the Book of Judges.

Following these, the fifth song is in the Second Book of Kings, when *David spoke to the Lord the words of this song, in the day that the Lord delivered him out of the hand of all his enemies, and out of the hand of Saul, and he said: 'The Lord is to me as a rock and a defence and my deliverer; my God will be my keeper.'* If, then, you also have been able to reflect as to who are these enemies whom David vanquishes and overthrows in the First and Second Books of Kings, and how he became worthy to receive the help of the Lord and to be delivered from enemies like that, then you yourself also will be able to sing this fifth song.

The sixth song is in the First Book of Paralipomenon, when David has just appointed Asaph and his brethren to sing the praises of the Lord; and the song begins like this: *Praise ye the Lord and confess Him, and call upon Him by His name; make known His will among the peoples. Sing ye to Him and chant a hymn, relate all His wondrous doings that the Lord hath done*, etc. You must know, however, that the song in the Second Book of Kings is very much like the seventeenth Psalm; and the first part of the song in the First Book of Paralipomenon, as far as the place where it says: *And do no evil to my prophets*, resembles Psalm 104, while the latter part of it, after this passage, shows a likeness to the opening verses of Psalm 95, where we read: *Sing to the Lord, all the earth*, down to the place where the psalmist says, *because He cometh to judge the earth.*

If, therefore, we are to finish our enumeration of the songs, it will be obvious that the book of the ***Song of Songs*** must be put in the seventh place. But, if anyone thinks that the song of Isaias should be numbered with the others—though it does not seem very suitable that the song of Isaias should be put before the ***Song of Songs***, seeing that Isaias wrote much later—if, notwithstanding, anyone is of opinion that the prophetic utterances are to be adjudged according to their content rather than their date, he will then add that song as well, and say that *this* song that Solomon sang is the ***Song of Songs*** not only in relation to those that were sung before it, but also in respect of those that followed it in time. Whereas if anyone opines further that we ought to add from the Book of Psalms whatever is there called a song, or a song of a psalm, he will gather together a multitude of psalms that are older in time. For he will add to the others the fifteen Gradual Songs and, by assessing the virtue of each song separately and collecting from them the grades of the soul's advance, and putting together the order and sequence of things with spiritual understanding, he will be able to show with what stately steps the Bride, as she makes her entrance, attains by way of all these to the nuptial chamber of the Bridegroom, passing *into the place of the wonderful tabernacle, even to the House of God with the voice of joy and praise, the noise of one feasting.* So she comes, as we said, even to the Bridegroom's chamber, that she may hear and speak all these things that are contained in the **Song of Songs**.

Before we come to the actual text of the book, we may make this further enquiry. Why is it that Solomon, who served the will of the Holy Spirit in these three books, is called *Solomon, son of David, who reigned in Israel* in Proverbs, while in the second book the name Solomon does not appear and he says merely: *The words of Ecclesiastes, the son of David, king of Israel in Jerusalem,* calling himself son of David and king of Israel as in the first book, but writing 'words' here in place of 'proverbs,' and calling himself Ecclesiastes, where formerly he gave his name Solomon? And whereas in the former he mentioned only the nation over which he reigned, here he mentions both the nation and the seat of government, Jerusalem. But in the **Song of Songs** he writes neither the name of the nation, nor the place where he reigns, nor even that he is the king at all, nor yet that he had David for his father; he only says *the* **Song of Songs** *that is Solomon's own.* And although it is difficult for me both to be able to examine the differences in these books and arrive at any explanation of them, and also to expound them clearly and commit them to writing when they have been thus searched out, nevertheless, as far as our own intelligence and our readers' apprehension allow, we will try to unfold these matters briefly.

It is, I think, unquestionable that Solomon is in many respects a type of Christ, first in that he is called the Peaceable, and also because *the queen of the south . . . came from the ends of the earth to hear the wisdom of Solomon.* Christ is thus called the Son of David, and reigns in Israel; He reigns also over those kings from whom He gets the title *King of kings.* Again, He *who, being in the form of God, . . . emptied Himself, taking the form of a servant,* that He might gather the Church into one flock, is Himself the true Ecclesiast; for an ecclesiast takes his title from his function of assembling the ecclesia. And then again, who is so truly Solomon—that is, Peaceable, as Our Lord Jesus Christ, *who of God is made unto us wisdom and justice and peace?* Therefore in the first book, Proverbs, where he grounds us in ethical teaching, Solomon is called king in Israel—not in Jerusalem, as yet; because, although we be called Israel by reason of faith, we have not yet got so far as to reach the heavenly Jerusalem. When, however, we have made further progress, and have attained to fellowship with *the Church of the firstborn that is in heaven* and, having rid ourselves more thoroughly of our old natural concerns, have come to recognize the heavenly Jerusalem as our celestial Mother,

then Christ becomes our Ecclesiast too, and is said to reign not in Israel only, but also in Jerusalem. And when the perfection of all things has been achieved and the Bride, who has been perfected—in other words, the whole rational creation—is united with Him, *because He hath made peace through His blood, not only as to the things that are on earth, but also as to the things that are in heaven,* then He is called Solomon only, *when He shall have delivered up the kingdom to God and the Father, when He shall have brought to nought all principality and power. For He must reign until He hath put all His enemies under His feet and death, the last enemy, is destroyed.* Thus, when all things have been pacified and subjected to the Father, and God is all in all, then He will be called Solomon and nothing else—that is, the Peaceable, only.

Fittingly, therefore, and for the same reason as before, we find in this little book that was to be written about the love of the Bridegroom and the Bride, neither 'Son of David,' nor 'king,' nor any other term patent of a corporeal connotation; thus the Bride now perfected may say of Him with reason: *And if we have known Christ after the flesh for a while, but now we know Him so no longer.* Let no one think that she loves anything belonging to the body or pertaining to the flesh, and let no stain be thought of in connection with her love. So the **Song of Songs** is simply Solomon's; it belongs neither to the Son of David, nor to Israel's king, and there is no suggestion of anything carnal about it. And let it not surprise you, seeing that Our Lord and Saviour is One and the Same, that we should speak of Him first as a beginner, in Proverbs; then as advancing, in Ecclesiastes; and lastly as more perfect in the **Song of Songs**, when you see the same things written in the Gospels where He is said, for us and among us, to advance. *Jesus advanced,* it is written, *in age and wisdom with God and men.*

It is, I think, because of all these things that neither 'Son of David' nor 'King of Israel' is written; and also for this further reason that in the **Song of Songs** the Bride had progressed to the point where there was something greater than the kingdom of Jerusalem. For the Apostle says there is a heavenly Jerusalem, and speaks of believers coming thither; but the same Paul calls this Bridegroom, to whom the Bride now hastens, *the High Priest,* and writes of Him not as being in heaven, but as *passing into* and beyond all *the heavens;* whither also His perfected Bride follows Him; cleaving to Him and *joined to Him,* she has ascended thither, for she has been made *one spirit* with Him.

Hence too it seems to me that this was the reason why, when He said to Peter, who could not follow Him at first: *Whither I go, ye cannot come now,* He added: *but thou shalt follow hereafter.* And we gather from the Book of Numbers that there may be something greater than Israel too. For there the whole of Israel is numbered and reckoned in twelve tribes, as under a fixed number; but the tribe of Levi, being of greater eminence than the others, is accounted extra to this number and never thought of as being one of Israel's number; for the writer says: *This is the visit of inspection in which the children of Israel were reckoned according to their households; the visitation of them yielded a total of six hundred and three thousand, five hundred and fifty. And the Levites were not included in this number, as the Lord commanded Moses.* You see how the Levites are set apart from the children of Israel, as being of greater eminence, and are not reckoned among their number.

Further, the priests are described as being more eminent than the Levites; for this same Scripture tells us that *the Lord spoke to Moses, saying: 'Bring the tribe of Levi and make them stand in the sight of Aaron the priest, to minister to him.'* Do you see how here too he both speaks of the priests as superior to the Levites, and once more makes the Levites appear as more eminent than the children of Israel?

We have thought fit to discuss these matters rather more carefully, because we wanted by their means to demonstrate the reason why, in the very titles of his books, Solomon differentiated as necessity required, and signified one thing in Proverbs, another in Ecclesiastes, and yet another in the *Song of Songs*, as the title in each case shows. And the fact that in the *Song of Songs*, where now perfection is shown forth, he describes himself neither as son of David, nor as king, enables us to say further that, since the servant has been made the lord, and the disciple as the master, the servant obviously is such no longer: he has become as the lord. Neither does the disciple figure as a disciple when he has been made as the master; rather, the sometime disciple is in truth as the master now, and the sometime servant as the lord. This line of thought may be applied also to the case of the king and those over whom he reigns, *when the kingdom will be delivered up to God and the Father.*

But let us not overlook the further fact that some people write the title of this little book as **Songs of Songs**. That is, however, incorrect; it is called the *Song of Songs* in the singular, not in the plural.

Let these remarks on the actual heading or title of the book suffice for introduction. Now, with Our Lord's help, let us go on to consider the beginning of the work itself; yet—not to leave anything out—there is one other point about the title and heading of the book that seems to some people to require investigation. For *The **Song of Songs**, which is Solomon's own,* is taken by these persons as meaning *the* Song of the Songs of Solomon, as though he signalized this one song among his many songs. But how shall we accept an interpretation like this when, in the first place, the Church of

God has not adopted any further songs of Solomon to be read; and, in the second place, the Hebrews, by whom God's utterances were transmitted to us, have in their canon no other than these three books of Solomon that we also have in ours? Those who advance this view, however, urge in its support that in the Third Book of Kings we are told that Solomon's songs were many, they cite this to prove that this song is one of many. The passage in question runs: *And God gave to Solomon understanding and wisdom exceeding much and largeness of heart as the sand that is on the seashore. And Solomon became exceeding wise, surpassing the wisdom of all the ancients and of all the sages of Egypt, and surpassing Gethan the Zarite and Henan and Chalcat and Darala; and Solomon spoke three thousand parables, and his songs were five thousand.* They would, therefore, reckon this **Song**, of which we are treating, as of the number of these five thousand songs; but as to when or where those songs were sung, the churches of God have no experience, nor have they even any knowledge of them.

It would be toilsome and irrelevant to the matter in hand for us to enquire how many books are mentioned in the Divine Scriptures, of which nothing whatever has been handed down for us to read. Nor do we find that the Jews made use of lections of this kind; for either the Holy Spirit saw fit to remove them from our midst, because they contained some matters beyond human understanding; or else—in the case of those scriptures that are called apocrypha—because many things were found in them that were corrupt and contrary to the true faith, our predecessors did not see fit for them to be given a place, or admitted among those reckoned as authoritative.

It is beyond us to pass judgement on such matters. But it is common knowledge that the apostles and evangelists borrowed and put into the New Testament many things that we read nowhere in the Scriptures that we account canonical, but that are found none the less in the apocryphal writings, and are quite obviously taken from them. Not that the apocryphal writings are to be given a place in this way: we must *not overpass the everlasting limits which our fathers have set.* But it may be that the apostles and evangelists, being filled with the Holy Spirit, knew what was to be taken out of those writings and what must be rejected; whereas we, who have not such abundance of the Spirit, cannot without danger presume so to select.

In regard to the text before us, therefore, we keep to the statement which we explained above, especially as the writer himself makes a clear distinction by saying: *The **Song of Songs** that is Solomon's own.* For, if he had meant us to understand that this is the Song of Solomon's Songs, he would surely have said: The Song of the Songs that are Solomon's, or A Song from among the Songs of Solomon. But now his saying *that is Solomon's* shows that this **Song**, which we have in hand and which he was about to sing, is Solomon's, and for that reason has the title that he gave to it. . . .

Lines from the first verse of the *Song*

show me you whom my soul loves

where you pasture where you lie at midday
lest I begin to wander after the flocks of your
    companions
if you do not know yourself o fairest of
    women
go out and follow the tracks of the flocks
and pasture your kids beside the tents of the
    shepherds
to my cavalry in the Pharaoh's chariots I have
    likened you my friend
your cheeks are fair like the turtle dove's
your neck like necklaces
we will make you chains of gold inlaid with
    silver

From the translation by E. Ann Matter in The
Voice of My Beloved, *University of
Pennsylvania Press, 1990.*

St. Gregory of Nyssa (essay date late 4th century)

SOURCE: "The First Homily," in *Commentary on the "Song of Songs,"* translated by Casimir McCambley, Hellenic College Press, 1987, pp. 43-56.

[*In the following allegorical interpretation and explanation of its "mysteries," St. Gregory advises that the* Song of Songs *is a literary embodiment of the purity and chastity of Christian love. This essay is believed to have been written toward the end of the fourth century*]

Those of you who, according to the advice of St. Paul, have stripped off the old man with his deeds and desires as you would a filthy garment and have wrapped yourselves by the purity of your lives in the bright garments of the Lord which he displayed upon the mount of transfiguration; you who have put on the Lord Jesus Christ with his holy robe and have been transformed with him into a state which is free from passion and more divine, listen to the mysteries of the **Song of Songs**. Enter the inner chamber of the chaste bridegroom and clothe yourselves with the white garments of pure, chaste thoughts. Let no one bring passionate, fleshly thoughts or a garment of conscience unsuitable for the divine nuptials. Let no one be bound up in his own thoughts, or drag the pure words of the bridegroom and the bride down into earthly, irrational passions. Anyone who entertains such shameful illusions should be cast out from the company of those who share the nuptial joys to the place of weeping (Mt 22.10-13). I issue this warning before entering upon the mystical contemplation of the **Song of Songs**. Through the words of the **Song** the soul is escorted to an incorporeal, spiritual, and pure union with God. For God, who "wishes all to be saved and to come to the recognition of the truth" (1 Tim 2.4), shows the most perfect and blessed way of salvation here—I mean the way of love. For some there is salvation by fear: we contemplate the threat of punishment in hell and so avoid evil. Further, there are those who, because of the hope of the reward held out for a life piously lived, conduct themselves virtuously. They do not possess the good out of love but by the expectation of a recompense. On the other hand, the person who is hastening to spiritual perfection rejects fear. (Such a disposition is servile, and the person with this disposition does not remain with the master out of love. He does not run away out of fear of being scourged.) Rather, the person seeking perfection disdains even rewards: he does not want to give the impression that he prefers the gift to the one who bestows it. He loves "with his whole heart and soul and strength" (Dt 6.5), not any of the things that come from God, but him who is the source of all good things. This, then, is the attitude which he commands to the souls of all who listen to him, for he summons to us to share his own life.

The one who establishes this law is Solomon (3 Kg or 1 Kg 3.12; 5.9-14). According to the divine testimony, his wisdom has no measure. It has no comparison with respect to both all who proceeded him and all who are to come after him. Nothing escapes his notice. Do not suppose that I mean the same Solomon from Bersabee who offered upon the mountains the sacrifice of a thousand victims (3 Kg or 1 Kg: 11.6-8), who sinned by following the counsel of a Sidonian woman (3 Kg or 1 Kg 11.1-2). No, another Solomon [Christ] is signified here: one who is also descended from the seed of David according to the flesh, one whose name means peace, the true king of Israel and builder of God's temple. This other Solomon comprehends the knowledge of all things. His wisdom is infinite and his very essence is wisdom, truth, as well as every exalted, divine name and thought. [Christ] used Solomon as an instrument and speaks to us through his voice first in Proverbs and then in Ecclesiastes. After these two books he speaks in the philosophy set forth in the **Song of Songs** and shows us the ascent to perfection in an orderly fashion.

Not all periods of life according to the flesh are capable of every natural operation; nor do our lives advance in the same way at different periods. (The infant has no share of adult activities, nor is an adult taken up in its nurse's arms, but each time of life has its own proper activity.) So too one can see in the soul an analogy to the body's growth where there is a certain order and sequence leading to a life in accord with virtue.

For this reason, Proverbs teaches in one way and Ecclesiastes in another; the philosophy of the *Song of Songs* transcends both by its loftier teaching. The instruction in Proverbs provides words fit for the person who is still young, adapting its words of admonition to that period of life. "Hear, my son, your father's instruction and reject not your mother's teaching" (Pr 1.8). You see here that the soul is at a stage of life where it is tender and easily formed. Moreover, it still needs maternal instruction and paternal admonition. In order that the infant may listen more willingly to his parents and be more careful in his lessons, he is promised childish trinkets. Such trinkets are the gold chain shining around his neck and the crown entwined with pretty flowers. It is necessary to understand these things fully if the symbol's intent is to point to something better. Thus Proverbs begins the description of wisdom to the child in several different ways and expounds the ineffable beauty so as not to inspire any fear or constraint; rather, it draws the child by yearning and desire to participate in the good. The description of beauty somehow attracts the desire of the young to what is shown, fanning their desire for a participation in beauty.

In order that our affections may be further intensified after having changed our material inclinations to an immaterial state, Solomon adorns the beauty of wisdom with praise. Not only does he present its loveliness with words, but he also states the wealth contained in wisdom, whose Lord will surely dwell with us. The wealth is then seen in the showy adornments of wisdom. The adornment of her right hand is all the ages, since the Word says: "Length of existence and years of life are in her right hand" (Pr 3.16). And on her left hand she wears the precious wealth of the virtues together with the splendor of glory; "And on her left hand are wealth and glory" (3.16). Then Solomon speaks of the fragrance from the bride's mouth which breathes the good odor of righteousness: "From her mouth comes forth righteousness" (3.16).

In place of the natural redness of the bride's lips, he says, law and mercy blossom. In order that beauty might be fully attributed to such a bride, her gait is also praised: "In the paths of righteousness she walks" (8.20). In praising her beauty, Solomon also praises her great size which equals that of a flourishing plant shooting up into full bloom. This plant to which her height is compared, he says, is the tree of life which nourishes those who lay hold of her, a firm and stable column to those who lean upon her. I think that both examples refer to the Lord: He is our life and support. Thus the text reads: "She is a tree of life to those who lay hold of her" and for those who lean upon her as

upon the Lord she is firm. Strength is included along with the remaining praises, that the praise of wisdom's beauty might be completely filled with all good things. "For God founded the earth by wisdom and prepared the heavens by prudence" (Pr 3.19). All the elements in creation Solomon attributes to the power of wisdom and adorns her with many names, for he means the same thing by wisdom, prudence, sense perception, knowledge, apprehension, and the like.

Solomon next escorts the youth to a special dwelling and exhorts him to gaze at the divine bridal chamber. "Do not let her go, and she will cleave to you. Love her and she will guard you. Secure her and she will exult you. Honor her in order that she may embrace you, that she may give to your head a crown of graces, and may cover you with a crown of delight" (Pr 4.6-9). The youth now adorned with these nuptial crowns as a bridegroom is exhorted not to depart from wisdom: "Whenever you walk, bring her and let her be with you. Whenever you sleep, let her guard you in order that when you wake she may converse with you" (6.22). With these and other such exhortations Solomon has inflamed the desire of the one still young according to the inner man, and has shown Wisdom describing herself. In this way Solomon elicits the love of those listening to him. Besides this, Wisdom says: "I love those who love me" (8.17)—for the hope of being loved in return disposes the lover to a more intense desire. Along with these words Solomon added other counsels by clear and easily grasped utterances. He leads the youth to a more perfect state in the final verses of Proverbs where he calls "blessed" the union of love in that section pertaining to the praises of the brave woman. Then Solomon adds the philosophy contained in Ecclesiastes for the person who has been sufficiently introduced by proverbial training to desire virtue. After having reproached in that book men's attitudes towards external appearances, and after having said that everything unstable is vain and passing ("everything which passes is vanity" [Ec 11.8]). Solomon elevates above everything grasped by sense the loving movement of our soul towards invisible beauty. Having thus cleansed the heart with respect to external matters, Solomon then initiates the soul into the divine sanctuary by means of the *Song of Songs*. What is described there is a marriage; but what is understood is the union of the human soul with God.

Because of this, the son in Proverbs is named a bride, and Wisdom is changed into the role of a bridegroom so that a person might be espoused to God by becoming a pure virgin instead of a bridegroom. By clinging to the Lord he might become one spirit (1 Cor 6.17) through a union with what is pure and free from passion and have a pure mind instead of burdened with the flesh's weight (Dt 6.5). Since it is Wisdom speaking, love as much as you can with your whole heart and strength; desire as much as you can. I boldly add to these words: "Be passionate about it." This affection for incorporeal things is beyond reproach and free from lust as wisdom states in Proverbs when she prescribes passionate love . . . for the divine beauty.

But the text now before us gives the same exhortation. It does not merely offer advice regarding love, but through ineffable mysteries it philosophizes and offers an image of the pleasures of life as a preparation for its instruction. The image is one of marriage where the desire for beauty acts as intermediary. The bridegroom does not initiate the desire according to normal human custom, but the virgin anticipates the bridegroom without shame, openly makes her passion known, and prays that she may enjoy the bridegroom's kiss.

Those attending the betrothed virgin are the patriarchs, prophets, and givers of the Law. They bring divine gifts to the bride, her wedding gifts, as it were. (Some examples of these gifts are forgiveness of trespasses, forgetfulness of evil deeds, the cleansing of sins, transformation of nature, the exchange of corruptibility for incorruptibility, enjoyment of paradise, the dignity of God's kingdom, and joy without end.) When the virgin receives all these divine gifts from the noble bearers who bring them through their prophetic teaching, she both confesses her desire and hastens to enjoy the favor of the beauty of the One she so eagerly desires. The virgin's attendants and associates hear her and spur her on to an even greater desire. The bridegroom then arrives leading a chorus of his friends and well-wishers. These represent either the ministering spirits by whom men are saved or the holy prophets. Hearing the bride's voice, they exult and rejoice (Jn 3.29) at the consummation of the pure union by which the soul that clings to the Lord becomes one Spirit with Him, as the Apostle says (1 Cor 6.17).

I will take up again what I said at the start of this homily: let no one who is passionate, fleshly and still smelling of the foul odor of the old man (2 Cor 2.16) drag down the significance of the divine thoughts and words to beastly, irrational thoughts. Rather, let each person go out of himself and out of the material world. Let him ascend into paradise through detachment, having become like God through purity. Then let him enter into the inner sanctuary of the mysteries revealed in this book (the *Song of Songs*). If the soul is unprepared to hear this, let it listen to Moses who forbids us to ascend the spiritual mountain before washing the garments of our hearts and before purifying our souls with the fitting aspersions of our thoughts. As we apply ourselves to this contemplation, we must put aside thoughts of marriage as Moses commanded (Ex 19.15) when he ordered those being initiated to cleanse themselves from marriage. We must follow his prescriptions when we are about to approach the spiritual mountain of the knowledge of God: thoughts about women, along with material goods, are left with the

life below. If any irrational notion should be seen around this mountain, it is destroyed with firmer thoughts as by stones. Otherwise, we would hardly be able to hear the sound of that trumphet reverberating with a great and awesome sound which is beyond the capacity of those who hear it. This sound comes from the dark obscurity where God is and who burns with fire every material thing upon this mountain.

Now let us enter the Holy of Holies, *Song of Songs*. In the expression "Holy of Holies" we are taught a certain superabundance and exaggeration of holiness. Through the title *Song of Songs* the noble text also promises to teach us the mystery of mysteries. To be sure, there are many songs in the divinely inspired teaching by which we acquire great knowledge about God from David, Isaiah, Moses, and many others. However, we learn from the title *Song of Songs* that just as the songs of the saints surpass the wisdom of profane songs, so does the mystery contained here surpass the songs of the saints. Indeed, human understanding left to its own resources could neither discover nor absorb the *Song*'s mystery. The most acute physical pleasure (I mean erotic passion) is used as a symbol in the exposition of this doctrine on love. It teaches us of the need for the soul to reach out to the divine nature's invisible beauty and to love it as much as the body is inclined to love what is akin to itself. The soul must transform passion into passionlessness so that when every corporeal affection has been quenched, our mind may seethe with passion for the spirit alone and be warmed by that fire which the Lord came to cast upon the earth (Lk 12.49).

I have said enough about how those who hear these mystical words should have their souls disposed. Now the time has come to begin our interpretation of the divine words of the *Song of Songs*. First let us consider the significance of the title. It is not accidental, I think, that the book is ascribed to Solomon. This serves as an indication to readers to expect something great and divine. Solomon's reputation for wisdom is unexcelled, and everyone is impressed by it. Therefore, the mention of his name at the outset raises the reader's expectation to find something great and worthy of such a reputation.

In the art of painting different colors combine to represent the subject portrayed. However, the person looking at the image created by the skillful use of colors does not linger over the colors painted on the tablet; he beholds instead only the form which the artist has shown. Thus it is with the present scripture: we should not look at the material of the colors [i.e. the words]; rather, we should consider the image of the king expressed by them in the chaste concepts. For white, yellow, black, red, blue, or any other color, are these words in their obvious meanings—mouth, kiss, myrrh, wire, bodily limbs, bed, maidens, and so forth. The form constituted by these terms is blessedness, detachment, union with God, alienation from evil, and likeness to what is truly beautiful and good. These concepts testify that Solomon's wisdom surpassed the boundaries of human wisdom. What could be more paradoxical than to make nature purify itself of its own passions and teach detachment . . . in words normally suggesting passion . . . ? Solomon does not speak of the necessity of being outside of the flesh's impulses or of mortifying our bodily limbs on earth, or of cleansing our mouths of talk of passion; rather, he disposes the soul to be attentive to purity through words which seem to indicate the complete opposite, and he indicates a pure meaning through the use of sensuous language.

The text should teach us one thing by its introductory words: those introduced into the hidden mysteries of this book are no longer men, but they have been transformed in their nature through the Lord's teaching into something more divine. The Word testified to his disciples that they were more than men. He differentiated them from other men when he said to them: "Who do men say that I am" (Mk 8.27)? The *Song*'s text readily employs words whose obvious meaning indicates the enjoyment of carnal passion. Yet it does not fall into any improper meaning but leads us to the philosophy of divine things by means of chaste concepts. It shows that we are no longer to be men with a nature of flesh and blood; rather, it points to the life we hope for at the resurrection of the saints, an angelic life free from all passion.

After the resurrection, the body which has been transformed into incorruptibility, will again be joined to the soul. The passions now disturbing us because of the flesh will not be restored with those bodies; rather, we shall become tranquil. No longer will the flesh's prudence dispute with the soul. No longer will there be civil war with the passions set against the mind's law, where the soul is overcome and taken captive by sin. Nature will then be cleansed from all such things, and one spirit will be in both. (I mean both in the flesh and in the spirit), and every corporeal disposition will be banished from human nature. Thus the text of the *Song* exhorts us, even if we now live in the flesh, not to turn to it in our thoughts; rather we should only regard the soul and attribute all manifestations of affection in the text to the surpassing goodness of God as pure, undefiled offerings. For God alone is truly sweet, desirable and worthy of love. The present enjoyment of God is the starting point for a greater share of his goodness, and it increases our desire for him. Thus, in Moses (Ex 33.11) the bride loved the bridegroom. As the virgin says in the *Song*: "Let him kiss me with the kisses of his mouth." Moses conversed with God face to face, as scripture testifies (Dt 34.10), and he thereby acquired a still greater desire for these kisses after the theophanies. He sought God as if he had never seen him. So it is with all others in whom the desire for God is deeply embedded: they never cease to desire, but every enjoyment of God they turn into the kindling of a still more intense desire.

Even now the soul united to God never has its fill of enjoyment. The more it enjoys his beauty, the more its desire for him increases. The words of the bridegroom are spirit and life (Jn 5.24), and everyone who clings to the Spirit becomes spirit. He who attaches himself to life passes from death into life as the Lord has said. Thus the virginal soul desires to draw near to the fountain of spiritual life. The fountain is the bridegroom's mouth from which the words of eternal life well forth. It fills the mouth drawn to it, just as with the prophet when he drew in the spirit through his mouth (Ps 118.131). Since it is necessary for the person drawing water from a fountain to apply his mouth to his mouth, and since the Lord himself is a fountain as he says: "If anyone thirsts, let him come to me and drink" (Jn 7.37), so the thirsting soul wishes to bring its mouth to the mouth that springs up with life and says: "Let him kiss me with the kisses of his mouth" (1-2). He who wells up with life for all and wishes all to be saved desires every person to share this kiss, for this kiss purges away all filth.

It seems to me that the Lord was reproaching Simon the Leper when he said: "You gave me no kiss" (Lk 7.45). He meant by this: you would have been cleansed of disease if you had drawn purity with your mouth. But in all likelihood Simon was unworthy of love since he had an excess growth of flesh through his illness and remained unmoved in desire for God by reason of his disease. But once the soul has been cleansed and is no longer hindered by the leprosy of the flesh, it looks to the treasure house of all good things. A name for this treasure house is the heart. From it there comes to the breasts the wealth of divine milk by which the soul is nourished and draws grace in proportion to its faith. Therefore the soul exclaims: "Your breasts are better than wine," signifying by the breasts the heart. Nobody will err if he understands by the heart the hidden, secret power of God. One would rightly suppose that the breasts are the activities of God's power for us by which he nourishes each one's life and bestows appropriate nourishment.

We are indirectly taught another lesson through the philosophy of this book, namely that perception within us is two-fold—bodily and divine. As the Word says in Proverbs, "You will find perception of God" (Pr 2.5). A certain analogy exists between the activities of the soul and the sense organs of the body. This we learn from the present text. Wine and milk are distinguished by taste, while the intellectual and apprehending capacity of the soul grasps spiritual realities. A kiss is effected through the sense of touch; the lips of two persons make contact in a kiss. On the other hand, there is a certain sense of touch in the soul which takes hold of the Word and works in an incorporeal, spiritual way. As John says: "Our hands have handled the word of life" (1 Jn 1.1). Similarly, the scent of the divine perfumes is not perceived by the nose, but by a certain spiritual and immaterial power drawing in the good odor of Christ by an inhalation of the Spirit. Thus, the next part of the virgin's prayer in the *Song*'s first words says: "Your breasts are better than wine, and the scent of your perfumes is beyond all ointments" (1.1-2).

What is signified by these words is, in our opinion, neither trivial nor unimportant. Through the comparison of milk from the divine breasts with the enjoyment obtained from wine we learn, I think, that all human wisdom, science, power of observation and comprehension of imagination cannot match the simple nourishment of the divine teaching. Milk, the food of infants, comes from the breasts. On the other hand, wine, with its strength and warming capacity, is enjoyment for the more perfect. However, the perfection of the wisdom of the world is less than the childlike teaching of the divine world. Hence the divine breasts are better than human wine, and the scent of divine perfumes is lovelier than any fragrance.

The meaning seems to me to be as follows: We understand the perfumes as virtues—wisdom, justice, temperance, fortitude, and so forth. If we anoint ourselves with these aromas, each of us, according to our own capacity and choice, has a good odor. Each of us has his respective odor—one has wisdom or temperance, another has fortitude or justice, or anything else pertaining to virtue. Another person may have a good odor within himself compounded from all these perfumes. However, all of them together could not compare with that perfect virtue which the heavens contain. As the prophet Habakkuk says: "His virtue covered the heavens" (3.3). This is God's absolute wisdom, justice, truth, and all the rest. Therefore, the odor of the heavenly ointments, he says, holds a delight which is incomparable to any aroma known by us.

In what immediately follows, the soul-spouse again touches on a more sublime philosophy and shows that the divine power is both utterly transcendent and unable to be contained by human conceptions. The text says: "Your name is ointment poured forth" (1.3). To me something like the following is signified through this verse: the unlimited [divine] nature cannot be accurately contained by a name; rather, every capacity for concepts and every form of words and names, even if they seem to contain something great and befitting God's glory, are unable to grasp his reality. But starting from certain traces and sparks, as it were, our words aim at the unknown, and from what we can grasp we make conjectures by a kind of analogy about the ungraspable. Whatever name we may adopt to signify the

perfume of divinity, it is not the perfume itself which we signify by our expressions; rather, we reveal just the slightest trace of the divine odor by means of our theological terms. As in the case of jars from which perfume has been poured out, the perfume's own nature is not known. But from the slight traces left from the vapors in the jar we get some idea about the perfume that has been emptied out. Hence we learn that the perfume of divinity, whatever it is in its essence, transcends every name and thought. However, the wonders visible in the universe give material for the theological terms by which we call God wise, powerful, good, holy, blessed, eternal, judge, savior, and so forth. All these give some small indication of the divine perfume's quality. Creation retains the traces of this divine perfume through its visible wonders as in the example of a perfume jar. "Therefore, the young maidens have loved you and have drawn you" (1.3). The bridegroom states here the cause of their noble yearning and loving disposition. Who can help but love such a beauty provided that he has an eye capable of reaching out to its loveliness? The beauty grasped is great; but infinitely greater is the beauty of which we get a glimpse from the appearances.

Passion does not touch those who are still infants, for an infant is incapable of passion; neither is it a problem for those in extreme old age. So too with regard to the divine beauty: both the person who is still an infant tossed about by every wind of doctrine and the aged person approaching death are incapable of desire. The invisible beauty does not touch such people, but only the soul which has passed the state of infancy and has attained the flower of spiritual maturity. Such a soul the text calls young (1.3); it has no spot or wrinkle or the like; it is neither lacking in perception because of infancy nor enfeebled by old age. This soul obeys the greatest and first commandment of the Law—to love that divine beauty with all its heart and strength (Dt 6.5). The human mind is unable to find any description, example, or adequate expression of that beauty.

Therefore, such maidens have grown through their virtues and at the proper time have entered the bridal chamber of the divine mysteries. Now they love the bridegroom's beauty, and through love they draw him to themselves. For he is a bridegroom who repays the desire of those who love and says in the person of Wisdom "I love those who love me," and "I will give substance to those who love me." (The bridegroom himself is this substance.) "And I will fill their treasuries with good things" (Pr 8.17, 21). The souls, therefore, draw to themselves a desire for their immortal bridegroom and follow the Lord God, as it is written (Hos 11.10). The cause of their love is the scent of the perfume to which they eternally run; they stretch out to what is in front, forgetting what is behind. "We shall run after you toward the scent of your perfumes" (1.4).

Those who are not yet perfect in virtue and who are still young promise to run towards the goal which the scent of perfumes represents. For they say, "We shall run toward the scent of your perfumes." But the more perfect soul, having stretched forward more earnestly, has already obtained the goal for which the course is undertaken, and it is worthy of the treasures in the storehouse. For she says: "The king has brought me into his chamber" (1.4). She desired to touch the good with the very tip of her lips and touched the beauty only as much as the power of her prayer could reach. (She prayed [1.2] to become worthy of a kiss through the illumination of the Word.) Now, through what she has already achieved, she has passed to a more interior part of the mysteries with her mind, and she cries out that her passage has brought her only to the vestibule of goodness. By the first fruits of the Spirit of which she was made worthy by the kiss of her spouse she says that she searches the depths of God within the innermost sanctuary of paradise, and, as the great Paul said, sees things unseen and hears words not to be spoken (2 Cor 12.4).

The discourse now reveals an ecclesiastical concern, for those who were first instructed by grace and who became eyewitnesses of the Word did not keep the good just for themselves. They passed on the same grace to those who came after them. Because of this the maidens say to the bride who was the first to be filled with good things by coming face to face with the Word and who was made worthy of the hidden mysteries: "Let us rejoice and be glad in you" (1.4) for your joy is our common rejoicing. Because you love the Word's breasts more than wine, we shall imitate you and love your breasts more than human wine, for through them you feed those who are infants in Christ.

To make the intention of the passage even clearer, consider the following: John, who reclined upon the Lord's chest, loved the Word's breasts (Jn 13.25); and having placed his heart like a sponge, as it were, beside the fountain of life, he was filled by an ineffable transmission of the mysteries hidden in the heart of the Lord. John offers us the teat filled by the Word and fills us with the good things he got from the fountain of goodness, loudly proclaiming the Word who exists eternally. Thus we may now rightly say, "We will love your breasts more than wine," if we have become like the maidens and are no longer infants in mind, yoked to an infantile kind of vanity, and if we are not soiled through sin in an old age unto death. Therefore, let us love the flow of your teaching, for "righteousness has loved you" (1.4). This is the disciple whom Jesus loved, and Jesus is righteousness. The text applies a more beautiful and fitting name to the Lord than the prophet David did, for David says that "The Lord is righteous" (Ps 91.15). This text, however, calls him righteousness. Whatever is crooked he makes straight. May all our crookedness be made straight and all our rough-

ness, smooth, by the grace of our Lord Jesus Christ, to whom be glory forever and ever. Amen.

St. Bernard of Clairvaux (essay date c. 1136)

SOURCE: "Sermon 1" and "Sermon 2," in *On the "Song of Songs" I*, translated by Kilian Walsh, Irish University Press, 1971, pp. 1-15.

[*In the following three sermons, presented around 1136, St. Bernard explains the title of the* Song of Songs; *the kiss as a symbol of God's presence and as a sustainer of faith; and suggests an interpretive approach to this and to other biblical texts.*]

Sermon 1

ON THE TITLE OF THE BOOK

The instructions that I address to you, my brothers, will differ from those I should deliver to people in the world, at least the manner will be different. The preacher who desires to follow St Paul's method of teaching will give them milk to drink rather than solid food, and will serve a more nourishing diet to those who are spiritually enlightened: "We teach," he said, "not in the way philosophy is taught, but in the way that the Spirit teaches us: we teach spiritual things spiritually." And again: "We have a wisdom to offer those who have reached maturity," in whose company, I feel assured, you are to be found, unless in vain have you prolonged your study of divine teaching, mortified your senses, and meditated day and night on God's law. Be ready then to feed on bread rather than milk. Solomon has bread to give that is splendid and delicious, the bread of that book called the **Song of Songs**. Let us bring it forth then if you please, and break it.

Now, unless I am mistaken, by the grace of God you have understood quite well from the book of Ecclesiastes how to recognize and have done with the false promise of this world. And then the book of Proverbs—has not your life and your conduct been sufficiently amended and enlightened by the doctrine it inculcates? These are two loaves of which it has been your pleasure to taste, loaves you have welcomed as coming from the cupboard of a friend. Now approach for this third loaf that, if possible, you may always recognize what is best. Since there are two evils that comprise the only, or at least the main, enemies of the soul: a misguided love of the world and an excessive love of self, the two books previously mentioned can provide an antidote to each of these infections. One uproots pernicious habits of mind and body with the hope of self-control. The other, by the use of enlightened reason, quickly perceives a delusive tinge in all that the world holds glorious, truly distinguishing between it and deeper truth. Moreover, it causes the fear of God and the observance of his commandments to be preferred to all human pursuits and worldly desires. And rightly so, for the former is the beginning of wisdom, the latter its culmination, for there is no true and consummate wisdom other than the avoidance of evil and the doing of good, no one can successfully shun evil without the fear of God, and no work is good without the observance of the commandments.

Taking it then that these two evils have been warded off by the reading of those books, we may suitably proceed with this holy and contemplative discourse which, as the fruit of the other two, may be delivered only to well prepared ears and minds.

Before the flesh has been tamed and the spirit set free by zeal for truth, before the world's glamour and entanglements have been firmly repudiated, it is a rash enterprise on any man's part to presume to study spiritual doctrines. Just as a light is flashed in vain on closed or sightless eyes, so "an unspiritual person cannot accept anything of the Spirit of God." For "the Holy Spirit of instruction shuns what is false," and that is what the life of the intemperate man is. Nor will he ever have a part with the pretensions of the world, since he is the Spirit of Truth. How can there be harmony between the wisdom that comes down from above and the wisdom of the world, which is foolishness to God, or the wisdom of the flesh which is at enmity with God? I am sure that the friend who comes to us on his travels will have no reason to murmur against us after he has shared in this third loaf.

But who is going to divide this loaf? The Master of the house is present, it is the Lord you must see in the breaking of the bread. For who else could more fittingly do it? It is a task that I would not dare to arrogate to myself. So look upon me as one from whom you look for nothing. For I myself am one of the seekers, one who begs along with you for the food of my soul, the nourishment of my spirit. Poor and needy, I knock at that door of his which, "when he opens, nobody can close," that I may find light on the profound mystery to which this discourse leads. Patiently all creatures look to you, O Lord. "Little children go begging for bread; no one spares a scrap for them;" they await it from your merciful love. O God most kind, break your bread for this hungering flock, through my hands indeed if it should please you, but with an efficacy that is all your own.

Tell us, I beg you, by whom, about whom and to whom it is said: "Let him kiss me with the kiss of his mouth." How shall I explain so abrupt a beginning, this sudden irruption as from a speech in mid-course? For the words spring upon us as if indicating one speaker to whom another is replying as she demands a kiss—whoever she may be. But if she asks for or

demands a kiss from somebody, why does she distinctly and expressly say *with the mouth,* and even with *his own* mouth, as if lovers should kiss by means other than the mouth, or with mouths other than their own? But yet she does not say: "Let him kiss me *with his mouth;*" what she says is still more intimate: "with the kiss of his mouth." How delightful a ploy of speech this, prompted into life by the kiss, with Scripture's own engaging countenance inspiring the reader and enticing him on, that he may find pleasure even in the laborious pursuit of what lies hidden, with a fascinating theme to sweeten the fatigue of research. Surely this mode of beginning that is not a beginning, this novelty of diction in a book so old, cannot but increase the reader's attention. It must follow too that this work was composed, not by any human skill but by the artistry of the Spirit, difficult to understand indeed but yet enticing one to investigate.

So now what shall we do? Shall we by-pass the title? No, not even one iota may be omitted, since we are commanded to gather up the tiniest fragments lest they be lost. The title runs: "The beginning of Solomon's *Song of Songs.*" First of all take note of the appropriateness of the name "Peaceful," that is, Solomon, at the head of a book which opens with the token of peace, with a kiss. Take note too that by this kind of opening only men of peaceful minds, men who can achieve mastery over the turmoil of the passions and the distracting burden of daily chores, are invited to the study of this book.

Again, the title is not simply the word "**Song**," but "*Song of Songs*," a detail not without significance. For though I have read many songs in the Scriptures, I cannot recall any that bear such a name. Israel chanted a song to Yahweh, celebrating his escape from the sword and the tyranny of Pharaoh, and the twofold good fortune that simultaneously liberated and avenged him in the Red Sea. Yet even though chanted, this has not been called a "Song of Songs"; Scripture, if my memory serves me right, introduces it with the words: "Israel sang this song in honor of Yahweh." Song poured from the lips of Deborah, of Judith, of the mother of Samuel, of several of the prophets, yet none of these songs is styled a "Song of Songs." You will find that all of them, as far as I can see, were inspired to song because of favors to themselves or to their people, songs for a victory won, for an escape from danger or the gaining of a boon long sought. They would not be found ungrateful for the divine beneficence, so all sang for reasons proper to each, in accord with the Psalmist's words: "He gives thanks to you, O God, for blessing him." But King Solomon himself, unique as he was in wisdom, renowned above all men, abounding in wealth, secure in his peace, stood in no need of any particular benefit that would have inspired him to sing those songs. Nor does Scripture in any place attribute such a motive to him.

We must conclude then it was a special divine impulse that inspired these songs of his that now celebrate the praises of Christ and his Church, the gift of holy love, the sacrament of endless union with God. Here too are expressed the mounting desires of the soul, its marriage song, an exultation of spirit poured forth in figurative language pregnant with delight. It is no wonder that like Moses he put a veil on his face, equally resplendent as it must have been in this encounter, because in those days few if any could sustain the bright vision of God's glory. Accordingly, because of its excellence, I consider this nuptial song to be well deserving of the title that so remarkably designates it, the **Song of Songs**, just as he in whose honor it is sung is uniquely proclaimed King of kings and Lord of lords.

Furthermore if you look back on your own experience, is it not in that victory by which your faith overcomes the world, in "your exit from the horrible pit and out of the slough of the marsh," that you yourselves sing a new song to the Lord for all the marvels he has performed? Again, when he purposed to "settle your feet on a rock and to direct your steps," then too, I feel certain, a new song was sounding on your lips, a song to our God for his gracious renewal of your life. When you repented he not only forgave your sins but even promised rewards, so that rejoicing in the hope of benefits to come, you sing of the Lord's ways: how great is the glory of the Lord! And when, as happens, texts of Scripture hitherto dark and impenetrable at last become bright with meaning for you, then, in gratitude for this nurturing bread of heaven you must charm the ears of God with a voice of exultation and praise, a festal song. In the daily trials and combats arising from the flesh, the world and the devil, that are never wanting to those who live devout lives in Christ, you learn by what you experience that man's life on earth is a ceaseless warfare, and are impelled to repeat your songs day after day for every victory won. As often as temptation is overcome, an immoral habit brought under control, an impending danger shunned, the trap of the seducer detected, when a passion long indulged is finally and perfectly allayed, or a virtue persistently desired and repeatedly sought is ultimately obtained by God's gift; so often, in the words of the prophet, let thanksgiving and joy resound. For every benefit conferred, God is to be praised in his gifts. Otherwise when the time of judgment comes, that man will be punished as an ingrate who cannot say to God: "Your statutes were my song in the land of exile."

Again I think that your own experience reveals to you the meaning of those psalms, which are called not Songs of Songs but Songs of the Steps, in that each one, at whatever stage of growth he be, in accord with the upward movements of his heart may choose one of these Songs to praise and give glory to him who empowers you to advance. I don't know how else these words could be true: "There are shouts of joy and victory in the tents of the just." And still more that beautiful and salutary exhortation of the Apostle: "With psalms and hymns and spiritual canticles, singing and chanting to the Lord in your hearts."

But there is that other song which, by its unique dignity and sweetness, excels all those I have mentioned and any others there might be; hence by every right do I acclaim it as the **Song of Songs**. It stands at a point where all the others culminate. Only the touch of the Spirit can inspire a song like this, and only personal experience can unfold its meaning. Let those who are versed in the mystery revel in it; let all others burn with desire rather to attain to this experience than merely to learn about it. For it is not a melody that resounds abroad but the very music of the heart, not a trilling on the lips but an inward pulsing of delight, a harmony not of voices but of wills. It is a tune you will not hear in the streets, these notes do not sound where crowds assemble; only the singer hears it and the one to whom he sings—the lover and the beloved. It is preeminently a marriage song telling of chaste souls in loving embrace, of their wills in sweet concord, of the mutual exchange of the heart's affections.

The novices, the immature, those but recently converted from a worldly life, do not normally sing this song or hear it sung. Only the mind disciplined by persevering study, only the man whose efforts have borne fruit under God's inspiration, the man whose years, as it were, make him ripe for marriage—years measured out not in time but in merits—only he is truly prepared for nuptial union with the divine partner, a union we shall describe more fully in due course. But the hour has come when both our rule and the poverty of our state demand that we go out to work. Tomorrow, with God's help, we shall continue to speak about the kiss, because today's discourse on the title sets us free to resume where we had begun.

Sermon 2

VARIOUS MEANINGS OF THE KISS

During my frequent ponderings on the burning desire with which the patriarchs longed for the incarnation of Christ, I am stung with sorrow and shame. Even now I can scarcely restrain my tears, so filled with shame am I by the lukewarmness, the frigid unconcern of these miserable times. For which of us does the consummation of that event fill with as much joy as the mere promise of it inflamed the desires of the holy men of pre-christian times? Very soon now there will be great rejoicing as we celebrate the feast of Christ's birth. But how I wish it were inspired by his birth! All the more therefore do I pray that the intense longing of those men of old, their heartfelt expectation, may be enkindled in me by these words: "Let him kiss me with the kiss of his mouth." Many an upright man in those far-off times sensed within himself how profuse the graciousness that would be poured upon those lips. And intense desire springing from that perception impelled him to utter: "Let him kiss me with the kiss of his mouth," hoping with every fiber of his being that he might not be deprived of a share in a pleasure so great.

The conscientious man of those days might repeat to himself: "Of what use to me the wordy effusions of the prophets? Rather let him who is the most handsome of the sons of men, let him kiss me with the kiss of his mouth. No longer am I satisfied to listen to Moses, for he is a slow speaker and not able to speak well. Isaiah is 'a man of unclean lips,' Jeremiah does not know how to speak, he is a child; not one of the prophets makes an impact on me with his words. But he, the one whom they proclaim, let him speak to me, 'let him kiss me with the kiss of his mouth.' I have no desire that he should approach me in their person, or address me with their words, for they are 'a watery darkness, a dense cloud'; rather in his own person 'let him kiss me with the kiss of his mouth;' let him whose presence is full of love, from whom exquisite doctrines flow in streams, let him become 'a spring inside me, welling up to eternal life.' Shall I not receive a richer infusion of grace from him whom the Father has anointed with the oil of gladness above all his rivals, provided that he will bestow on me the kiss of his mouth? For his living, active word is to me a kiss, not indeed an adhering of the lips that can sometimes belie a union of hearts, but an unreserved infusion of joys, a revealing of mysteries, a marvellous and indistinguishable mingling of the divine light with the enlightened mind, which, joined in truth to God, is one spirit with him. With good reason then I avoid trucking with visions and dreams; I want no part with parables and figures of speech; even the very beauty of the angels can only leave me wearied. For my Jesus utterly surpasses these in his majesty and splendor. Therefore I ask of him what I ask of neither man nor angel: that he kiss me with the kiss of his mouth.

Note how I do not presume that it is with his mouth I shall be kissed, for that constitutes the unique felicity and singular privilege of the human nature he assumed. No, in the consciousness of my lowliness I ask to be kissed with the kiss of his mouth, an experience shared by all who are in a position to say: 'Indeed from his fullness we have, all of us, received.'

I must ask you to try to give your whole attention here. The mouth kisses signifies the Word who assumes human nature; the nature assumed receives the kiss; the kiss however, that takes its being both from the giver and the receiver, is a person that is formed by both, none other than "the one mediator between God and mankind, himself a man, Christ Jesus." It is for this reason that none of the saints dared say: "let

him kiss me with his mouth," but rather, "with the kiss of his mouth." In this way they paid tribute to that prerogative of Christ, on whom uniquely and in one sole instance the mouth of the Word was pressed, that moment when the fullness of the divinity yielded itself to him as the life of his body. A fertile kiss therefore, a marvel of stupendous self-abasement that is not a mere pressing of mouth upon mouth; it is the uniting of God with man. Normally the touch of lip on lip is the sign of the loving embrace of hearts, but this conjoining of natures brings together the human and divine, shows God reconciling "to himself all things, whether on earth or in heaven." "For he is the peace between us, and has made the two into one." This was the kiss for which just men yearned under the old dispensation, foreseeing as they did that in him they would "find happiness and a crown of rejoicing," because in him were hidden "all the jewels of wisdom and knowledge." Hence their longing to taste that fullness of his.

You seem to be in agreement with this explanation, but I should like you to listen to another.

Even the holy men who lived before the coming of Christ understood that God had in mind plans of peace for the human race. "Surely the Lord God does nothing without revealing his secret to his servants, the prophets." What he did reveal however was obscure to many. For in those days faith was a rare thing on the earth, and hope but a faint impulse in the heart even of many of those who looked forward to the deliverance of Israel. Those indeed who foreknew also proclaimed that Christ would come as man, and with him, peace. One of them actually said: "He himself will be peace in our land when he comes." Enlightened from above they confidently spread abroad the message that through him men would be restored to the favor of God. John, the fore-runner of the Lord, recognizing the fulfillment of that prophecy in his own time, declared: "Grace and truth have come through Jesus Christ." In our time every christian can discover by experience that this is true.

In those far-off days however, while the prophets continued to foretell the covenant, and its author continued to delay his coming, the faith of the people never ceased to waver because there was no one who could redeem or save. Hence men grumbled at the postponements of the coming of this Prince of Peace so often proclaimed by the mouth of his holy prophets from ancient times. As doubts about the fulfillment of the prophecies began to recur, all the more eagerly did they make demands for the kiss, the sign of the promised reconcilement. It was as if a voice from among the people would challenge the prophets of peace: "How much longer are you going to keep us in suspense? You are always foretelling a peace that is never realized; you promise a world of good but trouble on trou-

A medieval manuscript depicting Christ and the Church kissing.

ble comes. At various times in the past and in various different ways this same hope was fostered by angels among our ancestors, who in turn have passed the tidings on to us. 'Peace! Peace!' they say, 'but there is no peace.' If God desires to convince me of that benevolent will of his, so often vouched for by the prophets but not yet revealed by the event, then let him kiss me with the kiss of his mouth, and so by this token of peace make my peace secure. For how shall I any longer put my trust in mere words? It is necessary now that words be vindicated by action. If those men are God's envoys let him prove the truth of their words by his own advent, so often the keynote of their predictions, because unless he comes they can do nothing. He sent his servant bearing a staff, but neither voice nor life is forthcoming. I do not rise up, I am not awakened, I am not shaken out of the dust, nor do I breathe in hope, if the Prophet himself does not come down and kiss me with the kiss of his mouth."

Here we must add that he who professes to be our mediator with God is God's own Son, and he is God. But what is man that he should take notice of him, the son of man that he should be concerned about him?

Where shall such as I am find the confidence, the daring, to entrust myself to him who is so majestic? How shall I, mere dust and ashes, presume that God takes an interest in me? He is entirely taken up with loving his Father, he has no need of me nor of what I possess. How then shall I find assurance that if he is my mediator he will never fail me? If it be really true, as you prophets have said, that God has determined to show mercy, to reveal himself in a more favorable light, let him establish a covenant of peace, an everlasting covenant with me by the kiss of his mouth. If he will not revoke his given word, let him empty himself, let him humble himself, let him bend to me and kiss me with the kiss of his mouth. If the mediator is to be acceptable to both parties, equally dependable in the eyes of both, then let him who is God's Son become man, let him become the Son of Man, and fill me with assurance by this kiss of his mouth. When I come to recognize that he is truly mine, then I shall feel secure in welcoming the Son of God as mediator. Not even a shadow of mistrust can then exist, for after all he is my brother, and my own flesh. It is impossible that I should be spurned by him who is bone from my bones, and flesh from my flesh.

We should by now have come to understand how the discontent of our ancestors displayed a need for this sacrosanct kiss, that is, the mystery of the incarnate word, for faith, hard-pressed throughout the ages with trouble upon trouble, was ever on the point of failing, and a fickle people, yielding to discouragement, murmured against the promises of God. Is this a mere improvisation on my part? I suggest that you will find it to be the teaching of the Scriptures: for instance, consider the burden of complaint and murmuring in those words: "Order on order, order on order, rule on rule, rule on rule, a little here, a little there." Or those prayerful exclamations, troubled yet loyal: "Give those who wait for you their reward, and let your prophets be proved worthy of belief." Again: "Bring about what has been prophesied in your name." There too you will find those soothing promises, full of consolation: "Behold the Lord will appear and he will not lie. If he seems slow, wait for him, for he will surely come and he will not delay." Likewise: "His time is close at hand when he will come and his days will not be prolonged." Speaking in the name of him who is promised the prophet announces: "Behold I am coming towards you like a river of peace, and like a stream in spate with the glory of the nations." In all these statements there is evidence both of the urgency of the preachers and of the distrust of those who listened to them. The people murmured, their faith wavered, and in the words of Isaiah: "the ambassadors of peace weep bitterly." Therefore because Christ was late in coming, and the whole human race in danger of being lost in despair, so convinced was it that human weakness was an object of contempt with no hope of the reconciliation with God through a grace so frequently promised, those good men whose faith remained strong eagerly longed for the more powerful assurance that only his human presence could convey. They prayed intensely for a sign that the covenant was about to be restored for the sake of a spiritless, faithless people.

Oh root of Jesse, that stands as a signal to the peoples, how many prophets and kings wanted to see what you see, and never saw it!

IV. Happy above them all is Simeon, by God's mercy still bearing fruit in old age! He rejoiced to think that he would see the long-desired sign. He saw it and was glad: and having received the kiss of peace he is allowed to go in peace, but not before he had told his audience that Jesus was born to be a sign that would be rejected. Time proved how true this was. No sooner had the sign of peace arisen than it was opposed, by those, that is, who hated peace; for his peace is with men of good-will, but for the evil minded he is "a stone to stumble over, a rock to bring men down." Herod accordingly was perturbed, and so was the whole of Jerusalem. Christ "came to his own domain, and his own people did not accept him." Those shepherds, however, who kept watch over their flocks by night, were fortunate for they were gladdened by a vision of this sign. Even in those early days he was hiding these things from the learned and the clever, and revealing them to mere children. Herod, as you know, desired to see him, but because his motive was not genuine he did not succeed. The sign of peace was given only to men of good-will, hence to Herod and others like him was given the sign of the prophet Jonah. The angel said to the shepherds: "Here is a sign for you," you who are humble, obedient, not given to haughtiness, faithful to prayer and meditating day and night on God's law. "This is a sign for you," he said. What sign? The sign promised by the angels, sought after by the people, foretold by the prophets; this is the sign that the Lord Jesus has now brought into existence and revealed to you, a sign by which the incredulous are made believers, the dispirited are made hopeful and the fervent achieve security. This therefore is the sign for you. But as a sign what does it signify? It reveals mercy, grace, peace, the peace that has no end. And finally, the sign is this: "You will find a baby, wrapped in swaddling clothes and lying in a manger." God himself, however, is in this baby, reconciling the world to himself. He will be put to death for your sins and raised to life to justify you, so that made righteous by faith you may be at peace with God. This was the sign of peace that the Prophet once urged King Achez to ask of the Lord his God, "either from the depths of Sheol or from the heights above." But the ungodly king refused. His wretched state blinded him to the belief that in this sign the highest things above would be joined to the lowest things below in peace. This was achieved when Christ, descending into Sheol, saluted its dwellers with a holy kiss, the pledge of peace, and then going up to heaven, enabled the spirits there to share in the same pledge in joy without end.

I must end this sermon. But let me sum up briefly the points we have raised. It would seem that this holy kiss was of necessity bestowed on the world for two reasons. Without it the faith of those who wavered would not have been strengthened, nor the desires of the fervent appeased. Moreover, this kiss is no other than the Mediator between God and man, himself a man, Christ Jesus, who with the Father and Holy Spirit lives and reigns as God for ever and ever. Amen.

St. Bernard of Clairvaux (essay date c. 1136)

SOURCE: "Sermon 31," in On the "Song of Songs" II, translated by Kilian Walsh, Cistercian Publications, 1976, pp. 124-33.

[See annotation to previous excerpt]

Sermon 31

THE VARIOUS WAYS OF SEEING GOD

Tell me, you whom my soul loves, where you pasture

your flock, where you make it lie down at noon?" The Word, who is the Bridegroom, often makes himself known under more than one form to those who are fervent. Why so? Doubtless because he cannot be seen yet as he is. That vision is unchanging, because the form in which he will then be seen is unchanging; for he is, and can suffer no change determined by present, past or future. Eliminate past and future, and where then is alteration or any shadow of a change? For whatever evolves out of the past and does not cease to move toward future development, passes through the instant that is the present, but one cannot say: it is. How can one say: it is, when it never remains in the same state? That alone truly is, which is neither altered from its past mode of being nor blotted out by a future mode, but "is" alone is predicated of it impregnably and unchangeably, and it remains what it is. No reference to the past can deny that it is from all eternity, nor any reference to the future that it is for all eternity. In this way it proves that it truly is, that is, it is uncreated, interminable, immutable. When he therefore who exists in this manner—who, furthermore, cannot be one moment in this form, another in that—is seen just as he is, that vision endures, as I have said, since no alteration interrupts it. This is the moment when that one denarius mentioned in the Gospel is given in the one vision that is offered to everyone who sees. For as he who is seen is immutable in himself, he is present immutably to all who contemplate him; to these there is nothing more desirable that they wish to see, nothing more enticing that they could see. Can their eager appetite, then, ever grow weary, or that sweetness ebb away, or that truth prove deceptive, or that eternity come to a close? And if both the ability and will to contemplate are prolonged eternally, what is lacking to total happiness? Those who contemplate him without ceasing are short of nothing, those whose wills are fixed on him have nothing more to desire.

But this vision is not for the present life; it is reserved for the next, at least for those who can say: "We know that when he appears we shall be like him, for we shall see him as he is." Even now he appears to whom he pleases, but as he pleases, not as he is. Neither sage nor saint nor prophet can or could ever see him as he is, while still in this mortal body; but whoever is found worthy will be able to do so when the body becomes immortal. Hence, though he is seen here below, it is in the form that seems good to him, not as he is. For example, take that mighty source of light, I speak of that sun which you see day after day; yet you do not see it as it is, but according as it lights up the air, or a mountain, or a wall. Nor could you see even to this extent if the light of your body, the eye, because of its natural steadiness and clearness, did not bear some degree of likeness to that light in the heavens. Since all the other members of the body lack this likeness, they are incapable of seeing the light. Even the eye itself, when troubled, cannot approach the light, be-cause it has lost that likeness. Just as the troubled eye, then, cannot gaze on the peaceful sun because of its unlikeness, so the peaceful eye can behold it with some efficacy because of a certain likeness. If indeed it were wholly equal to it in purity, with a completely clear vision it would see it as it is, because of the complete likeness. And so when you are enlightened you can see even now the Sun of Justice that "enlightens every man who comes into this world," according to the degree of the light he gives, by which you are made somehow like him; but see him as he is you cannot, because not yet perfectly like him. That is why the Psalmist says: "Come to him and be enlightened, and your faces shall never be ashamed." That is very true, provided we are enlightened as much as we need, so that "with our unveiled faces contemplating the glory of God, all grow brighter and brighter as we are turned into the same image, as by the spirit of the Lord."

Note that we must approach gently, not intrude ourselves upon him, lest the irreverent searcher of majesty be overwhelmed by glory. This approach is not a movement from place to place but from brightness to brightness, not in the body but in the spirit, as by the Spirit of the Lord; evidently by the spirit of the Lord, not by ours, although in ours. The brighter one becomes, the nearer is the end; and to be absolutely bright is to have arrived. For those thus arrived in his presence, to see him as he is means to be as he is, and not to be put to shame by any form of unlikeness. But, as I have said, this is for the next life.

In the meantime this immense variety of forms, these countless species of creatures, what are they but rays emanating from the Godhead, showing that he from whom they come truly is, but not fully explaining what he is. Hence what you see is what emanates from him, not himself. Nevertheless, though not seeing himself but what comes from him, you are made aware beyond all doubt that he exists, and that you must seek him. Grace will not be wanting to the seeker, nor ignorance excuse the negligent. All have access to this kind of vision. According to the Apostle Paul, it is common to everyone who has the use of reason: "The invisible attributes of God have been clearly perceived in the things that have been made."

Another kind of vision is that by which in former times the Fathers were often graciously admitted to sweet communion with God, who became present to them, though they did not see him as he is but only in the form he thought fitting to assume. Nor does he appear to all in a similar manner, but as the Apostle says: "in many and various ways," still remaining one in himself, in accord with his word to Israel: "The Lord your God is one God." This manifestation, though not apparent to everybody, took place exteriorly, and consist-ed of images or the spoken word. But there is another form of divine contemplation, very different from the former because it takes place in the interior, when God himself is pleased to visit the soul that seeks him, provided it is committed to seeking him with all its desire and love. We are told what the sign of such a visit is by one who experienced it. "Fire goes before him and burns up his adversaries round about." The fire of holy desire ought to precede his advent to every soul whom he will visit, to burn up the rust of bad habits and so prepare a place for the Lord. The soul will know that the Lord is near when it perceives itself to be aflame with that fire, and can say as the Prophet did: "He has sent a fire from on high down into my bones, and enlightened me;" and again: "My heart became hot within me and in my meditation fire burst forth."

When the Beloved who is thus sought for pays a visit in his merciful love to the soul that is filled with longing, that prays often, even without intermission, that humiliates itself in the ardor of its desire, that soul may fittingly say with St Jeremiah: "You are good, O Lord, to those who hope in you, to the soul that seeks you." And that soul's angel, one of the friends of the Bridegroom, and by him commissioned to be the minister and witness of that secret and mutual exchange—that angel, I say, must be dancing with joy! Does he not participate in their gladness and bliss, and turning to the Lord, say: "I thank you, Lord of majesty, because 'you have granted him his heart's desire, not denied him what his lips entreated'"? He is everywhere the soul's tireless attendant, never ceasing to lure it on and guide it with constant inspirations, as he whispers: "Take delight in the Lord, and he will give you the desire of your heart;" and again: "Wait for the Lord and keep his way." Or: "If he seems slow, wait for him; he will surely come, he will not delay." Turning to the Lord, he says: " 'As a hart longs for flowing streams, so that soul longs for you, O God.' It has yearned for you in the night, and your Spirit within it watched for you from morning onwards." And again: "All the day this soul reaches out to you; grant what it wants because it is shouting after you; relent a little and show your mercy. Look down from heaven and see, and visit this desolate spirit." This loyal groomsman, watching without envy over this interchange of love, seeks the Lord's glory rather than his own; he is the go-between for the lover and his beloved, making known the desires of one, bearing the gifts of the other. He quickens the soul's affections, he conciliates the Bridegroom. Sometimes too, though rarely, he brings them into each other's presence, either snatching her up to him, or leading him down to her: for he is a member of the household, a familiar figure in the palace, one who has no fear of being rebuffed, who daily sees the face of the Father.

Be careful, however, not to conclude that I see something corporeal or perceptible to the senses in this union between the Word and the soul. My opinion is that of the Apostle, who said that "he who is united to the Lord becomes one spirit with him." I try to express with the most suitable words I can muster the ecstatic ascent of the purified mind to God, and the loving descent of God into the soul, submitting spiritual truths to spiritual men. Therefore let this union be in the spirit, because "God is a spirit," who is lovingly drawn by the beauty of that soul whom he perceives to be guided by the Spirit, and devoid of any desire to submit to the ways of the flesh, especially if he sees that it burns with love for himself.

One who is so disposed and so beloved will by no means be content either with that manifestation of the Bridegroom given to the many in the world of creatures, or to the few in visions and dreams. By a special privilege she wants to welcome him down from heaven into her inmost heart, into her deepest love; she wants to have the one she desires present to her not in bodily form but by inward infusion, not by appearing externally but by laying hold of her within. It is beyond question that the vision is all the more delightful the more inward it is, and not external. It is the Word, who penetrates without sound; who is effective though not pronounced, who wins the affections without striking on the ears. His face, though without form, is the source of form, it does not dazzle the eyes of the body but gladdens the watchful heart; its pleasure is in the gift of love and not in the color of the lover.

Not yet have I come round to saying that he has appeared as he is, although in this inward vision he does not reveal himself as altogether different from what he is. Neither does he make his presence continuously felt, not even to his most ardent lovers, nor in the same way to all. For the various desires of the soul it is essential that the taste of God's presence be varied too, and that the infused flavor of divine delight should titillate in manifold ways the palate of the soul that seeks him. You must already have noticed how often he changes his countenance in the course of this love-song, how he delights in transforming himself from one charming guise to another in the beloved's presence: at one moment like a bashful bridegroom manoeuvring for the hidden embraces of his holy lover, for the bliss of her kisses; at another coming along like a physician with oil and ointments, because weak and tender souls still need remedies and medicines of this kind, which is why they are rather daintily described as maidens. Should anybody find fault with this, let him be told that "it is not the healthy who need the doctor, but the sick." Sometimes, too, he joins up as a traveller with the bride and the maidens who accompany her on the road, and lightens the hardships of the journey for the whole company by his fascinating conversation, so that when he has parted from them they ask: "Did not our hearts burn within us as he talked to us on the road? " A silver-tongued companion who, by the spell of his words and manners, persuades everyone, as if in a sweet-smelling cloud arising from the ointments, to follow him. Hence they say: "We will run after you in the odor of your ointments." At another time he comes to meet them as a wealthy father of a family "with bread enough and to spare" in his house; or again like a magnificent and powerful king, giving courage to his timid and poverty-stricken bride, stirring up her desire by showing her the ornaments of his glory, the riches of his wine-presses and storehouse, the produce of his gardens and fields, and finally introducing her into his private apartments. For "her husband's heart has confidence in her," and among all his possessions there is nothing that he thinks should be hidden from her whom he redeemed from indigence, whose fidelity he has proved, whose attractiveness wins his embraces. And so he never ceases, in one way or another, to reveal himself to the inward eye of those who seek him, thus fulfilling the promise that he made: "Be assured I am with you always to the end of time."

On all these occasions he is kind and gentle, full of merciful love. In his kisses he shows that he is both loving and charming; with the oil and the ointments that he is boundlessly considerate and compassionate and forgiving; on the journey he is gay, courteous, ever gracious and ready to help; in the display of his riches and possessions he reveals a kingly liberality, a munificent generosity in the bestowal of rewards. Through the whole context of this song you will find images of this nature to delineate the Word. Hence I feel that the Prophet was thinking on these lines when he said: "Christ the Lord is a spirit before our face; under his shadow we shall live among the nations," because now we see in a mirror dimly and not yet face to face. So it will be while we live among the nations; among the angels it will be otherwise. For then we shall enjoy the very same happiness as they; even we shall see him as he is, in the form of God, no longer in shadow.

Just as we say that our ancestors possessed only shadows and images, whereas the truth itself shines on us by the grace of Christ present in the flesh, so also no one will deny that in relation to the world to come, we still live in the shadow of the truth, unless he wishes to deny what the apostle asserts: "our knowledge is imperfect and our prophecy is imperfect;" or when he says: "I do not reckon myself to have got hold of it yet." Why should there not be a distinction between him who walks by faith and him who walks by sight? Hence the just man lives by faith, the blessed rejoices in the vision; the holy person here below lives in the shadow of Christ, the holy angel above is glorified in the splendor of his shining countenance.

That the faith is shadowy is a blessing, it tempers the light to the eye's weakness and prepares the eye for the light; for it is written: "He cleansed their hearts by faith." Faith therefore does not quench the light but protects it. Whatever it may be that the angel sees, is preserved for me by the shadow of faith, stored up in its trusty breast, until it be revealed in due time. If you cannot yet grasp the naked truth is it not worthwhile to possess it wrapped in a veil? Our Lord's Mother herself lived in the shadow of faith, for she was told: "Blessed are you who believed." Even the body of Christ was a shadow for her, as implied in the words: "The power of the Most High will cover you with its shadow." That is no mean shadow which is formed by the power of the Most High. Assuredly there was power in the flesh of Christ that overshadowed the Virgin, since by means of the envelope of his vivifying body she was able to bear his majestic presence, and endure the unapproachable light, a thing impossible to mortal woman. That was power indeed by which every opposing might was overcome. Both the power and the shadow put the demons to flight and became a shelter for men: an invigorating power surely, a shadow radiating coolness.

We therefore who walk by faith live in the shadow of Christ; we arc fed with his flesh as the source of our life. For Christ's flesh is real food. And perhaps for that reason he is now described here as appearing in the guise of a shepherd, when the bride addresses him as though one of the shepherds: "Tell me where you pasture your flock, where you make it lie down at noon." The Good Shepherd who lays down his life for his sheep! He gives them his life, he gives them his flesh; his life their ransom, his flesh their food. How wonderful! He is their shepherd, their food, their redemption. But this sermon is getting too long, the subject is extensive and contains great truths that cannot be explained in a few words. This necessitates that we break off rather than finish off. Since the matter is merely suspended we must keep it alive in our memories, so as to resume soon again where we have left off, and continue it with the aid of our Lord Jesus Christ, the Church's Bridegroom, who is God blessed for ever. Amen.

R. Abraham b. Isaac ha-Levi TaMaKH (essay date c. 14th century)

SOURCE: An introduction and "Chapter I," in *Commentary on the Song of Songs,* translated by Leon A. Feldman, Van Gorcum & Comp., 1970, pp. 50-3, 57-75.

[*In the following commentary, written sometime in the fourteenth century, the author provides both a literal interpretation of the* Song's *"plain meaning," and a parallel "occult interpretation" in which the* Song *is construed as an allegory of Jewish exile.*]

HERE BEGINS THE COMMENTARY OF R. ABRAHAM HA-
LEVI B. R. ISAAC TaMaKH . . . :

The wise king has said: "Honor not thyself in the presence of a king and stand not in the place of the great."
This precept should suffice to keep us from overreach-
ing ourselves, particularly in conjectural matters; so
were we instructed by God speaking through the greatest of prophets: "Lest they break through unto the Lord
to gaze." It is very dangerous, indeed, to probe into
matters which are the very foundation of our faith; it
is also presumptuous to write books for the instruction
of others when the author is not worthy of the task.
However, if one fulfills these two conditions—not to
probe into matters of faith and not to delude himself
into attempting to instruct others—he may be excused,
regardless of his status, for preserving for his own use
a record of what he has achieved in interpreting matters which he is likely to forget.

In this manner I have permitted myself to compose, as
best I can, a commentary on this matchchless song, the
Song of Songs, since I do not know of anyone who
has ever written a commentary, containing both the
plain meaning and the occult interpretation, which
harmonizes the language with the context.

Lines from the second verse of the *Song*

I am the flower of the field
  and the lily of the valley
like a lily among thorns
  so my friend among daughters
like the apple tree among trees of the woods
  so my beloved among sons
under the shadow of the one I had loved I sat
and his fruit sweet to my throat
he brought me into the wine cellar
he has disposed charity in me
support me with flowers, surround me with
  apples
  for I languish with love
his left arm under my head and
  his right are will embrace me

From the translation by E. Ann Matter in The
Voice of My Beloved, *University of
Pennsylvania Press, 1990.*

I have humbly set myself the task of establishing the
plain meaning in conformity with phraseology and
context and of reconciling, to the best of my ability,
the occult interpretation with the figures of speech. For
each verse I have indicated first its plain meaning and
then its occult allusion, except that in a number of
instances I have found it necessary to group together
the plain meaning of several consecutive verses, post-

poning the occult interpretation in accordance with the
requirements of the relationship of those verses one to
another.

I do not pretend to claim originality for all my comments. I have made selections from the most penetrating of my predecessors; I have made additions where
they missed a point; I have felt free to make emenda-
tions where I disagreed. When I reached a certain level
in my comprehension of this poetic song and began to
worry about retaining it all in my memory, I wrote
down my observations with God's help before I should
forget them.

Our Sages (may their memory be for a blessing!) and
most of our commentators are in general agreement
that the occult meaning of this book alludes to the
deliverance of Israel from its [several] exiles. They
differ in their interpretations of individual verses, some
commentators making ascriptions which are diametrically opposed to those of others. I have consistently
pursued my own course when it seemed just and accurate in the face of conflicting opinions. It devolved
upon me to reconcile the various sections of the book
with the several redemptions of Israel and to harmonize the metaphors with their analogues, after elucidating the former.

I aver that this book is based upon our holy nation's
plea to the Creator to deliver us from our present exile
and to direct us to do what is right in His sight. God,
in leading us along the right path, expresses His assurance that we shall be delivered as He delivered our
ancestors from previous exiles. The book describes
those redemptions and pledges the start and completion of our own. Such is the book's pattern.

The book has the following divisions:
  1:1-1:8 describes our present exile.
  1:9-5:1 describes the period from the exodus from
Egypt to the end of the First Temple.
  5:2-6:9 deals with the period from the end of the
Babylonian exile to the end of the Second Temple.
  6:10-8:13 speaks of the start and completion of our
own deliverance.
  8:14, the last verse, repeats the theme of the opening
verse—a characteristic of great poetry—and constitutes
a plea to the Creator to release us from the pit of our
exile and to restore His presence to our Temple (may
it be speedily rebuilt in our time!).

**1. THE *SONG OF SONGS* WHICH IS SOLOMON'S [SHELO-
MO'S]:**

We have already indicated in our Introduction that King
Solomon—may he rest in peace!—referred in this book
to Israel's redemption from both the Egyptian exile,
which occurred before his time, and from future exiles,
which he foresaw with the aid of the Holy Spirit. And

because the children of Israel offer up many songs of praise to the Creator—blessed be He!—for many deeds of redemption, he called it **Song of Songs**, namely, a song containing the songs of Israel.

"Which is Solomon's" can be interpreted simply as a reference to Solomon's [Shelomo's] authorship of the book and allegorically—as stated in the Midrash—as a reference to God, who is equated with peace [Shalom]. This accords with our statement in the Introduction that these are Israel's songs to God. The author compares the holy nation's love for the Creator to the true love of a maiden for her lover, a love in which there is desire only for the beloved and which values at naught any delights which are not bound up with her beloved. He also likens God's love for the chosen people—when He turns His efforts to redeem them from their exiles as well as during times of peace—to the feeling of a lover for his faultless bride who pleases him above all women. Another reason for calling the book **Song of Songs** is that, while its obvious subject is love, its chief purpose—the song of its songs—is, as he says, to strengthen the love and desire of the beloved people for their lover. Our Sages have therefore proclaimed it as the greatest of all songs.

2. **LET HIM KISS ME WITH THE KISSES OF HIS MOUTH,**

FOR THEY LOVE IS BETTER THAN WINE:

We have stated earlier that whereas the revealed subject of the book is the relationship between the lover and his beloved, its allegorical content is Israel's turning towards God and His response. This verse describes the beloved's yearning for reunion with her lover. She praises his love for its two chief delights—one physical, the other spiritual—which she compares to wine and fragrance. These delights round out man's nature, or, in the words of our Sages, "wine and fragrance make one wise" because "wine maketh glad the heart," strengthens the natural warmth, develops the body, prolongs its creative powers, and turns food and drink into healthful blood, while fragrance sustains the spirit. She praises her lover because his love possesses these two important qualities; therefore *thy love is better than wine* and *thine ointments have a goodly fragrance.* This is the simple meaning.

The occult interpretation of this verse is an expression of the chosen people's deep desire, their prayer that the Divine Presence join them as of old, although they live in exile at the present time. In the past they knew how *much better was* [God's] *love than wine*—a simile which contains an allusion to the seventy nations of the world. It is better for them to please God than to please the entire world. The Targum likewise interprets the verse as meaning: Your love is better for us than for the seventy nations.

3. **THINK OINTMENTS HAVE A GOODLY FRAGRANCE;**

THY NAME IS AN OINTMENT POURED FORTH;

THEREFORE DO THE MAIDENS LOVE THEE:

Thine ointments have a goodly fragrance, whoever longs for the fragrance, i.e. the good, let him betake himself to the goodly ointments, the fragrant ointments which the Psalmist calls "precious oil." One obtains pleasure from the oil's fragrance only when it is poured forth, for only then is its odor wafted to the nostrils. Therefore the verse stresses *thy name is an ointment poured forth.*—(Incidentally, oil [Shemen] occurs here in the feminine gender, something not found elsewhere; house [Bayit], always masculine, appears as a feminine noun on one occasion: "For her house sinketh down unto death.")—A good name is compared to precious oil, as it is written, "Better fame than precious oil." Our Sages, in a comment on the verse, "I shall make thy name great," compare a good reputation to a flask of foliatum oil.

There are some who regard *turaq* as the name of a city; they interpret the phrase to mean, "thy name is like an ointment from Turaq," a particularly fine ointment. Others make no distinction between *turaq* and *huraq.*—(Cf. *tukku* which is equated by some commentators with *hukku.*)—The simile is completed by a phrase which gives the reason for the lover's appeal, *therefore do the maidens love thee,* since his love is so desirable, it is not surprising that the young ladies long for him.

4. **DRAW ME AFTER THEE; LET US HASTEN; THE KING HAS BROUGHT ME INTO HIS CHAMBERS; WE SHALL BE GLAD AND REJOICE IN THEE; WE SHALL CELEBRATE THY LOVE MORE THAN WINE; RIGHTLY DO THEY LOVE THEE:**

The beloved's voice is now heard: When you draw me, that means, by your promise of love, I shall then hasten towards you. *The king has brought me into his chambers,* when this has come to pass, my joy of you will be complete. *We shall celebrate thy love more than wine,* this is a return to the wine simile above. *Rightly have they loved thee:* this is an additional reason for her love; it is not because of her desire alone that she loves him, but because of his qualities and his righteousness. It is well known that all lovers of righteousness are attracted to him. The author uses the term *rightly* to indicate that they are acting under the influence of righteousness, that they themselves are the symbol of righteousness.

The occult interpretation is that the [Israelite] people are praying to God to extricate them from the depth of their exile; that they will come running toward him to rejoice in the Sacred One of Israel by entering His rooms and temple. Thus they will remember His love, namely, His redemptive acts. *Rightly do they love thee:*

Rightly [Mesharim] is a reference to the patriarchs; cf. the words of the Sages: What is the Book of Yashar? It is the book of Abraham, Isaac and Jacob, who are called righteous [Yesharim]. From them have we inherited the love of God. In this verse Israel reminds God of the patriarchs' merit [in loving Him].

5. I AM DARK YET COMELY, MAIDENS OF JERUSALEM;
DARK AS THE TENTS OF QEDAR,
COMELY AS SOLOMON'S CURTAINS:

The young maiden always addresses her remarks to the most exalted young women because she, too, is of high rank. Therefore she uses the phrases *maidens of Jerusalem* or daughters of *Zion,* since they are known for their high qualities. She tells them that, although she is dark, they should not be surprised by her lover's desire for her because she is also comely. Her form is attractive and her appearance is as fine as the tents of Qedar, which, although black without, are full of precious stones and pearls; cf. the statement in the Midrash. *Like Solomon's* [Shelomo's] *curtains,* they are also more beautiful within than without in order to provide delight when lying down.

The occult interpretation has the chosen people declare that although they are blackened with exile—from lack of effort in performing their proper tasks and may— seem to be rejected by God, they possess the beauty of complete faith in Him, i.e., they are willing to suffer afflictions and even self-sacrifice for His sake. Lack of effort is compared to blackness, which is temporary, while strength of faith is like beauty of form and appearance, which is a permanent bodily characteristic. *Like the tents of Qedar, like Solomon's* [Shelomo's] *curtains,* my outward actions may not seem as perfect [Shalem] as my inner beliefs, but my heart's strong faith in God is as beautiful in His sight as *the tents of Qedar* and *Solomon's curtains.*

6. DO NOT SCORN ME BECAUSE I AM DARK, FOR THE SUN HATH TANNED ME; MY MOTHER'S SONS WERE SO ANGRY WITH ME THAT THEY MADE ME KEEPER OF THE VINEYARDS; BUT I DID NOT LOOK AFTER MY OWN VINEYARD:

Do not scorn me [tir'uni] is derived from the same root as "to gaze upon thee with scorn." The young woman says to the aforementioned maidens, *do not scorn me because I am dark;*—(this is a repetition, in stronger terms, of her previous remark. The second and third letters of the root are repeated . . . to strengthen its meaning. Sometimes, however, the repetition of the letters weakens the root. . .).

The maiden explains that they should not scorn her for her color, because it is not her natural hue; *she was tanned by the sun*—a temporary blemish. *My mother's*

sons were angry with me, those who should have acted fraternally were angry with me and alienated me. *They made me keeper of the vineyards,* because of this labor and the sun's scorching rays, *I did not look after my own vineyard,* since I was not permitted to guard my own.

According to the occult interpretation, the people apologize for their lagging, which was caused by the punishing rays of the sun of their exile. *My mother's sons were angry with me* is a plain allusion to their exile in the lands of Edom and Ishmael, who are their kin and who should therefore have dealt kindly with them; then they would not have departed from God's ways. But they became angry with them and made them *keeper of the vineyards;* they forced them into foreign worship so that they were unable to perform their own duty in the service of God.

7. TELL ME, MY BELOVED, WHERE THOU FEEDEST THE FLOCKS, WHERE THOU MAKEST THEM LIE DOWN AT NOON: WHY SHOULD I BE EMBARRASSED AMONG THEY COMPANIONS FLOCKS?

It is the practice of shepherds to pasture their flocks in the morning and in the evening and to have them lie in the shade at noon, the hottest part of the day. The maiden asks her lover to tell her where he will feed his flock and where he will take them for their noontime rest; she will meet him there. Should she wander among strangers' flocks, she would be embarrassed by their suspicion that all is not well between the lovers.—(The term *'otia,* literally, to be "veiled," is used instead of *mitbayeshet,* because the one who is embarrassed veils his face from everyone's gaze.)—

Its occult meaning is that the people pray to their Redeemer to teach them His ways so that they may follow them and find Him. Why should they suffer shame in their exile among the foreign nations?—(*Thy companions' flock* is, of course, a simile.)—Up to this point we have heard, on the one hand, the maiden speaking to her lover, and, on the other, the chosen people's prayer to God.

8. IF THOU KNOWEST NOT, O FAIREST OF WOMEN,
FOLLOW THE SHEEP TRACKS AND PASTURE THY KIDS BESIDE THE SHEPHERDS' TENTS:

Reciprocating her love, the lover responds to her plea, with which she is completely preoccupied, and says to her, "*if you do not know* where I am, *follow the flocks* and look for the shepherd who seeks the highest ground; there you will find me." He speaks of her *kids*—and not of her flocks—because, being delicate and gentle, she cannot feed a large flock; she tends several kids only for pleasure.

The occult interpretation is that this is God's response to the prayers of His people: If you do not know the Lord's ways, follow those of the Holy Flock, i.e., the patriarchs in their wanderings.

Pasture thy kids, teach the youth who are ignorant of God's ways. *Beside the shepherds' tents,* the teachings of the shepherds, the pious scholars of old, who follow His ways. There is also an allusion here to God's guidance and supremacy.

9. I compare thee, my love, to a mare in
   Pharaoh's chariots:

The lover tells his beloved that he compares her rich ornamentation to that observed on Pharaoh's own mare, the best of all horses—Egyptian in origin—which drew Pharaoh's chariots.

The occult interpretation is that here—as mentioned—begins the story of the deliverance from Egypt. In speaking of Pharaoh's mare, this verse identifies the country from which Israel was delivered, and adds that the people were adorned by possessing important and distinguished personalities.

10. Beautiful are thy cheeks with circlets,
    thy neck with strings of pearls:

Here are mentioned several of the maiden's jewels. These jewels also allude to distinguished personalities, viz. Moses, Aaron and his sons, Joshua, and the tribal chiefs.

11. Circlets of gold shall we make for
    thee,
    with studs of silver:

"Since these *circlets* and other jewels are so becoming to you," says the lover, "I shall bedeck you with even more beautiful ornaments—of gold, for richness and beauty, with insets of silver, for attracting attention."

According to the hidden meaning, God decides to complete the people's praiseworthy act of obedience to their leaders by bestowing upon them the perfection of the Torah. The commandments themselves are compared to gold and the narrative portions to silver insets which attract the reader's attention.

12. While the king is at his table,
    my nard sendeth forth its fragrance:

The maiden, upon finding her lover and sensing his desire for her, draws nearer to him so that he may breathe her fragrance and be even more attracted to her. She calls him *king,* as before, because of her admiration for him.

The occult interpretation is that when the people be-

came aware of God's interest in them, they drew nearer to Him through their good deeds and prayers. Their fragrant nard was their promise that "all that God hath spoken we shall do."

13. My beloved is unto me like a cluster
    of myrrh that lieth between my breasts:

The maiden assures her beloved that his delight in her fragrance need never cease; the bouquet of myrrh is always between her breasts, even while she sleeps.

This is an allusion to the people's promise to obey God's will and to God's assurance to Moses—in His omniscience—that the people's faith in Him and in Moses will continue forever.

14. My beloved is unto me like a cluster
    of henna from the vineyards of Ein-Gedi:

The maiden repeats the theme of the previous verse, varying the name of the flower and its source, which is unequaled. She tells her lover that she has a *cluster of henna* which she picked *from the vineyards of Ein-Gedi* because there is none better than what is found there.

The occult interpretation follows the Targum. This is an allusion to the people's practice, during their sojourn in the wilderness, of pressing the libation wine from the grapes of Ein-Gedi.

15. Thou art beautiful, my beloved, thou
    art beautiful;
    thine eyes are like doves:

A short while ago her beloved praised her by stating how her ornaments brought out her beauty. This is not, however, the highest form of praise for a woman. Now that they are so close, his awareness of her beauty compels him to praise her for her own, unadorned self. His praise of her *dove-like eyes* is a metaphor describing their power to awaken love in his heart, a metaphor more applicable to doves than to any other creatures.

Its occult interpretation: In praising the virtues of the holy nation, God had singled out its leaders, who are its adornments. Now He praises the people for themselves, because their virtues are part of their nature and they do not have to learn them from their leaders despite their greatness and importance. These leaders are their *eyes,* as stated in Scripture: "From the eyes of the community." It was they who aroused the people's love for God, just like the doves who evince great activity in matters of love.

16. Thou art handsome, my lover, and
    pleasant;
    and our couch is leafy:

The maiden reciprocates her lover's endearments, praising him, too, in order to consummate their mutual desire, implied in the ending of the verse.

17. THE BEAMS OF OUR HOUSES ARE CEDARS, OUR PANELS CYPRESSES:

The beams are the heavy supports for the lighter panels which rest on them.—(The latter word is derived from the root "to run," because they run across the beams; cf. the Targum and the Midrash: Rabbi Yohanan stated that the Torah teaches us to use cedars for supporting the roof, costly though they are, and cypresses, which are less expensive, for panels.)—

Martin Luther (lecture date 1539)

SOURCE: "Lectures on the *Song of Solomon,*" translated by Ian Siggins, in *Luther's Works,* Vol. 15, edited by Jaroslav Pelikan and Hilton C. Oswald, Concordia Publishing, 1972, pp. 191-210.

[*In the following excerpt from a series of lectures delivered in 1539, Luther provides a close exegesis of the first chapter of the* Song of Songs. *Luther attributes the* Song *specifically to Solomon, suggesting that the work deals with Solomon's government and his people's relationship with God.*]

DR. MARTIN LUTHER'S PREFACE TO THE *SONG OF SONGS*

Many commentators have produced all manner of interpretations of this song of King Solomon's—and they have been both immature and strange. But to get at the simplest sense and the real character of this book, I think it is a song in which Solomon honors God with his praises; he gives Him thanks for his divinely established and confirmed kingdom and government; he prays for the preservation and extension of this his kingdom, and at the same time he encourages the inhabitants and citizens of his realm to be of good cheer in their trials and adversities and to trust in God, who is always ready to defend and rescue those who call upon Him.

Moses did the same in Ex. 15. He composed his song about the work being performed at that moment in the Red Sea; and all the songs found in Holy Scripture deal with the stories of their own times. Of this sort are the song of Deborah in Judg. 5, the song of Hannah in 1 Sam. 2, and a good many others, including the majority of the psalms, with the exception of those which contain prophecies about Christ. Doubtless, therefore, Solomon, too, wrote his song about his own kingdom and government, which by the goodness of God he administered in the finest, happiest peace and the highest tranquillity. All this will become clear from the text itself too.

Moreover, since every kingdom, principality, or state which has the Word and true worship of God is forced to sustain many affliction—to be a laughingstock and abomination to the whole world, to dwell in the midst of enemies, and every single hour to await death like a sheep bound for the slaughter, such a kingdom or state is deservedly called "the people of God" and has every right to place this song and Solomon's state, before itself as an example, to praise God in the same manner, to glory and rejoice in God, and to proclaim and marvel at His divine mercy and power, by which He protects His own against the snares of the devil and the tyranny of the world.

We use the psalms of David and the writings of the prophets in this way as examples, even though we are not David or the prophets, but because we have the same blessings in common with them—the same Word, Spirit, faith, and blessedness—and because we sustain the same dangers and afflictions on account of God's Word. So we rightly take over their voices and their language for ourselves, praising and singing just as they praised and sang. Thus any state in which there is the church and a godly prince can use this song of Solomon's just as if it had been composed about its own government and state.

And so from this **Song of Songs**, which Solomon sang about only his own state, there springs as it were a common song for all states which are "the people of God," that is, which possess the Word of God and worship reverently, which acknowledge and truly believe that the power of governments is established and ordained by God and that through this power God preserves peace, justice, and discipline, punishes the guilty, defends the innocent, etc. They praise and proclaim God with thanksgiving for these great benefits.

Again, godly governments and states place no hope or trust at all in riches, power, wisdom, or other human defenses that are neither stable nor lasting, but they console, admonish, and arouse themselves to flee for refuge to God in all their afflictions and dangers and to trust in Him as their true and only Helper and Preserver, who never deserts His people when they suffer persecution for the sake of His name and Word. For it is certainly the case that a people which is zealous in godliness and loves the Word is always exposed to many evils with which it is assaulted by the devil and the world.

This is why this poem is called the **Song of Songs**, since it deals with matters of the loftiest and greatest kind, namely, with the divinely ordained governments, or with the people of God. It does not treat a story of an individual, as other songs in Holy Scripture do, but an entire permanent kingdom, or people, in which God untiringly performs a host of staggering miracles and displays His power by preserving and defending it against all the assaults of the devil and the world.

What is more, he does not sing of these exalted matters in the common words that people ordinarily use, but he illustrates and adorns his theme with lofty and figurative words to such an extent that when the crowd hears them, it supposes that the subject treated is something very different. For this is the custom with kings and princes: they compose and sing amatory ballads which the crowd takes to be songs about a bride or a sweetheart, when in fact they portray the condition of their state and people with their songs. This is precisely what "Teuerdank" has done in joining "Ehrenreich" to Maximilian as his bride. Or if they speak about hunting, they want to signify by this language that the enemy has been routed and put to flight and that they have gained the victory, as when they say, "The wild boar is speared, the savage beast is taken," and other things of the same sort.

Solomon proceeds in just this fashion in this song of his. He uses magnificent words—words that are worthy of so great a king—in describing his concerns. He makes God the bridegroom and his people the bride, and in this mode he sings of how much God loves that people, how many and how rich are the gifts He lavishes and heaps upon it, and finally how He embraces and cherishes the same people with a goodness and mercy with which no bridegroom has ever embraced or cherished his bride. And thus Solomon begins by speaking in the person of the whole people as the bride of God: "He is kissing me."

DR. MARTIN LUTHER'S BRIEF BUT ALTOGETHER LUCID EXPOSITION OF THE *SONG OF SONGS*

We take up this book for exposition not from any fondness for display of erudition, like some who lavish every effort upon the obscure books because, of course, on the one hand it provokes praise for their cleverness to have dared address subjects which others flee on account of their obscurity and on the other hand because in the obscure books each of them is free to make divinations and to indulge in speculations or private musings; rather, we take it up in order that after the absurd opinions which have so far obscured this little book have been rejected, we may demonstrate another, more suitable view, useful for life and for a right appreciation of the good gifts of God.

For we know that the purpose of the whole Scripture is this: to teach, reprove, correct, and train in righteousness, so that the man of God may be perfect for every good work, as Paul says in 2 Tim. 3:16-17. Those who fail to observe this purpose, even if they create the impression of erudition among the unlettered by their divinations, nevertheless are ignorant of the true essence of Scripture. Their learning is not unlike bodies infected with dropsy—inflated by inordinate swelling, they give an appearance of vigor, but the swelling is all corrupt and noxious. In the course of this exposition, therefore, we shall direct our reflections to the end that this book, too, may instruct us with doctrine useful for life, and secondly, with consolations.

For we shall never agree with those who think it is a love song about the daughter of Pharaoh beloved by Solomon. Nor does it satisfy us to expound it of the union of God and the synagog, or like the tropologists, of the faithful soul. For what fruit, I ask, can be gathered from these opinions? So even if this book, amidst all the variety of Scripture, has had its place in the shadows until now, yet by pursuing a new path, we shall not depart from the substance of the thought even if we may perhaps err here and there in details. Accordingly, my view is as follows.

There are three books of Solomon in Holy Scripture. The first, Proverbs, deals mostly with the home and sets forth general precepts for behavior in this life. It does so not as the philosophers of the Gentiles do, but it is diffused throughout with that weightier doctrine of faith and the fear of God, which the Gentiles did not perceive.

The second, Ecclesiastes, is a political book, which gives instruction not only to all in general but especially to the magistrate: namely, that the man who governs other men should himself fear God, perform with vigor the tasks that lie before him and not allow himself to be so discouraged either by the difficulty of the task or by the ingratitude of men that he fails to perform his office.

The third is the book before us, which is entitled "**Song of Songs.**" It rightly belongs with Ecclesiastes, since it is an encomium of the political order, which in Solomon's day flourished in sublime peace. For as those who wrote songs in Holy Scripture wrote them about their own deeds, so in Solomon this poem commends his own government to us and composes a sort of encomium of peace and of the present state of the realm. In it he gives thanks to God for that highest blessing, external peace. He does it as an example for other men, so that they too may learn to give thanks to God in this way, to acknowledge His highest benefits, and to pray for correction should anything reprehensible befall the realm.

CHAPTER ONE

1. *The* Song of Songs.

The book derives its title either from the subject matter, because it deals with the greatest of all human works, namely, government; or else from the style, because it is written in the fashion of grand oratory.

For the poem is entirely figurative, and figures of speech produce grand oratory.

2. *He kisses me.*

He speaks according to the custom of the people of that day. Among us kisses are held in less esteem. However, kisses are signs of love and favor. And so he says *The Lord kisses me,* that is, "He shows favor to this government, He kisses it, He honors it with all manner of blessings and love."

Now, to declare that a realm which to outward appearance was suffering all sorts of afflictions is God's own concern, that it is loved and cherished by God, is certainly the voice of faith. To outward appearance it is not obvious that He kisses the synagog, but rather that He wounds it and hates it. But he adds:

With the kisses of His mouth!

This means that God honors this people with His Word. And certainly this is the treasure which deserves to be extolled first in the political realm, for without it government cannot endure. Paul, too, extols God's gift to this people in Rom. 3:2: "The Jews are entrusted with the oracles of God." Similarly Ps. 147:19 says: "He declares His Word to Jacob, etc." He did not do so to every nation. For it is the Word which distinguishes the godly from the ungodly. It is also through the Word's agency that we come to regard everything we possess either in the domestic or the political realm to be gifts of God and sheer signs of the divine will and favor towards us. Granted that everyone else abounds in all good things, they nevertheless do not understand them to be the gifts of God and therefore cannot avoid abusing them to their own destruction.

For Your breasts are more delightful than wine.

Breasts refer to doctrine, by which souls are fed so that "the man of God may be perfect for every good work" (2 Tim. 3:17). He compares doctrine with wine, of which Holy Scripture declares that it makes the heart glad (Ps. 104:15). Wine is thus metaphorically used for all the world's delights and gratifications.

And this is, so to speak, the voice of an outstanding faith, which declares, "I prefer Your Word to all the pleasures of the world." For we must refer everything to the Word.

3. *For Your name is oil poured out.*

These are very meaningful figures and symbols. *Your name,* that is, "the knowledge of You," is like oil, since it yields a pleasing aroma and is spread abroad through the Word. And this blessing is not hidden away in a corner but is published throughout my whole realm, and it spreads its aroma also to neighboring peoples, like an ointment that is poured out.

So that Your best anointing oils are fragrant.

That is, "where Your Word is, there Your blessings are recognized." For the godly know through the Word that they enjoy the gifts of God and abound in them. But if these are taken away, they know that they are being tried by God, and they bear their cross patiently.

Therefore the maidens love You.

It is a Hebraism that cities are called "mothers" and "daughters." Here he calls Jerusalem a maiden. So the meaning is this: "Through the agency of Your Word it comes about that those who are the godly men on every hand in my kingdom are attracted by these great blessings, set their affections on You, and love You."

So far he has been commending his government for the special reason that it possesses the Word of God. It is therefore an ungodly thing that the external Word is nowadays despised by many who through diabolical revelation boast of the Spirit apart from the oral Word. And yet they know neither what the Spirit nor what the Word really is!

4. *Draw me after You.*

To know and to be able to do are two different things. When we therefore possess the Word, we are not immediately able to follow it, but our flesh, the world, and Satan draw us away from the Word again. Now, therefore, he adds this prayer: "You have given us Your Word, and I thank You for it. Now grant that we may also perform what the Word teaches and follow it in our lives."

No manner of life is without its special burden. Marry a wife: immediately you will discover a flood of ills! You will find things which displease you in your wife and in your children, and the care of the stomach will occupy you. Similarly those who are in government experience a host of evils, for Satan is nowhere inactive. Prayer, then, is all that remains; by prayer let us overcome the various hazards and rocks on which we run aground. For God allows us to be tested by such ills so that the glory of the Word may be demonstrated and the divine power magnified in our weakness. Otherwise there would be no way to demonstrate His glory and mercy.

We shall make haste.

This is emphatic. He does not say "we shall walk" but "we shall run." "If You breathe Your Spirit upon me, then I shall be glad to perform the task of prince, teacher, husband, pupil, etc. Unless You inspire, no one will accomplish anything, no matter how great his zeal and care, especially not in government." Thus we see the most flourishing states ruined rather than sustained by the wisdom of the greatest men.

The King has brought me into His chambers.

He alludes to the way of a groom and his bride and figuratively shows that prayer is heard, for he is picturing God's highest goodwill toward us. "God," he says, "consoles me in the evils I experience in government and reveals Himself to be willing and favorable—just as when a groom brings his bride into his chamber, he certainly does not do so from hatred of the bride!"

In this way he represents that sublime affection which God holds toward those who pray, in that He hears, consoles, cherishes, and enriches them with His own gifts and powers so that each may be able to execute his office more fitly.

We will now exult and rejoice in You;

Thanksgiving follows heeded prayer. "Now I shall exult because You do not forsake me but receive me in Your mercies."

His words *in You* are emphatic. It is as if he were saying: "Outside Your solace and aid one experiences nothing but toils, afflictions, unendurable burdens, griefs, lamentations, etc."

We will recall Your breasts more than wine.

This is part of his thanksgiving, that is: "We shall be grateful, we shall remember Your remembrance, how You love us, seeing that You give us Your breasts." For "to recall" means to preach, to praise, to give thanks. As before, he calls all physical and fleshly joys "wine."

The upright love You.

Twisted men, bent on their own advantage, want to live a life in which they suffer no inconveniences. But if inconveniences do befall them, they are offended and complain with utter impatience.

By contrast, when the upright suffer difficulties and inconveniences, they bear them patiently and pray. Accordingly, when they have been delivered, they acknowledge God's sheer goodwill and love towards them, and so they love God the more fervently.

Next, therefore, Solomon addresses his discourse to the instruction of such crooked men, so that they, too, may learn to triumph over present evils by the same means, namely, by endurance and prayer. For the normal response of those who have been tested and whose

prayers have been answered is to teach and instruct others also, as Ps. 116:10 testifies: "I have believed, therefore have I spoken."

ABOUT THE COURSE AND ORDER OF THE BOOK AS A WHOLE

Now, this is the order and course of this song, that it alternates consolations, complaints, prayers, and exhortations. For just as events occur in any legally established state—indeed, just as this life of ours is lived—so Solomon proceeds in this book. He lays out a sort of image of the state and the common life in which by turns consolation follows affliction and new affliction follows consolation as the night the day. Thus in public affairs new storms, new disturbances, and alarms arise constantly, and when they are dispersed, the ensuing period of quiet does not prevail longer, but straightway other tumults and calamities follow. Those who are experienced in government will testify to this state of affairs.

For instance, a rebellion of the people beset David at first. Scarcely had that disaster been put to rights when lo and behold, another ensued, the graver for its being less expected. His most beloved son, Absalom, takes up hostile arms against his father. He is not satisfied with banishing his father from the realm; he violates the royal concubines and also his father's wives. Thus government is like dangerous navigation on a stormy sea.

Consequently Solomon frequently repeats his consolations and exhortations to give encouragement to the hearts of rulers, so that they do not retreat or despair, discouraged by their difficulties, but may learn to lift themselves up by prayer in this manner and to hope for deliverance. And when deliverance has come about, the soul must in this way be prepared again not to succumb to subsequent vicissitudes. For just as valleys follow mountain ridges and the day follows the night, so deliverance follows affliction in constant interchange, and fresh disaster again follows deliverance. Anyone who has observed this rule will understand a good part of this book. And if someone wants to add some allegories later, it takes no effort to invent them!

5. *I am very dark, but comely, O daughters of Jerusalem.*

I have suggested earlier that after his thanksgiving he begins an address.

O daughters of Jerusalem, that is, "You states and adjoining towns, do not be scandalized if everything here is not flourishing."

I am very dark. "Although I am a state founded by God and adorned with the Word of God, yet I seem to be most wretched in appearance, there is no success, and there are very few who desire and maintain public peace. I seem to be not a state but some sort of rabble of seditious men. Do not be offended by this appearance. Turn your attention not to my blackness, but to the kiss which God offers me, and then you will see that I am comely and lovable. For although outwardly I suffer all manner of vexation, yet I am desirable on account of the Word and faith."

The church, too, is similarly undesirable in appearance. It seems to be lacerated and wretchedly afflicted and exposed to the taunts of all men. But this is our consolation: that our salvation is anchored in the Word and faith, not in outward appearance.

Like the tents of Kedar and like the tents of Solomon.

The tents of Kedar, that is, of the Arabs, are cheap and ugly. By contrast, *the tents of Solomon* are regal and very beautiful.

For this reason I consider that the sentence should be divided as follows: *I am very dark . . . like the tents of Kedar.* "I seem to be like some crowd of Arabs who have no government. For there are many in my people who do not believe the Word. There are many, too, who do not obey the government. It looks more like a jumble of men than a well-ordered state." But nonetheless, *I am comely . . . like the tents of Solomon.* When one takes the inward aspect into account, one will nevertheless discover in that state many godly men who do obey and are good and faithful members of the state, etc.

6. *Do not gaze at me because I am swarthy.*

He continues to exhort in the face of scandals. He warns: "Do not stare at the part of me in which I am ugly, but fix your eyes on my beauty and grace, consider my virtues, not my vices."

Moreover, the man who has learned this lesson should discover in the long run that he has learned and known the greatest art of all. For it is inbred in us that we are more disturbed by some single vice than by all the remaining virtues. Thus today those who are adjudged the wisest men in the world are offended by the many evils, which they undeservedly impute to the Gospel. Yet the magnitude of the blessings we have received from the Gospel both privately in men's hearts and consciences and publicly in state and household, is appreciated by no one or by very few. For before the revelation of the Gospel, what station of life was there, I ask, that men could assess correctly? Not husband, not wife, not children, not magistrates, not citizens, not menservants, not maidservants were sure that they were established in a way of life that was approved by God. So they all took refuge in the works of the monks.

Similarly, before the light of the Gospel was given, was the use of the arts rightly displayed or recognized? This is clear in the instruction of the young. The proper use of grammar, dialectic, or rhetoric was simply not apparent, so far removed was the possibility of their being taught correctly. If these things happened in the trivial arts, how much more in the weightier arts! The case of theology speaks for itself. Even if the professors of law did have some sort of knowledge of their discipline and its use, yet the deadliest thing of all was that very few of them believed they were in a station of life approved by God. The same could be said of the physicians.

Formerly no one took any notice of these terrible afflictions. Now utterly ungrateful men, forgetting the blessings now present, notice only the bad things. Our inability to enjoy the sight of these great blessings is the just desert of such sheer ingratitude, as it is written (Is. 26:10): "The ungodly will not see the glory of God." But the godly both see the abundant gifts of God and are grateful for them.

Moreover, this rule ought to be observed most diligently in private life as well: if a man banishes the blackness from his eyes, he will see a world full of God's mercy. Thus we read in Ps. 107:43: "Who is wise and will heed these things and understand the mercies of the Lord?" So in everyday human converse you will discover that no man is so bad that he does not possess innumerably many endowments.

The heart, therefore, should be trained to admire the virtues in individual people rather than to be offended by their vices, if any. If someone has vices, the same man has his virtues too—he must, for he cannot abuse all the capacities which he has received from nature! This argument will certainly help to preserve peace of heart. For if you direct your gaze only on the vices and the calamities which occur every day, the heart is necessarily tempted by impatience and hatred. Accordingly, since those evils and those troubles cannot be changed, change yourself and adopt a different outlook; keep your heart free and ignore the distresses at hand. As that excellent saying, which we have often used in Ecclesiastes, advises: "Let it go as it is going, since it wants to go as it is going." But the present benefits and blessings are so numerous and so great that the godly man may easily forget the evils in comparison with them.

Because the sun has scorched me.

The sun signifies tribulation, as Christ indicates in the parable of the seed scorched by the sun (Matt. 13:6). Similarly we read in Ps. 121:6: "The sun shall not smite you by day, nor the moon by night."

Thus he is saying: Lest you be scandalized by any

blackness whatsoever, I ask you now not to regard me as responsible for it. It is the sun that has blackened me. In other words, wherever the divine Word and ordinance are found, wherever there is some form of government, there the sun will come and inflict blackness. That is, the devil rises in opposition so that that Word or that state will appear on the verge of total failure. But do not be perturbed, Satan will not prevail.

My mother's sons were angry with me.

It is inevitable in the state not only that there are many tribulations but also that the children rage against their mother, that is, against the state, contrary to the mandate and Word of God. The person who holds governmental authority therefore should be aware that he has been set over seditious citizens, who require only a suitable occasion to stir up sedition, with the result that the very people who ought to have provided help in the administration have a single eye towards overturning and disrupting it. David found this out, and so did the Romans; and I believe that this is the special complaint of all godly princes today.

They made me keeper of the vineyards; but my own vineyard I have not kept!

Here is a grievous lament. He admits that he has the right, power, and title of king; but, he says, the administration is in the hands of others. The vineyard is the people. "I have been set over this people as king and prince. What do I do?" *My own vineyard I have not kept!*

He thus openly confesses that it is impossible to maintain the state by human judgment but that all human wisdom falls far short of what would suffice to sustain so great a task. The reason is obvious: however many good, pious, and wise princes there may be, they could still not alleviate all vices. The malice of the world is so great! And the very men who are in the vineyard oppose and resist and refuse to be ruled.

Then what is to be done? Must one despair of the state on account of such prodigious difficulties and troubles? No, but as far as possible this blackness should be banished from sight, and the mind should busy itself with meditation on the blessings of God, which He both promises in His Word and also displays. Next, one should follow the example of this king in taking refuge in prayer.

7. *Tell me, You whom my soul loves.*

This is a prayer in which he confesses that he lacks the wisdom and strength for administering the state well. In this vein Duke Frederick of Saxony told Staupitz that he knew less and less how to administer his duchy and yet that there was no one to whom he could safely

entrust any matter. Similarly Cicero, after the civil war, uttered this cry brimming with indignation and despair: "Oh! that I should have been reputed wise in vain!" Therefore, in accord with Solomon's example, godly princes should pray and say: "O God, Creator and Governor of all, whom my soul loves, show me how the vineyard committed to me is to be tended, etc."

Where You pasture Your flock, where You rest at noon.

Forsaken by his own wisdom and strength, he yearns for God as the Colleague of his reign. "Show me where I may find You, so that You may administer the state together with me. In government I stray as if in night and black fog; You rest at noon. O that I were permitted thus to reign 'at noon,' that is, in complete peace!"

For why should I be like one who is veiled beside the flocks of Your companions?

Veiling was a sign of mourning, as a covered head was among the Romans. So he is praying: "Rescue me from these afflictions. Reduce my cares by Your help, and the things which weary and disgust me by Your presence."

"Give me heart so that I shall not despair nor succumb to such difficulties. And do this *beside the flocks of Your companions.* I am in a place of eminence amidst the flock of Your companions. They are those who to this day are ruled by Your Word and Spirit. For their sake, I ask, grant success and tranquillity." In this manner he reverts to prayer and to the Word in his great difficulties.

8. *If you do not know, O fairest among women.*

We have heard the lament in which the magistrate complains of the difficulty of administering the state, since even the mother's daughters are hostile. He therefore now portrays the person of the bridegroom consoling those who experience such enormous difficulties and troubles. It is as if he were saying: "You complain about your state, even though there is not a single state in the whole world which can be compared with yours, so does it overflow with all God's highest endowments.

"You have the Word of God, the prophets, saintly judges, saintly kings; do you not recognize this your beauty and fairness?"

But this is the way it goes, in temptation we forget all His gifts because we are intent upon our immediate sorrow or emotion. For temptation swallows everything up, with the result that you see, feel, think, and expect nothing but evil. Even the most learned in Holy Writ, when they are tempted, need someone who will bring them consolation from Holy Writ. So it is necessary that in temptation we should be reminded of the things which have been given us, as Paul says in 1 Cor. 2. Now he adds still further advice.

Follow in the tracks of the flock, and go to pasture with your kids beside the shepherds' tents.

"I can give you no other advice than that you go out and pasture your own sheep, that you exercise your own administrative role, unconcerned about the fact that you also have goats in your flock, that is, evil, shameless, disobedient, seditious citizens. Do not let evil men make you anxious, for pastures exist for the sake of the sheep, and the state is established principally for the sake of good men."

But what does He mean when He specifies in *the tracks of the flock?* No doubt He means that he should pay special attention to the example of his forefathers, the saintly judges, kings, and prophets, etc., who were the flock of God, with the result that when he sees that they, too, underwent various trials, he will endure the present disruptions with greater equanimity. David consoles himself this way in Ps.77:11: "I will call to mind the deeds of the Lord; yea, I will remember Thy wonders of old."

Thus there is no consolation, no solace against evils except the Word of God. "For whatever was written in former days" (Paul says in Rom. 15:4) "was written for our instruction, that by steadfastness and by the encouragement of the Scriptures we might have hope." Christ nailed to the cross, John beheaded, Moses at death's door when his own people wanted to stone him, etc.—they console us so that we bear more calmly the world's outrageous ingratitude, so that we fulfill our office with singleness of purpose and are unconcerned about the goats.

9. *I have compared you, My love, to My cavalry of Pharaoh's chariots.*

This is an amplification of the foregoing consolation. But since there are some periods of war and others of peace, he also divides this amplification into two sections.

This first section should be addressed to a period of affliction and the cross. In tribulation it seems to you that you have been abandoned and defeated. But I have compared you to My cavalry; that is, in My sight you are like a victorious cohort which is equipped to do battle, as are the chariots of Pharaoh, the mightiest of all kings. I think that mention is made of Pharaoh because of all those known to the Jews he was the most powerful king.

This is a consolation of faith, a consolation which is a

matter neither of experience nor of sight, for in Solomon's eyes his government is like a worm. Why? Because burdened and disturbed by evils and by its awareness of these evils, it deserts the Word and ignores all of its gifts. But if you look to the Word, all these assertions are perfect truth. It is therefore a most ample promise that God calls the government His friend; but it is not obvious. In appearance it seems rather as if God has deserted it.

10. *Your cheeks are comely like earrings, and your neck like strings of jewels.*

This is the second section of the amplification, dealing with the time of peace. For then the Word of God, which is lost or barely retained in tribulation, is present with us, then we are delighted by the gifts of the Spirit, which in the time of the cross are completely obliterated by our awareness of evils.

We translate *earrings* because these ornaments are divided from each other and arranged in beautiful array. The Hebrew word elsewhere means "lines," or "rows." Moreover, *earrings* and "necklaces" are gifts of the Holy Spirit in the Word. They adorn our neck; that is, the Word is in public use, it is taught, read, heard, and the abundance of the divine promises is possessed everywhere.

11. *We will make you ornaments of gold, studded with silver.*

Ornaments of gold is the same word which we before translated "earrings." But here it denotes the growth of the ornamentation. It is as if He were saying: "We shall augment this adornment and make even golden ornaments for you. The Word will grow more abundant for you if you make use of it."

For the Word is the sort of treasure which grows with handling and distribution but rots with hoarding. It has to be in constant use, for the more it is taught, heard, and learned, the more readily and the more clearly it is understood.

Those ornaments will not be of gold alone, but they will be set off by studs of silver, or vermiculated; that is, the use of the Word is manifold and varied.

In this manner he tells us that as he exercises himself in God's Word and in the examples set forth in the Word, the result is that he finds he has been taught equanimity and is not anxious about the goats that are in his flock. The person who has faith sees and experiences these things. To the person who does not believe, such rich consolations are a game and a joke.

12. *The King is still on His couch.*

The effect of the words of comfort is that that person in government believes the consolation, and this is the unique strength of faith. For the outcome usually is that the heart, conquered by calamity and present grief, is unable to accept the Word, which promises things so different from experience. Yet faith, however afflicted, remains attentive to the Word and is built up by the Word.

So in this passage he says *The King is still on His couch.* It is as if he were saying: "In my temptation I felt that God had withdrawn very far from me. Therefore I pleaded that He would show me where He pastured His flock. But He has not gone away; He is at hand and reclines at His feast, that is, He cares for me, loves me, protects me, preserves me. He is not planning how to destroy, afflict, or torture me, as I used to feel in my temptation."

My nard gave forth its fragrance.

"My prayer was carried to Him when approach was easy and He still reclined at the feast. Therefore it pleased and delighted Him, and it was heard."

13. *My Beloved is to me a bag of myrrh that lies between my breasts.*

Now he adds his commendation of the comfort and enlarges on the consolation with images of sweetness. "God is not far away, but He dwells in the midst of our life and is like a bag of myrrh in my bosom and in my embraces. That is, He cares for me, protects and comforts me, etc. In short, His feeling for me is like that of a bridegroom for his bride."

It is to be noted, however, that these realities are not palpable. Rather, this consolation remains in the figure of a fragrance. These things are perceived only by smell, in order to express the mystery of faith, namely, that God dwells among His people through a fragrance, that is, through His Word and His name. The faith must needs be great which can believe these things regarding God, that He is between the breasts, that is, that He is very near and close to us, is not angry, etc.

14. *My Beloved is to me a cluster of balsam in the vineyards of Engedi.*

This is a figurative commendation of the consoling discovery that God loves, cherishes, protects, etc., as above.

I think *cluster of Copher* is balsam, and I think so because he adds the words *in the vineyards of Engedi,* which is a city in the tribe of Judah by the Dead Sea, where there are balsam gardens. Accordingly, it is my opinion that the tree was called *Copher* in antiquity, that more recently, however, the name "balsam" has

been given it for its value, because balsam is far superior to all other ointments.

15. *Behold, you are beautiful, my love; behold, you are beautiful.*

After trial, when the consolation of the Word has taken hold of the heart, we not only feel that God loves and cherishes us, but we also feel that we please God, that we delight God, and that God takes care of us. In this way conscience and the Spirit give mutual testimony. Conscience feels that it pleases God, and so it praises God. The Holy Spirit approves this faith and in turn commends us. That is what you see expressed by this passage.

Your eyes are the eyes of doves.

The dove has a reputation for simplicity. Accordingly, he is commending the simplicity of faith, because it does not change its mind in tribulation as those do who are without the Word, whose eyes are not dovelike but harlotlike. Their eyes are turned now to this attitude, now to that. We constantly observe this in the enemies of the Gospel. But faith persists in one and the same simple regard for the promises of God and retains a strong hope for its own well-being in the most extreme dangers.

16. *Behold, you, too, are beautiful, my beloved, truly lovely.*

Here is abundance of consolation. The Holy Spirit bears witness in the heart so that we are convinced we are pleasing and beautiful to God. The result therefore is that we in turn also confess that God is beautiful; that is, that He delights us, etc. However, this beauty is not obvious in time of tribulation.

17. *Our couch is green; the beams of our house are cedar, our rafters are pine.*

All these features are allegorical, and by them he signifies the happiness which he has drawn from consolation. In every state it is the case that at every possible danger the government seems to threaten to fall into destruction and ruin.

This is the mood Solomon expresses here. It is as if he were saying: "Formerly I used to think that the whole realm was on the brink of being overthrown. It seemed to be not a kingdom or a state at all but some ancient edifice which would be toppled by the slightest blast of the winds. But now, after the consolation I have received, I see that my government is as firmly established as a house built of cedar, of a material that does not crumble but endures for the longest time. I see also that it is adorned like a bed bedecked with flowers." Just as in temptation no end of trial is in sight, so those who believe the consolation foresee perpetual joy. As he says in Ps. 30:6: "I said in my prosperity, 'I shall never be moved.'"

Robert Lowth (lecture date 1787)

SOURCE: "Lecture XXX: The *Song of Solomon* not a Regular Drama" and "Lecture XXXI: Of the Subject and Style of Solomon's Song," in *Lectures on the Sacred Poetry of the Hebrews,* Vol. II, 1787. Reprint by Garland Publishing, Inc., 1971, pp. 287-308, 309-44.

[*In the following lectures, Lowth considers the* Song of Songs *as a form of dramatic poetry and suggests, after consideration of other Hebrew poetry, that the work should be read allegorically.*]

Thus much with suffice for that inferior species of Dramatic Poetry, or rather that Dramatic form which may be assumed by any species of poem. The more perfect and regular Drama, that I mean which consists of a plot or fable, will demand a more elaborate investigation.

There are only two poems extant among the writings of the Hebrews which can, on the present occasion, at all be brought into question, the **Song of Solomon**, and the book of Job; both eminent in the highest degree for elegance, sublimity, and I am sorry to add obscurity also. The almost infinite labours of the learned have left us but little new to say upon this subject: I shall, however, proceed to inquire, with some degree of minuteness, into the form and structure of each of these poems, and into the reasons which may be alledged in favour of their claim to the appellation of regular Dramas. The opinions of other critics shall not pass unregarded, if any remarks or even conjectures occur, which may be likely to throw any light upon the present subject, or to explain or illustrate their principal beauties.

The **Song of Songs** (for so it is entitled either on account of the excellence of the subject, or of the composition) is an Epithalamium, or Nuptial Dialogue; or rather, if we may be allowed to give it a title more agreeable to the genius of the Hebrew, a *Song of Loves.* It is expressive of the utmost fervour as well as the utmost delicacy of passion, it is instinct with all the spirit and all the sweetness of affection. The principal characters are Solomon himself and his bride, who are represented speaking both in dialogue, and in soliloquy when accidentally separated. Virgins also, the companions of the bride, are introduced, who seem to be constantly upon the stage, and bear a part in the dialogue: mention too is made of young men, friends of the bridegroom, but they are mute persons. This is exactly conformable to the manners of the Hebrews,

who had always a number of companions to the bridegroom, thirty of whom were present in honour of Sampson, at his nuptial feast. In the New Testament, according to the Hebrew idiom, they are called, "children (or sons) of the bride-chamber," and "friends of the bridegroom;" there too we find mention of ten virgins, who went forth to meet the bridegroom, and conduct him home: which circumstances, I think, indicate that this poem is founded upon the nuptial rites of the Hebrews, and is expressive of the forms or ceremonial of their marriages. In this opinion, indeed, the harmony of commentators is not less remarkable, [*It may seem a bold undertaking, to contradict the opinion of all the commentators which has been so long established, that the principal personages of the* **Canticles** *are a bride and bridegroom during the nuptial week. As I cannot, however, reconcile the matter to my mind, I shall briefly assign the reasons of my dissent from this opinion. The first is, that no direct mention is made, during the course of this long poem, of the ceremony of marriage; nor of any one of the circumstances which attend that ceremony. Again, who can possibly imagine a bridegroom so necessitated to labour, as not to be able to appropriate a few days in his nuptial week, to the celebration of his marriage; but be compelled immediately to quit his spouse and his friends for whole days, in order to attend his cattle in the pastures? Nay, at this time of festival, he even does not return at night, but leaves his bride, to whom he appears so much attached, alone and unhappy. Or if such instances might occur in particular cases, certainly they do not afford a proper subject for a nuptial song. At the same time the bridegroom is supposed to have the care of a vineyard, and his brothers are displeased with him for having neglected it; this is so contrary to every idea of nuptial festivity, that unless we could suppose it meant in the way of burlesque, it is impossible to conceive it to have any relation to the celebration of a marriage.*]

There is still less reason to think, that the poem relates to the state of the parties betrothed before marriage; and there are not the smallest grounds for supposing it the description of any clandestine amour, since the transaction is described as public and legal, and the consent of parents is very plainly intimated.

It remains therefore to explain my own sentiments and these are, that the chaste passions of conjugal and domestic life are described in this poem, and that it has no relation to the celebration of nuptials. It may seem improbable to some readers, that conjugal and domestic life should afford a subject for an amorous poem; but those readers have not reflected how materially the manners of the Orientals are different from ours. Domestic life among us is, in general, a calm and settled state, void of difficulties, perplexities, suspicions, and intrigues; and a state like this rarely affords matter for such a poem. But in the East, from the nature of polygamy, that state admits more of the per-plexities, jealousies, plots, and artifices of love; the scene is more varied, there is more of novelty, and consequently greater scope for invention and fancy.] than their disagreement concerning the general econo-my and conduct of the world, and the order and ar-rangement of the several parts. The present object of inquiry, however, is only whether any plot or fable be contained or represented in this poem; and upon this point, the most probable opinion is that of the celebrat-ed Bossuet, a critic, whose profound learning will ever be acknowledged, and a scholar whose exquisite taste will ever be admired. I shall endeavour, as briefly as possible, to explain his sentiments concerning the form and conduct of this poem, whence we shall probably be enabled to decide in some measure concerning the equity of its claim to the tide of a regular Drama.

It is agreed on all parts, that the nuptial feast, as well as every other solemn rite among the Hebrews, was hebdomadal. Of this circumstance M. Bossuet has availed himself in the analysation of the poem, and he accordingly divides the whole into seven parts, corre-sponding to the seven days of its supposed duration. [*In addition to what I remarked above, there is this circumstance, which militates against the conjecture of Bossuet, namely, that, though the nuptial banquet continues for seven days, no time appears in this poem appropriated to the banquet itself. Either the bride and bridegroom are separated from, and in quest of each other, or they are enjoying a wished-for solitude; and wherever they converse with the Virgins, it is in the street or in the field, and never with the guests, or at a banquet.*] The vicissitudes of day and night are marked with some degree of distinctness; he therefore makes use of these as indexes, to point to the true division of the parts. The nuptial banquet being concluded, the bride is led in the evening to her future husband; and here commences the nuptial week; for the Hebrews, in their account of time, begin always at the evening. The bridegroom, who is represented in the character of a shepherd, goes forth early in the morning to the accus-tomed occupations of a rural and pastoral life; the bride presently awaking, and impatient of his absence, breaks out into a soliloquy full of tenderness and anxiety, and this incident forms the exordium of the poem. The early departure of the bridegroom seems to be accord-ing to custom; hence that precaution so frequently and so anxiously repeated not to disturb his beloved:

"I adjure you, O ye daughters of Jerusalem,
"By the roes and the hinds of the field,
"That ye disturb not, neither awake
"The beloved, 'till herself be inclined."

Nor less frequent is the following exclamation of the Virgins:

"Who is she, rising up out of the desert!

"Who is she, that is seen like the morning!"

In these terms they seem to greet the bride when she first comes out of her chamber: and these several ex-pressions have some allusion to the early time of the morning. The night is also sometimes mentioned in direct terms, and sometimes it is indirectly denoted by circumstances. If therefore any reader, admitting these indications of time, will carefully attend to them, he cannot, I think, but perceive, that the whole of the work consists of seven parts or divisions, each of which occupies the space of a day. The same critic adds, that he can discover the last day to be clearly distinguished as the sabbath; for the bridegroom does not then, as usual, go forth to his rural employments, but proceeds from the marriage-chamber into public with his bride. Such are the sentiments of this learned person; to which I am inclined to accede, not as absolute demonstration, but as a very ingenious and probable conjecture upon an extremely obscure subject: I follow them therefore as a glimmering of light, which beams forth in the midst of darkness, where it would be almost unreason-able to hope for any clearer illumination.

This opinion is the most favourable of all to those who account the **Song of Solomon** a regular Drama; for this arrangement seems to display, in some measure, the order and method of a theatrical representation. But if they make use of the term Dramatic according to the common acceptation of the word, this poem must be supposed to contain a fable, or entire and perfect plot or action, of a moderate extent, in which the in-cidents are all connected, and proceed regularly from one another, and which, after several vicissitudes, is brought to a perfect conclusion. But certainly the bare representation of a nuptial festival cannot in any re-spect answer to this definition. We are, it is true, very imperfectly instructed in the particular rites and cere-monies of the Hebrew marriages; but we have no rea-son to suppose, that in their common and usual form they were possessed of such variety and vicissitude of fortunes and events, as to afford materials for a regular plot or fable. The whole was one even tenour of joy and festivity. An unexpected incident might indeed sometimes occur to interrupt the usual order, and to produce such a change of fortune, as might afford a basis for a Dramatic story; and if any such incident is to be found in the poem at present under our consid-eration, it will establish its claim to that appellation. But the truth is, the keenest inspection of criticism can, throughout the whole, discover no such incident or circumstance; the state of affairs is uniformly the same from the beginning to the end; a few light fluctuations of passion excepted, such as the anxiety of absence, and the amenity and happiness which the lovers enjoy in each others presence. The bride laments the absence of her beloved; she seeks, she finds him, she brings him home; again he is lost, she seeks him again, but with different success; she complains, languishes, indites messages to be delivered to him, she indulges her passion in a full and animated description of his person. All this, however, bears no resemblance to a regular plot, nor affords the piece any fairer title to the appellation of a perfect Drama, than the Dramatic Eclogues of Theocritus and Virgil, in which the loves, the amusements, and the emulations of shepherds are depicted, and which no critic has ever classed with the regular fables of Euripides and Terence. Thus far therefore we may safely admit, that the *Song of Solomon* possesses indeed the Dramatic form, and therefore belongs properly to that inferior species, which was mentioned in the former part of this Lecture; but that it cannot, upon any fair grounds of reason, be accounted a regular Drama.

There is however one circumstance in which this poem bears a very near affinity to the Greek Drama: the chorus of Virgins seems in every respect congenial to the tragic chorus of the Greeks. They are constantly present, and prepared to fulfil all the duties of advice and consolation: they converse frequently with the principal characters; they are questioned by them, and they return answers to their inquiries; they take part in the whole business of the poem, and I do not find that upon any occasion they quit the scene. Some of the learned have conjectured, that Theocritus, who was contemporary with the seventy Greek translators of the Scriptures, and lived with them in the court of Ptolemy Philadelphus, was not unacquainted with the beauties of this poem, and that he has almost literally introduced some passages from it into his elegant Idylliums. It might also be suspected, that the Greek tragedians were indebted for their chorus to this poem of Solomon, were not the. probabilities on the other side much greater, that the Greeks were made acquainted with it at too late a period; and were it not evident, that the chorus of the Greeks had a very different origin, were it not evident indeed that the chorus was not added to the fable, but the fable to the chorus.

Having, in my last Lecture, briefly explained what appeared to me most probable, among the great variety of opinions which have prevailed, concerning the conduct and economy of the *Song of Solomon*, a question next presents itself for our investigation, not less involved in doubt and obscurity, I mean the real nature and subject of the poem. Some are of opinion, that it is so be taken altogether in a literal sense, and others esteem it wholly allegorical. There is no less disagreement also among those who consider it as allegorical; some conceive it to be no more than a simple allegory, while others place it in that class which I have denominated mystical, that, namely, which is founded upon the basis of history. I would gladly, from the first, have considered this question as foreign to my undertaking, and would have avoided it as involved in the deepest obscurity, had I not, in the former part of these Lectures, been under the

necessity of remarking the connexion between the different kinds of allegory and the principles of the Sacred Poetry; had I not also found it necessary to advert to all the peculiarities of the parabolic style, the most obvious property of which is to express by certain images, chiefly adopted from natural objects, the analogy and application of which is regularly preserved, those ideas and doctrines which are more remote from common apprehension. This I cannot help considering as a matter of the utmost importance, in enabling us to understand properly the poetry of the Hebrews; and upon this point much of the present argument will be found to depend.

I shall on this, as well as upon the last occasion, proceed with that cautious reserve which I think prudent and necessary on so obscure a subject; and since certainty is not to be obtained, I shall content myself with proposing to your consideration what appears least improbable. In the first place then I confess, that by several reasons, by the general authority and consent of both the Jewish and Christian churches; and still more, by the nature and analogy of the parabolic style, I feel irresistibly inclined to that side of the question which confiders this poem as an entire allegory. Those, indeed, who have considered it in a different light; and who have objected against the inconsistency and meanness of the imagery, seem to be but little acquainted with the genius of the parabolic diction; for the removal, therefore, of these difficulties, which I find have been the cause of offence to many persons, I shall beg leave to trespass upon your attention, while I explain somewhat more accurately the nature of this allegory and its analogy with other productions of the Hebrew poets.

The narrowness and imbecility of the human mind being such, as scarcely to comprehend or attain a clear idea of any part of the Divine nature by its utmost exertions; God has condescended, in a manner, to contrast the infinity of his glory, and to exhibit it to our understandings under such imagery as our feeble optics are capable of contemplating. Thus the Almighty may be said to descend, as it were, in the Holy Scriptures, from the height of his majesty, to appear on earth in a human shape, with human senses and affections, in all respects resembling a mortal—"with human voice and human form." This kind of allegory is called anthropopathy, and occupies a considerable portion of theology, properly so called, that is, as delivered in the Holy Scriptures. The principal part of this imagery is derived from the passions; nor indeed is there any one affection or emotion of the human soul which is not, with all its circumstances, ascribed in direct terms, without any qualification whatever, to the supreme God; not excepting those in which human frailty and imperfection is most evidently displayed, anger and grief, hatred and revenge. That love also, and that of the tenderest kind, should bear a part in this Drama, is highly natural and perfectly consistent. Thus, not only the fondness of paternal affection is attributed to God, but also the force, the ardour, and the solicitude of conjugal attachment, with all the concomitant emotions, the anxiety, the tenderness, the jealousy incidental to this passion.

After all, this figure is not in the least productive of obscurity; the nature of it is better understood than that of most others; and although it be exhibited in a variety of lights, it constantly preserves its native perspicuity. A peculiar people, of the posterity of Abraham, was selected by God from among the nations, and he ratified his choice by a solemn covenant. This covenant was founded upon reciprocal conditions; on the one part love, protection, and support; on the other faith, obedience, and worship pure and devout. This is that conjugal union between God and his church; that solemn compact so frequently celebrated by almost all the Sacred writers under this image. It is indeed a remarkable instance of that species of metaphor which Aristotle calls analogical; that is, when in a proposition consisting of four ideas, the first bears the same relation to the second as the third does to the fourth, and the corresponding words may occasionally change their places without any injury to the sense. Thus in this form of expression God is supposed to bear exactly the same relation to the church as a husband to a wife; God is represented as the spouse of the church, and the church as the betrothed of God. Thus also, when the same figure is maintained with a different mode of expression, and connected with different circumstances, the relation is still the same; thus the piety of the people, their impiety, their idolatry, and rejection, stand in the same relation with respect to the sacred covenant; as chastity, modesty, immodesty, adultery, divorce, with respect to the marriage contract. And this notion is so very familiar and well understood in Scripture, that the word adultery (or whoredom) is commonly used to denote idolatrous worship, and so appropriated does it appear to this metaphorical purpose, that it very seldom occurs in its proper and literal sense.

Let us only observe how freely the sacred poets employ this image, how they dwell upon it, in how many different forms they introduce it, and how little they seem to fear exhibiting it with all its circumstances. Concerning the reconciliation of the church to Almighty God, and its restoration to the divine favour, amongst many images of similar nature, the elegant Isaiah introduces the following:

> For thy husband is thy maker;
> JEHOVAH, God of Hosts, is his name:
> And thy Redeemer is the Holy One of Israel;
> The God of the whole earth shall he be called.

And in another passage in the form of a comparison:

> For as a young man weddeth a virgin,
> So shall thy Restorer wed thee;
> And as the bridegroom rejoiceth in his bride,
> So shall thy God rejoice in thee.

The same image a little diversified, and with greater freedom of expression, as better adapted to the display of indignation, is introduced by Jeremiah, when he declaims against the defection of the Jews from the worship of the true God. Upon the same principle the former part of the prophecy of Hosea ought also to be explained; and whether that part of the prophecy be taken in the literal and historical sense, or whether it be esteemed altogether allegorical, still the nature and principles of this figure, which seems consecrated in some measure to this subject, will evidently appear. None of the Prophets, however, have applied the image with so much boldness and freedom as Ezekiel, an author of a most fervid imagination, who is little studious of elegance, or cautious of offending; insomuch, that I am under some apprehension of his incurring no inconsiderable share of censure from those over-delicate critics who have been emitted from the Gallic schools. [*Nothing can be more disgusting to any person of common sense, than the arrogant pretences of our neighbours on the continent to superior refinement and civilization; and I confess, on a fair investigation, I am utterly at a loss to find in what this boasted superiority consists. Is it seen in their enlarged and liberal notions of civil government, in their toleration and general information on politics and religion, in the mildness of their punishments and the equity of their laws? Is it marked by their progress in the great and useful sciences, by their Bacons and their Boyles, their Newtons and their Lockes? Does it appear in the sublimity, the grandeur, the elegance of their poets? Or is it demonstrated by still more certain marks of civilization, by the general cleanliness, decency, and industry of the common people? Is it seen in the convenience and grandeur of their public roads, and the accommodations afforded to travellers in every part of the kingdom? Does it appear in the face of the country, the high state of cultivation, and the success and improvement of agriculture? Or lastly, is it demonstrable from the morals of the people at large, from the independence, the dignity, the probity, particularly of the trading classes of society? I know no other marks of civilization than these; and if the admirers of Gallic frippery cannot answer these questions to my satisfaction, I shall continue to give but little credit to their pretensions to extraordinary refinement and politeness.*

That diversity of manners, that delicacy of conversation, which is observed by some nations, and the coarseness of others, results chiefly from the degree of intercourse which subsists between the sexes. In countries where the intercourse is free and familiar, where the sexes meet commonly in mixed companies, they accustom themselves to a greater modesty and delicacy in their conversation, which modesty is easily transferred to their composition. Such a people, therefore, with whom entertainments would seem languid and dull without the company of young women, though perhaps not free from licentiousness in their manners, will yet be chaste and delicate in their expressions. Hence arises, in a great degree, that extreme delicacy in the people of modern Europe, which can scarcely bear some of the passages in Virgil, and the chastest of the ancient poets. The case is quite different with the people of the East: for the men having scarcely any society with the unmarried women, or with the wives of others, converse together without being restrained by the blushes of females, or with their own wives, whom they regard in a very inferior light, and consequently treat with all the insolence of familiarity: the women also converse chiefly with each other; and as they are familiarly situated, are probably not less licentious. It is not extraordinary, therefore, if greater freedom of speech should prevail in those countries, and if this, when transferred into their poetry, should be found to offend our ears, which are accustomed to so much greater delicacy in conversation.]

His great freedom in the use of this image is particularly displayed in two parables, in which he describes the ingratitude of the Jews and Israelites to their great Protector, and their defection from the true worship under imagery assumed from the character of an adulterous wife, and the meretricious loves of two unchaste women. If these parables (which are put into the mouth of God himself with a direct allegorical application, and in which it must be confessed, that delicacy does not appear to be particularly studied) be well considered, I am persuaded, that the **Song of Solomon** (which is in every part chaste and elegant) will not appear unworthy of the divine sense in which it is usually taken, either in matter or style, or in any degree inferior either in gravity or purity to the other remains of the Sacred Poets. To these instances I may add the forty-fifth Psalm, which is a sacred Epithalamium, of the allegorical application of which, to the union between God and the church, I do not find that any doubt has hitherto been entertained; though many suspect it, and not without good reason, to have been produced upon the same occasion, and with the same relation to a real fact as the **Song of Solomon**. Neither ought we to omit, that the writers of the New Testament have freely admitted the same image in the same allegorical sense with their predecessors, and have finally consecrated it by their authority.

[*What* CHARDIN *relates of the Persian poetry, may perhaps not be unworthy of the reader's notice in this place. "Debauchery and licentiousness," says he, "are the common topics of these compositions; but I must not omit remarking, that the most serious of their poets treat of the sublimest mysteries of theology, under the most licentious language, in the way of allegory, as*

Afez in his Kafel." Voyage de Chardin, 4to. tom. ii. cap. xiv. But respecting this matter see the arguments on both sides elegantly stated by the learned Sir William JONES. *Poes. Asiaticae Comment.cap. ix.*]

These reasons appear to me sufficient to remove those objections founded on the meanness of the imagery, which render many critics averse to the allegorical explanation of this poem. I shall not attempt to confirm this opinion by any internal evidence from the poem itself, as I do not scruple to confess myself deterred by the great difficulty of the undertaking. For though induced by the most ancient authority, and still more by the analogy of this with other similar allegories contained in the Hebrew writings, I am fully persuaded of the truth of what I have advanced; yet I am still apprehensive that it would be extremely difficult to establish the hypothesis by direct arguments from the internal structure of the work itself.

[*Our author has treated this very difficult subject with more modesty and more address than any of the commentators; and indeed has said all that could be said, exclusive of the theological arguments in favour of the allegorical sense. I question, however, whether he will be able to remove all doubt from the mind of a cool and attentive reader; the reasons of my scepticism on this matter, I will, as a person earnestly desirous of the truth, endeavour briefly to explain; and I shall hold myself greatly indebted to that man, who shall, upon rational principles, undertake to remove my scruples.*

With regard to the authority of the ancient Christian church, in a question merely depending upon the exposition of a passage in Scripture, I hold it of very little importance, not only because the exposition of Scripture does not depend upon human authority, but because the fathers, as well on account of their ignorance of the Hebrew language, as of the principles. of polite literature in general, were very inadequate to the subject, eagerly pursuing certain mystical meanings, even with respect to the clearest passages, in the explanation of which, the most enlightened of the modern commentators have refuted them. The time of the fathers was so very distant from the period when this poem was composed, that it is impossible they should have been possessed of any certain tradition concerning its purport and meaning. I should entertain very different sentiments, if I could find any mention of the **Song of Songs** *in the New Testament; but on the most diligent examination, I have not been able to discern the slightest allusion to that poem.*

The authority of the Synagogue is of still less importance in my eyes, since in other respects we have found it so little deserving of confidence in its attempts at expounding the Scriptures. Such of the Jewish writers as have treated of the **Canticles** *lived so many ages* *after the time of Solomon, after the total destruction of the commonwealth and literature of the Hebrews, that they knew no more of the matter than ourselves.*

With regard to the analogy of other poems, all that can be said is, that it was indeed possible enough for Solomon to celebrate the Divine love in terms analogous to the descriptive of the human affections: but it is impossible to determine by that analogy, what kind of love he intended to be the subject of this poem. Shall we pretend to say, that his attention was wholly employed upon Sacred Poetry, and that he never celebrated in verse any of the human affections? Or, because some of the Hebrew poems celebrate the Divine goodness in terms expressive of the human passions, does it follow, that on no occasion those terms are to be taken in their literal sense?

Our author has prudently declined examining the arguments which are usually taken from the poem itself, and from its internal structure, for the purpose of establishing the allegory. It is indeed very improbable, that in so long a poem, if it were really allegorical, no vestiges, no intimation should be found to direct us to apply it to the Divine love; nothing, which does not most clearly relate to the human passion: and that too, considering it as the production of one of the Hebrew writers, who are accustomed to mix the literal sense with the allegorical in almost all their compositions of this kind. In so long an allegory one should also expect a deeper moral than usual, and one not generally obvious to be indicated: but no sober commentator has ever been able to deduce from the **Canticles** any other than this trite sentiment, that God loves his church, and is beloved by it. That this simple sentiment should be treated so prolixly, and nothing more distinctly revealed concerning it, who can credit, but upon the soundest basis of argument or proof? But in support of it we have only the bare position, that the Hebrew writers sometimes make use of allegorical expressions to denote the Divine love.

I am aware of the objections which are started by those who rest the matter upon theological arguments (though I cannot find that these are of great weight or utility in the present debate: for they seem rather calculated to silence than convince). They assert, that though the book has never been quoted by Christ or his Apostles, it was yet received into the Sacred Canon, and is therefore to be accounted of Divine original: and that there does not appear any thing in it Divine, or worthy of sacred inspiration, unless it be supposed to contain the mystery of the Divine love. Lest, however, they should seem to have proved too much, and lest they should dismiss the reader prepossessed with some doubts concerning the Divine authority of the book, I will venture to remind these profound reasoners, that the chaste and conjugal affections so carefully implanted by the Deity in the human

heart, and upon which so great a portion of human happiness depends, are not unworthy of a muse fraught even with Divine inspiration. Only let us suppose, contrary to the general opinion concerning the **Canticles**, *that the affection, which is described in this poem, is not that of lovers previous to their nuptials, but the attachment of two delicate persons, who have been long united in the sacred bond, can we suppose such happiness unworthy of being recommended as a pattern to mankind, and of being celebrated as a subject of gratitude to the great author of happiness? This is indeed a branch of morals which may be treated in a more artificial and philosophical manner; and such a manner will perhaps be more convincing to be understanding, but will never affect the heart with such tender sentiments as the* **Song of Solomon**; *in which there exists all the fervour of passion, with the utmost chastity of expression, and with that delicacy and reserve, which is ever necessary to the life and preservation of conjugal love. Let us remember, moreover, that Solomon, in his Proverbs, has not disdained very minutely to describe the felicities and infelicities of the conjugal state.*

Notwithstanding all that this learned writer has so ably advanced against the allegorical import of this exquisite Idyllium, I cannot be prevailed upon entirely to relinquish the idea. That compositions of a similar kind are still extant amongst the Asiatics is certain. The Loves of Megnoun and Leileh have been celebrated in the Arabic, Persic, and Turkish languages, with all the charms of poetic rapture, whilst the impassioned lovers themselves are regarded in the same allegorical light, as the bridegroom and bride in the **Song of Songs**. *Exclusive, however, of this consideration, there appear to stand forth in the composition it self indisputable traits of an allegorical sense. For, though (from our imperfect knowledge of the extraneous manners, arts, local peculiarities, and literature, of so singular a people, at so distant a period) we be now unable to apply the thing signified to its proper sign, yet a variety of images obtrude themselves upon us that evidently contain a symbolical meaning.—*JEHOVAH *having chosen the Jewish nation as his peculiar people, and being frequently, by the Prophets* AFTER *Solomon, represented as their* HUSBAND, *and they personified as his* WIFE; *might not the consecration (2* CHRON. *vii.) of the Temple, as an habitation for the Lord to dwell in, and there receive them to himself, have suggested to Solomon the idea of a* CONJUGAL UNION, *and induced him to adapt an allegory to it?—As to the allegation, that this poem is not cited in the New Testament; it will, upon this ground, be of the less weight; for our Saviour, in the parables of the ten Virgins and the Marriage Supper, has adopted (if not from it) the same allegory, as well as in other passages [*MARK *ix. 15,&c.] and is himself not only pointed out to the Jews expressly in the character of a bridegroom, by John Baptist [*JOHN *iii.] but referred to, under it, by St. Paul*

[EPH. v &c.] and more particularly in the Apocalyps. How far this conjecture may be supported, I will not venture a present to pronounce, but thus much it may be proper to observe, that such images as the tents of Kedar compared to the complexion of a young female; the tower of David to her neck; Tirza to her beauty, and Jerusalem to her comeliness; the filb-pools of Hesbbon by the gates of Betbrabbin, to her eyes; the tower of Lebanon looking towards Damascus, to her nose; the mount of Carmel, to her head; with others of a similar kind, would, I think, have never selected, to exemplify the beauties of a BRIDE, in any composition that was not allegorical.]

But if, after all, it be allowed that this work is of the allegorical kind, another question remains, namely, to which of the three classes of allegory already specified it properly belongs. The first of these, you will recollect, was the continued metaphor; the second the parable, strictly so called; and the third, the mystical allegory, which, under the veil of some historical fact, conceals a meaning more sacred and sublime. I must confess, that I am clearly of the same opinion with those who assign this production to the latter class of allegories; the reason of which will be evident, if it be admitted that there is any thing in the poem at all allegorical; since there can scarcely be any doubt that it relates in a literal sense to the nuptials of Solomon. Those also who are conversant with the writings of the Hebrew poets will easily perceive how agreeable the conduct of this poem is to the practice of those writers, who are fond of annexing a secret and solemn sense to the obvious meaning of their compositions, and of looking through the medium of human affairs to those which are celestial and divine. The subject of the **Canticles** appears to be the marriage feast of Solomon (who was both in name and in reality the Prince of Peace); his bride is also called *Solomitis*, the same name with a feminine termination; through the latter Jews have strangely disguised and obscured it by a vicious pronunciation: for Solomon and Solomitis have evidently the same relation to each other, as the Latin names Caius and Caia. This circumstance of the names was not to be disregarded, since they seem to have a very strict connexion, and to afford a very distinct intimation of the latent meaning: for to what purpose innovate the usual practice of the Hebrews, by assigning to the wife of Solomon the same name, unless from a regard to the force and meaning of the word? Unless it was meant to indicate, that the name of Solomon himself was not without importance, not without some further aim than merely the distinction of the person? Who this wife of Solomon was, is not clearly ascertained: but some of the learned have conjectured, with an appearance of probability, that she was the daughter of Pharaoh, to whom Solomon was known to be particularly attached. May we not therefore, with some shadow of reason, suspect, that under the allegory of Solomon chusing a wife from the Egyptians, might

be darkly typified that other Prince of Peace, who was to espouse a church, chosen from amoung the Gentiles?

Concerning the explanation of this allegory, I will only add, that, in the first place, we ought to be cautious of carrying the figurative application too far, and of entering into a precise explication of every particular: as these minute investigations are seldom conducted with sufficient prudence not to offend the serious part of mankind, learned as well as unlearned. Again, I would advise, that this production be treated according to the established rules of this kind of allegory, fully and expressly delivered in the Sacred Writings, and that the author be permitted to be his own interpreter. In this respect the errors of critics and divines have been as numerous as they have been pernicious. Not to mention other absurdities, they have taken the allegory not as denoting the universal state of the church, but the spiritual state of individuals; than which, nothing can be more inconsistent with the very nature and ground-work of the allegory itself, as well as with the general practice of the Hebrew poets of these occasions.

It remains to offer a few remarks upon the style of this poem. I formerly intimated that it was of the pastoral kind; since the two principal personages are represented in the character of shepherds. This circumstance is by no means incongruous to the manners of the Hebrews, whose principal occupation consisted in the care of cattle; nor did they consider this employment as beneath the dignity of the highest characters. Least of all, could it be supposed inconsistent with the character of Solomon, whose father was raised from the sheepfold to the throne of Israel. The pastoral life is not only most delightful in itself, but, from the particular circumstances and manners of the Hebrews, is possessed of a kind of dignity. In this poem it is adorned with all the choicest colouring of language, with all the elegance and variety of the most select imagery. "Every part of the **Canticles**," says a modern writer,[Bossuet]:

> abounds in poetical beauties; the objects, which present themselves on every side, are the choicest plants, the most beautiful flowers, the most delicious fruits, the bloom and vigour of spring, the sweet verdure of the fields, flourishing and well-watered gardens, pleasant streams, and perrenial fountains. The other senses are represented as regaled with the most precious odours, natural and artificial; with the sweet singing of birds, and the soft voice of the turtle; with milk and honey, and the choicest of wine. To these enchantments are added all that is beautiful and graceful in the human form, the endearments, the caresses, the delicacy of love; if any object be introduced which seems not to harmonize with this delightful scene, such as the awful prospect of tremendous precipices, the wildness of the mountains, or the haunts of the lions;

its effect is only to heighten by the contrast the beauty of the other objects, and to add the charms of variety to those of grace and elegance.

In the following passage the force and splendour of description in united with all the softness and tenderness of passion:

> Get thee up my companion.
> My lovely one, come away:
> For lo! the winter is past,
> The rain is over, is gone,
> The flowers are seen on the earth;
> The season of the song is come,
> And the voice of the turtle is heard in our
> land:
> The fig-tree puts forth its green figs,
> And the vine's tender grapes yield a fragrance:
> Arise, my companion, my fair one, and come.

The following comparisons abound in sweetness and delicacy:

> How sweet is thy love, O my sister, O spouse,
> How much better than wine is thy love,
> And the odour of thy perfumes than all
> spices!
> Thy lips, O spouse, distil honey from the
> comb,
> Honey and milk are under thy tongue,
> And the scent of thy garments is like
> the fragrance of Lebanon.

There are some others which demand a more accurate investigation.

> Thy hair is like a flock of goats,
> That browse upon Mount Gilead.

The hair of the goats was soft, smooth, of a yellow cast; like that of the bride; her beautiful tresses are compared with the numerous flocks of goats which covered this flourishing mountain from the top to the bottom.

> Thy teeth are like the shorn flock
> Which have come up from the washing place,
> All of which have twins,
> And none among them is bereaved.

The evenness, whiteness, and unbroken order of the teeth, is admirably expressed.

> Like the twice-dyed thread of crimson are thy
> lips,
> And thy language is sweet.

That is, thin and ruby-coloured, such as add peculiar graces to the sweetness of the voice.

> Like the slice of a pomegranate.
> Are thy cheeks amidst thy tresses.

Partly obscured, as it were, by her hair, and exhibiting a gentle blush of red from beneath the delicate shade, as the seeds of the pomegranate (the colour of which is white tinged with red) surrounded by the rind.

> Thy neck is like the tower of David
> Built for an armoury;
> A thousand shields are hung up against it,
> All bucklers for the mighty.

The neck is described as long, erect, slender, according to the nicest proportion; decorated with gold, gems, and large pearls. It is compared with some turret of the citadel of Sion, more lofty than the rest, remarkable for its elegance, and not less illustrious for its architecture than for the trophies with which it was adorned, being hung round with shields and other implements of war.

> Thy two breasts are like two young kids,
> Twins of the gazal, that browse among the
> lilies.

Delicate and smooth, standing equally prominent from the ivory bosom. The animal with which they are compared is an animal of exquisite beauty, and from that circumstance it derives its name in the Hebrew. Nothing can, I think, be imagined more truly elegant and poetical than all these passages, nothing more apt or expressive, than these comparisons. The discovery of these excellencies, however, only serves to increase our regret for the many beauties which we have lost, the perhaps superior graces, which extreme antiquity seems to have overcast with an impenetrable shade.

H. H. Rowley (essay date 1952)

SOURCE: "Interpretation of the *Song of Songs*," in *The Servant of the Lord and Other Essays on the Old Testament,* Rev. ed., Basil Blackwell, 1965, pp. 197-245.

[*In the following essay originally published in 1952, Rowley provides a brief historical survey of scholarship on the* Song of Songs, *outlining the allegorical, historical, Christian, and dramatic readings of the work, and considering its function and meaning.*]

There is no book of the Old Testament which has found greater variety of interpretation than the ***Song of Songs***. Nor can it be said that there is any real agreement amongst scholars to-day as to the origin and significance of the work. In the title it is ascribed to Solomon, but no weight can be attached to that tradition, and writers of all schools now recognize it to be without authority. It is generally believed, however, that it was owing to the fact that it was wrongly ascribed to Solomon that it secured its place in the Canon of Scripture, and owing to the allegorical interpretation it received that it maintained itself there. We know that in the first century A.D. there was some disagreement amongst the Rabbis as to whether it ought to have a place in the Canon, and there is preserved for us the opinion expressed by Rabbi Akiba, that "the world itself was not worth the day on which this book was given to Israel". The very extravagance of this utterance is perhaps an indication of the depth of the division of opinion, and it may well be that the ascription to Solomon turned the scale.

There is little reason to doubt that what caused some to urge its exclusion from the Canon was the sensuousness of its images, and its apparently erotic character. Indeed, we are told that the same Rabbi Akiba pronounced a curse on those who treated this book as a common ditty and sang passages from it at banquets. Clearly, there were some who so treated the song, and who thereby brought it into discredit.

How, then, was its credit restored? By the Rabbis it was interpreted allegorically, and this is the first type of interpretation at which we must look, apart from the plain erotic interpretation, to which we shall return. We find a trace of this allegorical interpretation in the Mishnah, where 3:11 is quoted, "Go forth, ye daughters of Zion, and behold King Solomon with the crown wherewith his mother crowned him in the day of his espousals, and in the day of the gladness of his heart", and then the strange comment is added, "*In the day of his espousals*—this is the giving of the Law; *and in the day of the gladness of his heart*—this is the building of the Temple." Other traces of an allegorical interpretation are found in the Talmud, and in the Targum the text is expanded by a running commentary, which interprets the whole song in terms of Israel's history, taking it as an allegory, which under the figures of human love set forth the story of God's dealings with His chosen people.

Along this path Rabbinical scholarship pressed, and ingenuity was strained to find the most unlooked-for of meanings. Thus the verse "A sachet of myrrh is my beloved to me, Between my breasts it lies" was found by Rashi and Ibn Ezra to be a reference to the Shekinah, between the cherubim that stood over the Ark; the Targum supposed "Come, O my beloved, be thou like a gazelle, Or a young hart on the spicy mountains" to be a reference to Mount Moriah, and the two breasts to be the two Messiahs, ben David and ben Ephraim, while Moses ibn Tibbon saw Moses and Aaron in the two breasts; Rashi thought "On my bed by night I sought him whom my soul loveth, I sought him but I found him not" referred to the years of wandering in the wilderness; pseudo-Sa'adia believed "Black am I but comely, O daughters of Jerusalem" to mean that

Israel was black by reason of the making of the Golden Calf, but comely by reason of receiving the Ten Commandments, while Moses ibn Tibbon explained the verse to mean black in this world and fair in the world to come; and Ibn Ezra supposed "thy navel" to refer to the Great Sanhedrin, and in the "mixed wine" found the Law, while "thy belly is an heap of wheat" he supposed to refer to the Little Sanhedrin.

It is of interest to observe that so recently as 1909 a Roman Catholic scholar of the highest reputation as a philologist and grammarian revived this old Jewish view of the *Song* and interpreted the book throughout in terms of Israel's history. He finds in the first half the story of Israel from the Exodus to the time of Solomon, and in the second half the story of Israel's defection from God, leading to the Exile, followed by the renewal of the divine favour, and the return from the Exile, with the restoration of the Temple and the walls of Jerusalem. At many points he follows the old Jewish interpreters, but at others he produces fresh flights of fancy. Thus, the verse already quoted, "On my bed by night I sought him whom my soul loveth, I sought him but I found him not," is said to be a reference to the capture of the Ark by the Philistines; while the verses "We have a little sister, and she hath no breasts. What shall we do for our sister, In the day when she shall be spoken for? If she be a wall we will build upon her A battlement of silver; And if she be a door we will fashion upon her A board of cedar. I am a wall, And my breasts are towers" are found to refer to the restoration of the walls of Jerusalem.

Few, however, have been the Christian scholars who have interpreted the *Song* in terms of Israel's history. In the fourteenth century the Franciscan Nicolaus de Lyra, whose biblical work so greatly influenced Luther that men sang "Si Lyra non lyrasset, Luther non saltasset", i.e., "If Lyra had not piped, Luther had not danced", and who is said by an unreliable tradition to have been himself of Jewish descent, supposed the first six chapters to recount the history of Israel, and the last two chapters to deal with the Christian Church, humble and weak amongst her enemies prior to Constantine's day.

But, speaking generally, while the Church took over from the Rabbis the allegorical method of interpretation, it was re-applied to fit the Christian interests, and the *Song* was held to be an allegory of the dealings of Christ with His Church, or of the faithful soul with the Divine Logos. With some important exceptions, which we shall note presently, this view has held the field until modern times, and it is represented in the chapter headings of the Authorized Version. In recent years it has still found some advocates, indeed, and in 1925 it was re-presented by a French writer [E. Tobac], who suggests that while it was God's love for Israel that primarily filled the thought of the writer, the inspiring

Spirit intended it equally to set forth the relations with the Church.

Some of the early Fathers of the Church interpreted particular phrases in the *Song* in relation to the Virgin Mary, and in the twelfth century this became a favourite line of interpretation that was greatly extended. It requires no great powers of imagination to see how, once this principle of interpretation was accepted, the Virgin Mary could be read into many texts. Thus Richard of St. Victor comments on the verse "Thou art all fair, my love; And there is no spot in thee" with the words "The Blessed Virgin Mary was wholly fair, because she was sanctified in the womb; and also after she was born she committed no sin, either mortal or venial." Needless to say, this particular variety of interpretation has not flourished in Protestant circles, though its influence persists in Roman Catholic works.

There have, however, been many strange extravagances of interpretation in all schools of allegorists, and the bold sensuousness of the figures of the *Song* has been transmuted in the hands of the allegorists into the vehicle of their own ideas. A few samples may be quoted in illustration. Origen held the verse "Black am I but comely, O daughters of Jerusalem" to mean black with sin but comely through conversion; Philo Carpasius and Cyril of Alexandria believed "A sachet of myrrh is my beloved to me, Between my breasts it lies" to refer to the Scriptures of the Old and New Testaments, between which stands Christ, while Justus Urgellensis found the breasts to denote the learned teachers of the Church, and pseudo-Cassiodorus thought the verse referred to the Crucifixion of Christ, which the believer keeps in eternal remembrance between his breasts, i.e. in his heart, and which is as myrrh to him; the last-named writer interpreted "The voice of the turtle-dove is heard in the land" of the preaching of the Apostles, and Philo Carpasius of the preaching of Paul; Cyril of Alexandria took "On my bed by night I sought him whom my soul loveth, I sought him but I found him not" to refer to the women who sought Christ on the Resurrection morning; Cyril of Jerusalem saw in the words "King Solomon made himself a palanquin" a reference to the Cross, and in its "silver pillars" an allusion to Judas's thirty pieces of silver, and in "the crown wherewith his mother crowned him in the day of his espousals" a reference to the crown of thorns; Justus Urgellensis referred "A garden enclosed is my sister, my bride; A spring enclosed, a fountain sealed" to the Virgin Mary, and pseudo-Cassiodorus to the Church; pseudo-Athanasius believed "I have come to my garden, my sister, my bride, I have gathered my myrrh and my spices" to declare the incarnation of our Lord; Philo Carpasius and Cyril of Alexandria believed the words "Eat, O friends, and drink, Yea, drink abundantly, O beloved" to refer to the Last Supper, while "I was asleep" is then held to mean on the Cross, and "but my heart is waked" to announce the Harrowing of

Hell; Philo Carpasius took "Thy navel is a circular goblet, Wherein mixed wine is not lacking" to refer to the sanctuary of the Church, and Hengstenberg to the cup from which the Church revives the thirsty with its refreshing draught; Bishop Wordsworth found "There are sixty queens and eighty concubines, And young women without number" to signify that the sectarians should outnumber the true Church, while Epiphanius found here a reference to the eighty heresies. With this last we may compare J. Durham's view that "Take us the foxes, the little foxes, That spoil the vineyards" is clear guidance to the secular authorities to co-operate with the Church in stamping out every heresy and schism, however small it might seem.

Elizabeth Cady Stanton, in her feminist commentary on the Bible, asserts a secular reading of the *Song*:

The name of God does not appear in the this Song, neither is the latter ever mentioned in the New Testament. This book has no special religious significance, being merely a love poem, an epithalamium, sung on nuptial occasions in praise of the bride and the groom. The proper place for this books is before either Proverbs or Ecclesiastes, as it was written in Solomon's youth, and is a more pardonable outburst for his early days than for his declining years. The Jewish doctors advised their young people not to read this book until they were thirty years old, when they were supposed to be more susceptible to spiritual beauties and virtues than to the mere attractions of face and form.

The Church, as an excuse for retaining this book as a part of "Holy Scriptures," interprets the Song as expressive of Christ's love for the Church; but that is rather far-fetched, and unworthy of the character of the ideal Jesus. The most rational view to take of the Song is, it was that of a luxurious king to the women of his seraglio.

Elizabeth Cady Stanton, The Woman's Bible, *European Publishing Company, 1898.*

Enough has been said to indicate what a wide field for fancy the method opened up, and how impossible it is by this means to reach any agreement as to what the *Song* really meant. The necessity to find a meaning for every detail led to this great variety of forced interpretations, which had to be brought to the *Song* rather than found in it. To free the interpretation from this necessity the view that the *Song* is a parable, rather than an allegory, has been advanced. This view has been particularly developed in a series of publications by D. Buzy, who observes that a parable requires only a general correspondence. It is not, therefore, necessary to attach any particular significance to geographical or historical allusions. What the *Song* describes, according to Buzy, is the bond between Yahweh and Israel, but with a plenary sense which extends to Christ and the Church, to Christ and the individual soul, and to the Virgin Mary. This view is declared to be an evasion by A. Robert, who prefers to describe the *Song* as an allegorical midrash.

To understand what is meant by this, we need to define the term midrash. Robert defines it as any research into the meaning of Scripture in the light of the Bible as a whole. He therefore argues that the *Song* carries its own key and that its figures can be paralleled elsewhere in relation to Yahweh and Israel, though he fails to adduce evidence of Yahweh's concubines elsewhere. He holds that the two heroes of the *Song* are Yahweh and Israel personified as husband and wife, and holds that the use of such terms as wife, king, shepherd, flock, vineyard, garden, Lebanon, springtime blossoming, night, and dream support this view. Robert is followed by A. Feuillet, who adduces such terms as marriage, shepherd, flock, lost sheep, morning, noon, night, dew, feast, the formula seek-find, the mountain (which is identified with the Temple mount), sleep, awaking, wild beasts as symbols of enemies, and argues that these evoke theological ideas. To these R. E. Murphy replies that while some of these terms have theological implications in their context elsewhere in the Bible, there is nothing in the terms themselves to require those implications a context where nothing suggests it. Moreover, we are soon carried back to the eisegesis of the older allegorists. "Rise up, my love, my fair one, and come away" is said to be a summons to captive Zion to return from the Babylonian exile; "the flowers appear on the earth" is interpreted by Hos. 14:6-8; "the time of singing is come, and the voice of the turtle is heard in our land" is held to refer to the time of glad songs so often promised in Is. 40-55; "O my dove, that art in the clefts of the rock" is explained as an allusion to the Babylonian exiles on the strength of Is. 42:7; 49:9, and Lam. 3:7; "Take us the foxes, the little foxes, that spoil the vineyards" is treated as a reference to the Samaritans, Ammonites, Arabs, and Philistines, who were installed in Judaea in place of the exiles. None of this springs naturally from the passages, and, as Murphy observes, it is incoherent. Equally fanciful is the interpretation of "I said, I will climb up into the palm tree, I will take hold of the branches thereof" as a reference to the liberties taken by the rivals of Yahweh in Ezek. 23:3-21.

It is, indeed, undeniable that the relation between God and His people is often represented in the Old Testament under the figure of marriage, especially in the prophets. Thus Jeremiah, speaking in the name of God, says "I remember your early devotion, The love of your bridal days; How through the words you followed me, Through lands unsown," and Israel's worship of other gods is constantly spoken of under the figure of adultery. Moreover, in the New Testament Christ is spoken of as the Bridegroom, and the Church as His Bride. All of this is readily conceded. But there is

nothing on all fours with the allegorical interpretation of the *Song of Songs*. For wherever the figure is used elsewhere, it is plainly symbolic, whereas here there is no hint whatever of allegory, and the whole *Song* can be read through without of itself suggesting any of the varied meanings the allegorists have read into it.

Some further varieties of allegorical interpretation should perhaps be mentioned, though they have exercised little influence on the stream of interpretation. So far as I know, the medieval Jew Abravanel was the first to advocate the view that the Bride represented Wisdom. He saw in the characters of the *Song* not God and Israel, but Solomon and Wisdom. He therefore found it necessary to regard only the Bride as an allegorical figure, and supposed that Solomon spoke in his own proper person as the Bridegroom. Abravanel was followed by his son, Leon Hebraeus, who held that Solomon likened Wisdom to a beautiful woman in the *Song of Songs*. A few others have followed this line of interpretation, including E. F. C. Rosenmüller, and the view has found a new advocate in recent years in the person of G. Kuhn, who, however, while identifying the Bride with Wisdom, finds in the Bridegroom not the Solomon of history, but a type of the seeker after wisdom. In a very different way Luther, who held that Solomon spoke in his own proper person, found the Bride to be symbolical, for in his view she symbolized Solomon's kingdom, and the *Song* is a hymn of praise for the loyalty of his subjects and the peaceful state of his realm.

Yet another type of allegorical treatment is given to the *Song* by Cocceius, who finds in it a detailed prophecy of the history of the Church, with an anti-papal turn. The divisions of the *Song* he finds to correspond with the periods of the history of the Church, and his interpretation becomes particularly full and detailed with the pre-Reformation and the Reformation period, and the coming triumph of Protestantism in which he believes the *Song* culminates. He explains "terrible as bannered hosts" of John Wiclif, and the Shulammite as that part of Bohemia which made peace with the Roman Church, while 7:5 he connects with Luther.

It is not surprising that the whole allegorical view, which is so varyingly applied at the impulse of obviously subjective factors, is generally abandoned in modern times, though not a few writers have adopted a modified form of it. They have supposed the *Song* to have a double meaning. Primarily, they suppose, it deals with human love, but a deeper, mystical meaning also penetrates it. This view must not be confused with that of the older allegorical interpreters, who sometimes treated first of the literal meaning of the text and then of its allegorical meaning. To them the literal meaning belonged merely to the form and not to the essential significance of the work, and they were far from suggesting that a double meaning attached to the text. But here a double meaning is found. Lane compared the *Song* with some Moslem songs he heard in Cairo, which were full of sensuous images, and which were understood erotically by the common people, but which were really intended to convey a spiritual meaning. Beside this we may place R. A. Nicholson's observation on the medieval poet Ibnu'l-Fárid.: "The double character of Islamic mystical poetry makes it attractive to many who are out of touch with pure mysticism. Ibnu'l-Fárid would not be so popular in the East if he were understood entirely in a spiritual sense. The fact that parts of the Díwán cannot be reasonably understood in any other sense would not, perhaps, compel us to regard the whole as spiritual, unless that view of its meaning were supported by the poet's life, the verdict of his biographers and commentators, and the agreement of Moslem critical opinion." On the view that the *Song of Songs* belongs to this type of poetry, the earthly figures which filled the superficial thought of the writer were also intended to be types of higher and holier things. Just as our Lord found a deeper meaning in the sign of Jonah, or in the Brazen Serpent, so, it is held, may the *Song of Songs* have a hidden meaning. But this idea rests on some confusion of thought. That we, for our profit, may rightly find in the images of the *Song*, as in all experience, analogies of things spiritual, does not mean that it was written for this purpose, or that the author had any such idea in mind. That Jesus found an analogy of the Cross in the Brazen Serpent can scarcely be held to prove that the purpose for which the Brazen Serpent was made was to prefigure the Cross. Nor can the fact that Eastern literatures provide other well-authenticated cases of apparently erotic poetry having an esoteric meaning prove that the *Song of Songs* is such a poem, in the absence of the slightest indication in the poem itself, and in the complete absence of agreement amongst those who find an esoteric meaning in it as to what that meaning is.

In the nineteenth century the view that the *Song* is a drama gained wide currency. The idea is older than that century, indeed, for Cornelius a Lapide had already termed it such, and Milton had called it a "divine pastoral drama," while even so anciently as in the third century A.D. Origen had applied the word "drama" to it. It was in the nineteenth century, however, that the view was particularly elaborated, and became especially popular. It still flourishes, indeed, for two of the most recent commentaries, [Pouget and Guitton, *Le Cantique des Cantiques*, 1934, and A. Hazan, *Le Cantique des Cantiques enfin expliqué*, 1936] though in wholly different ways, adhere to it.

The dramatic view has taken more than one form, however. Of the various forms it has assumed two have enjoyed especial popularity. According to one of these there are in the drama two characters, Solomon and a Shulammite shepherd girl. The king saw her and fell in love with her, and took her from her country home to make her his bride in Jerusalem, with the result that he was lifted from a merely physical attraction to a true and pure love. The most notable advocate of this view was Delitzsch [in *Biblischer Commentar über die poetischen Bücher des Alten Testaments,* iv, *Hoheslied und Koheleth,* 1875 (English translation by M.G. Easton as *Commentary on the* Song of Songs *and Ecclesiastes,* 1877)]. Its difficulties, however, were numerous, as its critics were not slow to point out. For it would be surprising to find Solomon acting as a shepherd, and still more so to find the closing scene in the girl's native village. Moreover, while in 3:6-11 Solomon is the bridegroom, in other passages he seems to be distinguished from the bridegroom. Thus, in 8:11f. the bridegroom says that Solomon is welcome to his vast estate. To get his thousand pieces of silver he has to expend two hundred, whereas the bridegroom without any such outlay has all he can desire in his bride. Similarly, in the passage "There are threescore queens, and fourscore concubines, And young women without number. But my dove, my perfect one, is alone," the lover seems to contrast his bride with the royal harem. To these considerations Harper adds the observation "We think few will find themselves able to believe that a voluptuary like Solomon could be raised to the height of pure love by the beauty of the Shulammite."

Hence another form of the dramatic view has been much more popular. This is associated especially with the name of H. Ewald, though it rests on the ideas of Jacobi and S. Löwisohn, and has been worked out by later scholars with some divergence of detail from Ewald's view. He found three principal characters— Solomon, the Shulammite maiden, and her rustic lover. On this view, the maiden resisted the king's advances, and though he carried her off to the royal palace, she was still true to her rustic swain, until the king, failing to win her affection, allowed her to return to her true love. The book is thus turned into the story of the triumph of pure love over the blandishments of a Court. Some of the advocates of this view have turned the Daughters of Jerusalem into a sort of Greek Chorus, and so have still more filled out the dramatic form of the work.

Of other varieties of dramatic view we may note that of Renan, who found a complete cast, consisting of some ten individual performers, and two choruses, one of men and one of women, and that of one of the most recent advocates of a dramatic theory, A. Hazan, who offers a complete rendering for the stage in dramatic verse, and who finds, in addition to the Fair Maid and her Shepherd lover, the King and the favourite lady of his harem, and a number of minor characters.

It must be recognized that scholars of the highest standing have accepted the dramatic view, and Ewald's theory stands in the work that has been regarded for more than a generation as the standard Introduction to the

Old Testament in English. Nevertheless, its popularity has greatly declined. So much has to be read between the lines, and such complicated stage directions have to be supplied, that its critics feel almost as much has to be brought to the book on this interpretation as on the allegorical. Despite the fact that analogies for the omission of the stage directions can be found, it is probable that the ingenuity of the dramatic interpretation belongs rather to the editors than to the author. Who, for instance, would suppose, as Pouget and Guitton do, that the dialogue in 1:15-2:3 is a dialogue at cross-purposes, the king praising the maiden, and her replies having reference, not to him, but to her absent lover:

> Solomon: How beautiful art thou, my love,
>   how beautiful!
>   Thy eyes are doves.
> The Shulammite: How beautiful art thou, my
>   Beloved, how lovely!
>   Our bed is verdant.
> Solomon: The beams of our house are cedar,
>   The rafters are cypress.
> The Shulammite: I am a narcissus of Sharon,
>   A lily of the valley.
> Solomon: Like a lily among thorns
>   Is my beloved among the youthful
> maidens.
> The Shulammite: Like an apple tree in the
> midst of the forest
>   Such is my Beloved among men.

Surely it is much more natural to see in this passage a dialogue between two lovers, who are mutually praising each other.

We have already seen that in the first century A.D. there were some who sang the *Song* as an ordinary song, giving it its plain sense as an erotic poem. At the end of the fourth century this view was taken by Theodore of Mopsuestia, who maintained that when Solomon's subjects criticized his marriage with an Egyptian he boldly sang of his love in this *Song*. More than a century after his death, he was anathematized, and his views were condemned as unfit for Christian ears. In the twelfth century an anonymous French Rabbi revived this view, and held that Solomon sang of his favourite wife. One of the early Reformers, Sebastian Castellio (Châteillon), presented a similar view, and declared that the *Song* should be excluded from the Canon since it dealt merely with earthly affections—a view which Calvin strongly reprobated, and which led to Castellio's departure from Geneva. Later Grotius adopted these views, and maintained that Solomon concealed all the intimacies of love under innocent terms. It is true that Grotius also gave the *Song* a mystical meaning, but he does not seem to have attached great weight to this, or to have devoted so much pains to the unfolding of this meaning as to the unfold-

ing of the erotic sense. In the eighteenth century Whiston declared that the *Song* was written by Solomon "when He was become Wicked and Foolish, and Lascivious, and Idolatrous," and thought so immoral a book had no rightful place in the Canon, and in the nineteenth century E. Reuss similarly regarded the work as merely profane poetry, which ought not to be included in the Canon of Scripture.

Not all who have rejected the allegorical view, and found the theme of the *Song* to be only human love, have felt it to be a thing evil and unworthy of a place in the Bible. The poet Herder found its theme to be pure love, and found beauty and worth enshrined in it. He did not regard it as a single composition, but as a collection of detached and separate poems. This view has found a number of followers, of whom we may note J. C. C. Döpke and A. Bernstein. It has also exercised a considerable influence upon many later students of the *Song*, who have, however, embodied also elements of other theories yet to be examined. To these we shall have occasion to return.

Meanwhile, scholars who themselves retained the allegorical view of the *Song* were preparing the way for a fresh line of approach. At the end of the seventeenth century Bossuet, who held, like many who had preceded him from the time of Origen, that the occasion of the *Song* was the marriage of Solomon with Pharaoh's daughter, observed that amongst the Jews the customary period for the celebration of a wedding was seven days. He then found the *Song* to fall into seven divisions, which he believed to correspond to the seven days of the feast. In this he was followed by Calmet and Lowth, both of whom held firmly that the *Song* had also an esoteric meaning. Lowth said: "May we not with some shadow of reason suspect that, under the allegory of Solomon choosing a wife from the Egyptians, might be darkly typified that other Prince of Peace, who was to espouse a Church chosen from among the Gentiles?"

In 1860 Renan noted the similarity of the *Song* to modern Syrian wedding poetry, and in 1873 Wetzstein, who was a German consul in Syria, published a study of modern marriage customs in Syria. It is customary for the celebrations to last seven days, during which the bridegroom and his bride are crowned, and treated as king and queen. Poems called *wasfs* are sung in their honour, describing their physical beauty, and also songs of war, while the bride performs a sword dance with a naked sword.

Not for twenty years did this study bear fruit, save for a brief note by B. Stade, until K. Budde presented the theory, with a force and persuasiveness that immediately secured the adhesion of C. Siegfried and dominated the discussion of the book for a quarter of a century, that we have here a collection of poems sung in connexion with the simple wedding ceremonies of the people. Customs are very tenacious, and it is said that the modern marriage customs of Syria may be not very different from those of two thousand years ago, and in any case they seem to throw much light on this book. For the descriptions of the charms of the bride and the bridegroom found in the *Song* have much of the character of the *wasfs,* while 6:10, 7:1-6 (E.V. 6:10, 13-7:5) may belong to the bride's sword dance.

It is not to be supposed, however, that this view has passed without criticism. While it has gathered to itself a long list of supporters, from the first it has had criticism, and it is now falling somewhat out of fashion. It is pointed out that there are here no war songs, and that the whole collection is insufficient to last for seven days. To this it is replied that we have only a selection of the amorous poems used on such occasions, rather than a complete cycle. O. Gebhardt, however, disputes the relevance of the assumption on which the whole view rests. He observes that the Syrian peasants of Transjordan are a mixed race, the result of frequent invasions, and their customs have no bearing on Jewish poetry. To this we may add that a recent student of marriage conditions in Palestine says that it is uncertain whether the custom described by Wetzstein exists in Palestine, and adds that most writers on wedding customs in Palestine say nothing of a "king's week," of which she herself saw no sign in the village she describes. Moreover, Rothstein has pointed out that the Shulammite is never called "queen" in the *Song*, as on Budde's view she ought to have been.

Hence a few writers, while recognizing that the marriage-cycle theory has contributed something to the understanding of the *Song*, and while finding in the poems it contains songs akin to the *wasfs* already mentioned, hesitate to accept the theory of Budde. The *wasf,* indeed was not limited to marriage celebrations, and Dalman has adduced some Arabic pre-nuptial *wasfs.* It is therefore held that we have in the *Song* a collection of love lyrics rather than merely marriage songs. This view, which runs back to the already noted view of Herder, has been adopted by E. Reuss, P. Haupt, M. Jastrow, W. Staerk, O. Eissfeldt, H. Wheeler Robinson, R. H. Pfeiffer, A. Bentzen, W. J. Lowther Clarke, R. Gordis, N. K. Gottwald, J. Winandy, A. S. Herbert, and W. Rudolph.

I am inclined to agree to some extent with this view. I am not persuaded that the marriage-week theory is soundly based, or that the songs as a whole had anything to do with a wedding occasion. They appear rather to be a series of poems in which a lover enshrined the love he gave and the love he received. But, unlike some of those who have treated the book as a collection of amorous poems, I am not able to distribute the poems amongst several authors. W. O. E. Oesterley, for instance, who finds in the book twenty-eight separate songs, some of which may be connected with the marriage week, and some of which are of liturgical origin, says that "unity of authorship is quite out of the question". Of this I am not persuaded. The repetitions that occur leave the impression of a single hand, and there is a greater unity of theme and of style than would be expected in a collection of poems from several hands, and from widely separated ages. It is probable, too, that there is artistry in the arrangement of the pieces, and it may be, as M. Thilo holds, that they trace the development of love to its consummation in marriage. I am not able, however, with Thilo, to find in the work an ethical or social tract, teaching a loftier view of woman then prevailed in contemporary society. That it presents a high conception of human love I am ready to agree. But I do not believe that it had the slightest didactic purpose. Love is ever content to express itself, and we need ask no other purpose of the *Song*. Its author was an artist, who created in these poems masterpieces of beauty. It is true that they are bolder in their images than our taste fancies, yet just because the love they sing is the true and pure love of two ardent lovers, they are infused with a spirit which perfects their artistry.

During the last generation, however, yet another view is gaining ground. This is associated with the name of Professor T. J. Meek, who in 1922 first published his theory. He believes the book was from the beginning a religious composition, but not connected with the worship of Yahweh. Instead he believes it was a liturgy of the Adonis-Tammuz cult. We have surviving texts from Babylonia, where the cult flourished, and these are held to exhibit so marked a similarity to the *Song of Songs* as to establish its character beyond dispute. The cult is also known to have been widely prevalent in Syria, and the Old Testament contains ample evidence that it existed in Israel. Thus in Ezek. 8:14 we read of women weeping for Tammuz, and Is. 27:10 f.2 gives further evidence of the cult.

It was, indeed, a very ancient cult, going back to the time before the Israelites entered Palestine, and it seems to have retained its hold on the common people throughout almost the whole period of the Old Testament. It was linked to the fertility rites which the prophets so often denounced in all their forms. In the Adonis-Tammuz cult someone represented the god and someone the goddess. The death of the god and his descent to the underworld, followed by the descent of the goddess in search of him, with the consequent languishing of Nature, and their subsequent release and return to the upper world, were all represented in a ritual drama. The rites then culminated in the marriage and union of those who represented the god and goddess, to the accompaniment of the ritual dance and much licentiousness. It was not regarded as mere licentiousness, however, but was believed to be an essential factor in the achievement of the annual miracle of reproduction in Nature. For by sympathetic magic all of this human acting was believed to effect the union of the god and goddess represented, and thus to release the powers of fertility in all Nature. The omission of these rites would therefore entail the direst consequences for the whole community.

Meek propounded the view that the *Song of Songs* is a thinly disguised survival of a liturgy of this cult. There had, indeed, been some anticipations of this view, though Meek was unaware of them when in 1920 he first presented his theory. In 1906 Erbt had given a cultic interpretation to the *Song* in terms of the astral theory of the Pan-Babylonian school. Its association with the ideas of that school was, however, sufficient to restrict the range of its influence, and little was heard of it.

The next form in which this view appeared connected it with Egypt. This was presented in 1914 by O. Neuschotz de Jassy, who developed the thesis that the *Song* is a liturgy of the Osiris cult. Again, however, the view commanded no attention. In a letter to its author Loisy expressed his doubt as to whether it would immediately command acceptance, but thought it worthy of discussion. Little discussion was given to it, however, and it left no ripple on the waters of scholarship. In 1919 Ebeling published an Accadian text, or series of fragments of texts, belonging to a liturgy of the Babylonian Tammuz cult, and this was not long in reopening the issue in the new form which Meek gave to it. Many Babylonian liturgies of the Tammuz cult had already been published prior to the appearance of this text, but Meek was at once struck with the similarities between the *Song of Songs* and passages here. The view of Meek does not depend on this particular text, however, for our knowledge of the Tammuz cult of Babylonia, and of the kindred rites of the Osiris cult of Egypt and the Adonis cult of Syria, is considerable, and it is upon that knowledge, rather than upon the text which directed Meek to it, that the theory rests. It should be added that since Meek's theory was formulated the Ras Shamra texts have been published, and our knowledge of the North Syrian forms of the cult and the mythology on which it rests has been greatly enriched.

Not a few scholars have announced their adhesion to this view. They include M. L. Margolis, W. H. Schoff, E. Ebeling, S. Minocchi, L. Waterman, W. Wittekindt, D. S. Margoliouth, N. H. Snaith, Graham and May, W. O. E. Oesterley, F. Dornseiff, M. Haller, I. Engnell, G. Widengren, H. Schmökel, H. Ringgren, and J. W. Wevers. Not all of these scholars content themselves with merely accepting the views of Meek, indeed. Several of them give some distinct originality of form to their presentation of it. Thus Waterman, instead of holding with Meek that the old Tammuz liturgy has been revised to bring it into accord with Yahwism, believed that it was reduced to the level of folk poetry,

and then made into an allegory of the political relations between the two Israelite kingdoms in the period following the Disruption. Again Snaith analysed the *Song* into alternating passages from two cycles, the one having associations with the spring and the other with the autumn, and brought it into connexion with the stories of the rape of the maidens of Shiloh and the sacrifice of Jephthah's daughter, while Oesterley found in the *Song* diverse elements, some of which are fragments of the old Tammuz liturgies, and others of which belong to the wedding celebrations of simple peasants. The most detailed working out of the theory in a complete commentary on the *Song* has been provided by Wittekindt, who believes it is a Jerusalem liturgy prepared for the celebration of the wedding of Ishtar and Tammuz at the spring new moon.

On the other hand, the critics of this view have been slow to expose its weaknesses. Two, indeed, in the persons of Umberto Cassuto and Nathaniel Schmidt, appeared promptly to enter a caveat, and to expose some of the difficulties of the theory, and later Ricciotti briefly criticized it, while Dürr subjected Wittekindt's work to a very brief critical review. Most of those who have remained unconvinced have been content with rejection rather than reply.

There is, indeed, to-day a growing tendency to find in various parts of the Old Testament ritual survivals, and it is in full harmony with this tendency that the *Song of Songs* should be ritually interpreted. Moreover, there is a growing recognition of references to the Adonis-Tammuz cult in the Old Testament. But this does not establish the thesis that a Tammuz liturgy is preserved in the Bible. For none of these references recognized the cult as a legitimate one. They are merely the evidence that it was popularly practised, and are on the same footing as the innumerable references to Baal worship in the Old Testament. These amply prove that that worship had a strong hold on the people, without leading us to expect to find a ritual of its practice in the Canon.

Here, indeed, we find the first serious difficulty Meek's theory has to face. The Adonis-Tammuz cult was inextricably connected with the immoral fertility rites, which the prophets so frequently denounced. When, then, can this liturgy be supposed to have been brought into the Canon? It cannot have been brought in in pre-exilic days, for there is no evidence for the existence of a Canon at that time. Nor is it likely to have been received into the sacred corpus until late post-exilic days, for in the first century A.D. there was still some dispute amongst the Rabbis as to whether it was properly to be regarded as canonical, and the seriousness of the doubt may be reflected in Rabbi Akiba's extravagant opinion. It may well be, as Meek points out, that the reference to the Tammuz cult in Deutero-Zechariah shows that the cult retained its hold over the people until a late post-exilic period, but it is highly unlikely that in the age when Judaism was developing its exclusiveness its leaders would recognize as canonical a work associated with the fertility cult.

This difficulty Meek resolves in a diametrically opposite way to that of Neuschotz. The latter boldly maintained that the Rabbis knew full well the character of the *Song*, and that this explains why they declared its sacredness. This is to meet the difficulty by evading it. That it was sacred to one cult could provide no reason why it should be incorporated in the Canon of another, and vigorously hostile, cult.

Meek, however, supposes that in the *Song* we have not the Tammuz liturgy in its original and offensive form, but that it has been revised to harmonize it with the Yahweh cultus. Neuschotz had expressly denied any such revision, and had declared that the *Song* has remained what it was from the beginning. Moreover, Waterman, while holding that we have not the liturgy in its original form, supposed it to have undergone a totally different revision from that assumed by Meek. So far from the revision having been undertaken in the interests of the Yahweh cult, he believed that it secularized all the older religious elements. The Solomon of the *Song* he held to be not Tammuz, the hero of the liturgy, but the villain of the piece, and would-be destroyer of love, striving to get the maiden into his power and make her forget her lover. But in the secularization of the poem its religious significance was changed for a political meaning, and the struggle between Israel and Judah depicted.

It is clear, therefore, that Meek had failed to convince even one who was largely impressed by his theory of this alleged revision. And in truth we look in vain in the *Song* for any real indication of the Yahweh cult. Indeed, Meek himself observes: "Rather strikingly Yahweh never once appears in the book. When the liturgy was incorporated into the Yahweh cult, it was deemed sufficient to transfer the titles to him without adding his name." Surely this was a strange procedure, which left traces of the rejected cult everywhere in the book, but which left the new cult into which it was absorbed unmentioned. An intelligent reviser would have taken care that the Yahwism whose interests the book was now to serve would be unequivocally displayed in it, and not left to the reader to supply.

It is true that Schoff attempts to supply Meek's deficiency, and to explain the nature of the alleged revision. The name of David has long been connected with the divine name Dod, and both Meek and Schoff adopt this view, and identify Dod with Tammuz. They also identify Shelem, from whom they hold Solomon to have been named, with the same god. From this Schoff concludes that both David and Solomon recognized the Tammuz cult, and he suggests that the abortive

effort of Adonijah to secure the throne was part of a puritan move to abolish this worship. Naturally, therefore, he holds that when the Temple was built the Tammuz cult found a place in it. He says: "There is nothing intrinsically impossible, therefore, in the presence of the Tammuz cult in the temple or in the survival in some form of its ceremonial."

With all this no fault can be found. For there can be no doubt that many practices found a home in the Temple, though later conscience condemned them, and it is highly probable that the popular Tammuz rites were observed through long periods even in the Jerusalem sanctuary. Nor would the mere survival of a Tammuz liturgy from Jerusalem appear at all incredible. It is its survival in the Canon of the Old Testament which needs to be shown to be probable.

Nor does Schoff's alleged double revision succeed in this task. For the first revision he supposes the *Song* to have undergone was merely an adaptation to the conditions of the Temple. He has made an elaborate study of the Offering-lists in the *Song*, and claims that one hundred and thirty-four of the terms have reference to the Tammuz cult, and one hundred and twenty-six to the early sanctuaries. The impressiveness of this conclusion vanishes on examination, however.

We may take as an example his lists for chap. I, where he finds the Tammuz cult in *wine, vineyards, flock, kids, king, vineyard, doves,* and *couch,* and the early sanctuaries in *ointments, chambers, tents, curtains, veil, steed, chariot, circlets, pearls, beads, studs, gold, silver, table, myrrh, beams, cedar, panels, cypress.* It is at once clear that, if this analysis of the reference of the terms is justified, the revision was not to bring the work into accord with the fundamental religious ideas of Yahwism, but merely to adapt the still unchanged fertility rite to the Temple *venue.* It was in no sense a revision that accommodated the Tammuz ritual to Yahwism, or that could for a moment satisfy the objections of the prophets to the fertility cult, and it can hardly be supposed that such a revision would have sufficed to win for the ritual recognition from the later leaders of Judaism.

Nor is the case improved by the second revision which Schoff supposes the work to have undergone, to adapt it to the Second Temple. For here he finds seven terms to indicate the extent of the revision, but as two of them are duplicates, they are reduced to five. These are *spikenard, henna, palanquin, saffron,* and *aloes.* It is hardly fair to ascribe to the supposed reviser such complete incompetence for his task. For not one of the five terms even points to the Second Temple at all. Moreover, four of the five terms of this alleged revision are found only in the *Song of Songs,* and while the fifth *(aloes)* is found in the Pentateuch, it is in the Balaam oracles. But even if all five terms pointed unequivocally to the Temple, they would still be quite unrelated to the essential ideas of Yahwism. The fundamental *differentiae* between the fertility cult and Yahwism were not to be found in these things, and a revision which consisted merely in rubbing a little ointment on the older ritual, and which failed to bring out the real qualities of the faith in whose interest it was carried through, would to exist in the mind of the interpreter rather than in the achievement of the reviser.

Nor can we be satisfied that Schoff's analysis rests on any substantial ground. For Meek finds two of the five terms which Schoff regards as marks of the second revision to belong to the old fertility cult—viz., *henna* and *palanquin*—and Wittekindt agrees, so far as *henna* is concerned. And since Schoff is himself doubtful of *aloes,* the marks of this revision become woefully slight to account for the strange acceptance of a Tammuz ritual into the Canon of Judaism.

Furthermore, in Schoff's first list are some terms which Meek regards as marks of the Tammuz cult, viz., *myrrh, cedar, cypress,* and several which Wittekindt holds to belong to that cult, e.g., *myrrh, table, steed, pearls, wall, windows, lattice.* The alleged revision is therefore both doubtful in itself, and altogether inadequate to give to the **Song** a definitely Yahwistic character.

The triviality of this alleged revision is the more surprising, since when Hebrew writers elsewhere used material which they had taken over from non-Yahwistic sources, they displayed an altogether greater skill in assimilating it to their own religious ideas. Thus, while there may be some connexion between the Creation story in Gen. I and the Babylonian Creation Epic, all the cruder elements have gone, and to the whole there is given a nobility which belongs to the Hebrew writer and not to his source. If Tiamat survives, it is as the innocuous *tᵉhôm,* and the majestic God is not left to the reader's imagination to supply, but is dominant in the story.

Again, the ingenuity with which Tammuz is imported at every point by the advocates of this theory can only cause grave doubts as to the soundness of the theory. If a writer cannot mention such common things of experience as *shepherd, vine, vineyard, dove, gazelle, apple, cedar, palmtree, garden,* or *hyacinth,* to name some things from Meek's list of alleged allusions to the Tammuz cult, without being held to be writing of that cult, the way of letters for all but devotees of Tammuz is made very hard; and when to these we add some further terms from Schoff's list, *flock, kids, king, couch, fruit, flowers, blossoms, bed, lions, leopard, sister, bride, honey, milk, spring, fountain, waters, dew, maidens, moon, sun, nuts,* and *dance,* the poet's case becomes desperate indeed. For how could one write a love lyric in any language if

such terms must be excluded from his vocabulary? The fact that these terms occur in relation to the Tammuz cult is no proof that they could only have relation to that cult. If the method of this theory should be applied to the whole of the Old Testament with something of the energy with which Cheyne applied his Jerachmeel theory, or the astral theorists their ideas, there would soon be little of it left without connexion with the Tammuz cult.

Two further points made by Meek in support of his theory have to be examined. The first is his claim that the word *zāmîr* in 2:12 is an indication that we have here a liturgy, since this is a technical term for such a liturgy, and the second is the allegedly significant fact that the **Song** belongs to the Passover liturgy of the Jews. So far as the first is concerned, Schmidt has replied that the word had certainly a wider use, while it is not certain that it means any kind of a song in **Cant.** 2:12. Meek dismisses the suggestion of Ehrlich and others that it here means *the pruning of vines,* on the ground that pruning is not done so late in the spring, and Snaith asks: "Who ever pruned when the flowers were in blossom?" But Snaith finds in the **Song** two alternating groups of passages, the one having associations with the spring and the other with the autumn. He believes the **Song** is intimately connected with the two ritual dances of maidens and youths celebrated outside Jerusalem in Mishnaic times, the one on the fifteenth of Ab, and the other on the Day of Atonement. The former group, he says, has associations with the spring, but its setting is in the time of the fruits of the gardens in the height of summer. It may then be relevantly recalled that in the Gezer Calendar *yrhw zmr* follows the mouth of general harvest, and precedes the harvest of summer fruits. Since all the other items of this calendar are connected with agricultural operations, it is probable that this is also, and that it is to be rendered the two months of vine-pruning, the reference being to the second pruning.

The other point, which is made by both Meek and Schoff, is the claim that it is significant that the **Song** belongs to the Passover liturgy of the Jews, since the Passover is a spring festival, while the Adonis festival was also observed in the spring. Schoff observes that its incorporation in the Passover liturgy clearly indicates that it has been brought down from the primitive spring festival. Meek, however, admits that this practice was officially adopted only in the Middle Ages, and this admission robs the practice of any evidential value for the original use and purpose of the **Song**. Against it may be set the statement of Theodore of Mopsuestia that neither Jews nor Christians had ever read the book in public. As Schmidt observes, we can hardly suppose that Ecclesiastes was written as a vintage hymn, or Ruth as a Pentecostal story, and we are therefore scarcely bound to suppose that the **Song** was written for a spring festival.

It should however, be added that Wittekindt repeats the argument of Meek, but disputes his admission that our evidence for the reading of the book at Passover is only late. He discounts the statement of Theodore of Mopsuestia, and finds significance in the fact that Hippolytus expounded **Cant**. 3:1-4 at Easter, and that the Targum expounds part of the *Song* in relation to the first Passover and the Exodus from Egypt. That this interpretation cannot naturally be got out of the *Song* itself is held to point to the fact that behind the Targum lies the already existing custom of reading the book at Passover, and Wittekindt therefore concludes that this practice may go back to the beginning of the Christian era. A very slight study of the history of the interpretation of the *Song* should suffice to show that innumerable meanings which cannot naturally be got out of the *Song* have been read into it, and that they are evidence for nothing whatever but the fancy of the interpreters, while for Hippolytus' choice of Easter for the exposition of **Cant**. 3:1-4 we need look no farther than the nature of the interpretation given to the *Song* in the Early Church. Moreover, even if it were proved conclusively that the *Song* was read at Passover as early as the beginning of the Christian era, this would not establish any community of origin between Passover and the *Song*. For, as Dürr points out, Passover was kept at the full moon, whereas Wittekindt finds the origin of the *Song* in the wedding of the Sun god and the Moon goddess that was celebrated at the spring new moon. Whenever the reading of the *Song of Songs* at Passover began, its choice for reading at that festival was natural, since the *Song* is full of the springtime, and since the spring is not merely the season of Adonis, but the time of love all the world over.

The case for the Adonis-Tammuz liturgy theory, therefore, does not seem to be adequately supported, and we cannot regard the *Song of Songs* as the liturgy of a pagan cult that was abhorred of the prophets. At the same time, it may be freely allowed that many of the allusions in the *Song* may genuinely refer to elements of the Adonis-Tammuz cult, whether found in the practice of the poet's contemporaries, or inherited in speech from an earlier age, and we owe a real debt to Meek and his associates for the light they have shed on some things in the *Song*, even though they have failed to carry conviction in their main thesis. For we must distinguish between the finding of allusions to the Tammuz cult and the acceptance of the *Song* as a cult liturgy. On Budde's view it is a cycle of popular marriage songs, and on the view above adopted it is a series of love lyrics. Now, since it is agreed that Adonis-Tammuz rites were deeply imbedded in the popular superstition, popular songs or lyrical poems, themselves essentially sensuous, would readily contain allusions to those rites. Our own poetry abounds in allusions to a mythology the poets did not seriously accept. An instance taken at random is from Milton's *L'Allegro:*

But come, thou Goddess fair and free
In heaven yclept Euphrosyne,
And by men, heart-easing Mirth,
Whom lovely Venus at a birth
With two sister Graces more
To ivy-crowned Bacchus bore.

If our own poets can thus deck their poems with allusions to an ancient and outgrown mythology, it can occasion no surprise that Hebrew poets should adorn the songs in which they expressed their love with allusions to the mythology that had long flourished in the land, and that doubtless still flourished all around them. For these poems were not composed for the Canon, but to express the warm affection of lovers' hearts.

From this brief résumé of the history of the exegesis of the *Song* it will be clearly observed that there is as yet no generally accepted view of the interpretation it should be given. In the present century there have been serious advocates of the old Jewish allegorical view, of the Christian allegorical view, of the dramatic theory, of the wedding-cycle theory, of the Adonis-Tammuz liturgy theory, and of the view that we have a collection of amorous poems, whether from a single author or from several. All interpreters agree in recognizing the high poetic quality of the *Song*, and in recognizing, too, that its metaphors show a freedom and boldness we should not allow ourselves to-day. The view I adopt finds in it nothing but what it appears to be, lovers' songs, expressing their delight in one another and the warm emotions of their hearts. All of the other views find in the *Song* what they bring to it.

One question still arises. In adopting a view which has so much in common with the anathematized view of Theodore of Mopsuestia, are we not proposing that which is "unfit for Christian ears," and does not this view mean that the *Song*, as Castellio and Whiston said, in quite unworthy of a place in the Canon? I do not think so. The view that it was written for use in connexion with the fertility rites, and that it has been very thinly disguised, would seem to make it very unworthy of a place there. But if we have songs that express pure human love, and the mutual loyalty of lovers to one another, even though the physical side of their love is expressed with a frankness we should not emulate, I do not think the *Song* is undeserving of inclusion in the Canon. For there is no incongruity in such a recognition of the essential sacredness of pure human love. The Church has always consecrated the union of man and woman in matrimony, and taught that marriage is a divine ordinance, and it is not unfitting that a book which expresses the spiritual and physical emotions on which matrimony rests should be given a place in the Canon of Scripture.

Lines from the third verse of the *Song*

on my bed through the nights
I sought him whom my soul loves
   I sought him and I did not find
I will arise and go around the city
   through the streets and the courtyards
I will seek him whom my soul loves
   I sought him and I did not find
the watchmen found me who guard the city
   have you seen him whom my soul has
   loved?
when I had hardly passed by them
   I found him whom my soul loves
I held him nor will I let him go
   until I lead him into the house of my
   mother
and into the chamber of her who bore me

From the translation by E. Ann Matter in The
Voice of My Beloved, *University of
Pennsylvania Press, 1990.*

Richard N. Soulen (essay date 1967)

SOURCE: "The *Wasfs* of the *Song of Songs* and Hermeneutic," in *Journal of Biblical Literature,* Vol. LXXXVI, No. II, June, 1967, pp. 183-90.

[*In the following essay, Soulen focuses on the function and effect of imagistic, descriptive passages, or* wasfs, *in chapters 4 and 7 of the* Song of Songs.]

In order to justify another look at the *Song of Songs* one need not resort to the kind of hyperbole recently employed by the Catholic scholar A. Feuillet [in "Einige scheinbare Widersprüche des Hohenliedes," *Biblische Zeitschrift,* 1964]: "Es gibt kein erregenderes Problem als das des Hohenliedes." An earlier remark of his [from "La formule d'appartenance mutuelle (II, 16) et les interprétations divergentes du Cantique des Cantiques," *Revue Biblique,* 1961] would suffice: "L'exégèse du **Cantique des Cantiques** ne cesse de faire l'objet des plus vives controverses." One of these controversies centers around the proper interpretation of its imagery, particularly the images of certain curiously interesting songs found in chs. 4-7. These poems are recognized as examples of a particular genre of erotic love poetry differing from other poems in the *Song of Songs* anthology in that they describe in detailed and fanciful fashion the features of the female and male physique, the latter being less frequent. Since the similarity between these poems in the *Song of Songs* and modern Arabic poetry was first discovered in the last century, they have been commonly referred to by the technical Arabic term, *wasf,* signifying "description." The imagery of the biblical *wasf* (occurring only in the *Song of Songs*) is of hermeneutic interest to us because (1) their interpretation demands and hence clearly illustrates hermeneutic principles active in the process of interpretation, and (2) new hermeneutic principles for interpreting this imagery suggest themselves from current discussions concerning the nature of language and poetic imagination.

Our discussion will deal primarily with the imagery of the descriptive poems in chs. 4 and 7 with the hope of discovering the function and purpose of the images they contain. Certain tangential and often belabored questions will not be considered. We are siding with those who find in the *Song of Songs* a collection of loosely connected love poems revealing no architectonic design whether to serve the purposes of allegory, pure drama, or cultic myth and ritual. Whether the *Song* as a whole or the *wasfs* individually are the product of folk poetry or the technical genius of a stylist is for the most part immaterial.

The question at hand simply put is: What do the images of these *wasfs* seek to accomplish, singly or collectively? To what end is this type of poetic imagination? Is it to aid perception, that is, to give the auditor a visual representation of his beloved's attributes by drawing forth visual parallels to the contour or color of her physical characteristics (hair, nose, neck, etc.)? If this be the case, one must be careful to note that the subject matter conveyed is the physical appearance of the maiden herself. Further, if this is the intent, then the weight of the metaphor lies on the cognitive process of perception and thereby tests the hearer's skill of abstraction and comparison. The hermeneutic principle involved in this method of interpretation is that of the biblical literalist or realist, as it comes to life, for example, in the work of Lercy Waterman [*The Song of Songs*].

Waterman's thoroughgoing rejection of interpretations which spiritualized or allegorized the *Song* left him with a hermeneutic of realism that contorted the object of comparison (the maiden) into grotesque and comic proportions: a girl with a neck like a tower is a Brobdingnagian; her teeth, like sheep herded together, are jumbled; and, her hair, like a small flock of goats on a sprawling mountain side, is patchy and bizzare. From the perspective of realism Waterman was forced by his own logic to conclude that the purpose of the *Song* was to humiliate Solomon by depicting him as one rebuffed by a humble if not downright ugly girl from the north. The aim of the images then was to create in the imagination real but in this case ridiculous parallels to a ridiculous physical appearance.

M. H. Segal applies the same principle [in "Song of Songs," *Vetus Testamentum,* 1962] but omits any seriousness of intention. He sees the songs as abounding in playfulness and gentle raillery:

> Only as playful banter can be rationally explained the grotesque description by the lover to the damsel of her neck as 'like the tower of David built for an armoury', of her nose 'as the tower of Lebanon which looketh toward Damascus', and of her head like Mount Carmel and similar comical comparisons of her other limbs.

Realism as an interpretive principle also underlies the approach of B. S. J. Isserlin. Building on an earlier suggestion by A. M. Honeyman that [the] word חלפּׂות in 4⁴ should be translated "coursed masonry," Isserlin interprets the passage (that the damsel's neck is like the tower of David) to refer to the real appearance of the young girl's *necklace.* A parallel is said to exist between the strings of beads and the strata or courses of masonry which, when topped with warriors' shields, reminds the onlooker of a multi-stringed necklace topped with a string of round beads. Isserlin calls attention to a necklace of this type on a famous sculpture from Arsos in Cyprus which is dated around the 6th century B.C. He then argues that this is the period in which this poem was written. That the verse says nothing of a necklace or that the image of the tower is also applied to the nose and breast are facts overlooked by his interpretive principle at work, viz., the perspective of realism.

The recent commentary by Gillis Gerleman [in *Das Hohelied*] seeks to transcend the realist's limitations. He notes that the poems are the products of emotion, a joyous capitulation to the senses. They do not examine the beloved critically; they simply feast on what is seen. Objects are viewed fancifully, not concretely. The striking figures, he suggests, are not used to make more tangible a mental impression, but are designed to increase the song's effect upon the hearer's mind and emotions. He adds further, "Here there is very little to do with outline and contour. Everything pertains to movements and dynamic events."

Unfortunately, Gerleman does not make use of his own insights as consistently as is here suggested he should. Enamoured with what he believes are parallels from ancient Egyptian art, Gerleman resorts to the perspective of realism when interpreting the imagery of the *wasfs* in question. The figures of Egyptian sculpture and bas relief, he suggests, are really the objects in the poet's mind and therefore can be used to explain the imagery of the descriptive songs. The maiden's eyes are as doves because the contour of sculpted eyes is like that of a dove; the navel is like a "round vessel" which, though unlike real life, is an accurate (realistic) description of the navel as seen in Egyptian statuary;

so also the hair of certain sculpted figures, with their geometric design of vertical and diagonal lines, etched deeply in stone to represent long strands and curls, is like wandering (?) goats on a mountain slope. In 4¹ and 6⁵ where the same comparison to goats is used, Gerleman finds the *tertium comparationis* to be in their color (black) rather than in the pattern of the flock. But when the figure changes to a king caught in a maiden's hair Egyptian art is again in mind, viz., the ornamental figures which were occasionally used to bedeck a woman's coiffure. "This much seems certain to me in any case," writes Gerleman, "metaphorical or not—the image owes its existence to art."

Approached in this way, however, the very purpose of the *wasf* is altered. The poems no longer have as their subject matter the writer's beloved or even how he feels about her; instead it has in mind certain stylized art forms of Egypt! The hearer or reader of the poem is confronted with imagery which must call to mind characteristics not intrinsic to the objects themselves but to other and less well-known quantities neither mentioned nor obvious, viz., Egyptian ornamental art and sculpture. Yet, still more is expected of the hearer, for he is invited to draw parallels between the pictorial image and Egyptian art (not first of all the maiden or the suitor), not for the beauty of the art itself, but (presumably) because the subjects of the art were divine or imperial personages and who for that reason enhanced the particular artistic forms involved. This oblique and metaphorical reference to Egyptian art is then intended to glamorize the beloved, not the art itself—a semantic trick effective only with the cultured few. In spite of his own insights into the function of the imagery of the songs, Gerleman's interpretation in these instances is driven by a hermeneutic of realism, perhaps due to his interest in Egyptian culture and motivated by a desire to correlate that knowledge with his studies in the **Song of Songs**, even though it contradicts his stated understanding of the nature and purpose of the imagery employed. Since knowledge of Egyptian art would be prerequisite to understanding the poems as he conceives them, his hermeneutic also forces him to the conclusion that the poems were aristocratic in origin and not popular poetry (*Volksdichtung*)—a conclusion necessary from his assumptions, but one which, less widely accepted, further weakens his case.

Gerleman's method again raises the question of the appropriate hermeneutic principle for understanding the poetic imagery of the *wasf.* It is suggested here that Gerleman is hermeneutically correct in so far as he sees the purpose of the *wasf* as presentational rather than representational. Its purpose is not to provide a parallel to visual appearance or, as we shall see, primarily to describe feminine or masculine qualities metaphorically. The *tertium comparationis* must be seen instead in the feelings and sense experiences of the poet himself who then uses a vivid and familiar imagery to present to his hearers knowledge of those feelings in the form of art.

An interpretation of the wasf which starts with this perspective but ends up with a hermeneutic reminiscent of rationalistic idealism is that of Thorleif Boman (*Hebrew Thought compared with Greek*). The ancient Hebrew poet, Boman begins, was characteristically disinterested in the appearances of persons and things; his concern was with his impression of their qualities. Thus, the connection between a tower and a woman's neck (as elsewhere her nose and breast) lies within their dynamic quality. A tower rising above its surroundings and a woman holding high (haughty) her neck are alike in that both strike the onlooker with awe and meekness by giving the impression of unapproachableness and inaccessibility. This initial phenomenological interest in the images, however, gives way to a total concern for the qualities themselves. To Boman the *wasf* is a "simple riddle, easy to solve," since it simply seeks to describe the dominant qualities of the object in mind. Boman divides the images of the ***Song of Songs*** into the three principal groupings of the bride's qualities: her inaccessibility, pride, purity, and virginity (represented by images such as the tower and fortress); her power of attraction and charm (images of flowers, palm trees, colors, and jewels); and her feminine voluptuousness and bodily vigor (images of edible animals and grains).

Boman's analysis, suggestive and convincing though it is in general, is weakened, not by an inconsistent principle of interpretation as with Gerleman, but by the overapplication of a given principle, viz., that images refer metaphorically to qualities and not to appearances. Thus, to maintain his principle of interpretation he alters those extended images which convey contradictory qualities by identifying the contradicting image as an insertion. For example, according to Boman the quality of impregnability conveyed by the word "battlement" in 8^9 is contradicted by the modifying phrase "of silver." This latter phrase is then omitted by Boman for material (and metric) reasons as an insertion. But, contrariwise, in his consideration of $5^{10\text{-}16}$ precious substances (including gold which like silver is soft) are now interpreted as images indicative of "superior physical endowment." Thus, Boman's practice of attributing qualities to images is purely arbitrary and reverses the usual role of metaphor. In 8^9 the object of comparison (the maiden) defines the metaphor rather than the metaphor illuminating the qualities of the maiden, and this is even more the case of $5^{10\text{-}16}$ where the presumption of youthful vigor and strength in the lad is used to determine what the metaphor means.

The danger to which Boman all but permits himself to succumb is to make the "simple riddle, easy to solve" into an analytic poem which needs a cognitive key of equivalents. Thus the discussion shifts from the impressions given by the qualities to the qualities themselves. Of course these aspects are but two parts of a whole: something (a quality) must be present to give an impression, and both are of concern in the *wasf.* But on which rests the *tertium comparationis?* What is being conveyed? The quality possessed or the impression given? One is abstract, the other existential. Boman's analysis encourages the reduction of images and metaphors to mere statements: "My beloved is pure, innocent, healthy, etc." But poetic imagination intends more than that! Poetry is not just a declaratory statement the long way around. The image in its poetic mode is, as Ezra Pound has said, "an emotional and intellectual complex in an instant of time."

What is suggested here then is that that interpretation is most correct which sees the imagery of the *wasf* as a means of arousing emotions consonant with those experienced by the suitor as he beholds the fullness of his beloved's attributes (or so the maiden as she speaks of her beloved in $5^{10\text{-}16}$). Just as the sensual experiences of love, beauty, and joy are vivid but ineffable, so the description which centers in and seeks to convey these very subjective feelings must for that reason be unanalytical and imprecise. The writer is not concerned that his hearers be able to retell in descriptive language the particular qualities or appearance of the woman described; he is much more interested that they share his joy, awe, and delight. The poet is aware of an emotional congruity between his experience of his beloved's manifold beauty and his experience of the common wonders of life. With this in mind he sets out to convey his discovery in lyrical imagery by creating in his hearers an emotion congruent with his own in the presence of his beloved. It should be obvious that comparisons of the female body to jewels, bowls of wine, heaps of wheat, and so on, are not intended to aid a mental image of the maiden's appearance or merely to draw parallels to her qualities; they, and others like them, seek to overwhelm and delight the hearer, just as the suitor is overwhelmed and delighted in her presence. Likewise, the point of comparison between the maiden's hair and a flock of goats on the slopes of Gilead has nothing to do with Egyptian sculpture, color, motion, or with the quality of either the hair or the flock; it lies simply in the emotional congruity existing between two beautiful yet otherwise disparate sights. "Bowls of wine," "hills of myrrh," "mountains of frankincense," "heaps of wheat"—just as milk, honey, oil, and fruit elsewhere in the poems—titillate the senses, not the capacity to reason. Each in its own way triggers the imagination, each is a Pavlovian bell. Metaphorical hyperbole (heap, mountain, hill, all-bearing twins, etc.) is the language of joy—the impression the author receives at the sight of his beloved. This is not to suggest that all of the metaphors and similes "mean" precisely the same thing. "Meaning" here can refer only to what the images "effect" or "set in motion." Most images appeal to sight, but some to taste, some to fragrance, and, as poetry, all to hearing. But because each, true to metaphor, reaches out beyond itself and invites participation, it is an event of language. In other words, it is something which "happens" to the hearer. From his own prior understanding of the bounty and goodness of creation—of sight, of fragrance, and of savor—the hearer participates in the varied and erotic experiences of the suitor, though at second hand: through art.

In short, a *wasf* is not a thought problem "easily solved"; it is a celebration of the joys of life and love and at the same time an invitation to share that joy. Only from this perspective is the intent of the poet preserved and the object of love not made grotesque and ludicrous.

Chaim Rabin (essay date 1973-74)

SOURCE: "The *Song of Songs* and Tamil Poetry," in *Studies in Religion,* Vol. 3, No. 3, 1973/74, pp. 205-19.

[*In the following essay, Rabin explores the connections between the* Songs of Songs *and Indian—specifically Tamil—poetry.*]

1. MONKEYS AND PEACOCKS

Letters written by Mesopotamian merchants between 2200 and 1900 B.C. often mention the country of *Melukkha* with which they traded. The late Benno Landsberger conclusively proved that this was Northwest India, where at that time the Indus civilization was flourishing.

In various places in Mesopotamia a few dozen of the typical Indus culture seals have been found, with pictures representing, as usual, religious motifs. Some appear to be local imitations. Motifs common to the Indus civilization and to Sumero-Akkadian culture have been pointed out, including some occurring on the seals found in Mesopotamia. It is therefore probable that such objects were brought in not as knicknacks, but because of their religious symbolism by people who had been impressed by Indus religion.

In the scenes depicted on Indus seals animals play an important role. Many of these still have a part in Indian religious symbolism. One of these is the Hanuman monkey, now associated with Rāma. Objects representing this monkey have been found in Mesopotamia, some dating from the period mentioned. We have also two literary references to the importation of monkeys. One is a 'letter,' of which four copies exist:

To Lusalusa, my mother, from Mr. Monkey. Ur is the delightful city of the god Nanna, Eridu the prosperous city of the god Enki. Here I am sitting outside the doors of the Great Music-Hall. I am obliged to feed on garbage—may I not die from it! I don't get any bread or beer. Send me a special courier—urgently!

The other is a Sumerian proverb: 'All Eridu prospers, but the monkey of the Great Music-Hall sits in the garbage-heap.' Thus the poor young monkey had been exhibited in public, but when the populace tired of the novelty, it was thrown out and had to fend for itself, no doubt to be replaced by some other sensation.

A similar story is told in the Buddhist Jātakas. These are collections of stories, mostly of evident folkloristic origin, purporting to describe former rebirths of the Buddha and his friends or opponents. The *Bāveru-Jātaka,* with omission of most of the dialogue byplay, runs:

Once upon a time, when Brahmadatta was reigning in Benares, the Bodhisatta came to life as a young peacock. When he was fully grown, he was exceedingly beautiful and lived in a forest. At that time some merchants came to the kingdom of Bāveru, bringing on board ship with them a foreign crow. At this time, it is said, there were no birds in Bāveru. [The natives admire the crow and buy it for a hundred pieces of money.] The natives took it and put it in a golden cage and fed it with kinds of fish and meat and wild fruits. In a place where no other birds existed, a crow endowed with ten evil qualities attained the highest gain and glory.

The next time these merchants came to the kingdom of Bāveru, they brought a royal peacock which they had trained to scream at the snapping of the fingers and to dance at the clapping of the hands. [The natives buy the peacock for one thousand pieces.] Then they put it into a cage ornamented with the seven jewels [there follow details of feeding]. Thus did the royal peacock receive the highest gain and glory. From the day of its coming, the gain and honour paid to the crow fell off, and no one wanted even to look at it. The crow, no longer getting food either hard or soft, went off crying softly 'caw caw' and settled on a garbage-heap.

Before the crested peacock had appeared,
Crows were with gifts of fruit and meat
        revered.
The sweet-voiced peacock to Bāveru came,
The crow at once was stripped of gifts and
        fame.

There is no need to spell out the parallels in these two tales, the second of which was 'published' some two thousand years after the first. Indeed they complement each other: the Eridu story supplies the fact that the animal was publicly exhibited, which is merely hinted at in the Jātaka, while the latter may provide some indication why the monkey of Eridu was cast out. The subject is typically Indian, exemplifying the doctrine of illusion (*māyā*). In fact one wonders whether the co-existence of the proverb and the letter in Sumerian does not point to an original form in which the prose story was summed up, Indian fashion, by some lines of poetry.

On the factual side, we know that maritime connection between Mesopotamia and India lapsed after the destruction of the Indus civilization, and the name of Babylon (Bāveru) would hardly have been known, since trade, when at last it was resumed, went via South Arabia. The Jātaka story must, therefore, ultimately date from before 2000, an example of the extraordinary retentiveness of Indian tradition.

Signs have been detected also of the importation of peacocks, or at least of ivory statuettes of peacocks, in the pre-2000 trade. The selection of monkeys and peacocks for export may of course have been the result of commercial flair; but one wonders whether it did not also derive from the Indian tendency, still in existence, to honour foreign visitors by presenting them with objects of religious significance. The story of the monkey may show further the acquaintance of the Babylonians of the time with the religious meaning of the animal, assuming that the story is in fact Indian.

Monkeys and peacocks are mentioned as imports to the Middle East in 1 Kings 10:22: 'because the king had Tarshish ships in the sea with the ships of Hiram. Once every three years the Tarshish ships would arrive, carrying gold and silver, ivory, and monkeys and peacocks.' This passage has caused modern commentators much difficulty, because peacocks existed then only in India, and it was considered unthinkable that in ca 950 B.C. ships should have crossed the Indian Ocean. The destination of the ships in 1 Kings 10:22 was thought to be the same as *Ophir,* mentioned in 1 Kings 10:11, 1 Kings 22:49, and elsewhere, as a land where gold and *algummim* wood could be obtained; and this land was sought mostly in South Arabia or East Africa. It was proposed to read for *tukkiyyīm* (peacocks') *sukkiyyīm,* an African people mentioned as allies of Egypt in 2 Chronicles 12:3, the assumption being that they were brought by Solomon as slaves. Another suggestion is that of W.F. Albright to take *tukkī* as a loan from Egyptian *kwy,* a kind of monkey, with the feminine article *t'* before it.

However, if *tukkiyyīm* did not originally mean 'peacocks,' how did it come to mean this? It is unlikely that peacocks could be brought alive to the West by caravan; the royal bird only began to appear there again when the Ptolemics reopened the passage through the Red Sea. There was no special reason why 'monkeys'

should have made anyone think of 'peacocks,' but, even if we assume that someone in the Hellenistic period guessed that Solomon's expeditions went to India, the very word *tukkiyyīm* should have precluded the identification as peacocks, for by then another word, *tawwās,* Greek *taōs,* had become established. The tradition must therefore go back to an older stage; and once we go back beyond the Hellenistic period, there is no compelling reason why another date should be preferred to the Solomonic one, especially as no one seems to doubt that Solomon's ships got as far as *Ophir,* wherever that was. The combination of monkeys and peacocks, with its echo of Indian export practices of a thousand years earlier, could hardly have been thought up by someone unless such journeys had really taken place.

In 1 Kings 10:1-13, next to the monkeys and peacocks, we find the story of the visit of the Queen of Sheba to Solomon, when she presented to him, among other things, a quantity of perfume 'such as had never arrived in Jerusalem on any other occasion.' Since perfumes and spices came mainly from India (in antiquity cinnamon also was used as a perfume), we can see here another reflection of the India trade. There is another Indian characteristic in this story: the queen ostensibly comes 'to try him [Solomon] with riddles.' We find no other reference to South Arabians as possessors of wisdom, but Indians were well known in the ancient world for their skill in disputation. In the Jātaka there is the story of girls whose parents teach them one thousand conundrums (*vāda*) and tell them to marry the first man who can answer them all. Perhaps the version of the story in the Ethiopian *Kebra Nagast,* where the queen bears Solomon a son, forms part of the original Indian story which provided the pattern for this part of the account of the queen's visit. The real reason for the visit is hinted at in the final words: that the queen returned after Solomon 'had given her all her wishes which she had asked from him.' She had thus come to negotiate, and we can guess what the issue was: if Solomon and Hiram had been bypassing South Arabia and were trading directly with India, the blow to Sabaean commerce must indeed have been painful. That this was the connection is perhaps suggested by the word 'because' at the beginning of verse 22, which may have got separated from the Queen of Sheba episode in the process of redaction. It may be surmised that Solomon agreed to withdraw port facilities at Ezion Geber from the Phoenicians in return for a share in the caravan trade. The failure of Jehoshaphat to re-establish the Red Sea route (1 Kings 22:49) shows that by then Phoenicians were not there to provide guidance.

The very fact that the economic-political reason for the queen's visit became obliterated is proof that the story itself is genuine and old, and went through stages of reworking. A genuine trait is also the existence of the queen herself: in Assyrian accounts of fights with the desert Arabs we find several such 'queens.' This archaic institution, apparently religious in character, is hardly a thing to be freely invented by a later storyteller. Although Jacqueline Pirenne's dating of the beginnings of South Arabian epigraphy in the fifth century B.C. is now generally accepted, we have evidence of a Sabaean state earlier than that, in such figures as Kariba'il, king of the land of Saba' in the time of Sanherib (ca 685 B.C.) and It'amra of the land of Saba' in the time of Sargon (715 B.C.). The queen of Solomon's time would thus belong to an earlier stage when the Sabaeans had 'queens,' as other Arabs had in the eighth and seventh centuries.

The singular of the word for 'peacocks,' *tukkiyyīm*, would in Hebrew be *tukkī*. This has been equated by various authors since the eighteenth century with the Tamil word *tōkai*, pronounced *tōgey*, meaning a peacock, a peacock's tail, or anything hanging down. Tamil is a Dravidian language which in ancient times was spoken in the entire south of the Indian peninsula, though now there is a split between Tamil spoken in the east, and Malayalam spoken in the west. Tamil possesses a body of ancient poetry, usually called Sangam ('Academy') poetry, thought to belong to the first century B.C. and the first century A.D. Modern historians follow the opinion of the anthropologist F. von Fürer-Haimendorf in connecting the coming of the Dravidians to South India with the beginning of the iron-using megalith culture, and date the event between 500 and 300 B.C. Tamil tradition dates its history back to well before the year 1000 B.C., and in particular sees the extant Sangam poetry as the product of the Third Sangam, which had been preceded many centuries previously by two earlier Sangams whose output far exceeded that of the Third. The Tamils also claim that there were prosperous cities which disappeared when the east coast of South India receded. The question is once again wide open, since Scandinavian scholars claim to have deciphered the Indus culture script as representing the Tamil language. Since the Indus culture has also been shown to have extended at least as far as the northern boundary of what is now Dravidian India, identification of the bearers of that culture as Dravidians would make it quite tenable to assume continuous Dravidian occupation of at least parts of South India during the second millennium B.C. This would also imply the possession of an artistic and literary culture, so that there may be some substance in the Tamils' claims that the Sangam literature was preceded by a long development.

Additional evidence for contact with Tamils early in the first millennium B.C. is to be found in the names of Indian products in Hebrew, and partly in other Semitic languages. Among these we must single out for mention the perfume-incense *ahaloth* (p1) 'eagle-wood' (in English Bibles 'aloe-wood'), from Tamil

akil, now pronounced *ahal*. This is used to perfume a man's garment, and bedding by holding these objects over a metal plate on which powdered eagle-wood is burning, as is the practice in India today; and quite unlike the use made of South Arabian incense woods, which were used to impart a scent to the air, not to objects. It was surely necessary to observe this practice in India in order to learn the use of the substance. The opportunity to do so resulted from the fact that the outward journey to India had to be carried out during the summer monsoon and the return journey during the winter monsoon, so that travellers had an enforced stay in India of about three months. This situation is described in a Tamil epic of the third century A.D., *Shilapadikāram* by Ilangō Adigal: 'In different places of Puhār the onlooker's attention was arrested by the sight of the abodes of Yavanas [Greeks and Romans], whose prosperity was never on the wane. On the harbour were to be seen sailors come from distant lands, but for all appearances they lived as one community.' Such a stay, especially if repeated, gave the traveller an opportunity to learn about local customs, beliefs, and art.

While the doubling of the *k* in *tukkī* is possibly due to a Hebrew sound-law, compensatory doubling, the attentive reader will have noticed that the intervocalic *k* of *tōkai* appears in Hebrew as *k*, and that of *akil* as *h*. We would suggest that the reason for this difference is that the name of the eagle-wood was learnt from stevedores at the dockside, while the word for the peacock was acquired from upper-class natives, whose speech was phonetically more conservative. Although the meaning 'peacock' is very well attested in Sangam poetry. its etymology shows that the meaning 'hanging down' is the original one. The word is rare, and restricted to poetry, and the peacock is usually referred to by other names. Thus *tōkai* is most probably a kenning restricted to poetry, and could only be learnt from educated Tamils, and possibly only in connection with literary activities. It would thus attest that Solomon's emissaries met people familiar with Tamil literature. We have another, somewhat later, instance of such a sociolinguistic doublet. While King Ashoka about 250 B.C. writes *keral* the name of the country Kerala, now pronounced in Tamil *tcheral,* the western words for 'rice' (Greek *orytza,* Hebrew *orez*) reflect the pronunciation *aritchi* for what was etymologically *ari-ki.* Ashoka, of course, learnt the name of Kerala from royal ambassadors.

2. The Mountains of Perfumes

The name of King Solomon is also connected with the ***Song of Songs***, where his name is repeatedly mentioned and details of his court life alluded to. In this case, too, modern criticism has strenuously denied any real connection of the poem with the time of Solomon. The various theories current about it are well known, and can be found in introductions to the Old Testament and to commentaries. Most modern theories assume that the poem was originally written as an ordinary love story or collection of love songs or wedding songs, and that its inclusion in the Bible is the result of allegorical reinterpretation. This does not really affect whatever view one holds about the literary genre: in order to be effective an allegory must make sense on the literal plane, and must be written in a style which the reader or listener can identify as befitting the subject of the literal meaning. Hence, even if the work were intended by its author to be an allegory, it had to be recognized by his contemporaries as love poetry or wedding songs, and we are entitled to study it as such. Nor do most theories point to certain dating of the original composition. The one exception is the theory that the work was originally a hymn to Ishtar, or influenced by Ishtar hymns: this presupposes a dating in the period when Assyro-Babylonian culture exerted a direct influence on ancient Israel, or before 589 B.C. This is some centuries earlier than the time assumed by theories which, on the basis of assumed Greek and Persian words and Mishnaic Hebrew features, date it in the last centuries of the Second Temple. The 'Ishtar' theory would even allow for a date in the time of Solomon, as Babylonian influence was strong in the preceding Canaanite period, and Canaanite literary influence seems to have been noticeable in the period of Solomon. Since no theory seems so far to have found wide acceptance, we may be allowed to propound a new theory, based on the economic activities of Solomon's reign which we discussed in the first part of this article.

Three features set the **Song of Songs** apart from ancient oriental love poetry. Though perhaps occasional traces of these can be found elsewhere, they do not recur in the same measure and not in this combination:

1 The woman expresses her feelings of love, and appears in fact as the chief person in the **Song**. Not only are fifty-six verses clearly put into the woman's mouth as against thirty-six into the man's (omitting all cases where the attribution is debatable), but there is a marked difference between the woman's 'lines' and the man's. While most of what he says are descriptions of her beauty, she expresses deep and complicated emotions. It is surely significant that there are a number of occasions when he speaks in her imagination, but never she in his. Indeed one gains the impression that his words are not infrequently mere cue lines for her answers. A case could be made out for the theory that everything the lover says is imagined by her, even if this is not expressly stated, just as it is certain that the words put into the mouth of the 'maidens of Jerusalem' are imagined by her. Such a theory would remove the difficulties of the sequence of passages by transferring it to the stream of consciousness of the girl. However this more extreme assumption is not essential for our the-

ory. Even without it, the freedom with which a woman expresses her most hidden emotions is enough to place the **Song of Songs** apart.

2 Nature plays a role not only in the similes, but in the fact that the phenomena of growth and renewal are constantly referred to and form the background against which the emotional life of the lovers moves. Moreover, where actual physical fulfillment is hinted at, it is either placed in 'natural' locations far removed from dwellings and intoxicating by their beauty, such as the forest, high rocks, and flowering vineyards, or clothed in an agricultural simile, the fertilization of the date palm. The prophets often refer to nature, but mainly as something inimical and terrifying; here nature is friendly, even the high crag in 2:14 holding a friendly promise. All this is familiar enough to us, but we are apt to forget that such an attitude to nature was achieved in the West only in the eighteenth century.

3 While the lover, whether intended as a person or as a dream figure, speaks in a proper masculine, aggressive manner, the dominant note of the woman's utterances is longing, reaching out for a lover who is far away and approaches her only in her dreams. She herself is aware that her longing is sinful, that it will bring her into contempt, and in her dream the 'watchmen' punish her and expose her to shame by taking away her outer garment. She must assert her chastity—note that the simile used, 'city wall,' is reminiscent of the 'watchmen of the city walls' in 5:7. Ancient eastern love poetry generally expresses desire, not longing, and to find parallels we have to go to seventh century Arabic poetry and to the troubadours; however there it is the man who longs and the woman who is unattainable.

There is, however, one body of ancient poetry that exhibits the three features which we have enumerated, and that is the Sangam poetry of the Tamils. Though this poetry has in recent years formed the subject of much research and there are some partial translations, it will be sufficient for our purposes to quote three poems from an easily accessible source, the *Golden Anthology of Ancient Tamil Literature* by Nalladai R. Balakrishna Mudaliar. Each poem is, in the original Sangam collections, accompanied by a prose introduction and summary, which are here quoted in extract only. I have also made slight changes in Mudaliar's rendering of the poems, mainly to make them easier to follow.

A *Mudaliar* I,17
INTRODUCTION A young suitor goes in search of wealth with a view to hasten the day of marriage with his beloved. The maiden pines at the separation from him.

Her confidante says:—
'The young ones of the deer on the lovely slopes of the mountains, having drunk their fill of sweet milk

flowing in abundance from the udders of their mother, frolic in the cool shade of the high mountain slopes. Such is the country of thy lover, o maiden, but alas, his heart is harder than the mountains.'

The maiden replies:—
'Yes, iron-willed is he in achieving his object. Since I was not aware of this, I now foolishly languish.'

B *Mudaliar* I,18
INTRODUCTION A maiden is in love with a highland chief, and her confidante says to the girl's fostermother, intending to reveal to her the cause of her mistress's languishment:—

'Hail, o mother, listen with love! Whenever his big luminous mountain disappears from her sight, that mountain where the people dig up yams and leave long pits that are quickly filled again by fresh golden Vengai flowers falling into them [a symbol for the chief's generosity], her eyes, wide and long like full-blown Vengai flowers falling on the rocks, fill with tears.'

C *Mudaliar* II,45
INTRODUCTION A young hero elopes with his beloved. As the young couple traverse a barren tract, he says:—

'O maiden, the sun has faded. On the bamboo-grown hillocks, you can hear the ringing of the clear-toned bells, tied by the cowherds for adornment around the necks of cows. Look over there! My nice little village is coming into sight. When the clouds with their thunder, that drives the snakes into their holes, rise on the right and melt in showers—on such a morning and in such a scenery the blue, jewel necked peacock magnificently spreads its plumes and dances. So too, O maiden, hasten thy steps, that thy flower-decked locks may be loosened, and be spread out by the breeze that blows.'

The last of these three poems has been quoted here to illustrate the link between love's fulfillment (the loosening of the woman's hair) and flight into nature. It has a close parallel in *Song of Songs* 7:12-13:

'Come, my lover, let us go into the open land, let us spend the nights in villages, let us rise early to go out to the vineyards, that we may see whether the vines have flowered, the vine-blossoms have opened, the pomegranate trees have budded—there I will give you my love; whether the mandrakes spread their scent, while right in front of our door are all delicacies, this year's and last year's—my love which I have stored up for you.'

The other two poems are only samples of the many in the *Golden Anthology*; there are many others in the complete Sangam collection in which women in love express their longing for their betrothed or for men with whom they have fallen in love, perhaps without the man knowing it. Only rarely is the cause of sepa-

ration stated in the poem itself; but the introductions clearly indicate causes deeply rooted in the Tamils' social system and code of honour: the man must acquire glory and wealth, he must fulfil his duties towards his feudal lord and towards his people. Marriage fetters, and is therefore delayed. Here the man's world conflicts with the world of the woman, whose desire is to have her man with her, symbolized in the *Song of Songs* by bringing him 'to the house of my mother.' This conflict is poignantly expressed in another Tamil Sangam poem (Mudaliar I, 93-4):

INTRODUCTION A young woman whose beloved has gone in search of wealth, says:—
'I did his manhood wrong by assuming that he would not part from me. Likewise he did my womanhood wrong by thinking that I would not languish at being separated from him. As a result of the tussle between two such great fortitudes of ours, my languishing heart whirls in agony, like suffering caused by the bite of a cobra.'

As in the Tamil poems the lovelorn maiden speaks to her 'confidante,' and her problems are discussed with her mother or foster mother, so the maiden of the *Song of Songs* appeals to 'the maidens of Jerusalem,' and her mother and her lover's mother are mentioned; but in neither is there a mention of the maiden's father. The world of men is represented by 'King Solomon,' surrounded by his soldiers, afraid of the night, having many wives and concubines, and engaged in economic enterprises. Significantly Solomon's values are mentioned only to be refuted, perhaps even ridiculed: his military power is worth less than the crown his mother (!) put on him on his wedding day; the queens and concubines have to concede first rank to the heroine of the *Song*; and she disdainfully tells Solomon to keep his money.

Since the Sangam poetry is the only source we have for information about its period, we can only surmise that the recurring theme of young men leaving their villages and towns to gain wealth and fame and leaving their women behind corresponded to reality, in other words that the theme of longing grew out of the conditions of the society which produced these poems. This is also why the cause for the lover's absence need not be explicitly mentioned in the Tamil poems, and is at most hinted at in the elaborate symbolic language of flowers and other similes. Have we any hints in the *Song of Songs* for the non-availability of the lover?

In 2:17, and again in 8:14, the lover is told: 'until the day blows cool and the shadows flee, turn away (8:14: depart, flee), my lover, and resemble a deer or a young gazelle on the mountains.' The mountains are further qualified in 2:17 as 'cleft mountains,' and in 8:14 as 'mountains of perfume.' In 2:8-9 the lover once more is said to resemble a deer or a young gazelle, as he

The poem set in a floral design for a wedding ceremony.

'jumps along the mountains, leaps along the hills.' The phrase 'until the day blows cool, and the shadows flee' recurs in 4:6-8. Until that time, he says, 'I shall go away to the mountain of myrrh and to the hill of incense . . . with me, O bride, from Lebanon, with me from Lebanon thou shalt come, thou shalt look down from the summit of Amanah, from the summits of Senir and Hermon, from lairs of lions, from mountains of tigers.' We can hardly believe that he is actually inviting his beloved to come with him on such perilous and difficult journeys: clearly he is merely suggesting to her (or she is suggesting to herself) that she think of him as he traverses those places, and wait for him until he will 'leap along the mountains' to return to her 'when the day will blow cool,' i.e., in winter? Possibly 'when the shadows flee' means when the noon shadows grow long; in any case the reference seems to be to winter time.

But the dreamlike quality of these verses need not prevent us from extracting the hard information they contain: that the lover must cross mountains, and that on those mountains, or beyond them, are to be found myrrh, incense, and perfumes or balsam. All these lead us in the same direction, to South Arabia, the land of myrrh and incense. Also balsam, which in the time of the Mishnah grew on the shores of the Dead Sea, has its homeland in South Arabia, and was apparently grown in Palestine only after the Babylonian Exile. We have thus an indication that the young man was absent on travels with a caravan. Of course he did not have to traverse the summits of Amanah and Hermon to reach Jerusalem from any direction: the caravan route from the north passed only within sight of these mountains; but he did have to traverse mountains, and, in South Arabia, to pass mountain roads between steep crags ('cleft mountains'); and it was on the slopes of such mountains that the much sought-after aromatic woods grew ('mountains of perfume'). But, when coming from South Arabia, one had to pass one mountain: one of the hills that overlook Jerusalem from the east between the city and the Judaean desert. Beyond those mountains shepherds graze their flocks for part of the year. There, on the mountain aptly called Mount Scopus or 'mountain of those who look out,' it is possible to see a caravan approaching at a considerable distance. 'Who is she that is coming up from the desert, like pillars of smoke, perfumed with myrrh and incense, and all the powders of the perfume merchant?' The dust raised by the caravan rises like smoke from a fire, but the sight of the smoke also raises the association of the scent the caravan spreads around it as it halts in the market and unpacks its wares. We may well have an allusion to the same tryst in the enigmatic passage 1:7-8: 'Tell me, you whom my soul loves, where do you pasture, where do you make your animals lie down at noon? . . . If you do not know, most beautiful of women, go out in the wake of the sheep and goats, and pasture your kids at the places where the shepherds stay.' To tell someone to look for a flock where there are flocks, makes little sense, but the passage gains information value if the first 'pasture' refers to camels that are rested at noon near the encampments of the local shepherds.

This brings us to another question of relevance to our theory. Because of the repeated use of the Hebrew verb *ra'ah* 'to pasture' and its participle meaning 'shepherd' most commentators think that the **Song of Songs** depicts a kind of shepherd idyll. But what kind of a shepherd is the lover, who 'has gone down to his garden, to the flowerbeds of perfume (or balsam), to pasture in the gardens, to gather lilies?' In an agricultural society such wanton destruction of valuable property would not have endeared him to his fellows, or for that matter to the contemporary reader. The reference is again to the perfume gardens of South Arabia, and the verb 'to pasture' may have some technical meaning connected with the management of camels (which perhaps it also has in 1:7). In the next verse the lover is called 'he that pastures among the lilies,' and the same phrase (in fact the whole verse) appears also in 2:16. There it is immediately explained by the words 'resemble, my lover . . . a young gazelle,' and the meaning is made clear by 4:5: 'like two young ones, twins of a deer, that pasture among the lilies.' 'He that pastures among the lilies' is a kenning for the young deer or gazelle, and the lover is called a young deer, or rather a young mountain-goat, because he spends his time upon the 'cleft mountains' and the 'mountains of perfume.' On the other hand, there is in those verses a certain amount of word play with the different meanings of *ra'ah* and the various kinds of gardens. Thus also the suggestion made to the girl in 1:8: 'pasture your goat-kids upon the places where the shepherds stay' may be meant playfully, or may even hide an idiomatic phrase meaning something like 'to hang about.' For similar reasons we can also discount 1:6, 'my brothers were angry with me, they appointed me as one who guards the vineyards,' as a description of actual agricultural activities. The dreams in which the maiden walks about the streets of a walled town, the appeals to 'the maidens of Jerusalem,' and the familiarity with Jerusalem landmarks and details of the royal court show that the heroine lived in Jerusalem. Of course, in biblical times people living within city walls engaged in agriculture, so that the heroine would have been familiar with its ways, but there is no reference to any real agricultural pursuits, such as sowing and harvesting. The references to vineyards, date palms, and the like are eclipsed by references to untamed nature—hardly a peasant's outlook.

The verses 4:12-14 betray a knowledge of expensive and rare spices which would have been most unusual in a simple peasant boy: '[You are] a locked garden, my sister, my bride, a locked water-place (?), a sealed spring, the irrigation channels of which are a plantation of pomegranates with fruit of delicacies, camphor-like substances and spikenard-like substances, spikenard and Indian saffron, canna and cinnamon, with all incense-producing woods myrrh and eaglewood, with all flower-heads of perfume.' This reads so much like the bill of goods of a South Arabian caravan merchant that we are tempted to believe that the author put this in as a clue. Be it what it may, it provides the atmosphere of a period when Indian goods like spikenard, curcuma, and cinnamon, as well as South Arabian goods like incense and myrrh, passed through Judaea in a steady flow of trade. This can hardly relate to the Hellenistic period when Indian goods were carried by ship and did not pass through Palestine: it sets the *Song of Songs* squarely in the First Temple period.

This conclusion, reached from our analysis of the contents, conflicts with the argument that the *Song* contains linguistic forms indicating a date in the Hellenistic period. The word *appiryōn* in 3:9, denoting some piece of furniture with a 'saddle' and a part for reclining, is supposed to be derived from Greek *phoreion* 'sedan-chair'; and in 4:4, 'like the tower of David is your neck, built for *talpiyyōth*,' the last word is said to be Greek *telōpia* 'looking into the distance.' The phonetic similarity between the Greek and Hebrew words is somewhat vague, and this writer considers both attributions to be unlikely, but even acceptance of these words as Greek does not necessitate a late dating for

the *Song of Songs*, since Mycenaean Greek antedates the Exodus. Neither word occurs elsewhere in the Bible, so that we cannot say whether in Hebrew itself these words were late. In contrast to this, *pardēs* 'garden, plantation' occurs, apart from 4:13, only in Nehemiah 2:8, where the Persian king's 'keeper of the *pardēs*' delivers wood for building, and in Ecclesiastes 2:5 next to 'gardens.' The word is generally agreed to be Persian, though the ancient Persian original is not quite clear. If the word is really of Persian origin, it would necessitate post-exilic dating. It seems to me, however, that this word, to which also Greek *paradeisos* belongs, may be of different origin.

The *Song of Songs* also exhibits some phenomena which are thought to connect it with Mishnaic Hebrew, the form of Hebrew written in the latest part of the Second Temple period—its earliest document may be the Copper Scroll from Qumran—and probably spoken during most of the Second Temple period. The main point is the subordinating particle *she*-for Classical Hebrew *asher* (in the *Song of Songs* *asher* occurs only in the title, which hardly forms part of the original work). However, *she*-, in the form *sha*-, occurs in one of the earliest extant documents of Hebrew, the Song of Deborah in Judges 5. It seems to have been current over part of the Hebrew language area, and to have persisted as a form used in familiar language and in dialects, being ousted from the written idiom only with the emergence of the official Classical Hebrew of the time of David and Solomon. Its appearance in the *Song of Songs* is thus more likely to be a stylistic matter than an indication for dating. Besides, the difference between *asher* and *she*- was well known in later times, and it can hardly be believed that a poet who wanted to give his work the appearance of having been written in the time of Solomon would have spoiled this by introducing an easily identified word betraying his own speech. It is not impossible, however, that our entire system of linguistic criteria for the dating of Hebrew texts needs revision. O. Loretz [in *Qohelet und der alte Orient* (1964)] adduces rather attractive evidence for influence of Babylonian and Assyrian literature upon the thought and language of Ecclesiastes. Largely because of the word *pardēs* he does not see a possibility of dating the book before the end of the sixth century B.C. This, however, would be the least likely time both for such profound Babylonian influence and for a Hebrew so deviant from the Classical prose style to occur. If we accept Loretz's evidence, we ought to date the book of Ecclesiastes much earlier. Then the features taken to indicate late composition would rather have to be explained as signs of the book having been written before the Classical standardization, or in a milieu which resisted this standardization.

It is thus possible to suggest that the *Song of Songs* was written in the heyday of Judaean trade with South Arabia and beyond (and this may include the lifetime of King Solomon) by someone who had himself travelled to South Arabia and to South India and had there become acquainted with Tamil poetry. He took over one of its recurrent themes, as well as certain stylistic features. The literary form of developing a theme by dialogue could have been familiar to this man from Babylonian-Assyrian sources (where it is frequent) and Egyptian literature (where it is rare). He was thus prepared by his experience for making a decisive departure from the Tamil practice by building what in Sangam poetry were short dialogue poems into a long work, though we may possibly discern in the *Song of Songs* shorter units more resembling the Tamil pieces. Instead of the vague causes for separation underlying the moods expressed in Tamil poetry, he chose an experience familiar to him and presumably common enough to be recognized by his public, the long absences of young men on commercial expeditions.

I think that so far our theory is justified by the interpretations we have put forward for various details in the text of the *Song of Songs*. In asking what were the motives and intentions of our author in writing this poem, we must needs move into the sphere of speculation. He might, of course, have been moved by witnessing the suffering of a young woman pining for her lover or husband, and got the idea of writing up this experience by learning that Tamil poets were currently dealing with the same theme. But I think we are ascribing to our author too modern an outlook on literature. In the light of what we know of the intellectual climate of ancient Israel, it is more probable that he had in mind a contribution to religious or wisdom literature, in other words that he planned his work as an allegory for the pining of the people of Israel, or perhaps of the human soul, for God. He saw the erotic longing of the maiden as a simile for the need of man for God. In this he expresses by a different simile a sentiment found, for instance, in Psalm 42:2-4: 'Like a hind that craves for brooks of water, so my soul craves for thee, O God. My soul is athirst for God, the living god: when shall I come and show myself before the face of God? My tears are to me instead of food by day and by night, when they say to me day by day: Where is your god?' This religious attitude seems to be typical of those psalms that are now generally ascribed to the First Temple period, and, as far as I am aware, has no clear parallel in the later periods to which the *Song of Songs* is usually ascribed.

We may perhaps go one step further. In Indian legend, love of human women for gods, particularly for Krishna, is found as a theme. Tamil legend, in particular, has amongst its best known items the story of a young village girl who loved Krishna so much that in her erotic moods she adorned herself for him with the flower-chains prepared for offering to the god's statue. When this was noticed, and she was upbraided by her father, she was taken by Krishna into heaven. Expressions of intensive love for the god are a prominent feature of mediaeval Tamil Shaivite poetry. The use of such themes to express the relation of man to god may thus have been familiar to Indians also in more ancient times, and our hypothetical Judaean poet could have been aware of it. Thus the use of the genre of love poetry of this kind for the expression of religious longing may itself have been borrowed from India.

Marvin H. Pope (essay date 1977)

SOURCE: An introduction in *Song of Songs*, Doubleday & Company, Inc., 1977, pp. 17-229.

[*In the following essay, Pope contends that the emphasis in the* Song of Songs *on expressions of love might link the work to the occasion of a funeral feast.*]

LOVE AND DEATH

It has been recognized by many commentators that the setting of Love and Passion in opposition to the power of Death and Hell in 8:6c,d is the climax of the **Canticle** and the burden of its message: that Love is the only power that can cope with Death. Throughout the **Song** the joys of physical love are asserted, but this singular mention of Death and his domain, Sheol, suggests that this fear may be the covert concern of the **Canticle**, the response to inexorable human fate with the assertion of Love as the only power that frustrates the complete victory of Death. The sacred marriage was a celebration and affirmation of this vital force. The inevitable circumstance in which Life and Love come into stark confrontation with Death is in mortuary observances, not only in the wake and burial but in the ongoing concern to commune with the departed and provide for their needs in the infernal realm with offerings of food and drink.

The sacral meal with ritual drinking of intoxicating beverage, music, song, dance, and sexual license was a feature of religious praxis in the Near East from early times. Glyptic art of ancient Mesopotamia presents vivid scenes of such festivities. Seals from the Royal Cemetery at Ur depict banquet scenes with celebrants imbibing from large jars through drinking tubes while a bed with cross bands is presented by an attendant. The cross bands, or saltire, are the symbol and attribute of the great goddess of love and war. The saltire of the love goddess adorning the couch (perhaps also serving to brace it) suggests the use to which it will shortly be put and this is graphically confirmed in other scenes which show the bed occupied by a copulating couple. Beneath the love couch is sometimes depicted the scorpion, symbol of tile goddess Išara, or the dog related to the goddess Gula. Both these goddesses, Išhara and Gula, are, according to H. Frankfort, "aspects of that great goddess of fertility whose union with a male god, consummated at the New Year's festival, insured the prosperity of the community; for the fertility of nature depended upon this act." The dog under the love couch depicted on a Mesopotamian seal of the Early Dynastic III period (ca. 2500 B.C.), recalls the canine beneath the couch which is common on Hellenistic funerary sculptures but which has not been plausibly explained. A recently published Ugaritic text, however, when correlated with observations by a couple of Fathers of the Church concerning accusations against the early Christians, throws light on the persistent canine at the connubium and the funeral feast. The Ugaritic text (UG 5.1) describes a banquet given by El, the father of the gods, in which a dog has an important but unspecified role. The highlights of the affair are given here in translation without notes. . . .

> El offered game in his house,
> Venison in the midst of his palace.
> He invited the gods to mess.
> The gods ate and drank,
> Drank wine till sated,
> Must till inebriated.
>
> . . . . .
>
> 'Astarte and Anat arrived
> 'Astarte prepared a *brisket* for him,
> And Anat a shoulder.
> The Porter of El's house chided them:
> "Lo, for the dog prepare a *brisket*.
> For the cur prepare a shoulder."
> El his father he chided.
> El sat (in) (his pl)ace,
> El sat in his *mrzh.*
> He drank wine till sated,
> Must till inebriated.
>
> . . . . .
>
> An apparition accosted him,
> With horns and a tail.
> He floundered in his excrement and urine.
> El collapsed, El like those who descend into
>   Earth.
> Anat and 'Astarte went roaming.

There is a gap of a couple of lines on the obverse of the tablet and the text continues for several lines on the reverse, with mention of the return of the goddesses and the administration of various medicines, including juice of green olives, to relieve the deity's crapulence.

The mention of special pieces of meat for the dog, the same cuts prepared by the goddesses for their father, recalls the allegations against the early Christians regarding the role of the dog in their festal meals. Tertullian in chs. 7 and 8 of his *Apology* in rebutting the charges that Christians in their reprobate feasts murdered and ate infants and climaxed the celebration with an incestuous sexual orgy, mentions dogs as "the pimps

of darkness" procuring license for these impious lusts by putting out the lights in a rather bizarre fashion. Tertullian ridiculed the charges simply by recounting the alleged proceedings:

> Yet, I suppose, it is customary for those who wish to be initiated to approach first the father of the sacred rites to arrange what must be prepared. . . . Now, you need a baby, still tender, one who does not know what death means, and who will smile under your knife. You need bread, too, with which to gather up his juicy blood; besides that, candlesticks, lamps, some dogs and bits of meat which will draw them on to overturn the lamps. Most important of all, you must come with your mother and sister.

These rites were alleged to have been performed for the purpose of gaining eternal life, to which charge Tertullian retorted:

> For the time being, believe it! On this point I have a question to ask: If you believed it, would you consider the acquisition of eternal life worth attaining with such a (troubled) conscience? Come, bury your sword in this baby, enemy though he be of no one, guilty of no crime, everybody's son; or, if that is the other fellow's job, stand here beside this (bit of) humanity, dying before he has lived; wait for the young soul to take flight; receive his fresh blood; saturate your bread with it; partake freely! Meanwhile, as you recline at table, note the place where your mother is, and your sister; note it carefully, so that, when the dogs cause the darkness to fall, you may make no mistake—for you will be guilty of a crime unless you commit incest.

Marcus Minucius Felix tells us a bit more about these alleged initiation rites for Christian novices:

> An infant covered with a dough crust to deceive the unsuspecting is placed beside the person to be initiated into the sacred rites. This infant is killed at the hands of the novice by wounds inflicted unintentionally and hidden from his eyes, since he has been urged on as if to harmless blows on the surface of the dough. The infant's blood—oh, horrible—they sip up eagerly; its limbs they tear to pieces, trying to outdo each other; by this victim they are leagued together; by being privy to this crime they pledge themselves to mutual silence. These sacred rites are more shocking than any sacrilege.

Minucius Felix continues:

> On the appointed day, they assemble for their banquets with all their children, sisters, and mothers—people of both sexes and every age. After many sumptuous dishes, when the company at the table has grown warm and the passion of incestuous lust has been fired by drunkenness, a dog which has

been tied to a lampstand is tempted by throwing a morsel beyond length of the leash by which it is bound. It makes a dash, and jumps for the catch. Thus, when the witnessing light has been overturned and extinguished, in the ensuing darkness which favors shamelessness, they unite in whatever revolting lustful embraces the hazard of chance will permit. Thus, they are all equally guilty of incest, if not indeed, yet by privity, since whatever can happen in the actions of individuals is sought for by the general desire of all.

Dogs figure in cultic symbolism and funerary rites of many cultures and there is no warrant to consider the topic in detail here since dogs play no part in the *Song of Songs*. The practice of putting pieces of meat on or around a corpse, as among the Parsees is easily understood as intended to distract the dogs from attacking the corpse. There is a rabbinic story about the death of King David and the cutting of an animal's carcass to keep the hungry dogs from attacking the corpse. Other references to food for dogs at funerals and weddings occur in rabbinic literature. An Anatolian funerary relief from Thasos, dating to the fifth century B.C., shows a dog under the banquet couch with muzzle to the ground, as if eating while a stela from Piraeus, also of the fifth century B.C., shows the dog reclining under the banquet couch and gnawing at a hefty hunk of meat. The meat in this instance could be explained as a sop. An early Corinthian crater, however, shows leashed dogs underneath the couches of the celebrants which suggests that the details related by Tertullian and Minucius Felix as to the function of the dogs as "the pimps of darkness" in sacral sexual orgies, for all its similarities to a Rube Goldberg mechanism, may have been an ancient artifice.

It is of interest to observe that the earliest representation of the dog under the couch, ca. 2500 B.C., is in a scene with two couples copulating in different positions and suggestive at least of the sort of group activity of which the later Christians were accused. Scenes of group sex involving three or more participants are not uncommon in the glyptic art of ancient Mesopotamia. The dog continued on funeral reliefs down to late antiquity, as on the urn of Iulia Eleutheris in the Thermen Museum in Rome showing mourners engaged in *conclamtio mortis* while beneath the bier reposes the persistent canine.

The dog played an important role in the funerary cults at Palmyra and Hatra. At Hatra there appears to have been a sanctuary dedicated to the infernal deity Nergol as a dog (*nrgwl klb'*).

The term *mrzh* applied in the Ugaritic text to the place where El imbibed to the point of delirium, diarrhea, and enuresis, and finally to a state resembling death, is of particular interest and importance for the understanding of the nature and purpose of the bacchanalian banquet. This word occurs twice in the Old Testament, Amos 6:7 and Jer 16:5, and the *RSV* renderings "revelry" in the first instance and "mourning" in the second, reflect the long standing puzzlement as to the precise meaning of the term. In Amos 6:4-7 the dissolute luxury of the proceedings is explicit:

> The lie on ivory beds,
> Sprawled on their couches,
> Eating rams from the flock,
> Bullocks from the stall.
> They chant to the tune of the lyre,
> Like David they improvise song.
>
> They drink wine from bowls,
> Choicest oils they smear,
> But are not sickened at Joseph's ruin.
> Therefore they will go at the head of the
> 　　exiles,
> And the sprawlers, banquet cease.

The "sprawlers' banquet," *marzēah sĕrûhîm*, is ambiguous. The root *srh* I is applied to an overhanging curtain in Exod 26:12 and to a spreading vine in Ezek 17:6, and possibly to a flowing headdress in Ezek 23:15. There is also a root *srh* II apparently meaning "be putrid," or the like, in Jer 49:7 and Sir 42:11.

The couch *(mēsib)* of the king whereon he enjoys, among other things, the fragrance of his lady's perfume, 1:12, in its feminine form *mēsibbah* is the post-Biblical Hebrew equivalent of the Greek term *symposion,* in which the revelers sprawl on couches.

The expression "marzēah-house," *bêt marzēah*, is used in Jer 16:5:

> Thus says YHWH:
> Do not enter the *marzēah-house*,
> Do not go to mourn,
>
> Do not lament for them.
> For I have removed my peace from this
> 　　people.

LXX here rendered *bêt marzēah* as *thiasos*, a term which designates a company assembled to celebrate a festival in honor of a deity, or a mourning feast. Jeremiah goes on (Jer 16:6-9) to describe the funeral celebration which will not take place:

> Great and small will die in this land
> And they will not be buried.
> None shall mourn or lament;
> None shall gash himself,
> None be made bald for them.
> None shall provide a mourning meal
> To comfort him for the dead,
> Nor make him drink the cup of consolation

For his father and his mother.
You shall not enter the drinking-house

To sit with them,
To eat and to drink.
For thus says YHWH of Hosts,
The God of Israel:
Behold, I am banishing from this place.
Before your eyes, and in your days,
The sound of exultation,
The sound of joy,
The sound of the groom,
And the sound of the bride.

The terms "*marzēaḥ*-house," *bêt marzēaḥ*, and "drinking-house," *bêt mišteh*, appear to be roughly synonymous in the passage just cited, as designations of a place in which banquets were held in both mourning and revelry for the dead, with drunkenness and sacral sexual intercourse. The mention of ivory beds, feasting, music and song, wine bibbing, and perfume oil in Amos 6:4-7 and of mourning and lamentation, eating and drinking, the sounds of exultation and joy, and the sounds of groom and bride in Jer 16:6-9 are all features of the funeral feast in the *marzēaḥ* (-house), or the drinking-house.

The drowning of sorrow in the cup of consolation is a practice older than the Irish wake. The rabbis felt it necessary to reform the custom and control the tendency to alcoholic excess at funeral feasts. Ten cups were permitted to be drunk in the house of mourning, but then four extra cups were added as special toasts to various notables, civic and religious leaders, and one in honor of Rabban Gamaliel, so that some became intoxicated and the limit of ten cups was restored. At the festival of Purim, however, it was permissible to drink until one could not tell the difference between Haman and Mordecai. The example of the father of the gods of Ugarit, reeling in drunken delirium, wallowing in excrement and urine, and collapsing as if dead, was on occasion emulated by the Israelites, to judge from the prophet's animadversion, Isa 28:7-9:

These, too, reel with wine,
With drink they stagger;
Priest and prophet stagger with drink,
Dazed with wine,
Reeling with drink.

They stagger in————,
Totter in————;
All the tables full of vomit,
Excrement without place.

The mention of tables full of vomit and excrement in the last couplet suggests that similar terms may have originally stood in lines f and g where MT has the bizarre readings *br'h*, vocalized as *bārô'eh*, "in the

seer," and *pělîliyyāh*, "judicial decision," as the setting of their staggering. With very slight change of *br'h* one may restore *bhr'*, "in excrement." The word *here'* was considered obscene and the less offensive term *so'āh*, "excretion," was imposed in Isa 36:23=II Kings 18:27. It is harder to guess what term may have been changed to *pělîliyyāh*, but the context suggests the common connection and parallel of solid and liquid excreta, as in Isa 36:12 and Ugaritic *hr'* and *ṯnt*, "excrement" and "urine." Isaiah's allusion to priests and prophets reeling among tables strewn with vomit and excrement, and the appalling picture of the drunken father of the gods wallowing in his own filth recall the rabbinic derision of the coprophilia ascribed to the cult of Baal Peor whose worship was alleged to include ceremonial defecation. A Jew was forbidden to relieve himself before the idol, even with the intention of degrading it, since this was the alleged mode of worshiping Baal Peor. A story is told of a certain Jew who entered the shrine of Baal Peor, defecated and wiped himself on the idol's nose and the acolytes praised his devotion saying, "no man ever served this idol thus." It is difficult to know whether this story is based on direct knowledge of such worship or was suggested by one of the meanings of the verb *p'r* in Jewish Aramaic.

While the coprological aspects of the cult of Baal Peor were not especially attractive, there were other features which had potent appeal and to which the Israelites succumbed at the first encounter with the Moabites at Shittim, and frequently thereafter. The "sacrifices" to which the Moabite women invited their Israelite cousins featured a contact sport which made it possible for Phinehas to skewer an Israelite man and a Moabite woman with a single thrust of the spear. Now these festivities are explicitly identified as funeral feasts in Ps 106:28:

They yoked themselves to Baal Peor,
And ate the sacrifices of the dead.

These sacrifices of the dead characterized by sacral sexual intercourse are identified by the rabbis as *marzēḥîm* in the Sifre, the same term applied to the setting of El's potation and self-pollution. Midrashic comment further related the *marzēaḥ* to the Mayumas festival, a celebration which featured wife-swapping. Mayumas festivals were observed along the Mediterranean, especially in port cities like Alexandria, Gaza, Ashkelon and Antioch, with such licentiousness that the Roman rulers felt constrained to ban them. Rabbi Hanan apparently alluded to such rites in his comment that "it was done in the cities of the Sea what was not done in the generation of the Flood." The equation of Marzēaḥ and Mayumas is also made in the mosaic map of the sixth-century church at Madeba which labels the Transjordanian area in which the Baal-Peor apostasy occurred as "*Betomarseas* (i.e. Beth Marzēaḥ) alias *(ho kai)* Maioumas." Several scholars have recently treated the term *marzēah* in detail, and only a brief summary with a few supplementary observations need be given for the present concern to understand the nature of the *marzēah* and suggest a relationship to the *Song of Songs*.

Considerable information on the *marzēah* comes to us from Palmyra in the form of dedicatory inscriptions and tessarae decorated with banquet scenes and bearing inscriptions mentioning the term *mrzh*. J. T. Milik has brought together the Semitic and Greek epigraphic materials dealing with these celebrations by gods and mortals with chapters on the vocabulary of the Palmyrene tessarae and inscriptions, and other data on the religious associations at Palmyra, Dura, Hatra, Syria, Phoenicia, and among the Nabateans. This work is a veritable treasure-trove of information on the funeral feasts, with data which may be correlated with the Ugaritic materials to provide new and provocative insights which may have relevance for the understanding of the *Song of Songs*. Some data from Milik's study will be briefly noticed in supplements to the commentary which had been completed before Milik's work appeared. There is much in Milik's study which will stimulate further research and discussion.

The members of the association were termed in Aramaic *bny mrzh'*, "children of the *mrzh*," and specific deities were sometimes designated, e.g., *bny mrzh nbw*, "members of the mrzh of Nabu." The most popular association at Palmyra was apparently associated with Bel (Baal), to judge from the numerous tessarae which mention the priests of Bel. Each *mrzh* had a chief, Phoenician *rb mrzh*, Aramaic *rb mrzh'*, Greek *symposiarchēs*. The priests of Bel at Palmyra were organized in a college headed by the chief priest, *archiereus kai symposiarchēs*, who served also as eponym for dating the acts of the association. The symposiarch of the priests of Bel was also chief of all other symposia of the city and had charge of the "house of distribution," *bt qsm'*. . . . An inscription erected in recognition of the services of a certain Yarhai Agrippa in the year A.D. 243 notes that in his leadership of the symposia he "served the gods and presided over the distribution (*qsm'*) a whole year and supplied old wine for the priests a whole year from his house."

The Akkadian documents from Ugarit which mention the *marzēah* suggest that it was an important institution. The king Niqmepa bequeathed "a house of the *marzēah*-men" to the *marzēah*-men and their children. A house of the *marzēah*-men of (the god) Šatran was taken over for official use, but another house was given in its place. A vineyard of Ištar was divided between the *marzēah*-men of the city of Ari and those of the city of Siyanni. In a fragmentary Ugaritic alphabetic text (2032) there are five or six occurrences of the phrase *mrzh'n* [. . .] and in line 2 occur the words *šd*

kr [. . .], "field vineya[rd]." Eissfeldt proposed the restoration *mrzh 'n[t]* and suggested that the text may deal with the bequest of several vineyards to the *marzēah* (Kultverein) of Anat.

The connection between the *marzēah* and the funeral feast, attested in both biblical and rabbinic references, is confirmed by Ugarit data. Although there are no explicit references to the funeral character of the sacrificial banquet in which all the gods become drunk but El sits in his *mrzh* and topes till he sinks down as if dead, and although there are no hints of sexual activities in connection with this occasion which centers on El's hangover and its medicinal relief, there are elsewhere hints of sexual activity in connection with funeral feasts at Ugarit. The so-called Rephaim Texts, thus designated because of the frequent occurrence of the term (*rpum* in the nominative case and *rpim* in the oblique cases), which in biblical usage is connected with the departed dead, denizens of the netherworld, supply all the elements of a *marzēah*, a funeral feast to which the gods and the deified dead are invited to join with the mourners in a seven-day celebration with flesh and wine and with hints, at least, of sexual activity. The Rephaim Texts apparently belong to the Aqht Epic and fit into the action following the murder of Daniel's son Aqht. In spite of the fragmentary state of the texts and numerous lexical and grammatical uncertainties, it is apparent that Daniel invites the Rephaim to a *mrz'*, a variant form of *mrzh*, in a shrine (*atr*, "place") in his house.

From the various strands of evidence, we gather that the *marzēah* was a religious institution which included families and owned houses for meetings and vineyards for supply of wine, that the groups met periodically to celebrate seven-day feasts with rich food and drink and sometimes with sexual orgies. The biblical and rabbinic identification of these revels as funeral feasts is illustrated by a wealth of sepulchural sculpture depicting the deceased as participating in the banquet. The charge that the early Christians in their initiation rites immolated infants and ate their flesh and drank their blood is of interest in light of the cannibalistic language of the Eucharist in which the bread and wine are Christ's flesh and blood. The eating of the flesh and drinking of the juices of deceased loved ones is a primitive practice and is attested also at Ugarit. In a brief vignette inscribed on the back of a lexical text, the goddess Anat is depicted as consuming the flesh and blood of her brother consort (Baal):

> Anat went and waxed mad (?)
> At the beauty of her brother,
> And at the handsomeness of her brother,
>
> For he was fair.
> She ate his flesh without a knife,
> She drank his blood without a cup.

While we are not informed whether Anat's beauteous brother was alive or dead when she thus consumed him, we may reasonably assume that he was defunct and that this was a mourning rite motivated by what anthropologists have termed "morbid affection." M. Astour related Anat's cannibalism to the raw flesh feasts of the Dionysiac and Orphic orgies. It is apparent that the Christian Eucharist and Love-Feast, as well as the Jewish Qiddush, represent radical reformations of the ancient funeral feasts with elimination of such gross features as cannibalism, drunkenness, and sexual license. Paul's rebuke of unseemly behavior at the sacred meals and the charges ridiculed by Tertullian and Minucius Felix suggest that there were those who resisted reform and persisted in the old ways and this is confirmed by the repeated condemnations of other fathers of the Church.

In his first letter to the Christians at Corinth the Apostle Paul was distressed about licentious conduct in the festal meals when they partook of "spiritual" (pneumatic) food and drink, I Corinthians 10-11. Paul cited in censure of the Christian misbehavior the example of the Israelites' mode of worship of the Golden Calf: "The people sat down to eat and drink and rose up to sport (*paizein*)," I Cor 10:7. The kind of sport implied by the Hebrew term in Exod 32:6 (*lĕsahēq*) is clear from Isaac's uxorious play in Gen 26:8. Paul explicitly inveighed against fornication in these pneumatic feasts and cited as a warning the fate of the twenty-three thousand (give or take a thousand; cf. Num 25:9) who fell in a single day, with obvious reference to the affair at the shrine at Baal Peor, Numbers 25. We are told in Ps 106:28 that the cult of Baal Peor involved the eating of sacrifices for the dead. The rabbis further identify the festivities of Baal Peor as *marzĕhîm* and relate them to the infamous Mayumas festivals, a correlation supported by the Madeba Map which labels the area in which the scandal occurred as Marzēah-House, alias Mayumas.

The etymology of the term *marzēah* remains unclear. Joseph Qimhi, followed by his son David, connected the word with Arabic *mirzih* alleged to signify a vehement voice or loud cry as in mourning or revelry. Eissfeldt posited a meaning "unite" for the root *rzh* and took the word to designate a cultic union, "Kultverein." B. Porten regarded Eissfeldt's distinction between two supposed homonyms *rzh,* "shout," and *rzh,* "unite," to be arbitrary. The basic meaning of *rzh* in Arabic is to fall down from fatigue or other weakness and remain prostrate without power to rise; it may be used of a man, a camel, or a grapevine. A *marzah* is a place where a camel collapses from fatigue and a *mirzah* is a prop for a fallen grapevine. The collapse of El in his *mrzh* and the *mirzāh* of sprawled ones Amos 6:7 comport with this sense of the term. The celebrants at a *marzih, thiasos,* or symposium recline on couches and after several rounds of drink would, no doubt, be aptly

described as sprawling, or perhaps even more relaxed to the state of comatose stupor.

Whatever the etymology, it is apparent that the *marzih designated a bacchanalian celebration roughly synonymous with the Greek *thiasos* and *symposion.* The "Marzēah House" is thus virtually synonymous with the "Banquet House," *bêt mišteh* literally "house of drinking." Rabbi Aqiba anathematized those who trilled verses of the *Song of Songs* in "drinking houses" and this has been understood to mean that the good rabbi objected to the singing of snatches of the most holy song in the wine shops or taverns The banquet house, or drinking house, however, was not a tavern or pub, but rather a place for sacral feasting and drinking, as evidenced by Belshazzar's feast in the *bêt mištĕyā',* Dan 5:10, with the appropriation of the holy vessels, taken from the Jerusalem Temple for sacral drinking in praise of the heathen gods by the king and his nobles and courtesans, Dan 5:1-4,10. The more explicit term "house of the drinking of wine," *bêt mišteh hayyayin,* is used in Esther 7:8 when the king returned to the wine-fest and found Haman prostrate on the couch with Esther, Haman apparently being in a drunken stupor and unaware of his predicament. In the festival of Purim which is supposed to celebrate and commemorate the deliverance of the Jews through the elimination of their enemy Haman by the counterplot of Mordecai and Esther, it is nevertheless permissible and even obligatory to become more than moderately inebriated. It has been suggested that Purim is in reality a disguised "feast of the dead," related to the Persian All Souls' Day, *Farvardigan,* and that the feasting and gift-giving are survivals of offerings to the dead. The avoidance of the name of the God of Israel in the Book of Esther was explained as due to this original connection with the cult of the dead. It is of interest in this connection that Esther and the **Canticle** are the only biblical books which make no mention of the ineffable name.

The unique term "house of wine" in *Song of Songs* 2:4 is manifestly an elliptical expression for "house of the drinking of wine," as in Esther 7:8, since a musty wine cellar would hardly be an appropriate setting for the activity envisaged:

> He brought me into the wine house,
> His intent toward me Love.

Other details of the **Canticle** also are suggestive of orgiastic revelry. The lady requests stimulants to renew her jaded desire, 2:5,

> Sustain me with raisin cakes,
> Brace me with apples,
> For faint from love am I.

These raisin cakes survive today in Purim pastries called

Hamantaschen (corrupted from German *Mohntaschen,* "poppy pockets," from the practice of stuffing them with poppy seeds). These cuneiform tarts have nothing to do with Haman's three-cornered hat or his ears, but probably originally represented the pubes of Queen Esther=Ishtar, Queen of Heaven. The mandrakes mentioned in 7:14[13E] give further hint of interest in stimulation. The repeated adjuration, 2:7, 3:5, 8:4, relating to the arousal of love when it is willing, suggests protracted and repeated amative activity. The reference in 7:10[9E] to the fine wine gliding over the lips of sleepers (if one follows MT against the versions) is understandable on the supposition that one could continue to imbibe even in sleep, or while unconscious, by means of a drinking tube or with an attendant to dribble the wine through the lips In competitive drinking, contestants may recline and drink through tubes for maximum intake and effect. The dead too were provided with drink through tubes leading into the tombs. Thus the "sleepers" over whose lips the wine drips may refer to the funerary libation. It is striking, and perhaps no accident, that this verse evoked for the rabbis the image of deceased scholars whose lips move in the grave whenever a saying is cited in their name.

The references to myrrh, spice, honey, wine, and milk in a single verse of the **Canticle,** 5:1, are suggestive of the funeral feast since all these elements are associated with funerary rites and sacrifices. Myrrh and spices were used in anointing the corpse for burial. Spices were also used as condiments in the savory stew for the funeral meal. Ezek 24:10 mentions the mixing of spices in the preparation of the pottage symbolic of Babylon's evil:

> Heap the wood,
> Kindle the fire,
> Prepare the meat,
> Mix the spices,
> Let the bones cook.

(The emendation of *weharqah hammerqāhāh,* "mix the spices," on the basis of LXX *kai elattōthē ho zōmos,* "and let the liquor be boiled away," is a dubious procedure.) Libations for the dead in Homeric times included honey wine, and milk, as when Ulysses poured to the congregation of the dead libations of honey and milk and sweet wine (*Odyssey* xi 28f) and Achilles laid beside Patroclus' bier jars of honey and oil (*Iliad* xxiii 172). In all parts of the Aryan world honey was a food sacred to the dead. In India the *pitaras,* "fathers," were supplied rice soup mixed with honey, similar to the mead of barley water and honey served by the peasants of White Russia to their ancestors. In Greece honey cakes, *melitoutta,* were given to the dead and were believed also to appease the infernal watchdog Cerberus. Honey cakes continue as an essential part of the commemorative funeral meal among Lithuanian and Russian peasants. Herodotus reported (i 198)

that the Babylonians buried their dead in honey. The Spartans reportedly brought home the body of King Agesipolis preserved in honey and that of King Agesilaus in wax. A first-century epitaph from Crete bids the parents of three defunct brothers bring offerings of honeycomb and incense.

The open invitation of 5:1ef,

> Eat, friends, drink,
> Be drunk with love!

suggests the sort of climax to be expected in a thoroughly inebriated mixed group. Similar invitations are given in the Ugaritic texts, as when El says to his erstwhile spouse Asherah:

> Eat, yea drink!
> Eat from the tables meat,
> Drink from the jars wine;
> From a gold cup the blood of the vine.
>
> Lo, the affection of King El will arouse you,
> The Bull's love will excite you.

Or the invitation to the votaries in the ritual portion of the "Birth of the Beautiful Gods"

> Eat of the food, Ay!
> Drink of the foaming wine, Ay!
> Peace. O King,
> Peace, O Queen,
> O entrants and archers.

These invitations recall the frescoes of the catacombs and some of the uninhibited scenes which create the impression of a cosy drinking party, as described by F. van der Meer:

> Above the heads of the serving girls, who are hastening to supply the guests, stand the words: 'Agape, mix my wine! Eirene, give me some warm water!—phrases which certainly do not elevate the ladies Love and Peace to the status of heavenly allegories; incidentally these ladies make their appearance no less than four times—the painter was obviously repeating a stereotype.

Among the slogans in these scenes of Christian love feasts for the dead were the cry *Refrigera bene* which van der Meer rendered "Take good refreshment, eat and drink!" and *eis agapen,* "To the heavenly feast" (literally "to love") and above all *In pace.* According to van der Meer,

> The people who chiselled these mystical allusions did their work in the midst of pagans and in the midst of persecution; but that reverent atmosphere is now definitely a thing of the past. The food upon

the tables, once a thing so full of meaning, has achieved vestigial survival, but those at the table now have manners more suited to a pothouse, while the crude decorations represent nothing more than the husks of an ancient symbolism which now garnish the wine jugs of an ordinary, and distinctly convivial, wake!

Sepulchural gardens were common in the Graeco-Roman world, adjacent to the tombs, hence the technical term "garden tomb," *kēpotafion, cepotafium.* Strabo described the district west of Alexandria as containing many gardens *(kēpoi)* and tombs *(tafai).* Jocelyn M. C. Toynbee cites several inscriptions and documents referring to funerary gardens. Of particular interest is an inscription found near Rome, dating probably to the second century, set up by the parents in memory of their ten-year-old son. The text includes a prayer to Osiris to give the dead lad cool water. The parents made for the boy "an eternal bridal chamber" *(aiōnion nymphōna)* and for themselves in expectation of their death a garden tomb *(kēpotafion).* Toynbee wondered whether the "eternal bridal chamber" was "for mystic marriage with the god." Extensive evidence associating sacral sexual rites with mortuary celebrations should relieve somewhat the puzzlement at the designation of a tomb as an "eternal bridal chamber." Toynbee goes on to cite some of the very interesting Latinized versions of Greek funerary terminology. In addition to *cepotafium* and the diminutive *cepotafiolum,* there are the Latin terms *hortus, horti,* and *hortulus.* These sepulchural plots are frequently described as surrounded by an enclosure-wall *(murus, maceria).* The enclosed garden is reminiscent of the *gan / l nā'ûl,* the *hortus conclusus,* of **Canticles** 4:12.

In addition to the general words for buildings used in the funerary inscriptions in association with the gardens, such as edifice *(aedificia)* and monument *(monumenta),* there are words that refer specifically to the places where the funerary feasts were celebrated. There are references to dining rooms *(cenacula),* eating houses *(tabernae),* summer houses *(tricliae),* bars or lounges *(diaetae),* sun terraces *(solaria),* storehouses *(horrea),* and even, in one case, apparently, rooms to let(?) or brothels(?) *(stabula* and *meritoria).* In the sepulchural gardens were paths *(itinera).* Water was supplied by cisterns *(cisternae),* basins *(piscinae),* channels *(canales),* wells *(putei),* and pools *(lacus).* The funerary garden is variously described as a small estate *(praedolium),* a field *(ager),* or as orchards *(pomaria* or *pomariola).* One tomb was adorned with vines, fruit trees, flowers, and plants of all kinds, another with trees, vines and roses, and yet another with a vineyard and enclosure-walls. The funerary terminology is strikingly similar to certain expressions of the **Canticle**.

The garden-tomb setting and terminology of the Graeco-Roman mortuary cult recalls the reprimand of Second (or Third?) Isaiah, depicting Israel's God as constantly waiting and making overtures to an unresponsive people addicted to abominable rites in the funerary gardens:

> I was available to those who did not ask,
> Accessible to those who did not seek.
> I said, "Here I am! Here I am!"
> To a nation that did not call on my name.
> I spread my hands all day
> To a rebellious people
> Who walk in a no-good way,
> Following their own devices,
> A people who provoke me
> To my face, constantly,
> Sacrificing in the gardens,
> Burning incense on bricks,
> Sitting in the tombs,
> Spending the night in crypts,
> Eating pig meat,
> Carrion broth in their vessels.
> They say, "Stand back;
> Don't touch me, I'm holy to you."
> These are smoke in my nose,
> A fire that burns all day.
> Lo, it is written before me:
> "I will not be quiet, I will requite
> I will requite in the bosom
> Your crimes and your fathers' crimes
> Together," says the Lord.
> "Because they burned incense on the
>   mountains,
> Disgraced me on the hills,
> I will measure out their wage
> Promptly on their lap."

The Qumran Isaiah Scroll offers in 65:3d a reading radically different from MT. In place of MT's "and burning incense on the bricks," the Qumran text presents the provocative reading *wynqw ydym 'l h'bnym,* "and they suck / cleanse hands upon / as well as the stones." In view of the well-attested euphemistic use of "hand" for phallus and the possibility that *'l h'bnym* in Exod 1:16 refers to genitalia in general or testicles in particular, the verb *ynqw,* could be connected either with *ynq,* "suck," or *nqy,* meaning "cleanse" in the factitive or D stem. Fellatio would inevitably be suggested by *ynq.* It is hard to imagine how cleansing hands could be bad.

An Old Babylonian text published by J. J. Finkelstein (1966) has a bearing on the present concern with mortuary meals. Finkelstein's masterly treatment of the document established its "Sitz im Leben," that is, the reason it was written and the manner in which it was used. The text lists the ancestors of Ammisaduqa, last king of the First Dynasty of Babylon, and includes collectively "the dynasties of the Amorites, the Haneans, the Gutium, the dynasty not recorded on this tablet, and the soldier(s) who fell while on *perilous campaigns* for their (his) lord, princes, princesses, all persons from East to West who have neither caretaker *(pāqidum)* nor attendant *(sāhirum)*. All these are invited:

> Come ye, e(a)t this, (drin)k this, (and)
> Ammisaduqa, son of Ammiditana, the king of
>   Babylon, bless ye.

The restorations of the imperatives *aklā*, "eat ye," and *šityā*, "drink ye," in lines 39-40 are suggested by the traces of the poorly preserved signs as well as by the unmistakable context of the whole as a *kispu* offering which consisted of food and drink for the dead.

> The nature and function of the text as a whole is hardly open to doubt: it is the invocation to an actual memorial service to the dead, the central action of which was the offering to the *etemmū*—ghosts or spirits of the dead—of the *kispu*, which consisted of food and drink.

It is no ordinary *kispu* ceremony, however, of the standard sort held semi-monthly on the first and sixteenth day.

> The inclusion of the spirits of other than the dead ancestors, including even the ghosts of anyone and everyone "from East to West," who otherwise has none to offer them the *kispum*, suggests that the occasion was an extraordinary one, but the text itself offers no clue as to what it might have been. The performance might still have been scheduled for the first or sixteenth day of the month, but this would have been coincidental with some other momentous occasion which called for a more inclusive mortuary "feast." One might think of the coronation of the new king as an occasion suitable for such an expression of royal "largesse"—when perhaps even the living population received something above their normally miserable fare. What could be more appropriate for Ammisaduqa, as the newly crowned *šar mīšarim*, than to demonstrate his concern for his people's welfare by a special food distribution to all—to the dead as well as the living?

The present writer ventures to suggest that the occasion in question was a sort of Hallowmas, a feast for All Saints and Souls.

The affirmation 8:6c,d "For Love is strong as Death, / Passion fierce as Hell," has been generally recognized as the theme and message of the ***Song of Songs***. This is also the assurance of Paul's praise of love in I Cor 13:8: "Love never quits" *(hē agapē oudepote ekpiptei)*. "There are three things that last, Faith, Hope, Love— and Love is the greatest." The nature of the Love *(hē agapē)* which Paul commended to the Corinthians had little in common with the sort of love feasts which they were wont to celebrate. Nevertheless, these pagan love feasts were also a response to death with the assertion of life in its most basic modes of expression, eating, drinking, and copulation, all requisite for the continuation of life. Mother Earth, from whom man comes and to whom he returns, she who creates, nourishes, destroys, and takes man back into her ample womb, was worshiped at the ancestral graves with love feasts and commemorative rites to ensure the continuation of life. It is no accident that tombstones and memorial stelae are sometimes distinctly phallic in form, as often with the Greek *herma*, and that the term *yād*, "hand," in Ugaritic and Hebrew is applied to the phallus and in Hebrew to a memorial stela, while the terms for "memory" and "phallus" appear to be related to the same root, **dkr, zkr*. . . .

The Epistle of Jude inveighs against impious persons who had sneaked into the Christian community and had perverted the grace of God to an excuse for fornication and unnatural lust. These people are described, Jude 12, as "reefs *(spilades)* in your love feasts *(en tads agapais humon)*." In a parallel passage, II Peter 2:13, they are called "blots *(spiloi)* and blemishes *(momoi)* who revel in their love feasts" (choosing the variant *agapais* over *apatais*, "dissipations"). The charges and invectives laid on these subversives, Jude 8-26; II Peter 2:4-22, stress sexual licentiousness. The point of interest here is the explicit connection of this sort of conduct with the love feasts. Passing over the question of the relation of the Agape and the Eucharist (on which see the excellent treatment by A. J. Maclean in *ERE,* s.v. Agape), it will suffice to stress the original and essential character of these celebrations as mortuary meals, continuing the ancient and well-nigh universal practice of providing refreshment for the dead and sharing it with them in a communal and commemorative meal. Such celebrations from time immemorial had not infrequently featured orgiastic revelry, drunkenness, gluttony, cannibalism, incest, and sundry other excesses. In the early church the cult of the martyrs evolved quite naturally from the need to offer a tolerable substitute for these irrepressible practices. . . . As long as the offerings, whether to ancestors or martyrs, remained moderately decent affairs, there was no need to prohibit them. The charge that Christians offered food and wine to appease the shades of the martyrs Augustine rebutted with the argument that the altars were built to God in honor of the martyrs and not to the martyrs as if they were gods; honor was paid to the martyrs merely to encourage others to emulate them and share in their merits. It was doubtless difficult for newcomers to Christianity to appreciate the subtle difference between outwardly similar procedures in offerings to the ancestors and the martyrs. The toleration of the memorials for the martyrs was probably a concession to recent converts who were reluctant to relinquish the pleasures of the old-time revels. The trouble came when the grosser features of the pagan celebrations were carried over into the Christian love feasts, as the protests of early Christian writers attest. Augustine was tolerant toward the harmless sort of devotion to the saints and martyrs which his mother practiced, but not toward the drunken carousels carried on in some circles. When his mother Monica first came to Milan, she went to church with a basket of food and wine for the graves of the saints, as she had been accustomed to do in Africa, but was informed by the porter that this practice had been banned by the bishop. Augustine well understood the reasons for this ban imposed by Ambrose, since these meals for the saints were too much like pagan *parentalia* and served as an excuse for drunkenness. There were those who worshiped at the tombs, set food before the dead, drank to excess, and then attributed gluttony and drunkenness to religion. One should not judge Christianity, Augustine argued, by the behavior of the masses, who remained superstitious or were so enslaved to sensual pleasures that they forgot their promises to God. In his sermons Augustine tried to persuade the people that such excesses were pagan and did not derive from the stock and vine of justice of our patriarchs. Sir 30:18, which compares the placing of food on graves to putting dainties before a mouth that is closed, was explained as referring to a sick person who refuses food, since the Patriarchs kept no *parentalia*. Tobit 4:7, however, commands the deposit of food and pouring of wine on the graves of the just, but not on those of the wicked, and from this Augustine deduced that the faithful may perform this sort of *memorial* for their relatives provided it is done with pious intention. Those who persisted in heathen revelry, however, were blasted by Augustine: "The martyrs hate your wine jugs and cooking pots and your gluttony."

> There they bring bread and wine to the grave and call the dead by name. How often after his death they must have called out the name of the wealthy glutton when they got drunk in his mausoleum, and yet not a drop fell on his parched tongue.

Similarly Zeno of Verona inveighed in the style of the prophet Amos:

> God is displeased by those who run along to the gravesides, offer their lunch to stinking corpses and then in their desire to eat and drink suddenly, with pot and glass, conjure up martyrs at the most unfitting places.

The Donatists, in particular, were charged with utter wantonness, as

> those gangs of vagabonds who bury their own selves upon their graves in loathsome promiscuity, seducing one another into all manner of vice.

Madden in her summation modestly concluded that

> out of the pagan customs in honor of the dead, abuses developed in the festivals held to honor the memory of the martyrs. It became necessary to take measures against these abuses. The allusions to the traces of these customs relating to the honoring of the dead show that this phase of paganism had a strong hold on the hearts of the people, even after they had become Christians.

It is beyond the scope of this present effort to attempt any systematic treatment of funeral cults in the ancient world. The preceding discussion was intended merely to suggest that certain features of the **Song of Songs** may be understood in the light of the considerable and growing evidences that funeral feasts in the ancient Near East were love feasts celebrated with wine, women, and song. The Greek term *agapē*, Love, attached to these feasts certainly included *eros* as well as *philia*, to judge from the condemnations of drunkenness, fornication, and other excesses in the New Testament and the Church Fathers. The appearance of some of the characteristic terms of the **Canticle** in the Ugaritic mythological and ritual texts, especially in connection with the term *marzih*, and in the inscriptions from Palmyra which confirm and elucidate the connection of the *marzih / thiasos / symposion* with the funeral feast, opens new possibilities, yet to be fully tested and exploited, for the understanding of the cultic origins of the **Canticles**. This approach seems capable of explaining the **Canticles** better than any other and is able to subsume aspects of other modes of interpretation as enfolding elements of truth. The connection of the **Canticle** with the funeral feast as expressive of the deepest and most constant human concern for Life and Love in the ever present face of Death adds new insight and appreciation of our pagan predecessors who responded to Death with affirmations and even gross demonstrations of the power and persistence of Life and Love:

> Kî ʿazzāh kammawet ʾah bāh
> Hoti krataia hōs thanatos agapē
> Quia fortis est ut mors dilectio
>
> For Love is strong as Death.

Phyllis Trible (essay date 1978)

SOURCE: "Love's Lyrics Redeemed," in *God and the Rhetoric of Sexuality*, Fortress Press, 1978, pp. 144-65.

[*In the following essay, Trible explores thematic and structural links between the* Song of Songs *and the book of Genesis.*]

Love is bone of bone and flesh of flesh. Thus, I hear

the *Song of Songs*. It speaks from lover to lover with whispers of intimacy, shouts of ecstasy, and silences of consummation. At the same time, its unnamed voices reach out to include the world in their symphony of eroticism. This movement between the private and the public invites all companions to enter a garden of delight.

Genesis 2-3 is the hermeneutical key with which I unlock this garden. That narrative began with the development of Eros in four episodes: the forming of the earth creature, the planting of a garden, the making of animals, and the creation of sexuality. Alas, however, the fulfillment proclaimed when 'îš and 'iššâ became one flesh disintegrated through disobedience. As a result, Yahweh God drove out generic man and invisible woman from the garden, and "at the east of the garden of Eden he placed the cherubim, and a flaming sword which turned every way, to guard the way to the tree of life." Clearly, Genesis 2-3 offers no return to the garden of creation. And yet, as scripture interpreting scripture, it provides my clue for entering another garden of Eros, the *Song of Songs*. Through expansions, omissions, and reversals, this poetry recovers the love that is bone of bone and flesh of flesh. In other words, the *Song of Songs* redeems a love story gone awry. Taking clues from Genesis 2, then, let us acquire first an overview of the form and content of the *Song*.

READING THE MUSICAL SCORE

Expanding upon the lyrics of eroticism in Genesis 2, three human voices compose this new *Song*. They belong to a woman, a man, and a group of women, the daughters of Jerusalem. Independent of logical progression or plot development, these voices flow freely and spontaneously to yield a series of metaphors in which many meanings intertwine simultaneously. At times, the standard, the figurative, and the euphemistic converge so compellingly that one cannot discern where vehicle ends and tenor begins. Often the language is elusive, holding its treasures in secret for the lovers themselves. Occasionally the identity of the speaker is uncertain, creating a problem for observers but not for participants who know that in Eros all voices mingle. Hence, the poetry of the *Song* resists calculations and invites imagination. The visual must be heard; the auditory, seen. Love itself blends sight, sound, sense, and non-sense. In these ways, the voices of the *Song of Songs* extol and enhance the creation of sexuality in Genesis 2.

Of the three speakers, the woman is the most prominent. She opens and closes the entire *Song*, her voice dominant throughout. By this structural emphasis her equality and mutuality with the man is illuminated. The arrangement recalls the stress placed upon the woman at the conclusion of Genesis 2: although equal

with the man in creation, she was, nonetheless, elevated in emphasis by the design of the story. In the *Song of Songs*, accent upon the female is further increased by the presence of the daughters of Jerusalem. As a foil and complement to the lovers, this group aids the flow of the action. Women, then, are the principal creators of the poetry of eroticism.

Strikingly, God does not speak in the *Song*; nor is the deity even mentioned. This divine absence parallels the withdrawal of Yahweh God in Genesis 2 precisely where the poem of eroticism emerged. After making the woman and bringing her to the transformed earth creature, the deity disappeared from scene one. Then the earth creature spoke for the first time:

> This, finally, bone of my bones
>   and flesh of my flesh.
> This shall be called 'iššâ
>   because from 'îš was differentiated this.

Just as the tenor of this poem continues in the *Song of Songs*, so appropriately does its setting. Yahweh God, who created male and female, withdraws when lovers discover themselves, speak the revelation, and become one flesh.

The cyclic design of Genesis 2 is also reflected and developed in the *Song*. Originally, the creation of humanity found its fulfillment in the creation of sexuality: the earth creature became two, male and female, and those two became one flesh. With such an erotic completion, the *Song of Songs* begins, continues, and concludes. As a symphony of love, it unfolds in five major movements of varying lengths. At the conclusions of the first four sections, the woman utters a refrain that both separates and joins these movements. It begins, "I adjure you, O daughters of Jerusalem." Clusters of verbal motifs that precede this refrain further interrelate the five movements, yielding an ebb and a flow among the images of the *Song*. An examination of the beginnings and endings of these movements shows the cyclic pattern of the overall composition.

The introductory movement extends from 1:2 to 2:7. By speaking first *about* her lover, rather than directly *to* him, the woman invites us to enter their circle of intimacy:

> O that he would kiss me with the kisses of
>   his mouth!

With the words of her mouth she reaches many; for the kisses of her mouth she desires only one. And by the end of the movement her yearnings are realized:

> His left hand is under my head,
>   and his right hand embraces me!

This verse appears again at the conclusion of the fourth movement, thus providing one of the many verbal links between sections. Since, with these words, the woman's desire has been fulfilled, she completes the introductory movement by imploring the daughters of Jerusalem to let love happen according to its own rhythm:

> I adjure you, O daughters of Jerusalem,
>   by the gazelles or the hinds of the field,
> that you stir not up nor awaken love
>   until it please.

Having begun the first movement by seeking the touch of her lover's mouth, the woman commences the second by invoking the speech of his lips:

> The voice of my lover!
>   Behold, he comes,
> leaping upon the mountains,
>   bounding over the hills.

She concludes this section by seeking and finding her man:

> Upon my bed by night
>   I sought him whom my *nephesh* loves;
> I sought him, but found him not;
>   I called him, but he gave no answer.
> "I will rise now and go about the city,
>   in the streets and in the squares;
> I will seek him whom my *nephesh* loves."
>   I sought him but found him not.
> The watchmen found me,
>   as they went about in the city.
> Him whom my *nephesh* loves, have you seen?
> Scarcely had I passed them,
>   when I found him whom my *nephesh* loves.
> I held him, and would not let him go
>   until I had brought him into my mother's
>   house,
>   and into the chamber of her that conceived
>   me.

The motifs of the search, the watchmen, and the mother's house surface again in various combinations in the conclusions of the third and fourth movements. Coming together here in the encounter of love, they allow the woman to close this second movement exactly as she did the first. Thus, she implores the daughters of Jerusalem to let love happen according to its own rhythm.

She opens the third movement with a question about her lover:

> What is that coming up from the wilderness,
>   like a column of smoke,
> perfumed with myrrh and frankincense,

> with all the fragrant powders of the
> merchant?

To end this section, she returns, with variations, to two of the themes at the conclusion of the second movement: the seeking, but not the finding, of the lover and her discovery by the watchmen, who this time not only fail to help but actually assault her:

> My *nephesh* failed because of him.
> I sought him, but found him not;
>   I called him, but he gave no answer.
> The watchmen found me,
>   as they went about in the city;
> they beat me, they wounded me,
> they took away my mantle,
>   those watchmen of the walls.

Exact verbal correspondences between the endings of movements two and three establish parallelism in their structure and content. The differences between them, on the other hand, sustain the tempo and flow of the poetry. Point and counterpoint shape the rhythm of love:

> *3:1-3a (Second Movement)*
> Upon my bed by night
>   I sought him whom my *nephesh* loves;
> <u>I sought him but found him not;</u>
>   <u>I called him but he gave no answer.</u>
> "I will rise now and go about the city,
>   in the streets and in the squares;
> I will seek him whom my *nephesh* loves."
> I sought him but found him not.
> <u>The watchmen found me,</u>
>   <u>as they went about in the city.</u>

> *5:6b-7 (Third Movement)*
> My *nephesh* failed because of him.
> <u>I sought him, but found him not;</u>
>   <u>I called him, but he gave no answer.</u>
> <u>The watchmen found me,</u>
>   <u>as they went about in the city;</u>
> they beat me, they wounded me,
>   they took away my mantle,
>   those watchmen of the walls.

At the very end of the third movement, the woman alters the refrain of adjuration to fit the situation that now exists. Since, contrary to the ending of the second movement (3:4), she does not find her lover, she enlists the daughters of Jerusalem in her search:

> I adjure you, O daughters of Jerusalem,
>   if you find my lover,
> that you tell him
>   I am sick with love.

The words "I am sick with love" repeat a line from the

closing sentiments of the first section, thereby showing another interplay among the motifs of the poem. Although these words led to fulfillment in the first movement, here they but long for consummation.

Linked closely to the third movement, the fourth commences with questions by the daughters, who are responding to the woman's plea in the preceding refrain of adjuration:

> What is your lover more than another lover,
>   O fairest among women?
> What is your lover more than another lover
>   that you thus adjure us?

This interrogative style parallels the woman's question at the beginning of the third section. And the closing speech of the fourth movement belongs again to the woman. She caresses the man with her voice:

> O that you were like a brother to me,
>   that nursed at my mother's breast!
> If I met you outside, I would kiss you,
>   and none would despise me.
> I would lead you and bring you
>   into the house of my mother,
>   and into the chamber of her that conceived
>   me.
> I would give you spiced wine to drink,
>   the juice of my pomegranates.
> His left hand is under my head,
>   and his right hand embraces me!

Like the end of the third section, this conclusion also returns, with variations, to motifs first appearing at the end of the second movement: finding the lover and bringing him to the house of the mother who conceived her. In the second movement, the woman sought the help of the watchmen and then spoke about her actions toward her lover. Now in the fourth, she addresses her intentions to him directly. Though her reference to "none would despise me" may allude to the watchmen who have since assaulted her, that group is not involved in this ending. Once again, however, exact verbal correspondences between the conclusions of two movements confirm the parallelism in their structure and content, while, on the other hand, differences between them enhance the rhythm of the poetry:

3:3b-4 (Second Movement)
Him whom my *nephesh* loves,
   have you seen?

Scarcely had I passed them when <u>I found him</u>
   whom my *nephesh* loves.
I held him and would not let him go
   until <u>I had brought him</u> <u>into my mother's</u>
<u>house,</u>

<u>and into the chamber of her that conceived</u>
<u>me.</u>

8:1-2a (Fourth Movement)
O that you were like a brother to me,
   that nursed at my mother's breast!
If <u>I found you</u> outside, I would kiss you,
   and none would despise me.
<u>I would lead you and bring you</u> <u>into my</u>
<u>mother's house</u>
<u>and into the chamber of her that conceived</u>
<u>me.</u>

The word *kiss* in the speech of the woman to the man recalls the opening line of the first movement, "O that he would kiss me with the kisses of his mouth." The touch she desired, she now gives: "If I found you outside, I would kiss you." Moreover, in the beginning of the first section, she declared that his "love is better than wine," and at its end she reported that "he brought me to the *house* of wine." Now, immediately after leading her lover to the *house* of her mother, she says:

> I would give you spiced wine to drink,
>   the juice of my pomegranates.

These allusions to the introductory movement are confirmed by the ensuing words of the woman. They repeat verbatim her last statement in the opening section:

> His left hand is under my head
>   and his right hand embraces me!

With this description the woman ceases to address the man directly and returns to the pattern of third-person narration that she has consistently used at the end of all the preceding movements. Thus she wavers between distance and intimacy.

Finally, the refrain of the fourth movement echoes, with variation, the adjurations of the first and second. Though the gazelles and the hinds of the fields are missing, the rhythm of love is again affirmed:

> I adjure you, O. daughters of Jerusalem,
>   that you stir not up nor awaken love until it
>   please.

Like the third and fourth movements, the fifth begins with a question. Perhaps the daughters ask it, since they similarly introduced the fourth movement.

> Who is that coming up from the wilderness,
>   leaning upon her lover?

To conclude this unit, the woman speaks, as indeed she has done at the close of each section. In all these instances, she has referred to the man in the third person, though in the fourth movement she also addressed him directly. In this final movement, however, distance and ambivalence vanish altogether. Intimacy triumphs. The woman summons her man to love:

> Make haste, my lover,
>   and be like a gazelle
> or a young stag
>   upon the mountains of spices.

No refrain of adjuration follows these closing words: with the consummation of Eros it is unnecessary. Thus, the daughters of Jerusalem disappear, and we, the readers, must also withdraw. Just as the first words of the woman at the very beginning of the *Song* invited us to enter the circle of intimacy, so her last words deny us further participation. In the end she speaks directly and only to her lover, the bone of her bone and the flesh of her flesh. The man of Genesis 2 once left his father and mother to cleave to his woman; now the woman of the *Song* bids her man make haste, and in this bidding all others are left behind. The circle of intimacy closes in exclusion when two become one.

As a symphony of love, the *Song of Songs* unfolds in five major movements: 1:2-2:7; 2:8-3:5; 3:6-5:8; 5:9-8:4; 8:5-14. The beginnings and endings of these sections demonstrate the interweaving of cyclic patterns in the overall structure. Through the convergence of form and content, these patterns recall cyclic designs throughout Genesis 2. Moreover, several themes in Genesis 2:21-24 have also enhanced our reading of this musical score: the creation and consummation of sexuality; an erotic poem; emphasis upon the female in the design of the literature; and the absence of God when female and male unite. Building upon this interpretation, let us explore leitmotifs within the *Song of Songs* that further reflect and elucidate Genesis 2-3.

EXPLORING VARIATIONS ON A THEME

A garden *(gan)* in Eden locates the tragedy of disobedience in Genesis 2-3. But the garden itself signals delight, not disaster, and that perspective reverberates in the *Song of Songs*. The woman is the garden *(gan)*, and to the garden her lover comes. This vocabulary appears first in the third movement when the man describes love withheld:

> A garden locked is my sister, my bride,
>   a garden locked, a fountain sealed.

Immediately the woman responds, offering her garden to him:

> Awake, O north wind,
>   and come, O south wind!
> Blow upon *my* garden,
>   let its fragrance be wafted abroad.

> Let my lover come to *his* garden,
>   and eat its choicest fruits.

The man accepts the invitation, claiming her garden as his own:

> I come to *my* garden, my sister, my bride.

This imagery of intercourse continues in the fourth movement. Answering questions from the daughters of Jerusalem, the woman says:

> My lover has gone down to his garden,
>   to the beds of spices,
> to pasture in the gardens,
>   and to gather lilies.

And in the fifth movement, the last words of the man address the woman with the same motif:

> O you who dwell in the gardens,
>   my companions are listening for your voice;
> let me hear it.

Male and female first became one flesh in the garden of Eden. There a narrator reported briefly their sexual union. Now in another garden, the lovers themselves praise at length the joys of intercourse. Possessive adjectives do not separate their lives. "My garden" and "his garden" blend in mutual habitation and harmony. Even person and place unite: the garden of eroticism is the woman.

In this garden the sensuality of Eden expands and deepens. Emerging gradually in Genesis 2-3, all five senses capitulated to disobedience through the tasting of the forbidden fruit. Fully present in the *Song of Songs* from the beginning, these senses saturate the poetry to serve only love. Such love is sweet to the taste, like the fruit of the apple tree. Fragrant are the smells of the vineyards, the perfumes of myrrh and frankincense, the scent of Lebanon, and the beds of spices. The embraces of lovers confirm the delights of touch. A glance of the eyes ravishes the heart, as the sound of the lover thrills it. Taste, smell, touch, sight, and hearing permeate the garden of the *Song*.

Plants also adorn this place of pleasure—"every tree that is pleasant to the sight and good for food." Again, what the storyteller in Genesis reported succinctly, the voices in the *Song* praise extensively. They name not only the trees, but also the fruits and the flowers. For instance, in the first movement the woman describes herself to the man:

> I am a lotus of the plain,
>   a lily of the valleys.

The word *lily* suggests to the man an extravagant comparison, to which even the thorns and thistles of the earth contribute:

> As a lily among brambles,
>   so is my love among women.

The woman replies in kind:

> As an apple among the trees of the wood,
>   so is my lover among men.

Yet her comparison does not stop there. She expands upon images from the plant world to portray the joy her lover embodies:

> In his shadow I delight to rest
>   and his fruit is sweet to my taste.
> He brought me to the house of wine
>   and his emblem over me was love.
> Strengthen me with raisin cakes,
>   refresh me with apples,
> for faint with love am I.

Throughout the *Song of Songs* other members of the plant world further specify "every tree pleasant to the sight and good for food": the mandrake, the fig tree, the pomegranate, the cedar, the palm, and "all trees of frankincense." And among these many plants, no tree of disobedience grows. Instead, the lovers offer an open invitation to eat freely of every tree of the garden, as well as to drink from its fountain of delight. In their world of harmony, prohibition does not exist:

> Eat, O friends, and drink:
>   drink deeply, O lovers!

The invitation to drink follows a description of the abundance of water that fills the garden:

> a garden fountain, a well of living water,
>   and flowing streams from Lebanon.

This imagery recalls the subterranean stream that watered the earth before creation (Gen. 2:6) and clearly invites comparison with the river flowing out of Eden to nourish that garden. In both settings, food and water enhance life.

Animals as well inhabit these two gardens. In Genesis 2:18-20 their creation was marked with ambivalence. Closely identified with the earth creature, they were, nevertheless, a disappointment, for among them "was not found a companion fit for it." Indeed, the power which the earth creature exercised in naming the animals underscored their inadequacy for humankind. Yet, conversely, the animals provided a context for the joy of human sexuality. In Genesis 3, however, the ambivalence of their creation yielded completely to the villainous portrayal of the serpent. The most clever of all wild animals beguiled the naked couple to become their perpetual enemy. In the garden of Eden, then, the animals lived in tension with the human creatures.

But in the garden of the *Song of Songs* this tension disappears. No serpent bruises the heel of female or male; no animals are indicted as unfit companions for humankind. To the contrary, the beasts of the field and the birds of the air now become synonyms for human joy. Their names are metaphors for love. Scattered throughout the movements of the poetry, these creatures are often used for physical descriptions of the lovers. In the opening poem of the second movement, for example, the woman limns her mate:

> leaping upon the mountains,
>   bounding over the hills,
> My lover is like a gazelle,
>   or a young stag.

To these images she returns in the closing lines of the *Song*. In other places she compares her lover's black hair to a raven and his eyes to "doves beside springs of water." Similarly, the man depicts the beauty of the woman in animal metaphors:

> Behold, you are beautiful, my love,
>   behold, you are beautiful!
> Your eyes are doves
>   behind your veil.
> Your hair is like a flock of goats,
>   moving down the slopes of Gilead.
> Your teeth are like a flock of shorn ewes
>   that have come up from the washing,
> Each having its twin,
>   and not one of them is bereaved. . . .
>
>
> Your two breasts are like two fawns,
>   twins of a gazelle,
>   that feed among the lilies.

The mare, the turtledove, and the lions and the leopards also dwell in this garden where all nature extols the love of female and male. Clearly, the *Song of Songs* banishes the ambivalence toward animals that Genesis 2 introduced, just as it knows nothing of the villainous serpent in Genesis 3. Even the little foxes that spoil the vineyards can be captured by love. Thus, all animals serve Eros.

Work and play belong together in both the garden of creation and the garden of eroticism. To till and keep the garden of Eden was delight until the primeval couple disobeyed, causing the ground to bring forth thorns and thistles and work to become pain and sweat. In the first movement of the *Song of Songs*, the woman transforms the pain of work into pleasure. At the command of her mother's sons, she keeps vineyards under the scorching sun; yet, undaunted by this experience of forced labor, she associates it with play:

> The sons of my mother were angry at me;
>   they made me keeper of the vineyards.
> My own vineyard I have not kept!

Identifying herself with a vineyard, the woman hints that her lover is *its* keeper. Such playfulness directs her to the man, with another allusion to work:

> Tell me, you whom my *nephesh* loves,
>   where do you pasture?

The man may well be a shepherd, but for the woman his occupation is the play of intercourse. After all, he pastures among the lilies, and she herself is a lily. By analogy, the man is also a king, but he neither rules nor dispenses wisdom. Instead, he provides luxury for the sake of love. Hence, throughout the garden of the *Song*, sexual play intertwines with work, redeeming it beyond the judgments of Genesis 3:16-19.

Familial references offer still another study in contrasts. Although in Genesis 2 the creation of male and female was totally independent of parents, in the *Song of Songs* the births of the lovers are linked to their mothers, though the fathers are never mentioned. Seven times, at least once in every movement, the word *mother* appears in the poetry. The man calls his love the special child of the mother who bore *(yld)* her, even as the woman cites the travail of the mother who bore *(yld)* him. Appropriately, both these references allude to the beauty of birth; they know nothing at all of the multiplication of pain in childbearing. Moreover, in yearning for closeness with her lover, the woman wishes that he were a brother nursing at the breast of her mother. Again, she parallels the desire for sexual union with her own conception; thus, she wants to lead the man

> into the house of my mother,
> and into the chamber of her
>   that conceived me.

This entry into the mother's house for intercourse suggests its opposite in Genesis 2:24. There the man broke up a family for the sake of sexual union. He left his father and mother to cleave to his woman. Standing alone, without parents, the woman was highlighted as the one to whom he must come. In the *Song*, the woman is emphasized, by contrast, as the one who brings the man into her mother's house. From different perspectives, two other passages in the *Song* also mention the mother. The woman identifies her brothers as "sons of my mother," and later she beholds King Solomon

> with the crown with which his mother
>   crowned him

on the day of his wedding,
on the day of the gladness of his heart.

Unquestionably, these seven references to mother, without a single mention of father, underscore anew the prominence of the female in the lyrics of love. Once again, then, the *Song of Songs* expands and varies a theme present in Genesis 2-3.

Belonging to a historical rather than a primeval setting, the *Song* also extends the witnesses to love beyond the human inhabitants of Eden. Certain groups are hostile, for not all the world loves a lover. Specifically, the woman encounters anger from her brothers and physical assault from the watchmen of the city. But other witnesses celebrate the happiness and beauty of the lovers: kings; queens and concubines; warriors, indeed, an army with banners; merchants with their fragrant powders; shepherds; and the daughters of Jerusalem. Moreover, the woman herself exults that other women, as well as men, adore her mate. In their attraction for him, she finds joy, not jealousy:

> your name is oil poured out;
>   therefore, *the maidens* love you.
> Draw me after you, let us make haste.
>   The king has brought me into his chambers.
> We will exult and rejoice in you;
>   we will extol your love more than wine;
>   rightly do *they* [masculine] love you.

Similarly, the man rejoices that other men, as well as women, delight in his partner:

> O you who dwell in the gardens,
> *my companions* [masculine] are listening for
>   your voice;
> let me hear it. . . .

> *The maidens* saw her and called her happy;
> *the queens and concubines* also, and they
>   praised her.

Throughout the *Song*, Eros is inclusive; the love between two welcomes the love and companionship of many. Only at the end does exclusion close this circle of intimacy.

On two occasions the woman expresses intimacy by the formula "My lover is mine, and I am his." This interchange of pronouns parallels the union of "my garden" with "his garden." Love is harmony. Neither male nor female asserts power or possession over the other. In light of Genesis 3:16, a third expression of this idea is particularly striking. The woman says, "I am my lover's and for me is his desire." Her use of the word *desire (t*šûqâ)* echoes, in contrast, the divine judgment upon the first woman: "Your desire *[t*šûqâ]* shall be for your man, but he shall rule over you." In

Eden, the yearning of the woman for harmony with her man continued after disobedience. Yet the man did not reciprocate; instead, he ruled over her to destroy unity and pervert sexuality. Her desire became his dominion. But in the **Song**, male power vanishes. His desire becomes her delight. Another consequence of disobedience is thus redeemed through the recovery of mutuality in the garden of eroticism. Appropriately, the woman sings the lyrics of this grace: "I am my lover's and for me is his desire."

A further hint of redemption comes in the way the word *name* is used in the two gardens. When the transformed earth creature called the woman *'iššâ* (and himself *'îš*), he did not name her but rather rejoiced in the creation of sexuality. But when the disobedient man called his woman's *name (šēm)* Eve, he ruled over her to destroy their one flesh of equality. On the other hand, the opening lines of the **Song of Songs** convert the motif of the name to the service of sexual fulfillment. The woman herself utters this word in a pun of adoration for the man:

> For better is your love than wine;
>   your anointing oils are fragrant;
> oil [*šemen*] poured out is your *name* [*šᵉmekā*].

Rather than following her man out of the garden, this woman bids him bring her to his palace of pleasure: "Draw me after you, let us make haste." For her, naming is ecstasy, not dominion. A new context marks a new creation.

Love redeemed meets even death unflinchingly. Although the threat of death belonged to the creation of Eros, it was through human disobedience that death became the disintegration of life. Harmony gave way to hostility; unity and fulfillment to fragmentation and dispersion. In the closing movement of the **Song of Songs**, this tragedy is reversed. Once again, eroticism can embrace the threat of death. The woman says

> Let me be a seal upon your heart,
> Like the seal upon your hand.
> For love is fierce as death,
> Passion is mighty as Sheol;
> Its darts are darts of fire,
> A blazing flame.

But she does more than affirm love as the equal of death. She asserts triumphantly that not even the primeval waters of chaos can destroy Eros:

> Many waters cannot quench love,
>   neither can floods drown it.

As a "garden fountain, a well of living water *[mayîm hayyîm]*," a woman in love prevails over the many waters *(mayîm rabbîm)* of chaos. With such assur-

ances, the poetry moves inexorably to its consummation.

COMPLETING THE *SONG*

Using Genesis 2-3 as a key for understanding the **Song of Songs**, we have participated in a symphony of love. Born to mutuality and harmony, a man and a woman live in a garden where nature and history unite to celebrate the one flesh of sexuality. Naked without shame or fear, this couple treat each other with tenderness and respect. Neither escaping nor exploiting sex, they embrace and enjoy it. Their love is truly bone of bone and flesh of flesh, and this image of God male and female is indeed very good. Testifying to the goodness of creation, then, eroticism becomes worship in the context of grace.

In this setting, there is no male dominance, no female subordination, and no stereotyping of either sex. Specifically, the portrayal of the woman defies the connotations of "second sex." She works, keeping vineyards and pasturing flocks. Throughout the **Song** she is independent, fully the equal of the man. Although at times he approaches her, more often she initiates their meetings. Her movements are bold and open: at night in the streets and squares of the city she seeks the one whom her *nephesh* loves. No secrecy hides her yearnings. Moreover, she dares to describe love with revealing metaphors:

> My lover put his hand to the latch,
>   and my womb trembled within me.

Never is this woman called a wife, nor is she required to bear children. In fact, to the issues of marriage and procreation the **Song** does not speak. Love for the sake of love is its message, and the portrayal of the female delineates this message best.

Though love is fulfilled when the woman and the man close the circle of intimacy to all but themselves, my imagination posits a postlude to the poetry. In this fantasy "the cherubim and a flaming sword" appear to guard the entrance to the garden of the **Song**. They keep out those who lust, moralize, legislate, or exploit. They also turn away literalists. But at all times they welcome lovers to romp and roam in the joys of eroticism:

> <u>Arise, my love, my fair one,</u>
>   <u>and come away;</u>
> for lo, the winter is past,
>   the rain is over and gone.
> The flowers appear on the earth,
>   the time of pruning has come,
> and the voice of the turtledove
>   is heard in our land.
> The fig tree puts forth its figs,

and the vines are in blossom;
they give forth fragrance.
<u>Arise, my love, my fair one,</u>
<u>and come away.</u>

Thus far we have studied two portrayals of male and female in the Old Testament. Genesis 2-3 depicted a tragedy of disobedience; the **Song of Songs**, a symphony of eroticism. . . .

Lines from the fourth verse of the *Song*

how fair you are, my friend

how fair you are
your eyes of doves
besides that which lies within
your hair like a flock of goats
which have come up from Mount Galaad
your teeth like a flock of shearlings
that have come up from a washing
all pregnant with twins
and no one barren among them
your lips like a band of scarlet
and your speech is sweet
like grains of pomegranates so your cheeks
besides that which lies within
like a tower of David your neck
which is built with bulwarks
a thousand shields hang from it
all the armor of strong men
your two breasts like two kids
twins who pasture among the lilies
until the day breathes and the shadows lean
I will go to the mountains of myrrh and to the
hill of frankincense
you are all fair, my friend
and there is no spot in you

From the translation by E. Ann Matter in The
Voice of My Beloved, *University of
Pennsylvania Press, 1990.*

Robert Alter (essay date 1985)

SOURCE: "The Garden of Metaphor," in *The Art of Biblical Poetry,* Basic Books, Inc., Publishers, 1985, pp. 185-203.

[In the following essay, Alter conducts a close formal analysis of the Song of Songs *as poetry, exploring the work's imagery and metaphor. Alter finds the* Song *a rare instance in biblical poetry of "uninhibited self-delighting play" and "elegant aesthetic form."]*

The **Song of Songs** comprises what are surely the most exquisite poems that have come down to us from an-

cient Israel, but the poetic principles on which they are shaped are in several ways instructively untypical of biblical verse. When it was more the scholarly fashion to date the book late, either in the Persian period (W. F. Albright) or well into the Hellenistic period (H. L. Ginsberg), these differences might have been attributed to changing poetic practices in the last centuries of biblical literary activity. Several recent analysts, however, have persuasively argued that all the supposed stylistic and lexical evidence for a late date is ambiguous, and it is quite possible, though not demonstrable, that these poems originated, whatever subsequent modifications they may have undergone, early in the First Commonwealth period.

The most likely sources of distinction between the **Song of Songs** and the rest of biblical poetry lie not in chronology but in genre, in purpose, and perhaps in social context. Although there are some striking love motifs elsewhere in biblical poetry—in Psalms, between man and God, in the Prophets, between God and Israel—the **Song of Songs** is the only surviving instance of purely secular love poetry from ancient Israel. The erotic symbolism of the Prophets would provide later ages an effective warrant for reading the **Song of Songs** as a religious allegory, but in fact the continuous celebration of passion and its pleasures makes this the most consistently secular of all biblical texts—even more so than Proverbs, which for all its pragmatic worldly concerns also stresses the fear of the Lord and the effect of divine justice on the here and now. We have no way of knowing the precise circumstances under which or for which the **Song of Songs** was composed. A venerable and persistent scholarly theory sees it as the (vestigial?) liturgy of a fertility cult; others—to my mind, more plausibly—imagine it as a collection of wedding songs. What I should like to reject at the outset is the whole quest for the "life-setting" of the poems—because it is, necessarily, a will-o'-the-wisp and, even more, because it is a prime instance of the misplaced concreteness that has plagued biblical research, which naively presumes that the life-setting, if we could recover it, would somehow provide the key to the language, structure, and meaning of the poems.

The imagery of the **Song of Songs** is a curious mixture of pastoral, urban, and regal allusions, which leaves scant grounds for concluding whether the poems were composed among shepherds or courtiers or somewhere in between. References in rabbinic texts suggest that at least by the Roman period the poems were often sung at weddings, and, whoever composed them, there is surely something popular about these lyric celebrations of the flowering world, the beauties of the female and male bodies, and the delights of lovemaking. The Wisdom poetry of Job and Proverbs was created by members of what one could justifiably call the ancient Israelite intelligentsia. Prophetic verse was produced by individuals who belonged—by sensibility and in several signal instances by virtue of social background as well—to a spiritual-intellectual elite. The psalms were tied to the cult, and at least a good many of them were probably created in priestly circles (the mimetic example of short prayers embedded in biblical narrative suggests that ordinary people, in contradistinction to the professional psalm-poets, may have improvised personal prayers in simple prose). It is only in the ***Song of Songs*** that there is no one giving instruction or exhortation, no leader or hierophant, no memorializer of national experience, but instead the voices of two lovers, praising each other, yearning for each other, proffering invitations to enjoy. I shall not presume to guess whether these poems were composed by folk poets, but it is clear that their poetic idiom is one that, for all its artistic sophistication, is splendidly accessible to the folk, and that may well be the most plausible explanation for the formal differences from other kinds of biblical poetry.

To begin with, semantic parallelism is used here with a freedom one rarely encounters in other poetic texts in the Bible. Since virtually the whole book is a series of dramatic addresses between the lovers, this free gliding in and out of parallelism—the very antithesis of the neat boxing together of matched terms in Proverbs—may be dictated in part by the desire to give the verse the suppleness and liveliness of dramatic speech. Thus the very first line of the collection: "Let him kiss me with the kisses of his mouth, / for your love is better than wine." The relation of the second verses to the first is not really parallelism but explanation—and a dramatically appropriate one at that, which is reinforced by the move from third person to second: your kisses, my love are more delectable than wine, which is reason enough for me to have declared at large my desire for them.

In many lines, the second verset is a prepositional or adverbial modifier of the first verset—a pattern we have encountered occasionally elsewhere but which here sometimes occurs in a whole sequence of lines, perhaps as part of an impulse to apprehend the elaborate and precious concreteness of the object evoked instead of finding a matching term for it. Here, for example, is the description of Solomon's royal palanquin:

1 Who is this coming up from the desert
   like columns of smoke
2 Perfumed with myrrh and frankincense
   of all the merchant's powders?
3 Look, Solomon's couch,
   sixty warriors round it
   of the warriors of Israel,
4 All of them skilled with sword,
   trained in war,
5 Each with sword on thigh,
   for terror in the nights.
6 A litter King Solomon made him

   of wood from Lebanon.
7 Its posts he made of silver,
   its bolster gold,
   its cushion purple wool,
8 Its inside decked with love
   by the daughters of Jerusalem.

The only strictly parallelistic lines here are 4 and 7. For the rest, the poet seems to be reaching in his second (and third) versets for some further realization of the object, of what it is like, where it comes from: What surrounds Solomon's couch? Why are the warriors arrayed with their weapons? Who is it who has so lovingly upholstered the royal litter?

Now, the picture of a perfumed cloud ascending from the desert, with a splendid palanquin then revealed to the eye of the beholder, first with its entourage, afterward with its luxurious fixtures, also incorporates narrative progression; and because the collection involves the dramatic action of lovers coming together or seeking one another (though surely not, as some have fancied, in a formal drama), narrativity is the dominant pattern in a number of the poems. Such narrativity is of course in consonance with a general principle of parallelistic verse in the Bible, as one can see clearly in single lines like this: "Draw me after you, let us run—/ the king has brought me to his chambers." The difference is that in the ***Song of Songs*** there are whole poems in which all semblance of semantic equivalence between versets is put aside for the sake of narrative concatenation from verses to verses and from line to line. I will quote the nocturnal pursuit of the lover at the beginning of Chapter 3, with which one may usefully compare the parallel episode in 5:2-8 that works on the same poetic principle:

1 On my bed at night
I sought the one I so love,
I sought him, did not find him.
2 Let me rise and go round the town,
in the streets and squares
3 Let me seek the one I so love,
I sought him, did not find him.
4 The watchmen going round the town found
   me—
"Have you seen the one I so love?"
5 Scarce had I passed them
when I found the one I so love.
6 I held him, would not loose him,
till I brought him to my mother's house,
to the chamber of her who conceived me.

In this entire sequence of progressive actions, the only moment of semantic equivalence between versets is in the second and third versets of the last line, and the focusing movement there from house to chamber is subsumed under the general narrative pattern: the woman first gets a tight grip on her lover, then brings him to her mother's house, and finally introduces him into the chamber (perhaps the same one in which she was lying at the beginning of the sequence).

This brief specimen of narrative reflects two other stylistic peculiarities of the *Song of Songs*. Although the collection as a whole makes elaborate and sometimes extravagant use of figurative language, when narrative governs a whole poem, as in 3:1-4 and 5:2-8, figuration is entirely displaced by the report of sequenced actions. There are no metaphors or similes in these six lines, and, similarly, in the description of the palanquin coming up from the desert to Jerusalem that we glanced at, the only figurative language is "like columns of smoke" at the beginning (where the original reading may in fact have been "*in* columns of smoke") and "decked with love" at the end (where some have also seen a textual problem). The second notable stylistic feature of our poem is the prominence of verbatim repetition. Through the rapid narrative there is woven a thread of verbal recurrences that, disengaged, would sound like this: I sought the one I so love, I sought him, did not find him, let me seek the one I so love, I sought him, did not find him, the one I so love, I found the one I so love. This device has a strong affinity with the technique of incremental repetition that is reflected in the more archaic layers of biblical poetry (the most memorable instance being the Song of Deborah). In the *Song of Songs*, however, such repetition is used with a degree of flexibility one does not find in the archaic poems, and is especially favored in vocative forms where the lover adds some item of enraptured admiration to the repetition: "Oh, you are fair, my darling, / oh, you are fair, *your eyes are doves.*" One finds the increment as well in the explanatory note of a challenge: "How is your lover more than another, / fairest of women, // how is your lover more than another, / *that thus you adjure us?*" One notices that there is a sense of choreographic balance lacking in the simple use of incremental repetition because in both these lines an initial element ("my darling," "fairest of women") is subtracted as the increment is added. In any case, the closeness to incremental repetition is not necessarily evidence of an early date but might well reflect the more popular character of these love poems, folk poetry and its sophisticated derivatives being by nature conservative in their modes of expression.

The most telling divergence from quasi-synonymous parallelism in the *Song of Songs* is the use of one verset to introduce a simile and of the matching verses to indicate the referent of the simile: "Like a lily among brambles, / so is my darling among girls. // Like an apple tree among forest trees, / so is my lover among lads." The same pattern appears, with a very different effect, in some of the riddle-form proverbs. In the *Song of Songs*, such a pattern makes particular sense because, more than in any other poetic text of the Bible,

what is at issue in the poems is the kind of transfers of meaning that take place when one thing is represented in terms of or through the image of something else, and the "like . . . / so . . ." formula aptly calls our attention to the operation of the simile. With the exception of the continuously narrative passages I have mentioned, figurative language plays a more prominent role here than anywhere else in biblical poetry, and the assumptions about how figurative language should be used have shifted in important respects.

The fact is that in a good deal of biblical poetry imagery serves rather secondary purposes, or sometimes there is not very much of it, and in any case "originality" of metaphoric invention would not appear to have been a consciously prized poetic value. Let me propose that outside the *Song of Songs* one can observe three general categories of imagery in biblical poems: avowedly conventional images, intensive images, and innovative images. Conventional imagery accounts for the preponderance of cases, and the Book of Psalms is the showcase for the artful use of such stock images. Intensive imagery in most instances builds on conventional metaphors and similes, with the difference that a particular figure is pursued and elaborated through several lines or even a whole poem, so that it is given a kind of semantic amplitude or powerfully assertive pressure. Intensive imagery occurs sometimes in Psalms, fairly often in Job, and is the figurative mode par excellence of prophetic poetry. Innovative imagery is the rarest of the three categories, but it can occur from time to time in any genre of biblical verse simply because poetry is, among other things, a way of imagining the world through inventive similitude, and poets, whatever their conventional assumptions, may on occasion arrest the attention of their audience through an original or startling image. The highest concentration of innovative imagery in the Bible is evident in the Book of Job, which I would take to be not strictly a generic matter but more a reflection of the poet's particular genius and his extraordinary ability to imagine disconcerting realities outside the frame of received wisdom and habitual perception. Let me offer some brief examples of all three categories of imagery in order to make this overview of biblical figuration more concrete, which in turn should help us see more clearly the striking difference of the *Song of Songs*.

Stock imagery, as I have intimated, is the staple of biblical poetry, and Psalms is the preeminent instance of its repeated deployment. Here is an exemplary line: "Guard me like the apple of Your eye, / in the shadow of Your wings conceal me." Both the apple of the eye as something to be cherished and the shadow of wings as a place of shelter are biblical cliches, though the two elements are interestingly connected here by a motif of darkness (the concentrated dark of the pupil and the extended shadow of wings) and linked in a pattern of intensification that moves from guarding to hiding.

There may be, then, a certain effective orchestration of the semantic fields of the metaphors, but in regard to the purpose of the psalm, the advantage of working with such conventional figures is that our attention tends to be guided through the metaphoric vehicle to the tenor for which the vehicle was introduced. In fact, as Benjamin Hrushovski has recently argued, there is a misleading implication of unidirectional movement in those very terms "tenor" and "vehicle," coined for critical usage by I. A. Richards some six decades ago, and when we return to the **Song of Songs** we will see precisely why the unidirectional model of metaphor is inappropriate. In the frequent biblical use, however, of stock imagery, the relation between metaphor and referent actually approaches that of a vehicle—that is, a mere "carrier" of meaning—to a tenor. In our line from Psalms, what the speaker, pleading for divine help, wants to convey is a sense of the tender protection he asks of God. The apple of the eye and the shading of wings communicate his feeling for the special care he seeks, but in their very conventionality the images scarcely have a life of their own. We think less about the dark of the eye and the shadow of wings than about the safeguarding from the Lord for which the supplicant prays.

Since I have pulled this line out of context, let me refer with a comment on the whole poem to the use of cliché in just one other fairly typical psalm, Psalm 94. In the twenty-three lines of this poem, which calls quite impressively on the Lord as a "God of retribution" to destroy His enemies, there are only four lines that contain any figurative language. How minimal and how conventional such language is will become clear by the quoting in sequence of these four isolated instances of figuration: "The Lord knows the designs of man, / that they are mere breath;" ". . . until a pit is dug for the wicked;" "When I thought my foot had slipped, / Your faithfulness, Lord, supported me;" "But the Lord is my stronghold, / and my God is my sheltering rock." Pitfall, stumbling, and stronghold occur time after time in biblical poetry, and their role in this otherwise nonfigurative poem is surely no more than a minor amplification of the idea that security depends upon God. The metaphor of breath or vapor may to the modern glance seem more striking, but it is in fact such a conventional designation for insubstantiality in the Bible that modern translations that render it unmetaphorically as "futile" do only small violence to the original.

We have seen a number of instances of intensive imagery in our discussion of prophetic poetry and of structures of intensification, but since the focus of those considerations was not on figurative language, one brief example from the prophets may be useful. Here is Deutero-Isaiah elaborating a metaphor in order to contrast the ephemerality of humankind and the power and perdurability of God:

> All flesh is grass,
> all its faithfulness like the flower of the field.
> Grass withers, flower fades
> when the Lord's breath blows on them.
> Grass withers, flower fades,
> and the word of the Lord stands forever.

The metaphor of grass for transience is thoroughly conventional, but the poet gives it an intensive development through these three lines in the refrain-like repetition of the key phrases; the amplification of grass with flower (a vegetal figure that involves beauty and still more fragility and ephemerality, as flowers wither more quickly than grass); and in the contrast between grass and God's breath-wind-spirit *(ruah)*. God's power is a hot wind that makes transient growing things wither, but God's spirit is also the source of His promise to Israel, through covenant and prophecy, which will be fulfilled or "stand" *(yaqum)* forever while human things and human faithfulness vanish in the wilderness of time. One sees how a cliché has been transformed into poignantly evocative poetry, and here the frame of reference of the metaphor, ephemeral things flourishing, interpenetrates the frame of reference of Israel vis-à-vis God as the pitfalls and strongholds of Psalms do not do to the objects or ideas to which they allude.

Finally, the Job poet abundantly interweaves with such intensive developments of conventional figures forcefully innovative images that carry much of the burden of his argument. Sometimes the power of these images depends on an elaboration of their implications for two or three lines, as in this representation of human life as backbreaking day labor tolerable only because of the prospect of evening / death as surcease and recompense: "Has not man a term of service on earth, / and like the days of a hireling his days? // Like a slave he pants for the shadows, / like a hireling he waits for his wage." Sometimes we find a rapid flow of innovative figures that in its strength from verset to verset seems quite Shakespearian, as in these images of the molding of man in the womb: "Did You not pour me out like milk, / curdle me like cheese? / / With skin and flesh You clothed me, / with bones and sinews wove me?" The brilliantly resourceful Job poet also offers a more compact version of the innovative image, in which an otherwise conventional term is endowed with terrific figurative power because of the context in which it is set. Thus, the verb *sabo'a,* "to be satisfied" or "sated," is extremely common in biblical usage, for the most part in literal or weakly figurative utterances, but this is how Job uses it to denounce the Friends: "Why do you pursue me like God, / and from my flesh you are not sated?" In context, especially since Job has just been talking about his bones sticking to his flesh and skin, the otherwise bland verb produces a horrific image of cannibalism, which manages to say a great deal with awesome compression about the perverted nature of the Friends' relationship to the stricken Job.

The innovative image by its forcefulness strongly colors our perception of its referent: once we imagine the Friends cannibalizing Job's diseased and wasted flesh, we can scarcely dissociate the words they speak and their moral intentions from this picture of barbaric violence. What remains relatively stable, as in the two other general categories of biblical imagery, is the subordinate relation of image to referent. We are never in doubt that Job's subject is the Friends' censorious behavior toward him, not cannibalism, or the shaping of the embryo, not cheese-making and weaving. By contrast, what makes the *Song of Songs* unique among the poetic texts of the Bible is that, quite often, imagery is given such full and free play there that the lines of semantic subordination blur, and it becomes a little uncertain what is illustration and what is referent.

It should be observed, to begin with, that in the *Song of Songs* the process of figuration is frequently "foregrounded"—which is to say, as the poet takes expressive advantage of representing something through an image that brings out a salient quality it shares with the referent, he calls our attention to his exploitation of similitude, to the artifice of metaphorical representation. One lexical token of this tendency is that the verbal root *d-m-h,* "to be like," or, in another conjugation, the transitive "to liken," which occurs only thirty times in the entire biblical corpus (and not always with this meaning), appears five times in these eight brief chapters of poetry, in each instance flaunting the effect of figurative comparison. Beyond this lexical due, the general frequency of simile is itself a "laying bare" of the artifice, making the operation of comparison explicit in the poem's surface structure.

The first occurrence of this verb as part of an ostentatious simile is particularly instructive because of the seeming enigma of the image: "To a mare among Pharaoh's chariots / I would liken you, my darling." Pharoah's chariots were drawn by stallions, but the military stratagem alluded to has been clearly understood by commentators as far back as the classical Midrashim: a mare in heat, let loose among chariotry, could transform well-drawn battle lines into a chaos of wildly plunging stallions. This is obviously an instance of what I have called innovative imagery, and the poet—or, if one prefers, the speaker—is clearly interested in flaunting the innovation. The first verset gives us a startling simile, as in the first half of a riddle-form proverb; the second verset abandons semantic parallelism for the affirmation of simile making ("I would liken you" or, perhaps, "I have likened you") together with the specification in the vocative of the beloved referent of the simile. The lover speaks out of a keen awareness of the power of figurative language to break open closed frames of reference

and make us see things with a shock of new recognition: the beloved in poem after poem is lovely, gentle, dovelike, fragrant, but the sexual attraction she exerts also has an almost violent power to drive males to distraction, as the equine military image powerfully suggests.

It is not certain whether the next two lines, which evoke the wreaths of jewels and precious metals with which the beloved should be adorned, are a continuation of the mare image (referring, that is, to ornaments like those with which a beautiful mare might be adorned) or the fragment of an unrelated poem. I would prefer to see these lines as an extension of the mare simile because that would be in keeping with a general practice in the *Song of Songs* of introducing a poetic comparison and then exploring its ramifications through several lines. A more clear-cut example occurs in these three lines, which also happen to turn on the next occurrence of the symptomatic verb *d-m-h:*

> Hark! My lover, here he comes!
> bounding over the mountains,
> loping over the hills.
> My lover is like a buck
> or a young stag.
> Here he stands behind our wall,
> peering in at the windows,
> peeping through the lattice.

This poem, which continues with the lover's invitation to the woman to come out with him into the vernal countryside, begins without evident simile: the waiting young woman simply hears the rapidly approaching footsteps of her lover and imagines him bounding across the hills to her home. What the middle line, which in the Hebrew begins with the verb of likening, *domeh,* does is to pick up a simile that has been pressing just beneath the verbal surface of the preceding line and to make it explicit—all the more explicit because the speaker offers overlapping alternatives of similitude, a buck *or* a young stag. The third line obviously continues the stag image that was adumbrated in the first line and spelled out in the second, but its delicate beauty is in part a function of the poised ambiguity as to what is foreground and what is background. It is easy enough to picture a soft-eyed stag, having come down from the hills, peering in through the lattice; it is just as easy to see the eager human lover, panting from his run, looking in at his beloved. The effect is the opposite of the sort of optical trick in which a design is perceived at one moment as a rabbit and the next as a duck but never as both at once, because through the magic of poetic likening the figure at the lattice is simultaneously stag and lover. What I would call the tonal consequence of this ambiguity is that the lover is entirely assimilated into the natural world at the same time that the natural world is felt to be profoundly in consonance with the lovers. This perfectly sets the stage for his invitation to arise and join him in the freshly blossoming landscape, all winter rains now gone.

A variant of the line about the buck occurs in another poem at the end of the same chapter, and there is something to be learned from the different position and grammatical use of the verb of similitude:

> My lover is mine and I am his,
>   who browses among the lilies.
> Until day breathes and shadows flee,
> Turn, and be you, my love, like a buck,
>   or a young stag
>   on the cleft mountains.

The verb "browses," *ro'eh,* which when applied to humans means "to herd" and would not make sense in that meaning here, requires a figurative reading from the beginning. The only landscape, then, in this brief poem is metaphorical: the woman is inviting her lover to a night of pleasure, urging him to hasten to enjoy to the utmost before day breaks. The lilies and the "cleft mountains"—others, comparing the line to 8:14, render this "mountains of spice," which amounts to the same erotic place—are on the landscape of her body, where he can gambol through the night. What is especially interesting in the light of our previous examples is that the verb of similitude occurs not in the speaker's declaration of likeness but in an imperative: "be you, my love, like *[demeh le]* a buck." The artifice of poetry thus enters inside the frame of dramatic action represented through the monologue: the woman tells her man that the way he can most fully play the part of the lover is to be like the stag, to act out the poetic simile, feeding on these lilies and cavorting upon this mount of intimate delight.

Of the two other occurrences of the verb *d-m-h* in the *Song of Songs,* one is a variant of the line we have just considered, appearing at the very end of the book and possibly detached from context. The other occurrence provides still another instructive instance of how this poetry rides the momentum of metaphor:

> This stature of yours is like the palm,
>   your breasts like the clusters.
> I say, let me climb the palm,
>   let me hold its branches.
> Let your breast be like grape clusters,
>   your breath like apples,
> Your palate like goodly wine
>   flowing for my love smoothly,*
>   stirring* the lips of sleepers.

The speaker first announces his controlling simile, proclaiming that his beloved's stately figure is like *(damte le)* the palm. The second verset of the initial line introduces a ramification—quite literally, a "branching out"—of the palm image or, in terms of the general poetics of parallelism, focuses it by moving from the tree to the fruit-laden boughs. The next line is essentially an enactment of the simile, beginning with "I say," which Marvin Pope quite justifiably renders as "methinks" because the verb equally implies intention and speech. The simile ceases to be an "illustration" of some quality (the stately stature of the palm tree in the woman) and becomes a reality that impels the speaker to a particular course of action: if you are a palm, what is to be done with palm trees is to climb them and enjoy their fruit. The last two lines of the poem sustain the sense of a virtually real realm of simile by piling on a series of images contiguous with the initial one but not identical with it: from clusters of dates to grape clusters, from branches to apples, from the breath of the mouth and from grapes to wine-sweet kisses.

Another reflection of the poetics of flaunted figuration that contributes to the distinctive beauty of the *Song of Songs* is the flamboyant elaboration of the metaphor in fine excess of its function as the vehicle for any human or erotic tenor. In terms of the semantic patterns of biblical parallelism, this constitutes a special case of focusing, in which the second or third verset concretizes or characterizes a metaphor introduced in the first verset in a way that shifts attention from the frame of reference of the referent to the frame of reference of the metaphor. Let me quote from the exquisite poem addressed to the dancing Shulamite in Chapter 7 the vertical description of the woman, ascending from feet to head.

> 1 How lovely your feet in sandals,
>   nobleman's daughter!
> 2 Your curving thighs are like ornaments,
>   the work of a master's hand.
> 3 Your sex a rounded bowl—
>   may it never lack mixed wine!
> 4 Your belly a heap of wheat,
>   hedged about with lilies.
> 5 Your two breasts like two fawns,
>   twins of a gazelle.
> 6 Your neck like an ivory tower,
>   your eyes pools in Heshbon
> 7 Your nose like the tower of David,
>   by the gate of Bat-Rabbim.
> 8 Your head on you like crimson wool,
>   looking out toward Damascus.
>   the locks of your head like purple,
>   a king is caught in the flowing tresses.

This way of using metaphor will seem peculiar only if one insists upon imposing on the text the aesthetic of a later age. A prime instance of what I have called the misplaced concreteness of biblical research is that proponents of the theory of a fertility-cult liturgy have felt that the imagery of metallic ornament had to be explained as a reference to the statuette of a love goddess and the looming architectural imagery by an invoking of the allegedly supernatural character of the female addressed. This makes only a little more sense than to claim that when John Donne in "The Sunne Rising" writes, "She is all States, and all Princes, I, / Nothing else is," he must be addressing, by virtue of the global imagery, some cosmic goddess and not sweet Ann Donne.

Our passage begins without simile for the simple technical reason that the second verset of line 1 is used to address the woman who is the subject of the enraptured description. After this point, the second (or, for the triadic lines, the third) verset of each line is employed quite consistently to flaunt the metaphor by pushing its frame of reference into the foreground. The poet sets no limit on and aims for no unity in the semantic fields from which he draws his figures, moving rapidly from artisanry to agriculture to the animal kingdom to architecture, and concluding with dyed textiles. (In the analogous vertical description of the lover the imagery similarly wanders from doves bathing in watercourses and beds of spices to artifacts of gold, ivory, and marble, though the semantic field of artifact dominates as the celebration of the male body concentrates on the beautiful hardness of arms, thighs, and loins.) There is nevertheless a tactical advantage in beginning the description with perfectly curved ornaments and a rounded bowl or goblet, for the woman's beauty is so exquisite that the best analogue for it is the craft of the master artisan, an implicit third term of comparison being the poet's fine craft in so nicely matching image with object for each lovely aspect of this body.

That implied celebration of artifice may explain in part the flamboyant elaboration of the metaphors in all the concluding versets. It should be observed, however, that the function of these elaborations changes from line to line in accordance with both the body part invoked and the position of the line in the poem. In line 2, "the work of a master's hand" serves chiefly as an intensifier of the preceding simile of ornament and as a way of foregrounding the idea of artifice at the beginning of the series. In lines 3-5, as the description moves upward from feet and thighs to the central erogenous zone of vagina, belly, and breasts, the elaborations of the metaphor in the second versets are a way of being at once sexually explicit and decorous through elegant *double entente.* That is, we are meant to be continuously aware of the sexual details referred to, but it is the wittily deployed frame of reference of the metaphor that is kept in the foreground of our vision: we know the poet alludes to the physiology of love-making, but we "see" a curved bowl that never runs dry; the wheat-like belly bordered by a hedge of lilies is an ingenious superimposition of an agricultural image on an erotic one, since lilies elsewhere are implicitly associated with pubic hair; the bouncing, supple, symmetrical breasts are not just two fawns but also, in the focusing elaboration, a gazelle's perfectly matched twins.

The geographical specifications of the final versets in lines 6 and 7 have troubled many readers. It seems to me that here, when the poet has moved above the central sexual area of the body, he no longer is impelled to work out a cunning congruity between image and referent by way of *double entente,* and instead he can give free rein to the exuberance of figurative elaboration that in different ways has been perceptible in all the previous metaphors. If, as his eye moves to neck and face, the quality of grandeur rather than supple sexual allure is now uppermost, there is a poetic logic in the speaker's expanding these images of soaring architectural splendor and making the figurative frame of reference so prominent that we move from the dancing Shulamite to the public world of the gate at Bat-Rabbim and the tower of Lebanon looking toward Damascus. As the lover's gaze moves up from the parts of the body usually covered and thus seen by him alone to the parts generally visible, it is appropriate that the similes for her beauty should be drawn now from the public realm. In a final turn, moreover, of the technique of last-verset elaboration, the triadic line 8 introduces an element of climactic surprise: the Shulamite's hair having been compared to brilliantly dyed wool or fabric, we discover that a king is caught, or bound, in the tresses (the Hebrew for this last term is a little doubtful, but since the root suggests running motion, the reference to flowing hair in context seems probable). This amounts to a strong elaboration of a relatively weak metaphor, and an elaboration that subsumes the entire series of images that has preceded: the powerful allure of sandaled feet, curving thighs, and all the rest that has pulsated through every choice of image now culminates in the hair, where at last the lover, through the self designation of king, introduces himself into the poem, quite literally interinvolves himself with the beloved ("a king is caught in the flowing tresses"). Up till now, she has been separate from him, dancing before his eager eye. Now, after a climactic line summarizing her beauty, he goes on to imagine embracing her and enjoying her (the climbing of the palm tree that I quoted earlier). It is a lovely illustration of how the exuberant metaphors carry the action forward.

Such obtrusions of metaphorical elaboration are allied with another distinctive mode of figuration of these poems, in which the boundaries between figure and referent, inside and outside, human body and accoutrement or natural setting, become suggestively fluid. Let me first cite three lines from the brief poem at the end of Chapter 1:

> While the king was on his couch,
>   my nard gave off its scent.
> A sachet of myrrh is my lover to me,

between my breasts he lodges.
A cluster of cypress is my lover to me,
  in the vineyards of Ein Gedi.

The first line is without figuration, the woman simply
stating that she has scented her body for her lover. But
the immediately following metaphoric representation
of the lover as a sachet of myrrh—because he nestles
between her breasts all night long—produces a delightful confusion between the literal nard with which she
has perfumed herself and the figurative myrrh she cra-
dles in her lover. Thus the act and actors of love become intertwined with the fragrant paraphernalia of
love. The third line offers an alternative image of a
bundle of aromatic herbs and then, in the second verset, one of those odd geographical specifications. . . .
I have not followed the New JPS and Marvin Pope in
translating the second verset as "from the vineyards,"
because it seems to me that the Hebrew has an ambiguity worth preserving. Presumably the metaphor is
elaborated geographically because the luxuriant oasis
at Ein Gedi was especially known for its trees and
plants with aromatic leaves, and so the specification
amounts to a heightening of the original assertion. At
the same time the initial Hebrew particle *be,* which
usually means "in," leaves a teasing margin for imagining that it is not the cypress cluster that *comes from*
Ein Gedi but the fragrant embrace of the lovers that
takes place *in* Ein Gedi. Though this second meaning
is less likely, it is perfectly consistent with the syntax
of the line, and the very possibility of this construal
makes it hard to be sure where the metaphor stops and
the human encounter it represents begins. There is, in
other words, an odd and satisfying consonance in this
teasing game of transformations between the pleasure
of play with language through metaphor and the pleasure of love play that is the subject of the lines. That
same consonance informs the beautiful poem that takes
up all of Chapter 4, ending in the first verse of Chapter
5. It will provide an apt concluding illustration of the
poetic art of the *Song of Songs*.

1 Oh, you are fair, my darling,
  oh, you are fair, your eyes are doves.
2 Behind your veil, your hair like a flock of
  goats
    streaming down Mount Gilead.
3 Your teeth are like a flock of ewes
  coming up from the bath,
4 Each one bearing twins,
  none bereft among them.
5 Like the scarlet thread your lips,
  your mouth is lovely.
6 Like a pomegranate-slice your brow
  behind your veil.
7 Like the tower of David your neck,
  built in rows.
8 A thousand shields are hung on it,
  all the heroes' bucklers.

9 Your two breasts are like two fawns,
  twins of the gazelle,
    browsing among the lilies.
10 Until day breathes
  and shadows flee
11 I'll betake me to the mount of myrrh
  and to the hill of frankincense.
12 You are all fair, my darling,
  there's no blemish in you.
13 With me from Lebanon, bride,
  with me from Lebanon, come!
14 Descend from Amana's peak,
  from the peak of Senir and Hermon,
15 From the dens of lions,
  from the mounts of panthers.
16 You ravish my heart, bride,
  you ravish my heart with one glance of
    your eyes,
  with one gem of your necklace.
17 How fair your love, my sister and bride,
  how much better your love than wine,
  and the scent of your ointments than any
    spice!
18 Nectar your lips drip, bride,
  honey and milk under your tongue,
  and the scent of your robes like Lebanon's
    scent.
19 A locked garden, my sister and bride,
  a locked pool, a sealed-up spring.
20 Your groove a grove of pomegranates
  with luscious fruit,
    cypress with nard.
21 Nard and saffron, cane and cinnamon,
  with all aromatic woods,
22 Myrrh and aloes,
  with all choice perfumes.
23 A garden spring,
  a well of fresh water,
    flowing from Lebanon.
24 Stir, north wind,
  come, south wind,
25 Breathe on my garden,
  let its spices flow.
26 "Let my lover come to his garden,
  and eat its luscious fruit."
27 I've come to my garden, my sister and
    bride,
I've plucked my myrrh with my spice,
28 Eaten my honeycomb with my honey,
  drunk my wine with my milk.
29 "Eat, friends, and drink,
  be drunk with love."

As elsewhere in the *Song of Songs*, the poet draws his
images from whatever semantic fields seem apt for the
local figures—domesticated and wild animals, dyes,
food, architecture, perfumes, and the floral world. Flamboyant elaboration of the metaphor, in which the metaphoric image takes over the foreground, governs the

first third of the poem, culminating in the extravagant picture of the woman's neck as a tower hung with shields. The very repetition of *ke* ("like"), the particle of similitude, half a dozen times through these initial lines, calls attention to the activity of figurative comparison as it is being carried out. There is a certain witty ingenuity with which the elaborated metaphors are related to the body parts: twin-bearing, newly washed ewes to two perfect rows of white teeth and, perhaps, shields on the tower walls recalling the layered rows of a necklace.

What I should like to follow out more closely, however, is the wonderful transformations that the landscape of fragrant mountains and gardens undergoes from line 11 to the end of the poem. The first mountain and hill—rarely has a formulaic word-pair been used so suggestively—in line 11 are metaphorical, referring to the body of the beloved or, perhaps, as some have proposed, more specifically to the *mons veneris.* It is interesting that the use of two nouns in the construct state to form a metaphor ("mount of myrrh," "hill of frankincense") is quite rare elsewhere in biblical poetry, though it will become a standard procedure in post-biblical Hebrew poetry. The naturalness with which the poet adopts that device here reflects how readily objects in the **Song of Songs** are changed into metaphors. The Hebrew for "frankincense" is *levonah,* which sets up an intriguing *faux raccord* with "Lebanon," *levanon,* two lines down. From the body as landscape—an identification already adumbrated in the comparison of hair to flocks coming down from the mountain and teeth to ewes coming up from the washing—the poem moves to an actual landscape with real rather than figurative promontories. If domesticated or in any case gentle animals populate the metaphorical landscape at the beginning, there is a new note of danger or excitement in the allusion to the lairs of panthers and lions on the real northern mountainside. The repeated verb "ravish" in line 16, apparently derived from *lev,* "heart," picks up in its sound *(libavtini)* the interecho of *levonah* and *levanon* and so triangulates the body-as-landscape, the external landscape, and the passion the beloved inspires.

The last thirteen lines of the poem, as the speaker moves toward the consummation of love intimated in lines 26-29, reflect much more of an orchestration of the semantic fields of the metaphors: fruit, honey, milk, wine, and, in consonance with the sweet fluidity of this list of edibles, a spring of fresh flowing water and all the conceivable spices that could grow in a well-irrigated garden. Lebanon, which as we have seen has already played an important role in threading back and forth between the literal and figurative landscapes, continues to serve as a unifier. The scent of the beloved's robes is like Lebanon's scent, no doubt because Lebanon is a place where aromatic trees grow, but also with the suggestion, again fusing figurative

with literal, that the scent of Lebanon clings to her dress because she has just returned from there. "All aromatic woods" in line 21 is literally in the Hebrew "all the trees of *levonah,*" and the echo of *levonah-levanon* is carried forward two lines later when the locked spring in the garden wells up with flowing water *(nozlim,* an untranslatable poetic synonym for water) from Lebanon—whether because Lebanon, with its mountain streams, is the superlative locus of fresh running water, or because one is to suppose some mysterious subterranean feed-in from the waters of wild and mountainous Lebanon to this cultivated garden. In either case, there is a suggestive crossover back from the actual landscape to a metaphorical one. The garden at the end that the lover enters—and to "come to" or "enter" often has a technical sexual meaning in biblical Hebrew—is the body of the beloved, and one is not hard put to see the physiological fact alluded to in the fragrant flowing of line 25 (the same root as *nozlim* in line 23) that precedes the enjoyment of luscious fruit.

What I have just said, however, catches only one side of a restless dialectic movement of signification and as such darkens the delicately nuanced beauty of the poem with the shadow of reductionism. For though we know, and surely the original audience was intended to know, that the last half of the poem conjures up a delectable scene of love's consummation, this garden of aromatic plants, wafted by the gentle winds, watered by a hidden spring, is in its own right an alluring presence to the imagination before and after any decoding into a detailed set of sexual allusions. The poetry by the end becomes a kind of self-transcendence of *double entente:* the beloved's body is, in a sense, "represented" as a garden, but it also turns into a real garden, magically continuous with the mountain landscape so aptly introduced at the midpoint of the poem.

It is hardly surprising that only here in biblical poetry do we encounter such enchanting interfusions between the literal and metaphorical realms, because only here is the exuberant gratification of love through all five senses the subject. Prevalent preconceptions about the Hebrew Bible lead us to think of it as a collection of writings rather grimly committed to the notions of covenant, law, solemn obligation, and thus the very antithesis of the idea of play. There is more than a grain of truth in such preconceptions (one can scarcely imagine a Hebrew Aristophanes or a Hebrew *Odyssey*), but the literary art of the Bible, in both prose narrative and poetry, reflects many more elements of playfulness than might meet the casual eye. Only in the **Song of Songs,** however, is the writer's art directed to the imaginative realization of a world of uninhibited self-delighting play, without moral conflict, without the urgent context of history and nationhood and destiny, without the looming perspectives of a theological world-view. Poetic language and, in particular, its most characteristic procedure, figuration, are manipulated as pleasurable substance: metaphor transforms the body into spices and perfumes, wine and luscious fruit, all of which figurative images blur into the actual setting in which the lovers enact their love, a natural setting replete with just those delectable things. There is a harmonious correspondence between poem and world, the world exhibiting the lovely tracery of satisfying linkages that characterizes poetry itself. In the fluctuating movement from literal to figurative and back again, both sides of the dialectic are enhanced: the inventions of the poetic medium become potently suffused with the gratifying associations of the erotic, and erotic longing and fulfillment are graced with the elegant aesthetic form of a refined poetic art.

Carol Meyers (essay date 1986)

SOURCE: "Gender Imagery in the *Song of Songs*," in *The Hebrew Annual Review,* Vol. 10, 1986, pp. 209-23.

[*In the following essay, Meyers offers a feminist reading of the* Song of Songs, *considering the use of architectural and faunal imagery in the* Song's *treatment of gender. She finds in the poem a rare insight into the private, "domestic realm" of ancient Israel.*]

I. Introduction: Imagery in the Song

In no other book of the Hebrew Bible does the imagery figure so prominently as it does in the *Song of Songs*. The rich and extravagant array of figurative language boldly draws the reader into the world so joyously inhabited by the ancient lovers. The poetic craft of the unknown author or authors succeeds at a descriptive level in conveying the lushness of the natural settings and also the beauty that the female and male characters each find in the physical appearance of the other. At the same time the sensual language of the *Song* creates its own erotic tension, drawing the audience into the heightened emotions of the lovers themselves.

Small wonder, then, that this extraordinary poetry of love has been the object of so much attention. In past ages, concern with the presence of frequent and explicit attention to the human body and also to freely expressed passion led to the development of extensive allegorical treatments of the *Song*. The outpouring of such interpretations over the centuries probably attests to the ongoing attractions of the language of love on a physical level as much as it does to the spirituality of those who engaged in allegorical explanation. The interpreter must willy-nilly absorb the words at their primary level of meaning before proceeding to comprehend the higher and hidden levels that constitute the object of the allegorist's task.

The rise of critical biblical scholarship rescued the *Song* from the fanciful twists and turns of spiritualized interpretation. Yet modern scholarly approaches have confronted the *Song* with that, to a great extent, have been as unwilling to explore the use of physical imagery as were those of the traditional exegetes. Critical treatments, for example, have been preoccupied with dating the work as a whole or certain passages within it, with finding the locale, with identifying the characters, and with figuring out the relationship of the *Song* to Solomon, who is mentioned by name in the superscription and six other times in the text itself.

In short, while modern interpreters have readily accepted the fact that the *Song* speaks to us of human love, they have rarely explored that language as such. To be fair, the focus on matters other than the love poetry, as a genre worthy of exploration on that level, has been in keeping with the general direction of biblical scholarship in the nineteenth and twentieth centuries. The critical tools honed and sharpened in the analysis of the pentateuchal, prophetic, and historiographic literature of the Bible have been inadequate to deal with a biblical book that differs in essential ways from the rest of the scriptural corpus. The poems, after all, are fundamentally secular in their celebration of human love. Biblical scholarship oriented towards religious meaning and development, not surprisingly, has been disadvantaged in its approach to literature that extols emotion derived from human response to another human rather than to God.

Recently, however, scholars trained in literary analysis as such, rather than in the peculiar brand of literary criticism developed for or linked to the study of sacred writings, have begun to examine the *Song of Songs*. In so doing, they have explored its figurative languages and have liberated the rich imagery as well as the poetic craft from the inescapable though unintentional constraint imposed by the methodological predisposition of both traditional allegorists and critical exegetes. Alter's exuberant chapter on "The Garden of Metaphor" in his book on biblical poetry and Falk's insightful work, which includes both translation and analysis, are noteworthy examples of exposition sensitive to the complex role of sensory metaphors in the *Song*.

Scholarship emerging from the study of literature *qua* literature is not the only recent development that has looked anew at the *Song*. Feminist interests in biblical studies, adumbrated in the nineteenth century by the energetic work of activist Elizabeth Cady Stanton (1895, 1898) and also by the eloquent treatment of C. D. Ginsburg (1857), have naturally been drawn to the one biblical book in which female behavior and status stand apart from the largely male orientation of the rest of the biblical canon. Trible's work is notable in this respect. The celebration of human love is inherently a matter of gender. Hence any consideration of gender in the biblical world would anticipate, in turning to the *Song*, a work replete with images depicting explicitly male or explicitly female attributes.

Among the various genres of love poetry that have been identified in the *Song of Songs*, the descriptive songs or *wasfs* provide the most obvious materials for the consideration of gender imagery. The term *wasf*, which means "description" in Arabic, is used to designate those passages that depict the attractions of the human body. The female and the male body are each portrayed in the *Song* through a graphic series of verbal images. In addition to the explicit attention to gender in the *wasfs*, various other passages allude to attributes of one or the other of the human lovers.

The images in the *wasfs* have caused great difficulty for scholars of nearly all methodological persuasions. For the literary critic as for all those dealing with the literal, erotic meaning of the *Song*'s language, some of the terms and phrases used to convey attributes of the human body are seen as bizarre or strange. Rather than seize on the apparent strangeness as an aspect demanding closer or different scrutiny, critics have paid scant attention to images that startle or shock or that seem inappropriate to what seems to be the task of depicting physical attractiveness. As Falk points out, even scholars familiar with the Hebrew original and also with other ancient Near Eastern love poetry find certain images peculiar and tend to dismiss them as appealing to an ancient aesthetic that is not present in contemporary standards of taste.

The striking imagery depicting body parts in the *Song*'s *wasfs* calls for special consideration of the function of metaphor. Soulen (1967) shows how the sparks of association called forth instantly, without need or time for contemplation and reflection, by the *Song*'s comparisons provide the excitement and stimulation that contribute to the *Song*'s success. If the visual offerings of the biblical poet are not familiar to us, the scholar should explore them so that they become vivid and offer us the same associative potential that existed for the inhabitants of an ancient landscape for whom the images drawn from that environment were commonplace.

Our particular concern here with gender imagery in the *Song of Songs* will be with the gender of the objects used in the metaphoric figures. The ancient poet drew from a wide range of semantic fields in the images used to indicate aspects of the male's or female's body, behavior, and attractiveness. Some of those fields are patently neutral with respect to gender. Images drawn from the world of food, for example, betoken no special nuances for understanding gender. The nourishing sweet aspects of pomegranates or nectar, of honey or milk are not related to any inherently gendered qualities. Floral images are likewise apparently neutral.

Images drawn from the natural world predominate. Indeed, the *Song* is sometimes referred to as nature poetry because of the richness and variety in the allusions to flora and fauna, to vineyards and gardens, and to uncultivated landscapes. One would think that images drawn from the non-human world might be generally neutral with respect to gender, even though in Hebrew all the forms are gendered. Such, however, is not necessarily the case. Vineyards and gardens in the *Song* apparently have nuances of female sexuality and have been examined in this way. There is also potential for discerning the *Song*'s gender imagery in the faunal world, for the *Song*, is replete with animal imagery. We shall examine some of those images below.

But there are some images in the *Song* drawn from settings other than the natural world. Few as they may be, they offer better potential for dealing with gender than do those supplied by nature. Thus, we turn first to the architectural images, found chiefly in the *wasfs*.

II. Architectural Imagery

The poet uses his or her familiarity with various architectural structures mainly in the description of the human body; and it is the female body that is more frequently depicted through such imagery. The fact that of the four *wasfs* in the *Song*, three are descriptive of the female and only one of the male may mean a more limited opportunity for the poet to have indulged in architectural imagery in portraying the male. Yet there is a sample of architectural language in the one *wasf* dealing with the male, and it its strikingly different from the architectural figures in those describing the female.

The images examined here will not be explored for the purpose of identifying the particular way in which they function as metaphors in developing the poet's awe for the beloved. Rather, these images are striking for the gender associations that they hold independently of the comparative purposes to which they have been put. All of these images have caused considerable difficulty for the exegete. Part of the problem lies in the use of rare terms or *hapax legomena*. But it is our contention that the application of images across the convention of gender lines in these instances is as much a cause of the exegetical consternation as is the apparent remoteness of the images themselves.

The first passage to be considered is the most complex. In 4:4, the female's neck is likened to a "tower." The visual aspect of this comparison has been the subject of much scholarly discussion, all of which may be important for establishing the metaphorical dynamics of the image. The expansion of the image in the three phases developing upon the original simile of verse 4a ("your neck is like the tower of David") has evoked considerable interpretation. The expression *bānûy l talpîyyôt*, for example, is explained variously as a ziggurat or stepped tower, or as coursed masonry. Other explanations assume, because of the content of the following two lines, that weapons are involved.

While purely architectural possibilities may be present in the verse, the military nuances should not be rejected. A tower, after all, is first and foremost a military structure. Its height is greater than that of surrounding buildings. It thereby gives those on top of it a vantage point from which to see whatever may threaten them. Whether as an isolated structure in the field or as the stronghold of a city, a tower represents strength and protection. Built wider and taller than ordinary walls, towers stand above the surrounding landscape, be it urban or rural, signifying an advantage to its occupants.

Because, in this verse, the tower is associated with David, the military might of an urban tower is probably the dominant aspect of the image. David is the warrior *par excellence* in the Israelite tradition. The Hebrew word *migdāl* ("tower") is linked in the Bible with a number of Palestinian sites in reference to their fortified appearance; and several Jerusalem towers are mentioned by name. None of those references are to a "tower of David." Thus, its use here would seem to be not necessarily a reference to any existing structure, but rather to an abstraction: the (military) might of an architectural form.

The language of the rest of the verse intensifies the notion of military power. The word for "shield," *māgēn,* is clearly a military term that itself is intensified by the quantitative information "thousand." Similarly, another term for "shield," *sēlet,* appears with "warriors" or "mighty men" and completes the depiction of the tower. The visual aspect of the imagery may well be beauty. The similarity of the language to that of Ezek 27:10-11, where beauty and splendor are produced by towers hung with shields and helmets, is surely relevant; and the overall intention of a *wasf* to celebrate the physical qualities of the person being described should not be ignored. Yet the very repetition of military terms remains an unmistakable and prominent part of the poetic terminology.

A second passage contributes further to the tower imagery. In 7:5, the female's nose (face?) is likened to a "tower of Lebanon." This could be either a tower on the mountains of Lebanon or the towering mountains of Lebanon themselves. In either case, the military advantage of the *migdāl* is emphasized by the relational information of the next phrase: "overlooking Damascus." Damascus, itself on a high plateau, was a major military threat to Israel between the reign of Solomon and the Assyrian conquest in 732 B.C.E. The Aramean rulers in Damascus alternately allied themselves with

or opposed various Judean and Israelite rulers. The military vantage point of a tower above Damascus provides a strong suggestion of strategic advantage and hence of military power.

The tower image appears also in 7:4, in the first clause of the verse, where the female's neck is likened to a tower. Since it is within another *wasf*-type passage, it may be a reprise or alternate version of the 4:1-5 description where "neck" and "tower" are linked. In this instance, the tower image is not so developed as in chapter 4. Yet it is accompanied by a series of related comparisons of bodily parts to public features. The "pools" in Hebron to which the woman's eyes are likened are most likely artificial pools—reservoirs—constructed for military, not agricultural, purposes. And the "gate" of Bat Rabbim is part of the military defenses of a city and also a public place, a place frequented by males and not by females. The architectural image of a tower in 7:4 is surely again, along with gates and pools, derived from the world of military structures.

Nearly at the end of the *Song* the tower image appears once more. The military context for the architectural reality of this usage, which comes in a simile referring to the two breasts of the female, is evident because of the related architectural terminology in the passage. The towers here are part of a wall system. The beloved herself is equated to a wall, with her breasts being compared to its towers. Similarly, in the previous verse the young sister of the desired female is said to be a wall upon which "battlements" or "buttresses" or "turrets" are built. The passage also mentions a board of cedar, which apparently refers to a plank of some sort used in military operations connected with siege.

At the end of this short catalogue of military architecture, the female asserts that she—and here the Hebrew *môs'ēt šālôm* is difficult—brings about or finds "peace." The one to whom all the military allusions have been made secures the opposite of what they represent. Well-being is the outcome, rather than war, danger, or hostility. Despite the appearance of "peace" after the last instance of military architectural terminology, the *Song* as a whole presents a significant corpus of images and terms derived from the military—and hence the male—world. Without exception, these terms are applied to the female. Since military language is derived from an aspect of ancient life almost exclusively associated with men, its use in the *Song* in reference to the woman constitutes an unexpected reversal of conventional imagery or of stereotypical gender association.

III. Faunal images

Our discovery that the military, and consequently the masculine, aspect of architectural imagery is part of the depiction of the female and not the male is echoed in the way the poet uses animal imagery. In examining the usage of the many faunal metaphors, we have sought to determine first whether the metaphors are applied to the humans and, if so, whether they are used for both males and females or for only one gender. When only one gender is depicted by an animal image, we have endeavored to ascertain whether the animal image conveys a characteristic associated with behavior stereotypical of one gender more than the other.

Over a dozen kinds of animals appear in the *Song*. Some are part of the setting and are not used to develop the imagery of any of the characters. Others are used conventionally; they are found, for example, in the description of a character's occupation as shepherd of kids of sheep. Two others, while associated with only one gender, are used figuratively in similes depicting hair. In these cases, a particular visual feature of the animal—the blackness of the raven in relation to the male's dark hair, and the movement of goats on a hillside in relationship to the female's flowing hair—is its contribution to the figurative usage.

For two other animals, those most often mentioned, the imagery serves to enhance the depictions of both the male and the female. One of these is the dove. The eyes of each of the lovers are compared to doves, though only the female as a person is metaphorically related to a dove. The general association of doves with love and peace is surely a dominant enough motif in ancient art and literature to provide an understanding of the force of this comparison. Because of the connection of doves with love and love goddesses in the Near Eastern world, a female aspect to the dove may be supposed, in which case the metaphoric use of the dove for the female and not the male would conform to gender stereotyping.

The other animal appearing in the faunal imagery portraying both the male and the female is the gazelle (sĕbî). For the male, the gazelle is paired with the deer ('ayyāl) three times in a stock phrase. The grace and free movement of these wild creatures would seem to underlie the poet's choice. This pair is used in two other places: neither is descriptive of one of the lovers, and both come in an apostrophic address to "daughters of Jerusalem." For the female, the tenderness and softness and perhaps suppleness of these young animals have led the poet to use them in a simile celebrating the attractiveness of her breasts.

Three other animals remain in the faunal catalogue of the *Song*. Two of these are the lions and leopards of 4:8. Like the military towers and battlements of the architectural imagery, these wild animals have posed vexing problems for commentators. The difficulty lies in the fact that the female is the one associated with the wild beasts and with their wild habitations in the highest peaks of Lebanon, the mountains of Amana,

Senir, and Hermon. Nothing would be further from a domestic association for a female. Nor does the wildness, danger, might, strength, aggressiveness, and other dramatic features of these predators fit any stereotypical female qualities. Even for a female lion, the salient aspect of her behavior in biblical passages lies not in nurturing the young but in teaching them to catch prey.

The lion, which appears frequently in the figurative language of the Bible, is consistently a superior, terrifying, powerful, and majestic animal. These qualities underlie the common portrayal of Yahweh in figures using lions. All the figurative biblical appearances of the lion underscore the masculinity of the imagery, insofar as the attributes of aggression and power are stereotypical male qualities. Similarly, the depictions of lions in Near Eastern art, with certain exceptions to be mentioned below, are in the male world of the hunt or the hero. Little wonder, then, that the *Song*'s image of the female emerging from the dens and lairs of leopards and lions has been troublesome and that exegetes (see the examples cited by Pope, 1977) have gone to considerable—and preposterous—lengths in attempting to deal with it.

The final faunal image has been similarly perplexing. In 1:9 the female is likened to a mare. In this case, the animal is female, so the gender of the animal is not at the root of the problem. Rather, the context is apparently enigmatic, for the mare is portrayed in a battle scene, amidst Pharaoh's chariots. However, the ancient midrashic commentators as well as several recent ones have recognized the military ploy alluded to in this image. The female horse set loose among the stallions of the chariotry does violence to the military effectiveness of the charioteers. The female has a power of her own that can offset the mighty forces of a trained army. The military allusions and significance found in the architectural imagery used for the female are here also part of the poet's unconventional use of a figure drawn from the animal world and used to portray the female.

IV. Discussion

Both the architectural and faunal images in the *Song of Songs* contain depictions of the female that are counter to stereotypical gender conceptions. These images convey might, strength, aggression, even danger. Before considering the role of such striking figurative language, I would like to point out that military language in relationship to the female appears in two other instances in the *Song*. Although they both involve difficult readings of the Hebrew text, their significance as war terminology linked with females is nonetheless apparent.

The first text is the comparison of the beloved in 6:4 initially to two cities and then to the terror of awesomeness *('āyummāh)* of *nidgālôt.* The latter word appears in the Hebrew Bible only here and in the reprise below in verse 10. The many ingenious solutions proposed by commentators are reviewed by Pope (1977). Perhaps the banners of an army are intended (from *degel,* "flag" or "banner"); or maybe awful trophies of war that is, human limbs or heads, are implied (on the basis of a possible mythological background for the term, as Pope, 1977). Either way, the language of war appears in this elaboration of the female.

Somewhat less obscure is the depiction In 7:6. One of the Hebrew words *(rĕhātîm)* is problematic; but the overall sense is clear. The most powerful human—the king—is somehow imprisoned or raptured by the female, perhaps in her tresses. The reversal of conventional gender typing is again apparent.

How are we to interpret the frequent use of military and/or male language in depiction of the female and its virtual absence for the male? Our analysis must set this reversing of conventional or traditional gender imagery alongside other unusual aspects of gender portrayal in the *Song of Songs.*

In the patriarchal world of ancient Israel and in the biblical literature that is its legacy, an androcentric perspective prevails. The Hebrew Bible, it has been said (Bird, 1974), is a "man's book" where women appear for the most part simply as adjuncts of men, significant only in the context of men's activities. The society depicted in the Bible is portrayed primarily from a male perspective, in terms of male accomplishments and in relation to a God for whom andromorphic imagery predominates. Yet in the *Song,* such characteristics disappear and in fact the opposite may be true; that is, a gynocentric mode predominates.

A number of features of the *Song,* as Trible has pointed out, reverse the male dominance of the rest of scripture. First, of the three voices in the poem (male; female; a group), the female is most prominent: she speaks more often, and she initiates exchanges more often. Second, the third voice consists of females, the daughters of Jerusalem, who play a strong supporting role in the ebb and flow of emotions. Third, the word "mother" occurs *seven* times in the *Song,* whereas the male parent, the father, is not mentioned at all. Fourth, the motifs and structures of the *Song* can be seen as a development or midrash on the Eden story, where the action and initiative shown for the female also are more prominent than for the male.

Another item should be added to this list. The poem twice mentions *bēt-'ēm* "mother's house." Nowhere does the masculine equivalent appear, although the poet does speak of the male in relation to "his" house. The appearance of "mother's house" is striking in view of the overriding importance of "father's house" in the

Bible. The latter phrase denotes a major social construct in ancient Israel. It refers to the family household, which was the primary economic and social unit during the formative period of Israelite existence and which continued thereafter as the dominant frame of reference for family life.

In light of the importance of the concept of "father's house" in Israelite society and the frequent use of that phrase in the Hebrew Bible, the appearance of "mother's house" startles the reader. The normal masculine-oriented terminology for family and/or household derives from lineage concerns, from descent and property transmission reckoned along patrilineal lines. But here in the *Song* we encounter a situation devoid of such concerns. Perhaps, then, it is no accident that without the public orientation of lineage reckoning, the internal functional aspect of family and home life is rightly expressed by "mother's house" rather than by "father's house."

This last point arises from a consideration of the social world or setting of the *Song of Songs.* In the varied and intermingled landscapes of the *Song* one can hardly isolate a setting. Yet, even though one catches glimpses of urban and palatial (public) life, there can be no doubt that two other settings predominate: the rural or pastoral, and the domestic. These two are not alternative settings but rather complementary ones. A peasant household, with its members coming and going about their daily business, forms the human and natural context for the lovers' trysts and longings. The prevailing rural atmosphere is also an important feature and one that sets this biblical book apart from all other parts of the Hebrew canon.

Even if the extraordinary literary quality of the *Song*'s poetry bespeaks the talents of educated and therefore perhaps upper-class poets, the love genre is one that transcends social class. The language of love is an everyday language, one that permeates all social settings. I have pointed out elsewhere . . . that the Bible as a whole is an elitist, urban, male-oriented document. Only in a work that emanates from a situation—love—in which females play a part to males can anything else be expected in an androcentric setting. In the *Song* we find that one exception: a love-world that is dependent upon females as well as males. Despite its literary sophistication, this one biblical book is truly folk literature. It has no national focus and so, as Alter puts it, is "splendidly accessible to the folk," a fact which alone may explain the significant formal as well as thematic differences between the *Song* and all other examples of biblical poetry.

How might female participation in folk culture be reflected in the *Song*? Anthropologists and cultural historians, now recognize that, despite the near universal androcentricity of human culture, there is an underlying sub-culture in which women's roles are not subordinate and may even dominate. In pre-modern societies, the domestic realm is recognized as a female realm. Women, even if appearances seem otherwise to external observers, control the basic functions of that arena of life: the technologies, the procreation, the spirituality, the socializing processes. As long as agrarian societies are organized in non-statist forms, the family household tends to be the dominant economic and social unit; and in such cases, the female's role is hardly secondary or subordinate.

The *Song of Songs*, set apart from the stratifying consequences of institutional and public life, reveals a balance between male and female. The domestic setting allows for the mutual intimacy of male and female relationships to be expressed. The *Song* has a preponderance of females, but that situation does not obtain at the cost of a sustained sense of gender mutuality. Neither male nor female is set in an advantageous position with respect to the other. Some images may be limited to one gender; but there is also a long list of images or phrases that are used interchangeably and that create the mood of shared love. In the erotic world of human emotion, there is no subordination of female to the male.

Yet even within this spirit of erotic mutuality and shared love, the predominance of female characters and language and also the presence of strong (masculine) figurative language in reference to females cannot be ignored. These two special features of the *Song* are related to its exceptional status as, perhaps uniquely among the books of the biblical canon, a "popular" work, a compendium of love songs arising from the non-official and non-public arena of daily life. Precisely because it is set apart from the national and the institutional settings that constitute the compelling religious and historical originality of the biblical corpus, the *Song* depicts that aspect of life in which the female role was primary. Public life looms large in the Bible, and females consequently are virtually invisible. But where private life can be seen apart from the myopic focus on the people Israel, one glimpses a life with lively female prominence. The idea of female power projected by the military architectural imagery and by some of the animal figures is stunningly appropriate to the internal world of Israelite households, where women exercised strong and authoritative positions. . . .

The military structures set forth in relation to the woman, and the association of lions and leopards with the female beloved, are strong and innovative metaphors. They should no more be taken literally, as supposed indications of mythic female warriors or of primeval huntresses, than should the graphic equivalent of the *Song*'s military and faunal symbols of female might. I refer now to the artistic convention of depicting certain Near Eastern goddesses—often deities of love and war—holding implements of war or surmounted on ferocious beasts, notably lions.

Gender was not a constraint on power in the world of the gods. Nor, if we listen to the words of might in the *wasfs* and other passages portraying the beloved female, was gender a constraint on power in the intimate world of a couple in love. From a social perspective, the domestic realm is the setting for such love, and therein exists the arena in which female power is expressed. Luckily for feminists, who often despair of discovering meaningful material in the man's world of the official canon, a single biblical book has preserved this non-public world and allows us to see the private realm that dominated the social landscape for much of ancient Israel's population.

Marcia Falk (essay date 1990)

SOURCE: "Contexts, Themes, and Motifs," *Love Lyrics from the Bible*, HarperCollins, 1990, 137-61.

[*In the following essay, revised from an original 1982 publication, Falk addresses issues of setting, theme, and motif in the* Song of Songs *that have arisen from her translation of the work. She finds the* Song *"extraordinarily rich with sensual imagery."*]

Woven into the tapestry of the *Song* are recurrent patterns that suggest the presence of literary conventions, analogous in some ways to the Petrarchan conventions of Renaissance poetry. To uncover and illuminate recurrent material in the *Song* may draw us closer to the distant cultural source of this poetry, while also deepening our appreciation of the individual poems and of the collection as a whole. The following discussions are intended to reveal patterns in the text by illuminating settings and ambiance (which I call "contexts"), underlying premises and ideas ("themes"), and repeated images and symbols ("motifs"). These categories were not fixed in my mind prior to translating; rather, they emerged during the process and, especially, aftersards, when I was able to step back from the text once again and see its contours from a new vantage point.

FOUR BASIC CONTEXTS

Context as setting is not equally dominant in all the poems of the *Song*; some poems depend crucially on setting for their arguments or moods, while others seem not to "take place" anywhere in particular, but to focus more on internal (psychological) space. Yet even when the setting of a poem is undefined, ambiance or atmosphere is present to some degree. Context changes often in the *Song*, from poem to poem and sometimes within poems, creating kaleidoscopic shifts of patterns. Out of this movement we can isolate four basic contexts that, either separately or in combination, color most of the poems in the *Song*:

(a) the cultivated or habitable countryside;
(b) the wild or remote natural landscape and its elements;
(c) interior environments (houses, halls, rooms);
(d) city streets.

(a) All the love dialogues and many of the love monologues take place, at least in part, in the countryside. The pastures of poem 3, the grove of poem 6, the valley and thicket of poem 7, the blossoming spring landscapes of poems 9, 21, and 24, the rocks and ravines of poem 10, the hills of poems 12, 15, and 31, the gardens of poems 18, 19, and 31, and the shade of the quince tree in poem 27 are all tempting and conducive sites for love. Either of the lovers may take the initiative in these settings, which themselves seem to invite lovemaking. The poems which share these lush pastoral contexts tend to portray young, idealized love: the pleasure of anticipation finds at least as much expression here as does the experience of fulfillment. Although the lovers are often separated in the countryside, reunions are expected. Thus, in the benign and receptive rural landscape, invitations to love are playful, suffused with feelings of happy arousal.

The countryside also sets the scene, as background if not foreground, for other types of poems—2, 11, and 30—that are not love monologues or dialogues. In each of these, the country is represented by the vineyard, a special kind of place (discussed below as a separate motif). . . . [T]he tone of these poems is quite different from that of the love monologues just mentioned.

(b) Although nature is generally receptive to the human lovers of the *Song*, another kind of natural context lends a very different ambiance to several poems. This is the landscape of wild, remote, sometimes dangerous nature: the desert/wilderness of poems 14 and 26, the mountain lairs of poem 16, the seas and rivers of poem 28, and the staring eye of the heavens in poems 2 and 20. These elements of nature suggest distant or overwhelming forces, which evoke anxiety or a sense of urgency, as in poems 16 and 28, or create a miragelike atmosphere, as in poems 14 and 26, or suggest mystery, as in poems 2 and 20. Although these natural elements are sometimes central images rather than complete settings, their effect in the poems is always strong; the poems that share this ambiance have a different mood from others in the collection, a mood permeated by awe. In contrast to the countryside setting, this context does not support intimacy; here nature can keep the lovers apart or be a fearsome backdrop to their union. The expression of love is not playful but reverent, sometimes even overwhelmed. Not just *I-Thou* love is expressed in

this context, but a variety of emotional experiences, balancing the more predictable range found in the countryside.

(c) Interior environments take several forms in the *Song*—the king's chambers in poems 1 and 5, the winehall in poem 8, the speaker's bedroom in poems 13 and 19, and the mother's house in poems 13 and 25—are all associated with lovemaking. In addition, poem 9 opens with a woman inside her house, listening for the voice of her lover, and poem 24 closes with an anticipated return from the countryside to the doorways of the lovers' home, where, the speaker promises, lovemaking will reach its climax. The interior environment often encourages the modes of dreams and fantasies, and the imagination seems to have its freest reign here.

Associated twice with the interior context of the home is the mother. The mother's house is the most intimate and protected environment in the *Song*; for this reason, the speakers of poems 13 and 25 want to lead their beloveds out of the streets and back to this private place, where they will be completely free to express their love.

The supportive bond of love between mother and child, which is implied in these poems (and in others not set in this context: 14, 20, 27), is in sharp contrast to some of the sibling relationships portrayed in the *Song*. In poem 2, for example, the "mother's sons" seem to have punished their sister for being sexually active; agian in 29, the brothers want to protect their sister from, or punish her for, having erotic experience. . . . Siblings, however, are not always portrayed as hostile; in poem 25 the speaker says that *if* her lover *were* her brother, she would fel free to kiss him in the public streets, which implies that sibling affection, besides being considered natural, is assumed by the speaker to be socially acceptable. And of course, the metaphorical phrase "my sister, my bride" (poems 17 and 18) also suggests that affection was an inherent aspect of sibling relationships. . . .

Strikingly, no mention of a father—or of the father's home—appears anywhere in the *Song*. Rather, male figures (with the exception of male lovers, and "the king" when used as a metaphor for the lover) play more distant roles, making their appearances in more public places. Public society, as we shall see next, creates a sharply different context from the microcosm of the home.

(d) Of all the contexts of the *Song*, the public domain of the city is the one least sympathetic to the lovers. Thus, the city watchmen or guards are of no help to the woman searching for her beloved in poem 13; in poem 19 these same figures violate the female lover. The speaker of poem 25 senses the city's danger: she knows she cannot kiss her beloved in the streets without exposing herself to ridicule. The city women (literally, "daughters of Jerusalem" or "daughters of Zion") are another group of spectators whose attitude toward the lovers is less than sympathetic: in poems 8, 13, and 25 they must be adjured not to disturb the lovemaking; in poem 19 they offer to help the woman find her beloved only after she entices them with a description of his charms. In poem 2, the city women are the hostile audience of a rural woman whose dark beauty they scorn. (In poem 14, the only other poem in which the daughters of Jerusalem appear, they play a different role. This poem is set in the desert rather than the city, and the women here are associated not with the public streets but with the entourage of the king. I have therefore distinguished them in this context by referring to them, in a more literal translation, as "Jerusalem's daughters.") Like the city guards, the city women provide a foil against which the intimate world-of-two emerges as an ideal; their presence contributes to the conflict and tension that often emerge in poems having urban settings. (I shall explore these ideas further in the ensuing discussions of themes).

Related to the subject of contexts are proper place-names, which appear frequently in the Hebrew text. In Hebrew these names often have considerable resonance, but in translation they lose a great deal. The places named in the Hebrew include: Jerusalem/Zion, Ein Gedi, Lebanon, Mount Gilead, Amana, Senir, Hermon, Tirza, Heshbon, Bat-Rabbim, Damascus, Carmel, and Baal-Hamon. I retained specific names in the translations when I thought they had clear associations for a contemporary English reader, or when I felt that specificity added to, rather than detracted from, the point of the poem. For example, in poem 20 I chose to use the names "Tirza" and "Jerusalem" instead of referring generally to "cities," because the musicality of the one, alongside the familiarity of the other, contributed, I felt, to the poem's atmposphere. More often than not, though, I interpreted the meanings of place-names for the English reader, as in the example of "the slopes" for Mount Gilead. . . . I did not strive for consistency in making these choices; as elsewhere, my decisions were based on the demands of the individual poems and what I believed would allow maximum expression in English verse.

FIVE THEMES AND THEIR VARIATIONS

The themes I analyze here were isolated for various reasons: to point out conceptual connections among poems, to explain otherwise enigmatic material, and to illuminate the intellectual and emotional fabric from which the poems in the *Song* are cut. This analysis does not attempt to cover all the thematic material in the *Song*, but treats instead what plays a significant, though not necessarily obvious, role. The following five themes not only recur but overlap, representing interwoven threads of meaning in over half the poems of the *Song*:

(a) beckoning the beloved (poems 1, 9, 10, 16, 24, 31);
(b) banishment of the beloved—the theme of secret love (poems 12, 15, 31);
(c) search for the beloved (poems 3, 13, 19);
(d) the self in a hostile world (poems 2, 29, 30);
(e) praise of love itself (poems 23, 28).

(a) Beckoning the beloved, a classic theme in the Western courtly love tradition, is central in many of the love monologues and dialogues in the *Song*. Unlike the poetry of courtly love, however, in the *Song* both female and male speakers beckon—or make invitations to—the beloved. As might be expected, beckoning is often accompanied by praise; as a part of courting, beckoning is enhanced by the lavishing of compliments. Poems that share this theme portray the idealism and romanticism of courtship and often have a mood of wondrous expectation about them. Their tone tends to be flirtatious and often coy, though sometimes they are also quite passionate.

The literary devices used to beckon the beloved are various. Sometimes praise and entreaties suffice, as in poems 1, 10, and 31. The speakers of poems 9 and 24 describe the lush countryside in an effort to induce their beloveds to join them there. The argument of these poems is that of the classic spring song: all of nature is mating—why not we too? Poem 16, in contrast, depicts an ominous landscape; the speaker urges his beloved to leave the danger, to "come away" with him.

A linguistic feature associated with the theme of beckoning is the frequent use of verbal imperatives. "Take me away" (literally, "pull me") says the speaker of poem 1. In poems 9, 10, 16, and 24, the speakers use verbal imperatives to extend invitations, which I rendered consistently with the verb "come." I chose this verb in part to suggest thematic similarity among these poems, and partly because more literal translations ("get up," "show me," "go") lack the delicate evocativeness of the Hebrew. The first half of poem 31, which also uses an imperative, seemed to me so imploring in tone that I rendered the imperative as a request: "will you let me hear you?"

In part, the pathos of these poems derives from the pain of the implied separation of the lovers and the strength of their desire to be united. Again, as distinct from the later poetry of the Western tradition, in these poems emotions are shared equally by both lovers, and may be expressed at different moments by either one of them. This mutuality only intensifies the pathos of separation in the *Song*. Separation is involved in other themes as well, and is crucial, as we shall see next, to the theme of secret love.

(b) In poems 12 and 15 and in the second half of 31, the male lover / beloved either is chased away or voluntarily leaves the woman. Poems 12 and 31 may seem particularly puzzling, because the female speaker refers to her beloved with an endearing love name as she banishes him. In poem 31, she is responding to her lover's tender invitation, and one hardly expects her to be unfeeling. In fact, in neither poem is her tone angry or even aloof; yet she is firm in her commands: as in the passages of beckoning, verbal imperatives are used ("turn round" and "go," in my translation). What are we to make of this?

The key to these poems lies, I believe, in viewing the romance as secret, an affair that can be consummated only at night, when the lovers are not exposed to public scrutiny. By chasing her beloved away in poems 12 and 31, the woman is not rejecting him, only exercising caution. The male speaker acts from the same motivation at the close of poem 15.

This interpretation accounts for otherwise enigmatic statements that most standard Bible translations attempt to circumvent. For example, in the second stanza of poem 31 the female speaker responds to her lover's invitation with the rather abrupt-sounding command *b*ᵉ*rah,* which means, literally, "flee." Perhaps because this seems, on first reading, out of tone with the rest of the passage, the standard translations alter the meaning: the King James and Revised Standard Versions render *b*ᵉ*rah* as "make haste," and *The New American Bible* reads "come into the open." But there is no mistaking the meaning of the biblical Hebrew text. The word *b*ᵉ*rah* is neither rare nor ambiguous; it means nto "come" or even "make haste," but "run away—flee."

So too in the second stanza of poem 12, the female speaker tells her beloved to *sov*—literally, "turn," the implication being "turn away from me." *Sov,* in this passage, seems to be analogous to *b*ᵉ*rah* in poem 31, as we can see from reading further in each poem. Both commands are followed by elaborate instructions form the speakers: lines reading, literally, "make yourself, my beloved, like a gazelle or young stag on the split mountains" in poem 12, and "my beloved, make yourself like a gazelle or young stag on the mountains of spices" in poem 31. These lines—so similar as to sound almost like a refrain—seem to link the meaning and intention of the women's speech in the two poems.

Finally, the same Hebrew lines that precede *sov* in poem 12—literally, "until the day breathes and the shadows disappear" (in my translation, "Until the day is over / And the shadows flee")—also precede the statement made by the male speaker at the end of poem 15. In the latter, the speaker voluntarily resolves to go away to the mountains / hills (here they are "the mountain of myrrh" and "the hill of frankincence," rendered together in my translation as "the hills / of fragrant bloom") "until the day breathes and the shadows disappear" (in my translation, "Until / the day is over, / shadows gone"). Thus, the closing of poem 15 seems also to be linked to the endings of poems 12 and 14; indeed, the situation of all three passages seems the same. In all three, the male lover is expected to remove himself from his beloved by running away to the hills; but the qualifying phrase "until the day is over" in poems 12 and 15 limits the duration of the separation. Underlying the explicit speech of all three poems is the unspoken understanding that the man will return to this beloved later—at night, when they will be out of public view.

My reading of the phrase "until the day breathes" as "until the day is over" supports the above interpretation. Some scholars, however, take this phrase to mean "until the day breaks." Mine, I believe, is the simpler reading, in that it assumes the shadows are ordinary sun-shadows whose departure suggests day's end. Moreoever, in a hot Mediterranean climate the day indeed seems to breathe at dusk, when the afternoon wind rises and the air begins to cool.

In our discussin of contexts, we saw that the public domain is unsympathetic to the lovers and that the city is the setting most threatening to the love relationship. Now we see that sometimes even in the countryside, where both male and female speakers express the desire to meet, the lovers feel that their rendezvous must be kept secret, confined to nighttime. This may be because of fear of public censure, or it may be a kind of fiction, part of a lovers' game. In either case, the theme of secret love explains otherwise baffling statements in at least three poems in the **Song**, and may deepen our understanding of other poems as well. For example, beckoning may now be seen as a counterpoint to secrecy: one lover coaxes while the other cautiously hides away. This explains the shyness and coyness of the hidden lover, and the fervor of the one extending the invitation.

The role of the public, as it relates to the theme of secret love, has implications for the interpretation of yet other kinds of poems. It is especially important to the next two themes.

(c) Searching for the beloved is the explicit theme of poems 13 and 19. Both poems open in the bedroom and then move into the city streets, where the speaker encounters the public world. In her search for her beloved, the female speaker of each poem first comes upon the city watchmen, who in poem 13 are unresponsive, and in poem 19 are actually brutal. These are the only two poems in which the figures of the guards appear, and it is difficult to speculate about their actual role in the society. However, as representatives of the public domain—groups of people outside the love relationship—they conform to a general pattern in the *Song*: they represent the real world, so to speak, against which the ideal world-of-two is contrasted.

The city women constitute another such group that appears in several poems of the *Song*. Although never as threatening as the male guards, these figures are often aloof and sometimes hostile spectators, situated outside the love relationship. When their aid is solicited to find the lost beloved in poem 19, they respond at first with reluctance and suspicion: what's so special about your lover that we should bother to help you find him? But after the woman replies with a lengthy and detailed description of him, the women are eager to participate in the search. At this point, the speaker turns them away, affirming that she knows where to find her beloved after all. The closing of this poem suggests that the search for the beloved, frenzied though it seems, may be only a fiction or a game. In other terms, the search may be a metaphorical way of describing the loss that is felt whenever the beloved is not near, even if his whereabouts are known. Alternately, the conclusion of the poem may be a bluff, a desperate fantasy or wish. In either case, when the city women are ready to offer help, they are perceived as intruders. This perception may also explain why, in poem 13, the women are adjured not to wake or rouse the lovers, that is, not to disturb them in their lovemaking. . . .

If we take the view that the urban searches in poems 13 and 19 are fictions or metaphors for feelings of loss, rather than actual odysseys into the streets, we may gain insight into the pastoral search that is the theme of poem 3. Here the speaker directly addresses her beloved with the request to know where she can find him while he is tending his flock, which is to say, during the daytime. The question, one deduces, is asked at night when the lovers are together and by themselves. The tone of the dialogue is coy rather than frantic, which is appropriate to a lovers' game. It is misguided to find the response of the male speaker cold or harshly evasive. The question itself is asked playfully, and the response implies that the woman is not really in need of an answer: "*If* you don't know," says the man—implying that she knows perfectly well where he may be found.

While the woman addresses her beloved directly in this poem, she also makes reference to other individuals outside the intimate relationship. She does not, she says, want to go about begging directions from her lover's friends. The friends here play a role similar to that of the city women in other poems. Though they may not be hostile, neither can they be expected to be of much help. They too represent the public domain which is repeatedly in conflict with the lovers' wish to be united.

(d) In poems 2 and 30, which make symbolic reference to erotic experience but are not specifically addressed to the beloved, we see yet another aspect of the role of figures outside the love relationship. Both these poems are monologues addressed to representatives of the public domain: the city women in one instance, King Solomon in the other. While neither Solomon nor the city women speak in these poems, we are invited to deduce their attitudes from the defiant and even indignant tones of the monologues.

The purpose of the postures struck by the speakers of these poems is self-assertion; both speakers present themselves in contrast to the outside world. Thus in poem 2, the speaker asserts that she is black *and* beautiful, even though others—the city women—may consider her dark skin unattractive. In poem 30, the speaker argues that his vineyard—a symbol for his beloved—is more valuable to him than the vineyard of the king. In both poems, the security provided by the love relationship gives the speakers confidence and even a measure of audacity, with which they are able to confront the public world.

Similarly, the female speaker in the dialogue poem 29 replies to the speech of her overprotective brothers with a declaration of her lover's regard for her. The men in this poem seem to have a punitive attitude toward their younger sister, who responds to them with a proud defiance of their authority. (The brothers referred to in poem 2 may have a similar attitude toward their sister.)

Indignation, defiance, fear, and hostility are emotions that have their parts in the *Song*, emerging often, as we have seen, in connection with the public domain. We find in the *Song* that self-love, like love of the other, meets often with challenges from the outside world but finds constant support in the intimate world-of-two.

(e) Explicit in only two poems, but implied in almost all the poems in the collection, is praise of love itself. As the opening lines of poem 23 exclaim, "Of all pleasure, how sweet / Is the taste of love!" While poem 23 does not pursue this thought explicitly, shifting instead to praise of the beloved, poem 28 is devoted almost entirely to praise of love. In this sense, poem 28 is unique in the collection, and distinguishes itself further by its use of hyperbole and singular imagery. It is the only poem in the *Song* that mentions death, pitting death against love in a contest for power. Love does not necessarily conquer death, the poem expounds, but neither is it conquered by it. Love blazes despite all attempts to put it out.

The opening lines of poem 23 and the middle stanzas

of poem 28 make two different statements about love: whereas the one proclaims the sensual joy of love, the other asserts its power. These two appreciations represent the emotional range of the text. The themes treated above indicate that the fabric of the *Song* is not smooth and even-textured, but knotted with tension and struggle. These aspects of particular love relationships are proclaimed to be the nature of love itself in poems 23 and 28. Taken as a whole, the *Song* eloquently expresses some of the paradoxes of erotic love: conflict that intensifies passion, painful separation that heightens the pleasure of union, intimate bonding with the other that gives the individual courage to stand alone.

SIX CENTRAL MOTIFS

Interwoven among the dominant themes of the *Song* are other, more delicate strands of meaning: images and symbols embroidered into the design of the tapestry. These are what I call motifs; the following recur most often and seem most prominent:

> (a) flora and fauna, and artifice, as
>   complementary sources of imagery;
> (b) the vines and the vineyard, as a special
>   place and as metaphors and symbols;
> (c) the garden, as a special place and as an
>   extended metaphor;
> (d) eating and drinking as erotic metaphors;
> (e) regality and wealth, as metaphors, figures,
>   and foils;
> (f) sensuality and the senses.

(a) The references to flora and fauna in the *Song* are so many and various that the *Song* has come to be thought of as nature poetry. It is true that "'nature poetry' is a clumsy term," as the poet Wendell Berry points out, "for there is a sense in which most poetry is nature poetry; most poets, even those least interested in nature, have found in the world an abundant stock of symbols and metaphors." But in the *Song*, flora and fauna are essential: they abound everywhere, in foregrounds and backgrounds, as real, metaphorical, and symbolic. Plants and animals appear as depictions of the natural landscape (as in poems 3, 6, 9, 16, 19, 21, 24, 27, and 31), as metaphors for the beloved (for example, in poems 4, 5, 7, 9, 10, 12, 18, 23, and 31), and as metaphors for parts of the human body (the best examples of these are in the *wasfs*). The animals in the *Song* include the mare, dove, gazelle, deer, nightingale ("songbird," in my translation), turtledove ("dove," in my translation), fox, lion, leopard, and raven. Most of these are identifiable by their biblical Hebrew names, although the standard English Bibles give somewhat differing translations for a few—for example, "stag" or "hart" for deer, "jackal" for fox. The plants mentioned in the *Song* are even more numerous—over twenty-five varieties of trees, shrubs, flowers, herbs,

fruits, nuts, spices, and nectars—and their identification is more problematic. Because botanical images are so numerous and recurrent in the *Song*, I will comment on their identification, interpretation, and translation before discussing their relationship to the world of artifice.

Like most botanical references in the Bible, those in the *Song* are difficult to identify because their biblical names do not necessarily correspond to modern Hebrew usage. For example, while today the word *tappuah* means "apple," it must have referred to something else in biblical times, because apples were not indigenous to ancient Israel. The translations in standard English Bibles and other versions of the *Song* tend to be misleading because the translators have hardly investigated the original referents of biblical plant names. And when modern versions do depart from the traditional renderings, they often do no more than guess at the meanings of these words; they rarely go so far as to attempt to determine the impact these images might have had in their original poetic contexts.

I believe that faithful translation of botanical imagery in the *Song* has three stages: first, accurate identification of the referent of the biblical Hebrew plant name to the extent possible; second, interpretation of the effect of the image in its original poetic context; finally, choice of an English word or phrase that will both evoke the original landscape and ahve an analogous effect in the new context of the English poem.

I was greatly assisted in the first stage by the findings of the research institute Neot Kedumim (the Gardens of Israel). The staff members at Neot Kedumim have done important work in the field of biblical botany; by consulting native speakers of languages that are cognate with Hebrew but that, unlike Hebrew, have retained the same common botanical names over the centuries, they have succeeded in identifying many of the plants named in the Bible. In addition, by cultivating and studying the terrain of present-day Israel, they have been able to make reasonable conjectures about the vegetation of biblical times. I considered the information provided by Neot Kedumim to be authoritative in most cases, and I used it as the basis for the next two stages, the interpretation of effect and the choice of English analogues. . . .

[W]hen a flower was used in the *Song* as a metaphor, I tried first to determine the point of the comparison: was it visual beauty, or fragrance, or perhaps texture that was being called to mind? I then searched for an equivalent image in English, one that would have similar impact on the modern reader. When using specific names, I tried, as often as possible, to name in English the same plants named in the Hebrew; but if these plants had accrued, over the centuries, inappropriate associations (as with myrrh and frankincense), or if the

English names sounded archaic or awkward, I found alternate expressions. In addition, I sometimes substituted descriptions for specific names (such as "sweet fruit tree growing wild" for *tappuah . . .*) and sometimes named plants of closely related species or having similar characteristics. I did not translate botanical images consistently from poem to poem, but let the demands of the individual poems guide my decisions. For example, I translated the oft-mentioned *šošannah* (narcissus) at different moments as "narcissus," "lily," "daffodil," "wildflower," and sometimes simply "flower"; in some cases I used different translations within a single poem, in order to stress a particular point in English. . . . Although I translated these images with considerable flexibility, I tried throughout to respect the integrity of the original landscape by never naming plants that could not have been part of it; I also did not name plants that would be totally unfamiliar to modern English readers.

The decisions I made in translating botanical images were difficult because these images, more than most others, convey specific, culture-bound information that resists migration. Plants tend not to be hardy travelers, so one must take pains when carrying them across to new terrain, lest their vitality be endangered.

Although plant and animal images are found throughout the **Song**, they are by no means the exclusive source of metaphor. Even in the *wasfs,* which rely heavily on natural imagery, metaphors are drawn from the realms of artifice—art, craft, and architecture—and these seem to mingle freely with metaphors from nature. Thus in the *wasf* of poem 19, the man's hair is black as a raven, his eyes are like doves, his cheeks like spices, his lips like flowers, and his stature or appearance like cedars in the mountains; but his arms are cylinders of gold studded with jewels, his belly is a slab of ivory inlaid with gems, and his legs are marble columns set on gold stands—all images evoking sculptural and architectural forms. Similarly, in the *wasf* of poem 15, the woman's lips are like threads of silk and her neck like a tower adorned with shields, images of artifice and architecture that are interspersed among images from nature—doves, goats, sheep, pomegranates, fawns. So too in the *wasf* of poem 22, thighs like spinning jewels suggest the artisan's handicraft, and the towerlike neck and face connote architectural grandeur, but the natural landscape—of wheat, flowers, pools, and mountains—lends images for other parts of the body.

In addition, the artifice of military society provides images for some poems in the **Song**. The tower in poem 15 is hung with the shields of warriors; the wall, door, and turrets of poem 29 suggest the structure of a fortress; sixty sword-bearing warriors in poem 14 attend the procession of the king. It is fascinating to note that military imagery in the **Song** applies more

often to descriptions of a female than of a male—one more example of the **Song**'s reversal of our stereotypical expectations.

Finally, the argument of poem 4 makes explicit what is implied throughout the **Song**: while the beloved is perceived as naturally beautiful, the speaker sees no harm adding artificial adornment; artifice does not compete with nature but complements it. Similar to other contrasts we have observed—such as between public and private domains or separation and union of lovers—the relationship between the natural world and the world of human artifacts is mutually intensifying and contributes to the density of the **Song**'s texture.

(b) The words *gefen,* "vine," and *kerem,* "vineyard," appear in eight poems in the **Song**, often more than once in each. I have translated these words in various ways—"vine," "vineyard," "grapevine," "grapes"—depending on the needs of the English poems. For the sake of this discussion, however, I will revert to a stricter distinction between the two Hebrew words. *Gefen* appears in poems 9, 21, 23, and 24; *kerem,* in poems 2, 5, 11, 24, and 30.

In poems 9, 21 and 24, *gefen* refers to the grapevine in the stage of budding or early fruit, when it gives forth fragrance. All three of these poems are spring songs, and the *gefen* is one of the details in the springtime landscape. In all three, moreover, the budding vines are associated with erotic experience, invited or anticipated by one of the lovers. In poem 23, *gefen* appears in the phrase *eškᵉlot haggefen,* "clusters of the vine"; here the reference is to the mature fruit, and I have rendered it "clusters of grapes." The poet evokes the smooth round fruit of the vine as a metaphor for the beloved's breasts.

The word *kerem* is also used in various ways. In poem 24 it refers to a vineyard, which, like the fields where the henna blooms, is an appealing site for the lovers. In poem 5 it is associated with Ein Gedi, where, according to the poem, *kofer,* "henna" ("blossoms," in my translation), is found. Because Ein Gedi is an oasis in the desert and henna does not grow on vines, the *kerem* of poem 5 seems to be not a vineyard but a general place of vegetation, and I have rendered it here as "oasis."

While in both poems 5 and 24 *kerem* refers to a place of vegetation, a wider range of meanings is suggested in poems 2, 11, and 30, because it is impossible to interpret these poems coherently without a symbolic reading. In each of these poems, *kerem* is mentioned several times, and once in each it is in the first-person-possessive: "my vineyard" in poems 2 and 30, "our vineyards" in poem 11. In poems 2 and 30 an emphatic modifier, *šelli,* "mine," follows the possessive *karmi,* "my vineyard." The female speaker of poem 2 says that she has been made to watch the vineyards (although the Hebrew does not specify whose these are, we may deduce from the context that they belong to the speaker's brothers) and meanwhile she has not watched her own. The male speaker of poem 30 says that Solomon has a prosperous vineyard but that his, the speaker's, own vineyard is more precious to him than Solomon's. Both poems suggest that the vineyard is to be understood as more than a literal place; at least when referred to in the possessive form, it seems to be also a symbol for female sexuality. Thus when the woman speaks of her vineyard, she refers to herself; when the man speaks of his own vineyard, he refers to his beloved. In poem 2, the woman alludes to not having guarded her own sexuality; in poem 30, the speaker asserts that his beloved is not to be shared with anyone else.

Poem 11 contains the most cryptic of all the references to *kerem,* because here it is unclear who is speaking and to whom. But once again the poem makes most sense if we understand the *kerem* symbolically: the foxes (a masculine noun in the Hebrew) are raiding the vineyards and therefore must be caught; if the "little foxes" are young men, might the vineyards be young women?

It should not be disconcerting to find *kerem* used in several different ways in the collection. The accumulated meanings enhance the resonance of each occurrence of the motif, and from this layering comes textual richness.

(c) The garden, like the vineyard, appears in several different poems in the *Song,* sometimes as a location and sometimes as a metaphor for the female beloved. Even when it refers to a location, however, it is generally associated with the woman, and it sometimes simultaneously symbolizes her.

In poem 31, the garden is the place where the female beloved is situated; in the penultimate stanza of poem 19, it is a place entered by a male. The walnut orchard of poem 21 is literally a "walnut garden," to which the speaker "goes down" ("walking," in my translation) to observe the opening of the flowers. In poem 19, the male "has gone down" to "his garden" to feed his sheep and gather flowers. The links between these two passages—the same verb and the similar references to flowers or flowering—make a strong argument for viewing the otherwise unidentifiable speaker of poem 21 as male. The association of the garden with the female beloved in poem 31 further suggests a symbolic level of meaning in poems 19 and 21: the garden represents the female beloved, who is "gone down to" by the male; the gathering and eating of flowers may be read as the male's erotic play on the woman's body, and the opening of the flowers as the woman's response.

In poem 18, the garden is *explicitly* erotic, functioning as an extended metaphor that describes the beloved. The word *gan,* "garden," appears five times in the Hebrew poem, three times in the possessive ("my garden" and "his garden"). Like the vineyard in poems 2 and 30, the garden in poem 18 can belong to either the woman or the man, but it seems to refer in both cases to the woman herself or to her sexuality. Thus the female speaker calls upon the winds to breathe on *ganni,* "my garden," invoking her beloved to come to *ganno,* "his garden." These two references are, of course, to the same garden, and to avoid confusion in the English I omitted the phrase "his garden" here. In the following stanza the male speaker replies that he has come to "my garden," thus accepting the gift that the woman has offered.

As in poem 19, the male speaker in poem 18 gathers plants (this time spices rather than flowers) in his garden, and also feasts there. Because poem 18 is controlled by an extended metaphor in which the female is compared to the garden itself, to the water that flows in it, and to all the varieties of vegetation (fruits, flowers, woods, spices) that grow in it, the activities of the male in the garden—entering, gathering, and eating—are also to be seen as erotic. The use of the garden as an extended metaphor in poem 18 . . . suggests ways to view the motif of eating and drinking in other poems as well.

(d) The Hebrew word-root *,kl,* "eat," appears three times in the *Song,* all in poem 19, where I have translated it variously as "share," "taste," and "feast"—verbs that build in intensity as they approach the poem's climax. The female speaker in the poem expresses the wish that her beloved will come to his garden and eat ("share") its choice fruits; the male speaker replies that he has come to gather spices, to eat ("taste") his honey and drink his wine and milk. At the conclusion of the poem, a third voice invites the two lovers to eat ("feast") and drink, even to the point of intoxication ("drink deeply," in my translation). Clearly, eating and drinking are symbols of erotic experience; the association of eating and drinking with the garden, and with the activity of gathering in particular, suggests that eroticism is implied also in other settings where eating and drinking occur.

For example, in the penultimate stanza of poem 19, the woman says that her beloved has gone down to his garden *lir'ot,* "to pasture" (in my version, "to feed his sheep"), and to gather flowers. In the last stanza she refers to him as *haro'eh baššošannim,* "the one who pastures among the flowers," an appellation that appears in poem 12 as well (I translate the phrase, in both instances, "Who leads his flock to feed / Among the flowers"). The Hebrew word for pasturing, or feeding one's flocks, also appears in poem 3: there the female speaker asks her beloved where he pastures ("where you feed your sheep," in my version), and the male speaker replies by telling her to pasture her own flocks among the fields of the other "ones who pasture" ("the shepherds," in my translation). In all these cases where the word-root *r'h* appears, there is an implied second level of meaning. Because pasturing is associated with the garden, with flowers, and with gathering—all of which have erotic connotations, the more so when they appear in combination—there is the strong suggestion that pasturing means not only feeding one's flock but feeding oneself in the act of love. Because the garden and its flowers are, as we have seen, often associated with the female body, pasturing is usually symbolic of male sexual activity. The one who pastures in the flowers is always a male (although poem 3 contains a reference to a woman who pastures, flowers are not mentioned in that instance).

Other, more direct references to the activities of eating and drinking, however, are not restricted to males; these too have erotic associations. In poem 7, the female speaker says that her beloved's fruit is sweet to her palate ("I taste your love," in my translation); here the male is compared to a fruit tree, and the speaker finds pleasure in dwelling in his shadow and tasting his fruit. In poem 8, the female speaker asks to be refreshed and sustained with raisincakes and quinces—an unusual request from one who is "sick with love." It seems that her hunger is not so much for cakes and fruits as for her lover's embraces, about which she fantasizes in the succeeding lines.

The food in the *Song* most emphatically associated with lovemaking is wine. More than once it is mentioned by way of complimenting a beloved: for example, that her mouth is like good wine (poem 23), or that her lovemaking is better than wine (poem 17), or that *his* lovemaking is better than wine (poem 1). The speaker of poem 17 goes on to praise his beloved in detail, not failing to mention the taste of honey and milk on her tongue, thus making explicit the association between lovemaking and food. Honey and milk (probably a "fixed pair," a convention of oral poetry) are linked with wine in poem 18 as well. In both poems, honey and milk lend added sweetness to the imagery of the wine and reinforce its erotic overtones.

The imagery of wine is perhaps nowhere more erotic, however, than in poem 25, where it is in parallel position to the nectar of pomegranates. The speaker of this poem offers to take her beloved to her mother's home, where she will give him spiced wine and the juice of her pomegranate to drink. The pomegranate, long recognized as a fertility symbol in ancient culture, is mentioned in connection with females several times in the *Song*: as a fruit of the gardens in poems 18 and 21, and as a metaphor for the woman's forehead in the *wasfs*. In poem 25 it seems to be a symbol, like the vineyard, of the woman's sexuality, an image that the

first person possessive, "my pomegranate," emphasizes. The lines that follow are the same as those that follow the request for food in poem 8 (which, incidentally, takes place in a winehall); and in both instances, the allusions to feasting lead into the woman's fantasy of her beloved's embrace. Feasting, it seems, always has erotic overtones in the *Song*, and wine is the most intoxicating temptation to the feast.

(e) Like the other motifs discussed here, regality is treated in various ways in the *Song*, but unlike the others, its connotations can be either positive or negative. Thus, when the beloved is compared to a king, as in poems 1 and 5, the regal image is clearly a compliment, a way of expressing affection and esteem. This is also the effect of calling the woman a princess in poem 22, and of stating, in the same poem, that she captures kings in the tresses of her hair—as if to say that her beauty is capable of attracting *anyone*. In poem 2, the image of King Solomon's tapestries also has positive associations: it is a metaphor for the speaker's black and lovely skin.

But in other poems, regality acts as a foil for the speaker or the beloved. The most vehement assertion is in poem 30, in which the speaker contrasts his own vineyard with the king's and proclaims his own to be superior. Similarly, but without the tone of defiance, the speaker of poem 20 sets his beloved against a backdrop of sixty queens, and proclaims her so remarkable that even the regal figures sing her praises. In both poems, the speaker contrasts the uniqueness of his beloved with the multitude of the regal holdings. The vineyard in poem 30 yields great wealth for its owner (the Hebrew specifies a thousand pieces of silver); in poem 20, the queens, concubines ("brides," in my translation), and young women, who are all possessions of the king, number in the scores. But these large numbers, signifying affluence and luxury, cannot compete, in the speaker's eyes, with his one, own beloved. He would not, he declares in poem 30, trade his beloved for all of Solomon's harem.

Wealth cannot compete with love, suggest the speakers of these poems. The female speaker of poem 28 asserts even more emphatically that a man is to be scorned if he attempts to buy love in the marketplace. Even were he to offer, as the Hebrew indicates, "all the wealth of his house," he could never purchase love with money.

Wealth, however, like regality, has more than one connotation in the *Song*. In poem 4 the speaker offers to adorn his beloved with gold and silver, gifts offered in the spirit of love. In poem 14, the poem in which regality is most central, the splendors of wealth—gold, silver, and cedar—adorn the king's wedding procession. The exquisite appeals of the imagery—the smells of the incense, the colors of the carriage—make regality and wealth seem enthralling; as fervently as they are elsewhere scorned, they are here celebrated. This discrepancy in attitudes toward the figure of the king attests again to the benefit of reading the poems of the *Song* as discrete units rather than parts of a unified whole.

(f) It should by now be apparent that the *Song* is a text extraordinarily rich with sensory imagery. By far the most prevalent sensory material in the text is visual (especially in the *wasfs*); in addition, references to sight and to visions recur in several places (in poem 20; also in poem 17, where a flash of the beloved's eyes thrills the heart). References to smell are also abundant, as in the many mentions of flowers, fruits, spices, perfumes, and even the aroma of the Lebanon mountains. The sense of taste is evoked in several poems, always seeming to suggest erotic experience. Sound is used less metaphorically, but the sounds of voices are important erotic enticements (as in poems 9, 10, 19, and 31); and, of course, sound-plays are essential in the construction of the Hebrew verse itself, alliteration being a common poetic device. The sense of touch is evoked with every wish for the lover's embrace (for example, in the couplets preceding the adjuration in poems 8 and 25) and is further implied in some of the more elusive metaphors (breasts "like fawns" in poems 15 and 22, and like "clusters of grapes" in poem 23). Finally, synesthesia is used to striking effect in poem 1, where a name, as remembered or heard, is associated with a fragrance. . . .

While I have not treated each of the senses as a separate motif, their importance is, I hope, apparent from the discussions of the other motifs to which they relate. Indeed, there is probably nothing more essential to appreciation of poetic effect in the *Song* than a readiness to respond to sensuality.

E. Ann Matter (essay date 1990)

SOURCE: "The Woman Who is the All: The Virgin Mary and the *Song of Songs*," in *The Voice of My Beloved: The Song of Songs in Western Medieval Christianity,* University of Pennsylvania Press, 1990, pp. 151-77.

[*In the following essay, Matter explores medieval Christian interpretations of the* Song of Songs *which associate the figure of the Bride with the Virgin Mary.*]

The female gender of one of the voices of the *Song of Songs*, so much more obvious in Latin than in English, elicited little comment from the medieval exegetes who worked in the allegorical and tropological modes. Of course, as both *Ecclesia* and *anima* are feminine nouns in Latin, there was no linguistic difficulty in putting the words of the Bride in the mouth of the Church or

of the human soul. But a logical consequence of medieval fascination with the *Song of Songs* was an association of the Bride with a human, a woman, although a highly idealized figure, the Virgin Mary. This form of personification begins early in the Latin *liturgical* tradition, and gradually becomes a part of *Song of Songs* commentary. In the history of western Christian interpretation, *use* of the *Song of Songs* in praise of the Virgin is a precursor, and to some extent a determinant, of a tradition of exegesis in the mariological mode. The confluence of marian liturgies and mariological *Song of Songs* exegesis is another interesting example of both the continual inner transformation and the outward expansion of the commentary genre.

The *Song of Songs* in Liturgies of the Virgin

Veneration of the Virgin Mary in western Christianity is closely linked to theological speculation about the humanity and divinity of Jesus Christ. The paradox of divine incarnation is, of course, a central tenet of Christian doctrine. Periods of high christology, especially those linked to eucharistic formulations, tended to be accompanied by liturgies in honor of the Virgin Mary. Three events in the Virgin's life became the focus of major devotions: her special nativity, her bodily assumption into heaven (both testified to by extra-canonical Christian writings), and her ritual purification according to Jewish law after the birth of Jesus (testified to by the Gospel of Luke). Liturgies for the feasts of the Nativity, Assumption, and Purification of the Virgin Mary had developed uses of the *Song of Songs* by the seventh century. These references to the *Song of Songs* became especially prominent, and received elaborate comment tending toward commentary, in the theologically expansive Carolingian Church. The Assumption of the Virgin Mary was the feast which especially brought about a transformation of the liturgical use of the *Song of Songs* to a marian level of interpreting the text.

Perhaps because of a desire to link liturgical practice to the formative figures of Latin Christianity, two of the most influential Carolingian treatises about the Virgin Mary are pseudonymous, bearing attributions to Augustine and Jerome. Jaroslav Pelikan has pointed out that when tracing theological elements of the early Middle Ages, it is often "more difficult than current conventional wisdom among theologians suggests to tell the difference between the 'pious fraud' of pseudonymity and just plain forgery." In any case, and however they may be judged by modern readers, the anonymous homily *De Assumptione Beatae Mariae Virginis,* which circulated as a work of Augustine, and the pseudonymous work of Paschasius Radbertus known as *Cogitis me* ("You Compel Me"), which was transmitted as Epistle 9 of Jerome, were far more widely read than anything either Jerome or Augustine actually

A twelfth-century representation of Christ and the Church; each holds a scroll with a quotation from the Song.

wrote about the Virgin Mary. This fact has a certain irony which is compounded by the probability that Augustine would have disapproved of the unapologetic use of the **Song of Songs** as a canonical reference to the Assumption of the Virgin.

Cogitis me is probably the earlier treatise, and it certainly makes the more important connection between the **Song of Songs** and the Feast of the Assumption. It is by far the most popular of a number of mariological works written by the ninth-century monk and sometimes abbot of Corbie, Paschasius Radbertus. The text opens with a conscious literary conceit, claiming that it is a letter of Jerome to his friends Paula and Eustochium, nuns in Bethlehem, when it actually was written by Radbertus for his friends and childhood protectors, Theodrada and Irma, nuns of Soissons. Like Jerome's friends, Theodrada and Irma were a mother-daughter pair dedicated to the life of Christian contemplation. Their relationship to Radbertus was extremely close, since Radbertus had been left as a foundling at the monastery, a house dedicated to the Virgin Mary,

where Theodrada (a cousin of Charlemagne) was abbess. He received monastic tonsure at this house before moving to Corbie, where Theodrada's brothers, Adalard and Wala, were abbots in the first third of the ninth century.

Posing as a famous figure from biblical or even classical antiquity was a common enough practice among Carolingian literary figures, especially those, like Radbertus, who had some contact with the ways of the court. But the pseudepigrahical attribution of *Cogitis me* to Jerome had more serious consequences than those, for example, of Charlemagne posing as David or Alcuin playing Horace, for the text passed enthusiastically through the Middle Ages with only one ripple of dissent when Hincmar, Bishop of Reims, had a luxury copy written for his cathedral chapter shortly after the death of Radbertus. To medieval eyes, *Cogitis me* was received as Jerome's elegant testimony to the Feast of the Assumption.

Cogitis me is, moreover, an exemplary document for discerning the influence of particular liturgies on Carolingian theology, end on the changing genre of **Song of Songs** interpretation. This is particularly so because Radbertus's text stays quite close to one important liturgical source, the Antiphoner of Compiègne, a manuscript from the monastery of Saint-Corneille associated by tradition with Charles the Bald. Quotations from the **Song of Songs** in the *Cogitis me* can usually also be found in this liturgical tradition, in a series of antiphons and responses to the Common of Virgins, to the Nativity of the Virgin Mary, and, especially, to the Assumption. These liturgical uses brought with them the earliest associations of the **Song of Songs** with the Virgin Mary, a *devotional* tradition with roots at least as far back as Ambrose.

The liturgy has always provided an arena for the ritual adaptation of sacred texts. In the monastic tradition, the liturgy was not limited to the Mass, but included the continual round of monastic offices, each of which drew antiphonary material from the Bible. This daily liturgical discipline provided a social and intellectual context in which adaptation of the **Song of Songs** for marian feasts flourished. A striking example of this process can be seen in a composite version of **Song of Songs** 6:9 and 6:3 which in the Antiphoner of Compiègne appears as an antiphon for the Vespers of the Feast of the Assumption of Mary:

> quae est ista quae ascendit
> quasi aurora consurgens
> pulchra ut luna electa ut sol
> terribilis ut castrorum acies ordinata

> Who is this who ascends
> like the rising dawn
> beautiful as the moon, chosen as the sun

terrible as a battle line drawn up from the
camps?

This is not a known Vetus Latina text. In fact, it is
extremely close to the Vulgate texts from which it is
drawn, varying in only one small but important word:
"ascendit" for "progreditur." The change from "goes
forth" to "ascends" emphasizes the connection of the
verses to the Feast of the Assumption. Radbertus must
have been quite familiar with this liturgy, for he quotes
this peculiar, "marianized" composite both in the deliberately pseudepigraphical *Cogitis me* and in the first
of his Assumption sermons, a text which is accidentally pseudepigraphical, having been incorporated into the
series of sermons attributed to Ildefonsus of Toledo.
Other quotations from the *Song of Songs* in *Cogitis
me* also show the influence of the liturgical tradition of
the Antiphoner of Compiègne by particular combinations of verses, or minor textual variants. Scrutiny of
these passages suggests how the liturgical tradition led
Radbertus to speak of the Virgin Mary as the Bride of
the *Song of Songs*; but the theological use which
Radbertus found for *Song of Songs* texts in his treatises on the Virgin marks the beginning of a new mode
of exegesis.

The complexity of this movement from liturgical use
to a mode of exegesis is evident in the way Radbertus
quotes a crucial passage for marian exegesis of the
Song of Songs 4:12b-13:

> Whence it is sung about her in those same **Canticles**:
> "A garden enclosed, a fountain sealed, your shoots
> a paradise." Truly a garden of delights, in which are
> planted all kinds of flowers, and the good scents of
> virtues; and so enclosed that it cannot be violated
> or corrupted by any trick of deceit. Therefore, a
> fountain sealed with the seal of the whole Trinity,
> out of which flows the fountain of life, "in whose
> light we all see light," (Psalm 35:10, Vulgate) since
> according to John, "He is the one who sheds light
> on every man coming into this world." (John 1:9).
> In the shoot springing forth from her womb is the
> paradise of the heavenly citizen.

In this passage, Mary and Jesus are described by pastoral images of the *Song of Songs* which become
metaphors of salvation: she is a garden, a fountain, out
of which springs Christ, the Logos, the paradise of the
blessed. Although the imagery is highly laudatory of
the Virgin Mary, it nevertheless makes clear that her
major virtue lies in being the spotless source of the
incarnate God. The function of the *Song of Songs* here
resonates clearly with the commentary genre as it had
developed to the ninth century. The tropological or
moral understanding of the *Song of Songs* greatly informs this treatise, in the sense that the Virgin becomes a spiritual model offered to the religious women
for whom the treatise was written, perhaps in a conscious echo of Jerome's Epistle 22 to Eustochium.

Cassian's allegorical mode is also evident here, mediated through an understanding of Mary as the Church,
the "garden enclosed" of many earlier Latin commentaries on the *Song of Songs*. This subtle mixture of
allegory in the service of theology, an approach which
could be properly called "mariological" as well as
"marian," is the spirit in which Radbertus quotes the
"hortus conclusus" passage here. The same attitude is
also found in Radbertus's defense of the virginity of
Mary *in partu,* and in his commentary on the epith-
alamial Vulgate Psalm 44, "My heart proffers a good
word."

Although Radbertus had set the stage for a mariological reading of the *Song of Songs*, it was not until the
twelfth century that this mode of exposition was fully
realized. Liturgies of the Virgin Mary are also very
close to the first systematic mariological exposition of
the *Song of Songs*, the *Sigillum Beatae Mariae* of
Honorius Augustodunensis. In fact, the liturgy can be
said to have sparked this text, since the *Sigillum* begins with a demand "discipuli ad magistrum" why Luke
10:38 (the story of Mary and Martha) and the *Song of
Songs* are read in the Assumption liturgy "about holy
Mary, since in no way do they appear clearly to pertain
to her." The *Sigillum* is made up of short commentaries on this Gospel and the Epistle of the Assumption,
followed by a complete, line-by-line, exposition of the
antiphonal text for the feast, the *Song of Songs*, understood as depicting the love between God and the Virgin Mary.

Valerie Flint has suggested that the *Sigillum* was written early in Honorius's career, perhaps about 1100, in
England, perhaps Worcester. It is a composite work,
woven together from a number of sources. The first
section, on the Gospel, is a reworking of a homily
attributed to Anselm, actually written by Ralph
d'Escures, abbot of Saint-Martin of Séez in Normandy.
The Ecclesiastes interpretation is adapted from another
pseudo-Anselmian sermon, changing the reference from
Christ and the Church to the Virgin Mary. This change
of reference also characterizes the major part of the
treatise, the mariological commentary on the *Song of
Songs*, an interpretation of some ingenuity and great
complexity of sources.

Honorius begins this exposition of the *Song of Songs*
with an analogy between Mary and the Church which
works on several levels:

> The glorious Virgin Mary manifests the type of the
> Church, which is shown to be both virgin and
> mother. Indeed, she [the Church] is proclaimed
> mother since she is fecundated by the Holy Spirit;
> through her every day children of God are born in
> baptism. She is, moreover, called virgin because,
> inviolably serving the integrity of faith, she is not
> corrupted by heretical perverseness. So Mary was a
> mother bringing forth Christ, remaining a virgin after

the parturition. Therefore all things which are written about the Church may be sufficiently appropriately read even about her [Mary]. Thus it says: "Let him kiss me from the kiss of his mouth." This very one whom kings and prophets were not worthy to see or hear, the Virgin was not only worthy to carry in her womb, but even, when born, to frequently give him kisses, receiving many from his sacred mouth. "For your breasts are better than wine." He who pastures the angels in the bosom of the Father, here sucks at the breast of the virgin mother.

The allegorical fluidity of this passage is remarkable. Subject and object, signified and signifier, slip back and forth even as the mode of interpretation shifts in mid-sentence. As far as the **Song of Songs** is concerned, Honorius seems to presume that the allegorical interpretation includes the mariological, since "all things which are written about the Church may be sufficiently appropriately *(satis congrue)* read even about her," that is, Mary. There is also a hint of the kiss of mystical union, several decades before Bernard of Clairvaux's third sermon on the **Song of Songs**, in the rapture with which the Virgin's kisses on the mouth of Christ are described. Finally, an apocalyptic vision of Christ, the shepherd of the angelic flock in the bosom of the Father, is seen in the child nursing at the breast of the virgin mother. As we have seen, these modes of understanding appear in a more highly developed form in Honorius's long **Song of Songs** commentary, but they are already present in this text from the beginning of his career, adapted to the Virgin Mary.

The *Sigillum* is thus important evidence of the transition from marian use to mariological interpretation of the **Song of Songs**. Indeed, this is a biblical, rather than a liturgical, commentary. The text of the **Song of Songs** is the Vulgate (including "progreditur" instead of "ascendit" at 6:9), and the exposition proceeds from verse to verse, each chapter expounding one chapter of the **Song of Songs**. Yet the *Sigillum* is related to what seems to be a homiletical tradition, perhaps falling between the activities of the choir and the chapter, and testifying to a tradition of spoken reflection on the **Song of Songs** on feasts of the Virgin.

The homiletical tone of this explanation is evident also in a series of rubrics which begin near the end of the second chapter of the *Sigillum.* The rubrics identify changes of voice in the text, while suggesting a line of interpretation: "The prayer of the Virgin for converts," "The praise of the Son for the Mother," "The praise of the Father for the Virgin," "The words of the Virgin hoping for Christ to come into her," "On the solicitude of the Virgin for the Church of the Jews." This last rubric is one of several which speak of the intercession of the Virgin Mary for the conversion of the Jews. In general, these titles stress the intercessory powers of the Virgin, and suggest a devotional context in which

the miracles of the Virgin were a part of a growing cult.

The *Sigillum Beatae Mariae* bears witness to a type of devotion to the Virgin that flourished especially among the Benedictines of Western England. Honorius tells five miracles of the Virgin in this text, four of them (the Jewish boy, Theophilus, Mary the harlot, the salvific belt) near the beginning and another (the miraculous revelation to a holy hermit of the date of the Virgin's Nativity) at the end. Flint has shown that several of these miracles can be traced to the Worcester Passionale, a compilation of mariological texts which also included the *Cogitis me.* Not surprisingly, Honorius alludes to the *Cogitis me* immediately after the story of the hermit. Traces of Paschasius Radbertus are found throughout the commentary, even, perhaps, in a reference to the "hortus conclusus" of 4:12 as the virginity of Mary at the moment of the birth of Christ. The religious life looms large in the *Sigillum,* here again, Mary is represented as the "primum exemplum virginitatis." Her virginity is, moreover, the source of the truly miraculous birth which Christ "reserved" for himself:

> God makes human beings in four ways: from the earth, as Adam; from man alone, as Eve; from man and woman, as us; from woman alone, Christ, since he reserved the privilege for himself.

The *Sigillum,* written at the very beginning of the twelfth century, shows equal influence of the ancient marian liturgical tradition and the growing cult of the Virgin. This century is, of course, the period in which is found the greatest increase in outright devotion to the Virgin, with both liturgical and literary responses. Even in the twelfth century, marian understanding of the **Song of Songs** was still linked to the liturgy; an even stronger connection was forged between the **Song of Songs** and the celebration of the Feast of the Assumption by the twelfth-century standardization of verses from the **Song of Songs** in the monastic office of the day and its octave. A number of twelfth-century sermons for the Assumption reinforce the general marian understanding of the **Song of Songs** while expanding on the liturgical use of one verse, as does the *Sermo de Assumptione Beatae Virginis* of Hugh of Saint-Victor, written for a certain Gerlandus, abbot of a monastery dedicated to the Virgin Mary.

Commentary on liturgical uses of the **Song of Songs** is especially interesting in its consistent application of dialogue to the text. Of course, the voices of the **Song of Songs** always speak either in monologue or dialogue, and we have already noted a tradition of rubrics in Latin Bibles which tended to emphasize this feature of the text. But the antiphonal nature of liturgy, where biblical verses respond to one another, creates an atmosphere of aural awareness of the **Song of Songs** which is lost to modern readers. When Paschasius Radbertus and Hugh of Saint-Victor wrote homilies on the Assumption, it can be said without exaggeration that they had verses from the *Song of Songs* ringing in their ears. Honorius's *Sigillum* also obviously began from a liturgical, spoken knowledge of the *Song of Songs*, and underlined a dialogical mood through its structure—questions and answers between students and a master. This spoken, responsory nature of the earliest marian interpretation of the *Song of Songs* fades as twelfth-century authors begin consciously to model their works on the commentary genre, becoming more oriented towards mariology than marian devotion. But this is a gradual process.

The Virgin Mary in *Song of Songs* Commentary

It is with the exegesis of Rupert of Deutz that mariological exposition of the *Song of Songs* takes the form classic to the commentary genre. Rupert was born near Liège around the year 1075, and spent much of his career in zealous support of monastic reform, especially in the Benedictine houses in the German Empire. He was certainly the paramount Latin Christian writer between Anselm of Canterbury and Bernard of Clairvaux. John Van Engen has called him "the most prolific of all twelfth century authors," and has shown that he was greatly influenced by the systematic approach to the Bible characteristic of the "masters of the Sacred Page." Rupert's exegesis is squarely and consciously in the midst of the development of theology as a school discipline. He wrote many biblical commentaries, beginning with . . . the Apocalypse and the *Song of Songs*. Rupert's second exegetical work *Commentaria in Canticum Canticorum (de Incarnatione Domini)* dates from around 1125. This text is extremely innovative in that it uses Cassian's modes to move the explication of the text beyond the bounds of Cassian's system.

Rupert's title proclaims his theological purpose, a reading of the *Song of Songs* as a love poem on the mystery of the incarnation of Christ. But here the *Song* is consistently understood to be in honor of the *vehicle* of this mysterious incarnation, the Virgin Mary. Rupert interprets the entire text of the *Song of Songs* with reference to the Virgin. Although abstracted from liturgical use, the commentary in some ways continues the dialogical nature of earlier marian exposition on the *Song of Songs*; much of it is written in the second person, addressing Mary directly, or even in the first person, allowing her to speak for herself in the words of the poems. This treatise, the shortest of Rupert's exegetical works, is much longer than the marian interpretations of the *Song of Songs* we have considered thus far. This is a fully developed monastic commentary heavily dependent on several treatises in the allegorical mode: the ninth-century *Song of Songs* catena of Angelomus of Luxeuil, the *Song of Songs* commen-

tary of Gregory the Great, and also Jerome's *Interpretatio hebraicorum nominum*. We have already seen easy shifts of understanding of the *Song of Songs* from the Church to the Virgin, but none that developed the new understanding at this theological level. Rupert consistently used sources from the prevailing ecclesiological tradition of the *Song of Songs* to elaborate a full theology of the Virgin Mary which he found in the text.

In spite of the precedent set by treatises based on the liturgies of the Virgin, both Rupert and his contemporaries seemed very aware of the novelty of this particular interpretation as a biblical commentary, for, as Van Engen says, "it was one thing to write a treatise honoring the Blessed Virgin which drew upon selected verses of the *Song* hallowed by liturgical usage; it was quite another to interpret the entire *Song* with reference to Mary." The testimony of a letter of Rupert extant in a twelfth-century schoolbook suggests that this innovation in the *Song of Songs* commentary genre was actually the center of some controversy. The dispute seems to have revolved around the question of whether it was proper to assume that things understood *generaliter* about the Church are meant to refer *specialiter* to the Virgin Mary. Rupert's reply rejects the use of the scholastic terms "genus" and "species" in dealing with this question, and defends his interpretation with reference to the precedent of *Cogitis me*. The letter ends with the explanation that Rupert had only hoped to "add a little something" *(aliquid supererogare)* to the work of the Fathers, since the treasures of Scripture properly belong to all who have the will *(voluntas)* and the skills *(facultas)* to look for them. In this case, the "little something" added is a devotional work, gathering testimony of many voices in honor of Mary, "the only beloved of Christ" *(unicae dilectae Christi Mariae)*.

In the dedicatory epistle to Thietmar of Verden, Rupert presents his mariological commentary as a devotional meditation on the Divine Word, Christ, who lives in the human heart and who was incarnated on earth. He describes this meditation as dictated "as much as possible in contemplation of the face of our lady, Mary holy and ever-virgin," perhaps in meditation on a devotional image, and offers the work as a bell *(tintinabulum)* to an old friend whose "ringing" preaching of the Gospel Rupert still remembers.

The prologue, which dedicates the work to Abbot Cuno of Siegburg, describes it as a spiritual battle like that of Jacob with the angel, a proper wrestling match with the mysteries God has placed in Scripture. In the development of this battle metaphor, Mary appears as both the courtly lady and the armorer:

> Therefore, O Lady, Godbearer, true and uncorrupt
> mother of the Word eternally God and man, Jesus

Christ; armed not with my but with your merits, I wish to wrestle with this same man, that is, with the Word of God, and to wrench out a work on the *Song of Songs* which it would not be unseemly to call *De incarnatione Domini,* to the praise and glory of that Lord, and to the praise and glory of your blessedness.

Some years earlier, Rupert explains, he had been inspired by the Virgin to attempt a verse work on the *Song,* a project he found himself unable to carry through. It is worth noting that Peter Heliae did eventually accomplish Rupert's youthful goal in a long unpublished verse commentary on the *Song of Songs* dating from around 1148. But Rupert's meditation on the *Song of Songs,* however passionate and direct, is still in focus and structure an unmistakable prose commentary. The prologue relates the *Song of Songs* to seven biblical songs (which are not those of Origen), and then offers a structural division of the *Song of Songs* into four (rather unequal) parts punctuated by the repeated refrain:

> adiuro vos filiae Hierusalem
> > per capreas cervosque camporum
> ne suscietis neque evigilare faciatis
> > dilectam quoadusque ipsa veldt

> I adjure you, daughters of Jerusalem
> > by the goats and the stags of the field
> neither arouse nor cause to awaken
> > my beloved until she wishes.

This commentary thus conceives the *Song of Songs* to be divided at 2:7, 3:5, and 8:4 by an injunction to let the beloved sleep.

Furthermore, Rupert says he will base his interpretation on a foundation of historical or actual deeds:

> For, indeed, the mystical exposition will be more firm, nor will it be allowed to fluctuate, if it is held to be built on the history of certain times or rationally demonstrable things.

With respect to the division of the text, this rhetorical structure seems to be Rupert's original, if not terribly influential, insight. Its relationship to the treatise, however, is partial. The commentary is actually divided into seven books, only the first two of which are marked by the rhetorical exclamation beginning "I adjure you, daughters of Jerusalem." Books three to seven take the text roughly a chapter at a time, but across the chapter divisions; the third "adiuro vos" comes without special notice in the middle of the last book.

With respect to Rupert's concern to base the *expositio mystica* in history or "real deeds," the commentary presents a challenge equal to its structure. The opening verse, "Let him kiss me with the kiss of his mouth," is immediately placed in the mouth of the Virgin Mary, whose state of spiritual rapture is described by two biblical verses: "what eyes have not seen and ears have not heard and the heart of man has not reached" (I Corinthians 2:9), and "Behold the handmaid of the Lord, do unto me according to your word" (Luke 1:38). Here it seems to be the *historical* sense that speaks of the Virgin Mary, or rather, that is the spiritually elevated moment of her speaking these words. Likewise, the "little foxes" of 2:15 refer to Herod, whom Jesus called "that fox" (Luke 13:32); again, the words are placed in Mary's mouth. The rhetorical shift here is from "spoken about" to "speaking," a movement that is directly tied to content, since both of these passages also relate directly to the birth of Jesus.

Other places, in contrast, seem to have a sense of universal history, relating Mary both to Eve before her and to the Church which she helped to found. For example, the interpretation of 1:11, "my nard gave forth its fragrance," relates Eve's "stink of pride" to Mary's sweet-smelling nard of humility. Far more complex is the interpretation of 4:12-15, where the "garden enclosed" is described in lush detail. The verse is immediately likened to the paradise planted by God:

> That one is the ancient paradise, the earthly paradise; this one is the new paradise, the celestial paradise. And the planter of each is the one and the same Lord God. In that one he placed the man he had formed, in this one he formed the man who with him in the beginning was God. "From [that] soil he brought forth all trees that are beautiful to the sight, and sweet to the taste, and the tree of life in the middle of paradise." He blessed this soil, this his earth, and he brought forth from it the seeds of all graces and the models *(exemplaria)* of all virtues. And that tree of life is Christ, God and man, the lord of the celestial paradise.

The repetition of the words *hortus conclusus* in the text of the *Song of Songs* indicates to Rupert that the verses speak of Mary, who was *conclusa,* "closed," both when she conceived, and at the moment of the birth of Jesus.

The interpretation of the garden continues with a series of juxtapositions to the four cosmological corners of the earth: the four parts of paradise, "the four sacraments necessary for salvation" (Christ's incarnation, passion, resurrection, ascension), the four evangelists (man, ox, lion, eagle), the four rivers (Nile, Ganges, Tigris, Euphrates). Each of these sets of four, on a different order of reality, stands in a special relationship to the Virgin, who is represented by the garden divided into four parts. The structure is established in reference to the salvation history which was so elaborately developed in the second *Song of Songs* commentary of Honorius.

Analysis of any part of Rupert's commentary on the *Song of Songs "de incarnatione Domini"* brings us up against many traditional elements of the *Song of Songs* commentary genre. Rupert interprets the text, although in relation to the Virgin Mary, by means of Cassian's allegorical and tropological modes. Mary is totally identified with the female speaker of the *Song of Songs*, and then she is interpreted according to the standard modes of *Song of Songs* exegesis. According to the allegorical mode, Mary becomes here not only the symbol of the Church, but the embodiment of it. On the tropological level, she is also the model of monastic virtues: virginity, humility, and obedience.

These dual roles were conceived and forged in a period of great contemplative emphasis on the Virgin Mary, by a man who freely admitted to using the Virgin as a focus for contemplation on the incarnation of Christ. In some ways, then, Rupert's treatise can be seen to participate in developing trends of the cult of the Virgin. Even more, considered from the point of view of *Song of Songs* commentary, Rupert's work is evidence of the great complexity which the commentary genre had achieved by the twelfth century. This flexible multivalence in the service of marian doctrine may have had a direct impact on Honorius (in whose long commentary are found many of the same themes), and a more dispersed influence on other commentators, including those who did specifically choose a consciously mariological mode of interpretation, rather than just marian content. The importance of Rupert's example is seen, for example, in the late twelfth-century commentary of Alan of Lille.

Like Honorius, Alan is a twelfth-century figure who defies simple categorization. He was thoroughly a man of the schools, having studied at Paris and perhaps at Chartres; yet he died a Cistercian, in fact, a monk of Cîteaux. An early work, the *De planctu Naturae,* in which Lady Nature *(Natura)* laments the disaster humanity has made of creation, became a set school text and was regularly studied into the age of printing. This treatise served as an introduction to a more refined and difficult allegory of *Natura,* the *Anticlaudianus.* Alan's youthful fame was based on these books and a number of other school texts.

Yet Alan experienced a sort of conversion when he went to teach in Montpellier, and encountered the spiritual battle which pitted the Cathars and Waldensians against the Cistercian Order. In this tumultous spiritual environment, he began to write catechetical works, eventually commenting on the Our Father, various creeds, and the *Song of Songs*. These are also teaching texts, but focused on "practical" rather than "speculative" theology, and tied to the *cloister* schools. G. R. Evans has written about Alan:

No doubt if he had been born a little later, he would

have become one of the Friars Preachers. The Dominican Order in the thirteenth century would have been able to make use of his talents as a scholar and a teacher in a way that no single Order or school could do in the twelfth.

But, of course, Alan was not born a bit later. He was an example of a counter-movement in twelfth-century Christian history, a movement from the schools to the monasteries. He is by no means alone in this twelfth-century pattern, which can also be seen in the lives of Honorius Augustodunensis and Peter Abelard. Evidently, the monastic life of prayer and study still held appeal to late twelfth-century intellectuals, and was able to absorb Alan's talents as a teacher and preacher. In this environment, especially considering his opposition to the Cathars, it is little wonder that Alan turned to exegesis of the *Song of Songs*. In doing so, he participated in a literary tradition which by this time had developed a highly complex articulation of bodily language for the love between God and the orthodox Church, the individual soul, and the type of both, the Virgin Mary.

Alan may have commented on the Bible in a systematic way, in either a cloister or a cathedral school. A set of unpublished glosses on the songs of the Old and New Testaments makes use of the rhetorical framework of the *accessus ad auctores* found in Honorius: *titulus, materia, intentio, modus agendi.* This scholastic compilation may have been recorded by Alan's pupils, or it may have been Alan's own work book, one of the sources from which he made exegetical lectures. *In Cantica Canticorum ad laudem Deiparae Virginis Mariae elucidatio,* the only one of his biblical commentaries to survive, was probably one of those lectures. Significantly, it was written down only at the special request of the prior of Cluny, and is extant in copies from important monastic houses: Klosterneuburg, Fleury, and St. Marien. This text, which probably dates from Alan's years at Cîtreaux, thus provides an unusual glimpse into his *monastic* teaching plan, and the role played in it by the *Song of Songs*.

Alan's *Elucidatio* on the *Song of Songs* makes references to both the spiritual elite and the life of contemplation, in specifying the difference between the Bridegroom's "manifest" teaching through the windows and the "more obscure" teaching through the lattices of *Song of Songs* 2:9. The Church in the world is also a major concern of the treatise, often leading to a type of exegetical preaching, as in this open condemnation of the "little foxes" of *Song of Songs* 2:15:

> "Catch for us the little foxes, who destroy the vineyards." By "foxes," which are tricky animals living in caves in the earth, the heretics are

understood; by "vineyards," the Churches are understood. The heretics demolish these same vineyards by any means they can. Inasmuch as they decry Christ and his mother, they work to weaken [var. sicken] the faith of the Church. Therefore, these can be the words of the faithful to Christ and to the Virgin: "catch for us," that is, pull down to our service, "the foxes," that is, the heretics, "little," on account of imbecility; since as much as they struggle against the Church, so much will they be sickened. "Who destroy the vineyards," that is, they draw away from ecclesiastical faith.

This passage demonstrates the extreme rhetorical clarity of Alan's style, a style especially adapted for teaching. The commentary is systematic, straightforward, and, as the relation of the "little foxes" to heretics suggests, somewhat traditional in its interpretations. Even the addition of the Virgin Mary to the interpretation is always in tandem with Christ and/or the Church. Alan's calm, didactic voice contrasts rather sharply with the breathless devotional tone of Rupert's commentary, yet it is clear that the two treatises are closely connected at the level of content.

Alan, for example, repeats Rupert's argument about the way in which the *Song of Songs* refers to the Virgin Mary:

> Thus, although the song of love, that is, the wedding hymn of Solomon, rather specially and spiritually refers to the Church, nevertheless, it relates most specially and spiritually to the Virgin, as we will explain (insofar as we can) by divine command. Therefore, the glorious Virgin, hoping for the presence of the spouse, desiring the glorious conception announced by the angel, striving for the divine Incarnation, says: "Let him kiss me with the kiss of his mouth."

In his interpretation of 1:14, "behold you are fair/your eyes of doves," Alan is yet more explicit about the way the Virgin functions in the multiple levels of meaning of the *Song of Songs*, "as the divine Scriptures should be understood not according to the letter, but according to the spirit, and spiritual mystery should be seen in them." In one sense, the Virgin's part in the narrative of the *Song of Songs* is on the allegorical level, it has to do with this world, with the incarnation of Christ on earth. Yet, the anagogical sense is also evoked with the phrase "behold you are fair," understood as "having to do with the age to come" *(ad futurum saeculum pertinet),* since the Virgin represents human perfection. Alan sets his interpretation within both the accepted commentary tradition and the developing framework of marian devotion. For instance, *Song of Songs* 1:16, "the beams of our house are of cedar," is understood as both the body of Christ (which is the Church), and the body of Mary. With an open quotation from the Pseudo-Au-

gustinian sermons, Alan makes an explicit connection to the Assumption:

> For just as we believe that the body of Christ was not dissipated by decay, as it is written "You will not give your Holy one to see corruption," (Psalm 15:10, Vulgate), thus it is probable that the body of Mary is alien to the corruption of decay: Thus Augustine says in the sermon *De Assumptione Virginis:* "We believe not only the flesh which Christ assumed, but even the flesh from which he assumed flesh, to have been assumed into heaven."

In the exposition of *Song of Songs* 4:8, "come from Lebanon / come, you will be crowned," Alan combines the traditional place-name allegories with yet another manifestation of late twelfth-century marian devotion, the celebration of the Coronation of the Virgin:

> From these mountains, then, the glorious Virgin is crowned: when the princes of this world are converted to the faith, and received into eternal beatitude, and they withdraw into the company and the praise of the Virgin. From the peaks of these mountains she is crowned, when by the princes subject to the catholic faith she is praised and glorified in Christ.

This passage indicates that the concept of the Coronation of the Virgin, a devotion which grew rapidly in the late twelfth century, is closely linked to the eschatological expectation of the glorified Church, "when the princes of this world are converted to the faith, and received into eternal beatitude." This association is made explicit by a number of manuscript illuminations in which the crowned Church and the crowned Virgin are distinguishable only through accompanying motifs. Alan's imagery is extremely flexible; at some points, the Virgin and the Church seem to have become symbolically merged:

> For the Virgin Mary is similar to the Church of God in many ways. Just as the Church of God is the mother of Christ in its members through grace; thus the Virgin is the mother of Christ, of its head through human nature. And just as the Church is without spot or wrinkle, even so is the glorious Virgin.

As Riedlinger notes, this comes close to the doctrine of the Immaculate Conception of Mary, a concept which did not become dogma until the nineteenth century.

The *Elucidatio* of Alan of Lille shows the full complexity of mariological *Song of Songs* commentary. The Mary of this treatise is rather like one of the allegorical personifications of Alan's *De planctu Naturae* and *Anticlaudianus,* far abstracted from any human woman. Alan even stresses Mary's elevation by portraying a very different biblical figure, Mary Magdalene, as acting out some narrative parallels between the Gospels and the *Song of Songs*. So it is *Mary Magdalene* who mourns, "widowed for her spiritual man, that is, Christ"; the *Magdalene's* search for Christ at the tomb is recollected from the *Song of Songs* 3:1 "on my bed through the nights/I sought him whom my soul loves"; it is to the garden in which *this* Mary sought him that Christ descends in *Song of Songs* 6:1. As for the Virgin Mary, her appearance in the *Song of Songs* has much the same function as Alan's *Natura:* to urge the human gaze upwards, "from history to the mystical sense." She is the model and the inspiration for the mystical life.

CRITICAL REFLECTIONS ON THE DEVELOPMENT OF MARIAN EXEGESIS

This discussion of medieval readings of the *Song of Songs* in relation to the Virgin Mary suggests that the tradition is not just "marian," relating to Mary, or even "mariological," having to do with doctrinal definitions regarding Mary, but also specifically linked to worship. The liturgical background of this mode of *Song of Songs* exegesis brings a level of specific devotional participation into the commentary tradition, participation in the growing cult of the Virgin. Marian commentary on the *Song of Songs* is a special case of the transformation of a primary genre into a secondary genre, of what Bakhtin has described as the ability of secondary genres to:

> absorb and digest various primary (simple) genres that have taken form in unmediated speech communication. These primary genres are altered and assume a special character when they enter into complex ones. They lose their immediate relation to actual reality and to the real utterances of others.

Of course, liturgy is in itself a formalized type of speech genre. Though not so flexible as other forms of spoken discourse, it is nevertheless an oral, performative, form of communication and, hence, in spite of repeated medieval efforts at standardization, open to myriad adaptations. When a verse from the *Song of Songs* was sung as an antiphon for the Assumption of the Virgin, it was transformed from God's voice speaking to humans (the "direct communication" of biblical revelation) to human voices speaking to heaven (to the Virgin Mary and to God) in praise and petition. I have suggested . . . that the direct address of liturgical language greatly influenced the voice of early marian commentaries on the *Song of Songs*. Yet, as this conception of the *Song of Songs* was "digested" by the commentary tradition, the immediacy of liturgical communication was changed into a far more mediated literary form. The antiphons of the Virgin still rang in the ears of Rupert and Alan, but their sound was muted; they had become simply another source for mariological commentary.

The interpretations considered in this [essay], therefore, are the most striking example of *Song of Songs* commentary as a secondary or "complex" genre. Here, the image of the Virgin Mary has no one fixed form, but changes shape from liturgy to commentary, from verse to verse. Mary is seen as at once the Church and the soul, the Bride, mother, and child of God. She is seen in the historical, allegorical, tropological, and anagogical levels of understanding the *Song of Songs*. Ann Astell has described marian interpretation of the *Song of Songs* as "historicized allegory." . . . [T]here is no tradition of *Song of Songs* commentary specifically in the anagogical mode, but the Virgin Mary, as type of both the Church and the soul, incorporates this level of understanding rather explicitly. Mariological exegesis of the *Song of Songs*, in fact, incorporates the entire tradition of *Song of Songs* commentary throughout the Latin Middle Ages, absorbing every level of understanding which it had inherited. These works are not necessarily the most structurally or rhetorically complicated interpretations of the *Song of Songs* (Rupert and Alan, for example, do not come close to the elaborate structure of Honorius's second exposition), but they are conceptually and typologically more complex, resonating with a whole other world of Christian spirituality, devotion to the Virgin.

Perhaps mariological commentaries on the *Song of Songs* also signal the waning, even the exhaustion, of the commentary tradition, as they look out to concerns which go beyond the limits of a monastic literary genre. By the twelfth century, a complex allegorical understanding of the *Song of Songs* had spread into numerous traditions of popular devotion to the Virgin, traditions visible over subsequent centuries and even into our own. Devotion to the Virgin Mary is still an important, some would say a growing, aspect of western Christianity. The "Marian Year" proclaimed by Pope John Paul II from the Feast of the Assumption, 1987 to the same feast of 1988 reflects the enormous amount of belief in and veneration of the Virgin in twentieth-century Christianity, a religious phenomenon which is only beginning to be analyzed from the perspective of the history of Christianity. The *Song of Songs* commentary genre came into confluence only briefly with this vibrant tradition of marian devotion. There are, actually, relatively few marian commentaries on the *Song of Songs*, mostly from one period—the twelfth century. These did not so much change the development of marian devotion as testify to one stage of it, one predominantly liturgical voice and its devotional and theological ramifications.

It should also be noted that even the earliest uses of verses from the *Song of Songs* in liturgies of the Virgin are evidence of a function of the *Song of Songs* throughout the Middle Ages on a different literary level from that of the commentary tradition, namely, as proof-texts or biblical tropes. This use was by no means totally divorced from the genre of **Song of Songs** commentary begun by Origen; in fact, it was often informed by the patterns and expectations which consistently structured the genre in time. But this use does indicate a different "horizon of expectations" against which the **Song of Songs** was also read, and which exerted greater influence on this form of commentary than on the traditional ecclesiological and tropological readings. The difficult relationship between broad reference and commentary is a sign of the continual outward expansion of the genre. It is also the most striking characteristic of . . . the influence of **Song of Songs** commentary on the vernacular literature of the later Middle Ages, both devotional and secular.

FURTHER READING

Astell, Ann W. *"The Song of Songs" in the Middle Ages.* Ithaca: Cornell University Press, 1990, 193 p.

Surveys commentary on the *Song of Songs* in the writings of Origen, Bruno of Segni, Saint Bernard of Clairvaux, and others.

Brenner, Althalya. *The Song of Songs.* Sheffield, England: JSOT Press, 1989, 106 p.

Concise introduction to the *Song of Songs*, covering such issues as authorship, historical context, interpretive theory, and liturgical reading.

Exum, Cheryl. "A Literary and Structural Analysis of the Song of Songs." *Zeitschrift für die Alttestamentliche Wissenschaft,* Vol. 85, 47-79.

Literary study of the *Song of Songs* which focuses on issues of form and style.

Fox, Michael V. *The "Song of Songs" and the Ancient Egyptian Love Songs.* Madison: The University of Wisconsin Press, 1985.

Compares the *Song of Songs* to ancient Egyptian love songs, seeking to establish a cultural affinity.

Gordis, Robert. *The Song of Songs and Lamentations: A Study, Modern Translation and Commentary.* Rev. ed., KTAV Publishing House, Inc., 1974.

Introduction and commentary address a variety of issues relating to the *Song of Songs,* including the work's date, structure, major themes, style, and its sources and historical references.

Jastrow, Morris, Jr. *"The Song of Songs," Being a Collection of Love Lyrics of Ancient Palestine.* Philadelphia: J.B. Lippincott, 1921, 241 p.

A translation and commentary, including essays outlining "Solomonic," allegorical, and dramatic readings.

Keel, Othmar. *"The Song of Songs": A Continental Commentary.* Translated by Frederick J. Gaiser. Minneapolis: Fortress Press, 1994, 308 p.

Translation and systematic analysis of the text. Illustrated.

Kramer, Samuel Noah. "The Sacred Marriage and Solomon's *Song of Songs.*" In *The Sacred Marriage Rite: Aspects of Faith, Myth, and Ritual in Ancient Sumer,* pp. 85-106. Bloomington: Indiana University Press, 1969.

Discusses the similarity of the *Song of Songs* to Sumerian love poetry.

Leclerq, Jean. *The Love of Learning and the Desire for God: A Study of Monastic Culture.* Translated by Catharine Misrahi. New York: Fordham University Press, 1982, 282 p.

Treats the place of the *Song of Songs* in monastic Old Testament scholarship.

Meek, Theophile James. "Canticles and the Tammuz Cult." *The American Journal of Semitic Languages and Literatures* XXIX, No. 1 (October, 1922): 1-14.

Contends that the *Song of Songs* likely has its source in the ancient Hebrew Tammuz cult.

Murphy, Roland E. *"Canticle of Canticles."* In *The Jerome Biblical Commentary,* edited by Raymond E. Brown et al., pp. 506-10. Englewood Cliffs, N.J.: Prentice-Hall, 1968.

Concise introductory essay and commentary; includes a brief bibliography.

———. "The Symbolism of the *Song of Songs,*" in *The Incarnate Imagination: Essays in Theology, the Arts and Social Sciences,* edited by Ingrid H. Shafer, pp. 229-34. Bowling Green: Bowling Green University Popular Press, 1988.

Comments on symbol and metaphor within the *Song of Songs,* and addresses the symbolism of the work as a whole.

———. *"The Song of Songs": A Commentary on the "Book of Canticles" or the "Song of Songs."* Minneapolis: Fortress Press, 1990, 237 p.

Introductory essay which provides a history of interpretation; also includes notes on style and structure, and a bibliography.

Parente, Paschal P. "The *Canticle of Canticles* in Mystical Theology." *Catholic Biblical Quarterly* 6 (1944): 142-58.

Considers the *Song of Songs* in the context of the Catholic doctrine of mystical marriage.

Pope, Marvin H. *"Song of Songs": A New Translation with Introduction and Commentary.* New York: Doubleday & Co., 1977, 743 p.

Substantial companion volume to the *Song of Songs;*

includes an historical survey of versions and interpretations, a bibliography, and detailed notes and commentary.

Schoff, Wilfred Harvey, ed. *"The Song of Songs": A Symposium.* Philadelphia: The Commercial Museum, 1924, 122 p.

Six essays addressing, among other issues, canonicity, Greek and Hindu analogies to the *Song of Songs,* and medieval Christian interpretations.

Turner, Denys. *Eros and Allegory: Medieval Exegesis of* the *"Song of Songs."* Kalamazoo: Cistercian Publications, 1995, 471 p.

An edition of medieval exegetical commentaries on the *Song of Songs*, with an introductory essay and bibliography.

Zhang, Lonxi. "The Letter of the Spirit: The *Song of Songs,* Allegoresis, and the *Book of Poetry.*" *Comparative Literature* 39, No. 3 (Summer, 1987): 193-217.

Explores "striking similarities" in allegorical readings of the *Song of Songs* and the Confucian *Book of Poetry.*

Vita Nuova

c. 1292

INTRODUCTION

Dante's *Vita Nuova* transformed European vernacular poetry by widening its scope to matters far beyond the troubadours' traditional love lyrics. In writing it, Dante also transformed himself from an occasional, if accomplished, composer of love poems into a serious poet devoted to his craft. Starting out as a rather haphazard collection of poems inspired by Dante's love for a woman he called Beatrice and written in the *dolce stil nuovo*, the extensive prose commentaries in the *Vita Nuova* recount the process by which Dante's feelings for Beatrice were converted into an intensely felt religious outlook.

Biographical Information

Dante Alighieri, the son of an impoverished nobleman of ancient lineage, wrote the *Vita Nuova* around 1292, when he was in his late twenties, during a period of impassioned study and self-reflection. The years of its composition are bracketed by his participation in the civic affairs of Florence. In 1289 Dante rode into pitched battle at Campaldino, where the Florentines defeated the Aretines, their commercial rivals. In 1295 he joined the guild of physicians and apothecaries so as to participate in the administration of Florence, which was then governed by the guilds. He later became one of the council of six priors, and his political prominence prompted the exile that left an indelible mark on the *Divina Commedia*. But neither his battle experience nor his interest in the governing of the city are as much as hinted at in the *Vita Nuova*. Here, Dante maintains a very narrow focus on his love for Beatrice, the poetry it inspired, and the religious experience it gave rise to. How reliable the book is as autobiography, however, is not entirely clear.

Plot and Major Characters

The story of the *Vita Nuova* begins in Dante's childhood, when, at the age of nine, he first glimpsed Beatrice, herself eight years old. Struck by her beauty, he fell in love. Nine years later he sees her again, and when she greets him his love is confirmed. However, in good troubadour fashion, Beatrice is forever beyond his reach: she marries and then dies a few years later. Her death occasions a crisis in Dante's

life and gives birth to poetry that will eventually lead to a religious and poetic conversion. After Beatrice's death, Dante temporarily consoles himself with a more casual love for a woman referred to only as *donna gentile,* or gentle lady. Upon reflection, Dante comes to understand this infatuation as a betrayal of Beatrice's memory, and ultimately the incident only serves to confirm his devotion and transform earthly love into a religious experience. Whether Beatrice really existed and whether it matters, has been a topic of some debate, but she is generally identified as Beatrice Portinari, a daughter of a nobleman, who married Simone de' Bardi and died young. Undoubtedly the most important character in the book is Dante himself, and the few events he recounts give rise to the intense self-reflection that was to shape his future as a poet.

Major Themes

The *Vita Nuova* has inspired centuries of critical debate regarding its true subject. Although ostensibly the autobiographical account of Dante's love for Beatrice, the story has struck generations of critics as difficult to take literally, in part because Beatrice is conspicuously absent from the story. Some critics explain that this state of affairs strikes the modern reader as odd because Dante's sensibility is so far removed from ours. Others maintain that the *Vita Nuova* is not in fact a love story at all, but rather a mystical affirmation of Dante's religious convictions, or a treatise on poetry focusing on Dante's transcendence of Provençal models and his transformation of vernacular love poetry into a far loftier vehicle of contemplation. Despite such disagreements, however, it is safe to say that love, poetry, and religious experience are the overarching themes of the book, while its main theme is the relationship between them.

Critical Reception

The *Divina Commedia* was received to great acclaim upon its publication, and the *Vita Nuova* has long basked in its reflected glory. Criticism has almost invariably been positive, although an occasional critic has taken exception to its sensibility, finding in it an overwrought imagination and sensitivity unbecoming a great poet. In later centuries, as the worldview of the poem has grown more foreign to their understanding, critics have found the *Vita Nuova* more enigmatic and have become more inclined to delve beneath its surface. Although still a favorite with younger readers, the love story tends to strike older readers as too trivial for a poet of Dante's stature. As a result, many have proposed that Beatrice is a symbol, although what she might be a symbol of is not very clear. The story of Dante's love for her is often taken as an allegory, particularly by critics reading the book in the light of Dante's later work. This strategy is supported by the fact that Dante himself gives a revisionist commentary on the *Vita Nuova* in the *Convivio*, which was written some ten or more years later. The more clearly allegorical *Divina Commedia*, in which Beatrice also plays a prominent role, has too worked to reinforce some critics' denials of the literal significance of the *Vita Nuova*.

PRINCIPAL ENGLISH TRANSLATIONS

Dante and the Circle of His Friends (includes *Vita Nuova;* translated by Dante Gabriel Rossetti)1861

Vita Nuova (translated by Theodore Martin) 1862
Vita Nuova (translated by Ralph Waldo Emerson) 1882?
Vita Nuova (translated by Charles Eliot Norton) 1892
Vita Nuova: Poems of Youth (translated by Barbara Reynolds) 1969

Vita Nuova (edited by Mark Musa) 1992
Vita Nuova (translated by Dino S. Cervigni and Edward Vasta) 1995

CRITICISM
Charles Eliot Norton (essay date 1859)

SOURCE: "*The New Life* of Dante," in *Medieval & Renaissance Texts & Studies,* Vol. 23, 1983, pp. 52-68.

[*In the following essay, origianlly written in 1859, Norton discusses the development of Dante's thought about Beatrice and the relationship of the* Vita Nuova *to his other works.*]

The year 1289 was one marked in the annals of Florence and of Italy by events which are still famous, scored by the genius of Dante upon the memory of the world. It was in this year that Count Ugolino and his sons and grandsons were starved by the Pisans in their tower prison. A few months later, Francesca da Rimini was murdered by her husband. Between the dates of these two terrible events the Florentines had won the great victory of Campaldino; and thus, in this short space, the materials had been given to the poet for the two best-known and most powerful stories and for one of the most striking episodes of the *Divina Commedia*.

In the great and hard-fought battle of Campaldino Dante himself took part. "I was at first greatly afraid," he says, in a letter of which but a few sentences have been preserved, "but at the end I felt the greatest joy—according to the various chances of the battle." When the victorious army returned to Florence, a splendid procession, with the clergy at its head, with the arts of the city each under its banner, and with all manner of pomp, went out to meet it. There were long-continued feasts and rejoicings. The battle had been fought on the 11th of June, the day of St. Barnabas, and the Republic, though already engaged in magnificent works of church building, decreed that a new church should be erected in honor of the Saint on whose day the victory had been won.

A little later in that summer, Dante was one of a troop of Florentines who joined the forces of Lucca in levying war upon the Pisan territory. The stronghold of Caprona was taken, and Dante was present at its capture; for he says, "I saw the foot-soldiers, who, having made terms, came out from Caprona, afraid when they beheld themselves among so many enemies" (*Inferno*, XXI, 94-96).

Thus, during a great part of the summer of 1289, Dante was in active service as a soldier. He was no lovesick idler, no mere home-keeping writer of verses, but was already taking his part in the affairs of the state which he was afterwards to be called on for a time to assist in governing, and he was laying up those stores of experience which were to serve as the material out of which his vivifying imagination was to form the great national poem of Italy. But of this active life, of these personal engagements, of these terrible events which took such strong possession of his soul, there is no word, no suggestion even, in the book of his *New Life*. In it there is no echo, however faint, of those storms of public violence and private passion which broke dark over Italy. In the midst of the tumults which sprang from the jealousies of rival states, from the internal discords of cities, from the divisions of parties, from the bitterness of domestic quarrels—this little book is full of tenderness and peace, and tells its story of love as if the world were the abode of tranquility. No external excitements could break into the inner chambers of Dante's heart to displace the love that dwelt within them. The contrast between the purity and the serenity of the *Vita Nuova* and the coarseness and cruelty of the deeds that were going on while it was being written is complete. Every man in some sort leads a double life—one real and his own, the other seeming and the world's—but with few is the separation so entire as it was with Dante.

But in these troubled times the *New Life* was drawing to its close. The spring of 1290 had come, and the poet, now twenty-five years old, sixteen years having passed since he first beheld Beatrice, was engaged in writing a poem to tell what effect the virtue of his lady wrought upon him. He had written but the following portion when it was broken off, never to be resumed:

So long hath Love retained me at his hest,
And to his sway hath so accustomed me,
That as at first he cruel used to be,
So in my heart he now doth sweetly rest.
Thus when by him my strength is
    dispossessed,
So that the spirits seem away to flee,
My frail soul feels such sweetness verily,
That with it pallor doth my face invest.
Then Love o'er me such mastery doth seize,
He makes my sighs in words to take their
    way,
And they unto my lady go to pray
That she to give me further grace would
    please
Where'er she sees me, this to me occurs,
Nor can it be believed what humbleness is
    hers.

Quomodo sedet sola civitas plena populo! facta est quasi vidua domina gentium!

(How doth the city sit solitary that was full of people! how is she become as a widow, she that

was great among the nations! [*Lamentations*, I, 1])

I was yet engaged upon this Canzone, and had finished the above stanza, when the Lord of justice called this most gentle one unto glory under the banner of that holy Queen Mary whose name was ever spoken with greatest reverence by this blessed Beatrice.

And although it might give pleasure, were I now to tell somewhat of her departure from us, it is not my intention to treat of it here for three reasons. The first is, that it is no part of the present design, as may be seen in the poem of this little book. The second is, that, supposing it were so, my pen would not be sufficient to treat of it in a fitting manner. The third is, that, supposing both the one and the other, it would not be becoming in me to treat of it, since, in doing so, I should be obliged to praise myself—a thing altogether blameworthy in whosoever does it—and therefore I leave this subject to some other narrator.

Nevertheless, since in what precedes there has been occasion to make frequent mention of the number nine, and apparently not without reason, and since in her departure this number appeared to have a large place, it is fitting to say something on this point, seeing that it seems to belong to our design. Wherefore I will first tell how it had place in her departure, and then I will assign some reason why this number was so friendly to her. I say, that, according to the mode of reckoning in Italy, her most noble soul departed in the first hour of the ninth day of the month; and according to the reckoning, in Syria, she departed in the ninth month of the year, since the first month there is Tismim, which with us is October; and according to our reckoning, she departed in that year of our indiction, that is, of the years of the Lord, in which the perfect number [the number ten] was completed for the ninth time in that century in which she had been set in the world; and she was of the Christians of the thirteenth century.

One reason why this number was so friendly to her may be this: since, according to Ptolemy and the Christian truth, there are nine heavens which move, and, according to the common astrological opinion, these heavens work effects here below according to their relative positions, this number was her friend, to the end that it might be understood that at her generation all the nine movable heavens were in most perfect conjunction. This is one reason; but considering more subtilely and according to infallible truth, this number was she herself—I speak in a similitude, and I mean as follows. The number three is the root of nine, since, without any other number, multiplied by itself, it makes nine—as we see plainly that three times three are nine. Then, if three is the factor by itself of nine, and the Author of Miracles by himself is three—Father, Son, and

Holy Spirit, who are three and one—this lady was accompanied by the number nine that it might be understood that she was a nine, that is, a miracle, whose only root is the marvellous Trinity. Perhaps a more subtle person might discover some more subtle reason for this; but this is the one that I see for it, and which pleases me the best.

After thus treating of the number nine in its connection with Beatrice, Dante goes on to say, that, when this most gentle lady had gone from this world, the city appeared widowed and despoiled of every dignity; whereupon he wrote to the princes of the earth an account of its condition, beginning with the words of Jeremiah which he quoted at the entrance of this new matter. The remainder of this letter he does not give, because it was in Latin, and in this work it was his intention, from the beginning, to write only in the vulgar tongue; and such was the understanding of the friend for whom he writes—that friend being, as we may suppose, Guido Cavalcanti, whom Dante, it may be remembered, has already spoken of as the chief among his friends. Then succeeds a Canzone lamenting the death of Beatrice, which, instead of being followed by a verbal exposition, as is the case with all that have gone before, is preceded by one, in order that it may seem, as it were, desolate and like a widow at its end. And this arrangement is preserved in regard to all the remaining poems in the little volume. In this poem he says that the Eternal Sire called Beatrice to himself, because he saw that this world was not worthy of such a gentle thing; and he says of his own life, that no tongue could tell what it has been since his lady went away to heaven.

Among the sonnets ascribed to Dante is one which, if it be his, must have been written about this time, and which, although not included in the *Vita Nuova*, seems not unworthy to find a place here. Its imagery, at least, connects it with some of the sonnets in the earlier portion of the book.

> One day came Melancholy unto me,
>   And said, "With thee I will awhile abide";
>   And, as it seemed, attending at her side,
>   Anger and Grief did bear her company.
> "Depart! Away!" I cried out eagerly.
>   Then like a Greek she unto me replied;
>   And while she stood discoursing in her
>   pride,
>   I looked, and Love approaching us I see.
> In cloth of black full strangely was he clad,
>   A little hood he wore upon his head,
>   And down his face tears flowing fast he
>   had.
> "Poor little wretch! what ails thee?" then I
>   said.
> And he replied, "I woful am, and sad,
> Sweet brother, for our lady who is dead."

About this time, Dante tells us, a person who stood to him in friendship next to his first friend, and who was of the closest relationship to his glorious lady, so that we may believe it was her brother, came to him and prayed him to write something on a lady who was dead. Dante, believing that he meant the blessed Beatrice, accordingly wrote for him a sonnet; and then, reflecting that so short a poem appeared but a poor and bare service for one who was so nearly connected with her, added to it a Canzone, and gave both to him.

As the months passed on, his grief still continued fresh, and the memory of his lady dwelt continually with him. It happened, that,

> on that day which completed a year since this lady was made one of the citizens of eternal life, I was seated in a place where, remembering her, I drew an Angel upon certain tablets. And while I was drawing it, I turned my eyes, and saw at my side certain men to whom it was becoming to do honor, and who were looking at what I did; and, as was afterward told me, they had been there now some time before I perceived them. When I saw them, I rose, and, saluting them, said, "Another was just now with me, and on that account I was in thought." When these persons had gone, I returned to my work, that is, to drawing figures of Angels; and while doing this, a thought came to me of saying words in rhyme, as for an anniversary poem for her, and of addressing them to those who had come to me. Then I said this sonnet, which has two beginnings:

FIRST BEGINNING.

> Unto my mind remembering had come
>   The gentle lady, with such pure worth
>   graced,
>   That by the Lord Most High she had been
>   placed
>   Within the heaven of peace, where Mary
>   hath her home.

SECOND BEGINNING.

> Unto my mind had come, indeed, in thought,
>   That gentle one for whom Love's tears are
>   shed,
>   Just at the time when, by his power led,
>   To see what I was doing you were brought.
> Love, who within my mind did her perceive,
>   Was roused awake within my wasted heart,
>   And said unto my sighs, "Go forth!
>   depart!"
>   Whereon each one in grief did take its
>   leave.
> Lamenting they from out my breast did go,
>   And uttering a voice that often led
>   The grievous tears unto my saddened eyes.
> But those which issued with the greatest woe,
>   "O noble soul," they in departing said,

"To-day makes up the year since thou to
   heaven didst rise."

The preceding passage is one of the many in the **Vita
Nuova** which are of peculiar interest, as illustrating
the personal tastes of Dante, and the common modes
of his life. "I was drawing," he says, "the figure of an
Angel"; and this statement is the more noticeable,
because Giotto, the man who set painting on its modern course, was not yet old enough to have exercised
any influence upon Dante. The friendship which afterwards existed between them had its beginning at a
later period. At this time Cimabue still held the field.
He often painted angels around the figures of the Virgin and her Child; and in his most famous picture, in
the Church of Sta. Maria Novella, there are certain
angels of which Vasari says, with truth, that, though
painted in the Greek manner, they show an approach
toward the modern style of drawing. These angels may
well have seemed beautiful to eyes accustomed to the
hard unnaturalness of earlier works. The love of Art
pervaded Florence, and a nature so sensitive and so
sympathetic as Dante's could not but partake of it in
the fullest measure. Art was then no adjunct of senti-
mentalism, no encourager of idleness. It was connected with all that was most serious and all that was most
delightful in life. It is difficult, indeed, to realize the
delight which it gave, and the earnestness with which
it was followed at this period, when it seemed, as by
a miracle, to fling off the winding-sheet which had
long wrapped its stiffened limbs, and to come forth
with new and unexampled life.

The strength and the intelligence of Dante's love of
Art are shown in many beautiful passages and allusions in the *Divina Commedia.* There was something
of universality, not only in his imagination, but also in
his acquisitions. Of the sources of learning which were
then open, there was not one which he had not visited;
of the fountains of inspiration, not one out of which he
had not drunk. All the arts—poetry, painting, sculpture, and music—were alike dear to him. His Canzoni
were written to be sung; and one of the most charming
scenes in the great poem is that in which is described
his meeting with his friend Casella, the musician, who
sang to him one of his own Canzoni so sweetly, that
"the sweetness still within me sounds."

"Dante took great delight in music, and was an excellent draughtsman," says Aretino, his second biographer; and Boccaccio reports, that in his youth he took
great pleasure in music, and was the friend of all the
best musicians and singers of his time. There is, perhaps, in the whole range of literature, no nobler homage to Art than that which is contained in the tenth and
twelfth cantos of the *Purgatory,* in which Dante represents the Creator himself as using its means to impress
the lessons of truth upon those whose souls were being
purified for the final attainment of heaven. The pas-

sages are too long for extract, and though their wonderful beauty tempts us to linger over them, we must
return to the course of the story of Dante's life as it
appears in the concluding pages of the *New Life.*

Many months had passed since Beatrice's death, when
Dante happened to be in a place which recalled the
past time to him, and filled him with grief. While standing here, he raised his eyes and saw a young and beautiful lady looking out from a window compassionately
upon his sad aspect. The tenderness of her look touched
his heart and moved his tears. Many times afterwards
he saw her, and her face was always full of compassion, and pale, so that it reminded him of the look of
his own most noble lady. But at length his eyes began
to delight too much in seeing her; wherefore he often
cursed their vanity, and esteemed himself as vile, and
there was a hard battle within himself between the
remembrance of his lady and the new desire of his
eyes.

At length, he says,

> The sight of this lady brought me into so new a
> condition, that I often thought of her as of one who
> pleased me exceedingly,—and I thought of her thus:
> "This is a gentle, beautiful, young, and discreet lady,
> and she has perhaps appeared by will of Love, in
> order that my life may find repose." And often I
> thought more amorously, so that my heart consented
> in it, that is, approved my reasoning. And after it
> had thus consented, I, moved as if by reason,
> reflected, and said to myself, "Ah, what thought is
> this that in so vile a way seeks to console me, and
> leaves me scarcely any other though?" Then another
> thought rose up and said, "Now that thou hast been
> in so great tribulation of Love, why wilt thou not
> withdraw thyself from such bitterness? Thou seest
> that this is an inspiration that sets the desires of
> Love before thee, and proceeds from a place no less
> gentle than the eyes of the lady who has shown
> herself so pitiful toward thee." Wherefore, I, having
> often thus combated with myself, wished to say some
> words of it. And as, in this battle of thoughts, those
> which spoke for her won the victory, it seemed to
> me becoming to address her, and I said this sonnet,
> which begins, "A gentle thought"; and I called it
> gentle because I was speaking to a gentle lady—but
> otherwise it was most vile.

A gentle thought that of you holds discourse
   Cometh now frequently with me to dwell,
   And in so sweet a way of Love doth tell,
   My heart to yield unto him he doth force.
"Who, then, is this," the soul says to the
   heart,
     "Who cometh to bring comfort to our
     mind?
    And is his virtue of so potent kind,
    That other thoughts he maketh to depart?"
"O saddened soul," the heart to her replies;

"This is a little spirit fresh from Love,
  Whose own desires he before me brings;
"His very life and all his power doth move
  Forth the sweet compassionating eyes
  Of her so grieved by our sufferings."

One day, about the ninth hour, there arose within me a strong imagination opposed to this adversary of reason. For I seemed to see the glorified Beatrice in that crimson garment in which she had first appeared to my eyes, and she seemed to me young, of the same age as when I first saw her. Then I began to think of her, and, calling to mind the past time in its order, my heart began to repent bitterly of the desire by which it had so vilely allowed itself for some days to be possessed, contrary to the constancy of reason. And this so wicked desire being expelled, all my thoughts returned to their most gentle Beatrice, and I say that thenceforth I began to think of her with my heart possessed utterly by shame, so that it was often manifested by my sighs; for almost all of them, as they went forth, told what was discoursed of in my heart—the name of that gentlest one, and how she had gone from us. . . . And I wished that my wicked desire and vain temptation might be known to be at an end; and that the rhymed words which I had before written might induce no doubt, I proposed to make a sonnet in which I would include what I have now told.

With this sonnet Dante ends the story in the **Vita Nuova** of the wandering of his eyes, and the short faithlessness of his heart; but it is retold with some additions in the *Convito* or *Banquet,* a work written many years afterward; and in this later version there are some details which serve to fill out and illustrate the earlier narrative. The same tender and refined feeling which inspires the **Vita Nuova** gives its tone to all the passages in which the poet recalls his youthful days and the memory of Beatrice in this work of his sorrowful manhood. In the midst of its serious and philosophic discourse this little story winds in and out its thread of personal recollection and of sweet romantic sentiment. It affords new insight into the recesses of Dante's heart, and exhibits the permanence of the gracious qualities of his youth.

Its opening sentence is full of the imagery of love.

Since the death of that blessed Beatrice who lives in heaven with the angels, and on earth with my soul, the star of Venus had twice shone in the different seasons, as the star of morning and of evening, when that gentle lady, of whom I have made mention near the close of the **New Life**, first appeared before my eyes accompanied by Love, and gained some place in my mind.

. . . And before this love could become perfect, there arose a great battle between the thought that sprang from it and that which was opposed to it,

and which still held the fortress of my mind for the glorified Beatrice [*Convito,* Tratt. ii c. 3].

And so hard was this struggle, and so painful, that Dante took refuge from it in the composition of a poem addressed to the Angelic Intelligences who move the third heaven, that is, the heaven of Venus; and it is to the exposition of the true meaning of this Canzone that the second book or treatise of the *Convito* is directed. In one of the later chapters he says (and the passage is a most striking one, from its own declaration, as well as from its relation to the vision of the *Divina Commedia*)—

The life of my heart was wont to be a sweet and delightful thought, which often went to the feet of the Lord of those to whom I speak, that is, to God for, thinking, I contemplated the kingdom of the Blessed. And I tell [in my poem] the final cause of my mounting thither in thought, when I say, "There I beheld a lady in glory"; [and I say this] in order that it may be understood that I was certain, and am certain, through her gracious revelation, that she was in heaven, whither I in my thoughts oftentimes went—as it were, seized up. And this made me desirous of death, that I might go there where she was [*Convito,* Tratt. ii. c. 8].

Following upon the chapter in which this remarkable passage occurs is one which is chiefly occupied with a digression upon the immortality of the soul—and with discourse upon this matter, says Dante, "it will be beautiful to finish speaking of that living and blessed Beatrice, of whom I intend to say no more in this book and I believe and affirm and am certain that I shall pass after this to another and better life, in which that glorious lady lives of whom my soul was enamored" [*Convito,* Tratt. ii. c. 9].

But it is not from the *Convito* alone that this portion of the **Vita Nuova** receives illustration. In that passage of the *Purgatory* in which Beatrice is described as appearing in person to her lover the first time since her death, she addresses him in words of stern rebuke of his fickleness and his infidelity to her memory. The whole scene is, perhaps, unsurpassed in imaginative reality; the vision appears to have an actual existence, and the poet himself is subdued by the power of his own imagination. He tells the words of Beatrice with the same feeling with which he would have repeated them, had they fallen on his mortal ear. His grief and shame are real, and there is no element of feigning in them. That in truth he had seemed to himself to listen to and to behold what he tells, it is scarcely possible to doubt. Beatrice says,

Some while at heart my presence kept him
  sound;
  My girlish eyes to his observance renting,
I led him with me on the right way bound.

When of my second age the steps
  ascending,
I bore my life into another sphere,
  Then stole he from me, after others
    bending.
When I arose from flesh to spirit clear,
  When beauty, worthiness, upon me grew,
I was to him less pleasing and less dear.

          [*Purgatory*, c. xxx. vv. 118-26]

But although Beatrice only gives utterance to the self-reproaches of Dante, we have seen already how fully he had atoned for this first and transient unfaithfulness of his heart. The remainder of the *Vita Nuova* shows how little she had lost of her power over him, how reverently he honored her memory, how constant was his love of her whom he should see never again with his earthly eyes. Returning to the *New Life*—"After this tribulation," he says,

at that time when many people were going to see the blessed image which Jesus Christ left to us as the likeness of his most beautiful countenance, which my lady now beholds in glory, it happened that certain pilgrims passed through a street which is almost in the middle of that city where the gentlest lady was born, lived, and died—and they went along, as it seemed to me, very pensive. And thinking about them, I said to myself, "These appear to me to be pilgrims from a far-off region, and I do not believe that they have even heard speak of this lady, and they know nothing of her; their thoughts are rather of other things than of her; for, perhaps, they are thinking of their distant friends, whom we do not know." Then I said to myself, "I know, that, if these persons were from a neighboring country, they would show some sign of trouble as they pass through the midst of this grieving city." Then again I said, "If I could hold them awhile, I would indeed make them weep before they went out from this city; for I would say words to them which would make whoever should hear them weep." Then, when they had passed out of sight, I proposed to make a sonnet in which I would set forth that which I had said to myself; and in order that it might appear more pity-moving, I proposed to say it as if I had spoken to them, and I said this sonnet, which begins, "O pilgrims."

I called them *pilgrims* in wide sense of that word; for pilgrims may be understood in two ways—one wide, and one narrow. In the wide, whoever is out of his own country is so far a pilgrim; in the narrow use, by pilgrim is meant he only who goes to or returns from the house of St. James. Moreover, it is to be known that those who travel in the service of the Most High are called by three distinct terms. Those who go beyond the sea, whence often they bring back the palm, are called *palmers*. Those who go to the house of Galicia are called *pilgrims*, because the burial-place of St. James was more distant from his country than that of any other of

the Apostles. And those are called *romei* who go to Rome, where these whom I call pilgrims were going.

O pilgrims, who in pensive mood move slow,
  Thinking perchance of those who absent
    are,
  Say, do ye come from land away so far
  As your appearance seems to us to show?
For ye weep not, the while ye forward go
  Along the middle of the mourning town,
  Seeming as persons who have nothing
    known
  Concerning the sad burden of her woe.
If, through your will to hear, your steps ye
  stay,
  Truly my sighing heart declares to me
  That ye shall afterwards depart in tears.
For she her Beatrice hath lost: and ye
  Shall know, the words that man of her may
    say
  Have power to make weep whoever hears.

Some time after this sonnet was written, two ladies sent to Dante, asking him for some of his rhymes. That he might honor their request, he wrote a new sonnet and sent it to them with two that he had previously composed. In his new sonnet, he told how his thought mounted to heaven, as a pilgrim, and beheld his lady in such condition of glory as could not be comprehended by his intellect; for our intellect, in regard to the souls of the blessed, is as weak as our eyes are to the sun. But though he could not clearly see where his thought led him, at least he understood that his thought told of his lady in glory.

Beyond the sphere that widest orbit hath
  Passeth the sigh that issues from my heart,
  While weeping Love doth unto him impart
  Intelligence which leads him on his path.
When at the wished-for place his flight he
  stays,
  A lady he beholds, in honor dight,
  And shining so, that, through her splendid
    light,
  The pilgrim spirit upon her doth gaze.
He sees her such that his reporting words
  I understand not, for he speaketh low
  And strange to the sad heart which makes
    him tell;
He speaketh of that gentle one, I know,
  Since oft he Beatrice's name records;
  So, ladies dear, I understand him well.

This was the last of the poems which Dante composed in immediate honor and memory of Beatrice, and is the last of those which he inserted in the *Vita Nuova*. It was not that his love grew cold, or that her image became faint in his remembrance; but, as he tells us in a few concluding and memorable words, from this time forward he devoted himself to preparation for a work in which the earthly Beatrice should have less part, while the heavenly and blessed spirit of her whom he had loved should receive more becoming honors. The lover's grief was to find no more expression; the lamentations for the loss which could never be made good to him were to cease; the exhibition of a personal sorrow was at an end. Love and grief, in their double ministry, had refined, enlarged, and exalted his spirit to the conception of a design unparalleled in its nature, and of which no intellectual genius, unpurged by suffering, and unpenetrated in its deepest recesses by the spiritualizing heats of emotion, would have been capable of conceiving. Moreover, as time wore on, its natural result was gradually to withdraw the poet from the influence of temporary excitements of feeling, resulting from his experience of love and death, and to bring him to the contemplation of life as affected by the presence and the memory of Beatrice in its eternal and universal relations.

He tells us in the *Convito* that,

> after some time, my mind, which neither such consolation as I could give it, nor that offered to it by others, availed to comfort, determined to turn to that method by which others in grief had consoled themselves. And I set myself to read that book, but little known, of Boethius, in which in prison and exile he had consoled himself. And hearing, likewise, that Tully had written a book, in which, treating of friendship, he had offered some words of comfort to Laelius, a most excellent man, on the death of Scipio, his friend, I read this also. And although at first it was hard for me to enter into their meaning, I at length entered into it so far as my knowledge of language, and such little capacity as I had, enabled me; by means of which capacity, I had already, like one dreaming, seen many things, as may be seen in the *New Life*. And as it might happen that a man seeking silver should, beyond his expectation, find gold, which a hidden chance presents to him, not, perhaps, without Divine direction, so I, who sought for consolation, found not only a remedy for my tears, but also acquaintance with authors, with knowledge, and with books.

Nor did these serious and solitary studies withdraw him from the pursuit of wisdom among men and in the active world. Year by year, he entered more fully into the affairs of state, and took a larger portion of their conduct upon himself.

His heart kept fresh by abiding recollections of love, his faith quickened by and intermingled with the tenderest hopes, his imagination uplifted by the affection which overleaped the boundaries of the invisible world, and his intellect disciplined by study of books and of men, his experience enlarged by constant occupation

in affairs, his judgment matured by the quick succession of important events in which he was involved— every part of his nature was thus prepared for the successful accomplishment of that great and sacred design which he set before himself now in his youth. Heaven had called and selected him for a work which even in his own eyes partook somewhat of the nature of a prophetic charge. His strength was to be tested and his capacity to be approved. Life was ordered for the fulfillment of his commission. The men to whom God intrusts a message for the world find the service to which they are appointed one in which they must be ready to sacrifice everything. Dante looked forward, even at the beginning, to the end, and saw what lay between.

The pages of the *New Life* fitly close with words of that life in which all things shall be made new, "and there shall be no more death, neither sorrow, nor crying, neither shall there be any more pain; for the former things are passed away." The little book ends thus:

> Soon after this, a wonderful vision appeared to me, in which I saw things which made me purpose to speak no more of this blessed one until I could more worthily treat of her. And to attain to this, I study to the utmost of my power, as she truly knoweth. So that, if it shall please Him through whom all things live, that my life be prolonged for some years, I hope to speak of her as never was spoken of any woman. And then may it please Him who is the Lord of Grace, that my soul may go to behold the glory of its lady, the blessed Beatrice, who in glory looks upon the face of Him, *qui est per omnia saecula benedictus* [who is Blessed forever]!

In 1320, or perhaps not till 1321, the *Paradiso* was finished; in 1321, Dante died.

Dante Gabriel Rossetti (essay date 1893)

SOURCE: An introduction to *Dante and His Circle: With the Italian Poets Preceeding Him,* edited and translated by Dante Gabriel Rossetti, revised edition, Roberts Brothers, 1893, pp. 1-24.

[*In this introduction to his translation of the poem, Rossetti argues that the* Vita Nuova *laid the foundation for some of the most salient features of the* Divina Commedia.]

The *Vita Nuova* (the Autobiography or Autopsychology of Dante's youth till about his twenty-seventh year) is already well known to many in the original, or by means of essays and of English versions partial or entire. It is, therefore, and on all accounts, unnecessary to say much more of the work here than it says for itself. Wedded to its exquisite and intimate beauties are personal peculiarities which excite wonder and conjecture, best replied to in the words which Beatrice herself is made to utter in the *Commedia*: "Questi *fù tal* nella sue vita nuova." Thus then young Dante *was*. All that seemed possible to be done here for the work was to translate it in as free and clear a form as was consistent with fidelity to its meaning; to ease it, as far as possible, from notes and encumbrances; and to accompany it for the first time with those poems from Dante's own lyrical series which have reference to its events, as well as with such native commentary (so to speak) as might be afforded by the writings of those with whom its author was at that time in familiar intercourse. . . .

It may be noted here, however, how necessary a knowledge of the *Vita Nuova* is to the full comprehension of the part borne by Beatrice in the *Commedia*. Moreover, it is only from the perusal of its earliest and then undivulged self-communings that we can divine the whole bitterness of wrong to such a soul as Dante's, its poignant sense of abandonment, or its deep and jealous refuge in memory. Above all, it is here that we find the first manifestations of that wisdom of obedience, that natural breath of duty, which afterwards, in the *Commedia*, lifted up a mighty voice for warning and testimony. Throughout the *Vita Nuova* there is a strain like the first falling murmur which reaches the ear in some remote meadow, and prepares us to look upon the sea.

Boccaccio, in his Life of Dante, tells us that the great poet, in later life, was ashamed of this work of his youth. Such a statement hardly seems reconcilable with the allusions to it made or implied in the *Commedia*; but it is true that the *Vita Nuova* is a book which only youth could have produced, and which must chiefly remain sacred to the young; to each of whom the figure of Beatrice, less lifelike than love-like, will seem the friend of his own heart. Nor is this, perhaps, its least praise. To tax its author with effeminacy on account of the extreme sensitiveness evinced by this narrative of his love, would be manifestly unjust, when we find that, though love alone is the theme of the *Vita Nuova*, war already ranked among its author's experiences at the period to which it relates. In the year 1289, the one preceding the death of Beatrice, Dante served with the foremost cavalry in the great battle of Campaldino, on the eleventh of June when the Florentines defeated the people of Arezzo. In the autumn of the next year, 1290, when for him, by the death of Beatrice, the city as he says "sat solitary," such refuge as he might find from his grief was sought in action and danger: for we learn from the *Commedia* that he served in the war then waged by Florence upon Pisa, and was present at the surrender of Caprona. He says, using the reminiscence to give life to a description, in his great

way:

> I've seen the troops out of Caprona go
>   On terms, affrighted thus, when on the spot
> They found themselves with foemen
>   compass'd so.

(Cayley's *Translation*)

A word should be said here of the title of Dante's autobiography. The adjective *Nuovo, nuova*, or *Novello, novella*, literally *New*, is often used by Dante and other early writers in the sense of young. This has induced some editors of the *Vita Nuova* to explain the title as meaning *Early Life*. I should be glad on some accounts to adopt this supposition, as everything is a gain which increases clearness to the modern reader; but on consideration I think the more mystical interpretation of the words, as *New Life* (in reference to that revulsion of his being which Dante so minutely describes as having occurred simultaneously with his first sight of Beatrice), appears the primary one, and therefore the most necessary to he given in a translation. The probability may be that both were meant, but this I cannot convey.

Kenneth McKenzie (essay date 1903)

SOURCE: "The Symmetrical Structure of Dante's *Vita Nuova*," in *PMLA*, Vol. XVIII, No. 3, 1903, pp. 341-55.

[*In this essay, McKenzie reviews the critical debate about the symmetrical arrangement of the lyrics of the* Vita Nuova *and argues that Dante's arrangement throws light on the process of composition.*]

At the beginning of the *Vita Nuova* Dante tells us that he proposes to copy into the little book words which he finds written in the book of his memory under the rubric *Incipit Vita Nova;* thus he brought together lyrics that he had already written, and connected them by a narrative and analysis in prose. The *Vita Nuova* belongs, then, to the class of writings made up of alternating prose and verse. As in the case of the *Convivio*, this method of composition was perfectly natural under the circumstances; Dante doubtless intended to do for his own early poems what had been done for certain *troubadours* by the compilers of some of the Provençal anthologies, in which a prose biography is interspersed with specimens of the poet's verse. This has been pointed out by Pio Rajna [in *Lo schema della Vita Nuova*], who further suggests [in the article "Per le 'Divisioni' della *Vita Nuova*, in *Strenna Dantesca*, edited by Bacci and Passerini] that the analytical *divisioni* may have been modeled on certain works of St. Thomas. The prose explanations in the Provençal anthologies are called *razos*, and Dante uses the word *ragione* with the same meaning. In at least one respect, however, the *Vita Nuova* differs in form from the other works of this type; for the poems do not simply follow one another chronologically or according to the exigencies of the narrative, but are arranged in a symmetrical plan. The credit for having made this plain belongs to Professor C. E. Norton, who pointed it out in 1859. But more than twenty years earlier Gabriel Rossetti had explained the essential features of the symmetrical arrangement in a letter to Charles Lyell, dated January 13, 1836, which . . . reads in part as follows:

> The interpretation of the *Vita Nuova* depends upon knowing what portions of it are to be taken first, and what portions are to be taken last. This enigmatic booklet contains thirty-three compositions (*vide* your Index), relating to the thirty-three cantos of each section of the *Commedia*. These poetic compositions are to be divided into three parts, according to the three predominant canzoni. The central canzone, which is "Donna pietosa," is the head of the skein, and from that point must the interpretation begin; then one must take, on this side and on that, the four lateral sonnets to the left, and the four to the right (the last one to the right has been somewhat altered by Dante, but it is in fact a sonnet). On this side and on that follow the two canzoni, placed symmetrically; and the one explains the other. And thus, collating the ten compositions to the right with the ten to the left, we come finally to the first and the last sonnets of the *Vita Nuova*, which contain two visions. . . . The central part, which constitutes the Beatrice Nine, consists or nine compositions.

It is to be noted here that Rossetti, seeing clearly the symmetrical arrangement of the poems, made it a part of his system of interpreting Dante's works; and also that he gave the number of the lyrics in the *Vita Nuova*, which in reality is thirty-one, as thirty-three. As he indicated, he derived this number from the first edition of Lyell's translation of Dante's lyrical poems. Lyell numbers continuously the lyrics of the *Vita Nuova*, and includes among them Guido Cavalcanti's reply to the first sonnet; he also counts separately the alternative beginnings of the eighteenth sonnet, and thus arrives at thirty-three numbers. In his second edition he changes his system of numbering. A few years later Rossetti published a statement of his discovery, still giving the number of poems as thirty-three, and now stating definitely that one of them is by Cavalcanti. He divides the poems into three groups, the first and the last each containing eleven brief compositions, while in the centre are eight sonnets and *tre sole canzoni solenni*. The first *canzone* and the last treat respectively the life and death of Beatrice, while the central one contains the germ of the fiction of the whole book. Now, if we put *ten* in place of *eleven*, this scheme agrees essentially with the one to be explained presently. Rossetti perhaps repeated his statement in the unpublished portion of his *Beatrice di Dante*, of which

only the first part was printed. The manuscript was turned over to Aroux; and Rossetti was displeased to find his theories carried by this writer to an extreme that he himself could not approve. The ideas expressed in the following passage on the *Vita Nuova* seems to have been derived by Aroux from Rossetti; the number thirty-three, in particular, he would hardly have found elsewhere:

> Ce bizarre opuscule contient trente-trois compositions poétiques. Ce nombre est exactement en rapport avec celui de chacune des trois parties de la *Comédie*. Leur disposition symétrique est telle, qu'elles se trouvent exactement divisées par onze, et que parmi elles, dominant le tout, se déploient trois Canzoni solennelles, dont celle du milieu contient le germe de toute la fiction de l'ouvrage, fiction qui va se développant de droite et de gauche.

Buried in Rossetti's manuscript and in this book by Aroux, which well deserves the epithet *bizarre* that its author applies to the *Vita Nuova*, the symmetrical arrangement awaited a new discoverer. But as a curious example of the persistence of error, we may note that Dr. Edward Moore [in *Studies in Dante*], apparently following Aroux for the moment, gives "the number of the poetical compositions of the *Vita Nuova*" as thirty-three.

In 1859 Professor Charles Eliot Norton published *The New Life of Dante: An Essay, with translations*. In an appendix was a note "On the Structure of the *Vita Nuova*" reprinted in the subsequent editions of the complete translation. Before going further, we must see how the theory of symmetrical arrangement is deduced. The book contains thirty-one lyrics, arranged in the following order:

5 sonnets
1 *ballata*
4 sonnets
1 *canzone*
4 sonnets
1 *canzone*
3 sonnets
1 stanza
1 *canzone*
1 sonnet
1 imperfect *canzone*
8 sonnets

The three *canzoni* are longer and more elaborate than the other poems, having respectively 70, 84, and 76 verses; the second is the longest, and occupies the central position, with fifteen poems on each side of it. The fourth *canzone*, with 26 verses, the *ballata*, with 44, and the second and fourth sonnets—*sonetti rinterzati*, with 20 verses each—are nearer in length to the ordinary sonnets than to the *canzoni*. The stanza, according to Dante's statement, was the beginning of a *canzone,* the composition of which was interrupted by the death of Beatrice; it has 14 lines, and metrically it is so nearly like a sonnet that it may be called one. We may, then, reduce our scheme to this:

> 10 minor poems, all sonnets but one.
>> CANZONE I
>
> 4 sonnets
>> CANZONE II
>
> 4 sonnets
>> CANZONE III
>
> 10 minor poems, all sonnets but one.

Moreover, the first and third *canzoni* correspond strikingly to one another. The first, called *figliuola d'amore* ("daughter of love"), is in praise of the living Beatrice, who is desired in Heaven; Dante speaks,

> Donne e donzelle amorose, con vui,
> Che non è cosa da parlarne altrui.

The third, called *figliuola di tristizia* ("daughter of sorrow") is in praise of the dead Beatrice, who has gone to Heaven, and contains these words, referring to the former *canzone*:

> E perché mi ricorda che io parlai
> De la mia donna, mentre che vivian,
> Donne gentili, volontier con vui,
> Non voi' parlare altrui.

Meanwhile in the central *canzone,* while Beatrice was still alive, Dante describes to certain ladies a vision of her death:

> Io dissi: "Donne, dicerollo a vui."

This is the arrangement of the lyrics primarily according to their form, as Professor Norton explains it in the three editions of his translation. In the third edition he shows also how a different numerically symmetrical division can be made out, according to subject; this had apparently never been noticed before. The first ten poems concern Dante's own experiences as a lover; after them he takes up a "new and more noble theme," the praise of his lady. The tenth poem of the second group is interrupted by the death of Beatrice, and again Dante takes up a "new subject." Finally, after the third group of ten, we come to the final sonnet, which is distinct from the rest, and is called "una cosa nuova." This last poem, like the *canzoni* which begin the second and third groups, is addressed to "gentle ladies." This scheme: 10 + 10 + 10 + 1, recalls the grouping into three canticles of the cantos in the *Divina Commedia*: (1 + 33) + 33 + 33.

Since pointed out by Professor Norton, the symmetrical grouping of the shorter poems around the *canzoni* has until recently always been accepted as a fact . . . Two writers have used it as an important element in their theories—John Earle in his interpretation of the *Vita Nuova* ["Dante's *Vita Nuova,*" *Quarterly Review,* July 1986] and G. Federzoni in discussing the date of its composition [in *Studi i Diporti Danteschi*]. . . . But in 1901 a violent attack was made on the whole theory of symmetrical arrangement by Michele Scherillo [in "La Forma architettonica della *Vita Nuova,*" *Giornale Dantesco,* 9]; and as a number of critics have since declared the theory "demolished," it is a matter of some interest to determine whether anything of it remains.

Scherillo's chief argument is simply a general denial that any symmetry exists. The self-evident fact that the four poems of intermediate length do not occupy symmetrical positions with reference to each other, seems to him a fatal weakness. Indeed, he declares that the presence of a fourth *canzone,* even a short one, is sufficient alone to overthrow the whole scheme of pretended symmetry. Counting up lines, he finds that the first ten poems have 182, the last ten 152. The stanza, although very like a sonnet, is not one, strictly speaking, for one of its lines has only seven syllables. The first and third *canzoni,* although they correspond in subject, fail to do so in metrical structure ; their rhymes are not similarly arranged, and although each has five fourteen-line stanzas, one has a six-line *commiato* in addition. The structure is, then, lop-sided. And why, continues Scherillo, is there no symmetry in the arrangement of the prose paragraphs? In reply to this, it is only necessary to recall that the numbering of the paragraphs was not done by Dante, and is not found either in the manuscripts or the early editions; but in any case we should not expect the prose commentary to be treated like the verse.

After reading these arguments, one is tempted simply to ask: "What of it?" For, as a matter of fact, they leave absolutely untouched the essential part of the theory—twenty-eight short poems arranged symmetrically around three *canzoni,* which are in every way written on a different scale from the rest. This much of symmetry, even if no more could be found, is too remarkable to be the result of chance. Scherillo thinks, however, that if Dante had intended any symmetry at all, he would have carried it out more thoroughly, as in the *Divina Commedia,* and would not have admitted irregularities. But we must remember that the scheme of the *Commedia* was surely arranged before any considerable part of the verses was written, whereas the *Vita Nuova,* was made up out of materials already at hand; and, moreover, a counting-up of lines does not make cantos and canticles exactly equal. Unfortunately, Scherillo, the great value of whose researches, particularly on the *Vita Nuova,* no one will wish to deny, seems in this case to be actuated by a feeling of personal or "patriotic" hostility against foreign critics. Commenting on Dr. Moore's accidental misstatement that there are thirty-three lyrics in the *Vita Nuova*, he remarks that "arithmetic is surely not a matter of individual opinion, even in England." His own arithmetic, however, is sufficiently individual to concoct this equation (3 X 10) + 3 = 43. To sum up, then, he declares that anyone who believes that Dante had the intention of arranging the *Vita Nuova* symmetrically shows "deplorable ingenuousness and lack of critical training." It seems to me however, that these deplorable qualities are shown rather by attempting to deny what is evident.

But the theory of symmetry has been carried further. The central *canzone*, it has been said, should be, both in subject and in form, the most important poem in the book. Thus Earle maintains that if the *Vita Nuova* were biography, the third *canzone*, written in connection with the death of Beatrice, would occupy the central position, and not a subordinate one; hence, he argues, the facts, even if true, are of no importance; the symbolism is the thing. Precisely, returns Scherillo, who in general disagrees totally with Earle; if there were any symmetry, the third *canzone*, not the second, would necessarily be the center. But do not both critics neglect Dante's distinct statement that he does not intend to treat of the death of Beatrice? Written after Dante's eyes "had wept for some time," the third *canzone* tells of his grief for Beatrice's death; but we need not necessarily connect it closely with the actual event, and we must remember its striking correspondence with the first *canzone*. In any case, as Professor Norton says, the second *canzone*, the most elaborate and important poem of the whole, serves to connect the life of Beatrice with her death, and rightfully holds the central position in the scheme. Federzoni agrees with this, and goes further; he believes that when the poems were brought together the second *canzone* was written especially to occupy the central position. But the existence of a scheme does not depend on the relative importance of the three *canzoni*.

The second symmetrical grouping pointed out by Professor Norton exists simultaneously with the first in a very striking way, and cannot be entirely accidental; but just how far Dante arranged the double symmetry it is difficult to say. Of course, the second scheme depends, to some extent, on the first. The symbolic numbers *three* and *ten* are evident in both schemes. With a little ingenuity the number *nine,* which is so important in the *Vita Nuova*, can be found also; Rossetti noticed that between the first and third *canzoni* are nine poems; Federzoni noticed the same thing, and also that between the first vision-sonnet and the first *canzone*, and again between the third *canzone* and the final vision-sonnet, there are also nine poems so that this scheme, with *three nines,* results: 1 + 9 + 1 + 9 + 1 + 9 + 1. However, to such ingenuities as this, little

importance should be attached.

Various other schemes of dividing the *Vita Nuova* according to subject have been proposed, but the only one containing the element of symmetry is by Federzoni. After adopting the division into three parts as proposed by Rossetti, he makes in each of these three parts, three subdivisions, or nine in all, as follows: First Part, announcement—awakening of love—vicissitudes of love; Second Part, praise of Beatrice—presentiment of her death—death of Beatrice; Third Part, love for the *donna gentile*—reawakening of the first love—announcement of a grand vision. In this scheme, striking correspondences can easily be found. But even if we accept this partition as exhaustive and accurate, it is hardly possible to prove that Dante had any such elaborate arrangement in mind when he distributed the lyrics symmetrically.

Assuming much or little of symmetrical arrangement, then, but assuming that it exists as a part of Dante's plan, in connection with the visions and the symbolic numbers—why did the poet wish "to produce an effect of symmetry that is not to be found in life?" Does this in itself necessarily prove that the *Vita Nuova* is made up of imaginary incidents, or that it has only a symbolic meaning? By no means. We must remember that in his earlier literary work Dante was influenced chiefly by Provençal models. The *troubadours* were satisfied to lavish all their artifices on single poems; would not Dante think it a mark of superior power to be able to combine such separate poems into a symmetrically organic whole? The symmetry of construction in the *Divina Commedia* cannot be found in earlier descriptions of visits to the other world; it is one of Dante's original contributions, as distinguished from what he derived by imitation. So in the *Vita Nuova*, out of materials already at hand, he wove together facts and fancies, experiences and imaginations, into an organic art work to which he subsequently gave an allegorical interpretation.

Some Dante scholars will say that this last statement implies too much belief in the historical accuracy of the *Vita Nuova*, others that it implies too little; but it seems to me to indicate the only rational basis for interpreting the book in connection with Dante's other works. If a study of the *troubadours* teaches us anything on this subject, it is that Dante founded his book on real events, which he worked into a narrative with various literary artifices. In this connection we must take account of the symmetrical construction of the book, which is one of these artifices; others are the modes of expression, such as the personification of love, and the use of the vision as a literary form. The art and symbolism do not, then, depend primarily on the invention of significant incidents, but on making incidents, whether real or invented, conform to the chosen scheme. In the *Convivio*, with a different point of view, Dante gives an allegorical interpretation of the last part of the *Vita Nuova*, which has led many to believe that the book had no other meaning. But Dante tells us that although the true and fundamental meaning of any work is the allegorical, the literal meaning must come first. So he wrote his poems as they were suggested to him from time to time by circumstances, without thinking either of an allegorical interpretation or of a scheme for symmetrical arrangement. Indeed, it was probably not until after the death of Beatrice, the episode of the Donna Pietosa, and the renewal of his faithfulness to Beatrice's memory, that the idea came to him of collecting his scattered verses into a book which should give a connected account of his New Life. The symmetrical structure of the book is strong evidence that he arranged the poems and wrote the prose all at one time. Hence it follows that his mental attitude when he wrote the prose governed the selection and interpretation of the poems. For instance, the first sonnet, which was doubtless written, as Dante says, in 1283, describes a vision in which Love shows Beatrice to Dante, and then goes away weeping. In the prose description of this vision, however, Love carries Beatrice away towards Heaven. We find added, then, an idea which is not inconsistent with the words of the sonnet, but which surely was not in Dante's mind originally. The addition was presumably made for the purpose of making this first sonnet correspond with the last one in the book, which also describes a vision, and connects Love, Beatrice and Heaven. Thus the book as a whole gains in unity and symmetry. So also the name of Beatrice, aside from one exceptional case, is not mentioned in the verses written during her life; but in the prose it is frequently mentioned, and she is spoken of at the very beginning as glorified in Heaven. It would be possible, then, to find an allegorical meaning in the prose and not in the verse, if such an interpretation were otherwise desirable.

Following a similar line of reasoning, Federzoni maintains that several of the poems were written, not when they purport to have been, but simultaneously with the prose, or even later, in order to fit into the symmetrical scheme. The second *canzone* in particular, he thinks, judging both from its subject and from its style as compared with the accompanying prose, could not have been written until after Dante's final and complete return to Beatrice, as related in the *Purgatorio*, xxx and xxxi. Now since Dante dates his great vision in 1300, Federzoni thinks that the *Vita Nuova* must have been composed either in or shortly before that year. But this conclusion rests on a misapprehension; just as the vision was a conventional literary form, so the date 1300 was chosen for external reasons, and not because Dante had any particular inner experience that time. The idea of the *Divina Commedia* developed gradually, and certainly had not reached its final form until long after the *Vita Nuova* was finished. Thus the most probable date for the composition of the *Vita Nuova*

still remains between 1293 and 1295; but so far as the fictitious date 1300 goes, the *Divina Commedia* might have been conceived long before. Federzoni's arguments from the style of the second *canzone* will appeal to a reader who is predisposed to agree with them; but they are largely subjective, and their validity is disputed.

That Dante, not finding all the poems that he needed for his scheme, may have written some for particular positions in the *Vita Nuova* while he was writing the prose, is not in itself impossible. Yet we must notice that he excuses the omission of a poem on the death of Beatrice, and does not furnish the poem. On the other hand he does not use all the poems already written ; and one factor in determining his choice was no doubt the symmetrical scheme. Thus the first *canzone* of the *Convivio*, "Voi che intendendo il terzo ciel movete," relates the events of the last part of the *Vita Nuova*. Provided the scheme had allowed another long *canzone*, this one would naturally have found a place there, if, as seems probable, it was written before the *Vita Nuova* was finished. By being reserved for the *Convivio*, it received a different interpretation from what it would have had in the *Vita Nuova*. It is not necessary to discuss here which of the extant poems attributed to Dante were contemporaneous with the *Vita Nuova*, and might have found a place in it if the poet had so willed. But evidently in studying this question the symmetrical scheme of the book should not be neglected.

In conclusion, what are we to say of the artistic value of this artifice which is so foreign to our modern methods? Let us answer the question with this other, asked by an American poet [Sydney Lanier]: "Is love less love because the lover in the very heavenly excess of his devotion shall wreathe it about with all the flowers his fancy can gather under the whole heaven of poetry?"

Karl Vossler (essay date 1907-10),

SOURCE: "The Ethical and Political Background of the *Divine Comedy*," in *Mediaeval Culture: An Introduction to Dante and His Times, Vol. I,* translated by William Cranston Lawton, 1929. Reprint by Frederick Ungar Publishing Co., 1958, pp. 175-354.

[*In this excerpt from an essay originally written in 1907-10, Vossler examines the intensity of Dante's passion for Beatrice, which he considers too extreme to be accepted at face value.*]

There is some ground for the surmise that Dante in early youth came into close relations with the Franciscans. His religious and political convictions and sentiments, which, as we have seen, were closely allied to the tendencies of the order; a tradition mentioned by the commentator Francesco da Buti (1354-1406), and current in the Franciscan order; a passage, somewhat dubious, to be sure, in the *Commedia* (*Inferno*, XVI, 106 sqq.), and finally, perhaps, the fact that the poet was buried beside the Church of St. Francis in Ravenna—all seem to point in that direction.

If it be taken for granted that Dante, perhaps at the age of fourteen, was sent to the school of the Minorite Brothers in Santa Croce in Florence, then this fertile conjecture serves to throw light on many obscure points and inconsistencies in the development of the poet's character. His upbringing in that school would undoubtedly have tended to a one-sided development of feeling and of imagination. It would have given a fresh, artificial, and somewhat perilous predominance to precisely those powers in the soul of the young poet to which Nature had already assured the ascendancy.

This error in education—supposing that it was committed—avenged itself. An overheated monastic atmosphere of sensitiveness and dreaminess environed and weakened his all too emotional spirit. And, lo! at the slightest contact with his troublesome age, it took fire. A sensuous and supersensuous love, morbid, intensified by fashion, took hold of him.

The story of this love he glorified poetically in the *Vita Nuova*. Here, like Goethe in his *Werther*, he summed up a complete series of inward experiences. Beyond this, the comparison with *Werther* might be misleading. We will carry it no further, then, than to say that the *Vita Nuova*, like *Werther*, is only with great caution to be utilized as an authority for the inner biography of its poet. Its value for the outer life of Dante can never be fully determined. Even the answer to the question whether his Beatrice was actually the daughter of Folco Portinari and became the wife of Simone de' Bardi will depend on the temperament of the inquirer.

Vision and reality, things dreamed of and things experienced, have been melted together in this enigmatic little book, and can hardly be separated again.

If we consider the external circumstances and events therein narrated, they present themselves as a meaningless and yet, no doubt, deliberately planned series of the most diverse incidents. A chance meeting the poet with Beatrice—she is in her ninth year and is wearing a red dress—a second meeting, nine years later; she wears a white dress. But in reality, that is, apparently, the poet lauds not her, but another lady. The latter goes on a journey; a friend of Beatrice dies; Dante also makes a journey, evidently only in order to have a vision on the way. Barely returned, he again,

for appearance sake, sings the praises of another lady. Beatrice refuses him her greeting. Beatrice's father dies; Beatrice herself dies. It is not her death, but Dante's dream of her approaching decease, that is poetically elaborated. Another incipient attachment disturbs his remembrance of the dead. Finally, however, Beatrice is victorious; that is, not she, but her glorified image of light. No action: a dream, an intention, a wish, constitute the drama.

But if we study these events for their value as inner emotions, the book as a whole attains, as if by a magic touch, a certain unity that is perhaps not artistically moulded, but is evidently felt and intended; and its name is Beatrice. It is the beloved maiden's figure and the worshipful devotion of the poet modestly veiled and inwardly deepened. The many minor incidents, the apparent digressions, the death of her friend and of her father, everything that anticipates or distracts from Beatrice, is nothing but the external re-flux of pious love which circles about and within itself like a whirlpool, blurs the outlines of every vision, and dissolves all sensuousness. The apotheosis of woman is accomplished in symmetrical chapters, symbolically numbered. Her picturesque environment is merely the cloud on which she soars aloft.

Dante's true intention in this little book remains indeed an enigma. Investigators have not determined which of all his imaginable purposes deserves the preference. [As Benedetto Croce remarks in his *Poetry of Dante*,]

> Was it the wish to erect a monument to his dead beloved and at the same time to his own past youth? Was it not rather the desire to bring together a number of poems composed by him on various occasions, and to give them a higher significance, so as to entrust them under better auspices and with more dignity to posterity? Or again, was it the necessity to light a beacon for his own journey through earthly life, that should forevermore point out to him the haven in the recollection, in the idealization, or in the discovery of a source of happiness enjoyed and not wholly lost, which he might some day recover, as he eventually did in the *Commedia*? Or, finally, was it all these various purposes intertwined one with another?

We do not know.

A notable, attractive, and ingenious effort to explain the *Vita Nuova* as a composition that had sprung out of a social necessity has been made by Rudolf Borchardt. He considers it a self-defense of the young poet who wished to regain his reputation, to restore his lessened importance, in an aristocratic, literary, and courtly circle of ladies and gentlemen. If it be considered that in the *Convivio*, and even in the *Commedia*, the purpose of a social rehabilitation is active, we shall hardly venture, in the case of a man so sensitive about his honour as Dante was, to reject this surmise without full consideration.

If Dante's purpose was self-defense before the world, the actual inward result for him was a relapse. His first contact with his age led to his flight from that age. His sensuousness is not overcome, only mystically dulled; his self-love is not crushed, only religiously purified. He studiously avoided coming to an understanding with those passions which he was compelled to recognize later as the strongest in his nature: his pride and his sensuousness. Inspired by uncontrolled sensuousness, he had been a dreamy worshipper,

So not to venture on mere virtuous deeds.

His uncontrolled pride had made him choose as his lady-love an angel who lifted him above all mankind.

> . . . The pot,
> Itself of iron, would fain with silver tongs
> Out of the fire be lifted, so that it
> May fancy 'tis itself a silver pot.

The manner in which the Dante of the *Vita Nuova* treats his visions and the sacred mystery of his heart is neither altogether artistically naive nor morally faultless. There is something conventional in this youthful work, and for that reason it is passionately enjoyed by all modern æsthetes.

Only the theoretical, not the moral, inadequacy of his youthful dreaminess was recognized and overcome by the poet himself. He lit up the cloudy and shapeless desires of youth. The hot surging of his blood he quieted, at least to some degree. He had looked straight in the eye of that secret power which, at a certain period of life, lays hold on us all, and, half sexually, half metaphysically, bewilders and entrances us with the yearning for love and death. He descended into the underworld of his own nature, and more fortunate than Orpheus, released out of the struggling night of impulses an ideal shape, the heavenly Beatrice.

To the man already growing old, she was a consolation and a guiding star. In the *Vita Nuova*, he shaped for himself, out of death and womanhood, a faith and a hope. And Beatrice again saw to it that vulgarity and cynicism, the characteristic vices of decadent mediævalism, were kept away from him.

Robert Hall comments on the importance of the *Vita Nuova* in the *Commedia*:

Without the *Vita Nuova,* the *Commedia* would still be the major work of literature that it is, but our understanding of the antecedent pscyhological events in Dante's mind—the origin and nature of his love for Beatrice—would be seriously diminished, as would indeed our comprehension of the *dolce stil nuova* as a poetical manner.

Robert A. Hall, Jr., *A Short History of Italian Literature,* Linguistica, 1951.

J. E. Shaw (essay date 1929)

SOURCE: "The Character of the *Vita Nuova*," in *Essays on the "Vita Nuova,"* 1929. Reprinted by Kraus Reprint Corporation, 1965, pp. 163-228.

[*In this essay, Shaw, repudiating the generally accepted view that the* Vita Nuova *is an allegory, proposes an interpretation based on a literal reading of the historical events recounted in the narrative.*]

That a boy of nine should fall ecstatically in love will always seem impossible to those who cannot imagine it, and with them argument is superfluous, nor will they be persuaded even by the citation of historically authentic examples. Those, however, whose imagination presents the matter as not impossible may be asked to consider that a love of the particular kind in question is more likely to have its beginnings before the age of fourteen than after. A little boy who, like Dante, may have passed his first years without any intimate acquaintance with girls, and who is, in his innocence, ignorant of the physiological nature of the attraction of sex, may be astonishingly affected by the apparition of a graceful and otherwise charming little girl, who is likely to seem to him an inexplicably dazzling creature. A powerful impression made at such an early age may be preserved and develop in after years, especially if the two never come to know one another well and if the little girl grows to be a gracious young lady, whom the young man is able to see every now and then without ever conversing with her. On the other hand, an infatuation begun after the age of puberty is likely to be soon forgotten for others of the same kind. And when the Beatrice of seventeen, recently married to one of the wealthiest noblemen of the city, beautiful and radiant with the prospects of a happy life, greeted the young man who, as a child, and before he was sent to school, had been a neighbour of hers—greeted him with the friendliness of an old acquaintance—she confirmed the impression she had made as a little child, by substituting for it another fully in harmony with it.

That Dante should, after this event, have been content with being spoken to by her, whenever they met, has also seemed incredible, but only to those who, although amazed at the precociousness of the young lover, still insist on thinking of this as the story of an ordinary love affair. Before the first greeting Beatrice had been the lady of his mind and of his dreams, and the kindly greeting, repeated more than once, heightened the glamour of that peculiar relation to him. If he had had the courage to approach her the spell would have been broken, the peculiarity of the charm would have been obliterated by commonplace conversation. The importance of the lady's salutation was one of the traditional conventions, but it was a convention that was founded on real human experience. The poets were, as a rule, inferior socially to the ladies whom they courted. Let anyone who can, remember the time when he was a presentable and ambitious young man but with no conspicuous social position; let him remember being greeted in public cordially, as an old acquaintance, by a beautiful, wealthy young lady of the highest rank; let him remember how the warm blood rushed through his happy body, flattering the elemental snob that is in every man, fortifying his self-respect and glorifying the gracious person who affected him so "virtuously"; and he will have no difficulty in understanding why the salutation of the lady became important. With Dante, however, the pardonable element of flattery must have been less effective than the realization that this adorable person was the same who, as a little child, had so affected his imagination that he had thought of her as an angel and had often sought occasion to look at her and wonder. She was more glorious now than ever, and she was kind to him.

The impressions made upon Dante by his first meeting with Beatrice and by her greeting him nine years later ought not to seem incredible in themselves, but if we also consider that the *Vita Nuova* was composed after her death, after Dante's temporary unfaithfulness to her memory, after the "forte imaginazione" ("convincingly imagined event") recorded in chapter thirty-nine, and immediately after the "mirabile visione" ("miraculous vision") mentioned in the last chapter, all reason for doubting the sincerity of the literal account vanishes. For he evidently composed the *Vita Nuova* under the influence of a flood of recollections which became transfigured in his memory by the new light in which he was reviewing his young life. In this new light all the incidents recollected assumed a predestined continuity, and a consequently heightened significance. He believed that he had been miraculously guided, and that Beatrice had been the guide providentially ordained for him. He had never been well acquainted with her, so that no conflicting material circumstances hampered his imagination as it transfigured her. The wondering admiration with which he remembered looking upon her as a child, the happiness of being greeted by her when she smiled upon him later, were memories that transcended the reality of the events.

The new light in which he is seeing the incidents he remembers envelops all of them and transforms them without altering them substantially. Let us face the difficulty of the "ladies of the defense," which, I think, constitutes the most reasonable of the objections to the credibility of the story. Dante tells us that, inspired by Love, he twice selected a lady to be the ostensible object of his affection, in order to conceal his love for Beatrice; but we cannot help believing that these ostensible affections were real love affairs which had a value of their own for him. Why do we believe that? Because we are told that the courting of the first lady lasted for "years and months" and we are allowed to read a poem which seems to be a very genuine lamentation over her departure. As for the second lady, Love is represented to us as actually carrying the heart of the poet away from the first lady, who had possessed it, to present it to the second, and we are told that the courting of this second lady was so ardent that Beatrice herself was shocked by it. In other words it is Dante himself who gives us the information which produces the belief in question. It is not that he is vainly trying to conceal the facts: no one can suppose him to be as clumsy an artist as that. He is conveying to us the meaning which the events had for him at the time in question as well as the meaning they have for him at the time of writing, but he is especially concerned that we shall see these events as he is seeing them now.

His first acquaintance with love had been that which a child may have who is endowed with a vivid imagination and a religious up-bringing. It was transformed, after his meeting with Beatrice at the age of eighteen, into a passion more suitable to his age, partly sensuous, although unconsciously so. The fascination of the glorious creature of his mind was accompanied by a yearning for something unknown, a longing which could not be satisfied, both because its object was inaccessible and because the nature of the satisfaction longed for was not apparent. It affected his health and so aroused curiosity in his friends. He would have been anxious to defeat that curiosity even if there had been no convention of secrecy, because his emotion was too chaste and precious to be revealed, and because of natural timidity: he was aware that his was not an ordinary love such as was fashionable. He wrote no poetry about it, except the first enigmatic sonnet which won him the sympathy of a more experienced poet—considered eccentric by the rest—who smiled understandingly and foresaw the tumultuous awakening of the senses, which was sure to bring trouble to this very young and delicate-minded lover.

The lady "of the defence," who appealed directly to his innocent senses, provided his vague longings with an accessible object, and gave him the opportunity to indulge in an ordinary, fashionable love. He became a "regular" lover such as could be understood by those about him. The satisfaction he must have felt on thus becoming "a man of the world" will be realized by all those who have suffered from being considered "odd," from not being "in the swim" with the young men who are their natural companions. His health was restored, he became happy, but although his ideal passion for "the lady of his mind" must, I think, have become less ardent, it was revived from time to time by his meetings with Beatrice, when he would give himself up completely to his earlier dreams, the dreams which could not be realized by the lady he was actually courting. He must have missed the latter when she left the city, but his affection for her was not such that no substitute for it could be found. The next lady "of the defence" was courted with a boldness born of successful experience, and we know the result: the smiling salutation of Beatrice, which had hitherto satisfied the cravings of his better self, was withdrawn, and with it went all the delightful fancies he had cherished as his most precious possession, his mental life of love, which made him superior to others. Before this time he had had no clear understanding of the nature of love, he had only known that there were different kinds, and that the superior kind was beyond the reach of most: he now began to realize that the love he had lost was the only real kind for him, and that the satisfactions he had so easily grasped were mere imitations of it.

Now that he is writing the *Vita Nuova* he sees that, in these as in all matters, he was guided by a higher power. The other affections were necessary stages of experience: without them he might never have reached his understanding of noble love, which, after the withdrawal of the salutation, appeared to him in an entirely new form. His saying that "Amore" prompted him to assume those disguises of his chief interest is only a figurative way of saying that his amorous inclinations, unstudied hitherto, were operating in a predestined direction. That these love affairs were really disguises of his best love is no doubt true, but his saying that he embraced them for that purpose is only partly true, and is due, no doubt, to his desire to adopt the Provençal conventions of secrecy and the "stalking horse." In the same way he had adopted the other convention of the importance of the lady's salutation although that importance was far from being merely conventional in his case. By adopting these conventions he was able to give an orthodox, traditional coloring, acceptable to his readers, to the otherwise unusual circumstances he was recording.

The recurrence of the number nine in the dates of events with which Beatrice is concerned is neither incredible nor astonishing. That any number should recur frequently in the dates of anyone's life is a coincidence which has often been noticed, but the nines of Beatrice, which are never mentioned in the verse, are for the most part purposely excogitated by the author, and that without any concealment. Free as he was to use the year, month, day, and hour of any event, it was not difficult for him to find another nine when he was determined to do so. We may smile at his earnestness in discovering these nines, but his motive is obvious enough. The mystical prestige of nine and its square

root three was traditional and a matter of common knowledge. However their significance might be interpreted, their association with a series of incidents emphasized the providential character of those incidents, and Dante was already convinced that the events to which he attaches the number nine were really providentially predestined. It did not matter much to him what particular significance might be found in the recurrence of the number, as is shown by his own deprecatory interpretation in chapter twenty-nine, but he desired that recurrence to reflect his own impression that the events were not accidental, and that Beatrice was a miraculous creature.

It would not be fair to ignore the fact that evidence of the allegorical character of the *Vita Nuova* has been apparent to some in the twenty-fifth chapter. It has been thought that the right of a poet to use the figure of personification is too obvious to justify an elaborate defense of that right, and that Dante is really conveying, in a guarded manner, the information that he is using allegory. It is also argued that, where he says "grande vergogna sarebbe a colui che rimasse sotto vesta di figura o di colore rettorico, e poscia, domandato, non sapesse denudare le sue parole da cotale vesta, in guisa che avessero verace intendimento" [*Vita Nuova*, xxv, 10], he is speaking of something more than mere figurative, metaphorical language, especially since in the *Convivio* the "verace intendimento" is declared to be the allegorical meaning of the poems expounded there. It is contended, too, that the examples cited from Virgil, Lucan, Horace and Ovid are taken from authors of *scritture* which, according to *Convivio*, I, ı, 2, are to be explained as allegorical, and that therefore their use in *Vita Nuova* xxv implies that allegory is being discussed although it is not mentioned.

Let us not fall into the common error of taking for granted in the *Vita Nuova* the theories and opinions set forth in the *Convivio*. Here in *Vita Nuova* xxv, the examples referred to are all specific examples of personification, and are cited as instances of the use of "figura o colore rettorico" ("figure or color of rhetoric"). It is more important that the impression of naïveté produced in us by the defense of the right to personify Love is due to a prejudice of ours: the contemporary reader would not receive any such impression. The Italian lyric preceding Dante is full of arguments as to whether Love is a god or not, and as to whether Love subsists by itself apart from the lover or not, as well as of attempts to define love existing in the lover. It was inevitable that, in this youthful work, the author should declare his position with regard to these matters. He foresaw this necessity when, in chapter twelve, he put off the explanation of why he had personified his *ballata,* until it could be included in the explanation of why he personified love, a matter which needed to be treated at some length. It needed to be treated because it involved the larger question as to the author's views on the nature of love, views which would stamp him as adhering to this or that set of recognized opinions, and here, as Marigo has noted [reference not available], Dante is explaining that he is not averroistic enough to believe that intellectual love can subsist apart from the lover, and not enough of a realist—in the controversy between realists and nominalists—to hold that a universal idea can subsist apart from the substance that individualizes it. His personifying Love, he says, is merely the use of a recognized figure of speech, a practice justified in the vulgar verse by the example of ancient poets in the classical tongue.

He himself knows what he is doing and is able to give his reasons, but there are those who imitate others in the use of this and other figures of speech without having any definite ideas as to the meaning and limitations of such figures, and they ought to be ashamed. These are the persons who, he says, write verses dressed in figurative language, but are unable to strip them of their clothing, that is, are unable to distinguish between the figure and the real meaning. The expression "veste di figura o di colore rettorico" ("dressed in a figure or color of rhetoric") is a repetition of the expression "figura o colore rettorico" used before in the same paragraph with regard to the examples of personification: only those who are determined to find a reference to allegory can see it in these words. The *Vita Nuova* gives us no information whatever as to what the author knew or thought about the use of allegory, but if, as is possible, he was acquainted with the Aquinian doctrine on that subject, he could not be thinking of allegory when he was writing this chapter, for St. Thomas makes it clear that figures like these belong to the literal sense and not to the allegorical: "Per literalem sensum potest aliquid significari dupliciter, scilicet secundum proprietatem locutionis, sicut cum dico: 'homo ridet,' vel secundum similitudinem seu metaphoram sicut cum dico: 'pratum ridet'. . . . . et ideo sub sensu literali includitar parabolicus, seu metaphoricus."

There are no good reasons for supposing that the *Vita Nuova* is an allegory, but there are good reasons for believing that it is not. I will not dwell on the importance of Dante's own description of the book, when comparing it with the *Convivio*, as youthful and unsophisticated, nor on the conviction which the narrative carries to many readers that the author is saying all that he means and concealing nothing except what would be self-praise. As far as the poems are concerned, they are indeed easily distinguishable, for the most part, from the previous and contemporary love-lyric, because of their greater beauty and originality, but they nevertheless belong to the great stream which originated in southern France and flooded, rather than flowed into, northern France, Italy and Germany. There is no characteristic of Dante's poetry that can be isolated and classified which does not find its counterpart in other poems by Italians, French or Germans, including the religious idealization of the lady and the mystical quality of love for her. Unless all or much of this poetry can be shown to be allegorical, it is improbable that Dante's verses were made with an allegorical intention.

Against the supposition that, in composing the *Vita Nuova,* Dante undertook to allegorize the contents of the poems is to be set the evidence of the twenty-fifth chapter. In that chapter the author defends his personification of Love, and condemns the unintelligent use of figures of speech. He explains that verse in the vulgar tongue was first devised in order to be understood by ladies, and implies that this is still its purpose, by declaring that it should have no other subject than love because that was its original subject. He refers to the Provençal and the early Italian poets, showing that he considers his own verse as of the same kind essentially as theirs. His desire to be understood by his readers is obvious, he abounds in explanation, but he says no word about allegory in his own verse or that of others, and least of all in the examples of personification that he cites: Love is nothing but love, just as Juno is nothing but the goddess, Aeolus is Aeolus and Rome is Rome. It follows, I think, that Beatrice is nothing but Beatrice, and to me it is inconceivable that the author should explain so much and say nothing about a hidden meaning pervading the whole work, if there were any.

On the other hand there are two little bits of allegory in the *Vita Nuova*, and these the author explains after drawing our attention to them. The dream described in the first sonnet requires interpretation, and Dante tells us that it is prophetic of the death of Beatrice. It is true that he leaves the other details to us, implying that any good interpretation will do, but there is no concealment; and when he chooses to read a symbolical meaning into the apparition of Beatrice and Giovanna, in chapter twenty-four, he does so plainly and complacently, far-fetched as the interpretation is, since it is childishly based on the name of the second lady.

The prose of the *Vita Nuova*, besides being a connecting narrative, is an explanation of what the reader may fail to understand in the poems and of much that he could not fail to grasp. It is elaborate with its *divisioni,* but except in the case of those poems that were not written for Beatrice, but which the poet thinks—or would have us think—were not written without some thought of her; and except for the obscure words "Ego tanquam centrum" which the sequel is expected to make clear, there is no hint of any hidden meaning; and even in the case of these exceptions there is only a presence of concealment: it is learned criticism that has made a mystery of the figure of the circle and its center.

Of the sonnet in chapter fourteen Dante says that the

meaning will be clear to all, except perhaps to some who are less experienced servants of Love than himself. To this latter kind of reader it is no use trying to explain why Love is said to destroy all the faculties except those of sight, and why the physical organs of sight—the eyes—are not needed in the presence of the lady. Of eight other poems he says either that they are sufficiently explained by the preceding *ragione,* which has described the occasion of their writing, or else that there is nothing to explain. If the **Vita Nuova** contains a connected allegory, the author has buried it so deep in silence that no one but the Archangel will ever rouse it.

In previous essays I have attempted to describe the rise of Dante's adult passion for Beatrice, after she had denied him the salutation which was the sign of her favor and had been the source of happiness in the private life of his phantasy. There remains to explain how he ceased to crave the satisfaction of a not unworthy human passion and became content with worshipping his lady. "Content," however, is a poor adjective to apply to a poet who is not conscious of any renunciation, but to whom the solution of his problem has brought ecstatic happiness ("beatitudine") in the triumph of a new understanding of his love and beloved.

In chapter thirteen he describes what he calls in the next chapter the "battaglia de li diversi pensieri," the conflict of thoughts which resulted in a clear view of his own humiliation. He was reduced to the ranks of the many conventional servants of Love who can only cry for mercy, and his lady was not the conventional lady who might ultimately be affected by the constant cry. "Volendo dire d'Amore, non so da qual parte pigli matera, e se la voglio pigliare da tutti, convene che io chiami la mia inimica, madonna la Pietade; e dico 'madonna' quasi per disdegnoso modo di parlare." It was a despicable situation: his love had before been precious for its singularity and it had been secret; now it could no longer be concealed and appeared commonplace as well as hopeless. His humiliation is acutely emphasized by the derision of Beatrice and her friends in the next chapter: he realizes that their view of him is that he is a lover of a well-known kind, hiding under a cloak of sentimentality a desire he is unwilling to confess. Why—he asks himself in chapter fifteen— why does he still seek her presence only to become an object of ridicule? It is because his passion is so powerful that it causes him to forget the rebuffs which have been peculiarly bitter to the proudest poet that ever lived. He has been hoping that his verses will be brought to her attention, as he tells us at the end of the fourteenth chapter, and now he writes one more sonnet—which is to be the last—in which he makes a full confession for her ears. He has four new things to say: "La prima delle quali si è che molte volte io mi dolea, quando la memoria movesse la fantasia a imaginare quale Amore mi facea." He grieves often over the

difference between his former feeling for her and the violence of his present passion, which makes him appear contemptible in her eyes. "La seconda si è che Amore spesse volte m'assalia sì forte, che 'n me non rimanea altro di vita se non un pensero che parlava di questa donna." Violent as his passion is it is altogether sincere; it leaves alive in him no other thought than of her; it is not a common craving. "La terza si è che quando questa battaglia d'Amore mi pugnava cosi, io mi movea quasi discolorito tutto per vedere questa donna, credendo che mi difendesse la sue veduta da questa battaglia . . ." It is not only the forgetfulness of previous disappointments, mentioned in the previous sonnet and repeated here, that causes him to seek her presence, but an instinctive confidence that she can protect him from the violence of his passion: he trusts in her for that. "La quarta si è come cotale veduta non solamente non mi difendea, ma finalmente disconfiggea la mia poca vita." But his confidence is unaccountably misplaced, his appeal to her goodness is strangely disappointed.

And now that he has said all he has to say he resolves to write no more. He will preserve his self-respect by remaining silent: the love of a poet who, though in love, is silent, of one who has ceased to sing because he is misunderstood, is bound to be at least respected. . . .

[F]rom the time when, after the vision of chapter twelve, he had begun seriously to enquire into the nature of love, he had compared the views of Cavalcanti and Guinizelli and had inclined to prefer the doctrine of the latter that love is the goodness in the heart of the lover seeking the goodness in the lady. It was inevitable that in pondering over the singularity of his lady and asking himself why his love was unacceptable to her, he should be impressed by the peculiar quality of Guinizelli's lady, who is the educator of her lover, and whose relation to him is like that of God to the angel who moves the sphere. It seems certain that, before the conversation with the ladies of chapter eighteen, Dante had reached the conclusion, at least subconsciously, that the reason why his love was unacceptable to Beatrice was that it was a passion which demanded correspondence and placed her on an equality with him. Beatrice was certainly not inferior to Guinizelli's ideal lady: to offer to her an earthly love would always be futile; to crave correspondence was insulting; to hope for it was ridiculous. Nothing but humble worship was her due, and if he were to write of her again it would have to be not as a suppliant lover but as a worshipper.

What was it that enabled Dante not so much to be reconciled to this new relation between him and Beatrice as to embrace it with joy? He was grieving not only over the loss of her favor but over the change in his own feeling for her; he remembered with grief the wonder of his early experiences when her salutation

Figure of Dante from an illuminated manuscript page.

used to kindle in him the "fiamma di caritade" that exalted him above himself. The thought that when all claims upon her were removed she might be as much to him as she had ever been was grateful and comforting. Another thought, which may have come to him with startling effect, as great ideas often do, was also born of his recollections. Her early and glorious apparition; the good influence coming from her which had enveloped his youth and protected him from vice and triviality; the fact that this powerful influence had been exercised by means of occasional momentary meetings, a smile and a word of greeting; was not all this miraculous? Might she not have been born on Earth to be his guardian angel, might he not have been resisting the will of Providence by entreating her for love of an inferior though innocent kind? If so she might still be far more to him than she had ever been before. This thought, which is a natural concomitant of Guinizelli's view both of Love and of the Lady, was of a kind to fire the imagination of the poet. What made it even dazzlingly attractive was the implication it carried of something else, something which Dante never dared, in this book, to declare openly: the implication that he

himself was a predestined being, the object of a special providence. After all the humiliation which he had suffered, an idea such as this, even if only entertained as possible, would more than rehabilitate that self-respect that was so dear to him. He would never again need to cry for pity: "Madonna la Pietà," that conventional hypocrite, might go hide her head.

That Dante came to be convinced of the truth of these ideas is certain, but it is not clear whether his conversion to them was complete before his interview with the ladies of chapter eighteen, or whether that interview served to precipitate conclusions which were already in solution in his mind. The ladies are sympathetic and curious. They know much about Dante; they know that Beatrice is his beloved; they have witnessed many of his *sconfitte* ("defeats"). He had not been able to conceal his passion as he had his early mystical devotion to her. Their interest in his case must have brought home to him the danger he had not quite avoided of becoming one of the many lovers who furnish an interesting subject for social conversation. He is anxious to persuade them that he is not a dejected lover in need of sympathy. On the contrary he is *beato*, but his happiness comes from a different source now that his lady is no longer kind. And when they press him to know whence comes this happiness, it may be the necessity of finding an answer that prompts him to utter the conclusion to which his reflections have been leading him. His *beatitudine,* he says, consists in the praise of his lady. But when his questioner is quick to point out that this doubtful *beatitudine* has not yet found expression in his verse, he has nothing to say. As he retreats from their presence he is glad that he has had the wit to answer right, but he wishes he had already justified his assertion, and he is thinking of nothing but the "nuova matera" ("new subject") to which he is committed. After much hesitation and thought there comes forth the joyful song of magnificent praise which his conversion has made possible, the song which declares that Beatrice is allowed to remain on earth for the protection of one who will sing her praise in hell if he happen to be among the lost. The spontaneous beauty of the poem, the first words of which were uttered as if the poet's tongue had been "per sé stessa mossa" ("moved by itself") testify to the vividness of his new intuition.

Needless to say a conversion like this would only have been possible for one to whom the life of the imagination was as real as the life of material circumstance, nor would it have been possible for anyone who had not, like Dante, been accustomed from childhood to think and feel religiously.

When the poem had become "alquanto divolgata tra le genti" the new inspiration did not pass unnoticed. Dante was requested to state explicitly his views on the nature of love, and he complied in the sonnet that endorses the theory of Guinizelli, and then followed it with another in which the singularity of Beatrice is triumphantly affirmed. She is not to be associated as an equal with other gentle ladies, she can make capable of love even those who are born incapable, and all those who come within her influence share it with Dante to some extent. She, like the Virgin Mary, is elevated above all the rest, without pride and inspiring no jealousy.

It is not astonishing that she should be endowed with miraculous powers. The conversion I have been describing is a religious conversion and implies faith in miracles. Guinizelli's ideal lady is also gifted with supernatural powers, and this gentle creature who has been placed upon earth for a special divine purpose is quite naturally a miracle worker, but her miracles are of a spiritual kind unknown to herself: she is unconscious of her mission, she goes her way thinking herself no better than her fellows, radiant with heavenly beauty.

Only her adoring poet knows but does not dare to say openly why she is here on earth. He knows that when her mission is accomplished she will return to her home in heaven. The stanza of chapter twenty-seven with its peaceful, joyful contentment is a sign to the reader that her mission is fulfilled, and she is gone.

The "nuova materia che appresso viene" ("the new subject which is approaching") is the logical sequel to that which had begun with "Donne che avete." Beatrice, who had been entrusted with a holy mission on Earth such as makes it not unnatural to speak of her with words that suggest a comparison with Christ and the Virgin Mary, has now gone to gladden the angels and saints who had besought God for her presence. The mourning of the poet is shot through with gleams of light descending from her: "sol nel mio lamento Chiamo Beatrice, e dico: 'or se' tu morta?' E mentre ch'io la chiamo, me conforta." "Ma qual ch'io sia la mia donna il si vede, E io ne spero ancor da lei mercede." The difference in the "nuova materia" is that now Beatrice knows that she was Dante's guardian angel on earth and that she is his saint in heaven, whereas while she pursued her way on earth she was unconscious of her mission. Direct communication with her was impossible while she lived, but now it is possible through ecstatic vision. She comforts him, she watches over him and rescues him from the temptation of the *donna gentile:* she draws him to her. It is impossible for him to imagine her now that she is pure spirit; the sighs which rise to her and seek her "beyond the heaven that widest whirls" bring back only the dimmest understanding of her new condition, but he still holds her by the womanhood she still preserves: he knows that she is still guarding and guiding him. Perhaps he gazed upon her without let in the "mirabile visione."

She is still a woman, she has never become a symbol of anything. It is true that Dante says of her: "No la ci tolse qualità di gelo/ Nè di calore, come l'altre face", but that is a figure of speech which he would have known how to "denudare . . . in guisa che [avesse] verace intendimento". In the canzone "Quantunque volte" he says plainly that his lady was overtaken by the cruelty of death, and almost the last words of the *Vita Nuova* are: "io spero di dicer di lei quello che mai non fue detto d'alcuna," where "alcuna" can mean nothing but "alcuna donna".

By the "character" of the *Vita Nuova* I mean the purpose of the author as it is executed in the book. That purpose can be understood clearly in the light of the "moment" of the work. It was when he had been rescued from a worldly affection which threatened to defeat the protecting influence of his saint in heaven, that, full of contrition for his ingratitude, he wrote the *Vita Nuova* as a confession of his indebtedness to Beatrice. This no doubt was part of his purpose, but there was more.

The "forte imaginazione" of chapter xxxix recalls him to Beatrice by presenting her to his memory as he first saw her when she was a child; the sonnet "Oltre la spera" of chapter xli (xlii) is an attempt to contemplate her as she is now, a saint in heaven; the intervening chapter, xl (xli), dwells on the desolation caused by her death when she was an adult woman. These chapters, with the last, which mentions the "mirabile visione," correspond to the "moment" of the *Vita Nuova*.

His thoughts at this time, concentrated upon Beatrice, travel from the memory of her as a child, through the recollection of her life and death, to the vision of her as a saint. He is reading, rapidly but absorbed, the book of his memory from which he is to transcribe the contents of the *libello*. He sees himself bewildered at the first apparition, but cherishing the memory of it; permanently enthralled by the kindly salutation; adoring the image in his memory and living a double life; desperate over the loss of his lady's kindness; passionately and hopelessly in love; struggling to reconcile his experience with the known theories of love; realizing at last the exceptional character of Beatrice, and the astonishing dignity of her relation to him; blissfully happy in the new understanding of the lady and his love for her; crushed by her sudden death; lured, after a time, into forgetfulness of her by the affectionate sympathy of a living woman.

Convinced again, and now more than ever, by the loving intervention of the saint who watches over him from above, acknowledging that he is her special charge, communing with him and offering herself to him in the spirit; convinced that in all his life of love he has been miraculously led; weeping over his own past ignorance, he is drawn gropingly upward to meet his Beatrice, by the new knowledge ("intelligenza nova") that has enabled him to read his own story. And then comes the vision that is too marvellous to describe.

The story which Dante has thus been enabled to read aright is to be told: it is too important to be withheld. It is punctuated with incidents which have been the occasion of poems. The author is a poet of love, and the expression of his love has always been in verse, as is only proper. The poems, then, arranged in the proper order, should tell the story of his love, but would they? Dante well knows that they would not. Some of them are too conventional to express clearly anything important. Others refer too definitely to extraneous circumstances which would distract the readers' attention from the proper subject. More important still: most of them were written without the knowledge the poet now has of the significance of the events concerned. The poems, then, must be carefully selected, and those chosen to make up the book must be interpreted, whenever it is necessary, so as to remove too material suggestions that jar with the religious atmosphere which the story has in the mind of the author, and so as to imply the significance which he now sees in the incidents. Whether the idea of connecting the poems by narrative and explanatory prose was derived from Boethius, Raimbaut d'Aurenga, or the biographer of Bertran de Born, or from no one at all, it was at any rate necessary for Dante's purpose.

His chief purpose is to so tell the story of his astonishing experience that the stages by which he was led to understand the miraculous power of his lady, and to have for her a finer kind of love than had hitherto been conceived, should be apparent to the reader. In this way he was giving a better answer than had hitherto been imagined—and perhaps he thought it was a final answer—to the question so often asked and answered before: What is fine love? The "alquanti grossi" who had first sung of love in verse had only played with the question; even his friend Cavalcanti had reached a false conclusion, in spite of his zeal for scientific truth, and since the *Vita Nuova* is dedicated to him it may be that he was the reader whom Dante chiefly had in mind. It was Guido Guinizelli who had had the right intuition when he vindicated, although hesitatingly, the right of fine sexual love to be compared to the worship of God. Dante was now proving by his own experience that love may be not only good and truly ennobling but even holy, stronger than death, and blessed by God, the "sire de la cortesia" to whom the poet's last words confidently appeal.

Dante's theory of love is here in its infancy. No other than fine sexual love is considered. Sensual love is ignored and so is the love of knowledge for its own sake. This fine sexual love is not yet identified with the love for God, still less is there any hint of the essential unity of all love. The doctrine of Guinizelli is restated and the manner in which potential love is aroused to actuality is clearly defined, otherwise there is no doctrine but only illustration in the experience of the author. And yet there can be no doubt that here we have the seed out of which will grow Dante's great theory of love which is already elaborate in the *Convivio* and the *Monarchia* and is the backbone of the *Commedia*; for Beatrice is, while on earth, the unconscious means of grace to Dante; she is "in altissimo grado di bontade", and love for her implies the love of goodness. Nevertheless it should be clearly understood that this book is not a miniature *Commedia* any more than it is a *Pilgrim's Progress*. It is not a story of salvation from sin and of rescue from its consequences. The episode of the *Donna Gentile*, at the end of the book, is the only instance of what might be called a temporary lapse from grace. Otherwise, if the purpose of the book had been similar to that of the *Commedia*, we should have seen Dante, after the death of Beatrice, and especially at the end of the story, turning to God in grateful adoration; but in the last chapters as elsewhere there is no word of gratitude to God, the thoughts of the poet are concentrated upon his Beatrice, the memories of her and the yearning to be with her: the last words of the book as the first are about Beatrice, and Dante's love for Beatrice is the only subject of the whole work.

The *Vita Nuova* is the story of how Dante, the poet of Love, singled out by an inscrutable Providence, was led by Beatrice, a lady endowed for his sake with miraculous powers for good, to free himself first from the conventional superficiality of other poets of love, and then from the serious naturalism of still other poets, and to experience a finer because holier kind of sexual love than had hitherto been dreamt of.

Charles S. Singleton (essay date 1949)

SOURCE: "*Vita Nuova,*" in *An Essay on the "Vita Nuova,*" 1949. Reprinted by The Johns Hopkins University Press, 1977, pp. 78-109.

[*In the following excerpt, Singleton examines the relationship between the* Vita Nuova *and Provençal love poetry, discerning that Dante's use of medieval mysticism in his book's conception of love distinguishes it from the Provençal tradition.*]

The three visions foretelling the death of Beatrice all bear the mark of a number *nine* and point thus to special meaning in that number. They would seem also, by being *three*, to stress the presence of some special meaning for the root of nine as well. The poet's gloss on the death of Beatrice and on the number nine (chapter XXIX) does much to confirm this: three is the "factor" by itself of nine, three is the sign of the "factor" of miracles which is the Holy Trinity.

Furthermore, it is precisely in terms of a number three that the center of the *Vita Nuova* may be located. The middle of the work is plainly marked by the second of three *canzoni,* the poem in which the death of Beatrice (her unreal death) shows a certain resemblance to the death of Christ.

Nor is this all in the way of a symmetrical arrangement of the poems to be noted in the Book of Memory. In all there are thirty-one poems in the *Vita Nuova.* Here again must not an eye alert to the meanings in numbers see the sign of the Trinity which is Three and One?

Moreover, in contrast with the three *canzoni,* all of the other poems in the book are shorter poems, minor forms or fragments: most are sonnets, but there are *three* exceptions: one ballata, one stanza of an unfinished *canzone,* and another poem made up of two stanzas only of a *canzone.* Among such as these, therefore, the three longer poems can have prominence by a length

alone and acan be used as markers to divide the others into groups. That they are used as such becomes evident with the first *canzone,* for that poem is explicitly said to mark the end of the poet's first subject matter and beginning of his second. This *canzone* thus leaves behind itself a certain number of shorter poems which thereby become a group to themselves. One notices, too, that these poems are ten in number and that all but one are sonnets.

Such clear signs of a deliberate design at the beginning can well prompt us to look at the end. There we are not surprised, I imagine, by what we discover: the end balances exactly the beginning; the last *canzone* is followed by ten poems jsut as the first is preceded by ten; and in this final group the poems are all sonnets but one. Hence, the first and the third of the three *canzoni* stand at equal distance respectively from beginning and end, marking off the shorter poems into a first group and a third.

What of the center? There the pattern is clearly confirmed. For between the first and the third *canzoni* there are nine poems. And, in this group of nine, the poem which is at the exact center is the second of the three *canzoni,* which thus becomes necessarily the central poem in respect to a number nine as well as to a number three.

It is all undeniably part of a conscious design in the arrangement of the poems of the *Vita Nuova,* amounting to a sort of external architecture, a kind of façade which, for all its evidence, appears to have escaped the notice of readers of the book until around the middle of the last century. It had, at any rate, to be rediscovered then. By now, the introductions to most editions of the *Vita Nuova* make oa point of it, usually seeing the whole design as one to be represented by the figures 10; I; 4-II-4; III, 10 (Roman numerals being the *canzoni*). But, given the exceptional importance of the number nine in this work, it would seem much more significant to consider the first and the last groups of the shorter poems as made up of nine plus one. This would require that we count the first poem of the *Vita Nuova* as an introductory one, much as we count the first canto of *Inferno*; and that we consider the last poem of the book as a kind of epilogue which, given its nature, it may well be. Such a pattern seems more meaningful for the *Vita Nuova* in that it can be stated in terms of nine and three and one: 1, 9; I; 4-II-4; III; 9, 1. Or more simply, and with perhaps even greater suggestiveness, as 1;9;1;9;1;9;1, since in this way the mysterious number nine is more clearly seen to occur three times.

This is more than a matter of extrinsic ornament. Here on the surface are ripples and eddies which are all so many signs of what we know already to lie deeper in the current of the action. As such signs, they make their own contribution to what is the principal intention of the whole form of the Book of Memory: the revealing through signs that Beatrice is a miracle, that she is herself a number nine which, like miracles, is the product of three times three.

By looking intently at such a miraculous object of love, we were able to trace a line of progression from love to charity. Now, if we begin once more at these surface signs of miracle and proceed to sound the deeper currents of the action, we shall see, by keeping our eyes this time on the subject of love, that there is yet another line of progression to be followed out. It too, like the other, is a line reaching upward. The subject of love is no miracle. The subject of love is the poet. The Book of Memory is his, his is the new life in love.

The progression which we must now follow out is that of this new life itself. In it, we may note at once, the number three is revealed again. For before the end is reached, the poet has found three subject matters for his poems. And these subject matters, marked off as three even in the surface design, are revealed, in their turn, to be stages in the new life, three stages.

In this manuscript Book of Memory the poems are, after all, the primary text; the rest is either a gloss to the poems or a gloss on that gloss. Hence, if there are three stages in the poet's love, that fact ought to be visible first in the poems. And so it is, although were there no gloss in prose to point out that fact, we might easily fail to see it.

But it is much easier to see that there are three subject matters for the poems than it is to give them names. The "gloss" in the Book of Memory does not tell specifically what their names might be. It makes, however, a rather clear suggestion of them. For instance, in the prose of chapter XVII we are told that when the poet had finished the last three of the first group of poems, he felt that these had been the "narrators" of all that he needed to say of his own "state" in love; and that the time, therefore, had come for him to find a new subject matter for his poems so that, as the Book of Memory has recorded it, the change comes first in respect to the poems. And this is as near as the prose ever comes to supplying a name for what has been the first subject matter of the poems: it is, we see, the state of the poet.

But do we expect lyric poems to be about anything else? Does a lyric poet actually ever write about anything other than his own inner state?

It would seem that he does, and the following chapter tells us as much. For something happened, something which made the poet realize that his poems must be no longer about himself. It takes the whole of that chapter XVIII to tell the "reason" of this, a chapter containing no poem of its own, but presenting what is surely one of the most charming episodes of the whole story:
. . .

> Inasmuch as from my aspect many persons had understood my heart's secret, certain ladies, who had come together, finding pleasure in each other's company, knew my heart very well, since every one of them had been present at many of my defeats; and I, passing near them as one led by fortune, was called by one of these gentle ladies. The lady who had called me was a lady of very gracious speech; so that when I was come before them and saw well that my most gentle lady was not with them, reassuring myself I greeted them and asked them what might be their pleasure. The ladies were many, among whom were some who were laughing among themselves. Others there were who were watching me, expecting me to speak. There were others who spoke among themselves. Of these one, turning her eyes toward me and calling me by name, spoke these words: "To what end do you love this your lady, since you cannot endure her presence? Tell us this, for certainly the end of such a love must be most strange." And when she had spoken these words to me, not only she but all the others began visibly to await my reply. Then I said these words to them: "My ladies, the end of my love was once the greeting of this lady, whom perchance you have in mind, and in that dwelt beatitude, for it was the end of all my desires. But when it pleased her to deny it to me, my lord Love, through his grace, put all my beatitude in that which cannot fail me." Then these ladies began to speak among themselves; and as sometimes we see rain fall mingled with beautiful snow, so it seemed to me to hear their words issue mingled with sighs. And when they had spoken among themselves a while, that same lady who had first spoken to me said these words to me: "We pray you that you tell us wherein resides this your beatitude." And I, replying to her, said thus: "In those words which praise my lady." Then she who was speaking to me replied to me: "If you were telling us the truth, those words which you spoke to us in setting forth your condition you would have used with another intention." Whereupon, thinking on these words, I left them as one ashamed, and came away saying to myself: "Since there is so much beatitude in those words which praise my lady, why have my words been of anything else?" And therefore I proposed henceforth to take as the subject of my words whatever might be in praise of this most gentle lady; and thinking much on this, it seemed to me that I had undertaken too lofty a subject for me, so that I did not dare to begin; and thus I remained some days desiring to write and afraid to begin.

This then, is the "reason" for the first *canzone*, for its subject matter, and for the second group of poems in the *Vita Nuova* which follows it. And this is, at the same time, also the reason for bringing the first group of poems to an end. The poet had come to see that he ought to write no more poems about himself. That subject, he felt, was exhausted. From now on he would write only in praise of his lady. It is a change in inspiration, the discovery of a new *direction* for his attention as poet. No longer will the eye of the poet focus upon himself and the effects of love on him. It will now turn to "madonna" and sing in praise of her and of her alone.

We know that, beginning especially with Guinicelli, two themes became predominant in the Italian love lyric, and we have seen what these were. Dante, like the others, had used them in poems. Now, in view of what we shall see to be the particular grouping of the poems according to subject in the *Vita Nuova*, we shall hardly fail to wonder if those same two themes have not become precisely the first two "subject matters" of the book. If they have, then we ought to observe that the *Vita Nuova* was, for one thing, a way of using poems probably already written on established themes before it was conceived as a whole made up of poems and prose.

The possibility of those two themes being the first two "subjects" of the poems in the *Vita Nuova* can at least serve to sharpen our view of what the first two subjects of the poems are. The two themes in the tradition were of the nature of two focuses, as we have seen. One theme turned the light of attention on the poet and the state of the poet, finding him done almost to death by the miraculous *virtù* of the object of love. Now is this theme not exactly the subject of the first group of poems in the *Vita Nuova*? We see that it is, and most clearly in the last three of those ten poems. The first of these is that sonnet written on the occasion of the wedding feast where, when Beatrice had walked into the room, the poet (as he afterwards told the friend who took him there) had suddenly stood on the verge of death. And the other two of the three poems are also on this same theme: the threat of death to the lover. The second is fairly representative of all three:

> *Ciò che m'incontra, ne la mente more,*
> quand'i' vegno a veder voi, bella gioia;
> e quand'io vi son presso, i'sento Amore
> che dice: "Fuggi, se'l perir t'è noia."
> Lo viso mostra lo color del core,
> che, tramortendo, ovunque pò s'appoia;
> e per la ebrietà del gran tremore
> le pietre par che gridin: Moia, moia.
>   Peccato face chi allora mi vide,
> se l'alma sbigottita non conforta,
> sol dimostrando che di me li doglia,
> per la pietà che'l vostro gabbo ancide,
> la qual si cria ne la vista morta
> *de li occhi, ch'hanno di lor morte voglia.*

What befalls me dies in my mind when I come to see you, beautiful joy; and when I am near you, I fed Love who says: "Flee, if to perish is irksome to you." My face shows the hue of my heart, which, fainting, leans for support wherever it may; and in the drunkenness of the great trembling the very stones seem to cry out: "Die, die." Then whoever beholds me sins if he does not comfort my frightened soul, showing that at least he feels sorry for me because of the pity which your mockery kills, and which is begotten in the dead light of my eyes which have desire of their own death.

And as for the *new* "matter" which the poet found after finishing these three sonnets, what is it if not precisely that other of the two established themes, that theme in praise of the lady of which we have seen outstanding examples already in the poems of Guinicelli and Cavalcanti? It seems indeed probable that, before the *Vita Nuova* as a whole was conceived, Dante would already have written a number of sonnets on just this matter, sonnets such as that in chapter XXVI of the *Vita Nuova*:

> *Tanto gentile e tanto onesta pare*
> la donna mia quand'ella altrui saluta,
> ch'ogne lingua deven tremando muta,
> e li occhi no l'ardiscon di guardare.
> Ella si va, sentendosi laudare,
> benignamente d'umiltà vestuta;
> e par che sia una cosa venuta
> da cielo in terra a miracol mostrare.
>   Mostrasi sì piacente a chi la mira,
> che dà per li occhi una dolcezza al core,
> che'ntender no la può chi no la prova:
> e par che de la sua labbia si mova
> un spirito soave pien d'amore,
> che va dicendo a l'anima: Sospira

So gentle and so modest my lady seems when she greets another that every tongue trembles and grows mute and eyes do not dare to look at her. She goes along, hearing herself praised, benignly clothed in humility; and she seems a thing come from heaven to earth to show a miracle. She is a sight so pleasant to anyone who sees her that through the eyes she sends a sweetness to the heart which cannot be understood by one who does not experience it; and from her face there seems to move a gentle spirit full of love that keeps saying to the soul: "Sigh."

Better than any other of the second group, that sonnet represents the second "matter" found by the poet, a matter which is also a manner.

But when poems are no longer single scattered things but have a place in a Book of Memory, then the very order of their occurrence in such a book can give them a new significance, especially if grouping is also a part of that order. For in that case (as a gloss in prose can make clear) the mere fact that one group follows another may also have special meaning. Poems become groups of poems for having a common subject matter.

As subject matters emerge, a second can be new merely by leaving another behind. And change in matter is change in manner: the full implications of which fact we shall not understand without examining the kinds of love from which manners may arise.

The balance in outward arrangement noted between the first and third *canzone* is maintained at the deeper level of subject matters. For just as the first *canzone* is the beginning of the second subject matter and the end of the first, so now is the third *canzone* the end of the second matter and the beginning of the third.

But what is this third matter? Actually, the sign of entrance into it are the words from Jeremiah announcing the widowhood of the city, as the prose of chapter xxx (is this number, made up of three tens, another sign at this critical point?), which reconsiders those words and gives their reason, tells us: . . .

> When she had departed from this world, all the aforesaid city remained as a widow bereft of all dignity; wherefore, still weeping in this desolate city, I wrote to the princes of the earth somewhat of its condition, taking that beginning of Jeremiah the prophet which says: Quomodo sedet sola civitas [How doth the city sit solitary]. And I say this so that no one will wonder that I have cited it above as an entrance to the new subject matter which follows.

Our name for this third matter ought not to be simply "The Death of Beatrice," but rather, "After the Death of Beatrice." For the poems in it do not continue to look exclusively at the *object* of love, and any fitting label for the new matter ought to allow for a certain return to the focusing of the poems on the poet himself. This third matter does begin with the cruel proclamation of Beatrice's death; but as it is developed by the poems of the third group we realize that, like the first matter, this third is again concerned with the lover and with the effects of love on him. Once more the poems tend to be *narratori* of the state of the poet. Not that the theme of praise is really abandoned, but it is no longer the exclusive focus. The third matter is a blending of the other two themes into a new one which includes them both and which, by doing so, transcends them. It is as a synthesis following on a thesis and an antithesis. It becomes the two themes in one, showing the poet at first thrown back upon himself and able to see only himself now that Beatrice is gone; and, then, ending in forgetfulness of self, in the triumph of a love which has found the way to a transcendental place of rest, ending in a poet's resolve to praise his lady as no lady was ever praised by poet.

Thus, for the three subject matters for poems in the *Vita Nuova*, one might propose the following names:

I. The effects of love on the poet.
II. In praise of his lady.
III. After the death of his lady.

But these, in any case, are only names for the subject matters of poems, not for stages in love. As their causes, however, the stages come first. For it is not, after all, the writing of poems which makes a New Life, but the actual and very real upward progression of the way of love in the poet who is the lover. However, that our attention should first have fallen upon poems and subject matters of poems is just as the Book of Memory would have it. The poems are the first text. Then, from the gloss to the poems, we learn that before the three subjects for poems were found, there were three changes in the way of love which made for three stages in love. Can the stages be named?

There are some fairly evident markers to guide us in the quest of the answer. It is not hard, for instance, to say where the first stage in love begins to end. That stage as such does not have, as does the first subject, any precise signpost like a *canzone* to mark its end; but that end can only be somewhere near the end of the corresponding subject matter for poems; and in this regard the denial of Beatrice's greeting appears to be the capital event. The fact is evident enough from what the poet says to the ladies who are so curious over the end of his love: . . .

> My ladies, the end of my love was once the greeting of this lady, whom perchance you have in mind, and in that dwelt beatitude, for it was the end of all my desires. But when it pleased her to deny it to me, my lord Love, through his grace, put all my beatitude in that which cannot fail me.

It is clear from these words how much a part of the change from one stage of love to another the denial of Beatrice's greeting is.

The poet, we recall, had brought this cruel moment upon himself. He had been far too assiduous in his efforts to make of the second "screen-lady" a cover for his love of Beatrice, and his attentions had resulted in much gossip on the part of malevolent people throughout the city. Whereupon, Beatrice, who was ever the queen of all virtues and the enemy of all evil things (of which this kind of gossip is one), one day refused the beatitude of her greeting to him who had brought about this unseemly talk.

Then we read in chapter xii that on the advice of the God of Love the poet wrote a *ballata* to his lady explaining how all this had come about, how it was all a mistake, how he had really been hers all the while. Nor are we given any reason to believe that Beatrice did not receive this poem. But if she did receive it, was there no jot of mercy in her? Why did she not forgive her lover? Why do we not read in the following chapter that Beatrice restored the greeting which it cost her so little to give and in which dwelt her lover's beatitude?

Merely to raise the question is to feel at once how irrelevant it is. There is only one reason why Beatrice's greeting was not restored, and this reason is not envisaged by such questions as those. It is simply that the denial of her greeting is a step in the upward way of love. It is because the lover must learn to do without that greeting that, in spite of all his explanations, it is never restored to him. He is being taught that the beatitude and end of love is not really to be sought in such things as this, that true *salute* ("well-being, salvation") does not reside there. If love is to ascend, these things must be left behind for other things.

This is precisely a lesson which the poet seems to have learned by the time the ladies ask him about the end of his love. At just what moment between the refusal of her greeting and this meeting with those inquisitive ladies he had understood that, in spite of all apologies, the greeting was not to be restored to him, we do not know. But when we hear his reply to those ladies, it is evident that he already knows that this will be so. And, in knowing this, he has already stepped from the first stage of love to the second.

Moreover, we can see, from that same reply to the ladies, that this step from one to the other stage means primarily a change in his love (and of course an awareness of change) with respect to the *place* of the end of love. At first, the place of that end had been in the greeting of Beatrice. The greeting in itself we may take to be more than just an end for his love. It is a good symbol of any love which is turned toward satisfactions from without, any love which is interested in some return from the beloved, interested in reward. Such a love as this looking for some return from the beloved is one which the ladies who question the poet would not find at all unusual; nor, indeed, would it be unusual in the whole tradition of courtly love of which these questioning ladies are, in this instance, the mouthpiece. In *troubadour* love, the lover might always *hope* for reward from his lady, for some sign of "mercy" on her part, were this no more than a passing smile or a greeting. In fact, in that degree of refinement to which the conception of courtly love had by this time attained in Italy, some such sign of *mercè* was quite all in the way of reward that the lover might dare to expect.

The question which the ladies address to the poet assumes in fact that love will seek some reward from the beloved. That is why they are puzzled about the poet's love now, because they have all been present on occasions when it was evident that he was unable to endure even the presence of Beatrice. What can the end of love be, if the lover is never in a condition to receive a reward from the beloved? . . .

> To what end do you love this your lady, since you cannot endure her presence? Tell us this, for certainly the end of such a love must be most strange.

The ladies are thus bound to be all the more puzzled by the poet's answer to their question, which declares that the end and happiness of love is no longer in any reward which might come from Beatrice. Now, he says, thanks to the God of Love, the end and happiness of his love is put where it cannot fail him. Neither the ladies nor the tradition of *troubadour* love had ever heard of any such love as this. Where can the end of such a love as this be? "In those words which praise my lady," the poet replies.

It is the *place* of the end of love that counts. For the poet, now, the place of the end of his love could not have suffered a more radical transfer than this. And change there, moreover, must necessarily mean a change in the *direction* from which love's happiness comes, because the end of love is happiness. We must look at the matter in terms of direction, then, and it should now be clear that as long as all happiness came from the greeting of Beatrice, the direction of happiness was from the outside in. But now, if the happiness which is the end of love is in words which praise the beloved, the direction of the happiness of love must be the direction of just those words which arise in the poet and flow out toward the beloved. This is a complete reversal. Happiness now comes from within and flows from the inside out. What kind of love is this?

If we will turn for a moment to listen to Richard of St. Victor (d. 1173), a mystic whose work was well known to Dante, on the degrees of that love which is properly called *caritas*, we shall discover, I think, the right name for this second degree of love which the poet has reached in the *Vita Nuova*. Richard writes of what charity is (and is not) in terms of the direction of love: . . .

> For how shall one who does not love, who does not feel the power of love, speak of love? Now of other subjects abundant matter appears in books; but of this one, it is either entirely within or it is nowhere, because it does not transpose its hidden sweetness from the outside to the inside, but transmits it from the inside out. He alone, therefore, speaks of that subject worthily who, as his heart dictates, so composes his words.

Here let us remember that already in the line of progression from love to charity followed with regard to the object of love we had come to a point in the ascent where love was seen to become charity: where a God

of Love was removed from the action, where all the
authority of love was transfered to Beatrice, and Love
itself was redefined.

Now, in the changes in a New Life in love as seen in
the subject of love, we have come to a point at which
we again see love becoming charity: where the new
direction of love, in fact, is no longer to be distinguished from that of charity, if we may allow Richard's distinctions in terms of the direction of love to
define that new direction for us. This we may surely
do, for the happiness of love which may not fail the
poet is a happiness arising within him and flowing
outward, even as charity.

As is well known, love which is charity is a disinterested love having its final perfection in Heaven. Charity seeks no reward but, at the same time, charity is
never without reward. The love of the blessed in Heaven
finds its happiness in the contemplation of God and in
praise of Him. In Heaven happiness arises within the
soul and flows out to the Beloved. Evidently love of
Beatrice in the new direction has reached a stage analogous to that.

Once more let us remember that, in that other line of
progression from love to charity which was followed
with respect to the object of love, charity was reached
when the God of Love (who was the symbol of *troubadour* love) was removed from the action. Now in
that parallel progression of the New Life as seen in the
subject of love, we may observe in turn that when the
greeting of Beatrice (which is likewise a sign of *troubadour* love) is removed from the action, a kind of
love which may be called charity is reached. For a
greeting as the end of love is the unmistakable symbol
of a love which had never attained to disinterested-
ness, of a love ever hopeful of some *mercè* from the
beloved. And that, precisely, is a predominant feature
of *troubadour* love. However refined that love became,
it continued to look for reward, some reward, from
without. Now when the happiness of the poet's love
has become a happiness arising freely within himself
and flowing out from within, his love has ascended to
a level above *troubadour* love—above because it is
toward the perfection of love as love will be in Heav-
en—even though it is here still a love in this life.

A new direction in love means a new subject matter
for poems of love. And this, if style be faithful to
inspiration, means a new style in poetry.

Later on, in *Purgatory* XXIV, Dante will tell us as
much and will give to this matter a dramatic cast,
causing a poet of the older generation met there, a
certain Bonagiunta from Lucca, to recognize in that
first poem written to give expression to this new direction in love in the *Vita Nuova* (and to recognize in a
redefinition of that direction) a style which is both

new and sweet: *dolce stil nuovo.*

"Tell me," says Bonagiunta to Dante, who is standing
before him on the terrace of the gluttons, "do I here
behold him who produced the new rhymes beginning
"Donne ch'avete intelletto d'amore?" This, as we know,
is the first verse of the first *canzone* in the *Vita Nuova*,
that first expression in verse of the second stage in the
New Life in love as the Book of Memory has recorded
it.

Dante replies to Bonagiunta's question with a definition in striking agreement with the one we heard Richard of St. Victor give of charity:

> E io a lui: "I' mi son un che quando
>   Amor mi spira, noto, e a quel modo
>   ch'e' ditta dentro vo significando."

> And I to him: "I am one who, when Love inspires
> me, take note and, in the manner in which he dictates
> within, I proceed to signify."

To which the older poet replies:

> "O frate, issa vegg'io," diss'elli, "il nodo
>   che'l Notaro e Guittone e me ritenne
>   di qua dal dolce stil novo ch'i'odo!

> Io veggio ben come le vostre penne
>   di retro al dittator sen vanno strette,
>   che de le nostre certo non avvenne."

> "O friend, now I see," he said, "the knot which kept
> the Notary and Guittone and me short of that sweet
> new style which I hear. I see well how your pens
> follow closely after the dictator, which certainly did
> not happen to ours."

Now (now that he is in Purgatory where all souls are
being schooled in the true nature of love which is
charity), Bonagiunta understands what that knot was
that kept him and the others he has named from attain-
ing to that style (and understanding) of poetry which
the first of the longer poems of the *Vita Nuova* represents. One even suspects that Bonagiunta is aware of
the place of that poem in the Book of Memory. For
only there is it the first of the poems on a new matter,
only in its special place there does it represent a new
style, because only there is it the expression of a
changed direction in love. What the changed direction
was we have seen, and we have found a definition and
a name for it in Richard of St. Victor. The redefinition
of it here in *Purgatory* only confirms our understanding. All of which means, if it means anything, that the
first poem of the second group of poems in the *Vita
Nuova* is the expression of a love which has found the
direction of charity. And all this Bonagiunta seems
now to understand too.

We, in turn, may be expected to realize that the author of the poems of the **Vita Nuova** was himself at one time also "on the other side of the knot," had also kept company at one time with the poets of another generation. In fact, as long as he had written of a love which depended for its happiness on some return from without (on a beloved's greeting), he had written in the "old" style.

Thus we see that the order of the poems themselves in the Book of Memory, being the direct consequence of the order of the poet's love, makes a judgment on the relative merits of two styles. For since, as the Book of Memory has it, the order of love is an ascending one, any *new* matter for poems, merely by succeeding another, is of necessity more lofty than the preceding. If the ascent is toward perfection of love, then a second step must be nearer to the goal than the first. It must be more noble. And this the gloss in prose in the Book affirms it to be, telling us in chapter *xvii* that love at the second stage is a more noble matter for poems than at the first: . . .

> When I had composed these three sonnets in which I had spoken of this lady, since they were the narrators of nearly all my condition, thinking to be silent and write no more because it seemed to me that I had manifested enough of myself even though I should henceforth refrain from writing to her, it behooved me to take up a new and more noble subject matter than the last had been.

But it did not prove to be true that the poet's happiness had been put where it might not fail him. A second stage of love was not to be the last. He could not know that his love had not yet reached the place of its rest, which is the place of its greatest perfection, that his happiness had not yet attained to that place beyond change where it might endure.

The poet, in the first stage of the new life in love, had found all the happiness of his love to be in the greeting from his lady. Then, through the painful privation of that greeting, he had found the happiness to be within himself, welling up there and overflowing in praise of his lady. He had thought that such happiness as this might never be taken from him. How might it be, if he now bore its source within himself, if his love now resembled the love of the blessed in Heaven, being all contemplation of the Beloved and all praise of her? Is not self-sufficiency an inalienable attribute of such love as this?

But he could not then know that he had another even more painful lesson to learn. In the exultation of a new love which was already incipient charity, the poet had forgotten what must not be forgotten when the object of love is a mortal creature. For what if contemplation should be deprived of its object? Can the praise continue? Then will the happiness of love continue to arise within? What if Beatrice should die?

Apparently the motive force of a love which ascends, and which is transformed by changes in the place of its end, is privation itself. First it was the greeting which was taken from the poet, and this loss had brought him to the second stage of love. Then the loss became infinitely more: the loss was Beatrice herself. True, love in the second stage had no longer looked to the outside for any reward. But in contemplation of the Beloved it had, nevertheless, continued to look to the outside, to depend on an object of sensual contemplation, on the miraculous beauty of a living woman. However, when the poet had thought that such a happiness could not fail him, he had forgotten one thing: that death exists in the world. Then one day certain terrible words from Jeremiah took their place in the Book of Memory, and the poet knew that Beatrice was dead. Can even a disinterested love survive such privation as this?

The third matter for poems in the **Vita Nuova** is not, like the first and second, a theme already established in the tradition. Neither Guinicelli nor Cavalcanti had written poems on the death of the beloved. Of death in love they had written, but that was rather of the death which constantly menaced the lover in the overwhelming brightness of his lady's presence.

But the last subject matter of the poems in the **Vita Nuova** is the death of the Beloved. One should therefore know that, in the order given by a Book of Memory, not only is an evaluation made of two traditional themes for poetry, but these themes are surmounted there by a third which is not traditional and which gives a new significance to the other two as steps toward it.

Our modern mind is little given to considering events in terms of a final cause; of a cause, that is, which lies at the end of an event. We are much more inclined to think of a cause as preceding what is caused, as being at the beginning rather than at the end. But the structure of a work of art (perhaps of any work of art) may still bring us to think in terms of that end cause to which medieval thought so readily turned. In the **Vita Nuova**, for instance, we must see the death of Beatrice, the last of three subject matters, as the cause of the other two. Actually, one feels little difficulty in allowing this in a sense, since it amounts only to saying something like this: if the last step in a flight of three steps reaches that point in space for which a stairway is intended, that point and hence that last step may be said to be the cause of the other two. This is, strictly speaking, not only a matter of order, but of their nature. The first would not only not be first, it would not even be the same step, if it were the only one; and even a first and a second step are different steps for having a step beyond them.

In the third stage, where is the place of the end of love? If the third subject matter is to be called "After the death of Beatrice," what shall the name of the third stage be, if that name, as in the case of the other two, is to be determined with regard to the place of the end of love?

In the third, the end is above. The final, the most noble resting place, and the last stage of the poet's new life in love is in Heaven. When we know the whole course of that new life (in so far as it is recorded in the Book of Memory) and can look back down over the ascending way, we feel certain that the only way in which that final place could have been attained was through the death of Beatrice.

Domenico Vittorini (essay date 1958)

SOURCE: "Lights and Shadows in Dante's *Vita Nuova*," in *High Points in the History of Italian Literature*, David McKay Company, Inc., 1958, pp. 42-52.

[*In this essay, Vittorini examines disjunctions between the lyrics and the prose of the* Vita Nuova, *arguing that, while the poems more closely represent Dante's actual experience, the prose tries to make them conform to an ideal of courtly love.*]

It is well known that the *Vita Nuova*, written after the death of Beatrice, is a book of memories in which Dante rethinks the events of his youth in the light of what that young girl meant to him or, at least, of what he believed she meant to him after the episode of the *Donna Gentile*.

The meeting with the latter took place immediately after the first anniversary of Beatrice's death. The struggle between the pale image of the dead girl and the young woman who attracted the poet and enveloped him in an ardent upsurge of love and passion lasted "several days," to quote Dante. If the final words of the *Vita Nuova*, referring to Beatrice, "I hope to utter praises of her such as were never uttered of any other woman," are understood to be not only a promise of writing the *Divine Comedy*, but also an indication of a complete and absolute return to the love of the early youth of the poet, one is led to believe that the work was written around 1292. At least the prose was written at that time, for the poet had been setting his feelings in verse since 1283, the date of the first sonnet "A ciascun alma presa e gentil core."

Three planes of reality are projected in the *Vita Nuova*: that of "actual" life, that is, the relations that Dante actually had with Beatrice and other women; that of poetry, which reflects those experiences relatively close-ly to the time in which they occurred; and that of prose, which reflects them as Dante felt them after the death of Beatrice.

Critics, by using the terms "reality," "realistic," and "realism," find considerable difficulty in differentiating between man's actual experience and its subsequent phase, when actual experience becomes art material. Paradoxically, actual life is not "real in art" until the poet relieves it in his stirred soul and causes it to blossom forth into sentiment, thought, and beauty by infusing into it a new life, a life that is real in the artistic plane. Art transforms the "actual" into the "real," to clarify the thought of De Sanctis and Croce, through the variations which life undergoes in being transposed from the level of experience to that of artistic expression. It seems, therefore, preferable to make use of the term "actual" to indicate the experience of the man in the poet, and the term "real" to refer to the changes that experience undergoes in the artistic works of the poet.

The plot of the *Vita Nuova* is very simple, and the action that develops in it emerges very clearly through the delicate shadings that the poet consciously gives to it. Dante fell in love with Beatrice at the age of nine; this love grew greatly when he was eighteen. Love filled the poet's life, but not to the extent of excluding from his heart interest in other young women, so much so that in the city he was criticized beyond the bounds of courtesy. Beatrice refused to greet him, but he continued to write poems about his great love for her. First, he sang of the effects that love had upon him; then, in search of "new material," he emerged from his egocentricity and exalted Beatrice's beauty and virtues. Beatrice died, and the poet's entire world sank into darkness. About a year after her death, Dante, sitting in his garden and thinking of the dead girl, beheld a young woman at a window gazing upon him with infinite tenderness and compassion. He fell in love with her and wrote poems for her which revealed to her his passionate sentiments. Dante was fully conscious that he was betraying Beatrice by yielding to that love, but that feeling came to him in all its naked truth only when he wrote the prose for the *Vita Nuova*. Beatrice's victory acquired the seal of reality through the words quoted above, which, even if repeated unendingly, will never lose the charm that glows in them.

Dante expressed his love in the forms that the Provençal tradition offered and prescribed at that time to poets of the grand style: the woman endowed with angelic perfection, the marvelous effects which she had on the one who loved her, absence or, at least, suppression of passion, perfect love born of admiration and worship of a woman's spiritual and physical qualities that were capable of raising the poet to God. These forms of courtly love in the *Vita Nuova* are accompanied by many conventional elements: Dante sees Beatrice for the first time when both are only nine years old; he sees her again after nine years, at the ninth hour of the day; he dreams of her rejecting his love "at the first hour of the last nine hours of the night." It should be observed that all these farfetched devices are found in the prose which, in terms of actual experience, is infinitely more conventional than the poetry. In the prose, Dante tells us that on the ninth day of his illness, he had in a dream a foreboding of Beatrice's death. Beatrice died on the ninth day of June, the ninth month of the year 1290, a date that the poet fabricated by invoking the help of foreign calendars. Beatrice appeared to him in the dream "almost in the ninth hour." In the nineteenth chapter the poet even explains to the reader why the number nine returns so persistently in the life of his lady: "to make it known that she was a nine, that is, a miracle whose root is found only in the wondrous Trinity."

This is the unimportant part of the *Vita Nuova* which, in varying degree, is found in all courtly poets of the time. It constitutes what poets of the grand style absorbed from the culture of their epoch. The living part is found where convention is broken down by a sincere and piercing cry in which the poet's torment has been so powerful as to break through the fetters of the traditional forms and to emerge from them in all its human truth. It is thus that were written the unforgettable pages of the little book in which the poet goes beyond the culture and doctrine of Dante, man of the thirteenth century.

It is natural to wonder to what point the "actual," that is, the historical and literal truth of Dante's love affairs has penetrated the convention of courtly love that envelops the *Vita Nuova* and makes of it one of the most perfect texts of ideal love. Only an attentive and objective reading of this work will enable us to answer such a question. Since the prose was written later and in a different mood from that which inspired the poetry, it is legitimate, in fact, dutiful, to read the poems independently of the prose. Only thus will we be able to see how the true experience of Dante as a man was reflected in vivid contrast on the two different planes of poetry and of prose in the book of Dante's youth. This way of reading will allow us to see how the poetry has preserved many fragments of true life which the prose attempted to exclude or eclipse when the poet looked in retrospect at the love affairs of his youth and saw them as a heap of extinguished ashes, without body or reality, in sharp contrast with the vivid light that enveloped the memory of his love of Beatrice. In showing these contrasts, our desire is not to be disrespectful of the poet, but only to know Dante better as a young man and to bring into relief the artistic process that guided him when he penned the *Vita Nuova.*

Nothing leads to a better understanding of authors than to know their aesthetic ideas; not those prevalent during their lifetime, which they may or may not have followed, but their specific tenets, and especially those that one can reconstruct in the work that one wishes to study. In the beginning of the *Vita Nuova*, precisely in the second chapter, the poet wrote: "Since to dwell on passions and deeds of such an extreme youthfulness seems to be a type of literature worthy of the people, I shall leave them; and, omitting many things which could be taken from the pattern whence these derive, I shall come to those words which are indelibly written in my memory under more important headings. This is the artistic creed of the poet at the time he composed his *Vita Nuova*. He believed that the contemplation and depicting of passions were not worthy of his art, for they represented the relativity of man and not the ideal and rational part of him. This latter part was found in the depths of his being and constituted the "more important headings" of the poet's life. What he omitted in the book of his youth was the element of passion, the memory of other loves, whatever they may have been, that accompanied his love of Beatrice. He left the elements of passion to the *fabula*, to popular art that was interested in sensuality, unbridled laughter, and loose metrical forms.

This was the plan which he had proposed for himself, but it is quite true that it was never possible for him to carry it out in full. Had he succeeded, the *Vita Nuova* would not be the first psychological novel in Italian literature. Traces of the human love are numerous, and they are still visible in the *Vita Nuova*. By way of example, the poem "Con l'altre donne mia vista gabbate" (XIV) shows us that Beatrice laughed at the poor poet who could not control his trembling with emotion as she approached him. The prose attributes the mockery to the other women, who were with Beatrice, and not to her, lessening in this way the impact of the situation and presenting it in the prose on a more ideal plane than the one projected in the poem.

The divine sonnet "I' mi sentii svegliar dentro lo core" (XXIV) loses much of its charm in the prose by a play on words of the name of Giovanna, Cavalcanti's lady, and the name Primavera, given to her by her friends because of the freshness of her beauty. In the sonnet the poet had written that he felt an unusual joy awakening in his heart in the guise of water gushing from a spring. His heart had unconsciously had the presentiment of the approaching of Beatrice and Giovanna. But in the prose Dante begins to rave about the fact that Giovanna bore that name because she walked ahead of Beatrice, not differently from St. John, who was the forerunner of Christ. And it was precisely for this reason that the girl had received the name of Primavera. She will come first (*prima verrà*), preceding Beatrice. Here the courtly system seriously damaged the poem or at least detracted from the poetic resonance that remains with the reader after having perused it.

The episode of the *Donna Gentile* is also presented on two different planes. Although both poetry and prose unite in revealing to us the struggle in the poet's heart between the image of Beatrice and the fascination of the *Donna Gentile* who showed compassion and love to the grieving poet, the prose removes every vestige of humanity from the poet's feelings. In the poem, in a very human way, the heart of Dante as a man is shown as it slowly surrendered to the young girl's love. The poet confesses its capitulation, "and then he sighs." The struggle between heart and soul, instinct and reason, is beautifully developed in the sonnet "Gentil pensero che parla di vui" (XXXVIII). But in the prose the need of conforming to the schema of courtly love causes reason to triumph, suppressing the heart's longings, and the poet calls the *Donna Gentile*'s thoughts "most vile." Actually, the sonnet addressed to the young girl is replete with love for her, and Dante reveals in it all his sentiments with the melody and grace that are typically his when he listens to the voice of his heart. The above-mentioned examples should convince us of the effective and real existence of the two planes of reality reflected in the poetry and the prose.

These contrasts can be seen and documented even more readily in the sonnets dedicated to women who were called "women of the foil." Following the custom of Provençal poets who, in order to conceal the identity of the lady who was the object of their love, pretended to dedicate themselves to serve another lady of the court, Dante tells us that he concealed his love for Beatrice through three women to whom he gave homage and for whom he wrote sonnets on various occasions. It should be observed that the convention of the "woman of the foil" does not suit Dante very well. Such a woman was the victim of the understanding of two lovers who wanted to keep their relationship a secret, and who would agree as to which woman the lover would court in order to throw off all the suspicions of the people of their courtly group. It is natural for the lady not to be troubled by the feigned courtship which the man bestows on another woman. If this be so, it is not understandable why Beatrice, instead, was angered to the point of refusing her greeting to Dante when the poet dedicated his attentions to the three "women of the foil." Moreover, such understanding presupposed a true love or passion between two lovers, while in Dante's case only one was in love, the poet himself. The real truth of the matter is quite different. Dante met the three young ladies, fell in love with them, and wrote poems about them which, later, while composing the prose of the *Vita Nuova*, he was determined to reduce to the schema of courtly love by forcing them to express his homage to Beatrice. In the prose, through devious ways, he succeeds, at least in part, in his very difficult task. But it was not possible to destroy or remove the initial and substantial contradiction between his feelings for the three young girls and his love for Beatrice. The attentive reader will discover such a contradiction with lucid clarity, and he can conclude only that when Dante assembled the poems which constitute the central part of the *Vita Nuova*, those loves, of whatever nature they might have been, had become meaningless to him. At that time the only and true reality was his love for the dead Beatrice. Even the *sirventese* that Dante, in the sixth chapter, tells us that he wrote in honor of the sixty most beautiful women of Florence, does not place Beatrice at the top of his thoughts, for she occupied only the ninth place, which most certainly must not have flattered her vanity as a woman.

The prose in the fifth chapter refers to the woman in whom Dante concealed his love for several years. Their relationship was born out of mere chance, when, one day in church, Dante's eyes, which were turned in Beatrice's direction, met with those of this woman. Dante relates that "immediately I thought of making this woman a foil for the truth; and I showed so much attention to her that those who discussed me believed her to be my secret love. With this woman I succeeded in hiding myself for several years and months." There is no doubt whatsoever that, according to the prose, this woman served only as a mask for his love for Beatrice. In the seventh chapter we are informed that, since this woman had to leave Florence, Dante felt obliged to write a sonnet in which he proposed to "make a complaint about it." If he had not shown grief, the poet tells us, "people would have immediately noticed my concealment." But the poem contains this verse:

> Sì che, volendo far come coloro
> Che per vergogna celan lor mancanza,
> Di fuor mostro allegranza
> E dentro de lo core struggo e ploro.

> Thus, wanting to be like those
> Who for shame hide their loneliness,
> Outwardly, I display happiness
> While within I cry, consumed by longing.

These words tell the very opposite of what the occasion of the woman's departure called for. The poet should have displayed sorrow instead of "happiness." The prose tells us that the sonnet was included in the *Vita Nuova* "because my lady [Beatrice] was the immediate cause of certain words which are found in the sonnet." In reality, what the poet writes in the prose shows him struggling desperately to attain unity of love in his *Vita Nuova*, but the attempted union between the actual and the artistic reality shows lacerations and breaks. One can only repeat that Dante's love for the "woman of the foil" was no longer alive when he wrote the prose of the *Vita Nuova*, though it had been a real love.

Even the sonnets in the eighth chapter fit very imperfectly into the schema of courtly love. The two sonnets, which are very beautiful, are none other than the expression of the poet's grief over the death of a young girl whose beauty and gentleness Dante admired. Love itself, personified, cries over her death, and the poet sees Love standing, his head bowed, over the beautiful image of the dead girl. She possessed a gay nature, and possessed that which, with the exception of honor, merits the highest exaltation in a woman—beauty. The poet sings that Death

> di pietà nemica,
> Di dolor madre antica,
> Giudizio incontestabile, gravoso,
>
> hai partita cortesia
> E ciò chè in donna da pregiar, vertute;
> In gaia gioventute
> Distrutta hai l'amorosa leggiadria.
>
> enemy of pity,
> Ancient mother of grief,
> Heavy and unquestionable judgment,
>
> you have destroyed courtesy
> And what is praiseworthy in a woman, virtue:
> In her gay youth
> You have destroyed the lovable charm.

In the prose the poet informs us that the two sonnets are included in the *Vita Nuova* because he remembered that "he had once seen her," the young deceased person, in the company of his gentle lady, Beatrice. In the prose, the poet's feelings are denied to the young woman and are directed toward Beatrice. Even if the poet cried, he states, he did so only because he once saw her in Beatrice's company, and if he proposed to "say several words regarding her death," he did so in compensation for having seen her in his lady's company. Yet, the memory of the young girl and her death are very much alive in the poems. In the prose they are obscured by the literary preoccupation to which the poet has subjected himself.

Chapter nine leads one to similar conclusions. Here, too, it is impossible to harmonize the poetry and the prose. The poetry, studied, as we have suggested, independently of the prose, shows us the end of a love affair, while a new interest appears in Dante. Basically, it shows the poet's passing from an old to a new love. According to the poetry, Dante tells us that he left the city against his will. Naturally enough it was Florence, but the poet does not mention it by name, preferring the romantic haze of the unknown. He was on horseback, he informs us, and he encountered Love dressed in a pilgrim's clothing like the poet. Love, too, was dispirited and unhappy with the sadness that accompanies the end of every human experience. Love reflected the poet's mood; it was the poet himself—his

heart aglow with love. Love informed him that he was taking his heart "to serve a new pleasure." The poet transfused himself to such an extent in the thought of the new love that he felt completely identified with it. In spite of all the efforts displayed in the prose, the sonnet has nothing to do with Beatrice. Perhaps it would be more accurate to say that Beatrice has nothing to do with the sonnet. If Dante's love for Beatrice had been more alive in his heart at the writing of the sonnet, one cannot understand why Love was so sad, spiritless, and so full of sighs. Dante's feelings for Beatrice were not really in danger. The love which becomes obscured in the sonnet is that which he felt for another woman when a new interest was aroused in the poet's heart, and he freely sang of its joy:

> Allora presi di lui sì grande parte
> Ch'elli disparve, e non m'accorsi come.
>
> Then I took from it such a great part
> That it disappeared, without my awareness.

The prose tried in vain to change the sonnet's meaning. Referring it to the occasion when Dante left Florence, possibly for a military expedition, the prose attributes the poet's sadness to the fact that he will no longer be able to see Beatrice, but this element is completely foreign to the sonnet's theme. This poem remains strictly love poetry, strangely and violently inserted in the magic circle occupied only by his love for Beatrice. It is because of such contrast that the idealistic pattern of the *Vita Nuova* is cut across by elements that show us the love theme plunged in the immediacy of life, without transportations of any kind. This part forms a beautiful underground spring that flows silently but powerfully under the conventional framework of the *Vita Nuova*.

Who can ever forget the words with which Dante described the curiosity of friends and gossipers who wanted to know who the woman was that had destroyed him so, and he "smilingly looked at them and said nothing"? Of course, the most perfect sonnets in the *Vita Nuova*, "Tanto gentile e tanto onesta pare" and "Ne gli occhi porta la mia donna amore," are rooted in the idea of perfection which was so dear to the Provençal and courtly poets. However, that idea became luminous and beautiful only because it was enriched by the human tenderness that it acquired in passing through Dante's soul. It is due to this fact if the blinding light of the absolute, diffused throughout the work, is often made varied, arising from the remembrance of actual life, life as actually lived. Who will complain and accuse the poet for not having adhered literally to the cultural precepts of his time? The soul of true poets is too great to remain constrained and oppressed by the narrow circle prescribed by the culture of their times.

Maurice Valency (essay date 1958)

SOURCE: "New Life," in *In Praise of Love: An Intro-duction to the Love-Poetry of the Renaissance,* The Macmillan Company, 1958, pp. 256-72.

[*Valency argues that the* Vita Nuova *is the work in which Dante first moved beyond the conventional "dolce stil nuovo" (sweet new style) into a visionary idealism that found its mature expression in the* Divina Commedia.]

The action of the *Vita Nuova* developed as naturally out of the songs of the *dolce stil* as the drama of true love out of the *troubadour chansons*. We have no dif-ficulty in identifying the plot of Dante's early master-piece. It is the old story, adapted conformably with the new setting and the new age in which it was rooted.

The *Vita Nuova* reflects in detail the changes which had come over the chivalric tradition in its process of naturalization in the Italian cities. It is urban in its environment and bourgeois in its tone. In its breadth of action it is narrow, but far deeper and higher in its spiritual scope than its Provençal counterpart, and in-finitely more imaginative, occult, and mysterious. As narrative, unquestionably, the prose is somewhat static and uncertain; the work belongs principally to the lyric genre. Its affinities are with the introspective novel or the bourgeois tragedy, certainly not with chivalric ro-mance. If we think of the narrative possibilities of the *troubadour* fantasy of true love—the story of Ca-bestanh, for example, or the story of Bertran de Born— the story of Beatrice seems almost too simple to be useful. Yet in its basic outline the story is the same as that of all other stories of true love, and the characters are the same. Somewhere in Dante's story the *gilos* exists, although he plays no part in the action and is never mentioned, and because of him and the ever-present *losengiers—maldicenti,* Cino calls them—the action proceeds in mystery, insofar as it may be said to proceed at all.

The figures which so strangely people the *Vita Nuova* doubtless inhabited all the poetry of the *dolce stil,* but it is rarely that we are made aware of any outward reality in these songs, and we do not observe them. It is in the *razos*—the *ragioni*—of Dante's book that the material action takes place. The songs around which the narrative is arranged have no action; they differ in no way—save perhaps in quality—from the *sonetti, ballate,* and *canzoni* of the other writers of this school. Even in Dante's *ragioni,* the realistic touches are few. The story which binds the songs together gives rather the illusion than the reality of a true and intense expe-rience.

Out of the songs of the *Vita Nuova* Dante developed a psychic drama which appears, indeed, to have con-sequences on every plane save that of material reality. From the microcosmic standpoint the love which is the subject of the work is treated as a perturbation of the soul which ends in spiritual illumination. As we have seen, this was essential in the new style. In its macro-cosmic aspect, this love is an aspiration of universal magnitude which involves in the *amours* of a Floren-tine young man, God Himself, the angelic host, the saints, the calendar, and the entire cosmic mechanism. Played on this scale, the plot of love's drama no longer has to do with the more or less comprehensible efforts of a young lover to engage the interest of a haughty lady in despite of her husband and the surrounding busybodies. It becomes a play of dreams and spirits, of fleeting contacts of unutterable significance, visions and premonitions of disaster, symbols and portents of occult character—a mystical experience of great depth and moment. The relation of the *Vita Nuova* to the rest of the literature of the new style seems unequivocal. It made explicit, rationalized, and interpreted, insofar as it was possible, in a more or less orderly narrative sequence what was already intrinsic and implicit in the stilnovist poetry up to the period of its composition. It is a synthesis and an epitome, not an innovation.

As a record of the ascent of the spirit through love, it is true, the *Vita Nuova* went no further than the initial stages. It is in the *Convivio* that Dante recorded the necessary preparations, and in the *Comedy*, the actual adventure of the soul. The *Vita Nuova*, however, laid the substantial groundwork for the *Comedy*. It preced-ed it as Lady Vanna precedes Lady Beatrice, and per-haps at no greater distance, for Dante was certainly of mature years when he put this work together, and the final prose indicates that he was already thinking of the greater work.

But while it seems quite clear that the one work grew out of the other, Dante's two masterpieces belong to entirely different levels of poetic development, just as the love which each work celebrates is in a different stage of evolution. Love appears in the *Vita Nuova* simultaneously with the first appearance of "the glori-ous lady of my mind who was called Beatrice by many who knew not how she was called," and then and there takes up its residence in the poet's soul. The final wish of the poet is addressed to Love, "the Lord of Courte-sy," that it may please him to let his soul see the glory of his lady who now gazes gloriously into the face of God. Between these two stages is unfolded the story of the carnal love of Beatrice.

The *Vita Nuova* records the adventure of the heart. The *Comedy* records the voyage of the soul. Heart and soul are, indeed, present in both ventures, but in differ-ent emphasis. In the *Vita Nuova* the willing spirit goes as far as the heart can send it. The sigh with which the heart explores the reaches of heaven in search of its beloved proceeds from the heart and returns to the heart, a spirit bearing incomprehensible tidings. But the *Comedy* is the adventure of the highest soul, the intellect, and, led by beauty, it reaches beyond the stars, in knowledge more and more precise, as far as thought can reach.

The *Vita Nuova* describes the first movements of that love which seeks the stars. It was normal that this love should see heaven first of all in the sparkle of a woman's eyes. Only when this light had failed did Love cause the gaze of the poet to turn upward where the true stars have their being. Before the death of Beatrice there had been some premonitions, but it was only when she was dead that the intellect came truly into play in the desperate effort to comprehend, and now there began for the lover another story and another life. The *Vita Nuova* has really only two phases. They are both governed by the same love—the love of the living woman and the love of the dead, the love of the spirit in the body and the love of the bodiless spirit. The intellect is deeply concerned in this love, which possesses all of the soul; but, even in its second phase, it is still, in St. Bernard's words, the love of the spirit according to the flesh. It is only in the *Paradiso*, in the last cantos, that the poet achieves the love of the spirit according to the spirit.

The term *Vita Nuova* was left ambiguous, like so many other things in this cryptic work. Very likely the poet himself was unwilling to be limited with regard to its meaning, and no one has since succeeded in defining what Dante left indefinite. The poet informs us in the opening lines that there is a chapter-heading in the book of his memory—if indeed *mente* in this place means memory and not mind or soul—a Latin rubric which reads *Incipit vita nova*. When Dante wrote these lines, he had, conceivably, other chapters in mind also; at any rate, in his later works, he referred to this as his *Vita Nuova*, and the work took on an independence which perhaps it was not at first intended to have.

At this time *nuovo* in Italian meant young, strange, wonderful, early, beautiful, rare and nine, as well as new, and the *stilnovisti* used it in all of these senses. The possibilities for rhetorical equivocation were therefore endless. *Vita Nuova* as a title really tickled the mind; it had precisely the kind of ambiguity which suited the closed style in which much of this work is couched. The work dealt with the poet's early life, his youth, an extraordinary youth ruled by an extraordinary love; a period spent in the contemplation of a miracle of feminine beauty the earthly manifestations of which occurred in a periodicity of nine, the number of perfection, yet not so perfect a number as the divine number, the decad. The title, however, lent itself to a more deeply pious connotation since, after the time of Augustine, new life was often used to signify the life of the spirit regenerated in Christ, and Dante himself made an analogy between Beatrice and Christ in the

Vita Nuova.

To the love-theory of the *dolce stil*, the *Vita Nuova* added only one idea that was new—the love of the disembodied spirit. This idea was largely developed in the prose. The poetry summed up the *dolce stil* authoritatively both in substance and in form. The songs and sonnets which Dante arranged for this work represented pretty well the entire range of the new poetry, from the merest gallantry to the ultimate intuition of divine love. As they are evidently pieces written at various times over a considerable period, they have no intrinsic principle of sequence, and fall chiefly into two categories, songs written to a living lady, and songs which lament her death. It is by no means certain that any of these songs was written especially for the *Vita Nuova*, though it seems quite probable that a few were written to round out the poetic frame of the work. It is the prose which gives narrative sequence to these songs, marshals them in a meaningful pattern, and in a sense re-writes them in the service of a unified concept.

The more closely we read the songs of the stilnovist canon, the more obvious it becomes that there is nothing absolutely new in the *Vita Nuova* except the scheme itself. All the poetic materials can be identified without difficulty in the work of Dante's contemporaries or predecessors. The lady is a miracle, an angel from heaven who is awaited in heaven; her beauty dazzles the world; her salutation is a benediction; her death a public calamity and the occasion of universal mourning—by this time these were all well-established elements of amatory poetry. In the same way the poet's timidity, his inner torment, his relations with the god of love, his visions, his intuitions, his sorrow and his joys are familiar themes; their novelty lies only in the skill with which they are developed poetically. The verse exemplifies most of the poetic modes that were current at the time in Dante's circle—the song of praise, the complaint, the plea for pity, the reproach, the excuse; the vision, the *planh*, together with some didactic forms which do not have to do directly with courtship.

The prose narrative is a work of art of the highest poetic value. In themselves, the songs are tolerably simple and clear, but the narrative develops to the full the visionary quality which distinguishes the *dolce stil*. By means of the prose the songs are set in a strange world in which personages, symbols, and events occur and recur as in a dream. The difference between this prose and the *razos* of the *troubadours* is very marked. The *troubadours* employed an objective technique in the narratives with which they "explained" the songs in their anthologies; it is chiefly in the songs themselves that we find the subjective element. Since Dante was explaining his own songs, his *ragioni* have an intimate and personal character which is foreign to the *troubadour* songbooks, and the result is an integrated work of "autobiographical" character, quite unlike anything which had been written in the lyric tradition up to that time.

Central in the plan of the *Vita Nuova* is the conception of the principal character, the lover. He is nameless, of course, and unlocalized, but the year of his birth is established with precision. He speaks in verse in the first person, as all lovers do in the forms related to the *canso*, but he speaks in the first person in prose as well, so that the temptation is irresistible to identify the character and the author, and to assume that the extraordinary spiritual happenings which the *Vita Nuova* relates really took place more or less as they were set forth. It would be impertinent at this stage of the discussion to suggest that the *Vita Nuova* is obviously a work of the imagination, a sort of novel like *Fiammetta*, were it not that ever since Boccaccio wrote his life of Dante, in 1364, it has been traditional to ascribe a certain historicity to these events and to assume that the daughter of that Folco Portinari who died on 31 December, 1289, the Bice Portinari who married Simone de' Bardi, was in fact identical with the Bice of the sonnet "I mi sentii svegliar" and the Beatrice of the *Vita Nuova*. Perhaps she was. But the fact is that the tradition which connects the glorious Beatrice, the "blessing of Florence," with the wife of a Florentine merchant is based chiefly on the testimony of a "trustworthy person" almost three-quarters of a century after the event; and, from a scholarly point of view, this is disturbing. From every other standpoint, the tradition is as strong as steel. Whatever validity it may have as fact, its validity as legend is beyond discussion.

But whatever the relation may have been between Dante and the daughter of Folco Portinari, it is clear that the Beatrice of the *Vita Nuova* is not a woman but a poetic concept, marking a stage of that spiritual evolution which the *stilnovisti* so often and so carefully described. With this idealized Beatrice, the daughter of Folco would have had in any case only the remotest connection. In the same way the gentle and timid youth, of whose exterior semblance we catch an occasional glimpse as he pauses in the street to speak respectfully to a group of ladies or sits bemused drawing pictures of angels, can hardly be confused with the stern figure which Boccaccio drew. Whatever his connection with Dante, the lover of the *Vita Nuova* is a poetic construction of more or less conventional cut, exactly as is Beatrice. Both are personages designed to play a certain action in a drama conceived according to the patterns of the stilnovist lyric, and this is their principal reality. Much the same may be said of Petrarch's Laura, and, in general, of all the ladies who in the following years became the subject of the Renaissance lyric sequences of love.

In the *Vita Nuova* the lover has, naturally, more solid-

ity as a character than the lady. Like almost all the *troubadour* ladies, Beatrice is depicted in terms of the ideal. She has little to distinguish her as an individual; we know only that she was of the color of pearl, perfect and pitiless. The lover, as always, is much more interested in himself than in the lady. He describes his comings and goings with some realism, and his inner life in great detail. Nevertheless this personage, while individualized in some degree, is at bottom an archetype like the other; both may be found in almost any song of the *dolce stil* pretty much as Dante portrays them, the lady remote and coolly radiant, the lover troubled and feverish. They are reciprocally conceived counterparts in the relation of form and potency: the one is made for the other as love for the gentle heart.

As these characters rarely meet, only that action which takes place within the lover's soul may be called truly dramatic. The thread of the narrative, as Dante devised it, involves mainly three stages, all of them traditionally the subject of poetry—the enamorment and courtship; the death of the lady; and its sequel—the lover's temporary infidelity and his return to the true way of love. These phases of the story are developed largely in the prose. It seems obvious that a good many of the poems would be equally appropriate to one or another section of the narrative.

The numerological system by which Dante governed the arrangement of the songs among the prose *ragioni* is chiefly interesting because of the manner in which it points the stages of the narrative. The system is not immediately apparent to the reader, and the numerological schemes of such later sequences as Scève's *Delie* would seem to derive rather from the more obvious number symbolism of the *Comedy* than from the *Vita Nuova*. The sections of the *Vita Nuova* were, indeed, not numbered by the author, but by his editors, and it was not until the time of Norton that the numerology of the *Vita Nuova* became the subject of close study.

By the time of Dante, numerology had long aroused interest in scholastic circles. In the wake of the Pythagorean traditions which identified form with number, Augustine had written [in *De libero arbitrio*], "Divine wisdom is seen in the numbers impressed on all things," and after him various patristic writers had written on the properties and virtues of certain numbers; but the church had no abiding interest in this type of symbolism, and the subject never acquired any degree of precision. Nevertheless, the Creator was believed to have apportioned the rhythms and quantities of the universe according to the virtues of numbers, and Dante also proportioned his work in accordance with a hidden numerological principle. This principle, symbolically meaningful, served also an artistic purpose. It was a principle of design and imposed upon the units of the work an extrinsic order which added yet another dimension of significance.

For the formal principle of the *Vita Nuova*, Dante chose the number nine. As he tells us in *Vita Nuova* XXIX, this number was closely associated with Beatrice because the nine spheres of heaven were perfectly related at the moment of her generation, and for this and other reasons she was herself a nine, a miracle, *cosa nova*. All manifestations of Beatrice in the *New Life* of Dante are conformable, or are made conformable, with the number nine. Presumably the perfect life of Beatrice was completely expressed in harmonies of nine, but all we know of it is her comings and goings in the life of Dante, both in the flesh and in the three visions which center upon her, so that the *Vita Nuova* is in reality Dante's life of nine, his life, so to speak, of Beatrice.

The consequence of this numerological conception is to give a cosmic dimension to the entire Dante-Beatrice relationship, every event of which is precisely timed in accordance with a supernatural schedule in which the stars themselves are concerned. Thus the life of Dante and Beatrice is conceived of as having design, rhythm, and purpose, like a poem, and the *Vita Nuova* is the poet's transcription of a love-poem composed by no less a poet than God Himself.

Dante's transcription, however, comes somewhat short of perfection. The numerical basis of the *Comedy* is three, and it is all marvelously built of threes. But the *Vita Nuova* was a compilation. It naturally offered a certain resistance to the superposed design, and the result is a little uncertain. For the poetry, apparently, ten and not nine is the principle of arrangement. There are three decads of poems and a final sonnet: three and one, a trinity. Of Beatrice's number nine, we are constantly reminded in the prose, and this number vibrates curiously with the poetic arrangement in tens. The poems themselves have still another principle of order. They are founded in the main on the fourteen-line stanza, all the sonnets and the three *canzoni*.

The distribution of the poems among the prose *ragioni* is carefully ordered so as to point the three stages of the love-story, of which the first has to do with earthly love, the second with death, and the third with the love of the spirit. The adult Beatrice first appears and speaks in *Vita Nuova* III. The consequence is the first vision of Love, and this event is at once announced in a sonnet addressed to the *fedeli d'amore*, the brotherhood of the gentle heart. In the tenth section the *gentilissima* expresses her dislike for the ways of *fin amor* by withholding her salutation. This motivates a *ballata* of apology, an apology which is also a declaration of love. In the fourteenth section, the lover is reduced to tears by Beatrice's mockery, her *gabbo*, and some sections later he resolves henceforth to write only in praise of Beatrice, and no longer about himself. He thus enters upon a "new and more noble matter." The first example of his new matter is the *canzone* "Donne ch'avete," in which the death of Beatrice is foreshadowed, and this song initiates the second decad of poems.

"Donne ch'avete," to which Dante gave the honor of representing the sweet new style in *Purgatorio* XXVI, is in fact a compendium of all that is most characteristic of the stilnovist manner. The lady of the song is not said to be an angel, it is true. But her soul shines on earth so brightly that it is visible in heaven, which would be perfect if she were there; her power is such that any woman appears noble who accompanies her; in her presence Love chills all evil thoughts; whoever can bear to look at her face becomes at once noble or else dies; whoever receives her greeting is filled with peace and forgets all wrongs; and God has granted that whoever speaks with her cannot come to a bad end. This lady is of the color of the pearl, a masterpiece of nature; it is by her pattern that beauty is measured, and from her eyes move flaming spirits of love which reach the hearts of all who gaze upon her. Nothing more appropriate could have been selected to exemplify the new style, and if this is what Dante set down at Love's dictation, we can only marvel at Love's thoroughness. He covered the ground.

Nevertheless there is in "Donne ch'avete" an unmistakable feeling of grandeur, and if we look closely it becomes evident that it centers upon the second strophe. Here we feel the pure strong thrust of the imagination, and the song gains suddenly a higher level:

> An angel cries out in the divine Intelligence and says: "Lord, in the world is seen a marvel in the act which proceeds from a soul which gleams as far as here." Heaven, which has no defect save the lack of her, asks her of its Lord, and all the saints implore this favor. Only Pity takes our part, for God says, and it is of my lady that he means to speak: "My beloved ones, now suffer in peace that the lady of your hope may dwell for as long as it may please me down yonder where there is one who expects to lose her, and who will say in hell: 'O ye ill-fated! I have seen the hope of the blessed in heaven.'"

In these lines one may see, as one chooses, a prophecy of the *Comedy*, or simply a compliment of more than ordinary magnificence. In either case this remarkable conceit, which ranges over the entire universe, taking hell, earth, heaven, and God Himself to witness the wonder of the lady, is of the very essence of the new style. Its pedantry makes us smile—the angel speaks to the Almighty as if He were in a classroom. Yet the audacity of the conception makes us marvel. This, too, is characteristic of the new style. It has scale.

Ten sections later, in the twenty-eighth chapter of the *Vita Nuova*, occurs the death of the most gentle lady, and the *canzone* "Li occhi dolenti" (Section XXXI) initiates the third decad of poems. It is in the thirty-fifth section that the other gentle lady distracts the poet from his devotion to the ideal Beatrice; but in the thirty-ninth section, the vision of the beatified Beatrice dressed in her first colors rescues him from his dilemma, and he determines henceforth to be faithful to this love alone. He is then rewarded with the final and indescribable vision which ends the last decad.

From every point of view, artistic, conceptual, and numerical, the entire design is composed around the *canzone* "Donna pietosa," in which for the second time the death of Beatrice is foreshadowed. This song, by any reckoning, occupies the precise center of the composition. It is the fifth poem of the second decad, and it occupies a central position between the other two *canzoni* of the **Vita Nuova**, the first of which looks forward to the death of Beatrice and the second of which, "Li occhi dolenti," looks back upon it. "Donna pietosa" has eighty-four lines. Its exact midpoint is the line in which the death of Dante himself is foreseen:

> Visi di donne m'apparve crucciati
> Che mi dicean pur: Morra' ti, morra' ti.

The *New Life* therefore centers upon death.

The true beginning of the new life is death, to which love is the prelude—this is the "meaning" of the **Vita Nuova**. It is the sight of Beatrice as an infant angel which first arouses love in the poet, and the vision of this resplendent child clothed in crimson, the color of charity, recalls him in the end to that love which is the earnest of his beatitude. Between the two visions is comprehended the brief life of Beatrice on earth, the prelude to the eternity of Beatrice in heaven. It is love which puts Dante in the way of salvation. It is death which rescues him from the folly of sensual desire. Death shows him the way that leads from the vanity of *fin amor* to that intellectual love of beauty, the ultimate object of which is God. In the **Vita Nuova** this process is not completed. It is begun. And therefore the rubric with which the book begins very properly reads: *Incipit vita nova.*

Thus the "vain imagining" of Dante in the *canzone* "Donna pietosa," when, after many signs and portents, he sees his lady's soul borne aloft by angels singing Hosanna, does not depress him. The dream of death, on the contrary, brings him joy and peace. It is in this mood that he sees his lady, still alive and healthy, pass by in the street, preceded by her friend Vanna, Cavalcanti's lady, and it occurs to him that Vanna in more than one sense is the precursor of Beatrice.

There is not much difference in the first part of the **Vita Nuova** between Beatrice and the lady Vanna whom Cavalcanti had created in his love-songs. It is only after the vision of death in "Donna pietosa" that the character of love is changed for Dante. His conversion is accomplished through the simplest and most traditional means; it is classic. During a period of illness, he experiences the sudden realization that Beatrice is mortal and will die, and with that it comes to him that he too will die one day. With this vivid realization of death comes a crucial change in his attitude toward Beatrice. From this point on, Beatrice begins to teach him the lesson which is summed up for him ultimately at the gates of paradise:

> Never did nature and art present to you any pleasure so great as the fair members in which I was enclosed and which are now scattered in dust,
>
> And if the highest pleasure thus failed you by my death, what mortal thing ought then to have drawn you to desire it?
>
> Truly, at the first arrow of deceitful things, you should have risen up after me who was such no longer. (*Purgatorio*, XXXI)

In Cavalcanti's conception, love was never free of the sensual appetite. Therefore in "Donna mi prega" love is said to be kindled by a dark ray from Mars, for love of this sort overshadows the intellect and arouses the endless conflict of mind and heart. This conflict Dante resolved in the death of the earthly Beatrice. In dying, Beatrice kindled a beacon in the sky toward which a more rational desire than sensual love could rise, and thus she initiated that movement of the soul which was to end, for Dante, only in the presence of the Heavenly Father. The lover of Vanna was earthbound, sad and restless. But the beauty of Beatrice led her lover first to the summit of human goodness, thence through knowledge to that place where the soul at last comes to rest.

The idea that man could ascend to God in this manner through the pure love of a woman had occurred in turn to Guinizelli and to Cavalcanti, but neither had devised the means—probably because, bound as they were to the *troubadour* tradition, they were unwilling to relinquish the lover's guerdon. For Dante the guerdon was not essential; at the end of the first decad of poems in the **Vita Nuova**, he put it from his mind. His guerdon was in any case no more than Beatrice's salutation. This was, he tells us, his only happiness; and in giving it up he found another happiness within himself, the joy of devoting himself to her praise. Many *troubadours,* as we have seen, had gone over this ground in the past; what was new was that for Dante not only the guerdon but the lady herself was expendable. "Donne ch'avete" therefore involves a declaration of independence from the tyranny of sensual love, even the purest. The lady shone in this world with celestial light; she was irresistible, it was true, but only for a time. It was logical therefore to worship the source rather than the mirror of this splendor. This would perhaps not be possible without aid from above, but this aid was immediately forthcoming. Indeed, it was Beatrice herself who, by denying Amor, indicated the way of charity.

We are thus able to understand why, immediately after the vision of death in the *Vita Nuova*, Dante interpolated the episode of Vanna and Beatrice and the sonnet "I mi sentii svegliar" together with the digression explaining why Vanna was called Primavera. It is because at this point in the narrative it becomes evident that Cavalcanti's lady was in fact the historical precursor of the lady of Dante's devising. The one concept, indeed, follows the other both logically and chronologically, and in this passage Dante serves notice that with respect to the angelic lady he has overgone his "first friend" and made something new and wonderful. The somewhat astonishing analogy of Beatrice and Christ, which is further developed in *Purgatorio* XXXI, now becomes comprehensible also. After the living Beatrice, who did not differ essentially from Cavalcanti's lady Vanna, there comes the ideal Beatrice, glorified and blessed, the savior of man through the New Life of love.

In this progression, the final step led inevitably to another and more exalted poetry. The *Comedy* of Dante Alighieri is obviously rooted in the lyric tradition. Without the lady of the *troubadour* song, without *Bon Vezi*, without Vanna, there could have been no Beatrice. Step by step in the course of two centuries Beatrice took form, and now through the perfection of Beatrice the well-schooled lover was able to intuit the perfection toward which the cosmos strives. Through the love of her beauty, he was able to achieve the supreme vision of the world which follows in all its various aspects from the comprehension of the universal Beatrice. This revelation was the guerdon which the lady bestowed upon her lover in the fullness of time. So love "restored in one day all the wrongs he had done elsewhere"—

> q'Amors
> Restaura tot en un dia
> Qant qe a mesfait alhors . . .

and here, at last, Love and the lady transcended the third heaven.

In this manner, the successive transformations of the lady of the song reached their apogee and came to an end. There was to be no more. The Renaissance added some Platonic touches, but in the main these patterns controlled the progress of the idealistic lyric until the middle of the seventeenth century, certainly, and perhaps much longer. The most gentle lady had, in all conscience, gone as far as she could. Since the *troubadours* themselves had begun at the top of the scale of perfection, the succeeding degrees could be but few. But these steps were the most difficult and, to encompass them, the art of pleasing ladies had to be transformed into a branch of theology. Out of the perfect lady of the *troubadours* was born the angelic lady, Cavalcanti's star, an angel in the flesh. Of this sort were Vanna, Cino's Selvaggia, Dante's Pargoletta, Sennuccio's Lisetta, and the countless others who were to appear in the course of the next centuries. Beatrice, however, held greater promise. In the *Vita Nuova*, Dante's lady shed her fleshly aspect and became pure spirit. It was then no longer possible to love the beauty of Beatrice in the flesh; it had to be loved in its spiritual aspect exclusively, the beauty of a blessed soul in heaven, a pure ideal. The ultimate step in the idealization of the lady of the song was, accordingly, her effacement from the earth.

The love of the earthly Beatrice led Dante, as he tells us, to a life of virtue, humility, and charity, and this simply in anticipation of his guerdon, the salutation in which was all his beatitude. Love had done as much, or almost as much, for the troubadour lover. But the love of the heavenly Beatrice, the true Beatrice, led Dante to God. The process which begins with the premonition of the death of Beatrice in the *Vita Nuova* ends only when in Paradise Beatrice steps aside, and the lover whom she has led to the Empyrean sees standing in her place the glorious elder who points the way to the seat of the All-Highest. From this moment on, Beatrice recedes further and further still from her lover's eyes until she takes her appointed place in the heavenly rose of which she forms a part; and her splendor, hitherto dazzling, is seen to be but a ray of the supreme and eternal light.

Mark Musa (essay date 1973)

SOURCE: "An Essay on the *Vita Nuova*: Aspects," in *Dante's "Vita Nuova,"* translated by Mark Musa, Indiana University Press, 1973, pp. 106-34.

[*In this excerpt, Musa analyzes the various appearances of Love personified, in which two different forms of love present themselves.*]

[In the *Vita Nuova*, the god of Love] is presented far more vividly than any of the other characters seen by the protagonist—who, for the most part, come through to the reader as shadowy shapes indeed. The first three times Love makes his entrance onto the stage of the *Vita Nuova*, not only are his clothes described but also his gestures and movements; and in all four of his appearances Love's voice is heard. This character, on whom a spotlight is focused, is made to behave in a way that must puzzle any reader. Love speaks Italian sometimes, sometimes Latin, and sometimes he even shifts languages in the midst of a visit. The accouterments of this actor in the scenes in which he plays his different roles vary, being those of a terrifying deity, a shabby traveler or a guardian angel. And so do his moods change, not only from scene to scene but within the same scene: from the radiant happiness of majesty, or the poised tranquility of beatitude, Love will fall into bitter weeping. Or, again, in his relationship toward the lover he may shift from kindly counselor to sublimely haughty lord, to impatient monitor, to chatty conspiratorial advisor. What can be the true significance of this mysterious, protean figure of Love, who four times appears on stage at a given moment to address the lover?

The god of Love first appears to the lover on the evening after he has received Beatrice's first greeting and returned home, ecstatic, to fall into a sweet sleep (III). He dreams he sees Love holding a sleeping lady in his arms; the figure speaks to the lover, in Latin, words that are mainly incomprehensible, and then ascends to Heaven. In Chapter IX the protagonist sees the figure of Love walking toward him along a country road; Love offers him practical advice as to maintaining the stratagem of the screen-lady. In Chapter XII, just as in Chapter III, Love appears to him during his sleep, a sleep into which he has fallen grieving bitterly over the loss of his lady's greeting. In Chapter XXIV, which immediately follows the prophetic vision of Beatrice's death, the lover is sitting thoughtful in "a certain place" when he sees Love coming from the direction "where his lady was." Then Beatrice appears with another lady, and he listens to Love's comments about them.

Now this last vision is followed by an "essay" (XXV) which begins with an explanation of the author's treatment of Love; though he mentions only the scene in Chapter XXIV, his words are surely meant to apply to all of the appearances of Love. But anyone familiar with the *Vita Nuova*, who is interested in the significance of the figure of Love, knows that in this chapter he will find no clue to the proper interpretation of this mysterious figure. The chapter treats instead the problem of poetic license, involving particularly the device of personification (a treatment promised us somewhat cryptically in Chapter XII). And it is puzzling that precisely after the last appearance of Love Dante would refer to this figure for no other reason than a rhetorical one. Perhaps there is a more important purpose underyling this chapter, whose threefold structure can be briefly summcd up.

First, he admits that, while perfectly aware of Love's being only an accident in a substance, he has treated it as if it were a substance—in fact, he has attributed to the figure of Love qualities properly human. Rather abruptly he turns to a consideration of the recent phenomenon of poets writing in the vernacular, stating that they should be allowed poetic license equal to that of thc poets of antiquity: in particular, the animization or personification of abstract entities. (Curious, that of

the many poetic figures recognized by medieval rhetoric, Dante specifies only the concretization of the abstract.) Finally, he illustrates the poetic license in question with quotations from the classical poets.

But he concludes the second part by allowing this poetic license to the vernacular poet only on one condition: . . .

> . . . it is fitting that the vernacular poet do the same—not, of course, without some reason, but with a motive that later can be explained in prose.

And he repeats this warning toward the end of the chapter: . . .

> For, if any one should dress his poem in images and rhetorical coloring and then, being asked to strip his poem of such dress in order to reveal its true meaning, would not be able to do so—this would be a veritable cause for shame.

This warning by the author amounts to a claim that he himself would be capable of offering the "verace intendimento" of the figure of Love, if asked to do so. To the reader who cannot ask the author to do so, these words are frustrating. But I believe they were intended to serve as a challenge to the reader, to inspire in him confidence that the device exploited is not mere ornamentation (as is the case, so the author tells us, with some poets known to him and Cavalcanti): there is indeed a "verace intendimento" which could be unmysteriously explained, and knowing this, the reader of the *Vita Nuova* must try, and hope, to find it. And perhaps the author is also suggesting—this would be most important—that because this significance can be ultimately made clear, no detail of his figurative presentation should be overlooked.

Of the four visions the first I find the most difficult; the simplest is the last, and with this I shall begin. In Chapter XXIV the first words of Love are a joyful command to the lover that he bless the day he became Love's captive, whereupon the lover, too, is filled with joy. Then he sees the "miraculous Beatrice" coming toward him, preceded by her friend Giovanna, called also Primavera. He hears Love speak portentous words comparing the Lady Giovanna, who comes before Beatrice, with John the Baptist proclaiming the approach of Christ. Love ends by saying: "E chi volesse sottilmente considerare, quella Beatrice chiamarebbe Amor per molta simiglianza che ha meco." ("Anyone of subtle discernment would call Beatrice Love, because she so greatly resembles me.") Thus, Love is comparing Beatrice indirectly to Christ and directly to himself.

We can surely assume, whatever the special significance we attribute to the figure of Love that, in each

Gustave Doré's engraving of Dante.

of the four visions in question, he always represents in some way the protagonist's love for Beatrice. And I suggest that here he represents the lover's total potential capacity for loving Beatrice as she should be loved: recognizing her Christlike nature which can only be unselfishly adored. This figure, which may be called by the formula "The Greater Aspect" of Dante's love for Beatrice, we shall see again as we go back to the other visions in the **Vita Nuova**.

But if we turn next to the other *imaginazione* (IX) among the four scenes, we will find the sharpest of contrasts. The lover himself is in a mood of dejection since he is forced to undertake a journey away from his city and from his lady; and the figure he suddenly sees coming toward him has the form of a pilgrim lightly and poorly clad—he, too, seeming dejected, staring at the ground, occasionally turning his glance toward a beautiful stream, swift and very clear, which flows alongside the path he is traveling. He advises the lover to choose a new screen-lady since the first one has left the city, and he urges him to be as ardently adept in his dissimulation with the second lady as he has been with the first. Surely this figure can only represent the "Lesser Aspect" of the protagonist's love, the lover's feelings at the moment, which are untouched by the transcendental. The lover's emotional state is

reflected in the epithet "disbigottito" applied to Love— who appears dressed as a pilgrim, since the lover himself happens to be a pilgrim at the present moment. Moreover, Love is poorly dressed; with this latter detail it is as if the poet would symbolize in Love's outward appearance the inner misery he himself is experiencing. And we learn that Love is playing the role of the lover's accomplice in the foolish game of the screen-ladies. The advice he offers, of a practical, even cynical nature, is of the sort to appeal to the childishly scheming lover.

There are two other indications that the Love who figures in this scene is none other than a reflection of the protagonist's own limited feelings: one concerned with Love's entrance on stage, the other with his disappearance. Love disappears, not as a person, not as a figure disappears, but as a substance melts. There is nothing left of Love for the lover to see, we are told, because Love has become so much a part of him. The manner of his appearance or, rather, the reason for his appearance also is connected with his being a part of the lover: after speaking of his anguish at leaving Florence and Beatrice, the lover adds, as if it were the most natural thing imaginable: "e *però* lo dolcissimo segnore . . . ne la mia imaginazione apparve come pellegrino. . . ." The significance of the causal *però* is obvious: It was the intensity of his feelings that caused his love to take on form and shape, reflecting his own mood, before his eyes.

In Chapter XII Love appears to the protagonist in his sleep; he sees Love sitting near his bed dressed in the whitest of raiment, deep in thought. After looking for some time at the lover, the figure sighs and says "Fili mi, tempus est ut pretermictantur simulacra nostra" ("My son, it is time to do away with our false ideals"). The lover notes that Love is weeping, and senses that he is waiting for him to say something. He can only ask: "Segnore della nobilitade, e perché piangi tu?" ("Lord of all virtues, why do you weep?"). He hears the answer: . . .

> I am like the center of a circle, equidistant from all points on the circumference; you, however, are not.

Finding these words obscure, the lover gathers courage to ask Love to explain them. Love answers, this time in Italian: "Non dimandare più che utile ti sia" ("Do not ask more than is useful to you").

The figure of the young man sitting dressed in purest white will remind any reader of the young man dressed in a long white garment sitting at the door of Christ's sepulchre. This suggestion, together with the solemnity of his Latin words, can only mean that, of the two Aspects of Love already discussed, the figure now on the stage of the lover's mind represents the Greater Aspect, that transcends the lover's own feelings on this occasion. And Love's first words of tender re-proach are those of a father to a son.

Most critics have seen in Love's first words announc-ing the necessity of abandoning "*simulacra nostra*" a reference to the device of the screen-ladies; and to them the possessive pronoun *nostra* amounts to a con-fession of complicity on the part of Love, who had encouraged the protagonist to continue this device. But it is surely impossible to imagine that the noble figure here portrayed could ever have played this puerile role; it is not he but the shabbily dressed pilgrim figure of Chapter IX, the Lesser Aspect, who had done so. And to imagine that this aider—and abettor—of the lover's game of screen-ladies would suddenly appear like an angel and, addressing him as "Fili mi," confess that they had both been wrong to play this game, is absurd. As for the possessive adjective *nostra* I see in this not a true plural but the well-known pedagogic device ("Fili mi") recorded from antiquity, of replacing the second person singular by the first person plural as if to in-clude the speaker along with the person addressed, the teacher with the pupil. This is a sympathetic and a patronizing device. Thus, assuming that *simulacra* is an illusion to the screen-ladies, the Greater Aspect would be here reproaching the lover for his weakness (that the Lesser Aspect had encouraged).

But I do not believe that the word *simulacra* refers specifically to the lover's use of screen-ladies, though such an allusion may well be included within the ref-erential range of this word. In classical Latin the word *simulacrum*, in its philosophical application, was used of an imitation as opposed to the original, of an ap-pearance as opposed to what is real. Thus, it could apply to any of the attitudes or actions of the young lover which were only false imitations of what true love for Beatrice should be. And if Love uses the word *simulacra* at this moment of the lover's development, while he is plunged in grief because of the loss of Beatrice's greeting, he must intend it to be a condem-nation, particularly, of the superficiality of a love that would seek its happiness in something transient, in a reward that could be arbitrarily bestowed or withdrawn. The greeting of Beatrice had seemed to the young lover to represent the ultimate in bliss ("mi *parve* allora vedere tutti li termini de la beatitudine"), but it was only a seeming, a *simulacrum*. Thus, Love's first words would seek to teach the lover, mourning the destruc-tion of his happiness, the vanity of that happiness it-self.

At this point one could hardly expect on the part of the protagonist immediate understanding of the rebuke, and immediate agreement with Love's suggestion. It would not be unreasonable, however, to expect at least a desire to understand: the lover might have asked his lord to explain what was implied by the word *simulacra* so that he should know just what it was he should avoid.

But if we read carefully from the beginning of the vision, it would seem as if he has not heard the words of admonition: . . .

> About half-way through my sleep I seemed to see in my room a young man sitting near the bed dressed in the whitest of garments and, from his expression, he seemed to be deep in thought, watching me where I lay; after looking at me for some time, he seemed to sigh and to call to me, saying these words: *Fili mi, tempus est ut pretermictantur simulacra nostra* ("My son, it is time to do away with our false ideals.") Then I seemed to know who he was for he was calling me in the same way that many times before in my sleep he had called me; and as I watched him, it seemed to me that he was weeping piteously, and he seemed to be waiting for me to say something to him; so, gathering courage, I began to address him, saying: "Lord of all virtues, why do you weep?"

The lover has heard the first two words, of course: "Fili mi", for they have served to make him recognize his lord. (Thus, between the vision in Chapter III and this one, there must have been other times when Love appeared to the sleeping lover, addressing him in pa-ternal terms.) He also notes that Love, silent again, is weeping and seems to be waiting for him to speak. And thus encouraged, he speaks—but, for some strange reason, only to inquire about Love's tears, not to com-ment on Love's message, his words of admonition, as would seem to be the normal thing to do. According to what we are offered of the protagonist's thought pro-cesses, he must have taken in only the first two words, missing the message itself: "Tempus est ut . . . ." Once he was sure that it was Love speaking, his attention passed from Love's words to his tears and to his wait-ing attitude, and he evidently believed that his puerile question was what Love was waiting to hear. But, of course, if he had understood Love's admonition, he would not have needed to ask him why he wept.

Love weeps because of the *simulacra*. Love weeps because the lover had put an exaggerated value on a mere greeting. He also weeps because, once this was refused, the lover collapsed utterly and childishly, in-stead of learning from this experience the obvious les-son—which he was to learn only later, thanks to his Muse (XVIII). If the lover did not understand the reason for Love's tears, little wonder that he did not under-stand Love's enigmatic answer, "Ego tanquam cen-trum circuli . . ."—words which have baffled genera-tions of critics of the *Vita Nuova*.

As for the interpretation of these words that the lover did not understand, surely, given the context, the com-parison they offer between Love and the young lover is a comparison between the two kinds of Love that must be distinguished: the lover's love, though tending toward the center is still on the circumference of the circle (where the *simulacra* are), while Love, the Greater Love, is, was, and always will be the irradiating center. And not only has Love, with his geometrical metaphor, set the *simulacra* in perspective, he has, in his self-definition, revealed his divine nature: in defining himself he uses a common Patristic definition of God. (And the *Paradiso* will end with the adoration of the perfection of the circle, to the movement of the three circles that are the Trinity and therefore the One.)

After the lover has been told not to ask more about what he obviously does not understand ("Non dimandare più che utile ti sia") he starts talking about himself. He laments the loss of Beatrice's greeting and asks for an explanation of it. Love tells him that Beatrice's rejection was due to the scandalous rumors about his relationship with the second screen-lady. He then proceeds to offer the lover a means of ingratiating himself with Beatrice once more, describing in some detail the kind of poem he should write her, one which would implore her forgiveness and appeal to Love himself as a witness to his loyalty: . . .

> "Since she has really been more or less aware of your secret for quite some time, I want you to write a certain poem, in which you make clear the power I have over you through her, explaining that ever since you were a boy you have belonged to her; and, concerning this, call as witness him who knows, and say that you are begging him to testify on your behalf; and I, who am that witness, will gladly explain it to her, and from this she will understand your true feelings and, understanding them, she will also set the proper value on the words of those people who were mistaken. Let your words themselves be, as it were, an intermediary, whereby you will not be speaking directly to her, for this would not be fitting; and unless these words are accompanied by me, do not send them anywhere she could hear them; also be sure to adorn them with sweet music where I shall be present whenever this is necessary." Having said these words he disappeared, and my sleep was broken.

But how can Love speak this way? The white-robed figure, reminiscent of St. Mark's angelic guard at the tomb of Christ, who at the beginning had been concerned only with transcendental values, is now interested in giving practical advice—encouraging the lover, in fact, to seek again the kind of happiness that can only fail, to concern himself again with *simulacra*? And the elegant speaker of sententious, epigrammatic Latin engages in this long-winded chatter? It is clear that with the introduction of this note of familiarity the atmosphere of deep seriousness, of awesome majesty that surrounded the figure of Love at the beginning has entirely disappeared.

It is, of course, the Lesser Aspect that gives this worldly advice, so easy (alas) for the young lover to understand: in the lover's mind the god has turned into the *Amore* of Chapter ix, who is on a plane no higher than that of the lover himself. The last words that we hear the Greater Aspect speak are the peremptory "Non dimandare più che utile ti sia"—which, however, being in Italian, prepare for the shift to the Lesser Aspect, serving as a hinge on which the two parts of the vision turn. That we have to do now with the *Amore* of Chapter ix is shown, not only by the tone of Love's words and the nature of his advice, but also by the fact that in his explanation of Beatrice's decision, when speaking of the lady chosen as the second screen, he calls her ". . . la donna la quale *io ti nominai* nel cammino de li sospiri . . . ," thereby identifying himself with the shabby, dejected figure of the pilgrim-Love. And if it is clear from these words that the one who abets the lover in his superficial program of wooing must be the same as the figure in Chapter IX, it should be just as clear that he cannot possibly be the one who appeared on stage saying, "Fili mi, tempus est . . . ." There has been a shift of identity. And since such a vision as this is comparable to a dream, in which one figure may easily turn into another, this shift in the lover's mind needs no psychological justification.

Now that we have recognized the possibility of a shift from the one to the other aspect of Love when this figure appears on stage to speak to the lover, it is only natural to wonder if this will be realized in the next appearance of Love to be considered—that is, the first of the four appearances of Love in the **Vita Nuova**. As the lover is sleeping sweetly, after having received Beatrice's first greeting, a marvelous vision comes to him in which he sees first a flame-colored cloud, then a figure in the cloud, whose aspect is frightening to look upon, yet expresses the deepest happiness. He speaks to the lover at length, though only a few of his words such as "Ego dominus tuus" are understandable to him. As he speaks, the lover sees that this awesome figure is holding in his arms a sleeping female figure, naked except for a crimson cloth in which she is loosely wrapped. Slowly the lover recognizes her as his lady; he also notes that the lordly man (who we know must be Love) holding the lady has in his hand a burning object; and he hears the words "Vide cor tuum." After some time has passed Love awakens the lady and cunningly forces her to eat of the burning object. This she does, reluctantly. After another passage of time Love's joy turns to bitterest grief and weeping he folds his arms about the lady and ascends with her toward Heaven. The lover's anguish at their departure breaks his sleep.

This figure who comes during the first of the last nine hours of the night, in the midst of a cloud the color of flame (suggesting the burning bush in which God appeared to Moses), who speaks in Latin and announces his lordship over the lover, and whose aspect is both radiant and terrifying is, obviously, the Greater Aspect of Love. At the end he ascends to Heaven; thus, the figure who appears with Beatrice and who departs with her must represent the same Aspect. And it must also be this divine being who, in the middle of the episode, says to the lover "Vide cor tuum." But I believe that in the lines following these words, in the interval of time that elapsed between Love's last words and the lady's awakening, there has been a shift from the Greater to the Lesser Aspect. "Vide cor tuum" is followed by "E quando elli era stato alquanto, pareami che disvegliasse questa che dormia. . . ." After the lady is made to eat the heart reluctantly, there is another pause in the action before the figure of Love, now weeping, will disappear: "Appresso ciò poco dimorava che la sue letizia si convertìa in amarissimo pianto"— a pause allowing for a second shift of Aspect, back to the first again. That the author has taken pains twice to indicate a lapse of time must be significant; and that his intention has been to set off this central action, to differentiate it from what precedes and what follows, is highly likely. And these two breaks could serve not only as dividers but to allow time for something to happen during the intervals in which nothing seems to happen.

Beatrice asleep in Love's arms is Beatrice dead, already in glory, pure spirit. When she is awakened she becomes a woman of flesh and blood, and her nakedness takes on warmth in the imagination. Perfect Love could not desire such a return to the carnal. Perfect Love could not try to force, to seduce the Beloved into an act against her nature, as the figure of Love does here: . . .

> And after some time had passed, he seemed to awaken the one who slept, and he forced her cunningly to eat of that burning object in his hand; she ate of it timidly.

When the figure of Perfect Love returns once more to the lover's imagination, the figure can only weep. He weeps because the lover's heart which he had declared to be in his possession ("Vide cor tuum") has been given over to the Lesser Love, which would make carnal the spiritual and, because of its covetousness, could envisage arousing covetousness in the miraculous Beatrice. It is difficult to understand the attitude of those critics who find sublimity in Love's gruesome act of forcing the lady to eat the lover's heart.

Now that the four visions have been discussed in the order: 4-3-2-1 (for reasons which should have become rather clear), let us sum up the sequence again in its original order. The figure of love capable of representing either the Greater or the Lesser Aspect, appears for the first time in Chapter III at its most dynamic and paradoxical: shifting from the Greater to the Lesser, back to the Greater Aspect again. The sonnet that the

lover writes describing the vision with a minimum of detail, he sends to his literary friends challenging them to discover its significance. And in the chapter immediately following we are told that for some time after his vision his digestive system was so upset that his friends were concerned about his haggard appearance. The literary maneuver may be a sign that the meaning of the vision was not clear to the poet-protagonist (not that such a sign is necessary), and the bad health which followed suggests that the memories of it must have tortured him.

In Chapter IX Love appears in abject form as the symbol of the protagonist-lover's superficial dalliance with the screen ladies. There are two details in the description of this figure which were passed over in the first discussion of Chapter IX and which are very important for establishing a link with the preceding vision. First, the pilgrim-Love is carrying the lover's heart in his hand, taking it, he says to the new screen-lady. Now, in Chapter III it is clearly the Greater Love that comes on stage with the young lover's heart in his possession; but I suggested that in the central episode of this vision the lover had given it over to the Lesser Love— who, in Chapter IX, still has it. The second link with the vision of Chapter III is of a different sort: in the second quatrain of the sonnet ("Cavalcando l'altrier . . .") following the prose narrative, the figure of Love, who will advise the lover about the second screen lady, is described as having suffered a change: "Ne la sembianza mi parea meschino,/ come avesse perduto segnoria." The "segnoria" that has been lost is the majesty of the radiant figure who presented himself to the lover saying, "Ego dominus tuus," in his first appearance. In the chapter that follows, the lover earnestly puts into practice the god's advice: the first of two times he will carry out the suggestion of the Lesser Love.

Nine chapters after his first appearance the Greater Love returns to the stage of the *Vita Nuova*, again waking the lover, again speaking Latin. This time there is no vague reference to "molte cose" spoken by Love which the lover did not understand. Apparently he said to him only two things in Latin, then turned to Italian to rebuke him sharply. The peremptory words, with the sudden shift from Latin to Italian, serve a purpose ultimately similar to the "lapses of time" indicated in Chapter III, only that whereas the latter allow for something unexpected to happen, for something to emerge out of the interval of time, the rebuke in Italian comes as a sharp announcement of change already on its way.

The obvious connection between the Lesser Love who will come to dominate the stage in Chapter XII, and the pilgrim-Love of Chapter IX has already been pointed out—a connection insisted on by Love himself (". . . la donna la quale *io ti nominai* nel cammino de li sospiri"). I would add that there is also a connection between this figure in Chapter XII, now giving elaborate instructions as to the means of winning back Beatrice's favor, and the one in Chapter III who, in the central episode, was intent on seducing Madonna: that Love who forced the lady with all his art to eat the lover's burning heart. And it is the influence of the Lesser Aspect that continues beyond the vision described: in the *ballata*, concluding the chapter, which the lover dutifully wrote at this figure's command. And it is surely in order that the influence of the Lesser Love should prolong itself beyond the vision that the poem closing the chapter represents this fulfillment of Love's worldly advice rather than sets forth a "recapitulative" version of the vision—the only vision of Love's appearance not described in verse, as was pointed out but not explained in the first part of this essay.

But it becomes clear in the following chapter that the first part of the vision, in which the Greater Love had spoken words the lover did not understand, had also made a strong impression on him. For this chapter is devoted to a "battle of the thoughts" about the nature of love: . . .

> After this last vision, when I had already written what Love commanded me to write, many and diverse thoughts began to assail and try me, against which I was defenseless; among these thoughts were four that seemed to disturb most my peace of mind. The first was this: the lordship of Love is good since he keeps the mind of his faithful servant away from all evil things. The next was this: the lordship of Love is not good because the more fidelity his faithful one shows him, the heavier and more painful are the moments he must live through. Another was this: the name of Love is so sweet to hear that it seems impossible to me that the effect itself should be in most things other than sweet, since, as has often been said, names are the consequences of the things they name: *Nomina sunt consequentia rerum.* The fourth was this: the lady through whom Love makes you suffer so is not like other ladies, whose heart can be easily moved to change its attitude. And each one of these thoughts attacked me so forcefully that it made me feel like one who does not know what direction to take, who wants to start and does not know which way to go. And as for the idea of trying to find a common road for all of them, that is, one where all might come together, this was completely alien to me: namely, appealing to Pity and throwing myself into her arms. While I was in this mood, the desire to write some poetry about it came to me, and so I wrote this sonnet which begins: "All my thoughts."

The problem he is struggling with is basically the eternal theme of the paradoxical nature of love. Still, it can be no coincidence that the only time he concerns himself with this *topos* is after the vision which contains conflicting aspects of Love. Perhaps the first of the four thoughts that comes to him, which stresses moral values, represents an attempt to think in terms of the Greater Aspect. The second thought, obviously, can apply only to the Lesser Aspect. The third merely describes the familiar oxymoric nature of love, with a touch of scholastic coloring. Whether the last thought is simply the conventional regret that the lady is unyielding, or whether it contains the recognition of the uniqueness of his lady Beatrice, is not too clear. But at least it is undeniable that the lover has been struggling with the problem of the nature of love after a second vision opposing Love's two natures.

In my treatment of the vision in Chapter XXIV, a number of fine details were left undiscussed, since I was faced with the problem of establishing for the first time the identity of the figure of Love. To understand the full significance of this vision the reader should examine carefully the opening lines of the chapter, that set the stage for Love's appearance: . . .

> After this wild dream I happened one day to be sitting in a certain place deep in thought, when I felt a tremor begin in my heart, as if I were in the presence of my lady. Then a vision of Love came to me, and I seemed to see him coming from that place where my lady dwelt, and he seemed to say joyously from within my heart: "See that you bless the day that I took you captive; it is your duty to do so." And it truly seemed to me that my heart was happy, so happy that it did not seem to be my heart because of this change. Shortly after my heart had said these words, speaking with the tongue of Love, I saw coming toward me a gentlewoman, noted for her beauty, who had been the much-loved lady of my best friend.

The "vana imaginazione" mentioned in the opening line is the prophetic vision of Beatrice's death. That a connection exists between that vision, described in terms suggesting the Crucifixion, and this one in which Beatrice is indirectly compared to Christ, is obvious. In fact, the lover might not have been capable of having this last vision of Love until after having experienced the one prophetic of her death; this is surely suggested by the words of Love himself that describe the significance of the name of Beatrice's companion, Primavera. He tells the lover: . . .

> The one in front is called Primavera only because of the way she comes today; for I inspired the giver of her name to call her Primavera, meaning 'she will come first' (*prima verrà*) on the day that Beatrice shows herself after the dream of her faithful one . . . .

Thus Love had planned this vision in advance, a plan which involved his inspiring one of Giovanna's friends to give her the nickname Primavera—intending this vision to take place after the vision of Beatrice's death, after the "vane imaginazione."

We are also told, in the opening sentence of the chapter, that the lover's heart began to tremble just before the appearance of Love; the fact that this tremor was of the sort he was accustomed to have when in the presence of his lady, prepares the way for the assimilation of Beatrice to Love at the conclusion of the vision. But this assimilation had already been suggested by degrees: the figure who appears in Chapter III, enveloped in a flame-colored cloud, will reappear in Chapter XII clothed in a garment of purest white; thus, Beatrice's two colors, red and white, belong to the god of Love.

Finally, there is the remarkable fusion between the god and the lover-protagonist, a fusion that takes place almost immediately: he sees Love only briefly, coming from a certain direction; when he hears him speak, the words of Love come from the lover's heart. In the three visions preceding that of Chapter XXIV the Lesser Aspect of Love had been represented: Chapter IX was exclusively concerned with this Aspect, while Chapters III and XII contained a shift from the Greater to the Lesser. And in all three cases this Aspect had been taken as being identical with the lover's feelings at the moment, so far below the level of the Greater Aspect that he could not understand him in the two cases when this being spoke to him. Here, in Chapter XXIV, as we have seen, there is no shift from the Greater to the Lesser; at the same time, however, there is no contrast between the mood of the god and that of the lover-at-the-moment. He has understood him completely, for now the god is speaking from within the lover's heart. For the first time the lover's feelings of the moment have been raised to the height of the Greater Aspect.

And after this high point reached in Chapter XXIV we shall not see the figure of Love again. But surely the young lover does. In that final vision which he withholds from us, which inspired him to stop writing about his love for Beatrice until he could do so more worthily, he must have seen Beatrice in glory; already in Chapter XLI he had caught a glimpse of

> . . . a lady held in reverence,
> splendid in light, and through her radiance
> the pilgrim spirit looks upon her being.

And if he sees, at the end, the celestial radiance of Beatrice, how could the figure of Love be absent from his imagination—Love who had proclaimed the Christlike nature of Beatrice and her likeness to himself. And this time, too, the lover must have been raised to the level of the Greater Aspect, never again to sink below it.

Robert Hollander (essay date 1974)

SOURCE: "*Vita Nuova*: Dante's Perceptions of Beatrice (1974)," in *Medieval & Renaissance Texts & Studies,* Vol. 23, 1983, pp. 372-89.

[*Hollander examines Dante's use of* vedere *and various terms related to seeing to reach a better understanding of the final vision of Beatrice in heaven, which the* Vita Nuova *refers to but withholds from the reader.*]

If one were asked to guess how many times Beatrice appears to Dante in the *Vita Nuova* one might, in view of Dante's fondness for the number, very well guess nine times. Since that is probably the correct answer it is at least a little surprising that no *dantista*—at least none known to this writer—has even made any effective attempt at a count. There are various objects of various kinds of "seeing" in the *Vita Nuova*, as will be described below. This discussion will be dominantly concerned with the appearances of Beatrice. An "appearance of Beatrice" is defined simply as what is recorded of a single particular awareness of Beatrice as actually being in Dante's presence, whether this awareness come from actual encounter, dream, or fantastic imagining. It is likely that from Dante's point of view one of the most important subjects of the *Vita Nuova* is its record of Beatrice's appearances. For this reason it does not matter whether a single event is described once or twice (i.e., in prose *and* in verse). What we wish to determine, first of all, is the number of her appearances to Dante. It may then be fruitful to study the qualities of these appearances. In order that the following survey he complete and clear, it will include specific apparitions of others to Dante as well as specific "non-apparitions" of Beatrice—occasions on which Dante expects or hopes to see her but does not.

1. Beatrice appears to Dante (they are both in their ninth year) dressed in crimson (II, 3).

2. Nine years to the day later, dressed in white, between two *gentili donne*, she appears to Dante and grants him her salutation (III, 1).

3. That same day Dante, while sleeping, has a *maravigliosa visione* of Beatrice held in the arms of Amore, a vision which is the subject of the first poem of the *Vita Nuova* (III, 3-7, 10-12).

4. In church Dante sees Beatrice but is thought to be admiring the lady who sits in his line of sight; she will serve as his *schermo de la veritade* (V,1).

    4a. Dante sees the corpse of *una donna giovane e di gentile aspetto molto* whom he had seen several times in the company of Beatrice (VIII, 1-2).

    4b. Amore appears in Dante's imagination and announces the name of a second "screen lady," as is recounted in the following sonnet (IX, 3-6, 9-12).

5. Beatrice, "passando per alcuna parte," denies Dante her *dolcissimo salutare* because of the gossip concerning Dante's infatuation with the second "screen lady" (x, 2).

    (5a. We are told that whenever Beatrice appeared Dante was filled with charity; here no specific occasion is alluded to (xi, 1).)

    5b. Amore appears in Dante's sleep, as he had done many times before, and urges Dante to justify himself against slanderous gossip by means of verse addressed to Beatrice (xii, 3-9).

6. A friend takes Dante along to a marriage feast where he sees Beatrice among the ladies (xiv, 4).

    6a. Dante, finding himself in the company of certain ladies, is relieved not to find Beatrice among them so that he can discuss the nature of his love with them (xviii, 2).

    6b. Dante goes to the funeral of Beatrice's father; he overhears departing ladies describe Beatrice's grief, but does not see or hear her himself (xxii, 3-5).

7. Dante, ill in his room, has wild imaginings of Beatrice's death and ascent to Heaven; his *erronea fantasia* is so strong that he even sees women covering Beatrice's head with a white veil and the last rites being administered to her; the central canzone recounts these imaginings (xxiii, 4-10, 17-28).

8. Dante sees Beatrice preceded by Guido's Giovanna after imagining that Amore had appeared to cheer him; the two episodes are united when they are recounted in a sonnet (xxiv, 2, 3-5, 7-9).

    8a. A year after her death, Dante, sketching an angel, has a thought of Beatrice which he records in the "anniversary poem" (xxxiv, 1-3).

    8b. Dante sees a *gentile donna* looking compassionately at him (xxxv, 2). &. He sees her several more times (xxxvi, 2).

9. In his imagination Dante seems to see Beatrice, as young as she was at their first encounter, and, as then, dressed in crimson; he repents his desire for a new love (xxix, 1-2).

    9a. In a sonnet Dante describes the heavenly voyage of his *pensero/sospiro*; it ascends to Beatrice, and though Dante's earthbound intelligence cannot understand what his heavenly thought comprehends of Beatrice's miraculous being, he does know that it is fully occupied with Beatrice alone, since he frequently hears it say her name (xli, 3-7, 10-13).

The final vision of chapter xlii will be discussed later.

In the prose of the *Vita Nuova* Dante makes use of three different modes of seeing:

    1) actual seeing

    2) seeing in dream

    3) imaginary or fantasized seeing.

For each of these modes of seeing there is a specialized vocabulary of vision and/or appearance. There are no observable inconsistencies in Dante's use of these three vocabularies. None, at least, if we confine our investigation to their use in the prose of the work. As will be pointed out later, there are a number of inconsistencies between various interjoined *prose* and *poesie*. Since it is the prose, written as a self-conscious unit, which gives us our best clues as to Dante's intentions in the *Vita Nuova*, it is only logical that it should here receive the major share of our attention.

Let us begin by examining Nicolò Mineo's assertion [in *Profetismo e Apocalittica in Dante*] that Dante uses the terms *visione*, *imaginazione*, and *fantasia* without apparent distinction. *Imaginazione* and *fantasia* are in fact used almost interchangeably to denote the third mode of seeing. In describing things seen *imaginazione* is used a total of seventeen times, *fantasia*, eight. The appearances of Beatrice to which they refer are items 7 and 9 in the preceding list; the appearances of Amore to which they refer are 4b and 8. In all four cases Dante explicitly informs his reader that the scene he describes occurred in his own mind and nowhere else—that it is a fantasy, an imagining, something limited to his own consciousness. *Visione*, on the other hand, *pace* Mineo, has two uses, neither of which is to be confused with the uses of *fantasia* and *imaginazione* in our third mode. The word is used only seven times in the *libello* ["little book"], and only thrice after the initial cluster of four which describes Dante's dream of Beatrice in the arms of Amore (item 3). In this first case the word joins with another, *sonno* ["dream"], to make the nature of the *visione* clear: it is a seeing in dream. The next time the word is used (item 5b), it describes Amore's appearance in a dream. Again it is accompanied by *sonno*. Items 3 and 5b are, strictly speaking, the only two dreams recorded in the *Vita Nuova*. One kind of *visione*, then, is that which occurs in dream. Our examination of the second kind lies ahead of us.

Thus far we have accounted for two kinds, or modes, of seeing in the *Vita Nuova*. But as our initial catalogue of Beatrice's appearances to Dante makes clear, a third kind of seeing has the lion's share: actual seeing. Six of Beatrice's appearances to Dante are of this nature: items 1, 2, 4, 5, 6, and 8. Is there a characteristic vocabulary at work here too? It is again simpler to proceed by means of a catalogue.

(1) Beatrice's first appearance to Dante: *apparire* is used five times, *vedere* once.

(2) Beatrice's second appearance: again *apparire*.

(4) Dante sees Beatrice in church: *vedere*.

(5) When Beatrice denies Dante her *salutare* her actions are described directly, and there is no verb of appearance or perception used, simply direct narrative description.

(6) Dante sees Beatrice at the wedding feast: *vedere*.

(8) Dante sees Giovanna followed by Beatrice: *vedere* is used for both sightings.

From this description it is evident that in the *Vita Nuova* even common words like *vedere* and *apparire* are also used "technically" in a vocabulary of appearance and vision that is impressively careful. To summarize these findings as briefly as possible: the *Vita Nuova* yields the following schema of modes of appearance and seeing (this table refers only to appearances of Beatrice to Dante):

KINDS OF SEEING
1) in actuality (1,2,4,5,6,8)
2) in dream (3)
3) in fantasy (7,9)

DESIGNATIVE TERMS
[1] —
[2] *sonno* and *visione*
[3] *imaginazione* and *fantasia*

MODAL TERMS
[1] *apparire* or vedere
[2] *parere, parea, vedere, apparire*
[3 *parere, parea, vedere, apparire*]

Discussion of Dante's final vision will return to this schema.

We set out to investigate the number and quality of Beatrice's appearances to Dante. She appears to him nine times in three different modes. Each of these modes has its own vocabulary of appearance and vision. Dante most likely limited his reports of her "formal" appearances to nine consciously—Beatrice is a nine. And for this reason, it might be argued, the references to his having seen her on other occasions or generic references to the fact that he has seen her are limited to being just that—references—they are not formally "appearances of Beatrice." Similarly, apparitions of Amore and of the *gentile donna*, though they variously share the modes of appearance and seeing in which Dante perceives Beatrice, are not to be considered as having as significant a function in the work as the apparitions of Beatrice. Their function is that of a supportive scaffolding for Dante's major purpose, which is to be *scriba Beatricis* ("Beatrice's recorder")—not of what she says, of what she is. Yet Dante's treatment of Amore deserves closer attention. For it too reveals the consis-

tency of Dante's distinction-making process in the *Vita Nuova*.

Caught between the conventions of thirteenth-century love poetry (as represented by his early lyrics) and the requirements of his own new poetic life (as represented by the prose of the *Vita Nuova*), Dante is forced to a somewhat ungainly compromise. Until we reach the twenty-fifth chapter of the work we must be prepared to encounter Amore in one of two guises: either as an actual "character" or as an internalized agency of Dante's being. Descriptions of his external behaviors occur in only four places in the prose. The following description proceeds in the order of Dante's composition, that is, from the earlier poems to the accompanying prose.

1. (3) In the first sonnet of the *Vita Nuova* Amore appears to Dante holding Beatrice in his arms. The verbs used to describe his appearance and Dante's beholding are *apparire* and *vedere* (III, 11, 12). In short, without the accompanying prose the action of the sonnet might be taken by a reader as either being or pretending to be the recounting of actual events. Dante's prose description of these events, however, makes it clear that the whole experience occurred during his sleep. The words used to describe the appearance of Amore ("uno segnore di pauroso aspetto") and Beatrice, as well as Dante's perceptions of them, carefully separate seeing in dream and appearance in dream from actual seeing and actual appearance.

1a. [(4a) In the sonnet "Piangete, amanti, poi che piange Amore" (VIII, 4-6) Dante sees Amore weeping ("ch'io 'l vidi lamentare in forma vera"—v, 10) over the dead form of the "donna giovane e di gentile aspetto molto." In the prose (VIII, 1-3) Amore is not mentioned at all. He has momentarily been excused from the fiction.]

2. (4b) In the sonnet "Cavalcando l'altr'ier per un cammino" (IX, 9-12) Dante finds Amore on the road ("trovai Amore in mezzo de la via"—v, 3). Once again in the sonnet Amore performs as an actual "character." In the prose (IX, 1-7) he is again described periphrastically and appears only in Dante's imagination.

3. (5b) The *ballata* which follows Dante's second and last dream in the *Vita Nuova* (XII, 3-9) does not involve Amore as a "character" who interacts with Dante. In the prose, where he does appear, he is once more not called by name, and once again (as in item 3) is presented as having been seen in dream.

4. (8) In the sonnet "Io mi senti' svegliar dentro a lo core" (XXIV, 7-9) Dante sees Amore coming toward him ("e poi vidi venir da fungi Amore"—v, 3). Though in the sonnet he appears as an actual "character," in the accompanying prose he is described as being in-

stead "una imaginazione d'Amore" (XXIV, 2). His appearance is thus sharply contrasted with those of Giovanna and Beatrice, who are *seen*, since they are actually present, both in the sonnet (XXIV, 8) and in the prose (XXIV, 3).

What emerges from this summary is a perhaps surprising fact: not once in the prose of the **Vita Nuova** is Amore treated as having actual existence; he is allowed this only in four of the sonnets, which had been previously composed. One of the aesthetic and rational problems of the **Vita Nuova** is Dante's rather confusing treatment of Amore. It is a problem which he himself partly acknowledges in the brilliant if self-serving twenty-fifth chapter of the work, one of the most brilliant passages of literary criticism written between the time of Servius and Macrobius and the close of the thirteenth century. The proximate cause of Dante's examination of poetic license in this passage is the contradiction raised by Amore's actualistic behavior in the sonnet of XXIV after what Dante has said of him in the preceding prose. Amore as internalized mechanism of Love runs the length of the **Vita Nuova**. He first appears in Chapter II and he is heard of for the last time in the final sonnet (XLI, 10). As a "character" he is essentially taken off after his appearance in the last dream recorded in the work (XII, 3-9). One can sense Dante's growing embarrassment with his presence as "character" in several passages. The only time after XII that he is treated as "character" is in the sonnet (XXIV, 7-9) that is the cause of his final dismissal as "character." It is as though his re-appearance in the *monna Vanna / monna Bice* sonnet were the last straw. And if we study his first appearance, which is conjoined with that of Beatrice, we can see that the author of the prose **Vita Nuova** never wanted him to be taken literally: the Amore who takes control of Dante's soul does so "per la vertù che li dava la mia imaginazione" (II, 7). This is the first use of the word *imaginazione* in the work, and it sharply contrasts with the four uses of *apparire* and the use of *vedere* which describe the appearance of Beatrice. It is of some use to understand that the Dante of the **Vita Nuova** was as careful in keeping distinctions between fiction modeled on "history" and fiction that is "fabula"—the *bella menzogna* of *Convivio*—as was the author of the *Commedia*.

Fiction that is modeled on history—medieval *argumentum*—is the basic fictive mode both of the **Vita Nuova** and of the *Commedia*. This does not necessarily mean that either Dante (or the present writer) believed that the actions recorded in either work actually occurred in history, but only that this is their fictional convention. Dante did not labor under the delusion that he had actually visited the afterworld. The question of his sense of the historicity of Beatrice is more complicated. While there may be almost enough documentation to suggest hat the **Vita Nuova** records historical events in a historical relationship, whether or not Beatrice was Bice Portinari, whether or not she existed at all, is not terribly important. The next step taken by critics who take that first step is, however, generally the wrong one: if she is not "real," she must be "allegorical." While questions concerning her actual existence are not terribly important, what is centrally important is to grasp the significance of Dante's treatment of her as actual. The same remark may be applied (and with some force) to the *Divina Commedia*. Dante was ahead of his contemporaries in this too, for he realized the aesthetic and intellectual superiority of a convention of fiction that is mimetic in nature, partly because he was a Thomist on this point, at least, and understood the implications for a poet of the priority of knowledge held through the senses and partly because he was the kind of man and poet who could not think without reference to the senses, for whom *nomina sunt consequentia rerum* (XIII, 4).

There are many apparitions or sightings in the **Vita Nuova**. It is at least likely that the numerologically inclined Dante gave some of these a numerological structure. It is also likely that such a structure would involve Beatrice rather than anyone else, and that its number would be a nine. However, an agreement can be reached that Dante records nine appearances of Beatrice in the **Vita Nuova** (six in actuality, two in fantasy, one in dream), it is also true that this accountancy does not include his most important vision of Beatrice, the *mirabile visione* that concludes the *libello*. This vision is unlike all the previous nine sightings in many respects. One of the more important of these is that it is undescribed. In the preceding chapter Dante tells us that his thought ("il mio pensero"—XLI, 3) flew up beyond the *primo mobile* (and thus into the Empyrean), saw a *donna* honored there (it can only have been Beatrice), but that what it had seen is beyond the capacity of Dante's intellect and that his thought spoke wholly of his lady (XLI, 3-7). The sonnet, the last poem of the work, is in basic accord with the prose and makes the identity of Beatrice specific (XLI, 13). This chapter does not technically record a sighting of Beatrice by Dante. The point it makes is that he was then incapable of seeing with heavenly vision. But if Dante is unable to understand, within the fiction, the implications of what his *pensero* returns from heaven with, his readers have perhaps received enough training at this stage in the work to understand what the character cannot. The play is taken out of our hands before we have time to give the problem much thought, for, suddenly, in chapter XLII, Dante has been able to follow his thought to Heaven. His intellect, as though trained by the near-vision of "Oltre la spera che più larga gira," has finally been granted what has always been the goal of the pilgrimage in love that is the **Vita Nuova**. To put this another way, his intellect has finally achieved comprehension of the new life.

The language with which Dante describes the fact of

the vision is interesting: "Appresso questo sonetto *apparve* a me una mirabile *visione*, ne la quale io *vidi* cose che mi fecero proporre di non dire più di questa benedetta infino a tanto che io potesse più degnamente *trattare* di lei" (XLII, 1—italics added). As has been previously noted, up to this moment in the *Vita Nuova* Dante has distinguished three vocabularies of appearance and vision. Now he brings together his vocabularies of seeing in dream (*visione*) and of actual seeing (*vedere*). (Since *apparire* has been assimilated by each of these two categories before, it is not clear at first which one it joins here.) Is the *mirabile visione* to be understood as dream seeing, or as actual seeing? The correct answer is probably neither, though more the latter than the former. On two previous occasions, when he recorded dreams, Dante has clearly told us they were dreams. Since he does not do so now, we have no reason to suppose that the vision is a dream. With regard to actual seeing in the *Vita Nuova*, it is limited, naturally enough, to perceiving the things apparent on this earth, which is to see through a glass darkly. And while the ability to discern what is actually before the eyes of the earthly beholder is essentially the same ability which enables the organs of sight to see face to face, the objects seen in the mystical vision, even when they are presented to mortal sight, are unrecognizable unless the beholder has undergone that change which Paul was believed to have referred to in I Corinthians 13:12. Dante's *mirabile visione* is not a vision in a dream, a Macrobian veiled presentation of the truth, as were the first two dreams; nor is it to be confounded with perception of earthly reality (the preceding sonnet makes that absolutely clear); it should most likely be taken as the result of a *raptus*, of a sudden seeing *in gloria*, with heavenly sight. The words *apparire, visione,* and *vedere* have gained an exalted context and new meanings.

Visione has a biblical counterpart—there are many fewer than one might think to choose from in the New Testament—that might well have been in Dante's mind. In all of St. Paul's works the word *visio* occurs only once: "Si gloriari oportet (non expedit quidem), veniam autem ad visiones et revelationes Domini" (2 Cor. 12:1). It is this passage which leads into the description of his *raptus*: "Scio hominem in Christo ante annos quattuordecim, sive in corpore nescio sive extra corpus nescio, Deus scit, raptum huiusmodi usque ad tertium caelum" (12:2). All one can claim is that if the experience recorded in *Vita Nuova* XLII is to be thought of as Pauline *raptus*, the word *visione* is likely to come from the same source. This does not seem an unlikely hypothesis, especially since Paul, in possession of knowledge it is not lawful to utter, continues as follows: "Nam, etsi voluero gloriari, non ero insipiens, veritatem enim dicam; parco autem, ne quis me existimet supra id quod videt in me aut aliquid audit ex me" (12:6). His disclaimers are at least likely to be behind those of Dante, who intends "di non dire più di

questa benedetta infino a tanto che io potesse più degnamente trattare di lei" (XLII, 1).

The verb *trattare* may also have a Pauline context here. Paul's use of the verb is indeed its single occurrence in the New Testament. He urges Timothy to show himself to God as an "operarium inconfusibilem, recte tractantem verbum veritatis" (2 Tim. 2:15). The last four words describe Dante's desire in Chapter XLII rather well. *Trattare*, however, has a more immediate context in the *Vita Nuova* that should not be overlooked. It is used a total of fourteen times. Its first use has reference to writing about Beatrice (v, 3) as an earthly being, and does not seem to have any unusual overtone. The second *trattare* of the *Vita Nuova* is used in a technical sense to describe the middle three stanzas of the *canzone* "Donne ch'avete intelletto d'amore." The subject of these three stanzas is the desire of the angels in Heaven to have Beatrice in their midst. Their request is spoken to by no less a being than God Himself, in His only speaking part in the *Vita Nuova* (the influence of Guinizelli's "Al cor gentil" is probably felt here). It seems possible that Dante's use of the word might reflect not only his technical sense of the division of a *canzone*, but the subject treated in that part of the *canzone*—things heavenly.

The next occurrence of the word (two uses in XX and one, retrospectively, in XXI) is entirely without such overtones. Here Dante, in the most overtly Guinizellian poem of the collection ("Amore e 'l cor gentil sono una cosa"), treats "philosophically" (and not "theologically") the nature of Amore. The next use (XXV, 3), in a discussion of love poetry as written by vernacular and "lettered" poets, seems to have the same meaning—a "philosophical" treatment of a subject in verse. Then, however, *trattare* enters the work for the penultimate time in a highly charged cluster (used six times in ten lines—XXVII, 2). Beatrice is dead and Dante will not "treat" her death. For the purposes of this investigation it is important to see that again the subject—though it is *not* treated—is "theological." The next chapter explains that Beatrice was a nine, or miracle (XXIX, 3). And in this chapter the second reason Dante gives for not treating Beatrice's death looks strangely familiar if it is seen in the perspective of chapter XLII: "ancora non sarebbe sufficiente a trattare come si converrebbe di ciò" (XXVIII, 2)—"infino a tanto che io potesse più degnamente trattare di led" (XLII, 1). To treat of Beatrice is to treat of high things indeed. Of the fourteen uses of *trattare* in the *Vita Nuova* nine (and here no further numerological point is intended) indicate the treatment of celestial *materia* ("subjects"). Three elements are involved in this heightened use of *trattare*: a thought of Beatrice desired in Heaven, the fact of Beatrice's death (and thus her implied presence in Heaven), and the final vision of Beatrice in Heaven. In the *Vita Nuova* the only "treatment" we are allowed to read is the first. The second is refused and the third only promised.

After the many purely technical and "philosophical" uses of *trattare* in the *Convivio*, the verb—now with "theological" overtones—reappears (like so much else in the *Vita Nuova*) in the *Commedia: Inferno* I, 8; *Paradiso* IV, 27; *Paradiso* XXV, 95. While all three uses are to the point here, the last one is particularly interesting. Dante's final response to St. James is to say that his Hope is based on scriptures in both Testaments (Isaiah 61:7, 10 and Revelation 7:9-17). Both these passages tell of the souls of the blessed sitting in Glory. Dante refers to the second of the two as follows: "là dove tratta de le bianche stole" (cf. Rev. 7:14: "Hi sunt qui venerunt de tribulatione magna et laverunt stolas suas et dealbaverunt eas in sanguine Agni"). Is not this precisely where and how we may presume Dante saw Beatrice in the *mirabile visione*? Seated in the presence of God in the sure and certain hope of the resurrection. At least one may now advance this fairly common view of Beatrice's heavenly situation with a particular text in view: Revelation 7:9-17. For where Paul does not recount his "visiones et revelationes Domini" ("visions and revelations of God"), John explicitly describes what Paul must have seen. In a sense it is he who offers one like Dante, who wanted to know what Paul saw, the only canonical description available. If Dante had previously thought of the form of his experience of the final vision in terms of a *raptus Pauli*, its content could come only from John's Apocalypse.

It is not until *Paradiso* XXXI, 70-93, that Dante will actually see Beatrice sit in Glory. That is very likely what his *pensero / sospiro* saw in the thirty-first and final poem of the *Vita Nuova*. And what she is said to gaze upon in the last line of the *Vita Nuova*, "la faccia di colui *qui est per omnia secula benedictus*," is what she gazes upon now: "sorrise e riguardommi; / poi si tornò a l'etterna fontana" (Par. XXXI, 92-93). Dante coming closer to seeing God by seeing Beatrice see God is a common element in both passages.

And so, if Dante ostensibly maintains a Pauline official silence about the content of the *mirabile visione* at the conclusion of the *Vita Nuova*, he also conspires, overtly as well as tacitly, to let all but *li più semplici* ("the most simple, innocent") of the *Vita Nuova*'s readers have a fairly sure idea of what his memory retained of the vision, both its form (Pauline) and its content (Johannine). If we had nothing else, the two little verbs that tell us Beatrice's condition and activity in Paradise—she knows and she gazes—are really enough to let the major fact about her be a most salient one. "E di venire a ciò io studio quanto posso, sì com'ella *sae* veracemente . . . quella benedetta Beatrice, la quale gloriosamente *mira* ne la faccia di colui *qui est per omnia secula benedictus*." In the first twenty-seven chapters of the *Vita Nuova* Beatrice is described in the "historical past," that is, by the past absolute. In the next fourteen chapters Dante looks back to the dead Beatrice in the same tense. After the *mirabile visione* a small grammatical miracle not only resurrects her from the dead, it even stands as a rebuke to the backward-looking intention of the entire *libello*: "*Incipit vita nuova*. Sotto la quale rubrica io trovo scritte le parole le quali è mio intendimento d'assemplare in questo libello." The liver of the new life must not be content to be the historian of his first awakening. As long as Dante is only able to live in his memory of past events he cannot live the new life. His new life may be said to be truly undertaken once he can speak of Beatrice in the present, as the living soul *in Gloria* who will draw him on up. The *incipit* of the *Vita Nuova* is the unvoiced *explicit* as well.

For these reasons it seems proper to look upon Dante's final vision of Beatrice as the first one, as an experience of such different order from that of her previous nine appearances that it should be set aside from these in our minds (as it certainly seems to have been in Dante's) as a kind of epilogue that transcends the rest of the work and which serves, as many have said before, as prologue to the great poem.

P. J. Klemp (essay date 1984)

SOURCE: "The Women in the Middle: Layers of Love in Dante's *Vita Nuova*," in *Italica,* Vol. 61, No. 3, Autumn, 1984, pp. 185-94.

[*In the following essay, Klemp explores the the ways in which Dante had revised his understanding of his love for Beatrice by the time he wrote the* Convivio.]

One reason why Dante's contemporary readers, like his modern ones, find his poems difficult is because he is a revisionist author whose later works reinterpret earlier ones. In the *Vita Nuova*, for example, we meet a "donna gentile" whose identity is not revealed. The *Convivio* then reflects on Dante's earlier writings, including the *Rime* and *Vita Nuova*, and insists that this donna gentile is Filosofia. Finally, the *Purgatorio* looks back on all of these works and transforms the well-meaning donna into a vain creature. Dante's acts of revisionist literary history prevent us from discussing any of the writings in isolation. The *Purgatorio* blurs and undermines the *Vita Nuova*, in effect erasing all of its moral lessons. But the *Convivio* redefines our view of the earlier work, teaching us how to read it well. I will examine the *Convivio*'s instructions about allegory to see how Dante uses them, retrospectively, to reveal a structural pattern in the *Vita Nuova*. Throughout the *Vita Nuova*, Dante playfully reminds his readers that they cannot identify his real love any better than they can comprehend his book of memory. After he writes his first poem about love ("A ciascun' alma presa"), he lets his friends read it: "A questo sonetto fue risposto da molti e di diverse sentenzie." Dante happily notes that all of his readers missed "Lo verace giudicio" (III, 15).

Flagrant revisionism accounts for many misinterpretations. The *Convivio* explains that in much of his early poetry—particularly the *Rime* and *Vita Nuova*—Dante wrote about "la mia condizione sotto figure d'altre cose" ("my condition under the cover of other things"). The early works contain nothing to suggest such an allegorical reading, but this does not prevent Dante from identifying the flaws that turn his readers into misreaders:

> né li uditori erano tanto bene disposti, che
> avessero sì leggiere le fittizie parole apprese;
> né sarebbe data loro fede a la sentenza vera,
> come a la fittizia, però che di vero si credea
> del tutto che disposto fosse a quello amore
> [Beatrice], che non si credeva di questo
> [Filosofia].
>
> (II.xii.8)

Readers receive the blame for loving fiction and attending to matters amatory, while the author glosses over his part in the revisionism that misleads us. If, however, we become educable readers by following his revisionism, this statement from the *Convivio* alerts us to the parallel paths of love and literary interpretation. As Giuseppe Mazzotta argues [in *Dante, Poet of the Desert*], the *Vita Nuova*, like the *Convivio*, is a story of "self-reading": "Dante suggests—along with the more conventional metaphoric bond between love and poetry—the profound links which connect love and interpretation." Dante indicates that, as a lover and as a writer, he must first mislead us in order to help us discover the truth, and this explains much of his revisionism. The key decoys to lead us astray in the *Vita Nuova* are the ladies whom Dante pretends to love in order to maintain the secrecy of his love for Beatrice.

He describes the first lady as a "schermo de la veritade" ("a screen or defense of the truth," V, 3); the second, another "simulato amore" ("pretended love") is also a screen or defense (IX, 6). Just as Dante hides his love behind a screen in the *Vita Nuova*, so in the *Convivio* he discusses literary interpretation in terms of layers or coverings. He describes the relationship of the allegorical and literal levels as "una veritade ascosa sotto belle menzogna" ("a truth hidden beneath a beautiful lie," II.i.3). It appears, then, that the *Convivio* encourages us to revise our view of the *Vita Nuova*'s structure by recognizing its parallels with the fourfold method of interpretation. Because poetry is born of love in the *Vita Nuova*, Dante's book of memory—revised by his statements in the *Convivio*—illustrates the correspondence between the pattern of the love experience and the pattern of allegorical discourse.

Many episodes in the *Vita Nuova* seem to be extraneous or confusing unless we recognize the correspondence between the four levels of polysemous writing and the book's four central women (the screen-ladies, the mortal Beatrice, Filosofia, and the spiritual Beatrice). Why, for instance, does Dante bother to introduce any screen-ladies? Scholars have frequency ignored these characters. One critic writes: "We will skip over the chapters where Dante uses the screen-woman." Less extreme, [Robert Hollander] underestimates their importance: "apparitions of Amore and of the *gentile donna* . . . are not to be considered as having as significant a function in the work as the apparitions of Beatrice." Without the screen-ladies, as I will argue, there can be no vision of Beatrice. The functions of the screen-ladies will lead to another question: why does Dante's relationship with Beatrice proceed so erratically? They meet at the age of nine (II). She reappears nine years later, for no apparent reason, and greets him, whereupon he retreats (III). And then she shuns him because of nasty rumors (X). They are reconciled before her death occurs in Chapter XXVIII, but he eventually finds another lady, Filosofia. Finally, he has a vision of the spiritual Beatrice wearing the "vestimenta sanguigne" ("bloodlike garment") of their first meeting, "e pareami giovane in simile etade in quale io prima la vidi" ("and she seemed as young to me as when I first saw her," XXXIX, 1). Have we been going around in circles, only to end up at Dante's and Beatrice's meeting when they were nine years old? No, we have instead learned that the pattern of the women in Dante's life, like the pattern of fourfold allegorical interpretation, is arranged in concentric circles. Since the women offer different kinds of love—simulated, earthly, philosophical, and divine—one layer of love leads to the next only when they are placed in their proper order.

Sequence is crucial to Dante's view of life and literature, or what the *Convivio* calls matters "naturale ed artificiale" (II.i.12). He repeatedly uses the words "impossibile ed inrazionale" to characterize the craftsman who builds an ark before he has prepared the wood, or a house before he has established its foundation (II.i.10-12). Hence an allegorist attempts the impossible if he presents the allegorical level before the literal, because he must lead his readers from the concrete "sobietto" ("subject") to the more abstract "forma" ("form") (II.i. 10). In the same section of the *Convivio*, he tells us that "sempre lo litterale dee andare innanzi" ("the literal must always come first") for one simple reason: "però che in ciascuna cosa che ha dentro e di fuori, è impossibile venire al dentro se prima non si viene al di fuori" (8-9). If the craftsman confuses this sequence, his efforts are also irrational: "Ancora, posto che possibile fosse, sarebbe inrazionale, cioè fuori d'ordine, e però con molta fatica e con molto errore si procederebbe" (13). As is well known, the correct sequence is the literal level, composed of "le parole fittizie" (3), which contains all other meanings (8); the allegorical, "una veritate ascosa sotto belle menzogna" (3); the moral, characterized by its ability to teach (5); and, finally, the anagogical, or "sovrasenso" ("transcendent meaning") dealing with "le superne cose de l'etternal gloria" ("the supernal things of eternal glory") (6). Only when this sequence is in its proper order can the allegorical writer, and presumably his reader, proceed beyond fictions toward a heavenly vision.

The narrative equivalent of this sequence appears in Chapter V of the *Vita Nuova*. Beatrice has already entered Dante's life, inexplicably disappeared for nine years, and returned—as "una maravigliosa visione" ("a miraculous vision," III, 3)—to greet him. He promptly retreats to the loneliness of his room. Their relationship remains ambiguous until, in Chapter V, two new women are introduced sitting in a church, Dante tells us that "io era in luogo dal quale vedea la mia beatitudine," Beatrice (V, 1). She is, significantly, an earthly obstacle placed between Dante and the divine "regina de la gloria" ("queen of glory"), the Madonna, about whom words are being spoken, Dante's mind lingers on the mortal woman when yet another buffer appears: "nel mezzo di lei [Beatrice] e di me per la retta linea sedea una gentile donna" ("on the straight line between her and me sat a gentle lady"). With the screen lady's appearance, the layers of love are assuming their proper order, leading Dante and Beatrice to establish a love relationship after a nine-year delay.

This seating arrangement or sequence (Dante, the screen-lady, Beatrice, and the Madonna) helps to explain the erratic movement of Chapters II and III, with all of their entrances, greetings, departures, and retreats. To use the language of the *Convivio*, before the church scene Dante the author has yet to establish his concrete foundation or subject, which is not merely love, but first the lowest form of love (the "simulato amore" or "simulacra," if—as Charles S. Singleton argues—Amore's statement in Chapter XII refers to the screen-ladies). The layers of love are as important as the layers of allegory, for a craftsman would find it impossible and irrational to begin with the higher love. His pattern of exposition resembles that of the allegorist, who cannot begin with the "sovrasenso." One must move from layer to layer, eventually recognizing that each layer (except the last), however enticing it looks initially, can in fact lead to the next. So Dante's early love for Beatrice in Chapter II is not only premature, but also impossible and irrational. He must begin at the beginning, so he requires the buffer of a "bella menzogna" to hide "una veritate"—that is, a screen-lady to conceal his love for Beatrice.

When Amore uses an enigmatic analogy taken from geometry, he endorses the idea of love as a circle to be penetrated: " 'Ego tanquam centrum circuli, cui simili modo se habent circumferentie partes; tu autem non

sic' " (XII, 4). If we recall the *Convivio*'s explanation of allegory moving from the outside to the inside, where we find the "sovrasenso" (II.i.9), we recognize its correspondence to the pattern of the love experience in the *Vita Nuova*. Amore, the personified essence of love, is located in the center, and the women's different loves form concentric circles around him. Dante's journey will consist of moving from the outermost circle to the center. Before the appearance of the first screen lady, the craftsman behind the *Vita Nuova* shows us the consequences of moving too quickly to an inner circle of love without first passing through the outer circle. Dante the lover must proceed from the lower (outside) to the higher (inside) kinds of love, from a "simulato amore" to a real love—and ultimately to *the* real love, as Amore later yields to God. Before the layers fall into place in the church scene, all we find are Dante's and Beatrice's abrupt entrances and exits, "con molta fatica e con molto errore" ("with much toil and many errors").

Although Dante's line of vision in the church scene could potentially extend through two loves (the screen-lady and Beatrice) and arrive at the highest love present (the Madonna), it does not. Filosofia and the spiritual Beatrice will later help him make this leap. In church, however, his vision stops with Beatrice, an earthly love whom he assumes to be the final truth. He is ironically trapped by the very weaknesses that the *Convivio* later attributes to his readers: a love of matters amatory and a reluctance to face "la sentenza vera" ("the true meaning," II.xii.8). Earthly love is, at this point, the highest love that he can acknowledge. As his journey momentarily returns to a series of erratic movements, Dante vacillates between two layers of love, simulated and true. One screen lady replaces another (IX-X), and Dante finds himself separated from Beatrice (IX) or shunned by her (IX). These forward and backward movements resemble those of an inexperienced writer or reader of allegory who, like this lover, lacks perspective. Just as a naive writer or reader might lack a clear vision of the "sovrasenso" to which all his efforts lead, so the lover in the *Vita Nuova* lacks an educator (Filosofia will arrive later) and a sincere commitment to the highest love.

In these early parts of the *Vita Nuova*, Dante briefly mentions—though he does not seem to understand—that Beatrice is linked to higher levels of reality, just as the allegorical sense is linked to the moral and anagogical. The famous *canzone* in Chapter XIX, "Donne ch'avete intelletto d'amore," illustrates Dante's limited perspective. Beatrice, he tells us, is "quanto de ben pò far nature" (line 49), referring to the world of the senses in which the lovers live. But she is also "disiata in sommo cielo" (line 29); while this poem's other speakers (the angel, God, and Amore) all understand what this divine perspective implies, Dante the lover does not. They recognize that Beatrice will become a spiritual being. Dante lets them speak, but he continues to focus on Beatrice's physical appearance:

> Color di perle ha quasi, in forma quale
> convene a donna aver, non for misura.
>
> (lines 47-48)

Even when he hints at her higher powers, Dante describes them in amatory terms that are deeply rooted in a physical being and not in a soul:

> De li occhi suoi, come ch'ella li mova,
> escono spirti d'amore inflammati,
> che feron li occhi a qual che allor la guati,
> e passan sì che 'l cor ciascun retrova:
> voi le vedete Amor pinto nel viso,
> la 've non pote alcun mirarla fiso.
>
> (lines 51-56)

Although the lover does not comprehend the spiritual significance of the eyes, a theme to be explored in the *Convivio* and *Commedia*, Beatrice is associated with heavenly beings throughout the *Vita Nuova*. While she is alive, however, Dante cannot understand the hints that her life has greater significance, for he is incapable of seeing beyond this earthly layer of love. He lacks an awareness of the corresponding levels of allegory, the moral and anagogical senses, even though outside sources remind him of Beatrice's connections with the spiritual world. Homer echoes through his mind: "'Ella non parea figliuola d'uomo mortale, ma di deo'" ("She appeared to be the daughter not of mortal man, but of God," II, 8; the verb here is very important, as we shall see when Filosofia enters Dante's life). Even people on the street notice: "'Questa non è femmina,'" they say, "'anzi è uno de li bellissimi angeli del cielo'" ("That is not a woman, but one those most beautiful angels of heaven," XXVI, 2). Once Dante faces Beatrice's mortality in Chapter XXIII, his vision begins to improve slightly, as Amore tries to lead him toward God. As in the church scene, Dante again sees Beatrice through the veil of another woman. Giovanna, Guido Cavalcanti's lover, approaches Dante, "E appresso lei, guardando, vidi venure la mirabile Beatrice. Queste donne andaro presso di me così l'una appresso l'altra" (XXIV, 3-4). Although Dante sees no significance in this episode or in the arrangement of the two ladies, Amore does:

> Quella prima è nominate Primavera solo per questa venuta d'oggi; chè io mossi lo imponitore del nome a chiamarla così Primavera, cioè prima verrà lo die che Beatrice si mosterrà dopo la imaginazion del suo fedele. E se anche vogli considerare lo primo nome quo, tanto è quanto dire "prima verrà," però che lo suo nome Giovanna è da quello Giovanni lo quale precedette la verace luce, dicendo: "Ego vox clamantis in deserto: parate viam Domini."
>
> (XXIV, 4)

When we read Amore's typological analysis, we should remember that although John leads us to Christ, we must not stop there. For Christ states that He is in turn the means by which we arrive at a higher love: "Ego sum via, et veritas, et vita. Nemo venit ad Patrem, nisi per me" (John 14:6). After listening to Amore's analogy and etymologies, Dante decides to write a poem but to withhold material that might offend Cavalcanti. This reaction indicates that Dante has grasped little of Amore's lesson about symbolic relationships and layers of love.

When Dante learns of Beatrice's death in Chapter XXVIII, we might assume that his love for her would progress immediately to the spiritual layer. That it does not is less a sign of his ignorance than of his natural inability to skip levels. As we learn from the *Convivio*'s explanation of the strict sequence of senses in allegorical discourse, the moral level must bridge the allegorical and the most difficult "sovrasenso." Dante shows us that he has the beginnings of knowledge, which will eventually lead to revelation, when he describes Beatrice's departure:

> lo segnore de la giustizia chiamoe questa
> gentilissima a gloriare sotto la insegna di
> quella regina benedetta virgo Maria, lo cui
> nome fue in grandissima reverenzia ne le
> parole di questa Beatrice beata.
>
> (XXVIII, 1)

We are immediately reminded of Mary's earlier roles in the *Vita Nuova*, both as a comforter of a distressed Dante (XII) and—more importantly—as "la regina de la gloria" ("the queen of glory") about whom he and Beatrice heard during the church scene (V, 1). When Dante gives further thought to Beatrice, he prematurely tries to interpret her existence in anagogical terms, as a sign of the highest things: "ella era uno nove, cioè uno miracolo, la cui radice, cioè del miracolo, è solamente la mirabile Trinitade" (XXIX, 3). The difficulty Dante experiences in trying to grasp this concept is revealed by the sentence's convolutions and repetitions, as he repeatedly pauses and attempts to explain his point ("cioè . . . cioè").

Even if Dante understood Beatrice's symbolic relationship to the Trinity, his vision is incapable of penetrating the deeper, divine layers of love. Just as he will require Matelda to act as a transition between Virgil and Beatrice in the *Commedia*, so he needs an intermediary in the *Vita Nuova*. Filosofia fills this role, providing further evidence that Dante the lover is about to explore deeper layers of love and the corresponding levels of allegory. His first vision of Filosofia is, significantly, indirect: "Allora vidi una gentile tonne giovane e belle molto, la quale da una finestra mi riguardava" ("Then I saw a young and very beautiful gentlewoman, who was looking at me from a window,"

XXXV, 2). By now, we have grown accustomed to seeing women only through someone or something, with Giovanna walking and the first screen-lady sitting between Dante and Beatrice. Also consistent is Dante's behavior, for he reacts as he did to Beatrice's greeting (III) and rejection (XII): "mi partio dinanzi da li occhi di questa gentile" (XXXV, 3). Although he turns away, he does connect Filosofia with Beatrice:

> Avvenne poi che là ovunque questa donna
>   [Filosofia]
> mi vedea, sì si facea d'una vista pietosa e
>   d'un
> colore palido quasi come d'amore; onde molte
>   fiate
> mi ricordava de la mia nobilissima donna
>   [Beatrice],
> che di simile colore si mostrava tuttavia.
>
>   (XXXVI, 1)

Later, in the *Convivio*, Dante revises this event and conveniently forgets the guilt and sorrow that accompany this new lady:

> Per che io, scutendomi levare dal pensiero del
> primo amore a la virtù di questo, quasi
> maravigliandomi apersi la bocca nel parlare de
> la proposta canzone ["Voi, che 'ntendendo il
> terzo ciel movete"], mostrando la mia
>   condizione
> sotto figure d'altre cose.
>
>   (II.xii.8)

In the *Vita Nuova*, we initially hear nothing about Dante being raised from one love to the next; instead, we hear sighs, groans, and cries of self-condemnation (XXXVII). He resolves to love Filosofia in Chapter XXXVIII, a necessary action—though he does not realize it, as in the *Commedia* he does not comprehend Matelda's role—if he is ever to reach the immortal Beatrice. If we recall Dante's Homeric description of Beatrice in Chapter II ("'Ella non *parea* figliuola d'uomo mortale, ma di deo'" ("'She did not *seem* to be the daughter of a mortal man, but of God'"; italics added), a statement in the *Convivio* clearly indicates that Filosofia is a higher love. Dante describes her, without falling back on Homer, in these words: "questa donna *fu* figlia di Dio, regina di tutto, nobilissima e bellissima Filosofia" ("that lady *was* God's daughter, queen of everything, most noble and beautiful," II.xii.9; italics added). We know that Beatrice also descends from God, but in Dante's estimation after their first meeting, she merely *seemed* to have divine origins. Filosofia, on the other hand, does not at first sight *seem* to be God's daughter; she *is* indeed of heavenly origin, and she will lead Dante to an awareness that Beatrice shares her lineage.

Dante's new love is described as "savia" ("wise,"

XXXVIII, 1), a word that is never to my knowledge applied to Beatrice in the *Vita Nuova*. Hence we see Filosofia as a representative of the moral, instructive sense of allegory, which will lead Dante to the highest sense and highest love. For someone who has undergone a difficult education about the layers of love and allegory, Dante has remarkably little empathy with people who are also looking through veils to find the highest love. In Chapter XL, Dante watches many pilgrims pass by on their way to see "quella imagine benedetta la quale Iesu Cristo lascio a noi per essemplo de la sue bellisima figura". Again we see the use of layers, for the pilgrims cannot see the real Christ, so they turn to an image. Why, Dante wonders naively, are they not thinking about Beatrice and feeling grief for her loss? He fails to recognize that, like him, they must approach the highest love indirectly. Only through a veil may we approach the Son in this life; only through the Son may we reach the Father.

Dante's description of his thought or sign as "lo peregrino spirito" ("the pilgrim spirit") in the sonnet in Chapter XLI (line 8) is a small sign of his increased empathy with the pilgrims of the preceding chapter. They share the same journey, an ascent through various veils or layers toward a vision of heaven. The ending of the *Vita Nuova* is wide-open and filled with anticipation because, while we expect Dante to reach the highest love or an awareness of allegory's "sovrasenso," this "peregrino spirito" is not allowed a direct vision of God. And even the vision of the immortal Beatrice is, as we have come to expect, indirect: he sees her "per lo suo splendore" (line 7). Furthermore, when his spirit returns to convey its message from heaven, language becomes as inadequate as vision:

> Vedela tal, che quando 'l mi ridice,
>   io no lo intendo, sì parla sottile
>   al cor dolente, che lo fa parlare.
>
>   (lines 9-11)

Dante decides not to write about Beatrice until he can write more nobly. As Mark Musa argues [in *Dante's "Vita Nuova"*], the *Vita Nuova* presents "the glory of Beatrice, and the slowly-increasing ability of the lover to understand it—who must confess at the end, however, that he has not truly understood it." The supreme things, a clear awareness of divine love and the anagogical significance of life, evade him in the end, but the *Paradiso*'s vision of Beatrice and the Trinity awaits him. It is significant, therefore, that the final vision of the *Vita Nuova* involves neither Dante nor screens, but rather the "benedetta Beatrice, la quale gloriosamente mira ne la faccia di colui *qui est per omnia secula benedictus*" (XLII, 3).

Harold Bloom considers current reader-responses to Beatrice:

The figure of Beatrice, in my own experience as a reader, is now the most difficult of all Dante's tropes, because sublimation no longer seems to be a human possibility. What is lost, perhaps permanently, is the tradition that moves between Dante and Yeats, in which sublimated desire for a woman can be regarded as an enlargement of existence. One respected feminist critic has gone so far as to call Beatrice a "dumb broad," since she supposedly contemplates the One without understanding Him. . . . Dante, like tradition, thought that God's Wisdom, who daily played before His feet, was a woman. . . .

Beatrice is now so difficult to apprehend precisely because she participates both in the allegory of the poets and in the allegory of the philosophers. Her advent follows Dante's poetic maturation, or the vanishing of the precursor, Virgil. In the allegory of the poets, Beatrice is the Muse, whose function is to help the poet remember. Since remembering, in poetry, is the major mode of cognition, Beatrice is Dante's power of invention, the essence of his art.

> Harold Bloom, "Introduction," *Modern Critical Views: Dante,* Chelsea House Publishers, 1986.

María Rosa Menocal (essay date 1991)

SOURCE: "Synchronicity: Death and the *Vita Nuova,*" in *Writing in Dante's Cult of Truth from Borges to Boccaccio,* Duke University Press, 1991, pp. 11-50.

[*Menocal argues in this excerpt that the* Vita Nuova's *real subject is Dante's search for a viable poetry and that he ultimately succeeds when he adopts an absolute literalness.*]

I

The story of the **Vita Nuova** is deceptively simple. The artist as a very young man falls hopelessly in love with an equally youthful Beatrice, and over a precisely marked period of years—the numbers will all turn out, in retrospect, to have been key markers—he acts out all the conceits of what we have come to call "courtly" love. In this endlessly suffering pursuit, hopeless beyond fulfillment, he sings the anguishes of such love and gives his readers a number of poems that are as lovely hymns to his ancestor troubadours as any those father figures ever wrote themselves. The living Beatrice in the first half of the book is thus the provocation of and the evocation in much marvelously self-serving and self-loving poetry, poetry that, in the strong vernacular tradition that fathered it, is primarily fascinated with itself and with the love object always just beyond its reach. The poetry itself is spun from that desire fueled and sustained by perpetual failure and endless seeking. The young poet playing the lover, then, indulges himself endlessly, has sleepless nights (some with remarkable dream visions), is physically ill, pines away . . . and sure enough, love poetry comes

forth from the ordeal, as it is supposed to. All is well. Until, in a kabbalistically inscribed twist of events, Beatrice dies, and with her, for that young poet, so does inspiration. Without the absent object of desire, the young man is left without song—but he will not give in to such a fate. And it is Beatrice's death that provokes the realization that there is more to both life and poetry than that, than desire never fulfilled, than poetry that is its own center.

It is the dead Beatrice who is not only the focus of Dante's new life as a poet, but also, perhaps, a keen metaphor for his own first life and death as a poet. The new poet emerges from the crucible of her death a far abler reader of the text than the young troubadour who fell in love with Beatrice: he has turned to the truths that lie in the poetry itself, truths that were there before but that he could not read because he could not decipher the language they were written in. The centrality and necessity of death for this sort of revelation—a revelation rooted in both synchronistic and kabbalistic truths that taunt the modern reader—was keenly understood (and mocked, not so gently, perhaps) by Borges: his incarnation of Beatrice is a Beatriz who is not only dead but seems never to have been alive, but whose portraits reign over the house that shelters the Aleph, in the dark pit of the basement, that Aleph, that magic looking-glass that enables one to see, and thus write, the literature of the cosmos.

II

It has been, at least in part, the tremendously authoritative power of Charles Singleton's reading of the **Vita Nuova** as an authentic and all-powerful religious conversion that has kept us in the intervening years from seeing the full extent to which Dante's so-called prologue to the *Commedia* is first and foremost his manifesto of literary conversion. By this I mean—and this will be the point of this chapter—that the **Vita Nuova** is first and last about writing, that other conversions and other "themes" are ancillary to this principal, *literal* story, that of the artist as a young man. I will argue, in fact, that to convince the reader of the literal truth of that story—a literal truth we have taken, by and large, as a metaphor—is the very point of Dante's narration of this remarkably failed love story. It is quite remarkable that one of the dominant clusters of themes of Dante criticism vis-à-vis the *Commedia* in recent years, that of tracing out the almost unending instances of self-reflection, literary conversions, literary invention reinscribed in the text, in sum, Dante's preoccupation with his work and his craft and his text, has been far less visible in readings of this text. This is true despite the fact that almost everyone views the **Vita Nuova** as the important—if at times arcane and impenetrable—prolegomenon to the masterpiece. While a number of key critics have certainly understood and explored the metaliterary dimensions of the **Vita Nuova**, I want to suggest that what we call metaliterary is, in the case of this text, the plainly literary as well, the story at the surface as well as just below it, and that the combination, which is a species of kabbalistic writing, has by and large evaded our modern critical readings.

Clearly, on many points and at many key junctures, my reading of this text will intersect and parallel previous readings, especially Singleton's powerful and canonical model. But the difference, I think, is fundamental, rather than merely one of emphasis or tone: to say that the story is about literature at the surface and that the conversion story is about a crucial change in an ideology of writing is apparently to situate the *Vita Nuova* within a category of texts somewhat outside the bounds of conventional criticism. Indeed, this shift renders it highly accessible to the modern reader—precisely the opposite of what Singleton's reading does. The Christian conversion story, on the other hand, one in which an ideology of writing and literature is ancillary to the specific detail of Christian belief, is, as Singleton himself was the first to point out, profoundly distanced from us, from all readers since the Council of Trent, in fact, and remarkably difficult if not impossible to recapture. However, Dante's story about arriving at strong—indeed, categorical—opinions about what is "right" and "wrong" in literature possesses a clearly transcendental importance and is readable within various historical constructs, including our own.

In fact, Dante in the *Vita Nuova* is unabashedly, shockingly concerned with texts and writing, with how one reads the text of life and then makes it literature. The work begins with the invocation of the *Libro della memoria* ("book of memory") and the narrator's thus establishing himself as an author, a writer. This explicit self-characterization, abundantly ratified throughout the work, is sealed at the end of the work, when the author-narrator reveals his future plans and tells us what he will write in the future—a future which is post-conversionary, of course, because he learned how to read a certain language. One of the major effects of the prose-poetry format of the *Vita Nuova* is the continual affirmation, with each poem "transcribed" from the old text to the new, that the protagonist is, of course, a Poet. The story of the Poet rises most consistently to the surface, presented without allegorical or symbolic intermediary. As Ezra Pound says, emerging from the critical/philological constraints of 1910 (not far different from our own in many ways), "Saving the grace of a greatly honored scholar, to speak of the *Vita Nuova* as 'embroidered with conceits' is errant nonsense. The *Vita Nuova* is strangely unadorned . . . . It is without strange, strained similes . . . . The 'Lord of the terrible aspect' is no abstraction, no figure of speech. There are those who can not or will not understand these things."

Indeed, to believe in the literal truth of the literary story of the *Vita Nuova* is, first of all, to begin to account for the otherwise unaccountably strange power of the story; it is rendered readable, what some might call "relevant" (if the latter had not become, in recent years, a term of opprobrium among so many), not just to the modern critic and reader but, crucially, to other writers, writers who, after Dante, struggled with his very deeply seated and in many ways very rigid views on the proper nature and function of poetry and literature. While the import of the specifics of an individual's faith may indeed, as Singleton recognized, dissolve into history, a strong poet's vision of poetry is never impenetrable or insignificant, even in its detail. In this text, then, as much as at the heart of the *Commedia*, Dante is a literary historian and theoretician; but here, in this more primitive story of his conversion, we have a starkly kabbalistic story as well, one in which the poet stands far less adorned, naked, vulnerable. The young artist has bared his soul and told us of his massive disappointments—his failures, really—and how he turns things around. As has been recently pointed out, Dantology has been a slave to Dante himself, a Dante who has convinced us, through the most remarkable rhetoric, of what his texts are about—and in this case, the authorially guided emphasis on the positive future has indeed obscured how much death and a dead past are the obsessions of a text thus deceptively entitled. In this, as in much else, Dante is a kabbalist, reading and interpreting "with excessive audacity and extravagance." What is at stake everywhere in the *Vita Nuova* is the Book, its reading and its rewriting, and, of course, it is Beatrice's death that constitutes the indispensable heart of the conversion (and this is equally true whether we read it as principally poetic, theological or amorous). Above all, the *Vita Nuova*, the story so charmingly called the "New Life," is in fact the story of the death—the purposeful and necessary death—for Dante of the old ways of reading and writing, the old kind of Literature, that had proved so disappointing.

III

The momentous break that marks the beginning of lyric poetry in the European vernaculars has been an obsessive fascination for critics since Dante himself first made it a legitimate object of study in his *De Vulgari Eloquentia*. It is one of a number of literary-historical subjects about which the braggart claim can be made that more has been written about it than about any other. Of the many entangled issues in this domain, I wish to single out the two major metaliterary ones that seem to me to have been of greatest concern to Dante the author of the *Vita Nuova*: the issue of the "new life" or new beginning for poetry that is so starkly raised by the conspicuous establishment of the vernaculars of eleventh- and twelfth-century Europe as a new beginning in literary cycles, and the deeply solipsistic nature of that newly minted poetry itself.

One can, paradoxically, dispense with any extended review of the "origins" debate(s), for when and where the story of lyric poetry in the European vernaculars "actually" begins (a matter, of course, of some considerable dispute) is not nearly so important in this discussion as the fact that it does have a discernable beginning, that it is and was perceived as a major rupture vis-à-vis its "classical" antecedents. Indeed, whatever the provocations and contingencies at its beginning, the denouement of the story invariably includes the remarkable invention that did indeed take place as part of the cluster of innovations conveniently tagged as "twelfth century": the vernaculars were born and prospered as literary languages, as the prime matter of a literature perceived (then, as well as now) as "new." It is difficult to overestimate the importance, difficulty, and implications of such an event, and it is supremely important to remember that, unlike the biological analogy that gives rise to the "birth" metaphor, a death is the implacable contingency of such creation: the displacement and substitution of a new language almost invariably constitutes, despite the wishes of many, the death of the one being replaced. Even more dramatically and with greater pain, of course, a number of paternal figures are supplanted by others. Dante, of course, was not only fully aware of these issues but both disturbed and fascinated by them: even his discussion of Latin as never having been a natural language at all but rather a *koine,* an artificial construct, smacks of self-justification, the defense against some unheard but deeply sensed reproach. His discussion of the inevitable evolution of natural and living languages, as opposed to those that are dead in their immutability—and the embarrassing but lurking hint that the same may hold for the poetry of such languages—leaves in no doubt his sensitivity to the issues of transitions and replacements that are both birth *and* death.

Thus, the specific historical conditions of the rupture are by and large irrelevant here. Almost any of the models that have been proposed for such origins share the characteristics that are critical for the perspective necessary for this reading of the *Vita Nuova*: a linguistic rupture that involves the canonization of a language previously spoken but not canonized, and the concomitant invention of poetic norms for a complex written poetry springing, in different measures and ways, from both an oral tradition (the spoken and probable sung vernacular languages and songs) and a written tradition or traditions. Dante's descriptive metaphors of heritage are unambiguous: the mother's language (her lullabies and love songs alike, those models of sung and unwritten literature) is being elevated to the status of what is otherwise the father's, and the father's, the classical, is then, of course, replaced as the model by the child's, by this "new" language of poetry. Of course, there is an important paradox in all of this: the establishment of this new form, when it is sufficiently entrenched to be considered canonical (as

was certainly the case soon enough with both Provençal and Mozarabic lyrics, for example), itself becomes a new norm, a new canon, a new father figure to be either followed or replaced. Thus, a Dante acutely aware of the literary history of which he is a product (and out of which, in many ways, he is trying to write himself) has not one but two major ancestral historical forms that have given him birth as a poet: firstly, the classical, since he is still, of course, a reader of that tradition; and secondly, and no less critically, those first several centuries of the vernacular or *troubadour* writings which, by the turn of the fourteenth century, are themselves quite legitimately a tradition. Historical foreshortening should not obscure the fact that the latter was in its own right no less oppressively canonical for a writer like Dante. Dante, then, stands at what may be a unique kind of crossroads in terms of poetic ancestry: because he is still remarkably close to the Latin tradition, certainly enough so that it is a fundamental part of his linguistic and poetic upbringing, it has paternal authority and will constitute, when he writes in Italian, a model he is rejecting. But—and this is the peculiarity and perhaps the paradox—he has imbibed a considerable and powerful vernacular tradition as well (certainly the *De Vulgari* is an homage, among other things, to that part of his ancestry), one which was itself eminently canonical and well established, in many crucial ways decaying and at an end, dead in the death of static and artificiality, by the time Dante began his writing career. Thus, although the extant vernacular tradition also defined itself, in great measure, as breaking from that same classical patronage, it too was a past for Dante; it too has been indispensable in his creation, and it too, inevitably, must be left behind.

If Dante embraces the first of the two salient characteristics of the *troubadours,* the substitution and recreation of a new poetic language deriving from the maternal tongue, ultimately he is deeply troubled by its second distinguishing feature, by what we insist on calling "courtly love" but is far more advantageously described as poetic solipsism. Dispensing, once again, with the seemingly interminable discussions of many often irrelevant ancillary aspects of the "courtly love" debate, and focusing on those readings that coincide with Dante's own interpretations of his antecedents, one can indulge in the simple assertion that the greatest obsession of *troubadour* poetry is itself. The poetry appears, on the first level, to be about an inaccessible love object; but when one apprehends, as most poets have, that the love is inaccessible because only then can the poetry be generated, then the true, the consummated objects of love are revealed: language itself and the music and poetry that are its receptacles. Given the historical nature of the dramatic linguistic break that is being executed and the new language that is being forged and molded as one goes along, it is scarcely surprising—perhaps even inevitable that the creator will be more intrigued by his own creation than even normally. The circular and solipsistic (and some would eventually say sterile and pristine) nature of the poetic ideology is striking: since the generation and writing of the poem itself depends on lack of fulfillment, only an unfulfilled love can exist within the borders of this poetry—since poetry itself is the real desired object. The circle is a tightly closed one (as Zumthor has so well pointed out), the poetry often starkly hermetic, the love perforce a dead end, "sans issu" ("without issue, or offspring"), as the *Tristan* poet will tell us, and the ultimate adoration is of the lyrical form *per se,* of this poetic language quite literally in the making. While these features are abundantly clear from the earliest Provençal examples (one need only remember Guillaume's "Farai un vers de dreyt rien" [I will make a poem from absolutely nothing]), the phenomenon reaches its peak and glory in what is called, appropriately and in full recognition of the tight hermetic circle, the *trobar clus*, perhaps best rendered as "*self-enclosed poetry.*" The master craftsman here is, of course, Arnaut Daniel, who, among other things, appears to have invented what is certainly one of the most difficult of lyrical forms, the *sestina*. The essence of Arnaut's accomplishment is best conveyed by the high priest of his cult in the modern period, Ezra Pound, who first learned about him in his truncated studies in Romance philology at the University of Pennsylvania, but who, shortly after abandoning that formal academic training, expended considerable independent effort on the translation of most of Arnaut's eighteen known extant songs, writing in 1918, "I have completely rewritten, or nearly finished completely rewriting all Arnaut Daniel." Two years later Pound published his essay of admiration on "il miglior fabbro" ("the better maker, craftsman"), delighting there in Arnaut's two salient characteristics: the stunning musicality of his verses and their hermeticism. Pound's translations, which are not, in fact, as complete as he had claimed, in turn also feast on these qualities of Arnaut's poetry (the very qualities which make him so perfect an exemplar, because of the high pitch of focus and the distillation—some might say exaggeration—of obsession with self and lyricism), and Pound's renditions are sparkling mosaics of almost meaningless beautiful sounds. As one critic of those translations has put it: "One winds up with the opposite of a literal trot: a free rendering that corresponds more with the original in terms of sound than in sense of imagery."

That, then, distilled through the later, far more iconoclastic philologist-become-poet, is the ancestor whom Dante too would hold up, in the considerably different, retrospective light of the *Purgatorio*, as exemplary of the tradition that had preceded him and molded him, although, crucially, the *tone* of Dante's apparent praise has not been much listened to . . . But no matter, for the time being: Dante's high estimation of Arnaut's craftsmanship and of the essential apprenticeship provided by the full range of the vernacular traditions is everywhere apparent. The *De Vulgari*, certainly, makes it abundantly clear that the Provençal corpus, and the Sicilian one closely linked to it, constitute explicit role models, and from the opening pages of the *Vita Nuova* there is no doubt that a crucial part of the story told is that the young Dante Alighieri has apprenticed himself to the rich (and by then venerable, over two centuries old) traditions of the highly self-reflective love lyrics of the Romance vernaculars. His own earliest efforts are so unmistakably (and self-consciously) a part of that tradition that they include, among other things, *sestine* to equal Arnaut's own best examples of the *trobar clus*. But the young artist ends up being far from satisfied with the poetics of predecessors who were once attractive, in part, because they stood as revolutionaries with respect to their ancestors (who were Dante's own, at the same time), predecessors who taught him, quite literally, how to write in the *parlar materno*, the mother tongue. His conversion from their poetics to his own thus becomes the meticulously chronicled story of the *Vita Nuova*; this follows the archetypical structures of autobiographies in beginning at the end of the story, a story which is that of how the author came to be able to understand what he had already written and then go on to write his new kind of literature—that literature of the New Life.

The confusion here, in part, is that of the occasional doubling between historical author and the author who is the poet of the story of the *Vita Nuova*. The role played out by the protagonist is that of authorship itself, and this conflation, a making explicit of what is always implicit, is part of Dante's kabbalistic enterprise: what is written is literally true and precedes any other reality. Among other things, that mysterious book from which the author Dante is taking his text is very much the kabbalistic text of reality. As in the *Commedia*, there is a tension between author and protagonist, the younger author, which is parallel to the tension between poet and pilgrim in the later text. After all, one is bent on usurping the other, quite literally taking his place, and the reader too suffers at least some of the anxieties and fears that naturally attend to such mergers of personalities within the self as we follow the not always gradual merger—at times a death struggle—between the two. At the end, after an apparently full assimilation of the implications of the conversion, we have the new author as he sits down to—in this case—rewrite, copy, recount, the story of how the old life came to be the New Life—all, of course, inevitably, from the light of the New Life which has recast the meanings and intentions of what was read and written in the old. All, of course, rooted in the death of the old. Freccero, in words about the *Commedia* which are no less applicable to the *Vita Nuova*, notes that "the paradoxical logic of all such narratives is that the beginning and end must logically coincide in order for the author and his persona to be the same." In the case of the *Vita Nuova* it is critical to note that the coincidence or convergence that unifies the beginning and end of the text is, furthermore, a congruence of emphasis on the process of writing: the first chapter gives us the author sitting down with a "book of memory" at hand and about to give the reader what we may best call a version of that text, and the last chapter ends with an invocation of a text to come, the text that is the logical and necessary result of the conversion just recounted—as it turns out, the *Commedia*. And in the *Vita Nuova*, it is worth repeating, the persona of the author, most markedly at the points of resolution and convergence, is the Poet. The conversion which is the fulcrum of change involves the movement, at least in theory a radical one, from poetry that serves itself primarily and a solipsistic love in the process, poetry as music and verbal hermeticism, in other words, to a poetry whose meaning and unequivocal truth exists a *priori* outside itself and its own frame of reference, a poetry pre-inscribed in the cosmos. The poet in this new universe is not the creator but the agent of revelation, at times even unknowingly so: the meaning of magic and sequences and visions may not be known until a startling revelation makes it transparent. This, of course, is exactly what is indicated in the recounting of the *Vita Nuova*'s seemingly impenetrable first dream and in the author's annoying denial of an explanation for his puzzled readers, saying: "Lo verace giudicio del detto sogno non fue veduto allora per alcuno, ma ore è manifestissimo a li più semplici" (The true meaning of the dream I described was not perceived by anyone then, but now it is completely clear even to the least sophisticated [chapter 3]). This is, from certain necessary perspectives, the story of a Platonic conversion: the harnessing of the primitive power of music—Poetry—to serve the needs of a kind of reason—Truth. But this is thus a species of reason that would be easily dismissed by almost any Platonist, for it is a reason which reflects not only transcendental Truths—which may or may not be true in an Aristotelian paradigm—but which is grounded in a shocking belief in the necessary truth of textuality itself and in the synchronicity that more traditional rationalists squirm away from uneasily.

IV

The major dramatic turn of events, what can be fairly described as the literary conversion, in the *Vita Nuova* is drawn out over nine chapters, from 19 to 28, thus beginning just before the midpoint of this text of forty-two chapters. The first two of these contain two of the poems generally described as "stilnovistic," "Donne che avete intelletto d'amore" and "Amor e 'l cor gentil son una cosa," and even if we had no other indicators, we might well suspect we are on the threshold here of an important shift or event, because these are the poems in which Dante's immediate poet-ancestors most starkly reverberate. If the poems, as well as the actions narrated, of the first eighteen chapters are reflexes of the earlier "courtly" traditions of Provence and Sicily,

these two poems, following both chronology and taste, approach Dante himself: they are kissing cousins to and resonances of the poet's contemporaries and near-contemporaries, Guinizelli and especially the powerful and enigmatic Cavalcanti, to whom the *Vita Nuova* is dedicated and who is called here the "primo amico." In the chronology of a poetic autobiography, then, the alert reader would anticipate a threshold: narrator and protagonist must soon merge, since the last of the poetic antecedents, those still lurking about in the authorial present, are rapidly falling behind.

But from a narrative, structural point of view the text is still at this point adhering to the initially established (preconversion) format. One must pause here to consider carefully the peculiar structure of this text: "Everyone knows" that the *Vita Nuova* is a prose-poetry text—and it is then described as either a hybrid or a *sui generis*. But far fewer seem to have noticed that what is of utmost importance is the variable nature of the prose-poetry relationship, the shifting relationship of three different voices vis-à-vis each other that is of interest, since in fact a major formal conversion will occur in this central cluster of chapters as well. The first part of the text is composed so that those chapters that contain poems (not all of them do, of course) include two very different prose voices which frame the lyric voice between them. There is the initial narrator, who has been telling us the story all along and is the generally unchallenged voice in the structurally simpler chapters that contain no poetry. This is the voice which is the autobiographical "I," necessarily already knowing the outcome but attempting to narrate the events "innocently" as he goes along, with a sense of fidelity to his preinscribed text. (This narrator appears also to have an often acute sense of the reader's expectations of suspense and dramatic outcome from something that has been marked off in the preexisting text and announced as the point at which a new life began.) This Dante narrates the events which, in these chapters at least, occasion or inspire a poem, introduced at the end of that chapter's events and following immediately thereafter. And these poems are—and here lies, finally, some considerable strangeness—in turn followed by a brief and usually completely straightforward and formal description of the poem itself, that poem that has just been presented. This second prose section of the chapter is normally called a *divisione*.

Thus, in the first movement of the text, roughly its first half, in each chapter that presents a poem (or more than one poem, as is the case in some chapters), there are three formally distinct presentations of what might be crudely described as the "same material": a prose narration of "what happened"; the poem(s) that formed the lyrical reaction to the event(s); and finally, and most mysteriously for almost all critics, a pseudo-scientific and remarkably banal explication of the poem's structure and "divisions" (i.e., its formal fundamental formal characteristics—that is why these blurbs are called *divisioni*, of course). In the invariable order of these three components, this last is a miniature and accurate, but essentially quite primitive, *explication de texte*. The first problem in knowing just what to make of these little expositions of the poems that precede them is their transparent limitations: they rarely go beyond telling the reader what he can see for himself (even "li più semplici," as Dante would have it). Traditional criticism has scarcely gone beyond pointing out the conspicuous similarity these *divisioni* bear to mechanical scholastic procedure—and Boccaccio, as editor of the **Vita Nuova**, acts out this reading by shifting these highly formal and starkly positivistic glosses to the margins. But there is a no less puzzling feature, one that seems largely to have gone by the wayside in most readings: these unadorned little expositions, beginning about halfway through the text, are either eliminated altogether or are fully integrated into the quite different voice of narration that *precedes* the poem. The text's second movement is thus substantially altered, structurally and tonally, from its first: after chapter 27, in which the *canzone* stands starkly alone, without any *divisione*, each chapter that houses a poem finishes with that poem—and the voice of mock Scholasticism, that droning voice of the self-evident gloss, the simple student at his rote best, is either gone altogether or transformed, absorbed into the "crowd of Dantes" of the storyteller. But I am getting ahead of the story here.

In chapters 19 and 20 we are still playing by the old rules: Dante has given us his remarkable "philosophical" or *stilnovista* poems and the reader is still given a *divisione* after each. The subsequent chapter, 21, exists almost exclusively to give us yet a third sonnet in what would be called the "sweet new style" in the retrospective clarity of the *Purgatorio*, and it too is followed by an exposition of its outward form. But the action of the story starts to pick up again in chapter 22 when Beatrice's father dies, a prefiguration of the more significant death that is to follow. If, however, Beatrice alive is in part an emblem of the old poetry, then her father's death is much more than mere foreshadowing of her own, since the death of the old poetry's father is a literalization of transparent significance. In chapter 23, Dante dreams that Beatrice herself has died, and once again there are at least two sayers of textual truth that mark events: the "annunciation" of what is "really" to happen and the literalization of the dream itself, the synchronicity playing itself out. And, in a relentless accumulation of images destroying the past, Dante's multiple literary pasts, there is yet another death—or, more appropriately, a disappearance—in chapter 24, in which we see for the last time the figure of Love.

Love had played a significant role in the first half of the book, the literally personified metaphor for Love as a separate entity and persona. His fourth and last

appearance here is both spectral and explicitly intended to clarify that he is disappearing because there is no longer any need for him, no longer any call, in the development of the artist's poetic ideology, for this kind of poetic prop. The narrator tells us that Love himself clarifies his own insufficiency, and quotes him as saying: "E chi volesse sottilmente considerare, quella Beatrice chiamerebbe Amore per molta simiglianza che ha meco" (Anyone of subtle discernment would call Beatrice Love, because she so greatly resembles me [chapter 24]). It is of considerable significance that this revelation comes on the heels of Beatrice's first death, so to speak, for that is what one must make of Dante's first knowledge of her death in a dream. Beatrice herself is no longer that dying kind of love poetry any more, the kind that needed agents like Love, elaborate and mediated poetic imagery, to be meaningful. It is crucial to remember here that the older, the first, the now-vanishing Beatrice had such needs, and in that purposefully cryptic first dream, with that engaging but teasingly difficult sequence of the burning and then eaten heart, she had exhibited some awareness of the nature of her limitations, at least in life. It is perhaps at this point, and not at the end of chapter 3, when Dante taunts us with the "obviousness" of the meaning of that numerically critical dream, that we can speak with some modicum of assurance about what it might in fact have so "obviously" signified. But again I get ahead of the story, for the meaning of the dream is explicitly dependent on the revelations of the conversion.

Returning, then, to the dismissal of Love from the story, the reader is left to conclude that mediation and metaphor in poetry have flown out the window—and in case it was not clear from Love's dramatic last annunciation and bowing out of the scene, Dante devotes the following chapter, the liminal twenty-fifth, to a clear prose discussion of the nature and purposes of poetry. It is a passage which includes a round dismissal of his vernacular antecedents, saying, "E la cagione per che alquanti ebbero fame di sapere dire, è che quasi fuoro li primi che dissero in lingua di sì" (The reason why a few ungifted poets acquired the fame of knowing how to compose is that they were the first who wrote poetry in the Italian language [chapter 25]). Even more to the point, the chapter ends with the following succinct statement on what real poetry ought to be: "Però che grande vergogna sarebbe a colui che rimasse cose sotto vesta di figura o di colore rettorico, e poscia, domandato, non sapesse denudare le sue parole da cotale vesta, in guisa che avessero verace intendimento" (For, if anyone should dress his poem in images and rhetorical coloring and then, being asked to strip his poem of such dress in order to reveal its true meaning, would not be able to do so—this would be a veritable cause for shame [chapter 25]). Once again, one is compelled to remark on the extent to which the Dante of the **Vita Nuova** is cultivating varieties of transparency; here, certainly, masking is not only dropped, it is denounced. (There is thus some irony in noting that so much criticism of the work has remained attached to the language of metaphor that is being banished from the "new life": in fact, the details of the "love story," paradoxically, start to fade and are increasingly subservient to the reflections on the nature of writing and literature that are at the core of this story of the "new life.") At this critical turning point we glimpse a Dante who has figured out the simplest solution to an impossibly complicated problem: how to limit and control the insufficiency and treachery of poetic language. The "solution" is, however, not an invention but a revelation, the kabbalistic insight that Truth is already there to be read and then rewritten—and it is only then that poetry can have any kind of exactitude of meaning, that it can say the Truth.

This revelation goes a very long way to explaining the meaning of the mysterious *divisioni* themselves, which, like the figure of Love, are no longer necessary in the new life. The last of the old-life *divisioni,* in fact, will appear in the next chapter, 26. (This, of course, is the number that will resonate strongly in the cantos of the *Purgatorio* devoted, once again explicitly, to poetic theory. It seems to me an exemplary case of the kind of synchronicity, as opposed to numerology, that Dante is involved with, for chapter 26 is important in the texts because of their internal harmony and correspondence, rather than because of any externally determined other "meaning.") The narrator tells us, from his perspective of knowing how it all came out and how it all fit together, things he could barely discern while he was living through them: Beatrice actually dies while Dante is writing the *canzone* that will stand alone in chapter 27—and we remember that in its transparency this becomes the first poem in the book not to have to be followed by a simple gloss, a poem that seems itself to reject the empty formal conceits of Scholasticism. Chapter 28, when Dante finds out about Beatrice's death in the original sequence of events, follows, and this is the last of the nine in this liminal and conversionary sequence. It is followed, appropriately, by the famous chapter that sets out the meaning of the number nine and concludes with the observation, rather precious for the modern reader, that Beatrice *is* a nine:

> Ma più sottilmente pensando, e secondo la infallibile veritate, questo numero fue ella medesima . . . questa donna fue accompagnata da questo numero del nove a dare ad intendere ch'ella era uno nove, cioè uno miracolo.... Forse ancora per più sottile persona si vederebbe in ciò più sottile ragione; ma questa è quella ch'io ne veggio, e che più mi piace.

> If anyone thinks more subtly and according to infallible truth, it will be clear that this number was she herself . . . then this lady was accompanied by the number nine so that it might be understood that

she was a nine, or a miracle. Perhaps someone more subtle than I could find a still more subtle explanation, but this is the one which I see and which pleases me the most. (chapter 29)

It is thus that in this seemingly bizarre chapter we find what is perhaps the most direct, the most unabashed and naked presentation not only of "what Beatrice means to me" (to paraphrase Eliot's famous essay on Dante) but, far more importantly, of what Dante has become; he has become a simple reader of the simplest truths inscribed, preinscribed, in a universe that can make sense only when we can become such readers. Then, at that point of breakthrough, the sense is complete, almost too simple, for the good reader—he who is not subtle, who has discarded the mediations and the conceits of all those other poetics. Initially, in fact, Beatrice's death leaves the Dante trained in the classical traditions, that earlier poet, stunned and poetryless. As Mazzotta has noted, "Now that she is physically dead, the metaphors for her seem to be another empty fiction. If the question while Beatrice was alive was whether she is and how she is unique, now that she is dead the question is finding the sense of metaphors that recall her." Once again, the problem can be reduced, at least initially, to one of the nature of expression chosen and the rejection of an expressive mode, a poetics, that was insufficient to deal with fundamental truths that are inscribed in texts we must first learn how to even read. What Mazzotta is calling rhetoric here I have called poetics, but the fact that they might indeed be taken for the same thing is exactly what Dante has in mind: the elimination of both or either as a category of expression separate or separable from other categories of truth and knowledge. There is a certain pathos, I think, in realizing that it is exactly when the poet's soul is most naked, when he reveals the most outrageous of truths, that his readers, at least in this century, have thrown the most elaborate of veils on his simple revelations. She *was* a nine, she *was* a miracle—no likes about it.

The differences, then, between the old life and the new life include the fact that poems in the new life, after the living Beatrice's death, need no *divisioni* or pseudoscientific explication, as did those in the old, now discarded days and poems once reigned over by an inaccessible love object, the living Beatrice, and a mediating Love figure. In those old days the author was just like all the other poets, in other words, all those in the tradition from which he came, a tradition within which, according to the *Vita Nuova* (and as a follow-up of sorts to the *De vulgari*), poems need the prop of commentary in order to have any really unassailable "truth value"—those things that are measurable and provable such as the number of stanzas and the kind of rhyme and where the first part ends and the next begins. The old poetry adored the empty glossing of form, but in the aftermath of death and its revelations, in the aftermath of the conversion—and in some great measure that *is* the conversion—it is clear that for him who can read and then rewrite the universe the poems themselves have absolute truth value, they are stripped of the trappings that begged for that kind of commenary and made it necessary, and they are so simply and so clearly about transcendental other truths that they can and must stand by themselves. Beatrice *is* love. Poetry *is* truth. The old Beatrice is dead, and the new writer, forged by the pain of the failure of the first Beatrice, will now revel in the vision of Beatrice who will need no Love as a figure to mediate between her and the absolute value of love itself. And just as she *is* a nine, as the newly converted Dante loses no time in telling us, so poetry, real and worthwhile poetry, is as rationally true as what others call scientific language. Here, clearly, is the merger between the disparate components characterized in the preconversion part of the text by the three different and incomplete voices: the narrative, the lyric, and the commenting. These observations, of course, have been made by a number of critics vis-à-vis the *Commedia* and its development of the motion of the inseparability of theology and poetry, but the **Vita Nuova**'s explicit turning to the primary truth of (certain kinds of) texts has been far less recognized, although, oddly enough, it is expressed with an embarrassing directness that has faded in the *Commedia* itself. Freccero's observation that, contrary to what Auerbach maintained, "the theological principles that seem to underlie Dante's formal pattern are themselves in turn derived from literary principles" is, if anything, even more applicable to the **Vita Nuova**, where on the most literal level—which is the level now invested with absolute truth value—the writer and his literary texts are invariably primary. This, then, is a new life indeed, and in the last half of the book, in the chapters remaining after the banishment of the past, we see an author preparing for the full significance, only partially divined (for that is the very nature of such belief in the kabbala of writing), of his newfound faith and practice. This is succinctly put in the famous last paragraph, of course, as "io spero dicer di lei quello che mai non fue detto d'alcuna" (I hope to write of her that which has never been written of any other woman [chapter 42]). Here all the components come together in the terseness and incantatory repetition of a synchronistic text: the hope that the reveleatons will continue and that the writing, the saying of truths of the universe that is the poetry, will flow from that.

v

Poi che fuoro passati tanti die, che appunto erano compiuti li nove anni appresso l'apparimento soprascritto di questa gentilissima ne l'ultimo di quest) die avvenne che questa mirabile donna apparve a me vestita di colore bianchissimo, in mezzo a due gentili donne, le quali erano di più lunge etade; e passando per una via, volse li occhi verve quella parse ov'io era molto pauroso, e per la sue ineffabile cortesia, la quale è oggi meritata nel grande secolo, mi salutoe molto virtuosamente, tanto che me parve allora vedere tutti li termini de la beatitudine. L'ora che lo suo dolcissimo salutare mi giunse, era fermamente none di quello giorno; e pero che quella fu la prima volta che le sue parole si mossero per venire a li miei orecchi, presi tanta dolcezza che come inebriato mi partio da le gent), e ricorsi a lo solingo luogo d'una mia camera, e puosimi a pensare di questa cortessima E pensando di led, mi sopragiunse uno soave sonno, ne lo quale m'apparve una maravigliosa visione: che me parea vedere ne la mia camera una nebula di colore di fuoco, dentro a la quale io discernea una figura d'uno segnore di pauroso aspetto a chi la guardasse; e pareami con tanta letizia, quanto a sé, che mirabile cosa era; e ne le sue parole dicea molte cose, le quali io non intendea se non poche; tra le quali intendea queste: *Ego dominus tuus*. Ne le sue braccia mi parea vedere una persona dormire nude, salvo che involta mi parea in uno drappo sanguigno leggeramente; la quale io riguardando molto intentivamente, conobbi ch'era la donna de la salute, la quale m'avea lo giorno dinanzi degnato di salutare. E ne l'una de le mani mi parea che quest) tenesse una cosa la quale ardesse tutta, e pareami e he mi dicesse queste parole: *Vide cor tuum*. E quando elk era stato alquanto, pareami che disvegliasse questa che dormia; e tanto si sforzava per suo ingegno, che le facea mangiare questa cosa e he in mano li ardea, la quale ella mangiava dubitosamente. Appresso cio poco dimorava che la sue letizia si convertia in amarissimo pianto; e cosi piangendo, si ricogliea questa donna ne le sue braccia, e con essa mi parea che si ne gisse verve lo cielo; once io sostenea si grande angoscia, che lo mio deboletto sonno non poteo sostenere, anzi si ruppe e fui disvegliato. E mantenente cominciai a pensare, e trovai che l'ora ne la quale m'era questa visione apparita, era la quarta de la notte state; si che appare manifestamente e ch'ella fue la prima ore de le nove ultime ore de la notte. Pensando io a cio che m'era apparuto, propuosi di farlo sentire a molti li quali erano famosi trovatori in quello tempo: e con cio fosse cosa che io avesse già veduto per me medesimo l'arte del dire parole per rima, propuosi di fare uno sonetto, ne lo quale io salutasse tutti li fedeli d'Amore; e pregandoli che giudicassero la mia visione, scrissi a loro cio che io avea nel mio sonno veduto. E cominciai allora questo sonetto, lo quale comincia: *A ciuscan'alma presa.*

A ciascun'alma presa e gentil core
nel cui cospetto ven lo dir presente,
in cio che mi rescrivan suo parvente,
salute in lor segnor, cioè Amore.
    Già eran quasi che atterzate l'ore
del tempo che onne stella n'è lucente,
quando m'apparve Amor subitamente,
cui essenza membrar mi dà orrore.
    Allegro mi sembrava Amor tenendo

meo core in mano, e ne le braccia avea
madonna involta in un drappo dormendo.
   Poi la sveglieva, e d'esto core ardendo
lei paventosa umilmente pascea:
appresso air lo ne vedea piangendo.

Questo sonneto si divide in due part); che ne la
prima parse saluto e domando risponsione, ne la
seconda significo a che si dee rispondere. La seconda
parse comincia quivi: *Già eran.*

A questo sonetto fue risposto da molti e di diverse
sentenzie; tra li quali fue risponditore quell) cui io
chiamo primo de li miei amici, e disse allora uno
sonetto, lo quale comincia: *Vedeste, al mio parere,
onne valore.* E questo fue quasi lo principio de
l'amistà tra lui e me, quando elk seppe che io era
quelli che li avea cio mandato. Lo verace giudicio
del detto sogno non fue veduto allora per alcuno,
ma ore è manifestissimo a li più semplici.

After so many days had passed that precisely nine years
were ending since the appearance, just described, of
this most gracious lady, it happened that on the last
one of those days the miraculous lady appeared, dressed
in purest white, between two ladies of noble bearing
both older than she was; and passing along a certain
street, she turned her eyes to where I was standing
faint-hearted and, with that indescribable graciousness
for which today she is rewarded in the eternal life, she
greeted me so miraculously that I seemed at that moment to behold the entire range of possible bliss. It
was precisely the ninth hour of that day, three o'clock
in the afternoon, when her sweet greeting came to me.
Since this was the first time her words had ever been
directed to me, I became so ecstatic that, like a drunk-
en man, I turned away from everyone and I sought the
loneliness of my room, where I began thinking of this
most gracious lady and, thinking of her, I fell into a
sweet sleep, and a marvelous vision appeared to me. I
seemed to see a cloud the color of fire and, in that
cloud, a lordly man, frightening to behold, yet he
seemed also to be wondrously filled with joy. He spoke
and said many things of which I understood only a
few; one was *Ego dominus tuus.* I seemed to see in his
arms a sleeping figure, naked but lightly wrapped in a
crimson cloth; looking intently at this figure, I recognized the lady of the greeting, the lady who earlier in
the day had deigned to greet me. In one hand he seemed
to be holding something that was all in flames, and it
seemed to me that he said these words: *Vide cor tuum.*
And after some time had passed, he seemed to awaken
the one who slept, and he forced her cunningly to eat
of that burning object in his hand; she ate of it timidly.
A short time after this, his happiness gave way to bitterest weeping, and weeping he folded his arms around
this lady, and together they seemed to ascend toward
the heavens. At that point my drowsy sleep could not
bear the anguish that I felt; it was broken and I awoke.

At once I began to reflect, and I discovered that the
hour at which that vision had appeared to me was the
fourth hour of the night; that is, it was exactly the first
of the last nine hours of the night. Thinking about
what I had seen, I decided to make it known to many
of the famous poets of that time. Since just recently I
had taught myself the art of writing poetry, I decided
to compose a sonnet addressed to all of Love's faithful
subjects; and, requesting them to interpret my vision,
I would write them what I had seen in my sleep. And
then I began to write this sonnet, which begins: *To
every captive soul.*

> To every captive soul and loving heart
>   to whom these words I have composed are
>   sent
> for your elucidation in reply,
> greetings I bring for your sweet lord's sake,
>   Love.
> The first three hours, the hours of the time
> of shining stars, were coming to an end,
> when suddenly Love appeared before me
> (to remember how he really was appalls me).
>
> Joyous, Love seemed to me, holding my heart
>   within his hand, and in his arms he had
>   my lady, loosely wrapped in folds, asleep.
> He woke her then, and gently fed to her
> the burning heart; she ate it, terrified.
> And then I saw him disappear in tears.

This sonnet is divided into two parts. In the first
part I extend greetings and ask for a response, while
in the second I describe what it is that requires the
response. The second part begins: *The first three
hours.*

This sonnet was answered by many, who offered a
variety of interpretations; among those who
answered was the one I call my best friend, who
responded with a sonnet beginning: *I think that you
beheld all worth.* This exchange of sonnets marked
the beginning of our friendship. The true meaning
of the dream I described was not perceived by
anyone then, but now it is completely clear even to
the least sophisticated. (chapter 3)

If we follow Dante, and we have reached a certain
level of clarity and vision, then, as he suggests tanta-
lizingly, here and there throughout the work, certain
things are now perfectly clear. First and foremost among
the mysteries that ought to be clear now is that of the
first dream, that garbled and vaguely terrifying vision
that produced the first of the text's poems. Dante's
almost taunting line about even the "simplest" of readers "now" (in the light of revelation) grasping it clearly still resonates—and a leery reader, a would-be interpreter remembers that none of the other poets appealed
to at the time, not even the great Cavalcanti, got it

right. In fact, it is fair to say that it is a problem more often avoided than not, despite its excruciating interpretative problem of the discrepancy between the enduring opacity of the dream and the assertion that, in a visionary light, it would become transparent. Certainly none of the interpretations offered to date gives one that "bingo" smart of recognition that a dream's "transparent" decipherment should certainly provoke, although the most recent meditation on it by Harrison is other-wise satisfying in its richness and density, thus mimicking appreciatively the text's and the dream's singular qualities. But Dante's dismissive little line invites us to call his bluff.

We must view the dream retrospectively, of course, realizing first and foremost that the Love who is the mysterious protagonist in that first dream has been utterly abandoned. That Love who once was verging on omnipotence for the struggling young poet, that tradition, as Singleton so aptly named it, has been banished from the scene, quite effectively killed off. In his second appearance, Love was the spokesman, a mediator, in fact, among several explicitly false "loves," the *donne schermo*, thus making his association with the older poetry as explicit as possible. It was Love who wept once again in his third appearance, one in which he was explicitly aware of his imminent banishment: he weeps, as does any lover who knows he is about to be abandoned, but he is also gracious enough, in Dante's depiction, to urge a new sincerity in Dante's poetry—thus, of course, sealing his own doom and final departure in chapter 24, as we have already seen. But this Love, this conceit of a spiritually solipsistic tradition and often intensely hermetic poetry, is still at the peak of his powers in the third chapter, in the dream and its retelling, a sequence of events provoked by the drunken ecstasy of Beatrice's greeting. In fact, since in the story that is the moment at which the young artist, overcome by classic first love, will write his first poem, Love's power could be no stronger—he is the poetry revered and emulated by the virtually mad young man about to write his first poem. Madness was her greeting and its revision in his provocatively difficult dream.

The first "obvious" interpretation, then, is that the author's statement, made in the light of the most severe kind of disdain, is subtly ironic: what is obvious to him when he has buried the poetics of Love is precisely that the dream has no meaning—certainly no "clear" meaning. One can, of course, point to all sorts of the bits and pieces of the dream that are true and that are interpretable: the color symbolism, the mysterious Latin, the burning heart, and so forth. One can talk about the young, misguided poet's heart being burned by Love and eaten by his Lady—i.e., step by step the original artist is destroyed by the trappings of his ancestors' poetry. One can, in fact, construct a number of more or less elaborate and more or less

sophisticated interpretations of the dream—but none that is or would have been transparent and obvious, let alone to the most simple. The only thing that is transparent and obvious, especially to the simple, is that the vision *qua* vision—or *qua* prophetic dream—is a garbled one. Inevitably, the poem written to reflect the incoherent vision is able to be formally lovely without shedding any light, any meaning, on the puzzle of the dream vision. And in much of this there is little question that it derives from that fine troubadour tradition of self-referentiality and obsession with the poetry itself, beginning with the evocation of an audience that is (what else?) exclusively other poets. That the "message" of the poem, beyond the evident interest in poetry and its encoding and decoding, should be hermetic is the best possible "proof," I believe, of Singleton's claim that this Love is a troubadour, and that the lyrics of the preconversion *Vita Nuova* are meant to be seen as examples and specimens of that parent with whom he had such a love-hate relationship. Finally, it is imperative to note that this is an incoherence that Dante as author is ascribing to a poetic history which he has clearly renounced for himself. What is it that we can always see so clearly at the end of the road? Our mistakes, of course, and the shallowness of so many a first love.

There can be little question, in the cruel light of that early morning, that dawn from which Dante is recounting his past, that his first love was, indeed, a failure. And since his persona, his character, was explicitly that of the artist as a young man, the Poet in the making, rather than independently or primarily a lover, then, crucially, it is not that the change in love drags with it a change in poetry, but rather that a change in attitude about what poetry is will necessarily entail writing about a different kind of love. The love written about and dictated by troubadour poetry is what the young Poet is in the *Vita Nuova*: self-serving, self-involved, self-pitying, unproductive of anything other than a love poetry, which may be marvelous in its forms—the cherished object of the structural gloss—but which is not a part of a larger universe of meaning. But for Dante such poetry and such a lover were simply no longer sufficient—in fact, were never sufficient or rewarding in the first place. One of the dark undercurrents of the *Vita Nuova*—detected by Borges in the resonances of the *Commedia*—is the great chasm of Beatrice's insufficiencies. In a particularly moving passage of his *Essay*, Singleton says that Dante is rejecting a love which knows no rest or satisfaction, necessarily a hopeless love, a love without possibility of peace. "Troubadour love was really always that—a love without peace" (99).

This is precisely the ease, of course, except that it is critical to note that this is because it is an explicitly and hermetically literary concept of love. It may, because of the charms of the writing of it, the seduction of its expression in lyrics, go on to influence people, of course—but the poets themselves do not hold it up as anything more than poetic, certainly not as a socio-logical or a theological theory of love developed out-side the context of the need for poetic inspiration and production. It is a theory of love which transparently serves artistic needs primarily and social ones second-arily, if at all, and a broad range of readers would argue it is highly negative and destructive when it is applied as a social principle. And that too is the story of the *Vita Nuova*, the failure, the heartbreak, even the tragedy of transferring what can only be lyrical to all other parts of life, including the narrative: garbled dreams, dead young women. And the point, finally, is that Dante rejects it as a literary principle as well because his young love of Beatrice was so catastroph-ically painful; but instead of retreating to a novelistic stance, he moves forward to the kabbalistic vision within which realities and lyricism cannot be separated from each other and literature functions in a moral universe that is no different from the moral universe of individuals. Literature, writing, is *real*. Beatrice *is* a nine. The Book of Memory *exists*. The ideology reject-ed is a poetics that does not recognize this, that cannot read or accept these truths about texts and their rela-tionship to life—an ideology that is founded on a no-tion of fiction as something that has its own rules and that is epistemologically different from reality. Dante, a kabbalist in this sense as well, rejects such a notion and kills off Love and the rather foolish and weepy young man who believed in him, a false god indeed. And Beatrice, finally, most painfully, had to go as well; she will he written about again when a Dante fully liberated from the old traps and trappings can both fully decipher and then say what she can mean in the newly revealed universe. The newly minted Dante has many hints which he has dutifully passed on to us, but he has a great deal more contemplation to go until all the harmonies and all the congruences, all those nines, are clear enough to he reinscribed. He licks his wounds and bides his time.

Alas, the modern reader, with few exceptions, cannot accept the radical notion that Beatrice is a nine as anything other than a literary statement, understanding literature as a construct that is starkly different episte-mologically from the construct we privilege as "reali-ty." This is so despite the fact that the statement is delivered in the *Vita Nuova* precisely as an example of how poetry is *not* fiction hut rather the ultimate, the very expression of Truth—mystical, kabbalistic, per-haps, but Truth nevertheless. If we were not, for better or worse, so deeply entrenched in a universe of reason and positivism anti their derivatives, we would be less inclined, perhaps, to talk about the fiction of not being a fiction, to remember that most famous of lines about the *Commedia*, hut rather about the destruction of fic-tion and the elevation of Truth as the principles of Poetry. That too is what the *Vita Nuova* is about. The

severe difficulty lies in determining whether we must deal with all of this as a fiction, whether, to put it differently, we reject the most fundamental premise of Dante's text by interpreting it as a fiction. But Dante himself is trying to reconcile something which we, as heirs of a remarkably powerful positivism and ratio-nalism, are greatly tempted to call mysticism, with a belief in the possibility not only of writing the Truth but having such written truth be revelatory and even conversionary for others. Thus, the "miracles" he de-scribes in the *Vita Nuova* are miracles for him, true for him and part of what he is trying to tell us: that there is (or can be, if we can learn how to read it) great transcendent Truth in what the unbeliever and the blind might take to be pedestrian "reality" or reduce to the banal parameters of the "factual" or "nonfactual." Moreover, in the writing of the events and the experi-ences, the "facts" are turned back into the Truth (a Truth we are unable to account for outside of litera-ture) they once were in the first Book. There are thus three separate "versions" of the events, of any event: those that are written kabbalistically, those that take place, which may seem to be pedestrian and unexcep-tional, and the third reinscribing in a literary text. The latter must be the right kind of literary text: that which is written by someone who is first and foremost a strong and able reader, able to properly interpret the events of the life that is lived "factually" as manifestations of events that in fact are already inscribed in the first Book, and then is able to write a text that lets us see the truth of one through the other. This is an experi-encing and subsequent writing of a reality and Truth that cannot be understood, let alone described and re-written, in positivist terms, in the terms that require an "understanding" that is limited by either rationalist discourse or precepts.

Dante, in other words, is a full step ahead of the many philosophers—all post medieval, of course—who have said that when the truth is understood it can no longer be said. Dante, prewriting Vico, believed that when the truth was understood it could be said—it must be said—and in a poetry that is more truthful than any facts can be. I believe his answer to the belief in the unsayability of truth would be that that is true only in a system that has classified the mystical and the "real" inappropriately, divided them from each other inap-propriately. What is True, in a text such as the *Vita Nuova* (and since the story of it is held up to be ex-emplary, by sheer dint of being True, in all texts), is that which lies between the pedestrian and ultimately meaningless "facts" of any possible encounters with a Bice Portinari—or any other woman, for that matter—and what renders such facts true and meaningful: how they reveal to us and act out what was and is always written in the greater text. The literary text, then, is the expression of the interpretation of one through the other. That is the lesson about writing and Truth—which ought, in fact to be inseparable—that Dante learns in the trials and tribulations recounted in the *Vita Nuova*.

Synchronicity is everywhere strewn along those paths, and that, first and foremost, is the meaning of such things as numbers and their obvious, if at times problematic conjunction with each other and with other meanings. Although the "meanings" of numbers according to external systems of symbolism are undeniably there and potent, though sometimes difficult to pin down and decipher in any absolute or neat system, the meanings of such coincidences of numbers is, more importantly, internal-markers along Dante's path that critical events or revelations are at hand, deeply personal, ultimately, and perhaps not fully interpretable according to formalized, external systems of numerology. They are, however, unmistakably and intensely meaningful personally, and they are inscribed in the text and in the universe of Truth precisely because there is an intersection between the details of a personal life and its potential banalities and cosmic Truth, on the one hand, and sense and order on the other. But neither the inattentive nor the unbeliever will be able to read such Truths. And the elaborate constellation of numbers which in part seem to make "sense" and in part do not is part of that greater text manifesting itself, leaving its markers in real life, although they can only serve as such markers if and when someone can read them. It is clear, for example, that even the "obvious" correspondence of the number nine with Beatrice's appearances and her very person are not perceived or understood by Dante until after the revelation is at hand; it is then, retrospectively, that he is able to understand that she was marked in certain specific ways as significant, unusual, a recurring indicator of the way his writing must turn. The additional fact that there are unavoidable links thus established between Beatrice and Christ caused modern critics some consternation, until Singleton was able to explain the ways in which, in an earlier mode of Christianity, such a tie between personal and universal salvation was in no way blasphemous. But one is also tempted to add, of course, that in many, if not most non-Western religions (and, not surprisingly, in the more universalistic, mystical branches of the Western ones, including the Christianity of the Gospels), the discovery of God within the individual is not only not blasphemous but altogether expected, the revelation that is actively sought in a lifetime. But because Dante is difficult to classify as a mystic, according to the ways in which we have come to label mysticism—i.e., principally by an assumption of a lack of linear coherence—we have discarded this as an additional interpretation of the facts set out in the *Vita Nuova*—that Beatrice is, for him, the Christ, and that Christ, rather than Beatrice, is the metaphor. And yet, Dante dearly is setting out for us in this text a mode of first reading and then writing the Truth that lies at the far end of the traditional and caricatured view we have of the mystical experience as unsayable, but is, if anything, even further removed

from that positivist dichotomy of fact versus fiction with which we perforce operate in our times and in our culture. In the new life, when the old gods and the first loves are dead, Truth is strange, and it is everywhere to be read, and poetry is its handmaiden.

FURTHER READING

Ahern, John. "The New Life of the Book: The Implied Reader of the *Vita Nuova*." *Dante Studies* 110 (1992): 1-16.

> Argues that the *Vita Nuova* addresses a variety of distinct audiences.

Bloom, Harold. "Introduction." In *Dante: Modern Critical Views,* edited by Harold Bloom, pp. 1-9. New York: Chelsea House, 1986.

> Suggests that Beatrice is a difficult character for the modern reader to accept because she is charged with such a high degree of symbolic meaning.

Durling, Robert M. and Ronald L. Martinez. "Early Experiments: *Vita Nuova* 19." In *Time and the Crystal: Studies in Dante's "Rime Petrose,"* pp. 53-70. Berkeley: University of California Press, 1990.

> Examines Dante's experimental use of Neoplatonic and Boethian elements in the *Vita Nuova*, focusing on the first canzone.

Hall, Robert A. *A Short History of Italian Literature.* Ithaca: Linguistica, 1951, 420 p.

> Argues that the *Vita Nuova* is more important "in Dante's own life and in Italian literature than any of his other writings" because it lays the groundwork for the *Commedia*.

Kleiner, John. "Finding the Center: Revelation and Reticence in the *Vita Nuova*." *Texas Studies in Literature and Language* 32 (Spring, 1990): 85-100.

> Finds a contrary tendency in the *Vita Nuova* to both reveal and conceal Beatrice.

Mazzotta, Giuseppe. "Introduction." In *Dante, Poet of the Desert: History and Allegory in the "Divine Comedy,"* pp. 3-13. Princeton: Princeton University Press, 1979.

> Argues that Dante's sense of history is informed by sacred history, hinging on salvation.

———. "The Light of Venus and the Poetry of Dante: *Vita Nuova* and *Inferno* XXVII." In *Dante: Modern Critical Views*, edited by Harold Bloom, pp. 189-204. New York: Chelsea House, 1986.

> Discusses the ways classical rhetoric is used in several of Dante's works, including the *Vita Nuova*.

Scott, J. A. "Notes on Religion and the *Vita Nuova*."

Italian Studies 20 (1965): 17-25.
> Compares Dante's experience of love to that of Christian baptism.

————. "Dante's 'Sweet New Style' and the *Vita Nuova*." *Italica* 42, No. 1 (1965): 98-107.
> Discusses the relationship of the *Vita Nuova* to more traditional poetry.

Singleton, Charles S. "*Vita Nuova* XII: Love's Obscure Words." *The Romanic Review* 36 (April 1945): 89-102.
> Proposes that the personification of Love, who appears to Dante in a dream, foretells Beatrice's death.

Sturm-Maddox, Sara. "The Pattern of Witness: Narrative Design in the *Vita Nuova*." *Forum Italicum* 12, No. 2 (Summer 1978): 216-32.
> Argues that the prose commentary tests "the sentiments and solutions proclaimed in the poems in terms of a life experience."

Vincent, E. R. "The Crisis in the *Vita Nuova*." In *Centenary Essays on Dante*, pp. 132-42. Oxford: Clarendon Press, 1965.
> Takes a stance against generations of critics who read the *Vita Nuova* as the account of a religious conversion, insisting that the crisis is entirely secular in nature.

Wheelock, James T. S. "A Function of the *Amore* Figure in the *Vita Nuova*." *Romanic Review* 68, No. 4 (November 1977): 276-86.
> Explores the difficulties in Dante's attempt to reconcile "the profane poetic tradition of Provence" with a thoroughly Christian frame of reference.

Witte, Karl. "Dante's Trilogy." In *Essays on Dante, Being Selections from the Two Volumes of 'Dante-Forschungen',* translated and edited by C. Mabel Lawrence and Philip H. Wicksteed, pp. 61-96. Boston and New York: Houghton, Mifflin, 1898.
> Gives a line-by-line comparison of Dante's accounts of his experience in the *Vita Nuova* and the *Convivio*.

Additional coverage of Dante's life and career is contained in the following source published by Gale Research: *Classical and Medieval Literature Criticism*, Vol. 3.

CLASSICAL AND MEDIEVAL LITERATURE CRITICISM

INDEXES

How to Use This Index

The main references

Calvino, Italo
1923-1985.....CLC 5, 8, 11, 22, 33, 39,
73; SSC 3

list all author entries in the following Gale Literary Criticism series:

BLC = *Black Literature Criticism*
CLC = *Contemporary Literary Criticism*
CLR = *Children's Literature Review*
CMLC = *Classical and Medieval Literature*
    Criticism
DA = *DISCovering Authors*
DAB = *DISCovering Authors: British*
DAC = *DISCovering Authors: Canadian*
DAM = *DISCovering Authors Modules*
    DRAM: Dramatists module
    MST: Most-studied authors module
    MULT: Multicultural authors module
    NOV: Novelists module
    POET: Poets module
    POP: Popular/genre writers module

DC = *Drama Criticism*
HLC = *Hispanic Literature Criticism*
LC = *Literature Criticism from 1400 to 1800*
NCLC = *Nineteenth-Century Literature Criticism*
PC = *Poetry Criticism*
SSC = *Short Story Criticism*
TCLC = *Twentieth-Century Literary Criticism*
WLC = *World Literature Criticism, 1500 to the*
    Present

The cross-references

See also CANR 23; CA 85-88;
obituary CA 116

list all author entries in the following Gale biographical and literary sources:

AAYA = *Authors & Artists for Young Adults*
AITN = *Authors in the News*
BEST = *Bestsellers*
BW = *Black Writers*
CA = *Contemporary Authors*
CAAS = *Contemporary Authors*
    Autobiography Series
CABS = *Contemporary Authors*
    Bibliographical Series
CANR = *Contemporary Authors New*
    Revision Series
CAP = *Contemporary Authors Permanent*
    Series
CDALB = *Concise Dictionary of American*
    Literary Biography
CDBLB = *Concise Dictionary of British*
    Literary Biography

DLB = *Dictionary of Literary Biography*
DLBD = *Dictionary of Literary Biography*
    Documentary Series
DLBY = *Dictionary of Literary Biography Yearbook*
HW = *Hispanic Writers*
JRDA = *Junior DISCovering Authors*
MAICYA = *Major Authors and Illustrators for*
    Children and Young Adults
MTCW = *Major 20th-Century Writers*
NNAL = *Native North American Literature*
SAAS = *Something about the Author Autobiography*
    Series
SATA = *Something about the Author*
YABC = *Yesterday's Authors of Books for Children*

Literary Criticism Series
Cumulative Author Index

A. E. . . . . TCLC 3, 10
  See also Russell, George William

Abasiyanik, Sait Faik 1906-1954
  See Sait Faik
  See also CA 123

Abbey, Edward 1927-1989 . . . . . . CLC 36, 59
  See also CA 45-48; 128; CANR 2, 41

Abbott, Lee K(ittredge) 1947- . . . . . . CLC 48
  See also CA 124; CANR 51; DLB 130

Abe, Kobo 1924-1993 . . . . . CLC 8, 22, 53, 81
  See also CA 65-68; 140; CANR 24;
  DAM NOV; MTCW

Abelard, Peter c. 1079-c. 1142 . . . CMLC 11
  See also DLB 115

Abell, Kjeld 1901-1961 . . . . CLC 15
  See also CA 111

Abish, Walter 1931- . . . . CLC 22
  See also CA 101; CANR 37; DLB 130

Abrahams, Peter (Henry) 1919- . . . . . CLC 4
  See also BW 1; CA 57-60; CANR 26;
  DLB 117; MTCW

Abrams, M(eyer) H(oward) 1912- . . . CLC 24
  See also CA 57-60; CANR 13, 33; DLB 67

Abse, Dannie 1923- . . . . CLC 7, 29; DAB
  See also CA 53-56; CAAS 1; CANR 4, 46;
  DAM POET; DLB 27

Achebe, (Albert) Chinua(lumogu)
  1930- . . . . . CLC 1, 3, 5, 7, 11, 26, 51, 75;
  BLC; DA; DAB; DAC; WLC
  See also AAYA 15; BW 2; CA 1-4R;
  CANR 6, 26, 47; CLR 20; DAM MST,
  MULT, NOV; DLB 117; MAICYA;
  MTCW; SATA 40; SATA-Brief 38

Acker, Kathy 1948- . . . . CLC 45
  See also CA 117; 122

Ackroyd, Peter 1949- . . . . CLC 34, 52
  See also CA 123; 127; CANR 51; DLB 155;
  INT 127

Acorn, Milton 1923- . . . . CLC 15; DAC
  See also CA 103; DLB 53; INT 103

Adamov, Arthur 1908-1970 . . . . . . CLC 4, 25
  See also CA 17-18; 25-28R; CAP 2;
  DAM DRAM; MTCW

Adams, Alice (Boyd)
  1926- . . . . CLC 6, 13, 46; SSC 23
  See also CA 81-84; CANR 26; DLBY 86;
  INT CANR-26; MTCW

Adams, Andy 1859-1935 . . . . TCLC 56
  See also YABC 1

Adams, Douglas (Noel) 1952- . . . CLC 27, 60
  See also AAYA 4; BEST 89:3; CA 106;
  CANR 34; DAM POP; DLBY 83; JRDA

Adams, Francis 1862-1893 . . . . NCLC 33

Adams, Henry (Brooks)
  1838-1918 . . . . . . TCLC 4, 52; DA; DAB;
  DAC
  See also CA 104; 133; DAM MST; DLB 12,
  47

Adams, Richard (George)
  1920- . . . . CLC 4, 5, 18
  See also AAYA 16; AITN 1, 2; CA 49-52;
  CANR 3, 35; CLR 20; DAM NOV;
  JRDA; MAICYA; MTCW; SATA 7, 69

Adamson, Joy(-Friederike Victoria)
  1910-1980 . . . . CLC 17
  See also CA 69-72; 93-96; CANR 22;
  MTCW; SATA 11; SATA-Obit 22

Adcock, Fleur 1934- . . . . CLC 41
  See also CA 25-28R; CAAS 23; CANR 11,
  34; DLB 40

Addams, Charles (Samuel)
  1912-1988 . . . . CLC 30
  See also CA 61-64; 126; CANR 12

Addison, Joseph 1672-1719 . . . . LC 18
  See also CDBLB 1660-1789; DLB 101

Adler, Alfred (F.) 1870-1937 . . . . . . TCLC 61
  See also CA 119

Adler, C(arole) S(chwerdtfeger)
  1932- . . . . CLC 35
  See also AAYA 4; CA 89-92; CANR 19,
  40; JRDA; MAICYA; SAAS 15;
  SATA 26, 63

Adler, Renata 1938- . . . . CLC 8, 31
  See also CA 49-52; CANR 5, 22; MTCW

Ady, Endre 1877-1919 . . . . TCLC 11
  See also CA 107

Aeschylus
  525B.C.-456B.C. . . . . CMLC 11; DA;
  DAB; DAC
  See also DAM DRAM, MST

Afton, Effie
  See Harper, Frances Ellen Watkins

Agapida, Fray Antonio
  See Irving, Washington

Agee, James (Rufus)
  1909-1955 . . . . TCLC 1, 19
  See also AITN 1; CA 108; 148;
  CDALB 1941-1968; DAM NOV; DLB 2,
  26, 152

Aghill, Gordon
  See Silverberg, Robert

Agnon, S(hmuel) Y(osef Halevi)
  1888-1970 . . . . CLC 4, 8, 14
  See also CA 17-18; 25-28R; CAP 2; MTCW

Agrippa von Nettesheim, Henry Cornelius
  1486-1535 . . . . LC 27

Aherne, Owen
  See Cassill, R(onald) V(erlin)

Ai 1947- . . . . CLC 4, 14, 69
  See also CA 85-88; CAAS 13; DLB 120

Aickman, Robert (Fordyce)
  1914-1981 . . . . CLC 57
  See also CA 5-8R; CANR 3

Aiken, Conrad (Potter)
  1889-1973 . . . CLC 1, 3, 5, 10, 52; SSC 9
  See also CA 5-8R; 45-48; CANR 4;
  CDALB 1929-1941; DAM NOV, POET;
  DLB 9, 45, 102; MTCW; SATA 3, 30

Aiken, Joan (Delano) 1924- . . . . CLC 35
  See also AAYA 1; CA 9-12R; CANR 4, 23,
  34; CLR 1, 19; DLB 161; JRDA;
  MAICYA; MTCW; SAAS 1; SATA 2,
  30, 73

Ainsworth, William Harrison
  1805-1882 . . . . NCLC 13
  See also DLB 21; SATA 24

Aitmatov, Chingiz (Torekulovich)
  1928- . . . . CLC 71
  See also CA 103; CANR 38; MTCW;
  SATA 56

Akers, Floyd
  See Baum, L(yman) Frank

Akhmadulina, Bella Akhatovna
  1937- . . . . CLC 53
  See also CA 65-68; DAM POET

Akhmatova, Anna
  1888-1966 . . . . CLC 11, 25, 64; PC 2
  See also CA 19-20; 25-28R; CANR 35;
  CAP 1; DAM POET; MTCW

Aksakov, Sergei Timofeyvich
  1791-1859 . . . . NCLC 2

Aksenov, Vassily
  See Aksyonov, Vassily (Pavlovich)

Aksyonov, Vassily (Pavlovich)
  1932- . . . . CLC 22, 37
  See also CA 53-56; CANR 12, 48

Akutagawa Ryunosuke
  1892-1927 . . . . TCLC 16
  See also CA 117

Alain 1868-1951 . . . . TCLC 41

Alain-Fournier . . . . TCLC 6
  See also Fournier, Henri Alban
  See also DLB 65

Alarcon, Pedro Antonio de
  1833-1891 . . . . NCLC 1

Alas (y Urena), Leopoldo (Enrique Garcia)
  1852-1901 . . . . TCLC 29
  See also CA 113; 131; HW

Albee, Edward (Franklin III)
  1928- . . . . . . CLC 1, 2, 3, 5, 9, 11, 13, 25,
  53, 86; DA; DAB; DAC; WLC
  See also AITN 1; CA 5-8R; CABS 3;
  CANR 8; CDALB 1941-1968;
  DAM DRAM, MST; DLB 7;
  INT CANR-8; MTCW

Alberti, Rafael 1902- . . . . CLC 7
  See also CA 85-88; DLB 108

Albert the Great   1200(?)-1280.... **CMLC 16**
See also DLB 115

Alcala-Galiano, Juan Valera y
See Valera y Alcala-Galiano, Juan

Alcott, Amos Bronson   1799-1888 .. **NCLC 1**
See also DLB 1

Alcott, Louisa May
1832-1888 .... **NCLC 6; DA; DAB;
DAC; WLC**
See also CDALB 1865-1917; CLR 1, 38;
DAM MST, NOV; DLB 1, 42, 79; JRDA;
MAICYA; YABC 1

Aldanov, M. A.
See Aldanov, Mark (Alexandrovich)

Aldanov, Mark (Alexandrovich)
1886(?)-1957 .... **TCLC 23**
See also CA 118

Aldington, Richard   1892-1962...... **CLC 49**
See also CA 85-88; CANR 45; DLB 20, 36,
100, 149

Aldiss, Brian W(ilson)
1925- .... **CLC 5, 14, 40**
See also CA 5-8R; CAAS 2; CANR 5, 28;
DAM NOV; DLB 14; MTCW; SATA 34

Alegria, Claribel   1924-........... **CLC 75**
See also CA 131; CAAS 15; DAM MULT;
DLB 145; HW

Alegria, Fernando   1918-........... **CLC 57**
See also CA 9-12R; CANR 5, 32; HW

Aleichem, Sholom .... **TCLC 1, 35**
See also Rabinovitch, Sholem

Aleixandre, Vicente
1898-1984 .... **CLC 9, 36; PC 15**
See also CA 85-88; 114; CANR 26;
DAM POET; DLB 108; HW; MTCW

Alepoudelis, Odysseus
See Elytis, Odysseus

Aleshkovsky, Joseph   1929-
See Aleshkovsky, Yuz
See also CA 121; 128

Aleshkovsky, Yuz .... **CLC 44**
See also Aleshkovsky, Joseph

Alexander, Lloyd (Chudley)   1924- .. **CLC 35**
See also AAYA 1; CA 1-4R; CANR 1, 24,
38; CLR 1, 5; DLB 52; JRDA; MAICYA;
MTCW; SAAS 19; SATA 3, 49, 81

Alfau, Felipe   1902-............... **CLC 66**
See also CA 137

Alger, Horatio, Jr.   1832-1899 ..... **NCLC 8**
See also DLB 42; SATA 16

Algren, Nelson   1909-1981 .... **CLC 4, 10, 33**
See also CA 13-16R; 103; CANR 20;
CDALB 1941-1968; DLB 9; DLBY 81,
82; MTCW

Ali, Ahmed   1910- .... **CLC 69**
See also CA 25-28R; CANR 15, 34

Alighieri, Dante   1265-1321 .... **CMLC 3, 18**

Allan, John B.
See Westlake, Donald E(dwin)

Allen, Edward   1948-............. **CLC 59**

Allen, Paula Gunn   1939-.......... **CLC 84**
See also CA 112; 143; DAM MULT;
NNAL

Allen, Roland
See Ayckbourn, Alan

Allen, Sarah A.
See Hopkins, Pauline Elizabeth

Allen, Woody   1935-.......... **CLC 16, 52**
See also AAYA 10; CA 33-36R; CANR 27,
38; DAM POP; DLB 44; MTCW

Allende, Isabel   1942- .... **CLC 39, 57; HLC**
See also CA 125; 130; CANR 51;
DAM MULT, NOV; DLB 145; HW;
INT 130; MTCW

Alleyn, Ellen
See Rossetti, Christina (Georgina)

Allingham, Margery (Louise)
1904-1966 .... **CLC 19**
See also CA 5-8R; 25-28R; CANR 4;
DLB 77; MTCW

Allingham, William   1824-1889 ... **NCLC 25**
See also DLB 35

Allison, Dorothy E.   1949-......... **CLC 78**
See also CA 140

Allston, Washington   1779-1843.... **NCLC 2**
See also DLB 1

Almedingen, E. M. .... **CLC 12**
See also Almedingen, Martha Edith von
See also SATA 3

Almedingen, Martha Edith von   1898-1971
See Almedingen, E. M.
See also CA 1-4R; CANR 1

Almqvist, Carl Jonas Love
1793-1866 .... **NCLC 42**

Alonso, Damaso   1898-1990 .... **CLC 14**
See also CA 110; 131; 130; DLB 108; HW

Alov
See Gogol, Nikolai (Vasilyevich)

Alta   1942-...................... **CLC 19**
See also CA 57-60

Alter, Robert B(ernard)   1935-...... **CLC 34**
See also CA 49-52; CANR 1, 47

Alther, Lisa   1944-.............. **CLC 7, 41**
See also CA 65-68; CANR 12, 30, 51;
MTCW

Altman, Robert   1925-............. **CLC 16**
See also CA 73-76; CANR 43

Alvarez, A(lfred)   1929-.......... **CLC 5, 13**
See also CA 1-4R; CANR 3, 33; DLB 14,
40

Alvarez, Alejandro Rodriguez   1903-1965
See Casona, Alejandro
See also CA 131; 93-96; HW

Alvarez, Julia   1950-.............. **CLC 93**
See also CA 147

Alvaro, Corrado   1896-1956 .... **TCLC 60**

Amado, Jorge   1912-..... **CLC 13, 40; HLC**
See also CA 77-80; CANR 35;
DAM MULT, NOV; DLB 113; MTCW

Ambler, Eric   1909-............ **CLC 4, 6, 9**
See also CA 9-12R; CANR 7, 38; DLB 77;
MTCW

Amichai, Yehuda   1924- ...... **CLC 9, 22, 57**
See also CA 85-88; CANR 46; MTCW

Amiel, Henri Frederic   1821-1881 .. **NCLC 4**

Amis, Kingsley (William)
1922-1995 ..... **CLC 1, 2, 3, 5, 8, 13, 40,
44; DA; DAB; DAC**
See also AITN 2; CA 9-12R; 150; CANR 8,
28; CDBLB 1945-1960; DAM MST,
NOV; DLB 15, 27, 100, 139;
INT CANR-8; MTCW

Amis, Martin (Louis)
1949- .... **CLC 4, 9, 38, 62**
See also BEST 90:3; CA 65-68; CANR 8,
27; DLB 14; INT CANR-27

Ammons, A(rchie) R(andolph)
1926- .... **CLC 2, 3, 5, 8, 9, 25, 57**
See also AITN 1; CA 9-12R; CANR 6, 36,
51; DAM POET; DLB 5, 165; MTCW

Amo, Tauraatua i
See Adams, Henry (Brooks)

Anand, Mulk Raj   1905-........ **CLC 23, 93**
See also CA 65-68; CANR 32; DAM NOV;
MTCW

Anatol
See Schnitzler, Arthur

Anaya, Rudolfo A(lfonso)
1937- .... **CLC 23; HLC**
See also CA 45-48; CAAS 4; CANR 1, 32,
51; DAM MULT, NOV; DLB 82; HW 1;
MTCW

Andersen, Hans Christian
1805-1875 .... **NCLC 7; DA; DAB;
DAC; SSC 6; WLC**
See also CLR 6; DAM MST, POP;
MAICYA; YABC 1

Anderson, C. Farley
See Mencken, H(enry) L(ouis); Nathan,
George Jean

Anderson, Jessica (Margaret) Queale
.... **CLC 37**
See also CA 9-12R; CANR 4

Anderson, Jon (Victor)   1940- .... **CLC 9**
See also CA 25-28R; CANR 20;
DAM POET

Anderson, Lindsay (Gordon)
1923-1994 .... **CLC 20**
See also CA 125; 128; 146

Anderson, Maxwell   1888-1959 ..... **TCLC 2**
See also CA 105; DAM DRAM; DLB 7

Anderson, Poul (William)   1926- .... **CLC 15**
See also AAYA 5; CA 1-4R; CAAS 2;
CANR 2, 15, 34; DLB 8; INT CANR-15;
MTCW; SATA-Brief 39

Anderson, Robert (Woodruff)
1917- .... **CLC 23**
See also AITN 1; CA 21-24R; CANR 32;
DAM DRAM; DLB 7

Anderson, Sherwood
1876-1941 .... **TCLC 1, 10, 24; DA;
DAB; DAC; SSC 1; WLC**
See also CA 104; 121; CDALB 1917-1929;
DAM MST, NOV; DLB 4, 9, 86;
DLBD 1; MTCW

Andouard
See Giraudoux, (Hippolyte) Jean

Andrade, Carlos Drummond de ...... **CLC 18**
See also Drummond de Andrade, Carlos

Andrade, Mario de   1893-1945..... **TCLC 43**

Andreae, Johann V(alentin)
1586-1654 . . . . **LC 32**
See also DLB 164

Andreas-Salome, Lou 1861-1937 . . . **TCLC 56**
See also DLB 66

Andrewes, Lancelot 1555-1626 . . . . **LC 5**
See also DLB 151

Andrews, Cicily Fairfield
See West, Rebecca

Andrews, Elton V.
See Pohl, Frederik

Andreyev, Leonid (Nikolaevich)
1871-1919 . . . . **TCLC 3**
See also CA 104

Andric, Ivo 1892-1975 . . . . **CLC 8**
See also CA 81-84; 57-60; CANR 43;
DLB 147; MTCW

Angelique, Pierre
See Bataille, Georges

Angell, Roger 1920- . . . . **CLC 26**
See also CA 57-60; CANR 13, 44

Angelou, Maya
1928- . . . . **CLC 12, 35, 64, 77; BLC; DA;**
DAB; DAC
See also AAYA 7; BW 2; CA 65-68;
CANR 19, 42; DAM MST, MULT,
POET, POP; DLB 38; MTCW; SATA 49

Annensky, Innokenty Fyodorovich
1856-1909 . . . . **TCLC 14**
See also CA 110

Anon, Charles Robert
See Pessoa, Fernando (Antonio Nogueira)

Anouilh, Jean (Marie Lucien Pierre)
1910-1987 . . . . . . **CLC 1, 3, 8, 13, 40, 50**
See also CA 17-20R; 123; CANR 32;
DAM DRAM; MTCW

Anthony, Florence
See Ai

Anthony, John
See Ciardi, John (Anthony)

Anthony, Peter
See Shaffer, Anthony (Joshua); Shaffer,
Peter (Levin)

Anthony, Piers 1934- . . . . **CLC 35**
See also AAYA 11; CA 21-24R; CANR 28;
DAM POP; DLB 8; MTCW; SAAS 22;
SATA 84

Antoine, Marc
See Proust, (Valentin-Louis-George-Eugene-)
Marcel

Antoninus, Brother
See Everson, William (Oliver)

Antonioni, Michelangelo 1912- . . . . . **CLC 20**
See also CA 73-76; CANR 45

Antschel, Paul 1920-1970
See Celan, Paul
See also CA 85-88; CANR 33; MTCW

Anwar, Chairil 1922-1949 . . . . **TCLC 22**
See also CA 121

Apollinaire, Guillaume . . **TCLC 3, 8, 51; PC 7**
See also Kostrowitzki, Wilhelm Apollinaris
de
See also DAM POET

Appelfeld, Aharon 1932- . . . . **CLC 23, 47**
See also CA 112; 133

Apple, Max (Isaac) 1941- . . . . **CLC 9, 33**
See also CA 81-84; CANR 19; DLB 130

Appleman, Philip (Dean) 1926- . . . . . **CLC 51**
See also CA 13-16R; CAAS 18; CANR 6,
29

Appleton, Lawrence
See Lovecraft, H(oward) P(hillips)

Apteryx
See Eliot, T(homas) S(tearns)

Apuleius, (Lucius Madaurensis)
125(?)-175(?) . . . . **CMLC 1**

Aquin, Hubert 1929-1977 . . . . **CLC 15**
See also CA 105; DLB 53

Aragon, Louis 1897-1982 . . . . **CLC 3, 22**
See also CA 69-72; 108; CANR 28;
DAM NOV, POET; DLB 72; MTCW

Arany, Janos 1817-1882 . . . . **NCLC 34**

Arbuthnot, John 1667-1735 . . . . **LC 1**
See also DLB 101

Archer, Herbert Winslow
See Mencken, H(enry) L(ouis)

Archer, Jeffrey (Howard) 1940- . . . . **CLC 28**
See also AAYA 16; BEST 89:3; CA 77-80;
CANR 22; DAM POP; INT CANR-22

Archer, Jules 1915- . . . . **CLC 12**
See also CA 9-12R; CANR 6; SAAS 5;
SATA 4, 85

Archer, Lee
See Ellison, Harlan (Jay)

Arden, John 1930- . . . . **CLC 6, 13, 15**
See also CA 13-16R; CAAS 4; CANR 31;
DAM DRAM; DLB 13; MTCW

Arenas, Reinaldo
1943-1990 . . . . **CLC 41; HLC**
See also CA 124; 128; 133; DAM MULT;
DLB 145; HW

Arendt, Hannah 1906-1975 . . . . **CLC 66**
See also CA 17-20R; 61-64; CANR 26;
MTCW

Aretino, Pietro 1492-1556 . . . . **LC 12**

Arghezi, Tudor . . . . **CLC 80**
See also Theodorescu, Ion N.

Arguedas, Jose Maria
1911-1969 . . . . **CLC 10, 18**
See also CA 89-92; DLB 113; HW

Argueta, Manlio 1936- . . . . **CLC 31**
See also CA 131; DLB 145; HW

Ariosto, Ludovico 1474-1533 . . . . **LC 6**

Aristides
See Epstein, Joseph

Aristophanes
450B.C.-385B.C. . . . . **CMLC 4; DA;**
DAB; DAC; DC 2
See also DAM DRAM, MST

Arlt, Roberto (Godofredo Christophersen)
1900-1942 . . . . **TCLC 29; HLC**
See also CA 123; 131; DAM MULT; HW

Armah, Ayi Kwei 1939- . . . . **CLC 5, 33; BLC**
See also BW 1; CA 61-64; CANR 21;
DAM MULT, POET; DLB 117; MTCW

Armatrading, Joan 1950- . . . . **CLC 17**
See also CA 114

Arnette, Robert
See Silverberg, Robert

Arnim, Achim von (Ludwig Joachim von
Arnim) 1781-1831 . . . . **NCLC 5**
See also DLB 90

Arnim, Bettina von 1785-1859 . . . . **NCLC 38**
See also DLB 90

Arnold, Matthew
1822-1888 . . . . . **NCLC 6, 29; DA; DAB;**
DAC; PC 5; WLC
See also CDBLB 1832-1890; DAM MST,
POET; DLB 32, 57

Arnold, Thomas 1795-1842 . . . . . . **NCLC 18**
See also DLB 55

Arnow, Harriette (Louisa) Simpson
1908-1986 . . . . **CLC 2, 7, 18**
See also CA 9-12R; 118; CANR 14; DLB 6;
MTCW; SATA 42; SATA-Obit 47

Arp, Hans
See Arp, Jean

Arp, Jean 1887-1966 . . . . **CLC 5**
See also CA 81-84; 25-28R; CANR 42

Arrabal
See Arrabal, Fernando

Arrabal, Fernando 1932- . . . **CLC 2, 9, 18, 58**
See also CA 9-12R; CANR 15

Arrick, Fran . . . . **CLC 30**
See also Gaberman, Judie Angell

Artaud, Antonin (Marie Joseph)
1896-1948 . . . . **TCLC 3, 36**
See also CA 104; 149; DAM DRAM

Arthur, Ruth M(abel) 1905-1979 . . . . **CLC 12**
See also CA 9-12R; 85-88; CANR 4;
SATA 7, 26

Artsybashev, Mikhail (Petrovich)
1878-1927 . . . . **TCLC 31**

Arundel, Honor (Morfydd)
1919-1973 . . . . **CLC 17**
See also CA 21-22; 41-44R; CAP 2;
CLR 35; SATA 4; SATA-Obit 24

Asch, Sholem 1880-1957 . . . . **TCLC 3**
See also CA 105

Ash, Shalom
See Asch, Sholem

Ashbery, John (Lawrence)
1927- . . . . . . **CLC 2, 3, 4, 6, 9, 13, 15, 25,**
41, 77
See also CA 5-8R; CANR 9, 37;
DAM POET; DLB 5, 165; DLBY 81;
INT CANR-9; MTCW

Ashdown, Clifford
See Freeman, R(ichard) Austin

Ashe, Gordon
See Creasey, John

Ashton-Warner, Sylvia (Constance)
1908-1984 . . . . **CLC 19**
See also CA 69-72; 112; CANR 29; MTCW

Asimov, Isaac
1920-1992 . . . **CLC 1, 3, 9, 19, 26, 76, 92**
See also AAYA 13; BEST 90:2; CA 1-4R;
137; CANR 2, 19, 36; CLR 12;
DAM POP; DLB 8; DLBY 92;
INT CANR-19; JRDA; MAICYA;
MTCW; SATA 1, 26, 74

Astley, Thea (Beatrice May)
1925- . . . . **CLC 41**
See also CA 65-68; CANR 11, 43

Bennett, (Enoch) Arnold
　　1867-1931 . . . . TCLC **5, 20**
　　See also CA 106; CDBLB 1890-1914;
　　DLB 10, 34, 98, 135

Bennett, Elizabeth
　　See Mitchell, Margaret (Munnerlyn)

Bennett, George Harold　1930-
　　See Bennett, Hal
　　See also BW 1; CA 97-100

Bennett, Hal . . . . CLC **5**
　　See also Bennett, George Harold
　　See also DLB 33

Bennett, Jay　1912- . . . . CLC **35**
　　See also AAYA 10; CA 69-72; CANR 11,
　　42; JRDA; SAAS 4; SATA 41, 87;
　　SATA-Brief 27

Bennett, Louise (Simone)
　　1919- . . . . CLC **28**; BLC
　　See also BW 2; DAM MULT; DLB 117

Benson, E(dward) F(rederic)
　　1867-1940 . . . . TCLC **27**
　　See also CA 114; DLB 135, 153

Benson, Jackson J.　1930- . . . . CLC **34**
　　See also CA 25-28R; DLB 111

Benson, Sally　1900-1972 . . . . CLC **17**
　　See also CA 19-20; 37-40R; CAP 1;
　　SATA 1, 35; SATA-Obit 27

Benson, Stella　1892-1933 . . . . TCLC **17**
　　See also CA 117; DLB 36, 162

Bentham, Jeremy　1748-1832 . . . . . NCLC **38**
　　See also DLB 107, 158

Bentley, E(dmund) C(lerihew)
　　1875-1956 . . . . TCLC **12**
　　See also CA 108; DLB 70

Bentley, Eric (Russell)　1916- . . . . CLC **24**
　　See also CA 5-8R; CANR 6; INT CANR-6

Beranger, Pierre Jean de
　　1780-1857 . . . . NCLC **34**

Berendt, John (Lawrence)　1939- . . . . CLC **86**
　　See also CA 146

Berger, Colonel
　　See Malraux, (Georges-)Andre

Berger, John (Peter)　1926- . . . . . . CLC **2, 19**
　　See also CA 81-84; CANR 51; DLB 14

Berger, Melvin H.　1927- . . . . CLC **12**
　　See also CA 5-8R; CANR 4; CLR 32;
　　SAAS 2; SATA 5

Berger, Thomas (Louis)
　　1924- . . . . CLC **3, 5, 8, 11, 18, 38**
　　See also CA 1-4R; CANR 5, 28, 51;
　　DAM NOV; DLB 2; DLBY 80;
　　INT CANR-28; MTCW

Bergman, (Ernst) Ingmar
　　1918- . . . . CLC **16, 72**
　　See also CA 81-84; CANR 33

Bergson, Henri　1859-1941 . . . . TCLC **32**

Bergstein, Eleanor　1938- . . . . CLC **4**
　　See also CA 53-56; CANR 5

Berkoff, Steven　1937- . . . . CLC **56**
　　See also CA 104

Bermant, Chaim (Icyk)　1929- . . . . . . CLC **40**
　　See also CA 57-60; CANR 6, 31

Bern, Victoria
　　See Fisher, M(ary) F(rances) K(ennedy)

Bernanos, (Paul Louis) Georges
　　1888-1948 . . . . TCLC **3**
　　See also CA 104; 130; DLB 72

Bernard, April　1956- . . . . CLC **59**
　　See also CA 131

Berne, Victoria
　　See Fisher, M(ary) F(rances) K(ennedy)

Bernhard, Thomas
　　1931-1989 . . . . CLC **3, 32, 61**
　　See also CA 85-88; 127; CANR 32;
　　DLB 85, 124; MTCW

Berriault, Gina　1926- . . . . CLC **54**
　　See also CA 116; 129; DLB 130

Berrigan, Daniel　1921- . . . . CLC **4**
　　See also CA 33-36R; CAAS 1; CANR 11,
　　43; DLB 5

Berrigan, Edmund Joseph Michael, Jr.
　　1934-1983
　　See Berrigan, Ted
　　See also CA 61-64; 110; CANR 14

Berrigan, Ted . . . . CLC **37**
　　See also Berrigan, Edmund Joseph Michael,
　　Jr.
　　See also DLB 5

Berry, Charles Edward Anderson　1931-
　　See Berry, Chuck
　　See also CA 115

Berry, Chuck . . . . CLC **17**
　　See also Berry, Charles Edward Anderson

Berry, Jonas
　　See Ashbery, John (Lawrence)

Berry, Wendell (Erdman)
　　1934- . . . . CLC **4, 6, 8, 27, 46**
　　See also AITN 1; CA 73-76; CANR 50;
　　DAM POET; DLB 5, 6

Berryman, John
　　1914-1972 . . . . . . CLC **1, 2, 3, 4, 6, 8, 10,
　　　　　　　　　　　　　　13, 25, 62**
　　See also CA 13-16; 33-36R; CABS 2;
　　CANR 35; CAP 1; CDALB 1941-1968;
　　DAM POET; DLB 48; MTCW

Bertolucci, Bernardo　1940- . . . . CLC **16**
　　See also CA 106

Bertrand, Aloysius　1807-1841 . . . . NCLC **31**

Bertran de Born　c. 1140-1215 . . . . . CMLC **5**

Besant, Annie (Wood)　1847-1933 . . . TCLC **9**
　　See also CA 105

Bessie, Alvah　1904-1985 . . . . CLC **23**
　　See also CA 5-8R; 116; CANR 2; DLB 26

Bethlen, T. D.
　　See Silverberg, Robert

Beti, Mongo . . . . CLC **27**; BLC
　　See also Biyidi, Alexandre
　　See also DAM MULT

Betjeman, John
　　1906-1984 . . . CLC **2, 6, 10, 34, 43**; DAB
　　See also CA 9-12R; 112; CANR 33;
　　CDBLB 1945-1960; DAM MST, POET;
　　DLB 20; DLBY 84; MTCW

Bettelheim, Bruno　1903-1990 . . . . . . CLC **79**
　　See also CA 81-84; 131; CANR 23; MTCW

Betti, Ugo　1892-1953 . . . . TCLC **5**
　　See also CA 104

Betts, Doris (Waugh)　1932- . . . . CLC **3, 6, 28**
　　See also CA 13-16R; CANR 9; DLBY 82;
　　INT CANR-9

Bevan, Alistair
　　See Roberts, Keith (John Kingston)

Bialik, Chaim Nachman
　　1873-1934 . . . . TCLC **25**

Bickerstaff, Isaac
　　See Swift, Jonathan

Bidart, Frank　1939- . . . . CLC **33**
　　See also CA 140

Bienek, Horst　1930- . . . . CLC **7, 11**
　　See also CA 73-76; DLB 75

Bierce, Ambrose (Gwinett)
　　1842-1914(?) . . . . TCLC **1, 7, 44**; DA;
　　　　　　　　　　　　DAC; SSC **9**; WLC
　　See also CA 104; 139; CDALB 1865-1917;
　　DAM MST; DLB 11, 12, 23, 71, 74

Billings, Josh
　　See Shaw, Henry Wheeler

Billington, (Lady) Rachel (Mary)
　　1942- . . . . CLC **43**
　　See also AITN 2; CA 33-36R; CANR 44

Binyon, T(imothy) J(ohn)　1936- . . . . CLC **34**
　　See also CA 111; CANR 28

Bioy Casares, Adolfo
　　1914- . . . CLC **4, 8, 13, 88**; HLC; SSC **17**
　　See also CA 29-32R; CANR 19, 43;
　　DAM MULT; DLB 113; HW; MTCW

Bird, Cordwainer
　　See Ellison, Harlan (Jay)

Bird, Robert Montgomery
　　1806-1854 . . . . NCLC **1**

Birney, (Alfred) Earle
　　1904- . . . . CLC **1, 4, 6, 11**; DAC
　　See also CA 1-4R; CANR 5, 20;
　　DAM MST, POET; DLB 88; MTCW

Bishop, Elizabeth
　　1911-1979 . . . . . . CLC **1, 4, 9, 13, 15, 32**;
　　　　　　　　　　　　DA; DAC; PC **3**
　　See also CA 5-8R; 89-92; CABS 2;
　　CANR 26; CDALB 1968-1988;
　　DAM MST, POET; DLB 5; MTCW;
　　SATA-Obit 24

Bishop, John　1935- . . . . CLC **10**
　　See also CA 105

Bissett, Bill　1939- . . . . CLC **18**; PC **14**
　　See also CA 69-72; CAAS 19; CANR 15;
　　DLB 53; MTCW

Bitov, Andrei (Georgievich)　1937- . . . CLC **57**
　　See also CA 142

Biyidi, Alexandre　1932-
　　See Beti, Mongo
　　See also BW 1; CA 114; 124; MTCW

Bjarme, Brynjolf
　　See Ibsen, Henrik (Johan)

Bjornson, Bjornstjerne (Martinius)
　　1832-1910 . . . . TCLC **7, 37**
　　See also CA 104

Black, Robert
　　See Holdstock, Robert P.

Blackburn, Paul　1926-1971 . . . . . . CLC **9, 43**
　　See also CA 81-84; 33-36R; CANR 34;
　　DLB 16; DLBY 81

Black Elk 1863-1950 . . . . **TCLC 33**
See also CA 144; DAM MULT; NNAL

Black Hobart
See Sanders, (James) Ed(ward)

Blacklin, Malcolm
See Chambers, Aidan

Blackmore, R(ichard) D(oddridge)
1825-1900 . . . . **TCLC 27**
See also CA 120; DLB 18

Blackmur, R(ichard) P(almer)
1904-1965 . . . . **CLC 2, 24**
See also CA 11-12; 25-28R; CAP 1; DLB 63

Black Tarantula, The
See Acker, Kathy

Blackwood, Algernon (Henry)
1869-1951 . . . . **TCLC 5**
See also CA 105; 150; DLB 153, 156

Blackwood, Caroline 1931- . . . . **CLC 6, 9**
See also CA 85-88; CANR 32; DLB 14;
MTCW

Blade, Alexander
See Hamilton, Edmond; Silverberg, Robert

Blaga, Lucian 1895-1961 . . . . **CLC 75**

Blair, Eric (Arthur) 1903-1950
See Orwell, George
See also CA 104; 132; DA; DAB; DAC;
DAM MST, NOV; MTCW; SATA 29

Blais, Marie-Claire
1939- . . . . **CLC 2, 4, 6, 13, 22; DAC**
See also CA 21-24R; CAAS 4; CANR 38;
DAM MST; DLB 53; MTCW

Blaise, Clark 1940- . . . . **CLC 29**
See also AITN 2; CA 53-56; CAAS 3;
CANR 5; DLB 53

Blake, Nicholas
See Day Lewis, C(ecil)
See also DLB 77

Blake, William
1757-1827 . . . . **NCLC 13, 37; DA; DAB;**
DAC; PC 12; WLC
See also CDBLB 1789-1832; DAM MST,
POET; DLB 93, 163; MAICYA;
SATA 30

Blake, William J(ames) 1894-1969 . . . **PC 12**
See also CA 5-8R; 25-28R

Blasco Ibanez, Vicente
1867-1928 . . . . **TCLC 12**
See also CA 110; 131; DAM NOV; HW;
MTCW

Blatty, William Peter 1928- . . . . **CLC 2**
See also CA 5-8R; CANR 9; DAM POP

Bleeck, Oliver
See Thomas, Ross (Elmore)

Blessing, Lee 1949- . . . . **CLC 54**

Blish, James (Benjamin)
1921-1975 . . . . **CLC 14**
See also CA 1-4R; 57-60; CANR 3; DLB 8;
MTCW; SATA 66

Bliss, Reginald
See Wells, H(erbert) G(eorge)

Blixen, Karen (Christentze Dinesen)
1885-1962
See Dinesen, Isak
See also CA 25-28; CANR 22, 50; CAP 2;
MTCW; SATA 44

Bloch, Robert (Albert) 1917-1994 . . . **CLC 33**
See also CA 5-8R; 146; CAAS 20; CANR 5;
DLB 44; INT CANR-5; SATA 12;
SATA-Obit 82

Blok, Alexander (Alexandrovich)
1880-1921 . . . . **TCLC 5**
See also CA 104

Blom, Jan
See Breytenbach, Breyten

Bloom, Harold 1930- . . . . **CLC 24**
See also CA 13-16R; CANR 39; DLB 67

Bloomfield, Aurelius
See Bourne, Randolph S(illiman)

Blount, Roy (Alton), Jr. 1941- . . . . . **CLC 38**
See also CA 53-56; CANR 10, 28;
INT CANR-28; MTCW

Bloy, Leon 1846-1917 . . . . **TCLC 22**
See also CA 121; DLB 123

Blume, Judy (Sussman) 1938- . . . **CLC 12, 30**
See also AAYA 3; CA 29-32R; CANR 13,
37; CLR 2, 15; DAM NOV, POP;
DLB 52; JRDA; MAICYA; MTCW;
SATA 2, 31, 79

Blunden, Edmund (Charles)
1896-1974 . . . . **CLC 2, 56**
See also CA 17-18; 45-48; CAP 2; DLB 20,
100, 155; MTCW

Bly, Robert (Elwood)
1926- . . . . **CLC 1, 2, 5, 10, 15, 38**
See also CA 5-8R; CANR 41; DAM POET;
DLB 5; MTCW

Boas, Franz 1858-1942 . . . . **TCLC 56**
See also CA 115

Bobette
See Simenon, Georges (Jacques Christian)

Boccaccio, Giovanni
1313-1375 . . . . **CMLC 13; SSC 10**

Bochco, Steven 1943- . . . . **CLC 35**
See also AAYA 11; CA 124; 138

Bodenheim, Maxwell 1892-1954 . . . **TCLC 44**
See also CA 110; DLB 9, 45

Bodker, Cecil 1927- . . . . **CLC 21**
See also CA 73-76; CANR 13, 44; CLR 23;
MAICYA; SATA 14

Boell, Heinrich (Theodor)
1917-1985 . . . . **CLC 2, 3, 6, 9, 11, 15, 27,**
32, 72; DA; DAB; DAC; SSC 23; WLC
See also CA 21-24R; 116; CANR 24;
DAM MST, NOV; DLB 69; DLBY 85;
MTCW

Boerne, Alfred
See Doeblin, Alfred

Boethius 480(?)-524(?) . . . . **CMLC 15**
See also DLB 115

Bogan, Louise
1897-1970 . . . . **CLC 4, 39, 46, 93; PC 12**
See also CA 73-76; 25-28R; CANR 33;
DAM POET; DLB 45; MTCW

Bogarde, Dirk . . . . **CLC 19**
See also Van Den Bogarde, Derek Jules
Gaspard Ulric Niven
See also DLB 14

Bogosian, Eric 1953- . . . . **CLC 45**
See also CA 138

Bograd, Larry 1953- . . . . **CLC 35**
See also CA 93-96; SAAS 21; SATA 33

Boiardo, Matteo Maria 1441-1494 . . . . **LC 6**

Boileau-Despreaux, Nicolas
1636-1711 . . . . **LC 3**

Boland, Eavan (Aisling) 1944- . . . **CLC 40, 67**
See also CA 143; DAM POET; DLB 40

Bolt, Lee
See Faust, Frederick (Schiller)

Bolt, Robert (Oxton) 1924-1995 . . . . **CLC 14**
See also CA 17-20R; 147; CANR 35;
DAM DRAM; DLB 13; MTCW

Bombet, Louis-Alexandre-Cesar
See Stendhal

Bomkauf
See Kaufman, Bob (Garnell)

Bonaventura . . . . **NCLC 35**
See also DLB 90

Bond, Edward 1934- . . . . **CLC 4, 6, 13, 23**
See also CA 25-28R; CANR 38;
DAM DRAM; DLB 13; MTCW

Bonham, Frank 1914-1989 . . . . **CLC 12**
See also AAYA 1; CA 9-12R; CANR 4, 36;
JRDA; MAICYA; SAAS 3; SATA 1, 49;
SATA-Obit 62

Bonnefoy, Yves 1923- . . . . **CLC 9, 15, 58**
See also CA 85-88; CANR 33; DAM MST,
POET; MTCW

Bontemps, Arna(ud Wendell)
1902-1973 . . . . **CLC 1, 18; BLC**
See also BW 1; CA 1-4R; 41-44R; CANR 4,
35; CLR 6; DAM MULT, NOV, POET;
DLB 48, 51; JRDA; MAICYA; MTCW;
SATA 2, 44; SATA-Obit 24

Booth, Martin 1944- . . . . **CLC 13**
See also CA 93-96; CAAS 2

Booth, Philip 1925- . . . . **CLC 23**
See also CA 5-8R; CANR 5; DLBY 82

Booth, Wayne C(layson) 1921- . . . . . **CLC 24**
See also CA 1-4R; CAAS 5; CANR 3, 43;
DLB 67

Borchert, Wolfgang 1921-1947 . . . . . **TCLC 5**
See also CA 104; DLB 69, 124

Borel, Petrus 1809-1859 . . . . **NCLC 41**

Borges, Jorge Luis
1899-1986 . . . **CLC 1, 2, 3, 4, 6, 8, 9, 10,**
13, 19, 44, 48, 83; DA; DAB; DAC;
HLC; SSC 4; WLC
See also CA 21-24R; CANR 19, 33;
DAM MST, MULT; DLB 113; DLBY 86;
HW; MTCW

Borowski, Tadeusz 1922-1951 . . . . . . **TCLC 9**
See also CA 106

Borrow, George (Henry)
1803-1881 . . . . **NCLC 9**
See also DLB 21, 55

Bosman, Herman Charles
1905-1951 . . . . **TCLC 49**

Bosschere, Jean de 1878(?)-1953 . . . **TCLC 19**
See also CA 115

Boswell, James
1740-1795 . . . . . . **LC 4; DA; DAB; DAC;**
WLC
See also CDBLB 1660-1789; DAM MST;
DLB 104, 142

Bottoms, David 1949- . . . . **CLC 53**
See also CA 105; CANR 22; DLB 120;
DLBY 83

Boucicault, Dion 1820-1890 . . . . . . **NCLC 41**

Boucolon, Maryse 1937-
See Conde, Maryse
See also CA 110; CANR 30

Bourget, Paul (Charles Joseph)
1852-1935 . . . . **TCLC 12**
See also CA 107; DLB 123

Bourjaily, Vance (Nye) 1922- . . . . **CLC 8, 62**
See also CA 1-4R; CAAS 1; CANR 2;
DLB 2, 143

Bourne, Randolph S(illiman)
1886-1918 . . . . **TCLC 16**
See also CA 117; DLB 63

Bova, Ben(jamin William) 1932- . . . . **CLC 45**
See also AAYA 16; CA 5-8R; CAAS 18;
CANR 11; CLR 3; DLBY 81;
INT CANR-11; MAICYA; MTCW;
SATA 6, 68

Bowen, Elizabeth (Dorothea Cole)
1899-1973 . . . . . . **CLC 1, 3, 6, 11, 15, 22;**
SSC 3
See also CA 17-18; 41-44R; CANR 35;
CAP 2; CDBLB 1945-1960; DAM NOV;
DLB 15, 162; MTCW

Bowering, George 1935- . . . . **CLC 15, 47**
See also CA 21-24R; CAAS 16; CANR 10;
DLB 53

Bowering, Marilyn R(uthe) 1949- . . . **CLC 32**
See also CA 101; CANR 49

Bowers, Edgar 1924- . . . . **CLC 9**
See also CA 5-8R; CANR 24; DLB 5

Bowie, David . . . . **CLC 17**
See also Jones, David Robert

Bowles, Jane (Sydney)
1917-1973 . . . . **CLC 3, 68**
See also CA 19-20; 41-44R; CAP 2

Bowles, Paul (Frederick)
1910- . . . . **CLC 1, 2, 19, 53; SSC 3**
See also CA 1-4R; CAAS 1; CANR 1, 19,
50; DLB 5, 6; MTCW

Box, Edgar
See Vidal, Gore

Boyd, Nancy
See Millay, Edna St. Vincent

Boyd, William 1952- . . . . **CLC 28, 53, 70**
See also CA 114; 120; CANR 51

Boyle, Kay
1902-1992 . . . . . **CLC 1, 5, 19, 58; SSC 5**
See also CA 13-16R; 140; CAAS 1;
CANR 29; DLB 4, 9, 48, 86; DLBY 93;
MTCW

Boyle, Mark
See Kienzle, William X(avier)

Boyle, Patrick 1905-1982 . . . . **CLC 19**
See also CA 127

Boyle, T. C. 1948-
See Boyle, T(homas) Coraghessan

Boyle, T(homas) Coraghessan
1948- . . . . **CLC 36, 55, 90; SSC 16**
See also BEST 90:4; CA 120; CANR 44;
DAM POP; DLBY 86

Boz
See Dickens, Charles (John Huffam)

Brackenridge, Hugh Henry
1748-1816 . . . . **NCLC 7**
See also DLB 11, 37

Bradbury, Edward P.
See Moorcock, Michael (John)

Bradbury, Malcolm (Stanley)
1932- . . . . **CLC 32, 61**
See also CA 1-4R; CANR 1, 33;
DAM NOV; DLB 14; MTCW

Bradbury, Ray (Douglas)
1920- . . . . **CLC 1, 3, 10, 15, 42; DA;**
DAB; DAC; WLC
See also AAYA 15; AITN 1, 2; CA 1-4R;
CANR 2, 30; CDALB 1968-1988;
DAM MST, NOV, POP; DLB 2, 8;
INT CANR-30; MTCW; SATA 11, 64

Bradford, Gamaliel 1863-1932 . . . . . **TCLC 36**
See also DLB 17

Bradley, David (Henry, Jr.)
1950- . . . . **CLC 23; BLC**
See also BW 1; CA 104; CANR 26;
DAM MULT; DLB 33

Bradley, John Ed(mund, Jr.)
1958- . . . . **CLC 55**
See also CA 139

Bradley, Marion Zimmer 1930- . . . . . **CLC 30**
See also AAYA 9; CA 57-60; CAAS 10;
CANR 7, 31, 51; DAM POP; DLB 8;
MTCW

Bradstreet, Anne
1612(?)-1672 . . . . . . **LC 4, 30; DA; DAC;**
PC 10
See also CDALB 1640-1865; DAM MST,
POET; DLB 24

Brady, Joan 1939- . . . . **CLC 86**
See also CA 141

Bragg, Melvyn 1939- . . . . **CLC 10**
See also BEST 89:3; CA 57-60; CANR 10,
48; DLB 14

Braine, John (Gerard)
1922-1986 . . . . **CLC 1, 3, 41**
See also CA 1-4R; 120; CANR 1, 33;
CDBLB 1945-1960; DLB 15; DLBY 86;
MTCW

Brammer, William 1930(?)-1978 . . . . **CLC 31**
See also CA 77-80

Brancati, Vitaliano 1907-1954 . . . . . **TCLC 12**
See also CA 109

Brancato, Robin F(idler) 1936- . . . . . **CLC 35**
See also AAYA 9; CA 69-72; CANR 11,
45; CLR 32; JRDA; SAAS 9; SATA 23

Brand, Max
See Faust, Frederick (Schiller)

Brand, Millen 1906-1980 . . . . **CLC 7**
See also CA 21-24R; 97-100

Branden, Barbara . . . . **CLC 44**
See also CA 148

Brandes, Georg (Morris Cohen)
1842-1927 . . . . **TCLC 10**
See also CA 105

Brandys, Kazimierz 1916- . . . . **CLC 62**

Branley, Franklyn M(ansfield)
1915- . . . . **CLC 21**
See also CA 33-36R; CANR 14, 39;
CLR 13; MAICYA; SAAS 16; SATA 4,
68

Brathwaite, Edward Kamau 1930- . . . **CLC 11**
See also BW 2; CA 25-28R; CANR 11, 26,
47; DAM POET; DLB 125

Brautigan, Richard (Gary)
1935-1984 . . . . **CLC 1, 3, 5, 9, 12, 34, 42**
See also CA 53-56; 113; CANR 34;
DAM NOV; DLB 2, 5; DLBY 80, 84;
MTCW; SATA 56

Braverman, Kate 1950- . . . . **CLC 67**
See also CA 89-92

Brecht, Bertolt
1898-1956 . . . . . . **TCLC 1, 6, 13, 35; DA;**
DAB; DAC; DC 3; WLC
See also CA 104; 133; DAM DRAM, MST;
DLB 56, 124; MTCW

Brecht, Eugen Berthold Friedrich
See Brecht, Bertolt

Bremer, Fredrika 1801-1865 . . . . . **NCLC 11**

Brennan, Christopher John
1870-1932 . . . . **TCLC 17**
See also CA 117

Brennan, Maeve 1917- . . . . **CLC 5**
See also CA 81-84

Brentano, Clemens (Maria)
1778-1842 . . . . **NCLC 1**
See also DLB 90

Brent of Bin Bin
See Franklin, (Stella Maraia Sarah) Miles

Brenton, Howard 1942- . . . . **CLC 31**
See also CA 69-72; CANR 33; DLB 13;
MTCW

Breslin, James 1930-
See Breslin, Jimmy
See also CA 73-76; CANR 31; DAM NOV;
MTCW

Breslin, Jimmy . . . . **CLC 4, 43**
See also Breslin, James
See also AITN 1

Bresson, Robert 1901- . . . . **CLC 16**
See also CA 110; CANR 49

Breton, Andre
1896-1966 . . . . . **CLC 2, 9, 15, 54; PC 15**
See also CA 19-20; 25-28R; CANR 40;
CAP 2; DLB 65; MTCW

Breytenbach, Breyten 1939(?)- . . **CLC 23, 37**
See also CA 113; 129; DAM POET

Bridgers, Sue Ellen 1942- . . . . **CLC 26**
See also AAYA 8; CA 65-68; CANR 11,
36; CLR 18; DLB 52; JRDA; MAICYA;
SAAS 1; SATA 22

Bridges, Robert (Seymour)
1844-1930 . . . . **TCLC 1**
See also CA 104; CDBLB 1890-1914;
DAM POET; DLB 19, 98

Bridie, James . . . . **TCLC 3**
See also Mavor, Osborne Henry
See also DLB 10

Brin, David 1950- . . . . **CLC 34**
See also CA 102; CANR 24;
INT CANR-24; SATA 65

Buchner, (Karl) Georg
1813-1837 .... NCLC 26

Buchwald, Art(hur) 1925-.......... CLC 33
See also AITN 1; CA 5-8R; CANR 21;
MTCW; SATA 10

Buck, Pearl S(ydenstricker)
1892-1973 .... CLC 7, 11, 18; DA; DAB;
DAC
See also AITN 1; CA 1-4R; 41-44R;
CANR 1, 34; DAM MST, NOV; DLB 9,
102; MTCW; SATA 1, 25

Buckler, Ernest 1908-1984.... CLC 13; DAC
See also CA 11-12; 114; CAP 1;
DAM MST; DLB 68; SATA 47

Buckley, Vincent (Thomas)
1925-1988 .... CLC 57
See also CA 101

Buckley, William F(rank), Jr.
1925- .... CLC 7, 18, 37
See also AITN 1; CA 1-4R; CANR 1, 24;
DAM POP; DLB 137; DLBY 80;
INT CANR-24; MTCW

Buechner, (Carl) Frederick
1926- .... CLC 2, 4, 6, 9
See also CA 13-16R; CANR 11, 39;
DAM NOV; DLBY 80; INT CANR-11;
MTCW

Buell, John (Edward) 1927-........ CLC 10
See also CA 1-4R; DLB 53

Buero Vallejo, Antonio 1916- ... CLC 15, 46
See also CA 106; CANR 24, 49; HW;
MTCW

Bufalino, Gesualdo 1920(?)-........ CLC 74

Bugayev, Boris Nikolayevich 1880-1934
See Bely, Andrey
See also CA 104

Bukowski, Charles
1920-1994 .... CLC 2, 5, 9, 41, 82
See also CA 17-20R; 144; CANR 40;
DAM NOV, POET; DLB 5, 130; MTCW

Bulgakov, Mikhail (Afanas'evich)
1891-1940 .... TCLC 2, 16; SSC 18
See also CA 105; DAM DRAM, NOV

Bulgya, Alexander Alexandrovich
1901-1956 .... TCLC 53
See also Fadeyev, Alexander
See also CA 117

Bullins, Ed 1935- .. CLC 1, 5, 7; BLC; DC 6
See also BW 2; CA 49-52; CAAS 16;
CANR 24, 46; DAM DRAM, MULT;
DLB 7, 38; MTCW

Bulwer-Lytton, Edward (George Earle Lytton)
1803-1873 .... NCLC 1, 45
See also DLB 21

Bunin, Ivan Alexeyevich
1870-1953 .... TCLC 6; SSC 5
See also CA 104

Bunting, Basil 1900-1985.... CLC 10, 39, 47
See also CA 53-56; 115; CANR 7;
DAM POET; DLB 20

Bunuel, Luis 1900-1983 .. CLC 16, 80; HLC
See also CA 101; 110; CANR 32;
DAM MULT; HW

Bunyan, John
1628-1688 ...... LC 4; DA; DAB; DAC;
WLC
See also CDBLB 1660-1789; DAM MST;
DLB 39

Burckhardt, Jacob (Christoph)
1818-1897 .... NCLC 49

Burford, Eleanor
See Hibbert, Eleanor Alice Burford

Burgess, Anthony
. CLC 1, 2, 4, 5, 8, 10, 13, 15, 22, 40, 62,
81, 93; DAB
See also Wilson, John (Anthony) Burgess
See also AITN 1; CDBLB 1960 to Present;
DLB 14

Burke, Edmund
1729(?)-1797 .... LC 7; DA; DAB; DAC;
WLC
See also DAM MST; DLB 104

Burke, Kenneth (Duva)
1897-1993 .... CLC 2, 24
See also CA 5-8R; 143; CANR 39; DLB 45,
63; MTCW

Burke, Leda
See Garnett, David

Burke, Ralph
See Silverberg, Robert

Burke, Thomas 1886-1945 .... TCLC 63
See also CA 113

Burney, Fanny 1752-1840 .... NCLC 12, 54
See also DLB 39

Burns, Robert 1759-1796............ PC 6
See also CDBLB 1789-1832; DA; DAB;
DAC; DAM MST, POET; DLB 109;
WLC

Burns, Tex
See L'Amour, Louis (Dearborn)

Burnshaw, Stanley 1906-..... CLC 3, 13, 44
See also CA 9-12R; DLB 48

Burr, Anne 1937- .... CLC 6
See also CA 25-28R

Burroughs, Edgar Rice
1875-1950 .... TCLC 2, 32
See also AAYA 11; CA 104; 132;
DAM NOV; DLB 8; MTCW; SATA 41

Burroughs, William S(eward)
1914- .... CLC 1, 2, 5, 15, 22, 42, 75;
DA; DAB; DAC; WLC
See also AITN 2; CA 9-12R; CANR 20;
DAM MST, NOV, POP; DLB 2, 8, 16,
152; DLBY 81; MTCW

Burton, Richard F. 1821-1890.... NCLC 42
See also DLB 55

Busch, Frederick 1941- ... CLC 7, 10, 18, 47
See also CA 33-36R; CAAS 1; CANR 45;
DLB 6

Bush, Ronald 1946- .... CLC 34
See also CA 136

Bustos, F(rancisco)
See Borges, Jorge Luis

Bustos Domecq, H(onorio)
See Bioy Casares, Adolfo; Borges, Jorge
Luis

Butler, Octavia E(stelle) 1947- ..... CLC 38
See also BW 2; CA 73-76; CANR 12, 24,
38; DAM MULT, POP; DLB 33;
MTCW; SATA 84

Butler, Robert Olen (Jr.) 1945-..... CLC 81
See also CA 112; DAM POP; INT 112

Butler, Samuel 1612-1680 .... LC 16
See also DLB 101, 126

Butler, Samuel
1835-1902 ...... TCLC 1, 33; DA; DAB;
DAC; WLC
See also CA 143; CDBLB 1890-1914;
DAM MST, NOV; DLB 18, 57

Butler, Walter C.
See Faust, Frederick (Schiller)

Butor, Michel (Marie Francois)
1926- .... CLC 1, 3, 8, 11, 15
See also CA 9-12R; CANR 33; DLB 83;
MTCW

Buzo, Alexander (John) 1944-...... CLC 61
See also CA 97-100; CANR 17, 39

Buzzati, Dino 1906-1972 .... CLC 36
See also CA 33-36R

Byars, Betsy (Cromer) 1928-....... CLC 35
See also CA 33-36R; CANR 18, 36; CLR 1,
16; DLB 52; INT CANR-18; JRDA;
MAICYA; MTCW; SAAS 1; SATA 4,
46, 80

Byatt, A(ntonia) S(usan Drabble)
1936- .... CLC 19, 65
See also CA 13-16R; CANR 13, 33, 50;
DAM NOV, POP; DLB 14; MTCW

Byrne, David 1952-................ CLC 26
See also CA 127

Byrne, John Keyes 1926-
See Leonard, Hugh
See also CA 102; INT 102

Byron, George Gordon (Noel)
1788-1824 ..... NCLC 2, 12; DA; DAB;
DAC; WLC
See also CDBLB 1789-1832; DAM MST,
POET; DLB 96, 110

C. 3. 3.
See Wilde, Oscar (Fingal O'Flahertie Wills)

Caballero, Fernan 1796-1877..... NCLC 10

Cabell, James Branch 1879-1958 ... TCLC 6
See also CA 105; DLB 9, 78

Cable, George Washington
1844-1925 .... TCLC 4; SSC 4
See also CA 104; DLB 12, 74; DLBD 13

Cabral de Melo Neto, Joao 1920-... CLC 76
See also DAM MULT

Cabrera Infante, G(uillermo)
1929- .... CLC 5, 25, 45; HLC
See also CA 85-88; CANR 29;
DAM MULT; DLB 113; HW; MTCW

Cade, Toni
See Bambara, Toni Cade

Cadmus and Harmonia
See Buchan, John

Caedmon fl. 658-680............. CMLC 7
See also DLB 146

Caeiro, Alberto
See Pessoa, Fernando (Antonio Nogueira)

Cage, John (Milton, Jr.) 1912- . . . . . CLC 41
See also CA 13-16R; CANR 9;
INT CANR-9

Cain, G.
See Cabrera Infante, G(uillermo)

Cain, Guillermo
See Cabrera Infante, G(uillermo)

Cain, James M(allahan)
1892-1977 . . . . CLC 3, 11, 28
See also AITN 1; CA 17-20R; 73-76;
CANR 8, 34; MTCW

Caine, Mark
See Raphael, Frederic (Michael)

Calasso, Roberto 1941- . . . . CLC 81
See also CA 143

Calderon de la Barca, Pedro
1600-1681 . . . . LC 23; DC 3

Caldwell, Erskine (Preston)
1903-1987 . . . . CLC 1, 8, 14, 50, 60;
SSC 19
See also AITN 1; CA 1-4R; 121; CAAS 1;
CANR 2, 33; DAM NOV; DLB 9, 86;
MTCW

Caldwell, (Janet Miriam) Taylor (Holland)
1900-1985 . . . . CLC 2, 28, 39
See also CA 5-8R; 116; CANR 5;
DAM NOV, POP

Calhoun, John Caldwell
1782-1850 . . . . NCLC 15
See also DLB 3

Calisher, Hortense
1911- . . . . CLC 2, 4, 8, 38; SSC 15
See also CA 1-4R; CANR 1, 22;
DAM NOV; DLB 2; INT CANR-22;
MTCW

Callaghan, Morley Edward
1903-1990 . . . . . CLC 3, 14, 41, 65; DAC
See also CA 9-12R; 132; CANR 33;
DAM MST; DLB 68; MTCW

Callimachus
c. 305B.C.-c. 240B.C. . . . . CMLC 18

Calvino, Italo
1923-1985 . . . . . CLC 5, 8, 11, 22, 33, 39,
73; SSC 3
See also CA 85-88; 116; CANR 23;
DAM NOV; MTCW

Cameron, Carey 1952- . . . . CLC 59
See also CA 135

Cameron, Peter 1959- . . . . CLC 44
See also CA 125; CANR 50

Campana, Dino 1885-1932 . . . . TCLC 20
See also CA 117; DLB 114

Campanella, Tommaso 1568-1639 . . . . LC 32

Campbell, John W(ood, Jr.)
1910-1971 . . . . CLC 32
See also CA 21-22; 29-32R; CANR 34;
CAP 2; DLB 8; MTCW

Campbell, Joseph 1904-1987 . . . . CLC 69
See also AAYA 3; BEST 89:2; CA 1-4R;
124; CANR 3, 28; MTCW

Campbell, Maria 1940- . . . . CLC 85; DAC
See also CA 102; NNAL

Campbell, (John) Ramsey
1946- . . . . CLC 42; SSC 19
See also CA 57-60; CANR 7; INT CANR-7

Campbell, (Ignatius) Roy (Dunnachie)
1901-1957 . . . . TCLC 5
See also CA 104; DLB 20

Campbell, Thomas 1777-1844 . . . . NCLC 19
See also DLB 93; 144

Campbell, Wilfred . . . . TCLC 9
See also Campbell, William

Campbell, William 1858(?)-1918
See Campbell, Wilfred
See also CA 106; DLB 92

Campos, Alvaro de
See Pessoa, Fernando (Antonio Nogueira)

Camus, Albert
1913-1960 . . . . CLC 1, 2, 4, 9, 11, 14, 32,
63, 69; DA; DAB; DAC; DC 2; SSC 9;
WLC
See also CA 89-92; DAM DRAM, MST,
NOV; DLB 72; MTCW

Canby, Vincent 1924- . . . . CLC 13
See also CA 81-84

Cancale
See Desnos, Robert

Canetti, Elias
1905-1994 . . . . CLC 3, 14, 25, 75, 86
See also CA 21-24R; 146; CANR 23;
DLB 85, 124; MTCW

Canin, Ethan 1960- . . . . CLC 55
See also CA 131; 135

Cannon, Curt
See Hunter, Evan

Cape, Judith
See Page, P(atricia) K(athleen)

Capek, Karel
1890-1938 . . . . . . TCLC 6, 37; DA; DAB;
DAC; DC 1; WLC
See also CA 104; 140; DAM DRAM, MST,
NOV

Capote, Truman
1924-1984 . . . . . . CLC 1, 3, 8, 13, 19, 34,
38, 58; DA; DAB; DAC; SSC 2; WLC
See also CA 5-8R; 113; CANR 18;
CDALB 1941-1968; DAM MST, NOV,
POP; DLB 2; DLBY 80, 84; MTCW

Capra, Frank 1897-1991 . . . . CLC 16
See also CA 61-64; 135

Caputo, Philip 1941- . . . . CLC 32
See also CA 73-76; CANR 40

Card, Orson Scott 1951- . . . . CLC 44, 47, 50
See also AAYA 11; CA 102; CANR 27, 47;
DAM POP; INT CANR-27; MTCW;
SATA 83

Cardenal (Martinez), Ernesto
1925- . . . . CLC 31; HLC
See also CA 49-52; CANR 2, 32;
DAM MULT, POET; HW; MTCW

Carducci, Giosue 1835-1907 . . . . TCLC 32

Carew, Thomas 1595(?)-1640 . . . . LC 13
See also DLB 126

Carey, Ernestine Gilbreth 1908- . . . . CLC 17
See also CA 5-8R; SATA 2

Carey, Peter 1943- . . . . CLC 40, 55
See also CA 123; 127; INT 127; MTCW

Carleton, William 1794-1869 . . . . . . NCLC 3
See also DLB 159

Carlisle, Henry (Coffin) 1926- . . . . . . CLC 33
See also CA 13-16R; CANR 15

Carlsen, Chris
See Holdstock, Robert P.

Carlson, Ron(ald F.) 1947- . . . . CLC 54
See also CA 105; CANR 27

Carlyle, Thomas
1795-1881 . . NCLC 22; DA; DAB; DAC
See also CDBLB 1789-1832; DAM MST;
DLB 55; 144

Carman, (William) Bliss
1861-1929 . . . . TCLC 7; DAC
See also CA 104; DLB 92

Carnegie, Dale 1888-1955 . . . . TCLC 53

Carossa, Hans 1878-1956 . . . . TCLC 48
See also DLB 66

Carpenter, Don(ald Richard)
1931-1995 . . . . CLC 41
See also CA 45-48; 149; CANR 1

Carpentier (y Valmont), Alejo
1904-1980 . . . . CLC 8, 11, 38; HLC
See also CA 65-68; 97-100; CANR 11;
DAM MULT; DLB 113; HW

Carr, Caleb 1955(?)- . . . . CLC 86
See also CA 147

Carr, Emily 1871-1945 . . . . TCLC 32
See also DLB 68

Carr, John Dickson 1906-1977 . . . . . . CLC 3
See also CA 49-52; 69-72; CANR 3, 33;
MTCW

Carr, Philippa
See Hibbert, Eleanor Alice Burford

Carr, Virginia Spencer 1929- . . . . CLC 34
See also CA 61-64; DLB 111

Carrere, Emmanuel 1957- . . . . CLC 89

Carrier, Roch 1937- . . . . . CLC 13, 78; DAC
See also CA 130; DAM MST; DLB 53

Carroll, James P. 1943(?)- . . . . CLC 38
See also CA 81-84

Carroll, Jim 1951- . . . . CLC 35
See also AAYA 17; CA 45-48; CANR 42

Carroll, Lewis . . . . NCLC 2, 53; WLC
See also Dodgson, Charles Lutwidge
See also CDBLB 1832-1890; CLR 2, 18;
DLB 18, 163; JRDA

Carroll, Paul Vincent 1900-1968 . . . . CLC 10
See also CA 9-12R; 25-28R; DLB 10

Carruth, Hayden
1921- . . . . . . CLC 4, 7, 10, 18, 84; PC 10
See also CA 9-12R; CANR 4, 38; DLB 5,
165; INT CANR-4; MTCW; SATA 47

Carson, Rachel Louise 1907-1964 . . . CLC 71
See also CA 77-80; CANR 35; DAM POP;
MTCW; SATA 23

Carter, Angela (Olive)
1940-1992 . . . . . . CLC 5, 41, 76; SSC 13
See also CA 53-56; 136; CANR 12, 36;
DLB 14; MTCW; SATA 66;
SATA-Obit 70

Carter, Nick
See Smith, Martin Cruz

Carver, Raymond
1938-1988 . . . **CLC 22, 36, 53, 55; SSC 8**
See also CA 33-36R; 126; CANR 17, 34;
DAM NOV; DLB 130; DLBY 84, 88;
MTCW

Cary, Elizabeth, Lady Falkland
1585-1639 . . . . **LC 30**

Cary, (Arthur) Joyce (Lunel)
1888-1957 . . . . **TCLC 1, 29**
See also CA 104; CDBLB 1914-1945;
DLB 15, 100

Casanova de Seingalt, Giovanni Jacopo
1725-1798 . . . . **LC 13**

Casares, Adolfo Bioy
See Bioy Casares, Adolfo

Casely-Hayford, J(oseph) E(phraim)
1866-1930 . . . . **TCLC 24; BLC**
See also BW 2; CA 123; DAM MULT

Casey, John (Dudley) 1939- . . . . **CLC 59**
See also BEST 90:2; CA 69-72; CANR 23

Casey, Michael 1947- . . . . **CLC 2**
See also CA 65-68; DLB 5

Casey, Patrick
See Thurman, Wallace (Henry)

Casey, Warren (Peter) 1935-1988 . . . **CLC 12**
See also CA 101; 127; INT 101

Casona, Alejandro . . . . **CLC 49**
See also Alvarez, Alejandro Rodriguez

Cassavetes, John 1929-1989 . . . . **CLC 20**
See also CA 85-88; 127

Cassill, R(onald) V(erlin) 1919- . . . **CLC 4, 23**
See also CA 9-12R; CAAS 1; CANR 7, 45;
DLB 6

Cassirer, Ernst 1874-1945 . . . . **TCLC 61**

Cassity, (Allen) Turner 1929- . . . . **CLC 6, 42**
See also CA 17-20R; CAAS 8; CANR 11;
DLB 105

Castaneda, Carlos 1931(?)- . . . . **CLC 12**
See also CA 25-28R; CANR 32; HW;
MTCW

Castedo, Elena 1937- . . . . **CLC 65**
See also CA 132

Castedo-Ellerman, Elena
See Castedo, Elena

Castellanos, Rosario
1925-1974 . . . . **CLC 66; HLC**
See also CA 131; 53-56; DAM MULT;
DLB 113; HW

Castelvetro, Lodovico 1505-1571 . . . . . **LC 12**

Castiglione, Baldassare 1478-1529 . . . **LC 12**

Castle, Robert
See Hamilton, Edmond

Castro, Guillen de 1569-1631 . . . . **LC 19**

Castro, Rosalia de 1837-1885 . . . . . **NCLC 3**
See also DAM MULT

Cather, Willa
See Cather, Willa Sibert

Cather, Willa Sibert
1873-1947 . . . . **TCLC 1, 11, 31; DA;**
DAB; DAC; SSC 2; WLC
See also CA 104; 128; CDALB 1865-1917;
DAM MST, NOV; DLB 9, 54, 78;
DLBD 1; MTCW; SATA 30

Catton, (Charles) Bruce
1899-1978 . . . . **CLC 35**
See also AITN 1; CA 5-8R; 81-84;
CANR 7; DLB 17; SATA 2;
SATA-Obit 24

Catullus c. 84B.C.-c. 54B.C. . . . . . **CMLC 18**

Cauldwell, Frank
See King, Francis (Henry)

Caunitz, William J. 1933- . . . . **CLC 34**
See also BEST 89:3; CA 125; 130; INT 130

Causley, Charles (Stanley) 1917- . . . . . **CLC 7**
See also CA 9-12R; CANR 5, 35; CLR 30;
DLB 27; MTCW; SATA 3, 66

Caute, David 1936- . . . . **CLC 29**
See also CA 1-4R; CAAS 4; CANR 1, 33;
DAM NOV; DLB 14

Cavafy, C(onstantine) P(eter)
1863-1933 . . . . **TCLC 2, 7**
See also Kavafis, Konstantinos Petrou
See also CA 148; DAM POET

Cavallo, Evelyn
See Spark, Muriel (Sarah)

Cavanna, Betty . . . . **CLC 12**
See also Harrison, Elizabeth Cavanna
See also JRDA; MAICYA; SAAS 4;
SATA 1, 30

Cavendish, Margaret Lucas
1623-1673 . . . . **LC 30**
See also DLB 131

Caxton, William 1421(?)-1491(?) . . . . . **LC 17**

Cayrol, Jean 1911- . . . . **CLC 11**
See also CA 89-92; DLB 83

Cela, Camilo Jose
1916- . . . . **CLC 4, 13, 59; HLC**
See also BEST 90:2; CA 21-24R; CAAS 10;
CANR 21, 32; DAM MULT; DLBY 89;
HW; MTCW

Celan, Paul . . . . . . **CLC 10, 19, 53, 82; PC 10**
See also Antschel, Paul
See also DLB 69

Celine, Louis-Ferdinand
. . . . **CLC 1, 3, 4, 7, 9, 15, 47**
See also Destouches, Louis-Ferdinand
See also DLB 72

Cellini, Benvenuto 1500-1571 . . . . **LC 7**

Cendrars, Blaise . . . . **CLC 18**
See also Sauser-Hall, Frederic

Cernuda (y Bidon), Luis
1902-1963 . . . . **CLC 54**
See also CA 131; 89-92; DAM POET;
DLB 134; HW

Cervantes (Saavedra), Miguel de
1547-1616 . . . . **LC 6, 23; DA; DAB;**
DAC; SSC 12; WLC
See also DAM MST, NOV

Cesaire, Aime (Fernand)
1913- . . . . **CLC 19, 32; BLC**
See also BW 2; CA 65-68; CANR 24, 43;
DAM MULT, POET; MTCW

Chabon, Michael 1965(?)- . . . . **CLC 55**
See also CA 139

Chabrol, Claude 1930- . . . . **CLC 16**
See also CA 110

Challans, Mary 1905-1983
See Renault, Mary
See also CA 81-84; 111; SATA 23;
SATA-Obit 36

Challis, George
See Faust, Frederick (Schiller)

Chambers, Aidan 1934- . . . . **CLC 35**
See also CA 25-28R; CANR 12, 31; JRDA;
MAICYA; SAAS 12; SATA 1, 69

Chambers, James 1948-
See Cliff, Jimmy
See also CA 124

Chambers, Jessie
See Lawrence, D(avid) H(erbert Richards)

Chambers, Robert W. 1865-1933 . . . **TCLC 41**

Chandler, Raymond (Thornton)
1888-1959 . . . . **TCLC 1, 7; SSC 23**
See also CA 104; 129; CDALB 1929-1941;
DLBD 6; MTCW

Chang, Jung 1952- . . . . **CLC 71**
See also CA 142

Channing, William Ellery
1780-1842 . . . . **NCLC 17**
See also DLB 1, 59

Chaplin, Charles Spencer
1889-1977 . . . . **CLC 16**
See also Chaplin, Charlie
See also CA 81-84; 73-76

Chaplin, Charlie
See Chaplin, Charles Spencer
See also DLB 44

Chapman, George 1559(?)-1634 . . . . . . **LC 22**
See also DAM DRAM; DLB 62, 121

Chapman, Graham 1941-1989 . . . . . . **CLC 21**
See also Monty Python
See also CA 116; 129; CANR 35

Chapman, John Jay 1862-1933 . . . . . **TCLC 7**
See also CA 104

Chapman, Walker
See Silverberg, Robert

Chappell, Fred (Davis) 1936- . . . . **CLC 40, 78**
See also CA 5-8R; CAAS 4; CANR 8, 33;
DLB 6, 105

Char, Rene(-Emile)
1907-1988 . . . . **CLC 9, 11, 14, 55**
See also CA 13-16R; 124; CANR 32;
DAM POET; MTCW

Charby, Jay
See Ellison, Harlan (Jay)

Chardin, Pierre Teilhard de
See Teilhard de Chardin, (Marie Joseph)
Pierre

Charles I 1600-1649 . . . . **LC 13**

Charyn, Jerome 1937- . . . . **CLC 5, 8, 18**
See also CA 5-8R; CAAS 1; CANR 7;
DLBY 83; MTCW

Chase, Mary (Coyle) 1907-1981 . . . . . . **DC 1**
See also CA 77-80; 105; SATA 17;
SATA-Obit 29

Chase, Mary Ellen 1887-1973 . . . . **CLC 2**
See also CA 13-16; 41-44R; CAP 1;
SATA 10

Chase, Nicholas
See Hyde, Anthony

Clarke, Arthur C(harles)
1917- ...... CLC **1, 4, 13, 18, 35; SSC 3**
See also AAYA 4; CA 1-4R; CANR 2, 28;
DAM POP; JRDA; MAICYA; MTCW;
SATA 13, 70

Clarke, Austin 1896-1974........ CLC **6, 9**
See also CA 29-32; 49-52; CAP 2;
DAM POET; DLB 10, 20

Clarke, Austin C(hesterfield)
1934- .... CLC **8, 53; BLC; DAC**
See also BW 1; CA 25-28R; CAAS 16;
CANR 14, 32; DAM MULT; DLB 53,
125

Clarke, Gillian 1937- .... CLC **61**
See also CA 106; DLB 40

Clarke, Marcus (Andrew Hislop)
1846-1881 .... NCLC **19**

Clarke, Shirley 1925- .... CLC **16**

Clash, The ·
See Headon, (Nicky) Topper; Jones, Mick;
Simonon, Paul; Strummer, Joe

Claudel, Paul (Louis Charles Marie)
1868-1955 .... TCLC **2, 10**
See also CA 104

Clavell, James (duMaresq)
1925-1994 .... CLC **6, 25, 87**
See also CA 25-28R; 146; CANR 26, 48;
DAM NOV, POP; MTCW

Cleaver, (Leroy) Eldridge
1935- .... CLC **30; BLC**
See also BW 1; CA 21-24R; CANR 16;
DAM MULT

Cleese, John (Marwood) 1939- ..... CLC **21**
See also Monty Python
See also CA 112; 116; CANR 35; MTCW

Cleishbotham, Jebediah
See Scott, Walter

Cleland, John 1710-1789 .... LC **2**
See also DLB 39

Clemens, Samuel Langhorne 1835-1910
See Twain, Mark
See also CA 104; 135; CDALB 1865-1917;
DA; DAB; DAC; DAM MST, NOV;
DLB 11, 12, 23, 64, 74; JRDA;
MAICYA; YABC 2

Cleophil
See Congreve, William

Clerihew, E.
See Bentley, E(dmund) C(lerihew)

Clerk, N. W.
See Lewis, C(live) S(taples)

Cliff, Jimmy.................... CLC **21**
See also Chambers, James

Clifton, (Thelma) Lucille
1936- .... CLC **19, 66; BLC**
See also BW 2; CA 49-52; CANR 2, 24, 42;
CLR 5; DAM MULT, POET; DLB 5, 41;
MAICYA; MTCW; SATA 20, 69

Clinton, Dirk
See Silverberg, Robert

Clough, Arthur Hugh 1819-1861.. NCLC **27**
See also DLB 32

Clutha, Janet Paterson Frame 1924-
See Frame, Janet
See also CA 1-4R; CANR 2, 36; MTCW

Clyne, Terence
See Blatty, William Peter

Cobalt, Martin
See Mayne, William (James Carter)

Cobbett, William 1763-1835 ..... NCLC **49**
See also DLB 43, 107, 158

Coburn, D(onald) L(ee) 1938- ...... CLC **10**
See also CA 89-92

Cocteau, Jean (Maurice Eugene Clement)
1889-1963 .... CLC **1, 8, 15, 16, 43; DA;**
DAB; DAC; WLC
See also CA 25-28; CANR 40; CAP 2;
DAM DRAM, MST, NOV; DLB 65;
MTCW

Codrescu, Andrei 1946- .... CLC **46**
See also CA 33-36R; CAAS 19; CANR 13,
34; DAM POET

Coe, Max
See Bourne, Randolph S(illiman)

Coe, Tucker
See Westlake, Donald E(dwin)

Coetzee, J(ohn) M(ichael)
1940- .... CLC **23, 33, 66**
See also CA 77-80; CANR 41; DAM NOV;
MTCW

Coffey, Brian
See Koontz, Dean R(ay)

Cohan, George M. 1878-1942 ..... TCLC **60**

Cohen, Arthur A(llen)
1928-1986 .... CLC **7, 31**
See also CA 1-4R; 120; CANR 1, 17, 42;
DLB 28

Cohen, Leonard (Norman)
1934- .... CLC **3, 38; DAC**
See also CA 21-24R; CANR 14;
DAM MST; DLB 53; MTCW

Cohen, Matt 1942- .... CLC **19; DAC**
See also CA 61-64; CAAS 18; CANR 40;
DLB 53

Cohen-Solal, Annie 19(?)- .... CLC **50**

Colegate, Isabel 1931- .... CLC **36**
See also CA 17-20R; CANR 8, 22; DLB 14;
INT CANR-22; MTCW

Coleman, Emmett
See Reed, Ishmael

Coleridge, Samuel Taylor
1772-1834 ..... NCLC **9, 54; DA; DAB;**
DAC; PC 11; WLC
See also CDBLB 1789-1832; DAM MST,
POET; DLB 93, 107

Coleridge, Sara 1802-1852 ...... NCLC **31**

Coles, Don 1928- .... CLC **46**
See also CA 115; CANR 38

Colette, (Sidonie-Gabrielle)
1873-1954 ...... TCLC **1, 5, 16; SSC 10**
See also CA 104; 131; DAM NOV; DLB 65;
MTCW

Collett, (Jacobine) Camilla (Wergeland)
1813-1895 .... NCLC **22**

Collier, Christopher 1930- .... CLC **30**
See also AAYA 13; CA 33-36R; CANR 13,
33; JRDA; MAICYA; SATA 16, 70

Collier, James L(incoln) 1928- ..... CLC **30**
See also AAYA 13; CA 9-12R; CANR 4,
33; CLR 3; DAM POP; JRDA;
MAICYA; SAAS 21; SATA 8, 70

Collier, Jeremy 1650-1726.......... LC **6**

Collier, John 1901-1980........... SSC **19**
See also CA 65-68; 97-100; CANR 10;
DLB 77

Collins, Hunt
See Hunter, Evan

Collins, Linda 1931-.............. CLC **44**
See also CA 125

Collins, (William) Wilkie
1824-1889 .... NCLC **1, 18**
See also CDBLB 1832-1890; DLB 18, 70,
159

Collins, William 1721-1759 .... LC **4**
See also DAM POET; DLB 109

Collodi, Carlo 1826-1890....... NCLC **54**
See also Lorenzini, Carlo
See also CLR 5

Colman, George
See Glassco, John

Colt, Winchester Remington
See Hubbard, L(afayette) Ron(ald)

Colter, Cyrus 1910- .... CLC **58**
See also BW 1; CA 65-68; CANR 10;
DLB 33

Colton, James
See Hansen, Joseph

Colum, Padraic 1881-1972........ CLC **28**
See also CA 73-76; 33-36R; CANR 35;
CLR 36; MAICYA; MTCW; SATA 15

Colvin, James
See Moorcock, Michael (John)

Colwin, Laurie (E.)
1944-1992 ....CLC **5, 13, 23, 84**
See also CA 89-92; 139; CANR 20, 46;
DLBY 80; MTCW

Comfort, Alex(ander) 1920-........ CLC **7**
See also CA 1-4R; CANR 1, 45; DAM POP

Comfort, Montgomery
See Campbell, (John) Ramsey

Compton-Burnett, I(vy)
1884(?)-1969 ...... CLC **1, 3, 10, 15, 34**
See also CA 1-4R; 25-28R; CANR 4;
DAM NOV; DLB 36; MTCW

Comstock, Anthony 1844-1915 .... TCLC **13**
See also CA 110

Comte, Auguste 1798-1857....... NCLC **54**

Conan Doyle, Arthur
See Doyle, Arthur Conan

Conde, Maryse 1937-.......... CLC **52, 92**
See also Boucolon, Maryse
See also BW 2; DAM MULT

Condillac, Etienne Bonnot de
1714-1780 .... LC **26**

Condon, Richard (Thomas)
1915- .... CLC **4, 6, 8, 10, 45**
See also BEST 90:3; CA 1-4R; CAAS 1;
CANR 2, 23; DAM NOV;
INT CANR-23; MTCW

Crane, Stephen (Townley)
1871-1900 . . . . . . **TCLC 11, 17, 32; DA;**
DAB; DAC; SSC 7; WLC
See also CA 109; 140; CDALB 1865-1917;
DAM MST, NOV, POET; DLB 12, 54,
78; YABC 2

Crase, Douglas 1944- . . . . **CLC 58**
See also CA 106

Crashaw, Richard 1612(?)-1649 . . . . . . **LC 24**
See also DLB 126

Craven, Margaret
1901-1980 . . . . **CLC 17; DAC**
See also CA 103

Crawford, F(rancis) Marion
1854-1909 . . . . **TCLC 10**
See also CA 107; DLB 71

Crawford, Isabella Valancy
1850-1887 . . . . **NCLC 12**
See also DLB 92

Crayon, Geoffrey
See Irving, Washington

Creasey, John 1908-1973 . . . . **CLC 11**
See also CA 5-8R; 41-44R; CANR 8;
DLB 77; MTCW

Crebillon, Claude Prosper Jolyot de (fils)
1707-1777 . . . . **LC 28**

Credo
See Creasey, John

Creeley, Robert (White)
1926- . . . . . **CLC 1, 2, 4, 8, 11, 15, 36, 78**
See also CA 1-4R; CAAS 10; CANR 23, 43;
DAM POET; DLB 5, 16; MTCW

Crews, Harry (Eugene)
1935- . . . . **CLC 6, 23, 49**
See also AITN 1; CA 25-28R; CANR 20;
DLB 6, 143; MTCW

Crichton, (John) Michael
1942- . . . . **CLC 2, 6, 54, 90**
See also AAYA 10; AITN 2; CA 25-28R;
CANR 13, 40; DAM NOV, POP;
DLBY 81; INT CANR-13; JRDA;
MTCW; SATA 9

Crispin, Edmund . . . . **CLC 22**
See also Montgomery, (Robert) Bruce
See also DLB 87

Cristofer, Michael 1945(?)- . . . . **CLC 28**
See also CA 110; DAM DRAM; DLB 7

Croce, Benedetto 1866-1952 . . . . . . **TCLC 37**
See also CA 120

Crockett, David 1786-1836 . . . . **NCLC 8**
See also DLB 3, 11

Crockett, Davy
See Crockett, David

Crofts, Freeman Wills
1879-1957 . . . . **TCLC 55**
See also CA 115; DLB 77

Croker, John Wilson 1780-1857 . . **NCLC 10**
See also DLB 110

Crommelynck, Fernand 1885-1970 . . **CLC 75**
See also CA 89-92

Cronin, A(rchibald) J(oseph)
1896-1981 . . . . **CLC 32**
See also CA 1-4R; 102; CANR 5; SATA 47;
SATA-Obit 25

Cross, Amanda
See Heilbrun, Carolyn G(old)

Crothers, Rachel 1878(?)-1958 . . . . . **TCLC 19**
See also CA 113; DLB 7

Croves, Hal
See Traven, B.

Crow Dog, Mary . . . . **CLC 93**
See also Brave Bird, Mary

Crowfield, Christopher
See Stowe, Harriet (Elizabeth) Beecher

Crowley, Aleister . . . . **TCLC 7**
See also Crowley, Edward Alexander

Crowley, Edward Alexander 1875-1947
See Crowley, Aleister
See also CA 104

Crowley, John 1942- . . . . **CLC 57**
See also CA 61-64; CANR 43; DLBY 82;
SATA 65

Crud
See Crumb, R(obert)

Crumarums
See Crumb, R(obert)

Crumb, R(obert) 1943- . . . . **CLC 17**
See also CA 106

Crumbum
See Crumb, R(obert)

Crumski
See Crumb, R(obert)

Crum the Bum
See Crumb, R(obert)

Crunk
See Crumb, R(obert)

Crustt
See Crumb, R(obert)

Cryer, Gretchen (Kiger) 1935- . . . . . . **CLC 21**
See also CA 114; 123

Csath, Geza 1887-1919 . . . . **TCLC 13**
See also CA 111

Cudlip, David 1933- . . . . **CLC 34**

Cullen, Countee
1903-1946 . . . . . . **TCLC 4, 37; BLC; DA;**
DAC
See also BW 1; CA 108; 124;
CDALB 1917-1929; DAM MST, MULT,
POET; DLB 4, 48, 51; MTCW; SATA 18

Cum, R.
See Crumb, R(obert)

Cummings, Bruce F(rederick) 1889-1919
See Barbellion, W. N. P.
See also CA 123

Cummings, E(dward) E(stlin)
1894-1962 . . . . . . **CLC 1, 3, 8, 12, 15, 68;**
DA; DAB; DAC; PC 5; WLC 2
See also CA 73-76; CANR 31;
CDALB 1929-1941; DAM MST, POET;
DLB 4, 48; MTCW

Cunha, Euclides (Rodrigues Pimenta) da
1866-1909 . . . . **TCLC 24**
See also CA 123

Cunningham, E. V.
See Fast, Howard (Melvin)

Cunningham, J(ames) V(incent)
1911-1985 . . . . **CLC 3, 31**
See also CA 1-4R; 115; CANR 1; DLB 5

Cunningham, Julia (Woolfolk)
1916- . . . . **CLC 12**
See also CA 9-12R; CANR 4, 19, 36;
JRDA; MAICYA; SAAS 2; SATA 1, 26

Cunningham, Michael 1952- . . . . **CLC 34**
See also CA 136

Cunninghame Graham, R(obert) B(ontine)
1852-1936 . . . . **TCLC 19**
See also Graham, R(obert) B(ontine)
Cunninghame
See also CA 119; DLB 98

Currie, Ellen 19(?)- . . . . **CLC 44**

Curtin, Philip
See Lowndes, Marie Adelaide (Belloc)

Curtis, Price
See Ellison, Harlan (Jay)

Cutrate, Joe
See Spiegelman, Art

Czaczkes, Shmuel Yosef
See Agnon, S(hmuel) Y(osef Halevi)

Dabrowska, Maria (Szumska)
1889-1965 . . . . **CLC 15**
See also CA 106

Dabydeen, David 1955- . . . . **CLC 34**
See also BW 1; CA 125

Dacey, Philip 1939- . . . . **CLC 51**
See also CA 37-40R; CAAS 17; CANR 14,
32; DLB 105

Dagerman, Stig (Halvard)
1923-1954 . . . . **TCLC 17**
See also CA 117

Dahl, Roald
1916-1990 . . . . . . **CLC 1, 6, 18, 79; DAB;**
DAC
See also AAYA 15; CA 1-4R; 133;
CANR 6, 32, 37; CLR 1, 7; DAM MST,
NOV, POP; DLB 139; JRDA; MAICYA;
MTCW; SATA 1, 26, 73; SATA-Obit 65

Dahlberg, Edward 1900-1977 . . . **CLC 1, 7, 14**
See also CA 9-12R; 69-72; CANR 31;
DLB 48; MTCW

Dale, Colin . . . . **TCLC 18**
See also Lawrence, T(homas) E(dward)

Dale, George E.
See Asimov, Isaac

Daly, Elizabeth 1878-1967 . . . . **CLC 52**
See also CA 23-24; 25-28R; CAP 2

Daly, Maureen 1921- . . . . **CLC 17**
See also AAYA 5; CANR 37; JRDA;
MAICYA; SAAS 1; SATA 2

Damas, Leon-Gontran 1912-1978 . . . **CLC 84**
See also BW 1; CA 125; 73-76

Dana, Richard Henry Sr.
1787-1879 . . . . **NCLC 53**

Daniel, Samuel 1562(?)-1619 . . . . **LC 24**
See also DLB 62

Daniels, Brett
See Adler, Renata

Dannay, Frederic 1905-1982 . . . . **CLC 11**
See also Queen, Ellery
See also CA 1-4R; 107; CANR 1, 39;
DAM POP; DLB 137; MTCW

D'Annunzio, Gabriele
1863-1938 . . . . **TCLC 6, 40**
See also CA 104

Delibes Setien, Miguel 1920-
See Delibes, Miguel
See also CA 45-48; CANR 1, 32; HW;
MTCW

DeLillo, Don
1936- ..... **CLC 8, 10, 13, 27, 39, 54, 76**
See also BEST 89:1; CA 81-84; CANR 21;
DAM NOV, POP; DLB 6; MTCW

de Lisser, H. G.
See De Lisser, Herbert George
See also DLB 117

De Lisser, Herbert George
1878-1944 .... TCLC 12
See also de Lisser, H. G.
See also BW 2; CA 109

Deloria, Vine (Victor), Jr. 1933-.... CLC 21
See also CA 53-56; CANR 5, 20, 48;
DAM MULT; MTCW; NNAL; SATA 21

Del Vecchio, John M(ichael)
1947- .... CLC 29
See also CA 110; DLBD 9

de Man, Paul (Adolph Michel)
1919-1983 .... CLC 55
See also CA 128; 111; DLB 67; MTCW

De Marinis, Rick 1934-.......... CLC 54
See also CA 57-60; CANR 9, 25, 50

Dembry, R. Emmet
See Murfree, Mary Noailles

Demby, William 1922-....... CLC 53; BLC
See also BW 1; CA 81-84; DAM MULT;
DLB 33

Demijohn, Thom
See Disch, Thomas M(ichael)

de Montherlant, Henry (Milon)
See Montherlant, Henry (Milon) de

Demosthenes 384B.C.-322B.C. ... CMLC 13

de Natale, Francine
See Malzberg, Barry N(athaniel)

Denby, Edwin (Orr) 1903-1983..... CLC 48
See also CA 138; 110

Denis, Julio
See Cortazar, Julio

Denmark, Harrison
See Zelazny, Roger (Joseph)

Dennis, John 1658-1734........... LC 11
See also DLB 101

Dennis, Nigel (Forbes) 1912-1989.... CLC 8
See also CA 25-28R; 129; DLB 13, 15;
MTCW

De Palma, Brian (Russell) 1940-.... CLC 20
See also CA 109

De Quincey, Thomas 1785-1859 ... NCLC 4
See also CDBLB 1789-1832; DLB 110; 144

Deren, Eleanora 1908(?)-1961
See Deren, Maya
See also CA 111

Deren, Maya .... CLC 16
See also Deren, Eleanora

Derleth, August (William)
1909-1971 .... CLC 31
See also CA 1-4R; 29-32R; CANR 4;
DLB 9; SATA 5

Der Nister 1884-1950........... TCLC 56

de Routisie, Albert
See Aragon, Louis

Derrida, Jacques 1930-........ CLC 24, 87
See also CA 124; 127

Derry Down Derry
See Lear, Edward

Dersonnes, Jacques
See Simenon, Georges (Jacques Christian)

Desai, Anita 1937-...... CLC 19, 37; DAB
See also CA 81-84; CANR 33; DAM NOV;
MTCW; SATA 63

de Saint-Luc, Jean
See Glassco, John

de Saint Roman, Arnaud
See Aragon, Louis

Descartes, Rene 1596-1650 .... LC 20

De Sica, Vittorio 1901(?)-1974 ..... CLC 20
See also CA 117

Desnos, Robert 1900-1945........ TCLC 22
See also CA 121

Destouches, Louis-Ferdinand
1894-1961 .... CLC 9, 15
See also Celine, Louis-Ferdinand
See also CA 85-88; CANR 28; MTCW

Deutsch, Babette 1895-1982 .... CLC 18
See also CA 1-4R; 108; CANR 4; DLB 45;
SATA 1; SATA-Obit 33

Devenant, William 1606-1649 ...... LC 13

Devkota, Laxmiprasad
1909-1959 .... TCLC 23
See also CA 123

De Voto, Bernard (Augustine)
1897-1955 .... TCLC 29
See also CA 113; DLB 9

De Vries, Peter
1910-1993 .... CLC 1, 2, 3, 7, 10, 28, 46
See also CA 17-20R; 142; CANR 41;
DAM NOV; DLB 6; DLBY 82; MTCW

Dexter, Martin
See Faust, Frederick (Schiller)

Dexter, Pete 1943-............ CLC 34, 55
See also BEST 89:2; CA 127; 131;
DAM POP; INT 131; MTCW

Diamano, Silmang
See Senghor, Leopold Sedar

Diamond, Neil 1941- .... CLC 30
See also CA 108

Diaz del Castillo, Bernal 1496-1584.. LC 31

di Bassetto, Corno
See Shaw, George Bernard

Dick, Philip K(indred)
1928-1982 .... CLC 10, 30, 72
See also CA 49-52; 106; CANR 2, 16;
DAM NOV, POP; DLB 8; MTCW

Dickens, Charles (John Huffam)
1812-1870 ...... NCLC 3, 8, 18, 26, 37,
50; DA; DAB; DAC; SSC 17; WLC
See also CDBLB 1832-1890; DAM MST,
NOV; DLB 21, 55, 70, 159; JRDA;
MAICYA; SATA 15

Dickey, James (Lafayette)
1923- .... CLC 1, 2, 4, 7, 10, 15, 47
See also AITN 1, 2; CA 9-12R; CABS 2;
CANR 10, 48; CDALB 1968-1988;
DAM NOV, POET, POP; DLB 5;
DLBD 7; DLBY 82, 93; INT CANR-10;
MTCW

Dickey, William 1928-1994 ...... CLC 3, 28
See also CA 9-12R; 145; CANR 24; DLB 5

Dickinson, Charles 1951-.......... CLC 49
See also CA 128

Dickinson, Emily (Elizabeth)
1830-1886 .... NCLC 21; DA; DAB;
DAC; PC 1; WLC
See also CDALB 1865-1917; DAM MST,
POET; DLB 1; SATA 29

Dickinson, Peter (Malcolm)
1927- .... CLC 12, 35
See also AAYA 9; CA 41-44R; CANR 31;
CLR 29; DLB 87, 161; JRDA; MAICYA;
SATA 5, 62

Dickson, Carr
See Carr, John Dickson

Dickson, Carter
See Carr, John Dickson

Diderot, Denis 1713-1784 .... LC 26

Didion, Joan 1934-..... CLC 1, 3, 8, 14, 32
See also AITN 1; CA 5-8R; CANR 14;
CDALB 1968-1988; DAM NOV; DLB 2;
DLBY 81, 86; MTCW

Dietrich, Robert
See Hunt, E(verette) Howard, (Jr.)

Dillard, Annie 1945-............ CLC 9, 60
See also AAYA 6; CA 49-52; CANR 3, 43;
DAM NOV; DLBY 80; MTCW;
SATA 10

Dillard, R(ichard) H(enry) W(ilde)
1937- .... CLC 5
See also CA 21-24R; CAAS 7; CANR 10;
DLB 5

Dillon, Eilis 1920-1994............ CLC 17
See also CA 9-12R; 147; CAAS 3; CANR 4,
38; CLR 26; MAICYA; SATA 2, 74;
SATA-Obit 83

Dimont, Penelope
See Mortimer, Penelope (Ruth)

Dinesen, Isak.......... CLC 10, 29; SSC 7
See also Blixen, Karen (Christentze
Dinesen)

Ding Ling....................... CLC 68
See also Chiang Pin-chin

Disch, Thomas M(ichael) 1940-... CLC 7, 36
See also AAYA 17; CA 21-24R; CAAS 4;
CANR 17, 36; CLR 18; DLB 8;
MAICYA; MTCW; SAAS 15; SATA 54

Disch, Tom
See Disch, Thomas M(ichael)

d'Isly, Georges
See Simenon, Georges (Jacques Christian)

Disraeli, Benjamin 1804-1881 .. NCLC 2, 39
See also DLB 21, 55

Ditcum, Steve
See Crumb, R(obert)

Dixon, Paige
See Corcoran, Barbara

Drury, Allen (Stuart) 1918-........ **CLC 37**
See also CA 57-60; CANR 18;
INT CANR-18

Dryden, John
1631-1700 .... **LC 3, 21; DA; DAB;**
DAC; DC 3; WLC
See also CDBLB 1660-1789; DAM DRAM,
MST, POET; DLB 80, 101, 131

Duberman, Martin 1930-........... **CLC 8**
See also CA 1-4R; CANR 2

Dubie, Norman (Evans) 1945-...... **CLC 36**
See also CA 69-72; CANR 12; DLB 120

Du Bois, W(illiam) E(dward) B(urghardt)
1868-1963 ...... **CLC 1, 2, 13, 64; BLC;**
DA; DAC; WLC
See also BW 1; CA 85-88; CANR 34;
CDALB 1865-1917; DAM MST, MULT,
NOV; DLB 47, 50, 91; MTCW; SATA 42

Dubus, Andre 1936-... **CLC 13, 36; SSC 15**
See also CA 21-24R; CANR 17; DLB 130;
INT CANR-17

Duca Minimo
See D'Annunzio, Gabriele

Ducharme, Rejean 1941- .... **CLC 74**
See also DLB 60

Duclos, Charles Pinot 1704-1772 ..... **LC 1**

Dudek, Louis 1918- .... **CLC 11, 19**
See also CA 45-48; CAAS 14; CANR 1;
DLB 88

Duerrenmatt, Friedrich
1921-1990 ...... **CLC 1, 4, 8, 11, 15, 43**
See also CA 17-20R; CANR 33;
DAM DRAM; DLB 69, 124; MTCW

Duffy, Bruce (?)-................. **CLC 50**

Duffy, Maureen 1933- .... **CLC 37**
See also CA 25-28R; CANR 33; DLB 14;
MTCW

Dugan, Alan 1923- .... **CLC 2, 6**
See also CA 81-84; DLB 5

du Gard, Roger Martin
See Martin du Gard, Roger

Duhamel, Georges 1884-1966 .... **CLC 8**
See also CA 81-84; 25-28R; CANR 35;
DLB 65; MTCW

Dujardin, Edouard (Emile Louis)
1861-1949 .... **TCLC 13**
See also CA 109; DLB 123

Dumas, Alexandre (Davy de la Pailleterie)
1802-1870 .... **NCLC 11; DA; DAB;**
DAC; WLC
See also DAM MST, NOV; DLB 119;
SATA 18

Dumas, Alexandre
1824-1895 .... **NCLC 9; DC 1**

Dumas, Claudine
See Malzberg, Barry N(athaniel)

Dumas, Henry L. 1934-1968 ..... **CLC 6, 62**
See also BW 1; CA 85-88; DLB 41

du Maurier, Daphne
1907-1989 .... **CLC 6, 11, 59; DAB;**
DAC; SSC 18
See also CA 5-8R; 128; CANR 6;
DAM MST, POP; MTCW; SATA 27;
SATA-Obit 60

Dunbar, Paul Laurence
1872-1906 ...... **TCLC 2, 12; BLC; DA;**
DAC; PC 5; SSC 8; WLC
See also BW 1; CA 104; 124;
CDALB 1865-1917; DAM MST, MULT,
POET; DLB 50, 54, 78; SATA 34

Dunbar, William 1460(?)-1530(?) .... **LC 20**
See also DLB 132, 146

Duncan, Lois 1934-................ **CLC 26**
See also AAYA 4; CA 1-4R; CANR 2, 23,
36; CLR 29; JRDA; MAICYA; SAAS 2;
SATA 1, 36, 75

Duncan, Robert (Edward)
1919-1988 .... **CLC 1, 2, 4, 7, 15, 41, 55;**
PC 2
See also CA 9-12R; 124; CANR 28;
DAM POET; DLB 5, 16; MTCW

Duncan, Sara Jeannette
1861-1922 .... **TCLC 60**
See also DLB 92

Dunlap, William 1766-1839 .... **NCLC 2**
See also DLB 30, 37, 59

Dunn, Douglas (Eaglesham)
1942-..................... **CLC 6, 40**
See also CA 45-48; CANR 2, 33; DLB 40;
MTCW

Dunn, Katherine (Karen) 1945-..... **CLC 71**
See also CA 33-36R

Dunn, Stephen 1939- .... **CLC 36**
See also CA 33-36R; CANR 12, 48;
DLB 105

Dunne, Finley Peter 1867-1936.... **TCLC 28**
See also CA 108; DLB 11, 23

Dunne, John Gregory 1932-........ **CLC 28**
See also CA 25-28R; CANR 14, 50;
DLBY 80

Dunsany, Edward John Moreton Drax
Plunkett 1878-1957
See Dunsany, Lord
See also CA 104; 148; DLB 10

Dunsany, Lord................. **TCLC 2, 59**
See also Dunsany, Edward John Moreton
Drax Plunkett
See also DLB 77, 153, 156

du Perry, Jean
See Simenon, Georges (Jacques Christian)

Durang, Christopher (Ferdinand)
1949-..................... **CLC 27, 38**
See also CA 105; CANR 50

Duras, Marguerite
1914- ...... **CLC 3, 6, 11, 20, 34, 40, 68**
See also CA 25-28R; CANR 50; DLB 83;
MTCW

Durban, (Rosa) Pam 1947-........ **CLC 39**
See also CA 123

Durcan, Paul 1944-............ **CLC 43, 70**
See also CA 134; DAM POET

Durkheim, Emile 1858-1917 ...... **TCLC 55**

Durrell, Lawrence (George)
1912-1990 .... **CLC 1, 4, 6, 8, 13, 27, 41**
See also CA 9-12R; 132; CANR 40;
CDBLB 1945-1960; DAM NOV; DLB 15,
27; DLBY 90; MTCW

Durrenmatt, Friedrich
See Duerrenmatt, Friedrich

Dutt, Toru 1856-1877.......... **NCLC 29**

Dwight, Timothy 1752-1817...... **NCLC 13**
See also DLB 37

Dworkin, Andrea 1946- .... **CLC 43**
See also CA 77-80; CAAS 21; CANR 16,
39; INT CANR-16; MTCW

Dwyer, Deanna
See Koontz, Dean R(ay)

Dwyer, K. R.
See Koontz, Dean R(ay)

Dylan, Bob 1941-...... **CLC 3, 4, 6, 12, 77**
See also CA 41-44R; DLB 16

Eagleton, Terence (Francis) 1943-
See Eagleton, Terry
See also CA 57-60; CANR 7, 23; MTCW

Eagleton, Terry................... **CLC 63**
See also Eagleton, Terence (Francis)

Early, Jack
See Scoppettone, Sandra

East, Michael
See West, Morris L(anglo)

Eastaway, Edward
See Thomas, (Philip) Edward

Eastlake, William (Derry) 1917-..... **CLC 8**
See also CA 5-8R; CAAS 1; CANR 5;
DLB 6; INT CANR-5

Eastman, Charles A(lexander)
1858-1939 .... **TCLC 55**
See also DAM MULT; NNAL; YABC 1

Eberhart, Richard (Ghormley)
1904- .... **CLC 3, 11, 19, 56**
See also CA 1-4R; CANR 2;
CDALB 1941-1968; DAM POET;
DLB 48; MTCW

Eberstadt, Fernanda 1960-........ **CLC 39**
See also CA 136

Echegaray (y Eizaguirre), Jose (Maria Waldo)
1832-1916 .... **TCLC 4**
See also CA 104; CANR 32; HW; MTCW

Echeverria, (Jose) Esteban (Antonino)
1805-1851 .... **NCLC 18**

Echo
See Proust, (Valentin-Louis-George-Eugene-)
Marcel

Eckert, Allan W. 1931- .... **CLC 17**
See also CA 13-16R; CANR 14, 45;
INT CANR-14; SAAS 21; SATA 29;
SATA-Brief 27

Eckhart, Meister 1260(?)-1328(?) .. **CMLC 9**
See also DLB 115

Eckmar, F. R.
See de Hartog, Jan

Eco, Umberto 1932-........... **CLC 28, 60**
See also BEST 90:1; CA 77-80; CANR 12,
33; DAM NOV, POP; MTCW

Eddison, E(ric) R(ucker)
1882-1945 .... **TCLC 15**
See also CA 109

Edel, (Joseph) Leon 1907-...... **CLC 29, 34**
See also CA 1-4R; CANR 1, 22; DLB 103;
INT CANR-22

Eden, Emily 1797-1869 .... **NCLC 10**

Enzensberger, Hans Magnus
1929- . . . . **CLC 43**
See also CA 116; 119

Ephron, Nora 1941- . . . . **CLC 17, 31**
See also AITN 2; CA 65-68; CANR 12, 39

Epsilon
See Betjeman, John

Epstein, Daniel Mark 1948- . . . . **CLC 7**
See also CA 49-52; CANR 2

Epstein, Jacob 1956- . . . . **CLC 19**
See also CA 114

Epstein, Joseph 1937- . . . . **CLC 39**
See also CA 112; 119; CANR 50

Epstein, Leslie 1938- . . . . **CLC 27**
See also CA 73-76; CAAS 12; CANR 23

Equiano, Olaudah
1745(?)-1797 . . . . **LC 16; BLC**
See also DAM MULT; DLB 37, 50

Erasmus, Desiderius 1469(?)-1536. . . . **LC 16**

Erdman, Paul E(mil) 1932- . . . . **CLC 25**
See also AITN 1; CA 61-64; CANR 13, 43

Erdrich, Louise 1954- . . . . **CLC 39, 54**
See also AAYA 10; BEST 89:1; CA 114;
CANR 41; DAM MULT, NOV, POP;
DLB 152; MTCW; NNAL

Erenburg, Ilya (Grigoryevich)
See Ehrenburg, Ilya (Grigoryevich)

Erickson, Stephen Michael 1950-
See Erickson, Steve
See also CA 129

Erickson, Steve . . . . **CLC 64**
See also Erickson, Stephen Michael

Ericson, Walter
See Fast, Howard (Melvin)

Eriksson, Buntel
See Bergman, (Ernst) Ingmar

Ernaux, Annie 1940- . . . . **CLC 88**
See also CA 147

Eschenbach, Wolfram von
See Wolfram von Eschenbach

Eseki, Bruno
See Mphahlele, Ezekiel

Esenin, Sergei (Alexandrovich)
1895-1925 . . . . **TCLC 4**
See also CA 104

Eshleman, Clayton 1935- . . . . **CLC 7**
See also CA 33-36R; CAAS 6; DLB 5

Espriella, Don Manuel Alvarez
See Southey, Robert

Espriu, Salvador 1913-1985 . . . . **CLC 9**
See also CA 115; DLB 134

Espronceda, Jose de 1808-1842 . . . **NCLC 39**

Esse, James
See Stephens, James

Esterbrook, Tom
See Hubbard, L(afayette) Ron(ald)

Estleman, Loren D. 1952- . . . . **CLC 48**
See also CA 85-88; CANR 27; DAM NOV,
POP; INT CANR-27; MTCW

Eugenides, Jeffrey 1960(?)- . . . . **CLC 81**
See also CA 144

Euripides c. 485B.C.-406B.C. . . . . **DC 4**
See also DA; DAB; DAC; DAM DRAM,
MST

Evan, Evin
See Faust, Frederick (Schiller)

Evans, Evan
See Faust, Frederick (Schiller)

Evans, Marian
See Eliot, George

Evans, Mary Ann
See Eliot, George

Evarts, Esther
See Benson, Sally

Everett, Percival L. 1956- . . . . **CLC 57**
See also BW 2; CA 129

Everson, R(onald) G(ilmour)
1903- . . . . **CLC 27**
See also CA 17-20R; DLB 88

Everson, William (Oliver)
1912-1994 . . . . **CLC 1, 5, 14**
See also CA 9-12R; 145; CANR 20; DLB 5,
16; MTCW

Evtushenko, Evgenii Aleksandrovich
See Yevtushenko, Yevgeny (Alexandrovich)

Ewart, Gavin (Buchanan)
1916-1995 . . . . **CLC 13, 46**
See also CA 89-92; 150; CANR 17, 46;
DLB 40; MTCW

Ewers, Hanns Heinz 1871-1943 . . . **TCLC 12**
See also CA 109; 149

Ewing, Frederick R.
See Sturgeon, Theodore (Hamilton)

Exley, Frederick (Earl)
1929-1992 . . . . **CLC 6, 11**
See also AITN 2; CA 81-84; 138; DLB 143;
DLBY 81

Eynhardt, Guillermo
See Quiroga, Horacio (Sylvestre)

Ezekiel, Nissim 1924- . . . . **CLC 61**
See also CA 61-64

Ezekiel, Tish O'Dowd 1943- . . . . **CLC 34**
See also CA 129

Fadeyev, A.
See Bulgya, Alexander Alexandrovich

Fadeyev, Alexander . . . . **TCLC 53**
See also Bulgya, Alexander Alexandrovich

Fagen, Donald 1948- . . . . **CLC 26**

Fainzilberg, Ilya Arnoldovich 1897-1937
See Ilf, Ilya
See also CA 120

Fair, Ronald L. 1932- . . . . **CLC 18**
See also BW 1; CA 69-72; CANR 25;
DLB 33

Fairbairns, Zoe (Ann) 1948- . . . . **CLC 32**
See also CA 103; CANR 21

Falco, Gian
See Papini, Giovanni

Falconer, James
See Kirkup, James

Falconer, Kenneth
See Kornbluth, C(yril) M.

Falkland, Samuel
See Heijermans, Herman

Fallaci, Oriana 1930- . . . . **CLC 11**
See also CA 77-80; CANR 15; MTCW

Faludy, George 1913- . . . . **CLC 42**
See also CA 21-24R

Faludy, Gyoergy
See Faludy, George

Fanon, Frantz 1925-1961 . . . . . **CLC 74; BLC**
See also BW 1; CA 116; 89-92;
DAM MULT

Fanshawe, Ann 1625-1680 . . . . **LC 11**

Fante, John (Thomas) 1911-1983 . . . **CLC 60**
See also CA 69-72; 109; CANR 23;
DLB 130; DLBY 83

Farah, Nuruddin 1945- . . . . **CLC 53; BLC**
See also BW 2; CA 106; DAM MULT;
DLB 125

Fargue, Leon-Paul 1876(?)-1947 . . . **TCLC 11**
See also CA 109

Farigoule, Louis
See Romains, Jules

Farina, Richard 1936(?)-1966 . . . . **CLC 9**
See also CA 81-84; 25-28R

Farley, Walter (Lorimer)
1915-1989 . . . . **CLC 17**
See also CA 17-20R; CANR 8, 29; DLB 22;
JRDA; MAICYA; SATA 2, 43

Farmer, Philip Jose 1918- . . . . **CLC 1, 19**
See also CA 1-4R; CANR 4, 35; DLB 8;
MTCW

Farquhar, George 1677-1707 . . . . **LC 21**
See also DAM DRAM; DLB 84

Farrell, J(ames) G(ordon)
1935-1979 . . . . **CLC 6**
See also CA 73-76; 89-92; CANR 36;
DLB 14; MTCW

Farrell, James T(homas)
1904-1979 . . . . **CLC 1, 4, 8, 11, 66**
See also CA 5-8R; 89-92; CANR 9; DLB 4,
9, 86; DLBD 2; MTCW

Farren, Richard J.
See Betjeman, John

Farren, Richard M.
See Betjeman, John

Fassbinder, Rainer Werner
1946-1982 . . . . **CLC 20**
See also CA 93-96; 106; CANR 31

Fast, Howard (Melvin) 1914- . . . . . . **CLC 23**
See also AAYA 16; CA 1-4R; CAAS 18;
CANR 1, 33; DAM NOV; DLB 9;
INT CANR-33; SATA 7

Faulcon, Robert
See Holdstock, Robert P.

Faulkner, William (Cuthbert)
1897-1962 . . . . . **CLC 1, 3, 6, 8, 9, 11, 14,**
18, 28, 52, 68; DA; DAB; DAC; SSC 1;
WLC
See also AAYA 7; CA 81-84; CANR 33;
CDALB 1929-1941; DAM MST, NOV;
DLB 9, 11, 44, 102; DLBD 2; DLBY 86;
MTCW

Fauset, Jessie Redmon
1884(?)-1961 . . . . **CLC 19, 54; BLC**
See also BW 1; CA 109; DAM MULT;
DLB 51

Faust, Frederick (Schiller)
1892-1944(?) .... **TCLC 49**
See also CA 108; DAM POP

Faust, Irvin 1924-................. **CLC 8**
See also CA 33-36R; CANR 28; DLB 2, 28;
DLBY 80

Fawkes, Guy
See Benchley, Robert (Charles)

Fearing, Kenneth (Flexner)
1902-1961 .... **CLC 51**
See also CA 93-96; DLB 9

Fecamps, Elise
See Creasey, John

Federman, Raymond 1928- ...... **CLC 6, 47**
See also CA 17-20R; CAAS 8; CANR 10,
43; DLBY 80

Federspiel, J(uerg) F. 1931-........ **CLC 42**
See also CA 146

Feiffer, Jules (Ralph) 1929-.... **CLC 2, 8, 64**
See also AAYA 3; CA 17-20R; CANR 30;
DAM DRAM; DLB 7, 44;
INT CANR-30; MTCW; SATA 8, 61

Feige, Hermann Albert Otto Maximilian
See Traven, B.

Feinberg, David B. 1956-1994...... **CLC 59**
See also CA 135; 147

Feinstein, Elaine 1930-............ **CLC 36**
See also CA 69-72; CAAS 1; CANR 31;
DLB 14, 40; MTCW

Feldman, Irving (Mordecai) 1928-.... **CLC 7**
See also CA 1-4R; CANR 1

Fellini, Federico 1920-1993..... **CLC 16, 85**
See also CA 65-68; 143; CANR 33

Felsen, Henry Gregor 1916- .... **CLC 17**
See also CA 1-4R; CANR 1; SAAS 2;
SATA 1

Fenton, James Martin 1949-....... **CLC 32**
See also CA 102; DLB 40

Ferber, Edna 1887-1968........ **CLC 18, 93**
See also AITN 1; CA 5-8R; 25-28R; DLB 9,
28, 86; MTCW; SATA 7

Ferguson, Helen
See Kavan, Anna

Ferguson, Samuel 1810-1886..... **NCLC 33**
See also DLB 32

Fergusson, Robert 1750-1774 .... **LC 29**
See also DLB 109

Ferling, Lawrence
See Ferlinghetti, Lawrence (Monsanto)

Ferlinghetti, Lawrence (Monsanto)
1919(?)- .... **CLC 2, 6, 10, 27; PC 1**
See also CA 5-8R; CANR 3, 41;
CDALB 1941-1968; DAM POET; DLB 5,
16; MTCW

Fernandez, Vicente Garcia Huidobro
See Huidobro Fernandez, Vicente Garcia

Ferrer, Gabriel (Francisco Victor) Miro
See Miro (Ferrer), Gabriel (Francisco
Victor)

Ferrier, Susan (Edmonstone)
1782-1854 .... **NCLC 8**
See also DLB 116

Ferrigno, Robert 1948(?)-.......... **CLC 65**
See also CA 140

Feuchtwanger, Lion 1884-1958 ..... **TCLC 3**
See also CA 104; DLB 66

Feuillet, Octave 1821-1890 ...... **NCLC 45**

Feydeau, Georges (Leon Jules Marie)
1862-1921 .... **TCLC 22**
See also CA 113; DAM DRAM

Ficino, Marsilio 1433-1499 .... **LC 12**

Fiedeler, Hans
See Doeblin, Alfred

Fiedler, Leslie A(aron)
1917- .... **CLC 4, 13, 24**
See also CA 9-12R; CANR 7; DLB 28, 67;
MTCW

Field, Andrew 1938-.............. **CLC 44**
See also CA 97-100; CANR 25

Field, Eugene 1850-1895 .... **NCLC 3**
See also DLB 23, 42, 140; DLBD 13;
MAICYA; SATA 16

Field, Gans T.
See Wellman, Manly Wade

Field, Michael .... **TCLC 43**

Field, Peter
See Hobson, Laura Z(ametkin)

Fielding, Henry
1707-1754 ...... **LC 1; DA; DAB; DAC;
WLC**
See also CDBLB 1660-1789; DAM DRAM,
MST, NOV; DLB 39, 84, 101

Fielding, Sarah 1710-1768 .... **LC 1**
See also DLB 39

Fierstein, Harvey (Forbes) 1954- ... **CLC 33**
See also CA 123; 129; DAM DRAM, POP

Figes, Eva 1932-................. **CLC 31**
See also CA 53-56; CANR 4, 44; DLB 14

Finch, Robert (Duer Claydon)
1900- .... **CLC 18**
See also CA 57-60; CANR 9, 24, 49;
DLB 88

Findley, Timothy 1930- ...... **CLC 27; DAC**
See also CA 25-28R; CANR 12, 42;
DAM MST; DLB 53

Fink, William
See Mencken, H(enry) L(ouis)

Firbank, Louis 1942-
See Reed, Lou
See also CA 117

Firbank, (Arthur Annesley) Ronald
1886-1926 .... **TCLC 1**
See also CA 104; DLB 36

Fisher, M(ary) F(rances) K(ennedy)
1908-1992 .... **CLC 76, 87**
See also CA 77-80; 138; CANR 44

Fisher, Roy 1930-................. **CLC 25**
See also CA 81-84; CAAS 10; CANR 16;
DLB 40

Fisher, Rudolph
1897-1934 .... **TCLC 11; BLC**
See also BW 1; CA 107; 124; DAM MULT;
DLB 51, 102

Fisher, Vardis (Alvero) 1895-1968.... **CLC 7**
See also CA 5-8R; 25-28R; DLB 9

Fiske, Tarleton
See Bloch, Robert (Albert)

Fitch, Clarke
See Sinclair, Upton (Beall)

Fitch, John IV
See Cormier, Robert (Edmund)

Fitch, Captain Hugh
See Baum, L(yman) Frank

FitzGerald, Edward 1809-1883 .... **NCLC 9**
See also DLB 32

Fitzgerald, F(rancis) Scott (Key)
1896-1940 .... **TCLC 1, 6, 14, 28, 55;
DA; DAB; DAC; SSC 6; WLC**
See also AITN 1; CA 110; 123;
CDALB 1917-1929; DAM MST, NOV;
DLB 4, 9, 86; DLBD 1; DLBY 81;
MTCW

Fitzgerald, Penelope 1916-... **CLC 19, 51, 61**
See also CA 85-88; CAAS 10; DLB 14

Fitzgerald, Robert (Stuart)
1910-1985 .... **CLC 39**
See also CA 1-4R; 114; CANR 1; DLBY 80

FitzGerald, Robert D(avid)
1902-1987 .... **CLC 19**
See also CA 17-20R

Fitzgerald, Zelda (Sayre)
1900-1948 .... **TCLC 52**
See also CA 117; 126; DLBY 84

Flanagan, Thomas (James Bonner)
1923- .... **CLC 25, 52**
See also CA 108; DLBY 80; INT 108;
MTCW

Flaubert, Gustave
1821-1880 .... **NCLC 2, 10, 19; DA;
DAB; DAC; SSC 11; WLC**
See also DAM MST, NOV; DLB 119

Flecker, Herman Elroy
See Flecker, (Herman) James Elroy

Flecker, (Herman) James Elroy
1884-1915 .... **TCLC 43**
See also CA 109; 150; DLB 10, 19

Fleming, Ian (Lancaster)
1908-1964 .... **CLC 3, 30**
See also CA 5-8R; CDBLB 1945-1960;
DAM POP; DLB 87; MTCW; SATA 9

Fleming, Thomas (James) 1927- .... **CLC 37**
See also CA 5-8R; CANR 10;
INT CANR-10; SATA 8

Fletcher, John 1579-1625............ **DC 6**
See also CDBLB Before 1660; DLB 58

Fletcher, John Gould 1886-1950... **TCLC 35**
See also CA 107; DLB 4, 45

Fleur, Paul
See Pohl, Frederik

Flooglebuckle, Al
See Spiegelman, Art

Flying Officer X
See Bates, H(erbert) E(rnest)

Fo, Dario 1926-.................. **CLC 32**
See also CA 116; 128; DAM DRAM;
MTCW

Fogarty, Jonathan Titulescu Esq.
See Farrell, James T(homas)

Folke, Will
See Bloch, Robert (Albert)

Follett, Ken(neth Martin) 1949- .... **CLC 18**
See also AAYA 6; BEST 89:4; CA 81-84;
CANR 13, 33; DAM NOV, POP;
DLB 87; DLBY 81; INT CANR-33;
MTCW

Fontane, Theodor 1819-1898..... **NCLC 26**
See also DLB 129

Foote, Horton 1916-.......... **CLC 51, 91**
See also CA 73-76; CANR 34, 51;
DAM DRAM; DLB 26; INT CANR-34

Foote, Shelby 1916- .... **CLC 75**
See also CA 5-8R; CANR 3, 45;
DAM NOV, POP; DLB 2, 17

Forbes, Esther 1891-1967......... **CLC 12**
See also AAYA 17; CA 13-14; 25-28R;
CAP 1; CLR 27; DLB 22; JRDA;
MAICYA; SATA 2

Forche, Carolyn (Louise)
1950- .... **CLC 25, 83, 86; PC 10**
See also CA 109; 117; CANR 50;
DAM POET; DLB 5; INT 117

Ford, Elbur
See Hibbert, Eleanor Alice Burford

Ford, Ford Madox
1873-1939 .... **TCLC 1, 15, 39, 57**
See also CA 104; 132; CDBLB 1914-1945;
DAM NOV; DLB 162; MTCW

Ford, John 1895-1973............ **CLC 16**
See also CA 45-48

Ford, Richard 1944-.............. **CLC 46**
See also CA 69-72; CANR 11, 47

Ford, Webster
See Masters, Edgar Lee

Foreman, Richard 1937-.......... **CLC 50**
See also CA 65-68; CANR 32

Forester, C(ecil) S(cott)
1899-1966 .... **CLC 35**
See also CA 73-76; 25-28R; SATA 13

Forez
See Mauriac, Francois (Charles)

Forman, James Douglas 1932-...... **CLC 21**
See also AAYA 17; CA 9-12R; CANR 4,
19, 42; JRDA; MAICYA; SATA 8, 70

Fornes, Maria Irene 1930-...... **CLC 39, 61**
See also CA 25-28R; CANR 28; DLB 7;
HW; INT CANR-28; MTCW

Forrest, Leon 1937- .... **CLC 4**
See also BW 2; CA 89-92; CAAS 7;
CANR 25; DLB 33

Forster, E(dward) M(organ)
1879-1970 ..... **CLC 1, 2, 3, 4, 9, 10, 13,
15, 22, 45, 77; DA; DAB; DAC; WLC**
See also AAYA 2; CA 13-14; 25-28R;
CANR 45; CAP 1; CDBLB 1914-1945;
DAM MST, NOV; DLB 34, 98, 162;
DLBD 10; MTCW; SATA 57

Forster, John 1812-1876 .... **NCLC 11**
See also DLB 144

Forsyth, Frederick 1938-...... **CLC 2, 5, 36**
See also BEST 89:4; CA 85-88; CANR 38;
DAM NOV, POP; DLB 87; MTCW

Forten, Charlotte L. .... **TCLC 16; BLC**
See also Grimke, Charlotte L(ottie) Forten
See also DLB 50

Foscolo, Ugo 1778-1827......... **NCLC 8**

Fosse, Bob .... **CLC 20**
See also Fosse, Robert Louis

Fosse, Robert Louis 1927-1987
See Fosse, Bob
See also CA 110; 123

Foster, Stephen Collins
1826-1864 .... **NCLC 26**

Foucault, Michel
1926-1984 .... **CLC 31, 34, 69**
See also CA 105; 113; CANR 34; MTCW

Fouque, Friedrich (Heinrich Karl) de la Motte
1777-1843 .... **NCLC 2**
See also DLB 90

Fourier, Charles 1772-1837 ...... **NCLC 51**

Fournier, Henri Alban 1886-1914
See Alain-Fournier
See also CA 104

Fournier, Pierre 1916-.......... **CLC 11**
See also Gascar, Pierre
See also CA 89-92; CANR 16, 40

Fowles, John
1926- ...... **CLC 1, 2, 3, 4, 6, 9, 10, 15,
33, 87; DAB; DAC**
See also CA 5-8R; CANR 25; CDBLB 1960
to Present; DAM MST; DLB 14, 139;
MTCW; SATA 22

Fox, Paula 1923-................. **CLC 2, 8**
See also AAYA 3; CA 73-76; CANR 20,
36; CLR 1; DLB 52; JRDA; MAICYA;
MTCW; SATA 17, 60

Fox, William Price (Jr.) 1926- ..... **CLC 22**
See also CA 17-20R; CAAS 19; CANR 11;
DLB 2; DLBY 81

Foxe, John 1516(?)-1587 .... **LC 14**

Frame, Janet .... **CLC 2, 3, 6, 22, 66**
See also Clutha, Janet Paterson Frame

France, Anatole .... **TCLC 9**
See also Thibault, Jacques Anatole Francois
See also DLB 123

Francis, Claude 19(?)- .... **CLC 50**

Francis, Dick 1920- .... **CLC 2, 22, 42**
See also AAYA 5; BEST 89:3; CA 5-8R;
CANR 9, 42; CDBLB 1960 to Present;
DAM POP; DLB 87; INT CANR-9;
MTCW

Francis, Robert (Churchill)
1901-1987 .... **CLC 15**
See also CA 1-4R; 123; CANR 1

Frank, Anne(lies Marie)
1929-1945 .... **TCLC 17; DA; DAB;
DAC; WLC**
See also AAYA 12; CA 113; 133;
DAM MST; MTCW; SATA 87;
SATA-Brief 42

Frank, Elizabeth 1945-............ **CLC 39**
See also CA 121; 126; INT 126

Frankl, Viktor E(mil) 1905-........ **CLC 93**
See also CA 65-68

Franklin, Benjamin
See Hasek, Jaroslav (Matej Frantisek)

Franklin, Benjamin
1706-1790 ..... **LC 25; DA; DAB; DAC**
See also CDALB 1640-1865; DAM MST;
DLB 24, 43, 73

Franklin, (Stella Maraia Sarah) Miles
1879-1954 .... **TCLC 7**
See also CA 104

Fraser, (Lady) Antonia (Pakenham)
1932- .... **CLC 32**
See also CA 85-88; CANR 44; MTCW;
SATA-Brief 32

Fraser, George MacDonald 1925-.... **CLC 7**
See also CA 45-48; CANR 2, 48

Fraser, Sylvia 1935-.............. **CLC 64**
See also CA 45-48; CANR 1, 16

Frayn, Michael 1933-....... **CLC 3, 7, 31, 47**
See also CA 5-8R; CANR 30;
DAM DRAM, NOV; DLB 13, 14;
MTCW

Fraze, Candida (Merrill) 1945-..... **CLC 50**
See also CA 126

Frazer, J(ames) G(eorge)
1854-1941 .... **TCLC 32**
See also CA 118

Frazer, Robert Caine
See Creasey, John

Frazer, Sir James George
See Frazer, J(ames) G(eorge)

Frazier, Ian 1951-................. **CLC 46**
See also CA 130

Frederic, Harold 1856-1898...... **NCLC 10**
See also DLB 12, 23; DLBD 13

Frederick, John
See Faust, Frederick (Schiller)

Frederick the Great 1712-1786...... **LC 14**

Fredro, Aleksander 1793-1876..... **NCLC 8**

Freeling, Nicolas 1927- .... **CLC 38**
See also CA 49-52; CAAS 12; CANR 1, 17,
50; DLB 87

Freeman, Douglas Southall
1886-1953 .... **TCLC 11**
See also CA 109; DLB 17

Freeman, Judith 1946-........... **CLC 55**
See also CA 148

Freeman, Mary Eleanor Wilkins
1852-1930 .... **TCLC 9; SSC 1**
See also CA 106; DLB 12, 78

Freeman, R(ichard) Austin
1862-1943 .... **TCLC 21**
See also CA 113; DLB 70

French, Albert 1943- .... **CLC 86**

French, Marilyn 1929-...... **CLC 10, 18, 60**
See also CA 69-72; CANR 3, 31;
DAM DRAM, NOV, POP;
INT CANR-31; MTCW

French, Paul
See Asimov, Isaac

Freneau, Philip Morin 1752-1832.. **NCLC 1**
See also DLB 37, 43

Freud, Sigmund 1856-1939 .... **TCLC 52**
See also CA 115; 133; MTCW

Friedan, Betty (Naomi) 1921-...... **CLC 74**
See also CA 65-68; CANR 18, 45; MTCW

Friedlaender, Saul 1932- .... **CLC 90**
See also CA 117; 130

Friedman, B(ernard) H(arper)
1926-....................... **CLC 7**
See also CA 1-4R; CANR 3, 48

Garnett, David 1892-1981 .... CLC 3
See also CA 5-8R; 103; CANR 17; DLB 34

Garos, Stephanie
See Katz, Steve

Garrett, George (Palmer)
1929- .... CLC 3, 11, 51
See also CA 1-4R; CAAS 5; CANR 1, 42;
DLB 2, 5, 130, 152; DLBY 83

Garrick, David 1717-1779 .... LC 15
See also DAM DRAM; DLB 84

Garrigue, Jean 1914-1972 .... CLC 2, 8
See also CA 5-8R; 37-40R; CANR 20

Garrison, Frederick
See Sinclair, Upton (Beall)

Garth, Will
See Hamilton, Edmond; Kuttner, Henry

Garvey, Marcus (Moziah, Jr.)
1887-1940 .... TCLC 41; BLC
See also BW 1; CA 120; 124; DAM MULT

Gary, Romain .... CLC 25
See also Kacew, Romain
See also DLB 83

Gascar, Pierre .... CLC 11
See also Fournier, Pierre

Gascoyne, David (Emery) 1916- .... CLC 45
See also CA 65-68; CANR 10, 28; DLB 20;
MTCW

Gaskell, Elizabeth Cleghorn
1810-1865 .... NCLC 5; DAB
See also CDBLB 1832-1890; DAM MST;
DLB 21, 144, 159

Gass, William H(oward)
1924- ... CLC 1, 2, 8, 11, 15, 39; SSC 12
See also CA 17-20R; CANR 30; DLB 2;
MTCW

Gasset, Jose Ortega y
See Ortega y Gasset, Jose

Gates, Henry Louis, Jr. 1950- ...... CLC 65
See also BW 2; CA 109; CANR 25;
DAM MULT; DLB 67

Gautier, Theophile
1811-1872 .... NCLC 1; SSC 20
See also DAM POET; DLB 119

Gawsworth, John
See Bates, H(erbert) E(rnest)

Gay, Oliver
See Gogarty, Oliver St. John

Gaye, Marvin (Penze) 1939-1984 ... CLC 26
See also CA 112

Gebler, Carlo (Ernest) 1954- .... CLC 39
See also CA 119; 133

Gee, Maggie (Mary) 1948- .... CLC 57
See also CA 130

Gee, Maurice (Gough) 1931- .... CLC 29
See also CA 97-100; SATA 46

Gelbart, Larry (Simon) 1923- ... CLC 21, 61
See also CA 73-76; CANR 45

Gelber, Jack 1932- .... CLC 1, 6, 14, 79
See also CA 1-4R; CANR 2; DLB 7

Gellhorn, Martha (Ellis) 1908- .. CLC 14, 60
See also CA 77-80; CANR 44; DLBY 82

Genet, Jean
1910-1986 ... CLC 1, 2, 5, 10, 14, 44, 46
See also CA 13-16R; CANR 18;
DAM DRAM; DLB 72; DLBY 86;
MTCW

Gent, Peter 1942- .... CLC 29
See also AITN 1; CA 89-92; DLBY 82

Gentlewoman in New England, A
See Bradstreet, Anne

Gentlewoman in Those Parts, A
See Bradstreet, Anne

George, Jean Craighead 1919- ...... CLC 35
See also AAYA 8; CA 5-8R; CANR 25;
CLR 1; DLB 52; JRDA; MAICYA;
SATA 2, 68

George, Stefan (Anton)
1868-1933 .... TCLC 2, 14
See also CA 104

Georges, Georges Martin
See Simenon, Georges (Jacques Christian)

Gerhardi, William Alexander
See Gerhardie, William Alexander

Gerhardie, William Alexander
1895-1977 .... CLC 5
See also CA 25-28R; 73-76; CANR 18;
DLB 36

Gerstler, Amy 1956- .... CLC 70
See also CA 146

Gertler, T. .... CLC 34
See also CA 116; 121; INT 121

Ghalib .... NCLC 39
See also Ghalib, Hsadullah Khan

Ghalib, Hsadullah Khan 1797-1869
See Ghalib
See also DAM POET

Ghelderode, Michel de
1898-1962 .... CLC 6, 11
See also CA 85-88; CANR 40;
DAM DRAM

Ghiselin, Brewster 1903- .... CLC 23
See also CA 13-16R; CAAS 10; CANR 13

Ghose, Zulfikar 1935- .... CLC 42
See also CA 65-68

Ghosh, Amitav 1956- .... CLC 44
See also CA 147

Giacosa, Giuseppe 1847-1906 ...... TCLC 7
See also CA 104

Gibb, Lee
See Waterhouse, Keith (Spencer)

Gibbon, Lewis Grassic .... TCLC 4
See also Mitchell, James Leslie

Gibbons, Kaye 1960- .... CLC 50, 88
See also DAM POP

Gibran, Kahlil
1883-1931 .... TCLC 1, 9; PC 9
See also CA 104; 150; DAM POET, POP

Gibran, Khalil
See Gibran, Kahlil

Gibson, William
1914- .... CLC 23; DA; DAB; DAC
See also CA 9-12R; CANR 9, 42;
DAM DRAM, MST; DLB 7; SATA 66

Gibson, William (Ford) 1948- ... CLC 39, 63
See also AAYA 12; CA 126; 133;
DAM POP

Gide, Andre (Paul Guillaume)
1869-1951 .... TCLC 5, 12, 36; DA;
DAB; DAC; SSC 13; WLC
See also CA 104; 124; DAM MST, NOV;
DLB 65; MTCW

Gifford, Barry (Colby) 1946- .... CLC 34
See also CA 65-68; CANR 9, 30, 40

Gilbert, W(illiam) S(chwenck)
1836-1911 .... TCLC 3
See also CA 104; DAM DRAM, POET;
SATA 36

Gilbreth, Frank B., Jr. 1911- .... CLC 17
See also CA 9-12R; SATA 2

Gilchrist, Ellen 1935- .. CLC 34, 48; SSC 14
See also CA 113; 116; CANR 41;
DAM POP; DLB 130; MTCW

Giles, Molly 1942- .... CLC 39
See also CA 126

Gill, Patrick
See Creasey, John

Gilliam, Terry (Vance) 1940- .... CLC 21
See also Monty Python
See also CA 108; 113; CANR 35; INT 113

Gillian, Jerry
See Gilliam, Terry (Vance)

Gilliatt, Penelope (Ann Douglass)
1932-1993 .... CLC 2, 10, 13, 53
See also AITN 2; CA 13-16R; 141;
CANR 49; DLB 14

Gilman, Charlotte (Anna) Perkins (Stetson)
1860-1935 .... TCLC 9, 37; SSC 13
See also CA 106; 150

Gilmour, David 1949- .... CLC 35
See also CA 138, 147

Gilpin, William 1724-1804 .... NCLC 30

Gilray, J. D.
See Mencken, H(enry) L(ouis)

Gilroy, Frank D(aniel) 1925- .... CLC 2
See also CA 81-84; CANR 32; DLB 7

Ginsberg, Allen
1926- ...... CLC 1, 2, 3, 4, 6, 13, 36, 69;
DA; DAB; DAC; PC 4; WLC 3
See also AITN 1; CA 1-4R; CANR 2, 41;
CDALB 1941-1968; DAM MST, POET;
DLB 5, 16; MTCW

Ginzburg, Natalia
1916-1991 .... CLC 5, 11, 54, 70
See also CA 85-88; 135; CANR 33; MTCW

Giono, Jean 1895-1970 .... CLC 4, 11
See also CA 45-48; 29-32R; CANR 2, 35;
DLB 72; MTCW

Giovanni, Nikki
1943- ...... CLC 2, 4, 19, 64; BLC; DA;
DAB; DAC
See also AITN 1; BW 2; CA 29-32R;
CAAS 6; CANR 18, 41; CLR 6;
DAM MST, MULT, POET; DLB 5, 41;
INT CANR-18; MAICYA; MTCW;
SATA 24

Giovene, Andrea 1904- .... CLC 7
See also CA 85-88

Gozzano, Guido 1883-1916 . . . . PC 10
See also DLB 114

Gozzi, (Conte) Carlo 1720-1806 . . NCLC 23

Grabbe, Christian Dietrich
1801-1836 . . . . NCLC 2
See also DLB 133

Grace, Patricia 1937- . . . . CLC 56

Gracian y Morales, Baltasar
1601-1658 . . . . LC 15

Gracq, Julien . . . . CLC 11, 48
See also Poirier, Louis
See also DLB 83

Grade, Chaim 1910-1982 . . . . CLC 10
See also CA 93-96; 107

Graduate of Oxford, A
See Ruskin, John

Graham, John
See Phillips, David Graham

Graham, Jorie 1951- . . . . CLC 48
See also CA 111; DLB 120

Graham, R(obert) B(ontine) Cunninghame
See Cunninghame Graham, R(obert)
B(ontine)
See also DLB 98, 135

Graham, Robert
See Haldeman, Joe (William)

Graham, Tom
See Lewis, (Harry) Sinclair

Graham, W(illiam) S(ydney)
1918-1986 . . . . CLC 29
See also CA 73-76; 118; DLB 20

Graham, Winston (Mawdsley)
1910- . . . . CLC 23
See also CA 49-52; CANR 2, 22, 45;
DLB 77

Grant, Skeeter
See Spiegelman, Art

Granville-Barker, Harley
1877-1946 . . . . TCLC 2
See also Barker, Harley Granville
See also CA 104; DAM DRAM

Grass, Guenter (Wilhelm)
1927- . . . . . CLC 1, 2, 4, 6, 11, 15, 22, 32,
49, 88; DA; DAB; DAC; WLC
See also CA 13-16R; CANR 20;
DAM MST, NOV; DLB 75, 124; MTCW

Gratton, Thomas
See Hulme, T(homas) E(rnest)

Grau, Shirley Ann
1929- . . . . CLC 4, 9; SSC 15
See also CA 89-92; CANR 22; DLB 2;
INT CANR-22; MTCW

Gravel, Fern
See Hall, James Norman

Graver, Elizabeth 1964- . . . . CLC 70
See also CA 135

Graves, Richard Perceval 1945- . . . . CLC 44
See also CA 65-68; CANR 9, 26, 51

Graves, Robert (von Ranke)
1895-1985 . . . . . . CLC 1, 2, 6, 11, 39, 44,
45; DAB; DAC; PC 6
See also CA 5-8R; 117; CANR 5, 36;
CDBLB 1914-1945; DAM MST, POET;
DLB 20, 100; DLBY 85; MTCW;
SATA 45

Gray, Alasdair (James) 1934- . . . . . . CLC 41
See also CA 126; CANR 47; INT 126;
MTCW

Gray, Amlin 1946- . . . . CLC 29
See also CA 138

Gray, Francine du Plessix 1930- . . . . CLC 22
See also BEST 90:3; CA 61-64; CAAS 2;
CANR 11, 33; DAM NOV;
INT CANR-11; MTCW

Gray, John (Henry) 1866-1934 . . . . TCLC 19
See also CA 119

Gray, Simon (James Holliday)
1936- . . . . CLC 9, 14, 36
See also AITN 1; CA 21-24R; CAAS 3;
CANR 32; DLB 13; MTCW

Gray, Spalding 1941- . . . . CLC 49
See also CA 128; DAM POP

Gray, Thomas
1716-1771 . . . . . . LC 4; DA; DAB; DAC;
PC 2; WLC
See also CDBLB 1660-1789; DAM MST;
DLB 109

Grayson, David
See Baker, Ray Stannard

Grayson, Richard (A.) 1951- . . . . CLC 38
See also CA 85-88; CANR 14, 31

Greeley, Andrew M(oran) 1928- . . . . CLC 28
See also CA 5-8R; CAAS 7; CANR 7, 43;
DAM POP; MTCW

Green, Anna Katharine
1846-1935 . . . . TCLC 63
See also CA 112

Green, Brian
See Card, Orson Scott

Green, Hannah
See Greenberg, Joanne (Goldenberg)

Green, Hannah . . . . CLC 3
See also CA 73-76

Green, Henry . . . . CLC 2, 13
See also Yorke, Henry Vincent
See also DLB 15

Green, Julian (Hartridge) 1900-
See Green, Julien
See also CA 21-24R; CANR 33; DLB 4, 72;
MTCW

Green, Julien . . . . CLC 3, 11, 77
See also Green, Julian (Hartridge)

Green, Paul (Eliot) 1894-1981 . . . . . . CLC 25
See also AITN 1; CA 5-8R; 103; CANR 3;
DAM DRAM; DLB 7, 9; DLBY 81

Greenberg, Ivan 1908-1973
See Rahv, Philip
See also CA 85-88

Greenberg, Joanne (Goldenberg)
1932- . . . . CLC 7, 30
See also AAYA 12; CA 5-8R; CANR 14,
32; SATA 25

Greenberg, Richard 1959(?)- . . . . CLC 57
See also CA 138

Greene, Bette 1934- . . . . CLC 30
See also AAYA 7; CA 53-56; CANR 4;
CLR 2; JRDA; MAICYA; SAAS 16;
SATA 8

Greene, Gael . . . . CLC 8
See also CA 13-16R; CANR 10

Greene, Graham
1904-1991 . . . . CLC 1, 3, 6, 9, 14, 18, 27,
37, 70, 72; DA; DAB; DAC; WLC
See also AITN 2; CA 13-16R; 133;
CANR 35; CDBLB 1945-1960;
DAM MST, NOV; DLB 13, 15, 77, 100,
162; DLBY 91; MTCW; SATA 20

Greer, Richard
See Silverberg, Robert

Gregor, Arthur 1923- . . . . CLC 9
See also CA 25-28R; CAAS 10; CANR 11;
SATA 36

Gregor, Lee
See Pohl, Frederik

Gregory, Isabella Augusta (Persse)
1852-1932 . . . . TCLC 1
See also CA 104; DLB 10

Gregory, J. Dennis
See Williams, John A(lfred)

Grendon, Stephen
See Derleth, August (William)

Grenville, Kate 1950- . . . . CLC 61
See also CA 118

Grenville, Pelham
See Wodehouse, P(elham) G(renville)

Greve, Felix Paul (Berthold Friedrich)
1879-1948
See Grove, Frederick Philip
See also CA 104; 141; DAC; DAM MST

Grey, Zane 1872-1939 . . . . TCLC 6
See also CA 104; 132; DAM POP; DLB 9;
MTCW

Grieg, (Johan) Nordahl (Brun)
1902-1943 . . . . TCLC 10
See also CA 107

Grieve, C(hristopher) M(urray)
1892-1978 . . . . CLC 11, 19
See also MacDiarmid, Hugh; Pteleon
See also CA 5-8R; 85-88; CANR 33;
DAM POET; MTCW

Griffin, Gerald 1803-1840 . . . . NCLC 7
See also DLB 159

Griffin, John Howard 1920-1980 . . . . CLC 68
See also AITN 1; CA 1-4R; 101; CANR 2

Griffin, Peter 1942- . . . . CLC 39
See also CA 136

Griffiths, Trevor 1935- . . . . CLC 13, 52
See also CA 97-100; CANR 45; DLB 13

Grigson, Geoffrey (Edward Harvey)
1905-1985 . . . . CLC 7, 39
See also CA 25-28R; 118; CANR 20, 33;
DLB 27; MTCW

Grillparzer, Franz 1791-1872 . . . . . . NCLC 1
See also DLB 133

Grimble, Reverend Charles James
See Eliot, T(homas) S(tearns)

Grimke, Charlotte L(ottie) Forten
1837(?)-1914
See Forten, Charlotte L.
See also BW 1; CA 117; 124; DAM MULT,
POET

Grimm, Jacob Ludwig Karl
1785-1863 . . . . NCLC 3
See also DLB 90; MAICYA; SATA 22

Grimm, Wilhelm Karl 1786-1859 .. **NCLC 3**
See also DLB 90; MAICYA; SATA 22

**Grimmelshausen, Johann Jakob Christoffel
von** 1621-1676 .... **LC 6**

Grindel, Eugene 1895-1952
See Eluard, Paul
See also CA 104

Grisham, John 1955- .... **CLC 84**
See also AAYA 14; CA 138; CANR 47;
DAM POP

Grossman, David 1954- .... **CLC 67**
See also CA 138

Grossman, Vasily (Semenovich)
1905-1964 .... **CLC 41**
See also CA 124; 130; MTCW

Grove, Frederick Philip .... **TCLC 4**
See also Greve, Felix Paul (Berthold
Friedrich)
See also DLB 92

Grubb
See Crumb, R(obert)

Grumbach, Doris (Isaac)
1918- .... **CLC 13, 22, 64**
See also CA 5-8R; CAAS 2; CANR 9, 42;
INT CANR-9

Grundtvig, Nicolai Frederik Severin
1783-1872 .... **NCLC 1**

Grunge
See Crumb, R(obert)

Grunwald, Lisa 1959- .... **CLC 44**
See also CA 120

Guare, John 1938- .... **CLC 8, 14, 29, 67**
See also CA 73-76; CANR 21;
DAM DRAM; DLB 7; MTCW

Gudjonsson, Halldor Kiljan 1902-
See Laxness, Halldor
See also CA 103

Guenter, Erich
See Eich, Guenter

Guest, Barbara 1920- .... **CLC 34**
See also CA 25-28R; CANR 11, 44; DLB 5

Guest, Judith (Ann) 1936- .... **CLC 8, 30**
See also AAYA 7; CA 77-80; CANR 15;
DAM NOV, POP; INT CANR-15;
MTCW

Guevara, Che .... **CLC 87; HLC**
See also Guevara (Serna), Ernesto

Guevara (Serna), Ernesto 1928-1967
See Guevara, Che
See also CA 127; 111; DAM MULT; HW

Guild, Nicholas M. 1944- .... **CLC 33**
See also CA 93-96

Guillemin, Jacques
See Sartre, Jean-Paul

Guillen, Jorge 1893-1984 .... **CLC 11**
See also CA 89-92; 112; DAM MULT,
POET; DLB 108; HW

Guillen (y Batista), Nicolas (Cristobal)
1902-1989 ..... **CLC 48, 79; BLC; HLC**
See also BW 2; CA 116; 125; 129;
DAM MST, MULT, POET; HW

Guillevic, (Eugene) 1907- .... **CLC 33**
See also CA 93-96

Guillois
See Desnos, Robert

Guiney, Louise Imogen
1861-1920 .... **TCLC 41**
See also DLB 54

Guiraldes, Ricardo (Guillermo)
1886-1927 .... **TCLC 39**
See also CA 131; HW; MTCW

Gumilev, Nikolai Stephanovich
1886-1921 .... **TCLC 60**

Gunesekera, Romesh .... **CLC 91**

Gunn, Bill .... **CLC 5**
See also Gunn, William Harrison
See also DLB 38

Gunn, Thom(son William)
1929- .... **CLC 3, 6, 18, 32, 81**
See also CA 17-20R; CANR 9, 33;
CDBLB 1960 to Present; DAM POET;
DLB 27; INT CANR-33; MTCW

Gunn, William Harrison 1934(?)-1989
See Gunn, Bill
See also AITN 1; BW 1; CA 13-16R; 128;
CANR 12, 25

Gunnars, Kristjana 1948- .... **CLC 69**
See also CA 113; DLB 60

Gurganus, Allan 1947- .... **CLC 70**
See also BEST 90:1; CA 135; DAM POP

Gurney, A(lbert) R(amsdell), Jr.
1930- .... **CLC 32, 50, 54**
See also CA 77-80; CANR 32;
DAM DRAM

Gurney, Ivor (Bertie) 1890-1937 ... **TCLC 33**

Gurney, Peter
See Gurney, A(lbert) R(amsdell), Jr.

Guro, Elena 1877-1913 .... **TCLC 56**

Gustafson, Ralph (Barker) 1909- .... **CLC 36**
See also CA 21-24R; CANR 8, 45; DLB 88

Gut, Gom
See Simenon, Georges (Jacques Christian)

Guterson, David 1956- .... **CLC 91**
See also CA 132

Guthrie, A(lfred) B(ertram), Jr.
1901-1991 .... **CLC 23**
See also CA 57-60; 134; CANR 24; DLB 6;
SATA 62; SATA-Obit 67

Guthrie, Isobel
See Grieve, C(hristopher) M(urray)

Guthrie, Woodrow Wilson 1912-1967
See Guthrie, Woody
See also CA 113; 93-96

Guthrie, Woody .... **CLC 35**
See also Guthrie, Woodrow Wilson

Guy, Rosa (Cuthbert) 1928- .... **CLC 26**
See also AAYA 4; BW 2; CA 17-20R;
CANR 14, 34; CLR 13; DLB 33; JRDA;
MAICYA; SATA 14, 62

Gwendolyn
See Bennett, (Enoch) Arnold

H. D. .... **CLC 3, 8, 14, 31, 34, 73; PC 5**
See also Doolittle, Hilda

H. de V.
See Buchan, John

Haavikko, Paavo Juhani
1931- .... **CLC 18, 34**
See also CA 106

Habbema, Koos
See Heijermans, Herman

Hacker, Marilyn
1942- .... **CLC 5, 9, 23, 72, 91**
See also CA 77-80; DAM POET; DLB 120

Haggard, H(enry) Rider
1856-1925 .... **TCLC 11**
See also CA 108; 148; DLB 70, 156;
SATA 16

Hagiwara Sakutaro 1886-1942 .... **TCLC 60**

Haig, Fenil
See Ford, Ford Madox

Haig-Brown, Roderick (Langmere)
1908-1976 .... **CLC 21**
See also CA 5-8R; 69-72; CANR 4, 38;
CLR 31; DLB 88; MAICYA; SATA 12

Hailey, Arthur 1920- .... **CLC 5**
See also AITN 2; BEST 90:3; CA 1-4R;
CANR 2, 36; DAM NOV, POP; DLB 88;
DLBY 82; MTCW

Hailey, Elizabeth Forsythe 1938- ... **CLC 40**
See also CA 93-96; CAAS 1; CANR 15, 48;
INT CANR-15

Haines, John (Meade) 1924- .... **CLC 58**
See also CA 17-20R; CANR 13, 34; DLB 5

Hakluyt, Richard 1552-1616 .... **LC 31**

Haldeman, Joe (William) 1943- ..... **CLC 61**
See also CA 53-56; CANR 6; DLB 8;
INT CANR-6

Haley, Alex(ander Murray Palmer)
1921-1992 .... **CLC 8, 12, 76; BLC; DA;
DAB; DAC**
See also BW 2; CA 77-80; 136; DAM MST,
MULT, POP; DLB 38; MTCW

Haliburton, Thomas Chandler
1796-1865 .... **NCLC 15**
See also DLB 11, 99

Hall, Donald (Andrew, Jr.)
1928- .... **CLC 1, 13, 37, 59**
See also CA 5-8R; CAAS 7; CANR 2, 44;
DAM POET; DLB 5; SATA 23

Hall, Frederic Sauser
See Sauser-Hall, Frederic

Hall, James
See Kuttner, Henry

Hall, James Norman 1887-1951 ... **TCLC 23**
See also CA 123; SATA 21

Hall, (Marguerite) Radclyffe
1886-1943 .... **TCLC 12**
See also CA 110; 150

Hall, Rodney 1935- .... **CLC 51**
See also CA 109

Halleck, Fitz-Greene 1790-1867 .. **NCLC 47**
See also DLB 3

Halliday, Michael
See Creasey, John

Halpern, Daniel 1945- .... **CLC 14**
See also CA 33-36R

Hamburger, Michael (Peter Leopold)
1924- .... **CLC 5, 14**
See also CA 5-8R; CAAS 4; CANR 2, 47;
DLB 27

Hamill, Pete   1935- . . . . CLC 10
See also CA 25-28R; CANR 18

Hamilton, Alexander
1755(?)-1804 . . . . NCLC 49
See also DLB 37

Hamilton, Clive
See Lewis, C(live) S(taples)

Hamilton, Edmond   1904-1977 . . . . CLC 1
See also CA 1-4R; CANR 3; DLB 8

Hamilton, Eugene (Jacob) Lee
See Lee-Hamilton, Eugene (Jacob)

Hamilton, Franklin
See Silverberg, Robert

Hamilton, Gail
See Corcoran, Barbara

Hamilton, Mollie
See Kaye, M(ary) M(argaret)

Hamilton, (Anthony Walter) Patrick
1904-1962 . . . . CLC 51
See also CA 113; DLB 10

Hamilton, Virginia   1936- . . . . CLC 26
See also AAYA 2; BW 2; CA 25-28R;
CANR 20, 37; CLR 1, 11, 40;
DAM MULT; DLB 33, 52;
INT CANR-20; JRDA; MAICYA;
MTCW; SATA 4, 56, 79

Hammett, (Samuel) Dashiell
1894-1961 . . . . CLC 3, 5, 10, 19, 47;
SSC 17
See also AITN 1; CA 81-84; CANR 42;
CDALB 1929-1941; DLBD 6; MTCW

Hammon, Jupiter
1711(?)-1800(?) . . . . NCLC 5; BLC
See also DAM MULT, POET; DLB 31, 50

Hammond, Keith
See Kuttner, Henry

Hamner, Earl (Henry), Jr.   1923- . . . CLC 12
See also AITN 2; CA 73-76; DLB 6

Hampton, Christopher (James)
1946- . . . . CLC 4
See also CA 25-28R; DLB 13; MTCW

Hamsun, Knut . . . . TCLC 2, 14, 49
See also Pedersen, Knut

Handke, Peter   1942- . . CLC 5, 8, 10, 15, 38
See also CA 77-80; CANR 33;
DAM DRAM, NOV; DLB 85, 124;
MTCW

Hanley, James   1901-1985 . . . CLC 3, 5, 8, 13
See also CA 73-76; 117; CANR 36; MTCW

Hannah, Barry   1942- . . . . CLC 23, 38, 90
See also CA 108; 110; CANR 43; DLB 6;
INT 110; MTCW

Hannon, Ezra
See Hunter, Evan

Hansberry, Lorraine (Vivian)
1930-1965 . . . . . . CLC 17, 62; BLC; DA;
DAB; DAC; DC 2
See also BW 1; CA 109; 25-28R; CABS 3;
CDALB 1941-1968; DAM DRAM, MST,
MULT; DLB 7, 38; MTCW

Hansen, Joseph   1923- . . . . CLC 38
See also CA 29-32R; CAAS 17; CANR 16,
44; INT CANR-16

Hansen, Martin A.   1909-1955 . . . . . TCLC 32

Hanson, Kenneth O(stlin)   1922- . . . . CLC 13
See also CA 53-56; CANR 7

Hardwick, Elizabeth   1916- . . . . CLC 13
See also CA 5-8R; CANR 3, 32;
DAM NOV; DLB 6; MTCW

Hardy, Thomas
1840-1928 . . . . . . TCLC 4, 10, 18, 32, 48,
53; DA; DAB; DAC; PC 8; SSC 2; WLC
See also CA 104; 123; CDBLB 1890-1914;
DAM MST, NOV, POET; DLB 18, 19,
135; MTCW

Hare, David   1947- . . . . CLC 29, 58
See also CA 97-100; CANR 39; DLB 13;
MTCW

Harford, Henry
See Hudson, W(illiam) H(enry)

Hargrave, Leonie
See Disch, Thomas M(ichael)

Harjo, Joy   1951- . . . . CLC 83
See also CA 114; CANR 35; DAM MULT;
DLB 120; NNAL

Harlan, Louis R(udolph)   1922- . . . . . CLC 34
See also CA 21-24R; CANR 25

Harling, Robert   1951(?)- . . . . CLC 53
See also CA 147

Harmon, William (Ruth)   1938- . . . . . CLC 38
See also CA 33-36R; CANR 14, 32, 35;
SATA 65

Harper, F. E. W.
See Harper, Frances Ellen Watkins

Harper, Frances E. W.
See Harper, Frances Ellen Watkins

Harper, Frances E. Watkins
See Harper, Frances Ellen Watkins

Harper, Frances Ellen
See Harper, Frances Ellen Watkins

Harper, Frances Ellen Watkins
1825-1911 . . . . TCLC 14; BLC
See also BW 1; CA 111; 125; DAM MULT,
POET; DLB 50

Harper, Michael S(teven)   1938- . . CLC 7, 22
See also BW 1; CA 33-36R; CANR 24;
DLB 41

Harper, Mrs. F. E. W.
See Harper, Frances Ellen Watkins

Harris, Christie (Lucy) Irwin
1907- . . . . CLC 12
See also CA 5-8R; CANR 6; DLB 88;
JRDA; MAICYA; SAAS 10; SATA 6, 74

Harris, Frank   1856-1931 . . . . TCLC 24
See also CA 109; 150; DLB 156

Harris, George Washington
1814-1869 . . . . NCLC 23
See also DLB 3, 11

Harris, Joel Chandler
1848-1908 . . . . TCLC 2; SSC 19
See also CA 104; 137; DLB 11, 23, 42, 78,
91; MAICYA; YABC 1

Harris, John (Wyndham Parkes Lucas)
Beynon   1903-1969
See Wyndham, John
See also CA 102; 89-92

Harris, MacDonald . . . . CLC 9
See also Heiney, Donald (William)

Harris, Mark   1922- . . . . CLC 19
See also CA 5-8R; CAAS 3; CANR 2;
DLB 2; DLBY 80

Harris, (Theodore) Wilson   1921- . . . . CLC 25
See also BW 2; CA 65-68; CAAS 16;
CANR 11, 27; DLB 117; MTCW

Harrison, Elizabeth Cavanna   1909-
See Cavanna, Betty
See also CA 9-12R; CANR 6, 27

Harrison, Harry (Max)   1925- . . . . . . CLC 42
See also CA 1-4R; CANR 5, 21; DLB 8;
SATA 4

Harrison, James (Thomas)
1937- . . . . CLC 6, 14, 33, 66; SSC 19
See also CA 13-16R; CANR 8, 51;
DLBY 82; INT CANR-8

Harrison, Jim
See Harrison, James (Thomas)

Harrison, Kathryn   1961- . . . . CLC 70
See also CA 144

Harrison, Tony   1937- . . . . CLC 43
See also CA 65-68; CANR 44; DLB 40;
MTCW

Harriss, Will(ard Irvin)   1922- . . . . . . CLC 34
See also CA 111

Harson, Sley
See Ellison, Harlan (Jay)

Hart, Ellis
See Ellison, Harlan (Jay)

Hart, Josephine   1942(?)- . . . . CLC 70
See also CA 138; DAM POP

Hart, Moss   1904-1961 . . . . CLC 66
See also CA 109; 89-92; DAM DRAM;
DLB 7

Harte, (Francis) Bret(t)
1836(?)-1902 . . . . TCLC 1, 25; DA; DAC;
SSC 8; WLC
See also CA 104; 140; CDALB 1865-1917;
DAM MST; DLB 12, 64, 74, 79;
SATA 26

Hartley, L(eslie) P(oles)
1895-1972 . . . . CLC 2, 22
See also CA 45-48; 37-40R; CANR 33;
DLB 15, 139; MTCW

Hartman, Geoffrey H.   1929- . . . . CLC 27
See also CA 117; 125; DLB 67

Hartmann von Aue
c. 1160-c. 1205 . . . . CMLC 15
See also DLB 138

Hartmann von Aue   1170-1210 . . . . CMLC 15

Haruf, Kent   1943- . . . . CLC 34
See also CA 149

Harwood, Ronald   1934- . . . . CLC 32
See also CA 1-4R; CANR 4; DAM DRAM,
MST; DLB 13

Hasek, Jaroslav (Matej Frantisek)
1883-1923 . . . . TCLC 4
See also CA 104; 129; MTCW

Hass, Robert   1941- . . . . CLC 18, 39
See also CA 111; CANR 30, 50; DLB 105

Hastings, Hudson
See Kuttner, Henry

Hastings, Selina . . . . CLC 44

Heppenstall, (John) Rayner
1911-1981 .... CLC **10**
See also CA 1-4R; 103; CANR 29

Herbert, Frank (Patrick)
1920-1986 ...... CLC **12, 23, 35, 44, 85**
See also CA 53-56; 118; CANR 5, 43;
DAM POP; DLB 8; INT CANR-5;
MTCW; SATA 9, 37; SATA-Obit 47

Herbert, George
1593-1633 .... LC **24**; DAB; PC **4**
See also CDBLB Before 1660; DAM POET;
DLB 126

Herbert, Zbigniew 1924- .... CLC **9, 43**
See also CA 89-92; CANR 36;
DAM POET; MTCW

Herbst, Josephine (Frey)
1897-1969 .... CLC **34**
See also CA 5-8R; 25-28R; DLB 9

Hergesheimer, Joseph
1880-1954 .... TCLC **11**
See also CA 109; DLB 102, 9

Herlihy, James Leo 1927-1993 ...... CLC **6**
See also CA 1-4R; 143; CANR 2

Hermogenes fl. c. 175- .... CMLC **6**

Hernandez, Jose 1834-1886 ...... NCLC **17**

Herodotus c. 484B.C.-429B.C.... CMLC **17**

Herrick, Robert
1591-1674 ..... LC **13**; DA; DAB; DAC;
PC **9**
See also DAM MST, POP; DLB 126

Herring, Guilles
See Somerville, Edith

Herriot, James 1916-1995 .... CLC **12**
See also Wight, James Alfred
See also AAYA 1; CA 148; CANR 40;
DAM POP; SATA 86

Herrmann, Dorothy 1941- .... CLC **44**
See also CA 107

Herrmann, Taffy
See Herrmann, Dorothy

Hersey, John (Richard)
1914-1993 .... CLC **1, 2, 7, 9, 40, 81**
See also CA 17-20R; 140; CANR 33;
DAM POP; DLB 6; MTCW; SATA 25;
SATA-Obit 76

Herzen, Aleksandr Ivanovich
1812-1870 .... NCLC **10**

Herzl, Theodor 1860-1904 .... TCLC **36**

Herzog, Werner 1942- .... CLC **16**
See also CA 89-92

Hesiod c. 8th cent. B.C.- .... CMLC **5**

Hesse, Hermann
1877-1962 .... CLC **1, 2, 3, 6, 11, 17, 25,**
69; DA; DAB; DAC; SSC **9**; WLC
See also CA 17-18; CAP 2; DAM MST,
NOV; DLB 66; MTCW; SATA 50

Hewes, Cady
See De Voto, Bernard (Augustine)

Heyen, William 1940- .... CLC **13, 18**
See also CA 33-36R; CAAS 9; DLB 5

Heyerdahl, Thor 1914- .... CLC **26**
See also CA 5-8R; CANR 5, 22; MTCW;
SATA 2, 52

Heym, Georg (Theodor Franz Arthur)
1887-1912 .... TCLC **9**
See also CA 106

Heym, Stefan 1913- .... CLC **41**
See also CA 9-12R; CANR 4; DLB 69

Heyse, Paul (Johann Ludwig von)
1830-1914 .... TCLC **8**
See also CA 104; DLB 129

Heyward, (Edwin) DuBose
1885-1940 .... TCLC **59**
See also CA 108; DLB 7, 9, 45; SATA 21

Hibbert, Eleanor Alice Burford
1906-1993 .... CLC **7**
See also BEST 90:4; CA 17-20R; 140;
CANR 9, 28; DAM POP; SATA 2;
SATA-Obit 74

Higgins, George V(incent)
1939- ....CLC **4, 7, 10, 18**
See also CA 77-80; CAAS 5; CANR 17, 51;
DLB 2; DLBY 81; INT CANR-17;
MTCW

Higginson, Thomas Wentworth
1823-1911 .... TCLC **36**
See also DLB 1, 64

Highet, Helen
See MacInnes, Helen (Clark)

Highsmith, (Mary) Patricia
1921-1995 .... CLC **2, 4, 14, 42**
See also CA 1-4R; 147; CANR 1, 20, 48;
DAM NOV, POP; MTCW

Highwater, Jamake (Mamake)
1942(?)- .... CLC **12**
See also AAYA 7; CA 65-68; CAAS 7;
CANR 10, 34; CLR 17; DLB 52;
DLBY 85; JRDA; MAICYA; SATA 32,
69; SATA-Brief 30

Highway, Tomson 1951- ...... CLC **92**; DAC
See also DAM MULT; NNAL

Higuchi, Ichiyo 1872-1896 .... NCLC **49**

Hijuelos, Oscar 1951- ...... CLC **65**; HLC
See also BEST 90:1; CA 123; CANR 50;
DAM MULT, POP; DLB 145; HW

Hikmet, Nazim 1902(?)-1963 .... CLC **40**
See also CA 141; 93-96

Hildesheimer, Wolfgang
1916-1991 .... CLC **49**
See also CA 101; 135; DLB 69, 124

Hill, Geoffrey (William)
1932- .... CLC **5, 8, 18, 45**
See also CA 81-84; CANR 21;
CDBLB 1960 to Present; DAM POET;
DLB 40; MTCW

Hill, George Roy 1921- .... CLC **26**
See also CA 110; 122

Hill, John
See Koontz, Dean R(ay)

Hill, Susan (Elizabeth)
1942- .... CLC **4**; DAB
See also CA 33-36R; CANR 29;
DAM MST, NOV; DLB 14, 139; MTCW

Hillerman, Tony 1925- .... CLC **62**
See also AAYA 6; BEST 89:1; CA 29-32R;
CANR 21, 42; DAM POP; SATA 6

Hillesum, Etty 1914-1943 .... TCLC **49**
See also CA 137

Hilliard, Noel (Harvey) 1929- ...... CLC **15**
See also CA 9-12R; CANR 7

Hillis, Rick 1956- .... CLC **66**
See also CA 134

Hilton, James 1900-1954 .... TCLC **21**
See also CA 108; DLB 34, 77; SATA 34

Himes, Chester (Bomar)
1909-1984 .... CLC **2, 4, 7, 18, 58**; BLC
See also BW 2; CA 25-28R; 114; CANR 22;
DAM MULT; DLB 2, 76, 143; MTCW

Hinde, Thomas .... CLC **6, 11**
See also Chitty, Thomas Willes

Hindin, Nathan
See Bloch, Robert (Albert)

Hine, (William) Daryl 1936- .... CLC **15**
See also CA 1-4R; CAAS 15; CANR 1, 20;
DLB 60

Hinkson, Katharine Tynan
See Tynan, Katharine

Hinton, S(usan) E(loise)
1950- .... CLC **30**; DA; DAB; DAC
See also AAYA 2; CA 81-84; CANR 32;
CLR 3, 23; DAM MST, NOV; JRDA;
MAICYA; MTCW; SATA 19, 58

Hippius, Zinaida .... TCLC **9**
See also Gippius, Zinaida (Nikolayevna)

Hiraoka, Kimitake 1925-1970
See Mishima, Yukio
See also CA 97-100; 29-32R; DAM DRAM;
MTCW

Hirsch, E(ric) D(onald), Jr. 1928-... CLC **79**
See also CA 25-28R; CANR 27, 51;
DLB 67; INT CANR-27; MTCW

Hirsch, Edward 1950- .... CLC **31, 50**
See also CA 104; CANR 20, 42; DLB 120

Hitchcock, Alfred (Joseph)
1899-1980 .... CLC **16**
See also CA 97-100; SATA 27;
SATA-Obit 24

Hitler, Adolf 1889-1945 .... TCLC **53**
See also CA 117; 147

Hoagland, Edward 1932- .... CLC **28**
See also CA 1-4R; CANR 2, 31; DLB 6;
SATA 51

Hoban, Russell (Conwell) 1925- .. CLC **7, 25**
See also CA 5-8R; CANR 23, 37; CLR 3;
DAM NOV; DLB 52; MAICYA;
MTCW; SATA 1, 40, 78

Hobbs, Perry
See Blackmur, R(ichard) P(almer)

Hobson, Laura Z(ametkin)
1900-1986 .... CLC **7, 25**
See also CA 17-20R; 118; DLB 28;
SATA 52

Hochhuth, Rolf 1931- .... CLC **4, 11, 18**
See also CA 5-8R; CANR 33;
DAM DRAM; DLB 124; MTCW

Hochman, Sandra 1936- .... CLC **3, 8**
See also CA 5-8R; DLB 5

Hochwaelder, Fritz 1911-1986 ...... CLC **36**
See also CA 29-32R; 120; CANR 42;
DAM DRAM; MTCW

Hochwalder, Fritz
See Hochwaelder, Fritz

Howell, James 1594(?)-1666 . . . . **LC 13**
　See also DLB 151

Howells, W. D.
　See Howells, William Dean

Howells, William D.
　See Howells, William Dean

Howells, William Dean
　1837-1920 . . . . **TCLC 7, 17, 41**
　See also CA 104; 134; CDALB 1865-1917;
　　DLB 12, 64, 74, 79

Howes, Barbara 1914- . . . . **CLC 15**
　See also CA 9-12R; CAAS 3; SATA 5

Hrabal, Bohumil 1914- . . . . **CLC 13, 67**
　See also CA 106; CAAS 12

Hsun, Lu
　See Lu Hsun

Hubbard, L(afayette) Ron(ald)
　1911-1986 . . . . **CLC 43**
　See also CA 77-80; 118; CANR 22;
　　DAM POP

Huch, Ricarda (Octavia)
　1864-1947 . . . . **TCLC 13**
　See also CA 111; DLB 66

Huddle, David 1942- . . . . **CLC 49**
　See also CA 57-60; CAAS 20; DLB 130

Hudson, Jeffrey
　See Crichton, (John) Michael

Hudson, W(illiam) H(enry)
　1841-1922 . . . . **TCLC 29**
　See also CA 115; DLB 98, 153; SATA 35

Hueffer, Ford Madox
　See Ford, Ford Madox

Hughart, Barry 1934- . . . . **CLC 39**
　See also CA 137

Hughes, Colin
　See Creasey, John

Hughes, David (John) 1930- . . . . **CLC 48**
　See also CA 116; 129; DLB 14

Hughes, Edward James
　See Hughes, Ted
　See also DAM MST, POET

Hughes, (James) Langston
　1902-1967 . . . . . **CLC 1, 5, 10, 15, 35, 44;**
　　BLC; DA; DAB; DAC; DC 3; PC 1;
　　SSC 6; WLC
　See also AAYA 12; BW 1; CA 1-4R;
　　25-28R; CANR 1, 34; CDALB 1929-1941;
　　CLR 17; DAM DRAM, MST, MULT,
　　POET; DLB 4, 7, 48, 51, 86; JRDA;
　　MAICYA; MTCW; SATA 4, 33

Hughes, Richard (Arthur Warren)
　1900-1976 . . . . **CLC 1, 11**
　See also CA 5-8R; 65-68; CANR 4;
　　DAM NOV; DLB 15, 161; MTCW;
　　SATA 8; SATA-Obit 25

Hughes, Ted
　1930- . . . . **CLC 2, 4, 9, 14, 37; DAB;**
　　DAC; PC 7
　See also Hughes, Edward James
　See also CA 1-4R; CANR 1, 33; CLR 3;
　　DLB 40, 161; MAICYA; MTCW;
　　SATA 49; SATA-Brief 27

Hugo, Richard F(ranklin)
　1923-1982 . . . . **CLC 6, 18, 32**
　See also CA 49-52; 108; CANR 3;
　　DAM POET; DLB 5

Hugo, Victor (Marie)
　1802-1885 . . . . **NCLC 3, 10, 21; DA;**
　　DAB; DAC; WLC
　See also DAM DRAM, MST, NOV, POET;
　　DLB 119; SATA 47

Huidobro, Vicente
　See Huidobro Fernandez, Vicente Garcia

Huidobro Fernandez, Vicente Garcia
　1893-1948 . . . . **TCLC 31**
　See also CA 131; HW

Hulme, Keri 1947- . . . . **CLC 39**
　See also CA 125; INT 125

Hulme, T(homas) E(rnest)
　1883-1917 . . . . **TCLC 21**
　See also CA 117; DLB 19

Hume, David 1711-1776 . . . . **LC 7**
　See also DLB 104

Humphrey, William 1924- . . . . **CLC 45**
　See also CA 77-80; DLB 6

Humphreys, Emyr Owen 1919- . . . . . **CLC 47**
　See also CA 5-8R; CANR 3, 24; DLB 15

Humphreys, Josephine 1945- . . . . **CLC 34, 57**
　See also CA 121; 127; INT 127

Hungerford, Pixie
　See Brinsmead, H(esba) F(ay)

Hunt, E(verette) Howard, (Jr.)
　1918- . . . . **CLC 3**
　See also AITN 1; CA 45-48; CANR 2, 47

Hunt, Kyle
　See Creasey, John

Hunt, (James Henry) Leigh
　1784-1859 . . . . **NCLC 1**
　See also DAM POET

Hunt, Marsha 1946- . . . . **CLC 70**
　See also BW 2; CA 143

Hunt, Violet 1866-1942 . . . . **TCLC 53**
　See also DLB 162

Hunter, E. Waldo
　See Sturgeon, Theodore (Hamilton)

Hunter, Evan 1926- . . . . **CLC 11, 31**
　See also CA 5-8R; CANR 5, 38;
　　DAM POP; DLBY 82; INT CANR-5;
　　MTCW; SATA 25

Hunter, Kristin (Eggleston) 1931- . . . **CLC 35**
　See also AITN 1; BW 1; CA 13-16R;
　　CANR 13; CLR 3; DLB 33;
　　INT CANR-13; MAICYA; SAAS 10;
　　SATA 12

Hunter, Mollie 1922- . . . . **CLC 21**
　See also McIlwraith, Maureen Mollie
　　Hunter
　See also AAYA 13; CANR 37; CLR 25;
　　DLB 161; JRDA; MAICYA; SAAS 7;
　　SATA 54

Hunter, Robert (?)-1734 . . . . **LC 7**

Hurston, Zora Neale
　1903-1960 . . . . **CLC 7, 30, 61; BLC; DA;**
　　DAC; SSC 4
　See also AAYA 15; BW 1; CA 85-88;
　　DAM MST, MULT, NOV; DLB 51, 86;
　　MTCW

Huston, John (Marcellus)
　1906-1987 . . . . **CLC 20**
　See also CA 73-76; 123; CANR 34; DLB 26

Hustvedt, Siri 1955- . . . . **CLC 76**
　See also CA 137

Hutten, Ulrich von 1488-1523 . . . . **LC 16**

Huxley, Aldous (Leonard)
　1894-1963 . . . . . **CLC 1, 3, 4, 5, 8, 11, 18,**
　　35, 79; DA; DAB; DAC; WLC
　See also AAYA 11; CA 85-88; CANR 44;
　　CDBLB 1914-1945; DAM MST, NOV;
　　DLB 36, 100, 162; MTCW; SATA 63

Huysmans, Charles Marie Georges
　1848-1907
　See Huysmans, Joris-Karl
　See also CA 104

Huysmans, Joris-Karl . . . . **TCLC 7**
　See also Huysmans, Charles Marie Georges
　See also DLB 123

Hwang, David Henry
　1957- . . . . **CLC 55; DC 4**
　See also CA 127; 132; DAM DRAM;
　　INT 132

Hyde, Anthony 1946- . . . . **CLC 42**
　See also CA 136

Hyde, Margaret O(ldroyd) 1917- . . . **CLC 21**
　See also CA 1-4R; CANR 1, 36; CLR 23;
　　JRDA; MAICYA; SAAS 8; SATA 1, 42,
　　76

Hynes, James 1956(?)- . . . . **CLC 65**

Ian, Janis 1951- . . . . **CLC 21**
　See also CA 105

Ibanez, Vicente Blasco
　See Blasco Ibanez, Vicente

Ibarguengoitia, Jorge 1928-1983 . . . . **CLC 37**
　See also CA 124; 113; HW

Ibsen, Henrik (Johan)
　1828-1906 . . . . **TCLC 2, 8, 16, 37, 52;**
　　DA; DAB; DAC; DC 2; WLC
　See also CA 104; 141; DAM DRAM, MST

Ibuse Masuji 1898-1993 . . . . **CLC 22**
　See also CA 127; 141

Ichikawa, Kon 1915- . . . . **CLC 20**
　See also CA 121

Idle, Eric 1943- . . . . **CLC 21**
　See also Monty Python
　See also CA 116; CANR 35

Ignatow, David 1914- . . . . . . **CLC 4, 7, 14, 40**
　See also CA 9-12R; CAAS 3; CANR 31;
　　DLB 5

Ihimaera, Witi 1944- . . . . **CLC 46**
　See also CA 77-80

Ilf, Ilya . . . . **TCLC 21**
　See also Fainzilberg, Ilya Arnoldovich

Immermann, Karl (Lebrecht)
　1796-1840 . . . . **NCLC 4, 49**
　See also DLB 133

Inclan, Ramon (Maria) del Valle
　See Valle-Inclan, Ramon (Maria) del

Infante, G(uillermo) Cabrera
　See Cabrera Infante, G(uillermo)

Ingalls, Rachel (Holmes) 1940- . . . . . **CLC 42**
　See also CA 123; 127

Ingamells, Rex 1913-1955 . . . . **TCLC 35**

Inge, William Motter
1913-1973 .... **CLC 1, 8, 19**
See also CA 9-12R; CDALB 1941-1968;
DAM DRAM; DLB 7; MTCW

Ingelow, Jean 1820-1897 .... **NCLC 39**
See also DLB 35, 163; SATA 33

Ingram, Willis J.
See Harris, Mark

Innaurato, Albert (F.) 1948(?)- .. **CLC 21, 60**
See also CA 115; 122; INT 122

Innes, Michael
See Stewart, J(ohn) I(nnes) M(ackintosh)

Ionesco, Eugene
1909-1994 .... **CLC 1, 4, 6, 9, 11, 15, 41,
86; DA; DAB; DAC; WLC**
See also CA 9-12R; 144; DAM DRAM,
MST; MTCW; SATA 7; SATA-Obit 79

Iqbal, Muhammad 1873-1938 ..... **TCLC 28**

Ireland, Patrick
See O'Doherty, Brian

Iron, Ralph
See Schreiner, Olive (Emilie Albertina)

Irving, John (Winslow)
1942- .... **CLC 13, 23, 38**
See also AAYA 8; BEST 89:3; CA 25-28R;
CANR 28; DAM NOV, POP; DLB 6;
DLBY 82; MTCW

Irving, Washington
1783-1859 ..... **NCLC 2, 19; DA; DAB;
SSC 2; WLC**
See also CDALB 1640-1865; DAM MST;
DLB 3, 11, 30, 59, 73, 74; YABC 2

Irwin, P. K.
See Page, P(atricia) K(athleen)

Isaacs, Susan 1943- .... **CLC 32**
See also BEST 89:1; CA 89-92; CANR 20,
41; DAM POP; INT CANR-20; MTCW

Isherwood, Christopher (William Bradshaw)
1904-1986 .... **CLC 1, 9, 11, 14, 44**
See also CA 13-16R; 117; CANR 35;
DAM DRAM, NOV; DLB 15; DLBY 86;
MTCW

Ishiguro, Kazuo 1954- ...... **CLC 27, 56, 59**
See also BEST 90:2; CA 120; CANR 49;
DAM NOV; MTCW

Ishikawa Takuboku
1886(?)-1912 .... **TCLC 15; PC 10**
See also CA 113; DAM POET

Iskander, Fazil 1929- .... **CLC 47**
See also CA 102

Isler, Alan .... **CLC 91**

Ivan IV 1530-1584 .... **LC 17**

Ivanov, Vyacheslav Ivanovich
1866-1949 .... **TCLC 33**
See also CA 122

Ivask, Ivar Vidrik 1927-1992....... **CLC 14**
See also CA 37-40R; 139; CANR 24

J. R. S.
See Gogarty, Oliver St. John

Jabran, Kahlil
See Gibran, Kahlil

Jabran, Khalil
See Gibran, Kahlil

Jackson, Daniel
See Wingrove, David (John)

Jackson, Jesse 1908-1983 .... **CLC 12**
See also BW 1; CA 25-28R; 109; CANR 27;
CLR 28; MAICYA; SATA 2, 29;
SATA-Obit 48

Jackson, Laura (Riding) 1901-1991
See Riding, Laura
See also CA 65-68; 135; CANR 28; DLB 48

Jackson, Sam
See Trumbo, Dalton

Jackson, Sara
See Wingrove, David (John)

Jackson, Shirley
1919-1965 .... **CLC 11, 60, 87; DA;
DAC; SSC 9; WLC**
See also AAYA 9; CA 1-4R; 25-28R;
CANR 4; CDALB 1941-1968;
DAM MST; DLB 6; SATA 2

Jacob, (Cyprien-)Max 1876-1944 ... **TCLC 6**
See also CA 104

Jacobs, Jim 1942- .... **CLC 12**
See also CA 97-100; INT 97-100

Jacobs, W(illiam) W(ymark)
1863-1943 .... **TCLC 22**
See also CA 121; DLB 135

Jacobsen, Jens Peter 1847-1885 .. **NCLC 34**

Jacobsen, Josephine 1908- .... **CLC 48**
See also CA 33-36R; CAAS 18; CANR 23,
48

Jacobson, Dan 1929- .... **CLC 4, 14**
See also CA 1-4R; CANR 2, 25; DLB 14;
MTCW

Jacqueline
See Carpentier (y Valmont), Alejo

Jagger, Mick 1944-............... **CLC 17**

Jakes, John (William) 1932- .... **CLC 29**
See also BEST 89:4; CA 57-60; CANR 10,
43; DAM NOV, POP; DLBY 83;
INT CANR-10; MTCW; SATA 62

James, Andrew
See Kirkup, James

James, C(yril) L(ionel) R(obert)
1901-1989 .... **CLC 33**
See also BW 2; CA 117; 125; 128; DLB 125;
MTCW

James, Daniel (Lewis) 1911-1988
See Santiago, Danny
See also CA 125

James, Dynely
See Mayne, William (James Carter)

James, Henry Sr. 1811-1882 ..... **NCLC 53**

James, Henry
1843-1916 ...... **TCLC 2, 11, 24, 40, 47;
DA; DAB; DAC; SSC 8; WLC**
See also CA 104; 132; CDALB 1865-1917;
DAM MST, NOV; DLB 12, 71, 74;
DLBD 13; MTCW

James, M. R.
See James, Montague (Rhodes)
See also DLB 156

James, Montague (Rhodes)
1862-1936 .... **TCLC 6; SSC 16**
See also CA 104

James, P. D. .... **CLC 18, 46**
See also White, Phyllis Dorothy James
See also BEST 90:2; CDBLB 1960 to
Present; DLB 87

James, Philip
See Moorcock, Michael (John)

James, William 1842-1910..... **TCLC 15, 32**
See also CA 109

James I 1394-1437 .... **LC 20**

Jameson, Anna 1794-1860...... **NCLC 43**
See also DLB 99

Jami, Nur al-Din 'Abd al-Rahman
1414-1492 .... **LC 9**

Jandl, Ernst 1925- .... **CLC 34**

Janowitz, Tama 1957- .... **CLC 43**
See also CA 106; DAM POP

Japrisot, Sebastien 1931-.......... **CLC 90**

Jarrell, Randall
1914-1965 .... **CLC 1, 2, 6, 9, 13, 49**
See also CA 5-8R; 25-28R; CABS 2;
CANR 6, 34; CDALB 1941-1968; CLR 6;
DAM POET; DLB 48, 52; MAICYA;
MTCW; SATA 7

Jarry, Alfred
1873-1907 .... **TCLC 2, 14; SSC 20**
See also CA 104; DAM DRAM

Jarvis, E. K.
See Bloch, Robert (Albert); Ellison, Harlan
(Jay); Silverberg, Robert

Jeake, Samuel, Jr.
See Aiken, Conrad (Potter)

Jean Paul 1763-1825 .... **NCLC 7**

Jefferies, (John) Richard
1848-1887 .... **NCLC 47**
See also DLB 98, 141; SATA 16

Jeffers, (John) Robinson
1887-1962 .... **CLC 2, 3, 11, 15, 54; DA;
DAC; WLC**
See also CA 85-88; CANR 35;
CDALB 1917-1929; DAM MST, POET;
DLB 45; MTCW

Jefferson, Janet
See Mencken, H(enry) L(ouis)

Jefferson, Thomas 1743-1826 .... **NCLC 11**
See also CDALB 1640-1865; DLB 31

Jeffrey, Francis 1773-1850....... **NCLC 33**
See also DLB 107

Jelakowitch, Ivan
See Heijermans, Herman

Jellicoe, (Patricia) Ann 1927- ...... **CLC 27**
See also CA 85-88; DLB 13

Jen, Gish .... **CLC 70**
See also Jen, Lillian

Jen, Lillian 1956(?)-
See Jen, Gish
See also CA 135

Jenkins, (John) Robin 1912- .... **CLC 52**
See also CA 1-4R; CANR 1; DLB 14

Jennings, Elizabeth (Joan)
1926- .... **CLC 5, 14**
See also CA 61-64; CAAS 5; CANR 8, 39;
DLB 27; MTCW; SATA 66

Jennings, Waylon 1937-........... **CLC 21**

Jensen, Johannes V. 1873-1950.... **TCLC 41**

Jensen, Laura (Linnea) 1948- ...... **CLC 37**
See also CA 103

Jerome, Jerome K(lapka)
1859-1927 .... **TCLC 23**
See also CA 119; DLB 10, 34, 135

Jerrold, Douglas William
1803-1857 .... **NCLC 2**
See also DLB 158, 159

Jewett, (Theodora) Sarah Orne
1849-1909 .... **TCLC 1, 22; SSC 6**
See also CA 108; 127; DLB 12, 74;
SATA 15

Jewsbury, Geraldine (Endsor)
1812-1880 .... **NCLC 22**
See also DLB 21

Jhabvala, Ruth Prawer
1927- .... **CLC 4, 8, 29; DAB**
See also CA 1-4R; CANR 2, 29, 51;
DAM NOV; DLB 139; INT CANR-29;
MTCW

Jibran, Kahlil
See Gibran, Kahlil

Jibran, Khalil
See Gibran, Kahlil

Jiles, Paulette 1943- .... **CLC 13, 58**
See also CA 101

Jimenez (Mantecon), Juan Ramon
1881-1958 .... **TCLC 4; HLC; PC 7**
See also CA 104; 131; DAM MULT,
POET; DLB 134; HW; MTCW

Jimenez, Ramon
See Jimenez (Mantecon), Juan Ramon

Jimenez Mantecon, Juan
See Jimenez (Mantecon), Juan Ramon

Joel, Billy .... **CLC 26**
See also Joel, William Martin

Joel, William Martin 1949-
See Joel, Billy
See also CA 108

John of the Cross, St. 1542-1591 .... **LC 18**

Johnson, B(ryan) S(tanley William)
1933-1973 .... **CLC 6, 9**
See also CA 9-12R; 53-56; CANR 9;
DLB 14, 40

Johnson, Benj. F. of Boo
See Riley, James Whitcomb

Johnson, Benjamin F. of Boo
See Riley, James Whitcomb

Johnson, Charles (Richard)
1948- .... **CLC 7, 51, 65; BLC**
See also BW 2; CA 116; CAAS 18;
CANR 42; DAM MULT; DLB 33

Johnson, Denis 1949- .... **CLC 52**
See also CA 117; 121; DLB 120

Johnson, Diane 1934- .... **CLC 5, 13, 48**
See also CA 41-44R; CANR 17, 40;
DLBY 80; INT CANR-17; MTCW

Johnson, Eyvind (Olof Verner)
1900-1976 .... **CLC 14**
See also CA 73-76; 69-72; CANR 34

Johnson, J. R.
See James, C(yril) L(ionel) R(obert)

Johnson, James Weldon
1871-1938 .... **TCLC 3, 19; BLC**
See also BW 1; CA 104; 125;
CDALB 1917-1929; CLR 32;
DAM MULT, POET; DLB 51; MTCW;
SATA 31

Johnson, Joyce 1935- .... **CLC 58**
See also CA 125; 129

Johnson, Lionel (Pigot)
1867-1902 .... **TCLC 19**
See also CA 117; DLB 19

Johnson, Mel
See Malzberg, Barry N(athaniel)

Johnson, Pamela Hansford
1912-1981 .... **CLC 1, 7, 27**
See also CA 1-4R; 104; CANR 2, 28;
DLB 15; MTCW

Johnson, Samuel
1709-1784 ..... **LC 15; DA; DAB; DAC;
WLC**
See also CDBLB 1660-1789; DAM MST;
DLB 39, 95, 104, 142

Johnson, Uwe
1934-1984 .... **CLC 5, 10, 15, 40**
See also CA 1-4R; 112; CANR 1, 39;
DLB 75; MTCW

Johnston, George (Benson) 1913- ... **CLC 51**
See also CA 1-4R; CANR 5, 20; DLB 88

Johnston, Jennifer 1930- .... **CLC 7**
See also CA 85-88; DLB 14

Jolley, (Monica) Elizabeth
1923- .... **CLC 46; SSC 19**
See also CA 127; CAAS 13

Jones, Arthur Llewellyn 1863-1947
See Machen, Arthur
See also CA 104

Jones, D(ouglas) G(ordon) 1929- .... **CLC 10**
See also CA 29-32R; CANR 13; DLB 53

Jones, David (Michael)
1895-1974 .... **CLC 2, 4, 7, 13, 42**
See also CA 9-12R; 53-56; CANR 28;
CDBLB 1945-1960; DLB 20, 100; MTCW

Jones, David Robert 1947-
See Bowie, David
See also CA 103

Jones, Diana Wynne 1934- .... **CLC 26**
See also AAYA 12; CA 49-52; CANR 4,
26; CLR 23; DLB 161; JRDA; MAICYA;
SAAS 7; SATA 9, 70

Jones, Edward P. 1950- .... **CLC 76**
See also BW 2; CA 142

Jones, Gayl 1949- .... **CLC 6, 9; BLC**
See also BW 2; CA 77-80; CANR 27;
DAM MULT; DLB 33; MTCW

Jones, James 1921-1977 .... **CLC 1, 3, 10, 39**
See also AITN 1, 2; CA 1-4R; 69-72;
CANR 6; DLB 2, 143; MTCW

Jones, John J.
See Lovecraft, H(oward) P(hillips)

Jones, LeRoi .... **CLC 1, 2, 3, 5, 10, 14**
See also Baraka, Amiri

Jones, Louis B. .... **CLC 65**
See also CA 141

Jones, Madison (Percy, Jr.) 1925- ... **CLC 4**
See also CA 13-16R; CAAS 11; CANR 7;
DLB 152

Jones, Mervyn 1922- .... **CLC 10, 52**
See also CA 45-48; CAAS 5; CANR 1;
MTCW

Jones, Mick 1956(?)- .... **CLC 30**

Jones, Nettie (Pearl) 1941- .... **CLC 34**
See also BW 2; CA 137; CAAS 20

Jones, Preston 1936-1979 .... **CLC 10**
See also CA 73-76; 89-92; DLB 7

Jones, Robert F(rancis) 1934- .... **CLC 7**
See also CA 49-52; CANR 2

Jones, Rod 1953- .... **CLC 50**
See also CA 128

Jones, Terence Graham Parry
1942- .... **CLC 21**
See also Jones, Terry; Monty Python
See also CA 112; 116; CANR 35; INT 116

Jones, Terry
See Jones, Terence Graham Parry
See also SATA 67; SATA-Brief 51

Jones, Thom 1945(?)- .... **CLC 81**

Jong, Erica 1942- ...... **CLC 4, 6, 8, 18, 83**
See also AITN 1; BEST 90:2; CA 73-76;
CANR 26; DAM NOV, POP; DLB 2, 5,
28, 152; INT CANR-26; MTCW

Jonson, Ben(jamin)
1572(?)-1637 .... **LC 6; DA; DAB; DAC;
DC 4; WLC**
See also CDBLB Before 1660;
DAM DRAM, MST, POET; DLB 62,
121

Jordan, June 1936- .... **CLC 5, 11, 23**
See also AAYA 2; BW 2; CA 33-36R;
CANR 25; CLR 10; DAM MULT,
POET; DLB 38; MAICYA; MTCW;
SATA 4

Jordan, Pat(rick M.) 1941- .... **CLC 37**
See also CA 33-36R

Jorgensen, Ivar
See Ellison, Harlan (Jay)

Jorgenson, Ivar
See Silverberg, Robert

Josephus, Flavius c. 37-100 ...... **CMLC 13**

Josipovici, Gabriel 1940- .... **CLC 6, 43**
See also CA 37-40R; CAAS 8; CANR 47;
DLB 14

Joubert, Joseph 1754-1824 .... **NCLC 9**

Jouve, Pierre Jean 1887-1976 ...... **CLC 47**
See also CA 65-68

Joyce, James (Augustine Aloysius)
1882-1941 .... **TCLC 3, 8, 16, 35, 52;
DA; DAB; DAC; SSC 3; WLC**
See also CA 104; 126; CDBLB 1914-1945;
DAM MST, NOV, POET; DLB 10, 19,
36, 162; MTCW

Jozsef, Attila 1905-1937 .... **TCLC 22**
See also CA 116

Juana Ines de la Cruz 1651(?)-1695 ... **LC 5**

Judd, Cyril
See Kornbluth, C(yril) M.; Pohl, Frederik

Julian of Norwich 1342(?)-1416(?) .... **LC 6**
See also DLB 146

Juniper, Alex
See Hospital, Janette Turner

Junius
See Luxemburg, Rosa

Just, Ward (Swift) 1935- .... **CLC 4, 27**
See also CA 25-28R; CANR 32;
INT CANR-32

Justice, Donald (Rodney) 1925- .. **CLC 6, 19**
See also CA 5-8R; CANR 26; DAM POET;
DLBY 83; INT CANR-26

Juvenal c. 55-c. 127 .... **CMLC 8**

Juvenis
See Bourne, Randolph S(illiman)

Kacew, Romain 1914-1980
See Gary, Romain
See also CA 108; 102

Kadare, Ismail 1936- .... **CLC 52**

Kadohata, Cynthia .... **CLC 59**
See also CA 140

Kafka, Franz
1883-1924 .... **TCLC 2, 6, 13, 29, 47, 53;**
DA; DAB; DAC; SSC 5; WLC
See also CA 105; 126; DAM MST, NOV;
DLB 81; MTCW

Kahanovitsch, Pinkhes
See Der Nister

Kahn, Roger 1927- .... **CLC 30**
See also CA 25-28R; CANR 44; SATA 37

Kain, Saul
See Sassoon, Siegfried (Lorraine)

Kaiser, Georg 1878-1945 .... **TCLC 9**
See also CA 106; DLB 124

Kaletski, Alexander 1946- .... **CLC 39**
See also CA 118; 143

Kalidasa fl. c. 400- .... **CMLC 9**

Kallman, Chester (Simon)
1921-1975 .... **CLC 2**
See also CA 45-48; 53-56; CANR 3

Kaminsky, Melvin 1926-
See Brooks, Mel
See also CA 65-68; CANR 16

Kaminsky, Stuart M(elvin) 1934- ... **CLC 59**
See also CA 73-76; CANR 29

Kane, Paul
See Simon, Paul

Kane, Wilson
See Bloch, Robert (Albert)

Kanin, Garson 1912- .... **CLC 22**
See also AITN 1; CA 5-8R; CANR 7;
DLB 7

Kaniuk, Yoram 1930- .... **CLC 19**
See also CA 134

Kant, Immanuel 1724-1804 ...... **NCLC 27**
See also DLB 94

Kantor, MacKinlay 1904-1977 ...... **CLC 7**
See also CA 61-64; 73-76; DLB 9, 102

Kaplan, David Michael 1946- ...... **CLC 50**

Kaplan, James 1951- .... **CLC 59**
See also CA 135

Karageorge, Michael
See Anderson, Poul (William)

Karamzin, Nikolai Mikhailovich
1766-1826 .... **NCLC 3**
See also DLB 150

Karapanou, Margarita 1946- .... **CLC 13**
See also CA 101

Karinthy, Frigyes 1887-1938 ..... **TCLC 47**

Karl, Frederick R(obert) 1927- ..... **CLC 34**
See also CA 5-8R; CANR 3, 44

Kastel, Warren
See Silverberg, Robert

Kataev, Evgeny Petrovich 1903-1942
See Petrov, Evgeny
See also CA 120

Kataphusin
See Ruskin, John

Katz, Steve 1935- .... **CLC 47**
See also CA 25-28R; CAAS 14; CANR 12;
DLBY 83

Kauffman, Janet 1945- .... **CLC 42**
See also CA 117; CANR 43; DLBY 86

Kaufman, Bob (Garnell)
1925-1986 .... **CLC 49**
See also BW 1; CA 41-44R; 118; CANR 22;
DLB 16, 41

Kaufman, George S. 1889-1961 ..... **CLC 38**
See also CA 108; 93-96; DAM DRAM;
DLB 7; INT 108

Kaufman, Sue .... **CLC 3, 8**
See also Barondess, Sue K(aufman)

Kavafis, Konstantinos Petrou 1863-1933
See Cavafy, C(onstantine) P(eter)
See also CA 104

Kavan, Anna 1901-1968 ...... **CLC 5, 13, 82**
See also CA 5-8R; CANR 6; MTCW

Kavanagh, Dan
See Barnes, Julian

Kavanagh, Patrick (Joseph)
1904-1967 .... **CLC 22**
See also CA 123; 25-28R; DLB 15, 20;
MTCW

Kawabata, Yasunari
1899-1972 ..... **CLC 2, 5, 9, 18; SSC 17**
See also CA 93-96; 33-36R; DAM MULT

Kaye, M(ary) M(argaret) 1909- ..... **CLC 28**
See also CA 89-92; CANR 24; MTCW;
SATA 62

Kaye, Mollie
See Kaye, M(ary) M(argaret)

Kaye-Smith, Sheila 1887-1956 ..... **TCLC 20**
See also CA 118; DLB 36

Kaymor, Patrice Maguilene
See Senghor, Leopold Sedar

Kazan, Elia 1909- .... **CLC 6, 16, 63**
See also CA 21-24R; CANR 32

Kazantzakis, Nikos
1883(?)-1957 .... **TCLC 2, 5, 33**
See also CA 105; 132; MTCW

Kazin, Alfred 1915- .... **CLC 34, 38**
See also CA 1-4R; CAAS 7; CANR 1, 45;
DLB 67

Keane, Mary Nesta (Skrine) 1904-
See Keane, Molly
See also CA 108; 114

Keane, Molly .... **CLC 31**
See also Keane, Mary Nesta (Skrine)
See also INT 114

Keates, Jonathan 19(?)- .... **CLC 34**

Keaton, Buster 1895-1966 .... **CLC 20**

Keats, John
1795-1821 .... **NCLC 8; DA; DAB;**
DAC; PC 1; WLC
See also CDBLB 1789-1832; DAM MST,
POET; DLB 96, 110

Keene, Donald 1922- .... **CLC 34**
See also CA 1-4R; CANR 5

Keillor, Garrison .... **CLC 40**
See also Keillor, Gary (Edward)
See also AAYA 2; BEST 89:3; DLBY 87;
SATA 58

Keillor, Gary (Edward) 1942-
See Keillor, Garrison
See also CA 111; 117; CANR 36;
DAM POP; MTCW

Keith, Michael
See Hubbard, L(afayette) Ron(ald)

Keller, Gottfried 1819-1890 ...... **NCLC 2**
See also DLB 129

Kellerman, Jonathan 1949- .... **CLC 44**
See also BEST 90:1; CA 106; CANR 29, 51;
DAM POP; INT CANR-29

Kelley, William Melvin 1937- ...... **CLC 22**
See also BW 1; CA 77-80; CANR 27;
DLB 33

Kellogg, Marjorie 1922- .... **CLC 2**
See also CA 81-84

Kellow, Kathleen
See Hibbert, Eleanor Alice Burford

Kelly, M(ilton) T(erry) 1947- .... **CLC 55**
See also CA 97-100; CAAS 22; CANR 19,
43

Kelman, James 1946- .... **CLC 58, 86**
See also CA 148

Kemal, Yashar 1923- .... **CLC 14, 29**
See also CA 89-92; CANR 44

Kemble, Fanny 1809-1893 .... **NCLC 18**
See also DLB 32

Kemelman, Harry 1908- .... **CLC 2**
See also AITN 1; CA 9-12R; CANR 6;
DLB 28

Kempe, Margery 1373(?)-1440(?) ..... **LC 6**
See also DLB 146

Kempis, Thomas a 1380-1471 .... **LC 11**

Kendall, Henry 1839-1882 .... **NCLC 12**

Keneally, Thomas (Michael)
1935- ...... **CLC 5, 8, 10, 14, 19, 27, 43**
See also CA 85-88; CANR 10, 50;
DAM NOV; MTCW

Kennedy, Adrienne (Lita)
1931- .... **CLC 66; BLC; DC 5**
See also BW 2; CA 103; CAAS 20; CABS 3;
CANR 26; DAM MULT; DLB 38

Kennedy, John Pendleton
1795-1870 .... **NCLC 2**
See also DLB 3

Kennedy, Joseph Charles 1929-
See Kennedy, X. J.
See also CA 1-4R; CANR 4, 30, 40;
SATA 14, 86

Kennedy, William 1928-... **CLC 6, 28, 34, 53**
See also AAYA 1; CA 85-88; CANR 14,
31; DAM NOV; DLB 143; DLBY 85;
INT CANR-31; MTCW; SATA 57

Kennedy, X. J.................. **CLC 8, 42**
See also Kennedy, Joseph Charles
See also CAAS 9; CLR 27; DLB 5;
SAAS 22

Kenny, Maurice (Francis) 1929-.... **CLC 87**
See also CA 144; CAAS 22; DAM MULT;
NNAL

Kent, Kelvin
See Kuttner, Henry

Kenton, Maxwell
See Southern, Terry

Kenyon, Robert O.
See Kuttner, Henry

Kerouac, Jack..... **CLC 1, 2, 3, 5, 14, 29, 61**
See also Kerouac, Jean-Louis Lebris de
See also CDALB 1941-1968; DLB 2, 16;
DLBD 3; DLBY 95

Kerouac, Jean-Louis Lebris de 1922-1969
See Kerouac, Jack
See also AITN 1; CA 5-8R; 25-28R;
CANR 26; DA; DAB; DAC; DAM MST,
NOV, POET, POP; MTCW; WLC

Kerr, Jean 1923-................. **CLC 22**
See also CA 5-8R; CANR 7; INT CANR-7

Kerr, M. E..................... **CLC 12, 35**
See also Meaker, Marijane (Agnes)
See also AAYA 2; CLR 29; SAAS 1

Kerr, Robert.................... **CLC 55**

Kerrigan, (Thomas) Anthony
1918-...................... **CLC 4, 6**
See also CA 49-52; CAAS 11; CANR 4

Kerry, Lois
See Duncan, Lois

Kesey, Ken (Elton)
1935-...... **CLC 1, 3, 6, 11, 46, 64; DA;
DAB; DAC; WLC**
See also CA 1-4R; CANR 22, 38;
CDALB 1968-1988; DAM MST, NOV,
POP; DLB 2, 16; MTCW; SATA 66

Kesselring, Joseph (Otto)
1902-1967................... **CLC 45**
See also CA 150; DAM DRAM, MST

Kessler, Jascha (Frederick) 1929-.... **CLC 4**
See also CA 17-20R; CANR 8, 48

Kettelkamp, Larry (Dale) 1933-.... **CLC 12**
See also CA 29-32R; CANR 16; SAAS 3;
SATA 2

Keyber, Conny
See Fielding, Henry

Keyes, Daniel 1927-.... **CLC 80; DA; DAC**
See also CA 17-20R; CANR 10, 26;
DAM MST, NOV; SATA 37

Khanshendel, Chiron
See Rose, Wendy

Khayyam, Omar
1048-1131........... **CMLC 11; PC 8**
See also DAM POET

Kherdian, David 1931-.......... **CLC 6, 9**
See also CA 21-24R; CAAS 2; CANR 39;
CLR 24; JRDA; MAICYA; SATA 16, 74

Khlebnikov, Velimir.............. **TCLC 20**
See also Khlebnikov, Viktor Vladimirovich

Khlebnikov, Viktor Vladimirovich 1885-1922
See Khlebnikov, Velimir
See also CA 117

Khodasevich, Vladislav (Felitsianovich)
1886-1939 .... **TCLC 15**
See also CA 115

Kielland, Alexander Lange
1849-1906 .... **TCLC 5**
See also CA 104

Kiely, Benedict 1919-.......... **CLC 23, 43**
See also CA 1-4R; CANR 2; DLB 15

Kienzle, William X(avier) 1928-.... **CLC 25**
See also CA 93-96; CAAS 1; CANR 9, 31;
DAM POP; INT CANR-31; MTCW

Kierkegaard, Soren 1813-1855.... **NCLC 34**

Killens, John Oliver 1916-1987..... **CLC 10**
See also BW 2; CA 77-80; 123; CAAS 2;
CANR 26; DLB 33

Killigrew, Anne 1660-1685.......... **LC 4**
See also DLB 131

Kim
See Simenon, Georges (Jacques Christian)

Kincaid, Jamaica 1949-... **CLC 43, 68; BLC**
See also AAYA 13; BW 2; CA 125;
CANR 47; DAM MULT, NOV;
DLB 157

King, Francis (Henry) 1923-..... **CLC 8, 53**
See also CA 1-4R; CANR 1, 33;
DAM NOV; DLB 15, 139; MTCW

King, Martin Luther, Jr.
1929-1968 .... **CLC 83; BLC; DA; DAB;
DAC**
See also BW 2; CA 25-28; CANR 27, 44;
CAP 2; DAM MST, MULT; MTCW;
SATA 14

King, Stephen (Edwin)
1947-...... **CLC 12, 26, 37, 61; SSC 17**
See also AAYA 1, 17; BEST 90:1;
CA 61-64; CANR 1, 30; DAM NOV,
POP; DLB 143; DLBY 80; JRDA;
MTCW; SATA 9, 55

King, Steve
See King, Stephen (Edwin)

King, Thomas 1943-........ **CLC 89; DAC**
See also CA 144; DAM MULT; NNAL

Kingman, Lee.................... **CLC 17**
See also Natti, (Mary) Lee
See also SAAS 3; SATA 1, 67

Kingsley, Charles 1819-1875..... **NCLC 35**
See also DLB 21, 32, 163; YABC 2

Kingsley, Sidney 1906-1995........ **CLC 44**
See also CA 85-88; 147; DLB 7

Kingsolver, Barbara 1955-...... **CLC 55, 81**
See also AAYA 15; CA 129; 134;
DAM POP; INT 134

Kingston, Maxine (Ting Ting) Hong
1940-................. **CLC 12, 19, 58**
See also AAYA 8; CA 69-72; CANR 13,
38; DAM MULT, NOV; DLBY 80;
INT CANR-13; MTCW; SATA 53

Kinnell, Galway
1927-........... **CLC 1, 2, 3, 5, 13, 29**
See also CA 9-12R; CANR 10, 34; DLB 5;
DLBY 87; INT CANR-34; MTCW

Kinsella, Thomas 1928-........ **CLC 4, 19**
See also CA 17-20R; CANR 15; DLB 27;
MTCW

Kinsella, W(illiam) P(atrick)
1935-............. **CLC 27, 43; DAC**
See also AAYA 7; CA 97-100; CAAS 7;
CANR 21, 35; DAM NOV, POP;
INT CANR-21; MTCW

Kipling, (Joseph) Rudyard
1865-1936 ...... **TCLC 8, 17; DA; DAB;
DAC; PC 3; SSC 5; WLC**
See also CA 105; 120; CANR 33;
CDBLB 1890-1914; CLR 39; DAM MST,
POET; DLB 19, 34, 141, 156; MAICYA;
MTCW; YABC 2

Kirkup, James 1918- .... **CLC 1**
See also CA 1-4R; CAAS 4; CANR 2;
DLB 27; SATA 12

Kirkwood, James 1930(?)-1989 ...... **CLC 9**
See also AITN 2; CA 1-4R; 128; CANR 6,
40

Kirshner, Sidney
See Kingsley, Sidney

Kis, Danilo 1935-1989 .... **CLC 57**
See also CA 109; 118; 129; MTCW

Kivi, Aleksis 1834-1872......... **NCLC 30**

Kizer, Carolyn (Ashley)
1925-.................. **CLC 15, 39, 80**
See also CA 65-68; CAAS 5; CANR 24;
DAM POET; DLB 5

Klabund 1890-1928.............. **TCLC 44**
See also DLB 66

Klappert, Peter 1942-............. **CLC 57**
See also CA 33-36R; DLB 5

Klein, A(braham) M(oses)
1909-1972 .... **CLC 19; DAB; DAC**
See also CA 101; 37-40R; DAM MST;
DLB 68

Klein, Norma 1938-1989 .... **CLC 30**
See also AAYA 2; CA 41-44R; 128;
CANR 15, 37; CLR 2, 19;
INT CANR-15; JRDA; MAICYA;
SAAS 1; SATA 7, 57

Klein, T(heodore) E(ibon) D(onald)
1947-...................... **CLC 34**
See also CA 119; CANR 44

Kleist, Heinrich von
1777-1811 .... **NCLC 2, 37; SSC 22**
See also DAM DRAM; DLB 90

Klima, Ivan 1931-................ **CLC 56**
See also CA 25-28R; CANR 17, 50;
DAM NOV

Klimentov, Andrei Platonovich 1899-1951
See Platonov, Andrei
See also CA 108

Klinger, Friedrich Maximilian von
1752-1831 .... **NCLC 1**
See also DLB 94

Klopstock, Friedrich Gottlieb
1724-1803 .... **NCLC 11**
See also DLB 97

Author Index

Kyprianos, Iossif
See Samarakis, Antonis

La Bruyere, Jean de 1645-1696...... **LC 17**

Lacan, Jacques (Marie Emile)
1901-1981 .... **CLC 75**
See also CA 121; 104

**Laclos, Pierre Ambroise Francois Choderlos
de** 1741-1803 .... **NCLC 4**

Lacolere, Francois
See Aragon, Louis

La Colere, Francois
See Aragon, Louis

La Deshabilleuse
See Simenon, Georges (Jacques Christian)

Lady Gregory
See Gregory, Isabella Augusta (Persse)

Lady of Quality, A
See Bagnold, Enid

**La Fayette, Marie (Madelaine Pioche de la
Vergne Comtes** 1634-1693....... **LC 2**

Lafayette, Rene
See Hubbard, L(afayette) Ron(ald)

Laforgue, Jules
1860-1887 .... **NCLC 5, 53; PC 14;
SSC 20**

Lagerkvist, Paer (Fabian)
1891-1974 .... **CLC 7, 10, 13, 54**
See also Lagerkvist, Par
See also CA 85-88; 49-52; DAM DRAM,
NOV; MTCW

Lagerkvist, Par .... **SSC 12**
See also Lagerkvist, Paer (Fabian)

Lagerloef, Selma (Ottiliana Lovisa)
1858-1940 .... **TCLC 4, 36**
See also Lagerlof, Selma (Ottiliana Lovisa)
See also CA 108; SATA 15

Lagerlof, Selma (Ottiliana Lovisa)
See Lagerloef, Selma (Ottiliana Lovisa)
See also CLR 7; SATA 15

La Guma, (Justin) Alex(ander)
1925-1985 .... **CLC 19**
See also BW 1; CA 49-52; 118; CANR 25;
DAM NOV; DLB 117; MTCW

Laidlaw, A. K.
See Grieve, C(hristopher) M(urray)

Lainez, Manuel Mujica
See Mujica Lainez, Manuel
See also HW

Lamartine, Alphonse (Marie Louis Prat) de
1790-1869 .... **NCLC 11**
See also DAM POET

Lamb, Charles
1775-1834 .... **NCLC 10; DA; DAB;
DAC; WLC**
See also CDBLB 1789-1832; DAM MST;
DLB 93, 107, 163; SATA 17

Lamb, Lady Caroline 1785-1828 .. **NCLC 38**
See also DLB 116

Lamming, George (William)
1927- .... **CLC 2, 4, 66; BLC**
See also BW 2; CA 85-88; CANR 26;
DAM MULT; DLB 125; MTCW

L'Amour, Louis (Dearborn)
1908-1988 .... **CLC 25, 55**
See also AAYA 16; AITN 2; BEST 89:2;
CA 1-4R; 125; CANR 3, 25, 40;
DAM NOV, POP; DLBY 80; MTCW

Lampedusa, Giuseppe (Tomasi) di ... **TCLC 13**
See also Tomasi di Lampedusa, Giuseppe

Lampman, Archibald 1861-1899 .. **NCLC 25**
See also DLB 92

Lancaster, Bruce 1896-1963........ **CLC 36**
See also CA 9-10; CAP 1; SATA 9

Landau, Mark Alexandrovich
See Aldanov, Mark (Alexandrovich)

Landau-Aldanov, Mark Alexandrovich
See Aldanov, Mark (Alexandrovich)

Landis, John 1950-............... **CLC 26**
See also CA 112; 122

Landolfi, Tommaso 1908-1979... **CLC 11, 49**
See also CA 127; 117

Landon, Letitia Elizabeth
1802-1838 .... **NCLC 15**
See also DLB 96

Landor, Walter Savage
1775-1864 .... **NCLC 14**
See also DLB 93, 107

Landwirth, Heinz 1927-
See Lind, Jakov
See also CA 9-12R; CANR 7

Lane, Patrick 1939-.............. **CLC 25**
See also CA 97-100; DAM POET; DLB 53;
INT 97-100

Lang, Andrew 1844-1912........ **TCLC 16**
See also CA 114; 137; DLB 98, 141;
MAICYA; SATA 16

Lang, Fritz 1890-1976 .... **CLC 20**
See also CA 77-80; 69-72; CANR 30

Lange, John
See Crichton, (John) Michael

Langer, Elinor 1939- .... **CLC 34**
See also CA 121

Langland, William
1330(?)-1400(?) ...... **LC 19; DA; DAB;
DAC**
See also DAM MST, POET; DLB 146

Langstaff, Launcelot
See Irving, Washington

Lanier, Sidney 1842-1881 .... **NCLC 6**
See also DAM POET; DLB 64; DLBD 13;
MAICYA; SATA 18

Lanyer, Aemilia 1569-1645 ...... **LC 10, 30**
See also DLB 121

Lao Tzu .... **CMLC 7**

Lapine, James (Elliot) 1949-....... **CLC 39**
See also CA 123; 130; INT 130

Larbaud, Valery (Nicolas)
1881-1957 .... **TCLC 9**
See also CA 106

Lardner, Ring
See Lardner, Ring(gold) W(ilmer)

Lardner, Ring W., Jr.
See Lardner, Ring(gold) W(ilmer)

Lardner, Ring(gold) W(ilmer)
1885-1933 .... **TCLC 2, 14**
See also CA 104; 131; CDALB 1917-1929;
DLB 11, 25, 86; MTCW

Laredo, Betty
See Codrescu, Andrei

Larkin, Maia
See Wojciechowska, Maia (Teresa)

Larkin, Philip (Arthur)
1922-1985 .... **CLC 3, 5, 8, 9, 13, 18, 33,
39, 64; DAB**
See also CA 5-8R; 117; CANR 24;
CDBLB 1960 to Present; DAM MST,
POET; DLB 27; MTCW

Larra (y Sanchez de Castro), Mariano Jose de
1809-1837 .... **NCLC 17**

Larsen, Eric 1941- .... **CLC 55**
See also CA 132

Larsen, Nella 1891-1964 ..... **CLC 37; BLC**
See also BW 1; CA 125; DAM MULT;
DLB 51

Larson, Charles R(aymond) 1938-.... **CLC 31**
See also CA 53-56; CANR 4

Las Casas, Bartolome de 1474-1566.. **LC 31**

Lasker-Schueler, Else 1869-1945 .. **TCLC 57**
See also DLB 66, 124

Latham, Jean Lee 1902-........... **CLC 12**
See also AITN 1; CA 5-8R; CANR 7;
MAICYA; SATA 2, 68

Latham, Mavis
See Clark, Mavis Thorpe

Lathen, Emma.................... **CLC 2**
See also Hennissart, Martha; Latsis, Mary
J(ane)

Lathrop, Francis
See Leiber, Fritz (Reuter, Jr.)

Latsis, Mary J(ane)
See Lathen, Emma
See also CA 85-88

Lattimore, Richmond (Alexander)
1906-1984 .... **CLC 3**
See also CA 1-4R; 112; CANR 1

Laughlin, James 1914-............ **CLC 49**
See also CA 21-24R; CAAS 22; CANR 9,
47; DLB 48

Laurence, (Jean) Margaret (Wemyss)
1926-1987 .... **CLC 3, 6, 13, 50, 62;
DAC; SSC 7**
See also CA 5-8R; 121; CANR 33;
DAM MST; DLB 53; MTCW;
SATA-Obit 50

Laurent, Antoine 1952- .... **CLC 50**

Lauscher, Hermann
See Hesse, Hermann

Lautreamont, Comte de
1846-1870 .... **NCLC 12; SSC 14**

Laverty, Donald
See Blish, James (Benjamin)

Lavin, Mary 1912-...... **CLC 4, 18; SSC 4**
See also CA 9-12R; CANR 33; DLB 15;
MTCW

Lavond, Paul Dennis
See Kornbluth, C(yril) M.; Pohl, Frederik

Lentricchia, Frank (Jr.) 1940-...... **CLC 34**
    See also CA 25-28R; CANR 19

Lenz, Siegfried 1926-............. **CLC 27**
    See also CA 89-92; DLB 75

Leonard, Elmore (John, Jr.)
    1925-................**CLC 28, 34, 71**
    See also AITN 1; BEST 89:1, 90:4;
    CA 81-84; CANR 12, 28; DAM POP;
    INT CANR-28; MTCW

Leonard, Hugh............. **CLC 19**
    See also Byrne, John Keyes
    See also DLB 13

Leonov, Leonid (Maximovich)
    1899-1994 .... **CLC 92**
    See also CA 129; DAM NOV; MTCW

Leopardi, (Conte) Giacomo
    1798-1837 .... **NCLC 22**

Le Reveler
    See Artaud, Antonin (Marie Joseph)

Lerman, Eleanor 1952-............. **CLC 9**
    See also CA 85-88

Lerman, Rhoda 1936-............. **CLC 56**
    See also CA 49-52

Lermontov, Mikhail Yuryevich
    1814-1841 .... **NCLC 47**

Leroux, Gaston 1868-1927....... **TCLC 25**
    See also CA 108; 136; SATA 65

Lesage, Alain-Rene 1668-1747....... **LC 28**

Leskov, Nikolai (Semyonovich)
    1831-1895 .... **NCLC 25**

Lessing, Doris (May)
    1919- ..... **CLC 1, 2, 3, 6, 10, 15, 22, 40,
    91; DA; DAB; DAC; SSC 6**
    See also CA 9-12R; CAAS 14; CANR 33;
    CDBLB 1960 to Present; DAM MST,
    NOV; DLB 15, 139; DLBY 85; MTCW

Lessing, Gotthold Ephraim
    1729-1781 .... **LC 8**
    See also DLB 97

Lester, Richard 1932-............. **CLC 20**

Lever, Charles (James)
    1806-1872 .... **NCLC 23**
    See also DLB 21

Leverson, Ada 1865(?)-1936(?) .... **TCLC 18**
    See also Elaine
    See also CA 117; DLB 153

Levertov, Denise
    1923- ......**CLC 1, 2, 3, 5, 8, 15, 28, 66;
    PC 11**
    See also CA 1-4R; CAAS 19; CANR 3, 29,
    50; DAM POET; DLB 5, 165;
    INT CANR-29; MTCW

Levi, Jonathan................ **CLC 76**

Levi, Peter (Chad Tigar) 1931-..... **CLC 41**
    See also CA 5-8R; CANR 34; DLB 40

Levi, Primo
    1919-1987 .... **CLC 37, 50; SSC 12**
    See also CA 13-16R; 122; CANR 12, 33;
    MTCW

Levin, Ira 1929-............... **CLC 3, 6**
    See also CA 21-24R; CANR 17, 44;
    DAM POP; MTCW; SATA 66

Levin, Meyer 1905-1981 .... **CLC 7**
    See also AITN 1; CA 9-12R; 104;
    CANR 15; DAM POP; DLB 9, 28;
    DLBY 81; SATA 21; SATA-Obit 27

Levine, Norman 1924-............. **CLC 54**
    See also CA 73-76; CAAS 23; CANR 14;
    DLB 88

Levine, Philip 1928-.. **CLC 2, 4, 5, 9, 14, 33**
    See also CA 9-12R; CANR 9, 37;
    DAM POET; DLB 5

Levinson, Deirdre 1931-........... **CLC 49**
    See also CA 73-76

Levi-Strauss, Claude 1908- .... **CLC 38**
    See also CA 1-4R; CANR 6, 32; MTCW

Levitin, Sonia (Wolff) 1934- .... **CLC 17**
    See also AAYA 13; CA 29-32R; CANR 14,
    32; JRDA; MAICYA; SAAS 2; SATA 4,
    68

Levon, O. U.
    See Kesey, Ken (Elton)

Lewes, George Henry
    1817-1878 .... **NCLC 25**
    See also DLB 55, 144

Lewis, Alun 1915-1944............ **TCLC 3**
    See also CA 104; DLB 20, 162

Lewis, C. Day
    See Day Lewis, C(ecil)

Lewis, C(live) S(taples)
    1898-1963 ..... **CLC 1, 3, 6, 14, 27; DA;
    DAB; DAC; WLC**
    See also AAYA 3; CA 81-84; CANR 33;
    CDBLB 1945-1960; CLR 3, 27;
    DAM MST, NOV, POP; DLB 15, 100,
    160; JRDA; MAICYA; MTCW;
    SATA 13

Lewis, Janet 1899-............... **CLC 41**
    See also Winters, Janet Lewis
    See also CA 9-12R; CANR 29; CAP 1;
    DLBY 87

Lewis, Matthew Gregory
    1775-1818 .... **NCLC 11**
    See also DLB 39, 158

Lewis, (Harry) Sinclair
    1885-1951 ..... **TCLC 4, 13, 23, 39; DA;
    DAB; DAC; WLC**
    See also CA 104; 133; CDALB 1917-1929;
    DAM MST, NOV; DLB 9, 102; DLBD 1;
    MTCW

Lewis, (Percy) Wyndham
    1884(?)-1957 .... **TCLC 2, 9**
    See also CA 104; DLB 15

Lewisohn, Ludwig 1883-1955...... **TCLC 19**
    See also CA 107; DLB 4, 9, 28, 102

Leyner, Mark 1956-............. **CLC 92**
    See also CA 110; CANR 28

Lezama Lima, Jose 1910-1976 ... **CLC 4, 10**
    See also CA 77-80; DAM MULT;
    DLB 113; HW

L'Heureux, John (Clarke) 1934-.... **CLC 52**
    See also CA 13-16R; CANR 23, 45

Liddell, C. H.
    See Kuttner, Henry

Lie, Jonas (Lauritz Idemil)
    1833-1908(?) .... **TCLC 5**
    See also CA 115

Lieber, Joel 1937-1971............ **CLC 6**
    See also CA 73-76; 29-32R

Lieber, Stanley Martin
    See Lee, Stan

Lieberman, Laurence (James)
    1935-.................... **CLC 4, 36**
    See also CA 17-20R; CANR 8, 36

Lieksman, Anders
    See Haavikko, Paavo Juhani

Li Fei-kan 1904-
    See Pa Chin
    See also CA 105

Lifton, Robert Jay 1926-.......... **CLC 67**
    See also CA 17-20R; CANR 27;
    INT CANR-27; SATA 66

Lightfoot, Gordon 1938-........... **CLC 26**
    See also CA 109

Lightman, Alan P. 1948- .... **CLC 81**
    See also CA 141

Ligotti, Thomas (Robert)
    1953-............... **CLC 44; SSC 16**
    See also CA 123; CANR 49

Li Ho 791-817.................... **PC 13**

Liliencron, (Friedrich Adolf Axel) Detlev von
    1844-1909 .... **TCLC 18**
    See also CA 117

Lilly, William 1602-1681........... **LC 27**

Lima, Jose Lezama
    See Lezama Lima, Jose

Lima Barreto, Afonso Henrique de
    1881-1922 .... **TCLC 23**
    See also CA 117

Limonov, Edward 1944-........... **CLC 67**
    See also CA 137

Lin, Frank
    See Atherton, Gertrude (Franklin Horn)

Lincoln, Abraham 1809-1865..... **NCLC 18**

Lind, Jakov .... **CLC 1, 2, 4, 27, 82**
    See also Landwirth, Heinz
    See also CAAS 4

Lindbergh, Anne (Spencer) Morrow
    1906-...................... **CLC 82**
    See also CA 17-20R; CANR 16;
    DAM NOV; MTCW; SATA 33

Lindsay, David 1878-1945........ **TCLC 15**
    See also CA 113

Lindsay, (Nicholas) Vachel
    1879-1931 ... **TCLC 17; DA; DAC; WLC**
    See also CA 114; 135; CDALB 1865-1917;
    DAM MST, POET; DLB 54; SATA 40

Linke-Poot
    See Doeblin, Alfred

Linney, Romulus 1930- .... **CLC 51**
    See also CA 1-4R; CANR 40, 44

Linton, Eliza Lynn 1822-1898.... **NCLC 41**
    See also DLB 18

Li Po 701-763................. **CMLC 2**

Lipsius, Justus 1547-1606 .... **LC 16**

Lipsyte, Robert (Michael)
    1938-............. **CLC 21; DA; DAC**
    See also AAYA 7; CA 17-20R; CANR 8;
    CLR 23; DAM MST, NOV; JRDA;
    MAICYA; SATA 5, 68

Lugones, Leopoldo 1874-1938 ..... **TCLC 15**
See also CA 116; 131; HW

Lu Hsun 1881-1936 ...... **TCLC 3; SSC 20**
See also Shu-Jen, Chou

Lukacs, George .... **CLC 24**
See also Lukacs, Gyorgy (Szegeny von)

Lukacs, Gyorgy (Szegeny von) 1885-1971
See Lukacs, George
See also CA 101; 29-32R

Luke, Peter (Ambrose Cyprian)
1919-1995 .... **CLC 38**
See also CA 81-84; 147; DLB 13

Lunar, Dennis
See Mungo, Raymond

Lurie, Alison 1926-........ **CLC 4, 5, 18, 39**
See also CA 1-4R; CANR 2, 17, 50; DLB 2;
MTCW; SATA 46

Lustig, Arnost 1926-.............. **CLC 56**
See also AAYA 3; CA 69-72; CANR 47;
SATA 56

Luther, Martin 1483-1546 .... **LC 9**

Luxemburg, Rosa 1870(?)-1919 .... **TCLC 63**
See also CA 118

Luzi, Mario 1914-................ **CLC 13**
See also CA 61-64; CANR 9; DLB 128

L'Ymagier
See Gourmont, Remy (-Marie-Charles) de

Lynch, B. Suarez
See Bioy Casares, Adolfo; Borges, Jorge
Luis

Lynch, David (K.) 1946-.......... **CLC 66**
See also CA 124; 129

Lynch, James
See Andreyev, Leonid (Nikolaevich)

Lynch Davis, B.
See Bioy Casares, Adolfo; Borges, Jorge
Luis

Lyndsay, Sir David 1490-1555 ...... **LC 20**

Lynn, Kenneth S(chuyler) 1923- .... **CLC 50**
See also CA 1-4R; CANR 3, 27

Lynx
See West, Rebecca

Lyons, Marcus
See Blish, James (Benjamin)

Lyre, Pinchbeck
See Sassoon, Siegfried (Lorraine)

Lytle, Andrew (Nelson) 1902-1995 .. **CLC 22**
See also CA 9-12R; 150; DLB 6; DLBY 95

Lyttelton, George 1709-1773........ **LC 10**

Maas, Peter 1929- .... **CLC 29**
See also CA 93-96; INT 93-96

Macaulay, Rose 1881-1958 ..... **TCLC 7, 44**
See also CA 104; DLB 36

Macaulay, Thomas Babington
1800-1859 .... **NCLC 42**
See also CDBLB 1832-1890; DLB 32, 55

MacBeth, George (Mann)
1932-1992 .... **CLC 2, 5, 9**
See also CA 25-28R; 136; DLB 40; MTCW;
SATA 4; SATA-Obit 70

MacCaig, Norman (Alexander)
1910- .... **CLC 36; DAB**
See also CA 9-12R; CANR 3, 34;
DAM POET; DLB 27

MacCarthy, (Sir Charles Otto) Desmond
1877-1952 .... **TCLC 36**

MacDiarmid, Hugh
.... **CLC 2, 4, 11, 19, 63; PC 9**
See also Grieve, C(hristopher) M(urray)
See also CDBLB 1945-1960; DLB 20

MacDonald, Anson
See Heinlein, Robert A(nson)

Macdonald, Cynthia 1928-...... **CLC 13, 19**
See also CA 49-52; CANR 4, 44; DLB 105

MacDonald, George 1824-1905..... **TCLC 9**
See also CA 106; 137; DLB 18, 163;
MAICYA; SATA 33

Macdonald, John
See Millar, Kenneth

MacDonald, John D(ann)
1916-1986 .... **CLC 3, 27, 44**
See also CA 1-4R; 121; CANR 1, 19;
DAM NOV, POP; DLB 8; DLBY 86;
MTCW

Macdonald, John Ross
See Millar, Kenneth

Macdonald, Ross..... **CLC 1, 2, 3, 14, 34, 41**
See also Millar, Kenneth
See also DLBD 6

MacDougal, John
See Blish, James (Benjamin)

MacEwen, Gwendolyn (Margaret)
1941-1987 .... **CLC 13, 55**
See also CA 9-12R; 124; CANR 7, 22;
DLB 53; SATA 50; SATA-Obit 55

Macha, Karel Hynek 1810-1846 .. **NCLC 46**

Machado (y Ruiz), Antonio
1875-1939 .... **TCLC 3**
See also CA 104; DLB 108

Machado de Assis, Joaquim Maria
1839-1908 .... **TCLC 10; BLC**
See also CA 107

Machen, Arthur.......... **TCLC 4; SSC 20**
See also Jones, Arthur Llewellyn
See also DLB 36, 156

Machiavelli, Niccolo
1469-1527 ...... **LC 8; DA; DAB; DAC**
See also DAM MST

MacInnes, Colin 1914-1976...... **CLC 4, 23**
See also CA 69-72; 65-68; CANR 21;
DLB 14; MTCW

MacInnes, Helen (Clark)
1907-1985 .... **CLC 27, 39**
See also CA 1-4R; 117; CANR 1, 28;
DAM POP; DLB 87; MTCW; SATA 22;
SATA-Obit 44

Mackay, Mary 1855-1924
See Corelli, Marie
See also CA 118

Mackenzie, Compton (Edward Montague)
1883-1972 .... **CLC 18**
See also CA 21-22; 37-40R; CAP 2;
DLB 34, 100

Mackenzie, Henry 1745-1831 .... **NCLC 41**
See also DLB 39

Mackintosh, Elizabeth 1896(?)-1952
See Tey, Josephine
See also CA 110

MacLaren, James
See Grieve, C(hristopher) M(urray)

Mac Laverty, Bernard 1942-....... **CLC 31**
See also CA 116; 118; CANR 43; INT 118

MacLean, Alistair (Stuart)
1922-1987 .... **CLC 3, 13, 50, 63**
See also CA 57-60; 121; CANR 28;
DAM POP; MTCW; SATA 23;
SATA-Obit 50

Maclean, Norman (Fitzroy)
1902-1990 .... **CLC 78; SSC 13**
See also CA 102; 132; CANR 49;
DAM POP

MacLeish, Archibald
1892-1982 .... **CLC 3, 8, 14, 68**
See also CA 9-12R; 106; CANR 33;
DAM POET; DLB 4, 7, 45; DLBY 82;
MTCW

MacLennan, (John) Hugh
1907-1990 .... **CLC 2, 14, 92; DAC**
See also CA 5-8R; 142; CANR 33;
DAM MST; DLB 68; MTCW

MacLeod, Alistair 1936- ..... **CLC 56; DAC**
See also CA 123; DAM MST; DLB 60

MacNeice, (Frederick) Louis
1907-1963 ...... **CLC 1, 4, 10, 53; DAB**
See also CA 85-88; DAM POET; DLB 10,
20; MTCW

MacNeill, Dand
See Fraser, George MacDonald

Macpherson, James 1736-1796 ...... **LC 29**
See also DLB 109

Macpherson, (Jean) Jay 1931-...... **CLC 14**
See also CA 5-8R; DLB 53

MacShane, Frank 1927-.......... **CLC 39**
See also CA 9-12R; CANR 3, 33; DLB 111

Macumber, Mari
See Sandoz, Mari(e Susette)

Madach, Imre 1823-1864........ **NCLC 19**

Madden, (Jerry) David 1933- .... **CLC 5, 15**
See also CA 1-4R; CAAS 3; CANR 4, 45;
DLB 6; MTCW

Maddern, Al(an)
See Ellison, Harlan (Jay)

Madhubuti, Haki R.
1942- .... **CLC 6, 73; BLC; PC 5**
See also Lee, Don L.
See also BW 2; CA 73-76; CANR 24, 51;
DAM MULT, POET; DLB 5, 41;
DLBD 8

Maepenn, Hugh
See Kuttner, Henry

Maepenn, K. H.
See Kuttner, Henry

Maeterlinck, Maurice 1862-1949 ... **TCLC 3**
See also CA 104; 136; DAM DRAM;
SATA 66

Maginn, William 1794-1842....... **NCLC 8**
See also DLB 110, 159

Mahapatra, Jayanta 1928-......... **CLC 33**
See also CA 73-76; CAAS 9; CANR 15, 33;
DAM MULT

Mahfouz, Naguib (Abdel Aziz Al-Sabilgi)
     1911(?)-
     See Mahfuz, Najib
     See also BEST 89:2; CA 128; DAM NOV;
     MTCW

Mahfuz, Najib . . . . **CLC 52, 55**
     See also Mahfouz, Naguib (Abdel Aziz
     Al-Sabilgi)
     See also DLBY 88

Mahon, Derek 1941- . . . . **CLC 27**
     See also CA 113; 128; DLB 40

Mailer, Norman
     1923- . . . . . . **CLC 1, 2, 3, 4, 5, 8, 11, 14,**
             28, 39, 74; DA; DAB; DAC
     See also AITN 2; CA 9-12R; CABS 1;
     CANR 28; CDALB 1968-1988;
     DAM MST, NOV, POP; DLB 2, 16, 28;
     DLBD 3; DLBY 80, 83; MTCW

Maillet, Antonine 1929- . . . . . . **CLC 54; DAC**
     See also CA 115; 120; CANR 46; DLB 60;
     INT 120

Mais, Roger 1905-1955 . . . . **TCLC 8**
     See also BW 1; CA 105; 124; DLB 125;
     MTCW

Maistre, Joseph de 1753-1821 . . . . **NCLC 37**

Maitland, Sara (Louise) 1950- . . . . . . **CLC 49**
     See also CA 69-72; CANR 13

Major, Clarence
     1936- . . . . **CLC 3, 19, 48; BLC**
     See also BW 2; CA 21-24R; CAAS 6;
     CANR 13, 25; DAM MULT; DLB 33

Major, Kevin (Gerald)
     1949- . . . . **CLC 26; DAC**
     See also AAYA 16; CA 97-100; CANR 21,
     38; CLR 11; DLB 60; INT CANR-21;
     JRDA; MAICYA; SATA 32, 82

Maki, James
     See Ozu, Yasujiro

Malabaila, Damiano
     See Levi, Primo

Malamud, Bernard
     1914-1986 . . . . . . **CLC 1, 2, 3, 5, 8, 9, 11,**
             18, 27, 44, 78, 85; DA; DAB; DAC;
             SSC 15; WLC
     See also AAYA 16; CA 5-8R; 118; CABS 1;
     CANR 28; CDALB 1941-1968;
     DAM MST, NOV, POP; DLB 2, 28, 152;
     DLBY 80, 86; MTCW

Malaparte, Curzio 1898-1957 . . . . . **TCLC 52**

Malcolm, Dan
     See Silverberg, Robert

Malcolm X . . . . **CLC 82; BLC**
     See also Little, Malcolm

Malherbe, Francois de 1555-1628 . . . . . **LC 5**

Mallarme, Stephane
     1842-1898 . . . . **NCLC 4, 41; PC 4**
     See also DAM POET

Mallet-Joris, Francoise 1930- . . . . . . **CLC 11**
     See also CA 65-68; CANR 17; DLB 83

Malley, Ern
     See McAuley, James Phillip

Mallowan, Agatha Christie
     See Christie, Agatha (Mary Clarissa)

Maloff, Saul 1922- . . . . **CLC 5**
     See also CA 33-36R

Malone, Louis
     See MacNeice, (Frederick) Louis

Malone, Michael (Christopher)
     1942- . . . . **CLC 43**
     See also CA 77-80; CANR 14, 32

Malory, (Sir) Thomas
     1410(?)-1471(?) . . . . . . **LC 11; DA; DAB;**
                                          DAC
     See also CDBLB Before 1660; DAM MST;
     DLB 146; SATA 59; SATA-Brief 33

Malouf, (George Joseph) David
     1934- . . . . **CLC 28, 86**
     See also CA 124; CANR 50

Malraux, (Georges-)Andre
     1901-1976 . . . . . . **CLC 1, 4, 9, 13, 15, 57**
     See also CA 21-22; 69-72; CANR 34;
     CAP 2; DAM NOV; DLB 72; MTCW

Malzberg, Barry N(athaniel) 1939- . . . **CLC 7**
     See also CA 61-64; CAAS 4; CANR 16;
     DLB 8

Mamet, David (Alan)
     1947- . . . . . . **CLC 9, 15, 34, 46, 91; DC 4**
     See also AAYA 3; CA 81-84; CABS 3;
     CANR 15, 41; DAM DRAM; DLB 7;
     MTCW

Mamoulian, Rouben (Zachary)
     1897-1987 . . . . **CLC 16**
     See also CA 25-28R; 124

Mandelstam, Osip (Emilievich)
     1891(?)-1938(?) . . . . . . **TCLC 2, 6; PC 14**
     See also CA 104; 150

Mander, (Mary) Jane 1877-1949 . . . **TCLC 31**

Mandiargues, Andre Pieyre de . . . . . . **CLC 41**
     See also Pieyre de Mandiargues, Andre
     See also DLB 83

Mandrake, Ethel Belle
     See Thurman, Wallace (Henry)

Mangan, James Clarence
     1803-1849 . . . . **NCLC 27**

Maniere, J.-E.
     See Giraudoux, (Hippolyte) Jean

Manley, (Mary) Delariviere
     1672(?)-1724 . . . . **LC 1**
     See also DLB 39, 80

Mann, Abel
     See Creasey, John

Mann, (Luiz) Heinrich 1871-1950 . . . **TCLC 9**
     See also CA 106; DLB 66

Mann, (Paul) Thomas
     1875-1955 . . . . **TCLC 2, 8, 14, 21, 35, 44,**
             60; DA; DAB; DAC; SSC 5; WLC
     See also CA 104; 128; DAM MST, NOV;
     DLB 66; MTCW

Manning, David
     See Faust, Frederick (Schiller)

Manning, Frederic 1887(?)-1935 . . . **TCLC 25**
     See also CA 124

Manning, Olivia 1915-1980 . . . . . . **CLC 5, 19**
     See also CA 5-8R; 101; CANR 29; MTCW

Mano, D. Keith 1942- . . . . **CLC 2, 10**
     See also CA 25-28R; CAAS 6; CANR 26;
     DLB 6

Mansfield, Katherine
     . . **TCLC 2, 8, 39; DAB; SSC 9, 23; WLC**
     See also Beauchamp, Kathleen Mansfield
     See also DLB 162

Manso, Peter 1940- . . . . **CLC 39**
     See also CA 29-32R; CANR 44

Mantecon, Juan Jimenez
     See Jimenez (Mantecon), Juan Ramon

Manton, Peter
     See Creasey, John

Man Without a Spleen, A
     See Chekhov, Anton (Pavlovich)

Manzoni, Alessandro 1785-1873 . . **NCLC 29**

Mapu, Abraham (ben Jekutiel)
     1808-1867 . . . . **NCLC 18**

Mara, Sally
     See Queneau, Raymond

Marat, Jean Paul 1743-1793 . . . . **LC 10**

Marcel, Gabriel Honore
     1889-1973 . . . . **CLC 15**
     See also CA 102; 45-48; MTCW

Marchbanks, Samuel
     See Davies, (William) Robertson

Marchi, Giacomo
     See Bassani, Giorgio

Margulies, Donald . . . . **CLC 76**

Marie de France c. 12th cent. - . . . . **CMLC 8**

Marie de l'Incarnation 1599-1672 . . . . **LC 10**

Mariner, Scott
     See Pohl, Frederik

Marinetti, Filippo Tommaso
     1876-1944 . . . . **TCLC 10**
     See also CA 107; DLB 114

Marivaux, Pierre Carlet de Chamblain de
     1688-1763 . . . . **LC 4**

Markandaya, Kamala . . . . **CLC 8, 38**
     See also Taylor, Kamala (Purnaiya)

Markfield, Wallace 1926- . . . . **CLC 8**
     See also CA 69-72; CAAS 3; DLB 2, 28

Markham, Edwin 1852-1940 . . . . . . **TCLC 47**
     See also DLB 54

Markham, Robert
     See Amis, Kingsley (William)

Marks, J
     See Highwater, Jamake (Mamake)

Marks-Highwater, J
     See Highwater, Jamake (Mamake)

Markson, David M(errill) 1927- . . . . **CLC 67**
     See also CA 49-52; CANR 1

Marley, Bob . . . . **CLC 17**
     See also Marley, Robert Nesta

Marley, Robert Nesta 1945-1981
     See Marley, Bob
     See also CA 107; 103

Marlowe, Christopher
     1564-1593 . . . . . **LC 22; DA; DAB; DAC;**
                                      DC 1; WLC
     See also CDBLB Before 1660;
     DAM DRAM, MST; DLB 62

Marmontel, Jean-Francois
     1723-1799 . . . . **LC 2**

Marquand, John P(hillips)
1893-1960 .... **CLC 2, 10**
See also CA 85-88; DLB 9, 102

Marquez, Gabriel (Jose) Garcia
See Garcia Marquez, Gabriel (Jose)

Marquis, Don(ald Robert Perry)
1878-1937 .... **TCLC 7**
See also CA 104; DLB 11, 25

Marric, J. J.
See Creasey, John

Marrow, Bernard
See Moore, Brian

Marryat, Frederick 1792-1848 .... **NCLC 3**
See also DLB 21, 163

Marsden, James
See Creasey, John

Marsh, (Edith) Ngaio
1899-1982 .... **CLC 7, 53**
See also CA 9-12R; CANR 6; DAM POP;
DLB 77; MTCW

Marshall, Garry 1934- .... **CLC 17**
See also AAYA 3; CA 111; SATA 60

Marshall, Paule
1929- .... **CLC 27, 72; BLC; SSC 3**
See also BW 2; CA 77-80; CANR 25;
DAM MULT; DLB 157; MTCW

Marsten, Richard
See Hunter, Evan

Martha, Henry
See Harris, Mark

Martial c. 40-c. 104 .... **PC 10**

Martin, Ken
See Hubbard, L(afayette) Ron(ald)

Martin, Richard
See Creasey, John

Martin, Steve 1945- .... **CLC 30**
See also CA 97-100; CANR 30; MTCW

Martin, Valerie 1948- .... **CLC 89**
See also BEST 90:2; CA 85-88; CANR 49

Martin, Violet Florence
1862-1915 .... **TCLC 51**

Martin, Webber
See Silverberg, Robert

Martindale, Patrick Victor
See White, Patrick (Victor Martindale)

Martin du Gard, Roger
1881-1958 .... **TCLC 24**
See also CA 118; DLB 65

Martineau, Harriet 1802-1876. .... **NCLC 26**
See also DLB 21, 55, 159, 163; YABC 2

Martines, Julia
See O'Faolain, Julia

Martinez, Jacinto Benavente y
See Benavente (y Martinez), Jacinto

Martinez Ruiz, Jose 1873-1967
See Azorin; Ruiz, Jose Martinez
See also CA 93-96; HW

Martinez Sierra, Gregorio
1881-1947 .... **TCLC 6**
See also CA 115

Martinez Sierra, Maria (de la O'LeJarraga)
1874-1974 .... **TCLC 6**
See also CA 115

Martinsen, Martin
See Follett, Ken(neth Martin)

Martinson, Harry (Edmund)
1904-1978 .... **CLC 14**
See also CA 77-80; CANR 34

Marut, Ret
See Traven, B.

Marut, Robert
See Traven, B.

Marvell, Andrew
1621-1678 ..... **LC 4; DA; DAB; DAC;**
PC 10; WLC
See also CDBLB 1660-1789; DAM MST,
POET; DLB 131

Marx, Karl (Heinrich)
1818-1883 .... **NCLC 17**
See also DLB 129

Masaoka Shiki. .... **TCLC 18**
See also Masaoka Tsunenori

Masaoka Tsunenori 1867-1902
See Masaoka Shiki
See also CA 117

Masefield, John (Edward)
1878-1967 .... **CLC 11, 47**
See also CA 19-20; 25-28R; CANR 33;
CAP 2; CDBLB 1890-1914; DAM POET;
DLB 10, 19, 153, 160; MTCW; SATA 19

Maso, Carole 19(?)- .... **CLC 44**

Mason, Bobbie Ann
1940- .... **CLC 28, 43, 82; SSC 4**
See also AAYA 5; CA 53-56; CANR 11,
31; DLBY 87; INT CANR-31; MTCW

Mason, Ernst
See Pohl, Frederik

Mason, Lee W.
See Malzberg, Barry N(athaniel)

Mason, Nick 1945- .... **CLC 35**

Mason, Tally
See Derleth, August (William)

Mass, William
See Gibson, William

Masters, Edgar Lee
1868-1950 ...... **TCLC 2, 25; DA; DAC;**
PC 1
See also CA 104; 133; CDALB 1865-1917;
DAM MST, POET; DLB 54; MTCW

Masters, Hilary 1928- .... **CLC 48**
See also CA 25-28R; CANR 13, 47

Mastrosimone, William 19(?)- ...... **CLC 36**

Mathe, Albert
See Camus, Albert

Matheson, Richard Burton 1926- ... **CLC 37**
See also CA 97-100; DLB 8, 44; INT 97-100

Mathews, Harry 1930- .... **CLC 6, 52**
See also CA 21-24R; CAAS 6; CANR 18,
40

Mathews, John Joseph 1894-1979... **CLC 84**
See also CA 19-20; 142; CANR 45; CAP 2;
DAM MULT; NNAL

Mathias, Roland (Glyn) 1915- ...... **CLC 45**
See also CA 97-100; CANR 19, 41; DLB 27

Matsuo Basho 1644-1694........... **PC 3**
See also DAM POET

Mattheson, Rodney
See Creasey, John

Matthews, Greg 1949- .... **CLC 45**
See also CA 135

Matthews, William 1942- .... **CLC 40**
See also CA 29-32R; CAAS 18; CANR 12;
DLB 5

Matthias, John (Edward) 1941- ...... **CLC 9**
See also CA 33-36R

Matthiessen, Peter
1927- .... **CLC 5, 7, 11, 32, 64**
See also AAYA 6; BEST 90:4; CA 9-12R;
CANR 21, 50; DAM NOV; DLB 6;
MTCW; SATA 27

Maturin, Charles Robert
1780(?)-1824 .... **NCLC 6**

Matute (Ausejo), Ana Maria
1925- .... **CLC 11**
See also CA 89-92; MTCW

Maugham, W. S.
See Maugham, W(illiam) Somerset

Maugham, W(illiam) Somerset
1874-1965 .... **CLC 1, 11, 15, 67, 93;**
DA; DAB; DAC; SSC 8; WLC
See also CA 5-8R; 25-28R; CANR 40;
CDBLB 1914-1945; DAM DRAM, MST,
NOV; DLB 10, 36, 77, 100, 162; MTCW;
SATA 54

Maugham, William Somerset
See Maugham, W(illiam) Somerset

Maupassant, (Henri Rene Albert) Guy de
1850-1893 ..... **NCLC 1, 42; DA; DAB;**
DAC; SSC 1; WLC
See also DAM MST; DLB 123

Maurhut, Richard
See Traven, B.

Mauriac, Claude 1914- .... **CLC 9**
See also CA 89-92; DLB 83

Mauriac, Francois (Charles)
1885-1970 .... **CLC 4, 9, 56**
See also CA 25-28; CAP 2; DLB 65;
MTCW

Mavor, Osborne Henry 1888-1951
See Bridie, James
See also CA 104

Maxwell, William (Keepers, Jr.)
1908- .... **CLC 19**
See also CA 93-96; DLBY 80; INT 93-96

May, Elaine 1932- .... **CLC 16**
See also CA 124; 142; DLB 44

Mayakovski, Vladimir (Vladimirovich)
1893-1930 .... **TCLC 4, 18**
See also CA 104

Mayhew, Henry 1812-1887 ...... **NCLC 31**
See also DLB 18, 55

Mayle, Peter 1939(?)- .... **CLC 89**
See also CA 139

Maynard, Joyce 1953- .... **CLC 23**
See also CA 111; 129

Mayne, William (James Carter)
1928- .... **CLC 12**
See also CA 9-12R; CANR 37; CLR 25;
JRDA; MAICYA; SAAS 11; SATA 6, 68

Mayo, Jim
See L'Amour, Louis (Dearborn)

Melmoth, Sebastian
See Wilde, Oscar (Fingal O'Flahertie Wills)

Meltzer, Milton 1915- . . . . **CLC 26**
See also AAYA 8; CA 13-16R; CANR 38;
CLR 13; DLB 61; JRDA; MAICYA;
SAAS 1; SATA 1, 50, 80

Melville, Herman
1819-1891 . . . . . **NCLC 3, 12, 29, 45, 49;**
DA; DAB; DAC; SSC 1, 17; WLC
See also CDALB 1640-1865; DAM MST,
NOV; DLB 3, 74; SATA 59

Menander
c. 342B.C.-c. 292B.C. . . . . **CMLC 9; DC 3**
See also DAM DRAM

Mencken, H(enry) L(ouis)
1880-1956 . . . . **TCLC 13**
See also CA 105; 125; CDALB 1917-1929;
DLB 11, 29, 63, 137; MTCW

Mercer, David 1928-1980. . . . . **CLC 5**
See also CA 9-12R; 102; CANR 23;
DAM DRAM; DLB 13; MTCW

Merchant, Paul
See Ellison, Harlan (Jay)

Meredith, George 1828-1909 . . . **TCLC 17, 43**
See also CA 117; CDBLB 1832-1890;
DAM POET; DLB 18, 35, 57, 159

Meredith, William (Morris)
1919- . . . . **CLC 4, 13, 22, 55**
See also CA 9-12R; CAAS 14; CANR 6, 40;
DAM POET; DLB 5

Merezhkovsky, Dmitry Sergeyevich
1865-1941 . . . . **TCLC 29**

Merimee, Prosper
1803-1870 . . . . **NCLC 6; SSC 7**
See also DLB 119

Merkin, Daphne 1954- . . . . **CLC 44**
See also CA 123

Merlin, Arthur
See Blish, James (Benjamin)

Merrill, James (Ingram)
1926-1995 . . . . **CLC 2, 3, 6, 8, 13, 18, 34,**
91
See also CA 13-16R; 147; CANR 10, 49;
DAM POET; DLB 5, 165; DLBY 85;
INT CANR-10; MTCW

Merriman, Alex
See Silverberg, Robert

Merritt, E. B.
See Waddington, Miriam

Merton, Thomas
1915-1968 . . **CLC 1, 3, 11, 34, 83; PC 10**
See also CA 5-8R; 25-28R; CANR 22;
DLB 48; DLBY 81; MTCW

Merwin, W(illiam) S(tanley)
1927- . . . **CLC 1, 2, 3, 5, 8, 13, 18, 45, 88**
See also CA 13-16R; CANR 15, 51;
DAM POET; DLB 5; INT CANR-15;
MTCW

Metcalf, John 1938- . . . . **CLC 37**
See also CA 113; DLB 60

Metcalf, Suzanne
See Baum, L(yman) Frank

Mew, Charlotte (Mary)
1870-1928 . . . . **TCLC 8**
See also CA 105; DLB 19, 135

Mewshaw, Michael 1943- . . . . **CLC 9**
See also CA 53-56; CANR 7, 47; DLBY 80

Meyer, June
See Jordan, June

Meyer, Lynn
See Slavitt, David R(ytman)

Meyer-Meyrink, Gustav 1868-1932
See Meyrink, Gustav
See also CA 117

Meyers, Jeffrey 1939- . . . . **CLC 39**
See also CA 73-76; DLB 111

Meynell, Alice (Christina Gertrude Thompson)
1847-1922 . . . . **TCLC 6**
See also CA 104; DLB 19, 98

Meyrink, Gustav . . . . **TCLC 21**
See also Meyer-Meyrink, Gustav
See also DLB 81

Michaels, Leonard
1933- . . . . **CLC 6, 25; SSC 16**
See also CA 61-64; CANR 21; DLB 130;
MTCW

Michaux, Henri 1899-1984 . . . . . . **CLC 8, 19**
See also CA 85-88; 114

Michelangelo 1475-1564. . . . . **LC 12**

Michelet, Jules 1798-1874 . . . . . . **NCLC 31**

Michener, James A(lbert)
1907(?)- . . . . **CLC 1, 5, 11, 29, 60**
See also AITN 1; BEST 90:1; CA 5-8R;
CANR 21, 45; DAM NOV, POP; DLB 6;
MTCW

Mickiewicz, Adam 1798-1855 . . . . . **NCLC 3**

Middleton, Christopher 1926- . . . . . . **CLC 13**
See also CA 13-16R; CANR 29; DLB 40

Middleton, Richard (Barham)
1882-1911 . . . . **TCLC 56**
See also DLB 156

Middleton, Stanley 1919- . . . . **CLC 7, 38**
See also CA 25-28R; CAAS 23; CANR 21,
46; DLB 14

Middleton, Thomas 1580-1627. . . . . . . **DC 5**
See also DAM DRAM, MST; DLB 58

Migueis, Jose Rodrigues 1901- . . . . . **CLC 10**

Mikszath, Kalman 1847-1910 . . . . . **TCLC 31**

Miles, Josephine
1911-1985 . . . . **CLC 1, 2, 14, 34, 39**
See also CA 1-4R; 116; CANR 2;
DAM POET; DLB 48

Militant
See Sandburg, Carl (August)

Mill, John Stuart 1806-1873 . . . . . **NCLC 11**
See also CDBLB 1832-1890; DLB 55

Millar, Kenneth 1915-1983 . . . . **CLC 14**
See also Macdonald, Ross
See also CA 9-12R; 110; CANR 16;
DAM POP; DLB 2; DLBD 6; DLBY 83;
MTCW

Millay, E. Vincent
See Millay, Edna St. Vincent

Millay, Edna St. Vincent
1892-1950 . . . . . **TCLC 4, 49; DA; DAB;**
DAC; PC 6
See also CA 104; 130; CDALB 1917-1929;
DAM MST, POET; DLB 45; MTCW

Miller, Arthur
1915- . . . . **CLC 1, 2, 6, 10, 15, 26, 47, 78;**
DA; DAB; DAC; DC 1; WLC
See also AAYA 15; AITN 1; CA 1-4R;
CABS 3; CANR 2, 30;
CDALB 1941-1968; DAM DRAM, MST;
DLB 7; MTCW

Miller, Henry (Valentine)
1891-1980 . . . . **CLC 1, 2, 4, 9, 14, 43, 84;**
DA; DAB; DAC; WLC
See also CA 9-12R; 97-100; CANR 33;
CDALB 1929-1941; DAM MST, NOV;
DLB 4, 9; DLBY 80; MTCW

Miller, Jason 1939(?)- . . . . **CLC 2**
See also AITN 1; CA 73-76; DLB 7

Miller, Sue 1943- . . . . **CLC 44**
See also BEST 90:3; CA 139; DAM POP;
DLB 143

Miller, Walter M(ichael, Jr.)
1923- . . . . **CLC 4, 30**
See also CA 85-88; DLB 8

Millett, Kate 1934- . . . . **CLC 67**
See also AITN 1; CA 73-76; CANR 32;
MTCW

Millhauser, Steven 1943- . . . . **CLC 21, 54**
See also CA 110; 111; DLB 2; INT 111

Millin, Sarah Gertrude 1889-1968 . . **CLC 49**
See also CA 102; 93-96

Milne, A(lan) A(lexander)
1882-1956 . . . . **TCLC 6; DAB; DAC**
See also CA 104; 133; CLR 1, 26;
DAM MST; DLB 10, 77, 100, 160;
MAICYA; MTCW; YABC 1

Milner, Ron(ald) 1938- . . . . . . **CLC 56; BLC**
See also AITN 1; BW 1; CA 73-76;
CANR 24; DAM MULT; DLB 38;
MTCW

Milosz, Czeslaw
1911- . . . **CLC 5, 11, 22, 31, 56, 82; PC 8**
See also CA 81-84; CANR 23, 51;
DAM MST, POET; MTCW

Milton, John
1608-1674 . . . . . . **LC 9; DA; DAB; DAC;**
WLC
See also CDBLB 1660-1789; DAM MST,
POET; DLB 131, 151

Min, Anchee 1957- . . . . **CLC 86**
See also CA 146

Minehaha, Cornelius
See Wedekind, (Benjamin) Frank(lin)

Miner, Valerie 1947- . . . . **CLC 40**
See also CA 97-100

Minimo, Duca
See D'Annunzio, Gabriele

Minot, Susan 1956- . . . . **CLC 44**
See also CA 134

Minus, Ed 1938- . . . . **CLC 39**

Miranda, Javier
See Bioy Casares, Adolfo

Mirbeau, Octave 1848-1917 . . . . **TCLC 55**
See also DLB 123

Miro (Ferrer), Gabriel (Francisco Victor)
1879-1930 . . . . **TCLC 5**
See also CA 104

Morgenstern, S.
See Goldman, William (W.)

Moricz, Zsigmond 1879-1942 . . . . . **TCLC 33**

Morike, Eduard (Friedrich)
1804-1875 . . . . **NCLC 10**
See also DLB 133

Mori Ogai . . . . **TCLC 14**
See also Mori Rintaro

Mori Rintaro 1862-1922
See Mori Ogai
See also CA 110

Moritz, Karl Philipp 1756-1793 . . . . . . **LC 2**
See also DLB 94

Morland, Peter Henry
See Faust, Frederick (Schiller)

Morren, Theophil
See Hofmannsthal, Hugo von

Morris, Bill 1952- . . . . **CLC 76**

Morris, Julian
See West, Morris L(anglo)

Morris, Steveland Judkins 1950(?)-
See Wonder, Stevie
See also CA 111

Morris, William 1834-1896 . . . . **NCLC 4**
See also CDBLB 1832-1890; DLB 18, 35,
57, 156

Morris, Wright 1910- . . . **CLC 1, 3, 7, 18, 37**
See also CA 9-12R; CANR 21; DLB 2;
DLBY 81; MTCW

Morrison, Chloe Anthony Wofford
See Morrison, Toni

Morrison, James Douglas 1943-1971
See Morrison, Jim
See also CA 73-76; CANR 40

Morrison, Jim . . . . **CLC 17**
See also Morrison, James Douglas

Morrison, Toni
1931- . . . . **CLC 4, 10, 22, 55, 81, 87;
BLC; DA; DAB; DAC**
See also AAYA 1; BW 2; CA 29-32R;
CANR 27, 42; CDALB 1968-1988;
DAM MST, MULT, NOV, POP; DLB 6,
33, 143; DLBY 81; MTCW; SATA 57

Morrison, Van 1945- . . . . **CLC 21**
See also CA 116

Mortimer, John (Clifford)
1923- . . . . **CLC 28, 43**
See also CA 13-16R; CANR 21;
CDBLB 1960 to Present; DAM DRAM,
POP; DLB 13; INT CANR-21; MTCW

Mortimer, Penelope (Ruth) 1918- . . . . **CLC 5**
See also CA 57-60; CANR 45

Morton, Anthony
See Creasey, John

Mosher, Howard Frank 1943- . . . . . . **CLC 62**
See also CA 139

Mosley, Nicholas 1923- . . . . **CLC 43, 70**
See also CA 69-72; CANR 41; DLB 14

Moss, Howard
1922-1987 . . . . **CLC 7, 14, 45, 50**
See also CA 1-4R; 123; CANR 1, 44;
DAM POET; DLB 5

Mossgiel, Rab
See Burns, Robert

Motion, Andrew (Peter) 1952- . . . . . . **CLC 47**
See also CA 146; DLB 40

Motley, Willard (Francis)
1909-1965 . . . . **CLC 18**
See also BW 1; CA 117; 106; DLB 76, 143

Motoori, Norinaga 1730-1801 . . . . **NCLC 45**

Mott, Michael (Charles Alston)
1930- . . . . **CLC 15, 34**
See also CA 5-8R; CAAS 7; CANR 7, 29

Mountain Wolf Woman
1884-1960 . . . . **CLC 92**
See also CA 144; NNAL

Moure, Erin 1955- . . . . **CLC 88**
See also CA 113; DLB 60

Mowat, Farley (McGill)
1921- . . . . **CLC 26; DAC**
See also AAYA 1; CA 1-4R; CANR 4, 24,
42; CLR 20; DAM MST; DLB 68;
INT CANAR-24; JRDA; MAICYA;
MTCW; SATA 3, 55

Moyers, Bill 1934- . . . . **CLC 74**
See also AITN 2; CA 61-64; CANR 31

Mphahlele, Es'kia
See Mphahlele, Ezekiel
See also DLB 125

Mphahlele, Ezekiel 1919- . . . . . **CLC 25; BLC**
See also Mphahlele, Es'kia
See also BW 2; CA 81-84; CANR 26;
DAM MULT

Mqhayi, S(amuel) E(dward) K(rune Loliwe)
1875-1945 . . . . **TCLC 25; BLC**
See also DAM MULT

Mr. Martin
See Burroughs, William S(eward)

Mrozek, Slawomir 1930- . . . . **CLC 3, 13**
See also CA 13-16R; CAAS 10; CANR 29;
MTCW

Mrs. Belloc-Lowndes
See Lowndes, Marie Adelaide (Belloc)

Mtwa, Percy (?)- . . . . **CLC 47**

Mueller, Lisel 1924- . . . . **CLC 13, 51**
See also CA 93-96; DLB 105

Muir, Edwin 1887-1959 . . . . **TCLC 2**
See also CA 104; DLB 20, 100

Muir, John 1838-1914 . . . . **TCLC 28**

Mujica Lainez, Manuel
1910-1984 . . . . **CLC 31**
See also Lainez, Manuel Mujica
See also CA 81-84; 112; CANR 32; HW

Mukherjee, Bharati 1940- . . . . **CLC 53**
See also BEST 89:2; CA 107; CANR 45;
DAM NOV; DLB 60; MTCW

Muldoon, Paul 1951- . . . . **CLC 32, 72**
See also CA 113; 129; DAM POET;
DLB 40; INT 129

Mulisch, Harry 1927- . . . . **CLC 42**
See also CA 9-12R; CANR 6, 26

Mull, Martin 1943- . . . . **CLC 17**
See also CA 105

Mulock, Dinah Maria
See Craik, Dinah Maria (Mulock)

Munford, Robert 1737(?)-1783 . . . . **LC 5**
See also DLB 31

Mungo, Raymond 1946- . . . . **CLC 72**
See also CA 49-52; CANR 2

Munro, Alice
1931- . . . **CLC 6, 10, 19, 50; DAC; SSC 3**
See also AITN 2; CA 33-36R; CANR 33;
DAM MST, NOV; DLB 53; MTCW;
SATA 29

Munro, H(ector) H(ugh) 1870-1916
See Saki
See also CA 104; 130; CDBLB 1890-1914;
DA; DAB; DAC; DAM MST, NOV;
DLB 34, 162; MTCW; WLC

Murasaki, Lady . . . . **CMLC 1**

Murdoch, (Jean) Iris
1919- . . . . . . **CLC 1, 2, 3, 4, 6, 8, 11, 15,
22, 31, 51; DAB; DAC**
See also CA 13-16R; CANR 8, 43;
CDBLB 1960 to Present; DAM MST,
NOV; DLB 14; INT CANR-8; MTCW

Murfree, Mary Noailles
1850-1922 . . . . **SSC 22**
See also CA 122; DLB 12, 74

Murnau, Friedrich Wilhelm
See Plumpe, Friedrich Wilhelm

Murphy, Richard 1927- . . . . **CLC 41**
See also CA 29-32R; DLB 40

Murphy, Sylvia 1937- . . . . **CLC 34**
See also CA 121

Murphy, Thomas (Bernard) 1935- . . . **CLC 51**
See also CA 101

Murray, Albert L. 1916- . . . . **CLC 73**
See also BW 2; CA 49-52; CANR 26;
DLB 38

Murray, Les(lie) A(llan) 1938- . . . . . **CLC 40**
See also CA 21-24R; CANR 11, 27;
DAM POET

Murry, J. Middleton
See Murry, John Middleton

Murry, John Middleton
1889-1957 . . . . **TCLC 16**
See also CA 118; DLB 149

Musgrave, Susan 1951- . . . . **CLC 13, 54**
See also CA 69-72; CANR 45

Musil, Robert (Edler von)
1880-1942 . . . . **TCLC 12; SSC 18**
See also CA 109; DLB 81, 124

Muske, Carol 1945- . . . . **CLC 90**
See also Muske-Dukes, Carol (Anne)

Muske-Dukes, Carol (Anne) 1945-
See Muske, Carol
See also CA 65-68; CANR 32

Musset, (Louis Charles) Alfred de
1810-1857 . . . . **NCLC 7**

My Brother's Brother
See Chekhov, Anton (Pavlovich)

Myers, L. H. 1881-1944 . . . . **TCLC 59**
See also DLB 15

Myers, Walter Dean 1937- . . . **CLC 35; BLC**
See also AAYA 4; BW 2; CA 33-36R;
CANR 20, 42; CLR 4, 16, 35;
DAM MULT, NOV; DLB 33;
INT CANR-20; JRDA; MAICYA;
SAAS 2; SATA 41, 71; SATA-Brief 27

Myers, Walter M.
See Myers, Walter Dean

Myles, Symon
See Follett, Ken(neth Martin)

Nabokov, Vladimir (Vladimirovich)
1899-1977 ..... CLC **1, 2, 3, 6, 8, 11, 15,
23, 44, 46, 64; DA; DAB; DAC; SSC 11;
WLC**
See also CA 5-8R; 69-72; CANR 20;
CDALB 1941-1968; DAM MST, NOV;
DLB 2; DLBD 3; DLBY 80, 91; MTCW

Nagai Kafu..................... TCLC **51**
See also Nagai Sokichi

Nagai Sokichi 1879-1959
See Nagai Kafu
See also CA 117

Nagy, Laszlo 1925-1978........... CLC **7**
See also CA 129; 112

Naipaul, Shiva(dhar Srinivasa)
1945-1985 .... CLC **32, 39**
See also CA 110; 112; 116; CANR 33;
DAM NOV; DLB 157; DLBY 85;
MTCW

Naipaul, V(idiadhar) S(urajprasad)
1932- .... CLC **4, 7, 9, 13, 18, 37; DAB;
DAC**
See also CA 1-4R; CANR 1, 33, 51;
CDBLB 1960 to Present; DAM MST,
NOV; DLB 125; DLBY 85; MTCW

Nakos, Lilika 1899(?)-............ CLC **29**

Narayan, R(asipuram) K(rishnaswami)
1906-.................. CLC **7, 28, 47**
See also CA 81-84; CANR 33; DAM NOV;
MTCW; SATA 62

Nash, (Frediric) Ogden 1902-1971 .. CLC **23**
See also CA 13-14; 29-32R; CANR 34;
CAP 1; DAM POET; DLB 11;
MAICYA; MTCW; SATA 2, 46

Nathan, Daniel
See Dannay, Frederic

Nathan, George Jean 1882-1958 ... TCLC **18**
See also Hatteras, Owen
See also CA 114; DLB 137

Natsume, Kinnosuke 1867-1916
See Natsume, Soseki
See also CA 104

Natsume, Soseki .... TCLC **2, 10**
See also Natsume, Kinnosuke

Natti, (Mary) Lee 1919-
See Kingman, Lee
See also CA 5-8R; CANR 2

Naylor, Gloria
1950- ..... CLC **28, 52; BLC; DA; DAC**
See also AAYA 6; BW 2; CA 107;
CANR 27, 51; DAM MST, MULT,
NOV, POP; MTCW

Neihardt, John Gneisenau
1881-1973 .... CLC **32**
See also CA 13-14; CAP 1; DLB 9, 54

Nekrasov, Nikolai Alekseevich
1821-1878 .... NCLC **11**

Nelligan, Emile 1879-1941....... TCLC **14**
See also CA 114; DLB 92

Nelson, Willie 1933-.............. CLC **17**
See also CA 107

Nemerov, Howard (Stanley)
1920-1991 .... CLC **2, 6, 9, 36**
See also CA 1-4R; 134; CABS 2; CANR 1,
27; DAM POET; DLB 5, 6; DLBY 83;
INT CANR-27; MTCW

Neruda, Pablo
1904-1973 ..... CLC **1, 2, 5, 7, 9, 28, 62;
DA; DAB; DAC; HLC; PC 4; WLC**
See also CA 19-20; 45-48; CAP 2;
DAM MST, MULT, POET; HW; MTCW

Nerval, Gerard de
1808-1855 ..... NCLC **1; PC 13; SSC 18**

Nervo, (Jose) Amado (Ruiz de)
1870-1919 .... TCLC **11**
See also CA 109; 131; HW

Nessi, Pio Baroja y
See Baroja (y Nessi), Pio

Nestroy, Johann 1801-1862...... NCLC **42**
See also DLB 133

Neufeld, John (Arthur) 1938- ...... CLC **17**
See also AAYA 11; CA 25-28R; CANR 11,
37; MAICYA; SAAS 3; SATA 6, 81

Neville, Emily Cheney 1919-....... CLC **12**
See also CA 5-8R; CANR 3, 37; JRDA;
MAICYA; SAAS 2; SATA 1

Newbound, Bernard Slade 1930-
See Slade, Bernard
See also CA 81-84; CANR 49;
DAM DRAM

Newby, P(ercy) H(oward)
1918- .... CLC **2, 13**
See also CA 5-8R; CANR 32; DAM NOV;
DLB 15; MTCW

Newlove, Donald 1928- .... CLC **6**
See also CA 29-32R; CANR 25

Newlove, John (Herbert) 1938-..... CLC **14**
See also CA 21-24R; CANR 9, 25

Newman, Charles 1938-.......... CLC **2, 8**
See also CA 21-24R

Newman, Edwin (Harold) 1919- .... CLC **14**
See also AITN 1; CA 69-72; CANR 5

Newman, John Henry
1801-1890 .... NCLC **38**
See also DLB 18, 32, 55

Newton, Suzanne 1936-........... CLC **35**
See also CA 41-44R; CANR 14; JRDA;
SATA 5, 77

Nexo, Martin Andersen
1869-1954 .... TCLC **43**

Nezval, Vitezslav 1900-1958 ...... TCLC **44**
See also CA 123

Ng, Fae Myenne 1957(?)-.......... CLC **81**
See also CA 146

Ngema, Mbongeni 1955- .... CLC **57**
See also BW 2; CA 143

Ngugi, James T(hiong'o)........ CLC **3, 7, 13**
See also Ngugi wa Thiong'o

Ngugi wa Thiong'o 1938-..... CLC **36; BLC**
See also Ngugi, James T(hiong'o)
See also BW 2; CA 81-84; CANR 27;
DAM MULT, NOV; DLB 125; MTCW

Nichol, B(arrie) P(hillip)
1944-1988 .... CLC **18**
See also CA 53-56; DLB 53; SATA 66

Nichols, John (Treadwell) 1940- .... CLC **38**
See also CA 9-12R; CAAS 2; CANR 6;
DLBY 82

Nichols, Leigh
See Koontz, Dean R(ay)

Nichols, Peter (Richard)
1927-.................. CLC **5, 36, 65**
See also CA 104; CANR 33; DLB 13;
MTCW

Nicolas, F. R. E.
See Freeling, Nicolas

Niedecker, Lorine 1903-1970.... CLC **10, 42**
See also CA 25-28; CAP 2; DAM POET;
DLB 48

Nietzsche, Friedrich (Wilhelm)
1844-1900 .... TCLC **10, 18, 55**
See also CA 107; 121; DLB 129

Nievo, Ippolito 1831-1861 .... NCLC **22**

Nightingale, Anne Redmon 1943-
See Redmon, Anne
See also CA 103

Nik. T. O.
See Annensky, Innokenty Fyodorovich

Nin, Anais
1903-1977 ...... CLC **1, 4, 8, 11, 14, 60;
SSC 10**
See also AITN 2; CA 13-16R; 69-72;
CANR 22; DAM NOV, POP; DLB 2, 4,
152; MTCW

Nishiwaki, Junzaburo 1894-1982 .... PC **15**
See also CA 107

Nissenson, Hugh 1933-........... CLC **4, 9**
See also CA 17-20R; CANR 27; DLB 28

Niven, Larry .... CLC **8**
See also Niven, Laurence Van Cott
See also DLB 8

Niven, Laurence Van Cott 1938-
See Niven, Larry
See also CA 21-24R; CAAS 12; CANR 14,
44; DAM POP; MTCW

Nixon, Agnes Eckhardt 1927-...... CLC **21**
See also CA 110

Nizan, Paul 1905-1940........... TCLC **40**
See also DLB 72

Nkosi, Lewis 1936-.......... CLC **45; BLC**
See also BW 1; CA 65-68; CANR 27;
DAM MULT; DLB 157

Nodier, (Jean) Charles (Emmanuel)
1780-1844 .... NCLC **19**
See also DLB 119

Nolan, Christopher 1965-.......... CLC **58**
See also CA 111

Noon, Jeff 1957-.................. CLC **91**
See also CA 148

Norden, Charles
See Durrell, Lawrence (George)

Nordhoff, Charles (Bernard)
1887-1947 .... TCLC **23**
See also CA 108; DLB 9; SATA 23

Norfolk, Lawrence 1963-.......... CLC **76**
See also CA 144

Norman, Marsha 1947- .... CLC **28**
See also CA 105; CABS 3; CANR 41;
DAM DRAM; DLBY 84

Olsen, Tillie
1913- ..... **CLC 4, 13; DA; DAB; DAC;**
SSC 11
See also CA 1-4R; CANR 1, 43;
DAM MST; DLB 28; DLBY 80; MTCW

Olson, Charles (John)
1910-1970 ..... **CLC 1, 2, 5, 6, 9, 11, 29**
See also CA 13-16; 25-28R; CABS 2;
CANR 35; CAP 1; DAM POET; DLB 5,
16; MTCW

Olson, Toby 1937- .... **CLC 28**
See also CA 65-68; CANR 9, 31

Olyesha, Yuri
See Olesha, Yuri (Karlovich)

Ondaatje, (Philip) Michael
1943- ... **CLC 14, 29, 51, 76; DAB; DAC**
See also CA 77-80; CANR 42; DAM MST;
DLB 60

Oneal, Elizabeth 1934-
See Oneal, Zibby
See also CA 106; CANR 28; MAICYA;
SATA 30, 82

Oneal, Zibby .... **CLC 30**
See also Oneal, Elizabeth
See also AAYA 5; CLR 13; JRDA

O'Neill, Eugene (Gladstone)
1888-1953 ...... **TCLC 1, 6, 27, 49; DA;**
DAB; DAC; WLC
See also AITN 1; CA 110; 132;
CDALB 1929-1941; DAM DRAM, MST;
DLB 7; MTCW

Onetti, Juan Carlos
1909-1994 .... **CLC 7, 10; SSC 23**
See also CA 85-88; 145; CANR 32;
DAM MULT, NOV; DLB 113; HW;
MTCW

O Nuallain, Brian 1911-1966
See O'Brien, Flann
See also CA 21-22; 25-28R; CAP 2

Oppen, George 1908-1984 .... **CLC 7, 13, 34**
See also CA 13-16R; 113; CANR 8; DLB 5,
165

Oppenheim, E(dward) Phillips
1866-1946 .... **TCLC 45**
See also CA 111; DLB 70

Orlovitz, Gil 1918-1973 .... **CLC 22**
See also CA 77-80; 45-48; DLB 2, 5

Orris
See Ingelow, Jean

Ortega y Gasset, Jose
1883-1955 .... **TCLC 9; HLC**
See also CA 106; 130; DAM MULT; HW;
MTCW

Ortese, Anna Maria 1914-........ **CLC 89**

Ortiz, Simon J(oseph) 1941- .... **CLC 45**
See also CA 134; DAM MULT, POET;
DLB 120; NNAL

Orton, Joe .... **CLC 4, 13, 43; DC 3**
See also Orton, John Kingsley
See also CDBLB 1960 to Present; DLB 13

Orton, John Kingsley 1933-1967
See Orton, Joe
See also CA 85-88; CANR 35;
DAM DRAM; MTCW

Orwell, George
..... **TCLC 2, 6, 15, 31, 51; DAB; WLC**
See also Blair, Eric (Arthur)
See also CDBLB 1945-1960; DLB 15, 98

Osborne, David
See Silverberg, Robert

Osborne, George
See Silverberg, Robert

Osborne, John (James)
1929-1994 ..... **CLC 1, 2, 5, 11, 45; DA;**
DAB; DAC; WLC
See also CA 13-16R; 147; CANR 21;
CDBLB 1945-1960; DAM DRAM, MST;
DLB 13; MTCW

Osborne, Lawrence 1958- .... **CLC 50**

Oshima, Nagisa 1932- .... **CLC 20**
See also CA 116; 121

Oskison, John Milton
1874-1947 .... **TCLC 35**
See also CA 144; DAM MULT; NNAL

Ossoli, Sarah Margaret (Fuller marchesa d')
1810-1850
See Fuller, Margaret
See also SATA 25

Ostrovsky, Alexander
1823-1886 .... **NCLC 30**

Otero, Blas de 1916-1979.......... **CLC 11**
See also CA 89-92; DLB 134

Otto, Whitney 1955-............... **CLC 70**
See also CA 140

Ouida .... **TCLC 43**
See also De La Ramee, (Marie) Louise
See also DLB 18, 156

Ousmane, Sembene 1923- .... **CLC 66; BLC**
See also BW 1; CA 117; 125; MTCW

Ovid 43B.C.-18(?)......... **CMLC 7; PC 2**
See also DAM POET

Owen, Hugh
See Faust, Frederick (Schiller)

Owen, Wilfred (Edward Salter)
1893-1918 ...... **TCLC 5, 27; DA; DAB;**
DAC; WLC
See also CA 104; 141; CDBLB 1914-1945;
DAM MST, POET; DLB 20

Owens, Rochelle 1936-............. **CLC 8**
See also CA 17-20R; CAAS 2; CANR 39

Oz, Amos 1939- ... **CLC 5, 8, 11, 27, 33, 54**
See also CA 53-56; CANR 27, 47;
DAM NOV; MTCW

Ozick, Cynthia
1928- .... **CLC 3, 7, 28, 62; SSC 15**
See also BEST 90:1; CA 17-20R; CANR 23;
DAM NOV, POP; DLB 28, 152;
DLBY 82; INT CANR-23; MTCW

Ozu, Yasujiro 1903-1963 .... **CLC 16**
See also CA 112

Pacheco, C.
See Pessoa, Fernando (Antonio Nogueira)

Pa Chin .... **CLC 18**
See also Li Fei-kan

Pack, Robert 1929-............... **CLC 13**
See also CA 1-4R; CANR 3, 44; DLB 5

Padgett, Lewis
See Kuttner, Henry

Padilla (Lorenzo), Heberto 1932-... **CLC 38**
See also AITN 1; CA 123; 131; HW

Page, Jimmy 1944-............... **CLC 12**

Page, Louise 1955-............... **CLC 40**
See also CA 140

Page, P(atricia) K(athleen)
1916- .... **CLC 7, 18; DAC; PC 12**
See also CA 53-56; CANR 4, 22;
DAM MST; DLB 68; MTCW

Page, Thomas Nelson 1853-1922.... **SSC 23**
See also CA 118; DLB 12, 78; DLBD 13

Paget, Violet 1856-1935
See Lee, Vernon
See also CA 104

Paget-Lowe, Henry
See Lovecraft, H(oward) P(hillips)

Paglia, Camille (Anna) 1947-....... **CLC 68**
See also CA 140

Paige, Richard
See Koontz, Dean R(ay)

Pakenham, Antonia
See Fraser, (Lady) Antonia (Pakenham)

Palamas, Kostes 1859-1943 .... **TCLC 5**
See also CA 105

Palazzeschi, Aldo 1885-1974....... **CLC 11**
See also CA 89-92; 53-56; DLB 114

Paley, Grace 1922-.... **CLC 4, 6, 37; SSC 8**
See also CA 25-28R; CANR 13, 46;
DAM POP; DLB 28; INT CANR-13;
MTCW

Palin, Michael (Edward) 1943-..... **CLC 21**
See also Monty Python
See also CA 107; CANR 35; SATA 67

Palliser, Charles 1947-............ **CLC 65**
See also CA 136

Palma, Ricardo 1833-1919........ **TCLC 29**

Pancake, Breece Dexter 1952-1979
See Pancake, Breece D'J
See also CA 123; 109

Pancake, Breece D'J............... **CLC 29**
See also Pancake, Breece Dexter
See also DLB 130

Panko, Rudy
See Gogol, Nikolai (Vasilyevich)

Papadiamantis, Alexandros
1851-1911 .... **TCLC 29**

Papadiamantopoulos, Johannes 1856-1910
See Moreas, Jean
See also CA 117

Papini, Giovanni 1881-1956...... **TCLC 22**
See also CA 121

Paracelsus 1493-1541.............. **LC 14**

Parasol, Peter
See Stevens, Wallace

Parfenie, Maria
See Codrescu, Andrei

Parini, Jay (Lee) 1948- .... **CLC 54**
See also CA 97-100; CAAS 16; CANR 32

Park, Jordan
See Kornbluth, C(yril) M.; Pohl, Frederik

Parker, Bert
See Ellison, Harlan (Jay)

Parker, Dorothy (Rothschild)
1893-1967 . . . . **CLC 15, 68; SSC 2**
See also CA 19-20; 25-28R; CAP 2;
DAM POET; DLB 11, 45, 86; MTCW

Parker, Robert B(rown) 1932- . . . . . . **CLC 27**
See also BEST 89:4; CA 49-52; CANR 1,
26; DAM NOV, POP; INT CANR-26;
MTCW

Parkin, Frank 1940- . . . . **CLC 43**
See also CA 147

Parkman, Francis, Jr.
1823-1893 . . . . **NCLC 12**
See also DLB 1, 30

Parks, Gordon (Alexander Buchanan)
1912- . . . . **CLC 1, 16; BLC**
See also AITN 2; BW 2; CA 41-44R;
CANR 26; DAM MULT; DLB 33;
SATA 8

Parnell, Thomas 1679-1718 . . . . **LC 3**
See also DLB 94

Parra, Nicanor 1914- . . . . **CLC 2; HLC**
See also CA 85-88; CANR 32;
DAM MULT; HW; MTCW

Parrish, Mary Frances
See Fisher, M(ary) F(rances) K(ennedy)

Parson
See Coleridge, Samuel Taylor

Parson Lot
See Kingsley, Charles

Partridge, Anthony
See Oppenheim, E(dward) Phillips

Pascoli, Giovanni 1855-1912 . . . . . . **TCLC 45**

Pasolini, Pier Paolo
1922-1975 . . . . **CLC 20, 37**
See also CA 93-96; 61-64; DLB 128;
MTCW

Pasquini
See Silone, Ignazio

Pastan, Linda (Olenik) 1932- . . . . . . **CLC 27**
See also CA 61-64; CANR 18, 40;
DAM POET; DLB 5

Pasternak, Boris (Leonidovich)
1890-1960 . . . . . . **CLC 7, 10, 18, 63; DA;**
DAB; DAC; PC 6; WLC
See also CA 127; 116; DAM MST, NOV,
POET; MTCW

Patchen, Kenneth 1911-1972 . . . **CLC 1, 2, 18**
See also CA 1-4R; 33-36R; CANR 3, 35;
DAM POET; DLB 16, 48; MTCW

Pater, Walter (Horatio)
1839-1894 . . . . **NCLC 7**
See also CDBLB 1832-1890; DLB 57, 156

Paterson, A(ndrew) B(arton)
1864-1941 . . . . **TCLC 32**

Paterson, Katherine (Womeldorf)
1932- . . . . **CLC 12, 30**
See also AAYA 1; CA 21-24R; CANR 28;
CLR 7; DLB 52; JRDA; MAICYA;
MTCW; SATA 13, 53

Patmore, Coventry Kersey Dighton
1823-1896 . . . . **NCLC 9**
See also DLB 35, 98

Paton, Alan (Stewart)
1903-1988 . . . . . . **CLC 4, 10, 25, 55; DA;**
DAB; DAC; WLC
See also CA 13-16; 125; CANR 22; CAP 1;
DAM MST, NOV; MTCW; SATA 11;
SATA-Obit 56

Paton Walsh, Gillian 1937-
See Walsh, Jill Paton
See also CANR 38; JRDA; MAICYA;
SAAS 3; SATA 4, 72

Paulding, James Kirke 1778-1860 . . **NCLC 2**
See also DLB 3, 59, 74

Paulin, Thomas Neilson 1949-
See Paulin, Tom
See also CA 123; 128

Paulin, Tom . . . . **CLC 37**
See also Paulin, Thomas Neilson
See also DLB 40

Paustovsky, Konstantin (Georgievich)
1892-1968 . . . . **CLC 40**
See also CA 93-96; 25-28R

Pavese, Cesare
1908-1950 . . . . . **TCLC 3; PC 13; SSC 19**
See also CA 104; DLB 128

Pavic, Milorad 1929- . . . . **CLC 60**
See also CA 136

Payne, Alan
See Jakes, John (William)

Paz, Gil
See Lugones, Leopoldo

Paz, Octavio
1914- . . . . **CLC 3, 4, 6, 10, 19, 51, 65;**
DA; DAB; DAC; HLC; PC 1; WLC
See also CA 73-76; CANR 32; DAM MST,
MULT, POET; DLBY 90; HW; MTCW

Peacock, Molly 1947- . . . . **CLC 60**
See also CA 103; CAAS 21; DLB 120

Peacock, Thomas Love
1785-1866 . . . . **NCLC 22**
See also DLB 96, 116

Peake, Mervyn 1911-1968 . . . . . . **CLC 7, 54**
See also CA 5-8R; 25-28R; CANR 3;
DLB 15, 160; MTCW; SATA 23

Pearce, Philippa . . . . **CLC 21**
See also Christie, (Ann) Philippa
See also CLR 9; DLB 161; MAICYA;
SATA 1, 67

Pearl, Eric
See Elman, Richard

Pearson, T(homas) R(eid) 1956- . . . . **CLC 39**
See also CA 120; 130; INT 130

Peck, Dale 1967- . . . . **CLC 81**
See also CA 146

Peck, John 1941- . . . . **CLC 3**
See also CA 49-52; CANR 3

Peck, Richard (Wayne) 1934- . . . . . . **CLC 21**
See also AAYA 1; CA 85-88; CANR 19,
38; CLR 15; INT CANR-19; JRDA;
MAICYA; SAAS 2; SATA 18, 55

Peck, Robert Newton
1928- . . . . **CLC 17; DA; DAC**
See also AAYA 3; CA 81-84; CANR 31;
DAM MST; JRDA; MAICYA; SAAS 1;
SATA 21, 62

Peckinpah, (David) Sam(uel)
1925-1984 . . . . **CLC 20**
See also CA 109; 114

Pedersen, Knut 1859-1952
See Hamsun, Knut
See also CA 104; 119; MTCW

Peeslake, Gaffer
See Durrell, Lawrence (George)

Peguy, Charles Pierre
1873-1914 . . . . **TCLC 10**
See also CA 107

Pena, Ramon del Valle y
See Valle-Inclan, Ramon (Maria) del

Pendennis, Arthur Esquir
See Thackeray, William Makepeace

Penn, William 1644-1718 . . . . **LC 25**
See also DLB 24

Pepys, Samuel
1633-1703 . . . . . **LC 11; DA; DAB; DAC;**
WLC
See also CDBLB 1660-1789; DAM MST;
DLB 101

Percy, Walker
1916-1990 . . . . **CLC 2, 3, 6, 8, 14, 18, 47,**
65
See also CA 1-4R; 131; CANR 1, 23;
DAM NOV, POP; DLB 2; DLBY 80, 90;
MTCW

Perec, Georges 1936-1982 . . . . **CLC 56**
See also CA 141; DLB 83

Pereda (y Sanchez de Porrua), Jose Maria de
1833-1906 . . . . **TCLC 16**
See also CA 117

Pereda y Porrua, Jose Maria de
See Pereda (y Sanchez de Porrua), Jose
Maria de

Peregoy, George Weems
See Mencken, H(enry) L(ouis)

Perelman, S(idney) J(oseph)
1904-1979 . . . **CLC 3, 5, 9, 15, 23, 44, 49**
See also AITN 1, 2; CA 73-76; 89-92;
CANR 18; DAM DRAM; DLB 11, 44;
MTCW

Peret, Benjamin 1899-1959 . . . . **TCLC 20**
See also CA 117

Peretz, Isaac Loeb 1851(?)-1915 . . . **TCLC 16**
See also CA 109

Peretz, Yitzkhok Leibush
See Peretz, Isaac Loeb

Perez Galdos, Benito 1843-1920 . . . **TCLC 27**
See also CA 125; HW

Perrault, Charles 1628-1703 . . . . **LC 2**
See also MAICYA; SATA 25

Perry, Brighton
See Sherwood, Robert E(mmet)

Perse, St.-John . . . . **CLC 4, 11, 46**
See also Leger, (Marie-Rene Auguste) Alexis
Saint-Leger

Perutz, Leo 1882-1957 . . . . **TCLC 60**
See also DLB 81

Peseenz, Tulio F.
See Lopez y Fuentes, Gregorio

Pesetsky, Bette 1932- . . . . **CLC 28**
See also CA 133; DLB 130

Peshkov, Alexei Maximovich 1868-1936
See Gorky, Maxim
See also CA 105; 141; DA; DAC;
DAM DRAM, MST, NOV

Pessoa, Fernando (Antonio Nogueira)
1888-1935 . . . . **TCLC 27; HLC**
See also CA 125

Peterkin, Julia Mood 1880-1961. . . . **CLC 31**
See also CA 102; DLB 9

Peters, Joan K. 1945-. . . . . **CLC 39**

Peters, Robert L(ouis) 1924-. . . . . **CLC 7**
See also CA 13-16R; CAAS 8; DLB 105

Petofi, Sandor 1823-1849. . . . . . . **NCLC 21**

Petrakis, Harry Mark 1923-. . . . . **CLC 3**
See also CA 9-12R; CANR 4, 30

Petrarch 1304-1374. . . . . **PC 8**
See also DAM POET

Petrov, Evgeny . . . . **TCLC 21**
See also Kataev, Evgeny Petrovich

Petry, Ann (Lane) 1908- . . . . . . **CLC 1, 7, 18**
See also BW 1; CA 5-8R; CAAS 6;
CANR 4, 46; CLR 12; DLB 76; JRDA;
MAICYA; MTCW; SATA 5

Petursson, Halligrimur 1614-1674 . . . . **LC 8**

Philips, Katherine 1632-1664. . . . . . . **LC 30**
See also DLB 131

Philipson, Morris H. 1926-. . . . . **CLC 53**
See also CA 1-4R; CANR 4

Phillips, David Graham
1867-1911 . . . . **TCLC 44**
See also CA 108; DLB 9, 12

Phillips, Jack
See Sandburg, Carl (August)

Phillips, Jayne Anne
1952- . . . . **CLC 15, 33; SSC 16**
See also CA 101; CANR 24, 50; DLBY 80;
INT CANR-24; MTCW

Phillips, Richard
See Dick, Philip K(indred)

Phillips, Robert (Schaeffer) 1938-. . . **CLC 28**
See also CA 17-20R; CAAS 13; CANR 8;
DLB 105

Phillips, Ward
See Lovecraft, H(oward) P(hillips)

Piccolo, Lucio 1901-1969. . . . . **CLC 13**
See also CA 97-100; DLB 114

Pickthall, Marjorie L(owry) C(hristie)
1883-1922 . . . . **TCLC 21**
See also CA 107; DLB 92

Pico della Mirandola, Giovanni
1463-1494 . . . . **LC 15**

Piercy, Marge
1936- . . . . **CLC 3, 6, 14, 18, 27, 62**
See also CA 21-24R; CAAS 1; CANR 13,
43; DLB 120; MTCW

Piers, Robert
See Anthony, Piers

Pieyre de Mandiargues, Andre 1909-1991
See Mandiargues, Andre Pieyre de
See also CA 103; 136; CANR 22

Pilnyak, Boris . . . . **TCLC 23**
See also Vogau, Boris Andreyevich

Pincherle, Alberto 1907-1990 . . . **CLC 11, 18**
See also Moravia, Alberto
See also CA 25-28R; 132; CANR 33;
DAM NOV; MTCW

Pinckney, Darryl 1953-. . . . . **CLC 76**
See also BW 2; CA 143

Pindar 518B.C.-446B.C. . . . . **CMLC 12**

Pineda, Cecile 1942-. . . . . **CLC 39**
See also CA 118

Pinero, Arthur Wing 1855-1934 . . . **TCLC 32**
See also CA 110; DAM DRAM; DLB 10

Pinero, Miguel (Antonio Gomez)
1946-1988 . . . . **CLC 4, 55**
See also CA 61-64; 125; CANR 29; HW

Pinget, Robert 1919- . . . . **CLC 7, 13, 37**
See also CA 85-88; DLB 83

Pink Floyd
See Barrett, (Roger) Syd; Gilmour, David;
Mason, Nick; Waters, Roger; Wright,
Rick

Pinkney, Edward 1802-1828 . . . . . **NCLC 31**

Pinkwater, Daniel Manus 1941-. . . . **CLC 35**
See also Pinkwater, Manus
See also AAYA 1; CA 29-32R; CANR 12,
38; CLR 4; JRDA; MAICYA; SAAS 3;
SATA 46, 76

Pinkwater, Manus
See Pinkwater, Daniel Manus
See also SATA 8

Pinsky, Robert 1940-. . . . . **CLC 9, 19, 38, 91**
See also CA 29-32R; CAAS 4;
DAM POET; DLBY 82

Pinta, Harold
See Pinter, Harold

Pinter, Harold
1930- . . . . . **CLC 1, 3, 6, 9, 11, 15, 27, 58,
73; DA; DAB; DAC; WLC**
See also CA 5-8R; CANR 33; CDBLB 1960
to Present; DAM DRAM, MST; DLB 13;
MTCW

Pirandello, Luigi
1867-1936 . . . . . . **TCLC 4, 29; DA; DAB;
DAC; DC 5; SSC 22; WLC**
See also CA 104; DAM DRAM, MST

Pirsig, Robert M(aynard)
1928- . . . . **CLC 4, 6, 73**
See also CA 53-56; CANR 42; DAM POP;
MTCW; SATA 39

Pisarev, Dmitry Ivanovich
1840-1868 . . . . **NCLC 25**

Pix, Mary (Griffith) 1666-1709 . . . . . . **LC 8**
See also DLB 80

Pixerecourt, Guilbert de
1773-1844 . . . . **NCLC 39**

Plaidy, Jean
See Hibbert, Eleanor Alice Burford

Planche, James Robinson
1796-1880 . . . . **NCLC 42**

Plant, Robert 1948- . . . . **CLC 12**

Plante, David (Robert)
1940- . . . . **CLC 7, 23, 38**
See also CA 37-40R; CANR 12, 36;
DAM NOV; DLBY 83; INT CANR-12;
MTCW

Plath, Sylvia
1932-1963 . . . . . **CLC 1, 2, 3, 5, 9, 11, 14,
17, 50, 51, 62; DA; DAB; DAC; PC 1;
WLC**
See also AAYA 13; CA 19-20; CANR 34;
CAP 2; CDALB 1941-1968; DAM MST,
POET; DLB 5, 6, 152; MTCW

Plato
428(?)B.C.-348(?)B.C. . . . . . **CMLC 8; DA;
DAB; DAC**
See also DAM MST

Platonov, Andrei . . . . **TCLC 14**
See also Klimentov, Andrei Platonovich

Platt, Kin 1911- . . . . **CLC 26**
See also AAYA 11; CA 17-20R; CANR 11;
JRDA; SAAS 17; SATA 21, 86

Plautus c. 251B.C.-184B.C. . . . . **DC 6**

Plick et Plock
See Simenon, Georges (Jacques Christian)

Plimpton, George (Ames) 1927-. . . . . **CLC 36**
See also AITN 1; CA 21-24R; CANR 32;
MTCW; SATA 10

Plomer, William Charles Franklin
1903-1973 . . . . **CLC 4, 8**
See also CA 21-22; CANR 34; CAP 2;
DLB 20, 162; MTCW; SATA 24

Plowman, Piers
See Kavanagh, Patrick (Joseph)

Plum, J.
See Wodehouse, P(elham) G(renville)

Plumly, Stanley (Ross) 1939- . . . . . . **CLC 33**
See also CA 108; 110; DLB 5; INT 110

Plumpe, Friedrich Wilhelm
1888-1931 . . . . **TCLC 53**
See also CA 112

Poe, Edgar Allan
1809-1849 . . . . **NCLC 1, 16, 55; DA;
DAB; DAC; PC 1; SSC 1, 22; WLC**
See also AAYA 14; CDALB 1640-1865;
DAM MST, POET; DLB 3, 59, 73, 74;
SATA 23

Poet of Titchfield Street, The
See Pound, Ezra (Weston Loomis)

Pohl, Frederik 1919- . . . . **CLC 18**
See also CA 61-64; CAAS 1; CANR 11, 37;
DLB 8; INT CANR-11; MTCW;
SATA 24

Poirier, Louis 1910-
See Gracq, Julien
See also CA 122; 126

Poitier, Sidney 1927-. . . . . **CLC 26**
See also BW 1; CA 117

Polanski, Roman 1933- . . . . **CLC 16**
See also CA 77-80

Poliakoff, Stephen 1952-. . . . . **CLC 38**
See also CA 106; DLB 13

Police, The
See Copeland, Stewart (Armstrong);
Summers, Andrew James; Sumner,
Gordon Matthew

Polidori, John William
1795-1821 . . . . **NCLC 51**
See also DLB 116

Pollitt, Katha 1949-. . . . . **CLC 28**
See also CA 120; 122; MTCW

Pollock, (Mary) Sharon
　　1936- . . . . **CLC 50; DAC**
　　See also CA 141; DAM DRAM, MST;
　　DLB 60

Polo, Marco　1254-1324 . . . . **CMLC 15**

Polonsky, Abraham (Lincoln)
　　1910- . . . . **CLC 92**
　　See also CA 104; DLB 26; INT 104

Polybius　c. 200B.C.-c. 118B.C. . . . . **CMLC 17**

Pomerance, Bernard　1940- . . . . **CLC 13**
　　See also CA 101; CANR 49; DAM DRAM

Ponge, Francis (Jean Gaston Alfred)
　　1899-1988 . . . . **CLC 6, 18**
　　See also CA 85-88; 126; CANR 40;
　　DAM POET

Pontoppidan, Henrik　1857-1943 . . . **TCLC 29**

Poole, Josephine . . . . **CLC 17**
　　See also Helyar, Jane Penelope Josephine
　　See also SAAS 2; SATA 5

Popa, Vasko　1922-1991 . . . . **CLC 19**
　　See also CA 112; 148

Pope, Alexander
　　1688-1744 . . . . . . **LC 3; DA; DAB; DAC;**
　　　　　　　　　　　　　　　　　　WLC
　　See also CDBLB 1660-1789; DAM MST,
　　POET; DLB 95, 101

Porter, Connie (Rose)　1959(?)- . . . . . **CLC 70**
　　See also BW 2; CA 142; SATA 81

Porter, Gene(va Grace) Stratton
　　1863(?)-1924 . . . . **TCLC 21**
　　See also CA 112

Porter, Katherine Anne
　　1890-1980 . . . . . . **CLC 1, 3, 7, 10, 13, 15,**
　　　　　　　　　　　　27; DA; DAB; DAC; SSC 4
　　See also AITN 2; CA 1-4R; 101; CANR 1;
　　DAM MST, NOV; DLB 4, 9, 102;
　　DLBD 12; DLBY 80; MTCW; SATA 39;
　　SATA-Obit 23

Porter, Peter (Neville Frederick)
　　1929- . . . . **CLC 5, 13, 33**
　　See also CA 85-88; DLB 40

Porter, William Sydney　1862-1910
　　See Henry, O.
　　See also CA 104; 131; CDALB 1865-1917;
　　DA; DAB; DAC; DAM MST; DLB 12,
　　78, 79; MTCW; YABC 2

Portillo (y Pacheco), Jose Lopez
　　See Lopez Portillo (y Pacheco), Jose

Post, Melville Davisson
　　1869-1930 . . . . **TCLC 39**
　　See also CA 110

Potok, Chaim　1929- . . . . **CLC 2, 7, 14, 26**
　　See also AAYA 15; AITN 1, 2; CA 17-20R;
　　CANR 19, 35; DAM NOV; DLB 28, 152;
　　INT CANR-19; MTCW; SATA 33

Potter, Beatrice
　　See Webb, (Martha) Beatrice (Potter)
　　See also MAICYA

Potter, Dennis (Christopher George)
　　1935-1994 . . . . **CLC 58, 86**
　　See also CA 107; 145; CANR 33; MTCW

Pound, Ezra (Weston Loomis)
　　1885-1972 . . . . . . **CLC 1, 2, 3, 4, 5, 7, 10,**
　　　　　　　13, 18, 34, 48, 50; DA; DAB; DAC; PC 4;
　　　　　　　　　　　　　　　　　　　　WLC
　　See also CA 5-8R; 37-40R; CANR 40;
　　CDALB 1917-1929; DAM MST, POET;
　　DLB 4, 45, 63; MTCW

Povod, Reinaldo　1959-1994 . . . . **CLC 44**
　　See also CA 136; 146

Powell, Adam Clayton, Jr.
　　1908-1972 . . . . **CLC 89; BLC**
　　See also BW 1; CA 102; 33-36R;
　　DAM MULT

Powell, Anthony (Dymoke)
　　1905- . . . . **CLC 1, 3, 7, 9, 10, 31**
　　See also CA 1-4R; CANR 1, 32;
　　CDBLB 1945-1960; DLB 15; MTCW

Powell, Dawn　1897-1965 . . . . **CLC 66**
　　See also CA 5-8R

Powell, Padgett　1952- . . . . **CLC 34**
　　See also CA 126

Power, Susan . . . . **CLC 91**

Powers, J(ames) F(arl)
　　1917- . . . . **CLC 1, 4, 8, 57; SSC 4**
　　See also CA 1-4R; CANR 2; DLB 130;
　　MTCW

Powers, John J(ames)　1945-
　　See Powers, John R.
　　See also CA 69-72

Powers, John R. . . . . **CLC 66**
　　See also Powers, John J(ames)

Powers, Richard (S.)　1957- . . . . **CLC 93**
　　See also CA 148

Pownall, David　1938- . . . . **CLC 10**
　　See also CA 89-92; CAAS 18; CANR 49;
　　DLB 14

Powys, John Cowper
　　1872-1963 . . . . **CLC 7, 9, 15, 46**
　　See also CA 85-88; DLB 15; MTCW

Powys, T(heodore) F(rancis)
　　1875-1953 . . . . **TCLC 9**
　　See also CA 106; DLB 36, 162

Prager, Emily　1952- . . . . **CLC 56**

Pratt, E(dwin) J(ohn)
　　1883(?)-1964 . . . . **CLC 19; DAC**
　　See also CA 141; 93-96; DAM POET;
　　DLB 92

Premchand . . . . **TCLC 21**
　　See also Srivastava, Dhanpat Rai

Preussler, Otfried　1923- . . . . **CLC 17**
　　See also CA 77-80; SATA 24

Prevert, Jacques (Henri Marie)
　　1900-1977 . . . . **CLC 15**
　　See also CA 77-80; 69-72; CANR 29;
　　MTCW; SATA-Obit 30

Prevost, Abbe (Antoine Francois)
　　1697-1763 . . . . **LC 1**

Price, (Edward) Reynolds
　　1933- . . **CLC 3, 6, 13, 43, 50, 63; SSC 22**
　　See also CA 1-4R; CANR 1, 37;
　　DAM NOV; DLB 2; INT CANR-37

Price, Richard　1949- . . . . **CLC 6, 12**
　　See also CA 49-52; CANR 3; DLBY 81

Prichard, Katharine Susannah
　　1883-1969 . . . . **CLC 46**
　　See also CA 11-12; CANR 33; CAP 1;
　　MTCW; SATA 66

Priestley, J(ohn) B(oynton)
　　1894-1984 . . . . **CLC 2, 5, 9, 34**
　　See also CA 9-12R; 113; CANR 33;
　　CDBLB 1914-1945; DAM DRAM, NOV;
　　DLB 10, 34, 77, 100, 139; DLBY 84;
　　MTCW

Prince　1958(?)- . . . . **CLC 35**

Prince, F(rank) T(empleton)　1912- . . **CLC 22**
　　See also CA 101; CANR 43; DLB 20

Prince Kropotkin
　　See Kropotkin, Peter (Alekseievich)

Prior, Matthew　1664-1721 . . . . **LC 4**
　　See also DLB 95

Pritchard, William H(arrison)
　　1932- . . . . **CLC 34**
　　See also CA 65-68; CANR 23; DLB 111

Pritchett, V(ictor) S(awdon)
　　1900- . . . . **CLC 5, 13, 15, 41; SSC 14**
　　See also CA 61-64; CANR 31; DAM NOV;
　　DLB 15, 139; MTCW

Private 19022
　　See Manning, Frederic

Probst, Mark　1925- . . . . **CLC 59**
　　See also CA 130

Prokosch, Frederic　1908-1989 . . . . **CLC 4, 48**
　　See also CA 73-76; 128; DLB 48

Prophet, The
　　See Dreiser, Theodore (Herman Albert)

Prose, Francine　1947- . . . . **CLC 45**
　　See also CA 109; 112; CANR 46

Proudhon
　　See Cunha, Euclides (Rodrigues Pimenta) da

Proulx, E. Annie　1935- . . . . **CLC 81**

Proust, (Valentin-Louis-George-Eugene-)
　　Marcel
　　1871-1922 . . . . **TCLC 7, 13, 33; DA;**
　　　　　　　　　　　　　　　　DAB; DAC; WLC
　　See also CA 104; 120; DAM MST, NOV;
　　DLB 65; MTCW

Prowler, Harley
　　See Masters, Edgar Lee

Prus, Boleslaw　1845-1912 . . . . **TCLC 48**

Pryor, Richard (Franklin Lenox Thomas)
　　1940- . . . . **CLC 26**
　　See also CA 122

Przybyszewski, Stanislaw
　　1868-1927 . . . . **TCLC 36**
　　See also DLB 66

Pteleon
　　See Grieve, C(hristopher) M(urray)
　　See also DAM POET

Puckett, Lute
　　See Masters, Edgar Lee

Puig, Manuel
　　1932-1990 . . . **CLC 3, 5, 10, 28, 65; HLC**
　　See also CA 45-48; CANR 2, 32;
　　DAM MULT; DLB 113; HW; MTCW

Purdy, Al(fred Wellington)
　　1918- . . . . **CLC 3, 6, 14, 50; DAC**
　　See also CA 81-84; CAAS 17; CANR 42;
　　DAM MST, POET; DLB 88

Purdy, James (Amos)
1923- .... **CLC 2, 4, 10, 28, 52**
See also CA 33-36R; CAAS 1; CANR 19,
51; DLB 2; INT CANR-19; MTCW

Pure, Simon
See Swinnerton, Frank Arthur

Pushkin, Alexander (Sergeyevich)
1799-1837 ..... **NCLC 3, 27; DA; DAB;
DAC; PC 10; WLC**
See also DAM DRAM, MST, POET;
SATA 61

P'u Sung-ling 1640-1715 .... **LC 3**

Putnam, Arthur Lee
See Alger, Horatio, Jr.

Puzo, Mario 1920- .... **CLC 1, 2, 6, 36**
See also CA 65-68; CANR 4, 42;
DAM NOV, POP; DLB 6; MTCW

Pym, Barbara (Mary Crampton)
1913-1980 .... **CLC 13, 19, 37**
See also CA 13-14; 97-100; CANR 13, 34;
CAP 1; DLB 14; DLBY 87; MTCW

Pynchon, Thomas (Ruggles, Jr.)
1937- ..... **CLC 2, 3, 6, 9, 11, 18, 33, 62,
72; DA; DAB; DAC; SSC 14; WLC**
See also BEST 90:2; CA 17-20R; CANR 22,
46; DAM MST, NOV, POP; DLB 2;
MTCW

Qian Zhongshu
See Ch'ien Chung-shu

Qroll
See Dagerman, Stig (Halvard)

Quarrington, Paul (Lewis) 1953- .... **CLC 65**
See also CA 129

Quasimodo, Salvatore 1901-1968 ... **CLC 10**
See also CA 13-16; 25-28R; CAP 1;
DLB 114; MTCW

Queen, Ellery .... **CLC 3, 11**
See also Dannay, Frederic; Davidson,
Avram; Lee, Manfred B(ennington);
Sturgeon, Theodore (Hamilton); Vance,
John Holbrook

Queen, Ellery, Jr.
See Dannay, Frederic; Lee, Manfred
B(ennington)

Queneau, Raymond
1903-1976 .... **CLC 2, 5, 10, 42**
See also CA 77-80; 69-72; CANR 32;
DLB 72; MTCW

Quevedo, Francisco de 1580-1645 .... **LC 23**

Quiller-Couch, Arthur Thomas
1863-1944 .... **TCLC 53**
See also CA 118; DLB 135, 153

Quin, Ann (Marie) 1936-1973 .... **CLC 6**
See also CA 9-12R; 45-48; DLB 14

Quinn, Martin
See Smith, Martin Cruz

Quinn, Peter 1947- .... **CLC 91**

Quinn, Simon
See Smith, Martin Cruz

Quiroga, Horacio (Sylvestre)
1878-1937 .... **TCLC 20; HLC**
See also CA 117; 131; DAM MULT; HW;
MTCW

Quoirez, Francoise 1935- .... **CLC 9**
See also Sagan, Francoise
See also CA 49-52; CANR 6, 39; MTCW

Raabe, Wilhelm 1831-1910 .... **TCLC 45**
See also DLB 129

Rabe, David (William) 1940- ... **CLC 4, 8, 33**
See also CA 85-88; CABS 3; DAM DRAM;
DLB 7

Rabelais, Francois
1483-1553 ...... **LC 5; DA; DAB; DAC;
WLC**
See also DAM MST

Rabinovitch, Sholem 1859-1916
See Aleichem, Sholom
See also CA 104

Racine, Jean 1639-1699 .... **LC 28; DAB**
See also DAM MST

Radcliffe, Ann (Ward)
1764-1823 .... **NCLC 6, 55**
See also DLB 39

Radiguet, Raymond 1903-1923 .... **TCLC 29**
See also DLB 65

Radnoti, Miklos 1909-1944 .... **TCLC 16**
See also CA 118

Rado, James 1939- .... **CLC 17**
See also CA 105

Radvanyi, Netty 1900-1983
See Seghers, Anna
See also CA 85-88; 110

Rae, Ben
See Griffiths, Trevor

Raeburn, John (Hay) 1941- .... **CLC 34**
See also CA 57-60

Ragni, Gerome 1942-1991 .... **CLC 17**
See also CA 105; 134

Rahv, Philip 1908-1973 .... **CLC 24**
See also Greenberg, Ivan
See also DLB 137

Raine, Craig 1944- .... **CLC 32**
See also CA 108; CANR 29, 51; DLB 40

Raine, Kathleen (Jessie) 1908- ... **CLC 7, 45**
See also CA 85-88; CANR 46; DLB 20;
MTCW

Rainis, Janis 1865-1929 .... **TCLC 29**

Rakosi, Carl .... **CLC 47**
See also Rawley, Callman
See also CAAS 5

Raleigh, Richard
See Lovecraft, H(oward) P(hillips)

Raleigh, Sir Walter 1554(?)-1618 .... **LC 31**
See also CDBLB Before 1660

Rallentando, H. P.
See Sayers, Dorothy L(eigh)

Ramal, Walter
See de la Mare, Walter (John)

Ramon, Juan
See Jimenez (Mantecon), Juan Ramon

Ramos, Graciliano 1892-1953 ..... **TCLC 32**

Rampersad, Arnold 1941- .... **CLC 44**
See also BW 2; CA 127; 133; DLB 111;
INT 133

Rampling, Anne
See Rice, Anne

Ramsay, Allan 1684(?)-1758 .... **LC 29**
See also DLB 95

Ramuz, Charles-Ferdinand
1878-1947 .... **TCLC 33**

Rand, Ayn
1905-1982 ...... **CLC 3, 30, 44, 79; DA;
DAC; WLC**
See also AAYA 10; CA 13-16R; 105;
CANR 27; DAM MST, NOV, POP;
MTCW

Randall, Dudley (Felker)
1914- .... **CLC 1; BLC**
See also BW 1; CA 25-28R; CANR 23;
DAM MULT; DLB 41

Randall, Robert
See Silverberg, Robert

Ranger, Ken
See Creasey, John

Ransom, John Crowe
1888-1974 .... **CLC 2, 4, 5, 11, 24**
See also CA 5-8R; 49-52; CANR 6, 34;
DAM POET; DLB 45, 63; MTCW

Rao, Raja 1909- .... **CLC 25, 56**
See also CA 73-76; CANR 51; DAM NOV;
MTCW

Raphael, Frederic (Michael)
1931- .... **CLC 2, 14**
See also CA 1-4R; CANR 1; DLB 14

Ratcliffe, James P.
See Mencken, H(enry) L(ouis)

Rathbone, Julian 1935- .... **CLC 41**
See also CA 101; CANR 34

Rattigan, Terence (Mervyn)
1911-1977 .... **CLC 7**
See also CA 85-88; 73-76;
CDBLB 1945-1960; DAM DRAM;
DLB 13; MTCW

Ratushinskaya, Irina 1954- .... **CLC 54**
See also CA 129

Raven, Simon (Arthur Noel)
1927- .... **CLC 14**
See also CA 81-84

Rawley, Callman 1903-
See Rakosi, Carl
See also CA 21-24R; CANR 12, 32

Rawlings, Marjorie Kinnan
1896-1953 .... **TCLC 4**
See also CA 104; 137; DLB 9, 22, 102;
JRDA; MAICYA; YABC 1

Ray, Satyajit 1921-1992 .... **CLC 16, 76**
See also CA 114; 137; DAM MULT

Read, Herbert Edward 1893-1968 .... **CLC 4**
See also CA 85-88; 25-28R; DLB 20, 149

Read, Piers Paul 1941- ...... **CLC 4, 10, 25**
See also CA 21-24R; CANR 38; DLB 14;
SATA 21

Reade, Charles 1814-1884 .... **NCLC 2**
See also DLB 21

Reade, Hamish
See Gray, Simon (James Holliday)

Reading, Peter 1946- .... **CLC 47**
See also CA 103; CANR 46; DLB 40

Reaney, James 1926- .... **CLC 13; DAC**
See also CA 41-44R; CAAS 15; CANR 42;
DAM MST; DLB 68; SATA 43

Rebreanu, Liviu 1885-1944 ...... **TCLC 28**

Rechy, John (Francisco)
1934- .... **CLC 1, 7, 14, 18; HLC**
See also CA 5-8R; CAAS 4; CANR 6, 32;
DAM MULT; DLB 122; DLBY 82; HW;
INT CANR-6

Redcam, Tom 1870-1933 .... **TCLC 25**

Reddin, Keith.................... **CLC 67**

Redgrove, Peter (William)
1932-.................... **CLC 6, 41**
See also CA 1-4R; CANR 3, 39; DLB 40

Redmon, Anne.................... **CLC 22**
See also Nightingale, Anne Redmon
See also DLBY 86

Reed, Eliot
See Ambler, Eric

Reed, Ishmael
1938- ... **CLC 2, 3, 5, 6, 13, 32, 60; BLC**
See also BW 2; CA 21-24R; CANR 25, 48;
DAM MULT; DLB 2, 5, 33; DLBD 8;
MTCW

Reed, John (Silas) 1887-1920 ...... **TCLC 9**
See also CA 106

Reed, Lou........................ **CLC 21**
See also Firbank, Louis

Reeve, Clara 1729-1807 .... **NCLC 19**
See also DLB 39

Reich, Wilhelm 1897-1957....... **TCLC 57**

Reid, Christopher (John) 1949-..... **CLC 33**
See also CA 140; DLB 40

Reid, Desmond
See Moorcock, Michael (John)

Reid Banks, Lynne 1929-
See Banks, Lynne Reid
See also CA 1-4R; CANR 6, 22, 38;
CLR 24; JRDA; MAICYA; SATA 22, 75

Reilly, William K.
See Creasey, John

Reiner, Max
See Caldwell, (Janet Miriam) Taylor
(Holland)

Reis, Ricardo
See Pessoa, Fernando (Antonio Nogueira)

Remarque, Erich Maria
1898-1970 .... **CLC 21; DA; DAB; DAC**
See also CA 77-80; 29-32R; DAM MST,
NOV; DLB 56; MTCW

Remizov, A.
See Remizov, Aleksei (Mikhailovich)

Remizov, A. M.
See Remizov, Aleksei (Mikhailovich)

Remizov, Aleksei (Mikhailovich)
1877-1957.................... **TCLC 27**
See also CA 125; 133

Renan, Joseph Ernest
1823-1892 .... **NCLC 26**

Renard, Jules 1864-1910 .... **TCLC 17**
See also CA 117

Renault, Mary.............. **CLC 3, 11, 17**
See also Challans, Mary
See also DLBY 83

Rendell, Ruth (Barbara) 1930- .. **CLC 28, 48**
See also Vine, Barbara
See also CA 109; CANR 32; DAM POP;
DLB 87; INT CANR-32; MTCW

Renoir, Jean 1894-1979 .... **CLC 20**
See also CA 129; 85-88

Resnais, Alain 1922-.............. **CLC 16**

Reverdy, Pierre 1889-1960 .... **CLC 53**
See also CA 97-100; 89-92

Rexroth, Kenneth
1905-1982 ...... **CLC 1, 2, 6, 11, 22, 49**
See also CA 5-8R; 107; CANR 14, 34;
CDALB 1941-1968; DAM POET;
DLB 16, 48, 165; DLBY 82;
INT CANR-14; MTCW

Reyes, Alfonso 1889-1959 .... **TCLC 33**
See also CA 131; HW

Reyes y Basoalto, Ricardo Eliecer Neftali
See Neruda, Pablo

Reymont, Wladyslaw (Stanislaw)
1868(?)-1925 .... **TCLC 5**
See also CA 104

Reynolds, Jonathan 1942-........ **CLC 6, 38**
See also CA 65-68; CANR 28

Reynolds, Joshua 1723-1792........ **LC 15**
See also DLB 104

Reynolds, Michael Shane 1937- .... **CLC 44**
See also CA 65-68; CANR 9

Reznikoff, Charles 1894-1976....... **CLC 9**
See also CA 33-36; 61-64; CAP 2; DLB 28,
45

Rezzori (d'Arezzo), Gregor von
1914- .... **CLC 25**
See also CA 122; 136

Rhine, Richard
See Silverstein, Alvin

Rhodes, Eugene Manlove
1869-1934 .... **TCLC 53**

R'hoone
See Balzac, Honore de

Rhys, Jean
1890(?)-1979 .... **CLC 2, 4, 6, 14, 19, 51;**
SSC 21
See also CA 25-28R; 85-88; CANR 35;
CDBLB 1945-1960; DAM NOV; DLB 36,
117, 162; MTCW

Ribeiro, Darcy 1922-............. **CLC 34**
See also CA 33-36R

Ribeiro, Joao Ubaldo (Osorio Pimentel)
1941-.................... **CLC 10, 67**
See also CA 81-84

Ribman, Ronald (Burt) 1932- .... **CLC 7**
See also CA 21-24R; CANR 46

Ricci, Nino 1959-................ **CLC 70**
See also CA 137

Rice, Anne 1941- .... **CLC 41**
See also AAYA 9; BEST 89:2; CA 65-68;
CANR 12, 36; DAM POP

Rice, Elmer (Leopold)
1892-1967 .... **CLC 7, 49**
See also CA 21-22; 25-28R; CAP 2;
DAM DRAM; DLB 4, 7; MTCW

Rice, Tim(othy Miles Bindon)
1944- .... **CLC 21**
See also CA 103; CANR 46

Rich, Adrienne (Cecile)
1929- .... **CLC 3, 6, 7, 11, 18, 36, 73, 76;**
PC 5
See also CA 9-12R; CANR 20;
DAM POET; DLB 5, 67; MTCW

Rich, Barbara
See Graves, Robert (von Ranke)

Rich, Robert
See Trumbo, Dalton

Richard, Keith.................... **CLC 17**
See also Richards, Keith

Richards, David Adams
1950-.................. **CLC 59; DAC**
See also CA 93-96; DLB 53

Richards, I(vor) A(rmstrong)
1893-1979 .... **CLC 14, 24**
See also CA 41-44R; 89-92; CANR 34;
DLB 27

Richards, Keith 1943-
See Richard, Keith
See also CA 107

Richardson, Anne
See Roiphe, Anne (Richardson)

Richardson, Dorothy Miller
1873-1957 .... **TCLC 3**
See also CA 104; DLB 36

Richardson, Ethel Florence (Lindesay)
1870-1946
See Richardson, Henry Handel
See also CA 105

Richardson, Henry Handel.......... **TCLC 4**
See also Richardson, Ethel Florence
(Lindesay)

Richardson, John
1796-1852 .... **NCLC 55; DAC**
See also CA 140; DLB 99

Richardson, Samuel
1689-1761 ...... **LC 1; DA; DAB; DAC;**
WLC
See also CDBLB 1660-1789; DAM MST,
NOV; DLB 39

Richler, Mordecai
1931-....... **CLC 3, 5, 9, 13, 18, 46, 70;**
DAC
See also AITN 1; CA 65-68; CANR 31;
CLR 17; DAM MST, NOV; DLB 53;
MAICYA; MTCW; SATA 44;
SATA-Brief 27

Richter, Conrad (Michael)
1890-1968 .... **CLC 30**
See also CA 5-8R; 25-28R; CANR 23;
DLB 9; MTCW; SATA 3

Ricostranza, Tom
See Ellis, Trey

Riddell, J. H. 1832-1906 .... **TCLC 40**

Riding, Laura.................... **CLC 3, 7**
See also Jackson, Laura (Riding)

Riefenstahl, Berta Helene Amalia 1902-
See Riefenstahl, Leni
See also CA 108

Riefenstahl, Leni.................. **CLC 16**
See also Riefenstahl, Berta Helene Amalia

Riffe, Ernest
See Bergman, (Ernst) Ingmar

Rosenthal, M(acha) L(ouis) 1917-... **CLC 28**
See also CA 1-4R; CAAS 6; CANR 4, 51;
DLB 5; SATA 59

Ross, Barnaby
See Dannay, Frederic

Ross, Bernard L.
See Follett, Ken(neth Martin)

Ross, J. H.
See Lawrence, T(homas) E(dward)

Ross, Martin
See Martin, Violet Florence
See also DLB 135

Ross, (James) Sinclair
1908-...............**CLC 13; DAC**
See also CA 73-76; DAM MST; DLB 88

Rossetti, Christina (Georgina)
1830-1894 ..... **NCLC 2, 50; DA; DAB;**
DAC; PC 7; WLC
See also DAM MST, POET; DLB 35, 163;
MAICYA; SATA 20

Rossetti, Dante Gabriel
1828-1882 .... **NCLC 4; DA; DAB;**
DAC; WLC
See also CDBLB 1832-1890; DAM MST,
POET; DLB 35

Rossner, Judith (Perelman)
1935-.................**CLC 6, 9, 29**
See also AITN 2; BEST 90:3; CA 17-20R;
CANR 18, 51; DLB 6; INT CANR-18;
MTCW

Rostand, Edmond (Eugene Alexis)
1868-1918 ...... **TCLC 6, 37; DA; DAB;**
DAC
See also CA 104; 126; DAM DRAM, MST;
MTCW

Roth, Henry 1906-1995 ...... **CLC 2, 6, 11**
See also CA 11-12; 149; CANR 38; CAP 1;
DLB 28; MTCW

Roth, Joseph 1894-1939.......... **TCLC 33**
See also DLB 85

Roth, Philip (Milton)
1933-...... **CLC 1, 2, 3, 4, 6, 9, 15, 22,**
31, 47, 66, 86; DA; DAB; DAC; WLC
See also BEST 90:3; CA 1-4R; CANR 1, 22,
36; CDALB 1968-1988; DAM MST,
NOV, POP; DLB 2, 28; DLBY 82;
MTCW

Rothenberg, Jerome 1931-....... **CLC 6, 57**
See also CA 45-48; CANR 1; DLB 5

Roumain, Jacques (Jean Baptiste)
1907-1944 .... **TCLC 19; BLC**
See also BW 1; CA 117; 125; DAM MULT

Rourke, Constance (Mayfield)
1885-1941 .... **TCLC 12**
See also CA 107; YABC 1

Rousseau, Jean-Baptiste 1671-1741 ... **LC 9**

Rousseau, Jean-Jacques
1712-1778 ..... **LC 14; DA; DAB; DAC;**
WLC
See also DAM MST

Roussel, Raymond 1877-1933 ..... **TCLC 20**
See also CA 117

Rovit, Earl (Herbert) 1927-........ **CLC 7**
See also CA 5-8R; CANR 12

Rowe, Nicholas 1674-1718.......... **LC 8**
See also DLB 84

Rowley, Ames Dorrance
See Lovecraft, H(oward) P(hillips)

Rowson, Susanna Haswell
1762(?)-1824 .... **NCLC 5**
See also DLB 37

Roy, Gabrielle
1909-1983 ..... **CLC 10, 14; DAB; DAC**
See also CA 53-56; 110; CANR 5;
DAM MST; DLB 68; MTCW

Rozewicz, Tadeusz 1921-........ **CLC 9, 23**
See also CA 108; CANR 36; DAM POET;
MTCW

Ruark, Gibbons 1941- .... **CLC 3**
See also CA 33-36R; CAAS 23; CANR 14,
31; DLB 120

Rubens, Bernice (Ruth) 1923-... **CLC 19, 31**
See also CA 25-28R; CANR 33; DLB 14;
MTCW

Rudkin, (James) David 1936- ...... **CLC 14**
See also CA 89-92; DLB 13

Rudnik, Raphael 1933-............ **CLC 7**
See also CA 29-32R

Ruffian, M.
See Hasek, Jaroslav (Matej Frantisek)

Ruiz, Jose Martinez .... **CLC 11**
See also Martinez Ruiz, Jose

Rukeyser, Muriel
1913-1980 .... **CLC 6, 10, 15, 27; PC 12**
See also CA 5-8R; 93-96; CANR 26;
DAM POET; DLB 48; MTCW;
SATA-Obit 22

Rule, Jane (Vance) 1931-......... **CLC 27**
See also CA 25-28R; CAAS 18; CANR 12;
DLB 60

Rulfo, Juan 1918-1986.... **CLC 8, 80; HLC**
See also CA 85-88; 118; CANR 26;
DAM MULT; DLB 113; HW; MTCW

Runeberg, Johan 1804-1877...... **NCLC 41**

Runyon, (Alfred) Damon
1884(?)-1946 .... **TCLC 10**
See also CA 107; DLB 11, 86

Rush, Norman 1933-.............. **CLC 44**
See also CA 121; 126; INT 126

Rushdie, (Ahmed) Salman
1947- ...... **CLC 23, 31, 55; DAB; DAC**
See also BEST 89:3; CA 108; 111;
CANR 33; DAM MST, NOV, POP;
INT 111; MTCW

Rushforth, Peter (Scott) 1945- ..... **CLC 19**
See also CA 101

Ruskin, John 1819-1900......... **TCLC 63**
See also CA 114; 129; CDBLB 1832-1890;
DLB 55, 163; SATA 24

Russ, Joanna 1937-.............. **CLC 15**
See also CA 25-28R; CANR 11, 31; DLB 8;
MTCW

Russell, George William 1867-1935
See A. E.
See also CA 104; CDBLB 1890-1914;
DAM POET

Russell, (Henry) Ken(neth Alfred)
1927- .... **CLC 16**
See also CA 105

Russell, Willy 1947-............. **CLC 60**

Rutherford, Mark .... **TCLC 25**
See also White, William Hale
See also DLB 18

Ruyslinck, Ward 1929-............ **CLC 14**
See also Belser, Reimond Karel Maria de

Ryan, Cornelius (John) 1920-1974 ... **CLC 7**
See also CA 69-72; 53-56; CANR 38

Ryan, Michael 1946- .... **CLC 65**
See also CA 49-52; DLBY 82

Rybakov, Anatoli (Naumovich)
1911- .... **CLC 23, 53**
See also CA 126; 135; SATA 79

Ryder, Jonathan
See Ludlum, Robert

Ryga, George 1932-1987 ..... **CLC 14; DAC**
See also CA 101; 124; CANR 43;
DAM MST; DLB 60

S. S.
See Sassoon, Siegfried (Lorraine)

Saba, Umberto 1883-1957 .... **TCLC 33**
See also CA 144; DLB 114

Sabatini, Rafael 1875-1950 ...... **TCLC 47**

Sabato, Ernesto (R.)
1911- .... **CLC 10, 23; HLC**
See also CA 97-100; CANR 32;
DAM MULT; DLB 145; HW; MTCW

Sacastru, Martin
See Bioy Casares, Adolfo

Sacher-Masoch, Leopold von
1836(?)-1895 .... **NCLC 31**

Sachs, Marilyn (Stickle) 1927- ..... **CLC 35**
See also AAYA 2; CA 17-20R; CANR 13,
47; CLR 2; JRDA; MAICYA; SAAS 2;
SATA 3, 68

Sachs, Nelly 1891-1970 .... **CLC 14**
See also CA 17-18; 25-28R; CAP 2

Sackler, Howard (Oliver)
1929-1982 .... **CLC 14**
See also CA 61-64; 108; CANR 30; DLB 7

Sacks, Oliver (Wolf) 1933- .... **CLC 67**
See also CA 53-56; CANR 28, 50;
INT CANR-28; MTCW

Sade, Donatien Alphonse Francois Comte
1740-1814 .... **NCLC 47**

Sadoff, Ira 1945-.................. **CLC 9**
See also CA 53-56; CANR 5, 21; DLB 120

Saetone
See Camus, Albert

Safire, William 1929-.............. **CLC 10**
See also CA 17-20R; CANR 31

Sagan, Carl (Edward) 1934-........ **CLC 30**
See also AAYA 2; CA 25-28R; CANR 11,
36; MTCW; SATA 58

Sagan, Francoise .... **CLC 3, 6, 9, 17, 36**
See also Quoirez, Francoise
See also DLB 83

Sahgal, Nayantara (Pandit) 1927-... **CLC 41**
See also CA 9-12R; CANR 11

Saint, H(arry) F. 1941- .... **CLC 50**
See also CA 127

St. Aubin de Teran, Lisa 1953-
See Teran, Lisa St. Aubin de
See also CA 118; 126; INT 126

Sainte-Beuve, Charles Augustin
1804-1869 . . . . NCLC 5

Saint-Exupery, Antoine (Jean Baptiste Marie Roger) de
1900-1944 . . . . TCLC 2, 56; WLC
See also CA 108; 132; CLR 10; DAM NOV;
DLB 72; MAICYA; MTCW; SATA 20

St. John, David
See Hunt, E(verette) Howard, (Jr.)

Saint-John Perse
See Leger, (Marie-Rene Auguste) Alexis
Saint-Leger

Saintsbury, George (Edward Bateman)
1845-1933 . . . . TCLC 31
See also DLB 57, 149

Sait Faik . . . . TCLC 23
See also Abasiyanik, Sait Faik

Saki . . . . TCLC 3; SSC 12
See also Munro, H(ector) H(ugh)

Sala, George Augustus . . . . NCLC 46

Salama, Hannu 1936- . . . . CLC 18

Salamanca, J(ack) R(ichard)
1922- . . . . CLC 4, 15
See also CA 25-28R

Sale, J. Kirkpatrick
See Sale, Kirkpatrick

Sale, Kirkpatrick 1937- . . . . CLC 68
See also CA 13-16R; CANR 10

Salinas, Luis Omar 1937- . . . CLC 90; HLC
See also CA 131; DAM MULT; DLB 82;
HW

Salinas (y Serrano), Pedro
1891(?)-1951 . . . . TCLC 17
See also CA 117; DLB 134

Salinger, J(erome) D(avid)
1919- . . . . . . CLC 1, 3, 8, 12, 55, 56; DA;
DAB; DAC; SSC 2; WLC
See also AAYA 2; CA 5-8R; CANR 39;
CDALB 1941-1968; CLR 18; DAM MST,
NOV, POP; DLB 2, 102; MAICYA;
MTCW; SATA 67

Salisbury, John
See Caute, David

Salter, James 1925- . . . . CLC 7, 52, 59
See also CA 73-76; DLB 130

Saltus, Edgar (Everton)
1855-1921 . . . . TCLC 8
See also CA 105

Saltykov, Mikhail Evgrafovich
1826-1889 . . . . NCLC 16

Samarakis, Antonis 1919- . . . . CLC 5
See also CA 25-28R; CAAS 16; CANR 36

Sanchez, Florencio 1875-1910 . . . . . TCLC 37
See also HW

Sanchez, Luis Rafael 1936- . . . . CLC 23
See also CA 128; DLB 145; HW

Sanchez, Sonia 1934- . . . CLC 5; BLC; PC 9
See also BW 2; CA 33-36R; CANR 24, 49;
CLR 18; DAM MULT; DLB 41;
DLBD 8; MAICYA; MTCW; SATA 22

Sand, George
1804-1876 . . . . . NCLC 2, 42; DA; DAB;
DAC; WLC
See also DAM MST, NOV; DLB 119

Sandburg, Carl (August)
1878-1967 . . . . CLC 1, 4, 10, 15, 35; DA;
DAB; DAC; PC 2; WLC
See also CA 5-8R; 25-28R; CANR 35;
CDALB 1865-1917; DAM MST, POET;
DLB 17, 54; MAICYA; MTCW; SATA 8

Sandburg, Charles
See Sandburg, Carl (August)

Sandburg, Charles A.
See Sandburg, Carl (August)

Sanders, (James) Ed(ward) 1939- . . . CLC 53
See also CA 13-16R; CAAS 21; CANR 13,
44; DLB 16

Sanders, Lawrence 1920- . . . . CLC 41
See also BEST 89:4; CA 81-84; CANR 33;
DAM POP; MTCW

Sanders, Noah
See Blount, Roy (Alton), Jr.

Sanders, Winston P.
See Anderson, Poul (William)

Sandoz, Mari(e Susette)
1896-1966 . . . . CLC 28
See also CA 1-4R; 25-28R; CANR 17;
DLB 9; MTCW; SATA 5

Saner, Reg(inald Anthony) 1931- . . . . CLC 9
See also CA 65-68

Sannazaro, Jacopo 1456(?)-1530 . . . . . . LC 8

Sansom, William
1912-1976 . . . . CLC 2, 6; SSC 21
See also CA 5-8R; 65-68; CANR 42;
DAM NOV; DLB 139; MTCW

Santayana, George 1863-1952 . . . . . TCLC 40
See also CA 115; DLB 54, 71; DLBD 13

Santiago, Danny . . . . CLC 33
See also James, Daniel (Lewis)
See also DLB 122

Santmyer, Helen Hoover
1895-1986 . . . . CLC 33
See also CA 1-4R; 118; CANR 15, 33;
DLBY 84; MTCW

Santos, Bienvenido N(uqui) 1911- . . . CLC 22
See also CA 101; CANR 19, 46;
DAM MULT

Sapper . . . . TCLC 44
See also McNeile, Herman Cyril

Sappho fl. 6th cent. B.C.- . . . . CMLC 3; PC 5
See also DAM POET

Sarduy, Severo 1937-1993 . . . . CLC 6
See also CA 89-92; 142; DLB 113; HW

Sargeson, Frank 1903-1982 . . . . CLC 31
See also CA 25-28R; 106; CANR 38

Sarmiento, Felix Ruben Garcia
See Dario, Ruben

Saroyan, William
1908-1981 . . . . . CLC 1, 8, 10, 29, 34, 56;
DA; DAB; DAC; SSC 21; WLC
See also CA 5-8R; 103; CANR 30;
DAM DRAM, MST, NOV; DLB 7, 9, 86;
DLBY 81; MTCW; SATA 23;
SATA-Obit 24

Sarraute, Nathalie
1900- . . . . CLC 1, 2, 4, 8, 10, 31, 80
See also CA 9-12R; CANR 23; DLB 83;
MTCW

Sarton, (Eleanor) May
1912-1995 . . . . CLC 4, 14, 49, 91
See also CA 1-4R; 149; CANR 1, 34;
DAM POET; DLB 48; DLBY 81;
INT CANR-34; MTCW; SATA 36;
SATA-Obit 86

Sartre, Jean-Paul
1905-1980 . . . . CLC 1, 4, 7, 9, 13, 18, 24,
44, 50, 52; DA; DAB; DAC; DC 3; WLC
See also CA 9-12R; 97-100; CANR 21;
DAM DRAM, MST, NOV; DLB 72;
MTCW

Sassoon, Siegfried (Lorraine)
1886-1967 . . . . CLC 36; DAB; PC 12
See also CA 104; 25-28R; CANR 36;
DAM MST, NOV, POET; DLB 20;
MTCW

Satterfield, Charles
See Pohl, Frederik

Saul, John (W. III) 1942- . . . . CLC 46
See also AAYA 10; BEST 90:4; CA 81-84;
CANR 16, 40; DAM NOV, POP

Saunders, Caleb
See Heinlein, Robert A(nson)

Saura (Atares), Carlos 1932- . . . . CLC 20
See also CA 114; 131; HW

Sauser-Hall, Frederic 1887-1961 . . . . CLC 18
See also Cendrars, Blaise
See also CA 102; 93-96; CANR 36; MTCW

Saussure, Ferdinand de
1857-1913 . . . . TCLC 49

Savage, Catharine
See Brosman, Catharine Savage

Savage, Thomas 1915- . . . . CLC 40
See also CA 126; 132; CAAS 15; INT 132

Savan, Glenn 19(?)- . . . . CLC 50

Sayers, Dorothy L(eigh)
1893-1957 . . . . TCLC 2, 15
See also CA 104; 119; CDBLB 1914-1945;
DAM POP; DLB 10, 36, 77, 100; MTCW

Sayers, Valerie 1952- . . . . CLC 50
See also CA 134

Sayles, John (Thomas)
1950- . . . . CLC 7, 10, 14
See also CA 57-60; CANR 41; DLB 44

Scammell, Michael . . . . CLC 34

Scannell, Vernon 1922- . . . . CLC 49
See also CA 5-8R; CANR 8, 24; DLB 27;
SATA 59

Scarlett, Susan
See Streatfeild, (Mary) Noel

Schaeffer, Susan Fromberg
1941- . . . . CLC 6, 11, 22
See also CA 49-52; CANR 18; DLB 28;
MTCW; SATA 22

Schary, Jill
See Robinson, Jill

Schell, Jonathan 1943- . . . . CLC 35
See also CA 73-76; CANR 12

Schelling, Friedrich Wilhelm Joseph von
1775-1854 . . . . NCLC 30
See also DLB 90

Schendel, Arthur van 1874-1946 . . . TCLC 56

Scherer, Jean-Marie Maurice 1920-
See Rohmer, Eric
See also CA 110

Schevill, James (Erwin) 1920-....... **CLC 7**
See also CA 5-8R; CAAS 12

Schiller, Friedrich 1759-1805 .... **NCLC 39**
See also DAM DRAM; DLB 94

Schisgal, Murray (Joseph) 1926-..... **CLC 6**
See also CA 21-24R; CANR 48

Schlee, Ann 1934-................ **CLC 35**
See also CA 101; CANR 29; SATA 44;
SATA-Brief 36

Schlegel, August Wilhelm von
1767-1845 .... **NCLC 15**
See also DLB 94

Schlegel, Friedrich 1772-1829.... **NCLC 45**
See also DLB 90

Schlegel, Johann Elias (von)
1719(?)-1749 .... **LC 5**

Schlesinger, Arthur M(eier), Jr.
1917- .... **CLC 84**
See also AITN 1; CA 1-4R; CANR 1, 28;
DLB 17; INT CANR-28; MTCW;
SATA 61

Schmidt, Arno (Otto) 1914-1979.... **CLC 56**
See also CA 128; 109; DLB 69

Schmitz, Aron Hector 1861-1928
See Svevo, Italo
See also CA 104; 122; MTCW

Schnackenberg, Gjertrud 1953-..... **CLC 40**
See also CA 116; DLB 120

Schneider, Leonard Alfred 1925-1966
See Bruce, Lenny
See also CA 89-92

Schnitzler, Arthur
1862-1931 .... **TCLC 4; SSC 15**
See also CA 104; DLB 81, 118

Schopenhauer, Arthur
1788-1860 .... **NCLC 51**
See also DLB 90

Schor, Sandra (M.) 1932(?)-1990 ... **CLC 65**
See also CA 132

Schorer, Mark 1908-1977 .... **CLC 9**
See also CA 5-8R; 73-76; CANR 7;
DLB 103

Schrader, Paul (Joseph) 1946-...... **CLC 26**
See also CA 37-40R; CANR 41; DLB 44

Schreiner, Olive (Emilie Albertina)
1855-1920 .... **TCLC 9**
See also CA 105; DLB 18, 156

Schulberg, Budd (Wilson)
1914- .... **CLC 7, 48**
See also CA 25-28R; CANR 19; DLB 6, 26,
28; DLBY 81

Schulz, Bruno
1892-1942 .... **TCLC 5, 51; SSC 13**
See also CA 115; 123

Schulz, Charles M(onroe) 1922-.... **CLC 12**
See also CA 9-12R; CANR 6;
INT CANR-6; SATA 10

Schumacher, E(rnst) F(riedrich)
1911-1977 .... **CLC 80**
See also CA 81-84; 73-76; CANR 34

Schuyler, James Marcus
1923-1991 .... **CLC 5, 23**
See also CA 101; 134; DAM POET; DLB 5;
INT 101

Schwartz, Delmore (David)
1913-1966 ... **CLC 2, 4, 10, 45, 87; PC 8**
See also CA 17-18; 25-28R; CANR 35;
CAP 2; DLB 28, 48; MTCW

Schwartz, Ernst
See Ozu, Yasujiro

Schwartz, John Burnham 1965- .... **CLC 59**
See also CA 132

Schwartz, Lynne Sharon 1939-..... **CLC 31**
See also CA 103; CANR 44

Schwartz, Muriel A.
See Eliot, T(homas) S(tearns)

Schwarz-Bart, Andre 1928-....... **CLC 2, 4**
See also CA 89-92

Schwarz-Bart, Simone 1938-........ **CLC 7**
See also BW 2; CA 97-100

Schwob, (Mayer Andre) Marcel
1867-1905 .... **TCLC 20**
See also CA 117; DLB 123

Sciascia, Leonardo
1921-1989 .... **CLC 8, 9, 41**
See also CA 85-88; 130; CANR 35; MTCW

Scoppettone, Sandra 1936-........ **CLC 26**
See also AAYA 11; CA 5-8R; CANR 41;
SATA 9

Scorsese, Martin 1942- .... **CLC 20, 89**
See also CA 110; 114; CANR 46

Scotland, Jay
See Jakes, John (William)

Scott, Duncan Campbell
1862-1947 .... **TCLC 6; DAC**
See also CA 104; DLB 92

Scott, Evelyn 1893-1963.......... **CLC 43**
See also CA 104; 112; DLB 9, 48

Scott, F(rancis) R(eginald)
1899-1985 .... **CLC 22**
See also CA 101; 114; DLB 88; INT 101

Scott, Frank
See Scott, F(rancis) R(eginald)

Scott, Joanna 1960- .... **CLC 50**
See also CA 126

Scott, Paul (Mark) 1920-1978.... **CLC 9, 60**
See also CA 81-84; 77-80; CANR 33;
DLB 14; MTCW

Scott, Walter
1771-1832 .... **NCLC 15; DA; DAB;**
DAC; PC 13; WLC
See also CDBLB 1789-1832; DAM MST,
NOV, POET; DLB 93, 107, 116, 144, 159;
YABC 2

Scribe, (Augustin) Eugene
1791-1861 .... **NCLC 16; DC 5**
See also DAM DRAM

Scrum, R.
See Crumb, R(obert)

Scudery, Madeleine de 1607-1701..... **LC 2**

Scum
See Crumb, R(obert)

Scumbag, Little Bobby
See Crumb, R(obert)

Seabrook, John
See Hubbard, L(afayette) Ron(ald)

Sealy, I. Allan 1951- .... **CLC 55**

Search, Alexander
See Pessoa, Fernando (Antonio Nogueira)

Sebastian, Lee
See Silverberg, Robert

Sebastian Owl
See Thompson, Hunter S(tockton)

Sebestyen, Ouida 1924-............ **CLC 30**
See also AAYA 8; CA 107; CANR 40;
CLR 17; JRDA; MAICYA; SAAS 10;
SATA 39

Secundus, H. Scriblerus
See Fielding, Henry

Sedges, John
See Buck, Pearl S(ydenstricker)

Sedgwick, Catharine Maria
1789-1867 .... **NCLC 19**
See also DLB 1, 74

Seelye, John 1931-................ **CLC 7**

Seferiades, Giorgos Stylianou 1900-1971
See Seferis, George
See also CA 5-8R; 33-36R; CANR 5, 36;
MTCW

Seferis, George .... **CLC 5, 11**
See also Seferiades, Giorgos Stylianou

Segal, Erich (Wolf) 1937- .... **CLC 3, 10**
See also BEST 89:1; CA 25-28R; CANR 20,
36; DAM POP; DLBY 86;
INT CANR-20; MTCW

Seger, Bob 1945-................. **CLC 35**

Seghers, Anna .... **CLC 7**
See also Radvanyi, Netty
See also DLB 69

Seidel, Frederick (Lewis) 1936-..... **CLC 18**
See also CA 13-16R; CANR 8; DLBY 84

Seifert, Jaroslav
1901-1986 .... **CLC 34, 44, 93**
See also CA 127; MTCW

Sei Shonagon c. 966-1017(?) ...... **CMLC 6**

Selby, Hubert, Jr.
1928- .... **CLC 1, 2, 4, 8; SSC 20**
See also CA 13-16R; CANR 33; DLB 2

Selzer, Richard 1928-............. **CLC 74**
See also CA 65-68; CANR 14

Sembene, Ousmane
See Ousmane, Sembene

Senancour, Etienne Pivert de
1770-1846 .... **NCLC 16**
See also DLB 119

Sender, Ramon (Jose)
1902-1982 .... **CLC 8; HLC**
See also CA 5-8R; 105; CANR 8;
DAM MULT; HW; MTCW

Seneca, Lucius Annaeus
4B.C.-65.............. **CMLC 6; DC 5**
See also DAM DRAM

Senghor, Leopold Sedar
1906- .... **CLC 54; BLC**
See also BW 2; CA 116; 125; CANR 47;
DAM MULT, POET; MTCW

Shone, Patric
See Hanley, James

Shreve, Susan Richards 1939-...... CLC 23
See also CA 49-52; CAAS 5; CANR 5, 38;
MAICYA; SATA 46; SATA-Brief 41

Shue, Larry 1946-1985............ CLC 52
See also CA 145; 117; DAM DRAM

Shu-Jen, Chou 1881-1936
See Lu Hsun
See also CA 104

Shulman, Alix Kates 1932-...... CLC 2, 10
See also CA 29-32R; CANR 43; SATA 7

Shuster, Joe 1914-............... CLC 21

Shute, Nevil...................... CLC 30
See also Norway, Nevil Shute

Shuttle, Penelope (Diane) 1947-..... CLC 7
See also CA 93-96; CANR 39; DLB 14, 40

Sidney, Mary 1561-1621 .... LC 19

Sidney, Sir Philip
1554-1586 ..... LC 19; DA; DAB; DAC
See also CDBLB Before 1660; DAM MST,
POET

Siegel, Jerome 1914- .... CLC 21
See also CA 116

Siegel, Jerry
See Siegel, Jerome

Sienkiewicz, Henryk (Adam Alexander Pius)
1846-1916 .... TCLC 3
See also CA 104; 134

Sierra, Gregorio Martinez
See Martinez Sierra, Gregorio

Sierra, Maria (de la O'LeJarraga) Martinez
See Martinez Sierra, Maria (de la
O'LeJarraga)

Sigal, Clancy 1926-............... CLC 7
See also CA 1-4R

Sigourney, Lydia Howard (Huntley)
1791-1865 .... NCLC 21
See also DLB 1, 42, 73

Siguenza y Gongora, Carlos de
1645-1700 .... LC 8

Sigurjonsson, Johann 1880-1919... TCLC 27

Sikelianos, Angelos 1884-1951 .... TCLC 39

Silkin, Jon 1930- .... CLC 2, 6, 43
See also CA 5-8R; CAAS 5; DLB 27

Silko, Leslie (Marmon)
1948- .... CLC 23, 74; DA; DAC
See also AAYA 14; CA 115; 122;
CANR 45; DAM MST, MULT, POP;
DLB 143; NNAL

Sillanpaa, Frans Eemil 1888-1964... CLC 19
See also CA 129; 93-96; MTCW

Sillitoe, Alan
1928-......... CLC 1, 3, 6, 10, 19, 57
See also AITN 1; CA 9-12R; CAAS 2;
CANR 8, 26; CDBLB 1960 to Present;
DLB 14, 139; MTCW; SATA 61

Silone, Ignazio 1900-1978 .... CLC 4
See also CA 25-28; 81-84; CANR 34;
CAP 2; MTCW

Silver, Joan Micklin 1935- .... CLC 20
See also CA 114; 121; INT 121

Silver, Nicholas
See Faust, Frederick (Schiller)

Silverberg, Robert 1935-........... CLC 7
See also CA 1-4R; CAAS 3; CANR 1, 20,
36; DAM POP; DLB 8; INT CANR-20;
MAICYA; MTCW; SATA 13

Silverstein, Alvin 1933-........... CLC 17
See also CA 49-52; CANR 2; CLR 25;
JRDA; MAICYA; SATA 8, 69

Silverstein, Virginia B(arbara Opshelor)
1937-........................ CLC 17
See also CA 49-52; CANR 2; CLR 25;
JRDA; MAICYA; SATA 8, 69

Sim, Georges
See Simenon, Georges (Jacques Christian)

Simak, Clifford D(onald)
1904-1988 .... CLC 1, 55
See also CA 1-4R; 125; CANR 1, 35;
DLB 8; MTCW; SATA-Obit 56

Simenon, Georges (Jacques Christian)
1903-1989 ...... CLC 1, 2, 3, 8, 18, 47
See also CA 85-88; 129; CANR 35;
DAM POP; DLB 72; DLBY 89; MTCW

Simic, Charles 1938-... CLC 6, 9, 22, 49, 68
See also CA 29-32R; CAAS 4; CANR 12,
33; DAM POET; DLB 105

Simmons, Charles (Paul) 1924-..... CLC 57
See also CA 89-92; INT 89-92

Simmons, Dan 1948-.............. CLC 44
See also AAYA 16; CA 138; DAM POP

Simmons, James (Stewart Alexander)
1933-........................ CLC 43
See also CA 105; CAAS 21; DLB 40

Simms, William Gilmore
1806-1870 .... NCLC 3
See also DLB 3, 30, 59, 73

Simon, Carly 1945-............... CLC 26
See also CA 105

Simon, Claude 1913-...... CLC 4, 9, 15, 39
See also CA 89-92; CANR 33; DAM NOV;
DLB 83; MTCW

Simon, (Marvin) Neil
1927-........... CLC 6, 11, 31, 39, 70
See also AITN 1; CA 21-24R; CANR 26;
DAM DRAM; DLB 7; MTCW

Simon, Paul 1942(?)- .... CLC 17
See also CA 116

Simonon, Paul 1956(?)- .... CLC 30

Simpson, Harriette
See Arnow, Harriette (Louisa) Simpson

Simpson, Louis (Aston Marantz)
1923-.................. CLC 4, 7, 9, 32
See also CA 1-4R; CAAS 4; CANR 1;
DAM POET; DLB 5; MTCW

Simpson, Mona (Elizabeth) 1957-... CLC 44
See also CA 122; 135

Simpson, N(orman) F(rederick)
1919-........................ CLC 29
See also CA 13-16R; DLB 13

Sinclair, Andrew (Annandale)
1935-........................ CLC 2, 14
See also CA 9-12R; CAAS 5; CANR 14, 38;
DLB 14; MTCW

Sinclair, Emil
See Hesse, Hermann

Sinclair, Iain 1943-.............. CLC 76
See also CA 132

Sinclair, Iain MacGregor
See Sinclair, Iain

Sinclair, Mary Amelia St. Clair 1865(?)-1946
See Sinclair, May
See also CA 104

Sinclair, May.................. TCLC 3, 11
See also Sinclair, Mary Amelia St. Clair
See also DLB 36, 135

Sinclair, Upton (Beall)
1878-1968 ...... CLC 1, 11, 15, 63; DA;
DAB; DAC; WLC
See also CA 5-8R; 25-28R; CANR 7;
CDALB 1929-1941; DAM MST, NOV;
DLB 9; INT CANR-7; MTCW; SATA 9

Singer, Isaac
See Singer, Isaac Bashevis

Singer, Isaac Bashevis
1904-1991...CLC 1, 3, 6, 9, 11, 15, 23,
38, 69; DA; DAB; DAC; SSC 3; WLC
See also AITN 1, 2; CA 1-4R; 134;
CANR 1, 39; CDALB 1941-1968; CLR 1;
DAM MST, NOV; DLB 6, 28, 52;
DLBY 91; JRDA; MAICYA; MTCW;
SATA 3, 27; SATA-Obit 68

Singer, Israel Joshua 1893-1944... TCLC 33

Singh, Khushwant 1915-........... CLC 11
See also CA 9-12R; CAAS 9; CANR 6

Sinjohn, John
See Galsworthy, John

Sinyavsky, Andrei (Donatevich)
1925-........................ CLC 8
See also CA 85-88

Sirin, V.
See Nabokov, Vladimir (Vladimirovich)

Sissman, L(ouis) E(dward)
1928-1976 .... CLC 9, 18
See also CA 21-24R; 65-68; CANR 13;
DLB 5

Sisson, C(harles) H(ubert) 1914-..... CLC 8
See also CA 1-4R; CAAS 3; CANR 3, 48;
DLB 27

Sitwell, Dame Edith
1887-1964 .... CLC 2, 9, 67; PC 3
See also CA 9-12R; CANR 35;
CDBLB 1945-1960; DAM POET;
DLB 20; MTCW

Sjoewall, Maj 1935-............... CLC 7
See also CA 65-68

Sjowall, Maj
See Sjoewall, Maj

Skelton, Robin 1925-............. CLC 13
See also AITN 2; CA 5-8R; CAAS 5;
CANR 28; DLB 27, 53

Skolimowski, Jerzy 1938-......... CLC 20
See also CA 128

Skram, Amalie (Bertha)
1847-1905 .... TCLC 25

Skvorecky, Josef (Vaclav)
1924-.......... CLC 15, 39, 69; DAC
See also CA 61-64; CAAS 1; CANR 10, 34;
DAM NOV; MTCW

Slade, Bernard................ CLC 11, 46
See also Newbound, Bernard Slade
See also CAAS 9; DLB 53

Spark, Muriel (Sarah)
1918- .... **CLC 2, 3, 5, 8, 13, 18, 40;**
DAB; DAC; SSC 10
See also CA 5-8R; CANR 12, 36;
CDBLB 1945-1960; DAM MST, NOV;
DLB 15, 139; INT CANR-12; MTCW

Spaulding, Douglas
See Bradbury, Ray (Douglas)

Spaulding, Leonard
See Bradbury, Ray (Douglas)

Spence, J. A. D.
See Eliot, T(homas) S(tearns)

Spencer, Elizabeth 1921- .... **CLC 22**
See also CA 13-16R; CANR 32; DLB 6;
MTCW; SATA 14

Spencer, Leonard G.
See Silverberg, Robert

Spencer, Scott 1945-.............. **CLC 30**
See also CA 113; CANR 51; DLBY 86

Spender, Stephen (Harold)
1909-1995 ...... **CLC 1, 2, 5, 10, 41, 91**
See also CA 9-12R; 149; CANR 31;
CDBLB 1945-1960; DAM POET;
DLB 20; MTCW

Spengler, Oswald (Arnold Gottfried)
1880-1936 .... **TCLC 25**
See also CA 118

Spenser, Edmund
1552(?)-1599 .... **LC 5; DA; DAB; DAC;**
PC 8; WLC
See also CDBLB Before 1660; DAM MST,
POET

Spicer, Jack 1925-1965 ...... **CLC 8, 18, 72**
See also CA 85-88; DAM POET; DLB 5, 16

Spiegelman, Art 1948- .... **CLC 76**
See also AAYA 10; CA 125; CANR 41

Spielberg, Peter 1929- .... **CLC 6**
See also CA 5-8R; CANR 4, 48; DLBY 81

Spielberg, Steven 1947- .... **CLC 20**
See also AAYA 8; CA 77-80; CANR 32;
SATA 32

Spillane, Frank Morrison 1918-
See Spillane, Mickey
See also CA 25-28R; CANR 28; MTCW;
SATA 66

Spillane, Mickey .... **CLC 3, 13**
See also Spillane, Frank Morrison

Spinoza, Benedictus de 1632-1677 .... **LC 9**

Spinrad, Norman (Richard) 1940-... **CLC 46**
See also CA 37-40R; CAAS 19; CANR 20;
DLB 8; INT CANR-20

Spitteler, Carl (Friedrich Georg)
1845-1924 .... **TCLC 12**
See also CA 109; DLB 129

Spivack, Kathleen (Romola Drucker)
1938- .... **CLC 6**
See also CA 49-52

Spoto, Donald 1941-.............. **CLC 39**
See also CA 65-68; CANR 11

Springsteen, Bruce (F.) 1949- ...... **CLC 17**
See also CA 111

Spurling, Hilary 1940-............ **CLC 34**
See also CA 104; CANR 25

Spyker, John Howland
See Elman, Richard

Squires, (James) Radcliffe
1917-1993 .... **CLC 51**
See also CA 1-4R; 140; CANR 6, 21

Srivastava, Dhanpat Rai 1880(?)-1936
See Premchand
See also CA 118

Stacy, Donald
See Pohl, Frederik

Stael, Germaine de
See Stael-Holstein, Anne Louise Germaine
Necker Baronn
See also DLB 119

Stael-Holstein, Anne Louise Germaine Necker
Baronn 1766-1817 .... **NCLC 3**
See also Stael, Germaine de

Stafford, Jean 1915-1979... **CLC 4, 7, 19, 68**
See also CA 1-4R; 85-88; CANR 3; DLB 2;
MTCW; SATA-Obit 22

Stafford, William (Edgar)
1914-1993 .... **CLC 4, 7, 29**
See also CA 5-8R; 142; CAAS 3; CANR 5,
22; DAM POET; DLB 5; INT CANR-22

Staines, Trevor
See Brunner, John (Kilian Houston)

Stairs, Gordon
See Austin, Mary (Hunter)

Stannard, Martin 1947-........... **CLC 44**
See also CA 142; DLB 155

Stanton, Maura 1946- .... **CLC 9**
See also CA 89-92; CANR 15; DLB 120

Stanton, Schuyler
See Baum, L(yman) Frank

Stapledon, (William) Olaf
1886-1950 .... **TCLC 22**
See also CA 111; DLB 15

Starbuck, George (Edwin) 1931-.... **CLC 53**
See also CA 21-24R; CANR 23;
DAM POET

Stark, Richard
See Westlake, Donald E(dwin)

Staunton, Schuyler
See Baum, L(yman) Frank

Stead, Christina (Ellen)
1902-1983 .... **CLC 2, 5, 8, 32, 80**
See also CA 13-16R; 109; CANR 33, 40;
MTCW

Stead, William Thomas
1849-1912 .... **TCLC 48**

Steele, Richard 1672-1729.......... **LC 18**
See also CDBLB 1660-1789; DLB 84, 101

Steele, Timothy (Reid) 1948-....... **CLC 45**
See also CA 93-96; CANR 16, 50; DLB 120

Steffens, (Joseph) Lincoln
1866-1936 .... **TCLC 20**
See also CA 117

Stegner, Wallace (Earle)
1909-1993 .... **CLC 9, 49, 81**
See also AITN 1; BEST 90:3; CA 1-4R;
141; CAAS 9; CANR 1, 21, 46;
DAM NOV; DLB 9; DLBY 93; MTCW

Stein, Gertrude
1874-1946 ..... **TCLC 1, 6, 28, 48; DA;**
DAB; DAC; WLC
See also CA 104; 132; CDALB 1917-1929;
DAM MST, NOV, POET; DLB 4, 54, 86;
MTCW

Steinbeck, John (Ernst)
1902-1968 ...... **CLC 1, 5, 9, 13, 21, 34,**
45, 75; DA; DAB; DAC; SSC 11; WLC
See also AAYA 12; CA 1-4R; 25-28R;
CANR 1, 35; CDALB 1929-1941;
DAM DRAM, MST, NOV; DLB 7, 9;
DLBD 2; MTCW; SATA 9

Steinem, Gloria 1934-............. **CLC 63**
See also CA 53-56; CANR 28, 51; MTCW

Steiner, George 1929-............. **CLC 24**
See also CA 73-76; CANR 31; DAM NOV;
DLB 67; MTCW; SATA 62

Steiner, K. Leslie
See Delany, Samuel R(ay, Jr.)

Steiner, Rudolf 1861-1925........ **TCLC 13**
See also CA 107

Stendhal
1783-1842 .... **NCLC 23, 46; DA; DAB;**
DAC; WLC
See also DAM MST, NOV; DLB 119

Stephen, Leslie 1832-1904 .... **TCLC 23**
See also CA 123; DLB 57, 144

Stephen, Sir Leslie
See Stephen, Leslie

Stephen, Virginia
See Woolf, (Adeline) Virginia

Stephens, James 1882(?)-1950...... **TCLC 4**
See also CA 104; DLB 19, 153, 162

Stephens, Reed
See Donaldson, Stephen R.

Steptoe, Lydia
See Barnes, Djuna

Sterchi, Beat 1949-............... **CLC 65**

Sterling, Brett
See Bradbury, Ray (Douglas); Hamilton,
Edmond

Sterling, Bruce 1954-.............. **CLC 72**
See also CA 119; CANR 44

Sterling, George 1869-1926....... **TCLC 20**
See also CA 117; DLB 54

Stern, Gerald 1925- .... **CLC 40**
See also CA 81-84; CANR 28; DLB 105

Stern, Richard (Gustave) 1928-... **CLC 4, 39**
See also CA 1-4R; CANR 1, 25; DLBY 87;
INT CANR-25

Sternberg, Josef von 1894-1969..... **CLC 20**
See also CA 81-84

Sterne, Laurence
1713-1768 ...... **LC 2; DA; DAB; DAC;**
WLC
See also CDBLB 1660-1789; DAM MST,
NOV; DLB 39

Sternheim, (William Adolf) Carl
1878-1942 .... **TCLC 8**
See also CA 105; DLB 56, 118

Stevens, Mark 1951- .... **CLC 34**
See also CA 122

Surtees, Robert Smith
    1803-1864 .... **NCLC 14**
    See also DLB 21

Susann, Jacqueline 1921-1974 .... **CLC 3**
    See also AITN 1; CA 65-68; 53-56; MTCW

Su Shih 1036-1101 .... **CMLC 15**

Suskind, Patrick
    See Sueskind, Patrick
    See also CA 145

Sutcliff, Rosemary
    1920-1992 .... **CLC 26; DAB; DAC**
    See also AAYA 10; CA 5-8R; 139;
    CANR 37; CLR 1, 37; DAM MST, POP;
    JRDA; MAICYA; SATA 6, 44, 78;
    SATA-Obit 73

Sutro, Alfred 1863-1933 .... **TCLC 6**
    See also CA 105; DLB 10

Sutton, Henry
    See Slavitt, David R(ytman)

Svevo, Italo .... **TCLC 2, 35**
    See also Schmitz, Aron Hector

Swados, Elizabeth (A.) 1951- .... **CLC 12**
    See also CA 97-100; CANR 49; INT 97-100

Swados, Harvey 1920-1972 .... **CLC 5**
    See also CA 5-8R; 37-40R; CANR 6;
    DLB 2

Swan, Gladys 1934- .... **CLC 69**
    See also CA 101; CANR 17, 39

Swarthout, Glendon (Fred)
    1918-1992 .... **CLC 35**
    See also CA 1-4R; 139; CANR 1, 47;
    SATA 26

Sweet, Sarah C.
    See Jewett, (Theodora) Sarah Orne

Swenson, May
    1919-1989 .... **CLC 4, 14, 61; DA; DAB;**
                                    DAC; PC 14
    See also CA 5-8R; 130; CANR 36;
    DAM MST, POET; DLB 5; MTCW;
    SATA 15

Swift, Augustus
    See Lovecraft, H(oward) P(hillips)

Swift, Graham (Colin) 1949- .... **CLC 41, 88**
    See also CA 117; 122; CANR 46

Swift, Jonathan
    1667-1745 ...... **LC 1; DA; DAB; DAC;**
                                    PC 9; WLC
    See also CDBLB 1660-1789; DAM MST,
    NOV, POET; DLB 39, 95, 101; SATA 19

Swinburne, Algernon Charles
    1837-1909 ..... **TCLC 8, 36; DA; DAB;**
                                    DAC; WLC
    See also CA 105; 140; CDBLB 1832-1890;
    DAM MST, POET; DLB 35, 57

Swinfen, Ann .... **CLC 34**

Swinnerton, Frank Arthur
    1884-1982 .... **CLC 31**
    See also CA 108; DLB 34

Swithen, John
    See King, Stephen (Edwin)

Sylvia
    See Ashton-Warner, Sylvia (Constance)

Symmes, Robert Edward
    See Duncan, Robert (Edward)

Symonds, John Addington
    1840-1893 .... **NCLC 34**
    See also DLB 57, 144

Symons, Arthur 1865-1945 .... **TCLC 11**
    See also CA 107; DLB 19, 57, 149

Symons, Julian (Gustave)
    1912-1994 .... **CLC 2, 14, 32**
    See also CA 49-52; 147; CAAS 3; CANR 3,
    33; DLB 87, 155; DLBY 92; MTCW

Synge, (Edmund) J(ohn) M(illington)
    1871-1909 .... **TCLC 6, 37; DC 2**
    See also CA 104; 141; CDBLB 1890-1914;
    DAM DRAM; DLB 10, 19

Syruc, J.
    See Milosz, Czeslaw

Szirtes, George 1948- .... **CLC 46**
    See also CA 109; CANR 27

Tabori, George 1914- .... **CLC 19**
    See also CA 49-52; CANR 4

Tagore, Rabindranath
    1861-1941 .... **TCLC 3, 53; PC 8**
    See also CA 104; 120; DAM DRAM,
    POET; MTCW

Taine, Hippolyte Adolphe
    1828-1893 .... **NCLC 15**

Talese, Gay 1932- .... **CLC 37**
    See also AITN 1; CA 1-4R; CANR 9;
    INT CANR-9; MTCW

Tallent, Elizabeth (Ann) 1954- ..... **CLC 45**
    See also CA 117; DLB 130

Tally, Ted 1952- .... **CLC 42**
    See also CA 120; 124; INT 124

Tamayo y Baus, Manuel
    1829-1898 .... **NCLC 1**

Tammsaare, A(nton) H(ansen)
    1878-1940 .... **TCLC 27**

Tan, Amy 1952- .... **CLC 59**
    See also AAYA 9; BEST 89:3; CA 136;
    DAM MULT, NOV, POP; SATA 75

Tandem, Felix
    See Spitteler, Carl (Friedrich Georg)

Tanizaki, Jun'ichiro
    1886-1965 ...... **CLC 8, 14, 28; SSC 21**
    See also CA 93-96; 25-28R

Tanner, William
    See Amis, Kingsley (William)

Tao Lao
    See Storni, Alfonsina

Tarassoff, Lev
    See Troyat, Henri

Tarbell, Ida M(inerva)
    1857-1944 .... **TCLC 40**
    See also CA 122; DLB 47

Tarkington, (Newton) Booth
    1869-1946 .... **TCLC 9**
    See also CA 110; 143; DLB 9, 102;
    SATA 17

Tarkovsky, Andrei (Arsenyevich)
    1932-1986 .... **CLC 75**
    See also CA 127

Tartt, Donna 1964(?)- .... **CLC 76**
    See also CA 142

Tasso, Torquato 1544-1595 .... **LC 5**

Tate, (John Orley) Allen
    1899-1979 .... **CLC 2, 4, 6, 9, 11, 14, 24**
    See also CA 5-8R; 85-88; CANR 32;
    DLB 4, 45, 63; MTCW

Tate, Ellalice
    See Hibbert, Eleanor Alice Burford

Tate, James (Vincent) 1943- ... **CLC 2, 6, 25**
    See also CA 21-24R; CANR 29; DLB 5

Tavel, Ronald 1940- .... **CLC 6**
    See also CA 21-24R; CANR 33

Taylor, C(ecil) P(hilip) 1929-1981 ... **CLC 27**
    See also CA 25-28R; 105; CANR 47

Taylor, Edward
    1642(?)-1729 ... **LC 11; DA; DAB; DAC**
    See also DAM MST, POET; DLB 24

Taylor, Eleanor Ross 1920- .... **CLC 5**
    See also CA 81-84

Taylor, Elizabeth 1912-1975 ... **CLC 2, 4, 29**
    See also CA 13-16R; CANR 9; DLB 139;
    MTCW; SATA 13

Taylor, Henry (Splawn) 1942- ...... **CLC 44**
    See also CA 33-36R; CAAS 7; CANR 31;
    DLB 5

Taylor, Kamala (Purnaiya) 1924-
    See Markandaya, Kamala
    See also CA 77-80

Taylor, Mildred D. .... **CLC 21**
    See also AAYA 10; BW 1; CA 85-88;
    CANR 25; CLR 9; DLB 52; JRDA;
    MAICYA; SAAS 5; SATA 15, 70

Taylor, Peter (Hillsman)
    1917-1994 ..... **CLC 1, 4, 18, 37, 44, 50,**
                                    71; SSC 10
    See also CA 13-16R; 147; CANR 9, 50;
    DLBY 81, 94; INT CANR-9; MTCW

Taylor, Robert Lewis 1912- .... **CLC 14**
    See also CA 1-4R; CANR 3; SATA 10

Tchekhov, Anton
    See Chekhov, Anton (Pavlovich)

Teasdale, Sara 1884-1933 .... **TCLC 4**
    See also CA 104; DLB 45; SATA 32

Tegner, Esaias 1782-1846 .... **NCLC 2**

Teilhard de Chardin, (Marie Joseph) Pierre
    1881-1955 .... **TCLC 9**
    See also CA 105

Temple, Ann
    See Mortimer, Penelope (Ruth)

Tennant, Emma (Christina)
    1937- .... **CLC 13, 52**
    See also CA 65-68; CAAS 9; CANR 10, 38;
    DLB 14

Tenneshaw, S. M.
    See Silverberg, Robert

Tennyson, Alfred
    1809-1892 .... **NCLC 30; DA; DAB;**
                                    DAC; PC 6; WLC
    See also CDBLB 1832-1890; DAM MST,
    POET; DLB 32

Teran, Lisa St. Aubin de .... **CLC 36**
    See also St. Aubin de Teran, Lisa

Terence 195(?)B.C.-159B.C. ...... **CMLC 14**

Teresa de Jesus, St. 1515-1582 ...... **LC 18**

Tomlin, Lily...................... **CLC 17**
See also Tomlin, Mary Jean

Tomlin, Mary Jean 1939(?)-
See Tomlin, Lily
See also CA 117

Tomlinson, (Alfred) Charles
1927- .... **CLC 2, 4, 6, 13, 45**
See also CA 5-8R; CANR 33; DAM POET;
DLB 40

Tonson, Jacob
See Bennett, (Enoch) Arnold

Toole, John Kennedy
1937-1969 .... **CLC 19, 64**
See also CA 104; DLBY 81

Toomer, Jean
1894-1967 ...... **CLC 1, 4, 13, 22; BLC;
PC 7; SSC 1**
See also BW 1; CA 85-88;
CDALB 1917-1929; DAM MULT;
DLB 45, 51; MTCW

Torley, Luke
See Blish, James (Benjamin)

Tornimparte, Alessandra
See Ginzburg, Natalia

Torre, Raoul della
See Mencken, H(enry) L(ouis)

Torrey, E(dwin) Fuller 1937-....... **CLC 34**
See also CA 119

Torsvan, Ben Traven
See Traven, B.

Torsvan, Benno Traven
See Traven, B.

Torsvan, Berick Traven
See Traven, B.

Torsvan, Berwick Traven
See Traven, B.

Torsvan, Bruno Traven
See Traven, B.

Torsvan, Traven
See Traven, B.

Tournier, Michel (Edouard)
1924-...................**CLC 6, 23, 36**
See also CA 49-52; CANR 3, 36; DLB 83;
MTCW; SATA 23

Tournimparte, Alessandra
See Ginzburg, Natalia

Towers, Ivar
See Kornbluth, C(yril) M.

Towne, Robert (Burton) 1936(?)-.... **CLC 87**
See also CA 108; DLB 44

Townsend, Sue 1946- .. **CLC 61; DAB; DAC**
See also CA 119; 127; INT 127; MTCW;
SATA 55; SATA-Brief 48

Townshend, Peter (Dennis Blandford)
1945- .... **CLC 17, 42**
See also CA 107

Tozzi, Federigo 1883-1920........ **TCLC 31**

Traill, Catharine Parr
1802-1899 .... **NCLC 31**
See also DLB 99

Trakl, Georg 1887-1914........... **TCLC 5**
See also CA 104

Transtroemer, Tomas (Goesta)
1931- .... **CLC 52, 65**
See also CA 117; 129; CAAS 17;
DAM POET

Transtromer, Tomas Gosta
See Transtroemer, Tomas (Goesta)

Traven, B. (?)-1969............. **CLC 8, 11**
See also CA 19-20; 25-28R; CAP 2; DLB 9,
56; MTCW

Treitel, Jonathan 1959- .... **CLC 70**

Tremain, Rose 1943-.............. **CLC 42**
See also CA 97-100; CANR 44; DLB 14

Tremblay, Michel 1942-...... **CLC 29; DAC**
See also CA 116; 128; DAM MST; DLB 60;
MTCW

Trevanian........................ **CLC 29**
See also Whitaker, Rod(ney)

Trevor, Glen
See Hilton, James

Trevor, William
1928- ..... **CLC 7, 9, 14, 25, 71; SSC 21**
See also Cox, William Trevor
See also DLB 14, 139

Trifonov, Yuri (Valentinovich)
1925-1981 .... **CLC 45**
See also CA 126; 103; MTCW

Trilling, Lionel 1905-1975 .... **CLC 9, 11, 24**
See also CA 9-12R; 61-64; CANR 10;
DLB 28, 63; INT CANR-10; MTCW

Trimball, W. H.
See Mencken, H(enry) L(ouis)

Tristan
See Gomez de la Serna, Ramon

Tristram
See Housman, A(lfred) E(dward)

Trogdon, William (Lewis) 1939-
See Heat-Moon, William Least
See also CA 115; 119; CANR 47; INT 119

Trollope, Anthony
1815-1882 ..... **NCLC 6, 33; DA; DAB;
DAC; WLC**
See also CDBLB 1832-1890; DAM MST,
NOV; DLB 21, 57, 159; SATA 22

Trollope, Frances 1779-1863 ..... **NCLC 30**
See also DLB 21

Trotsky, Leon 1879-1940......... **TCLC 22**
See also CA 118

Trotter (Cockburn), Catharine
1679-1749 .... **LC 8**
See also DLB 84

Trout, Kilgore
See Farmer, Philip Jose

Trow, George W. S. 1943-......... **CLC 52**
See also CA 126

Troyat, Henri 1911-.............. **CLC 23**
See also CA 45-48; CANR 2, 33; MTCW

Trudeau, G(arretson) B(eekman) 1948-
See Trudeau, Garry B.
See also CA 81-84; CANR 31; SATA 35

Trudeau, Garry B.................. **CLC 12**
See also Trudeau, G(arretson) B(eekman)
See also AAYA 10; AITN 2

Truffaut, Francois 1932-1984....... **CLC 20**
See also CA 81-84; 113; CANR 34

Trumbo, Dalton 1905-1976 .... **CLC 19**
See also CA 21-24R; 69-72; CANR 10;
DLB 26

Trumbull, John 1750-1831....... **NCLC 30**
See also DLB 31

Trundlett, Helen B.
See Eliot, T(homas) S(tearns)

Tryon, Thomas 1926-1991 .... **CLC 3, 11**
See also AITN 1; CA 29-32R; 135;
CANR 32; DAM POP; MTCW

Tryon, Tom
See Tryon, Thomas

Ts'ao Hsueh-ch'in 1715(?)-1763...... **LC 1**

Tsushima, Shuji 1909-1948
See Dazai, Osamu
See also CA 107

Tsvetaeva (Efron), Marina (Ivanovna)
1892-1941 .... **TCLC 7, 35; PC 14**
See also CA 104; 128; MTCW

Tuck, Lily 1938-................. **CLC 70**
See also CA 139

Tu Fu 712-770..................... **PC 9**
See also DAM MULT

Tunis, John R(oberts) 1889-1975 ... **CLC 12**
See also CA 61-64; DLB 22; JRDA;
MAICYA; SATA 37; SATA-Brief 30

Tuohy, Frank..................... **CLC 37**
See also Tuohy, John Francis
See also DLB 14, 139

Tuohy, John Francis 1925-
See Tuohy, Frank
See also CA 5-8R; CANR 3, 47

Turco, Lewis (Putnam) 1934- ... **CLC 11, 63**
See also CA 13-16R; CAAS 22; CANR 24,
51; DLBY 84

Turgenev, Ivan
1818-1883 .... **NCLC 21; DA; DAB;
DAC; SSC 7; WLC**
See also DAM MST, NOV

Turgot, Anne-Robert-Jacques
1727-1781 .... **LC 26**

Turner, Frederick 1943-........... **CLC 48**
See also CA 73-76; CAAS 10; CANR 12,
30; DLB 40

Tutu, Desmond M(pilo)
1931- .... **CLC 80; BLC**
See also BW 1; CA 125; DAM MULT

Tutuola, Amos 1920- ... **CLC 5, 14, 29; BLC**
See also BW 2; CA 9-12R; CANR 27;
DAM MULT; DLB 125; MTCW

Twain, Mark
..... **TCLC 6, 12, 19, 36, 48, 59; SSC 6;
WLC**
See also Clemens, Samuel Langhorne
See also DLB 11, 12, 23, 64, 74

Tyler, Anne
1941- .... **CLC 7, 11, 18, 28, 44, 59**
See also BEST 89:1; CA 9-12R; CANR 11,
33; DAM NOV, POP; DLB 6, 143;
DLBY 82; MTCW; SATA 7

Tyler, Royall 1757-1826........... **NCLC 3**
See also DLB 37

Tynan, Katharine 1861-1931 .... **TCLC 3**
See also CA 104; DLB 153

Tyutchev, Fyodor 1803-1873 ..... **NCLC 34**

Vesaas, Tarjei 1897-1970 . . . . **CLC 48**
See also CA 29-32R

Vialis, Gaston
See Simenon, Georges (Jacques Christian)

Vian, Boris 1920-1959 . . . . **TCLC 9**
See also CA 106; DLB 72

Viaud, (Louis Marie) Julien 1850-1923
See Loti, Pierre
See also CA 107

Vicar, Henry
See Felsen, Henry Gregor

Vicker, Angus
See Felsen, Henry Gregor

Vidal, Gore
1925- . . . . . **CLC 2, 4, 6, 8, 10, 22, 33, 72**
See also AITN 1; BEST 90:2; CA 5-8R;
CANR 13, 45; DAM NOV, POP; DLB 6,
152; INT CANR-13; MTCW

Viereck, Peter (Robert Edwin)
1916- . . . . **CLC 4**
See also CA 1-4R; CANR 1, 47; DLB 5

Vigny, Alfred (Victor) de
1797-1863 . . . . **NCLC 7**
See also DAM POET; DLB 119

Vilakazi, Benedict Wallet
1906-1947 . . . . **TCLC 37**

Villiers de l'Isle Adam, Jean Marie Mathias
Philippe Auguste Comte
1838-1889 . . . . **NCLC 3; SSC 14**
See also DLB 123

Villon, Francois 1431-1463(?) . . . . **PC 13**

Vinci, Leonardo da 1452-1519 . . . . . . **LC 12**

Vine, Barbara . . . . **CLC 50**
See also Rendell, Ruth (Barbara)
See also BEST 90:4

Vinge, Joan D(ennison)
1948- . . . . **CLC 30; SSC 22**
See also CA 93-96; SATA 36

Violis, G.
See Simenon, Georges (Jacques Christian)

Visconti, Luchino 1906-1976 . . . . **CLC 16**
See also CA 81-84; 65-68; CANR 39

Vittorini, Elio 1908-1966 . . . . . . **CLC 6, 9, 14**
See also CA 133; 25-28R

Vizinczey, Stephen 1933- . . . . **CLC 40**
See also CA 128; INT 128

Vliet, R(ussell) G(ordon)
1929-1984 . . . . **CLC 22**
See also CA 37-40R; 112; CANR 18

Vogau, Boris Andreyevich 1894-1937(?)
See Pilnyak, Boris
See also CA 123

Vogel, Paula A(nne) 1951- . . . . **CLC 76**
See also CA 108

Voight, Ellen Bryant 1943- . . . . **CLC 54**
See also CA 69-72; CANR 11, 29; DLB 120

Voigt, Cynthia 1942- . . . . **CLC 30**
See also AAYA 3; CA 106; CANR 18, 37,
40; CLR 13; INT CANR-18; JRDA;
MAICYA; SATA 48, 79; SATA-Brief 33

Voinovich, Vladimir (Nikolaevich)
1932- . . . . **CLC 10, 49**
See also CA 81-84; CAAS 12; CANR 33;
MTCW

Vollmann, William T. 1959- . . . . **CLC 89**
See also CA 134; DAM NOV, POP

Voloshinov, V. N.
See Bakhtin, Mikhail Mikhailovich

Voltaire
1694-1778 . . . . . **LC 14; DA; DAB; DAC;**
SSC 12; WLC
See also DAM DRAM, MST

von Daeniken, Erich 1935- . . . . **CLC 30**
See also AITN 1; CA 37-40R; CANR 17,
44

von Daniken, Erich
See von Daeniken, Erich

von Heidenstam, (Carl Gustaf) Verner
See Heidenstam, (Carl Gustaf) Verner von

von Heyse, Paul (Johann Ludwig)
See Heyse, Paul (Johann Ludwig von)

von Hofmannsthal, Hugo
See Hofmannsthal, Hugo von

von Horvath, Odon
See Horvath, Oedoen von

von Horvath, Oedoen
See Horvath, Oedoen von

von Liliencron, (Friedrich Adolf Axel) Detlev
See Liliencron, (Friedrich Adolf Axel)
Detlev von

Vonnegut, Kurt, Jr.
1922- . . . . . . **CLC 1, 2, 3, 4, 5, 8, 12, 22,**
40, 60; DA; DAB; DAC; SSC 8; WLC
See also AAYA 6; AITN 1; BEST 90:4;
CA 1-4R; CANR 1, 25, 49;
CDALB 1968-1988; DAM MST, NOV,
POP; DLB 2, 8, 152; DLBD 3; DLBY 80;
MTCW

Von Rachen, Kurt
See Hubbard, L(afayette) Ron(ald)

von Rezzori (d'Arezzo), Gregor
See Rezzori (d'Arezzo), Gregor von

von Sternberg, Josef
See Sternberg, Josef von

Vorster, Gordon 1924- . . . . **CLC 34**
See also CA 133

Vosce, Trudie
See Ozick, Cynthia

Voznesensky, Andrei (Andreievich)
1933- . . . . **CLC 1, 15, 57**
See also CA 89-92; CANR 37;
DAM POET; MTCW

Waddington, Miriam 1917- . . . . **CLC 28**
See also CA 21-24R; CANR 12, 30;
DLB 68

Wagman, Fredrica 1937- . . . . **CLC 7**
See also CA 97-100; INT 97-100

Wagner, Richard 1813-1883 . . . . **NCLC 9**
See also DLB 129

Wagner-Martin, Linda 1936- . . . . **CLC 50**

Wagoner, David (Russell)
1926- . . . . **CLC 3, 5, 15**
See also CA 1-4R; CAAS 3; CANR 2;
DLB 5; SATA 14

Wah, Fred(erick James) 1939- . . . . . . **CLC 44**
See also CA 107; 141; DLB 60

Wahloo, Per 1926-1975 . . . . **CLC 7**
See also CA 61-64

Wahloo, Peter
See Wahloo, Per

Wain, John (Barrington)
1925-1994 . . . . **CLC 2, 11, 15, 46**
See also CA 5-8R; 145; CAAS 4; CANR 23;
CDBLB 1960 to Present; DLB 15, 27,
139, 155; MTCW

Wajda, Andrzej 1926- . . . . **CLC 16**
See also CA 102

Wakefield, Dan 1932- . . . . **CLC 7**
See also CA 21-24R; CAAS 7

Wakoski, Diane
1937- . . . . . **CLC 2, 4, 7, 9, 11, 40; PC 15**
See also CA 13-16R; CAAS 1; CANR 9;
DAM POET; DLB 5; INT CANR-9

Wakoski-Sherbell, Diane
See Wakoski, Diane

Walcott, Derek (Alton)
1930- . . . . **CLC 2, 4, 9, 14, 25, 42, 67, 76;**
BLC; DAB; DAC
See also BW 2; CA 89-92; CANR 26, 47;
DAM MST, MULT, POET; DLB 117;
DLBY 81; MTCW

Waldman, Anne 1945- . . . . **CLC 7**
See also CA 37-40R; CAAS 17; CANR 34;
DLB 16

Waldo, E. Hunter
See Sturgeon, Theodore (Hamilton)

Waldo, Edward Hamilton
See Sturgeon, Theodore (Hamilton)

Walker, Alice (Malsenior)
1944- . . . . **CLC 5, 6, 9, 19, 27, 46, 58;**
BLC; DA; DAB; DAC; SSC 5
See also AAYA 3; BEST 89:4; BW 2;
CA 37-40R; CANR 9, 27, 49;
CDALB 1968-1988; DAM MST, MULT,
NOV, POP; DLB 6, 33, 143;
INT CANR-27; MTCW; SATA 31

Walker, David Harry 1911-1992 . . . . **CLC 14**
See also CA 1-4R; 137; CANR 1; SATA 8;
SATA-Obit 71

Walker, Edward Joseph 1934-
See Walker, Ted
See also CA 21-24R; CANR 12, 28

Walker, George F.
1947- . . . . **CLC 44, 61; DAB; DAC**
See also CA 103; CANR 21, 43;
DAM MST; DLB 60

Walker, Joseph A. 1935- . . . . **CLC 19**
See also BW 1; CA 89-92; CANR 26;
DAM DRAM, MST; DLB 38

Walker, Margaret (Abigail)
1915- . . . . **CLC 1, 6; BLC**
See also BW 2; CA 73-76; CANR 26;
DAM MULT; DLB 76, 152; MTCW

Walker, Ted . . . . **CLC 13**
See also Walker, Edward Joseph
See also DLB 40

Wallace, David Foster 1962- . . . . **CLC 50**
See also CA 132

Wallace, Dexter
See Masters, Edgar Lee

Wallace, (Richard Horatio) Edgar
1875-1932 . . . . **TCLC 57**
See also CA 115; DLB 70

Wallace, Irving 1916-1990....... CLC 7, 13
See also AITN 1; CA 1-4R; 132; CAAS 1;
CANR 1, 27; DAM NOV, POP;
INT CANR-27; MTCW

Wallant, Edward Lewis
1926-1962 .... CLC 5, 10
See also CA 1-4R; CANR 22; DLB 2, 28,
143; MTCW

Walley, Byron
See Card, Orson Scott

Walpole, Horace 1717-1797......... LC 2
See also DLB 39, 104

Walpole, Hugh (Seymour)
1884-1941 .... TCLC 5
See also CA 104; DLB 34

Walser, Martin 1927-............ CLC 27
See also CA 57-60; CANR 8, 46; DLB 75,
124

Walser, Robert
1878-1956 .... TCLC 18; SSC 20
See also CA 118; DLB 66

Walsh, Jill Paton.............. CLC 35
See also Paton Walsh, Gillian
See also AAYA 11; CLR 2; DLB 161;
SAAS 3

Walter, Villiam Christian
See Andersen, Hans Christian

Wambaugh, Joseph (Aloysius, Jr.)
1937- .... CLC 3, 18
See also AITN 1; BEST 89:3; CA 33-36R;
CANR 42; DAM NOV, POP; DLB 6;
DLBY 83; MTCW

Ward, Arthur Henry Sarsfield 1883-1959
See Rohmer, Sax
See also CA 108

Ward, Douglas Turner 1930-....... CLC 19
See also BW 1; CA 81-84; CANR 27;
DLB 7, 38

Ward, Mary Augusta
See Ward, Mrs. Humphry

Ward, Mrs. Humphry
1851-1920 .... TCLC 55
See also DLB 18

Ward, Peter
See Faust, Frederick (Schiller)

Warhol, Andy 1928(?)-1987........ CLC 20
See also AAYA 12; BEST 89:4; CA 89-92;
121; CANR 34

Warner, Francis (Robert le Plastrier)
1937- .... CLC 14
See also CA 53-56; CANR 11

Warner, Marina 1946-............ CLC 59
See also CA 65-68; CANR 21

Warner, Rex (Ernest) 1905-1986.... CLC 45
See also CA 89-92; 119; DLB 15

Warner, Susan (Bogert)
1819-1885 .... NCLC 31
See also DLB 3, 42

Warner, Sylvia (Constance) Ashton
See Ashton-Warner, Sylvia (Constance)

Warner, Sylvia Townsend
1893-1978 .... CLC 7, 19; SSC 23
See also CA 61-64; 77-80; CANR 16;
DLB 34, 139; MTCW

Warren, Mercy Otis 1728-1814... NCLC 13
See also DLB 31

Warren, Robert Penn
1905-1989 .... CLC 1, 4, 6, 8, 10, 13, 18,
39, 53, 59; DA; DAB; DAC; SSC 4; WLC
See also AITN 1; CA 13-16R; 129;
CANR 10, 47; CDALB 1968-1988;
DAM MST, NOV, POET; DLB 2, 48,
152; DLBY 80, 89; INT CANR-10;
MTCW; SATA 46; SATA-Obit 63

Warshofsky, Isaac
See Singer, Isaac Bashevis

Warton, Thomas 1728-1790 .... LC 15
See also DAM POET; DLB 104, 109

Waruk, Kona
See Harris, (Theodore) Wilson

Warung, Price 1855-1911........ TCLC 45

Warwick, Jarvis
See Garner, Hugh

Washington, Alex
See Harris, Mark

Washington, Booker T(aliaferro)
1856-1915 .... TCLC 10; BLC
See also BW 1; CA 114; 125; DAM MULT;
SATA 28

Washington, George 1732-1799...... LC 25
See also DLB 31

Wassermann, (Karl) Jakob
1873-1934 .... TCLC 6
See also CA 104; DLB 66

Wasserstein, Wendy
1950- .... CLC 32, 59, 90; DC 4
See also CA 121; 129; CABS 3;
DAM DRAM; INT 129

Waterhouse, Keith (Spencer)
1929- .... CLC 47
See also CA 5-8R; CANR 38; DLB 13, 15;
MTCW

Waters, Frank (Joseph)
1902-1995 .... CLC 88
See also CA 5-8R; 149; CAAS 13; CANR 3,
18; DLBY 86

Waters, Roger 1944-.............. CLC 35

Watkins, Frances Ellen
See Harper, Frances Ellen Watkins

Watkins, Gerrold
See Malzberg, Barry N(athaniel)

Watkins, Paul 1964-.............. CLC 55
See also CA 132

Watkins, Vernon Phillips
1906-1967 .... CLC 43
See also CA 9-10; 25-28R; CAP 1; DLB 20

Watson, Irving S.
See Mencken, H(enry) L(ouis)

Watson, John H.
See Farmer, Philip Jose

Watson, Richard F.
See Silverberg, Robert

Waugh, Auberon (Alexander) 1939-.. CLC 7
See also CA 45-48; CANR 6, 22; DLB 14

Waugh, Evelyn (Arthur St. John)
1903-1966 ...... CLC 1, 3, 8, 13, 19, 27,
44; DA; DAB; DAC; WLC
See also CA 85-88; 25-28R; CANR 22;
CDBLB 1914-1945; DAM MST, NOV,
POP; DLB 15, 162; MTCW

Waugh, Harriet 1944- .... CLC 6
See also CA 85-88; CANR 22

Ways, C. R.
See Blount, Roy (Alton), Jr.

Waystaff, Simon
See Swift, Jonathan

Webb, (Martha) Beatrice (Potter)
1858-1943 .... TCLC 22
See also Potter, Beatrice
See also CA 117

Webb, Charles (Richard) 1939-...... CLC 7
See also CA 25-28R

Webb, James H(enry), Jr. 1946-.... CLC 22
See also CA 81-84

Webb, Mary (Gladys Meredith)
1881-1927 .... TCLC 24
See also CA 123; DLB 34

Webb, Mrs. Sidney
See Webb, (Martha) Beatrice (Potter)

Webb, Phyllis 1927-.............. CLC 18
See also CA 104; CANR 23; DLB 53

Webb, Sidney (James)
1859-1947 .... TCLC 22
See also CA 117

Webber, Andrew Lloyd............. CLC 21
See also Lloyd Webber, Andrew

Weber, Lenora Mattingly
1895-1971 .... CLC 12
See also CA 19-20; 29-32R; CAP 1;
SATA 2; SATA-Obit 26

Webster, John 1579(?)-1634(?) .... DC 2
See also CDBLB Before 1660; DA; DAB;
DAC; DAM DRAM, MST; DLB 58;
WLC

Webster, Noah 1758-1843 .... NCLC 30

Wedekind, (Benjamin) Frank(lin)
1864-1918 .... TCLC 7
See also CA 104; DAM DRAM; DLB 118

Weidman, Jerome 1913-............ CLC 7
See also AITN 2; CA 1-4R; CANR 1;
DLB 28

Weil, Simone (Adolphine)
1909-1943 .... TCLC 23
See also CA 117

Weinstein, Nathan
See West, Nathanael

Weinstein, Nathan von Wallenstein
See West, Nathanael

Weir, Peter (Lindsay) 1944- .... CLC 20
See also CA 113; 123

Weiss, Peter (Ulrich)
1916-1982 .... CLC 3, 15, 51
See also CA 45-48; 106; CANR 3;
DAM DRAM; DLB 69, 124

Weiss, Theodore (Russell)
1916- .... CLC 3, 8, 14
See also CA 9-12R; CAAS 2; CANR 46;
DLB 5

Welch, (Maurice) Denton
1915-1948 . . . . TCLC 22
See also CA 121; 148

Welch, James 1940- . . . . CLC 6, 14, 52
See also CA 85-88; CANR 42;
DAM MULT, POP; NNAL

Weldon, Fay
1933- . . . . CLC 6, 9, 11, 19, 36, 59
See also CA 21-24R; CANR 16, 46;
CDBLB 1960 to Present; DAM POP;
DLB 14; INT CANR-16; MTCW

Wellek, Rene 1903-1995. . . . . CLC 28
See also CA 5-8R; 150; CAAS 7; CANR 8;
DLB 63; INT CANR-8

Weller, Michael 1942- . . . . CLC 10, 53
See also CA 85-88

Weller, Paul 1958- . . . . CLC 26

Wellershoff, Dieter 1925-. . . . . CLC 46
See also CA 89-92; CANR 16, 37

Welles, (George) Orson
1915-1985 . . . . CLC 20, 80
See also CA 93-96; 117

Wellman, Mac 1945- . . . . CLC 65

Wellman, Manly Wade 1903-1986 . . CLC 49
See also CA 1-4R; 118; CANR 6, 16, 44;
SATA 6; SATA-Obit 47

Wells, Carolyn 1869(?)-1942 . . . . . . TCLC 35
See also CA 113; DLB 11

Wells, H(erbert) G(eorge)
1866-1946 . . . . TCLC 6, 12, 19; DA;
DAB; DAC; SSC 6; WLC
See also CA 110; 121; CDBLB 1914-1945;
DAM MST, NOV; DLB 34, 70, 156;
MTCW; SATA 20

Wells, Rosemary 1943-. . . . . CLC 12
See also AAYA 13; CA 85-88; CANR 48;
CLR 16; MAICYA; SAAS 1; SATA 18,
69

Welty, Eudora
1909- . . . . . . CLC 1, 2, 5, 14, 22, 33; DA;
DAB; DAC; SSC 1; WLC
See also CA 9-12R; CABS 1; CANR 32;
CDALB 1941-1968; DAM MST, NOV;
DLB 2, 102, 143; DLBD 12; DLBY 87;
MTCW

Wen I-to 1899-1946 . . . . TCLC 28

Wentworth, Robert
See Hamilton, Edmond

Werfel, Franz (V.) 1890-1945 . . . . . . TCLC 8
See also CA 104; DLB 81, 124

Wergeland, Henrik Arnold
1808-1845 . . . . NCLC 5

Wersba, Barbara 1932-. . . . . CLC 30
See also AAYA 2; CA 29-32R; CANR 16,
38; CLR 3; DLB 52; JRDA; MAICYA;
SAAS 2; SATA 1, 58

Wertmueller, Lina 1928- . . . . CLC 16
See also CA 97-100; CANR 39

Wescott, Glenway 1901-1987. . . . . . CLC 13
See also CA 13-16R; 121; CANR 23;
DLB 4, 9, 102

Wesker, Arnold 1932- . . CLC 3, 5, 42; DAB
See also CA 1-4R; CAAS 7; CANR 1, 33;
CDBLB 1960 to Present; DAM DRAM;
DLB 13; MTCW

Wesley, Richard (Errol) 1945-. . . . . . CLC 7
See also BW 1; CA 57-60; CANR 27;
DLB 38

Wessel, Johan Herman 1742-1785 . . . . LC 7

West, Anthony (Panther)
1914-1987 . . . . CLC 50
See also CA 45-48; 124; CANR 3, 19;
DLB 15

West, C. P.
See Wodehouse, P(elham) G(renville)

West, (Mary) Jessamyn
1902-1984 . . . . CLC 7, 17
See also CA 9-12R; 112; CANR 27; DLB 6;
DLBY 84; MTCW; SATA-Obit 37

West, Morris L(anglo) 1916-. . . . . CLC 6, 33
See also CA 5-8R; CANR 24, 49; MTCW

West, Nathanael
1903-1940 . . . . . TCLC 1, 14, 44; SSC 16
See also CA 104; 125; CDALB 1929-1941;
DLB 4, 9, 28; MTCW

West, Owen
See Koontz, Dean R(ay)

West, Paul 1930- . . . . CLC 7, 14
See also CA 13-16R; CAAS 7; CANR 22;
DLB 14; INT CANR-22

West, Rebecca 1892-1983 . . CLC 7, 9, 31, 50
See also CA 5-8R; 109; CANR 19; DLB 36;
DLBY 83; MTCW

Westall, Robert (Atkinson)
1929-1993 . . . . CLC 17
See also AAYA 12; CA 69-72; 141;
CANR 18; CLR 13; JRDA; MAICYA;
SAAS 2; SATA 23, 69; SATA-Obit 75

Westlake, Donald E(dwin)
1933- . . . . CLC 7, 33
See also CA 17-20R; CAAS 13; CANR 16,
44; DAM POP; INT CANR-16

Westmacott, Mary
See Christie, Agatha (Mary Clarissa)

Weston, Allen
See Norton, Andre

Wetcheek, J. L.
See Feuchtwanger, Lion

Wetering, Janwillem van de
See van de Wetering, Janwillem

Wetherell, Elizabeth
See Warner, Susan (Bogert)

Whale, James 1889-1957 . . . . TCLC 63

Whalen, Philip 1923- . . . . CLC 6, 29
See also CA 9-12R; CANR 5, 39; DLB 16

Wharton, Edith (Newbold Jones)
1862-1937 . . . . . . TCLC 3, 9, 27, 53; DA;
DAB; DAC; SSC 6; WLC
See also CA 104; 132; CDALB 1865-1917;
DAM MST, NOV; DLB 4, 9, 12, 78;
DLBD 13; MTCW

Wharton, James
See Mencken, H(enry) L(ouis)

Wharton, William (a pseudonym)
. . . . CLC 18, 37
See also CA 93-96; DLBY 80; INT 93-96

Wheatley (Peters), Phillis
1754(?)-1784 . . . . LC 3; BLC; DA; DAC;
PC 3; WLC
See also CDALB 1640-1865; DAM MST,
MULT, POET; DLB 31, 50

Wheelock, John Hall 1886-1978. . . . CLC 14
See also CA 13-16R; 77-80; CANR 14;
DLB 45

White, E(lwyn) B(rooks)
1899-1985 . . . . CLC 10, 34, 39
See also AITN 2; CA 13-16R; 116;
CANR 16, 37; CLR 1, 21; DAM POP;
DLB 11, 22; MAICYA; MTCW;
SATA 2, 29; SATA-Obit 44

White, Edmund (Valentine III)
1940- . . . . CLC 27
See also AAYA 7; CA 45-48; CANR 3, 19,
36; DAM POP; MTCW

White, Patrick (Victor Martindale)
1912-1990 . . CLC 3, 4, 5, 7, 9, 18, 65, 69
See also CA 81-84; 132; CANR 43; MTCW

White, Phyllis Dorothy James 1920-
See James, P. D.
See also CA 21-24R; CANR 17, 43;
DAM POP; MTCW

White, T(erence) H(anbury)
1906-1964 . . . . CLC 30
See also CA 73-76; CANR 37; DLB 160;
JRDA; MAICYA; SATA 12

White, Terence de Vere
1912-1994 . . . . CLC 49
See also CA 49-52; 145; CANR 3

White, Walter F(rancis)
1893-1955 . . . . TCLC 15
See also White, Walter
See also BW 1; CA 115; 124; DLB 51

White, William Hale 1831-1913
See Rutherford, Mark
See also CA 121

Whitehead, E(dward) A(nthony)
1933- . . . . CLC 5
See also CA 65-68

Whitemore, Hugh (John) 1936-. . . . . CLC 37
See also CA 132; INT 132

Whitman, Sarah Helen (Power)
1803-1878 . . . . NCLC 19
See also DLB 1

Whitman, Walt(er)
1819-1892 . . . . . NCLC 4, 31; DA; DAB;
DAC; PC 3; WLC
See also CDALB 1640-1865; DAM MST,
POET; DLB 3, 64; SATA 20

Whitney, Phyllis A(yame) 1903-. . . . CLC 42
See also AITN 2; BEST 90:3; CA 1-4R;
CANR 3, 25, 38; DAM POP; JRDA;
MAICYA; SATA 1, 30

Whittemore, (Edward) Reed (Jr.)
1919- . . . . CLC 4
See also CA 9-12R; CAAS 8; CANR 4;
DLB 5

Whittier, John Greenleaf
1807-1892 . . . . NCLC 8
See also CDALB 1640-1865; DAM POET;
DLB 1

Whittlebot, Hernia
See Coward, Noel (Peirce)

Winchilsea, Anne (Kingsmill) Finch Counte
  1661-1720 . . . . **LC 3**

Windham, Basil
  See Wodehouse, P(elham) G(renville)

Wingrove, David (John) 1954- . . . . . . **CLC 68**
  See also CA 133

Winters, Janet Lewis . . . . **CLC 41**
  See also Lewis, Janet
  See also DLBY 87

Winters, (Arthur) Yvor
  1900-1968 . . . . **CLC 4, 8, 32**
  See also CA 11-12; 25-28R; CAP 1;
  DLB 48; MTCW

Winterson, Jeanette 1959- . . . . **CLC 64**
  See also CA 136; DAM POP

Winthrop, John 1588-1649 . . . . **LC 31**
  See also DLB 24, 30

Wiseman, Frederick 1930- . . . . **CLC 20**

Wister, Owen 1860-1938 . . . . **TCLC 21**
  See also CA 108; DLB 9, 78; SATA 62

Witkacy
  See Witkiewicz, Stanislaw Ignacy

Witkiewicz, Stanislaw Ignacy
  1885-1939 . . . . **TCLC 8**
  See also CA 105

Wittgenstein, Ludwig (Josef Johann)
  1889-1951 . . . . **TCLC 59**
  See also CA 113

Wittig, Monique 1935(?)- . . . . **CLC 22**
  See also CA 116; 135; DLB 83

Wittlin, Jozef 1896-1976 . . . . **CLC 25**
  See also CA 49-52; 65-68; CANR 3

Wodehouse, P(elham) G(renville)
  1881-1975 . . . **CLC 1, 2, 5, 10, 22; DAB;
  DAC; SSC 2**
  See also AITN 2; CA 45-48; 57-60;
  CANR 3, 33; CDBLB 1914-1945;
  DAM NOV; DLB 34, 162; MTCW;
  SATA 22

Woiwode, L.
  See Woiwode, Larry (Alfred)

Woiwode, Larry (Alfred) 1941- . . . **CLC 6, 10**
  See also CA 73-76; CANR 16; DLB 6;
  INT CANR-16

Wojciechowska, Maia (Teresa)
  1927- . . . . **CLC 26**
  See also AAYA 8; CA 9-12R; CANR 4, 41;
  CLR 1; JRDA; MAICYA; SAAS 1;
  SATA 1, 28, 83

Wolf, Christa 1929- . . . . **CLC 14, 29, 58**
  See also CA 85-88; CANR 45; DLB 75;
  MTCW

Wolfe, Gene (Rodman) 1931- . . . . **CLC 25**
  See also CA 57-60; CAAS 9; CANR 6, 32;
  DAM POP; DLB 8

Wolfe, George C. 1954- . . . . **CLC 49**
  See also CA 149

Wolfe, Thomas (Clayton)
  1900-1938 . . . . . **TCLC 4, 13, 29, 61; DA;
  DAB; DAC; WLC**
  See also CA 104; 132; CDALB 1929-1941;
  DAM MST, NOV; DLB 9, 102; DLBD 2;
  DLBY 85; MTCW

Wolfe, Thomas Kennerly, Jr. 1931-
  See Wolfe, Tom
  See also CA 13-16R; CANR 9, 33;
  DAM POP; INT CANR-9; MTCW

Wolfe, Tom . . . . **CLC 1, 2, 9, 15, 35, 51**
  See also Wolfe, Thomas Kennerly, Jr.
  See also AAYA 8; AITN 2; BEST 89:1;
  DLB 152

Wolff, Geoffrey (Ansell) 1937- . . . . . **CLC 41**
  See also CA 29-32R; CANR 29, 43

Wolff, Sonia
  See Levitin, Sonia (Wolff)

Wolff, Tobias (Jonathan Ansell)
  1945- . . . . **CLC 39, 64**
  See also AAYA 16; BEST 90:2; CA 114;
  117; CAAS 22; DLB 130; INT 117

Wolfram von Eschenbach
  c. 1170-c. 1220 . . . . **CMLC 5**
  See also DLB 138

Wolitzer, Hilma 1930- . . . . **CLC 17**
  See also CA 65-68; CANR 18, 40;
  INT CANR-18; SATA 31

Wollstonecraft, Mary 1759-1797 . . . . . . **LC 5**
  See also CDBLB 1789-1832; DLB 39, 104,
  158

Wonder, Stevie . . . . **CLC 12**
  See also Morris, Steveland Judkins

Wong, Jade Snow 1922- . . . . **CLC 17**
  See also CA 109

Woodcott, Keith
  See Brunner, John (Kilian Houston)

Woodruff, Robert W.
  See Mencken, H(enry) L(ouis)

Woolf, (Adeline) Virginia
  1882-1941 . . . . **TCLC 1, 5, 20, 43, 56;
  DA; DAB; DAC; SSC 7; WLC**
  See also CA 104; 130; CDBLB 1914-1945;
  DAM MST, NOV; DLB 36, 100, 162;
  DLBD 10; MTCW

Woollcott, Alexander (Humphreys)
  1887-1943 . . . . **TCLC 5**
  See also CA 105; DLB 29

Woolrich, Cornell 1903-1968 . . . . **CLC 77**
  See also Hopley-Woolrich, Cornell George

Wordsworth, Dorothy
  1771-1855 . . . . **NCLC 25**
  See also DLB 107

Wordsworth, William
  1770-1850 . . . . **NCLC 12, 38; DA; DAB;
  DAC; PC 4; WLC**
  See also CDBLB 1789-1832; DAM MST,
  POET; DLB 93, 107

Wouk, Herman 1915- . . . . **CLC 1, 9, 38**
  See also CA 5-8R; CANR 6, 33;
  DAM NOV, POP; DLBY 82;
  INT CANR-6; MTCW

Wright, Charles (Penzel, Jr.)
  1935- . . . . **CLC 6, 13, 28**
  See also CA 29-32R; CAAS 7; CANR 23,
  36; DLB 165; DLBY 82; MTCW

Wright, Charles Stevenson
  1932- . . . . **CLC 49; BLC 3**
  See also BW 1; CA 9-12R; CANR 26;
  DAM MULT, POET; DLB 33

Wright, Jack R.
  See Harris, Mark

Wright, James (Arlington)
  1927-1980 . . . . **CLC 3, 5, 10, 28**
  See also AITN 2; CA 49-52; 97-100;
  CANR 4, 34; DAM POET; DLB 5;
  MTCW

Wright, Judith (Arandell)
  1915- . . . . **CLC 11, 53; PC 14**
  See also CA 13-16R; CANR 31; MTCW;
  SATA 14

Wright, L(auraii) R. 1939- . . . . **CLC 44**
  See also CA 138

Wright, Richard (Nathaniel)
  1908-1960 . . . . **CLC 1, 3, 4, 9, 14, 21, 48,
  74; BLC; DA; DAB; DAC; SSC 2; WLC**
  See also AAYA 5; BW 1; CA 108;
  CDALB 1929-1941; DAM MST, MULT,
  NOV; DLB 76, 102; DLBD 2; MTCW

Wright, Richard B(ruce) 1937- . . . . . . **CLC 6**
  See also CA 85-88; DLB 53

Wright, Rick 1945- . . . . **CLC 35**

Wright, Rowland
  See Wells, Carolyn

Wright, Stephen Caldwell 1946- . . . . **CLC 33**
  See also BW 2

Wright, Willard Huntington 1888-1939
  See Van Dine, S. S.
  See also CA 115

Wright, William 1930- . . . . **CLC 44**
  See also CA 53-56; CANR 7, 23

Wroth, LadyMary 1587-1653(?) . . . . . **LC 30**
  See also DLB 121

Wu Ch'eng-en 1500(?)-1582(?) . . . . **LC 7**

Wu Ching-tzu 1701-1754 . . . . **LC 2**

Wurlitzer, Rudolph 1938(?)- . . . **CLC 2, 4, 15**
  See also CA 85-88

Wycherley, William 1641-1715 . . . . **LC 8, 21**
  See also CDBLB 1660-1789; DAM DRAM;
  DLB 80

Wylie, Elinor (Morton Hoyt)
  1885-1928 . . . . **TCLC 8**
  See also CA 105; DLB 9, 45

Wylie, Philip (Gordon) 1902-1971 . . . **CLC 43**
  See also CA 21-22; 33-36R; CAP 2; DLB 9

Wyndham, John . . . . **CLC 19**
  See also Harris, John (Wyndham Parkes
  Lucas) Beynon

Wyss, Johann David Von
  1743-1818 . . . . **NCLC 10**
  See also JRDA; MAICYA; SATA 29;
  SATA-Brief 27

Xenophon
  c. 430B.C.-c. 354B.C. . . . . **CMLC 17**

Yakumo Koizumi
  See Hearn, (Patricio) Lafcadio (Tessima
  Carlos)

Yanez, Jose Donoso
  See Donoso (Yanez), Jose

Yanovsky, Basile S.
  See Yanovsky, V(assily) S(emenovich)

Yanovsky, V(assily) S(emenovich)
  1906-1989 . . . . **CLC 2, 18**
  See also CA 97-100; 129

Yates, Richard   1926-1992 . . . . . CLC 7, 8, 23
    See also CA 5-8R; 139; CANR 10, 43;
    DLB 2; DLBY 81, 92; INT CANR-10

Yeats, W. B.
    See Yeats, William Butler

Yeats, William Butler
    1865-1939 . . . . . TCLC 1, 11, 18, 31; DA;
                                        DAB; DAC; WLC
    See also CA 104; 127; CANR 45;
    CDBLB 1890-1914; DAM DRAM, MST,
    POET; DLB 10, 19, 98, 156; MTCW

Yehoshua, A(braham) B.
    1936- . . . . CLC 13, 31
    See also CA 33-36R; CANR 43

Yep, Laurence Michael   1948- . . . . . . CLC 35
    See also AAYA 5; CA 49-52; CANR 1, 46;
    CLR 3, 17; DLB 52; JRDA; MAICYA;
    SATA 7, 69

Yerby, Frank G(arvin)
    1916-1991 . . . . CLC 1, 7, 22; BLC
    1; CA 9-12R; 136; CANR 16;
    DAM MULT; DLB 76; INT CANR-16;
    MTCW

Yesenin, Sergei Alexandrovich
    See Esenin, Sergei (Alexandrovich)

Yevtushenko, Yevgeny (Alexandrovich)
    1933- . . . . CLC 1, 3, 13, 26, 51
    See also CA 81-84; CANR 33;
    DAM POET; MTCW

Yezierska, Anzia   1885(?)-1970 . . . . . CLC 46
    See also CA 126; 89-92; DLB 28; MTCW

Yglesias, Helen   1915- . . . . CLC 7, 22
    See also CA 37-40R; CAAS 20; CANR 15;
    INT CANR-15; MTCW

Yokomitsu Riichi   1898-1947 . . . . . . TCLC 47

Yonge, Charlotte (Mary)
    1823-1901 . . . . TCLC 48
    See also CA 109; DLB 18, 163; SATA 17

York, Jeremy
    See Creasey, John

York, Simon
    See Heinlein, Robert A(nson)

Yorke, Henry Vincent   1905-1974 . . . CLC 13
    See also Green, Henry
    See also CA 85-88; 49-52

Yosano Akiko   1878-1942 . . TCLC 59; PC 11

Yoshimoto, Banana . . . . CLC 84
    See also Yoshimoto, Mahoko

Yoshimoto, Mahoko   1964-
    See Yoshimoto, Banana
    See also CA 144

Young, Al(bert James)
    1939- . . . . CLC 19; BLC
    See also BW 2; CA 29-32R; CANR 26;
    DAM MULT; DLB 33

Young, Andrew (John)   1885-1971 . . . . CLC 5
    See also CA 5-8R; CANR 7, 29

Young, Collier
    See Bloch, Robert (Albert)

Young, Edward   1683-1765 . . . . LC 3
    See also DLB 95

Young, Marguerite (Vivian)
    1909-1995 . . . . CLC 82
    See also CA 13-16; 150; CAP 1

Young, Neil   1945- . . . . CLC 17
    See also CA 110

Yourcenar, Marguerite
    1903-1987 . . . . CLC 19, 38, 50, 87
    See also CA 69-72; CANR 23; DAM NOV;
    DLB 72; DLBY 88; MTCW

Yurick, Sol   1925- . . . . CLC 6
    See also CA 13-16R; CANR 25

Zabolotskii, Nikolai Alekseevich
    1903-1958 . . . . TCLC 52
    See also CA 116

Zamiatin, Yevgenii
    See Zamyatin, Evgeny Ivanovich

Zamora, Bernice (B. Ortiz)
    1938- . . . . CLC 89; HLC
    See also DAM MULT; DLB 82; HW

Zamyatin, Evgeny Ivanovich
    1884-1937 . . . . TCLC 8, 37
    See also CA 105

Zangwill, Israel   1864-1926 . . . . TCLC 16
    See also CA 109; DLB 10, 135

Zappa, Francis Vincent, Jr.   1940-1993
    See Zappa, Frank
    See also CA 108; 143

Zappa, Frank . . . . CLC 17
    See also Zappa, Francis Vincent, Jr.

Zaturenska, Marya   1902-1982 . . . . CLC 6, 11
    See also CA 13-16R; 105; CANR 22

Zelazny, Roger (Joseph)
    1937-1995 . . . . CLC 21
    See also AAYA 7; CA 21-24R; 148;
    CANR 26; DLB 8; MTCW; SATA 57;
    SATA-Brief 39

Zhdanov, Andrei A(lexandrovich)
    1896-1948 . . . . TCLC 18
    See also CA 117

Zhukovsky, Vasily   1783-1852 . . . . NCLC 35

Ziegenhagen, Eric . . . . CLC 55

Zimmer, Jill Schary
    See Robinson, Jill

Zimmerman, Robert
    See Dylan, Bob

Zindel, Paul
    1936- . . . . . CLC 6, 26; DA; DAB; DAC;
                                                      DC 5
    See also AAYA 2; CA 73-76; CANR 31;
    CLR 3; DAM DRAM, MST, NOV;
    DLB 7, 52; JRDA; MAICYA; MTCW;
    SATA 16, 58

Zinov'Ev, A. A.
    See Zinoviev, Alexander (Aleksandrovich)

Zinoviev, Alexander (Aleksandrovich)
    1922- . . . . CLC 19
    See also CA 116; 133; CAAS 10

Zoilus
    See Lovecraft, H(oward) P(hillips)

Zola, Emile (Edouard Charles Antoine)
    1840-1902 . . . . . . TCLC 1, 6, 21, 41; DA;
                                          DAB; DAC; WLC
    See also CA 104; 138; DAM MST, NOV;
    DLB 123

Zoline, Pamela   1941- . . . . CLC 62

Zorrilla y Moral, Jose   1817-1893 . . NCLC 6

Zoshchenko, Mikhail (Mikhailovich)
    1895-1958 . . . . TCLC 15; SSC 15
    See also CA 115

Zuckmayer, Carl   1896-1977 . . . . CLC 18
    See also CA 69-72; DLB 56, 124

Zuk, Georges
    See Skelton, Robin

Zukofsky, Louis
    1904-1978 . . . . CLC 1, 2, 4, 7, 11, 18;
                                                      PC 11
    See also CA 9-12R; 77-80; CANR 39;
    DAM POET; DLB 5, 165; MTCW

Zweig, Paul   1935-1984 . . . . CLC 34, 42
    See also CA 85-88; 113

Zweig, Stefan   1881-1942 . . . . TCLC 17
    See also CA 112; DLB 81, 118

Literary Criticism Series
Cumulative Topic Index

This index lists all topic entries in Gale's *Classical and Medieval Literature Criticism, Contemporary Literary Criticism, Literature Criticism from 1400 to 1800, Nineteenth-Century Literature Criticism,* and *Twentieth-Century Literary Criticism.*

Topic Index

Topic Index

CMLC Cumulative Nationality Index

CMLC Cumulative Title Index

See "Ode to Aphrodite"
Odysseis (Homer)
    See *Odyssey*
Odysses (Homer)
    See *Odyssey*
Odyssey (*Odysseis*; *Odysses*) (Homer)   **1**:287, 293, 310, 312, 315-17, 319-20, 329, 338, 354, 362-63, 369-72, 375, 379, 388, 396-97, 400, 407-08
Oeconomicus (*On Household Economy*) (Xenophon)   **17**:323, 326, 345, 374, 375
Oedipous epi Kolōnōi (*Oedipus at Colonos*; *Oedipus Coloneus*; *Oedipus in Colonos*) (Sophocles)   **2**:289, 292, 296, 298, 300-01, 303-05, 312, 314-16, 318-19, 321, 325, 330, 335-36, 338-39, 342, 345-46, 349-52, 362-63, 367-70, 377, 388, 392, 398, 416-19, 421, 425-28
Oedipous Tyrannos (*King Oedipus*; *Oedipus*; *Oedipus Rex*; *Oedipus the King*) (Sophocles)   **2**:288-89, 292, 296, 300, 304-05, 309-10, 312-16, 319-21, 324-24, 337-40, 343-45,347, 349-51, 353, 355-57, 359-62, 369-78, 382, 384, 387, 389-92, 394, 409-10, 415-21, 423-29
Oedipus (Aeschylus)   **11**:122, 124, 138, 159-60
Oedipus (Seneca)   **6**:343-44, 366, 369, 373, 379-81, 388-89, 413, 415, 417, 420-22, 428, 432
Oedipus (Sophocles)
    See *Oedipous Tyrannos*
Oedipus at Colonos (Sophocles)
    See *Oedipous epi Kolōnōi*
Oedipus Coloneus (Sophocles)
    See *Oedipous epi Kolōnōi*
Oedipus in Colonos (Sophocles)
    See *Oedipous epi Kolōnōi*
Oedipus Rex (Sophocles)
    See *Oedipous Tyrannos*
Oedipus the King (Sophocles)
    See *Oedipous Tyrannos*
"Oenone" (Ovid)   **7**:311
Oetaeus (Seneca)
    See *Hercules oetaeus*
Of Natural and Moral Philosophy (Apuleius)   **1**:12-13
Offices (Cicero)
    See *De officiis*
De officiis (*Duties*; *Offices*; *On Duties*) (Cicero)   **3**:192-93, 196, 202-03, 214, 221, 228-29, 242, 245, 254-57, 288-89, 296-98
Ol. IX (Pindar)
    See *Olympian 9*
Ol. XI (Pindar)
    See *Olympian 11*
Old Cantankerous (Menander)
    See *Dyskolos*
Old Kalevala
    See *Kalevala*
"Old Love Is Best" (Sappho)   **3**:396
"Olden Airs" (Li Po)   **2**:178
Olympian 1 (*First Olympian*; *O. 1*; *Olympian Odes 1*) (Pindar)   **12**:263, 269, 295, 298-99, 301, 304-05, 307, 309, 319, 322, 334, 349, 354, 363, 367, 371-72, 377-81, 383
Olympian 2 (*Second Olympian*) (Pindar)   **12**:264, 271, 293, 298, 304, 319, 321, 351, 358, 363, 365, 367, 379, 383
Olympian 3 (*Third Olympian*) (Pindar)   **12**:266, 312, 319, 353, 363, 368-69, 378, 383-84
Olympian 4 (Pindar)   **12**:321, 354, 362-63, 365, 378, 380, 383

Olympian 5 (Pindar)   **12**:321, 353, 363, 365, 370, 377-79, 382-83
Olympian 6 (*Sixth Olympian*) (Pindar)   **12**:264, 267, 313, 353, 355, 364, 369, 378-84
Olympian 7 (*O. 7*; *Olympian VII*) (Pindar)   **12**:264, 267, 296, 298, 308-09, 313, 320, 348, 353, 362, 369, 372, 374, 378, 380, 382-83
Olympian VII (Pindar)
    See *Olympian 7*
Olympian 8 (*Eighth Olympian*; *O. 8*) (Pindar)   **12**:269, 289, 302, 326, 357, 359, 365, 369, 378-80, 382-83
Olympian 9 (*O. 9*; *Ol. IX*) (Pindar)   **12**:289, 300, 352, 355, 365-66, 368, 370, 372, 378, 381-84
Olympian 10 (*Tenth Olympian*) (Pindar)   **12**:272, 304, 309, 322, 352-53, 365-67, 378-79
Olympian 11 (*Eleventh Olympian*; *Ol. XI*) (Pindar)   **12**:264, 344, 352-53, 380
Olympian 12 (*Twelfth Olympian*) (Pindar)   **12**:309, 343
Olympian 13 (*Thirteenth Olympian*) (Pindar)   **12**:304, 320, 322, 338, 348, 353, 355-56, 362, 378, 380, 383-84
Olympian 14 (*Fourteenth Olympian*; *O. 14*) (Pindar)   **12**:294-95, 297, 301, 323, 325, 348, 352, 378, 383
Olympian Odes 1 (Pindar)
    See *Olympian 1*
Olynthiac I (*First Olynthiac*) (Demosthenes)   **13**:145, 148-9, 166, 171, 197
Olynthiac II (*Second Olynthiac*) (Demosthenes)   **13**:148, 151, 171, 180, 197
Olynthiac III (*Third Olynthiac*) (Demosthenes)   **13**:144, 146, 148-9, 151, 165, 171
Olynthiacs (Demosthenes)   **13**:138, 143, 149-51, 165, 169, 183, 189
"On a Picture Screen" (Li Po)   **2**:136
"On Anactoria" (Sappho)
    See "Ode to Anactoria"
On Ancient Medicine (Thucydides)   **17**:253
On Anger (Seneca)
    See *De ira*
On Animals (Albert the Great)
    See *De animalibus*
On Armaments (Demosthenes)   **13**:158
On Christian Doctrine (Augustine)
    See *De doctrina Christiana*
On Clemency (Seneca)
    See *De clementia*
On Consolation (Seneca)   **6**:344
On Divination (Cicero)
    See *De divinatione*
On Division (Boethius)
    See *Divisions*
On Duties (Cicero)
    See *De officiis*
On Forms (Hermogenes)
    See *On Types of Style*
On Free Will (Augustine)
    See *De libero arbitrio voluntatis*
On Friendship (Cicero)
    See *De amicitia*
On Gentleness (Seneca)   **6**:423
On Giving and Receiving Favours (Seneca)
    See *De beneficiis*
On Glory (Cicero)   **3**:177
On Good Deeds (Seneca)   **6**:427
On Grace and Free Will (Augustine)
    See *De gratia et libero arbitrio*
On Halonnesus (Demosthenes)   **13**:165

On His Consulship (Cicero)
    See *De consulatu suo*
On Household Economy (Xenophon)
    See *Oeconomicus*
On Ideas (Hermogenes)
    See *On Types of Style*
On Invention (Cicero)
    See *De inventione*
On Invention (*De inventione*) (Hermogenes)   **6**:170-72, 185-86, 188, 191, 198-202
On Laws (Cicero)
    See *De legibus*
On Mercy (Seneca)
    See *De clementia*
On Method (Hermogenes)
    See *On the Method of Deinotēs*
On Misconduct of Ambassadors (Demosthenes)
    See *On the Misconduct of the Embassy*
"On Nourishing Life" (Su Shih)   **15**:401
On Old Age (Cicero)
    See *De senectute*
On Order (Augustine)
    See *De ordine*
On Peace of Mind (Seneca)
    See *De tranquillitate animi*
On Providence (Seneca)
    See *De providentia*
On Qualities of Style (Hermogenes)
    See *On Types of Style*
On Sleep and Waking (Albert the Great)   **16**:16
On Staseis (Hermogenes)
    See *On Stases*
On Stases (*On Staseis*; *De statibus*) (Hermogenes)   **6**:158, 170-74, 185-86, 191, 196, 198-202
"On Taking Leave of Tzu-yu at Ying-chou: Two Poems" (Su Shih)   **15**:411
On the Affairs in the Chersonese (Demosthenes)
    See *On the Chersonese*
On the Best Kind of Orators (Cicero)
    See *De optimo genere oratorum*
On the Blessed Life (Cicero)
    See *Tusculan Disputations*
On the Categoric Syllogism (Apuleius)   **1**:12-13
On the Categorical Syllogism (Boethius)   **15**:27
On the Catholic Faith (Boethius)
    See *De fide catholica*
On the Causes and Properties of the Elements and of the Planets (Albert the Great)
    See *De causis et proprietatibus elementorum et planetarum*
On the Chersonese (*On the Affairs in the Chersonese*) (Demosthenes)   **13**:138, 146, 148-9, 152, 161, 166, 193, 195
On the Chief Good and Evil (Cicero)
    See *De finibus*
On the Christian Struggle (Augustine)   **6**:21
On the City of God (Augustine)
    See *De civitate Dei*
On the Crown (*De Coruna*; *Crown Speech*) (Demosthenes)   **13**:139, 143, 145, 147-52, 162, 166, 172-5, 179, 183-4, 189, 191-5, 197
On the Divine Unity and Trinity (Abelard)
    See *Theologia 'Summi boni'*
On the False Embassy (Demosthenes)
    See *On the Misconduct of the Embassy*
On the Fraudulent Embassy (Demosthenes)
    See *On the Misconduct of the Embassy*
On the Freedom of Rhodes (Demosthenes)
    See *For the Rhodians*

Title Index

CMLC Cumulative Critic Index

Abe Akio
Sei Shōnagon **6**:2

Abusch, Tzvi
Epic of Gilgamesh **3**:365

Adams, Charles Darwin
Demosthenes **13**:148

Adams, Henry
The Song of Roland **1**:166

Adcock, F. E.
Thucydides **17**:288

Addison, Joseph
Aeneid **9**:310
Iliad **1**:282
Ovid **7**:292
Sappho **3**:379
Sophocles **2**:293

Adler, Mortimer J.
Plato **8**:342

Adlington, William
Apuleius **1**:6

Aiken, Conrad
Murasaki, Lady **1**:423

Albert, S.M.
Albert the Great **16**:33

Alighieri, Dante
Aeneid **9**:297
Bertran de Born **5**:4
Seneca, Lucius Annaeus **6**:331
Sordello **15**:323

Ali-Shah, Omar
Khayyám **11**:288

Allen, Archibald W.
Livy **11**:334

Allen, Richard
Njáls saga **13**:358

Allinson, Francis G.
Menander **9**:204

Allison, Rev. William T.
The Book of Psalms **4**:371

Al-Nadīm
Arabian Nights **2**:3

Alphonso-Karkala, John B.
Kalevala **6**:259

Alter, Robert
The Book of Psalms **4**:451
Song of Songs **18**:283

Ambivius, Lucius
Terence **14**:302

Amis, Kingsley
Beowulf **1**:112

Anacker, Robert
Chrétien de Troyes **10**:144

Anderson, George K.
Beowulf **1**:98
The Dream of the Rood **14**:245

Anderson, J. K.
Xenophon **17**:342

Anderson, William S.
Juvenal **8**:59

Andersson, Theodore M.
Hrafnkel's Saga **2**:103

Apuleius, Lucius
Apuleius **1**:3

Aquinas, St. Thomas
Augustine, St. **6**:5
Averroës **7**:3
Plato **8**:217

Arendt, Hannah
Augustine, St. **6**:116

Aristophanes
Aeschylus **11**:73

Aristotle
Aeschylus **11**:73
Greek Historiography **17**:13
Hesiod **5**:69
Iliad **1**:273
Plato **8**:202
Sophocles **2**:291

Arnold, E. Vernon
Seneca, Lucius Annaeus **6**:362

Arnold, Edwin
Hesiod **5**:71
Iliad **1**:308
Odyssey **16**:208
Sappho **3**:384

Arnold, Mary
Poem of the Cid **4**:226

Arnold, Matthew
Aeneid **9**:316
Aristophanes **4**:54
Iliad **1**:300
Mabinogion **9**:146
The Song of Roland **1**:162
Sophocles **2**:311

Arnott, Geoffrey
Menander **9**:261

Arnott, W. G.
Menander **9**:253

Arnstein, Adolf
Meister Eckhart **9**:4

Arrowsmith, William
Aristophanes **4**:131

'Arùdì, Nizàmì-i-
Avicenna **16**:147

Ascham, Roger
Cicero, Marcus Tullius **3**:186

Ashe, Geoffrey
Arthurian Legend **10**:2

Asquith, Herbert Henry
Demosthenes **13**:135

Aston, W. G.
Murasaki, Lady **1**:416
Sei Sh nagon **6**:291

Athanasius
The Book of Psalms **4**:344

Atkins, J. W. H.
Aristophanes **4**:104

Atkinson, James C.
Mystery of Adam **4**:207

Auden, W. H.
Iliad **1**:347
Njáls saga **13**:330

Auerbach, Erich
Augustine, St. **6**:79
Inferno **3**:72, 95
Mystery of Adam **4**:193
Odyssey **16**:221
Poem of the Cid **4**:251

Critic Index

Haines, C. R.
Sappho **3**:397

Haley, Lucille
Ovid **7**:310

Hallam, Henry
Bacon, Roger **14**:16
Poem of the Cid **4**:225

Hallberg, Peter
Hrafnkel's Saga **2**:124
Njáls saga **13**:339

Hallett, Judith P.
Sappho **3**:465

Halleux, Pierre
Hrafnkel's Saga **2**:99, 102

Halverson, John
Beowulf **1**:131

Hamilton, Edith
Aeschylus **11**:128
Aristophanes **4**:109
Sophocles **2**:328
Terence **14**:322

Hamori, Andras
Arabian Nights **2**:51

Handley, E. W.
Menander **9**:243, 276

Hanford, James Holly
Razón de Amor **16**:337

Hanning, Robert
Marie de France **8**:158

Hanson-Smith, Elizabeth
Mabinogion **9**:192

Hardison, O. B., Jr.
Mystery of Adam **4**:203

Hardy, E. G.
Juvenal **8**:17

Hardy, Lucy
Boccaccio, Giovanni **13**:30

Harris, Charles
Kālidāsa **9**:81

Harrison, Ann Tukey
The Song of Roland **1**:261

Harrison, Robert
The Song of Roland **1**:220

Harsh, Philip Whaley
Menander **9**:216

Hart, Henry H.
Polo, Marco **15**:309

Hart, Thomas R.
Poem of the Cid **4**:306

Hartley, L. P.
Murasaki, Lady **1**:422

Hastings, R.
Boccaccio, Giovanni **13**:59

Hatto, A. T.
Gottfried von Strassburg **10**:259
Nibelungenlied, Das **12**:194

Havelock, E. A.
Catullus **18**:91

Havelock, Eric A.
Hesiod **5**:111, 150
Iliad **1**:382, 386

Hay, John
Khayyám **11**:261

Haymes, Edward R.
Nibelungenlied, Das **12**:244

Headstrom, Birger R.
Boccaccio, Giovanni **13**:35

Hearn, Lafcadio
Khayyám **11**:258

Hegel, G. W. F.
Aristophanes **4**:46
The Book of Job **14**:157
Inferno **3**:12
Plato **8**:225
Sophocles **2**:297

Heidegger, Martin
Plato **8**:295
Sophocles **2**:376

Heidel, Alexander
Epic of Gilgamesh **3**:310

Heine, Heinrich
Bertran de Born **5**:10

Heinemann, Frederik J.
Hrafnkel's Saga **2**:120, 123

Heiserman, Arthur
Apuleius **1**:46
Longus **7**:254
Xenophon **17**:351

Herder, Johann Gottfried von
The Book of Psalms **4**:355
Kālidāsa **9**:102

Herington, John
Aeschylus **11**:210

Hermann, Fränkel
Pindar **12**:305

Herodotus
Hesiod **5**:68

Herriott, J. Homer
Polo, Marco **15**:289

Hesse, Hermann
Arabian Nights **2**:28
Boccaccio, Giovanni **13**:32

Hewlett, Maurice
Hesiod **5**:83

Hickes, George
Cædmon **7**:78

Hieatt, Constance
The Song of Roland **1**:209

Higgins, W. E.
Xenophon **17**:352

Highet, Gilbert
Arabian Nights **2**:41
Beowulf **1**:97
Cicero, Marcus Tullius **3**:232, 241
The Dream of the Rood **14**:243
Juvenal **8**:40, 45
Pindar **12**:279
Romance of the Rose **8**:399

Hillebrandt, A.
Kālidāsa **9**:95

Hillgarth, J. N.
Llull, Ramon **12**:112

Hirsch, S. A.
Bacon, Roger **14**:23

Hirsch, Steven W.
Xenophon **17**:361

Hisamatsu, Sen'ichi
Sei Shōnagon **6**:292

Hobbes, Thomas
Odyssey **16**:189
Thucydides **17**:214

Hölderlin, Friedrich
Sophocles **2**:297

Hole, Richard
Arabian Nights **2**:4

Hollander, Lee M.
Njáls saga **13**:326

Hollander, Robert
Boccaccio, Giovanni **13**:67, 88
Vita Nuova **18**:362

Hollister, C. Warren
Anglo-Saxon Chronicle **4**:19

Holmes, Urban T., Jr.
Chrétien de Troyes **10**:150

Holyday, Barten
Juvenal **8**:4

Homann, Holger
Nibelungenlied, Das **12**:239

Honko, Lauri
Kalevala **6**:271

Hopkins, E. Washburn
Mahābhārata **5**:192

Horowitz, Irving L.
Averroës **7**:28

Hough, Lynn Harold
The Book of Psalms **4**:388

Hourani, George F.
Averroës **7**:36

Housman, Laurence
Khayyám **11**:278

Howard, Donald R.
Sir Gawain and the Green Knight **2**:221

Howes, Robert C.
The Igor Tale **1**:517

Hroswitha, Abess
Terence **14**:349

Hsu, Sung-peng
Lao Tzu **7**:182, 190

Huang Kuo-pin
Li Po **2**:164

Hueffer, Francis
Bertran de Born **5**:12

Hügel, Baron Friedrich von
Meister Eckhart **9**:27

Hugill, William Meredith
Aristophanes **4**:107

Hugo, Victor
Inferno **3**:22

Huizinga, Johan
Abelard **11**:6

Hulbert, James R.
Beowulf **1**:90

Hull, Denison Bingham
Iliad **1**:398

Hume, David
Cicero, Marcus Tullius **3**:188

Humphries, Rolfe
Juvenal **8**:58

Hunt, H. A. K.
Cicero, Marcus Tullius **3**:253

Hunt, J. William
Aeneid **9**:433

Huppé, Bernard F.
Augustine, St. **6**:92
Cædmon **7**:105
The Dream of the Rood **14**:278

Hutson, Arthur E.
Nibelungenlied, Das **12**:162

Hutton, Richard Holt
Khayyám **11**:271

Huxley, Aldous
Bhagavad Gītā **12**:54
Meister Eckhart **9**:68
Sappho **3**:398

Lyne, R. O. A. M.
Catullus **18**:148

Critic Index

Critic Index

Critic Index

Juvenal **8**:22

Wright, Thomas
Polo, Marco **15**:261

Wyckoff, Dorothy
Albert the Great **16**:54

Wyld, Henry Cecil
Layamon **10**:320

Wyld, M. Alice
Inferno **3**:50

Wynn, Marianne
Wolfram von Eschenbach **5**:326,
416

Yadin, Yigael
Josephus, Flavius **13**:239

Yarmolinsky, Avrahm
The Igor Tale **1**:496

Yates, Frances A.
Cicero, Marcus Tullius **3**:273
Llull, Ramon **12**:103

Yavetz, Zvi
Josephus, Flavius **13**:250

Young, Karl
Mystery of Adam **4**:190

Yourcenar, Marguerite
Murasaki, Lady **1**:455

Yoshikawa, Kojiro
Su Shih **15**:410

Yu-lan, Fung
Lao Tzu **7**:126

Yutang, Lin
Lao Tzu **7**:135

Zaehner, R. C.
Bhagavad Gītā **12**:67
Mahābhārata **5**:243

Zanker, G.
Callimachus **18**:50

Zedler, Beatrice H.
Averroës **7**:22

Zeydel, Edwin H.
Gottfried von Strassburg **10**:258
Wolfram von Eschenbach **5**:307

Zhirmunsky, Victor
Book of Dede Korkut **8**:96

Zimmer, Heinrich
Arabian Nights **2**:32
Bhagavad Gītā **12**:45
Sir Gawain and the Green Knight
2:187

Zweig, Stefan
Cicero, Marcus Tullius **3**:225

Critic Index

ISBN 0-8103-9981-4

90000

9 780810 399815